THE PAPERS

of

JOHN C. CALHOUN

JOHN C. CALHOUN

John Sartain's engraving was taken from a miniature portrait painted by James Wise in 1843. Wise's portrait was thought by Calhoun's family to be the best likeness of the statesman.

THE PAPERS

of

JOHN C. CALHOUN

Volume XVII, 1843–1844

Edited by

CLYDE N. WILSON

Shirley Bright Cook, *Associate Editor*

Alexander Moore, *Assistant Editor*

UNIVERSITY OF SOUTH CAROLINA PRESS, 1986

ea

Copyright © 1987 by the
University of South Carolina

*Publication of this book was made possible
by a grant from the National Historical Publications
and Records Commission.*

*International Standard Book Number: 0–87249–483–7
Library of Congress Catalog Card Number: 59–10351*

Manufactured in the United States of America

8/12/87

CONTENTS

▯

PREFACE

◫

Despite all the attention that has been devoted to it, the American political history of the 1840's—whether narrative, institutional, or intellectual—remains to be written in satisfactory detail and synthesis. This is apparent to any historian who has dipped into the primary sources with a desire to understand rather than simply to elaborate upon or confute the sometimes superficial and misleading generalizations that are already established. Indeed, this observation can be enlarged to cover the whole middle period of American history—say, from the end of the War of 1812 to the Kansas-Nebraska acts.

This constitutes part of the justification, if any is needed, for an ample publication of Calhoun documents. Calhoun and the circle of which he was the center constituted a substantial segment—though only one of several—of the political reality of the time. One cannot construct a satisfactory narrative of the period without incorporation of this circle. One cannot understand the developing democratic institutions of the period—especially party, parliamentary, and journalistic institutions—without taking account of Calhoun's role in and criticism of these institutions. And certainly, one cannot fully comprehend the mind of the time without attention to Calhoun. In that respect he is as essential, perhaps, as any of his contemporaries who were public actors. Observers of diverse times and sympathies have found something of enduring pertinence in Calhoun's thought.

As in previous volumes, this book has been made as inclusive as is possible. All documents written by Calhoun, including several pseudonymously published or unpublished essays, mainly on the defects on the emerging two-party system, have been presented. Everything addressed to Calhoun that has been found has also been included, with one exception: letters addressed to Calhoun in an official capacity as Secretary of State between March 6, 1844, when he was nominated and confirmed to that office, and April 1, 1844, when he took up the duties of the post, have been omitted, except for those that concern appointments to office. (There also exists a considerable correspondence dated prior to April 1, 1844, addressed to Calhoun's predecessors as Secretary of State, which was awaiting his reply when he took office. This also has been omitted, and both omitted categories of correspondence will be taken account of in the next volume.) We have included, however, a selection of documents neither to nor from John C. Calhoun, but taken from his family papers and from campaign literature, that relate intimately to Calhoun's activities or to his positions.

A portion of Calhoun's incoming correspondence for the later months of 1843, preserved at Clemson University, was damaged by fire at some unknown time, leaving many letters partially mutilated. These have been presented in necessarily unsatisfactory transcriptions in the belief that knowledgeable users of this book will understand the substance and drift of these letters from what survives.

Documentary editing, done properly, requires a long-range commitment of resources, talents, and efforts. Indispensable resources have been supplied by the Program for Editions of the National Endowment for the Humanities, by the National Historical Publications and Records Commission, and by the University of South Carolina. Shirley Bright Cook and Alexander Moore have expended efforts and talents beyond the call of duty. Lee R. Wilson also provided valuable assistance.

The brief period covered by this volume was, from the point of view of the political history of the United States, a time of dynamic flux and expansion from which much may be learned that is relevant to what came after. Possibly, the best history of the period will not be written until the primary documents relating to all of the segments that made up the diverse reality of the time are presented in as comprehensive and accessible a fashion as we have tried to present Calhoun's.

CLYDE N. WILSON

Columbia, August, 1985

INTRODUCTION

⫿

In the period of the Revolution, constitution making, and early Republic in which John C. Calhoun had his roots, political life was marked to a significant degree by a high and strenuous republican ideal in which public men were judged by their principles, foresight, and virtue (the last conceived in a Roman rather than a Victorian sense). But probably always a solid substratum of American politics has been temporizing and pragmatic, reflecting an aspect of national character which some have decried for its resistance to idealism and others have cherished for having providentially spared us many internal conflicts.

As American republican society established itself more securely and experienced an expansive confidence after 1815, it was perhaps inevitable that pragmatism would assert its relative strength. As America became more democratic, it also became more complacent. (From the Civil War era on, the long stretches of pragmatic accommodation would be interrupted less by episodes of high statesmanship than by messianic eruptions resulting in forced readjustments.) Most of Calhoun's national career, then, coincided with a period in which the public man's rather aristocratic striving for distinction was being substantially displaced by the perennial centrist pragmatism which has characterized innumerable political figures since.

The republican statesman found honor in foreseeing, grappling with, and resolving fundamental conflicts of values and interests. He sought to clarify and settle the issues, even should that prove quite demanding, and thus to secure the long-range welfare of his people. Such leaders were capable, for instance, of such impracticalities as making a Revolution over a trifling tax on tea. The pragmatic politician, on the other hand, presents an air of vigorous but compromising competence. He asserts ideas and values in vague and conventional terms and hopes not so much to lead as to please the people. He seeks to mute conflict by ignoring or redefining it, or even by raising false issues. His goal is to avoid divisive stands, appeal to as broad a base as possible, keep the lid on, acquire or retain power and its benefits, and muddle through. His vision is necessarily of the short term and his rhetoric undemanding.

A classic description of the practical politician's response to dilemma was given when an admirer of Calhoun described to him the stand of Silas Wright, New York's Democratic governor, on an issue that exploded a few years after the period of this volume, the Wilmot Proviso. Two influential party newspapers had declared, with equal authority and persistence, that they represented Wright's position. One said he was for the Proviso, the other declared him to be opposed. Both were right. As Calhoun's friend remarked: "He was *opposed* to the Wilmot Proviso being brought forward in Congress—but being introduced he was *in favor* of its being sustained. A parallel case to that of [his] *speaking against* the Tariff of '42 and *voting for* it."[1]

There is doubtless something to be said for and against both styles of politics, and it might be argued that the preference between them is less a choice of right and wrong than an expression of taste or judgment. The pragmatist may be considered to be in sensible pursuit of harmony. But, undoubtedly, John C. Calhoun, in both theory and practice, was a critic of the pragmatic style, especially as it interwove itself inextricably with the emergent institutional fabric of party politics. Whatever sins and errors might be justly charged to Calhoun's account by contemporaries or later commentators, an expedient pragmatism was not one of them. This was, in fact, one of the chief sources of his appeal to that outnumbered but not insignificant body of citizens who struggled during 1843 to secure for him a Presidential nomination from the Democratic party (an entity which Calhoun to the end of his days archaically referred to by an older label, "the Republicans"). To avow that Calhoun's public life was not characterized by short-term pragmatism is not necessarily to deny that he possessed and exercised at times the arts of a politician.

The course of the campaign of 1843–1844 gave Calhoun ample opportunity to criticize the emergent style in his correspondence and in public papers, some of them anonymous and not much noticed by later scholars—public papers which, like most of Calhoun's productions, were tactical in their occasions but not without a degree of enduring philosophical pertinence.[2] This critique was capsulized to

---

[1] From Fitzwilliam Byrdsall, June 6, 1847, John C. Calhoun Papers, Clemson University.

[2] See below in this volume the "Address" adopted by the South Carolina Democratic Convention, partly drafted by Calhoun, May 24, 1843; the letter to William Smith, July 3, 1843; the letter to William M. Corry and others, July 9, 1843; the essay by "Pendleton," August 12, 1843; the essays by "A Member of

a confidant as Calhoun was on the point of withdrawing his name from contention:

> If the people should ever become thoroughly acquainted with the principles of our Government, & fully competent for self Government, it will be by drawing into the Presidential canvass and fully discussing, all the great questions of the day. One of my strong objections to the caucus system is, that it stiffles [*sic*] such discussions, and gives the ascendency to intrigue & management over reason & principles.[3]

To a friend who had reported trickery in his State in the management of proceedings that were supposed to represent the will of the people, Calhoun wrote: "I fear the day for sagacious and patriotic statesmen has passed, and that the country is doomed to be the victim of juggling politicians."[4]

Calhoun would have been less than human had there been no element of personal frustration and disappointment in his revulsion from "juggling politicians." But his disdain for them and his efforts to provide a more inspiring alternative were long-standing—indeed can be said to have marked his whole career, as when he took pains to distance himself from part of his party's program while he was a Republican leader during the War of 1812 period and when he disagreed with both parties on the currency during the 1830's.[5] He had vigorously exposed the evasiveness and demagoguery of the Whig campaign of 1840. His distaste on similar grounds for Martin Van Buren (who seemed during 1843 to be the likely vanquisher of the efforts of Calhoun's friends to secure his Presidential nomination) was well known. Wright's mentor, Van Buren was as perfect an ex-

the Convention," August 16 and September 13, 1843; and Calhoun's address to his friends and supporters, December 21, 1843 (first draft) and January 29, 1844 (published version). Similar attitudes are amply reflected in correspondence and in documents by others as well. Tantalizingly, what may have been the most important of Calhoun's essays at this period has been lost. It is known (Calhoun to Virgil Maxcy, February 12, 1844, herein) that Calhoun drafted an "Address to the Republican party" in early 1844, which he wished to have published anonymously, and sent it to Virgil Maxcy a few weeks before Maxcy's death. Extensive searches have uncovered no trace of this document in either manuscript or published form.

[3] To Robert M.T. Hunter, October 24, 1843, herein. Among many other similar statements herein, see the letter to Orestes A. Brownson, February 1, 1844.

[4] To Colin M. Ingersoll, November 11, 1843, herein.

[5] Argued in Clyde N. Wilson, "John Caldwell Calhoun," in Joel Myerson, ed., *Antebellum Writers in New York and the South* (Vol. III of *Dictionary of Literary Biography*. Detroit: Gale Research Co., 1979), pp. 44–55.

ample of the pragmatic approach as could be found, though he was far from the only one on the scene, whether one looked North or South, among Democrats or Whigs.

While the pragmatic style was relatively less trenchant in the South, it was by no means absent. Calhoun did not differ from other Southern leaders so much in the intensity of his allegiance to the interests and institutions of the section, as he did in the candor and foresight which he displayed in dealing with threats to those interests. That is, if defending the regime of the South was evil, Calhoun took the lead not because he was more evil but because he was more of a statesman. In 1843, Calhoun was the candidate of a non-pragmatic minority of Southerners only. Even so, there was evidence that his popular base was growing, and that public sentiment was moving in his direction.

In Lexington District, South Carolina, an area not noted for its fire-eaters and large plantations, a visiting politician, seeking guidance on addressing the people, was given advice on public sentiment that unconsciously paraphrased the Calhoun campaign motto, which was "Free Trade, Low Duties, No Debt, Separation from Banks, Economy, Retrenchment, Strict Adherence to the Constitution." The local adviser added: "Our people like to hear Calhoun praised very highly."[6] And a Mississippi Senator approved of his successor's endorsement of Calhoun with the remark that "those who have been leading the party for the last few years, have certainly lost caste with the people. A new order of things is about to commence, and men are hereafter to be selected for their moral worth and their political consistency."[7]

The conventionality and caution of mainstream politics explains why historians seeking to understand particular periods have turned again and again to insurgent movements which, though representing minorities, give glimpses of intense and meaningful tendencies that lie beneath the great bland barrier of party regularity. The effort carried on from various quarters on behalf of Calhoun's nomination was such an insurgent movement. In few places outside his own State did his supporters constitute more than a minority of Democrats, but they were in many places not insignificant in numbers, talents, and intensity of feelings.

A gradually stiffening defense of Southern interests and substantial positions on such issues as the tariff and banking cannot be dis-

[6] Lemuel Boozer to Armistead Burt, January 2, 1843, Armistead Burt Papers, Duke University.

[7] Thomas H. Williams to Jesse Speight, October 16, 1843, Thomas H. Williams Collection, Chicago Historical Society.

counted in assessing the sources of Calhoun's support. But in this volume and elsewhere in the sources of the period is abundant evidence that the strongest element in such popularity as Calhoun had among Americans was his rejection of the pragmatic style, his symbolization of an earlier order. This conclusion can hardly be avoided unless we refuse to take the citizens of the 1840's at their word and assume that the sentiments they expressed were merely cynical or self-deceptive codes for some other ideas. The evidence is perhaps more persuasive among Calhoun's Northern "friends" than in the South. A New Yorker who found in Calhoun his ideal, juxtaposed him with other existing leaders: "A system of national Corruption introduced by van Buren and his adherents now pervades the whole country, and which enables a man to raise himself, to an exalted station, without ability, integrity[,] wisdom or virtue."[8]

The positive side of the same feeling was put by Orestes A. Brownson of Boston, who avowed his allegiance to Calhoun with youthful enthusiasm:

> In these days of venality and corruption, of selfishness and plunder, when patriotism is scouted, and civic virtue scarcely thought of, it is some consolation to find one, even in the ranks of the highest, who can be moved by more generous impulses than love of popularity, and follow the lead of a loftier ambition than the mere selfish possession of place and power. His example is full of moral grandeur, and with superb majesty rebukes the whole herd of selfish and intriguing aspirants.[9]

These were not eccentric, but rather typical statements of the period. The manner in which Calhoun's confidant, Robert M.T. Hunter of Virginia, retrospectively summarized the situation of 1843 is fully borne out by the documents:

> That Mr. Calhoun made little way in the canvass for the nomination is not surprising. But when we consider the number from the South who notwithstand[ing] the inducement of interest to sustain and support him actually opposed and disliked him, it is marvellous to find so many in all sections of the union admiring and sustaining him. In the city of New York itself his party was by no means small. This consisted for the most part of young men and of those of advanced views in politics who were generally independent in thought and action.

[8] From Robert R. Hunter, August 21, 1843, herein.
[9] *Brownson's Quarterly Review*, vol. I, no. 1 (January, 1844), p. 127. Brownson's involvement in behalf of Calhoun appears in a number of documents below. See also Joseph F. Gower and Richard M. Leliaert, eds., *The Brownson-Hecker Correspondence* (Notre Dame, Ind.: University of Notre Dame Press, 1979).

In New England too his friends though not so numerous as in the city of New York were neither few nor undistinguished. His friends there were chiefly to be found amongst the believers in free trade, states rights and the Democratic principles of reform in the country. Not the men who entertained these views merely as a scholastic, but in whom they constituted a real and a living faith.[10]

Calhoun's appeal to idealistic and reforming young Northerners such as Brownson in Boston, Francis Wharton in Philadelphia, and Fitzwilliam Byrdsall and many others in New York City (described by one cynical editor as "an association of philosophers and politicians")[11] merits more attention and explanation than it has received. One of the few historians who has dealt with it explicitly is Arthur M. Schlesinger, Jr., in *The Age of Jackson*. Schlesinger's description of the phenomenon is interesting as far as it goes, but his interpretive scheme requires that the phenomenon be minimized, perhaps more than is justified, as a temporary anomaly. Many of the young reformers remained Calhoun admirers long after the campaign of 1843, when quite different and more explosive issues dominated the scene. Contrary to Schlesinger, whose Jeffersonianism evolves to the Free Soil movement, it could be argued that it was Calhoun who most appealed to those reformers whose guiding ideals looked back to classical Jeffersonian republicanism. As a class they did not disappear in the North, but would steadily lose ground to reformers drawn from quite different social and ideological roots, who expressed an emergent nineteenth-century vision combining moral regulation and material progress. Put another way, those reform impulses that ended in the Free Soil movement and the Republican party of the late antebellum era reflected less the Jeffersonian dispensation than the contrary thrust of the moralistic Whig progressives that one Calhoun ally referred to derogatorily as the *"Decensy and all the virtue party."*[12]

The Calhoun campaign effort is abundantly documented herein—especially in regard to its personnel, position papers, private and public sentiments of the candidate as well as his supporters and opponents, its overt actions and subtler nuances, and its literary, journalistic, and organizational aspects. So rich are the materials that one

[10] Hunter's ms. memoir of Calhoun, pp. 245–246, Robert M.T. Hunter Papers, Virginia State Library.

[11] New York, N.Y., *Herald*, October 27, 1843, p. 2.

[12] Francis W. Pickens to George McDuffie, March 12, 1842, Francis Wilkinson Pickens Papers, South Caroliniana Library, University of South Carolina. For the discussion by Schlesinger, see *The Age of Jackson* (Boston: Little, Brown and Co., c. 1945), especially pp. 406–410.

hesitates to quote or cite a few documents and incidents for fear of detracting attention from many others equally interesting. The chapter introductions preceding each section of documents are designed to give a coherent narrative of the chief features of the campaign and of its course. The remarks which follow immediately below do not comprise a comprehensive history but can only give a suggestive outline of some aspects of an event which reveals much about the times and the political and social and intellectual terrain—about how Americans, or at least some of them, felt, and how they went about expressing their values and preferences in the public arena in a day of expanding democratic participation and progressive institutionalization of the two-party system.

Literary Efforts

Among campaign literature generated in Calhoun's behalf, the most significant items were two volumes published in 1843 by the leading American publisher, Harper and Brothers of New York City and which remain important in the canon of Calhoun documents. These were an anonymous *Life of John C. Calhoun*, in a pamphlet of over 70 pages, and an edition of *Speeches of John C. Calhoun*, prepared largely by the South Carolinian himself, in a substantial book of 554 pages. Many documents in this volume and the preceding volume of *The Papers of John C. Calhoun* relate to the preparation, publication, dissemination, description, and reception of these works.[13]

The New York *Herald* reported on March 11, 1843, that Harpers had that day published "a pamphlet, 'got up' in their usual neat style, with large type, and a beautiful portrait on steel," on the life of Calhoun, which could be purchased at the newspaper office for a shilling (12½ cents). Commented the *Herald* the next day: "The period of issuing this book is seasonable, and will give it a rapid sale." The work was available at Head's bookstore on East Bay in Charleston by March 23, on which day 400 copies were reported sold, many of them to ladies.[14] It was available in New Orleans by April 1, and doubtless

[13] Consult these titles in the indexes to *The Papers of John C. Calhoun*, vols. XVI and XVII. An interesting addendum to the information provided by the documents, to be approached with caution of course, is Joseph A. Scoville's autobiographical fiction, *Vigor. A Novel* (New York: Carleton, Publisher, 1864), written under the pseudonym of "Walter Barrett, Clerk." On p. 366 is a circumstantial account of the arrangements for publication of Calhoun's *Life* and *Speeches* in New York City.

[14] Charleston, S.C., *Mercury*, March 24, 1843, p. 2, and March 25, 1843, p. 2.

in other cities.[15]   As a literary production the *Life* was successful.   It was concisely and astutely written and relates the events of Calhoun's public life persuasively, presenting a high view of his talents, ethics, courage, disinterestedness, and adherence to the principles of the Republican party.[16]

The *Speeches of John C. Calhoun* was published in June.   It was available in Charleston by June 29 (though in only a small consignment), where it was greeted with the editorial comment that "it would be difficult to make up a volume better deserving the deep and thoughtful study of every political reader."[17]   It appears impossible to make any certain estimates about the readership of the *Life* and *Speeches*, though for both the success of distribution fell far behind the quality of content.   The best scrap of evidence available indicates a "circulation" of 18,000 copies of the *Life* by the publisher,[18] though all those copies were not necessarily sold or otherwise placed in the hands of individuals.   The circulation of the weighty volume of *Speeches* was doubtless smaller.

As indicated by documents herein, the *Speeches* provoked a controversy over whether its selection of contents deliberately slighted Calhoun's early "nationalist" policies.   The *Life* too was controversial, but it was over sixty years before it provoked a continuing contention among historians in regard to the identity of its author or authors. The editor's judgment on this difficult and controversial problem appears below in the chapter introduction which precedes the text of the *Life*.   The judgment essentially follows that of Charles M. Wiltse[19] and of James L. Anderson and W. Edwin Hemphill, who ably surveyed the literature of the controversy and analyzed the most perti-

[15] New Orleans, La., *Daily Picayune*, April 1, 1843, p. 2.

[16] For considered and sympathetic review-essays by contemporaries of the *Life of John C. Calhoun*, the *Speeches of John C. Calhoun*, or both, see [Orestes A. Brownson,] "Life and Speeches of John C. Calhoun," in *Brownson's Quarterly Review*, vol. I, no. 1 (January, 1844), pp. 105–131, reprinted in Henry F. Brownson, ed., *Works of Orestes A. Brownson* (20 vols. Detroit: T. Nourse, 1882–1887), 15:451–472; [Francis Wharton,] "Mr. Calhoun's Parliamentary Eloquence," in *United States Magazine and Democratic Review*, vol. XIV, no. 68 (February, 1844), pp. 111–130; and the following articles in *Southern Quarterly Review*: vol. III, no. 6 (April, 1843), pp. 496–531; vol. V, no. 10 (April, 1844), pp. 361–391; vol. VI, no. 11 (July, 1844), pp. 95–129; and vol. IX, no. 17 (January, 1846), pp. 204–236.   The writers of the *Southern Quarterly Review* articles have not been identified except for the last, who was Muscoe R.H. Garnett.

[17] Charleston, S.C., *Mercury*, June 29, 1843, p. 2.

[18] Harper & Brothers to Virgil Maxcy, June 13, 1843, herein.

[19] Charles M. Wiltse, *John C. Calhoun* (3 vols. Indianapolis: The Bobbs-Merrill Co., Inc., c. 1944, 1949, 1951), 1:401–402 and 3:110–112, 500.

nent sources for resolving it.[20]   The *Life* has been included in *The Papers of John C. Calhoun* not because it was, as some have contended, Calhoun's clandestine composition, but because it contains much information probably originating with Calhoun for which there are no earlier and better sources, and because nowhere else are Calhoun's views of his career and the course of American history reflected and developed in such considered, extended, and systematic form.

In addition to the *Life* and the *Speeches* and innumerable newspaper and magazine articles, Calhoun's campaign produced three other distinct works of a personal bearing, all of them pamphlets published by his New York City enthusiasts.   Early in 1843 appeared *John C. Calhoun, in His Personal, Moral and Intellectual Traits of Character.* This complimentary work was written from what later generations would refer to as a human-interest point of view.   Its author has not been identified, although it was issued from Parke Godwin's press in New York City and had first appeared in his newspaper.[21]

Late in the year 1843, unfortunately not long before Calhoun withdrew from the campaign, New Yorkers got out two more rather effective works.[22]   *Life and Character of the Hon. John C. Calhoun, with Illustrations* was aimed at a less sophisticated audience than the Harpers' biography.   Its text was adorned with somewhat crude and fanciful woodcuts, and emphasis was laid on the fact that Calhoun was the only Presidential candidate of that time whose family had taken a direct and creditable part in the Revolutionary War.   This was

[20] See James L. Anderson and W. Edwin Hemphill, "The 1843 Biography of John C. Calhoun: Was R.M.T. Hunter Its Author?" in *Journal of Southern History*, vol. XXXVIII, no. 3 (August, 1972), pp. 469–474.   Many manuscript sources that bear at least marginally on the question appear in the volume in hand and in the preceding volume of the Calhoun series.   One contemporary source not cited by Wiltse or by Anderson and Hemphill, which carries some slight weight, is the plain statement of Hunter's authorship, almost in passing, in the New York, N.Y., *Plebeian*.   This is the only contemporary *public* statement on the authorship that has been found, and persons involved with the *Plebeian* were undoubtedly close to Calhoun's more knowledgeable allies in New York. (*Plebeian* of unknown date, reprinted in the Mobile, Ala., *Register and Journal*, March 23, 1843, p. 2.)

[21] Fully cited and abstracted in *The Papers of John C. Calhoun*, 16:585.   The Saco, Me., *Maine Democrat* responded favorably to this work and to Calhoun with a long review-essay headed "Republican Simplicity."   (Reprinted in the Boston, Mass., *Post*, August 4, 1843, p. 1.)

[22] Complete citations and fuller descriptions of these two works appear below in this volume at the end of November, 1843, and some scattered documentary evidence about their preparation and fate can be found by consulting the titles in the index.

made clear by its subtitle: *Containing Notices of His Father and Uncles, and Their Brave Conduct During Our Struggle for Independence in the American Revolutionary War.* At about the same time appeared *The Calhoun Text Book,* a fairly ably put together collection of favorable comments from the nation's press on Calhoun's principles and prospects. The title pages of both of these works indicated that they aspired to be distributed in many cities, though to what degree this was achieved has not been discovered.

Possibly worth mentioning among Calhoun campaign literature are three other slight publications, all of them anonymous and even more ephemeral than those earlier mentioned because they were tactical pieces designed to influence delegates to conventions. The earliest of these was *An Appeal to the Democratic Party, on the Principles of a National Convention for the Nomination of President and Vice President of the United States,*[23] which was written by Robert Barnwell Rhett. This was followed by *The Compromises of the Constitution Considered in the Organization of a National Convention,* written by Rhett, and *Democratic National Convention,* written by Virgil Maxcy. Documents in this volume describe the preparation of the latter two publications and the use to which they were put by Calhoun supporters.[24] Generally speaking, the success of the literary efforts that accompanied Calhoun's campaign resembled the campaign itself—that is, they were failures or very limited successes which did not achieve their purpose or potential. To examine closely the differences in tone, approach, and intended effect between these publications and those that had been produced for Calhoun's first Presidential effort twenty years earlier could provide interesting suggestions about changes the two decades had wrought in the American public mind.[25]

[23] Cited and abstracted in *The Papers of John C. Calhoun,* 16:584–585.

[24] Consult the titles in the index.

[25] The earlier publications were: 1) *Measures, Not Men. Illustrated by Some Remarks upon the Public Conduct and Character of John C. Calhoun* (New York: Printed by E.B. Clayton, 1823), by "A Citizen of New York" who is usually identified as Joseph G. Swift, though the pamphlet is largely a revision of newspaper articles attributed to George M. Dallas which had appeared in the Philadelphia, Pa., *Franklin Gazette,* March 14 and 28, April 11, May 16, 22, and 30, June 11 and 27, and July 11, 1822. 2) *An Address to the Citizens of North-Carolina, on the Subject of the Presidential Election,* which appeared in two undated versions, one with no publisher indicated and the other printed by Bell & Lawrence of Raleigh. This essay was signed by "Carolina," whose identity is not established, though George McDuffie is the most likely author. 3) *Presidential Election* [Richmond?, 1823?], which was a collection of essays originally contributed to

Journalistic Efforts

Antebellum newspapers, broadly speaking, conveyed the substance of public events objectively, but they made no pretense of nonpartisanship. Most were to some degree or other party organs, and as the chief regular means of mass communication were indispensable links in the political process. Calhoun had support among some established presses, and others were started in the flush of his candidacy. Some newspapers boldly proclaimed "Calhoun" from their mastheads, like the Charleston *Mercury*, the Milledgeville *Federal Union* in the capital city of Georgia, and the Mobile *Alabama Tribune*. Others, like Charles G. Greene's Boston *Post*, were sympathetic, without a direct commitment.

The *Mercury*, a Rhett family enterprise, was an ably edited journal of national influence. During most of 1843 it was directed by Albert Rhett, younger brother of Robert Barnwell Rhett, until his sudden and untimely death.[26] The *Mercury* was in some respects an ideal campaign organ—it was financially sound and it spoke with eloquence, authority, and discretion. Thus it could provide useful leadership for other sympathetic papers, though its reputation as the voice of the most determined South Carolina State rights men limited its influence.

Efforts to achieve equal effectiveness in Virginia, Washington, and New York City met limited success. In Washington the Democratic regulars spoke to the people through *The Globe*, the Whigs through the *Daily National Intelligencer*, and the Tyler administration through the *Madisonian*. Calhoun's friends, with money from Charleston, adopted the Washington *Spectator*, published by John Heart, which had first appeared in June 1842. In March 1843 it proclaimed itself dedicated to the advancement of John C. Calhoun. Ideally, such a paper would publish daily, with less frequent editions distributed nationwide. But the *Spectator* did not become a daily until Novem-

---

the Richmond, Va., *Enquirer*, from May through December, 1823, by "Thomson," "Roanoke," and "Wythe." This 64-page work included only a selection of the pro-Calhoun essays that appeared in the *Enquirer* during this time period. Others by "Pendleton," "Mason," and "Wythe," were not collected in the pamphlet. Winfield Scott wrote the "Wythe" and "Pendleton" essays. The other pseudonyms have not been identified. 4) *An Address to the People of Maryland* (No place, no date), with no author, but probably by Virgil Maxcy.

[26] See John Milton Clapp, "The Death of Albert Rhett," in William Gilmore Simms, ed., *The Charleston Book: A Miscellany in Prose and Verse* (Spartanburg, S.C.: Reprint Co., 1983), pp. 149–153.

ber, shortly before the candidate withdrew. In fact, as Hunter observed later, it was impossible for Calhoun's friends to sustain the financial burden.[27]

It proved impossible also to secure a first-rate full-time editor, all those who would have been adequate being already needed where they were. Robert Barnwell Rhett remained in Washington between sessions of Congress and wrote most of the editorials, assisted by the able Virgil Maxcy and by others.[28] The *Spectator* struggled on until October 1844 when it became the *Constitution*. In that guise it carried on until December 1845, prolonged its life a few weeks by a move to Baltimore, and expired.

From Virginia, still the State of greatest prestige for most "Republicans," Thomas Ritchie maintained a national influence for Democratic regularity through the Richmond *Enquirer*. Calhoun's friends established an insurgent force of real though limited effectiveness in the Petersburg *Republican*, edited by Washington Greenhow,[29] and with other smaller papers. These journalistic struggles within the party were carried on with restraint, at least where they were under the direct influence of the principals. Ritchie generally bent over backward not to seriously offend Calhoun's friends and to assure the public that there would be resounding unity behind the party's nominee when the national convention was over.[30] Calhoun's friends did not go so far as to pledge such acquiescence, but they did handle Van Buren gently. Both groups felt that they needed each other for the later and larger battle with the Whigs and Henry Clay.

In the fiercely competitive arena of New York City journalism a number of efforts were made, with even less success than elsewhere. William Lyon Mackenzie, the late Canadian rebel, established in the fall of 1843 a paper called the *Examiner* which was anti-Van Buren and reputed to be a Calhoun organ.[31] But it closed quickly and never became an explicit ally of the South Carolinian. As is documented in the text of this volume, serious efforts were made to establish a New York City paper called the *Gazette* to speak for the Calhoun Democrats of the city, but despite some capital and talent this paper did not

[27] Hunter's ms. memoir of Calhoun, pp. 243–244.
[28] *Ibid.*
[29] Robert Greenhow was chief translator and librarian in the U.S. Department of State for some years. He was of the same family but not the same man as the editor of the Petersburg *Republican*, as has been erroneously stated in several secondary sources. Both Greenhows were acquainted with Calhoun.
[30] See especially the Richmond, Va., *Enquirer*, February 3, 1844.
[31] New York, N.Y., *Evening Post*, October 2, 1843, p. 2.

survive long.[32] After its disappearance, Duff Green returned from Europe with financial backing from a wealthy Philadelphian he had met there and established in New York the *Republic*.[33] This paper continued to flourish for a time and to promote the idea of a Calhoun nomination outside of the Democratic national convention, but it too floundered after awhile.

Among other papers that supported Calhoun forthrightly an incomplete and somewhat random list that comes readily to hand from the documents and press of the day is perhaps suggestive. It includes: the Warrenton, Va., *Flag of '98*; the Jackson, Miss., *Southern Reformer*; the Lafayette, La., *Signal*; the St. Clairsville, Ohio, *Gazette*; the Mount Clemens, Mich., *Patriot*; the Grand Rapids, Mich., *Enquirer*; the Portsmouth, N.H., *Gazette*; the Brooklyn, Conn., *Pennant*; the New Haven, Conn., *Republic*; and the Cumberland, Md., *Gazette*. At least occasionally sympathetic were the New York *Journal of Commerce* and the Alexandria, D.C., *Gazette*.

Organizational Efforts

The careful student will find herein in the letters and other documents of Calhoun's supporters a wealth of information pertaining to the nuts and bolts of political activity: the organization and activities of campaign committees, the working of conventions and other public meetings, fund-raising, the management of newspapers, and many other matters, including the value judgments of some Americans on such proceedings. It was the question of the working of political conventions and their relation or lack thereof to the will of the people that elicited the public papers by Calhoun mentioned above, as well as many other reactions. The documentation herein relates to most of the then States of the Union to some degree, but is most abundant in regard to the campaign activities carried on from Washington, Charleston, and New York City, and in Virginia and New England.

The young New Yorker Joseph A. Scoville attempted to conduct a central campaign committee from Washington during the early months of 1843. This effort proved abortive, but its surviving correspondence, which eventually found its way into Calhoun's papers at Clemson University, has been included herein. Thereafter, the center of effort shifted to a committee appointed by the South Carolina Democratic State Convention, which operated out of Charleston.

[32] Consult the newspaper's name in the index and see also the New York, N.Y., *Herald*, October 27, 1843, p. 2, and December 13, 1843, p. 2.

[33] Again, consult the index of this volume.

The key figure in this group was Franklin H. Elmore, former Representative from South Carolina and long-time president of the Bank of the State of South Carolina. The South Carolinian Benjamin F. Perry, who was not an admirer of Calhoun, wrote many years later that Elmore "was one of the most adroit managing public men. His talents were of a high order, and his power of controlling others unsurpassed. . . . He was a devoted follower of Mr. Calhoun, and yet had great influence over him."[34] The more important papers generated by the Charleston group are also found herein. Elmore's sister had married Dixon H. Lewis, a South Carolina native and an influence for Calhoun in Alabama. Elmore and Lewis, along with Robert Barnwell Rhett, Robert M.T. Hunter, and Virgil Maxcy, can be said to be Calhoun's chief lieutenants. Both Rhett and Maxcy worked in Washington and travelled in the North on Calhoun's behalf.

Calhoun's zealous New Yorkers have already been mentioned, and their activities are perhaps better documented herein than those of Calhoun's allies in any other State. Calhoun evoked also a perhaps surprising degree of support in New England. His "friends" probably did not achieve a majority among the Democrats in any State of the region, but they were not insignificant. There was a knot of supporters in Connecticut where the South Carolinian had numerous personal ties. There was some interest in New Hampshire and Maine, which seems to have centered around those who hoped to see Senator Levi Woodbury of New Hampshire receive a Vice-Presidential nomination. Woodbury's exact role in Calhoun's campaign is unclear, at least so far as the documents herein reveal.

In Massachusetts Calhoun was the favorite of a group of original Jackson Democrats who had refused to swallow Van Buren as well as certain young reformers. The former centered around Charles G. Greene's Boston *Post* and around David Henshaw, appointed Secretary of the Navy by President Tyler. Here, as elsewhere, Calhoun was inextricably and perhaps counter-productively tied up with the ill-fated administration. Among other Massachusetts Calhounites were the South Carolinian's old classmate Lemuel Williams, appointed by Tyler Collector of the Port of Boston, Daniel D. Brodhead, and the reformers Orestes A. Brownson and Benjamin F. Hallett.[35]

[34] Benjamin F. Perry, *The Writings of Benjamin F. Perry* (3 vols. Spartanburg, S.C.: Reprint Co., 1980), 2:223–224.

[35] The intricacies of factional Democratic politics in Massachusetts are described by Arthur B. Darling, *Political Changes in Massachusetts, 1824–1848. A Study of Liberal Movements in Politics* (New Haven: Yale University Press, 1925), pp. 284, 301, 303–306, 321–325, 330–331, 341, 343.

The campaign apparently was aided in New England by Edmund T. Bridge who, as an agent of the Post Office Department, was able to travel freely. This is one of the few examples of spoilsmanship in Calhoun's behalf that emerges clearly from the documents.

The Campaign in Perspective

It would be wrong to conceive of the campaign to secure for Calhoun the Presidential nomination of the Democratic party as centralized and managed in the manner of a twentieth-century campaign. Calhoun was, of course, interested in activities carried on in his name in the public arena, and those who carried them on could hardly do so without his consent and were obligated to defer to his suggestions. However, to Calhoun it was not his campaign, it was theirs. "I look on calmly," he wrote an old friend. "Personally, I care but little about the result. I have neither pride nor ambition to gratify."[36]

This was more than a hypocritical pose. If a ceremonial bow to the republican prejudice against Ambition was necessary for candidates, Calhoun did not maneuver behind the requirements of that convention; rather he defended the prejudice with an eloquence that suggests conviction and the desire to set an example that would help to preserve it. To a group of Cincinnati citizens whose invitation to visit their city he felt compelled to refuse, Calhoun wrote:

> There are then in my opinion, strong considerations, both of propriety and expediency, why the office of President of the United States should not be sought by personal canvass or the usual modes of electioneering. . . . the office, it seems to me, is too high and its duties too responsible to be the object of personal solicitation. Who, with the proper spirit, can contemplate the task of discharging its high duties without being inspired with a diffidence and awe . . . ? When I look at the country as it now is, and compare it with what it was when I first entered the councils of the Union, as it relates to . . . all the elements of greatness—and then look forward to what it will be when those who are now entering on the stage shall retire, provided our liberty, institutions, and union shall be preserved—and then reflect on the great and decisive influence which the powers vested in the President must have, in that respect, for good or evil, as they may be properly or improperly exercised, to me it seems to be the highest and most responsible office in the world—far too much so to be the object of personal solicitation, or sought by a personal canvass, or ever to be accepted on any other ground than that of duty.[37]

[36] To Micah Sterling, July 8, 1843, herein.
[37] To William M. Corry and others, July 9, 1843, herein.

Calhoun simply attempted, as far as the times allowed, to live up to the famous maxim of his long dead friend William Lowndes—the Presidency was neither to be pursued nor refused.

The campaign so elaborately documented herein was carried on over the course of the year 1843 by Calhoun's friends chiefly on an organizational issue—they needed to break what would in later times be called the "unit rule" in order that they could secure at least some national delegates from the many States in which they had strong but not majority support. After defeat on this issue in several key States Calhoun made up his mind to withdraw, a decision which can be traced through the papers of late 1843 and early 1844. The decision was prolonged because, in keeping with his attitude that the campaign was his supporters' and not his, he involved those supporters in the timing and terms with which the decision would be presented to the public.

Calhoun told his son: "I have written to my friends in Congress, that I cannot permit my name to go before the Convention, as it must now be constituted, and that I deem it my duty to inform them of the fact, in order, that they may take it into the estimate in making up their decision on the proper course to be pursued."[38] The dispersed authority of a republic and the individualistic pride of its citizens required this courtesy, as did his own position as a public man ethically obligated to justify his course of action. Calhoun did not consider that he was removing himself from a contest, for he had never entered himself into any contest. Rather, he owed it to the public to make clear that he could not allow his name to be associated with the Democratic national convention, for reasons which he also made clear.

Possibly the best-informed and most plausible analysis of Calhoun's last serious effort to secure a Presidential nomination was made three decades or so after the fact by Robert M.T. Hunter. Hunter had been deeply involved in the failed effort of Calhoun's friends to secure him the nomination. When he set down his recollections, Hunter had behind him the experience of the 1850's, Civil War, and Reconstruction, in which he had played a fairly prominent role, and he had had ample time for reflection on the events he referred to:

> Whether Mr. Calhoun ever regarded himself as having any real chance for the presidency I did not then & I do not now know. But then and now I have supposed that he did not really believe that he had any such chance. But Mr. Calhoun had a theory that no man could perform a first rate part in Federal politics or in the arena of

[38] To Andrew Pickens Calhoun, December 5, 1843, herein.

Washington if no one supposed that he was available then or could be so hereafter as a candidate for the presidency. He would therefore exert himself to keep what apparent claims or chances he might have for the presidency whether he really hoped for it or not. To keep up and increase if possible his power of usefulness was always a first rate object with him which in his eyes would have justified any exertion.[39]

Most of Calhoun's "friends" approved of his decision to withdraw—it confirmed the things they liked about him—though they were divided over what to do next, as Calhoun's correspondence and the press of the day make clear. If, indeed, as Hunter plausibly suggested, Calhoun did not really expect to become President or even to receive a nomination in 1844—that is, if the campaign were a demonstration rather than a real hope—it nevertheless did not lack meaning for those who participated in it nor does it lack instruction for historians. And, if indeed Hunter was right that Calhoun's real intent was to maintain influence over policy, then surely the judgment, almost conventional among some of his contemporaries and some historians, that Calhoun was obsessed by a devious pursuit of the Presidency, is rather far off the mark.

On his withdrawal, Calhoun vigorously criticized the course that the Democracy was taking, both in public and privately, ignoring advice to keep harmony for a later day. His condemnations were not muted—the developing party machinery was unconstitutional in spirit and a threat to the South and the small States; party leaders, especially those identified with the likely nominee Van Buren, were waffling dangerously and deceitfully on the tariff, abolition, and Texas. He scorned hinted proffers of a Vice-Presidential nomination. He discouraged the effort of Duff Green to promote a national convention in Philadelphia on July 4, 1844, which would secure Calhoun an independent nomination. Calhoun, in sum, behaved like a man who had a greater ambition to influence events and preserve a reputation for high-mindedness than he did to secure an office.

And it would seem that Calhoun's calculation was correct, that his withdrawal enhanced his stature in many quarters. For he was very soon called to what at the moment was the most important office in the Union after the Presidency—that of Secretary of State. The possibility of his nomination to that post by Tyler had been vented in the press repeatedly. As early as the spring of 1842 the colorful Dixon H. Lewis had discounted a rumor that Calhoun might go into Tyler's

[39] Hunter's ms. memoir of Calhoun, p. 244.

cabinet with the remark: "It is as hard for the *minor* to swallow the *major*, in the moral political & intellectual, as in the natural world."[40]

When the State Department became vacant in mid-1843, an overture was made to Calhoun, perhaps not for the first time, and was turned down.[41] The Virginian Abel P. Upshur, who undertook the office, called on Calhoun for advice quietly but repeatedly, and there is no doubt that Calhoun was well informed about the state of foreign relations and the administration's plans, including its initiative toward a treaty of annexation with the Texas Republic that was already under way in 1843. Then, on February 28, 1844, during a festive cruise of Washington notables on the Potomac on board a U.S. warship, a large gun exploded during a demonstration, killing Secretary Upshur and a number of others, including Virgil Maxcy who had been Calhoun's most intimate and trusted personal friend for over thirty years. It so happened, the South Carolina statesman's second son was also present at the disaster and left an eyewitness account.[42]

President Tyler wanted Calhoun for the office that had now so unexpectedly become vacant once more—he was all the more attractive in that he was no longer entangled in the Presidential issue. Tyler took steps to sound Calhoun out through George McDuffie. Calhoun's reply to the overture expressed great reluctance to take on such duties at his age.[43] But before the reply was received in Washington, Tyler had sent the South Carolinian's name to the Senate where it had been unanimously approved the same day, thus putting the appointment on a basis he knew Calhoun would not refuse—that of duty.

It seems that large segments of American opinion approved of the appointment, as is indicated by the correspondence herein and the press of the day. *Niles' National Register*, a Whiggish journal never overly enthusiastic about Calhoun, remarked: "This appointment, we have no doubt, will meet the cordial approbation of the country." In later issues of the *Register* this opinion was supported by the quotation of three and a half columns of sentiments to the same effect from other journals.[44]

There were a great many citizens who felt that Calhoun would see to the settlement of the Oregon question with Great Britain calmly

[40] Dixon H. Lewis to Joseph A. Scoville, April 27, 1842, Dixon Hall Lewis Papers, University of Texas.

[41] From Charles A. Wickliffe, June 20, 1843, herein.

[42] From 2nd Lt. Patrick Calhoun, February 28, 1844, herein.

[43] To George McDuffie, March 9, 1844, herein.

[44] *Niles' National Register*, vol. LXVI, no. 2 (March 9, 1844), p. 18; no. 4 (March 23, 1844), pp. 49–50; no. 5 (March 30, 1844), p. 60.

and wisely. There were many, also, for whom the need to fix Texas to the Union, for the security of both, was an urgent question. In 1844 they felt, as it was later to be put sardonically by Richard K. Crallé (who was to join Calhoun at the State Department as his Chief Clerk) that the two leading and opposing Presidential candidates Van Buren and Clay "very naturally decided that it was better that Texas should be lost to the country, at least for the present, than that the important contest pending between them should be disturbed by any new issue."[45] It followed that the matter must be settled before a new administration came in, and many believed Calhoun would give Tyler the added strength and skill needed to accomplish the job.

In the light of later history, it can easily be argued that the appointment of Calhoun as Secretary of State was unfortunate for all concerned. But at the moment many considered him a superb choice—precisely because the Union's foreign relations were at their most critical juncture since the War of 1812. It was just such a situation in which tradition called for high and far-seeing republican statesmanship rather than cautious and routine politics. So, in March 1844, reluctantly and without joy, and not for the first time in his long and eventful career, John C. Calhoun departed for the federal city to undertake new labors and political perils. He was now 62 and the times were changing rapidly.

[45] Comment by Crallé in his edition of *The Works of John C. Calhoun* (6 vols. Columbia, S.C.: printed by A.S. Johnston, 1851, and New York: D. Appleton & Co., 1853–1857), 5:319–320.

THE PAPERS

of

JOHN C. CALHOUN

Volume XVII

MARCH 1843

[][]

*In early March, 1843, Harper & Brothers of New York City published
an anonymous 74-page* Life of John C. Calhoun, Presenting a Condensed History of Political Events from 1811 to 1843. *In June, 1843,
the same publisher issued* Speeches of John C. Calhoun. Delivered in
the Congress of the United States from 1811 to the Present Time.
*Both of these works were, at least in the timing of their publication,
campaign literature. Many documents in this volume and the preceding volume of* The Papers of John C. Calhoun *relate to their preparation, publication, and dissemination.*

The Life *was widely available by the end of March in a pamphlet
priced at 12½ cents. It was also subsequently made available in book
form, bound together with the* Speeches *with a combined title page:*
Life of John C. Calhoun, Presenting a Condensed History of Political Events from 1811 to 1843. Together with a Selection from His
Speeches, Reports and Other Writings Subsequent to His Election as
Vice-President of the United States, Including His Leading Speech
on the Late War Delivered in 1811. *Both versions of the* Life *included
an engraving of Calhoun by A.L. Dick from Washington Blanchard's
miniature portrait.* (See *The Papers of John C. Calhoun, 12:frontis-
piece.*)

*Calhoun himself took the leading role in selecting and preparing
the materials for his* Speeches. *The authorship of the* Life *has been
the subject of controversy among later biographers and commentators,
some of whom have contended that it was an autobiography, ghost-
written by Calhoun. Calhoun, to the contrary, always referred to the*
Life *as having been written by Robert M.T. Hunter. Hunter himself,
in contemporary letters to his wife, took credit for half of the finished
book.* (See *The Papers of John C. Calhoun, 16:571–572, 585.*) *In fact,
the first chapter, part of the second chapter, and the last seven
paragraphs of the* Life *either closely paraphrase or adopt verbatim
material from a "Biographical Memoir of John Caldwell Calhoun"
written by Virgil Maxcy in 1830 and published in several newspapers
in 1831.* (See *The Papers of John C. Calhoun, 11:152.*) *If Hunter
adopted this extensive material and wrote half of the work himself,*

3

then very little, if any, could have been written by Calhoun. Probably, Hunter wrote the Life, *using previously published materials, enjoying the collaboration of other Calhoun intimates, and receiving, to an undetermined degree, Calhoun's supervision and approval.*

Thus, though not a clandestine autobiography, the Life *may fairly be described as an official biography incorporating some elements of a memoir by Calhoun. It contains some biographical details and accounts of circumstances for which there are no earlier or better sources. It constitutes, also, the best available account of Calhoun's career, to 1843, from Calhoun's own viewpoint, and is thus an important Calhoun document.*

[]

Life of John C. Calhoun, Presenting a Condensed History of Political Events from 1811 to 1843

CHAPTER I.

Including the Period from his Infancy until he entered Congress.

The object of the present memoir of JOHN CALDWELL CALHOUN is not to present a biography of the man, but to describe him as a statesman; to draw and to develop his character in that capacity, and to trace his eminent public services during a long career in one of the most eventful periods of human history. To dwell on a character like his, distinguished by every trait that should win esteem and command admiration, would be to the biographer a most attractive labour; but the pleasure of depicting a private life elevated by spotless purity and integrity, and a severe simplicity of tastes and habits, must be relinquished—except so far as occasional reference to his early history may become necessary—for the higher duty of portraying his intellectual features, and of explaining his motives and conduct as a public man. It is not our aim to commend him to public affection, or to enlist popular sympathy in his behalf, but rather to show to the world, not for his sake, but for its own instruction, the deep influence of this master-mind upon the great political events of his age. A fair and impartial review of the career of this eminent statesman in connexion with public affairs, is necessary to a thorough understanding of the course of our own government for nearly two thirds of its existence. Such a review, it is believed, would be no unacceptable offering at the present time. Throughout the whole period from 1811 up to the present time he has served the Union in the various capacities of Representative, Secretary of War, Vice-president, and Senator. He has taken a prominent and influential part in all the great questions which have arisen during that long interval; and, although he has asked a release from farther public service, it is not impossible that he may be destined to close his career as a statesman in another and a higher station. With faculties unclouded, with physical powers unimpaired, with a judgment matured by observation and experience, with an intrepidity untamed by the many trying vicissitudes of his extraordinary life, and with an activity whose energies are unabated by time, it is probable that the American people will not dispense with such services as he might render in the highest sphere open to American statesmen.

Mr. Calhoun is a native of South Carolina, and was born in Abbeville District on the 18th of March, 1782. His family is Irish on both sides. His father, Patrick Calhoun, was born in Donegal, in Ireland, but the family emigrated when Patrick was a child, first to Pennsylvania, where they remained some years, and then to the western part of Virginia, from whence they were driven by the Indians after Braddock's defeat. They removed finally to South Carolina in 1756, when Patrick settled on the place where the subject of this sketch was born, and which still continues in the family of his younger brother [Patrick Calhoun]. His mother, whose maiden name was [Martha] Caldwell, was born in Charlotte County, Virginia. They had five children, one daughter and four sons, of whom John was the youngest but one. He was called after his maternal uncle, Major John Caldwell, whom the Tories had murdered in cold blood, and in his own yard, after destroying his house by fire. If time permitted, it might be interesting here to trace the effect which the traditions of the stirring scenes of a pioneer's life might have had upon the mind and character of young Calhoun. His paternal and maternal family both being Whig, they were exposed not only to hostile Indian incursions, but also to Tory outrages. They maintained their foothold on the soil despite the conflicts of an almost constant border warfare, and adhered to their country amid the horrors of civil strife and in the face of foreign invaders. But they had need both of courage and constancy to bear them through the severe trials to which they were exposed. Of three maternal uncles able to bear arms, one perished as we have before described, another [James Caldwell] fell at the battle of Cowpens

5

with thirty sabre wounds, and a third [William Caldwell], taken prisoner by the English, was immured for nine months in the dungeons of St. Augustine. Nor was Patrick Calhoun, the father, indebted to anything less than a strong arm and a stout heart for his escape from the perils which surrounded him. Upon one occasion, with thirteen other whites, he maintained a desperate conflict for hours with the Cherokee Indians, until, overwhelmed by superior numbers, he was forced to retreat, leaving seven of his companions dead upon the field. Three days after, they returned to bury their dead, and found the bodies of twenty-three Indian warriors, who had perished in the same conflict. At another time, he was singled out by an Indian distinguished for his prowess as a chief and for his skill with the rifle. The Indian taking to a tree, Calhoun secured himself behind a log, from whence he drew the Indian's fire four times by holding his hat on a stick a little above his hiding-place. The Indian at length exhibited a portion of his person in an effort to ascertain the effect of his shot, when he received a ball from his enemy in the shoulder, which forced him to fly. But the hat exhibited the traces of four balls by which it had been perforated. The effect of this mode of life upon a mind naturally strong and inquisitive was to create a certain degree of contempt for the forms of civilized life, and for all that was merely conventional in society. He claimed all the rights which nature and reason seemed to establish, and he acknowledged no obligation which was not supported by the like sanctions. It was under this conviction that, upon one occasion, he and his neighbours went down within twenty-three miles of Charleston, armed with rifles, to exercise a right of suffrage which had been disputed: a contest which ended in electing him to the Legislature of the state, in which body he served for thirty years. Relying upon virtue, reason, and courage as all that constituted the true moral strength of man, he attached too little importance to mere information, and never feared to encounter an adversary who, in that respect, had the advantage over him: a confidence which many of the events of his life seemed to justify. Indeed, he once appeared as his own advocate in a case in Virginia, in which he recovered a tract of land in despite of the regularly-trained disputants who sought to embarrass and defeat him. He opposed the Federal Constitution,* because, as he said, it permitted other people than those of South Carolina to tax the people of South Carolina, and thus allowed taxation without representation, which was a violation of the fundamental principle of the Revolutionary struggle.

---

* Editor's note: Compare *The Papers of John C. Calhoun,* 1:xxiv.

6

We have heard his son say that among his earliest recollections was one of a conversation when he was nine years of age, in which his father maintained that government to be best which allowed the largest amount of individual liberty compatible with social order and tranquillity, and insisted that the improvements in political science would be found to consist in throwing off many of the restraints then imposed by law, and deemed necessary to an organized society. It may well be supposed that his son John was an attentive and eager auditor, and such lessons as these must doubtless have served to encourage that free spirit of inquiry, and that intrepid zeal for truth for which he has been since so much distinguished. The mode of thinking which was thus encouraged may, perhaps, have compensated in some degree the want of those early advantages which are generally deemed indispensable to great intellectual progress. Of these he had comparatively few. But this was compensated by those natural gifts which give great minds the mastery over difficulties which the timid regard as insuperable. Indeed, we have here another of those rare instances in which the hardiness of natural genius is seen to defy all obstacles, and develops its flower and matures its fruit under circumstances apparently the most unpropitious.

The section of the country in which his family resided was then newly settled, and in a rude frontier state. There was not an academy in all the upper part of the state, and none within fifty miles, except one at about that distance in Columbia county, Georgia, which was kept by his brother-in-law, Mr. Waddell [*sic*; Moses Waddel], a Presbyterian clergyman. There were but a few scattered schools in the whole of that region, and these were such as are usually found on the frontier, in which reading, writing, and arithmetic were imperfectly taught. At the age of thirteen he was placed under the charge of his brother-in-law to receive his education. Shortly after, his father died; this was followed by the death of his sister, Mrs. Waddell [*sic*; Catherine Calhoun Waddel], within a few weeks, and the academy was then discontinued, which suspended his education before it had fairly commenced. His brother-in-law, with whom he was still left, was absent the greater part of the time, attending to his clerical duties, and his pupil thus found himself on a secluded plantation, without any white companion during the greater portion of the time. A situation apparently so unfavourable to improvement turned out, in his case, to be the reverse. Fortunately for him, there was a small circulating library in the house, of which his brother-in-law was librarian, and, in the absence of all company and amusements, that attracted his attention. His taste, although undirected, led him to history, to the

7

neglect of novels and other lighter reading; and so deeply was he interested, that in a short time he read the whole of the small stock of historical works contained in the library, consisting of [Charles] Rollin's Ancient History, [William] Robertson's Charles V., his South America, and Voltaire's Charles XII. After despatching these, he turned with like eagerness to [Capt. James] Cook's Voyages (the large edition), a small volume of Essays by Brown [*sic*; Sir Thomas Browne], and [John] Locke on the Understanding, which he read as far as the chapter on Infinity. All this was the work of but fourteen weeks. So intense was his application that his eyes became seriously affected, his countenance pallid, and his frame emaciated. His mother, alarmed at the intelligence of his health, sent for him home, where exercise and amusement soon restored his strength, and he acquired a fondness for hunting, fishing, and other country sports. Four years passed away in these pursuits, and in attention to the business of the farm while his elder brothers were absent, to the entire neglect of his education. But the time was not lost. Exercise and rural sports invigorated his frame, while his labours on the farm gave him a taste for agriculture, which he has always retained, and in the pursuit of which he finds delightful occupation for his intervals of leisure from public duties.

About this time an incident occurred upon which turned his after life. His second brother, James, who had been placed at a counting-house in Charleston, returned to spend the summer of 1800 at home. John had determined to become a planter; but James, objecting to this, strongly urged him to acquire a good education, and pursue one of the learned professions. He replied that he was not averse to the course advised, but there were two difficulties in the way: one was to obtain the assent of his mother, without which he could not think of leaving her, and the other was the want of means. He said his property was small and his resolution fixed: he would far rather be a planter than a half-informed physician or lawyer. With this determination, he could not bring his mind to select either without ample preparation; but if the consent of their mother should be freely given, and he (James) thought he could so manage his property as to keep him in funds for seven years of study preparatory to entering his profession, he would leave home and commence his education the next week. His mother and brother agreeing to his conditions, he accordingly left home the next week for Dr. Waddell's, who had married again, and resumed his academy in Columbia county, Georgia. This was in June, 1800, in the beginning of his 19th year, at which time it may be said he commenced his education, his tuition having been previously very imperfect, and confined to reading, writing, and arithmetic in an ordinary country school. His progress here was so rapid that in two years he entered the junior class of Yale College, and graduated with distinction in 1804, just four years from the time he commenced his Latin grammar. He was highly esteemed by Dr. [Timothy] Dwight, then the president of the college, although they differed widely in politics, and at a time when political feelings were intensely bitter. The doctor was an ardent Federalist, and Mr. Calhoun was one of a very few, in a class of more than seventy, who had the firmness openly to avow and maintain the opinions of the Republican party, and, among others, that the people were the only legitimate source of political power. Dr. Dwight entertained a different opinion. In a recitation during the senior year, on the chapter on Politics in [William] Paley's Moral Philosophy, the doctor, with the intention of eliciting his opinion, propounded to Mr. Calhoun the question, as to the legitimate source of power. He did not decline an open and direct avowal of his opinion. A discussion ensued between them, which exhausted the time allotted for the recitation, and in which the pupil maintained his opinions with such vigour of argument and success as to elicit from his distinguished teacher the declaration, in speaking of him to a friend, that "the young man had talent enough to be President of the United States," which he accompanied by a prediction that he would one day attain that station.

An English oration was assigned to Mr. Calhoun at the Commencement. He selected for his thesis, "The qualifications necessary to constitute a perfect statesman," and prepared his oration, but was prevented from delivering it by a severe indisposition. After graduating, he commenced the study of the law, and devoted three years to that and miscellaneous reading, eighteen months of which were spent at Litchfield, Connecticut, where a celebrated law-school was kept at that time by Judge Reeves [*sic*; Tapping Reeve] and Mr. [James] Gould. He acquired great distinction at the school. It was there that he successfully cultivated, in a debating society, his talents for extemporary speaking. The residue of the time was spent in the offices of Mr. [Henry William] De Saussure, of Charleston (afterward chancellor), and of Mr. George Bowie, of Abbeville. Having spent seven years in preparation, according to his determination when he commenced his education, and having passed his examination for admission to the bar, he began the practice of law in his native district. He rose at once into full practice, taking a stand with the oldest and ablest lawyers on the circuit.

He continued but a short time at the bar. While he was yet a student, after his return from Litchfield to Abbeville, an incident occurred which agitated the whole Union, and contributed to give to Mr. Calhoun's life, at that early period, the political direction which it has ever since kept—the attack of the English frigate Leopard on the American frigate Chesapeake. It led to public meetings all over the Union, in which resolutions were passed expressive of the indignation of the people, and their firm resolve to stand by the government in whatever measure it might think proper to adopt to redress the outrage. At that called in his native district, he was appointed one of the committee to prepare a report and resolutions to be presented to a meeting to be convened to receive them on an appointed day [8/3/-1807]. Mr. Calhoun was requested by the committee to prepare them, which he did so much to their satisfaction, that he was appointed to address the meeting on the occasion before the vote was taken on the resolutions. The meeting was large, and it was the first time he had ever appeared before the public. He acquitted himself with such success that his name was presented as a candidate for the state Legislature at the next election. He was elected at the head of the ticket, and at a time when the prejudice against lawyers was so strong in the district that no one of the profession who had offered for many years previously had ever succeeded. This was the commencement of his political life, and the first evidence he ever received of the confidence of the people of the state—a confidence which has continued ever since constantly increasing, without interruption or reaction, for the third of a century; and which, for its duration, universality, and strength, may be said to be without a parallel in any other state, or in the case of any other public man.

He served two sessions [1808 and 1809] in the state Legislature. It was not long after he took his seat before he distinguished himself. Early in the session an informal meeting of the Republican portion of the members was called to nominate candidates for the places of President and Vice-president of the United States. Mr. Madison was nominated for the presidency without opposition. When the nomination for the vice-presidency was presented, Mr. Calhoun embraced the occasion to present his opinion in reference to coming events, as bearing on the nomination. He reviewed the state of the relations between the United States and Great Britain and France, the two great belligerents which were then struggling for mastery, and in their struggle trampling on the rights of neutrals, and especially ours; he touched on the restrictive system which had been resorted to by the government to protect our rights, and expressed his doubt of its efficacy, and the conviction that a war with Great Britain would be unavoidable. "It was," he said, "in this state of things, of the utmost importance that the ranks of the Republican party should be preserved undisturbed and unbroken by faction or discord." He then adverted to the fact, that a discontented portion of the party had given un-equivocal evidence of rallying round the name of the venerable vice-president, George Clinton (whose re-nomination was proposed), and of whom he spoke highly; but he gave it as his opinion, that should he be nominated and re-elected, he would become the nucleus of all the discontented portion of the party, and thus make a formidable division in its ranks should the country be forced into war. These persons, he predicted, would ultimately rally under De Witt Clinton, the nephew, whom he described as a man of distinguished talents and aspiring disposition. To avoid the danger, he suggested for nomination the name of John Langdon, of New-Hampshire, of whom he spoke highly both as to talents and patriotism. *

It was Mr. Calhoun's first effort in a public capacity. The manner and matter excited great applause; and when it is recollected that these remarks preceded the declaration of war more than three years, and how events happened according to his anticipations, it affords a striking proof of that sagacity, at so early a period, for which he has since been so much distinguished. It at once gave him a stand among the most distinguished members of the Legislature. During the short period he remained a member, he originated and carried through several measures, which proved in practice to be salutary, and have become a permanent portion of the legislation of the state.

CHAPTER II.

Including the period from his entering Congress until his appointment
as Secretary of War.

In the mean time, the growing difficulties in our foreign relations, especially with Great Britain, impressed the community at large with the belief that war with that formidable power was approaching. The impression naturally turned the attention of the people, in selecting

* Editor's note: This summary of Calhoun's speech in 1808 is apparently taken from the "Biographical Memoir of John Caldwell Calhoun," [by Virgil Maxcy], which appeared in the Washington, D.C., *United States' Telegraph*, April 25 and 26, 1831. No earlier version has been found.

candidates for Congress, to those whom they believed to be the most competent to serve them at so trying a period. The eyes of the congressional district in which Mr. Calhoun resided were turned towards him, and he was elected by an overwhelming majority over his opponent. This was in the fall of 1810, and he took his seat in the councils of the nation a year afterward, in the first session of the twelfth Congress, known as the war session, with his two distinguished colleagues, Mr. [Langdon] Cheves and Mr. [William] Lowndes, who, like himself, had been elected in reference to the critical condition of the country. His reputation had preceded him, and he was placed second on the Committee of Foreign Relations, which, in the existing state of our relations with the two great belligerents, was regarded as the most important of the committees, and was, accordingly, filled by members selected in reference to the magnitude of its duties. The other distinguished individuals who composed it were Peter B. Porter [of N.Y.], the chairman, and Felix Grundy, of Tennessee, on the Republican side, and John Randolph [of Va.] and Philip Barton Key [of Md.] on the other. It was, indeed, an eventful period of our history, and the duties which it imposed on the committee were of the most difficult and responsible character.

It is not easy, at this day, to estimate the magnitude of the crisis. Our present government had its origin just preceding the commencement of the Great Revolution in France, which, in its progress, involved her in a war without example or parallel in the history of the world, taking into estimate its cause, extent, duration, the immensity of force brought into conflict, the skill which directed it, the variety and magnitude of its incidents, and the importance of the stake at issue. England was the great antagonist power to France in this mighty struggle, whose shocks reached even our distant shores. From the beginning, our mutual rights were invaded by both sides, and our peace endangered; but so recently had our government been established, so hazardous was it to put it to the test of war, and especially in such a struggle, and so advantageous to our commerce and prosperity was our position as a neutral power, while all Europe was at war, that it became the fixed policy of the government to preserve peace and bear wrongs, so long as the one could be preserved and the other endured without sacrificing the honour and independence of the country. This pacific and wise policy was, with some slight exceptions, steadily pursued for more than fifteen years. At length came the Berlin and Milan Decrees on the part of France, and the hostile orders in council on the part of England, which forced on our government the embargo and other restrictive measures, adopted from an anxious desire of preserving peace, and in the hope of obtaining respect for our rights from one or other of the two belligerents. Experience soon proved how impotent these measures were, and how fallacious was our hope. The encroachments on our rights and independence continued to advance, till England at length pushed her aggressions so far that our commerce was reduced to a state of dependance as complete as when we were her colonies, and our ships were converted, at the same time, into a recruiting-ground to man her navy. Not a vessel of ours was permitted to reach Europe but through her ports, and more than 3,000 of our hardy seamen were impressed into her service, to fight battles in which they had no interest. Our independence, as far as the ocean was concerned, had become an empty name; but so hazardous was it to take up arms in the unprepared state of the country, and to be drawn into a struggle apparently so fearful and interminable between the two first powers on earth, that the stoutest and boldest might well have paused at taking the step.

It was in such a crisis of our affairs that Mr. Calhoun took his seat in Congress. To him it was not unexpected. He had little confidence from the beginning in the peaceful measures resorted to for the redress of our wrongs, and saw beforehand that the final alternatives would be war or submission, and had deliberately made up his mind, that to lose independence, and to sink down into a state of acknowledged inferiority, depending for security on forbearance, and not on our capacity and disposition to defend ourselves, would be the worst calamity which could befall the country. According to his opinion, the ability of the government to defend the country against external danger, and to cause its rights to be respected from without, was as essential as protection against violence within, and that, if it should prove incompetent to meet successfully the hazard of a just and necessary war, it would fail in one of the two great objects for which it was instituted, and that the sooner it was known the better. With these fixed opinions, his voice, on taking his seat, was for the most decisive course.

The President's [James Madison's] Message, at the opening of the session [of 11/1811–7/1812], was, in its general features, warlike, and yet there were expressions of an ambiguous character, which led many to doubt what course of policy was really intended by the administration. The portion which related to our affairs with other powers was referred to the Committee of Foreign Relations. The excitement in the country was intense, and party spirit never ran higher. All eyes were turned on the proceedings of the committee. They reported, at an early period of the session, resolutions strongly recommending immediate and extensive preparations to defend our rights and redress our wrongs by an appeal to arms. The debate was opened by the chairman, Mr. Porter, and he was followed on the same side by Mr. Grundy. It was allotted to Mr. Calhoun [on 12/12/1811] to follow Mr. Randolph, who, on the opposite side, succeeded Mr. Grundy in an able and eloquent speech. The discussion from the beginning excited profound interest, both in the body and the crowded audience daily assembled in the lobby and galleries, and this interest had increased as the discussion advanced. It was Mr. Calhoun's first speech in Congress, except a few brief remarks on the Apportionment Bill. The trial was a severe one; expectation was high. The question was of the greatest magnitude, and he to whom he had to reply, a veteran statesman of unsurpassed eloquence. How he acquitted himself, the papers of the day will best attest. The remarks of the Richmond Enquirer, then, as now, a leading journal on the Republican side, may be taken as an example. Mr. [Thomas] Ritchie, in his remarks on the speeches, after characterizing Mr. Randolph's, said: "Mr. Calhoun is clear and precise in his reasoning, marching up directly to the object of his attack, and felling down the errors of his opponent with the club of Hercules; not eloquent in his tropes and figures, but, like Fox, in the moral elevation of his sentiments; free from personality, yet full of those fine touches of indignation, which are the severest cut to the man of feeling. His speech, like a fine drawing, abounds in those lights and shades which set off each other: the cause of his country is robed in light, while her opponents are wrapped in darkness. It were a contracted wish that Mr. Calhoun were a Virginian; though, after the quota she has furnished with opposition talents, such a wish might be forgiven us. We beg leave to participate, as Americans and friends of our country, in the honours of South Carolina. We hail this young Carolinian as one of the master-spirits who stamp their names upon the age in which they live."

When Mr. Calhoun sat down, he was greeted by the great body of the party for his successful effort, and thenceforward took rank with the ablest and most influential members of the body. But, as clear as it appeared to him that the period had arrived when a resort to arms could no longer be avoided without sacrificing the honour and interest of the country, such was far from being the feeling of many, even of the Republican members of the body. Many, who saw the necessity, hesitated; some from the great hazard of war, others from the want of preparation, or the difficulty of selecting between the belligerents, when both had so grossly violated our rights; and not a few from a lingering confidence in the Non-importation Act, and other restrictive measures, as the means of redressing our wrongs. Mr. Calhoun, although he approved of the motive which had led to a resort to those measures in the first instance, and regarded them as wise temporary expedients, never had any confidence in them as instruments of avenging or redressing the wrongs of the country. Believing that they had accomplished all they ever could, and that a latent attachment to them was one of the principal impediments to a resort to arms, he did not hesitate to attack the whole system.

To realize the boldness and hazard of such a step, it must be borne in mind that the support or opposition to the system had been for many years the main test of party fidelity, and that party spirit was never higher than at the time. But as strongly as he was attached to the administration, to the Republican party, and their general policy, and opposed as he was to the Federalists, he did not hesitate, young as he was, when he believed duty and the interest of the country required it, to place himself above all party considerations, and to expose manfully the defects of a system which had been so long cherished and defended by the party to which he belonged. The following extracts from a speech delivered against it [on 6/24/1812] will give in his own language some of the most prominent objections which he urged against the system, and afford, at the same time, a fair specimen of his powers of reasoning and eloquence at that early period, and of the lofty and patriotic sentiments which actuated him in the line of policy that he advocated.

"The restrictive system," he said, "as a mode of resistance, or as a means of obtaining redress, has never been a favourite one with me. I wish not to censure the motives which dictated it, or attribute weakness to those who first resorted to it for a restoration of our rights. But, sir, I object to the restrictive system because it does not suit the genius of the people, or that of our government, or the geographical character of our country. We are a people essentially active; I may say we are pre-eminently so. No passive system can suit such a people; in action superior to all others, in patient endurance inferior to none. Nor does it suit the genius of our government. Our government is founded on freedom, and hates coercion. To make the restrictive system effective, requires the most arbitrary laws. England, with the severest penal statutes, has not been able to exclude prohibited articles; and Napoleon, with all his power and vigilance, was obliged to resort to the most barbarous laws to enforce his Continental system."

After showing how the whole mercantile community must become corrupt by the temptations and facilities for smuggling, and how the public opinion of the commercial community (upon which the system must depend for its enforcement) becomes opposed to it, and gives sanction to its violation, he proceeds

"But there are other objections to the system. It renders government odious. The farmer inquires why he gets no more for his produce, and he is told it is owing to the embargo, or commercial restrictions. In this he sees only the hand of his own government, and not the acts of violence and injustice which this system is intended to counteract. His censures fall on the government. This is an unhappy state of the public mind; and even, I might say, in a government resting essentially on public opinion, a dangerous one. In war it is different. Its privation, it is true, may be equal or greater; but the public mind, under the strong impulses of that state of things, becomes steeled against sufferings. The difference is almost infinite between the passive and active state of the mind. Tie down a hero, and he feels the puncture of a pin: throw him into battle, and he is almost insensible to vital gashes. So in war. Impelled alternately by hope and fear, stimulated by revenge, depressed by shame, or elevated by victory, the people become invincible. No privation can shake their fortitude; no calamity break their spirit. Even when equally successful, the contrast between the two systems is striking. War and restriction may leave the country equally exhausted; but the latter not only leaves you poor, but, even when successful, dispirited, divided, discontented, with diminished patriotism, and the morals of a considerable portion of your people corrupted. Not so in war. In that state, the common danger unites all, strengthens the bonds of society, and feeds the flame of patriotism. The national character mounts to energy. In exchange for the expenses and privations of war, you obtain military and naval skill, and a more perfect organization of such parts of your administration as are connected with the science of national defence. Sir, are these advantages to be counted as trifles in the present state of the world? Can they be measured by moneyed valuation? I would prefer a single victory over the enemy, by sea or land, to all the good we shall ever derive from the continuation of the Non-importation Act. I know not that a victory would produce an equal pressure on the enemy; but I am certain of what is of greater consequence, it would be accompanied by more salutary effects on ourselves. The memory of Saratoga, Princeton, and Eutaw is immortal. It is there you will find the country's boast and pride—the inexhaustible source of great and heroic sentiments. But what will history say of restriction? What examples worthy of imitation will it furnish to posterity? What pride, what pleasure, will our children find in the events of such times? Let me not be considered romantic. This nation ought to be taught to rely on its courage, its fortitude, its skill and virtue, for protection. These are the only safeguards in the hour of danger. Man was endued with these great qualities for his defence. There is nothing about him that indicates that he is to conquer by endurance. He is not incrusted in a shell; he is not taught to rely upon his insensibility, his passive suffering, for defence. No, sir; it is on the invincible mind, on a magnanimous nature, he ought to rely. Here is the superiority of our kind; it is these that render man the lord of the world. It is the destiny of his condition that nations rise above nations, as they are endued in a greater degree with these brilliant qualities."

But this is not the only instance in which Mr. Calhoun, at this early stage of his public life, manifested a spirit above party influence or control, that spirit which he has so often since exhibited, when duty and patriotism demanded it. No one appreciates more highly the value of party ties within proper limits, or adheres more firmly to his party within them, than he does. He never permits them to influence him beyond those necessary limits. Acting accordingly, he did not hesitate to give his cordial and warm support to a bill for the increase of the navy, reported by his able and distinguished colleague [Langdon Cheves], who was then chairman of the Naval Committee, although, at and previous to that time, the great body of the Republican party was and had been opposed to it. It was owing to the decided support which it received from Mr. Cheeves [sic], Mr. Calhoun, Mr. Lowndes, and Mr. [Henry] Clay, and its brilliant achievements afterward (even then confidently anticipated by them), that it has since become with the whole Union the favourite arm of defence.

As prominent as was the situation of Mr. Calhoun at the commencement of this eventful session, as the second on the most important committee, it became still more so in its progress. The chairman, Mr. Porter, withdrew from Congress, and Mr. C[alhoun] found himself at the head of the committee, which, in addition to its peculiar duties, was charged, by a vote of the House, with a large portion of those properly belonging to the Committee on Military Affairs. Few individuals with so little parliamentary experience have ever been placed in so responsible a situation. He had never before served in a deliberative body except for two short sessions in the Legislature of his own state, making together but nine weeks. With such limited experience, it is difficult to conceive a situation of the kind more arduous than that in which he was placed at the head of such a committee at such a period, when party spirit was at its height and the opposition under the guidance of leaders distinguished for their talents and experience; and yet, so ample were his resources, and so great his aptitude for business, that he not only sustained himself, but acquired honour and distinction for the ability with which he discharged the duties of his station.

It will not be attempted to trace Mr. Calhoun's course through this laborious and long-to-be-remembered session. It is sufficient to say that he exhibited throughout the same zeal and ability with which he commenced it. Near its close he reported* and carried through the bill declaring war against Great Britain—a war under all circumstances fairly entitled to its appellation as the second war of independence. The proceedings were in secret session, contrary to his opinion and wishes.

Such was the brilliant career of Mr. Calhoun during his first session, and that under the most responsible and trying circumstances. Much of his success is to be attributed to his early and wise determination not to come forward till he had laid the foundation in a solid education, and fully prepared himself to act his part in life. Without them, the mere force of natural talents could not have carried him successfully through the difficulties he had to encounter at the outset of his congressional career.

The declaration of war fixed the policy of the government for the time, and the discussions in Congress during its continuance turned, for the most part, on questions relating to the finances, the army, the navy, the mode of conducting the war, and its success and disasters. These gave rise to many warm and animated debates of deep interest and excitement at the time, and in most of which Mr. Calhoun took a prominent part, and fully sustained the reputation he had acquired for ability and eloquence; but as the subjects were generally of a temporary character, and have long since lost much of their interest, the object of this sketch does not require that they should be particularly noticed. They will, accordingly, be passed in silence, and the notice of the events of the period confined to those that may be regarded as exceptions to the ordinary party discussions of the day. This course is the more readily adopted, because it is believed that the whole country is disposed to do ample justice to the patriotism, the intelligence, and ability with which he performed his part during this eventful period of our history.

The first incident that will be noticed took place at the commencement of the session [of 11/1812–3/1813] immediately succeeding the declaration of war. South Carolina had in that Congress an unusual

* Editor's note: Compare *The Papers of John C. Calhoun*, 1:122–124.

number of men of talents: General D[avid] R. Williams, Langdon Cheves, William Lowndes, and the subject of this sketch, all of whom were entitled to prominent positions in the arrangement of committees. Mr. Calhoun was the youngest. The speaker [Henry Clay] was embarrassed. There was a difficulty in placing so many from one state, and that a small one, at the head of prominent committees, and Mr. Calhoun, with his characteristic disinterestedness, cheerfully assented to be placed second on that at the head of which he had served with so much distinction at the preceding session. Mr. [John] Smilie, an old and highly-respectable member from Pennsylvania, was placed at the head of the committee. At its first meeting the chairman, without previously intimating his intention, moved that Mr. Calhoun should be elected chairman. He objected, and insisted that Mr. Smilie should act as chairman, and declared his perfect willingness to serve under him; but he was, notwithstanding, unanimously elected, and the strongest proof that could be given of the highly satisfactory manner in which he had previously discharged his duty was thus afforded. In this conviction, and as illustrative of the same disinterested character, when the speaker's chair became vacant by the appointment of Mr. Clay as one of the commissioners to negotiate for peace, Mr. Calhoun was solicited by many of the most influential members of the party to become a candidate for it; but he peremptorily refused to oppose his distinguished colleague, Mr. Cheves, who was elected.

At an early period of the same session, a question out of the ordinary course, and which excited much interest at the time, became the subject of discussion, that of the merchants' bonds. The Nonimportation Act (one of the restrictive measures) was in force when war was declared. Under its operation a large amount of capital had been accumulated abroad, and especially in England, the proceeds of exports that could not be returned in consequence of the prohibition of imports. The owners, when they saw war was inevitable, became alarmed, and gave orders for the return of their property. It came back, for the most part, in merchandise, which was subject to forfeiture under the act. The owners petitioned for the remission of the forfeiture, and permission to enter the goods on paying the war duties. The secretary of the treasury, on the other hand, proposed to remit the forfeiture on condition that the amount of the value of the goods should be loaned to the government by the owners. Mr. Cheves, who was at the head of the Committee of Ways and Means, reported in favour of the petition, and supported his report by an able speech. The question had assumed much of a party character, but it did not deter Mr. Calhoun from an independent exercise of his judgment. He believed that the act never contemplated a case of the kind, and that to enforce, under such circumstances, a forfeiture amounting to millions, which would embrace a large class of citizens, would be against the spirit of the criminal code of a free and enlightened people. But wa[i]ving these more general views, he thought the only alternative was to remit the forfeiture, as prayed for by the owners, or to enforce it according to the provisions of the act: that, if the importation was such a violation as justly and properly incurred the forfeiture, then the act ought to be enforced; but if not, the forfeiture ought to be remitted; and that the government had no right, and if it had, it was unbecoming its dignity to convert a penal act into the means of making a forced loan. Thus thinking, he seconded the effort of his distinguished colleague, and enforced his views in a very able speech [on 12/8/1812]. The result was, that the forfeiture was remitted, and the goods admitted on paying duties in conformity to the course recommended by the committee.

There was another case in which, at this period, he evinced his firmness and independence. The administration still adhered to the restrictive policy, and even after the war was declared the President recommended the renewal of the Embargo. Mr. Calhoun, as has been shown, opposed, on principle, the whole system as a substitute for war, and he was still more opposed to it as an auxiliary to it. He held it, in that light, not only as inefficient and delusive, but as calculated to impair the means of the country, and to divert a greater share of its capital and industry to manufactures than could be, on the return of peace, sustained by the government on any sound principles of justice or policy. He thought war itself, without restrictions, would give so great a stimulus, that no small embarrassment and loss would result on its termination, in despite of all that could be done for them, while, at the same time, he expressed his willingness, when peace came, to protect the establishments that might grow up during its continuance, as far as it could be fairly done.

The Embargo failed on the first recommendation; but, at the next session, being recommended again, it succeeded. Mr. Calhoun, at the earnest entreaties of friends, and to prevent division in the party when their union was so necessary to the success of the war, gave it a reluctant vote.

But the time was approaching when an opportunity would be afforded him to carry out successfully his views in reference to the restrictive system, and that with the concurrence of the party. The disasters of Bonaparte in the Russian campaign, his consequent fall and dethronement in the early part of 1814, and the triumph of Great Britain, after one of the longest, and, altogether, the most remarkable contests on record, offered that opportunity, which he promptly seized. This great event, which terminated the war in Europe, left Great Britain, flushed with victory, in full possession of all the vast resources, in men, money, and materials, by which she had brought that mighty conflict to a successful termination, to be turned against us. It was a fearful state of things; but, as fearful as it was of itself, it was made doubly so by the internal condition of the country, and the course of the opposition. Blinded by party zeal, they beheld with joy or indifference what was calculated to appal the patriotic. Forgetting the country, and intent only on a party triumph, they seized the opportunity to embarrass the government. Their great effort was made against the Loan Bill—a measure necessary to carry on the war. Instead of supporting it, they denounced the war itself as unjust and inexpedient; and they proclaimed its farther prosecution, in so unequal a contest, as hopeless, now that the whole power of the British Empire would be brought to bear against us. Mr. Calhoun replied in a manner highly characteristic of the man, undaunted, able, and eloquent. None can read this speech [of 2/25/1814], even at this distance of time, without kindling under that elevated tone of feeling, which wisdom, emanating from a spirit lofty and self-possessed under the most trying circumstances, only can inspire. In order to show the justice and expediency of the war, he took an historical view of the maritime usurpations of Great Britain, from the celebrated order in council of 1756, to the time of the discussion, and demonstrated that her aggressions were not accidental, or dependant on peculiar circumstances, but were the result of a fixed system of policy, intended to establish her supremacy on the ocean. After giving a luminous view of the origin and character of the wrongs we had suffered from her, he clearly showed the flimsiness of the pretext by which she sought to justify her conduct, as well as that of the opposition to excuse her, and dwelt upon the folly of hoping to obtain redress by sheathing the sword or throwing ourselves on her justice. The following extract, taken from the conclusion, will afford an example of his lofty and animating eloquence:

"This country is left alone to support the rights of neutrals. Perilous is the condition, and arduous the task. We are not intimidated. We stand opposed to British usurpation, and, by our spirit and efforts, have done all in our power to save the last vestiges of neutral rights. Yes, our embargoes, non-intercourse, non-importation, and, finally, war, are all manly exertions to preserve the rights of this and other nations from the deadly grasp of British maritime policy. But (say our opponents) these efforts are lost, and our condition hopeless. If so, it only remains for us to assume the garb of our condition. We must submit, humbly submit, crave pardon, and hug our chains. It is not wise to provoke where we cannot resist. But first let us be well assured of the hopelessness of our state before we sink into submission. On what do our opponents rest their despondent and slavish belief? On the recent events in Europe? I admit they are great, and well calculated to impose on the imagination. Our enemy never presented a more imposing exterior. His fortune is at the flood. But I am admonished by universal experience, that such prosperity is the most precarious of human conditions. From the flood the tide dates its ebb. From the meridian the sun commences his decline. Depend upon it, there is more of sound philosophy than of fiction in the fickleness which poets attribute to fortune. Prosperity has its weakness, adversity its strength. In many respects our enemy has lost by those very changes which seem so very much in his favour. He can no more claim to be struggling for existence; no more to be fighting the battles of the world in defence of the liberties of mankind. The magic cry of 'French influence' is lost. In this very hall we are not strangers to that sound. Here, even here, the cry of 'French influence,' that baseless fiction, that phantom of faction now banished, often resounded. I rejoice that the spell is broken by which it was attempted to bind the spirit of this youthful nation. The minority can no longer act under cover, but must come out and defend their opposition on its own intrinsic merits. Our example can scarcely fail to produce its effects on other nations interested in the maintenance of maritime rights. But if, unfortunately, we should be left alone to maintain the contest, and if, which may God forbid, necessity should compel us to yield for the present, yet our generous efforts will not have been lost. A mode of thinking and a tone of sentiment have gone abroad which must stimulate to future and more successful struggles. What could not be effected with eight millions of people will be done with twenty. The great cause will never be yielded—no, never, never! Sir, I hear the future audibly announced in the past—in the splendid victories over the Guerriere, Java, and Macedonian. We, and all nations, by these victories, are taught a lesson never to be forgotten. Opinion is power. The charm of British naval invincibility is gone."

Such was the animated strain by which Mr. Calhoun roused the spirit of the government and country under a complication of adverse circumstances calculated to overwhelm the feeble and appal the stoutest. Never faltering, never doubting, never despairing of the

Republic, he was at once the hope of the party and the beacon light to the country.

But he did not limit his efforts to repelling the attacks of the opposition, and animating the hopes of the government and country. He saw that the very events which exposed us to so much danger, made a mighty change in the political and commercial relations of Continental Europe, which had been so long closed against foreign commerce, in consequence of the long war that grew out of the French Revolution, and of those hostile orders and decrees of the two great belligerents, which had for many years almost annihilated all lawful commerce between the Continent of Europe and the rest of the world. The events that dethroned Bonaparte put an end to that state of things, and left all the powers of Europe free to resume their former commercial pursuits. He saw in all this that the time had come to free the government entirely from the shackles of the restrictive system, to which he had been so long opposed; and he, accordingly, followed up his speech by a bill to repeal the Embargo and the Nonimportation Act. He rested their repeal on the ground that they were a portion of the restrictive policy, and showed that the ground on which it had been heretofore sustained was, that it was a pacific policy, growing out of the extraordinary state of the world at the time it was adopted, and, of course, dependant on the continuance of that state. "It was a time," he said [in his speech of 4/6/1814], "when every power on the Continent was arrayed against Great Britain, under the overwhelming influence of Bonaparte, and no country but ours interested in maintaining neutral rights. The fact of all the Continental ports being closed against her, gave to our restrictive measures an efficacy which they no longer had, now that they were open to her." He admitted that the system had been continued too long, and been too far extended, and that he was opposed to it as a substitute for war, but contended that there would be no inconsistency on the part of the government in abandoning a policy founded on a state of things which no longer existed. "But now," said he, "the Continental powers are neutrals, as between us and Great Britain. We are contending for the freedom of trade, and ought to use every exertion to attach to our cause Russia, Sweden, Holland, Denmark, and all other nations which have an interest in the freedom of the seas. The maritime rights assumed by Great Britain infringe on the rights of all neutral powers, and if we should now open our ports and trade to the nations of the Continent, it would involve Great Britain in a very awkward and perplexing dilemma. She must either permit us to enjoy a very lucrative commerce with them, or, by attempting to exclude them from our ports by her system of paper blockades, she would force them to espouse our cause. The option which would thus be tendered her would so embarrass her as to produce a stronger desire for peace than ten years' continuance of the present system, inoperative as it is now rendered by a change of circumstances." These views had the desired effect, and the bill passed.

The subsequent session (that of 1814–15) was the last of the war sessions. It was short, terminating on the 4th of March. It was one of much excitement, but was principally distinguished for the project of a bank, submitted by the administration, and intended for the relief of the financial difficulties of the government. Upon this measure Mr. Calhoun differed from the [James Madison] administration and a large portion of the party.

It so happened that he was detained at home by sickness, and did not take his seat for several weeks after the commencement of the session, and his place as chairman of the Committee of Foreign Relations was filled by the late secretary of state, Mr. [John] Forsyth [of Ga.]. He found, on his arrival, the plan of a bank agreed on, and he was especially requested by the secretary of the treasury [Alexander J. Dallas], with whom he had the kindest relations, and several members of the Committee of Ways and Means, to give it his particular attention, which he promised to do. His predisposition was strongly in favour of a bank of some kind. It was then generally thought to be indispensable to the prosecution of the war. With this disposition, and a strong desire to meet what were the views of the secretary and the administration, and of his friends on the Ways and Means, he took up the plan for examination. The whole subject of banking, theoretically and practically, was, in a great measure, new to him. He had never given it a serious and careful examination, and his mind, though favourably disposed to the plan, was open to the reception of truth.

The leading features of the plan were a bank of $50,000,000 of capital, to consist, with the exception of a few millions of specie, entirely of the stock issued by the government for loans made to carry on the war. It was not to pay specie during the war, not till three years after its termination, and was to lend the government, whenever required, $30,000,000, at six per cent., to carry on the war. With all his prepossessions in its favour, he was soon struck by the fact, that the great leading object was to create a machine for lending money, not on the means or credit of the bank, or the individuals to be incorporated, but of the government itself; for the bank would not be bound to pay its notes, and would have little or nothing on which to lend but the stock of the government. The whole contrivance was, virtually, under the specious show of a loan, for the government to borrow back its own credit at six per cent., for which it had already stipulated to pay a high interest—not less, on an average, than eight per cent. Those who had lent the government, alleging that they had loaned all they had, modestly proposed to lend it, on its own credit, as much as it might need to carry on the war, if it would incorporate them under the magic name of "a bank," exempt them from the payment of their debts as a corporation, give them the use of the public money, and not only endorse their notes by receiving them for its dues, but also pay them away as money in their disbursements.

It was impossible for a mind constituted as Mr. Calhoun's not to see the whole effects of the scheme, or to give its assent to it, by whomsoever contrived, or by whatever name called. To him, no alternative was left but to sacrifice his judgment, or to differ from the administration and many of his friends who were anxious to have his support; but, as responsible and painful as was the alternative, he did not hesitate.

When the bill came up he opposed it in a speech [of 11/16/1814], in which he briefly stated his objections; and such was its effect that, though the measure had the support of the [Madison] administration, and the whole of the Committee of Ways and Means but one, it was struck out, and the amendment he proposed was substituted by an overwhelming majority. His substitute was, that the government should use its own credit directly in the shape of treasury notes, to be issued to meet its wants, and to be funded in the bank in the form of stock at six per cent.; that the bank should be bound to pay its notes at all times, and should make the government no loans but short ones, in anticipation of its current revenue. By the issue of treasury notes, to be funded in the bank, he proposed to obtain the immediate supplies to carry on the government; and, by establishing a specie-paying bank, under proper restrictions, he hoped to sustain a strong position, from which the currency, then consisting, south of New-England, exclusively of the notes of suspended banks, might be restored to the specie standard on the return of peace. His substitute was, in its turn, defeated. Two other bills, differently modified, were successively introduced, and were both defeated—one by the casting vote of the speaker, Mr. Cheeves [*sic*], and the other by the President, who vetoed it on the ground that, as modified, it would not afford the relief required by the treasury.

The greater part of the session had been spent in these various attempts to pass a bill, and many who entirely agreed with Mr. Calhoun in his view of the subject, and had stood fast by him at first, now yielded to the pressure. Finally, a rally was made, a short time before the close of the session, to pass a bill, and it was again introduced in the Senate much improved in some of its objectionable features, but still defective enough to prevent him and the friends who stood by him from giving it their support. It speedily passed that body, and was sent to the House, where it was pressed through to its passage with all possible despatch. On the question of ordering it to the third reading [on 2/13/1815?], Mr. Calhoun made a few remarks, in which he warned the House against adopting a measure which a great majority decidedly disapproved, but for which they were prepared to vote under a supposed necessity, which did not exist. He concluded by saying that the bill was so objectionable that, were it not for the supposed necessity, if, for instance, the news of peace should arrive before its passage, it would not receive fifteen votes, and concluded by saying that he would reserve a full statement of his objections to the bill for the question on the passage to be taken the next day, when he intended to make a final stand against it, and appeal to the public for the vindication of his course. At the time there was not the slightest rumour or indication of peace, and no one expected it. On the contrary, every indication was, that the war would be pushed with vigour in the approaching campaign. The attack had been made on New-Orleans, and by every mail it was expected to hear of its fate; and yet, strange as it may seem, that very day, subsequent to the adjournment of the House, a despatch, sent on by a mercantile house in New-York, to be forwarded by the mail to the South to its agents, arrived in the city, with the intelligence that a vessel had come in after the departure of the mail, bringing the treaty of peace. The member to whom it was sent was so struck with the coincidence, that he informed Mr. Calhoun of the fact in confidence. By some means, a rumour got out that there was a late arrival at New-York bringing important intelligence. Next day the friends of the bill made an effort to push it through before the arrival of the mail in the afternoon. Mr. Calhoun moved to lay the bill on the table, saying that there was a hope that the mail from New-York, which would arrive in a few hours, might bring intelligence that would have an important bearing on the bill. The vote on his motion verified his prediction. The mail arrived with the treaty of peace. It was then proposed to him to modify the bill in conformity with his views, if he would withdraw his opposition. He refused, and demanded other and severer restrictions than those which he had heretofore proposed. An attempt was then made to take up the bill and pass it, which failed by a large majority.

It was thus his sagacity and firmness, under the most trying circumstances, against the whole weight of the administration, defeated a measure, which, if it had been adopted as first proposed, would have been followed by consequences more disastrous than could well be anticipated. He had the satisfaction to receive the thanks of many of the members for its defeat, who but a short time before were ready to denounce him for his resistance to it. It is now to be regretted that none of Mr. Calhoun's speeches against the measure were published. He declined publishing at the time on the ground that his object was to defeat the bill, but to do so without distracting the party or impairing confidence in the administration, on which the success of the war so much depended. For that reason, he not only avoided publishing, but bore patiently the denunciations daily levelled against him for his opposition to the bill. On all other measures of the session he gave the administration an active and hearty support. It was, indeed, a rule with him, when compelled to differ from his party on an important measure, to limit his opposition strictly to the measure itself, and to avoid, both in manner and matter, all that could by possibility give offence. By a rigid observance, too, of this rule, he succeeded in maintaining his individual opinion in reference to all important questions on which he differed from his party without weakening his standing with them.

The transition from a state of war to that of peace gave rise to many important questions, the most prominent of which grew out of the finances and the currency. At the succeeding session [of 12/1815–4/1816], Mr. Lowndes and Mr. Calhoun were placed at the head of the committees which had charge of these important subjects; Mr. Lowndes was made chairman of the Ways and Means, and Mr. Calhoun, from the prominence he had acquired at the preceding session on the Bank Question, was appointed chairman of that on currency. The most prominent question connected with the finances was that of the readjustment of the duties on the imposts. The duties had been doubled at the commencement of the war, and the question now presented was, how much they should be reduced. It was one that took in the whole range of the future policy of the government, and involved the consideration of many important subjects; the military and naval establishments, the debt, and the new direction given to a large amount of the capital and industry of the country in consequence of the war, the Embargo, the Non-importation, and Non-intercourse Acts, which preceded it. These, in turn, involved the question of our foreign relations in all their bearings. After a survey of the whole

27

ground, the Committee of Ways and Means reported the bill, with the full concurrence of the administration, which passed with but few changes, and has since been called the Tariff of 1816.

Few measures have been less understood or more misrepresented. It has been the general impression that the duties were adjusted by the bill mainly in reference to the protection of manufactures. Such is far from being the fact. With the exception of a few items, such as the minimum duty on coarse cottons, the duties on rolled iron, and, perhaps, one or two more, the duties would have been arranged substantially as they were if there had not been a manufacturing establishment in the whole country. It was in other respects a revenue bill, proposed and reported by the committee to whom the subject of revenue properly belonged, and regulated in its details, with the few exceptions referred to, by revenue considerations.

The first great question in the adjusting of the duties was, what amount of revenue would the future policy of the country require? And, in deciding that, the leading question was, whether the public debt should be rapidly or slowly paid? In this decision were involved, not only the question of the policy of freeing the government as soon as possible from debt, but also the collateral effects of such a process on the country under the particular circumstances of the case. In that view, the effects which raising the duties, with the view to the speedy discharge of the debt, would have in sustaining the manufacturing establishments which had grown up under the war, and the restrictive system preceding it, served to create a strong motive for adopting that policy, and for fixing the duties as high as they stand in the act. In conformity with this policy, an efficient sinking fund of $10,000,000 annually was provided for the payment of the principal and interest of the debt, with the proviso that all moneys remaining in the treasury at the end of each year exceeding $2,000,000 should be carried to its aid. It was in reference to these views, and the necessity of providing for the military and naval establishments on a scale sufficiently extended for the public service, that the details of the bill and the rates of the duties were mainly adjusted, and not solely or principally for the protection of manufactures, as has been erroneously supposed. If proof is required, conclusive evidence will be found in the bill itself, which imposes a much lower average rate of duties on what are now called the protected articles, that is, articles similar to those made at home, or which may come into competition with them, than upon the other descriptions.

Nor has the course of Mr. Calhoun in reference to it been less misunderstood or misrepresented than the measure itself. He has frequently been called the author of the protective system. Nothing is more untrue. He was not on the committee, and took no part in the discussion, except to make a short off-hand speech [on 4/4/1816] at the request of a friend, at a particular stage of the debate. He was engrossed with the duties of his own committee, and had bestowed but little attention to the details of the bill. He concurred in the general views and policy in which it originated, and the more readily because it would sustain the manufacturing establishments that had grown up under the war-measures of the government. Shortly after he came into Congress, he had anticipated, as has been stated, the difficulty that would be occasioned by the new direction which so considerable a portion of the capital and labour of the country had taken; and, while he professed a disposition at the time to do what could be legitimately done to support them on the return of peace, yet he used his best efforts to diminish the necessity, as far as practicable, by removing every remnant of the restrictive system during the war. He did not then, nor do we believe that he has since doubted that, in deciding whether the debt should be more speedily or more tardily discharged, the favourable effects which the former mode would have in sustaining the manufacturing establishments was, under the circumstances of the case, a legitimate and proper consideration. But truth and candour require us to say, that, as far as the details of the bill went beyond, and raised the duties above the revenue point, with the view to protection, as on our coarse cottons and rolled iron, he has long believed it to be unconstitutional, unjust, and unwise. The subject was new, and his attention was drawn to other subjects, and he did not take the proper distinction between duties for revenue and for protection, nor was it, as it is believed, taken at the time by any one. He who will examine Mr. Calhoun's remarks on the occasion will not fail to perceive that the support he gave the bill looked, not to what has since been called the protective policy, but almost wholly to considerations of a public character connected with the foreign relations of the country, and the danger resulting from war to a country, as ours was then, in a great measure, dependant on agriculture and commerce with foreign nations, without the requisite naval power to keep open in war the channels of trade with the rest of the world. In fact, it is difficult at this time, in the changed condition of the country and the world, to realize the circumstances under which the public men of that day acted, and the motives which guided them.

To do so, we must go back to the history of that period. A just and necessary war had been honourably terminated with the greatest power in the world, after a short but perilous struggle. The violent and unpatriotic course of the opposition [Federalists] during the war had so discredited it, that the name and doctrines of the Federal party, once so respectable, had become odious. After the war, they ceased to use their old name, or to avow their doctrines as a party; and the long struggle between them and their principles and policy, and the Republican party and their principles and policy, was supposed to have finally terminated in the ascendency of the latter. The impression was almost universal, that the danger to our popular system of government from the Federal consolidation doctrines was ended. The only cause of danger to the country and its institutions was then supposed to be from abroad. The overthrow of Bonaparte was followed throughout Europe by a powerful reaction against the popular principles on which our government rests, and to which, through the influence of our example, the French Revolution was traced. To counteract their influence and to put down effectually their revival in Europe, a league of all the great Continental monarchs was formed, called the Holy Alliance. Great Britain did not expressly accede to it, but countenanced and supported it. Our country of all the world stood alone in opposition, and became an object of the deepest jealousy. The Spanish provinces of South America, it is true, were in a revolutionary state, and struggling to form governments similar to ours. It was known that this formidable combination of crowned heads meditated hostile movements against them on political grounds, which could not be made without involving us. In such a state of the world, well might the patriots of that day be roused to the dangers from without, almost to the neglect of those from within. Had events taken the course which then seemed so probable, much that was then said and done, which now seems to require explanation, would have been regarded as profoundly wise. This is pre-eminently true of Mr. Calhoun's course. Always vigilant and solicitous for the safety and prosperity of the country, he kept his eyes steadily directed, at that critical period, to the point from which he and all then thought the country was menaced, and was active and zealous in giving such a direction to the policy of the government, for the time, as was best calculated to meet it. During this period, he spoke [on 1/31/1816] at large on the subject of defence against external danger, in a speech delivered on the subject of the repeal of the direct taxes, and which, for its eloquence, ability, and lofty and patriotic sentiments, gained him great applause. To the same cause may be traced his course, and that of the great body of the party at the time, on most of the subjects in reference to which different views are now entertained by them, and, among others, on that of internal improvements. On that subject, as well as upon the tariff, his views have been much misunderstood as well as misrepresented. Of these views a brief explanation may here be important.

During the war, while the coasting trade was interrupted, the whole internal commercial intercourse, and the military transportations and movements over our widely-extended country, had to pass through internal routes, then in a state far less perfect than at present, and the difficulties were immense. Great delay, uncertainty, and expense attended the concentration of any considerable force or supply on a point where the defence of the country or an attack on the enemy made it necessary. This greatly enfeebled our military operations, and contributed much to exhaust the means of the government. So great were the expense and difficulties, that it is estimated, for example, that much of the flour delivered at Detroit during the war cost $60 per barrel, and most of the cannon and ball transported to the lakes not less than 50 cents per pound.

At the commencement of the first session after the war, while the recollection of these things was fresh, Mr. Madison, in his opening message, among other things, invited the attention of Congress to the subject of internal improvements, and recommended Congress to call into exercise whatever constitutional power it might possess over the subject, and if that should not prove adequate, to apply for an amendment to the Constitution granting such additional powers as would be sufficient. Mr. Calhoun, acting, as he supposed, in strict conformity to this recommendation, reported a bill, at the next session, [that of 12/1816–3/1817,] to set apart and pledge the bonus of the United States Bank and their share of its dividends as a fund for internal improvement. It made no appropriation, nor did it intend to affirm that Congress had any power, much less to fix the limits of its power, over the subject; but to leave both, as well as the appropriations thereafter to be made, to abide the decision of Congress, in conformity with the President's views. Nor did Mr. C[alhoun] undertake to establish either in his speech [of 2/4/1817]. He declined both, and confined his remarks to the general benefit of a good system of internal improvements. When urged to assert the power of Congress, he refused, saying that, although he believed it possessed the power to a certain extent, he was not prepared to say to what limits it extended. He had not the least suspicion, in reporting and supporting the bill, that he went beyond the President's recommendation, or that he would have any difficulty in approving it, till the bill had passed both Houses, and was sent to him for his signature.

It was Mr. Madison's last session, and only a few days before its termination, when the bill was sent to him; and while it was still before him, Mr. Calhoun called to take his leave of him. After congratulating him on the success of his administration, and expressing the happiness he felt in having had the opportunity of co-operating with him in its most difficult period, that of the war, he took his leave. When he reached the door, Mr. Madison requested him to return. He did so, and took his seat; and for the first time Mr. M[adison] disclosed to him his constitutional objections to the bill. Mr. Calhoun expressed his deep regret, first, that he should entertain them, and, next, that he had not intimated them to him in time, saying that, if he had, he (Mr. Calhoun) would certainly not have subjected him to the unpleasant duty, at the very close of his administration, of vetoing a bill passed by the votes of his friends, nor himself to having the weight of his name and authority brought against him on such a subject. He then stated that he had introduced the bill, as he believed, in strict conformity to his recommendation, and if he had gone beyond, it was not intentional, and entreated him to reconsider the subject; but it was too late.

In this connexion, it is due to candour to state, that although Mr. Calhoun has never committed himself, in any speech or report, as to the extent of the constitutional powers of Congress over internal improvements, yet his impression, like that of most of the young men of the party at the time, was, that it was comprehended under the money-power of the government. Experience and reflection soon taught him this was an error—one, in all probability, originating with him, and others of his own age, in the precedent of the Cumberland Road, which may be regarded as the first departure by the Republican party from the true construction of the Constitution in reference to that dangerous power. Thus much it has been thought proper to state by way of explanation, and as due to that portion of our political history, and the part which Mr. Calhoun acted in relation to it.

The subject of the currency, as has been stated, was particularly intrusted to Mr. Calhoun. It was regarded as the most difficult and important question of the session. All the banks of the states south of New-England had, at an early period of the war, stopped payment, and gold and silver had entirely disappeared, leaving within their limits no other currency than the notes of banks that either would not or could not redeem them. Government was forced to submit, and not only to collect its taxes and dues, and make its disbursements, and negotiate its loans in their discredited and depreciated paper, but also to use them, at the same time, as the agents of the treasury and depositories of its funds. At first the depreciation was inconsiderable, but it continued to increase, though unequally, in the different portions of the Union to the end of the war. It was then hoped it would stop; but the fact proved far otherwise; for the progress of depreciation became more rapid and unequal than ever. It was greatest at the centre (the District of Columbia and the adjacent region), where it had reached 20 per cent., as compared with Boston; nor was there the least prospect that it would terminate of itself. It became absolutely necessary, in this state of things, for the government to adopt the rule of collecting its taxes and dues in the local currency of the place, to prevent that which was most depreciated from flooding the whole Union; for the public debtors, if they had the option, would be sure to pay in the most depreciated. But the necessary effect of this was to turn the whole import trade of the country towards the Chesapeake Bay, the region where the depreciation was the greatest. By making entry there, the duties could be paid in the local depreciated currency, and the goods then shipped where they were wanted. The result of the rule, though unavoidable, was to act as a premium for depreciation. It was impossible to tolerate such a state of things. It was in direct hostility to the Constitution, which provides that "all duties, imposts, and excises shall be uniform throughout the United States," and that "no preference shall be given by any regulation of commerce or revenue to the ports of one state over another." Thus the only question was, What shall be done?

The administration was in favour of a bank, and the President (Mr. Madison) recommended one in his Message at the commencement of the session [of 12/1815–4/1816]. The great body of the Republican party in Congress concurred in the views of the administration, but there were many of them who had, on constitutional grounds, insuperable objections to the measure. These, added to the Federal party, who had been against the war, and were, in consequence, against a bank, constituted a formidable opposition.

Mr. Calhoun, whose first lesson on the subject of banks, taken at the preceding session, was not calculated to incline him to such an institution, was averse, in the abstract, to the whole system; but perceiving then no other way of relieving government from its difficulties, he yielded to the opinion that a bank was indispensable. The separation of the government and the banks was at that time out of the question. A proposition of the kind would have been rejected on all sides. Nor was it possible then to collect the taxes and dues of the government in specie. It had been almost entirely expelled [from] the country; there appeared to be no alternative but to yield to a state of things to which no radical remedy could at that time be applied, and to resort to a bank to mitigate the evils of a system which in its then state was intolerable. This, at least, was the view which Mr. Calhoun took, and which he expressed in his speech [of 2/26/1816] on taking up the bill for discussion. It is said to have been one of the most elaborate and powerful he ever delivered. Unfortunately, it is lost. That published at the time is a meager sketch of what took three hours in the delivery, and such as it is, never passed under his review and correction, and omits almost entirely all that does not immediately refer to the bank.

The passage of the Bank Bill was followed by the joint resolution of 1816, which prohibited, after a certain day, the reception of the notes of any bank which did not pay specie. It received the decided support of Mr. Calhoun, and was the first step towards the separation of the government from the banking system. Through the joint agency of the two measures, the currency was brought to the specie standard, and the evil remedied.

During the same session a bill was passed changing the per diem pay of members of Congress into an annual compensation of $1,500. It proved to be exceedingly unpopular; so much so, that the greater part of the members who voted for it declined offering for re-election, and those who were again candidates, with few exceptions, were defeated at the polls. Mr. Calhoun voted for the bill, though he took but little part or interest in its passage. When he returned to his constituents, he found, for the first time, the tide of popular favour against him. So strong was the current, that his two predecessors, who had retired in his favour, General [William] Butler and Colonel [Joseph] Calhoun, the latter a near relative, were both violently opposed to him, and the former came out as a candidate against him. They were both men of great influence, the one residing at Edgefield, the other in Abbeville, and these two formed the Congressional district. Only a few faithful friends ventured openly to vindicate his vote. He was advised to appeal to the kind feelings of his constituents, and apologize for his course. This he peremptorily declined, declaring that he had voted for the measure because he believed it was right, and could not, as his opinion remained unchanged, apologize for that which his judgment approved. He added, at the same time, that all he asked was, that his constituents should give him a hearing in explanation of his vote. A day was appointed in each of the districts for him to address them at the courthouses. He met and addressed them accordingly. In his two speeches he confined himself to the merits of the question, without apology or appeal to sympathy, but with such force, candour, and manliness, that the tide was completely turned, and he was triumphantly re-elected.

At the next session of Congress a bill was introduced to repeal the act. It gave rise to an animated and interesting debate, in which Mr. Calhoun took part, and entered fully into the merits of the measure, and the reasons which governed him in voting for it. An estimate may be formed of the ability of the speech [of 1/17/1817] from the following compliment bestowed upon it by Mr. [Thomas P.] Grosvenor, of New-York, one of the ablest and most distinguished members of the House, on the opposite side in politics. To understand the allusion which he made, and to appreciate the full force of the compliment, it is proper to premise that there had been a personal difference between him and Mr. Calhoun in one of the secret sessions during the war, since which they had not been on speaking terms. Mr. Grosvenor said, "He had heard, with peculiar satisfaction, the able, manly, and constitutional speech of the gentleman from South Carolina." (Here Mr. Grosvenor, recurring in his own mind to their [sic] personal difference with Mr. Calhoun, which arose out of the warm party discussions during the war, paused for a moment, and then proceeded): "Mr. Speaker, I will not be restrained. No barrier shall exist which I will not leap over for the purpose of offering to that gentleman my thanks for the judicious, independent, and national course which he has pursued in this House for the last two years, and particularly upon the subject now before us. Let the honourable gentleman continue with the same manly independence, aloof from party views and local prejudices, to pursue the great interests of his country, and fulfil the high destiny for which it is manifest he was born. The buzz of popular applause may not cheer him on his way, but he will inevitably arrive at a high and happy elevation in the view of his country and the world."

He made another effort about the same time [on 1/9/1816?] on the treaty-making power, of which William Pinckney [sic; Pinkney], the distinguished advocate, at that time a member of the House from Maryland, and who followed in the debate, said, "The strong power of genius, from a higher region than that of argument, had thrown on the subject all the light with which it is the prerogative of genius to invest and illustrate everything;" and still more directly, "The gentleman from South Carolina (Mr. Calhoun) has exhausted the correct constitutional grounds of the question, and left me nothing but to recapitulate his arguments."

After taking an active and influential part in all the great questions which grew out of the transition from a state of war to that of peace, both at this and the preceding session, he began to turn his attention towards correcting the abuses which existed in the administrative branches of the government, and more especially towards the disbursements, in which great looseness and profusion had prevailed during the war. He had ever been the advocate of rigid economy and accountability in the use of the public money, and had resolved thenceforward to devote himself to their enforcement while he remained in Congress. The first thing that he struck at was the dangerous power which had been given to the President, of transfering appropriations, at his discretion, from one branch of service to another, in the war and navy departments; thereby converting, in effect, specific into general appropriations, and subjecting them, in a great measure, to his control. The evil had become so inveterate that it could not all at once be extirpated. The chairman of the Committee of Ways and Means, and the Secretary of the Treasury, both opposed the repeal of the act which authorized such transfers, but he nevertheless succeeded, against their opposition, in imposing important limitations on the power. This was among his last Congressional acts.*

CHAPTER III.

Including the Period during his Administration of the War Department.

Shortly before the meeting of Congress at the next session, he received an invitation from Mr. [James] Monroe to take a place in his cabinet as Secretary of War. It was unsolicited and unexpected. His friends, with some exceptions, advised against his acceptance, on the ground that Congress was the proper theatre for his talents; Mr. Lowndes concurred in this advice, and, among other reasons, urged that his improvement in speaking had been such that he was desirous to see the degree of eminence he would reach by practice. Indeed, the prevailing opinion at the time was, that his talent lay more in the power of thought than action. His great powers of analysis and generalization were calculated to make the impression, which was not uncommon at the time, that his mind was more metaphysical than practical, and that he would lose reputation in taking charge of a de-

* Editor's note: Compare *The Papers of John C. Calhoun*, 1:410–415.

partment, especially one in a state of such disorder and confusion as the war department was then. The reasons assigned by his friends served but to confirm Mr. Calhoun in the opinion that he ought to accept. He believed the impression of his friends was erroneous as to the character of his mind; but if not, if his powers lay rather in thinking and speaking than in execution, it was but the more necessary he should exercise them in the latter, and thereby strengthen them where they were naturally the weakest. He also believed that he could render more service to the country in reforming the great disbursing department of government, admitted to be in a state of much disorder, than he could possibly do by continuing in Congress, where most of the great questions growing out of a return to a state of peace had been discussed and settled. Under the influence of these motives, he accepted the proffered appointment, and entered on the duties of the department early in December, 1817.

Thus, after six years of distinguished services in Congress, during which Mr. Calhoun bore a prominent and efficient part in originating and supporting all the measures necessary to carry the country through one of the most trying and difficult periods of its existence, and had displayed throughout great ability as a legislator and a speaker, we find him in a new scene, where his talents for business and administration for the first time are to be tried. He took possession of his department at the most unfavourable period. Congress was in session, when much of the time of the secretary is necessarily occupied in meeting the various calls for information from the two Houses, and attending to the personal application of the members on the business of their constituents. Mr. [George] Graham, the chief clerk, an able and experienced officer, retired shortly afterward, and a new and totally inexperienced successor [Christopher Vandeventer] had to be appointed in his place. The department was almost literally without organization, and everything in a state of confusion. Mr. Calhoun had paid but little attention to military subjects in any of their various branches. He had never read a treatise on the subject, except a small volume of the Staff.

In this absence of information, he determined at once to do as little as possible at first, and to be a good listener and a close observer till he could form a just conception of the actual state of the department and what was necessary to be done. Acting on this prudent rule, he heard all and observed everything, and reflected on and digested all that he heard and saw. In less than three months he became so well acquainted with the state of the department, and what was required to be done, that he drew up himself, without consultation, the bill for organizing it on the bureau principle, and succeeded in getting it through Congress against a formidable opposition, who denounced it as wild and impracticable.* But, on the contrary, this organization has been proved to be so perfect, that it has remained unchanged through all the vicissitudes and numerous changes of parties till this time, a period of twenty-five years.

But that was only the first step. The most perfect system is of little value without able and faithful officers to carry it into execution. The President, under his advice, selected to fill the several bureaus such officers as had the confidence of the army for ability and integrity, and possessing an aptitude of talent for the service of the bureau for which they were respectively selected. With each of these Mr. Calhoun associated a junior officer, having like qualifications, for his assistant. But, to give effect to the system, one thing was still wanting—a code of rules for the department and each of its bureaus, in order to give uniformity, consistency, efficacy, and stability to the whole. These he prepared, with the assistance of the heads of the respective bureaus, under the provision of the bill for the organization of the department, which gave the secretary the power to establish rules not inconsistent with existing laws. They form a volume of considerable size, which, like the act itself, remains substantially the same, though, it is to be feared, too often neglected in practice by some of his successors. All this was completed in the course of a few months after the passage of the act, and the system put into active operation. It worked without a jar.

In a short time its fruits began to show themselves in the increased efficiency of the department and the correction of abuses, many of which were of long standing. To trace his acts through the period of more than seven years, during which Mr. Calhoun remained in the war-office, would be tedious, and occupy more space than the object of this sketch would justify. The results, which, after all, are the best tests of the system and the efficiency of an administration, must be taken as a substitute. Suffice it, then, to say, that when he came into office, he found it in a state of chaos, and left it, even in the opinion of opponents, in complete organization and order. An officer of high standing and a competent judge pronounced it the most perfectly organized and efficient military establishment for its size in the world. He found it with upward of $40,000,000 of unsettled accounts, many of them of long standing, going back almost to the origin of the government, and he reduced them to less than three millions, which con-

* Editor's note: Compare *The Papers of John C. Calhoun*, 2:lxi–lxix.

sisted, for the most part, of losses, and accounts that never can be settled. He prevented all current accumulation, by a prompt and rigid enforcement of accountability; so much so, that he was enabled to report to Congress in 1823, that "of the entire amount of money drawn from the treasury in 1822 for military service, including pensions amounting to $4,571,961[.]94, although it passed through the hands of 291 disbursing officers, there has not been a single defalcation, nor the loss of a single cent to the government." He found the army proper, including the Military Academy, costing annually more than $451 per man, including officers, professors, and cadets, and he left the cost less than $287; or, to do more exact justice to his economy, he diminished such parts of the cost per man as were susceptible of reduction by an efficient administration, excluding pay and such parts as were fixed in moneyed compensation by law, from $299 to $150. All this was effected by wise reforms, and not by parsimony (for he was liberal, as many supposed, to a fault) in the quality and quantity of the supplies, and not by a fall of prices; for in making the calculation, allowance is made for the fall or rise of prices; on every article of supply. The gross saving on the army was $1,300,000 annually, in an expenditure which reached $4,000,000 when he came into the department. This does not include the other branches of service, the ordnance, the engineer and Indian bureaus, in all of which a like rigid economy and accountability were introduced, with similar results in saving to the government.

These great improvements were made under adverse circumstances. Party excitement ran high during the period, and Mr. Calhoun came in for his full share of opposition and misrepresentation, which may be explained by the fact that his name had been presented as a candidate for the presidency. He was often thwarted in his views and defeated in his measures, and was made for years the subject of almost incessant attacks in Congress, against which he had to defend himself, but with such complete success, finally, as to silence his assailants. They had been kept constantly informed of every movement in his department susceptible of misconstruction or of being turned against him. One of the representatives, who boarded in the same house with his principal assailant, offered to disclose to Mr. Calhoun the channel through which his opponents in Congress derived the information on which they based their attacks. Mr. Calhoun declined to receive it. He said he did not object that any act of the department should be known to his bitterest enemies: that he thought well of all about him, and did not desire to change his opinion; and all that he regretted was, that if there was any one near him who desired to communicate anything to any member, he did not ask for his permission, which he would freely have given. He felt conscious he was doing his duty, and dreaded no attack. In fact, he felt no wish that these attacks should be discontinued. He knew how difficult it was to reform long-standing and inveterate abuses, and he used the assaults on the department and the army as the means of reconciling the officers, who might be profiting by them, to the measures he had adopted for their correction, and to enlist them heartily in co-operating with him in their correction, as the most certain means of saving the establishment and themselves. To this cause, and to the strong sense of justice which he exhibited on all occasions, by the decided support he gave to all who did their duty, and his no less decided discharge of his duty against all who neglected or omitted it, is to be attributed the fact that he carried through so thorough a reform, where there was so much disorder and abuse, with a popularity constantly increasing with the army. Never did a secretary leave a department with more popularity or a greater degree of attachment and devotion on the part of those connected with it than he did.

In addition to the ordinary duties of the department, he made many and able reports on the subject of our Indian affairs, on the reduction of the army, on internal improvements, and others. He revived the Military Academy, which he found in a very disordered state, and left it in great perfection; he caused a minute and accurate survey to be made of the military frontier, inland and maritime, and projected, through an able board of engineers, a plan for their defence. In conformity with this plan, he commenced a system for fortification, and made great progress in its execution, and he established a cordon of military posts from the lakes around our northwestern and southwestern frontiers to the Gulf of Mexico.

Another measure remains to be noticed, which will be regarded in aftertimes as one of the most striking and useful, although it has heretofore attracted much less attention than it deserves. In organizing the medical department, Mr. Calhoun, with those enlarged views and devotion to science which have ever characterized him, directed the surgeons at all the military posts extending over our vast country, to report accurately to the surgeon-general at Washington every case of disease, its character, its treatment, and the result, and also to keep a minute register of the weather, the temperature, the moisture, and the winds, to be reported in like manner to the surgeon-general. To enable them to comply with the order, he directed the surgeons at the various posts to be furnished with thermometers, barometers, and hygrometers, and the surgeon-general from time to time to publish the result of their observations in condensed reports, which were continued during the time he remained in the war department. The result has been, a vast mass of valuable facts, connected with the diseases and the climate of our widely-extended country, collected through the long period of nearly a quarter of a century. They have been recently collected and published in two volumes by Dr. Samuel Forney [*sic*; Forrey], of the United States army. The one is entitled "Medical Statistics," and the other "The Climate of the United States," in which many interesting facts are disclosed relative to the diseases and climate of the different portions of our country. This example has been already followed by England, on a still more enlarged scale, and will doubtless be imitated by all civilized nations, and will in time lead to most interesting discoveries in the sciences of medicine and meteorology generally. The honour of taking the first step in this important matter, and the discoveries to which it will lead, will, under the enlightened policy of Mr. Calhoun, belong to our country.

During the second term of Mr. Monroe's administration, the names of six candidates were presented to the people of the United States for the presidential office, Mr. [John Quincy] Adams, Mr. [William H.] Crawford, General [Andrew] Jackson, Mr. [Henry] Clay, Mr. [William] Lowndes, and Mr. Calhoun. The names of the two latter had been brought forward, the former by South Carolina, and the latter by Pennsylvania, and both nearly at the same time, without its being known to either that it was intended. They were warm and intimate friends, and had been so almost from their first acquaintance. They had both entered Congress at the same time, and had rarely ever differed in opinion on any political subject. Mr. Lowndes was a few years the oldest, and the first nominated. Mr. Calhoun's nomination followed almost immediately after. As soon as he heard of it, he called on Mr. L[owndes], and stated that it had been made without his knowledge or solicitation, and that he called to say that he hoped the position in which they had been placed by their friends towards each other would not affect their private and friendly relations. That he would regard it as a great misfortune should such be the effect, and was determined on his part to do everything to avoid it. Mr. Lowndes heartily reciprocated the same sentiment. It is unnecessary to state that they faithfully adhered to their resolution; and these two distinguished citizens of the same state, and nearly of the same age, set the noble and rare example of being placed by friends as rivals for the highest office in the gift of a great people, without permitting their mutual esteem and friendship to be impaired.

But, unfortunately for themselves, and, it may be said, for the country, the same harmony of feeling was not preserved between Mr. Calhoun and another of the candidates, Mr. Crawford. They had been long acquainted, and although residing in different states, they lived but a short distance apart, and had been long on friendly terms. It is difficult to trace the chain of causes by which they and their friends were brought into collision. Mr. Calhoun supported decidedly Mr. Monroe [in 1816] in his first election, when Mr. Crawford's name had been brought forward in opposition to him. He had acted as chairman of the Committee of Foreign Relations, while Mr. Monroe was Secretary of State, during Mr. Madison's time, and had, from his frequent and intimate intercourse with him, formed a high estimate of his character for honesty, fidelity, and patriotism, to which, adding his sound judgment, long public service and experience, his age, and revolutionary claims, it was natural, without disparaging the high qualifications of Mr. Crawford, he should give him the preference. Mr. Crawford's friends relied on a Congressional caucus for a nomination, to which Mr. Calhoun was opposed, and against which he long stood out with the leading friends of Mr. Monroe in Congress. They finally assented reluctantly to go into one, to avoid a split in the party. Mr. Monroe was nominated by a small majority, when, in the opinion of his friends, the majority of the people was overwhelming in his favour. It is not extraordinary that he and many of his other friends, with this impression, should have been confirmed in their objections to a caucus nomination, as calculated to be influenced by improper considerations, and thus, instead of concentrating the will of the people, as it was originally intended to do, becoming capable of being made the instrument of defeating it, and of imposing on the country a President not of its choice.

When Mr. Crawford's friends brought forward his name the second time [in 1824], they again relied on a caucus; while the friends of all the other candidates were in favour of leaving the election to a direct appeal to the sense of the people, as they all belonged to one party, and professed the same political creed. With his decided impression against a caucus, strengthened, as has been stated, by what occurred at the first election of Mr. Monroe, it is not at all surprising that Mr. Calhoun's friends should take a prominent stand against another appeal to a Congressional caucus: that, together with the latent feelings on both sides (of which both were perhaps unconscious), growing out of the stand he made in favour of Mr. Monroe and against Mr. Crawford, probably led to the regretted division between their friends, which continued, as usual, long after the cause had ceased, with such mischievous influence on the politics of the country and the party to which both belonged.

Time and experience have decided against a Congressional caucus; but it must be admitted, looking back to the scenes of that day, that much might be said for and against it. It is certainly highly desirable that the people should act directly in voting for a President, uninfluenced by the address and management of powerful combinations of individuals acting through a small body, and who, in making a nomination, may respect their own interest and feelings much more than the voice of the people, or even the party they represent. But, on the other hand, without the intermediate agency of some such body in so large a country, and with so many prominent citizens from which to make a selection, the danger of discord in the ranks of the majority, and, through it, of the triumph of a minority in the election, is great. The chance is between discord with all its consequences, and the dictation of party leaders with all its effects. Each is pregnant with mischief. It is the weak point of the government, and unless it be guarded with the utmost vigilance, must end, on the one hand, in interminable confusion, or, on the other, in rendering the election by the people merely nominal. Without such vigilance, the real election would degenerate into the dictation of caucus. It was on this difficult point that the friends of these two distinguished citizens split, and it is left to time and experience yet to decide which were right.

In the progress of the canvass the talented and lamented Lowndes died, in the prime of life, and Mr. Calhoun's friends in Pennsylvania, with his acquiescence, withdrew his name, rather than subject the state to a violent contest between them and the friends of General Jackson. They had maintained throughout the canvass the most friendly relations, and were both decidedly opposed to the caucus. On his withdrawal, he was taken up by the friends both of General Jackson and Mr. Adams for the Vice-presidency.

This memorable canvass terminated in returning General Jackson, Mr. Adams, and Mr. Crawford to the House of Representatives, from which three, by the provisions of the Constitution, one was to be elected. The electoral votes received by each stood in the order in which their names are placed. Mr. Calhoun was elected by the people Vice-president by a large majority. The House, voting by states, on the first ballot elected Mr. Adams. Mr. Clay, who was then a member of the body, voted for him, against, as it was believed, the sense of a majority of his constituents. That impression, connected with his previous relations, personal and political, with Mr. Adams, caused much excitement, and a strong determination on the part of many to organize forthwith an opposition to the new administration. Mr. Calhoun discountenanced an immediate move, on the ground that, although, in his opinion, the vote belonged to the state, and should be given to the candidate the state would elect if left to its choice, yet he was not prepared to say whether there might not be circumstances under which a member might assume the high responsibility of voting otherwise, and, for the justification of his conduct, throw himself on the state; but he thought it indispensable that the member assuming it should make out a strong case, and that he would owe it to himself and the country to place his relations and conduct towards the administration of him whom he had elected above all suspicion. His advice induced his friends to wait the development of events; but when Mr. Clay afterward took office, and Mr. Adams adopted, in its full extent, Mr. Clay's American System, opposition to the administration from himself and his friends followed as a matter of course.

CHAPTER IV.

Including the Period during which he was Vice-president.

Mr. Calhoun took his seat in the Senate as Vice-president on the 4th of March, 1825, having remained in the war department a few months more than seven years. There never was a department left in more perfect order. It literally almost moved of itself. When he took charge of the department, it was difficult to discharge its duties with less than fourteen or fifteen hours of severe daily labour; but when he left it, the secretary had little to do beyond signing his name and deciding on such cases as were brought up by the subordinate officers, and were not embraced in the numerous and comprehensive rules provided for their government. He had not, indeed, been long in office before those who doubted his executive talents were disposed to place them even above his parliamentary, great as they were acknowledged to be. He united, in a remarkable degree, quickness with precision, firmness with patience and courtesy, and industry with the higher capacity for arrangement and organization; and to these he added exemption from favouritism, a high sense of justice and inflexible devotion to duty. Taken together, they formed a combi-

44

nation so fortunate, that General [Simon] Bernard, who had been a favourite aid-de-camp of the Emperor Napoleon, and saw and knew much of him, and who was chief of the board of engineers while Mr. Calhoun was secretary, and had an equal opportunity of observing him, not unfrequently, it is said, compared his administrative talents to those of that extraordinary man.

The duties of the office of Vice-president, though it is one of high dignity, are limited, except giving a casting vote when the body is equally divided, to presiding in the Senate, which, in a body so small and courteous, and having so few and simple rules, affords but little opportunity for the display even of the peculiar talents necessary for Presidency in a deliberative body. The most eminent in filling such an office cannot leave much behind worth remembering. It is sufficient to say of him, that, as a presiding officer, he was impartial, prompt, methodical, and attentive to his duties. He always appeared and took his seat early in the session, and continued to preside till within a short time of its close; contrary to the practice of some of his immediate predecessors, who, by their long and frequent absence from their seat, had permitted the office to fall into some discredit. He was careful in preserving the dignity of the Senate, and raising its influence and weight in the action of the government. In putting questions, he changed the form of address from "Gentlemen" to the more simple and dignified address of "Senators," which has since been preserved, and adopted by the senators themselves in alluding to each other in debate. But the most important and memorable incident connected with the discharge of his duty as the presiding officer, and the most characteristic of the man, was the stand he took in favour of the rights of the body itself, and against his own power. He decided [in 1826], during a period of great excitement on the Panama Question, when party spirit ran high, and the debate was very warm and personal, that he had no right to call a senator to order *for words spoken in debate.* He rested his decision on the broad ground that, as the presiding officer, he had no power but to carry into effect the rules adopted by the body, either expressly or by usage, and that there was neither rule nor usage to authorize him to exercise the power in question. On the contrary, the rules of the Senate, by strong implication, limited the power of calling to order *for words spoken in debate* to the members themselves, to the exclusion of the presiding officer. And yet this decision, resting on so solid a foundation, subjected Mr. Calhoun to the fiercest attacks and the grossest abuse; and, what is more extraordinary, he was opposed by the members themselves, whose rights he maintained, with the exception of Mr. [Nathaniel] Macon, Mr. [Littleton W.] Tazewell, and a few others of the elder and more experienced, and his immediate personal friends. To understand how this should happen, it is necessary to advert to the existing state of the parties, and the circumstances under which the decision was made.

The circumstances under which Mr. Adams was elected, the part which Mr. Clay took in his election, and the prominent position to which he was appointed in his cabinet, laid the foundation of the opposition which finally overthrew his administration. This opposition was greatly strengthened by the bold Federal and consolidation doctrines avowed by Mr. Adams in his inaugural address, and by the wild measures of policy which he recommended. Among these was the project of sending commissioners to the Congress proposed to be convened at Panama of all the states that had grown up on the overthrow of the Spanish dominions on this Continent. This was a favourite measure of the administration. Mr. Calhoun was understood to be decidedly opposed to it, both on the ground of unconstitutionality and inexpediency; and it was on that question that the first attack was made on the administration. It commenced in the Senate; and, as he had not disguised his disapprobation, he was regarded in a great measure as the adviser and author of the attack, which, of course, subjected him to the fierce and united assaults of the administration and its friends. At the same time, the opposition in the Senate, though united against the administration, and its doctrines and policy, consisted of individuals who had but a short time before held political relations with men far from being friendly. They consisted of the friends of Mr. Crawford, General Jackson, Mr. Calhoun, and such portion of Mr. Clay's as disapproved of his connexion with Mr. Adams. With the exception of his own friends, and those of General Jackson, there was no indisposition, on the part of a large portion of the rest of the opposition, to see him sacrificed by the party in power. But as difficult and critical as was his position, it could not prevent him from a manly avowal of his opinion on a novel, and what he believed to be an important question, or from exposing himself to hazard when principle and duty required him to assert the rights of the body, though against his own power. But what added greatly to the excitement and abuse was the particular occasion upon which the decision was made. Mr. Randolph was then a member of the Senate, and gave full vent to his inimitably sarcastic power against the administration, and especially against the President and the Secretary of State, and their supporters in the body. It was too keenly felt by the last to permit them to do justice to the grounds on which Mr. Calhoun placed his decision, and the occasion was too favourable to be permitted to pass without a formal attack on him. A writer of great power (supposed to be the President himself) attacked his decision with much acrimony, under the signature of Patrick Henry. Finding it impossible to assail the decision with effect, or through the rules of the Senate or its usage, he was forced to assume the position that the Vice-president, in virtue of his office, derived the power of calling a senator to order *for words spoken in debate*, not from the body itself, but directly from the Constitution, and that, in exercising the power, he was wholly independent of its will. This gave the whole subject a new and highly important aspect; for if it could be successfully maintained, it would give the Vice-president supreme control over the freedom of debate in the Senate. To this a reply followed (supposed to be from Mr. Calhoun), in two numbers, under the signature of Onslow, that so completely demolished the argument of Patrick Henry as to turn the tide in his favour. The Senate itself became so well satisfied of the injustice done him, that on the revisal of the rules a year or two afterward, they gave him the power in question, with an almost unanimous approval of his decision. It was thus, by his fairness under these trying circumstances, that he preserved a right of the body, which he might have usurped, not only with safety, but with increased popularity for the time; but of which the Senate could not be divested without a surrender of the freedom of debate, and the right of making their own rules, secured to them by the Constitution itself.*

So vigorous was this first onset of the opposition, that the administration reeled under the force of the blow, and it became apparent that nothing but some bold step could save them from defeat, by the election of General Jackson, under whom the opposition, with the hearty concurrence of Mr. Calhoun and his friends, had unanimously rallied. The great strength of the administration lay in the various powerful interests rallied under the plausible name of Home Industry and the American System, of which the Secretary of State was the acknowledged head, and to which the President had given his adhesion. Their hope of holding power rested on a unanimous and zealous rally of that powerful combination in favour of the administration. The tariff was the great central interest, around which all the others revolved. The whole party, without schism, were united in its favour, while the opposition was greatly divided in reference to

* Editor's note: The complete exchange between "Patrick Henry" and "Onslow" is printed in *The Papers of John C. Calhoun*, vol. X.

it; a great portion of the party, North and West, being in its favour, while the South and Southwest were united almost to a man against it. In fact, the portion of the Union at that time most attached to a high protective tariff was the Middle and Western States, and yet its union with the South and Southwestern portion was indispensable to the election of General Jackson. The advantage this state of things afforded was perceived by those in power, and was not permitted to remain without an attempt to turn it to account.

For that purpose, a general convention was called to meet [in 7/-1827] at Harrisburg, the seat of government in Pennsylvania, and the friends of the tariff everywhere were invited to take into consideration the state of the manufacturing interest, and to devise measures for its farther promotion. The place was well chosen. Pennsylvania, though a thorough tariff state, was favourable to General Jackson's election, and its support was regarded as indispensable to his success. It met, and attempted to rally the whole interest by an elaborate report in favour of the protective system, accompanied by a scheme of high duties, to be presented to Congress at the next session for its action. It was thought, if the friends of General Jackson in the tariff states should oppose it, his defeat in those states would be certain; but if, on the contrary, they should support it, a schism between his Northern and Southern supporters would be equally certain, and with not less certainty would be followed by his defeat. But, as plausible as the calculation was, the tariff friends of General Jackson in New-York, Pennsylvania, New-Jersey, and the West, succeeded, as far as politics were concerned, in turning it against its projectors.

They succeeded in electing the speaker [Andrew Stevenson], and in obtaining the majority of the Committee of Manufactures in the House. Instead of adopting the Harrisburg scheme, this committee reported a thorough protective tariff, such as suited the states they represented, imposing duties even higher and more indiscriminately than those of the Harrisburg plan. They laid their duties without the slightest regard to the navigating and commercial interests of New-England, and so managed it as to induce the Southern members to resist all the amendments offered to render it acceptable to those who represented that interest, in the expectation of defeating the bill, either on its passage through the House or in the Senate, by the united votes of the members from those states and the South and Southwest. The expectation proved fallacious. The bill passed the House by a small majority, a large portion of the New-England members voting against it; but when it came to the Senate, where the relative united strength of the Southern and New-England States is much greater than in the House, it was ascertained that the bill could not pass unless it was modified so as to be acceptable to the senators from New-England favourable to the administration. It was so modified by the votes of the senators opposed to the administration from the Middle and Western States, contrary to the expectation of the South; for the bill, as modified, received the votes of the New-England senators in favour of the administration, which, added to those in favour of General Jackson from New-York, New-Jersey, Pennsylvania, and the Northwest, made a majority. It passed, accordingly, and became a law [as the Tariff of 1828]; but under such circumstances as not only to deprive the administration of the advantage they anticipated from the scheme, but to turn it directly against them.

Unfortunately, however, in this political manoeuv[e]ring in the presidential contest, equity, justice, the Constitution, and the public welfare were overlooked. The interest of the great body of the consumers and of nine tenths of the producing interests, including especially the growers of the great agricultural staples, rice, cotton, and tobacco, with those engaged in commerce, ship-building, and navigation, and all their connected interests, were sacrificed to promote the prosperity of a single interest, and that constituting but a small portion of the community. But the evil ended not with their sacrifice, as immense as it was. As bad as was the effect in its pecuniary bearing, it was far worse in its financial, political, and moral operation. Never, in that respect, was a measure of the kind passed under more adverse circumstances. Viewed in its financial aspect, it was worse than folly—it was madness itself. The public debt was nearly extinguished, under the wise policy adopted after the war. After its final discharge, one half nearly of the annual revenue applied to the payment of its principal and interest would be liberated, which, if a wise and just policy had been adopted, would have enabled the government to reduce the duties one half, and still leave a sufficient revenue to provide amply for all the public wants. Instead of that, and in the face of these consequences, the duties were greatly increased, so much so as to be, on an average, nearly fifty per cent. on the value of the imports. This led to a corresponding increase of the revenue, which, in turn, hastened proportionally the final discharge of the debt, when, by necessity, one of three consequences must follow: a vast increase of expenditures; a sudden reduction of the duties, to the ruin of the manufacturers; or else an immense surplus in the treasury, with all its corrupting influence. These obvious results were either not seen or disregarded by those who were governed by cupidity, or too intensely engaged in the presidential contest to look to consequences.

It is regarded as necessary to understand the history of the origin and passage of that disastrous measure, in order to have a just conception of the events which have since occurred, and the motives which governed Mr. Calhoun's course in reference to them. To it may be traced almost every important incident in our political history since that time, as far as our internal affairs are concerned. To it, too, may be ascribed the division in the Republican party, which separated Mr. Calhoun and the States' Rights portion from the other, and the disasters which have impaired the credit and standing of the country, and deranged and interrupted its currency, finances, commerce, and industrial operations. Mr. Calhoun, although not an actor at the time, was not an inattentive observer of what passed. His position as President of the Senate afforded great advantages for observation and reflection, of which he did not fail to avail himself from the time he first took his seat. Questions relating to the protective policy were constantly occurring in one form or another, and especially attracted his attention and excited reflection. He was not long in making himself master of that policy in all its bearings, economical and political, and in becoming thoroughly satisfied that it was unconstitutional, unjust, unequal, and oppressive in its character and tendency, and that it must, in the end, if it became the established and permanent policy, lead to the overthrow of our free and popular system of government. With this impression of the system, he watched with vigilance the progress of the tariff of 1828, from its incipient state at Harrisburg to the passage of the bill through the Senate. The results of his observation confirmed him in all his previous objections to the system, and strengthened his conviction of the dangers to which it exposed our institutions. For the first time he began to fear, from the part taken in the passage of the bill in the Senate by a considerable and influential portion of the party, that the leading object which he and his friends had in view in the presidential contest (a gradual and cautious reduction of the duties to the revenue standard preparatory to the discharge of the debt) might not be realized by a change of administration. He saw that the passage of the bill opposed great and almost insuperable difficulties to effecting what they desired; but neither he nor they permitted these misgivings to abate their zeal in support of General Jackson's election. They still hoped for the best from him; and how strongly Mr. C[alhoun] desired his election, an occurrence at the time will best illustrate.

The Senate was so nearly equally divided at one time, that it was believed that the friends of the administration would intentionally so arrange it as to make a tie, and throw the casting vote on the Vice-president, in order to defeat General Jackson's election. His friends became alarmed, and some of them intimated a desire that Mr. Calhoun should leave his seat to avoid the effect, stating as an inducement that, in the event of a tie, the bill would be defeated without his vote. He promptly refused, and replied that no consideration could prevent him from remaining and doing his duty by voting against it; but added, it should not hurt General Jackson's election, for in that event his name should be withdrawn from the ticket as Vice-president. Such was the interest he took in his success, and so strong, and, at the same time, so patriotic, was his opposition to the bill of abominations; and yet many have been so unjust as to attribute his after opposition to the bill to disappointed ambition. On the contrary, he was ready to sacrifice every object of ambition, at a time when not a cloud darkened his prospects, to defeat a measure he believed to be so fraught with mischief. He was then the second officer in the government, and stood, without opposition, for re-election to the same place, on the ticket of General Jackson, whose success was then certain; nor was there any other man in the party of equal prominence and popularity, except the general himself. Nothing was wanting on his part but to accommodate himself to the course of events, without regard to their effects on the country, to have attained the highest office, which lay within a single step from the place where he then stood. This he could not but plainly see; but his resisting temptation on this occasion is but one instance of self-sacrifice among many in a long life, the whole course of which abundantly proves that office, even the highest, has ever been with him subordinate to his sense of duty and the public welfare.

The entire South was justly indignant at the passage of so unjust and oppressive a measure, especially under the circumstances which attended it, and the question universally asked was, What is to be done? On his return home this question was often and emphatically asked him. He was not the man to evade it. He frankly replied that there was no hope from Congress; that in both houses there were fixed majorities in favour of the system, and that there was no hope of any speedy change for the better; but, on the contrary, things must grow worse, if no efficient remedy should be applied. He said that he could see but two possible remedies within the limits of the Constitution; one, the election of General Jackson, who, by bringing to bear systematically and steadily the patronage which the protective system placed in his hands, might reduce the duties down to the revenue standard; and the other, State Interposition or Veto, the high remedy pointed out in the Virginia and Kentucky resolutions as the proper one, after all others had failed, against oppressive and dangerous acts of the general government, in palpable violation of the Constitution. He gave it as his opinion that there was no hope from the judiciary, and, as the act stood, the constitutional question could not be brought before the courts, the majority having refused to amend the title of the bill so as to make it appear on the face of it that the duties were laid for protection and not for revenue, expressly with the view of preventing the courts from taking jurisdiction, and deciding on its constitutionality. He also stated that, although he regarded General Jackson's election as certain, yet he was constrained to say that the circumstances under which the act passed, and the part which many of his influential supporters took in its passage, made it doubtful whether the hopes entertained from his election would, as it regarded the protective system, be realized, and expressed his belief that South Carolina would in the end be obliged to resort to its ultimate constitutional remedy by state interposition, and the ruinous consequences which must inevitably result from the act to itself, to the South, and finally to the whole Union.

Many of the leading citizens of the state visited Mr. Calhoun at his residence, near the mountains in South Carolina, during the summer and autumn [of 1828] after his return from Washington, with all of whom he conversed freely, and expressed the same sentiments. But while he stated his conviction of the necessity of preparing in time for the worst, he always advised that there should be no precipitation, nor anything done to endanger the election of General Jackson, nor, indeed, afterward, till it was ascertained whether his administration would correct the evil before the public debt was finally discharged. He fixed on that as the period for invoking the high authority of the state, as one of the sovereign parties to the constitutional compact, to arrest the evil, not only because he thought that ample time ought to be allowed to see if anything would be done, but because he believed that so long as the money, however unjustly and unconstitutionally extorted from the people by the act of '28, was applied to the payment of the debt, it should be borne. But he thought, if the operation of the act should not then be arrested promptly, the vast surplus revenue which it would afterward pour into the treasury would be converted into the means of perpetuating it, and fixing the system on the country permanently and beyond the reach of any constitutional remedy.

He was the more deeply impressed with the danger from what had already occurred. A leading advocate of the measure in the Senate, Mr. [Mahlon] Dickerson, of New-Jersey, the chairman of the Committee on Manufactures, and since Secretary of the Navy, had already moved in anticipation of the payment of the debt, and with the view of strengthening the protective system, that five millions of dollars should annually be taken from the treasury and divided among the states. Such a proposition could not fail to arouse the attention and apprehension of one so sagacious and vigilant as Mr. Calhoun. He saw at once the full extent of the danger. No measure could be devised more insidious, corrupting, or better calculated to effect the object contemplated. The money proposed to be so divided would never return to the pockets of the tax-paying people from whom it was first taken. It would go to the State Legislatures, to be disposed of as they should think proper, and would constitute a fund, in the management of which there would be no responsibility, under the control of the majority of the Legislature, or, rather, of the few leaders of the majority for the time, to be converted by them into means of power and emolument for themselves, through their partisans and friends. The necessary effect would be, that the leaders for the time in all the State Legislatures, even of those most injured by the system, would be interested in its favour; as they, and their friends and partisans, would derive more from the administration and application of the fund than they had contributed to it, as tax-payers, under the duties from which it was derived. Seeing these consequences, he could not doubt that, if the measure was once adopted, it would absorb in its vortex the whole surplus revenue after the discharge of the debt, and unite the General and State Governments in support of a universal system of plunder. Under that state of things, he believed the evil would become remediless, and our free and popular institutions would sink into a mass of corruption. With this impression, he used his utmost influence against this incipient move. It was defeated for the time, but not without deep apprehension, on his part, that it would revive and finally prevail, unless the protective policy, from which this monstrous measure derived its origin as a legitimate offspring, was effectually and forever destroyed. It was this view of the subject that so strongly impressed him with the necessity of decisive action, should the coming administration fail to put it down, and confirmed him in the belief that the time for action should by no means be delayed beyond the final discharge of the public debt.

So deep was his conviction of the danger, that when he was requested by [William C. Preston] one of the members elected to the

Legislature of South Carolina, with whom he had conversed freely when on a visit to him, and who expected to be on the Committee of Federal Relations, to give him his views on the subject, he did not hesitate to draw them up in the shape of a report, in which he fully expressed himself as to the disease, the danger, and remedy; and, regardless of popularity, he gave him authority to state who was its author, should he think it would be of any service. The paper was reported by the committee with some, though not material alterations. Five thousand copies were ordered by the Legislature to be printed, under the title of "The South Carolina Exposition and Protest on the subject of the Tariff."

But while the Legislature were thus preparing to arrest, in the last resort, the obnoxious act, if it should become necessary, they showed, at the same time, their continued confidence in General Jackson. The presidential election came on at the same session, and the electors who were appointed by the Legislature gave their votes to General Jackson and Mr. Calhoun, who were elected by a large majority of the whole electoral college.

His [Jackson's] inaugural address was received with enthusiasm by the people of the state, and strong hopes were entertained that their expectations upon his election would be fully realized, and the necessity of resorting to the ultimate remedy of the Constitution avoided; but his first message, at the commencement of the next session, went far to extinguish their hopes.

Here we reach a period of history of which it will be difficult to treat without reviving some recollection of the unfortunate difference which, for a time, divided the Republican party, now so happily united in the defence of their common principles and of constitutional liberty. But, referring to the past, as we shall for its facts, and not for its feelings, we shall endeavour to give so much of this history as is indispensable to an explanation of Mr. Calhoun's connexion with political affairs, as it will hereafter be written by some impartial hand—an effort which, we trust, may not be unacceptable to the great actors of that day, if they should find it but a calm and dispassionate review of those trying and eventful scenes in which they bore so prominent a part. To suppose that any man would recoil from the truth of history is to attribute to him the meanest and most unmanly of fears—an injustice which no motives of false delicacy would make us even seem to offer to those whom we respect as friends. In discharging our duty as chroniclers, we shall not presume to decide upon the merits of past disputes, as our immediate object may be accomplished without entering upon that delicate ground. In stating the opinions and course of Mr. Calhoun, it is not always with a view of justifying them, and we may disapprove some features in the policy of President Jackson without doubting his motives, or disparaging his great abilities and eminent public services. Each of these great men is too deservedly proud of the past to wish to disguise or conceal any portion of that history upon which he rests his pretensions for fame; and the highest evidence of a noble nature is that candour which receives truth without offence whenever it is truthfully told. Now that the fires of old feuds have burned out, and the excitement of the time has passed away, we doubt not but that each will look upon the past without passion and with impartiality.

But to resume the thread of our narrative. The first message of the President, in December, 1829, did not remove the apprehensions which heretofore had weighed so heavily upon Mr. Calhoun's mind—apprehensions which then seemed the more exaggerated as he, perhaps, was the only man of the time who measured, in their full extent, the consequences of a system against which he was destined soon to peril his all in deadly strife. One of the paragraphs in this message declares that, "After the extinction of the public debt, it is not probable that any adjustment of the tariff, upon principles satisfactory to the people of the Union, will, until a remote period, if ever, leave the government without a considerable surplus in the treasury beyond what may be required for its current service." After discussing various modes of applying this surplus, the message thus again proceeds: "To avoid these evils, it appears to me that the most safe, just, and federal disposition which could be made of this surplus revenue would be its apportionment among the several states, according to their ratio of representation; and, should this measure not be found warranted by the Constitution, that it would be expedient to propose to the states an amendment authorizing it." These recommendations were not calculated to relieve the apprehensions of Mr. Calhoun as to the danger of a long continuance of the protective system and its union with distribution; a conjunction which, of all others, he regarded as the most formidable to the liberties of our people and the permanence of their free institutions; and, at the same time, they contributed to make a deep and lasting impression upon the people of South Carolina, and greatly increased their efforts to disseminate correct information as to the nature of the evil, and the absolute necessity of averting it by the separate action of the state, if not done by the General Government, all hope of which was now wellnigh gone. The next annual message recurred to the same topics. "In my first message," said President Jackson, "I stated it to be my opinion that 'it is not probable that any adjustment of the tariff, upon principles satisfactory to the people of the Union, will, until a remote period, if ever, leave the government without a considerable surplus in the treasury beyond what may be required for its current service.' I have had no cause to change that opinion, but much to confirm it." In another part of the same message he said, "Thus viewing the subject, I have heretofore felt it my duty to recommend the adoption of some plan for the distribution of the surplus funds, which may at any time remain in the treasury after the national debt shall have been paid, among the states, in proportion to the number of their representatives, to be applied by them to objects of internal improvement. Although this plan has met with favour in some portions of the' Union, it has also elicited objections, which merit deliberate consideration." These he proceeded to state and answer at great length. It soon became apparent that systematic movements were making in the leading tariff states to enforce this policy by the weight of their influence. The governors of New-York and Pennsylvania followed with similar recommendations, and their respective legislatures adopted strong resolutions in favour of the scheme. The door of hope from without seemed to be wellnigh closed. Unless the state should interpose to avert this system by her separate action, it appeared inevitable that the tariff of 1828, that "bill of abominations," would be perpetuated in connexion with a distribution of the surplus revenue after the payment of the debt, with all of its dangerous and corrupting consequences. South Carolina did not hesitate in her choice between these alternatives. Everywhere the subject of state remedies was agitated, and the elections throughout the state turned upon that deeply-exciting and important question.

In the mean time, the personal relations between Mr. Calhoun and the President had been impaired by various causes, and in the spring of 1830 the difference became serious and the rupture complete. Separated as they now were upon great public questions, and alienated also by private differences, it is not surprising that the President should have directed the whole weight of his immense popularity against Mr. Calhoun; nor had the latter any resource in the opposition, who, separated from him in principle and policy, bore down upon him with their whole strength and influence. These things, of themselves, seemed to constitute difficulties of sufficient magnitude to overpower him. On the whole expanse of the wide American Continent, there were, perhaps, but two spirits that could have encountered them; and these, strangely enough, were the two individuals who were destined to conduct the two parties in the tremendous contest that was approaching. But, undaunted at the prospect, and strong not only in the consciousness of his intellectual resources, but also in that high resolve which springs from a deep sense of wrong, Mr. Calhoun fearlessly assumed the responsibility of the movement in the great issue which South Carolina was preparing to make with the General Government; and, in obedience to the calls on him from various quarters, he unhesitatingly avowed his opinions on the complex and difficult questions arising out of it. It would be difficult to imagine a situation of more peril, or a greater example of self-abandonment and moral intrepidity. He and the state now stood alone in open, bold, and undaunted resistance against the scheme of a permanent distribution of the surplus revenue, sustained by a perpetual protective tariff. They were assailed with equal fierceness by the administration and opposition parties and they were deserted by all the Southern states, though most of them had adopted the strongest resolutions, declaring the tariff of '28 to be oppressive, unjust, unequal, and unconstitutional, and pledging themselves in the most positive manner to oppose it. Nothing but the deepest conviction of the truth and justice of their cause, and of the magnitude of the questions, could have sustained him under such difficulties, and in the face of so imposing a force.

He commenced the address [of 7/26/1831] containing the avowal of his opinion with a statement of his views on the question of the relation which the states bear to the General Government. After referring to the Virginia and Kentucky resolutions, the Virginia report and the decision of the Supreme Court of Pennsylvania in the case of [William] Cobbett, as containing a summary of his opinion, he said, "As many might not have an opportunity to refer to them, and as different opinions might be entertained as to their meaning, he would, to avoid all ambiguity, and that his sentiments might be fully known, state his opinions of the doctrine which he believed they embraced." With these preliminary remarks, he proceeded to give, in the first place, a concise summary of the doctrines they embraced, and in the next, his impression of the character and tendency of these doctrines, followed up by a calm, lucid, and able array of reasons in support of his opinion; and, finally, brought the whole to bear on the protective system, and the dangers to which it exposed our political institutions. He then showed that the period of the final payment of the debt was fast approaching, and that, if the threatened danger was not promptly met, the most disastrous consequences would follow; and, finally, if the government itself should fail to meet it, state interposition was the only adequate and constitutional remedy which could arrest it.

The following extract from this manly and able document contains
the doctrines of state interposition or nullification, with his impression
of its character and tendency:

"The great and leading principle is, that the General Government
emanated from the people of the several states, forming distinct political communities, and acting in their separate and sovereign capacity, and not from all of the people forming one aggregate political
community; that the Constitution of the United States is, in fact, a
compact, to which each state is a party, in the character already described; and that the several states or parties have a right to judge
of its infractions, and, in case of a deliberate, palpable, and dangerous
exercise of power not delegated, they have the right, in the last resort,
to use the language of the Virginia resolutions, *'to interpose for arresting the progress of the evil, and for maintaining, within their respective limits, the authorities, rights, and liberties appertaining to
them.'* This right of interposition, thus solemnly asserted by the State
of Virginia, be it called what it may, state-right, veto, nullification, or
by any other name, I conceive to be the fundamental principle of our
system, resting on facts historically as certain as our Revolution itself,
and deductions as simple and demonstrative as that of any political or
moral truth whatever; and I firmly believe that on its recognition depends the stability and safety of our political institutions.

"I am not ignorant that those opposed to the doctrine have always,
now and formerly, regarded it in a very different light, as anarchical
and revolutionary. Could I believe such in fact to be its tendency,
to me it would be no recommendation. I yield to none, I trust, in a
deep and sincere attachment to our political institutions, and the
union of these states. I never breathed an opposite sentiment; but,
on the contrary, I have ever considered them the great instrument of
preserving our liberty, and promoting the happiness of ourselves and
our posterity; and, next to these, I have ever held them most dear.
Nearly half my life has passed in the service of the Union, and whatever public reputation I have acquired is indissolubly identified with
it. To be too national has, indeed, been considered by many, even of
my friends, to be my greatest political fault. With these strong feelings of attachment, I have examined, with the utmost care, the
bearing of the doctrine in question; and so far from anarchical or revolutionary, I solemnly believe it to be the only solid foundation of our
system and of the Union itself, and that the opposite doctrine, which
denies to the states the right of protecting their several powers, and
which would vest in the General Government (it matters not through
what department) the right of determining, exclusively and finally,

the powers delegated to it, is incompatible with the sovereignty of the states and of the Constitution itself, considered as the basis of a Federal Union. As strong as this language is, it is not stronger than that used by the illustrious Jefferson, who said, to give to the General Government the final and exclusive right to judge of its powers, is to make '*its discretion,* and *not the Constitution, the measure of its powers;*' and that '*in all cases of compact between parties having no common judge, each party has an equal right to judge for itself, as well of the infraction as of the mode and measure of redress.*' Language cannot be more explicit, nor can higher authority be adduced.

"That different opinions are entertained on this subject, I consider but as an additional evidence of the great diversity of the human intellect. Had not able, experienced, and patriotic individuals, for whom I have the highest respect, taken different views, I should have thought the right too clear to admit of doubt; but I am taught by this, as well as by many similar instances, to treat with deference opinions differing from my own. The error may possibly be with me; but, if so, I can only say, that after the most mature and conscientious examination, I have not been able to detect it. But with all proper deference, I must think that theirs is the error who deny what seems to be an essential attribute of the conceded sovereignty of the states, and who attribute to the General Government a right utterly incompatible with what all acknowledge to be its limited and restricted character; an error originating principally, as I think, in not duly reflecting on the nature of our institutions, and on what constitutes the only rational object of all political constitutions."

The following are the three concluding paragraphs, which will exhibit the tone and feeling with which the address was written.

"In forming the opinions I have expressed, I have not been actuated by an unkind feeling to our manufacturing interest. I now am, and ever have been, decidedly friendly to them, though I cannot concur in all the measures which have been adopted to advance them. I believe considerations higher than any question of mere pecuniary interest forbid their use. But, subordinate to the higher views of policy, I regard the advancement of mechanical and chemical improvements in the arts with feelings little short of enthusiasm, not only as the prolific source of national and individual wealth, but as the great means of enlarging the domain of man over the material world, and thereby of laying the solid foundation of a highly-improved condition of society, morally and politically. I fear not that we shall extend our power too far over the great agents of nature; but, on the contrary, I consider such enlargement of our power as tending more certainly and powerfully to better the condition of our race, than any one of the many powerful causes now operating to that result. With these impressions, I not only rejoice at the general progress of the arts in the world, but on their advancement in our own country; and, as far as protection may be incidentally afforded in the fair and honest exercise of our constitutional powers, I think now, as I have always done, that sound policy, connected with the security, independence, and peace of the country, requires it should be; but we cannot go a single step beyond without jeopardizing our peace, our harmony, and our liberty—considerations of infinitely more importance to us than any measure of mere policy can possibly be.

"In thus placing my opinion before the public, I have not been actuated by the expectation of changing the public sentiment. Such a motive on a question so long agitated, and so beset with feelings of prejudice and interest, would argue, on my part, an insufferable vanity, and a profound ignorance of the human heart. To avoid, as far as possible, the imputation of either, I have confined my statement on the many and important points on which I have been compelled to touch, to a simple declaration of my opinion, without advancing any other reasons to sustain them than what appeared to me to be indispensable to the full understanding of my views; and if they should, on any point, be thought to be not clearly and explicitly developed, it will, I trust, be attributed to my solicitude to avoid the imputations to which I have alluded, and not from any desire to disguise my sentiments, nor the want of arguments and illustrations to maintain positions which so abound in both, that it would require a volume to do them anything like justice. I can only hope that truths which I feel assured are essentially connected with all we ought to hold most dear, may not be weakened in the public estimation by the imperfect manner in which I have been, by the object in view, compelled to present them.

"With every caution on my part, I dare not hope, in taking the step I have, to escape the imputation of improper motives, though I have, without reserve, freely expressed my opinions, not regarding whether they might or might not be popular. I have no reason to believe that they are such as will conciliate public favour, but the opposite, which I greatly regret, as I have ever placed a high estimate on the good opinion of my fellow-citizens. But, be that as it may, I shall, at least, be sustained by feelings of conscious rectitude. I have formed my opinions after the most careful and deliberate examinations, with all the aids which my reason and experience could furnish;

I have expressed these honestly and fearlessly, regardless of their effects personally, which, however interesting to me individually, are of too little importance to be taken into the estimate, where the liberty and happiness of our country are so vitally involved."

He followed up, the next year, this statement of his opinion by a letter [of 8/28/1832] addressed to General [James] Hamilton [Jr.], then governor of the state, at his request, in which he went into the same subjects more fully, and with additional force of argument and illustration. They both did much to enlighten the state on the subject discussed, and to sustain her in the arduous struggle into which she was preparing to enter.

In the mean time, the period selected for final and decisive action was rapidly approaching, and the excitement in the state became deeper and deeper. A strong party, under able leaders, had risen in the state against the course proposed to be taken. They admitted the tariff to be unconstitutional and oppressive, but disagreed as to the remedy, which they regarded as revolutionary, and not warranted by the Constitution. They assumed the popular name of the Union party. The whole weight of the General Government was thrown in their favour. The two parties were drawn up in fierce array against each other, and every nerve was strained on each side to gain the ascendency. The whole energy and talents of the state were aroused, and the people were incessantly addressed on both sides, through speeches, pamphlets, and newspapers, by the ablest men, in manly and eloquent arguments, making direct appeal to their understandings and patriotism, on all the questions involved in the issue.

At this stage, a gleam of light inspired the hope that the necessity of resorting to the extreme remedy of the Constitution would be unnecessary. President Jackson, in his message to Congress at the opening of the session in December, 1831, omitting for the first time all allusion to the scheme of distribution, announced the near approach of the period when the public debt would be finally paid, and recommended that provision should be made for the reduction of the duties and the relief of the people from unnecessary taxation, after the extinguishment of the debt. The message diffused general joy throughout the state. It was believed that the scheme of distribution was abandoned, and was hoped, late as it was, that most of the mischief anticipated from the surplus revenue, by a prompt and judicious reduction of the duties, might be still avoided. The delegation in Congress prepared to co-operate zealously with the friends of the administration in making such a reduction as would relieve the people

61

from unnecessary taxation, and save the country and government from the worst of all evils, an accumulating and corrupting surplus, collected in bank notes, or, what was the same thing, bank credit.

But this gleam of sunshine proved transient and illusory. It soon became apparent that neither side, administration or opposition, contemplated anything like an adequate reduction. In spite of every effort made by the delegation, and after spending the greater portion of the session on the subject, an inconsiderable reduction of some three or four millions of dollars only was effected. This still left a revenue more than twice as large as the usual and necessary expenditure of the government would require after the payment of the debt, and the duties at high protective rates, on what were called the protected articles; and as if, too, to extinguish all hope, this trifling reduction was announced by Mr. Clay on the part of the opposition, and the Secretary of the Treasury [Louis McLane] on that of the administration, as the final adjustment of the tariff, and the permanent system of revenue, after the payment of the debt. In a striking particular, the act making the reduction was even more unequal and worse than the tariff of '28. It exempted the manufacturing portion of the community almost literally from all taxes. It gave them a bounty on all they made by imposing duties on all similar articles imported, and all such as could come in competition with what they made, while it exempted them, as consumers, from paying taxes on almost all others, by admitting them duty free; so that, instead of abandoning the principle of protection, or guarding against the danger of a surplus, the act but perpetuated the protective policy, and left the country and the government exposed to all the evils of a large annual surplus.

Such an arrangement could not induce South Carolina to surrender the stand she had taken. On the contrary, it only aroused her to more active resistance, and energetic preparation to meet an issue, which now seemed almost inevitable. At this stage an incident occurred that tended greatly to confirm and animate her in her course.

From the commencement, the State Rights party had claimed the authority of the Virginia Resolutions, Mr. Madison's Report, and the Kentucky Resolutions, which they attributed to Mr. Jefferson, as sanctioning the doctrine of nullification and the course they proposed to take, while those who opposed denied that they authorized the interpretation put on them, or that Mr. Jefferson was the author of the Kentucky Resolutions. It became a point of great importance to establish which of the two were right. Both sides admitted the high authority of Mr. Jefferson, and that the report and resolutions contained the true political creed of the party. Mr. [Thomas] Ritchie, the experienced editor of the [Richmond] Enquirer and the associate of Mr. Jefferson, and most of the distinguished men who were his contemporaries in Virginia, was among the most influential of those who denied that these documents, or the opinions of Mr. Jefferson, authorized the doctrine of nullification. But, fortunately, the original manuscript of Mr. Jefferson, from which the Kentucky Resolutions were taken, was brought to light at this critical juncture, and left no doubt that Mr. Jefferson was their real author, and that he entertained the doctrines of nullification to the full extent, as interpreted by the State Rights party, which Mr. Ritchie had the candour to acknowledge as the following extract from the Enquirer of March, 1832, shows.

From the Richmond Enquirer, March 13th.

MR. JEFFERSON THE AUTHOR OF THE KENTUCKY RESOLUTIONS

"*Nullification—An Error corrected.*—We come before the public to correct an error into which we have betrayed them. Some of the politicians of South Carolina had maintained the opinion, that Mr. Jefferson was not only the friend, but the father of nullification; and their principal argument was, that he was the author of the Kentucky Resolutions of 1799, as well as those of 1798; and that in those of 1799 is to be found the memorable passage, 'The several states which formed that instrument, being sovereign and independent, have the unquestionable right to judge of its infraction; and that *a nullification by these sovereignties of all unauthorized acts, done under colour of that instrument, is the rightful remedy.*'

"We had a great curiosity to ascertain the truth of this opinion. We hunted up all the facts that were within our reach, weighed them as impartially as we could, and we arrived at a different conclusion from that of the State Rights politicians of South Carolina. We expressed our opinions in the 'Enquirer' of the 13th of September last.

"We have now to state our conviction *that we were wrong, and the South Carolinians were right as to Mr. Jefferson's opinions.* A small MS. book has been found among his papers, which, with other articles, contains two copies, in his own handwriting, that appear to have been the original of the Kentucky Resolutions. The first of these is blurred and much corrected, with passages struck out and others interlined. The other is a fair and later copy, judging from the colour of the paper and of the ink, of Mr. J[efferson]'s draught. We are indebted to his grandson [Thomas Jefferson Randolph] for the permission to examine these MSS., and compare them with the printed copies of the Kentucky Resolutions, and for the opportunity of correcting our own mistake, and of laying the following result before our readers."

Here follows Mr. Jefferson's original draught of the Kentucky Resolutions.

Never was a document more clear and explicit on any point than this in favour of the principles on which [South] Carolina had placed her right to interpose. Words could not make it more so. It says expressly, "That in all cases of an abuse of delegated powers, the members of the General Government being chosen by the people, a change by the people would be the constitutional remedy; but *where powers are assumed which have not been delegated, a* NULLIFICATION *of the act is the* RIGHTFUL REMEDY that every state has a natural right to, in cases not in the compact (casus non foederis), to nullify, of their own authority, all assumptions of powers within their limits; that without this right, they would be under the absolute and unlimited dominion of whoever might exercise this right of judgment for them; that, nevertheless, this Commonwealth (Kentucky), from motives of regard and respect for its co-states, has wished to communicate with them on the subject; that with them alone it proposes to communicate, they alone being parties to the compact, and solely authorized to judge, in the last resort, of the powers exercised under it—Congress being not a party, but merely the creature of the compact, and subject, as to its assumption of its powers, to the final judgment of those by whom, and for whose use, itself and its powers were created."

So fully does the above extract, and the whole draught, in fact, accord with the views taken by Mr. Calhoun in the statement of his opinion, and letter to General Hamilton, that, had it been possible for him to have had access to the manuscript, he might well have been suspected of plagiarism.

Supported by this high and explicit authority, the State Rights party moved forward with renovated energy and confidence in preparing for the great issue; but the difficulties were great. The Union party, thoroughly organized under able leaders, and animated by the greatest zeal, were supported not only by the whole influence of the General Government, but sustained and cheered by the concurring voice of both parties, and, it may almost be literally said, of the whole Union. Against this immense resistance, the State Rights party had to obtain a majority of two thirds of both houses of the Legislature to carry out its views, as, according to their opinion, the right of a state to declare an act of Congress unconstitutional, and therefore null and void, is derived from the fact that the Constitution is a compact to which the people of the states, in their sovereign capacity, are direct parties; and, of course, the right appertains to them in this capacity only, and can only be exercised by them, through a convention, in the same mode that the instrument was adopted, and not by the State Government. They regard the General and State Governments as co-ordinate governments, and the people of the states, severally, as the paramount sovereign authority. According to these views, in order to take the final step it would be necessary to call a convention of the people of the state; and for this purpose, by a provision of the Constitution of the state, two thirds of the Legislature were necessary; without that nothing could be done, and the cause would have to be abandoned. The election was pending, and the great struggle between the parties was, on one side, to carry two thirds of both houses, and on the other to defeat it. The magnitude of the issue was felt by both, and never was a political struggle more ardent; and, let it be added for the honour of both parties and the state, never before, in such a struggle, was the appeal more direct and solemn to the intelligence and patriotism of the people, and so free from all false issues, cant, or appeal to passion or prejudice.

It resulted in the triumph of the State Rights party. They returned more than the constitutional number to both houses. The Legislature met and called a Convention, which assembled and passed the Ordinance of Nullification, the 24th of November, 1832, accompanied by two addresses; one to the people of South Carolina, and the other to the people of their co-states of the Union, setting forth fully an explanation of the motives and principles which governed them as one of the parties to the constitutional compact, in the high and solemn act of sovereignty, which duty to themselves and to the Union compelled them to perform. They adjourned to meet in March, subsequent to the period at which, by the Constitution, the approaching session of Congress would terminate.

Congress met at the usual period, in December, and the President, in his Message, announced the final payment of the public debt, and recommended a reduction of the duties to the standard required for the revenue of the government economically and efficiently administered, to take place as soon as the faith of the government, and the preservation of the large capital invested in manufacturing establishments, would permit.

The time of Governor Hamilton having expired, General [Robert Y.] Hayne, then a senator in Congress, was elected his successor, and placed at the head of the government of the state at this momentous period. The proceedings of the Convention were reported to the Legislature, which met shortly after its adjournment, and an act introduced and passed to carry into effect the ordinance, to go into operation in February. That was followed by the proclamation of the President [on 12/10/1832], which asserted that the ordinance was subversive of the Constitution, and that the object of South Carolina was the destruction of the Union; and after giving his views of the Constitution, and the provisions of the existing laws applicable to the case, and declaring the course he would pursue, he warned all the people of the state against obedience to the ordinance, under the high penalty for treason against the United States. Governor Hayne issued his counter proclamation, repelling the charges of the President, and maintaining the grounds taken by the Convention, and replying to the reasons assigned for the grounds taken in the President's proclamation.

CHAPTER V.

Including the Period from his Resignation of the Vice-presidency
till the Admission of Michigan into the Union.

At this critical juncture, the Legislature elected Mr. Calhoun to fill the vacancy in the Senate occasioned by the election of General Hayne as governor. As trying as was the situation under such circumstances, he resigned without hesitation his place as Vice-president, and proceeded to Washington to take his seat in the Senate. Never was there, since the commencement of the government, a moment of more intense interest and anxiety throughout the whole Union, and never before was any public man placed in a situation more difficult and responsible. The expectation was general that he would be arrested as soon as he arrived in Washington; and on his way thither, wherever he stopped, crowds collected to see him. Nor was the excitement less when he arrived at the seat of government, where he had been so long and familiarly known. When he appeared in the Senate to take his seat as a member in a body over which he had so long and recently presided, the gallery and chamber were thronged with spectators. He repeated the constitutional oath in a firm and audible voice, and took his seat on the side and in the midst of his old political friends, of whom a large majority were now placed in hostile array to him. But as trying and responsible as was the occasion, he stood erect and unappalled, conscious of the purity of his motives, and strong in the depth of his conviction of the truth, justice, constitutionality, and magnitude of the question which South Carolina, in her confidence, had selected him as her chosen representative to defend.

Mr. Calhoun, a few days after he took his seat, in order to bring the whole subject under the early consideration of the Senate, offered [on 1/14/1833] a resolution, calling upon the President to lay before the body the ordinance and other documents connected with it, which had been transmitted to him by the executive of the state; but he forbore to press its adoption, on the statement of Mr. [Felix] Grundy, that there was reason to believe the President was preparing a message on the subject, which would be accompanied by the documents requested, and that the message would probably be sent the day after the next. Not expecting anything of importance the next day [*sic*; 1/16/1833], Mr. Calhoun delayed some time after the usual meeting of the body to take his seat. When he entered the chamber, he was surprised to find it crowded, and the Secretary of the Senate in the midst of reading the message, which he did not expect until the next day. It took strong ground against South Carolina, and recommended the adoption of the most decisive measures to coerce her obedience.

It was a trying moment. He had not the slightest anticipation that he would be called on to say anything when he entered the chamber, and was wholly unprepared; and, to add to his embarrassment, he had, for the long period of fifteen years (while he filled the war department and the place of Vice-president), been entirely out of the habit of public speaking. Nor could he avoid speaking, as it would look like shrinking not to give an immediate reply to the message. Under all these trying circumstances, he rose as soon as the reading was over, and replied, in a manly and effective speech, to the ground taken in the message. After he concluded, the message and documents were referred to the Committee on the Judiciary, of which Mr. Grundy was chairman and Mr. [Daniel] Webster a prominent member. They reported a bill, extending the jurisdiction of the courts of the United States greatly and beyond all former acts, and clothing the President with almost unlimited powers, both as to men and money.

In order to have a preliminary discussion, and to take the sense of the Senate on the principles involved in the issue, before the bill was called up, Mr. Calhoun prepared and moved [on 1/22/1833] the three following resolutions, which affirmed the grounds on which South Carolina placed her right, on the one side, and negatived, on the other, those assumed in the proclamation and message.

"Resolved, That the people of the several states composing these United States are united as parties to a constitutional compact, to which the people of each state acceded as a separate and sovereign community, each binding itself, by its own particular ratification; and that the Union, of which the said compact is the bond, is a Union *between the states* ratifying the same.

"Resolved, That the people of the several states, thus united by a constitutional compact, in forming that instrument, in creating a General Government to carry into effect the objects for which it was formed, delegated to that government, for that purpose, certain definite powers, to be exercised jointly, reserving, at the same time, each state to itself, the residuary mass of powers, to be exercised by its own separate government; and that, whenever the General Government assumes the exercise of powers not delegated by the compact, its acts are unauthorized, void, and of no effect; and that the said government is not made the final judge of the powers delegated to it, since that would make its discretion, and not the Constitution, the measure of its powers; but that, as in all other cases of compact among sovereign parties, without any common judge, each has an equal right to judge for itself, as well of the infraction as of the mode and measure of redress.

"Resolved, That the assertions, that the people of these United States, taken collectively as individuals, are now, or ever have been, united on the principle of the social compact, and, as such, are now formed into one nation or people, or that they have ever been so united in any one stage of their political existence; or that the people of the several states comprising the Union have not, as members thereof, retained their sovereignty; or that the allegiance of their citizens has been transferred to the General Government; or that they have parted with the right of punishing treason through their respective state governments; or that they have not the right of judging, in the last resort, as to the extent of the powers reserved, and, of consequence, of those delegated, are not only without foundation in truth, but are contrary to the most certain and plain historical facts, and the clearest deductions of reason; and that all exercise of power on the part of the General Government, or any of its departments, deriving authority from such erroneous assumptions, must of necessity be unconstitutional; must tend directly and inevitably to subvert the sovereignty of the states, to destroy the federal character of the

Union, and to rear on its ruins a consolidated government, without constitutional check or limitation, and which must necessarily terminate in the loss of liberty itself."

It is obvious, on the perusal, that if the principles offered by the resolutions be true, South Carolina would stand justified; and if those negatived be false, the bill could not be rightfully sustained; and such being the case, it was but fair that the principles should be settled prior to the discussion and action on the bill. But as reasonable as was the request of Mr. Calhoun, the Senate, under the influence of the committee, laid his resolutions on the table, and took up the bill for discussion. The debate was very able on both sides. Many of the old and sound Republicans, refusing to yield their long-cherished principles to party feelings or considerations, opposed the bill with great ability and vigour. Mr. Grundy, as chairman, claimed the right of closing the debate, and Mr. Calhoun reserved himself to reply to Mr. Webster, who was the great champion of the bill; but he was informed, through one of Mr. Webster's friends, that he would not speak before him. This left him no option, as he could not avoid speaking, and had therefore to submit. He spoke late, [on 2/15–16,] and conjecturing that Mr. Webster intended to speak to the principles involved, and not to the provisions of the bill, he spoke at large on a variety of points, which he thought required explanation in connexion with the course of South Carolina, and but slightly touched on the principles which he had affirmed or negatived in his resolutions, in order to deprive Mr. Webster of the advantages he aimed at in reserving himself for the reply. He was right in his conjecture. The moment he sat down, Mr. Webster rose to reply, but spoke, as he anticipated, not on the bill, but to the resolutions, without assailing or controverting any of the positions taken by Mr. C[alhoun] in his speech. This gave him a claim to be heard on his resolutions; and the Senate accordingly permitted him to call them up, and assigned a day in order to give him an opportunity of replying to Mr. Webster in their support.

When the day came [on 2/26/1833] the senate-chamber and gallery were crowded, and Mr. Calhoun replied in a speech which, for precision and force of argument, has rarely, if ever, been equalled. The great point at issue was, whether the Constitution is or is not a compact between the States. Mr. Webster, with that strength of understanding which belongs to him, saw clearly where the real issue lay, and had the fairness and candour to concede that if, in fact, the Constitution is a compact between the States, then the doctrines contended for by South Carolina necessarily followed, nullification, secession, and all. Mr. Calhoun, accordingly, mainly directed his efforts to establishing the fact, and with such success, that even the North American Quarterly Review, published in Boston, and at all times the champion of the principles supported by Mr. Webster, in an article reviewing the debate, admitted that Mr. Calhoun had successfully maintained his ground on that point. Mr. [John] Randolph, then in a feeble state of health, on his way to Philadelphia, was present in the senate-chamber, it is believed for the last time, when Mr. Calhoun spoke. He sat near the desk where Mr. C[alhoun] stood while addressing the Senate, and at the close openly and highly complimented him for the ability and success of his reply, which he regarded as unanswerable.

The bill passed, but while it was in progress, efforts were made in both Houses so to modify the duties as to terminate the controversy peaceably. Upon faith in these efforts, South Carolina postponed the time for carrying into effect her ordinance, from the first of February till after the adjournment of Congress on the fourth of March. Mr. [Gulian C.] Verplanck [Representative from N.Y.], in the early part of the session, had reported a bill in conformity with the message of the President at the opening of the session, proposing a very great reduction of the duties, but without surrendering the principle of protection, or, in many instances, reducing the duties to the revenue standard. Its progress was slow. It was detained a long time in committee of the whole, where many amendments, increasing the duties, were made. After it was reported to the House, it continued to drag along with difficulty. Many of the objectionable amendments made in the committee of the whole were concurred in, and the fate of the bill still continued doubtful, notwithstanding the steady and united support which it received from the State Rights party, objectionable as it was in many particulars. Their support was more than counterbalanced by the division in the ranks of the administration party.

In the mean time, Mr. Clay introduced a bill in the Senate, which received the sanction of that body, and was sent to the House, where Mr. Verplanck's bill still lingered near the end of the session. It was moved as a substitute to his bill, and carried by a large majority; Mr. Verplanck himself, and the leading friends of the administration who supported his bill, voting for it in despair, as it is believed, of the passage of his own. It received the sanction of the President, and has since been called the *Compromise Act*; and thus terminated this controversy, the most agitating and memorable that ever occurred under the government.

It is not deemed necessary to go into the origin or history of the act, or minutely into its provisions. The former have been given several times by Mr. Clay and Mr. Calhoun in their places in the Senate, and are generally known. It is sufficient to say that Mr. Calhoun, from the commencement, refused to go into any arrangement which did not explicitly surrender the principle of protection, but was willing to allow ample time for the gradual reduction of the duties on the protected articles, in order to save the manufacturers from ruin; but he insisted on a total repeal at once on all unprotected articles, in order to prevent, if possible, the great object of his dread from the first, a surplus revenue. Mr. Clay was, of course, on his part, solicitous, in making the changes necessary to a compromise, to give as slight a shock as possible to his long-cherished system. The result was the surrender of the protective principle and the establishment of the *ad valorem*, and a gradual reduction of duties on all protected articles, to terminate on the thirtieth of June, 1842, when no duty above 20 per cent. *ad valorem* should be laid; the immediate repeal of all duties on articles not similar to those manufactured in the country, and a moderate list of articles to be made permanently free of duty after the thirtieth of June, 1842, with provisions for cash duties and home valuation. Such are the general outlines of the provisions of the act which peaceably closed the controversy; and if faith and pledges had been observed with as much fidelity on the side of the tariff interest as it has been on the part of the opposite side, the possibility of its renewal would have forever been prevented.

Whatever opinion may have been entertained at one time of the views and motives of Mr. Calhoun, and the small but gallant party with which he acted, none now, not even the most prejudiced, doubts the purity and patriotism of his and their motives, however much they may differ from them as to principles and policy. So far from hostility to the Union, one of the leading objects was its preservation. The Union may be destroyed as well by *consolidation* as by *dissolution*—by the centripetal as well as the centrifugal tendency of the bodies of which it is composed. It is the duty of the patriot to resist both, and hold the government firmly to its allotted sphere. Against the former, state interposition is an all-sufficient remedy, and it remains to be seen whether experience will not prove that it is an indispensable one. It was, at least, so considered by the State of South Carolina, and that was one of the principal motives for resorting to it. Nor does it admit of a doubt but that her action did much to counteract the consolidating tendency of the Government. Had she not taken the stand she did, in all probability the distribution of the surplus revenue among the states and the protective policy would have become the established system of the Government. The scheme of distribution is almost a necessary consequence of that policy. They are most intimately connected, as the experience of the last few years shows, even with an empty treasury. With one full to overflowing, as was the case when the debt was paid and the state interposed, it was almost, if not altogether unavoidable, without state interposition. That the protective tariff would not have been overthrown without it, the inconsiderable reduction of 1832, and the fate of Mr. Verplanck's bill, notwithstanding all the pressing circumstances under which it was introduced and attempted to be passed, conclusively prove; and that it could not have been overthrown if the two, distribution and protection, had become united, may be fairly inferred. They would then have been beyond the reach of all ordinary and constitutional remedies, when either consolidation or despotism would have been the end of our political system.

But how different now is the situation of the government and the country in consequence of the course pursued. When the state first took its stand, the very existence of states' rights was almost forgotten in the Union. The party had greatly departed from the old standard of its faith both in theory and practice, and had imperceptibly embraced, to a great extent, the doctrines and policy of its opponents. If proof be required, the proclamation, the message recommending the Force Bill, the bill itself, and the arguments by which it was supported, afford conclusive evidence. That a great and cheering change has since taken place, all must admit; and that it may be attributed, in a great measure, to say the least, to the stand taken by South Carolina, cannot well be doubted.

It was expected that, among its other benefits, it had put an end forever to the protective policy, but the act of the last session has proved to the contrary. It is, however, to be hoped that the wound it has received will yet prove to be its death-blow, and that the act of the last session will be but a last spasmodic struggle preceding its final dissolution. Great has been the progress of truth in reference to this policy, both as to its character and operation, since the stand taken by South Carolina. That it is unjust, unequal, oppressive, and unconstitutional, the great body of the Democratic party are now agreed, and, being agreed, they can never cease their determined resistance to it until it is finally overthrown, without (what cannot be anticipated) an abandonment of their political faith.

Such is a sketch of this important part of Mr. Calhoun's public life. As long as it is, not a word has been added which was not regarded as necessary to a just understanding of his motives and conduct, in the most trying scene through which it has been his fortune to pass.

Congress adjourned on the third of March [1833], and he proceeded by public conveyance to Columbia to meet the Convention, which was to reassemble in a few days. The spring was unusually cold and backward. The snow lay several inches deep on the ground, and the Potomac was frozen. He took the stage at Alexandria, but the roads were so broken up in consequence of the frost that he had to take open mail-carts, in which he rode night and day without stopping, for a considerable portion of the way, in order to reach Columbia in time. He found the members of the Convention assembled. Knowing how firm and resolved the state was to maintain its rights, he anticipated some dissatisfaction at the compromise, which had induced him to proceed with the speed which he used. He was not mistaken; but, on explaining fully what had been done, and the reasons on which he and his colleague had acted, the Convention readily acquiesced in the adjustment. Let it be added, in conclusion, that the earliest opportunity was seized by both parties in the state, at the next session of the Legislature, after the closing of the controversy with the General Government, to meet like friends, and agree to disband their party organization, and forget their past differences, which both sides, to their lasting honour, have faithfully and honestly observed. The consequence of so patriotic and magnanimous a course has been a degree of harmony and unanimity in the state ever since, without example in any other member of the Confederacy.

This great subject of controversy was thus happily closed in the Union and the State of South Carolina; but the recess between the last and the next session was not permitted to pass without giving birth to another question of deep and abiding excitement: the withholding of the deposites of the public money from the Bank of the United States, and their transfer, by the authority of the President [Andrew Jackson], to certain state banks, selected for the purpose. To effect his object, he had removed Mr. [William J.] Duane for declining to comply with his order, and appointed Mr. [Roger B.] Taney Secretary of the Treasury in his place, in order to have it executed. The bank was made by its charter the fiscal agent of the government for the collection, distribution, and safe keeping of the public funds, unless otherwise ordered by the Secretary of the Treasury, and in that case it was provided he should report to Congress, if in session, immediately, and if not, at the commencement of the next session, his reasons for so doing. For that and other privileges, the bank paid a bonus for the charter of one million five hundred thousand dollars.

The President communicated the fact of the removal of the deposites in his message at the opening of the next session [in 12/1833], with his reasons, which were repeated and enlarged on by the Secretary of the Treasury in his Annual Report.

The subject gave rise to a long and animated discussion between the two great parties, both as to the right and expediency of the measure. Mr. Calhoun was not regarded as attached to either, and much interest was felt in the course he might take. He spoke first, and in a speech [of 1/13/1834] distinguished for its ability, admitted the right of the President to remove his secretary, though he regarded it, under the circumstances, an abuse of power; but denied not only the right of the secretary to withhold the deposites so long as the funds were safe and the bank performed faithfully its duties as a fiscal agent, but also the expediency of the act. But he did not confine himself to these points. He saw, at that early period, the radical defects of the banking system, and he resolved, though he disapproved of the act of the executive, that his position should not hereafter be mistaken as that of a partisan of the bank or the banking system. With that view, after discussing the questions immediately connected with the withholding of the deposites, and some other intermediate ones, he added:

"Nor is it more true that the real question is 'Bank or no Bank.' Taking the deposite question in the broadest sense; suppose, as it is contended by the friends of the administration, that it involves the question of the renewal of the charter, and, consequently, the existence of the bank itself, still the banking system would stand almost untouched and unimpaired. Four hundred banks would still remain scattered over this wide Republic, and on the ruins of the United States Bank many would rise to be added to the present list. Under this aspect of the subject, the only possible question that would be presented for consideration would be, Whether the banking system was more safe, more beneficial, or more constitutional with or without the United States Bank?"

"If," said Mr. C[alhoun], "this was a question of 'Bank or no Bank'—if it involved the existence of the banking system, it would, indeed, be a great question—one of the first magnitude; and, with my present impression, long entertained and daily increasing, I would hesitate—long hesitate—before I would be found under the banner of the system. I have great doubts, if doubts they may be called, as to the soundness and tendency of the whole system, in all its modifications. I have great fears that it will be found hostile to liberty and the advance of civilization—fatally hostile to liberty in our country, where the system exists in its worst and most dangerous form. Of all institutions affecting the great question of the distribution of wealth—a question least explored, and the most important of any in the whole range of political economy—the banking institution has, if not the greatest, one of the greatest, and, I fear, most pernicious influences on the mode of distribution. Were the question really before us, I would not shun the responsibility, as great as it might be, of freely and fully offering my sentiments on these deeply-important points; but as it is, I must content myself with the few remarks which I have thrown out."

"What, then, is the real question which now agitates the country? I answer, it is a struggle between the executive and legislative departments of the government; a struggle, not in relation to the existence of the Bank, but whether Congress or the President should have the power to create a bank, and, through it, the consequent control over the currency of the country. This is the real question. Let us not deceive ourselves. This league, this association, vivified and sustained by receiving the deposites of the public money, and having their notes converted, by being received everywhere by the treasury, into the common currency of the country, is, to all intents and purposes, a bank of the United States—the executive bank of the United States, as distinguished from that of Congress. However it might fail to perform satisfactorily the useful functions of the Bank of the United States, as incorporated by law, it would outstrip it—far outstrip it—in all its dangerous qualities, in extending the power, the influence, and the corruption of the government. It was impossible to conceive any institution more admirably calculated to advance these objects. Not only the selected banks, but the whole banking institutions of the country, and with it the entire money power, for the purpose of speculation, peculation, and corruption, would be placed under the control of the executive. A system of menaces and promises will be established: of menace of the banks in possession of the deposites, but which might not be entirely subservient to executive views, and of promise of future favours to those who may not as yet enjoy its favours. Between the two, the banks would be left without honour or honesty, and a system of speculation and stock-jobbing would commence, unequalled in the annals of our country."

Again: "So long as the question is one between a bank of the United States incorporated by Congress, and that system of banks which has been created by the will of the executive, it is an insult to the understanding to discourse on the pernicious tendency and unconstitutionality of the Bank of the United States. To bring up that question fairly and legitimately, you must go one step farther: you

must *divorce the government and the bank.* You must refuse all connexion with banks. You must neither receive, nor pay away bank-
notes; you must go back to the old system of the strong box, and of
gold and silver. If you have a right to receive bank-notes at all—to
treat them as money by receiving them in your dues, or paying them
away to creditors, you have a right to create a bank. Whatever the
government receives and treats as money, is money in effect; and if it
be money, then they have the right, under the Constitution, to regulate it. Nay, they are bound by high obligation to adopt the most
efficient means, according to the nature of that which they have recognised as money, to give it the utmost stability and uniformity of
value. And if it be in the shape of bank-notes, the most efficient
means of giving those qualities is a Bank of the United States, incorporated by Congress. Unless you give the highest practical uniformity to the value of bank-notes—so long as you receive them in
your dues, and treat them as money, you violate that provision of the
Constitution which provides that taxation shall be uniform throughout the United States. There is no other alternative, I repeat; you
must *divorce the government entirely from the banking system*, or, if
not, you are bound to incorporate a bank, as the only safe and efficient means of giving stability and uniformity to the currency. And
should the deposites not be restored, and the present illegal and unconstitutional connexion between the executive and the league of
banks continue, I shall feel it my duty, if no one else moves, to introduce a measure to prohibit government from receiving or touching
bank-notes in any shape whatever, as the only means left of giving
safety and stability to the currency, and saving the country from
corruption and ruin."

Again: "Were I," said Mr. C[alhoun], "to select the case best calculated to illustrate the necessity of resisting usurpation at the very
commencement, and to prove how difficult it is to resist it in any subsequent stage if not met at first, I would select this very case. What,
he asked, is the cause of the present usurpation of power on the part
of the executive? what the motive? the temptation which has induced it to seize on the deposites? What, but the large surplus
revenue? the eight or ten millions in the public treasury beyond the
wants of the government? And what has put so large an amount of
money in the treasury when not needed? I answer, the protective
system: that system which graduated the duties, not in reference to
the wants of the government, but in reference to the importunities
and demands of the manufacturers, and which poured millions of dollars into the treasury beyond the most profuse demands, and even the

extravagance of the government—taken—unlawfully taken—from the pockets of those who honestly made it. I hold that those who make are entitled to what they make against all the world except the government, and against it except to the extent of its legitimate and constitutional wants; and that for the government to take one cent more is robbery. In violation of this sacred principle, *Congress first* removed the money by high duties, unjustly and unconstitutionally imposed, from the pockets of those who made it, where it was rightfully placed by all laws, human and divine, into the treasury. The executive, in his turn, following the example, has taken them from that deposite, and distributed them among favourite and partisan banks. The means used have been the same in both cases. The Constitution gives to Congress the power to lay duties, with a view to revenue. This power, without regarding the object for which it was intended, forgetting that it was a great trust power, necessarily limited, by the very nature of such powers, to the subject and the object of the trust, was perverted to a use never intended, that of protecting the industry of one portion of the country at the expense of another; and, under this false interpretation, the money was transferred from its natural and just deposite, the pockets of those who made it, into the public treasury, as I have stated. In this, too, the executive followed the example of Congress. By the magic construction of a few simple words—'unless otherwise ordered'—intended to confer on the Secretary of the Treasury a limited power—to give additional security to the public deposites, he has, in like manner, perverted this power, and made it the instrument, by similar sophistry, of drawing the money from the treasury, and bestowing it, as I have stated, on favourite and partisan banks. Would to God, said Mr. C[alhoun], would to God I could reverse the whole of this nefarious operation, and terminate the controversy by returning the money to the pockets of the honest and industrious citizens, by the sweat of whose brows it was made, with whom only it can be rightfully deposited. But as this cannot be done, I must content myself by giving a vote to return it to the public treasury, where it was ordered to be deposited by an act of the Legislature."

These extracts contain an explanation, not only of Mr. Calhoun's views of the banking system at the time, but also of those which have governed his after course in reference to the banks, and most of the prominent questions since agitated. He believed that there was, at the time, a strong tendency in all the departments of the government to usurp power, and that it originated with Congress. It is, indeed, a settled opinion with him, which he has long entertained, and the reasons for which he recently explained in his speech on the veto [on 2/28/1842], that usurpations in the Federal Government almost necessarily originate with Congress; but that the powers which it gains by usurping those of the states or people, adds, not to its strength, but to that of the other departments, and especially of the executive, in whose hands it becomes the means of usurping in turn the powers of Congress, and controlling its proceedings. He accordingly attributed the great power and influence of the executive at this time, and its tendency to encroachment, to the previous encroachments of Congress, especially in passing the tariff of '28. That having been prostrated by the interposition of the State of South Carolina and the Compromise Act at the last session, he next turned his efforts to arresting, what he believed to be its natural consequence, the encroachments of the executive; and was thus, and to that extent, brought for the time to act with the opposition party, then called National Republicans. But he occupied throughout his own independent State Rights ground and principles, from which he in no instance departed. Wherever they led, he followed, without regarding whether they brought him to co-operate with the opposition or administration, or left him alone in the Senate to maintain and defend his own separate and peculiar position.

His course in the very case under consideration strikingly illustrates these remarks. He essentially differed on this important occasion from both of the great parties, administration and opposition. The former was in favour of the league of state banks as the fiscal agents and depositaries of the Government, and opposed both to a national bank and the divorce of government from the banks. The latter, on the contrary, were in favour of a national bank, and opposed to the league of banks and the divorce; while Mr. Calhoun and the State Rights party were in favour of the divorce, or what has since been called the Independent Treasury, and opposed to a national bank, and any connexion with the banking system in any way. It was in conformity to these views, and after consulting Mr. Calhoun and the prominent members of the party, that General [William F.] Gordon, then a distinguished representative from Virginia, introduced at the time a bill to establish the Independent Treasury. It failed. The public mind was not then prepared; but to him will belong the lasting honour of introducing one of the most important measures of modern times.

The removal of the deposites was not the only question of importance which was agitated during the session. Among others, the motion of Mr. Webster, who was then chairman of the Committee on

Finance, for leave to bring in a bill to recharter the Bank of the United States for six years, gave rise to an interesting discussion. Mr. Calhoun seized the opportunity, not to discuss the question of renewal, but that of the currency generally, which he showed, even then, to be deeply diseased, and to warn the Government and country of the approach of the catastrophe which has since befallen them. He pointed out the cause and character of the disease, and the remedy that should be adopted to prevent, if possible, the approaching shock, or at least to lessen its violence. His speech on the occasion [on 3/21/1834] is one of the ablest and most remarkable for its forecast he ever made. It is prophetic throughout, and was pronounced by one of the senators, himself a speaker of distinguished abilities and long experience, the ablest he ever heard. To appreciate its merits, it must be read.

Upon this occasion he exhibited, in a remarkable degree, that statesmanlike faculty which has enabled him to do so much to direct events, by always taking the nearest practicable step towards his object, instead of refusing to do anything unless he could effect what was the best in the abstract. The great ends in his system of life, whether public or private, he has ever held to be fixed by reason and general rules; but the time and mode of attaining them he regarded as questions of expediency, to be determined by the circumstances under which he is called to act. If things are now wrong, he who refuses to make any change for the better because he cannot obtain at once what he believes to be best in the abstract, is responsible for them as they exist, and should be classed rather with those who sustain the present wrongs than with those who pursue the right; for in practice, the effects of their action are the same; and yet he who makes the nearest attainable approach to the right is too often confounded with those who maintain the wrong, and postponed for others who, content to think correctly, are yet too timid to act if there be danger of misconstruction, and really contribute to the continuance of that which they condemn. This is a species of fear which Mr. Calhoun has never known. Seeing clearly his own ends, which have been long fixed by observation and reflection, he judges, with a rare sagacity, of the nearest practicable approach which can be made to them under the circumstances, and advances forward to the boundaries assigned by prudence without fear of the enemy, and halts when he has taken as much ground as he can occupy, without regard to the remonstrances of his followers, who take their counsels merely from zeal, and do not properly ascertain the limits upon human power, and the controlling force of events. It is thus that he is ever in progress; and although generally in advance of his party and the world, in a long life he has never been forced to abandon any forward movement, or recede from his end. He uses time to control circumstances, and directs them both to his great object, which he is ever on the march sooner or later to attain. This it is which makes him the master-statesman of his age, and thus he has been able to accomplish so much with such inconsiderable means.

Upon the occasion to which we now refer, he exhibited this states-manlike mode of thinking and acting in a remarkable degree. He sought no trial of skill in oratory where victories were to be barren of results to the country. He avoided all those topics of personal or party excitement, whose fleeting interest belonged to the time and not to the case; but, looking to the exigencies of the country, and not to the mere feelings of the day, he surveyed the whole ground with military precision, and made a masterly reconnoisance [sic] of the field. As abstract questions, he did not enter into the nature of the banking system, or its constitutional propriety. In discussing the disease, it was necessary to touch slightly upon the tendencies of the banking system; and these touches, like the line of Apelles, showed the master's hand, and his thorough acquaintance with the subject. He traced clearly the deep seat of the malady, and developed its probable progress and consequences unless corrected. He then addressed himself to the discovery of some remedy, which should be both safe and efficient. With the propriety and constitutionality of the banking system as abstract questions he had nothing to do, and upon them he only touched so far as they bore upon the remedy which he had in view. Banks were in existence, and through them the currency was indisputably deeply diseased. There was not the least probability of any successful effort to force the Government to abandon the use of paper. He contented himself, therefore, with showing that, if the Government could use paper, it could also regulate its value; and the question was to ascertain the best means of reaching that object. He proposed a continuance of the bank for twelve years, under severe restrictions, and upon conditions which would gradually diminish the volume of paper currency, so as to enable the Government, at the end of that period, to dispense with its use altogether, if it should choose to do so, without any shock to the community. In this point of view, it was of no importance whether the original charter was constitutional or not. Suppose it to be unconstitutional, it was a question whether we would rid ourselves of the evil gradually, and without injury to the community, or whether we should repeal it at once, at the sacrifice of all of its immense connected interests, and send the whole toppling down the abyss together. He thought there was a great difference between doing and undoing; and while he would never originate what he believed to be unauthorized by the Constitution, he would take his own time for repairing the breaches already made in it, and so conduct the process as to produce the least possible amount of suffering in the country. It was thus that he agreed to compromise an unconstitutional tariff by allowing time, so as to save vast and meritorious interests which were connected with it; and thus, too, he now sought (to use his own words) to "unbank the banks." Here, too, he exhibited an instance of that cautious process by which all real statesmen conduct their reforms, and proved his aversion to hazarding the vast interests of a community by any sudden change which was not justified by experience, but suggested only by theoretic opinions. It was clearly seen, both in this and his preceding speeches, that he disapproved the banking system, and saw, as far as mere reason without experience could point, that its tendencies were evil; and yet he forbore to strike at it until there was time to verify his reflection by experience, and the period should arrive when an effectual blow might be given. If the system were good, it was clear to him that it required severe restrictions and judicious regulation; if evil, he was equally decided that it ought to be removed gradually, so as to produce the least shock to the community. In either point of view, his course of conduct would be the same up to a certain period, to which he limited his prescription. The question of his future action he reserved for the time itself, to be determined by the lights of a more matured experience. It was not his object to amuse theorists or gratify a mere taste for speculation, but he sought a practical remedy for a disease under which the community was likely to suffer most intensely. As his suggestions were not taken, we can come to no certain conclusion as to what they would have led, but posterity will form its opinion as to their probable result. Of this, however, we feel assured, that the speech will always be considered as most remarkable for its political forecast.

So deeply was he impressed with the approaching danger, that when he understood Mr. Webster contemplated making the motion he afterward made, to renew the charter, he sent word through a friend of his, who had called on him, that he feared he was about to make a false move, and said that, although he and Mr. Webster were scarcely on speaking terms, in consequence of the occurrences of the last session, he would be glad to have a full conversation with him before he made his motion, if he would give him an opportunity by calling on him. The next morning he called. Mr. Calhoun stated his objection to the course he proposed, and what he thought ought to be done. Mr. Webster took time before he gave an answer, but informed Mr. Calhoun, when he called next day to learn his decision, that he concluded not to change his course. Mr. Calhoun expressed his regret, and on being asked by Mr. Webster whether he would oppose his motion, he replied no; but added that he believed the government and country were approaching a period of great peril, and that he felt that it would be due both to the public and himself to embrace the occasion to state at large the opinions and views he had expressed to him. He, in fact, regarded it as the critical moment; and when he saw that it was permitted to pass without doing anything to prevent the disorder into which the currency was falling, he made up his mind that what has since followed was inevitable.

In this connexion, and governed by the same views, he gave a decided support [in 1834] to what is called the Gold Bill, which raised the relative value of gold compared to silver, and the establishment of the branch mints, both of which he regarded as intimately connected with a return to a permanent and sound currency. The administration favoured both measures, and Mr. Clay opposed them. The discussion on both was conducted principally by him and Mr. Calhoun.

The proceedings of the Senate on the removal of the deposites was followed by the President's protest, which gave rise to a full and animated discussion in the Senate. Mr. Calhoun took decided ground against its reception. In the course of his argument [on 5/6/1834], he maintained the position that the Constitution vests all discretionary powers in Congress, to the exclusion of the executive and judiciary departments; and that neither of them, nor any office under the government, can exercise any power not authorized by law, but such as is expressly granted by the Constitution. To sustain this important position, he cited the provision in the Constitution which gives to Congress the power "to pass all laws necessary and proper for carrying into execution the foregoing" (that is, the powers granted to Congress), "*and all other powers vested by this Constitution in the government of the United States, or in any department or office thereof.*" The provision is express, and the position incontrovertible; and yet, strange as it may seem, it had been theretofore entirely overlooked, although it is one of the most important provisions in the whole instrument. It is the provision, in fact, which binds up all the parts in one, making of them one government, instead of consisting, as they would without it, of three hostile departments, each with the authority to assume whatever right it might think proper to carry into execution its share of the granted powers. One of the important con-

sequences of this provision of the Constitution is to subject the removing power to the regulation of law. The mere *fact* that the power
of removing from office is *not granted* by the Constitution to the President, is conclusive proof that it can only be exercised by the authority
of law, and, of course, subject to such limitation as it may impose. It
was, indeed, an investigation into the origin of that power which led
Mr. Calhoun to the examination of the Constitution, which ended in
making this important disclosure, as it may fairly be termed.

At the next session [that of 12/1834–3/1835] a special committee
of nine members was, on motion of Mr. Calhoun, raised, in order to
inquire into the extent of the executive patronage, the cause of its
great increase of late, and the expediency and practicability of reducing the same, and the means of doing it. After a minute and
laborious investigation, he made a full and able report [on 2/9/1835]
on all the points, of which 10,000 copies were ordered to be printed
by the Senate.

One of the leading objects which he had in view was to strike at
the surplus revenue. He anticipated it would be large, although the
Compromise Act had repealed the duties on more than one half of the
imports. But even that, aided by the gradual reduction on all the
residue, could not prevent the accumulation. He dreaded it, not only
because it would add greatly to the patronage of the executive by extending its control over the banks, and, through them, over the whole
community, but still more because it would be the source of boundless
speculation and corruption. To ascertain its probable extent, he
entered into a minute examination of the finances, and after exploring
the whole ground, he estimated the surplus at an average of not less
than nine millions of dollars annually for the whole period the Compromise Act had to run. As moderate as his estimate proved to be, it
was violently assailed, at the time, for its supposed extravagance.

But time rolled on, and at the opening of the next session [in 12/-
1835], his estimate, instead of proving extravagant, fell short of the
actual amount by millions, and that with a surplus daily increasing
with an accelerated velocity, under a new impulse, which was swelling it beyond all assignable limits. Here a brief explanation is necessary, in order to have a just conception of the danger to which the
government and country were exposed at this period.

The tariff of 1828 gave the first impulse to that great expansion of
the currency, which, under the influence of different causes, both
foreign and domestic, was still on the increase, and continued so till
just before the final explosion in 1837. So powerful was the first impulse, from the high duties imposed in 1828, that the currency was

doubled, in the manufacturing portions of the Union, in eighteen months from the passage of the act. On the accumulation of the surplus revenue from the same cause, after the payment of the public debt, a new impulse was given to the expansion. The surplus was deposited with the banks, and became, in fact, so much additional bank capital, in the least responsible and most dangerous form. This, with other causes, and especially the withdrawal of the deposites from the United States Bank, and the approaching termination of its charter [in 1836], gave a great additional impulse to the whole system. State banks were multiplied in all directions, with but little capital, and charters less guarded than ever. All these concurring causes tended greatly to increase the expansion, and, by necessary consequence, to produce a corresponding augmentation of prices, to which, however, there was an important exception. The price of all public lands which had been offered at public sales and not sold, was fixed by law at $1[.]25 per acre, and could not, of course, partake of the general rise. The quantity of such lands was great, not less, probably, than two hundred millions of acres, and thus a universal spirit of speculation, engendered by an inflated currency and high duties, was turned in that direction.

The facility of purchasing was not less than the quantity to be purchased. The deposites of the government in the state banks selected as its fiscal agents was upward of forty millions of dollars, consisting almost exclusively of bank-notes. From this vast source speculators and political partisans drew their funds, in the form of discount or loan, in exchange for which they gave their own promissory notes, and received the notes deposited by the government, or, what was the same, a credit in bank founded on them. These, in turn, were exchanged for the public lands, when they passed into the hands of the receivers, and were by them returned to the banks as new deposites, to take the same rapid round again and again, and sweeping away from the people, by means of their own funds, a corresponding amount of their land, and swelling, in the same proportion, the amount brought to the credit of the government by the banks, under the fallacious name of public money in the treasury, but which, in reality, was nothing more than the notes in bank given by speculators and partisans in exchange for the public lands.

In this operation every revolution but increased the force of the next, which, if left to operate unchecked, must end, as was manifest, in the entire absorption of the public domain and the universal explosion of the banking system, with the ultimate loss of what was due to the Government. It was about the time when these powerful causes began to operate with such effect as to be seen and felt by all, that the administration obtained a majority in the Senate, where it had for some time been in a minority; on which Mr. Calhoun, who had moved, as has been stated, at the preceding session, in anticipation of the danger, rose in his place [on 3/17/1836?] and said, that, as the friends of the administration were now in a majority, he left it to them to take the lead in providing a remedy for this alarming state of things.

All now felt that something must be done, and that promptly, to regulate and control the deposite banks, and to save the public funds and the national domain. Three remedies were proposed. The first was, to absorb the current revenue and the vast surplus already accumulated by the increase of the public expenditures; and, with that view, a resolution was actually introduced in the Senate and passed, calling on the executive to know how much could possibly be spent on military defences. The next was to vest what was not needed to meet the current expenses of the government in state stocks; and the other, to pass an act regulating and controlling the deposite banks, and to place the surplus in deposite in the treasury of the several states. The first two came from the friends of the administration, and the last was proposed by Mr. Calhoun as an amendment to the second.

It was the choice of evils. Something must be done. Anything was better than the continuance of the actual state of things. This all acknowledged. The objection to the first was great. So sudden and great an increase of expenditures when prices were so extravagant, and when, without a vast enlargement of the disbursing departments, there could be no efficient accountability, could not but end in much waste, loss, extravagance, and corruption, to say nothing of the great increase of patronage. But the great and decisive objection was, that expenditures sufficiently large to absorb the surplus would necessarily destroy, in their effects, the Compromise Act, and restore the protective system. It is easy to raise the expenditures, but very difficult to reduce them, of which the experience of the last five or six years affords abundant proof. The revenue at the time, though far beyond the wants of the government, was in the regular course of reduction under the compromise, which would, in the course of six years, bring it down to a sum only sufficient for the support of the Government with rigid economy. To have raised the expenditures sufficiently high to absorb the surplus, under such circumstances, would have required an unusual disbursement of between thirty and forty millions of dollars for the whole period, as experience has shown;

and, of course, a sudden reduction of nearly twenty millions, to bring down the expenditures to what, with proper management, would be necessary. So great and sudden a reduction would prove impracticable, and the certain result would be loans, debts, the violation of the compromise, and a renewal of the protective system. All this was urged against the scheme by Mr. Calhoun at the time. It was defeated, at least in a great degree; and it may well be asked, after the experience of the last two years, what would have been the consequences if it had not been, when even its partial effects have brought on the Government and country, to the extent they have, the very evils then anticipated by him.

The objection to vesting the surplus in state stocks was not less serious[.] Among so many other mischievous consequences, it would have been grossly partial; but the insurmountable objection was the danger of entangling the Government with the state stocks.

This scheme was in substance as much a deposite of the surplus revenue with the states as that proposed by Mr. Calhoun as an amendment to it. The latter placed the money with the states upon their promise to return it, if the General Government should require it, while the former exchanged the surplus for the obligations, by which the states, in another form, were bound to repay it; so that each scheme proposed to exchange the surplus for state credit in some form. With state stocks depreciating as they have since done, it would have been as unpopular and impossible to have used any means to recover the money by selling them, as it would have been to have recalled it directly from the states themselves. The difference was, that Mr. Calhoun's scheme bestowed upon the states all the patronage resulting from the use of the money, while the other gave it to the Secretary of the Treasury, in whom it vested an almost unlimited discretion, and to whom it gave the dangerous power of dealing in those stocks to large amounts. That this plan would have resulted in the entire loss of the money, with little or no benefit to the states, we may see from our past experience. The immense increase of executive patronage to which it would have led may also be estimated. But the endless train of mischiefs which would have followed in some of its remote consequences it would be difficult to measure, as we may readily perceive, when we come to consider the use which might have been made of such a power in the federal executive by those who have conceived the monstrous scheme of assuming the state debts. Indeed, the existence of such a power would naturally seem to suggest such a use of it, with the ideas now prevalent in the minds of many of our public men on the subject of state-indebtedness.

Nor was the last of the alternatives free from serious objections; but, under all circumstances, it was thought to be the least so by Congress, and it accordingly passed through both houses by a large majority. Mr. Calhoun made a very comprehensive and able speech [on 5/28/1836] against the first two, and explained his views of the substitute he offered.

This was not the only important measure that claimed his attention during the session. In the preceding recess the Abolitionists had for the first time regularly organized as a party, with a powerful press, and attempted, by systematic operations, to force its publications on the South, with a view of acting on its slave population. It carried deep excitement throughout that entire section. Everywhere meetings were held and the attempt denounced, and the other sections called upon to adopt measures to stay the evil. The President [Andrew Jackson], in his message at the opening of the session, called the attention of Congress to the subject, and recommended the adoption of efficient measures to prevent the circulation of their incendiary publications through the mail. Mr. Calhoun, although he appreciated and highly approved the patriotic motives of the President, could not agree with him to the full extent of his recommendation. He saw the danger of permitting Congress to assume the right of judging of what constituted an incendiary publication; for if it be conceded that it has the right of determining what is incendiary, and to prevent its circulation, it would, by necessary consequence, carry with it the right of determining what was not, and to enforce its circulation against the laws of such states as might prohibit them. With this impression, and in order to prevent the adoption of erroneous views, at the outset, on a subject so vitally important to the slave-holding states, he moved the reference of the portion of the message containing the recommendation to a special committee, of which he was appointed chairman.

The report he made [on 2/4/1836] took a very original and able survey of the whole ground, and conclusively proved, both by arguments drawn from the Constitution and the practice of the Government, that it belonged to the states separately to determine what is or is not calculated to affect or disturb its internal police, including its peace and safety, and to adopt the measures necessary for their security; and that it was the duty of the General Government not only to conform its acts, in reference to the mail or for the regulation of commerce, to the legislation of the states in such cases, but to aid in the execution of the laws of the states, as far as its power would permit, when it became necessary. The report was accompanied by a bill, drawn up in conformity with these views, and was ordered to the third reading by the casting vote of the Vice-president [Martin Van Buren], but finally failed.

This bill gave rise in the Senate to a very animated and interesting debate, principally between Mr. Calhoun and Mr. [John] Davis of Massachusetts, in which the arguments for and against are strongly presented on both sides. For original views of the Constitution and strength of argument, Mr. Calhoun's speech [of 3/9/1836] on the occasion ranks with his ablest, and is worthy of the study of all who desire to understand some of the most important provisions of that instrument.

During the same session he made another speech on the same subject [on 4/12/1836], distinguished for its foresight and knowledge of the Constitution. For the first time there began to pour in that flood of petitions on the subject of abolition which has since deluged Congress. The members from the non-slave-holding states on both sides, though adverse to the petitions, were opposed to taking strong and decided grounds against them; and their respective political friends in the South were naturally indisposed to force them to take higher grounds than they were inclined to do. The result was a sort of compromise, to receive the petitions, but not to refer or act upon them. Mr. Calhoun, whose rule has ever been to meet danger "on the frontier," to use his own expression, saw the peril of receiving the petitions, and determined to take a decided stand against it. He expected to stand alone; but with such force did he maintain his objections to receiving [in his speech of 2/6/1837], that he was supported by a large portion of the Southern senators, and the motion to receive was laid on the table. Since then, no petition of the kind has been received by the Senate.

The prominent question at the next session [of 12/1836–3/1837] was the Specie Circular. The President had issued an order in the recess prohibiting the receipt of bank-notes, or anything but specie in payment of the public lands. The opposition was unanimously opposed to it, both on the ground of expediency, and the want of authority on his part to issue such an order, while his friends and supporters were greatly divided, some sustaining, but the greater part opposing the measure. Mr. Calhoun agreed with those who denied the right of the President to issue the order, on the broad principle that neither the Constitution nor the laws conferred it, and that the executive had no power but what was conferred by the one or the other. Nevertheless, he declined voting for the bill to supersede the order, which was passed by a great majority, a large portion of the administration party voting for it. His reasons were, that the diseased state of the currency was beyond remedy, and whether the circular was repealed or not, the result would be the same. He regarded the catastrophe as inevitable, and that the only question was, at whose door the responsibility should be laid. He saw that if the circular should be rescinded, it would be charged on those by whose vote it was done; and as he felt conscious that he had done all that he could to arrest the approaching calamity, he was determined to avoid all responsibility, and therefore declined voting for the bill. He was entitled to the floor, and intended to offer his reasons at large; but when it came up on its passage, was accidentally prevented from speaking. On his return home in March [1837], several of his friends in Charleston, interested in trade and the banks, asked his opinion of the prospect ahead. His reply [on 3/17/1837] was, that the storm was approaching, and was just at hand, and his advice was to reef—reef—reef—quickly and closely, to avoid being wrecked. In two months the banks suspended payments, and the commerce and business of the country were prostrated.

During the same session an important question arose in reference to the admission of Michigan. She had been admitted at the preceding session on the condition of agreeing to the boundary between her and Ohio, as presented by the act for her admission. The Legislature of the state, in compliance with the act of Congress, called a convention of the people of the state, in order to determine whether the conditions should be accepted or not. The convention rejected the condition. Subsequently, an informal meeting or caucus was called by the party in favour of accepting it, without legal authority, or any other ceremony than is used for convening such meetings for ordinary political objects. It met, and agreed to the condition, which had been in due form considered and rejected by the convention legally and regularly called. The Committee on the Judiciary, to whom the subject was referred, reported in favour of admitting the state on the authority of the informal meeting or caucus, for it was, in fact, nothing more. Mr. Calhoun opposed the report in two speeches [on 1/2 and 1/5/1837] on the ground of the unconstitutionality and the danger of the precedent, in which he displayed, with great force of argument, that thorough knowledge of the Constitution for which he is remarkable. But, as powerful as was his resistance, it proved vain. The bill passed, and has made a precedent, the danger of which time only can disclose.

CHAPTER VI.

In which the Narrative is continued until the Termination of the
Second Session of the 27th Congress.

The suspension of the banks in the spring of '37 marks an important period in the life of Mr. Calhoun and the political history of the country. Fortunately, under the operation of the joint resolution of 1816, and the Deposite Act of the preceding year, in the passage of both of which he took a decided part, the act of suspension of itself entirely separated the Government and the banks. The former prohibited the Government from receiving the notes of suspended banks in the public dues; and the latter prohibited it from using such banks as the depositaries of the public money, or as the fiscal agents of the Government. Without these, the union of the Government with the banks would still have continued, and the former would have found itself reduced to the same condition that it was at the end of the war in 1815, of receiving and paying away the notes of discredited banks, and using them as its depositaries and agents in the management of its revenue.

The suspension, as has been stated, was not unexpected to Mr. Calhoun; and he was not long in making up his mind as to the course he would pursue. He resolved to resist the reunion of the Government and the banks in any form, and to oppose the establishment of a national bank. Indeed, he regarded it as the first occasion that ever occurred which offered an opportunity for carrying into execution what he had long believed to be the true policy of the country, the divorce of the Government from all connexion with banks; an opinion which he had first publicly and plainly indicated in 1834, in his speech on the removal of the deposites, already cited. He made known his determination to a few confidential friends long before the call of the extraordinary session [of 9–10/1837], and resisted decidedly all attempts to influence him to support a national bank.

With his course thus fixed, he went to Washington at the commencement of the extra session, resolved to await the development of the views of the two great parties before he should publicly make known his own, and to act with or against them, according as their course might agree or disagree with his own. He listened attentively to the reading of the President's [Martin Van Buren's] Message at the opening of the session, which explicitly opposed the establishment of a United States Bank, and the renewal of the union of the Government and the banks, and made up his mind, as soon as the reading was finished, that he would give it his support.

The impression got out that Mr. Calhoun would support the message. It caused much excitement; but as it was only a rumour, the development of his course in his place in the Senate was looked to with deep solicitude. It was not long before an occasion offered. The Committee on Finances reported, shortly after the message was received, a bill for the establishment of what was called a Sub-treasury, but without any provision for collecting the Government dues in specie.

Mr. Calhoun rose in his place [on 9/16/1837], and declared himself in favour of the entire separation of the Government from the banks, but denounced in strong terms the report of the committee for omitting what he regarded as essential to a separation; a provision for collecting the public dues in the constitutional currency, without which the measure they had reported would prove a perfect abortion. He declared that if that was what was meant by a sub-treasury, he washed his hands of all concern with it. His remarks made a deep sensation, and he was solicited by many of the friends of the administration to bring forward, in the shape of an amendment, a proposition to collect the public dues in specie. He replied that he had not intended to offer any proposition of his own; but, as they requested it, he would comply with their wishes. When the bill for the issue of treasury notes came up a few days after, he stated his opinion at large on the subject of the separation of the Government and the banks, in a speech, which made a permanent impression on the public mind, in reference to the whole banking system. He gave notice in his speech [on 9/18/1837] of his intention of moving an amendment, at the proper time, to the bill, for the gradual but permanent separation of the Government from the banks, but finally agreed to postpone his motion till the bill for the establishment of the Sub-treasury should come under consideration. When that came up, he moved his amendment, and made a second speech [on 10/3/1837] in which he traced the rise and progress of the banking system, and marked the several stages through which it had passed; he showed that it contained within itself the principle of its own destruction; and finally exposed the mischievous character and tendency of the system, economically, politically, and morally. His amendment prevailed, and the bill passed the Senate as amended, but failed in the House.

Such was Mr. Calhoun's course on this memorable occasion. All things considered, it has seldom been equalled for patriotism, magnanimity, sagacity, and boldness. We have seen him, in obedience to his principles, and what seemed to be his duty, separate himself from General Jackson and the party when in the plenitude of their power, and when he held the second office in the Government, with every prospect of reaching the highest. We have seen him, after his separation, instead of courting the opposition in order to maintain himself against the power and influence of the executive, again pursue a course in obedience to principle and duty, which brought him into direct conflict with both, and left him with his state alone to maintain the unequal struggle against a course of policy which, he believed, if not arrested, would prove ruinous to the Government and country. We have seen him, when the state, in pursuance of his course, had effected its object, availing himself of the aid of the opposition to bring down the power and influence of the executive department (originating in the encroachments of the Congress) within proper constitutional, legal limits. That done, we next see him, when the reaction of the very system to oppose which he separated from the party had prostrated them, and when the opposition with which he had for a time acted were preparing to rush on and overwhelm them in their weakness, and to re-establish their old doctrines and principles, rising up promptly, overcoming all personal feelings, forgetting all past differences, boldly repelling the assaults of his recent allies, and defending and protecting those from whom he had been so long separated, and by whom he had been much wronged, in stern obedience to his principles and to what he believed to be his duty: thus clearly showing, by his whole course throughout this eventful period, that *when they were at stake*, neither ambition, fear, enmity, friendship, nor popularity could bend him from his course.

The stand which he took drew down on him, as might be expected, the bitter denunciation and vengeance of the opposition, who had now assumed the name of Whigs. Among other things, they charged him with desertion, as if he had ever been of their party, and when, in fact, he had kept himself distinct from both the great parties from the time of his separation from General Jackson. That there might be no mistake on that point, he took the earliest opportunity in the Senate to avow what his position was. In his speech on Mr. Webster's motion, in 1834, to renew the charter of the United States Bank for six years, he said, "I am the partisan of no class, nor, let me add, of either political party. I am neither of the opposition nor administration. If I act with the former in any instance, it is because I approve of their course on the particular occasion, and I shall always be happy to act with them when I do approve. If I oppose the administration, if I desire to see power change hands, it is because I disapprove of the general course of those in authority."

To which he added: "But mine has not been, nor will it be, a systematic opposition. Whatever measure of theirs I deem right I shall cheerfully support, and I only desire that they will afford me more frequent occasions for support and fewer for opposition than they have heretofore done." He often avowed the same sentiments, and acted throughout in strict conformity to the principles here laid down; and when Mr. Clay, for the first time in the Senate, assumed the name of Whig for himself and the party, intending to comprehend under it all that did not support the administration, the State Rights as well as the national parties, Mr. Calhoun rose in his place [on 5/6/-1834], and disavowed the name, as applied to himself, and expressed himself contented with the name he bore. If to this it is added, he never, on any occasion, joined in their political meetings or party consultations, and always kept himself free on every question to follow the dictates of his own judgment, it must be obvious that the charge of desertion is wholly groundless. In truth, he never from the first permitted his party obligations to overrule his attachment to principles or duty, and throughout this trying period he availed himself of the aid of whatever party fell in with his course for the time, to effect the important objects he had in view, but without permitting them, in any instance, to divert him from his end.

At the next session [of 12/1837–7/1838], the Sub-treasury, or the reorganization of the treasury, with a view of collecting, safe keeping, and disbursing the public moneys through its own officers, without the agency of banks, again became the prominent question. The subject was again referred in the Senate to the Committee on Finance, which reported a bill much fuller in its details, and containing what is called the specie feature, that is, a provision for the gradual, but entire separation of the government from the banks, similar to that moved at the extra session by Mr. Calhoun. Mr. [William C.] Rives moved, as a substitute, to strike out the whole bill after the enacting clause, and to insert in lieu the use of the state banks as the depositaries and fiscal agents of the government, as formerly used, but with some additional modifications. The discussion took place on the amendment, and the argument principally turned on the respective merits of the two systems. Both sides put out their strength. The debate was animated and able. Mr. Calhoun took a prominent part, and greatly distinguished himself in the speech he delivered on the occasion [on 2/15/1838]. This drew down on him pointed personal attacks from the two great leaders of the opposition, Mr. Clay and Mr. Webster, with whom he had to contend single handed. The conflict excited deep and universal interest. It was called in the journals of the day the war of the giants; and it is no more than justice to him to say, that [in his speeches of 3/10 and 3/22/1838] he repelled their charges with signal success, and turned back the war with effect.

After the defeat of the amendment offered by Mr. Rives, and just before the question was put on the engrossment, a motion was made to strike out the specie feature, which succeeded by the united vote of the opposition and a considerable portion of the friends of the administration. The effect of the amendment would be for the government to collect the dues in the notes of the banks, and deposite them for safe keeping in its own safes and vaults, to which Mr. Calhoun had from the first avowed his hostility. He reserved his opposition until the bill had been perfected, according to the views of those who had made the amendment, and the question put on the engrossment, when he stated his objections in a short, but strong and decisive speech [on 3/24/1838], showing that it was liable to all the dangers and objections for which the pet-bank system was obnoxious, attended by additional dangers and objections peculiar to itself. The bill, nevertheless, passed the Senate, but the argument was not without its effects. The views of Mr. Calhoun were almost unanimously sustained by the party in the House and the country. The bill failed, and the session terminated in leaving things as they were.

It was during this session [on 12/27/1837] that Mr. Calhoun introduced his resolutions on the subject of abolition. He had always regarded this as the most mischievous species of political fanaticism, and the only question which could really endanger the Union. He saw the non-slave-holding states closely divided between two great parties, and a third growing up and organizing upon a principle which they believed of a higher importance than any involved in the political issues of the day. Should this sect continue to increase without opposition from either of the great parties, its influence might become strong enough to decide the political contests, and so formidable that it would be courted. As their ends could only be attained through consolidation, it was likely that they would join the party whose principles had that tendency. The best interests of the Union, and the integrity of the Republican party, seemed to require the line to be drawn at once between that party and the Abolitionists. He accordingly moved the following resolutions, which present so strongly his views of the relations of the General Government and of the states to this subject, that we shall extract them.

"Mr. Calhoun then submitted the following resolutions:

"Resolved, That, in the adoption of the Federal Constitution, the states adopting the same acted severally as free, independent, and sovereign states; and that each, for itself, by its own voluntary assent, entered the Union with the view to its increased security against all dangers, domestic as well as foreign, and the more perfect and secure enjoyment of its advantages, natural, political, and social.

"Resolved, That, in delegating a portion of their powers to be exercised by the Federal Government, the states retained severally the exclusive and sole right over their own domestic institutions and police, and are alone responsible for them; and that any intermeddling of any one or more states, or a combination of their citizens, with the domestic institutions and police of the others, on any ground or under any pretext whatever, political, moral, or religious, with a view to their alteration or subversion, is an assumption of superiority not warranted by the Constitution, insulting to the states interfered with, tending to endanger their domestic peace and tranquillity, subversive of the objects for which the Constitution was formed, and, by necessary consequence, tending to weaken and destroy the Union itself.

"Resolved, That this Government was instituted and adopted by the several states of this Union as a common agent, in order to carry into effect the powers which they had delegated by the Constitution for their mutual security and prosperity; and that, in fulfilment of this high and sacred trust, this Government is bound so to exercise its powers as to give, as far as may be practicable, increased stability and security to the domestic institutions of the states that compose the Union; and that it is the solemn duty of the Government to resist all attempts by one portion of the Union to use it as an instrument to attack the domestic institutions of another, or to weaken or destroy such institutions, instead of strengthening and upholding them, as it is in duty bound to do.

"Resolved, That domestic slavery, as it exists in the Southern and Western States of the Union, composes an important part of their domestic institutions, inherited from their ancestors, and existing at the adoption of the Constitution, by which it is recognised as constituting an essential element in the distribution of its powers among the states; and that no change of opinion or feeling on the part of the other states of the Union in relation to it can justify them or their citizens in open and systematic attacks thereon, with the view to its overthrow; and that all such attacks are in manifest violation of the mutual and solemn pledge to protect and defend each other, given by the states respectively on entering into the Constitutional compact which formed the Union, and, as such, is a manifest breach of faith, and a violation of the most solemn obligations, moral and religious.

"Resolved, That the intermeddling of any state or states, or their citizens, to abolish slavery in this district, or any of the territories, on the ground or under the pretext that it is immoral or sinful, or the passage of any act or measure of Congress with that view, would be a direct and dangerous attack on the institutions of all the slave-holding states.

"Resolved, That the union of these states rests on an equality of rights and advantages among its members; and that whatever destroys that equality tends to destroy the Union itself; and that it is the solemn duty of all, and more especially of this body, which represents the states in their corporate capacity, to resist all attempts to discriminate between the states in extending the benefits of the Government to the several portions of the Union; and that to refuse to extend to the Southern and Western States any advantage which would tend to strengthen or render them more secure, or increase their limits or population by the annexation of new territory or states, on the assumption or under the pretext that the institution of slavery, as it exists among them, is immoral or sinful, or otherwise obnoxious, would be contrary to that equality of rights and advantages which the Constitution was intended to secure alike to all the members of the Union, and would, in effect, disfranchise the slave-holding states, withholding from them the advantages, while it subjected them to the burdens of the Government."

These, with the exception of the last, passed the Senate with some slight modifications. In the course of a long and running debate [during 1/1838] on these resolutions, he examined the relations of our government to this subject. He showed those who viewed slavery only in the abstract, that they could never thus form a true conception of their duty in the existing state of things. It was not a question to be considered in the abstract, but in the concrete, and with a full view of all the circumstances connected with it. In a large portion of our country, two races had been thrown together in nearly equal numbers, and separated into castes by a natural line too strongly drawn ever to be effaced. The question was not as to what different state of things could be conceived as more desirable, but what was the best relation to establish between two such races thrown together under such circumstances. Under the institution of slavery, both races had prospered, and the black especially had made a more rapid advance in civilization than it had ever done before in the same space

96

of time and under other circumstances. These were facts to induce those to pause who were tempted, by considerations of abstract philanthropy, to overstep the bounds which were imposed on their action not only by the Constitution, but also by an enlightened spirit of benevolence itself. If other considerations were wanting, he pointed to the incidental political benefits arising from an institution which harmonized the relations between capital and labour, and thus introduced a spirit conservative of both interests, so far as Southern influence could be felt in the action of the General Government. The passage of these resolutions placed the Abolitionists in direct hostility to the Republican party, and led to a state of things which was far safer to the party and the Union than to have permitted so dangerous a sect to grow up unopposed. The Republicans, from all sections of the Union, found in these propositions a common ground where they could stand, without danger of schism upon the question which threatened most to divide them.

At the next session [of 12/1838–3/1839] the prominent subject of debate was Mr. Crittenden's bill to prevent the interference of certain Federal officers in elections. Mr. Calhoun spoke with much power and effect on the occasion [on 2/22/1839]. After discussing the subject fully against the bill on its merits, both as to its constitutionality and expediency, and showing that its effects would be the opposite of what was intended—that it would increase instead of diminishing the influence of the executive—he declared himself the fixed and strenuous friend of reducing the influence and patronage of that branch of the government within the narrowest limits consistent with the Constitution and the object for which it was created. He then proceeded to show that the legitimate means of effecting that was to restrict the revenue and expenditure to the legitimate and constitutional wants of the Government, and to hold the executive power strictly to its appropriate sphere. This led him into a very interesting account of the two hostile systems of policy, which had divided the country from the formation of the Government, of one of which Mr. Jefferson was the head and General Hamilton of the other. After tracing their rise and progress, he showed that the present struggle was but a continuation of the original conflict between them, and that an opportunity was now afforded for the first time since the Government went into operation, to put down effectually that of which Hamilton was the head—the old Federal and consolidation party; and to give the opposite—that of which Jefferson was the head, the old State Rights Republican party—a permanent ascendency. In conclusion he said, "It would be presumptuous in me, Mr. President, to advise those who are charged with the administration of the Government what course to adopt; but if they would hear the voice of one who desires nothing for himself, and whose only wish is to see the country prosperous, free, and happy, I would say to them, You are placed in the most remarkable juncture that has ever occurred since the establishment of the Federal Government, and, by seizing the opportunity, you may bring the vessel of state to a position where she may take a new tack, and thereby escape all the shoals and breakers into the midst of which a false steerage has run her, and bring her triumphantly into her destined port, with honour to yourselves and safety to those on board. Take your stand boldly; avow your object; disclose your measures, and let the people see clearly that you intend to do what Jefferson designed, but, from adverse circumstances, could not accomplish: to reverse the measures originating in principles and policy not congenial with our political system; to divest the Government of all undue patronage and influence; to restrict it to the few great objects intended by the Constitution; in a word, to give a complete ascendency to the good old Virginia school over its antagonist, which time and experience have proved to be foreign and dangerous to our system of Government, and you may count with confidence on their support, without looking to other means of success. Should the Government take such a course at this favourable moment, our free and happy institutions may be perpetuated for generations, but, if a different, short will be their duration." Had the course advised been early and openly avowed and vigorously pursued in time, very different might have been the termination of the last presidential election [of 1840]; and it may be added, that the advice is not less applicable to the coming than to the past election, and, if the Federal consolidation party is ever to be permanently put down, and the State Rights Republican party to gain the permanent ascendency, it can only be effected by its adhering steadily and in good faith to the course advised.

The next session, that of 1839–40, which immediately preceded the late presidential election, was distinguished for the number and importance of the subjects that were agitated and discussed, and, it may be added, the ability and animation of the discussions. Among the more prominent of these may be included the public lands; the assumption of state debts; Mr. Calhoun's resolutions in reference to the case of the Enterprise; the Bankrupt Bill [on which he spoke on 6/2/-1840], and the repeal of the salt-tax; in all of which Mr. Calhoun took a prominent part. His speeches on his resolutions [on 3/13/1840] and on the assumption of state debts [on 2/5/1840] are among the ablest he ever delivered, and are worthy of the attention of all who desire to understand the subjects which they discuss.

The presidential election having terminated in favour of the Whigs, the next session was principally occupied in the discussions connected with the public lands, preparatory to one of the leading objects of policy contemplated under the new administration. Mr. Calhoun made three speeches on the subject: one on the prospective Pre-emption Bill [on 1/12/1841]; another on an amendment to it proposed by Mr. Crittenden, as a substitute, to distribute the revenue from the public lands among the states [on 1/23/1841]; and, finally, one in reply to Mr. Webster and Mr. Clay [on 1/30/1841]. In these the whole policy of the public lands, and the various plans which were proposed in reference to them, were discussed. It is a subject which early attracted Mr. Calhoun's attention, and has engrossed much of his reflection.

As far back as February, 1837, he offered a substitute, in the form of an amendment to the bill, to suspend the sales of the public lands, in which he proposed to cede to the new states the portion of the public lands lying within their respective limits, on certain conditions, which he accompanied by a speech explanatory of his views and reasons. He followed up the subject in a speech delivered in January, 1839, on the Graduation Bill; and in May, 1840, an elaborate and full report was made from the Committee on Public Lands, and a bill introduced by him, containing substantially the same provisions with his original proposition. These, with his three speeches already referred to, contain a full view of his objects and reasons for the proposed cession.

There have been few measures ever presented for consideration so grossly misrepresented, or so much misconceived, as the one in question. It has been represented as a gift—a surrender—an abandonment of the public domain to the new states; and having assumed that to be its true character, the most unworthy motives have been attributed to the author for introducing it. Nothing is more untrue. The cession is neither more nor less than a conditional sale, not extended to the whole of the public domain, as represented, but to that portion in the new states respectively within whose limits they lie; the greater part of which are mere remnants, which have long since been offered for sale, without being sold.

The conditions on which they are proposed to be ceded or sold are drawn up with the greatest care, and with the strictest provisions to ensure their fulfilment; one of which is, that the state should pay 65 per cent. of the gross proceeds of the sale to the General Government, and retain only 35 per cent. for the trouble, expense, and responsibility attending their administration. Another is, that the existing laws, as they stand, except so far as they may be modified or authorized to be modified by the act of cession, shall remain unchanged, unless altered by the joint consent of the General Government and the several states. They are respectively authorized, if they should think proper, to adopt a system of graduation and pre-emption within well-defined and safe limits prescribed in the conditions; and the General Government is authorized to appoint officers in the several states, to whom its share of the proceeds of the sale shall be directly paid, without going into the state treasury; and these conditions are put under the guardianship of the courts, by providing, if they shall be violated, that all after rules by the state shall be null and void. So far from this being a gift, or an abandonment of the public lands to the new states, he has clearly proved, if there be truth in figures, that the Government would receive a greater amount of revenue from the lands in the new states, under the system he proposes, than under the present. These demonstrations are based on calculations which neither have nor can be impugned.

But his views extended far beyond dollars and cents in bringing forward the measure. He proposed to effect by it the high political objects of placing the new states on the same footing of equality and independence with the old, in reference to their domain; to cut off the vast amount of patronage which the public lands place in the hand of the executive; to withdraw them, as one of the stakes, from the presidential game; to diminish by one fourth the business of Congress, and with it the length and expense of its session; to enlist the Government of the new states on the side of the General Government; to aid in a more careful administration of the rest of the public domain, and thereby prevent the whole of it from becoming the property of the occupants from possession; and, finally, to prevent the too rapid extinction of Indian titles in proportion to the demand for lands from the increase of population, which he shows to be pregnant with great embarrassment and danger. These are great objects, of high political import; and if they could be effected by the measure proposed, it is justly entitled to be ranked among the wisest and most politic ever brought forward. That they can be effected, it is almost impossible for any well-informed and dispassionate mind deliberately to read the speeches and documents referred to, and to doubt.

CHAPTER VII.

Conclusion.

One of the first acts of the new administration [of William Henry Harrison] was to call an extra session in the spring of 1841. Flushed with success, and confident in their power to consummate their entire system of policy, the Whigs assembled at the commencement of this session [of 5–9/1841] with overwhelming majorities in each House of Congress. The Republicans came, under circumstances well calculated to dispirit them, and too weak in point of numbers to have made an efficient opposition except under the most skilful management. It soon became manifest, as the plan of the campaign was developed, that the majority were determined to sweep every thing by "coups-de-main," and would not depend upon address at the expense of time to take any post which could possibly be carried by storm. They commenced in the House of Representatives by wresting from the minority some of the most inestimable of the privileges of debate: privileges which the minority had enjoyed from the institution of the House of Representatives up to that time, and even during the war, when the opposition, by its factious course, seemed to have justly forfeited all respect, if it had not been deemed the sacred right of the tax-payer to be fully heard before new burdens were imposed upon him. But the minority were no longer allowed to debate questions in the Committee of the Whole until they were satisfied with the hearing.

The majority seized the power of arresting the debate whenever they chose, and thus, under the pretence of preventing factious delays, they acquired the means of terminating the discussion whenever it searched their purposes too deeply, or developed too strongly the consequences of their measures. Under this state of things, there was little left to the opposition but the mere vote; and the majority so completely acquired the whole sway in the lower House that it was by their grace only that their opponents could even remonstrate against their measures. In that body one overruling influence seemed to prevail, which did not emanate from within, but cast its shadow from without. Nor could even the fascinations of the splendid genius that controlled, relieve the dull, dreary, and depressing sense of dependance under which that House seemed to think and move. In the Senate, however, this tendency to the absolute power of a majority met with a severe and effective resistance. Determined never to yield up the arms which were necessary for the contest, they repelled every attempt to introduce "the gag." Foremost among the opposition stood Mr. Calhoun, and the parliamentary annals of the world hardly afford an instance of a more formidable array of intellectual force than that opposition then presented. Nothing could be more brilliant than its career through the whole of this short but eventful session.

The majority boldly assumed the old Federal positions upon the bank, the tariff, and the distribution of the proceeds of the public lands. Confident in their strength to carry it, they openly avowed their system. Profusion in public expenditure and special legislation seemed to be the order of the day. To the shattered victims of the war so long waged by the stock interests, a deliverance from all obligation for the past was declared in the Bankrupt Law; and the affiliated system of the bank, the tariff, and the distribution tempted them with an almost boundless prospect for future indulgence. The prodigal, the idle, the desperate, the visionary speculator, and even the cunning usurer, were each invited, by some appropriate hope, to join in the general foray, when the whole field of productive industry was to be given up to plunder. There seemed to be at last a prospect that Hamilton's system would prevail. With revenue decreasing daily, the Secretary of the Treasury [Thomas Ewing] proposed an annual expenditure of about $27,000,000, and recommended a distribution among the states of the proceeds of the public lands. This lavish expenditure was to be maintained from customs alone; and through the influence of another bank expansion, our people were to be tempted to buy freely under the ruinous rates of duties which were proposed. Entreaty and remonstrance were alike unavailing with the majority, which for a while pursued its course without regard to the rights of the states or the freedom of individual pursuits, which were overwhelmed in their way. The whole hope of an efficient resistance to these measures in Congress now rested on the Senate, where the necessary privileges of debate were still retained. Our history does not present us an instance of an opposition more distinguished for its ability, or more untiring in its energy. Its searching gaze seemed to read the hidden purpose with almost as much certainty as it followed the open movements of its adversary. The purposes and principles of the system proposed by the majority were so clearly exposed by skilful amendments or in vigorous debate, that the public attention was fully aroused and directed to the consequences: consequences which were so powerfully and accurately depicted, that even the authors of the measures would have been appalled had they been less reckless of the future. The natural affinity between the tariff and distribution, which Mr. Calhoun had proclaimed so long before, was now clearly proved by the course of the majority during this session. So essential did they deem the distribution in order to secure the permanence of the tariff, that they ventured upon the former measure at every hazard, and at a time, too, when the revenue was deficient, and there was scarcely a hope that the customs would afford money enough for the current expenses of the Government. This ominous combination, which Mr. Calhoun had sacrificed so much to avert, was now at hand, and he met it in a speech [of 8/24/1841], which is one of the finest specimens of his power and style. There are portions of that speech in which he traces the consequences of distribution with a spirit of inquiry so eager, so searching, so keen, that he forgets himself and the personal feelings of the contest in the contemplation of the vision of ruin before him, and seems to seek relief from his forebodings by unbosoming himself to the country. The majority now faltered, for the first time, under the appeals of the opposition, and incorporated a provision for suspending the distribution when the duties upon imports exceeded a certain rate—a provision to which we have since owed the suspension of that dangerous act. The condition of the finances, which seemed not to have been fully appreciated by the majority, together with the proviso of which we have spoken, rendered the distribution law practically inefficient. Their bank bills had been vetoed by the President [John Tyler], from whom they were soon alienated; the Bankrupt Law was generally odious, and it seemed to require nothing more than the absurd and extravagant Tariff Act of the succeeding session [of 1842] to consummate their ruin. Thus did the opposition come out of the contest with flying colours at the close of that eventful session. The part which Mr. Calhoun bore in this crisis is so justly and so thoroughly appreciated by the country, that no particular comment upon it is necessary.

Suffice it to say, that the discussions of the extra session and of that [of 12/1841–8/1842] which succeeded it were important and exciting. The most prominent of the extra session were upon the M'Leod case [on which Calhoun spoke on 6/11/1841], the Report of the Secretary of the Treasury [on which he spoke on 6/21/1841], and the Bankrupt Law. The debate on the [national] bank bills turned almost exclusively upon the details. At the succeeding session the principal subjects were the Treasury Note Bill, the Veto power, Mr. Clay's resolutions in reference to the revenue and expenditures, the Loan Bill, and the Tariff Bill. To Mr. Calhoun's speeches upon these subjects [on 1/25, 2/28, 3/16, 4/12, and 8/5/1842, respectively] we simply refer, because they are so recent as to be familiar to all, and not because they are less worthy of study than some others of a more distant date, from which we have extracted freely. Indeed, we have so often found occasion to recommend the perusal of the particular speech to which we were referring, that we were almost afraid of exciting the suspicion that our object was more to eulogize the statesman than to instruct the reader; and yet we are sure that all who study these speeches will acquit us of such a motive. We have recommended their perusal because we believed that they gave the best view of the state of public affairs, and of the mode in which a statesman would deal with such events, which has yet been furnished; nor did we know of any other models, either of statesmanship or oratory, in our own parliamentary annals, to which we could better invite the attention of the student. Indeed, we could scarcely direct him amiss among these speeches for specimens of luminous conceptions, or of that simple and natural order of propositions which constitutes a peculiar charm in style, and enables the orator to fascinate his audience, and carry them along with him. The English language affords no finer examples than are to be found in these speeches of the power of analysis in eliminating the truth of a case from circumstances which obscure and embarrass it. Nor are there any more attractive for novel and profound speculation, in which he sometimes deals when such lights and shadows are necessary to complete the picture which he is drawing.

In how many of the unexplored regions of human thought will the attentive reader be startled to find the trace of his footstep, and yet so rapid is he in his flight over his subject, that he scarcely takes time to set up his flag on the lands which he has found, or to perpetuate the evidences of his title to the honours of discovery.

Here, perhaps, we ought to leave the reader to draw his own conclusions as to the nature of the man and of his public services from the narrative which we have given; and yet we feel that it will be impossible for him to understand either fully, even with the aids which we have offered him, without a careful study of his speeches, reports, and other public addresses, in connexion with the history of the times; a study to which we again commend him, as well worthy of the time and labour which it may cost. For ourselves, we can truly say, that our estimate of his public services has increased with our opportunities for studying them, and that our admiration of his character has grown as his private and political history became more familiar to us. Indeed, it would almost seem to us, at times, that it belonged to the destiny of the American people to have reared up such a man, and that one of its necessities required him to pursue that long and stormy career, through which he has watched and helped to steer the ship of state with an eye that never winked and an energy that never tired. It required his indomitable will, and a nature thus rarely constituted, to have maintained this eager and incessant labour for the happiness of the American people, and to have led, for so long a period, the triumphal march of our glorious institutions. With a turn of mind naturally philosophical, his great power of analysis and his faculty of attentive observation early enabled him to form a system for the conduct of life, both in his private and public relations, and to determine within his own mind upon the true ends of human action; ends which he has pursued with a matchless constancy, while a knowledge of his ultimate destination and of the high objects of his journey has cheered him along through the thorny paths of public life. Of all the men whom we have ever seen, he seems to us to have surveyed most completely the whole ground of human action. To these advantages he adds another, which constitutes, perhaps, his highest quality as a statesman. It is the faculty of considering circumstances in their combinations, and of determining their relative power in propelling events. To analyze this combination, or "juncture" (as he sometimes calls it), and to determine the resultant of all these forces, is, in his opinion, the highest and rarest faculty of a statesman. If he values this power more than most others, it is because he has derived more benefit from its use, and well may he estimate highly that quality which, by affording him an insight into futurity far beyond the usual range of human vision, has given him such control over events. These were the gifts in whose strength he presented himself on the stage of the world in the very commencement of his public life, as one fully grown and armed for the trials which belonged to the time and the place. True to those noble instincts which spring more from a Divine source than from human reason, he ever leaned to liberty as against power, and early learned to resist those temptations which so often lead man to increase the power of the mass, which he is content to share as a member, at the expense of those separate and individual rights of which nature constituted him the peculiar guardian, and which were only given as the means of self-culture, and as indispensable to the moral elevation of his being.

His public life may be divided into two grand epochs: the first, in which he put forth his whole energies to enable his countrymen to maintain their independence against foreign aggression; and the second, in which he undertook the more difficult task of freeing their domestic legislation from those devices by which one was enabled to prey upon another. In each of these periods he has been emphatically "the man of his time," and he has ever regarded the tenets of the Republican party as indicating the best means of attaining these ends under our form of government. Of all men now living, he, perhaps, has contributed most to illustrate and establish that political creed. We are aware that we expose ourselves here to the sneers of some of those literal expositors of the law, who believe that man was made for the Sabbath and not the Sabbath for man. But we repeat the assertion, that in all the public exigencies in which he was called to act, he made the nearest practical approach to the great ends of the Republican party which human wisdom or foresight could then devise. In all the great measures of our government since he first entered Congress, his influence has been felt either in their origination or modification, and to this influence more than any other the Republican party is indebted for its present proud position before the world.

Morally considered, the great objects of the Republican party are simple and few. Its first is to preserve, as far as possible, the independence of individual action and pursuit; and it rejects all limitations upon this independence which are not essential to the great ends of social organization. It regards all of those powers which man wields in his aggregate or corporate capacity as so many limitations upon his individual rights, and it yields those which are indispensable to the institution of society as so many concessions which necessity has extorted from liberty. These are the terms upon which they would grant Government its powers; and they would administer the power thus limited with an equal regard for all who are entitled to share the benefits of the trust. Tried by these tests, Mr. Calhoun has nothing to fear, when the circumstances are considered under which he was called to act.

In the first epoch of his public life, we were forced to defend ourselves in a war with the most formidable nation of the globe, and with the only power whose arm was long enough to reach us in our distant position, and within the defences of so many natural barriers. In its commencement it was a war of independence, and it might become a contest for existence. In this state of things, it was in our aggregate power alone that we were to find the strength to resist foreign assaults, and every American patriot sought the means of increasing it as far as the limitations of the Constitution would permit. The war was a measure of the Republican party, and the unpatriotic course of the opposition devolved upon them alone the duty of devising the means to prosecute it. Under these circumstances, the Republican party deflected from the natural line of their direction, and sought to concentrate as much power in the Government as they then believed indispensable for the successful conduct of the war. How far they were right or wrong, it is not our province here to determine; but certain it is, that there was much in the overruling power of circumstances to justify their course and excuse their errors, if errors they may be called. With how much more justice may the same apology be made for Mr. Calhoun himself. The leading advocate of hostilities and the chairman of the committee which reported the declaration of war, with a deep responsibility to the country for the success of that contest, which he was accused of precipitating; young, ardent, and indignant at the course of foreign and domestic enemies, it is surprising that he was not less scrupulous of the Constitution in calling forth the means of defending it, and our people against foreign expositions of law and justice, which ultimately might have overturned all, unless arrested by our successful resistance. And yet, upon how many great occasions did he restrain the Republican party from aberrations from their principles.

It was he who opposed the restrictive system against the majority of the party. It was he, too, who took a prominent part in resisting the system of forced loans in the case of the merchants' bonds, and who defeated Mr. [Alexander J.] Dallas's vast scheme of a national bank to issue irredeemable paper, which was recommended by a Republican President [James Madison] and supported by the party. Session after session did he combat it, until he succeeded in restoring to the country a specie-paying paper, and something like uniformity in the medium in which its taxes were collected. And although the opinions of that day, growing out of the exigencies of the war, exaggerated the necessity for roads and canals as military defences, and called for the general use of a power which was given by the Constitution within the narrowest limits, it is remarkable that he has nowhere expressly affirmed the existence of such a power in the Federal Government.

His views of the proper use to be made of this power, if it existed, or could be obtained, when given [on 1/7/1819] in obedience to a call of the House of Representatives, were perhaps the ablest ever taken of the relation of this subject to our military defences, yet he cautiously abstained from deciding the constitutional question. This was before the Republican party had paused in that career in which they were concentrating power within to defend themselves against attacks from without. In a review of this period of his life, it may with truth be said, that all those acts for which he has been reproached as departures from the State Rights creed, were substitutes for much worse measures, which, but for him, his party would have adopted; and, although some of them were neither the wisest nor best, according to the present standard of information, they were each the nearest approach to the true Republican line of action which was permitted by the state of public knowledge and feeling at the time. But, whatever may have been the errors of the early part of his *public* life, he nobly redeemed them in the second period, which commenced from his election to the vice-presidency. It was during the interval then allowed for reflection that he first examined thoroughly the working of the machinery of the Government in its internal as well as its external relations. He was among the first of the Republican party to pause in that career by which power had been consolidated in the Federal Government, without due reflection upon its consequences to the states and the people. He saw that the distribution of the political powers of our system, as contemplated by the Constitution, had been deranged, and that vast affiliated stock interests had been permitted to grow up almost unconsciously, which threatened to absorb the whole power and influence of the Confederacy, and to substitute a government of the few for that of the many; and, worse than all, he saw many of the Republican party so deeply entangled in the consequences of past action, and so little aware of the mischiefs which threatened them, that it was impossible to receive their co-operation in the efforts which were necessary to save the Government from deep organic derangement, and the party itself from utter annihilation. His position gave him a deep interest in the unity of the party, if he had looked to himself alone; the road to office was open and easy; but the higher and more alluring path to fame lay along a steeper route and over rugged and difficult precipices. Between these alternatives he did not hesitate, but determined at once to strike the blows he believed to be necessary to save the country and restore the party to its pristine purity of faith and practice. We have given the history of the memorable contest in which, with unexampled odds against him, he maintained his foothold and accomplished his grand design.

We have seen the series of skilful movements and masterly combinations by which, with comparatively few forces, he occupied and manfully contested every inch of disputed territory, until he finally struck down the protective system with blows from which it never can entirely recover in the face of the formidable array against him, wielding the battle-axe of Richard or the cimeter [*sic*] of Saladin, as strength or skill might best serve his turn. Ever ready, cheerful, and confident, he sometimes obtained concessions from mere respect to his gallantry and prowess, which no force at his disposal could then have extorted. Experience now proved that he had not been a moment too soon in striking at the protective system. The Republican party had been gradually wasting under the assaults of their open enemies, and the moral influences of the stock interests. The banks, deprived for the time of their natural ally the tariff, were forced to take the field alone, and the difficulty which the Republicans experienced in coping with this single interest, proved how impossible it would have been for them to have resisted the whole affiliated system if its strength had been unimpaired, and its united forces directed against them. They now saw that Mr. Calhoun had been warring all along, not against them, but a common enemy, which, but for him, might have overwhelmed all together. Mr. Calhoun, who had left his ancient friends in their strength to reform, but not to destroy, now returned to them in their weakness to cheer, to animate, to rally, and defend them, and was prouder of their alliance upon principle in their period of adversity than he would have been of all the honours which they could have heaped upon him in their prosperity. It was not in his nature to regard the execrations which these stock interests poured out upon him. They had too often tried the temper of his steel not to know the force of the arm which wielded it, and it was perhaps with as much of despair as rage that privilege saw its ancient and well-trained adversary take the field with additional strength against it. Mr. Calhoun did not now direct his attention so much to mere affairs of outposts as to placing the party upon that solid platform of principle, in which he well knew that the whole battering train of the Federal hosts could never effect a breach. With a true military eye, he readily seized all the advantages of position, and under his advice mainly, they have, at every sacrifice, directed column after column upon this elevated post, where they now command the field, and from which, if not abandoned or lost by want of vigilance, they must ultimately recover the country.

He is now about to retire from the theatre of public life, neither wearied nor worn, but because his work is done, so far, at least, as senatorial life can afford him any useful part to play. If there be any new field of action worthy of his powers, and as yet untrodden by him, it is in that highest executive sphere, for which the character of his mind and the experience of his life have so eminently fitted him. It is, perhaps, only upon this theatre that his countrymen would not now exclaim, "Superfluous lags the veteran on the stage," and it is there that they will probably require him to consummate, as perhaps he alone can do, those great Republican reforms so cherished by the party, as destined to commend it to the grateful regards of posterity. We cannot better close this sketch than by extracting a portrait of Mr. Calhoun as a man and an orator, which was drawn by a friendly hand, it is true, but which we recognise as being so just and well executed that we gladly adopt it as our own.

In his person Mr. Calhoun is slender and tall. His countenance, at rest, is strikingly marked with decision and firmness. In conversation it is highly animated, expressive, and indicative of genius. His eyes are large, dark, brilliant, and penetrating, and leave no doubt, at first view, of a high order of intellect. His manners are easy, natural, and unassuming, and as frank as they are cordial and kind. In all his domestic relations his life is without a blemish. He has none of the cautious reserve and mystery of common politicians; for he has nothing to conceal or disguise. He is accessible to all, agreeable, animated, instructive, and eloquent in conversation, and communicates his opinions with the utmost freedom. Some politicians seek popularity by carefully avoiding responsibility. Whatever popularity Mr. Calhoun possesses has, on the contrary, been acquired by bold and fearless assumption of responsibility on all critical and trying occasions. His judgment is so clear and discriminating, that he seems to possess a sort of prophetic vision of future events, and on occasion when most men doubt and hesitate, he decides with confidence, follows up his decision with undoubting firmness, and has never failed in the end to be justified by time, the arbiter of all things.

Few men have been called upon to pass through scenes of higher political excitement, and to encounter more vigorous and unrelenting opposition than Mr. Calhoun; yet, amid all the prejudices which party feeling engenders, and all the jealousy of political rivals, and all the animosity of political opponents, no one has yet ventured to hazard his own reputation for judgment or sincerity so far as to doubt one moment his great and commanding talents.

As an orator, Mr. Calhoun stands in the foremost rank of parliamentary speakers. On first rising in debate, he always felt the anxiety of diffidence, arising from a sensibility which is almost always the companion of true genius. His manner of speaking is energetic, ardent, rapid, and marked by a solemn earnestness, which leaves no doubt of his sincerity and deep conviction. His style is pure, forcible, logical, and condensed; often figurative for illustration, never for ornament. His mind is well stored with the fruits of learning, but still better with those of observation and reflection. Hence depth, originality, and force characterize all his speeches. He lays his premises on a foundation too broad, solid, and deep to be shaken; his deductions are clear and irresistible; "the strong power of genius," to adopt the language of the eloquent [William] Pinkney, in referring to Mr. Calhoun's splendid speech on the treaty-making power, "from a higher region than that of argument, throws on his subjects all the light with which it is the prerogative of genius to invest and illustrate every-thing." And his speeches, full of the most elevated and patriotic sentiments, after conquering the understanding, take the heart en-tirely captive, and carry along his hearers, often unconsciously, and sometimes against their will, to the point he desires.

Mr. Calhoun had attained so high a reputation as a member of Congress, that it was thought by many that he was leaving his appro-priate field when he accepted the appointment of Secretary of War. On the contrary, his new situation only presented another theatre for the exercise of his great and diversified talents. The distinguishing feature of his mind, the power of analysis, was now to be exercised in the practical business of Government, and at once, as by enchantment, order, efficiency, and perfect accountability sprang from the chaos in which he found the department, and demonstrated that his energy in execution was equal to his wisdom in organizing, and left it doubtful whether his legislative talents were not surpassed by his practical ability in administration.

As a statesman, in the most enlarged and elevated sense of the term, Mr. Calhoun has no superior. A philosophical observer of men and of their affairs, he analyzes and reduces all things to their original elements, and draws thence those general principles, which, with in-conceivable rapidity and unerring certainty, he applies on all oc-casions, and banishes the perplexity and doubt by which ordinary minds are overwhelmed and confounded. By this wonderful faculty, he is enabled to decide at once, not only what measures are at present necessary for a government novel in its principles, and placed in cir-cumstances of which there is no precedent in the history of mankind, but, by discerning results through their causes, to look into futurity, and to devise means for carrying on our beloved country in a direct path to the high and glorious destiny which, under the guidance of wisdom and virtue, awaits her.

To the highest powers of mind Mr. Calhoun unites those elevated moral qualities, which are equally essential with ability to complete the character of a perfect statesman: inflexible integrity, honour with-out a stain, disinterestedness, temperance, and industry; a firmness of purpose which disdains to calculate the consequences of doing his duty; prudence and energy in action, devotion to his country, and in-extinguishable love of liberty and justice. To these great qualities, perhaps, we ought to add a lofty ambition; but it is an ambition that prefers glory to office and power, which looks upon the latter only as a means for acquiring the former, and which, by the performance of great and virtuous actions for the accomplishment of noble ends, aims at the establishment of a widely-extended and ever-[en]during fame. This ingredient, which enters into the composition of all great and powerful minds, seems intended by Providence to stimulate them to the highest pitch of exertion in the service of mankind; and if it be a defect, it is one which Mr. Calhoun shares, as well as all their high qualities, with the most perfect models of Greek and Roman excellence.

To those who have not been attentive observers of the life, character, and conduct of Mr. Calhoun, or who may have been alienated by political conflicts, the above portraiture may seem to derive some of its colouring from the partial pencil of friendship. If an intimate connexion of that kind for more than a quarter of a century may be supposed to tincture the writer's mind with partiality, it will be allowed, at the same time, that it affords the best possible opportunity of forming an accurate estimate of the moral and political character of the subject of this memoir. His *statements of fact and opinion he knows to be entirely authentic*; and after a deliberate review of every sentence and word he has written, he finds nothing which a reverence for justice and truth will allow him to alter.

PC in *Life of John C. Calhoun, Presenting a Condensed History of Political Events from 1811 to 1843* (New York: Harper & Brothers, 1843); PC in *Life of John C. Calhoun, Presenting a Condensed History of Political Events from 1811 to 1843. Together with a Selection from His Speeches, Reports, and Other Writings Subsequent to His Election as Vice-President of the United States, Including His Leading Speech on the Late War Delivered in 1811* (New York: Harper & Brothers, no date), pp. 3–74. NOTE: The text above has been reproduced as originally published except for the adding of a few editorial footnotes, the interpolation of brief explanatory material into the text within brackets, and the omission of eighteen footnotes which appeared in the original. These omitted footnotes all referred the reader to certain numbered documents that appeared in the companion *Speeches of John C. Calhoun*. For each of the omitted footnotes, information has been interpolated in the text above between brackets, giving the date under which the relevant document may be found in volumes of *The Papers of John C. Calhoun*. Interpolated dates and other brief aids have been supplied at a few other places in the above text in addition to the points at which the omitted footnotes appeared, for chronological clarity or other reasons. The *Life of John C. Calhoun* was copyrighted by the publisher.

MARCH 4–JUNE 30
1843

On his way home from Washington, a private citizen for the first time in thirty-four years, Calhoun received a complimentary welcome from the citizens of Norfolk and Portsmouth, who detained him two days. He refused a public observance in his honor, but he did receive callers in his lodgings, attend Christ Episcopal Church, and dine on board the U.S.S. Constitution. *The* Norfolk and Portsmouth Herald *reported: "Mr. Calhoun appears to be in fine health and excellent spirits. 'Time has not thinned that flowing hair,' which graced his head when he visited us in company with Lafayette, in November, 1824; but it has scattered its frosts on it with a liberal hand." All was not well in the Old Dominion, however, as the State Democratic Convention proved to be under the control of Thomas Ritchie, and thus of Martin Van Buren. Calhoun was to lament often the failure of Virginia to take her proper place at the head of the South.*

When Calhoun arrived at Fort Hill, he found the womenfolk in good health. Besides the spring work on the farm, he had to concern himself with settling his third son in college and with borrowing money, needed at least in part to pay off debts to his son-in-law. In March and again in June he visited his gold mine in Georgia.

Meanwhile, his friends were endeavoring to fund a Washington newspaper, the Spectator, *as a Calhoun organ, and to establish a functioning central campaign committee. All did not go smoothly. On the plus side, the Democracy of most of the States accepted his position that the national convention should be held in the spring of 1844 rather than the fall of 1843, as favored by the Van Buren-controlled Virginians and New Yorkers. However, the results of the Georgia State Convention were disappointing, funds were scarce, and there were problems in the publication and distribution to the people of his* Life and Speeches.

Invitations and urgings to take the campaign circuit, as all the other leading men of both parties were doing, deluged the South Carolinian. It was not only expedient, it was his duty, many said, to show himself to the people and to visit those portions of the Union he

113

had never seen or had not seen in many years. Calhoun was adamant as to the impropriety of such behavior. "I have never known any visit, by one in the position I occupy, that did not do more to weaken, than to strengthen him," Calhoun told a Northern friend in June. He believed that there was a quiet but influential body of citizens who regarded the Presidency as "too elevated . . . to be the object of personal solicitation and canvass." Rather than bow to the times, he would defer to the republican traditions of the Founders. In other ways he resisted expediency, declining the temptation to make even a slight verbal waffle on the tariff question, that would have won support without conceding anything of substance.

Late in June, a source close to the President, John Tyler, sounded Calhoun out as to whether "under any circumstances you would consent to take the State Department." The idea that Calhoun might become Secretary of State, the only high executive office of the Union he had not held except the Presidency, had been in the air for some time. It was reenforced by instability in the office. Daniel Webster resigned in May. He was replaced by the South Carolinian Hugh S. Legaré, who died a few weeks later. Calhoun's reply to the overture has not been found, but it must have been negative, for the President soon appointed his Secretary of the Navy and fellow State rights Virginian, Abel P. Upshur, to the office. Yet the association of Calhoun and the State Department remained in many minds, including evidently that of Ashbel Smith, an old friend who also happened to be the diplomatic representative of the Republic of Texas in London. At about the same time Calhoun received the hint about the State Department, he heard from Smith about the first "world convention" of abolitionists, then under way in the capital of the British Empire, and about evidence of British designs on Texas, designs that were ominous for the interests of the United States and the South.

▯

CIRCULAR [from the "Calhoun Central Committee"]

(Private)   [Washington, March, 1843]

I enclose you a Prospectus of a Newspaper, which the friends of Mr. Calhoun have selected to be the Central Organ of the Calhoun portion of the Democratic Party. The [Washington] Spectator will continue to be published Weekly, as heretofore, until a month previous to the meeting of the 28th Congress, when a Daily Paper will also be issued from the same Newspaper establishment.

The Spectator will publish every movement relating to Mr. Calhoun's growing prospects, and the proceedings of his friends in the various sections of the country.

Its Editorial columns will be under the charge of an old personal as well as political friend of Mr. Calhoun [that is, Virgil Maxcy?]. It is desirable that the Spectator should be circulated as extensively as possible; and means will be used to obtain Subscribers in every town in the Union. I am desired to send you a Prospectus for your own use, and also an additional number of [*blank space*] to be handed by you to well known friends. You will confer a favor by getting as many Subscribers as possible. Please give the same directions to those friends to whom you hand the other Prospectuses. They are numbered [*blank space*], and you will be expected to see that said numbers are returned to Mr. Heart, eventually, whether any names are subscribed or not.

I send you, also, [*blank space*] Receipts for subscriptions, which I have received from the Publisher of the Spectator, Mr. John Heart. You will please account to him for the same, at the prices named in the Prospectus, as I have informed him of the number of receipts that I send you.

Calling your early attention to the subject, which is important, I remain, with respect, &c., Your obedient servant, [*blank space.*]

Printed letter in Vi, Robert Mercer Taliaferro Hunter Papers; another copy in NcU, Theodore Washington Brevard Papers; another copy in DLC, Galloway-Maxcy-Markoe Papers. NOTE: This circular was made so that it could be dated, addressed, and signed by hand and the blanks filled in with appropriate numbers. The copy addressed to Hunter in Va. was dated on 3/4 from Washington and was signed by "Ja[me]s Broom, Secretary, Calhoun Central Committee." It contains an AEU by Broom as follows: "Please send a list of all the leading newspapers published in your State, Post offices & names. Also mark the Calhoun papers." The copy addressed to Theodore W. Brevard in Tuskegee, Ala., is dated 3/18 and signed by "J[oseph] A. Scoville, Sec[retar]y, Calhoun Central Committee." It bears an AEU as follows: "Send letters under cover to the Hon. D[ixon] H. Lewis at this place." The third copy cited, belonging to Virgil Maxcy, was not dated, addressed, or signed. Hunter received twenty copies of the prospectus and fifty receipts for subscriptions. Brevard received two copies of the prospectus and ten receipts. A copy of what appears to be the prospectus enclosed, or a later version of it, is found in ViU, Crallé-Campbell Papers. The printed prospectus is dated 3/13/1843 and appears over the name of John Heart. It informs the public that the *Spectator* "will be devoted to the spread of true Democratic principles, and will adopt for its motto the words of the Hon. John C. Calhoun— 'Free Trade; Low Duties; No Debt; Separation from Banks; Economy, Retrenchment, and strict adherence to the Constitution.' " The *Spectator* "will zealously urge upon the country the claims of the distinguished Southern Statesman for the Presidency. In doing this, it will not be unmindful of the integrity and safety of the Republican Party, and will manifest a proper regard for the pretensions of the prominent individuals who have been named for this high trust, and are identified with the advancement of these principles." The editor is described as "one of the ablest and most experienced political writers of the day." Prices for the paper, beginning at "five dollars per annum" for two copies, are listed and space is left for subscribers to sign their names and places of residence.

From MAT[T]HEW MCDONALD

Dahlonega [Ga.,] 7th March 1843

Dear Sir, I Rec[ei]v[e]d you[r]s of the 26th Febr[uar]y, and according to your Instructions I have this morning dismist all hands that was working on the new discov[e]ry. They have Bin dooing nothing Since I wrote you last. They [*sic*; The] Shoot that Smith & Hovis discovered was Small and has given out entirely[.] There is no opperation going on oanly what I am dooing in the old vein. I done Better last week than I have ever done[.] I made 218 dwts of Cleain Gold, and the prospect is fare for dooing equally as weell this week[.]

My Reason for let[t]ing those men Hovis & Smith work on, was that I did not in my opinion Believe it would last, and I wisht to See it well tested. They [*sic*; The] purson[s] whoom Mr. [Thomas G.] Clemson gave leases ar[e] still working. Mr. Griffin has Comenst [*sic*; commenced] piting[?] off in the Bank of the River But has not washt enny yet[.] He is doubtful of its paying. I am glad to heare you ar[e] Coming Soon as I am anxious to See you[.] They [*sic*; The] Deposits that is in the mint ar[e] in Mr. Clemson[']s name. I shal[l] make a deposit this week in your name. They [*sic*; The] horse I got from Clemson is dead. You[r]s Respectfully, Mathew McDonald.

Letter (written and signed for McDonald by someone else) in ScU-SC, John C. Calhoun Papers.

From H[ENRY] S[T]. G[EORGE] TUCKER, [Professor of Law]

University of Virginia, [*ca.* March 8, 1843]
My dear Sir, Your letter by your son [John C. Calhoun, Jr.] was handed me by him two days ago and I immediately introduced him to your old acquaintance Mrs. [Anne Evelina Hunter] Tucker, my son Randolph & the young ladies of my family. He remained with us till last night when his rooms were ready & he is now fixed in a dormitory in the district of the best boarding house in the University. We have been all much interested by his unpretending manners, his intelligence and evidently amiable disposition. I hope he will avail himself of our wishes to spend as much of his time with us as is agreeable. He seems well except the affection of the larinx [*sic*] produced by the *Uvula palati* which I think should be watched very carefully. I have recommended him to take the classes of mathematics & natural philosophy & those only. There is a class in mathematics just about as far advanced as he is, while the entire distinctness of the several subjects of Natural philosophy will enable him to fall in them, very conveniently. They are just commencing [*partial word canceled*] Pneumatics so that he can proceed with the Class without difficulty. I hope you will not fail to command my services in every thing respecting your son. The *request* is due to our ancient friendship and the result will show how readily my compliance will be yielded to one who has so long possessed my affection & esteem. Though we *have* differed I am not one of the school, which declares in the language of a late resolution [of a Democratic convention] in Richmond that those who do not agree with us "*forfeit forever* the confidence of the party.["] Though you are sick of politics let me say, *I* may fall under their ban; for I never can vote for [Martin] V[an] B[uren] as I believe he is under [Thomas H.] Benton[']s thumb and will leave no stone unturned to further Benton[']s fortunes.

The Convention in Richmond, of which I was not a member though I was present & not inactive ended I think in Smoke. They fixed the National Convention for the 4[t]h Monday in ["May" *canceled and* "Nov(embe)r" *interlined*], whereas the other States or many of them will not meet till May. My own opinion is to wrestle with them for the first if we have ["a" *canceled*] fair prospects; if not, then to give it the go-by & send our delegates to the general Convention in May where they do not cho[o]se to be represented. I design to write some essays but am now too unwell to do any thing. *Our* misfortune is we have *no press. Where can I get* any thing published[?] Mr. [Thomas] Ritchie—the impartial Mr. Ri[t]chie, would never suffer any thing to see the light which would thwart his own views: so that it is really hard to say what is to be done. I hope some measures are taking to get us a press.

And so [Henry A.] Wise is disappointed! Though ["it" *canceled*] he deserved it, I am sorry for him, as I have had in former days a personal regard for him; & there is no office I think more desirable [than that of U.S. Minister to France for which the Senate refused to confirm him]. Perhaps I may estimate ["it" *interlined*] the more, because it brings with it a trip across the water and I compare it with my place here of which I am heartily tired, as my health is sinking under it. Wise offers again [for election as Representative from Va.] & says "he appeals to the people unhesitatingly."

[Robert M.T.] Hunter has sent me a biographical sketch [of you], which has brought some former scenes before my eyes. When I remember the honour I once had in striving shoulder to shoulder [in the House of Representatives] with the subject of it and the beloved [William] Lowndes, it increases my anxiety for the success of our views in the coming contest. I am, my dear Sir, very sincerely your friend, H.S.G. Tucker.

ALS in ScCleA. NOTE: This undated letter was postmarked on 3/8. The date has been supplied from the postmark. On the same day Anna Maria Calhoun Clemson wrote from Fort Hill to her brother, Lt. Patrick Calhoun, that John C. Calhoun, Jr., and James Edward Calhoun were being withdrawn from the Hallowell School at Alexandria, D.C., because of "the falling off of the school especially in the classics . . . . I regret this change for their letters evinced a spirit of improvement & I fear changing the school which is always a drawback may check it especially as James comes home & runs the risk of falling into his old idle hunting habits." (ALS in ScU-SC, John C. Calhoun Papers.)

RESOLUTIONS ADOPTED BY A DEMOCRATIC DISTRICT CONVENTION AT CHARLESTON

[New Theater, March 11, 1843]
[*According to previous public notice, a mass meeting of Democrats of the "sixth Congressional District" of S.C. was convened. The meeting appointed a committee, headed by Franklin H. Elmore, to draw up a report and resolutions, both of which were adopted without dissent.*

The report praised Calhoun and nominated him for President. The resolutions were as follows:]

1. Resolved, That this meeting regards the selection of a proper candidate for the Presidency by the Democratic Republican Party, as of the highest importance to secure harmony and efficient co-operation; and that they will cheerfully submit this selection to a National Convention, to be organized upon principles of perfect fairness and equality and to meet at such a time as will afford to the people full opportunity to form an enlightened and deliberate judgment as to public men and measures.

2. Resolved, That the Constitution of the United States embodies the political wisdom of the ablest Statesmen and Patriots of the Revolution, and furnishes rules for practical government which command the confidence of the whole country; that a National Convention ought therefore to conform as nearly as possible to the spirit and principles of that Constitution, and cannot but fail in its objects when it departs from a guide so well established in the opinions of our entire people.

3. Resolved, That this Constitution prescribes for the Government the mode of executing the very duty which a National Convention is now required to discharge for the party, that is to say, the selection of the proper person to represent them as President; and therefore the rule prescribed in the Constitution for the choice of President and Vice President by the electors, furnishes the proper guide for casting the vote in the Democratic Republican Convention; that in conformity to this rule, the Delegates in such a Convention should consist of the same number and be entitled to vote *per capita* for their respective Candidates, as is prescribed by the Constitution of the United States.

4. Resolved, That a departure from so high an authority and the allowance of more than the ratio of one member to each Congressional District and two to each State at large, would be calculated to introduce confusion and uncertainty; and by the novelty and unsoundness of the principles which they would introduce, must tend to mar the harmony and confidence of the entire Democratic Republican Party.

5. Resolved, That the next Congress of the United States is looked to with the deepest interest and anxiety by all sections of the Union, as entrusted with the settlement of questions of the greatest moment; and that the meeting of a National Convention before the meeting of Congress would require the people to decide between candidates, before any opportunity shall have been afforded of seeing what mea-

sures were pursued by the different parties; and could not fail to sow the seeds of personal divisions, to imply distrust of the people, and to create doubts as to the sincerity and straight forwardness of the entire party.

6. Therefore Resolved, That this meeting can see no sufficient reason for changing the time already appointed for the meeting of the National Convention by the Democratic Republicans in the States of Kentucky, Maryland and Michigan; that this time has already been found the most advisable by former Conventions, and is the most suitable in every respect; that a change of the period of meeting without some urgent necessity (which does not in this case exist) would not only seem wanting in courtesy to those who were the first to name it, but might justly tend to infuse suspicions as to ulterior objects which every member of the party should strive to avert; that the Democratic Republicans of the Sixth Congressional District of South Carolina do therefore unanimously recommend to the whole party the month of May 1844, as the proper time for the meeting of the Convention.

7. Resolved, That the Democratic Republican Party throughout the Union be and they are hereby requested to take measures in their respective States for calling together a National Convention at the time above mentioned, to be organized upon the principles embodied in these resolutions.

8. Resolved, That a Committee of —— be appointed by the Chair, to be a Standing Committee, charged with the duty of carrying into effect all measures necessary to accomplish the objects of this meeting, with power to appoint all Sub Committees of correspondence, &c., which may be necessary for the purpose; and especially that said Committee take steps to procure the like action in all the Congressional Districts in this State.

9. Resolved, That this meeting entertaining the highest sense of the integrity, public virtue, and ability of the Hon. JOHN C. CALHOUN, and highly approving as they do, the firmness and efficiency with which he has throughout a life of public service maintained the principles of the Democratic Republican Party, do hereby cordially nominate him to the National Convention, as the candidate of their first choice for the Presidency of the United States.

PC in the Charleston, S.C., *Mercury*, March 13, 1843, p. 2; PC in the Washington, D.C., *Globe*, March 18, 1843, p. 3; PC in the Washington, D.C., *Spectator*, March 18, 1843, p. 2; PC in the Pendleton, S.C., *Messenger*, March 24, 1843, p. 1. NOTE: The report adopted stated in part that "while in the Democratic ranks there are many eminent statesmen, illustrious for their worth, patriotism and talents, there is one who is recommended to our confidence and support by qualifications which we conceive make him peculiarly the man for this crisis. By long services in elevated stations, by his great experience in public affairs, the surpassing abilities he has displayed, his profound knowledge of Government, unbending integrity, disinterested patriotism, and the unblemished purity of his private and public life, he stands forth a statesman of the highest order, commanding our warmest regard as a man, and our highest confidence as a patriot. In all the stations he has filled, whether at home as the farmer, or at Washington as Representative, Secretary of War, Vice President or Senator, simplicity of habits, frankness of manners, uprightness of principle and directness of conduct has marked his life. In every station, surrounded with difficulties, with a noble courage above all sense of fear, he has confronted the frowns of power, advocated the principles of constitutional liberty, asserted the rights of the people, vindicated his State and maintained the honor and interests of his whole country. Such a man is JOHN C. CALHOUN, whom we the people of the sixth Congressional District of South Carolina do now hereby recommend to the National Convention for their nomination as the candidate of the Democratic Republican party for President." The report and resolutions were "enthusiastically received and unanimously adopted" by the meeting, according to the *Mercury.* Similar meetings were held and resolutions passed in other parts of the State subsequently, as reported in the press: for instance, see the Greenville, S.C., *Mountaineer,* May 5, 1843, p. 2. In ScHi, Chesnut-Miller-Manning Papers, is a ms. copy of similar resolutions offered about 4/1843 at a meeting in Clarendon District.

From J[OHN] S. BARBOUR,
[former Representative from Va.]

Catalpa [Culpeper County, Va.,] March 12th 1843

My Dear Sir, I rec[eive]d your last letter (that of the 3rd) when I was confined to my chamber.

It will not be in my power to lend more than Eighteen thousand dollars & this will exceed by 2000$ two of the shares of my Children. The periods for the return of the principal will be ten years from next July for 8000$. Eight years from next February for 8000$ more, & the other 2000$ must be paid in about six years. Next Autumn there will be more funds in Bank & you can then *probably* obtain for four or five years the other Eight thousand dollars. But of this I can not write with any certainty. The funds of which I now speak are in hand & must be placed upon loan & at interest. The interest has to be paid each half year. The 15th Jan[uar]y & 15th July corresponding with our periods for Bank dividends. Colo[nel James] Byrne devised his whole estate *away from me* to my wife [Eliza A. Byrne Barbour] & children. My wife was his only child. I became Adm[inistrat]or with the will annexed & gave bond & security for 140,000$. My securities died & their Administrators cou[l]d not distribute their estates pending this liability for me. To relieve all difficulty, in Feb[ruar]y 1837, I delivered into the Richmond Court of Chancery, the whole assets of the estate. It was then contemplated to place the assets in the hands of a Trustee that the widow of Colo[nel] Byrne might draw her share of the profits without troubling me—a task that was thankless, vexatious & profitless. But she died soon after & my children being all minors they became by operation of Law *wards of the Court,* and practically the Court has since administered the estate to the uses of the Testator[']s will. It has continued under my direction very much as formerly. I report to the Judge every six months & my arrangements for lending the money have invariably been carried out by decree. Two of my children are now of legal age & their concurrence has usually been required & which is without hesitation given and will be given very cheerfully in your application. The Court sits the 5th May & the decree for the loan to you will be among its first acts & the money will immediately be lent.

Before that day & very shortly from this time I will go to Fauquier [County] & have the papers all arranged before hand. I shou[l]d have said that by petition the cause & its incidents were removed from the Richmond Chancery Court to that of Fauquier, according to a late act of Assembly for removing causes from the Old Chancery Courts. I have thought this full statement necessary to your distinct understanding of the subject. The whole *Interest* upon the principal belongs to my wife ["during life" *interlined*] but she has executed an instrument of writing filed in the cause & upon her privy examination has relinquished to her children as they come of age her right to the annual profits of the money retaining the Catalpa Lands & Slaves for her maintenance.

Your last letter (of the 3d March) expresses a wish for 3 of the shares. A word of explanation on that point. There will be enough for this if the aggregate sum in hand is considered. But last winter (& before I saw you) I was committed to let my sister have 5000$ of it. And I had gone so far as to file a paper to that effect in the records of the cause. They giving me ample security. I enclose you her last letter [*not found*] to show you the pressure of her necessity & that she holds me to the promise I made her & which (the Court Consenting) I am bound in good faith, as well as fraternal duty to fulfil.

Jack [that is, John S. Barbour, Jr.] & Sally join their best Respects for you. In great haste y[ou]rs Sincerely, J.S. Barbour.

ALS in ScCleA.

From Mat[t]hew McDonald

Dahlonega [Ga.,] March 14th 1843

Dear Sir, As I expect you have ar[r]iv[e]d at home and ar[e] anxious to heare how I am Coming on, I now will give you a Statement of my last week[']s work[;] it did not turn out as well as I antisapated it would when I last wrote you last [*sic*]. I made 117 dwts of Cleain Gold[.] I deposited it to day & the toll I rec[ei]v[e]d from Mr. Mills & Keenum[?] which made in all 132 dwts deposited. Mr. Griffin has Comenst [*sic*; commenced] washing this day in the Bank of the River for the first [time] Since Chris[t]mas. I do not know how he done as I have not Seen him this evening[.] I made yesterday on the Surphus [*sic*; surface] 20 dwts in the Quick. I doo not know what I have made to day as I have not pan[ne]d out[.] Ac[c]ording to your instructions ["all opperations" *interlined*] is Suspended on the veins and have Bin Since I Rec[ei]v[e]d your orders. Corne is get[t]ing Scarse[;] Corne meal is Selling for 75 c[e]nts per Bushel[.] I have this day engag[e]d what will doo the mine for 50 c[e]nts per Bush[el] by holling [*sic*; hauling] it myself fifteen miles. If you ar[e] not Coming Soon Wright [*sic*; write] me on the Rece[i]pt of this. My Best Respect to you all, Mathew McDonald.

Letter (written and signed for McDonald by someone else) in ScU-SC, John C. Calhoun Papers.

Agreement between Joseph A. Scoville and Harper & Brothers

New York [City,] March 15, 1843

Know all men by these Presents that I, Joseph A. Scoville do hereby assign & make over to Harper and Brothers such portion of an agreement which I hold (in relation to Publications) as relates to the publication of the Speeches of John C. Calhoun—viz[.] said agreement reads that after ten thousand copies have been sold by the Messrs. Harpers—they shall give the Copy right ["& Stereotype plates" *interlined*] to me on payment of one hundred Dollars—now I hereby assign said portion of that agreement—as security of my order on the Post Office Department for One hundred & fifty three dollars—when said draft is paid—this assignment shall be null and void and of no effect—but if said draft is not paid, then this assignment shall continue in full force—Said draft is dated April 1, 1843. Joseph A. Scoville.

ADS in NNC, Archives of Harper & Brothers, 1817–1914 (published microfilm, reel 1); FC in NNC, Archives of Harper & Brothers, 1817–1914 (published microfilm, reel 55).

To F[RANKLIN] H. ELMORE, *Charleston*

Fort Hill, 19th Feb: [*sic*; March] 1843

My dear Sir, I enclose a letter of introduction to the President [John Tyler], which I hope may reach you before you leave for Washington.

If I may infer from what I have seen of the State since I left Charleston, the movement there will be responded to with Zeal throughout the State.

Should you visit Washington, you must cheer up Mr. [Dixon H.] Lewis and our other friends there. There will be no difficulty in counteracting the Richmond movement, if our friends should take a firm and active stand against it. We have truth, justice & the Constitution on our side, and all that is wanting ["to ensure success" *canceled*] is Zeal, energy and discretion to ensure success. Yours truly, J.C. Calhoun.

ALS in ScU-SC, Franklin Harper Elmore Papers. NOTE: The date of this letter has been corrected because the postmark reads "MAR[CH] 20" and on 2/19/- 1843 Calhoun was in Washington.

To "Messrs. Emmitt, [S.R.?] McNevin, and O'Connor," New York City, 3/19. "It would have afforded me great pleasure [to have been able to accept your invitation] to participate in your celebration [of St. Patrick's Day by the Society of the Friendly Sons of St. Patrick of New York]—nothing that is of interest to Irishmen or the sons of Irishmen, is indifferent to me. I am proud of my descent from so generous and gallant a race." PEx in the Charleston, S.C., *Mercury*, May 9, 1843, p. 2; PEx in the Washington, D.C., *Globe*, May 13, 1843, p. 2; PEx in the Washington, D.C., *Spectator*, May 20, 1843, p. 2. [According to the Washington, D.C., *Daily National Intelligencer*, March 27, 1843, p. 1, Calhoun was also invited to the St. Patrick's day observance in Washington, and a letter from him in response to the invitation was read to the celebrants in that city on 3/17.]

To DUFF GREEN, [Washington?]

Fort Hill, 19th Feb. [*sic;* March] 1843
My dear Sir, I received your letter when I was about to take my departure from Charleston for my residence, where I arrived day before yesterday, which will explain why I have not answered it before.

I presume Judge [Abel P.] Upshur has already decided, so that it would be useless to write to him on the subject, to which your letter refers. I hope that his decision has been such as you desire, and in which I concur. I had a conversation with him a few days before I left Washington, in which the subject of a possible vacancy in the State Department was adverted to, and in which I stated to him in that event, if the office was tendered to him, I was of the impression he ought to accept. It would give him a commanding position, in which he might exert a very salutary influence over the important questions that are like to grow out of our foreign relations the next few years.

I am glad to learn, that your prospect is so good, and do hope, that your most sanguine expectations may be realized. You have struggled long and manfully against an adverse tide and deserve success. I have never doubted that your mountain property [near Cumberland, Md.] was of great [mining] value; but always feared, that you would not be able to hold on sufficiently long to realize your anticipations. I hope in that I may be mistaken.

What effect has the Richmond movement had? You see that it has been met with sperit by the Charleston Meeting, and will be by the whole State and I trust the entire South. If it should be met by my friends as it ought to be, it will react on its authors.

With kind regards to Mrs. [Lucretia Edwards] Green and your family I remain yours truly [J.C. Calhoun].

PC in Jameson, ed., *Correspondence,* pp. 525–526.

J[ames] E[dward] C[olhoun], Millwood, [Abbeville District, S.C.,] to Maria E. [Simkins] Colhoun, Edgefield Court House, 3/21. He received a letter yesterday "from Mr. J[ohn] C. Calhoun, in which, he withdraws his proposal to buy Negroes." ALI in ScU-SC, James Edward Colhoun Papers.

V[IRGIL] MAXCY to R[obert] M.T. Hunter,
Lloyds, Essex County, Va.

Washington, 23 March 1843

My dear Sir, I have duly received your favour of the (no date). I regret sincerely to hear, that you consider it in the slightest degree doubtful that you will succeed in your election [as Representative from Va.].

Under the present desponding state of our friends in Virginia, you must of course wait for further de[ve]lopments in other quarters to rally their spirits. I should think it all important to have a paper at Richmond.

The Report of the Charleston Committee is a complete answer to that of your [Va.] convention; and I have recommended to Mr. [Joseph A.] Scoville to consider it the text book & guide for the [Washington] Spectator.

I [am] sorry to perceive, that Mr. Scoville has led you into complete error in reference to the relations between me & the Spectator. About the time you are [*sic*] going away he settled, ["I underst" *canceled*] not only without my authority but against my positive protest of the utter incompatibili[ty] of my residence at a distance with the arrangement, that the title of the paper was to be transferred to me & that I was to be the depositary of the pecuniary contributions for its support. When it was pushed so far, that I was compelled to come to a downright peremptory refusal, he was equally free, after it was supposed I had gone to the country, in making me the Chairman of the central committee & Superintendant of the paper, that my name, as being a known friend of Mr. Calhoun, might be signed to all correspondence &c. &c. &c. How he made all this practicable in his mind, I am unable to say, nor whether it might not have been only intended as a decoy to subscribers, and as a means of reconciling Mr. Calhoun's friends to the actual state of the paper. A severe attack of bilious colic laid me in my bed, from which I was ["not" *interlined and then canceled*] able to arise only a few days ago and I now learn—& to be able to do this have delayed this answer—that Scoville ["advanced" *canceled and* "went to the north & sent on" *interlined*] enough money to keep [John] Heart from starving and the paper from stopping. Heart has conveyed the establishment to Scoville and he has issued subscription papers to every quarter of the union & as he said he could not get subscribers without its being distinctly understood, that it was set up to support Mr. Calhoun's election, he has run up aloft the Calhoun flag, which was ["contrary" *canceled*], as I supposed, against his wish as well as the judgment of his friends for the present, so far as I was made acquainted with them. All this as well as what related to me personally was done without my knowledge.

Scoville has been some days as [*sic*] is now here. He came to see me and his excuse was the necessity of the case, that as Mr. [Dixon H.] Lewis had rec[eive]d no funds, the paper would have stopped and that he is ready on the re-payment of the advances & his relief from the engagements he has been obliged to enter into, to transfer the paper and its management into whatever hands Mr. Calhoun & his friends may wish. ["He" *altered to* "Scoville"] tells me, Mr. Lewis, who, when Mr. Calhoun went away, I understood was to decide on the arrangements to be made with the paper & to effect them, approves of what he has done. I have not yet been able to see Mr. Lewis and I am not yet well enough to go to him, which is necessary, if I would communicate with him, as Mahomet was obliged to go to the mountain.

What under these circumstances ought to have been done? You shall learn my opinion, from what I have done.

Acting on my usual rule of making the best, of what can't be helped, I strongly advised Scoville, that he should rest satisfied with having, in order to get the subscription list well filled up, openly announced the paper to be for Calhoun and now to go on with its publication in the manner originally intended. Make it the receptacle of electioneering movements & intelligence in regard to all the republican candidates opposed to Mr. [Martin] Van Buren, treat him personally with respect & *occasionally* notice the proceedings of his friends also, as long as the Globe ["did" *canceled and* "does" *interlined*] the same in regard to Mr. Calhoun—fill the paper chiefly with extracts from others—and make the Charleston report in answer to that of the Virginia convention the guide & text book for his editorial comments. I say his editorial comments, for as yet there is no other Editor, nor can there be, till funds are gathered from Subscriptions to the paper or sent on from Charleston.

Notwithstanding all this, when he came here last night he showed me several pieces he had prepared for the next paper, in every one of which he had either a direct assault on Mr. Van Buren or a pointed & very unfavourable contrast bebetween [*sic*] his personal character & qualifications & those of Mr. Calhoun, the publication of which in the *Calhoun* paper, as the Spectator now avowedly is—at the seat of Government, would have operated as an invitation for the Globe to come out with similar attacks, and shut up its columns from the publication of every proceeding favorable to him, such as the Report of the Charleston Meeting, which he has re-published at length. Such things will do very ["well" *interlined*] even now, ["by way of warning" *interlined*] in the distant papers, but, ["it" *interlined*] seem[s] to me, ought to be avoided in this place, as long as the Globe is civil. At all events Scoville ought to wait till he gets orders from head quarters to be decidedly belligerent.

After he had read these pieces, I remonstrated with him against the course he seemed to have marked out for the paper and gave him my views at large and begged him to follow them at least until he should hear from Mr. Calhoun or some of his confidential friends in So[uth] Carolina, what course would meet their approbation.

From the above you will agree with me I think, that Scoville has more zeal, than discretion and that it will be well for you and other judicious friends of our cause, whose opinions would have weight with him, to give him frankly & fully your opinions as to what he ought to avoid.

What Scoville relies on for pecuniary means I know not except getting a large subscription list.

No Central Committee has yet been formed here. It seems almost impossible to get the proper materials, who are not Office-holders. Until the committee is formed Scoville means that a young man in the office [James Broom?] shall sign his name, ["with the" *canceled*] to correspondence with the title of Secretary. How would old ["Mr." *altered to* "Gen."] Van Ness [that is, John Peter Van Ness] do for Chairman, if he can be got up to the sticking point. He was the old Jackson Chairman [in D.C.].

I had written to Mr. [Levi] Woodbury before receiving your letter.

I ought to have added above, that Scoville seemed satisfied after I had fully presented my views to pursue the moderate course I had urged on him, until he should receive orders to begin the war from head quarters. When this time comes, an able & experienced Editor will be absolutely necessary. His next number will be out on Saturday & we shall then be able to judge whether he can be prudent. In what I have said of Mr. Scoville I wish it to be distinctly understood, that I have entire faith in his zeal, sincerity & good intentions. I think it would do great good, if you will write your views fully to him.

I think Mr. Calhoun ought to know the exact state of things here, that he may take such steps himself in relation to the paper or get some of his Carolina friends to do it as he shall think proper. I intended to have written him fully, but I am still feeble & will therefore beg you to forward this letter to him, which will save the necessity of my writing the substance of it over.

As soon as I can travel, which I now hope will be in a day or two, I shall go to West River, where I shall always be glad to hear from you. I shall be more useful in getting Maryland in a proper train, having got her committed to the [*one word altered to* "right course"] as to the convention, than I could be here, were it practicable for me to remain here. I have already taken steps to get the Columns of the leading Republican paper at Baltimore open on the subject of the Convention. ["This" *canceled and* "The Editor(')s" *interlined*] leaning is decidedly towards Calhoun. I shall see him personally in about six[?] days.

Lewis is still here, but as I said above I have not yet been able to go to see him. I think it would be well, if you would write to him here fully & without delay. [Thomas D.] Sumter [recently a Representative from S.C.] is still here & franks. I find he is hurt a little, that he was not requested to remain here & frank & assist in the correspondence of the paper. Can't you sooth[e] him a little without appearing to know his Carolina friends had neglected him.

I presume Scoville has already sent you subscription papers. With great respect I am Dear Sir, Truly Y[ou]r friend, V. Maxcy.

ALS in ScCleA. NOTE: The Baltimore newspaper referred to in the third to last paragraph cannot be identified with certainty.

To A[NDREW] P[ICKENS] CALHOUN, Faunsdale (Marengo County), Ala.

Fort Hill, 31st March 1843
My dear Andrew, On my return from the O'Barr mine day before yesterday, I found your letter of the 11th Inst[ant] among others, that had accumulated in my absence. The one, which you refer to, addressed to me in Charleston I have not yet received. I wrote you before I left Charleston, and since my return home and hope you have received both.

I agree with you, our debt to Mr. [Thomas G.] Clemson must be funded, and fortunately we have an excellent opportunity now of doing it. I wrote you before I left Washington, and in the letter from

Charleston & the one written since my return, that Mr. [John S.] Barbour would have from 16 to 20 thousand dollars to lend early in May at 6 per cent. I found a letter on my return from the mine from him, in which he says, that he will have $16,000 certainly to lend in May; that the court sits the 5th May, and that the decree for the loan will be among its first acts. That the periods for the loan will be ten years from July next for $8000, eight years from February next for $8000, and if the additional two thousand should be loaned, six years ["will be required" *interlined*] for its return. He thinks that there will probably be $8000 in the fall to be ["loaned to be" *interlined*] returned in three or four years.

There could not be a fairer opportunity for funding, ["and" *canceled and* "but" *interlined*] it is indispensable, that you should be here in time to execute the papers & attend to it. Should it be permitted to be lost, I know not what we shall do. You must not fail to give it your prompt attention; and if you have not already started, I hope you will not fail to ["make"(?) *canceled*] set out without delay. You may have to go to Virginia to receive the money, though I hope Mr. Clemson will [go] himself. The opportunity must not be lost. It will put us at our ease. Cotton cannot remain at the present depressed price, and on the next rise the debt may be paid off and the foundation laid for of [*sic*] a large fortune. I will write to Mr. Barbour positively, that ["I" *canceled and* "we" *interlined*] will take the loan, calculating certainly that you are coming. Bring ["with you" *interlined*] all the papers necessary for a settlement with Mr. Clemson, and also between you & myself up to this time.

As I will expect you, I will refrain from writing much, that I intended.

We are all well & all join in love to you, Margaret [Green Calhoun] & Duff [Green Calhoun]. Your affectionate father, J.C. Calhoun.

ALS in ScU-SC, John C. Calhoun Papers. NOTE: Writing on 3/8/1843 to her brother, Lt. Patrick Calhoun, Anna Maria Calhoun Clemson commented: "I fear Andrew exercises an undue influence over father in his business matters (because I do not consider him the man of business father does) & do not think the Alabama concern will turn out as profitable as they expected besides saddling father with a debt it will take his life time to get rid of. Andrew gets his living off it of course & so far it is profitable to *him* but neither father or Mr. Clemson have yet received the first cent that I know of & it is now the fifth year. Neither can Mr. C[lemson] get A[ndrew] to give the necessary papers to give security . . . ." (ALS in ScU-SC, John C. Calhoun Papers.)

To H[ENRY] ST. GEORGE TUCKER,
[Professor of Law, University of Virginia]

Fort Hill, 31st March 1843

My dear Sir, Absence from home on business since my return has prevented an earlier acknowledgment of your kind letter. I shall not fail to avail myself of your kind offer, in reference to my son [John C. Calhoun, Jr.], and shall ["to" *erased*] say to him, that he must regard you in the place of a Parent, while at the University. I am exceedingly uneasy about the affection of his Larinx [*sic*]. He writes me, that his disease was much aggrav[at]ed by exposure in the steam boat going down the Potomac on his way to the University, and that he has not yet recovered from the effects of the exposure. His letter has very greatly increased my anxiety about him. It is my desire, if the disease continues, that he should have the benefit of the best medical advise [*sic*] that can be obtained. You would exceedingly oblige me, if you would take the same steps in his case, in reference to this distressing disease, as if he were your own son.

You cannot have less confidence in a caucus, or convention to nominate a candidate for the Presidency, than I have. It is with extreme reluctance, that I would permit my name to go before any, however constituted; and ["is" *canceled and* "my reluctance is" *interlined*] insuperable ["against" *canceled*] to permitting it to go before one not as fairly constituted, as the nature of such an assemblage would admit. Nothing but the the [*sic*] circumstances, in which my friends are place[d], at this time, could induce me to yield to the authority of any convention. The proceedings of the Richmond meeting are little calculated to add to the authority of such meetings, whether State, or general. Its recommendations, if they should be adopted, would create a precedent, which, if not reversed, would transfer the control of the presidential election permanently to a few large non slave holding States, to the exclusion of Virginia & the whole South in the end. I regard the scheme as a cunning devise of the New York school of politicks and the course of Mr. [Thomas] Ritchie and his associates in adopting it, as base treason to Virginia and all the South. He & they have stuck Virginia, as a tail to N[ew] York, instead of placing her, in natural position, at the head of the South.

I agree with you, as to the importance of a press at Richmond. It is time, that the authority of the Enquirer & Ritchie should be checked. An able & judicious press there, with ["an" *canceled*] respectable subscription, would soon put a new face on things.

Mr. [Robert M.T.] Hunter afforded me an opportunity of reading your manuscript essay against conventions as the means of nominating a preside[n]tial candidate. There is very little in it, that I do not cordially approve, and I hope that at the proper time it will be published. It is calculated to awaken thought and to do much good. Yours sincerely, J.C. Calhoun.

ALS in PHC, Charles Roberts Autograph Collection; variant PC in Jameson, ed., *Correspondence*, pp. 526–528. NOTE: On 3/22/1843 John C. Calhoun, Jr., had written to an unidentified friend (possibly Joseph A. Scoville) describing his experiences and impressions at the University of Va. He stated that he had written twice to his father from the university, but had not yet received any reply. (ALS in NcD, John C. Calhoun Papers.)

From [Thomas J. Green, Castle of Perote, Mexico, *ca. 4/*——]. "Eight years of the prime of my life, and a considerable portion of my fortune, have been spent for the establishment of liberty in Texas; therefore my friends must see that I am too closely identified with her to take *my* liberty upon conditions which may compromise my political relations to her, and I hope they will avoid any promises of that kind." (Captured with Texan forces at the Battle of Mier on 12/26/1842, Green refused a release on the condition that he abandon hostilities against Mexico. He later published an extract from a letter he wrote to Calhoun at the time to explain why he did not accept the good offices of Calhoun and other leading citizens of the U.S. in securing his release. Green escaped, however, in 7/1843.) PEx in Thomas J. Green, *Journal of the Texian Expedition Against Mier; Subsequent Imprisonment of the Author . . . with Reflections upon the Present Political and Probable Future Relations of Texas, Mexico, and the United States* (New York: Harper and Brothers, 1845), p. 296.

To R[OBERT] M. T. HUNTER,
L[l]oyds, Essex County, Va.

Fort Hill, 2d April 1842 [*sic*; 1843]
My dear Sir, I had been at home but a few days, when business compelled me to leave ["home" *canceled*]. I did not return till the 28th March, when I found your two letters of the 10th & 17th of March among many others, that had been received in my absence.

The Richmond proceedings gave a heavy blow against (I will not

say us) the South and in their effects ["should they not be arrested,"
interlined] ag[ai]nst the Constitution itself. I have examined them
with care; and I cannot be mistaken, when I say, that should conventions to nominate the presidential candidates become the settled
practise, and should the Richmond resolutions form the precedent,
on which they are hereafter to be constituted, ["that" *canceled*] the
necessary consequence will be, that the great central non slave holding States will control the election, to the exclusion of the rest of the
Union, & especially the South. It would place permanently the control of the ballot box, the patronage of the Government & the veto in
the same hands, and those the least safe of any, in which they could
be placed. In other words, it would centralize the powers of the
Union, and establish the most intolerable despotism, by virtually subverting the constitution, as far as the election of the President is concerned, and substituting in its place, the worst possible mode that
could be devised. I regard the whole as a cunningly devised scheme
of the N[ew] York school, emanating from the brain of [Silas] Wright
[Senator from N.Y.] & ["intended" *canceled and* "designed" *interlined*] to lead to the result, to which it must, if the precedent ["be not"
canceled] it is intended to ["constitute" *canceled and* "form" *interlined*], be not arrested. And what is baser; what is calculated to
excite the deepest indignation in the bosom of any true hearted Virginian and son of the South is, that [Thomas] Ritchie and his associates should sink Virginia from her high and proud position of
standing at the head of the South, to make her the humble & dependent foll[ow]er of New York—to be her tail instead of the head of the
South.

It is not a new thing with him. He began ["it" *canceled and* "his
work" *interlined*] in 1829, after the election of Gen[era]l [Andrew]
Jackson. Had he not then deserted Virginia & the South for N[ew]
York, Gen[era]l Jackson would never have taken the course he did.
All that I ever anticipated from his election would have been realised,
and the flood of corruption which since broke in on the Government &
country, and the disasters which have followed would have been staid.
I trace all our misfortunes almost exclusively to the fact, that Virginia
has lost her true position in the Union, and that to the Wiles & cunning
of one man. I had hoped, that he would have returned, ["in" *canceled
and then interlined*] good faith, to the old Virginia school of politicks,
but of that I dispair [*sic*]. The omission of all mention of the Tariff
in [George C.] Dromgoole[']s address is ominous. It proves design
["to abandon our cause" *interlined*] on the most vital of all questions.

I write what I have, as preliminary to saying, that in my opinion, there is ["but" *interlined*] one of three courses left for our Virginia friends; to submit quietly to be placed, ["where" *canceled*] where the managers of the Convention have put the State, or rather intend to put the State; to break Mr. [Thomas] Ritchie and his associates down, or drive them openly into the camp, to which they truly belong. We ["are" *canceled and* "would be" *interlined*] safer with them there, than in our camp. They, in truth, belong to the N[ew] York & not to the Virginia school of politicks. If it is not intended to submit, a paper at Richmond, conducted with judgment, sperit and ability, is indispensible [*sic*]. It is the one thing needful. Such a paper backed by a general organization of our friends could not fail to accomplish the object intended. Break ground ag[ai]nst the time, in a decided, & sperited tone. Call on the friends of all, who are truly in favour of harmony and desire that the nomination should truly represent the voice of the party[,] to rally in favour of May 1844. Draw the attack ["of Mr. Ritchie" *interlined*] but when attacked carry the war into Africa. I fear our friends in your State are not prepared for so bold and decided a course; but I feel assured, that properly executed, it is the safest. We ought not to look too exclusively to the election. Our eyes must be kept on consequences to follow beyond.

As to our State, I have no idea, that she will acquiesce in the Virginia proceedings, if she should stand alone; and, if she should, I cannot consistently with my opinion of the principles involved and the consequences to follow permit my name to go before a convention to be held at the time and to be constituted, as the Richmond Resolutions recommend.

I am much gratified to learn, that you have determined to run again, and I do hope, that you will run with success. Your presence in the next Congress will be of great importance; and on the course of that Congress much—very much will depend. I do hope that the South will make the adjustment of the Tariff, strictly on revenue principles, a sine qua non. It will be impossible to reform the Government, so long as duties are laid for protection—["that" *canceled and* "so long as" *interlined*] what is ["the" *canceled*] a tax in the most oppres[s]ive form in one section, is a bounty, or regarded as a bounty, in the other. I shall be anxious to hear from you and to learn, as soon as possible, the result of your election. I am glad to see, that Hubbard [*sic*; Edmund W. Hubard] runs again [for the U.S. House of Representatives], and also [William] Smith. I hope [William O.] Goode will not give away to Dromgoole. I hope the day is not far distant, when Virginia will return to her old mode of self nomination, to the entire overthrow of the caucus system. Truly & sincerely, J.C. Calhoun.

ALS in ScCleA; variant PC in Jameson, ed., *Correspondence*, pp. 528–530. NOTE: For a detailed account of efforts and ideas of Calhoun's supporters in Va. at this time see James A. Seddon to Hunter, April 1, 1843 (ALS in Vi, Robert Mercer Taliaferro Hunter Papers; PC in Ambler, ed., *Hunter Correspondence*, pp. 63–64). Proceedings of the Va. State Democratic convention which elicited Calhoun's remarks are reported in full in the Richmond, Va., *Enquirer*, March 4, 7, and 14, 1843. The Convention adopted a resolution endorsing 11/1843 as the meeting date for the national convention and another stating that the party should elect four delegates from each Congressional district to the national convention. This latter resolution apparently was intended to embrace a report offered earlier by the Van Buren leader, George C. Dromgoole, which implied that the district delegates referred to should be elected by the party members in the State legislature (in all States) and that they should vote by unit rule in the national convention. Resolutions offered by Seddon were voted down on the floor. These provided for the meeting of the national convention in 5/1844 and that five delegates should be chosen [by party members] *in* each Congressional district.

FLORIDE [COLHOUN] CALHOUN to
Lt. Patrick Calhoun, "Fort Towson,
Choctaw Nation, Arkansaw"

Forthill, Aprill 3d 1843

My Dear Son, We have been delighted at hearing from you frequently. The last letter was to John [C. Calhoun, Jr.], and as it came here first, we read it, and forwarded it to him. He is now at the Virginia University, and appears thus far very well pleased. His throat I fear will give him much trouble. It has been very painful for some time. I miss him much, now that James [Edward Calhoun], is at home particularly, it appears as though he ought to be here too. James, is to go to the GreenWood School, as soon as I can get him ready, and William Lowndes [Calhoun], to Mr. [F.M.] Adams again. He keeps the Village Academy now, and has a full school already.

We are all well. Little [John] Calhoun [Clemson], has been sick, but is well again. Little Elizabeth Floride [that is, Floride Elizabeth Clemson], grows finely, and is a sweet little creature, and very pritty. Your Sister Anna [Maria Calhoun Clemson], is in good health again, and looks as well as I ever saw her. Mr. [Thomas G.] Clemson complains a great deal.

Your Uncle[']s [John Ewing Colhoun's] family have not yet returned from Columbia. He has gone for them. I think it probable they will delay, as the Varioloid is in the neighbourhood. All have been Inoculated here, even the Baby, and their arms are very sore, particularly William Lowndes. He had a fever, and three large places on one arm as large as a fourpence, and a red streak up to his shoulder. Your Father, and James, have just returned from the mines. They went during the inclement weather[;] we had a few days since more snow than I ever saw in Pendleton, and colder weather. I rather think the comet has had something to do with it, if it is one [it] is different from any I ever saw, it has more the appearance of a long streak of light through a star. When I first saw it, it reached nearly across the heavens, but is gradually diminishing. We have had quite a winter of disasters. First Anna[']s illness, then the house taking fire under the hearth. And lately Issey[']s, trying to burn us all up. She put a large coal of fire under William Lowndes['] pillow, fortunately the smell of the feathers led to the discovery in time to save the house. She was taken up immediately, and confessed the whole, but said after she put the fire under the pillow she became alarmed, and intended when she went to turn down the bed to take it out, but I told her that would have been too late. I intend shipping her off. The Negro[e]s all appeared shocked at the act, and said she ought to have been hung. I think her Father is at the bottom of all[;] as soon as the alarm was given of fire, he took up his hat and stick and ran off as hard as he could. Burn this letter as soon as read as I would not like any one to see this about Issey. We have kept it a profound secret. If it was known she would have to be hung. The Negro[e]s all beg to be remembered to you particularly Caty. When you come home again, you must bring her a nice dress pat[t]ern, or a large shawl. Your man Isaac is coming out a little, he walks a little faster. I am learning him to milk and cook, as I thought he never would make a house servant. I heard a few days since from your Aunt Maria [Simkins Colhoun], She is well, now at Edgefield. Your Uncle [James Edward Colhoun] is also well, at home. As I have nothing in the news way to communicate must conclude. All join me in love to you, and may God grant you health, and happiness, is the prayer of your devoted mother, Floride Calhoun.

ALS in ScU-SC, John C. Calhoun Papers.

L E W I S S. C O R Y E L L to James Broom,
"Sec[retar]y, Cal[houn] C[entral] C[ommittee],"
[Washington]

New Hope [Pa.,] 3d Apr[il] 1843
Dear Sir, Your Circular of Mar[ch] 4th ar[r]ived in my absence or
w[oul]d have been earlier replied to. You may rely on my prudence
and fidelity as may touch the accompan[y]ing papers. The sign is
["yet" *canceled and* "not" *interlined*] Right *yet* in Penn[sylvani]a.
There must be more efferves[c]ence, sober reason & Principle has yet
no actual power. And the weakness of [James] Buch[ana]n to perceive, and his want of tact, leaves us almost in dispair. He vainly
["relies" *canceled*] conceives himself in the hearts of the Poeple, and
under this delusion allows a clique of unprincipled demagogues to
direct his present which must distroy his future hopes which must be
["yet" *canceled*] *yet planted, nursed* & *husbanded* by *us*. And he
must, rely on Mr. [John C.] Calhoun[']s ray's of light and glory for
any more position than he now has—& had it not have been for our
Interest in Mr. C[alhoun] to be promoted by ["the" *changed to* "His"]
reelection to Senate, we c[oul]d have allowed him to have been defeated by the Porters & Co. [that is, the brothers, Governor David R.
Porter and Secretary of War James M. Porter] who are the most faithless hollow hearted Clique ever associated together & who now aspire
to rule & plunder the union as they have done Poor Penn[sylvani]a.

There has been a false moove in New Jersey or rather no move on
our part. I knew that the [Pottsville, Pa.] Emporium was for sale. I
wrote F[rancis] W. Pickens a loan of $1500 w[oul]d have possessed it
& given us the controul, ["sub rosa" *marginally interpolated*] and as it
was the Demo[cratic] Organ we c[oul]d have preserved every subscriber (& what would have astonished other States) could have by
our course have gradually & imperceptably have posses[s]ed the
hearts of the Democrats before we even hoisted Mr. Calhoun[']s flag
& this State, that stood absolutely Vibrating between [Martin] V[an]
B[uren] & C[alhoun,] could have been secured to the latter as firmly
as S.C. This was my game for I *know* our Election must go to the
House, the signs now are beginning to show that state of things most
clearly. Capt. [Robert F.] Stockton is not (as we think) to be trusted,
he and Jim Porter have long worked in unison. Caution and prudence
before the war opens, and death to the knife afterwards is our course.

Our strongest & most available argument is *one term*. This fact
has only to reach the Poeple to be successful, but then we have the

137

Politicians to cut down. They are every where before the poeple & prevent our efforts. Y[ou]r f[rien]d truly, Lewis S. Coryell.

[P.S.] You are now doing what if you had done at my suggestion 6 months or 4, ago we would have headed many a measure that will now an[n]oy us. Your general prospective will enable you to issue effective orders, and we ought to have a sign or token for the general staff, different from the Field Officers whose Valor, may make them essential, while yet they may lack discretion & prudence. Our steps must all be sure. There need be no provision for *retreat*—we conquer or die.

ALS in ScCleA.

CH[ARLES] AUG[USTUS] DAVIS to
Dixon H. Lewis, Washington,
"Private, *for the Committee*"

New York [City,] 5 Ap[ril] 1843
D[ea]r Sir, The policy I would advocate at this time, would be 1st a direct hostility ag[ains]t all party violence, or partizanship and party management, showing that "party distinction" was never intended to run to the extremes it has. True party Vigilance sh[oul]d be confined, by all good men, to preventing bad men from reaching power, thus carrying out the good old honest doctrine that *"when bad men combine good men sh[oul]d unite."*

There are so many people now seeking office and who can't get any & who feel that *they* have a better right to *place* than those who hold place, that the above doctrine will win them. And moreover I sincerely believe the Shortest and best way for them to get a living is by changing existing measures of Gov[ernmen]t, so that if they do not get *office* they will get *employment* & that is is far preferable.

2nd I would urge calmly but firmly a change of policy on the score of general prosperity—regarding *agriculture* and *commerce* as the first interests of the Country. Give all the incidental protection and aid to *other* interest[s] that can be given thro' revenue under a Tariff, *provided* the same in no way conflicts with *Commerce*, which is the great & active *agent* of Agriculture seeking for its productions the remotest markets in distant seas & countries.

Without an active and prosperous commercial marine we can have no navy to rely on and without a Navy what power have we to defend the most ingenuous *system of "protection* at home," from the rapacity of any "outside Barbarian" afloat who may be disposed to batter down our sea ports & cut up our coasting trade? We sh[oul]d be unable "to protect protection," and become what China has become or has witnessed.

3d as to Currency, I w[oul]d advance something like the doctrine contain[e]d in a short article inclosed. You can insert it [in the Washington Spectator] if you please—if not, no harm done. You are not responsible for *communications* even if you insert them.

I ["shall" *interlined*] send under cover some other articles which you can serve as y[ou]r judgment dictates.

But I urge as a matter of sound expediency that you preserve due caution in not letting your contributors be known. *Incognito* is a hoste—*identity* a mere *individual.* I can do you and our Cause little good if you do not comply with this request on my part. There is much up hill work here to put down prejudices, but they are disappearing gradually and in good time will be graded down to a level track. I have ["y(ou)r" *canceled and* "Mr. Broom(')s" *interlined*] favor of 27 Ult[im]o and [have] taken due note of its contents. Y[ou]r Ob[edien]t Ser[vant,] Ch: Aug. Davis.

ALS in ScCleA. NOTE: Endorsements on this letter indicate that it was received on 4/7 and answered on 4/22 by letter "No. 13."

M[ICAH] STERLING to "the Calhoun Central Committee," Washington

Watertown [N.Y.,] April 6, 1843
Gentlemen, You do well in counting upon me as one of the friends of J[ohn] C. Calhoun. I am so most sincerely and devotedly & have been so since the day we met at Yale.

I only regret that I am so located among the friends of [Martin] V[an] B[uren] that I can do comparatively but little towards promoting our great object. I shall be obliged to feel my way cautiously & slowly. It is not so all over the State[,] more particularly in the city of New York, where the mercantile interest feel a strong political preference for Mr. Calhoun.

An effort is now making at Albany to secure for Mr. Van Buren a Legislative nomination. My own opinion is, it will succeed, though our party are divided and almost distracted for other reasons than the

Presidential question. A short time will decide. It is true there is a great opposition to Mr. Van Buren's nomination in our own ranks—thousands wish he would retire. It would lead to reunion & I think secure the election of Mr. Calhoun. But if he goes for a nomination and all indications at present look like it, he will have a strong party in the State for him.

A majority of the old & leading politicians in the State of New York, I think are for him—but New York cannot decide the election. If the South presents, as I trust she will, an undivided front for Mr. Calhoun, he will most certainly get the nomination. Michigan has spoken well, in a united & strong voice. I had the proceedings published here, & think they will aid us much in getting Mr. Calhoun fairly before the People. Our party lines here are strongly drawn, and as the friends of Mr. V[an] B[uren] represent him as the choice of *the party*, it operates with great force to silence those whose preference is otherways.

It is hardly orthodox with many to prefer another man even before the nomination is made.

This principle should be combatted, & freedom and Independence of thought and action, at least till after the nomination is made, should be inculcated. Respectfully Yours &c, M. Sterling.

LS in ScCleA. NOTE: Endorsements on this letter read "Mr. Sterling, Watertown, No. 7," and "Ans[were]d Ap[ri]l 22, No. 19."

To JAMES ED[WARD] COLHOUN, Terrysville, Abbeville District, S.C.

Fort Hill, 8th April 1843
My dear Sir, It is a little uncertain, when I shall go to Georgia. Mr. [Thomas G.] Clemson may probably go over next week. It will however depend on information, that may be received from there. I delivered your message in reference to Authur's [*sic*; Arthur Simkins's] note, and he will leave it with your sister [Floride Colhoun Calhoun], ready to be delivered whenever you may send up for it. I shall ["attend to" *interlined*] your request in reference to Dr. [Frederick W.] Symmes['s] paper ["attended to" *canceled*]. I regret to hear of Polydore's attack. He is a very valuable negro, & his death would be a great loss to you.

Whether there will be an extra session or not, must depend on the state of the treasury and that again on the imports. If they should ["not" *interlined*] increase very considerably compared to what they were during the first quarter, a call[ed] session will be unavoidable; but I am of the impression that they will, and that it is doubtful whether one will be ["called" *interlined*] or not. I agree with you, that it is highly desirable, that the [Martin] Van Buren party should be compelled to show their hands on the Tariff and the sooner the better. He & his party have twice betrayed us on the Tariff. It was they, who passed ["that" *canceled and* "those" *interlined*] of '28 and '42, and they will be sure to betray us again, unless closely watched. That they intend it, I have no doubt. The fact, that Drumgole's [Representative from Va. George C. Dromgoole's] address [adopted by the Va. Democratic convention] had no reference to the Tariff is itself almost conclusive proof of their intention.

I understand the biographical sketch [of me] has had and is having a very extended circulation. The only real danger is the [national] Convention. That point must be watched with vigilance. I think, ["the time" *canceled*] on the question of time, we shall certainly succeed. That is ["an" *canceled*] important ["point" *canceled*], but the manner of constituting ["it" *canceled and* "the convention" *interlined*], and how the members shall vote are not less so. I trust we shall succeed in fixing them on fair principles; but I have made up my mind, that I will not permit my name to go before a convention, which is not calculated to bring out fully & fairly the voice of the party. I regard any other as a fraud on the people.

I hope you & Maria [Simkins Colhoun] will not fail to make us a visit during the summer. We shall be glad to see you. It will give you an opportunity to look at your mountain property. Pickens [District, S.C.,] is becoming quite a gold region. You ought to look to your property at this time. A good gold mine would be of service at a period of such low prices.

All join in love to you. Yours affectionately, J.C. Calhoun.

ALS in ScCleA; variant PC in Jameson, ed., *Correspondence*, pp. 530–531.

To J[AMES] ED[WARD] COLHOUN, Millwood, Abbeville [District, S.C.]

Fort Hill, 8th April 1843

My dear Sir, I received your letter by mail on Friday & and [*sic*] answered it by the mail of today before the arrival of George.

Things are going, I understand, at 12 Miles [Creek] as badly as they can. Your brother's [John Ewing Colhoun's] negroes were to have been sold on last sale day, but were not forthcoming, in consequence, I understand, of his not being returned till some time late in the day from Columbia. It offended the Sheriff [F.N. Garvin], I understand, and he has seized on all he could find & has taken them to Pickens to be detained till next sale day. The greater part, I learn, took to the woods. Your brother, is I am told, alone with two or three old negroes on the place only. His situation must be distressing. It is painful for me to think of it. Were it in my power, I would be happy to relieve him.

I will give the direction to George in relation to the letter ["of" *canceled and* "to" *interlined*] Dr. [Frederick W.] Symmes, which you request.

From what you state, I infer, that you are more forward with your crop than I am. I have in some corn, not more than 55 acres, and have not yet commenced on my cotton. The spring is very backward. The oak trees have scarcely commenced bud[d]ing. This day is quite cool with a prospect of a frost tonight.

The gold mania seems to be sp[r]eading all over the South. Every nook & corner will be searched for it, if the present hard times should continue. I doubt not that discoveries will be made in Abbeville. I recollect hearing my father [Patrick Calhoun] say a peice [*sic*] about the size of [a] guin[e]a[?], was found in the Calhoun settlement before the Revolution. I doubt, whether the specimen you sent contains metal of any discreption [*sic*]. All join in love. Affectionately, J.C. Calhoun.

[P.S.] It is [a] little uncertain when James [Edward Calhoun] will go to Greenwood. It will depend on the time the next quarter begins. He will go by Millwood, or spend the first vacation in part with you.

Mr. [Thomas G.] Clemson says that the specimen contains nothing but iron pyrites.

ALS in ScCleA. NOTE: This letter was addressed by Calhoun as if it was to be delivered by "George." The troubled affairs of John Ewing Colhoun (as well as other Calhoun family matters) are further discussed in a letter from Anna Maria Calhoun Clemson to Lt. Patrick Calhoun, 4/15/1843 (ALS in ScU-SC, John C. Calhoun Papers). See also *The Papers of John C. Calhoun*, 16:xxxi.

From P[ATRICK] G. BUCHAN

Rochester N.Y., 10th April 1843

Sir, You are probably aware of the present state of political feeling in this State and the doubt & distrust which at present distract the democratic party here. The real grounds of difference are somewhat different than appear on the surface and have more reference to the presidential election than the nick names [*sic*] of "conservatism" and "subterranean" seem to imply. From the commencement of the present session Mr. [Martin] Van Buren and his friends have been using every effort to secure the vote of this State for him at the great national caucus; the appointments of the Governor [William C. Bouck]—the efforts of his friends in the legislature as evinced by their action & the course of the State paper have all tended to the same object & could matters have proceeded as they wished and expected it would have ended with a legislative nomination for Mr. Van Buren this winter. All these efforts however have been met & counter[ed] & they have besides created a spirit of oppo[sition] to Mr. Van Buren which cannot be quelled. [I am] satisfied that Mr. V[an] B[uren] cannot procure the [vote of] this State in caucus, and I am just as cer[tain that] sh[oul]d he receive the nomination in the natio[nal convention] this State will cast its votes against him [in the] Election of 1844. The breach has beco[me too] wide to be healed—the leading men thro[ughout] the State are *marked* and *known* either [as for or] against Mr. Van Buren & they know what to expect in the event of his election. Never popular in the State he is now doubly unpopular from his supposed connection with the recent movements here.

There is a very strong feeling in your favor in the eastern part of the State and a desire on the part of Mr. Van Buren[']s opponents to concentrate their strength on you which will be developed in due season. In the western part that feeling is not so perceptible altho' you have many warm political friends here. With the exception of some old political hacks the opposition to Mr. Van Buren is pretty general in the democractic [*sic*] ranks. Still there is quite a want of union amongst us as to the individual on whom we shall concentrate our force—instead of a want of *union* I should have said an uncertainty as to the candidate. The name of General [Lewis] Cass has been favorably received by some, but even his strongest friends have no hope of using his name with any success. Mr. [James] Buchanan is not [tho]ught of—in this State at least—nor Col. [Richard M. John]son altho' he has many warm friends who [if th]ere were any prospects of success would [make] a demonstration in his favor. To secure

[suc]cess in our incipient movements it is necessary [tha]t we should unite on some candidate and that [at] an early period.

In reference to yourself the only drawback we feel here are [*sic*] your supposed views on the subject of the tariff & which in this section have been very much misrepresented. Could these be explained satisfactorily as I have no doubt they can, the democracy in the western part of this State would unite upon you with an unanimity & a force that would be overwhelming. In the first place ["then" *interlined*] altho' we have a few amongst us who are opposed to a tariff even for revenue & who would prefer that the government should be supported by direct taxation, I think I may safely say that the majority of the democracy here are in favor of a tariff *for revenue only* with discriminating duties *for the purposes of protection* & this they claim to be the democratic creed as set forth in the messages of [James] Madison, [James] Monroe, [Andrew] Jackson and even of President [John] Tyler. In opposition to this your views are represented to be in favor of a *"horizontal"* tariff—a tariff of equal duties on all articles—a tariff for revenue only it is true, but no discrimination in imposing such tariff for the protection of one article more than another—except that you are in favor of a discrimination for the *purposes of revenue only*—and it is broadly asserted that should you be el[ected] to the chief magistracy & a tariff bill should [be] passed by congress which obviously embodied [the] principle of protection you would not [hesitate] to interpose the *veto* power.

On this subject if your time perm[its I] should esteem it a great favor to hea[r your] views, even for my own satisfaction & [should you] have in your possession any of your print[ed] speeches on this subject you would oblige [me] by forwarding me a copy.

Your answer, if you find time to give it, I should publish in this section, should it become necessary[,] provided always, of course, that you give me that permission.

So far as New York is concerned I am satisfied that the vote in the western section will control the State. It did in 1840 against Mr. Van Buren & it will again. There is therefore more necessity for securing the west than any other portion of the State. Altho we are here always in a political minority & our voice is not heard in the State legislature yet the aggregate democratic vote is large. In this county [of Monroe] alone the democratic vote is 5220 making it the fifth county in the State in point of democratic votes except New York city. We have gradually reduced the whig majority from 2000 to 300 & with a candidate on whom we could all cordially unite we could carry the county. I have the honor to be Yours very respectfully, P.G. Buchan.

ALS in ScCleA; PC in Boucher and Brooks, eds., *Correspondence*, pp. 182–184. NOTE: A printed letterhead on the first sheet of this letter reads: "Buchan ["& Storrs" *canceled*], Attorneys, Solicitors and Counsellors, Rochester, N.Y., P.G. Buchan, ["W.C. Storrs" *canceled*]." This letter was partly burned at some time and is missing a lower corner of each page. Missing words have been supplied within brackets from the text of Boucher and Brooks.

From W[illia]m Butler, [former Representative from S.C.], Greenville, S.C., 4/10. "I have received by Mr. [Charles C.?] Pinckney the $241 which you sent. The short delay in returning the money, has caused me no sort of inconvenience, and ["I" *interlined*] should have regretted very much if you should have given yourself the least trouble about it." ALS in ScU-SC, John C. Calhoun Papers.

To CHARLES GOULD

Fort Hill, 10th April 1843

Dear Sir, I am much obliged to you for your kind feelings towards me.

The subject of your letter is one, which from a feeling of delicacy I rarely touch, ["and when I do," *canceled*] and when I do, I do it as lightly as possible. I believe in good faith, that it is an office not to be solicited nor declined; and that it ought to be left, under an enlightened & fair discussion, to the unbiased decession [*sic*] of the people of the Union.

Our affairs have been long progressing from bad to worse, and must, unless there should be more wisdom & patr[i]otism brought to their control, terminate in confusion and revolution. All I can say is, that if it be the will of the people to confide the reins to my hands, I shall do my best to arrest their downward course and restore the prosperity & character of the country. With great respect I am & &, J.C. Calhoun.

ALS in MH.

To A[NDREW] P[ICKENS] CALHOUN, [Marengo County, Ala.]

Fort Hill, 20th April 1843

My dear Andrew, Mr. [Thomas G.] Clemson left here yesterday to attend to the loan, which I expect to get of Mr. [John S.] Barbour. He left sooner than was ["necessary" *canceled and* "intended" *interlined*], in consequence of having made arrangement to purchase 30 negroes of your uncle John [Ewing Colhoun] to be sold next sale day. He is to give $6,500. I have made arrangement to borrow $4,500 of the Bank of the State and have undertaken to pay the balance in 4 & 5 months. He goes by Charleston to attend to the ["loan there" *interlined*]. If the Virginia loan should succeed, it will be applied to meet these engagements. Mr. Barbour wrote that the money was ready. All I fear ["that" *canceled*] is, that there may be some informality, especially in your power of attorney to me; as the loan is to be made under the decree of the court. I hope, however, there will be no difficulty. I write now principally to say, that it is uncertain how long Mr. Clemson will be absent; and that you had better postpone your visit, till you ["can" *canceled*] hear from me again. His presence will be necessary to our settlement. I will write you as soon as I can learn when he will be back.

We are all well. The season now is fine. My cotton is coming up. I hope you have got a good start.

All join in love to you, Margaret [Green Calhoun] & Duff [Green Calhoun]. Your affectionate father, J.C. Calhoun.

ALS in ScU-SC, John C. Calhoun Papers.

Geo[rge] C. Patterson, Middlebrook, Md., to D[ixon] H. Lewis, [Washington], 4/21. Patterson requests copies of "Mr. Calhoun's speech on the treaty" [of Washington] to distribute. "There is nothing I assure you wanting to secure the zeal of old Maryland in favour of Mr. Calhoun but an acquaintance with the man & his principles & if there is any honorable means by which I can bring about this desideratum I shall most cordially make use of them—in which service I shall be glad to receive your direction. It is true I am in the employ of Government (as Librarian to the [U.S.] House of Rep[resentative]s) but in espousing those principles which I honestly believe ought to govern the councils of the nation I feel that I am doing a service to my country, which I hold eminently higher than considerations of self advantage." He discusses his views of politics at length. ALS in ScCleA.

N[athan?] Preston, Hartford, Conn., to James "Broome," Washington, 4/24. Preston has received a letter and materials relating to the gathering of subscribers for the Washington *Spectator*. These were probably sent to him on the suggestion of his relative, Jos[eph] A. Scovill[e]. Although Preston is friendly to Calhoun's "prospects," because of his "present constant employment," he declines obtaining subscribers. He will return the materials to Scoville when he sees him. ALS in ScCleA.

CIRCULAR from [Joseph A. Scoville],
"Secretary, Calhoun Central Committee"

(PRIVATE AND CONFIDENTIAL)

CENTRAL COMMITTEE-ROOM
Washington, D.C. *April* 24, 1843

Sir: Will you send a reply to the following questions at your earliest convenience; and also communicate any additional information which you may deem of importance to be known to this committee?

How many leading or important Post Offices are there in your Congressional District?

How many of the Postmasters are Whigs?

How many are Calhoun men? Name them.

Name the Democratic papers published in your Congressional district. And where published. And editors['] and proprietors' names.

Name those friendly to Mr. Calhoun.—[To Martin] Van Buren, [Richard M.] Johnson, [Lewis] Cass, or [James] Buchanan for the Presidency.

Are you acquainted with any leading Democrats, who are friendly to Mr. Calhoun, residing in any of the county towns in your State? If so, please name them; and request them to correspond with this committee.

Will you send us a list of names of reliable friends of Mr. Calhoun in your county?

When does your County Convention meet? When does your State Convention meet?

The names of your State Central Committee? Name those friendly to Mr. Calhoun.

Name an Agent for the [Washington] Spectator in your county town. Yours, &c. [*space for signature*] Secretary Calhoun Central Committee.

Printed letter in Vi, Robert Mercer Taliaferro Hunter Papers. NOTE: This document was made so it could be addressed and signed by hand. The copy found is addressed to Hunter and is signed by J[oseph] A. Scoville. It also contains a ms.

P.S. by Scoville: "[Dixon H.] Lewis goes away tomorrow. Can you not come on here[?] *Penn*[sylvania] *has gone for May 1844*[.]" From the extant replies to this circular, it would appear to have been sent only to persons in northeastern States, the copy to Hunter being a sample.

From J[OHN] S. BARBOUR

Catalpa [Culpeper County, Va.,] April 26th 1843
My Dear Sir, I reached home last night from Fauquier & Rappa[hannock] Counties.

In Fauquier I applied to the Judge through my Counsel for the forms he would require in the Bonds from [my kinsman] Colo[nel J.B.] Hogan, which he declined to give. He said that he doubted his power to lend the funds of my children who are infants beyond the jurisdiction of his Court by process of attachment & execution.

Without intimating any other than a doubt of his power, he expressed a wish to have the question of power discussed in open Court. The Court opens the second of May, and the funds will be disposed of the 4th day of the Court, which will be the 5th of May. If the Court thinks it holds the power, it will be determined instantly & the sooner the money is put out the better—I presume for all parties. If put out during the session of the Court, a power will be given by decree to the borrower to check on the deposit in Bank, but should it not be done whilst the Court is open, it will be necessary to create a Commissioner to lend it according to the decree of the Court. And this may make additional Costs (to the assets within the power of the Court) a certain consequence of the delay. The Son of the Judge is a practising Lawyer in his Court, & he promised me at Rappahannock Superior Court to confer with his father on the difficulty that existed in his mind as to lending the money in another State. I shall hear from him (I expect) tomorrow or the next day, and hearing in advance what the difficulties are we shall be the better prepared to meet them. The Court sits at Fauquier fifteen days and I should be very glad that you would have some one here during the Court to close the loan.

The Court being in session, the decree can be modified to suit the condition of things (as ["things" *canceled and* "it" *interlined*] may exist,) which cannot be done in vacation. I was very desirous of drawing from the Judge an official decision through the call of a Commissioner in Chancery. Our act of assembly authorising even Master or Comm[issione]r in Chancery to send the Judge any question on which he doubts in vacation for his opinion & advice. The Comm[issione]r did not think that anything was before him to authorise or excuse such a call, and I had therefore to apply by my Counsel. [*Interpolation*: The Judge resides in the country a few miles from Warrenton ("else" *canceled*).] Had he been near me I w[oul]d have applied in person.

In a day or two you will hear again from me. With Great Respect y[ou]rs very truly, J.S. Barbour.

ALS in ScCleA.

Jesse Brush, New York [City], to Joseph A. Scovill[e], Washington, 4/27. Brush requests that he be sent copies of "the speeches made on the Oregon question by the Different members of the senat[e] and the one made by J.C. Calhoun in particular as the time is arriving when ther[e] will be some Occasion for the Democracy to express the[i]r preference's [*sic*] for the Different Candidates for the Presidency and I should like to become acquainted with some of their claims . . . ." Brush adds in a P.S.: "Burn this when read." (The recipient of the letter apparently wrote on it the name of Timothy Childs [Representative from N.Y.].) ALS in ScCleA.

To Joseph H. Hedges, [Philadelphia], 4/28. "I have not a spare copy left of my speech [of 8/5/1842] on the Tariff & cannot therefore comply with your request. But a volume containing many of my speeches have [*sic*] been printed, or is in the course of printing by the Harpers of N[ew] York, which, among others, will contain the one you desire to possess." ALS owned by Elmer O. Parker.

J. Fr[anci]s Hutton to J[oseph] A. Scoville, "S[ecretary], C[alhoun] C[entral] C[ommittee]," Washington

New York [City], April 28, 1843

Dear Scovill[e], Your favor of the 24th rec[eive]d. In answer to your questions, first, There are four Post Offices in [Staten Island,] the County of Richmond (one portion of the 2nd Congressional district) all of them unimportant. 2nd. Two of them have Whig Postmasters & two democratic. 3rd. One in favor of John C. Calhoun. 4th. There is but one weekly paper [the *Richmond County Mirror*] published in the County and it is neutral in politics, our Calhoun friends communicate with the democrats by pamphlet &c. The paper I mention is published and edited by F[rancis] L. Hagadorn[,] a Van Buren man but easily induced to support our cause by a little *public printing.* 5th. The following persons you ["may" *interlined*] rely upon with confidence as strong Calhoun men, and I trust you will communicate with them. *Henry C. Hedley* Esq[ui]r[e], *John C. Thompson, Gen-[era]l D[enyse] Denyse, Rob[er]t M. Hazard,* Bornt P. Winant, *Icssy*[?] *Dissossway* [*sic*; Israel Dissosway?], *Judge* [Jonathan] *Coddington,* John C. Reyser [*sic*; Ryerss], and a host beside but these are our leading democrats; those underlined are[,] if any choice could be made[,] the most reliable. 6th. Our County Convention will meet in August. For Agents of the Spectator in Richmond County I name for the town of Southfield Icssy[?] Dissosway [*sic*; and for the] Town of Castleton Jno. C. Thompson. Truly Yours in haste, J. Frs. Hutton.

ALS in ScCleA.

C[OLIN] M. I[NGERSOLL] to Jos[eph] A. Scoville, "Sec[retary], C[alhoun] C[entral] C[ommittee]," Washington, *"Private & Confidential"*

New Haven, Conn., Ap[ri]l 28, 1843
Dear Sir, I have been absent from this place for some days past, & found on my arrival here to day yours "Private & confidential." The matters therein contained shall be attended to as soon as I can find the time to set down & write you at length. On Monday I go to Hartford & shall suffer my name to go before the Senate for nomination to the Secretaryship. Our friends think it will be important for the cause that I get the office & they will I believe use their exertions to put me in the chair. I will send you the result, *if favorable,* which you can, if you choose, hand to the [Washington] Spectator, for publication. I am in much haste. Thinks look *well* ["here" *interlined*]. Rely upon it, we move *slow* but *sure.*

I think you may expect to hear Conn. speak for "May '44." The [New Haven] Register inclines that way. I will inform you if anything transpires at the seat of Gov[ernmen]t. Y[ou]rs, C.M.I.

ALI in ScCleA. NOTE: Ingersoll (1819–1903) was elected Clerk of the Conn. Senate on 5/3. He was Representative from Conn. during 1851–1857.

To J[OSEPH] A. SCOVILLE, Washington

Fort Hill, 28th April 1843

Dear Sir, If I do not answer your letters, you must not infer, that I do not appreciate your efforts, or want confidence in you; but because I deem it both proper & prudent, that I should write as few letters as possible.

I concur with you, both in reference to a press in N[ew] York and in Washington. Our cause is based on truth, justice and the Constitution, and only needs enlightened and able discussion to succeed. A Well established and well conducted paper at both points are almost essential. The Spectator is doing well. The last number is excellent. It ought never to attack, but in self-defence; & then with moderation, dignity and power. Purs[u]ing the course, I doubt not it will, I have no doubt, it will be well supported & patronized. It takes time for a paper to gain confidence & strength; but in the present state of things, ["if" *canceled*] a paper properly conducted at the seat of Gov[ernmen]t, cannot fail in the end to acquire both.

Our State Convention will now meet at Columbia in a few weeks, when I have no doubt proper measures will be devised to produce concert of action, and to give support to the cause.

Every thing looks well at the South. I received a letter from John Danthforth [*sic*] of N[ew] London, Con[necticu]t ["last week" *interlined*]. He gives a favourable account of a conversation he recently had with Gov[erno]r [Chauncey F.] Cleveland, and speaks favourably of the state of things in Conne[c]ticut. Do you know him? And also one ["of" *canceled*] from P.G. Buchan, of Rochester, N.Y., very sensible & favourable. He thinks, if my views on the Tariff could be fully understood and satisfactorily explained, I would carry the State. Do you know him? And if so, who is he? I also had one from an ardent young friend of N[ew] Orleans, Alexander Walker, who gives a very favourable account of the state of things in Louis[i]ana. It would be well to send him a number of the Spectator with some prospectus.

I hear nothing of the volume of speeches. What delays ["their" *canceled and* "its" *interlined*] appearance, and when will ["they" *canceled and* "it" *interlined*] be out? It is desirable that ["they" *canceled*] it should be as soon as possible. Every day now is important, in the way of giving information. How has the [published] life gone out? Has any effort been made to circulate it? With great respect I am & &, J.C. Calhoun.

ALS in ScCleA; PC in Jameson, ed., *Correspondence*, pp. 531–532.

[LEVI WOODBURY, Senator from N.H.,] to Joseph A. Scoville, Washington, "Confidential"

P[ortsmou]th [N.H.,] 28 Apr[il] 1843
Mr. Woodbury's respects to Mr. Scoville. The within article is much more than was expected from that quarter. It will put New York *November* hors de combat in this State! and accomplish all you desire as to *time* &c.

The Circular you sent me under date of Ap[ril] 24th may do good, but more out of this State than in it.

If it [be] addressed to Ab Greenleafe [*sic*; Abner Greenleaf] Es-q[ui]re or Rich[ard] Jenners Esq[ui]re or one to both, answers will be given doubtless in full.

As to a loan named in your former line, money cannot be got here for loan or labour, as unfortunately the times have forced me to be a borrower or suffer—& the latter seems likely to fall to be my lot. Please show the [Concord, N.H.,] Patriot to Mr. [Edmund T.] Bridge if he is in your city.

Mr. [Richard] Ela [a Clerk in the Treasury Department] will pay on his return or Mr. [McClintock] Young, Ch[ief] Clerk [of the Treasury Department] for him in his absence, to Mr. [John] Heart.

P.S. Be not too fast in New H[ampshire] in acts or hopes, and all may end well.

ALU in ScCleA. NOTE: An endorsement indicates that this letter was answered on 5/3.

From KER BOYCE

Charleston, April 29th 1843
My dear Sir, I fear you will think me a troublesom[e] correspond[ent], by [*sic*] my only apoligy [*sic*] is to see you at the helm of our government, and I may think many thing[s about] which you will differ with me from your great Experience and ability. Still I am urged on by that desire to see you, Elevated to suggest ["offer" *interlined and then canceled*] to you what I feel of benefit.

I had a conversation with Col. [Franklin H.] Elmore, last Ev[en]ing who is Just from Washington, and he agrees with me that you ought and that the people of the North have a right to see you, and should you be invited to Boston you ought not to refuse on your own a/c [*sic*; account] or that of your friends. I will not say any more on this subject as I know, I have ["been"(?) *canceled*] sayed anoghf [*sic*] on that subject but will allow you to hear from others better able to advise you on that subject than I can.

Gen[era]l [James] Hamilton [Jr.] stated to me he would Write the ad[d]ress for the Convention at Columbia and submit it to our Committee, a week before the Convention, but in a conversation with Col. Elmore, We have Come to the Conclusion that it would be prudent, and wise that you should give the the [*sic*] out lines of that ad[d]ress or one Compleat and send that to Col. Elmore[.] I hope ["it" *interlined*] is not asking two [*sic*] much at your hands. Of Course it would be Considered to be strictly Confideltial, as I hold all your letters on subjects relative to your letters [*sic*] on the Presidential Election[.] Col. Elmore, and myself fear our own Amiable[?] friends as to the Course of the Election. First[?] nominating a President & Vice President is assuming two much. This has been done not by the Consent of the Committee hear but by Mr. Stewart [*sic*; John A. Stuart]. This we will have to get over at the Convention as well as posiable [*sic*] by saying that We the party of South Carolina, feel it our duty not to nomi[n]ate the Vice Presidency but leave that to the Convention—for in that I feel as we had a trump Card. While I would go for [Levi] Woodbury before any others, but if it become necessary in the Convention to take Gen[er]al [Lewis] Cass or ["Dick Johnston" *canceled and* "(James K.) Polk" *interlined*,] Buckhannon, [*sic*; James Buchanan,] or Loose [*sic*] you, Whey [*sic*] I would Certainly take Either to secure your Election. Therefore It is Very imprudent to h[o]ist the flagg for any Man for Vice President. We must be prudent in any stand we take, which might look like dictation[,] for any thing we do that will give our Enemys a loop hole to hang on they will take hold with great evidity [*sic*] and turn it again[s]t you. For I look on the move in ["Collenton" *canceled and* "Beauforttown" *interlined*; as] Very imprudent on [*sic*; and?] one that will do you harm. Now My Dear Sir make up your mind to Visit Boston and let the people see the man who will become their Ideal after that sight. Y[ou]rs most Sinsarely, Ker Boyce.

ALS in ScCleA. NOTE: An AEU by Calhoun reads: "Ker Boyce[.] Ans[wer]ed 6th May[.] Requests the out lines of an address." The "imprudent" move at "Beauforttown" referred to by Boyce was reported in the Charleston, S.C., *Mercury*, March 22, 1843, p. 2. At a meeting of citizens of St. Helena's Parish at Beaufort on 3/20, chaired by Robert Barnwell Rhett, resolutions were adopted expressing the position that participation in a Democratic national nominating convention should be conditional on the tariff having "first been regulated consistently with justice to the South and the pledges of the party."

From JOHN GRIFFIN

Philadelphia, April 29, 1843

Dear Sir, I take the liberty of writing to you Those [*sic*] few lines not having the Honour of your Acquaintance only as the Son of my Countryman. I always had a regard for you as a Public Man of the first Standing [*one word or partial word canceled*] Second to none[.] I saw last night your [published] life for the first Time in my life time in this Country 29 years out of 45[.] I see by that, that you are full Blooded Irish on Both Sides as Good Game Blood as God Ever put in The Veins of Man[.] My Opinion is that you Should take a Tour North this Summer And let your friends have a Shake of the Hand with you[.] Your Chance for the Presidency is Verry Good if you will only make this move[.] Your Friends are More Numerous than you are a ware of[.] I my Self was original[l]y a [Andrew] Jackson Man & A [John] Tyler Man[.] Mr. Tyler[']s Prospect this ["Ty" *canceled*] Time last year ["was" *interlined*] verry Good But his Stock is Lowering in the Market True [*sic*] the miss Management of his Son Robert [Tyler] & an Upstart Companion of his Named [Job R.?] Tyson[.] When your Name Comes into the Convention your Chance will be two to one a gainst any other man in the Union[.] Van Buren is obnoxious to the Democracy only the old office holders.

My Motive for writing this letter to you is on The Score of your Orriginal & Lenial [*sic*] Blood[;] that Blood I Love where Ever I will Meet it[.] It has Governed the Britis[h] Empire For ages Past Both in the Field & the Cabinet[.] Like wise this Glorious Republic.

I wish you to Send me ["a" *canceled*] as large a Number of your Life as you think would be Proper for Distribution a Mong my Country Men[.] I Pledge you the honour of an Irish Man that I will Make Good youse [*sic*] of them[.] If you Should think well of this Direct them to the Care of Mr. Dennis Mealy[,] No. 4 South 4th St. an old Resident of this City for Upwards of 40 years & his old Uncle[,] Both from the same County that gave your Father & Mother Berth [*sic*,] Donegal[,] Gen. [Richard] Montgomery['s] Native County. I Remain With Great Respect your Friend, John Griffin[,] No. 4 Raspberry St.

ALS in ScCleA. NOTE: An AEU by Calhoun reads: "John Griffin, Irishman."

From S. W. JEWETT

Weybridge Vermont, 29 Ap[ri]l 1843
D[ea]r Sir, The private and political interest of this State prompts me
to write you. To commence, you are well aware that wool is the main
article of production in this State and where *our interest is, the people
will go,* so soon as they can be convinced. Now Sir if consistent I
would be happy to obtain your views on the present tariff so far as
relates to wool. You undoubtedly understand that enormous quantities of foreign wools are yearly imported, and sold here at very low
rates and unless we have more protection or something turns up to
turn the market for these cheap wools to some orther [*sic*] quarter, we
wool growers, must suffer, and of course other branches also. I send
you a paper [*not found*] in which is a communication from me, on
wool ["Tariff &c" *interlined*] by reading that & another that will
come out next week which I will send you, you will see my drift of
argument[.]

The facts are that thousands of our Best Merino Bucks have been
exported to foreign countries to improve their sheep, and those wools
now in large quantities are imported here from ½ to ¾ merino, and
sold here for almost 10 cents p[e]r lb. The manufacture[r]s understanding the value of this wool, better than our northern legislators,
so contrived to word the tariff as to evade the construction and about
all wools ["and" *canceled*] are admitted at the *Invoice price,* without
regard to the word "*coarse*" [or] "*fine*" [or] "*naturally*" &c[.]

Through our whig Editors the people are generally made to believe that you are for "*free trade*" out and out. The fact, to besure,
the better informed know to the contrary. Our State is on the poise
and nothing but the plain facts in regard to the matter of wool, if
rightly presented will give the democratic party the State this year.
Your colleague Mr. [William C.] Preston, moved that 20 p[e]r c[en]t
be added to all coarse wool, seconded by Mr. [Thomas H.] Benton
who made a short speech thereon; one of the [former] whig senators
of this State S[amuel] C. Crafts voted against it, (He being true to
his master Gov[ernor Charles] Paine an extensive manufacturer)[.]

Now Sir, you will not allow me to flatter, but so sure as you would
be inclined so to modify the Tariff as to give us a chance to compete
with these S[outh?] A[merican?] and other cheap foreign wool's [*sic,*]
so sure you would get the Nomination of the Highest Office in the gift
of the people, by the Committee of this State, *In my humble opinion.*

The facts are, in looking at the pictures as they are arranged and hung up in representation of the order of the Presidents it would not look right to see Martin Van buren in its order then follow two other Presidents then up comes Martin again[.]

Please, sir, give me an answer, and any thing you may write shall be confidential, or shall not be published, unless you neglect to advise me on the subject, but it would do us a favor if we could be assured by you, that you thought the present tariff inadequate, so far as relates ["to" *interlined*] these cheap wool's in protecting the wool growing districts. ["We 'democrats' mostly think" *canceled.*] Yours with great Respect and Esteem, S.W. Jewett.

ALS in ScCleA. NOTE: An AEU by Calhoun reads: "Mr. Jewett[,] Wants my views on the Tariff, & my opinion on the duty on coarse wool[,] not answered."

M[ICAH] STERLING to J[oseph] A. Scoville, Washington, "Confidential"

29th April [18]43, Watertown [N.Y.] My D[ea]r Sir, Yours of the 22d inst[ant] was duly rec[eive]d. I have no time now to answer you in full but you may expect to hear from me occasionally.

So, our P[ost]master [John F. Hutchinson] professes [to] be a *Calhoun man.* He was in 1840 a most violent [William Henry] Harrison man. He abandoned the Whigs to keep the P[ost] Office and will support [John] Tyler, [John C.] Calhoun or the Devil if he can thereby keep the Post office—at least so I think & so is his reputation here. But he has made up his mind, (so he told me some time since), that Calhoun would be our next President—of course he will be a Calhoun man if Tyler is out of the question. I have no great faith in him and would make him no promises but treat him kindly and make the most of him.

The truth is there is no feeling & no excitement here generally speaking upon the subject of the next Presidential election—and if the Committee are not prudent they will run ahead of Public sentiment. Democrats & Whigs are standing aghast at many of the late appointments and I am this day very credibly informed that Senator [Silas] Wright has written to a Political friend in this county that none who accepted office under Tyler would be any longer recognised as true Democrats!! This is as I anticipated.

Depend upon it, a strong attempt will be made to render Tylerism as odious as possible and then to identify Tylerism with Calhounism! The Committee must already be aware of this and guard themselves accordingly. But the but[t] of the joke is that the Friends of [Martin] V[an] Buren are so greedy for office that they readily accept office under Tyler and of course must shut up their mouths as to Tyler and become neutralised as to V[an] Buren.

I fear the Committee are going too fast. We must not fire all our guns & then let V[an] Buren come in & play oneup[?; *one word illegible*]. It is clear that V[an] Buren is beaten as to the time of holding the convention. Pennsylvania has settled that matter. No meeting can be advantageously held in this county of Democrats at present. We must not meet in county convention as the friends of Calhoun but as Democrats simply.

Tyler can do much for Calhoun. It is wholly out of the question as to his doing any thing for himself. But all who accept office under Tyler must eventually go for Calhoun, be neutralised or resign or be turned out.

But I am too much engaged to write further today. Yours truly, M. Sterling.

ALS in ScCleA.

Th[oma]s J. Agnew, New York [City], to Joseph A. Scoville, Washington, 5/1. Agnew replies briefly to Scoville's letter [of 4/24?], sending to him the name of Dan[ie]l C. Martin, of Newark, N.J., "a man to be relied on in every respect—and a true *Democrat*." Agnew encloses a copy of the New York Plebeian containing the proceedings of the Democratic party in his ward, the Second, and promises to send him the names of other men "who are of the right stamp." ALS in ScCleA.

W[ILLIA]M L. CLARK to Joseph A. Scoville, Washington, "Private"

New York [City,] May 1, 1843

Dear Joe, I have sent by to day[']s mail to Dixon H. Lewis, The Plebe[i]an containing the proceeding in the old "2nd" [ward.] You may rest easy in relation to *my* Ward as I shall in future take charge of it. It would have ammused [*sic*] you could you have witnessed our proceedings as we took them by surprise[;] the object of the meeting was to *censure* myself & McCaisky [*sic;* McClusky] and they admitted they had such resolutio[ns] in their pocket and said if we would allow them to offer the resolutions *prepar[ed]* they would withdraw the part that related to myself & McCaisky but we had about 100 of the right *Kind,* and you know we belong to the kind of animals that give and take[.] I refer you to the proceedings. We meet in Committee tomorrow night & the fight will then come of[f] whether the resolutions shall be re[s]cinded[.] It took us till 2 o[']clock AM to pass them & I think it will take them till 4 to repeal.

["I" *canceled*] As I mentioned to you I offered a resolution to invite J[ohn] C. C[alhoun] to visit our city which was laid on the table by [a] 5 [vote] maj[ori]ty. I shall bring it up again when the time arrives[.]

Will you request the Spectator to send their paper directed to Jno. P. Howard[,] Howard[']s Hotell. I will send you some more names when they *pay* up [and] also will send the funds Howard has paid me and I should like the paper sent. Man [that is, Emanuel B.] Hart is out openly for our man. The old Hunkers dare not call a mass meeting for Van [Buren] and their move in our ward was a fuller [*sic;* failure?]. We gave Bob Wetmore the scoundrell a dig and I will here state to you that if I believed as is reported such suckers are to remain in office should we be successful I would be the first to stop working[.] In haste yours, Wm. L. Clark.

[P.S.] Destroy this scrawl[.] They name me in our ward disorganizer and *Spartan*[.] Write me all the news[.]

ALS in ScCleA. NOTE: The Spartan Club was an Irish street gang in New York City, organized by Mike Walsh for political agitation.

SCHUYLER SAMPSON to J[oseph] A. Scoville, "Sec[re]t[ar]y C[alhoun] C[entral] Committee," Washington

Plymouth Mass., May 1 1843
Sir: I have received your circular of the 24th ult[imo]. I cannot now give you such an answer as is satisfactory to myself. I shall however make such communications from time to time as I am possessed of information which it may be well for you to know. Your first query will be replied to as the County instead of our Congressional District which is No. 10 and embraces most of the Counties of Plymouth and

Bristol. In this District Henry Williams has been chosen to Congress, and is said to be an ardent friend of Mr. [Martin] Van Buren. In this County (Plymouth) there are forty Post Offices. All the important ones are in the hands of the whigs. There are ten of the minor offices in the hands of the Democrats and are as follows—

Eel River—Nathan Whiting
North Bridgewater—Edward Southworth ["(Jr.)" *interlined*]
North Scituate—S.B. Merritt
West Scituate—Zattu Cushing
Kingston—Rufus B. Bradford
Halifax—Henry Pope
North Carver—William Barrows
Hanson—Jeremiah Loper
Marshfield—Proctor Bourne
North Middleborough—Morrill Robinson.

Plymouth, Hingham, Middleborough, Abington and all the important offices are in the hands of the whigs. If we could have a change in Plymouth P[ost] Office and have one of our friends in lieu of a Clay Whig who is a very incompetent officer it would help us much. As all our party are in favor of supporting the nominee of the National Convention, it is almost impossible to say who are, and who are not in favor of any particular candidate who has been named. In our Manufacturing towns Mr. Van Buren may be preferred—in our Commercial towns Mr. [John C.] Calhoun would be the favorite. The only Democratic Paper published in this County is the "Plymouth Rock." I should think the paper rather inclined toward Mr. Van Buren, but will support whoever is nominated at the National Convention to be held in May 1844. This time seems to be fixed for the Convention, whether New York falls in with it or not. I sent some time since a number of the "Plymouth Rock" to the [Washington] "Spectator" thinking they may exchange. The Editor and Proprietor is Gideon W. Young, a sound sterling Democrat. I shall take another opportunity to name persons in other Counties who are friendly to Mr. Calhoun. Our County Convention meets in the Autumn as also ["does" *interlined*] our State Convention. From the best information I now have all the State Committee are inclined to favor Mr. Van Buren except Charles G. Greene of Boston. I am the Chairman of the County Committee and have been for ten years. I am also Chairman of the Congressional District Committee and I believe I am its only member who favors Mr. Calhoun. I have received several Receipts, and Prospectus' for the Spectator. At present it is not expedient to name an agent for the Spectator here. I shall do all I can in this matter—there are various hindrances at present to do much. If the friends of the prominent candidates for a nomination to the Presidency all agree to support the nominee of the National Convention Mr. Calhoun will be triumphantly elected, and I am fully persuaded that the Democrats of this State will do so. The Districts of our State will this fall elect each a Delegate to attend the National Convention to be held in May 1844, three of which will certainly be in favor ["of Mr. Calhoun" *interlined*] and probably four among which will be the Delegates from this District. I am very respectfully Sir: Your Obedient Servant, Schuyler Sampson.

ALS in ScCleA. NOTE: Sampson was Collector of Customs at Plymouth.

W[illia]m L. Clark to J[oseph] A. Scoville, Washington, "Confidential"

New York [City], May 2, 1843

D[ea]r Sir, Will you inform me the course I should pursue to obtain for my brother John V. Clark a situation in the custom house[.] My object in getting him a situation is not only on a/c [account] of his connexion but for Political purposes as with him in our city for an auxilliary I could move to better advantage[.] You are aware of my position here as a Calhoun man and I assure you no steps shall be left to obtain for him our city[.] In every move that has taken place I started the same and shall continue so to do. In fact in my ward they think of reading me out for the course I have pursued as I have thaurted [*sic*] them in all their undertakings, viz[.] in both Committees and in two publick meetings in our ward[.] In fact I have made my arrangements so complete that I can command 200 when the occasion requires & *you know* it is done at no small expense[;] but such has [*sic*] been my feelings that I have mixed more with politics that [*sic*] I intended ever to do but enough of this[.] Will you request your friends in Washington to move in this matter for my sake[;] the situation of inspector will answer him well and I think as it is the first favour I ever asked it might be granted[.] As I am situated I would not ask Edward Curtis for the best office in his gift[;] to you I apply on the ground of old friendship and I pledge [to] the friends of Mr. Calhoun that you may see—That if this appointment is made they never will regret the little trouble it may give them & to yourself[.] I will repay the same at our first meeting or before should you request my *services.* Joe[,] make this a personal matter on *my* account and I will be *gratefull.* I wrote you yesterday in great haste stating how we progressed[;] tomorrow night the fight comes of[f] and we have a game to play that will require all our exertions[.] We intend to fill vacancies for one night and as a great many *suckers* under[?] the Common Council belong to our *Com[mit]tee* they will as a matter of course be absent[.] So I think upon that score you need not fear. [William] Dem[in]g[?] & myself are pulling in the same harnass [*sic*] and if you can get John his appointment it will give him satisfaction as well as myself[.] Should you deem it important I can get you a petition for him signed by the *Democracy* of both Candidates.

Man [Emanuel B.] Hart & myself were on Sunday talking of getting up a *Young Men[']s* mass meeting in the *Park*[;] how will it answer[?] The old Hunkers dare not but the *unter[r]ified* & *Subterraneans* know no fear.

I would be pleased to hear from you at your earliest leasure & command[.] Yours truly, Wm. L. Clark.

[P.S.] Charley Secor[?] is out [for?] Van Buren[.] After the appointments are made our cause will be [*one word canceled*] stronger.

["In" *canceled*] Ogden from Chemung Co[unty] & Strong from E[l]mira[?] are at Howard[']s and seem mightily pleased at the proceedings in our ward[.] I may come on to Washington this summer[.]

ALS in ScCleA.

From SIMEON B. JEWETT

[Clarkson, N.Y.,] 2 May 1843

Dear Sir, I am one of your supporters for the next presidency—as against Mr. [Martin] Van Buren or any other individual. The democracy of this State hold a convention in September next to determine the time they will go into a National Convention, and the mode in which the delegates to that convention shall be appointed.

I am fully satisfied from the already expressed opinion of the press and the people, May 1844 will be the time fixed upon for a National Convention and that the delegate[s] be appointed by Congressional Districts. I am confident Mr. Van Buren'[s] personal friends will be opposed to any such result, but they will be wholly incompetent to change it. There is a deep and strong feeling of preference daily maturing with the people, to stand aside for Mr. Van Buren, and to go into the support of yourself, which is based upon sound and democratic principles.

It would be exceedingly gratifying to the democracy of this State and the North generally, to welcome you there during the summer. Your presence would greatly aid their exertions, while I have no doubt it would be a matter of great pleasure with yourself to meet your democratic friends of the Northern States. It would be very gratifying to the democrats of Massachusetts could you be present the 17 June at the Bunker Hill celebration, to which I am informed you will be kindly invited. The democracy of this County are pleased to meet and become personally acquainted with their candidate for the presidency. The Western part of this State, my residence, being Clarkson[,] Monroe County, is much engaged in the promotion of your success. I am Your Ob[edient] Ser[vant,] Simeon B. Jewett.

ALS in ScCleA. Note: An AEU by Calhoun reads: "Mr. Jewett of N[ew] York." No correspondence concerning an invitation to Calhoun to the "Bunker Hill celebration" has been found.

"Cosine," Dexter, Jefferson County, N.Y., to [Joseph A. Scoville,] "Editor of the Spectator," Washington, [5/3]. "Cosine" avows his political adherence to Calhoun's Presidential campaign and describes the anti-Van Buren sentiment in the States along the Canadian border, from N.Y. to Michigan. A major part of his letter is a complaint against John F. Hutchinson, the postmaster of Watertown, N.Y., who, according to "Cosine," got his appointment as a Whig but now claims to be a Calhoun supporter. Hutchinson is "the jest & the but[t] of the whole town—the laughing stock of even boys." "Cosine" does not seek any appointment for himself, only the removal of Hutchinson, lest he damage Calhoun's prospects in the region. ALS in ScCleA.

O[restes] A. Brownson to Dixon H. Lewis, Washington

[Boston, May 4?, 1843]

Dear Sir, I owe you a thousand apologies, and if I could see you I could make a thousand[,] any one of which would be satisfactory to you. I have been out of health all the past year, and able to perform no more labor than what I was obliged to do to get the bare necessaries of life for myself and family. Let this be some [e]xcuse for me. Sickness and poverty are two hard masters, and I have had to serve both.

I want to write some for the Spectator, but I want to write as a correspondent, so that I may write as I please. I send you the enclosed [*not found*]. I hope you will insert it, for it tells the truth, but I do not wish you to endorse it. I understood from Mr. Colvill [*sic*; Joseph A. Scoville] that you did not hold yourselves responsible for correspondents. My belief is that Martin [Van Buren] must be frightened off the course. He cannot be elected without Mr. Calhoun's friends, and I wish him to feel that there [is] some uncertainty about his getting ["this" *altered to* "their"] support in case he gets the nomination. If you insert ["this"(?) *altered to* "the"] enclosed you will hear from me again. Yours with great Respect, O.A. Brownson.

ALS in ScCleA. Note: This undated letter has been provided with a date from its nearly illegible postmark.

O[restes] A. Brownson to Dixon H. Lewis, Washington

[Boston,] May the 5, 1843
Dear Sir, In addition to what I have said elsewhere, if you will contrive to get me in a few days a copy of Mr. Calhoun's Speeches, I will review them & his the Life in the Democratic Review.

Are not the Speeches published?

Mr. [Joseph A.] Scovill[e] requested me to write a review of the Life of Mr. Calhoun for the Spectator. I can not do it, as that paper is Mr. C[alhoun]'s organ. It is an awkward place in which to review his Life, and moreover I have not time to do it as I wish to, independent of my contributions to the Democratic Review.

Mr. Scovill[e] also requested me to furnish a ["feature"(?) *canceled*] column or two of matter a week for the Spectator. My will is good enough, but I find that my literary engagements are already so great, that I must not form any new ones, in my present state of health. But if the paper is open to me, so I can write when the *fit* is on me, you may perhaps hear from me quite often. I can no more write on compulsion than old Jack Falstaff could give reasons. You will get more out of me if you do not ask regular contributions than if you do.

Mr. Van Buren must not be president come what may; Mr. Calhoun must be, if possible. Here is my political creed. I have a deep seated, thorough, inveterate dislike to the Dutchman. I will cut my right hand off sooner than vote for him. Do in common charity give me an opportunity now and then to hit him under the fifth rib. It will improve my morale, especially my digestion. I have never forgiven him for embroiling General [Andrew] Jackson and Mr. Calhoun. I detest his namby-pamby betweentity [*sic*] Democracy, and his miserable policy of always floating on the surface of his party and taking any direction that it gives him. I could be eloquent in denouncing him.

But help me to a copy of the Speeches at the earliest possible moment. Yours truly, O.A. Brownson.

P.S. If you should feel that the publication of the communication I have sent would do harm to our cause throw [it] into the fire by all means, for we have too much at stake to risk any thing on the gratification of personal vanity. Soften any [e]xpression that you think too severe. O.A.B.

ALS in ScCleA.

From J[ohn] S. Barbour

Warrenton [Va.,] May 6th 1843

My Dear Sir, The Judge adhered to the opinion expressed the 19th April, and refused to allow the funds to be lent out of the State, or in any other way than on real estate security according to the terms of a decree made in Feb[ruar]y 1837. This had been departed from in two cases since that time, so far as to dispense with security on real estate. Your name has not been mentioned to the Court nor to any one else except to my wife [Elizabeth A. Byrne Barbour] & son [John S. Barbour, Jr.]. The decision of the Judge was made on the application of Colo[nel J.B.] Hogan, & it was urged by me in his case with all the zeal & exertion I could exert, & on your account much more than on his. Finding the Judge immoveable on this point I then endeavoured to obtain a decree paying to my wife 10,000$ of the money on deposit as interest due her and the Judge immediately said he w[oul]d do so if he could. Until late to day I hoped that this w[oul]d be done & then 5,000$ of that could be lent without the trouble of going before the Court[.]

The Judge made an order directing a master in Chancery to report to him on this point forthwith, and on the return of that report 5,000$ can be had on your Bond—possibly 7,000$. The period of this loan will be indefinite—["B" *canceled*] But six months['] notice ["upon a call for payment" *interlined*] shall be given. This money can be had the 1st Monday in July and there cannot be a doubt of it. Nor will it be necessary to come for it, or do any t[h]ing else than send the Bond on receipt of the money. This sum is no part of the trust within the power of the Court. The Judge intimated that he might hold a special Court before the 1st Monday in July. If so I will write again before I leave here. But there is no doubt of it on or before the 1st Monday in July.

I deeply regret this disappointment. All the spring the Judge was in Richmond & Fred[ericksbur]g, and was not in his circuit until a few days before the 19th April. It was not possible for me to know earlier, that any objection could arise—and the two precedents to which I have referred, justified me in the belief that real Estate security w[oul]d be dispensed with. I will write you before (or when) the Court adjourns[.] Mr. [Thomas G.] Clemson will explain all to you that I may have omitted.

In haste with Great Respect & Regard, Y[ou]rs faithfully, J.S. Barbour.

[P.S.] It was thought best to get Mrs. Barbour[']s written assent & my Son[']s to your having the funds in loan in preference to any other, & for this reason they were informed of your wishes. To no one else [was the subject mentioned]. Nor will it be mentioned when the 5,000 ["$" *interlined*] are had. If any thing further occurs I will write you instantly. No part of the money on deposit will be let out until the special term. J.S.B.

ALS in ScCleA. NOTE: An AEU by Calhoun reads: "Ans[were]d 8th June."

LEVI WOODBURY to [Joseph A. Scoville?, Washington,] "Private"

Portsmouth [N.H.], 6 May 1843
Dear Sir, I thank you for the friendly feelings exhibited in yours of the 3d inst[ant]. It will not be in my power to attend at Poughkepsiee, and probably it would injure the cause much, out as well as in my own State, were I to adopt a course so unusual in this region, as for a candidate for a high office ["or one of the candidates" *inter-*

lined] to take the field in person or exert an active part in the election. Nothing could be more fatal under our New H[ampshire] notions & habits.

But all, which can be suggested to friends, will be done cheerfully, where likely to do good.

The democratic papers in this State, a list of which you desire, are the New H[ampshire] Gazette at Portsm[ou]th, the Dover Gazette at Dover, the two Patriots at Concord, the Manchester Democrat at Manchester, the Argus at Newport, the Museum at Keene, the Dem[ocratic] Republican at Haverhill and the Coos County Democrat, at Lancaster. There is, also, one at Nashua, called, I believe, the Republican, & one at Guilford, the Belknap Gazette.

But nothing can be done here thro[ugh] the Press, except in *following* Conventions—State, County & District. The People here speak only that way & now our local divisions are very unfavorable to any new action or exertion & the Presses have got so committed on them, they fear any difference as to other matters. The [Charleston] Mercury as well as you overrate my influence at this moment—& at no time does any one man ever exercise half the *personal* influence in New England, which he often does South & West. Respectfully, Levi Woodbury.

ALS in ScCleA.

GEO[RGE] W. CHAYTOR to J[oseph] A. Scoville, Washington

Wilmington [Del.,] May ["8th" *changed to* "7th"] 1843
Dear Sir, Your communication of the 3rd inst[ant] would have met earlier attention had I not been absent from the city for several days & but just returned.

With regard to the [Wilmington?] Aurora it *will* support Mr. [John C.] Calhoun for the nomination. I have ever regarded Mr. C[alhoun] as one of our very ablest statesmen as well as one of the truest patriots of our country. It has ever been ["a" *canceled*] my desire to see him at the head of the government and if his friends are only true & *cautious*, I have not the least doubt but that *desire* will be realized. We have however much to contend with, & cunning and able opponents to frustrate. To do this, the greatest caution is necessary, both with regard to committees & presses. Since my residence in this State, I have ever made it a rule to bring his name before the people as much as possible, in all the address[es] which I have made. In fact so pointed was I in a speech made in this county [New Castle] last year, that the whig press attacked me openly as his champion in Delaware. I did this, the rather, as through me W[illia]m Hemphill Jones Esq[ui]r[e] was nominated for Congress in opposition to the Van Buren faction, & my object was to make him commit himself in favor of Calhoun—he being one of the strongest men of the Democratic party in the State—in which I partly succeeded.

Such being the case, it would be strange that a press under my controll would support any one else. The knowledge of this very fact is operating against the Aurora at present, and was the only cause why the paper was not issued at the time the prospectus named. The friends of [Martin] Van Buren are the *monied* portion of our community, and consequently have a great influence in such cases. I hope however to be able in a short time to make the necessary arrangements.

With regard to your organization in *every* State it seems to me you have overlooked little Del. as I know of ["not" *changed to* "no"] organization, except such as I have temperally made. The system, I am now about adopting, is to form each Hundred into private lodges, so as to effect the appointment of delegates to the national Convention, who are ["favorably known" *changed to* "favorable"] to Mr. C[alhoun] and I have not the least doubt that we shall be successfull.

The important post offices are at this place[,] Dover and Georgetown, but every office is of importance. The post masters of these named are all whigs, and under the immediate control of John M. Clayton; as is the case with nearly every office in the State—there is not a Calhoun man in any one of them to my knowledge. On this I will write you more at large hereafter.

There is not a *Democratic* paper in the State, though the [Wilmington] Gazette professes to be such. Its principle proprietor is a whig, and it is under the controll of the Van B[uren] faction. There is a paper to be started at George Towne to support [Lewis] Cass in opposition to the Aurora.

I am more or less acquainted with every leading Democrat in the State, and have pleasure in stating that there are some of them who seem of late to lean towards Calhoun. But not so decide[d]ly favorable as to be too far trusted ["at" *interlined*] present. In a few months I shall be able to give you a different account I hope. On this I shall again take occassion to be more full.

There has been no time fixed for a State Convention. There is no

167

Central Committee in the State, proper. I am the Chairman of the Corresponding Committee of the Democratic Association of this County & the only decided friend of Mr. C[alhoun] though Mr. Jones leans that way & may be obtained by proper means.

I have thus rapidly answered all our questions though not as fully as I could have wished owing to several letter[s] on my table which must be attended to to night. What-ever it is in my power to do, you may depend shall be done to forward the views of Mr. C[alhoun] & it would give me great pleasure to to hear further from you & cooperate with your Committee. With great respect &c I remain &c, Geo. W. Chaytor, M.D.

ALS in ScCleA. NOTE: It seems likely that the proposed newspaper, "the Aurora," was never published.

John Hogan, Utica, N.Y., to Dixon H. Lewis, Washington, 5/8. Hogan sends to Lewis a copy of a letter he has written to Democratic friends in Rochester and says that he has written twenty letters "this day" to different parts of the State where close elections [of State convention delegates] will take place. Hogan has had "to labour like a slave in the matter to rally our men & have them act in concert." ALS in ScCleA.

From EDMUND S. DERRY

New York [City,] May 9, 1843

Dear Sir, Without other introduction than that which the object of this communication may afford, I have taken the liberty of addressing you; trusting that my desire to serve you may form a sufficient apology for the want of a formal introduction, which under other circumstances, I should have felt bound to have procured, before claiming your attention.

As you may have perceived[,] a Strong and unconcealed determination exists in our City, to afford to you every facility and to secure to you every just advantage, in presenting your claims, to the Presidency, before the National Convention. The friends of Mr. [Martin] Van Buren have been greatly surprized at the numbers and daring of those who will support you—and they are much more cautious in developing their plans, than they had intended to be. Were they not fearful of the rapid spread of disaffection to Mr. V[an] Buren, the Albany recommendation would have been sternly carried into effect, but they have been alarmed at the supineness and bad judgment of their leaders and at the determination and vigilance of your friends—the most that they have yet attempted in this City, is the assural [*sic*] in part only, of that which had been decreed at Albany to be forced upon the People. It is well understood that the Syracuse Convention will yield to the assembling of the National Convention in May '44. The people already discover the weakness from which this concession so speedily springs, and they cannot avoid believing that, if Mr. Van Buren is unable to carry out the recommendation of his friends, as to an earlier day; if he withdraw submissively from that point, which until lately he was so strenuous to claim, his popularity has been most eggregiously [*sic*] over estimated. All acknowledge that the Albany movement was illy advised for Mr. Van Buren—but most serviceable to you.

The many advantages which now present themselves, by which the current of popular feeling in our City might be directed to your benefit—it would be shameful to allow to pass unimproved. We are wanting only in a system of action to enable us to obtain a strong foothold in our City. This we can have, if your friends were but properly organized—under the direction of some of your most trustworthy friends here—men of well known devotion to the Democratic party. There are many such who could be selected and in whom the most implicit confidence might safely be reposed. Strong in the number of such would be those of Irish birth and descent—with an influence controlling 5000 votes in the City, they are more ardent and ["they are equally" *canceled*] powerful ["than"(?) *canceled*] than any other body of our fellow citizens. Their admiration for your character and talents as freely expressed, they regard Mr. Van Buren as a mechanical President, one whose heart never yet betrayed, towards them a generous impulse, one who has made himself the confidant of their worst enemies and as one in no degree an admirer of their Country or themselves. They are devoted to you and so far as their adherence to the man whom they admire, can avail—it will neither secretly nor ["fearfu" *canceled*] timidly ["be" *interlined*] evinced—they need only to be shewn how they may prove their sincerity—and it will stand any test to which it may be submitted.

I know, from report, of your elevated disregard of these minor arrangements, which will become necessary, if your friends are to hope, in any decided manner, to urge, from this City your claims to the Presidency. I ask no confidence to be reposed in me—a stranger—but I am conscious that the present favorable state of affairs, should be rendered still more auspicious to you. Silent friends—men who will

169

vote for you or for committees ["favorable to" *canceled and* "to support" *interlined*] you are not the only ones who now should be got together. We require men who can plan and guide—men of influence and respectability, who will have your confidence and that of your friends throughout the States. Possibly we New Yorkers consider our City as of more importance than it really is—but we are vain enough to believe, that we exercise an influence beyond our own City[']s limits. If this be true—and of it you can determine—how essential is it that we should have a ["compact" *canceled*] body of good advisers ["here" *canceled*]—ready for any emergency which may arise, and to whom your friends would look for that direction which the future arrangements of the party may render necessary. I have waited to see whether your more immediate ["personal" *interlined*] friends would make any movement, towards establishing a concert of action—but I confess—that I have been surprized at their remissness. I am anxious to aid you and them so far as I can do it, but I know not with whom to consult, in confidence that I and those who may act with me will be directed ["in a manner" *interlined*] to meet your wishes. May I ask, (with a sincere apology for my lengthy epistle,) that you will furnish me with the names of some of those in this City, to whom you entrust the control of matters connected with the approaching presidential contest and such other *general* directions as you may ["com"(?) *canceled*] deem it adviseable to communicate to me. With much respect I have the honor to be Your obe[dient] Serv[an]t, Edmund S. Derry.

ALS in ScCleA. Note: An AEU by Calhoun reads: "Mr. Derry of N[ew] York[,] Ans[were]d 7th June."

To Ed[ward] Everett,
[U.S. Minister to Great Britain, London]

Fort Hill, 9th May 1843

My dear Sir, This will be handed you by the Rev[eren]d Mr. [Charles C.] Pinckney, to whom I take much pleasure in introducing you.

He is a highly respectable clergyman of the Episcopal C[h]urch; and when I ad[d], that his father is the son of Gen[era]l Thomas Pinckney, & the Nephew of Gen[era]l Charles Cotesworth Pinckney, I feel assured, I need not add another word to ensure your kind attention to him, while on his sojourn in London & England. With great respect yours truly, J.C. Calhoun.

ALS in MHi, Edward Everett Papers (published microfilm, reel 20, frame 266).

To Joseph H. Hedges, Philadelphia, 5/9. "I have no copy of the Speech to which you refer; but the Harpers of N[ew] York are publishing a volume of my speeches which will contain it, and which I presume will shortly be out." ALS in ScU-SC, John C. Calhoun Papers.

To R[OBERT] M. T. HUNTER, [Lloyds, Va.?]

Fort Hill, 9th May 1843

My dear Sir, I deeply regret to learn by the last mail the certainty of your defeat. I regret it every way; on your account, and the account of the cause & Country. Your presence in the next Congress was every way important. There is none whose absence would be more severely felt. But let me intreat you to be neither disgusted, nor discouraged. On the contrary rouse yourself to greater exertions and energy. The times call on every citizen, who loves his country, & every son of the South, who regards the safety of his section, to do his utmost. More depends for weal or woe on the turn, which events may now take, than can well be told.

I see the loss, as far as Congress is concerned, falls mainly on our friends. Things have been so managed, that yourself, & [William O.] Goode, & [Francis] Mallory & [William] Smith [all of whom had been Representatives from Va. during 1841–1843] are safriced [*sic;* sacrificed]. Was it designed? Was the arrangement of the Districts with that view? Is it a part of the wicked & foul policy of the N[ew] York school? Or was it accide[n]tal?

I must say, I fear it was the former. I know that [Thomas] Ritchie protests against it; but I have not the least faith in his protests. That he acts in strict concert with Albany I hold certain. The evidence is too strong to admit of doubt. And what is worse—what more infamous, he acts in strict subordination to the dictates of N[ew] York. He has put Virginia in a false position. Her true position is at the head of the South. He & his clique have selected the more humble one of sticking her on, as the tail [of] N[ew] York.

How do you account for the great strength which the whigs have exhibited at the election? Is it to be attributed to the tax bill? Or is it, that Virginia is politically demoralized? I fear there is much in the latter. There is ["in truth" *interlined*] much in her N[ew] York association to demoralize her. I fear unless vigorous efforts should be made to restore her to her true position, she will shortly be entirely lost to the State rights Republican side. If she is to be saved, it must be by the manly & vigorous efforts of ["the" *interlined*] younger portions of ["your" *canceled and* "her" *interlined*] population.

What is going to be the result of the election on the politicks of the State? Will it tend to throw the State more effectually into the hands of Ritchie, or not? What course will our friends take?

It seems to me, that [Henry A.] Wise's position is calculated to give him much increased strength. What will be his course? Will he act with our friends? It seems to me it is very important he should, and that pains ought to be taken to effect it. No one could do as much, in that respect, as yourself.

Write me fully & early on all points. Do not hesitate to make your letter full.

Our State Convention will meet on the 4th Monday in this month in Columbia. There is but one sentiment in the State as far as I am concerned. It will, I doubt not, take strong grounds on the subject of the Gen[era]l Convention. The more I reflect on the subject, the more I am satisfied of ["the" *canceled*] its dangerous tendency, and with my views, it will not be possible for me to permit my name to go before it, unless it should [be] satisfactorily formed on all essential points. Yours truly & sincerely, J.C. Calhoun.

ALS in DNA, RG 109 (War Department Collection of Confederate Records), Citizen File, R.M.T. Hunter.

From JOHN MCKEON,
[former Representative from N.Y.]

New York [City,] May 10, 1843

Dear Sir, I take great pleasure in presenting to you Mr. [Lathrop J.] Eddy of this City, one of your warm & I may add efficient supporters in this part of the Union. Mr. E[ddy] is a gentleman of character and standing and I commend him to your kind offices. With great respect I remain Your Obed[ient] S[ervant], John McKeon.

ALS in ScCleA.

From LATHROP J. EDDY

New York [City,] May 10th 1843

Sir, Enclosed you will find a letter of introduction with which the Hon. J[ohn] McKeon has been so kind as to favour me.

My anxiety to advance the interests of those great political principles of which I consider you the present most prominent & truthful representative, is my apology for the intrusion.

A majority of the younger democracy in this City & State conceive that if you are elected to the office of President, they will secure through your administration the perfection of political democracy [*ms. torn; one word missing*] we shall be resolute in securing jus[tice?] to you at the convention in '44.

But we meet with great opposition f[rom] the older members of our party who are desirous of restoring the [Martin] Van Buren dynasty and who at heart fear the bold support of democracy ["in its purity" *interlined*] which they have reason to know would characterize your administration.

Our first effort will be to obtain such a representation in our State Convention as will secure a Resolution to abide by the decision of the national Convention of '44; and in favour of the District representation in that convention.

You are doubtless advised of the strife in anticipation of such results, now existing in this City between the Free Trade Ass[ociatio]n & Young Men's General Com[mitte]e on the one side; and the Old Men's Com[mitte]e on the other.

But my object in now writing to you was not to give you information of our movements, but to urge on you the necessity of your visiting the north at an early day this Summer.

I am aware of the high stand taken by you in reference to a nomination—that it must to meet your views be the free will offering of the people and not the result of intrigue; and therefore you may feel reluctant to travel through the northern States at this period. But as chairman of the State Corresponding Com[mitte]e during the past year, I have had an opportunity of learning the feeling in the country in reference to you. A strong argument used against you and with much force, is that you have no feelings in common with us of the North—that your prepossessions & sympathies are exclusively Southern: and we find difficulty in meeting the assertion, made with truth, that, while in your public capacity, the interests of the whole Union have to a great degree been continually in your hands—you have allowed twenty two years to elapse without visiting those States where I believe a large numerical majority of your supporters reside, and whose interests you will be bound to protect if elected President. It is to remove this feeling—to satisfy the people by personal intercourse, that you are at heart American[,] that you regard the Union as a Union—and to ["remove" *interlined*] the lipservice which at best is all that Van Buren can obtain, by a service of the heart as well as the head, which we believe you could command.

As yet the north has only admired you in the distance—as a fearless supporter of democratic doctrines—but the intimate & almost social relation which must necessarily exist in a Republic between the people and their President, requires that we should know you more nearly & intimately, to call forth that ardour which is requisite to secure to you the support of the northern States, in opposition to the strong interest made for three northern candidates.

Consider Sir, that you come not on any personal mission, but at the command of your friends who have a right to require your cooperation [in] the furtherance of common sentiments.

You have very many & enthusiastic frie[nds] here & in the New England States, Pennsylvania[,] Mich[igan] &c, who will give you a cordial welcome.

Should you be desirous that any previous step be taken here, such as an invitation from a body of citizens, or a general meeting or otherwise, I shall be most happy to bring it about. I had proposed such a course to some of your supporters, but it was delayed until we could learn whether such a course would be gratifying to you. With high regard Yours &c, Lathrop J. Eddy.

ALS with En in ScCleA. Note: An AEU by Calhoun reads: "Mr. Eddy of New York introduced by Mr. McKeon."

N[oyes] Billings, Hartford, Conn., to [Joseph A. Scoville?], "Editor of the Spectator," Washington, 5/12. Billings requests a copy of "the Speech of Mr. Calhoun on the Tariff in Feb[ruar]y last [*sic*]" in order that he might refer to it. [Billings was a member of the Conn. House of Representatives.] ALS in ScCleA.

C[harles] A. Secor, New York [City], to Joseph A. Scoville, Washington, "Private," 5/12. Secor acknowledges receipt of Scoville's letter of 5/10 and avows that, despite lies "told you about my position," he is a loyal Calhoun supporter. He will represent his ward at the [N.Y. Democratic] Convention in Syracuse in September and will remain true to his pledges. He informs Scoville that "Micheal Walsh Esq[ui]r[e] is M[arshall] O. Robert['s] & R[obert] C. Wetmore[']s Cartman and does all the Carting for them for the Navy Yards. Now get the business from Robert if you can[,] Joe." ALS in ScCleA.

R[OBERT] M.T. H[UNTER] to Jos[eph] A. Scoville, Washington

[Lloyds, Va., May 13, 1843]

My dear Sir, I was so much away from home during my late canvass that I was unable to answer the letters which I received during that period. The unsuccessful termination of the canvass has diminished my chances of being useful to the cause but others will be found who can render more service. I wish I could ["go" *changed to* "visit"] Washington as you desire but I am so engaged just now with private business that it is impossible. I should have to learn the state of affairs from you and our other friends before I could be competent to advise. I have had nothing from [Dixon H.] Lewis since the first week after the last adjournment and nothing from ["any of" *interlined*] our friends except those in Va. We shall endeavor to organize here and do what we can to carry the State, but the last apportionment bill of our Legislature was a sad blow to the cause. We ought to avail ourselves of any favorable chance for a movement for [John C.] Calhoun. In Main[e,] N[ew] Hampshire and Connecticut our friends ought to move if they can [*one word changed to* "give"] the movement the proper direction but they should count beforehand and make no abortive efforts. As there is no central Committee in Washington the Committee in Charleston ought to open a general correspondence ["with the Calhoun Committees" *interlined*] throughout the Union. ["When" *changed to* "If"] we cannot obtain an expression of preference for Calhoun from a Convention or public meeting it will be something to get them to declare for May 1844 and a proper organization of the National Convention. And now for the [Washington] Spectator.

I fear that your prediction as to Southern Contributions will prove true. Subscribers are all we can hope in that quarter and I fear they will be few. Indeed the times are exceedingly hard and there is a great reluctance to taking papers. I sent some of the prospectus to persons who I thought could get subscribers but I do not know the result. I have a parcel of receipts for subscriptions[;] these I shall burn as it will be taxing you with too much postage to return them and my franking privilege I believe is out. Will you ascertain the construction of the Law at the P[ost] O[ffice] Dept. for me without calling my name? I am much obliged to you for your though[t]fulness of my interest in your preparation as to the Spectator. But the plan will not answer for many reasons both political and private. My attention to my ["private" *canceled*] affairs at home for a while is now indispensable and in a private point of view my defeat was fortunate to me. If I had now the command of money I could be of use to the cause in many ways, but I must do what I can with such means as I have. In your editorials you ought to beware of attacking your Democratic [*ms. torn; word missing*] Except when self defence makes it indispensable. Nor should you attack [Martin] Van Buren. There was an article in your last [*one word changed to* "in"] relation to V[an] B[uren]'s response to the I[ndian]a Committee which squinted that way. You ought to group all the evidence of public sentiment in favor of Mr. C[alhoun] or of the proper time and mode of the convention so to produce as much effect as possible. You ought also to make the Tariff question prominent and evidences of its hardships or of disaffection to it particularly in the commercial cities will be very useful. If you can possibly do so I should be very glad to see you *here*. The Rappahannock steamboat comes around once a week from Baltimore and if you would let me know[?] beforehand I would meet you at Laytons which is a stopping place on the river. Yours truly, R.M.T.H.

ALI in ScCleA.

From JAMES P. LOWRY

Houston (Texas), May 13th 1843

Dear Sir, In the year 1838 I saw and became acquainted with you in Washington City, and now take the liberty, upon that slight acquaintance, of asking at your hands a favor.

I have a friend, or relation in a mexican prison, in chains and subjected to the most servile labors, under task masters who are not, in the scale of human beings, above your slaves.

He has past the meridian of life & has a large and interesting family dependant on his personal exertions for subsistence. His name, John M. Bradley, a native of Abingdon Virginia. He was captured last fall in defending manfully what he regarded as an invasion, not only of his personal rights, but the rights of his adopted Country. The fortunes of war placed [him] in the hands of the Mexicans. If it is the policy of the United States Government and other civilized Gover[n]-ments to look tamely and quietly upon the violations of all civilized warfare committed by the dastardly and semi-barbarous Mexicans, I hope there are some philanth[r]opists who will at least use their individual exertions to ameliorate the condition of those who have had the misfortune to fall into their hands.

Then Sir, to you who has been my model in politics and for whose private virtues I have ever had the highest regard, I appeal for an interference in behalf of my friend. Write to the President [John] Tyler, or to Gen[era]l [Waddy] Thompson [Jr., U.S. Minister to Mexico], or to both and get them interested for him and I feel certain that by a concentration of their influence upon his case, his release can be effected, where if they continue the attempt to procure the discharge of all at once, they will fail on all. If you will attend to this application you will secure the gratitude of a most interesting family, and will always be regarded as a benefactor of mankind by your most Ob[edien]t Serv[an]t, James P. Lowry.

ALS in DNA, RG 59 (Records of the Department of State), Miscellaneous Letters of the Department of State, 1789–1906 (M-179:102, frames 19–22). NOTE: This letter was postmarked in Mobile, Ala., on 5/20.

From GEORGE BOOKER

Hampton Va., May 14th 1843

My Dear Sir, I know of no one in this section of the State, who is in correspondence with you. The lively interest I feel in your future prospects must be my apology for troubling you with a short letter upon the subject of our late elections. The Whigs have made a gallant effort to carry the State[;] the struggle was one of the severest I ever witnessed[.] It appears that we have lost ground since the last spring elections. Our majority on joint ballot will be about 20. Last year it was 42. We shall have 11 members of Congress—perhaps 3 of the seats contested, [Thomas W.] Gilmer's, [John W.] Jones'es [*sic,*] and [Archibald] Atkinson's the Norfolk district.

Upon the whole we look upon the result as descidedly [*sic*] favourable to your friends. Their strength will be considerably increased in the next assembly, and confidence will be inspired. Firmness has alone been wanting among your friends to insure the vote of the State for you in the National Convention.

The [Martin] Van Buren men have changed their tone very much[;] they talk about a late day for the National Convention and Compromise and Concession[.] They are evidently alarmed at the state of things, their organ the [Richmond] Enquirer is humbled & subdued. No one understands better than Mr. [Thomas] Ritchie the causes which have lead to this state of things. He knows that the Whigs have not increased in strength in any district of the State, that the jealousy between the Calhoun & Van Buren men[,] the seeds of which were plentifully sowed by the ill-timed and illiberal proceedings of the Richmond Convention in March[,] has produced these results.

The firm & descided tone of the Charleston Mercury[,] the Washington Spectator and other journals friendly to you are producing happy effects[.] We have nothing to loose [*sic,*] every thing to gain by a firm and descided stand.

Mr. [John] Tyler is here on a visit to his home. I understand that he is full of *hope* for the future.

You have seen Mr. Van Buren's electione[e]ring *essay* to the Indiana State Convention. Very Sincerely Y[ou]rs[?] Se[rvant], George Booker.

ALS in ScCleA. NOTE: An AEU by Calhoun reads: "Mr. Booker[,] Not answered."

From SIMEON B. JEWETT

14 May 1843, Clarkson[,] Monroe Co[unty,] N.Y. *Dear Sir,* I wrote you some days since & mailed the letter to Charleston, learning from some source you were there, or would be very soon.

Since the date of that letter, I have past [*sic*] through many portions of this State, and have had full & free interchange of views and wishes with many of our most influential and prominent democratic friends in relation to the time of holding the National Convention, and the manner of appointing delegates to that convention. Much to my surprise, but to my great satisfaction I learnt the feeling of the people to be entirely almost averse to the recommendations of the Legislative caucus at Albany the 17 of April last. The Convention which that caucus called to be held at Syracuse next September will fix the time of the National Convention May 1844, and what is equally, and perhaps of more importance to the success of the democratic cause, that convention will recommend the appointment of delegates by congressional districts.

The Stand taken by your friends and the opponents of Mr. [Martin] Van Buren have [*sic*] forced the friends of the latter to yield a reluctant assent. Many of the democratic journals over the State have taken decided and open ground against the *caucus* recommendations.

If the public feeling continues to increase, in the direction it has been running the last two months, with the same force, Mr. Van Buren will not get the nomination of this State, even at the Syracuse Convention—but on the contrary the democracy will nominate their distinguished Statesman of South Carolina.

In this State there are no other candidates before the public, but yourself and Mr. Van Buren—the contest will be between you two. Indeed there is no other candidate, that can get a single delegate.

You could render the democracy essential aid by a personal visit during July and August to Saratoga Springs and a trip upon the line of the Erie Canal, West to Niagara Falls. The great Mass of the people would be pleased to do honor to yourself. You would excite a deep interest which would materially aid the efforts of your friends. There can be no objection to your visiting the residence and family fire side of your opponent. Your Ob[edient] S[e]r[vant], Simeon B. Jewett.

ALS in ScCleA. NOTE: An AEU by Calhoun reads: "Mr. Jewett[,] Answered 7th June 1843."

To A[NDREW] P[ICKENS] CALHOUN,
Faunsdale (Marengo County), Ala.

Fort Hill, 16th May 1843

My dear Andrew, I wrote to you some time since, that Mr. [Thomas G.] Clemson had left for Virginia to attend to the loan, that Mr. [John S.] Barbour informed me I could have of funds coming to his minor children, and which would be lent under the decree[?] of the court in this month.

He has returned without succeeding, as the court decided against lending it out of the State, ["and" *canceled*] or lending it within it, except on Mortgage on real estate. The decision was made on the application of a relation of Mrs. Barbour from Alabama to whom it was proposed to loan a part of the funds, and my name did not appear connected with the subject. It is unfortunate we could not obtain the funds[;] it would have suited us every way.

In my letter, I advised you not to commence your journey here 'till you again heard from me, as it was quite uncertain when Mr. Clemson would be back, and I now write to say that it is so late in the season, that you had better now ["to" *canceled*] postpone ["it" *canceled and* "your visit" *interlined*] till your crop is sufficiently advanced ["as" *canceled*] not to make your presence necessary, & then to ["come" *canceled*] make your arrangement to come with Margaret [Green Calhoun] & your family prepared to spend the summer with us. We will all rejoice to have you with us, and you & she will find the relaxation and change of scene, in addition to the pleasure of the visit, not unfavourable to your health. If her sister [Eliza M. Green?] should be with you, we would expect her to accompany you. When you come, bring every thing necessary to a full settlement and closing [of] our transaction with Mr. Clemson, and among others a conveyance in blank of his third of the tract to us to be signed by him; and also all that is necessary for a full settlement between you & myself.

I am glad to hear that your crop has started so well, & that the price of land keeps up so high in the vincity [*sic*; vicinity]. It speaks much for the location. I trust we are now through the pressure, and with the rise, that must take place in Cotton, and our fall preparation to make the article, that we shall find no difficulty in making payments.

My crop of corn, cotton & small grain is very promising.

If the season holds out, I shall not fall short of 1000 weight in the seed[?] per acre round. I made last year from 50 acres, of which 8 or 10 were old & inferior nearly 12,500 pounds of pick cotton. The stand & the bud[?] in this year are better than the last.

[All join] their love to you, ["&" *canceled*] Margaret & [the family] with our respects to Miss Eliza [M. Green], if with you. Your affectionate father, J.C. Calhoun.

[P.S.] Let me know in your next when I may expect you.

ALS in ScU-SC, John C. Calhoun Papers.

To R[OBERT] M. T. HUNTER,
Lloyds (Essex County), Va.

Fort Hill, 16th May 1843

My dear Sir, I wrote you as soon as I heard of the result of your election and expressed my deep regret, at your defeat. I hope you have received my letter, and that you have not permitted your sperits to flag in consequence of defeat.

I now write principally to say, that I received by the last mail a letter from [John] H[e]art, from which I fear, that the Spectator concern is becoming confused and embarrassed. He is very discontented with [Joseph A.] Scoville's course, who I fear is rash and imprudent, though I cannot doubt his Zeal & honesty in the cause. I wrote to [Virgil] Maxcy, & enclosed, in confidence, H[e]art's letter, and said to him, that I relied on him and other friends at Washington to take steps to put the paper on some solid basis; and also informed him, that I would write to you & express a hope, that you would visit Washington as early as possible, & cooperate with him, which I now do. I regard it of vital importance, that some effectual step ["may" *canceled and* "should" *interlined*] be taken, to place it on such foundation. It took its cour[s]e without consulting me; but now that it has taken it, & come out for me, it would, indeed, be unfortunate, if it should fall, or be misconducted. I have no doubt, that ample funds could be had in this State to sustain it, if there was sufficient confidence inspired in its stability & good management. Measures have already been taken in Charleston, I understand with considerable success, to sustain it, & still more efficient, I hope, will be taken, when the Convention of the State meets on Monday next at Columbia. If some able & trust worthy editor cannot be obtained, it would probably be as well to leave it in the ["Hart" *canceled*] hands of Mr. H[e]art, for the present at least, who, as far as I know, is ["a" *interlined*] worthy man, of respectable understanding & much prudence. What are our friends doing in Virginia, or propose to do? And what is the prospect in the State? Will [Thomas] Ritchie and his clique be able to have every thing in their own way? I see he has endorsed [Martin] Van Buren's letter to the Indiana Committee. He is certainly easily pleased on the Tariff ["subject" *interlined*], if he is satisfied with it. It is studiously ambiguous, but it says enough to show, that there is but little difference between his opinion & Mr. [Henry] Clay's, as expressed in his Speech before he left the Senate.

I hope the Convention to meet next week at Columbia will put out an able address and take strong, ["&" *canceled*] but prudent grounds, on the subject of the Convention. It is time that we should show distinctly, on what grounds we intend to stand. If my friends would consult my feelings, they would not yield a single ["gr"(?) *canceled*] inch of principle, or a point of policy of any importance, to win victory. It is better, in my opinion, to be defeated maintaining the true & the right, than to succeed on any other ground. But I deem it not only the honest and patriotick course, but the one, which wisdom & policy dictate. So strong is my impression, in favour of its expediency, that I firmly believe, if we adhere inflexably to the right & true, victory is almost certain; and if not defeat is not less so.

Do write me fully on all points at your early convenience.

[Romulus M.] Saunders writes in good sperits, from North Carolina. All South is sound, and more united than it has been for many years. Truly, J.C. Calhoun.

ALS in ViU, Hunter-Garnett Papers (published microfilm, reel 3, frames 166–167).

Advertisement by the Board of Trustees of the Pendleton Male Academy, 5/19. The trustees announce that they have contracted with R[obert] M. Renick, a graduate of West Point, to conduct the Academy beginning in July. In addition to an English and classical curriculum, the Academy will offer courses in French, chemistry, surveying, civil engineering, and physics. The Trustees signing include: F[rancis] K. Huger, J[ohn] C. Calhoun, F[rederick] W. Symmes, J[oseph] V. Shanklin, J[esse] P. Lewis, Ja[me]s Stuart, R[obert] A. Maxwell, T[homas] M. Sloan, and O[zey] R. Broyles. PC in the Charleston, S.C., *Mercury*, May 30, 1843, p. 3, and several subsequent issues; PC in the Pendleton, S.C., *Messenger*, June 2, 1843, p. 3, and several subsequent issues.

To A[NDREW] P[ICKENS] CALHOUN, [Marengo County, Ala.]

Fort Hill, 21st May 1843

My dear Andrew, I wrote you immediately after Mr. [Thomas G.] Clemson's return, which was much sooner than expected, and I hope you got my letter in the due course of the mail, & in time for Margaret [Green Calhoun] to accompany you. Your letter of the 9th Inst[ant] gave the first intelligence we had, that she was in the family way, & near her confinement; and we would all very greatly regret not to have her with us, and for you & her to spend the summer with us; and I do hope that my last letter ["arrive(d) in time &" *interlined*] will induce you to reverse your decision.

I am gratified to hear, that your crop has started so finely. Mine has also made a fine start, and ["the cotton" *interlined*] was as forward on the 19th when I got your letter as yours was on the 9th when it was written. The start however has been bad generally in the State owing to dry weather.

We are all well & all join their love to you, Margaret & Duff [Green Calhoun], & their respects to Miss Eliza [M. Green] if with you. Your affectionate father, J.C. Calhoun.

ALS in ScU-SC, John C. Calhoun Papers.

From P. Roman Steck

Cumberland [Md.,] 21st May 1843

Sir: You will percieve [*sic*] by the papers accompan[y]ing this, that I have commenced a new paper in this place, for the purpose of advocating your claims for the next Presidency, which I hope will meet with your approbation.

The primary object in addressing this letter to you, is, to enquire, whether you will abide by the Decision of a Democratic National Convention? Your answer shall be *private*, or otherwise, as you may deem best.

The "Gazette" is the only paper friendly to your nomination in this, (notwithstanding your friends are more numerous than ["any" *canceled*] that of any other person spoken of for the Presidency) State, and any documents you will be kind enough to send ["you" *canceled*] me, will be very acceptable. Your Ob[edien]t Se[r]v[an]t, P. Roman Steck, Ed[itor,] Maryland Gazette.

ALS in ScU-SC, John C. Calhoun Papers. NOTE: This letter was addressed to Calhoun erroneously at Fort Hill, "York County, S.C."

Harper & Bro[ther]s to V[irgil] Maxcy, West River, Md.

New York [City,] May 22d 1843

D[ea]r Sir, Yours of the 18th by Col. B—— [Daniel D. Brodhead] is at hand.

Not hearing any thing about the proof sheets of the "Speeches" for so long a time—and being anxious to bring them out as early as possible—we put the stereotype plates to press, and commenced printing from them several days since. We are glad that there are so few Errors—and those as unimportant as they seem to be. They will be corrected however before printing off any more. The Speeches make

554 pp. and are all stereotyped. We have directed the remainder of the proof sheets to be forwarded to you—but presuming there will be but little or nothing to correct in them, we shall proceed with the printing, and endeavour to bring them out with as little delay as may be.

Our silence on the subjects referred to must be attributed to the agency of Mr. S—— [Joseph A. Scoville.] We communicated to and with him as occasion offered, and supposed that he had kept you advised of our movements. The directions referred to, as having been sent us through him, in relation to blanking out the pages, at the close of the Speeches, the running heads, &c. &c. (and we suspect other matters), were never communicated to us. It is now too late to make the alterations.

Upon the publication of the "Life" we sent it to the principal cities of the different States, and to all by whom it was ordered—and are prepared to supply further orders to any extent upon the most reasonable terms. We have been somewhat surprised that more have not been ordered. A considerable part of those sent to Washington remain yet unpaid for. A number of gentlemen have *talked* about taking quantities—but that's all. Had Col. Brodhead, for instance, been anxious to take some on with him to Boston, he could have been supplied—but he did not ask for them. The only way in which they can be scattered extensively is, *by gratuitous circulation,* and we hope something may yet be done in this way.

We are not sorry to learn, that we are to correspond directly with you hereafter—and shall be happy to hear from you frequently on the subject, and to have you make such suggestions as will tend to promote the object had in view in publishing the Life and Speeches of Mr. Calhoun. Respectfully, Y[ou]r Obliged Servants, Harper & Bro's.

LS in DLC, Galloway-Maxcy-Markoe Papers, vol. 47. Note: Part of this letter is written on a printed subscription blank dated 1/1843, which offers the *Life* at $80 per 1,000 copies "with Portrait," at $60 per 1,000 "with covers, without Portrait," and at $50 per 1,000 "without covers or Portrait."

From ALFRED SCHÜCKING

Washington, May 22d 1843

Dear Sir: Hearing that my present position here may be misrepresented to you, if I may suppose that you deem my course worthy of your attention, ["induces me" *canceled*] I am induced, to take the liberty of addressing these lines to you directly.

The establishment of the "German in America," a widely circulated German paper, of which I took charge in March last, has been removed to this place, and the paper is now published here in connection with the weekly "German National Gazette," a paper, which has declared itself in favour of Jno. Tyler as a Candidate for the next Presidency. Since the publication here in such a character *my name has been withdrawn from the paper*, as, with due deference to all that is estimable in the conduct of the present Executive, I do by no means consider him a fit individual to fill that exalted place.

The Germans also will not be forced into a predilection for him; all efforts to that effect are almost universally met with ridicule. On the contrary we have been called upon (amongst others by some very influential Germans of Richmond, Va., and of Philadelphia and New York) to place your name, highly esteemed by all Germans, at the head of our columns.

In truth, Sir, I am loth of eulogizing John Tyler, where I can not do so from conviction, and nothing would give me greater pleasure, than to be able to speak my heart[']s sentiments in giving vent to that *enthusiasm*, which nothing restrains me from ["to say" *canceled and* "saying," *interlined*] I entertain for you.

But I have no means at present, to gratify this desire, though I would with great pleasure embark a fortune in its accomplishment. The patronage which it is in the power of government to bestow, has, I believe, (for I speak without the advice of the publisher) solely forced him, to insist upon our declaration for Mr. Tyler. I am casting round for a total disconnection from this establishment, which (I can say without transgressing modesty) would seriously if not fatally injure it; and for the establishment under my exclusive control of a paper here, going hand in hand with the "*Spectator*." I can hardly look for this purpose to your friends here; for they seem now to look at me with distrust. But should you think it feasible & proper to influence them so as to come to my assistance, ["a" *canceled and* "one" *interlined*] thousand dollars would suffice to set up a paper here; the rest would be done by the Germans, who generally are very fond of you. In the mean while permit me to ask you to consider this letter as strictly confidential. Should you see fit to honour me with a communication, direct or by your friends here, I should be very happy to know that I am not looked at with distrust on account of my apparent course here. I am, Sir[,] very respectfully Your very humble & ob[e]d[ien]t serv[an]t, Alfred Schücking.

ALS in ScU-SC, John C. Calhoun Papers. NOTE: Calhoun endorsed this letter: "Mr. Shücking[,] German news paper[,] not ans[were]d."

From THOMAS P. TEALE

New York [City,] May 22nd 1843
Dear Sir, As president of a Democratic Republican Association in this city numbering nearly four hundred members I have been directed by a resolution of the association (perceiving that you are to be a candidate for the next Presidential term) to address you asking your sentiments upon the following important questions:

1st Your opinion in relation to a United States Bank

2nd On Tarriff [*sic*]

& 3rd[l]y On the sales by the Government of the public lands and the disposition of the proceeds thereof.

I am well aware My Dear Sir that you are a firm friend and an uncompromising Democrat. I have therefore taken the liberty thus to address you in plain and unsophisticated language, having at the same time unfeigned respect for all the public acts of your political life and the highest esteem for your private worth as a friend, a citizen and an inflexible supporter of Jeffersonian Democracy. It is the intention of this association Sir to use their utmost exertions to secure you if possible the delegation in this city and also in the adjacent counties.

Should you think this letter worthy of your consideration you will be kind enough to direct answer to me. With sentiments of highest regard and esteem I am your Ob[edien]t Serv[an]t, Thomas P. Teale, 147 Chapel St[.,] New York.

ALS in ScCleA. NOTE: An AEU by Calhoun reads: "Teale[,] Answered 7th June."

From R[OBERT] M. T. HUNTER

L[l]oyds, ["Essex" *interlined*; County, Va.,] May 23d 1843
My dear Sir, Your letter reached this place whilst I was in Washington to which place I had been suddenly summoned to a meeting of some of our friends, in order to rescue the management of our affairs from poor [Joseph A.] Scoville whose indiscretion was doing us much mischief. This and other matters were the subject of our consultations of which I will give you a full account in another letter if I should not find space in this after answering your enquiries.

I am much obliged to you my dear Sir for your sympathy and for the estimate which you place upon my services. But I do not think ["my defeat" *interlined and* "it" *canceled*] will ["be of" *canceled and* "produce" *interlined*] any serious injury to our prospects. My defeat was owing in part to the fact that this ["was" *changed to* "is"] notoriously a *Whig* district and partly to the fact that the Bank is much stronger in this district and I believe in the State than we had supposed ["& partly to the Tax bill" *interlined*]. I believe that the last Legislature gave me as [*one word canceled and* "unmanageable" *interlined*] a district as they believed it was safe to give me although I think their impression was that I would be reelected. The losses have undoubtedly fallen upon your friends but still there were so many circumstances which apparently justified the arrangement that we cannot make any complaint upon the subject. Notwithstanding all this you are undoubtedly gaining strength in Eastern Virginia and I am determined to fight it to the last. I shall take steps (if our friends will back me, as I think they will) to organize the State. You need not fear that I shall relax in my efforts ["so far as your prospects are concerned and which(?) I say this" *canceled*] during the present contest. [Thomas] Ritchie chuckles secretly (I have no doubt) at the prospect of having laid so many upon the shelf but he cannot stir a step in Va. without us if we are true to ourselves. The Whigs are far stronger in the State than he supposed. [Martin] Van [Buren] cannot carry this State, *you* are the only Republican who can. But you cannot do it without Ritchie's assistance for we cannot bring western Va. in ["to your support" *interlined*] without his aid. We must deal gently with him. The [Charleston] Mercury must not attack him. I have given the same directions to the [Washington] Spectator. I send by this mail to the Spectator some strictures upon his "Appeal to the Democracy" which will appear as editorial if [John] Heart will insert them as I presume he will. Do not suppose from all this that I mistake R[itchie]'s real feelings but I trust that *we shall yet make him help to elect you.* I had a long consultation with [Dabney S.?] Carr[?] of Baltimore and some of our N[ew] England friends. They are in high spirits and we hope to get you the nomination. [James A.] Seddon [later a Representative from Va.] and [William O.] Goode [former Representative from Va.] are full of fight. So are [Richard] Coke [Jr., former Representative from Va.,] and Roy[?]. We are thinking of a paper in Richmond, we can get it up but an *imprudent* paper would do us harm. I shall write to Seddon by this mail also. We must organize this State and start a paper too if Ritchie[']s course should make it necessary.

I have not heard from [Henry A.] Wise [Representative from Va.] since the adjournment. I heard during the canvass that he declared his preference for you after [John] Tyler. He will be for you but whether he will "act with our friends" is another matter. I shall write to him however and do all that I can to induce him to take the proper direction. I can scarcely say what direction Va. will take if V[an] B[uren] should be the candidate. The Whigs I think would carry the State in that event and years would elapse before our principles would regain their ascendancy. I feel the force of this in my canvass. The Richmond Convention had produced the impression in the State that V[an] B[uren] would be the candidate and the Bank[,] Tariff and Distribution have all gained ground. But if our friends do not despond I will not despair of the State. I have not had time as yet to sound them. But I am now at work.

Let me entreat you my dear Sir to say nothing yet awhile about refusing to permit your name to go before the Convention. Hear what I have now to say and I think you will agree with me that your prospects are brightening. I met in Washington [Daniel D.] Brodhead of Boston, and [Edmund T.] Bridge of Conn: whom you know. They were Representatives of your friends from N[ew] England and they and [Virgil] Maxcy sent for me to ["a" *interlined*] consultation. They say that you are growing daily in strength in New England. Our friends are about to get up a New England organization of which Massachusetts is to be the centre. We have 3 good men and true in ["the" *interlined*] Con[necticut] delegation. We shall take half the Maine delegation and carry [the] State in the Gen[era]l Convention. We shall carry ["in that convention" *interlined*] Mass. ["and" *canceled*,] Vermont, & perhaps Rhode Island. New Hampshire is doubtful. This Bridge is a "trump"[;] you have no idea how valuable he is. They consider it very important to make [Levi] Woodbury show his hand at the N[ew] Hampshire Convention. For that purpose Brodhead and [David] Henshaw have gone to see him. For that reason too it is not desirable that our papers should place his name at their head. What the Mercury has done cannot be undone but we ventured to take steps to prevent it in other cases. Besides all this they say that [former Vice-President Richard M.] Johnson is disposed to drive a trade with V[an] B[uren] and is willing to take the V[ice-]Presidency. To keep him in check it is desirable that we should keep the question of V[ice-]P[resident] open. And yet Scoville had undertaken ["as sec(re)t(ar)y"(?) *canceled*] to correspond in the name of a central committee which did not exist and to order our papers to hoist the Woodbury flag. These gentlemen do not doubt Woodbury[']s sincerity or his intention to support you ultimately, but he is so timid that he requires a little driving and in addition to this we must keep the question open. Tyler is for himself of course but several members of his Cabinet are now acting efficiently for us as I shall presently explain.

We found it indispensable to divorce Scoville from the Spectator and from all participation in the management of our affairs of which he had assumed the entire control for some weeks past.

His indiscretions and his misconduct in money affairs had been such that our friends would not contribute to the paper whilst he was there—and moreover they insisted that he should no longer [be] concern[ed] in the management of the campaign. Maxcy prom[i]sed to write you a full account of these matters. Suffice it for me to say that the Spectator is to be made over to a trustee (Maxcy I hope) who is to control its course. Heart will have ⅓d of its profits. The other ⅔ds to be in [Francis W.] Pickens['s] name but designed as a fund for the good of the cause. I promised Scoville to say to you that I did not doubt his Zeal or the sincerity of his attachment to you. I am sorry I cannot say more. But I think a certain portion of the profits ["of the paper" *interpolated*] should be given to him[,] perhaps ⅛. Maxcy however is against giving him so much. Some provision however ought to be made for him out of the paper as he relinquished his interest in his contract. This would not have availed him much as he had failed to comply with his part of the bargain. But he might have embarrassed us and I wish we had some letters from him which are in his possession. Beware how you write to him. As the matter now stands Heart will edit the paper for the present under general directions from Maxcy and myself. These gentlemen say that we shall be able to get money to sustain the paper and to pay an editor handsomely. Do you know one fit for the place? We are all looking out.

These gentlemen were anxious for me to go to Washington and act as the Ch[airma]n of the Central committee and conduct the correspondence. This was out of the question—nor could we even form a central committee in Washington. We shall still endeavor to get two or three to act. The result of the arrangement however was this— until the meeting of the next Congress I am to conduct the general correspondence. I promised to endeavor to get up a central committee in each State and get them to organize the State. When the necessity exists Maxcy and myself are to meet in Washington. And our friends generally will communicate with me to ascertain your wishes and obtain your directions. You know I urged the importance of a committee in each State before I left Washington and I supposed they had been formed. But if so I could not ascertain the fact in Washington or learn their names. It must still be done and in this matter I must beg your assistance. I think we can get along everywhere except in the West. I shall venture to write to Judge [Richard M.] Young ["of Illinois" *interlined*] tomorrow. To whom shall I write in Ohio? He must be *honest* and *faithful*. Is there any man amongst your friends there who could ["act as" *interlined*] secret agent of the P[ost] O[ffice]. [Postmaster General Charles A.] Wickliffe I am told does not like the present incumbent. We desire the organization for many reasons. But amongst others for this—we shall certainly carry our point as to the time of the Convention. We must carry the question as to districts also as we can do by proper exertions. For this purpose the central State committee must organize each Congressional district in reference to the delegate. And each District must send its delegate no matter how its State convention decides. We may then safely leave the manner of voting to the convention itself. In Missouri they seem to contemplate a district representation. In N.H. Bridge says it may be done because notwithstanding the Gen[era]l Ticket system there are districts laid off from each of which a candidate is always selected. Cannot this be done in Ga.[?] Have they no territorial divisions by which they distribute the representation equally over the State? You are near enough [to] them to put them in motion if you concur with me as to its importance. Let Mr. Ritchie discuss the "how" and the "when" of a convention[,] we will go to work and ["when" *canceled*] organize so as to elect one in our own way and we will hold it too at the right time. You will understand me when I ["say" *altered to* "tell"] you that Bridge says we have now extraordinary facilities for organizing N[ew] England. The Boston Post and some[?] other leading papers are ready to come out for us whenever he says the word. [Former] Gov[erno]r [of Vt., Cornelius P.] Van Ness has been acting with us and it is probable he will continue to do so. He is probably the collector of the Port of New York by this time. I saw him in Washington. He promises to assist me. If we get the patronage ["we shall" *canceled and* "it will" *interlined*] probably ["be" *interlined*] used ["it" *canceled*] in such masses that there will be too many to be shot down as deserters. They amuse themselves at the prospect of Vans [*sic*; Van Buren's] dismay if things go as they expect.

And now a little in relation to our difficulties. They beg and implore that you will not answer [William] Smith's letter in relation to R[hode] Island until Van B[uren] also answers. They are very much alarmed at the letter of which they heard either through Mr. [Thomas G.] Clemson or some one to whom he mentioned it. I hope you will take their advice in this matter.

They also think as I do that your So[uth] Ca[rolina] friends ought to be moderate in their expressions about a Convention and also in relation to V[an] Buren. They say as I also believe that you cannot be elected without a nomination by the convention but at the same time they think the prospect ["a" *canceled*] fair for your nomination. For that reason we ought not to produce the impression that we would resist the convention and we ought not to alienate the friends of V[an] B[uren]. Their chief fear seems to be that Johnson will transfer his strength to V[an] B[uren] for the sake of the V[ice-]P[residenc]y. I found that Gen[era]l [Nathan] Towson entertained the same suspicion which he derived in part from Gen[era]l [Duff] Green.

They also expressed a desire to draw from you the declaration that you would be willing to [support] "a discriminating ["Tariff" *canceled*] revenue Tariff which would yield a nett protection of 25 p[e]r cent to the manufacturers." They said that many of the manufacturers had declared their preference for you with ["this" *interlined*] declaration, over [Henry] Clay with all the protective Tariffs which could be given them. They did not explain but I think I understand their drift. They would use the generality of the phrase to insist that you would discriminate for protection whilst to the South it would be interpreted to mean a discrimination for ["protection" *canceled and* "revenue" *interlined*]. This would of course be inconsistent with your character and ultimately mischievous. But perhaps you might suggest some modification of this declaration which would be useful. I promised to write you upon these subjects and I have now redeemed my pledge.

I hope you will write to Maxcy to act as trustee for the Spectator. The trustee to control its course and to hold it ⅓ for Heart and ⅔ for Pickens. But of this ⅔ we can allow Scoville what is fair and reasonable and devote the rest to the cause. If we can get a good editor the subscriptions will be large but in the mean time Charleston must advance [some funds] through Maxcy to relieve the paper of its embarrassments—Brodhead will advance $500 for that purpose during this week & Bridge thinks he can procure 2 or 300 subscribers.

I shall write to you frequently to inform you of what we are doing and I hope you will keep me advised of your wishes in relation to the conduct of the campaign. I have undertaken a laborious task until the meeting of the next Congress and perhaps have agreed to assume

191

too much responsibility. But they insisted upon it as indispensable and forced upon me the responsibility. I shall always be subject to your correction however and if I had a daily mail I might get along better. My nephew [Muscoe R.H. Garnett?] who lives with me will assist me very much in the correspondence and he wields a pen which may occasionally be useful to the Spectator. I ["have advised" *canceled*] shall advise Heart to exchange with all of the ["Demo" *canceled*] Calhoun papers and with as many of the Democratic Journals in favor of other candidates than V[an] B[uren] as he can afford. This is one of the uses of the Spectator. It shows ["the editors of" *interlined*] these papers that we know and remember them.

The Speakership [of the next House of Representatives] was another subject of our consultations. They wished me to sound [Samuel] Beardsley [Representative from N.Y.] but Van Ness thinks this dangerous and promised to ascertain in N[ew] York whether he could be approached. They think we may make much out of this election but I confess[?] not yet see how it is to be done.

Will Pickens be at home this summer[?] If so he ought to write freely to Ohio where his correspondence used to be extensive.

Your friend Carr[?] will probably be the collector in Baltimore. He thinks the Richmond V[an] B[uren] men are alarmed at your [prospects?] as they were talking the other day when he was there of starting another man. Will [you] do me the favor to give me Gen[era]l [Alexander O.?] Anderson[']s address when you write again.

I fear I have bored you with too long a letter but I now leave much unsaid which I shall have to say in another letter.

I hope the Columbia convention has been prudent. Very faithfully your friend, R.M.T. Hunter.

P.S. Perhaps I have spoken too strongly aga[i]n[s]t Van B[uren]'s chance to carry Va. But with Ritchie's aid you would be much the stronger.

ALS in ScCleA; variant PEx in Boucher and Brooks, eds., *Correspondence*, pp. 184–186. NOTE: The dateline in this manuscript appears to have been written with a different pen and perhaps at a different time from all that follows it but also to have been written, probably, in Hunter's hand. In Calhoun's reply of 6/3 to Hunter the address of Gen. Romulus M. Saunders of N.C. was given to Hunter, but "Saunders" does not seem to be the name written in Hunter's request near the end of the text above. Rather, the request seems to refer to an "Anderson," possibly Alexander O. Anderson, former Senator from Tenn. Daniel Dodge Brodhead, who seems to have been one of Calhoun's most enthusiastic advocates in Mass., had been prominent in the formation of the original "Jackson party" in that State. During 1830–1838 he was Naval Agent of the Port of Boston under David Henshaw as Collector.

ADDRESS OF THE SOUTH CAROLINA
DEMOCRATIC CONVENTION

Address of the Convention of South Carolina,
Met at Columbia, on the 22d of May, 1843,
to the Democratic Republican party of the United States.
[Adopted May 24, 1843]

We have convened, Fellow-Citizens, to deliberate on the subject of the approaching Presidential election, and have given it that serious attention which its great importance demands at all times, but more especially in the present critical condition of the country. The result is, our unanimous determination to recommend to you JOHN CALD-WELL CALHOUN, as the candidate of the Democratic Republican Party, for next President. We are also unanimous in recommending, *that the General Convention of the party should be held in Baltimore, in May, 1844; that each State should appoint as many Delegates as she is entitled to members in the Electoral College; that two should be appointed at large, and the remainder by Districts, one from each Congressional District where there are such in a State, and where not, by the mode which the Republican Party of each State may deem best fitted to collect and express the opinions of the People; and that the members should vote per capita.*

We shall pass over all minor and subordinate considerations for recommending Mr. Calhoun, and proceed directly to state the leading and paramount reason for giving him our preference. We, then, rest our recommendation on his long, faithful, and important public services; on his acknowledged abilities, energy, firmness and sagacity; on his profound knowledge of the Constitution, and the genius and character of our admirable system of Government; on his high administrative talents; on his devoted attachment to free and popular institutions, and the principles and doctrines of the Republican Party; and finally, on the spotless purity of his life.

These are high qualifications, but not higher than he possesses, nor (as we believe) than a large majority of his fellow-citizens accord to him. They are those, which at all times should be regarded as paramount, in the selection of the Chief Magistrate, and as decisive, at such a period as the present, when the government is surrounded by perils and difficulties; when its character and credit are greatly sunk at home and abroad; when great abuses and corruption have crept into its administration; when the principles of the Constitution have been departed from; and when universal embarrassment prevails throughout the land. It is at such a period, that the great and only question should be, who is best qualified to carry the Government through its perils and difficulties; to correct its errors; reform its abuses; elevate its character and credit; re-establish the Constitution, and restore confidence and the prosperity of the country? Whoever he may be, he ought to be the man. Every subordinate consideration should yield.

Who, then, is the man for the present period? Without intending to underrate or disparage the high qualifications of the distinguished individuals of the party, whose names have been presented by their friends as candidates, we respond to the question, Mr. Calhoun is the man. We sincerely believe, that he unites in himself more fully, and in a higher degree, than any other individual, all the high qualities demanded by the occasion; and that his election would do more to redeem the character of the Government and country, and restore confidence and prosperity, than the election of any other man, or the occurrence of any other event.

It is not to be disguised that the deplorable condition of the country may be almost exclusively traced to errors and mismanagement of Government. It cannot be charged either to the Constitution, or the dispensations of Providence. On the contrary, His dispensations have not only been kind, but munificent, in abundant harvests and almost universal health; while to the violation or neglect of the provisions of the Constitution may be traced most of the evils that have befallen us. We then must mainly look for their remedy, to the correction of the errors of the Government, and the reformation of its abuses, and for that, to the election of the President, without whose lead, and enlightened and hearty co-operation, there can be no thorough and radical reform, or essential change in the course of Government, as experience has abundantly proved. What his lead and co-operation will be in the coming administration, depends on the individual to be elected, and that, as far as the party is concerned, on the candidate to be nominated; and hence, at this time, the great importance of making the proper selection.

It may be supposed, that the fact of Mr. Calhoun being a native of South Carolina has influenced us in making up an estimate of his qualifications, and that large deductions ought to be made on that account. We are not unaware how much opinion is liable to be biased by State attachments; and have made allowance for it, but it is possible, not enough. If, however[,] deduction is to be made on that account, from the weight of our opinion in his favor, there are other considerations, which ought at least to throw an equal weight in the opposite scale. If the fact, that we are of the State and vicinage of Mr. Calhoun, is calculated to warp our judgment and lessen the weight of our opinion in his favor, the same fact is calculated, in another view, to add to its weight. For, while it may bias our opinion in his favor, it gives us the opportunity to view his conduct, public and private, more closely and minutely, and to make up our opinion from actual observation and full and correct knowledge. When with such advantages, the jury of the vicinage, the whole State, renders an unanimous verdict in his favor, it ought to be entitled to full credence. We say unanimous, for there is, literally, but one party in this State, as far as he is concerned.

On this elevated ground, we rest our preference for Mr. Calhoun. To that, we might add many other reasons, entitled to much consideration, but of a subordinate character. Among them, that he belongs to a portion of the Union which has never yet had a President. The Central States, the Northern and Eastern, the Western and North-Western, all have had their Presidents; but the Southern or South-Western—the great exporting States, from the exchange of whose products with the rest of the world more than two-thirds of the revenue of the Union has been drawn, and which have ever furnished their full share of talents, patriotism, eloquence, and wisdom to the councils of the nation—have never yet had one.

In this connexion, there is another view not less entitled to consideration. The Presidents have heretofore been taken exclusively from the larger States. There is not an instance of one, in the long course of half a century, selected from the medium size, or smaller States. Is it to be inferred, from these remarkable facts, that the smaller and weaker States, and the least populous portions of the Union, are to be permanently excluded from its highest honors?—or rather has it been an accidental course of events, without aim or design? The latter, we hope, has been the case, but surely, on the first fitting occasion, generosity, the sense of justice and sound policy, require of the larger States, and more populous portions of the Union, that they should give a practical and substantial proof it has been in reality accidental, and not designed. And what occasion can be more fitting than the present?

If the high qualifications of Mr. Calhoun, strengthened by such long and important services, unanimously supported, as there is every reason to believe he will be, not only by his State, but the portion of the Union to which he belongs, cannot ensure his election, is it to be expected that any citizen hereafter belonging to it, however eminent his talents or great his services, or from the smaller States, will ever be elected? And would there not be strong grounds, for believing that their citizens are forever to be disfranchised, as far as the office of President is concerned, and that the office is to be a permanent monopoly of the larger States and more populous sections? To these[,] other reasons might be added of not less weight. We shall however allude to but one or two, and among them, his disinterested and magnanimous course in his party relations, of which a single instance will suffice.

It is well known, that he did not hesitate, regardless of consequences, in obedience to what he believed to be the true principles and policy of the Republican Party, to separate from the great body of the party in the plenitude of its power, and when the highest rewards and honors of the country were in his grasp. It is equally well known, that it subjected him, for the time, to the severest denunciations of those he separated from, and apparently forever blasted his political prospects, so far as office, power, and influence were concerned. He willingly sacrificed all to maintain his principles. Nor is it unknown, when the tide of events turned against his former friends, from whom he had separated, and when the party was at its greatest depression, and their old opponents ready to rush in and overwhelm them, as they believed forever, it was then that he, forgetting the past, and overlooking all personal considerations, regarding only his duty and his principles, unhesitatingly brought to them, at their utmost need, his powerful aid. If events have since turned—if the party is again in the ascendant, and more powerful than ever after its great fall, it may be surely said with truth, that the happy change is, in a great measure, to be attributed to him. It is true that in all this he sought neither gratitude nor reward; that, however, only enhances his title to both.

To this we add, that he was the first to discover, long in advance, the present dangers and disasters; to point out their causes, and warn against their approach; to use his utmost efforts, and peril his all to avert them; and, when actually arrived, to take the lead in the endeavor to pass through them in safety. In proof of all this, we refer to addresses, speeches, and reports for the last fifteen years. Now that which was then future is past, they look more like history than the anticipations of what was to come, and afford evidence of sagacity and foresight rarely equalled and never surpassed. Although he could not avert the dangers and disasters he anticipated, it cannot be doubted he did much to lessen them, and to prepare the way finally to overcome them; and now, when the question is, How shall they be overcome? who so well qualified to give a satisfactory answer—to undertake the task, and restore health and prosperity to the body politic, as he who has given such conclusive evidence of his thorough knowledge of the cause and nature of the disease to be remedied.

And, finally, may we not ask, without being thought to disparage the just merits of other candidates for the Presidency, which one of them do his past history and opinions more thoroughly identify with all the great articles of the Democratic creed than Mr. Calhoun? He, as far back as 1834, discountenanced the connexion of the Government with banks; and when in 1837, that connexion was broken asunder, he was amongst the first to advocate the necessity of the separation—to plant his foot, without fear of consequences, boldly in the front; and, under denunciations and obloquy unexampled for their bitterness in political warfare, to take up this great measure of reform, and by the force of his decision and genius, principally contributed to sustain and pass it through? Few men have been so efficient in saving the liberties of the country from that most dangerous of all the instruments of Federalism, a United States Bank. Next to Mr. [Thomas] Jefferson, no one who has lived under our Constitution has done more, if as much, to preserve its republican features, by exposing the dangers of consolidation, and resisting its encroachments. And when, in the lust for absolute power, it was madly proposed to mutilate the Constitution, by abolishing the great balance-wheel and conservative provision of the Veto, he was the most distinguished of all in that gallant resistance by which the attempt was frustrated. The best energies of his life have been spent in efforts to reform a degenerating Government, and restore it by economy and retrenchment, to its original simplicity and purity. He is the true representative of *the great essential principle of Democracy, freedom of human pursuits,* in the exemption of industry from unnecessary burdens and exactions. He recognizes no justice in tariffs taxing unequally the labor and capital of the farmer, the planter, the merchant, the mechanic, the shipmaster, and all other industrial pursuits, to give protection to and make the labor and capital of the manufacturer profitable. He believes that such injustice alienates affection between these classes of citizens, and causes deep dissatisfaction with and weakens the Government which sanctions it; that it causes fierce and angry struggles, by the efforts of the one to free themselves from wrongful burdens, and of the other to maintain or increase them; that out of these conflicts, occurring periodically, and mixing themselves up in all governmental questions, the best interests of the manufacturers themselves are far more deeply injured, from the unsettled condition of their existence, and the sudden and ruinous change to which it subjects their affairs, than they

197

could possibly be by that fair protection which an equal, moderate, and just system of revenue duties would afford, and which, if just, equal, and fair, would be permanent. A power has been claimed as existing in the Government, to give, *indirectly*, to the labor and capital of one class, or one section, a preference over those of another, which, at the same time it is acknowledged it would be oppressive to give *directly*; but he admits neither the constitutional right, the morality, nor the logic, by which a mere difference of mode, in perpetrating a wrong, can be used to change it into a right, and denies any rightful power in the federal legislature, directly or indirectly, primarily or incidentally, to draw the exactions of the Government from the people by duties on imports, otherwise than by a fair, equal, and bona fide tariff of revenue. Between a tariff of protection, and a tariff of revenue, *discriminating for protection,* he is able to see no difference in constitutional principle, and he holds the one as much as the other, repugnant to natural justice and the plainest principles of political economy, and in their tendency subversive of the very ends of civil society. He is not in favor of abolishing duties on imports for a system of direct or internal taxes, but for a system of duties on imports laid purely for revenue, and allowing discriminations only where true revenue principles call for it. He is in favor of burdening commerce and the labor which supports it with no more duties than are indispensable to the economical and necessary wants of the Government. He is unalterably opposed to all extravagance, corruption, and abuses in the expenditure of public money, the reform of which cannot be effected so long as the revenue is levied on the principles of protection, which acts as a bounty on large and influential classes, enlisting them in the support of extravagant expenditures as an excuse for high taxation. He believes that the Government has no power nor right to lay taxes, nor to collect revenue, nor to sell the public lands, for the purpose of distributing the proceeds, or any portion thereof, amongst the States; nor that it has any right or power, directly or indirectly, to assume the debts of the States; nor to carry on a system of Internal Improvements. Many of these are cardinal considerations, in comparison with which the Presidency sinks into insignificance, and no compromises of them can be bartered even for that high dignity.

Having now given our reasons for preferring Mr. Calhoun, we shall next proceed to state those that governed us in making the recommendations we have in reference to the General Convention.

Reason and discussion have already done much to settle most of the points connected with the Convention, and about which there was at first a difference of opinion. We regard the question as definitely settled, that Baltimore is to be the place where it is to be held, and shall therefore pass it over without further comment. The expression of opinion, so far as there has been one, is so strongly in favor of May, 1844, it is scarcely to be supposed, that those who prefer November will stand out against it. But four States, Tennessee, Missouri, Virginia, and New York, have expressed opinions in favor of the latter, while Maryland, Kentucky, Louisiana, Massachusetts, Pennsylvania, Michigan, Alabama, Mississippi, Rhode Island, and New Hampshire, have either expressed opinions in favor of, or given strong indications that they prefer, the former. Indeed the argument, to afford the people ample time to make up and express their opinion, and to mark the course of events and the conduct of public men during the first session of the next Congress, especially in reference to the Tariff and the expenditures of the Government, is so strong, that we do not see how it can well be resisted. But putting aside that and other reasons which might be urged in favor of the latter period, it seems to us, as a mere matter of courtesy, if time be requested by any considerable portion of the party, it should be granted, unless the period proposed be obviously unreasonably late, which cannot be alleged against that which we, with so large a portion of the party, have concurred on recommending. On this ground, if no other, we cannot believe that those highly respectable States which have fixed on an earlier day, will be so wanting in courtesy, as to refuse to yield to so reasonable a request, and persist in adhering to November. Under this impression, we shall not dwell longer on the reasons in favor of May.

We also regard it as substantially settled, that the Delegates, with the exception of the two proposed to be appointed by the Republican members of the Legislature, or a State Convention, are to be appointed by Districts. We are not aware that any State or portion of the party has expressed a preference for any other mode, except Pennsylvania, while most of the States and public meetings where the subject of the Convention has been agitated, including Virginia, have expressed opinions in its favor.

It is certainly gratifying to observe, that the tendency of a free and enlightened discussion is to unite and harmonize the party, instead of dividing and distracting it, as was feared by many would be the case; and it may be fairly anticipated, that the continuance of the discussion, in the same liberal and free manner, which has already contributed so much to settle the important points it has connected, with the Convention, will have the same salutary effect in settling the only two, that we regard as remaining in reality unsettled—the number of Delegates to be appointed from each District, and the mode of voting—whether *per capita*, that is, each member voting individually and his vote counting one, or by the majority, that is, the vote of the whole delegation of the State to be disposed of by a majority of the delegation. The recent Convention held at Richmond, recommended four Delegates from each Congressional District, and that a majority of the Delegates should dispose of the vote of the State in the Convention: in which the legislative caucus held at Albany has concurred, while all the other States, as far as we are informed, which have expressed an opinion, are in favor of one Delegate from each District, and the *per capita* mode of voting.

We have carefully and impartially examined and compared both, and with every respect for the source from which it emanates, we are compelled to say, that our objection is irresistibly strong against what, for brevity, we shall call the plan of the Richmond Convention, and in favor of what, with the same object, we shall call the Maryland plan, that State being the first which fully adopted and recommended it.

And here it is proper to premise, that as the nomination, if acquiesced in, would in effect be the election, so far as the voice of the party is concerned, we hold it, in the first place, to be indispensable, that the General Convention should conform, as nearly as may be, to the Electoral College, in the manner of constituting it, and the mode of voting and counting the votes. In the next, that every practicable means should be adopted, that the voice of the Convention shall utter the voice of the People, in contradistinction to political managers; and that the relative weight of the States, as fixed by the Constitution, in the election of President and Vice-President, should be preserved. These we regard as fundamental principles, by which every proposition, in relation to the General Convention ought to be tested. None but those who can stand that test, should be admitted. They are too obviously just and reasonable to require illustration. He would ill deserve the name of Republican, who objects to them. It is to their test we intend to bring the points of difference between the two plans, which may be regarded as still unsettled.

We object, then, to the mode of voting and counting recommended by the Richmond Convention, because it adopts a principle unknown to the Constitution, and which, combined with the number of delegates proposed to be appointed from each District, would in practice be destructive of the most important of all the compromises of the Constitution, or as we might with truth say, the fundamental compromise on which the whole rests. As strong as these assertions may appear, we shall, unless greatly deceived, establish their truth beyond controversy.

It is well known to all in the least conversant with our political history, that the greatest difficulty experienced in framing the Constitution, was to establish the relative weight of the States, in the government of the Union. The smaller States, placing themselves on the incontestible principle of the perfect equality of rights between all sovereign and independent communities, without regard to size or population, insisted on a like equality of weight in the government of the Union, while the larger and more populous, admitting the correctness of that principle, insisted that in a Federal Republic, composed of States of unequal size, and united for the common defence of the whole, the States which brought to the common stock of power and means the greater share, should in fairness and justice have a proportionate weight in the government. Such was the obstinacy, with which both sides maintained their ground, that it was at one time seriously apprehended the object of the Convention would fail, and its labors end in doing nothing. The alarm, which this caused, led to a compromise. The larger States agreed to an equality of representation in the Senate, and the smaller to representation in the House proportioned to population estimated in federal numbers. From these two elements, all the materials for constructing our beautiful and solid political fabric were drawn. The Electoral College for the choosing of President and Vice-President consists of the two blended, so as to give to each State the number of electors that she may have members in the two Houses of Congress.

The modes of voting, as prescribed by the Constitution, are in unison with these elements. As there are but two, so there are but two modes of voting known to the Constitution—the *per capita*, and that by a majority, corresponding with the two elements. When the States are intended to be regarded in their original equality, and independent and sovereign character, the mode of voting prescribed is by delegation, each delegation voting by itself, and the majority disposing of the vote of the State; but the vote of the State in such cases, without regard to the number of delegates, counts but one. Such was the mode of voting and counting in the formation and adoption of the Constitution, and such the mode prescribed for propositions to amend it, and in the election of President, when the choice devolves on the House, by the failure of the Electoral College to elect. But when the States are not intended to be so regarded, the vote and count is always *per capita*, and such is the mode, accordingly, prescribed for the two

Houses of Congress in all cases, except the instance cited, and also for the Electoral College, in voting for a President and Vice-President.

It is well known, that it was very difficult to agree on the mode of electing those distinguished officers, resulting from the same conflict between the large and small States, that endangered, as has been stated, the formation of the Constitution itself. That, too, ended in a compromise, which gave the larger States a preponderance in the election by the Electoral College, and the smaller a preponderance in case of a failure of choice, and the election devolving on the House.

It was thus, that this great and dangerous conflict among the States was settled by compromises, and that which endangered the formation of the Constitution was, by consummate wisdom and skill, made to furnish the elements out of which the Government was constructed; and what we are irreconcilably opposed to in the plan of the Richmond Convention is, that it confounds these elements by combining together incongruous modes of voting and counting—and thereby adopts a principle unknown to the Constitution, and in deadly conflict with the compromises upon which it rests, and on the observance of which, its balance depends. Our objection applies, not to the delegates of the General Convention voting by States, or that the vote of the States should be given by the majority, but what we do object to as blending incongruous methods is, that the vote of a State should be given by a majority, but counted *per capita*. It is that, which we pronounce to be unknown to the Constitution, and monstrous and destructive in its character. Virginia, or any other State, may take choice, to vote by majority, or *per capita*; but whichever she may select, she cannot complain if she should be subject to the mode of counting, which the Constitution, in conformity to its compromises, invariably prescribes for that mode. If she should insist on a majority of her delegates disposing of her vote, she must also submit to place herself on an equality with the smallest State, and count but one, as she would in the case of the Presidential election going to the House. If she desires to have her whole delegation counted, as in the House of Representatives on all other questions, she must vote *per capita*, and run, as there, the hazard of a division among her delegates. She cannot, without subverting the principles of the Constitution, enjoy the benefit of both modes, and exempt herself from their disadvantages. She cannot concentrate her whole strength, by disposing of her vote by a majority, without placing herself in the same scale with Delaware; or count her full number, without the hazard of a division in her delegation. Choose which she may, we for one shall not object, but we never can assent that she, or any other State, shall at the same time grasp the benefit of both, and exempt herself from their disadvantages. The advantages and disadvantages of whichever may be selected, must be taken together.

But we consider the plan of the Richmond Convention as dangerous in its practical bearings, as it is clearly unconstitutional in principle. It would tend almost irresistibly to concentrate the power of electing the President in the hands of the larger States and the more populous portions of the Union, and by necessary consequence, give them the almost exclusive control over the Executive Department of the Government, and, through its power and influence, over the whole Union. We must look at things as they are. The control of the nomination, if acquiesced in, would be in fact, as has been premised, the control of the election, as far as the party is concerned; and what could be better devised to concentrate their combined power in the General Convention, than the plan of the majority giving the vote of each State, and yet at the same time counting *per capita*, and thereby controlling its proceedings, and through it the nomination and election? And what could tend more powerfully than that, to destroy the balance of the Constitution, and convert our Federal Republic into a great consolidated and absolute Government, to be succeeded by all the disasters which must inevitably follow?

But it may be said, that the evil apprehended has already occurred in another form; that their strength is already concentrated on the Electoral College by changing the system of choosing electors by Districts, into that of the General Ticket, and that it is but right that they should have the same relative weight in the Convention, as they have in the Electoral College. It is, indeed, true that the system of choosing electors by general ticket, in its operation, as far as the concentration of power is concerned, has the same effect, as voting by majority, and counting *per capita*, and it is to be feared has already done much, and will do still more, to disturb the balance of the Government. But there is a great difference between them, so much so, that the general ticket can afford neither excuse nor precedent, for the plan of the Richmond Convention. If the two have the like effect in securing to the States a united vote, it is brought about in a very different manner. The General Ticket may defeat, to a certain extent, the intent of the Constitution, but it does not invade its principles, as to the manner of voting and counting. The electors still vote individually, and their votes are counted *per capita*. Bad as it is to get round the principles of the Constitution in practice, it is still worse to act in open defiance and contempt of them.

Nor is this the only difference. It is well known that at the commencement of the Government, and for many years afterwards, the District system of choosing Electors generally prevailed, and that it was changed to the general ticket, not voluntarily, through a conviction, that the latter was right and the former wrong, but reluctantly, and under a general conviction that the change was for the worse. It was caused in a great measure by compulsion, through the almost necessary operation of party conflicts. The system once commenced by any one party in a State, in order to secure victory by concentrating its united strength, almost necessarily compelled the opposite side, in order to avoid defeat, to imitate the bad example. Once started, the same cause, by its action and re-action, led to the almost universal adoption. It was a weapon forged for party warfare exclusively, and fit only for the purpose for which it was intended. But to introduce a weapon so intended, into a Convention of members of the same party, assembled, not in hostility, but for the peaceable and friendly purpose of producing and preserving harmony, union and concert, would be clearly, not only not authorized by the example of the general ticket, but without justification or excuse.

Another view remains, deserving the most serious consideration; going to show, that the introduction of the general ticket, so far from affording reason or precedent in favor of the plan proposed by the Richmond Convention, furnishes strong grounds against it. The very fact that it has been adopted in choosing electors, and that it has increased the relative weight of the larger States and more populous portions of the Union, in the Electoral College and the election of President, instead of a reason why their weight should be increased in the General Convention and the nomination of the candidate, is one of the strongest against it. It obviously makes it more important to the others, that what has been lost in the election, shall not be lost in the nomination also. If it be lost there too, all will be hopelessly lost. To understand the full force of the remark, it must be recollected, that the nomination is necessary to make the vote of the Electoral College *certain.* One indeed of the leading and avowed objects is to avoid division, *in order to prevent the election from going into the House,* where the vote is by States, and where the largest and the smallest, New York and Delaware, stand on the same level. The certain consequence of the nomination is to deprive the smaller States of the chance of this contingent advantage, given them by an express provision of the Constitution, in order to compensate for the advantage which the larger States have in the Electoral College. It forms one of the compromises in adjusting the relative weight of the States in the Executive Department, and not an unimportant one, as it came from the hands of its framers. We wish to be understood. We are not the advocates of carrying the election to the House. We know that there are strong reasons against it, and we are sincerely desirous of avoiding it, if it can be done on fair and equal terms; but we are not so blind as not to see, that as things now stand, if the smaller States and less populous sections, should surrender this contingent advantage, without securing in the nomination a compensation which would preserve the relative weight assigned them by the Constitution, they will virtually surrender all control over the Presidential election and the Executive Department. The plan of the Richmond Convention does not secure it; on the contrary, it is apparent from what has already been stated, that in going into a Convention on that plan, so far from securing compensation for surrendering their contingent advantage, the smaller States would have even less weight in the Convention, and nomination, than in the Electoral College and election.

But the case is still stronger. As weak as the mode of voting and counting would make them in the Convention, under the plan of the Richmond Convention, they would be made still more so, under that portion of it which recommends four Delegates to be appointed from each District, as we shall next proceed to show. Its obvious effect will be to give a much larger number of Delegates to the central and contiguous States, than to the exterior and remote; for the plain reason, that they could attend with far less relative inconvenience, expense and time. The most remote of their Delegates could go and return home in a few days, at the expense of a few dollars, and with but little sacrifice of time and convenience, owing to the nearness and great facilities which rail roads and steamboats afford for travelling in that portion of the Union. Such would not be the case with the Delegates from the exterior and more remote States. To them the expense, time and sacrifice would interpose formidable obstacles against attending. The result would be, that from the one there would be a full attendance, and from the other a thin one. One would send a host of five hundred or six hundred Delegates, and the other a handful, probably of scarcely an hundred. He has a very imperfect knowledge of our nature, who does not see in this a great relative increase of influence and weight to the States which should send the most, and diminution to those which should send the handful. The voice of the many would be almost sure to drown that of the few.

But this relative increase of weight in the Convention, of the central and contiguous States, would be in reality, but a relative increase of the weight of the larger members of the Union, as those having the greatest population are in fact, for the most part, the central and contiguous States, while the less populous generally, are the exterior and remote. The two causes then, though apparently operating among the different classes of States, would, in fact, unite and combine to increase the relative influence of the same States and portions of the Union, and would by their joint operation give them an overwhelming weight in the Convention, and th[r]ough it, over the nomination, the election and Executive Department.

We have now we trust conclusively shown, that the plan of the Richmond Convention, in the mode of voting and counting it recommends, instead of conforming to, departs wholly from the analogy of the Electoral College, and that it adopts a principle unknown to the Constitution, and which in its operation would destroy the relative weight of the States, as fixed by its compromises, in the election of President and Vice-President; and of course, not standing the test of the principles to which we proposed to bring it, should be rejected. So clear and just is this conclusion to our minds, that we hazard nothing in asserting, that no State would venture to propose, as an amendment to the Constitution, the mode of voting and counting recommended by the Richmond Convention, containing, at the same time, a provision to divest the smaller States of their contingent advantage, on the election devolving on the House; or that, if proposed, it would not receive the vote of a single State in the Union, so strong would be the sense of justice against it. And yet, if that plan should become the precedent, and General Conventions for nominating Presidents and Vice-Presidents, the established practice, it would, in effect, supersede the existing provisions in reference to those elections, and become, virtually, a part of the Constitution; as much so as if formally adopted as an amendment.

But if the mode of voting and counting recommended by that plan should be rejected, as it seems to us it clearly ought to be, and the *per capita* adopted, as it must be to conform to the Constitution, then the other portion of the plan, which recommends four Delegates to be appointed from each election District, must also be rejected. The reason is plain: it would be incompatible with the *per capita* mode of voting, which, in order to preserve the relative weight of the States, as fixed by the Constitution, makes it necessary, that each should have the same number of delegates in the General Convention, that it is entitled to in the Electoral College. Were it, however, possible to meet this objection to the number of delegates from each District, recommended by the Richmond Convention, it would fall under the test of the other principle premised, which requires, that every practicable means should be adopted, in order that the General Convention should utter truly the voice of the people, in contradistinction to that of mere politicians. To effect that, it is indispensable the delegates should, in all possible cases, be directly appointed by the people. The greater the number of intermediate bodies, the farther the appointment is removed from the people, the feebler will be their voice, and the more potential that of poli[ti]cal managers. It is that, which constitutes the great and fatal objection to appointing delegates by State Conventions, which themselves are always one, and sometimes two or three degrees removed from the people. However proper they may be, to make previous arrangements preparatory to their appointment, it is hazardous to leave that to them. If it be left to them, it would be vain to hope it would not become in time, the channel by which improper influences, and even corruption itself, might enter and control the proceedings of the Convention, and, through it, the nomination and election. No plan could be better devised, to give those who hold or expect to hold office the control of the election, and through them, give the President the power of nominating his successor. In other words, to divest the people of the control over the election, and to transfer it, and with it the control over the Executive Department, to those who hold or seek to hold office. There is a proclivity in all popular Governments to that result, which can be prevented only by the greatest caution and vigilance.

Such is the danger of appointing the Delegates by State Conventions; and our objection to the plan of the Richmond Convention, which proposes four Delegates to each District, is, that it has the same tendency, though less powerfully, to weaken the voice of the people, and strengthen that of political managers. To increase the number of Delegates to be appointed from each District, is but to increase the necessity of a caucus to make the nomination of the candidates. The greater the number to be appointed, the stronger the tendency to distraction and confusion, and the necessity of such caucus to make nomination; and the greater that necessity, the less will be the control of the people of the District over the appointment, and the greater that of political intriguers. The most effectual check to their control, and means of giving the appointment in reality to the people, is for each District to appoint one Delegate. Where one only is to be appointed, if the District is divided in reference to the Presidential candidates, the usual course will be, that some one prominent individual on the side of each of the two most popular candidates, shall offer for the place of Delegate, and will canvass the District in behalf of his particular favorite; than which no conceivable mode is better calculated to make known the qualifications of candidates, and thereby enable the people to come to an enlightened selection.

Having now stated frankly and fairly, though not as fully as we might, our objections to the plan of the Richmond Convention, it remains to set forth the reasons for our preference of the Maryland plan. It will not be necessary to be very elaborate, as the reasons against the former are, in fact, the great and conclusive reasons in favor of the latter, so striking is the contrast between the two.

We, then, are in favor of the Maryland plan, because the time it fixes on to hold the General Convention affords ample opportunity for the people to make up and develope their opinion in reference to the respective candidates, and enables them to mark the conduct of the prominent friends of the several candidates in the new Congress to be assembled in December next, on questions of vital importance and strong bearing on the future course of the Government. We add, that we are in its favor because it is a convenient and pleasant season of the year, which will be favorable to a full attendance of Delegates, especially from the distant States.

But we are especially in its favor, because its recommendations conform, as near as may be, to the great fundamental principles by which all propositions connected with the Convention ought to be tested. Taken as a whole, we are of opinion it has adopted the most efficient means that can be devised, in order that the voice of the Convention shall be the voice of the people, in contradistinction to the voice of politicians, and of preserving the relative weight of the States in the Presidential election, as fixed by the Constitution. It secures a compensation, at least in a great degree, by the appointment of the Delegates by Districts, and voting *per capita*, for the surrender, which the smaller States and less populous portions of the Union make, by going into a Convention, of their contingent advantage in case of the election devolving on the House. It is here proper to remark, in order to avoid misconstruction, that in insisting on preserving the relative weight of the smaller States, we are not actuated by the slightest feeling of opposition to the larger. We would not, if we could, subtract a grain from the relative weight assigned them by the Constitution. We hold, that the interest and the prosperity and happiness of each and all are best promoted by a rigid conformity in all things to the provisions of the Constitution, more especially that which touches its great compromises, and on which the balance of the Government depends; and it is principally because we believe it does that, that we give our adhesion to the Maryland plan.

We have now declared our views, explicitly and frankly, on the points in relation to the Convention which, as we believe, remain unsettled by the public voice. Our object is not to throw difficulties in the way of a General Convention, nor to distract or divide our common party. It is the reverse, to harmonize and unite; which, according to our conception, can only be done by a calm, manly appeal to reason, justice, equity, patriotism, and the Constitution. These are, we think, the only foundation on which the Republican party can or ought to stand; and a strict conformity to them in practice, the only means by which union and harmony can be preserved in our ranks.

The objections we have stated against the plan to which we are opposed, and the reasons given in favor of the one we support, are of a grave character, going to the principles of the Constitution, and some of its most sacred compromises, and which touch in its bearings, the very vitals of our political system. If they are true, they must, in the opinion of all who value the Government and the Constitution, settle the points of difference in favor of that which we, in common with so many other States, recommend. The question then is, are they true? That they are, is our solemn conviction, and all we ask is, that the reasons we have advanced in their favor should be carefully, impartially, and dispassionately weighed; if not assented to, the opposing reasons presented in the same spirit of truth and frankness, in which ours have been advanced. If we are wrong, we shall be happy to be put right. Truth is our first object. But as long as convinced that we are right, it cannot be expected, we shall surrender the ground on which they place us. To do so would be an abandonment of principle, and with us principles are of more importance than the Presidency; and we feel assured that Virginia, herself, the plan of whose Convention we have been constrained to oppose, would be the last to expect us to surrender our ground, unless convinced that it is erroneous. It is according to our view, the old ground on which she has made so many glorious battles for liberty, and on maintaining which, her influence and respectability as a State depend; and happy shall we be, at this critical and dangerous period of our political history, to find her standing side by side with us, in her old position, on the ramparts of the Constitution, ready to repel all assaults, from whatever quarter, on its sacred provisions, whether by open and direct attack, or by the still more dangerous hostility of covert undermining.

PC in *Proceedings of the Democratic State Convention, Composed of Delegates from the Several Districts and Parishes of the State of South-Carolina, Assembled at Columbia, on the 22d of May, 1843* (Columbia: printed at the South Carolinian Office, 1843), pp. 7–19; PC in the Charleston, S.C., *Mercury*, May 27, 1843, p. 2; PC in the Pendleton, S.C., *Messenger*, June 2, 1843, pp. 1–3; PC in the Washington, D.C., *Spectator*, June 3, 1843, pp. 1–2. NOTE: Although it cannot be proved by direct evidence, it is herein assumed that the portion of this address beginning with the fourteenth paragraph ("Reason and discussion . . .") and concerning the structure of the national convention was either written by Calhoun or was taken fairly directly from a draft prepared by him. The indirect evidence for this assumption is as follows: the invitation from Ker Boyce to Calhoun to prepare such a document, in Boyce's letter dated 4/29/1843 above; the mention by James Hamilton, Jr., of a "memorandum" sent by Calhoun to the convention, in Hamilton's letter of 6/4/1843 below; the apparent presence of Calhoun's style and thought in the portion of the address referred to; and the fact that Calhoun, in a number of letters below in this volume, sent out copies of the address as exactly representing his views on the convention question. If the conjecture of Calhoun's authorship is correct, then this document embodies one of the most considered statements he ever made on the nature and function of national political conventions, considered from the viewpoint of the Constitution and republican values. Given the fact that, as the "Address" itself observed, the political party convention system had de facto become a part of the constitutional electoral process, then the document assumes considerable significance. The "Address" was presented to the convention on 5/23 as a report of a committee of twenty-one. On 5/24 it was considered by the convention paragraph-by-paragraph and unanimously adopted. The members of the committee were Thomas N. Dawkins, Chairman; F[rancis] W. Pickens, S[amuel] W. Trotti, Ker Boyce, R[obert] F.W. Al[l]ston, J[ames] W. Harrison, H.J. Caughman, J[oseph] A. Black, F[ranklin] H. Elmore, Samuel Porcher, John S. Brisbane, J[ohn] L. Manning, E[dward] G. Palmer, J[ohn] J. Chappell, John Douglass, J[ohn] M. Felder, R[ichard] De Treville, J[ames] J. Caldwell, Edward Frost, G[eorge] W. Dargan, and John McQueen. In publishing the "Address," the *Mercury* stated, "We present to day the Address of the Convention at Columbia, reported by the Committee of 21, through their Chairman, General Dawkins, and unanimously adopted. It is an elaborate and powerful appeal to the Democratic Party of the United States, and we cannot doubt will exercise a great and salutary influence on their action, and on the issue of the presidential contest."

RESOLUTIONS ADOPTED BY
THE SOUTH CAROLINA
DEMOCRATIC CONVENTION

[Columbia, S.C., May 24, 1843]

The Committee of Fifteen, to whom it was referred, to report a plan for the representation of the people of this State in the General Convention of the Democratic Republican Party, and also to report upon all such matters in connexion with the said Convention, and the measures proper to be adopted for promoting the election of JOHN CALDWELL CALHOUN to the Presidency of the United States, as the said Committee may deem expedient,

Respectfully report, that they have had the several matters committed to them under consideration, and submit the following resolutions for the consideration of this Convention:

1. *Resolved,* That this Convention concurs with the Democratic Republican Party in the States of Maryland, Massachusetts, Rhode Island, Louisiana, Kentucky, Pennsylvania, New Hampshire, Michigan, Alabama, and Mississippi, in the appointment of a General Convention of the Democratic Republican Party of the United States, to assemble at Baltimore in the State of Maryland, in May, 1844, and that this Convention recommend the fourth Monday in that month as the day of meeting of the said General Convention.

2. *Resolved,* That in the opinion of this Convention, the Democratic Republican Party in the several States ought to appoint to the said General Convention as many Delegates from each State, as such State is entitled to in the Electoral College of the Union, under the Constitution; two of the Delegates for each State to be appointed for the said State at large, by a State Convention, or by Democratic Republican members of the Legislature of the said State, in Convention; the remaining delegates to be chosen, one for each Congressional District, by the people thereof, in those States which are divided into Congressional Districts, and where there are no such Districts, then to be chosen in such manner as the Democratic Republican Party in such State may deem most advisable, and best calculated to insure the true expression of the will of the people.

3. *Resolved,* That the vote in the said General Convention should be *per capita,* each delegate's vote counting for itself only; a rule consecrated by the genius and principles of the Constitution, and equally indispensible to securing a true expression of the popular will, and the protection of the just rights of minorities.

4. *Resolved,* That this Convention recommend to the people of the several Congressional Districts of this State to elect a delegate, each, to represent them respectively in the said General Convention; the said delegates to be chosen by the people of each of the said Districts in such manner as they may respectively determine upon: and that the delegates to this Convention be, respectively, appointed Committees to bring the subject of this resolution to the consideration of the people of their respective Districts and Parishes, at such time as will insure an election of delegates to the General Convention, on or before the first Monday in April next.

5. *Resolved,* That this Convention proceed to elect, by ballot, two Delegates to represent the State at large in the General Convention proposed to be held in May, 1844.

6. *Resolved*, That the Delegates to this Convention be respectively appointed Committees in their several Districts and Parishes, except in those Districts and Parishes where similar committees have already been, or hereafter may be appointed by the people thereof; which Committees shall be charged with all such matters, in connexion with the objects of this Convention, as may require attention after the adjournment of the said Convention: And that a Central Committee, to meet in the City of Charleston, and to consist of fifteen persons, be appointed by this Convention; which Central Committee shall also be charged with the duties assigned to the Committees for the several Districts and Parishes, with authority to correspond with the said Committees, and to take all necessary measures, for the general objects, which may require united, or general action: including the supply of all vacancies which may occur, by referring them to a State Convention, to be called by them if necessary, or in such other manner as may be necessary to ensure a representation of the will of the people.

PC in *Proceedings of the Democratic State Convention, Composed of Delegates from the Several Districts and Parishes of the State of South-Carolina, Assembled at Columbia, on the 22d of May, 1843* (Columbia: printed at the South Carolinian Office, 1843), pp. 19–21; PC in the Charleston, S.C., *Mercury*, May 26, 1843, p. 2; PC in the Pendleton, S.C., *Messenger*, June 2, 1843, pp. 1–3; PC in the Washington, D.C., *Spectator*, June 3, 1843, p. 2. NOTE: Pursuant to the fifth resolution, Franklin H. Elmore and Francis W. Pickens were elected delegates to the Baltimore Convention. The members of the Central Committee established by the sixth resolution were Jacob Bond I'On, Nathaniel Heyward, Ker Boyce, John S. Ashe, Edward Frost, James Rose, Henry Bailey, F[ranklin] H. Elmore, W[illia]m Aiken, Henry Gourdin, W[illia]m Dubose, John M. Felder, John L. Manning, W[illia]m M. Murray, and M.E. Carn.

From EPHRAIM CLARK

Stat[en] Island [N.Y.,] May 24th 1843

D[ear] Sir, From the very high opinion I have long entertained of your talents and political standing in our Country, I have been induced to address you for the purpose of consulting with and obtaining your advice relative to the most judicious course you would advise [sic] pursued in procuring your nomination as a Candidate for the Presidency of these United States. I am influenced in this matter by the purest motives, believing as I do that their [sic] is no gentleman in our Country having stronger claims, more capacity, or that would give a stronger vote, than him of whom I have the pleasure of addressing. I have taken some pains to ascertain the feelings of our prominent politicians on the Island and am happy to say that your majority over Mr. [Martin] Vanburen would be two to one, and some of the most prominent Whigs that left the Democratic party, driven away by Mr. Vanburen[']s nomination, have assured me that they would support Mr. Calhoun if nominated.

The political standing of the Island would be a very fair criterion to judge of the State. I am aware that there will be a most powerful effort made to obtain the nomination of Mr. Vanburen, which I most seriously deprecate, for if effected[,] without presuming to be a Prophet, Mr. [Henry] Clay will be our next President.

I have ever since I first deposited my vote in the ballot box supported the Democratic party which has been about twenty years and feel great pleasure in the reflection, that I have been uniform in my political principles and wish not to be driven or compel[l]ed to withhold my vote, but Mr. Vanburen would not be my choice and I believe we have the strongest evidence that he is not the choice of the majority of the people of this Country. We have had the assurance given us in the Election of Gen. [William H.] Harrison, and I presume I may venture to say his strength has not increased much since. Mr. Vanburen has lost the influence and fostering care of Gen. [Andrew] Jackson which influence evidently placed him at the head of this great nation.

I presume Sir you will excuse the liberty I have taken in my communication in as much as I am unknown to you. As a reference I will refer you to my neighbour the Hon. Ogden Edwards Esq. who permit me to say but a few Evenings ago at my House, passed a very handsome Eulogy upon your talents and political standing in this great republic. With sentiments of the highest respect I rem[ain] your Ob[edient] Ser[vant,] Ephraim Clark, M.D.

ALS in ScCleA. NOTE: An AEU by Calhoun reads "Dr. Clark[,] not Answered."

From ROB[ER]T R. HUNTER

New York [City,] 27 May 1843
Dear Sir, Since my interview with you at Washington last february, I have anxiously awaited the promised communication from you, and now rendered more anxious, by despair of its receipt, am induced to write you in order to awaken the recollection of that promise.

In observing the political movements and feelings in this part of our Country, I perceive with great satisfaction the favorable progress that you have of late made in public opinion, and cherish the hope that you are destined from the "signs of the times," to make still further progress.

The late attempt and failure of Mr. [Martin] Van Buren to obtain a nomination from the Legislature, will prove to him eventually a sword thrust in his political heart, and the Caucus nomination of him by his *personal* and political friends of the Legislature (among whom was my Brother of the Senate) was the most stupid, and most barefaced political fraud that was ever attempted to be practised upon the understanding of the American people, and proves weakness[,] not strength, and will certainly be abrogated by the people. You may rest assured that although the prospects of Mr. Van Buren to be the nominee of the Democratic Convention, are brighter than John Tyler's, whose credulousness has rendered him the victim of the most egregious dupery, yet they are by no means so bright as yours; he will hereafter meet with opposition from quarters where he now relies for support, and his loss will be your gain.

The principles of free trade with which you have identified yourself, are spreading fast, far and wide in the Country, and your opposition to those innumerable duties which have been laid to the oppression of the landed and mercantile Interests of the nation, daily gains you strength among the mercantile classes, and some of our most eminent merchants, heretofore strong friends of Mr. [Henry] Clay, now express their preference for you on this account.

I leave here in a few days for my summer residence at Sandy Hill, Washington County[,] N.Y.[,] where I will be pleased to hear from you. I contemplate making arrangements to have established a newspaper there this summer to support for the Presidency John C. Calhoun, a man, who whatever errors he may have been charged to have committed in public life, I believe has always loved his Country, and that he may have a glorious share in restoring its Government back to its true principles, is the sincere wish of yours truly, Robt. R. Hunter.

P.S. Our friends W[illia]m Lynn Brown of Philadelphia and [John] McKeon and [James] Kelly of this city, coincide with me in opinion that you should make a visit to Saratoga Springs this summer.

M[ordecai] M. Noah I am just informed is about to establish a weekly paper in this City to support you.

ALS in ScCleA. NOTE: An AEU by Calhoun reads: "R.R. Hunter of N[ew] York[,] An[swere]d 7th June."

From V[IRGIL] MAXCY

West River [Md.,] 27 May 1843

My dear Sir, About ten days ago I went over to Washington to meet Col. [Daniel D.] Brodhead of Boston & Mr. [Edmund T.] Bridge of Connecticut, the Agent of the Post master General [Charles A. Wickliffe] for New England. Events had occurred, which convinced both of these gentlemen (who are warmly interested in your election & have the entire confidence of Mr. [David] Henshaw & other leading friends at the north,) as well as myself of the absolute necessity of removing Mr. [Joseph A.] Scoville from all control over or connexion with the Spectator. A letter from Col. [Franklin H.] Elmore had informed me that Mr. [Dixon H.] Lewis & himself came to the same conclusion before they left Washington & that no pecuniary aid could be expected from Charleston until his connexion with the paper should cease. My letters some time since must have prepared you in some measure for this result. It would be tedious as well as unnecessary to trouble you with the details which have brought us to adopt unanimously the opinion respecting this matter above expressed. Supposing Mr. [Robert M.T.] Hunter could better than any of us bring about a separation between Scoville & [John] Heart upon amicable terms—& all of us desiring very much to consult him on various other matters, it was decided to send Heart down express to bring him up. I wrote him a strong letter & he came up immediately. He concurred with us in opinion as to the necessity of the proceeding we proposed. He undertook to break the matter to Scoville & succeeded in inducing him to surrender his contract with Heart and consent to leave the connexion quietly.

This being effected, Col. Brodhead was of opinion that he could raise considerable pecuniary contributions in aid of those from Charleston for the relief of the debts of the paper & securing the title & control of it, as well as procuring the services of Mr. [Richard K.] Crallé or some other able Editor till the meeting of the convention. He said he would contribute $500 out of his own purse & I engaged to add to the contributions I had already made to prevent the paper from stopping, the same sum. ["I hope our friends" *canceled.*] I only lament that the extreme depression of our tobacco & wheat deprives me of the means at present of contributing more. I had strong hopes of succeeding in a large sale of unproductive property in the course of the summer and had it succeeded succeeded [*sic*] I should not have hesitated a moment to put into the expense fund $5000 instead of $500 but all hope of this is postponed till next winter & ren-

215

dered doubtful altogether. Our friends however in Charleston & Boston I hope will be now ["stimulated" *with the* "la" *interlined*] into activity so as to make the paper at least tri-weekly.

We had some hope before Mr. Hunter arrived at Washington, that we should be able to induce him to come to Washington and without being formally the Editor, yet under the name of Chairman of the Central Committee, to write for, control & give direction to the course of the paper: and in case he would do this, we were prepared to guaranty to him $3000 to indemnify him for the pecuniary sacrifice of removing & keeping his family at Washington until the meeting of the convention. We had some reason to believe for half a day that he might atlength accede to our wishes. In the morning however he came to the conclusion, that he might by such a course lose his influence, if not lose caste, in Virginia, where he thought he could do more for the cause by remaining. Our next effort was to persuade him to consent to have letters, intended for the central committee, *addressed to him* at his residence in Virginia, to answer them & give such direction to the committee at Washington & the paper, as he should judge best. To induce ["him" *interlined*] to do this, I promised to aid him in any way I could, considering my ignorance, from absence from the country of the present attitude & relations of politicians—and especially, whenever he should desire it I would meet him at Washington to consult & advise with him ["and to receive and disburse moneys contributed to the expense fund, which I had before declined in the hope of getting some one at Washington, who could command confidence" *interlined*]. To diminish the burthen of his undertaking, it was agreed that your friends in all the States ought now as soon as possible to organize in each State by appointing a central ["committee" *interlined and then canceled*] & county committees—*the central committee of the State alone* to open a correspondence with the central general committee at Washington.

This arrangement with Hunter, who is so well & universally known & respected, I consider a great point gained. He has agreed to sign the Circulars & correspondence, which will give us the same advantage or nearly the same, as if he resided at Washington—as his name will inspire universal confidence in the prudence & discretion as well as high character of the power, which will control the direction of the Spectator ["and the movements of the Central Committee," *interlined*]—qualities, sadly wanting in Scoville—tho with all his faults, none of us doubt his zeal in your cause. The only thing now wanting is money to place the paper on a respectable footing of at least a triweekly paper—& exertions in all the States to extend the circulation.

Heart says with 500 subscribers only ["for the tri-weekly" *interlined*] he could get along—till they should increase.

Col. Brodhead and Mr. Bridge give the most encouraging accounts of the disposition of the republican party in New England, where they are organizing. They assure me that there will be a decided majority of delegates to the National convention in all the N[ew] England States, except perhaps in New Hampshire, where the question could be settled also in your favor, if [Levi] Woodbury would at once take an open & decided part. This he seems not disposed to do, until he ["makes" *canceled and* "is" *interlined*] sure of being taken up by your friends. As if taking an open & decided part were not the best way to ensure his being ultimately taken up as the Candidate for the Vice Presidency. Altho he has been more true than any ["of the" *interlined*] other prominent public men in the non-slaveholding States in the support of Southern principles & institutions, so far as I am informed as to their course & will probably be the man finally fixed on, it appears to me ["nevertheless" *interlined*] to be too early to cut off all the hopes of [Lewis] Cass & [James] Buchanan and that the question of the Vice Presidency ought to be kept open and subsidiary to the Presidency.

The principal object of the visit of Col. Brodhead & Mr. Bridge to Washington seemed to be to induce the Cabinet to take a more favorable course in the bestowment of patronage & to get the collectorship ["at Boston" *interlined*] & some other important offices filled with your friends. They assured me they had been successful & Mr. Bridge, who seems to have the entire confidence of the Postmaster General, was authorised to [*one or two words canceled and* "fill up" *interlined*] 60 post offices, and he has this confidence, tho' it is known by Mr. Wickliffe & the President [John Tyler] that he prefers you for the next President to all the other canddiates [*sic*] and both these gentlemen assure me that of those, who pretend to be friendly to Mr. Tyler's election, 19 of 20 ["in New England" *interlined*] are in fact in your favor.

Just before Gen[era]l [Duff] Green sailed for Europe he had a long interview with me, in which he urged me very strongly to persuade you to go to Saratoga, Boston—then westerly thro' New York to Ohio & thro' the Western States home and he almost convinced me, that it would produce a good political effect as well as re[c]ruit you from the wear & tear of constant political labours such as you have gone thro'. I almost half promised him I would write you on the subject: but I had given up the idea, until I had a visit last week from our old friend Lem[ue]l Williams, who now practices law in

Boston and is of a decided opinion, that a tour would have a good effect. And indeed I never knew any one who gained so many friends by personal acquaintance as you do: and altho' I have doubted on the subject heretofore I am now disposed, to think favorably of a tour, if you can reconcile your feelings to it. Gen[era]l Green informed me that a great many leading men in the West are warmly devoted to you & wish for your success. Amongst those he named was Jesse [B.] Thomas [former Senator from Ill.], who was formerly so much opposed to you. They want organization in the Western States and I hope some of your friends in So[uth] Ca[rolina], who have acquaintances in those States will write to them to put them in motion.

Gen. Green thought it very important that you should have some confidential friends from the West to attend the meeting, which is proposed in Illinois on the subject of the public lands, in order to influence them in favor of your plan of selling them.

Before leaving Washington, when I went there recently to meet Mr. Hunter, it was agreed, that he should address a circular to such persons in each of the States as he knew were attached to you [*one word canceled*] to urge them to get up a State organization of your friends & to appoint a central Committee in each State to correspond with him & the Central Committee at Washington. Letters ought to be written to the same effect by your friends in So[uth] Carolina.

One of the indiscretions, which Scoville committed & for which we were much displeased, was his exhibiting, from mere vanity a letter received from you. The same motive, a desire to be considered your correspondent, will affect many others. Hence you cannot be too cautious to ["what" *changed to* "whom"] & what you write.

I intended to have written you sooner, but did not like to plague you with the troubles I have had with Scoville, the Spectator &c. until I could, with the aid of others get matters put on a better footing. I hope you will approve of what has been done. The paper is certainly put under better auspices than we could have hoped for and its extensive success must now depend on the aid of your friends in the different States.

Should you come to ["Find"(?) *canceled*] the conclusion that it is best to take the tour so many of your friends desire, I must claim a visit of atleast one or two days as twice a week a steamboat from Baltimore comes directly to a landing on West River in sight of my house in 5 hours, besides touching at Annapolis on its way. And the rail road ["train" *interlined*] every day would bring you either from Washington or Baltimore to Annapolis ["every day" *interlined*]—12

218

miles from my house ["where I could meet you with my carriage" *interlined*]. Mrs. [Mary Galloway] M[axcy] & my daughter [Ann-Sarah Maxcy Hughes], who are with me all insist on this & join me in aff[ectiona]te regards to Mrs. [Floride Colhoun] Calhoun & yourself. Faithfully yours, V. Maxcy.

[P.S.] If I understand your opinions aright on the subject of duties, you have no constitutional objections to making different classes of duties, so as to give incidental aid to manufactures, provided they should be within the limits of a strictly *revenue* tariff. Col. Brodhead expressed a most decided opinion, that if this could be distinctly understood by the manufacturers in New England, that you would gain their support in preference to [Henry] Clay—as what they most desire is *permanence* & *steadiness* in the law, which can never be hoped for in a *protective* tariff.

Gen[era]l Green, it seems, is authorized by the President, to sound the British ministry on the subject of a commercial treaty on fair terms in conjunction with Mr. [Edward] Everett & thinks he will be able to induce them to send out a commission for that purpose to treat at Washington. And if such should be the case, that the President would be disposed to appoint you, as commanding the confidence of the South & [Daniel] Webster as commanding that of the north to meet the British mission at Washington & negotiate the Treaty—either independently of or in conjunction with Mr. [Abel P.] Upshur as Secretary of State. If thro such a treaty a permanent tariff could be fixed, that would satisfy north & south, thro' your instrumentality, it would undoubtedly have the effect with the manufacturers above anticipated by Brodhead & at the same time secure the mercantile interest, as well as agricultural in your support & place your election beyond a doubt. The whole tone of the Press in England & the speeches in Parliament favors very strongly the idea, that the British Government are prepared to relax their corn laws *in our favor*, excluding the continental nations who exclude her manufactures—and also her tobacco duties—if we will come down to a moderate tariff on her manufactures.

Gen. Green was of opinion from his observation in the western country, that if the fund arising from the sales of land on your plan could be devoted ["with your approbation" *interlined*] to making permanent contracts with the Post Master General for the transportation, of the mail & troops & munitions of war with companies, who would construct rail roads for the purpose, [it] would beyond all doubt carry the west in your favor.

ALS and ms. copy in ScCleA.

From W[ILLIA]M SMITH,
[former and future Representative from Va.]

Warrenton Springs Va., May 27th 1843

My dear Sir, Your highly esteemed favour of the 10th Ins[tan]t has been received, after some delay, in consequence of my attendance on a distant Court.

I sincerely thank you for your interest in my success, in my late contest for Congress. In becoming a candidate, I was governed alone by the wishes of my friends. Personally, I did not, at this time particularly, desire a seat in Congress. I knew enough of public life to be aware that merited distinction, (a mere locum tenens I never could be content to be) could only be won by unceasing labour, (unless associated with powers of mind of which I knew I was not master) & that labour my private interests would not allow me to bestow—so that I was really content to retire. I so advised my friends in Richmond; but, still protested against their schemes—procured a change & at last got a scheme, improved, it is true, but far from my liking. [Robert M.T.] Hunter ought to have been elected. I bet upon him. I can't account for his defeat. I could have done better, if I would have stooped to conciliate certain elements of discord among the Fed[eralist]s & softened or shaded my own notions. But I scorned the policy. I proclaimed my hostility to Banks & tariffs from the *house top*. And had I had time, the result here might have been otherwise. As it is, with the whole whig party against me, as far as it can ever be brought against me I reduced the majority of 901 in 1840 to 263 now.

I do not believe our scheme of apportionment, *as adopted* had any reference to results, other than to keep out the Whigs; & to advance certain personal interests of our friends: *As reported* the scheme had other views, I am sure, which were abandoned, I know. Nor, is our State falling away from her ancient principles. I believe she is as firm in them as ever. Her present political exhibit is, ["12" *changed to* "9"] members of Congress, 8 Senators & 16 Delegates, as majorities, giving strong assurance that she is sound & healthy. *And this condition will be more fully demonstrated in the two next annual elections.*

I strongly urged upon Mr. [Thomas] Ritchie, last winter, May 1844 as the period for our general convention. I was much dissatisfied, at the period fixed ["for" *changed to* "by"] our State convention;

because I saw no necessity for so early a day, but an urgent one for the later day; because it was ["designed" *canceled and* "calculated" *interlined*] to defeat the very object it was designed to secure[,] to wit, harmony; & because it could not stand, being opposed, as it seems to be understood by all of our ["friends" *interlined*] talked of, for the Presidency, except Mr. [Martin] Van Buren, who is himself, as I am bound to believe from a conversation I had with Maj[o]r [Abraham?] Van Buren, perfectly content with May 1844. At any rate, an earlier day than May 1844 will be abandoned, every where I have no doubt, but certainly in this State.

A good feeling prevails here among your friends & Mr. Van Buren's. The community, as far as the Democracy is concerned is divided between you & him. And I have no doubt when the time arrives for movements you will be sustained with active cordiality.

I have received from Mr. Van Buren an acknowledgment of my letter touching the R.I. affair, promising to respond in due season. I have addressed my queries to no one, other than you & him, although I shall do so in a few days.

I have recently located at Warrenton Va., with a view, to the improvement of some property adjoining the town, & a larger theatre for the prosecution of my professional career. With friends who prize me—with a wife & children who love me—with a country to protect me, I have determined to dedicate the next few years, God willing, with my health & energies unbroken & unimpaired, to the repair of my private fortunes—the happiness & comfort of my dear wife, & the moral & intellectual culture of my children, taking only such part in politics as may be regarded as a duty. In so doing I feel I shall be a better, certainly a happier if not a wiser man.

In conclusion, allow me to say, that your fortunes can never be without interest to me. In your aspirations I can but sympathize & that too, strongly, for I know they are the aspirations of a pure & lofty spirit, a spirit that loves his country & his kind. With ardent wishes for your health & happiness I am most truly Y[ou]r friend, Wm. Smith.

ALS in ScU-SC, John C. Calhoun Papers. NOTE: An AEU by Calhoun reads: "Hon: W. Smith, Answered the 6th June 1843 & informed him that I had furnished my answer on to his questions and would transmit it as soon as he informed me that he had received answers from any ["oth"(?) *canceled*] other." William Smith (1797–1887), lawyer, planter, and mail contractor, served as Governor of Va. during 1846–1849, Representative from Va. during 1841–1843 and 1853–1861, and president of the first Democratic State Convention in California in 1850. During the Civil War, when he was in his late sixties, he served as Governor of Va. and as a Major General in the Confederate States Army. On 2/10/1843 Smith wrote Van Buren proposing a set of questions regarding Van Buren's opinions on the "R.I. affair," that is, the Dorr disturbances. Van Buren replied on 3/18, acknowledging receipt and promising to answer at leisure, which he did in a long letter dated 7/1843. The Smith-Van Buren correspondence is found in DLC, Martin Van Buren Papers, series 2, letterbook 45 (Presidential Papers Microfilm, Van Buren Papers, roll 26). The similar letter addressed by Smith to Calhoun has not been found, but Calhoun incorporated Smith's questions into his reply, dated 7/3/1843 below. There are also extant three letters from Smith to James Buchanan, posing the same inquiry that had been posed to Calhoun and Van Buren. These are dated 2/10/1843, 6/3/1843, and 6/28/1843. They are found in PHi, in the James Buchanan Papers and the Cadwalader Collection (published microfilm of The James Buchanan Papers, roll 7, frames 511–513 and 584–585, and roll 45, frames 487–488). Buchanan's replies have not been found, although endorsements indicate that answers were written by him to Smith's letters and Smith summarized part of Buchanan's response in a letter below to Calhoun dated 6/28/1843.

From J A [ME] S A. M O R T O N

New York [City,] May 29th 1843

Respected Sir, It becomes my duty to address you as Corresponding Secretary of an Association just organized for the avowed support of Democratic principles, and of the Candidate of the May convention [in] 1844. Our organization is now completed & we have commenced in good earnest the support of those men calculated to carry out the ["do" *canceled*] measures advocated by Tho[ma]s Jefferson and ["at the same time" *canceled*] having the respect & admiration of what is here called the "Young Democracie." I need scarcely say that the majority if not all of our ass[ociatio]n are friends to the "So[uth] C[arolin]a Statesman." We number now some 300—all good men & true—& our endeavors shall prove worthy of the Cause. The object of addressing this letter to you is to acquaint you with our organization as individual effort without union would produce but little good. As to our course—Can it be mercenary? This is not written in order to publish your answer—but in order if possible to promote a concert of action on the part of your friends. Any suggestion calculated to benefit us as an ass[ociatio]n in support of the May Convention & whose predilections are in favor of yourself will meet with the attention deserving them from us as friends of your own. Very Resp[ectfull]y Y[ou]r Ob[edien]t Ser[van]t, Jas. A. Morton, 106½ W[est] Broadway, New York.

ALS in ScCleA. NOTE: An EU in an unknown hand reads, "Answered by Mr. Clemson[,] 7th June 1844."

Speeches of John C. Calhoun, published in 6/1843. This work was printed in 554 pages and was copyrighted by the publisher. It was edited by Calhoun himself, basing the texts on earlier printed versions with slight, occasional revisions. The materials included appear in 38 chapters or sections. The first is Calhoun's speech in the House of Representatives on 12/19/1811 [*sic;* 12/12]; the second is the first two of his "Onslow" letters [of 1826]; the third and fourth are the Fort Hill letter [of 7/26/1831] and the letter to James Hamilton, Jr., [of 8/-28/1832]. The other thirty-four items are speeches by Calhoun in the Senate from 1833 to 1843. The work was first published as *Speeches of John C. Calhoun. Delivered in the Congress of the United States from 1811 to the Present Time* (New York: Harper & Brothers, 1843). It was later reissued, bound with the *Life of John C. Calhoun* which had been earlier published by Harpers, under the combined title page, *Life of John C. Calhoun, Presenting a Condensed History of Political Events from 1811 to 1843. Together with a Selection from His Speeches, Reports, and Other Writings Subsequent to His Election as Vice-President of the United States, Including His Leading Speech on the Late War Delivered in 1811* (New York: Harper & Brothers, no date). In the latter version the work was preceded by a half-title page: "A Selection from the Speeches, Reports, and Other Publications of John C. Calhoun, Subsequent to His Election as Vice-President, (Including Also His First Speech in Congress in 1811), and Referred to in His 'Life.'"

ADVERTISEMENT by Harper & Brothers

New-York [City], June, 1843

It may not be inappropriate to set forth, briefly, the considerations which have induced the publishers to offer this volume [of *Speeches of John C. Calhoun*] to the public. The speeches which it contains afford the principal—it might almost be said, the only—means of knowing the political opinions of a citizen who, for a long succession of years, has occupied a conspicuous place before the people; who, as a high officer of the government at one time, and as a statesman and legislator both before and since that time, has taken a leading part in all the great political questions that have agitated the country; who has long possessed an almost paramount influence in one part of the Union, and been looked upon, in fact, as the chief representative of political opinion in that portion; and who, finally, has now retired from direct participation in the councils of the country, only to occupy the station of a candidate for the highest office in the gift of the people. The political doctrines of such a man cannot but afford interesting matter for attention and study; and it is believed that both friends and opponents of the distinguished person referred to will gladly avail themselves of this opportunity to make themselves acquainted with his views and principles.

The publishers have only to add, that in collecting the materials for the succeeding pages, they have resorted to the most authentic sources. [Signed:] H. & B.

PC in *Speeches of John C. Calhoun. Delivered in the Congress of the United States from 1811 to the Present Time* (New York: Harper & Brothers, 1843). NOTE: The above "Advertisement" appeared only in copies of the *Speeches* with the above cited title page. It did not appear when, later in 1843, the *Speeches* were bound together with the *Life of John C. Calhoun* (previously published by Harpers) and issued with a new title page. In the latter combined publication there appeared a different, undated, and unsigned "Advertisement," as follows: "Since Mr. Calhoun first took a leading part in the politics of the country and the administration of its government, a new generation of men has risen into life, who cannot appeal to their memories for the history of his public services. It was thought necessary, therefore, by his political friends, who desire to see his great abilities and high virtues placed in the widest sphere of usefulness, that a biographical sketch should be published to furnish information to the young, and to revive the recollections of those of more mature age; and to attain their object most effectually, it was deemed expedient that the sketch should be accompanied with a selection from his speeches, reports, and other writings, which would furnish the most authentic evidence of his opinions as well on subjects of high constitutional law as on the great measures of policy which divide and distinguish the two great parties of the country. Such a selection, to be practically useful to the public, must necessarily be very limited when taken in comparison with the whole body of Mr. CALHOUN's very numerous speeches, reports, and other writings, as a complete collection of them would be too bulky and expensive for general circulation. This selection, therefore, contains one speech only delivered prior to his becoming Vice-president, and, while many delivered subsequently have, in order to prevent the volume from being too large, been unavoidably excluded, it is particularly full on the subject of Banks, Independent Treasury, Currency, Tariff, Distribution of the Proceeds of the Public Lands, State Rights, and the principles and policy which should control in the administration of the government, those being the subjects which for some years past have agitated, and still continue to agitate, the public mind, and on which the people of the United States are interested in having exact and authentic information respecting Mr. CALHOUN's settled and matured opinions after the long experience of thirty-two years uninterruptedly devoted to their service." In his letter to Calhoun below, dated 8/29/1843, Virgil Maxcy indicated that he was the author of the second "Advertisement."

To an UNIDENTIFIED NORTHERNER

[Fort Hill, *ca.* June, 1843]

I have received numerous invitations to visit various portions of the Union, and especially the Northern, and given the subject that deliberate and favorable consideration which is due to the wishes of my friends; but must say, after viewing the subject on all sides, that my judgment is against it. I have never known any visit, by one in the position I occupy, that did not do more to weaken, than to strengthen him, and I can see no reason why the fact should not be the same in my case. There are many reasons why it should be so; and among them one of the strongest, in my opinion, is, that there is a large and influential, but quiet portion of the community, who regard the office of President as too elevated, and its responsibility too great, to be the object of personal solicitation or canvass. I must say, I participate in the impression. According to my opinion, the highest office in the Union ought to be the reward only of acknowledged services—services long and faithful, and evincing a thorough knowledge of our system of Government, and a deep devotion to the Constitution, the liberty and the happiness of the country. Thus thinking, I am adverse to taking any step that might be construed so as to place me in an attitude inconsistent with that opinion.

Believing that such would be the certain effect of a visit to the North, or any other section, at this time—that it would be regarded as a mere electioneering tour—I cannot, without doing violence to my feelings, comply with the wishes of my friends. It may appear fastidious, but, as such, in my opinion, would be the fact, I must respect it. If it was a mere matter of opinion, whether it would or would not contribute to the result which my friends desire, I would defer to their judgment, and cheerfully comply with their wishes. I should feel it due to them to make the visit, and should, moreover, take much pleasure in witnessing the great growth and improvement of our country, and in forming the acquaintance of those friends with whom I am now personally unacquainted, and in renewing that of those whom I have heretofore personally known. But as it is, I do hope they will excuse me; and I will thank you to make known to those who have expressed the desire to you, that I should make a visit to their portion of the Union, my reasons for declining to accede to their wishes, and to assure them, that, under different circumstances, it would have afforded me much pleasure to comply with them.

PEx in the Washington, D.C., *Spectator,* July 1, 1843, p. 2; PEx in the Alexandria, D.C., *Gazette and Virginia Advertiser,* July 3, 1843, p. 3; PEx in the Richmond, Va., *Enquirer,* July 7, 1843, p. 4; PEx in the Washington, D.C., *Globe,* July 14, 1843, p. 2; PEx in the Pendleton, S.C., *Messenger,* July 14, 1843, p. 1; PEx in the Petersburg, Va., *Republican,* July 14, 1843, p. 2; PEx in *Niles' National Register,* vol. LXIV, no. 20 (July 15, 1843), p. 316.

From ROB[ER]T L. DORR

Dansville [N.Y.,] June 3 [18]43

My D[ea]r S[i]r, It is a long time since I have heard from [you] dire[c]tly but many times & daily through the papers. It is with much satisfaction as you must probably be aware that I witness the tide setting in, in your favour so strongly in all parts of the U.S. I was as conscious that this would be the result as I have been for three or four years past of my own Existence. The letter of Mr. [Martin] Van Buren [to the Indiana Democrats?] so long, so argumentative, so evasive, so sophistical and uncertain in comparison to others, might & was well calculated, to please the Banking Gentry who are accustomed to this mode of proceeding in defending themselves ["& their iniquities" *interlined*], but has done the work of *self destruction* with the great body of the people. This is true! But I wish to tell you that as your cause advances with the people, my enemies multiply & become more savage & revengeful. The wireworkers of Albany, are using every effort to depress my fortunes, my character & my prospects, & because I have been open, unreserved in your favour since 1837, I have not the positive proof that it all proceeds from Albany but on putting many circumstances together, such is a rational conclusion. The men in this County [that is, Livingston] who are leagued with with [*sic*] what they call the Albany Regency, are very hostile to me, & without any assignable cause & loud in their denunciations against you—they have been incessant in getting up prosecutions against me in all of which I have succeeded against them— done all they could to injure my business & prejudice the community against me—& one of their principal actors has recently commenced a prosecution against me in the Supreme Court for slander—the cause of which originated in an aff[idavi]t I made, in a case pending in Chancery in which I was employed as counsel. He is the very impersonation of Bankism, full of duplicity & double dealing & most an [*sic*] admirable agent for the Albany Regency as might be supposed. My aff[idavi]t charged duplicity in that case. In not liking the revelation [he] has sought satisfaction in this way. They are constantly engaged in schemes to get the advantage & injure me. I never was sued before coming here, & have been sued at least ["14" *changed to* "15"] times, & succeeded in all; they have the village paper under their controul & will not allow an article from me since the rebellion in R[hode] Island—they have had the civil authority under their controul, & to cap the climax of abominations have stuck up a gambling shop next to my office—to create the impression abroad that I keep the company of blacklegs tho' I never enter the room. Should you be nominated for the Presidency or should you be *elected*, & I ["should" *canceled*] be *assassinated* you need not be surprised. Should not this Event take place, & my destruction ["is" *canceled*] not accomplished otherwise, you will discover that it will be owing to my good fortune. You may think that I am telling a pretty large story here to excite your sympathy or to establish a claim to favor in case you should be elected— *no such thing!* What I have stated as facts, are so, & the rest are my solemn convictions. Another circumstance, The Editor of the Village paper here, another fit representative of the Albany Regency, was persuaded to attack me, & my reputation without any cause whatever—& tho' a man of huge dimensions & myself small I had the satisfaction of pitching him head foremost out of my office—& that was ["satisfaction" *interlined*] enough. *They are bent upon my destruction!* Whether they will succeed or not remains to be seen. I endeavour to conduct myself with the greatest propriety—am temperate[,] sober, as moral as I know how to be, & thus far have proven myself competent to defend myself.

In case of serious difficulty I shall call on you for help—the combination is now too strong & formidable for me, & it is difficult to make the people understand the cause, if we should feel disposed, & much more, to believe it tho' solemnly asserted. None know the effects of political persecution so well as those who have experienced it & its extent. With Great respect, Robt. L. Dorr.

ALS in ScU-SC, John C. Calhoun Papers. NOTE: An AEU by Calhoun reads: "Mr. Dorr, Not ans[were]d." This letter was addressed to Calhoun at Fort Hill and was forwarded to Dahlonega, Ga. On one leaf of the letter, in Dorr's hand, is what appears to be an incomplete postscript: "I was about to say" . . . .

From REUBEN H. GRANT

Macon Miss., June 3rd 1843

Sir, excuse me from tresspasing [*sic*] on you. My excuse is like many more of your friends in Miss. We are anxious for your nomination for the Presidency and to secure to you this State and the South generally we deem it important that you should pay us a visit between this and november. You have indicated to me that you intended to visit us last fall. Please inform me if it will be convenient to visit us say by the first of October[.] Would you perfer [*sic*] us to get up meetings at different points and invite you[?] Mr. [Henry] Clay, [Martin] Van buren, [Richard M.] Johnson & [Lewis] Cass are traveling ["about" *canceled*] in different States amongst their friends[.] You must assist your friends[;] come amongst us and you will be received by them with every attention.

Should you perfer to inform me when you could visit Miss. your friends will Greet you in Tuscaloosa[,] Alabama, Columbus[,] Miss., Macon, Miss.[,] Jackson and other places which may suit your convenience[.] If you perfer meetings got up and invitations from the meetings, we will forthwith put them in motion. Your presence in Miss. will secure you her vote which is now considered doubtful but I am certain you have more friends here than any of them but they outmanage us. We want an impulse to action[;] nothing will be so ef[f]ectual as John C. Calhoun amongst us[.] I am with due respect your H[um]bl[e] S[ervan]t, Reuben H. Grant.

ALS in ScU-SC, John C. Calhoun Papers.

To R[OBERT] M. T. HUNTER, [Lloyds, Va.]

Fort Hill, 3d June 1843

My dear Sir, The mail of yesterday, brought me yours of the 23d of June [*sic*; May], and I am glad to find that you do not dispair of the old Commonwealth. The indication every ["every" *canceled*] where South of Virginia is favourable. In this State, there is perfect unanimity & much devotion to the cause. You have of course seen the address of our Convention, and I hope you approve of it. The Georgia Convention meets to day, and I had, before I received your letter, written to an influential member, and enclosed him the address of our Convention, and advised him strongly to adopt the principles throughout, even to districting. There will be no difficulty, as the [U.S. House of Representatives] districts of the bill vetoed by Governor [Charles J.] McDonald can be adopted, which I suggested to him. If Georgia, which is the largest & most influential of the General ticket States should adopt the District system, it will be decisive. I also wrote to Col. [Francis W.] Pickens and suggested the propriety of his writing for[th]with to Mr. [Levi] Woodbury, and urging him to exert himself to induce N.H. to adopt the same course. Her legislature meets this month, and no time is to be lost. Can you not put other springs in motion there? It is important, and every thing ought to be done, to obtain her concurrence. It would go far to settle the question.

I am glad, that you visited Washington, and have got [Joseph A.] Scoville out of the Spectator. All condemn his want of discretion; but I do not doubt his attachment. I agree with you, that he ought to be dealt with liberally; and you may say so to him. I have written ["to him" *interlined*] not more than two or three letters altogether, and they of a character, that can do no mischief, if published. I got a letter [*not found*] from [John] H[e]art on the difference between them, which I enclosed in the letter, I wrote to you or [Virgil] Maxcy on the subject; I do not recollect which. I wrote you both.

Col. Pickens writes me, that he has written you on the subject of taking charge of the Spectator, and that he was authorised by the Presiding officers of the [S.C.] Convention to offer you $4000. I do hope, you will find it consistent with your interest & feelings ["to accept the offer" *interlined*]. It would give the paper at once an established character, & wide circulation, and go far to decide the contest, and ["would" *interlined*] put myself & my friends, if possible, under still stronger obligations. I am sure you could not take a step, that would have greater influence on the contest, and the after history of the country. It would among other things supercede the necessity of establishing a press at Ritchmond [*sic*]. Your Nephew [Muscoe R.H. Garnett?] could be your coadjutor, and on your withdrawal take possession of the establishment; which, if we succeed, would give him a solid basis to commence with. You need not apprehend, that I shall take ["a" *canceled and* "any" *interlined*] hasty step relative to the [national] Convention. I am ["sinceriously"(?) *canceled and* "seriously" *interlined*] anxious to give it a fair trial, though I have no great confidence, that it can be made tolerable. [Thomas] Ritchie has put himself, and through his influence, ["to" *canceled*] put the State [of Va.] in a false position; in that of an associate, ["nominally" *canceled and then interlined*], with the other great central States, but in reality, as the tail of N[ew] York; and it is scarcely possible to bring him and

229

those with whom he acts, in and out of the State, to yield to any fairly arranged Convention. They rely on one constituted for the purpose of effecting their design, and will fight desperately for it. Hence, he will be dec[ide]dly opposed to the address of our Convention. He sees the blow & will struggle to parry it; but, if Virginia shall be true to herself, and my friends stand firm, it will be all ["in van" *canceled and* "in vain" *interlined*]. Her true position is at the head of the South (the weaker Section) and of the medium size and smaller States. It is the one suited to her political ["creed" *interlined*] and out of which, in fact, ["that" *canceled*] her creed grew; and the only one, in which she can maintain her high standing & influence in the Union. In any other, ["it" *canceled and* "she" *interlined*] must become contemptible and be entirely detached from the South. Her desertion of it since 1828, has caused all our disasters & compelled this State, reluctantly, to take the ground she deserted. We never sought it, and would be glad to yield it to her. If he should ever support me, it will be on compulsion, & because he can do no better. Believe what I say. I know him well and his ways, and to what he is wedded. I agree with you, that the true course will be, at the proper time, to go on and make appointments according to our plan ["to appoint" *canceled and* "of" *interlined*] delegates from Districts. I say, at the proper time; for we need not be in hurry. November is already abandoned; and so will the other parts of the plan of the Virginia Convention be, and for the same reason, because the majority is ag[ai]nst it, and in favour of the Maryland plan, and ["that" *canceled and* "in favour of it" *interlined*] because the Constitution & reason are on that side. They will see this and yield, or break up the Convention itself, under the cry of dictation. The last will ["certainly" *interlined*] be the course, if they dare attempt it.

I hope you do not err in supposing, that Gov[erno]r [Cornelius P.] Van Ness will be appointed collector of N[ew] York. It would be a great point, ["third" *canceled and* "second" *interlined*] only [in] importance to your taking charge of the Spectator, and Georgia & N.H. adopting the district system. It would give us a head and a leader, with great influence and skill, where one is most needed.

I do not think, that my friends ought to be uneasy about the Rhode Island question. The questions propounded by Mr. [William] Smith all, except the last, are couched in general terms, and relate to the Federal aspect of the subject. Thus ["thus" *canceled*] presented, they will puzzle Mr. [Martin] Van Buren and the other candidates ["to answer them" *interlined*] much more, than they will me. The last asks my opinion on the right of suffrage involved in the question.

On that, I am too orthodox to be injured. I have just concluded my answer to his questions, and it is now copying, to be sent. I hold the argument on all the points to be incontrover[ti]ble; and that neither of the others can venture to take different grounds, without shocking the sense of the Community. I feel bound to send it to him, but shall do it, under strict injunction not to publish, or to show it to anyone, till he gets the answers of the others, which I have no idea will be shortly. I would be glad, that you could see it.

I agree with you, that we ought to do nothing, that can fairly be avoided to alienate the friends of Mr. Van Buren; but while sarcasm, and every thing of the kind ought to be avoided, I hold, that whenever he, or his friends take false, or deceptive grounds, as on the tariff, it ought to be exposed to the publick, in a moderate and dignified way; and that we ought to be resolute not to be ["driven" *canceled and then interlined*] from our ground, when right. I say so, because, I do not in the least doubt, that he & his friends, including Ritchie, intend to betray us again on the Tariff question. They did so in '28 & '42, and if we permit ourselves to be betrayed the third time, like ["an" *canceled and* "third" *interlined*] apoplectick strok[e], it will be fatal. The worse possible result of the election would be for us to be wheedled by their deceptive arts to aid in his elevation, to be betrayed again on that vital question; not openly, for that they dare not, but by their incidental duties, combined with a permanent high rate of expenditures. Do you not notice, that Van Buren in his Indiana letter speaks of a rate of duty, which would give a revenue of at least $25,000,000, and that Ritchie says, that the Tariff of '42 must be essentially *modified. The Bill of abominations modified!* There is a volume in that.

On the subject of making ["any" *canceled and* "a" *interlined*] declaration on my part, in reference ["reference" *canceled*] to discrimination, I must be excused. I can make none. My sentiments on the Tariff stand of Record, and are such, ["as" *interlined*] I believe to be true. I maintained them in the worst of times, & ag[ai]nst fearful odds, and nothing can induce me to change or modify them. All that can be expected from me ["is" *interlined*], that I will not change the system of revenue, nor make too sudden a transition from ["a bad" *canceled and* "high" *interlined*] to low duties. To that, I am adverse and always have been.

It would be desirable to have the cooperation of [Samuel] Beardsl[e]y [Representative from N.Y.], but I should think, that there is another individual more likely to cooperate with us, and whose cooperation would be more important; I mean, Col. [Samuel] Young, the

[N.Y.] Secretary of State. I am not personally acquainted with him but should think, from all I know of him ["that" *interlined*] he is talented & independent, and from his position, not well inclined to the side of what is called the Regency. It would be well to learn what are his opinion & inclination, if you can do it through some safe & confidential channel.

Gen[era]l Saunders['s] address is Hon[ora]ble Romulus M. Saunders[,] Raleigh N.C.

Let me ["hear" *interlined*] from you as often & as fully as you can conv[en]iently. Truly, J.C. Calhoun.

[P.S.] I hear nothing about the publication of my speeches by the Harpers. What is the matter? It is very desirable, that they should be published early. I would be glad, that you would write to him and ascertain when they are to appear and let me know, as well as the cause of delay.

Ritchie I see is about to open his columns. The battery must be kept up on our side, especially on the address of our [S.C.] Convention. What pens can you put in motion?

ALS in ScCleA; variant PEx's (partly misdated) in Jameson, ed., *Correspondence*, pp. 532–536.

From W[ILLIAM] M. SMYTH

Grand Gulf, Mis[sissi]p[pi,] June 3, 1843
My D[ea]r Sir: You will recognise in the writer of this, the former editor of the Grand Gulf Adverti[s]er, and one of your old and consistent advocates. It is now some six years, since I had the pleasure of addres[s]ing you by letter. I now interrupt this *long silence*, to communicate to you the fact, that I am about commencing a new paper at the Capitol of this State, [Jackson,] which will zealously sustain you for the highest office in the gift of a free people; and for the record, that able and distinguished statesman, Mr. [Levi] Woodbury.

With proper exertions, there is no doubt but that this State will make known its decided preference for the ticket above named. But, I am sorry to say, that the friends of Mr. [Martin] Van Buren, here, as in other States, are, many of them, *secretly* at work to prevent a *fair* expression of the popular voice. This is all we ask, and this is what your friends will insist upon at all hazzards. It will be my great aim, however[?], in the discussion of this question, *not* to exasperate the feelings of Van Buren's friends, but by a course of moderation and fairness, to conciliate and make *converts* to our ranks. The course which some of our papers are pursuing, I think, very indiscrete, and calculated to do more injury than good. Although, I must admit, that the *systematic efforts* of some of the Van Buren organs is enough to give cause for the indignant expression of honest feeling. But, the "leading" papers of our side, should guard against such indiscretions.

Nothing but the deep interest I feel in the next presidential election, and the triumph of pure State rights principles, has ever induced me to engage in the publication of another paper. It is an unpleasant and ungrateful station, under any circumstances; but in this instance, I go into the enterprise with the utmost ardor, conscious that my cause is a *good one*, and that it must triumph.

I will send you a Prospectus of my paper in a few days. My paper will be issued the *4th of July next*. I start to-day to N[ew] O[rleans] to procure my type, &C. and now write in haste. Be pleased to let me hear from you soon—and at all times, when convenient, giving me such items of information as it is important I should be informed of, &C. Yours truly, &C., W.M. Smyth.

ALS in ScU-SC, John C. Calhoun Papers. NOTE: The Jackson, Miss., *Southern Reformer* was established by Smyth in 9/1843.

From J[AMES] HAMILTON, [JR.]

Oswichee Bend, Chattahoochee [River, Ala.,] June 4[t]h 1843
My Dear Sir, Some days after my arrival at this place I had the pleasure to receive your kind favor. I am very happy that you did send the memorandum to Col. [Franklin H.] Elmore for it is not by any means improbable it might have missed me, and the Convention might have been deprived of the import[ant] views which you presented for their consideration.

I am very sorry that Col. Elmore has made the Document so long, as I fear your ["own" *interlined*] admirable matter[?] will be over laid and unread. The great defect in all our public papers is their great length. Even those who have the greatest interest in them have neither time or patience to read them.

The Georgia Democratic Convention meets tomorrow. I went up [river] to Columbus and [*sic*] Evening of the last Week to see Major J[ohn] H. Howard[,] one of the staunchest & most intelligent of the

friends you have in Georgia[,] to confer with him at his earnest solicitation as to the best course for your friends to take in Convention.
I ["of" *canceled*] recommend[ed] a cordial adhesion to the Maryland
plan in the composition of the Convention and an emphatic negative
on the Virginia & New York schemes—and an open & out & out nomination of yourself as the Democratic Candidate—with an equally un-
faltering assignment of their Reasons for such a preference.

On leaving the next morning Major Howard requested me in conformity with this plan to send him up from this place the sketch of
an address and altho on my return home I had but three hours to do
my work on & to send it off by express to Columbus yet I adventured
on the work. But to tell you the truth I have no hope that the address will be adopted for altho it treats your opponents with respect
it takes such decidedly strong ground in your own favor that the timid
will be afraid to play the card, & the bold have too much cunning to
break down to [*sic*] bridge to enable them to retreat on [Martin] Van
Buren if need be. For altho they are aware that if they attempt to
run Van Buren the Whigs will carry the State, yet ["measure"(?) *canceled and* "many" *interlined*] of them after this peril is passed would
be quite willing that Van Buren should get the nomination of the
Baltimore [Convention]. That with the people of Georgia you are
decidedly in a majority I have no doubt. But ["however" *changed to*
"how"] far Howard may be able to control the old [William H.]
Crawford Party remains to be seen. If you see an address adopted
containing your nomination which goes the entire figure you may
infer that he has succeed[ed;] if on the other hand one of a half & half
temporising character is passed you may be certain he has failed.
[Matthew Hall] McAllister of Savannah who probably ["is" *canceled
and* "will be" *interlined*] the most talented & influential Man in the
position will support your nomination as he told me because you were
the only man in the Union who could beat Mr. [Henry] Clay before
the People of Georgia altho he confessed *personally* & politically he
prefer[r]ed Mr. Van Buren. You see the danger we run in having our
work well done. The Convention I apprehend will fear to speak out.
But if Howard carries[?] the address I prepared[,] "*he who runs may
lead*[?]."

My agency in the Document I pray you to hold in confidence as I
do not desire to be known as its Author and it is on all accounts best
that I should not.

In this State [of Ala.] I [*manuscript mutilated*]d Mr. [William R.]
King's friends with the [ho]pe of securing in some way his nomination
to the Vice Pres[i]d[enc]y are creating an impression that your chance

is entirely hopeless, and are thus paralysing the efforts of those who would be otherwise be [*sic*] zealous in your behalf.

I shall gladly embrace the occasion which a visit to attend the ["appeal" *interlined*] Court at Tuscaloosa ["in July" *interlined*] will afford me of doing you all the service there & at Columbus[,] Miss[iss]ippi where my business will call me in my power.

We are quite pleased with our situation here where our Crops are highly promising notwithstanding the long continued Drought. The accounts from Tal[l]apo[o]sa [Ala.] in relation to the Gold Mines are of the most encouraging kind. I am told they promise from their being vein & not surface mines far more than those you have been engaged in in Georgia. I propose visiting them during the next month as they are only 70 miles distant from this place. Would you like to transfer your miners on my securing a privilege & putting an equal number of hands with yours to that section? Can[']t you visit that section of this State this Summer & meet me there? or if not in your power can you give me any information to avoid my being cheated short of keeping out of the business entirely, which perhaps may be best[?] With sincere esteem my Dear Sir Yours faithfully, J. Hamilton.

P.S. Direct to Fort Mitchell Alabama & let me hear from you immediately.

ALS in ScCleA.

To DUFF GREEN, [London]

Fort Hill, 7th June 1843

Dear Sir, I hope you had a pleasant and safe voyage, and that the favorable change going on in reference to the credit of the country, will enable you to dispose of to advantage your valuable property.

The course of events, politically speaking and in reference to myself, as far as I am informed, since you left, is such as you, and my friends would desire. There is, I think, no danger of any State South of North Carolina. That State will be taken either by Mr. [Henry] Clay, or myself; and as I regard Clay's chance to be far from bright, I consider the prospect there to be in my favour. Virginia is a doubtful State, but my friends are sanguine. They think the prospect daily brightens. Of the other portions of the Union I will not speak, except to say, I hear nothing unfavorable.

On the subject of the commercial arrangement with England, I think Mr. [Daniel] Webster's developement was too sudden, and early. The papers in the various parts of the Union were not prepared to take their ground, and many have gone off in the direction of the [Washington] Globe. Even in this State, the [Charleston] Mercury rather fell into its tracts [*sic*; tracks?] under the apprehension, that Mr. Webster's object in the scheme, was to divide and distract the anti Tariff interest, by holding out the fal[l]acious hope of an arrangement, that could never be made. A friend wrote me from Charleston, to know my views, which I gave him, and hope they may have the effect of putting things right, in that quarter.

I must say, that I have not much hope, that anything satisfactory can be done, in the form of arrangement; although I do not doubt the sincerity of the Government on either side. The difficulties are great; but if an equal and fair arrangement can be made, I do not doubt its expediency. I am for free trade; free trade on both sides, if it can be had; but, *if not,* on one side. It is good in part, but better in whole, for the interest of both countries; and my advice, as far as I have an opportunity of giving it to my friends, is to push without the least relaxation for decided action on the part of Congress, at the next session; but at the same time, to throw no discouragement on the attempt to arrange the Duties by mutual agreement; and, I hope, they may take that course. It is, I hold, to be the most certain mode to effect the object they have in view; to strike off the Shackles of Commerce.

I do not concur in the opinion of yourself and other friends that I should travel this summer, or at any time during the Canvass. My judgement is strongly opposed to it. I have never known any one, occupying the position I do, that has not lost by it; and for which many and strong reasons might be assigned. Among them, I believe one of the strongest is, that there is a large, and quiet, but influential portion of the country, who regard the office, as too exalted and too responsible to be an object of personal solicitude, or Canvass [*sic*], and such I must say is my opinion and feeling. The highest office of the Union ought to be the reward of *acknowledged services*—services long and faithful, and, ensuring a thorough knowledge of our system of Gov[ernmen]t and deep devotion to the freedom and happiness of the Country. Under this impression, I have made up my mind to avoid anything, that looks like electioneering. I would rather lose the office, than to seek it by means unworthy, in my opinion, of its dignity, and high and responsible trusts. It may be fastidious, but as such are my feelings, I must yield obedience to them.

I shall be glad to hear from you, whenever it may be convenient.

PC in Jameson, ed., *Correspondence*, pp. 537–538; PEx in the London, England, *Times*, September 1, 1843, p. 5; PEx in the London, England, *Examiner*, September 23, 1843, p. 1.

To HUGH S. LEGARÉ, Acting Secretary of State

Fort Hill, 7th June 1843

My dear Sir, I transmit the enclosed [letter of 5/13/1843, from James P. Lowry to me], knowing nothing further of the case, than the facts it discloses.

My acquaintance with Mr. Lowrey [*sic*] is slight; but, as far as my information extends, his character is respectable. I can only add, if any thing can be done with propriety in reference to the case of his relation, I would be much gratified.

I avail myself of the occasion, to express the hope, that your temporary appointment to the State Department may become, permanent, if the post should be prefer[r]ed by you to that of Attorney General. With great respect yours truly, J.C. Calhoun.

ALS with En in DNA, RG 59 (Records of the Department of State), Miscellaneous Letters of the Department of State, 1789–1906 (M-179:102, frames 18–22).

From EDWARD DIXON

Alexandria [D.C.], June 8th 1843

My Dear Sir, A short time ago I sent you a number of the Alexandria Gazette containing in its columns a communication over the signature of "Justitia" setting forth the superiority of your claims and prospects to those of Mr. [Martin] Van Buren. Mr. [Thomas] Ritchie thought proper to notice the article, and in the paper which I send along with this letter, you will find my reply which is mild and conciliatory. Indeed, it should be the policy of your friends to pursue this conciliatory course towards Mr. Ritchie and the Van Buren party generally, while it is well enough to let them know occasionally that something is due to the opinions and wishes of that portion of the Republican party (constituting indeed the majority of its members) who have from the honest convictions of their minds and from the purest and most patriotic motives, enlisted under your banner. Mr. Ritchie, I presume, entertains a preference for Mr. Van Buren, though Gen[era]l [John R.] Wallace had a conversation with him a short time ago in which he expressed no such preference, but said that his feelings towards you had undergone an entire change. I sent you lately a number of the Democratic Warrenton [Va.] paper [*Flag of '98*] containing an article over the signature of "Americus" which was written, I suppose, by Major [William W.] Wallace who is your warm and steadfast friend and intends to advocate your claims through the medium of the press and in public speeches. This he will do with energy and ability.

A paper [the *Republican*] is about to be established in Petersburg [Va.] which will be edited by a Mr. [Washington] Greenhow who is a young man of great promise and will devote all his energies and talents to the support of your claims. I met with Mr. W[illia]m P. Taylor some time ago in Caroline County [Va.; "who" *canceled*] and he told me that James A. Seddon and some others had resolved to get up a Calhoun paper in Richmond. Whether this will ever be done or not, the threat, at least, will keep Ritchie in check. I have lately had a conversation with Mr. [Edgar] Snowden the Editor of the Alexandria Gazette and he expressed the kindest feelings towards you; he frequently expresses in his Editorials great respect and admiration for ["your" *interlined*] character and talents. You are his next choice to Mr. [Henry] Clay for the Presidency.

The fact that Mr. Ritchie has come into terms in regard to the time of holding the Democratic National Convention is considered very auspicious to your prospects. Indeed, no one seems now to have any idea that the Convention will be held before May 1844. Much, you know, depends upon the time of holding it. It is cheering to your friends ["to see" *canceled*] to see the rapid strides you are making in every quarter. In Virginia, that portion of the Republican party who reside in the country, a plain, ["industr" *canceled*] honest, industrious class of citizens, and who make but little noise about politics and have no ambitious or selfish feelings to gratify, generally prefer you to Mr. Van Buren or any body else for the Presidency. It is becoming more and more ["clea"(?) *canceled*] clearly demonstrated every day that you are the favorite of the ["Re" *canceled*] Republican party, and if the present state of public sentiment throughout the United States is to be regarded as furnishing any index to the future action of the People upon the subject of the Presidency, your friends may very reasonably indulge the hope of greeting you as our next President.

That an Almighty and gracious Providence may aid them in carry-ing out fully their wishes upon this subject is the earnest prayer of Your sincere friend, Edward Dixon.

ALS in ScU-SC, John C. Calhoun Papers.

Assignment by J[OSEPH] A. SCOVILLE to Harper & Brothers

New York [City], June 9, 1843

Know all men by these presents that I, Joseph A. Scoville do hereby assign and make over to Harper & Bros. my agreement with them in regard to the publication of the Life & Speeches of John C. Calhoun on the following conditions—I have this day received from them One Hundred and twenty dollars for which I have given my note at six months from this date. The conditions of this agreement are such—that if the above note is not paid at maturity, then the above assign-ment is good and in full force.

Or should said amount of one hundred and twenty Dollars be paid at any time previous to the date when said note falls due—then this assignment becomes null and void and of no effect. J.A. Scoville.

ADS in NNC, Archives of Harper & Brothers, 1817–1914 (published microfilm, reel 1); FC in NNC, Archives of Harper & Brothers, 1817–1914 (published micro-film, reel 55).

From M[ICAH] STERLING

Watertown [N.Y.,] June 9, 1843

My dear sir, I have a thousand things to say to you, & more than one object in writing to you. I conclude you of course know what is go-ing on among our Democratic friends in the Nation, and that we have reason to think the prospect of our success is flattering.

That Mr. [Martin] Van Buren has more of the political leaders & hackneyed politicians, in his favor than any other of the candidates is very probable, particularly in this State where his friends for a long time have headed and lead the Democracy.

Those men still taking the lead will probably carry this State for V[an] Buren, in spite of all that your friends can do—but you are strong in the South, and Western part of the State, and it is already clear that your friends will carry the day, as to the time of holding, and probably as to the mode of constituting the [national] Convention. But I am satisfied that you would succeed could you get into the house [of Representatives] and that you will go in if the convention does not prevent it. A most worthy and excellent friend, ["writes me" *canceled*] L. Beardsley, writes me from Ohio, that the plan will be for all to rally, & unite in the first place against Van Buren, and then go for the next strongest, and gives his opinion that you will be the man.

I am surrounded by the friends of V[an] Buren, tho' there is no hostile feeling to you, & the Whigs to a man prefer you to Van Buren, tho' many of them pretend to fear you on account of the Tariff and nullification.

The last bugbear was well explained, & laid at rest in a Biography of you lately published. The question of Slavery, you will of course expect, will operate against you in the minds of some northern men. I occasionally hear from the Committee at Washington who will do good, if they do not in their zeal overact.

My object in writing you now was to say that my son John Calhoun [Sterling], or myself, or both may spend next winter at the South. The health of neither of us is good, & I am inclined to think a Southern climate during the winter, might prove beneficial.

The health of John is however much improved of late, and I think bids fair, to become well established. Should he go to the South he would like a place as a teacher, in a private family or public School. I should go, & visit [John M.] Felder, [former Representative from S.C., Isaac H.] Bronson, [former Representative from N.Y.,] & perhaps yourself.

Is not yours a very healthy regeion [*sic*]. I think I have heard So. Write me soon & give my best regards to Mrs. [Floride Colhoun] Calhoun. Truly yours &c, M[icah] Sterling.

LS in ScU-SC, John C. Calhoun Papers. NOTE: This letter was addressed to Calhoun at Fort Hill and was forwarded to him at Dahlonega, Ga. An AEU by Calhoun reads: "Mr. Sterling, ans[were]d 8th July."

To A[NDREW] P[ICKENS] CALHOUN, [Marengo County, Ala.]

Fort Hill, 10th June 1843

My dear Andrew, I wrote you immediately after Mr. [Thomas G.] Clemson's return from Virginia, which was much earlier, than was expected, and informed you that he had got back. I learned by your letter of the 24th last month, that you had not got ["the" *interlined*] one from me ["written" *interlined*] after his return, which ought to have arrived about th[*manuscript torn*] time. I have been waiting for a we[ek] to hear of your having received it, and [to] learn when I might certainly exp[ect] you. Not having heard, I conclude, either my letter to you has miscarried or your reply to it to me; and in the uncertainty of the time for expecting you, I have concluded to leave home for Dahlonega this evening or tomorrow, to attend to my business there, which requires my presence. I shall be gone 8 or 10 days, and do hope on my return to get a letter from you, informing me certainly when I may expect you. I am exceedingly anxious to have our business with Mr. Clemson closed, as I am sure you must be. It is a large transaction, and ought not to be left open. I repeat what I said to you in my last, I wish you to bring all the papers requisite to a full settlement all round, including his, as well as our own.

The weather has been very dry till last night, when we had a fine rain. The Drought, tho pretty severe, I think, has done [no] lasting damage, except to the oat crop. [I w]rite in much haste, as I am preparing to [leav]e, and can add no more, except that [we] are all well and all desire their [lo]ve to you, Margaret [Green Calhoun] & Duff [Green Calhoun]. Your affectionate father, J.C. Calhoun.

ALS in ScU-SC, John C. Calhoun Papers. NOTE: The manuscript transcribed above is badly faded and is missing a fragment from its edges.

HARPER & BRO[THER]s to V[irgil] Maxcy, West River, Md.

New York [City], June 13th 1843

D[ea]r Sir, Yours of June 5th [*not found*] has just reached us.

Before receiving the parcel of proofs, accompanying your letter, we had finished printing a small edition of the Speeches, which we are now sending out to our customers. The errors pointed out, however, shall be carefully corrected before any more copies are printed, so that the subsequent editions will be entirely correct.

Your observations, in relation to your being disappointed in the circulation of the Life [of John C. Calhoun], we remarked upon in our letter to you a few days since—which we presume had not reached you at the time of your writing. In the conversation referred to, we wished simply to be understood, that our correspondents were more numerous than those of any other House in the Trade, and that it would afford us pleasure to use them in circulating the Memoir. This we have endeavoured to do, not only by advertising, but by sending the work unordered to our agents. [*"But"* canceled and *"And"* interlined] we supposed that the friends of the cause throughout the country would have seconded your and our efforts, by purchasing those thus sent out, and causing more to be ordered—as they did in the case of Gen[era]l [William Henry] Harrison's Life. But this, we are sorry to say, they have not yet done to any extent. Had but a few of Mr. C's friends acted as spiritedly as you have, the circulation would probably have met your expectations ere this. The copies referred to, for the members of the Legislature, were forwarded—but through some mismanagement somewhere it appears they did not get into their hands in time. We hope when Congress meets, some more efficient measures may be contrived and pursued. Some of the work ought to [be] franked and distributed gratuitously in the small villages and obscure places throughout the United States. Thus far the circulation of the Life has reached about 18000. Some of the members of Congress, we are sorry to say, reduced their subscriptions materially. It is sold at a very low price—and we hope it may still become extensively distributed. Nothing could afford us more pleasure. And any suggestions from you, having this object in view, will be thankfully received. In haste. Respectfully, Y[ou]r ob[e]d[ien]t Servants, Harper & Bros.

LS in DLC, Galloway-Maxcy-Markoe Papers, vol. 48.

From EDWARD DELONY

Clinton La., June 14[t]h 1843

Sir, It is pretended by some, and so contended, that the principles of free trade, as advocated by you, will lead to *direct taxation* as a means of raising a sufficient revenue for the support of government.

This opinion, I presume, must arise from a misconstruction of your views upon this great question of *free trade*; If I understand what you mean by *"free trade; low duties; no debt"* &C; it is to reduce the fiscal operations of the government to a simple, economical system, to incur *no debt*, by unnecessary expenditures, or appropriations, schemes of internal Improvements, funding systems or assumptions, unwarranted by the Constitution, but to bring the government back to the essential and natural object of its creation—a *simple agency* of the people of the several States, created by them for certain defined purposes and acting under certain specified powers—and not a *great patron* of corporate bodies, sectional or seperate interests and monopolies; The Government thus reformed to this simple and wholesome sphere, the expenses necessary to its support would be greatly reduced, so much so, indeed, as to carry down the duties for revenue to the lowest standard; The result of this state of things, as every body must see, would be *free trade* to all intents and purposes and which would cause a speedy development of the great and general benefits that would be derived from it by all classes, as well as by all the varied interests, of the american people.

Such Sir is my opinion of your views in regard to this interesting subject, though very briefly and imperfectly expressed, and in these views I cannot perceive any thing whatever tending in the least to the necessity of *direct taxation.*

But however well satisfied I may feel myself upon this subject, injustice may be done you by others and your friends misled into erroneous impressions as to the policy which would necessarily result from their construction of your views of *free trade.* I have the honor to be Very Respectfully Sir Y[ou]r fellow Citizen, Edward Delony.

ALS in ScU-SC, John C. Calhoun Papers.

From SAM[UE]L D. DENVON

Richmond [Va.,] June 14th [18]43
Dear Sir, Many Democrats of Richmond have Read Your letter [of 1/26/1843] to the Democratic Committee of Indianna and we Cannot fully Understand You. You say to the Committee You Abide by the decishin of a convention fairly formed[;] please answer us this question[:] will You or will You ["not" *interlined*] Abide by the deciscion of a Democratic Convention no matter weather You are the the nominee of said Convention or not. Your Compliance will Greatly oblige Many Democrats of Richmond. Your obed[i]ent Servant, Saml. D. Denvon.

P.S. Answer this by next Return mail. S.D.D.

ALS in ScU-SC, John C. Calhoun Papers. NOTE: This letter was addressed to Calhoun at Pendleton but was forwarded to him at Dahlonega, Ga. An AEU by Calhoun reads: "not answered."

From E[phraim] B. Wheeler

Rochester [N.Y.,] June 15 1843

D[ea]r Sir, Although a stranger to you allow me to say that I feel a deep interest in the next Presidential Election.

And as your name is associated with the names of other distinguished individuals for the first office in the gift of the people, I would respectfully ask are you in favor of the District System of appointing Delegates to the national convention in all parts of the union for the purpose of nominating candidates for the Office of President and Vice President?

My sole object is so to politically arrange my own section so that it shall co operate with the Democracy entire and in those operations I should also wish to learn should President [John] Tyler nominate to office any of the Democracy (your friends) of Western New York for any office in his gift—will the Senate confirm such nominations. If they will Western New York will be again Democratic! The young Democracy of this section are cooperating with the City of New York, and with the joint Cooperation of both sections we can fix the time & the manner of appointing our delegates, to the national convention.

The City of New York and the Democracy of the entire west are decidedly for the District System and a convention in May 1844 with that System you have a majority of the Empire State.

The young Democracy of this entire western section of the State and a great portion of the whigs will Come in to the rescue. In using the term a great portion of the whigs I mean the Democratic portion which was lost to the Democratic party under the reign of Terror (Anti Masonry)[.]

I wish to know your views before choosing Delegates to our State Convention which is in September next so that this section can appear in our State Convention with its wed[d]ing garment on to co operate in such a manner as shall be ["come" *canceled*] judicious and ensure union and success to our efforts and may God grant the victory Complete.

You will see by my name ["see" *canceled*] that I have been influential in obtaining from the Hon. John C. Spencer his letter to his friends in Western N[ew] York, which has been published generally, by this however I do not wish you to understand that I am or have been a whig. I am very far from it. I am a Democrat now[,] always have been and I pray God I ever shall be[.]

I have written this as your political friend to be confided to [yo]ur own bosom and shoul[d yo]u deem it of sufficient im[portan]ce to merit an answer I sha[ll] consider it equally confidential on my part and all communications which I send, giving you the situation of Western N[ew] York, politically. I remain Sir your friend and obedient Servant, E.B. Wheeler.

ALS in ScU-SC, John C. Calhoun Papers. NOTE: This letter was addressed to Calhoun at Charleston, S.C., and was forwarded thence to Pendleton. An AEU by Calhoun indicates that he answered it on 7/7.

From R[OBERT] M. T. HUNTER

L[l]oyds Essex [County,] Va., June 16th [1843]
My dear Sir, I have just received letters from [Levi] Woodbury and others in New England. I wrote to Woodbury before the meeting of the N[ew] Hampshire Convention to beg him to go to it and take an active part for you. I said that the nomination of [Martin] V[an] B[uren] by that Convention would be considered as a fatal blow to him and whatever might be the professions of those who made the movement such would be their design. But for him the Convention would have nominated V[an] B[uren]—as it was they made no nomination, and recommended May 1844 and a district representation. Under the circumstances this was a great victory. We shall carry the Democratic party of New England. Our friends are in high spirits. Colo[nel Daniel D.] Brodhead has sent $400 to the Spectator, the Charleston Committee $500 and Dr. Brodhead a poor clerk in Washington loaned it $350. For the present and for a short time it is out of danger.

Our friends in N[ew] England are about to organize. I am writing to our friends wherever I can rely upon them to beg them to get up an organization by Congressional districts. If we have (as we shall have) a district representation this organization is essential as a preliminary step and indeed through this organization we can force a district representation. Suppose we were to invite an election of delegates by the party at the polls, assimilating the mode to ["that of" *interlined*] the Congressional election, and that our strong men in each district would take the stump for you and rally the people to the polls. V[an] B[uren]'s ["friends" *interlined*] would be obliged to go in. He would certainly be beaten if he did not, he would probably be beaten if he did. I am doing my best to get up such an organization and especially in Va. We will beat down [Thomas] Ritchie[']s influence in that way if he resists us.

By the way [Washington] Greenhow is about to establish a Calhoun paper in Petersburg. Ritchie has so many well wishers amongst our own friends that we thought it most prudent to avoid the odor of opposition to the [Richmond] Enquirer and to hang upon his flanks until he opened himself so as to justify an attack upon his center. If the paper is sustained it will ultimately move to Richmond unless Mr. Ritchie should take a satisfactory course.

I had entertained some hopes of [Samuel] Young at one time and had written three weeks ago to friends in New York to ascertain his true position. For reply I received a paper in which he publishes his preference to V[an] B[uren] to silence there recent rumors. He is more of a N.Y. politician than V[an] B[uren] himself and our friends in Poughkeepsie made a mistake in endeavoring to identify him with our cause. He is one of those enemy-friends of V[an] B[uren], who are the most subtle of all politicians and win both office and hate from him without being grateful for the former or caring a rush for the latter. [Charles Augustus] Davis (Jack Downing) is now making a tour in western N.Y. and promises to give me the result of his observations upon his return. But it is hard to make a lodgment in that State. The keys of office would be more potent there at present than those to St. Peter[']s gate. I wish we had [Cornelius P.] Van Ness in the Custom House. But I hear nothing more of that for the present. I have a great many letters still to write. Most truly your friend, R.M.T. Hunter.

P.S. I have just received your letter of 3d June for which I am much obliged to you. I have not time now to answer it but will write by the next mail.

ALS in ScCleA; variant PC in Jameson, ed., *Correspondence*, pp. 865–866.

From TOMLINSON FORT,
[President of the State Bank of Ga.]

Milledgeville [Ga.,] 17th June 1843
Dear Sir, By this mail I forward you the [Milledgeville] Federal Union [newspaper], containing the proceedings of our Democratic State convention.

Mr. [John H.] Howard of Columbus, detained by indisposition, was not at the convention; but your letter to him was shewn to a few of your friends. I regret that our proceedings do not fully correspond with your views. They are in the best form we could have passed them with suitable unanimity, and I hope they will have a good effect at this juncture. I dread as much as any one can, the intrigues of a National Convention, but I see no way of avoiding that ordeal.

It may be interesting to you to know something of the present state of parties in Georgia. The Nullifiers of 1830 are the Whigs of 1843. There are a few exceptions including, Messrs. [Mark A.] Cooper, [Walter T.] Colquit[t], [Edward J.] Black[,] Howard &c, who ["are" *canceled*] united themselves with the Democrats in 1840. The number of this class is very small, but they are petted like a returned prodigal. By far the largest portion of the Democratic Party are the Union Party of 1830. They number at the polls at least thirty thousand. They have twice supported Mr. [Martin] Van Buren for President and are well inclined to do so again. It has required some effort to give the matter the direction it took in our convention. The Democratic Party as it is now constituted includes, three classes of politicians well known to each other, viz the old [John] Clark party, the Union men who with Mr. [John] Forsyth joined it in 1830[,] and the recruits of 1840—above mentioned. The old Clark men, and the new recruits have concurred in your support—the men of 1830 have proven untractable. Indeed they had before I was aware of it taken a decided course, and pushed it to the last with zeal and talent. Our majority however was very decided, and we have full faith in running you successfully should you run under a regular nomination.

In renewing a long neglected correspondence with you, I may without impropriety express the satisfaction I have had in giving my aid in organising the Democratic Party in your name. As principal proprietor of the Federal Union office and intimate friend of its Editors I have had it in my power to do something more than I could otherwise have accomplished. That paper has effected more than any thing else in this matter and I have the pleasure of stating that its present editors have the proper feeling on the subject. Expecting to continue in the present relation to that office, I ask the favor of you to let me know if you have particular views on the questions which may arise and especially if on any point of policy it is important to take a decided stand. This letter is of course *strictly Confidential.*

Mrs. [Martha Fannin] Fort desires her best respect[s] presented to yourself and family and I remain y[ou]r friend and ob[edien]t serv[an]t, Tomlinson Fort.

ALS in ScU-SC, John C. Calhoun Papers. NOTE: This letter was addressed to Calhoun at Pendleton and was forwarded to Dahlonega, Ga.

From W[ILLIAM] M. CORRY and Others

Cincinnati, June 19 1843

Sir, The undersigned have been appointed a Committee by a public meeting in this place held on the 31st Ult[imo] to invite you to visit this city and State, as soon as you can make it convenient.

The resolutions adopted on the occasion, and herewith transmitted will explain the sentiments and motives of the meeting.

Nothing, it seems to us, can be more natural or reasonable than the desire of the people of this country to see and to know personally, one of whom they have heard so often—one who has gained so much distinction in the councils of his country, and confer[r]ed so much on them—one whose clear perception and powerful defence of the great truths of political science at a time when they were overlooked, opposed, or unpopular, has contributed so much to render them at last triumphant. The people of the West and SouthWest already most important sections of the Union and rapidly advancing to entire political preponderance cannot but be grateful to one, who more than any other man has *protected* them during their political minority from the unequal and injurious action of the government, when it was subjected to the controul of other sections of the Union—and made subservient to a scheme for securing special priviledges [*sic*] to their labour and capital over the rest. In defeating this design we consider that you were first and foremost—and in the most trying emergency supported only by the noble and enlightened State you then represented. To your success then in divorcing the government from an alliance with ["a" *canceled*] special interests and in the subsequent separation of government from banks, a policy to which you gave completeness and an argument which on that question has never been answered nor equalled, the new States of the West and South are indebted for much of the progress they have already made in wealth and power, and much of the promise which now presides over their destiny.

We trust therefore that in calling you amongst us in order that we may render our living testimonials of gratitude[,] attachment and esteem, we shall present to you the not unpleasing spectacle of a prosperity and greatness[,] the offspring in a material degree of that policy which is more peculiarly your own than any other man's.

We invite you to a contemplation of these fruits of your labours, and the elements of future greatness in which our section of the Union abounds, that you may be stimulated to even further effort in accomplishing the high destinies of our common country.

We are aware that at a time like this when the people are engaged in a Presidential canvass, and your own name stands amongst the very first of those from whom they are expected to choose a chief magistrate, your visit might be by some attributed to a sinister motive—to the desire of popularity. But we think that the circumstances of the time more gravely considered forbid this imputation. Your recent retirement from long and arduous public service affords the first opportunity for many years in your power of making such a visit. And as it cannot be expected that your countrymen will long consent to your relinquishment of public affairs, the present interval affords perhaps the only opportunity that may arise, for surveying a region of the country whose progress and prospects afford the finest subjects of contemplation ever presented to the mind of a great statesman. If this be not enough to suppress any objection to your visit, your own peculiar public character and career ["and" *canceled*] would be more than enough. From the beginning to the ["f" *canceled*] very last acts of your public life you have too often deliberately encountered the popular errors of the day to be now obnoxious to the reproach of an ignoble or undue solicitude for ["mere" *canceled*] popular favour. Besides Sir, it is now an established custom of the country for her distinguished men to visit at the invitation of their friends the various sections of the Union: And in pursuance of that practice, almost every man whose name has been mentioned as deserving the highest public trusts ["of the people" *canceled*] has already been amongst us—so that it is now a common subject of enquiry and surprise that you also have not been here.

We might dwell much longer on the several reasons we have suggested for your compliance with our request, and urge many more—more than our limits allow, but will content ourselves with submitting these considerations to your mind believing them to be sufficient, and await with confidence a speedy and favourable answer. With sentiments of profound regard and attachment we are your friends, W.M. Corry, Ellwood Fisher, J.L. Vattier, Stephen Hulse, W[illiam] F. Johnson.

[Enclosure]

At a large and respectable meeting of the Democrats of Hamilton County for the purpose of inviting the Hon. John C. Calhoun to visit them and the State of Ohio, William H. Roche was called to the Chair, and George E. Pugh [later Senator from Ohio] elected Secretary.

On motion, W[illiam] M. Corry, Mark Buckingham, W[illia]m Hunter, W.M. McCarty, Charles Moore, W.S. Smith, and Peter Linn were appointed a Committee to report a preamble and resolutions expressive of the sense of the meeting—who, after a short absence, submitted the following:

Whereas the two political parties of the United States are now engaged in a violent contest not only about the manner in which the General Government is to be administered, and the persons who are to be entrusted with it, but concerning its very nature:

And whereas the Democratic party is decidedly in favour of that strict construction of the Constitution which will preserve the integrity of State Rights—confine the executive, legislative, and judicial departments of the General Government to their appointed orbits—and prevent inevitably the intrusion through either of them of vicious forms and projects upon the People:

And whereas the Democratic party, in pursuance of these principles, is unalterably opposed to each of the cardinal points of Whigism, to wit:

1. To any connexion of the banks and government,
2. To any distribution of the land-fund,
3. To any further limitation of the Veto power,
4. and, above all, to any protective tariff:

And whereas it is evident that the success of opposition to false opinions is infinitely more certain when the champions of the true are recognised and respected than when they fall into neglect—under which belief the Democrats of this County and the State at large have lately extended their hospitalities in succession to several prominent statesmen at present out of actual service:

And whereas the West, as much as any portion of the Union, has a deep interest in the establishment of those doctrines for which the Democratic party is now struggling against hosts of enemies:

And whereas John C. Calhoun has devoted the powers of a great mind to the support of these doctrines, and recommended them effectually, by his wisdom and eloquence, to the enlightened judgment of the country:

Therefore be it resolved,

1. That for the sake of the Cause, as well as respect for the Man, the Democracy of Hamilton County do hereby declare their high esteem for Mr. Calhoun as a Democrat who has done faithful service throughout an arduous and brilliant career in offices of the first importance.

2. That his suggestion and support of "the specie clause" went to the root of the evil of banking six years ago—that nothing else can restore to the South and the West the fair action of their intrinsic re-

sources, and to the country at large the integrity of the Constitution.

3. That his late speeches, in the Senate of the United States, on the Independent Treasury Scheme, the Land Bill, and the Veto Power, entitle him to pre-eminent rank as an expositor of the Constitution and a friend of the People.

4. That we regard, with the most vivid admiration and gratitude, the long and invincible defence of Free Trade which has been made by John C. Calhoun almost alone, and through evil report not less than good.

5. That the People of the West generally, and of Ohio in particular, have heretofore suffered extremely from the protective policy to the loss of many millions of dollars, and that the oppressive and scarcely tolerable action of the federal government by its means forces the Tariff Question into the greatest political issue of the day.

6. That the Democratic electors of Hamilton County, in order to show their deep sense of what is due to The Champion of Free Trade for exertions which are this moment felt at every fireside, do invite John C. Calhoun to visit them at Cincinnati as early as may be convenient to him.

7. That we seize this interval in Mr. Calhoun's incessant public employment, with pleasure, as affording him and us the first opportunity of meeting face to face in a region whose value and welfare have never left his thoughts—the Valley of the Mississippi.

8. That we feel the utmost desire to make the personal acquaintance of the statesman whose motto is—"Free Trade, low duties, no debt, separation from banks, economy, retrenchment, and a strict adherence to the Constitution."

9. That the spotless character of Mr. Calhoun presents the strongest guaranty, if any were wanting, of the purity of motive which has hitherto directed the whole course of his public life and will preside in future over the career which his country may assign him.

10. That a committee of five be appointed, by the Chair, to send the letter of invitation to Mr. Calhoun covering these resolutions.

11. That our proceedings be signed by the officers of the meeting, and published in the democratic papers.

Which preamble and resolutions were unanimously adopted.

In pursuance of the tenth resolution, the Chair appointed W[illiam] M. Corry, Ellwood Fisher, J.L. Vattier, W.F. Johnson, and Stephen Hulse a committee to forward this invitation to Mr. Calhoun.

Several gentlemen addressed the meeting—after which, on motion, it adjourned. [Signed:] W[illiam] H. Roche, Chairman; G[eorge] E. Pugh, Secretary.

LS with En in ScU-SC, John C. Calhoun Papers; PC in the Cincinnati, Ohio, *Daily Enquirer,* August 2, 1843, p. 2; PC in the Richmond, Va., *Enquirer,* August 15, 1843, p. 2; PC in the Washington, D.C., *Spectator,* August 19, 1843, p. 2; PC in the Charleston, S.C., *Courier,* August 25, 1843, p. 2; PC in the Pendleton, S.C., *Messenger,* August 25, 1843, p. 1; PC of En in the Cincinnati, Ohio, *Daily Enquirer,* June 5, 1843, p. 2; PC of En in the Petersburg, Va., *Republican,* June 22, 1843, p. 3.

From ASHBEL SMITH, [Chargé d'Affaires of the Republic of Texas in Great Britain]

London[,] 3 St James's Street, June 19, 1843
My dear Sir, Some months since I wrote to Mr. [Isaac] Van Zandt, the Texian Chargé d'Affaires at Washington, concerning the proceedings of certain parties in England, having for their *immediate* object the abolition of slavery in Texas. I requested Mr. Van Zandt to communicate my letters on this subject to yourself and a few other gentlemen, in confidence. I wished it to be in confidence so far as my name was concerned, inasmuch as I alluded to the British Government in connection with this ["subject" *canceled and* "matter" *interlined*]; and being the Representative of Texas to this Court, the publicity of my name would be disagreeable. For the same reason, please keep my name confidential.

Great efforts are making here to accomplish the abolition of slavery in Texas. An agent of the abolitionists in Texas [Stephen P. Andrews] is here now in London in close intercourse with the English Abolitionists, concerting the means of attaining this object. I have just had a long conversation with him. He is to have an interview to day at 4 o'clock with the Earl of Aberdeen [Secretary of State for Foreign Affairs] on this subject. I cannot undertake to say what active measures the British Government have taken, nor whether they have authorized any distinct propositions to be made by Capt. [Charles] Elliott [*sic*] their Chargé d'Affaires, to the Government of Texas, for the abolition of slavery in that country; but I am *certainly* assured on *unquestionable authority,* that it is the subject of official communication from Capt. Elliott to his Government, and that the British Government are fully cognizant of all that is done in relation to the matter.

Ample but hitherto vague promises are held out to the Texians for the abolition; the advantages of an immense emigration from

252

Europe which would give a value to our unsettled[?] lands ["is" *altered to* "are"] greatly insisted on. It is alleged that such an emigration from Europe would immediately take place upon slavery being abolished. I sincerely believe that the ultimate purpose is to make Texas a refuge for runaway slaves from the United States, & eventually a negro nation, a sort of Hayti on the continent, to be more or less [*two words canceled*] according to circumstances, under the protection of the British Government. Neither would European emigration flow into Texas on the abolition of slavery. Powerful parties here—both governments and individuals—would oppose it. They have their own colonies to which Governments wish to direct their emigrating population; and individuals are largely interested in speculation for ["colonizing"(?) *canceled and* "settling" *interlined*] portions of their colonial territories. Texas is not like the United States so known as to be above the influence of interested parties in Europe.

The abolition of slavery in Texas is deemed a small matter in itself considered. It is regarded as infinitely important as an entering wedge to the abolition of slavery in the United States—as a point d'appui for operations against the *institutions* of the *Southern* States.

I have been compelled to write to you in *great* haste, to be in time for the packet for[?] tomo[rrow] from Liverpool. You *may rely on the accuracy* of the few facts and opinions I have stated. By next mail I will write more fully to yourself or some of our Southern friends.

The abolition of slavery in Texas is fraught with infinite dangers in my opinion to the South. Will the South look to it?

With sentiments of the highest esteem, I am Your very obedient servant and friend, Ashbel Smith.

FC in TxU, Ashbel Smith Papers, Letterpress Book, [pp. 284–286]. Note: This document is faint and nearly illegible in places, and several words have been conjectured. In a letter of 5/23/1845 to Andrew J. Donelson (ALS in DLC, Andrew Jackson Donelson Papers), Calhoun stated that he received two letters from Ashbel Smith in 1843. The recipient's copy of neither has been found. The letter above was probably the second of the two. The recipient's copy of the letter above was sent by Calhoun to Secretary of State Abel P. Upshur, according to Upshur's letter to Calhoun below of 8/14/1843. The other of the two letters from Smith that Calhoun mentioned in 1845, which he indicated was received early in the year while he was still in the Senate, is entirely lost. Possibly this was, as suggested in Smith's first paragraph above, communicated indirectly through Isaac Van Zandt. In a later recollection, Smith stated: "These facts [about the World Antislavery Convention] were communicated to Mr. Van Zandt . . . as well as to our own [Texas] state department. My letters were in the hands of Mr. Calhoun, who, as he afterwards told me, placed them with Mr. Upshur." Ashbel Smith, *Reminiscences of the Texas Republic* (Galveston: Historical Society of Galveston, 1876), p. 54.

From S.W. Alexander, T.I. Bacon, and H.M. Law, Athens, [Ga.,] 6/20. They inform Calhoun that he has "been unanimously elected by the Phi Kappa Society to officiate as President at her ["next" *interlined*] annual meeting at the ensuing Commencement." LS in ScU-SC, John C. Calhoun Papers.

From C[HARLES] A. WICKLIFFE,
"(Private & confidential in part)"

Boston, June 20th 1843

My dear Sir, Poor [Hugh S.] Legare Died this morning after a short illness of an inflam[m]ation of Bowels.

I write this letter to you unknown to any man, to know of you if under any circumstances you would consent to take the State Department. The President [John Tyler] has not the slightest idea of this communication, and I write to be put in possession of your views confidentially, that I may speak not upon *authority* but upon *opinion*.

Will you write me at Washington. The President is quite ill to-day. I have had no conversation with him on this subject but ["fe" *canceled*] would feel most happy if you would think the position of S[ecretar]y of State and that which your friends have assigned you before the people not incompatable [*sic*]. Your friend, C.A. Wickliffe [Postmaster General].

ALS in ScU-SC, John C. Calhoun Papers. NOTE: Legaré, Attorney General, had been appointed Secretary of State ad interim on 5/9/1843, upon the resignation of Daniel Webster.

From JOHN L. WILSON,
[former Governor of S.C.]

New York [City,] 20th June 1843

My dear Sir, Where friendship is the motive few words are best, and I hope you will receive this short communication in the spirit which dictates it. I have witnessed at this place the late entry and departure of the President [John Tyler], on his pilgrimage to Bunker Hill. He has neither friends nor party here, but was received with great kindness in respect to the office he holds.

But sir, I consider it all important that you should come on to this place, as I am well warranted in saying you would be received in a most enthusiastic manner. The Irish here are in the ascendant, and your immediate ancestry being of that lineage would be no disadvantage to you. I have conversed with many, very many gentlemen; who have expressed their surprise that you have not determined to visit the north. [Brig.] General [John E.] Wool says, there is no man in the United States that could assemble the same number of persons, who would be anxious to see you and take you by the hand, as your individual self. He says, that is the feeling over the whole United States, and expresses his wish that you would visit the North. Young [Robert F.?] Stockton says the same thing and indeed every one I have conversed with.

You have many, very warm friends here. I believe a majority are in your favor. I have often heard persons speaking in reference to your election to the Presidency when some of the party would say they "did not know you, they never saw you." Give up the retirement of Fort Hill and pass through New York [City] on your way to Saratoga, thence to Boston, Providence, Hartford[,] your alma mater &c. &c. Be seen and known by the people who are willing to serve you.

I do not flatter myself that I can say any thing to change your purpose whatever it may be, or I would add more.

Accept the assurance of my respect & regard, John L. Wilson.

ALS in ScU-SC, John C. Calhoun Papers. NOTE: John Lyde Wilson (1784–1849) had been Governor of S.C. during 1822–1824 and was the author of *The Code of Honor; or Rules for the Government of Principals and Seconds in Duelling* (Charleston: 1838).

From P[ATRICK] G. BUCHAN

Rochester N.Y., 22 June 1843

Dear Sir, I rec[eive]d your letter of the 7[t]h inst[ant] yesterday & felt highly gratified ["by" *canceled*] with its contents. I saw Simeon B. Jewett Esq. of this county in New York City some weeks ago who informed me of the receipt of my letter by you & of the pressure of your engagements. I did not mean your letter for publication nor even for exhibition unless I sh[oul]d be contradicted on any political occasion as to your actual opinions.

Since I last wrote to you your cause has progressed nobly in this State—from a feeling of despondency amongst your political friends (with whom I am proud to rank myself) there has arisen a feeling of growing confidence in your ultimate success in the convention. The friends of Mr. [Martin] V[an] Buren took high grounds & even intimidation was not wanting, but now their fears are thoroughly aroused—they have discovered the growing influence of your friends & the progress of public opinion & their tone has become lower. If you see the Albany papers which I presume you do you must have noticed the subdued tone of their editors. Indeed I have it from a gentleman of high respectability who was in Albany a few days ago that in an interview he had then with [Edwin] Croswell [editor of the Albany *Argus*] Croswell stated that he had come to the conclusion that Mr. Van Buren[']s friends must drop him. There is yet much to be overcome, however, & our course here & *every where* must be of a ["ch" *canceled*] calm, judicious character. We all speak—must all speak of Mr. Van Buren highly—no denunciation must be used—if we did so we would split—disunion & bitterness w[oul]d be the consequence. We oppose his renomination on the ground of expediency. He has had enough—he is full of honors. He & his friends must be satisfied with what we have done for him.

I had a long conversation with Mr. Jewett on the subject of your visiting this State & his opinions coincide with mine. Whatever your feelings may be on that subject I must say & all our friends concur in the opinion that it is *absolutely necessary* for you to come here this summer—say—early in August, [*word fragment canceled*] visiting the city—Saratoga Springs—& the [Niagara] falls & returning by the western route. To postpone it till next year will never do. Then the party lines will be strictly drawn, party spirit will run high & every man will have taken sides & be counted on. Now—the enemy are in confusion—distrust & doubt reigns amongst them. In this part of the State you probably know that there are a great many old democrats, ardent admirers of yours among the whig ranks who became whigs thro' the medium of the Anti masonic party[,] subsequently transferred to the national republican party & it requires only a very little effort to bring them back. This is a singularly exciteable region & tho' it may sound odd to you I have no doubt that your *very appearance* here amongst us will have a great effect. It will bring them out. Those who spoke of you coldly before will then speak enthusiastically in your favor.

No person can charge you with popularity hunting in this movement. In the first place no one will ever charge you with being a demagogue & in the next place it is more than twenty years I understand since you have been in New York. Now, is it not the duty of a prominent Statesman like yourself in this country to make himself personally acquainted with every part of his country & especially so prosperous[,] so powerful & so populous a portion of our union as New York, and are we not fairly entitled to charge you with coldness & neglect in not coming amongst us before?

The fact is, *you must come.* Do not consider me impertinent or disrespectful in these remarks but set down my language to my zeal & anxiety for *the cause.* Distrust not your welcome—it will be enthusiastic every where.

I saw last Evening Major Bumphrey [*sic*; Harvey Humphrey?] the chairman of our [Democratic] county central committee. He is one of *us*, and is the Editor of the Rochester Daily Advertiser[,] our party paper. A majority of our committee are in your favor & are anxious that matters should be so arranged that you could pass through here during the sitting of our county convention[,] the time of holding which could be regulated accordingly. He requested me to write to you immediately on the subject. He will write you in a few days himself. You may rely on his Statements. He asked me strongly to impress upon you the necessity of visiting this part of the country *immediately.* As I feel anxious to send this off by this night[']s mail I must close & I can only add, once more, that on every account—for the sake of the Democracy, for our success, our union, our energy, our cause—*you must* come, *& come quickly.* I will not tax your valuable time by asking you to write me any answer to this letter but it w[oul]d be highly gratifying to us to know your determination. In haste—I have the honor to be Yours very respectfully & Sincerely, P.G. Buchan.

ALS in ScU-SC, John C. Calhoun Papers.

From T. Stower, Geo[rge] W. Dohnert, Francis Bodsford, Cha[rle]s Brown, and Chris[tophe]r Mason, Philadelphia, 6/22. As a committee of invitation appointed by "the Democracy of the City and County of Philadelphia in Town Meeting assembled," they invite Calhoun "to join them at the Festive board at a public Dinner" on 7/4. The committee members sign themselves as "Your friends and Democratic fellow Citizens." LS in ScU-SC, John C. Calhoun Papers.

From OCTAVIA WALTON LE VERT

Mobile, Alabama, June 24th 1843

My dear Mr. Calhoun, I introduce to your kind acquaintance, my friend, Mr. [James] Wise, whom I commend to you, not only as the first Miniature Painter in the Union but as a gentleman of merit and intellect.

Mr. Wise will show you, a Miniature he has painted of myself, I am persuaded it will afford you pleasure to look upon it, as it is such an admirable specimen of the Fine Arts, and the resemblance of one who cherishes the warmest and most affectionate friendship for you.

We hoped during the last Spring to have seen you in Mobile. I do trust, my dear friend, you will visit us. Believe me, no event that the tide of Time could bear on its bosom, would thrill our hearts with so much delight, as greeting you, in our own home; you should have a welcome warm from the heart, I assure you.

I have become quite the "Mother of a large family," and hope some day to present to you my *Three Graces.*

We have often had the pleasure of seeing your son, Mr. [Andrew Pickens] Calhoun, and thro' him have heard of your well bieng [sic].

Mamma, and Papa [that is, Sally Walker Walton and George Walton, Jr.] unite in many kind remembrances to you. Farewell, believe me, ever, your most true and devoted friend, Octavia Walton Le Vert.

ALS in ScCleA. Note: Octavia Walton Le Vert, who had married Dr. Henry Strachey Le Vert in 1836, became the author of *Souvenirs of Travel* (1857). Her grandfather, George Walton, signed the Declaration of Independence for Ga. and her father was mayor of Mobile during 1837–1839. On 10/5/1843, Anna [Maria Calhoun Clemson] wrote from Fort Hill to Maria [Simkins] Colhoun: ". . . we have staying with us a Mr. Wise a min[i]ature painter who brought father a letter from Mrs. Le Vert (the celebrated Miss Octavia Walton) & is taking his likeness. He has a picture of Mrs. Le Vert amongst others which is the most beautiful thing I ever saw both as to style & execution. I think his painting superior to anything I ever saw. He seems a retiring modest man devoted to his profession & will I hope take a good likeness of father." (ALS in ScU-SC, John C. Calhoun Papers.) The Petersburg, Va., *Republican,* November 21, 1843, p. 2, reported as follows: "We were much pleased on Saturday evening by a visit from Mr. Wise, of St. Louis, the celebrated miniature painter. Mr. Wise has just finished a picture of Mr. Calhoun, which Mr. Calhoun's family, and himself consider to be the best ever taken . . . . Mr. Wise has gone to the North for the purpose of superintending an engraving to be made from his portrait, which he expects to present to the public by next February."

From CHA[RLE]S H. POND

Milford (Con[n.]) June 27, 1843

D[ea]r Sir, Your esteemed favor of the 4th ult[im]o was duly received, & read with pleasure & approbation. It seems to be now generally agreed that the National Convention will be held in *May*, & the mode of choosing the delegates will be by districts in most of the States. So far, so good. As to the third point—the mode of voting in Convention will of course be fixed by that body & it should be per capita. Doubtless your friends will consider this a "sine qua non." This being obtained; I think the way will be clear for a fair, & I ardently hope a favorable nomination.

I like your views on the Tariff question. At the S[outh] & South West they are no doubt popular; but in the Middle & Northern States will be opposed by the manufacturers; who want some duties *beyond* the Compromise Act. From these quarters & sources your chief opposition will come. These things being taken for granted:—in true sincerity I ask whether it will not be best, all things considered, for your friends to aid the "arrangement" like that—or *similar* to that alluded to in Mr. [Daniel] Webster's Baltimore speech? I may not be able to survey the whole ground, but from what I do see, I now believe that it is important for you to have the Tariff subject *permanently* disposed of & put to rest. The whigs want to agitate—& *agitate* this matter; but it seems to me that your friends should fix it, & fix it firmly, & immovably if possible. This would help to disarm the whigs; many great manufacturers (whatever the smaller & political ones may think) & the friends of Peace—& all the friends of "moral suasion" as the phrase is, will naturally favor an international arrangement based on the principles of reciprocity. But the [Henry] Clay men & all ultra partizans will oppose it fiercely. If your friends have concluded to aid this "arrangement"—should they not move forthwith?: so that its moral effect may be felt as soon as possible & on the coming elections? I see no reason why President [John] Tyler should not favor the "arrangement"—whether he be a candidate himself, or whether he lend his influence to forward the claims of another prominent candidate. I well know that you understand this subject in its various bearings much better than I do, & probably your mind is made up, & for aught I know steps are ["are" *canceled*] being taken to reach the great point—still I have my opinion & in offering it, am willing that it should pass for what it is worth. It has at least one merit—it is sincere.

The death of Mr. [Hugh S.] Legare causes two important vacancies. I have this moment seen that Mr. [Abel P.] Upsher [*sic*] is appointed Sec[re]t[ar]y of State. I have also seen the name of the Hon. David Henshaw of Mass. mentioned for Sec[re]t[ar]y of the Navy. Lately I met Mr. H[enshaw] in Hartford & had a long talk with him on matters & things in general, & some things in *particular*. And I will add that he is an able & warm friend of our democratic institutions; that he is your fast & influential advocate, & in short—that he is just the man for you & for our country to be in Washington or elsewhere either as Sec[re]t[ar]y of the Navy or in any other responsible station. Remember (if you please) what I say—there is no mistake in this man; for on this subject I speak from "the book." *That* would be an excellent appointment. I am not in your secrets & I have no right to claim to be—But these things are said on the assumption that the President & you are friends. To me, things seem to be so shaping.

In a late [Washington] "Spectator" I read an able, long & capital article, or address, on the National Convention. Beautiful in style & rich in matter. I know not who wrote it—but I can *guess*—who wrote or dictated it. But be the author who he may, he wields a stiff & polished pen—which should be kept busy.

But as I have probably written more than you will have time or inclination to read I will stop—merely adding that I should feel honored in hearing from you occasionally. Your well wisher & old friend, Chas. H. Pond.

P.S. The "Pennant" a paper published in Brooklyn in the Eastern part of this State publishes your name for President.

ALS in ScU-SC, John C. Calhoun Papers.

From W[ILLIA]M SMITH

Warrenton Va., June 28, 1843

My dear Sir, I am in receipt of your highly esteemed favour of the 6th Ins[tan]t.

In my last, it was my purpose to inform ["you," *interlined*] that I had received a letter from Mr. [Martin] V[an] B[uren], apprizing me that he would in good season, respond to my interrogatories [on the R.I. question].

A few days ago, I received a similar letter from Mr. [James] Buchanan. In that letter, he says "I have declared myself a suffrage man. My opinion on this subject is very decided; & *accords with what I may say is the universal opinion of the Northern Democracy.* Why then agitate it[?] But 'luck's a Lord' & every thing seems to be running in favour of the Magician."

To this I responded by saying that I began to incline to his opinion; & that I doubted, if I should publish "the responses" when received.

I also added, that in my opinion, for some obvious public, & for some not less obvious private reasons, the friends of all our candidates, would in the sequel combine against Mr. Van Buren, in the Convention; & of course, defeat his nomination.

Benjamin V. Larkin formerly of this County [Fauquier], now of Columbia S.C. is indebted as per enclosed memorandum. May I trouble you to enclose it to some attorney, with a request to enquire as to Mr. Larkin[']s solvency, & then address me to this place[?]

Please, regard the extract from Mr. B[uchanan]'s letter as confidential. With great regard I am truly Y[ou]rs, Wm. Smith.

ALS in ScU-SC, John C. Calhoun Papers. NOTE: An AEU by Calhoun indicates that he answered this letter on 7/8 and forwarded the enclosed memorandum to W[illiam] F[ord] DeSaussure.

From JOHN A[LFRED] CALHOUN

Eufaula [Ala.,] June 29th 1843
Dear Uncle, For some time back I have been intending to write to you; but under a *somewhat vague* hope that I should be able to meet you this summer, I have delayed. The state of my business, as well as my family, will prevent me from doing myself the pleasure of a personal visit. A letter, therefore, affords me the only means of a conference with you on matters about which I have desired to confer with you.

Since my last to you, an active canvas[s] has been going on in our State, between your friends & Mr. [Martin] Van Buren's relative to your respective claims on the Democracy. The result of this agitation has been decidedly favourable to you. Your strength has been constantly on the increase. Even the *spoils* portion of the Democracy, with their natural instinct in favour of the rising sun, are coming to your side. In our Congressional District we have had more to contend with, from the new[?] spoils men than in any portion of the State. Here, was the center of all the corruptions of the land speculations— and although they have generally met with the fate which they deserved, in being totally broken up; yet the feelings which have been engendered by them still exists. The Democracy of this section of Alabama *was*, without exception, the most degraded of any in the whole South. But I am happy to say that a most favourable change has been going on, and is now most rapidly progressing, in favour of an elevated cast[?] of Democracy. Fortunate circumstances have placed me in a situtation [*sic*] greatly to promote this desirable end, which I havenot neglected. The late impeachment & turning out of

261

of [*sic*; John P. Booth] our Circuit Judge (the very head of this corrupt faction) has greatly promoted our ends. We had a trial of our strength a short time since in the nomination of our candidate for Congress. One of the candidates for nomination was in your favour, the other of Mr. Van Buren. We had a signal triumph, in the nomination of Mr. [James E.] Belser, of Montgomery—a devoted personal & political friend of yours. He speakes [*sic*] in the most enthusiastic strains of you. He became acquainted with you in Washington, during the last session of Congress, when he attended as the representative of our State in its claims against the general government. I have been greatly assisted in these movements by General [Reuben C.] Shorter, who met with you on your return from Washington during last Summer. He belonged to the old Union party in Georgia, and I think had no special fondness for you, until his accidentally meeting with you. He is now one of your most enthusiastic admirers. General Shorter and several others of the most leading Democrats in this Section of the State, have recently consulted me as to the propriety of starting an organisation of your friends ["into association" *interlined*] and placing their preference for you on the grounds of your Tariff principles. To this proposal I have informed them; that if such a movement can be made without distraction in our ranks, it would be well—but not otherwise. I *think that* the *Democrats* are *ready for such a move*—but it is concluded to be sure, that we are not mistaken, before any movement of this kind is made. Can I give your friends here any assurance that you will visit them at any time during next fall or winter? Your presence here would be hailed with great enthusiasm. I wish you could make it convenient to visit, quite extensively, through the United States, during this summer & Fall. If you could bring your *feelings* to approve of such a course, I am well assured that it would be of great service to you.

Our crops are good. The weather is rather too wet & our farms are somewhat grassy. My crop is good. If the rains which are now falling daily should continue much longer, it must be seriously injured.

Our county [Barbour] is quite healthy. I hear of no fever. My family are all in good health. My children (5 in number) are in excellent health.

With sentiments of the greatest respect I remain your Nephew most affectionately, John A. Calhoun.

N.B. I have been informed that you have sold your gold mine for one hundred thousand dollars. I should like to be sure that you have had this good fortune. Be pleased to let me know. J.A.C.

ALS in ScU-SC, John C. Calhoun Papers. NOTE: This letter was postmarked at Irwinton, Ala., on 6/29. An AEU by Calhoun reads: "J.A. Calhoun, 8th July answered."

From F[RANCIS] W. PICKENS

Edgewood [Edgefield District, S.C.] 29 June 1843
My dear Sir, I have just this moment returned from Abbeville & Laurense [sic; Districts] where I have been for two weeks, and for the last few days I have been in mud and water on my mills and mill dams. I went to examine mills in Laurense, and there to understand how to fix mine on a proper basis. I begin almost to think I was born for a miller and was spoiled when I turned my attention to any thing else. We are at present deluged with rains which will injure the cotton very much.

On my arrival I found yours enclosing [Robert M.T.] Hunter[']s &c. I deeply regret the situation of the Spectator, but I never encouraged the idea of starting such a paper but the contrary, as I knew it would draw the fire of the [Washington] Globe & [Richmond] Enquirer (and expressly said so) before we were prepared to develope, and they had a firm basis and large ["sup" *canceled*] subscription list and we had none. We would thus be run down in advance. I knew also your friends would not pay money or could not. You know that I was the only one of our delegation for the last two Winters that paid a cent. I never could get a dollar out of them except to subscribe for your life. Winter before last I advanced about $700 to the Pen[n]sylvania papers alone. I knew they would talk about the Spectator but do nothing, and it was impossible for just one or two to pay all. I wrote a letter to Hunter while at Columbia offering him $4,000 immediately if he would take charge of the paper as it was started, and left the letter with [Franklin H.] Elmore for him to sign & for the Pres[i]d[en]t & V[ice] Pres[i]d[en]ts of our convention to sign & enclose. I have heard not a word from them since. I re-c[eive]d a demand from Charleston for money for sustaining the paper, and expect to enclose $400 on day after to-morrow. If any others would do the same we could get along, but on my trip up through Abbevill[e] I tried several, amongst others Col. [James Edward] Colhoun & [George] McDuffie but could not get even a cent. Colhoun, I will do him the ["justice" *canceled*] justice to say, I believe has no funds of any kind. As to [Joseph A.] Scoville I never had any confidence in him or his judgement, but if Hunter will take

263

charge of it I have confidence in his character & talent, although I think he will always talk more than he will do. I will write to [Ker] Boyce immediately, & Connor [that is, Henry Workman Conner], & Gourdine [Henry Gourdin] on the Subject.

I wrote you before I left home as to McDuffie's health as I had heard of it, but found him much better and recovering; In fact I think he is as well as usual, and in high spirits, but more perfectly absorbed in Cotton than any human being I ever saw.

I left my children with their Aunt, but will send for them in a week. I wrote you as to a visit in August & the whooping cough. If Anna [Maria Calhoun Clemson] has any fears about her Children, I can say that not one of the Children had coughed for 4 days when I left them and they are pronounced entirely well.

I will go to Athens [Georgia] the first week in August, the commenceme[nt] is on the 1st Wednesday in August, and McDuffie is going too—he beg[g]ed me to take him in my carriage and I will do so as he has neither carriage nor horses nor servants. He said he had written you to go. I wish you could meet us there. It would be right, as they have nominated you. I hope you will go. I must now try for the next week to prepare myself for the occasion as it is the only time I will have. I understand it will be a great collection.

As to the Statue I have long since written to ["po"(?) *canceled*; Hiram] Powers and enclosed $1500—to begin with. I enclose you a letter from Connor on the subject; which you will be kind enough to send back.

I hope your [gold] mine is doing well in Ga. I hear they are doing first rate business in Abbeville and in this Dist[rict] on Saluda [River] in Gold—$5 per day to the hand.

Do say to Mr. [Thomas G.] Clemson that Mr. Hill came to see me on the River[?], and wishes to sell him his residence. It is not quite three miles from the Canebreak. It is an excellent two story house just finished with 8 rooms & 12 foot passage & 7 rooms [with] fireplaces, with brick under story and fine[?] c[e]llars, first rate framed barn and stables, and as good water as ever was with certain health &c—& 800 acres of land only 90 of it cleared. I told him I would let Mr. Clemson know as he desired it. He asks $6,000 but I think and feel certain it can be got for $5000, as he is very anxious to move nearer to his place on the [Savannah?] river, and wishes a plainer establishment as he is in debt. My own opinion is that it is far better than to build, and the buildings cost what he asks. It would suit Mr. C[lemson] exactly if he intends living at his place.

Present me kindly to cousin Floride [Colhoun Calhoun] & Anna. In haste but very truly, F.W. Pickens.

ALS in ScU-SC, John C. Calhoun Papers.

From W[ILLIAM] M. CORRY

Cincinnati, 30 June 1843

Dear Sir; The subject of your visit to the West is still enthusiastically discussed by your friends here, who insist that you shall be further pressed to make it.

Our meeting of the 31st Ult[im]o held at the Court House to give you the invitation, was called by one hundred and fifty citizens. You have received their proceedings, and perceive at once their opinions and their spirit.

Your friends in Cincinnati who can be relied on for action; and who are the prime movers of the Invitation, are for the most part young politicians of the straightest sect, whose tendency is at present very strong to the destruction of indirect taxes. They go now for a Tariff discriminating for revenue—and are satisfied that such a Tariff is the present fashion with the Democratic Party. They are likewise satisfied of the error, and disgusted with the iniquity of paper money. Their characters as well as their talents will soon give them the lead of the people, and the consequent direction of affairs. I think that when you were in the Senate last winter, they sent you a memorial originally transmitted to our State Legislature, and printed for circulation recommending the collection of the taxes in Ohio in gold and silver. These citizens are as anxious to see and to hear you as their declarations state.

There are many other men in the democratic party who feel also desirous that you should visit the West, who were with held from any public expression for fear of "distracting the Party." But it will not surprize you to learn of others who for *that reason* oppose any such movement, in this region. These are the Ultra Van Buren politicians, who lean instinctively to the strong side, and go with the majority on all occasions. They are the self styled conservators of the Party. But they abundantly over rate their power and mistake their position. They have become so cautious from long following of public opinion, that the People are far in advance, and the enemy almost up with them. They dread now the sentiments which are quite common in popular assemblies; They are jealous of the popular favorites. They have the aristocratic ["dread" *canceled and* "fear" *interlined*] of a "novus homo"; and must soon join the ranks of the sworn[?] foes to all improvement. They are now on the neutral ground of average tariffs—good banks, moderate measures, and easy victories.

But these gentlemen are not to be feared.

We apprehend that no division will be seen if you visit us, and we entreat you earnestly not to deny us that gratification. You will be warmly received by all who have any place for ability and virtue in the Party; or weight with the Public.

If we did not desire to repay any arrears of gratitude for the services of your past life[,] the good you could accomplish for the cause hereafter, gives the occasion great consequence. There is nothing in our judgment which would contribute so largely to the overthrow of the Tariff as your visit to the West. One speech on that subject from your mouth, would find enthusiastic response by the People, and the American System receive its death blow very near the spot of its origin. We know not how true opinions on the Great Question of the day can be so powerfully inculcated.

Such an effort would inspire your friends for the conflict of May 1844 & give them the resources which that conflict demands. The people are not now fixed in any Presidential preference. But they have seen your formidable rivals, and ask impatiently why you are never to meet them face to face? They will almost take your denial as a personal disappointment. Very truly and Respectfully Yours, W.M. Corry.

ALS in ScU-SC, John C. Calhoun Papers.

To [Professor] HENRY ST. GEORGE TUCKER, University of Virginia

Fort Hill [late June 1843?]

My dear Sir, I wrote to my son, [John C. Calhoun, Jr.,] a month since and requested him to let me know, what sum would be necessary to meet his expences, in addition to that required for travelling home; but owing to some unaccountable delay, I did not till the last mail receive his answer, though dated on the 16th of last month.

Not knowing whether he may not have left Charlotte[s]Ville (as it is vacation) I have taken the liberty of enclosing $70 in [South]

Carolina bills for him, and if he should be still in Charlotte[s]Ville ["I will thank you" *interlined*] to deliver it to him; and, if not, to inform him without delay, that you have it for him.

It will be sufficient for his purpose, if he should return by the usual route by Charleston; but I have suggested to him, whether it would not be better for his health, to return home on ["horse" *canceled and then interlined*] back. Should he conclude to do so, it will be necessary to purchase a horse, saddle & bridle; and, in that case, the sum transmitted may not be sufficient. May I ask you, in that case, to aid him in getting his ["equipment" *canceled and* "outfit" *interlined*] for the Journey, and to advance, if perfectly convenient, the additional fund, that may be necessary; or, if not, to say to whomever he may purchase his horse, that you will see him paid, on the return of my son in the fall to the University. I will take it as a great favour. The Horse need not be a high priced one. All that ["we" *canceled and* "would be" *interlined*] required is, that he should be sound, with good saddle gaits. The bridle & saddle may be plain & cheap.

I regret to give you any trouble, and would not take the liberty I have were I not assured of your disposition to oblige me.

I send you by the Mail that takes this a copy of the address of our [S.C. Democratic] Convention. Yours truly & Sincerely, J.C. Calhoun.

ALS in WHi.

JULY 1–SEPTEMBER 30
1843

ⅅ

The St. Louis painter James Wise stayed at Fort Hill in the fall of 1843 to execute a miniature portrait, later engraved, which Calhoun's family believed to be the best likeness of the statesman. That fall Wise visited Petersburg, where a newspaper editor paraphrased for the public Wise's impressions. "Mr. Calhoun resides on a large and valuable farm, chiefly devoted to the culture of cotton and corn; his house is large and commodious, and generally thronged with visitors. Mr. Calhoun rises by light in the morning, and on foot attends to the various duties of a farmer, which he performs with a degree of ability and energy surprising for a man in his situation, and at his age. Mr. Wise's remark to us was, 'he is the best Farmer I ever saw, he has an Overseer but could do as well without him, he does every thing himself.' His farm duties being performed, he retires to his study until the time for receiving his numerous visitors has arrived. . . . In the afternoon he walks the farm over again, and then passes the balance of his evening either in the social circle, or in writing." (Petersburg, Va., Republican, November 21, 1843, p. 2.)

The effort to make Calhoun the next Presidential nominee of the Democracy was in what would appear to be, in retrospect, its crucial phase. Calhoun's correspondence was heavy. He drafted a good many papers designed to set before the public the best possible arguments for the position his supporters were taking in regard to the all-important matter of the method for electing delegates to the national convention—that is, whether State delegations were to be selected by conventions of politicians and office holders and vote as a unit, or whether they were to come more directly from the people and be divided in fair proportion to the support each candidate had within the State. Calhoun's advice and inspiration were in demand as efforts, often halting and inadequate, went forward to establish viable newspapers in Washington and New York and to stimulate vigorous action on the part of the campaign committee headed by Franklin H. Elmore in Charleston. Still, another summer visitor, the Rev. James H. Thorn-

well, Professor of Sacred Literature at the South Carolina College, found Calhoun relaxed and ready for leisurely conversation on education, metaphysics, and theology.

"Our strength," Calhoun wrote to Robert M.T. Hunter of Virginia on August 6, "lies in principles & position, so much so, that if we had the aid of a single central paper, of established influence, . . . there would be no contest." "I shall abandon no principle, or any position, which I have heretofore assumed," Calhoun wrote on September 8 to Duff Green, who was in Europe for the dual purpose of raising capital for his many business projects and keeping an eye on the British abolitionists and their designs on Texas. "Whether victorious or defeated," Calhoun continued, "it shall be on my own ground. Victory thus won will be worth having, and defeat, if it should come, will not be an overthrow. But within these limits, I shall exercise as much conciliation, as is consistent with preserving them. Of the two, I would rather risk defeat than character."

Such an idealistically republican position appealed to many. As a New Yorker, by way of contrast, asked Calhoun of Van Buren, the front runner: "What great or good act, has he ever performed for this State, or the United States?" But Calhoun was well aware of the limitations faced by his bands of dedicated amateurs, lacking patronage and newspapers "of established influence." At the time he wrote Green, serious setbacks had already been suffered in the State conventions of Democrats meeting at Syracuse, New York, and Worcester, Massachusetts. The game was not yet up, and many hoped that the highhandedness of the opposition would ultimately create a reaction in Calhoun's direction. It is unlikely, however, that the South Carolinian cherished any unrealistic hopes. His goal, perhaps, was not so much to become President as it was to maintain a maximum of influence over the future course of policy.

Increasingly, Calhoun was called upon to be confidential adviser to the Secretary of State, Abel P. Upshur. Responding to his own awareness of approaching crisis and to a deluge of suggestions and urgings from Duff Green and many others, Upshur repeatedly called upon Calhoun for his views. "Ought we not to move immediately, for the admission of Texas into the Union . . . ?," he asked in August. "Should not the South demand it, as indispensable to their security?"

Meanwhile, Calhoun's national position generated a flurry of demands for likenesses to satisfy public curiosity and memorialize the statesman. In Italy, Hiram Powers was at work on a sculpture commissioned by South Carolina admirers. Around the time of the visit by Wise, another artist, William Henry Brown, took a silhouette.

269

Other portraits were under way, and a number of engravings were produced and broadcast. And, according to the Charleston Courier, a local artist was painting Calhoun's image on that city's magnificent new fire engine, which, it was reported, could shoot a solid stream of water more than two hundred feet.

〚

To W[illiam] Smith, [Warrenton, Va.]

Fort Hill, *July 3d,* 1843

Dear Sir: It is necessary, before replying to the several questions on which you ask my views, and the reasons and principles on which I rest them, that I should make a remark explanatory of what I understand to be your desire.

Your questions are all couched in general terms, without reference to any particular case, except the sixth and last, which refers to that of Rhode Island. I understand them all, however, to grow out of it, and to have relation to this case; and that, the more fully my answers meet and cover it, the more fully will your object, in propounding the questions, be met.

With this understanding, I shall proceed to reply to your inquiries, taking them in the order in which they stand in your letter.

Your first question is: "When the Federal Union was formed by the adoption of our present Constitution, did, or did not, each member thereof possess such a republican form of government as satisfied the Constitution, and which, it is declared, the United States shall guarantee to every State of the Union?"

I answer, yes, most certainly it did; and that, to suppose the contrary, that any State was admitted into the Union, whose government, at the time, was not republican, within its meaning, would be absurd in the extreme. The Constitution provides, in express terms, [*Footnote*: Const. of the U.S. Art(icle) 4, Sec(tion) 4.] that—"The United States shall guarantee to every State in the Union, a republican form of government; and shall protect each of them against invasion; and, on application of the Legislature, or of the Executive (when the Legislature cannot be convened), against domestic violence." To suppose, under the first of these provisions, that any State, whose government was not republican, within the meaning of the guarantee, would ratify the Constitution and enter into the Union, and that the other States would accept the ratification and admit her, is too absurd for belief. It would be to suppose, that the State, so ratifying, stipulated for the suppression of the very government under which it entered the Union, and that the Government of the State called the Convention for ratifying the Constitution, with the design that it should be suppressed; or that she was ignorant of what she was doing[.] It would also be to suppose, that the other States, in accepting the ratification, and admitting her into the Union, permitted that to be done, which was directly opposed to the guarantee; and which, under the duty it imposed on them, they would be bound to suppress; or that they, too, were ignorant of what they were doing. Absurdity could not go further.

On this ground I rest my answer to your first question. Others might be added; but this is deemed sufficiently strong of itself.

Your second question is in the following words: "When a State has been admitted into the Union, and shall call on the Federal Executive for protection, in the manner, and for the purpose prescribed in the section quoted, can he pause to inquire and judge whether such State has, or has not a republican form of government; and according to his opinion thereon, grant or withhold the aid demanded?"

Your question, as I understand it, presupposes a case of domestic violence, within the meaning of the Constitution; and also that the State has made application, in the form it prescribes, for protection; and that your object is, to know if, in my opinion, the Federal Government has a right to determine whether the Government of the State is republican or not; and if it be not, whether the fact would take the case out of the guarantee, and make it the duty of the Federal Government to withhold the protection? With this understanding, I shall proceed to reply to it.

I answer, yes; but to explain the reasons and principles on which my answer rests, and the restrictions to which the high and delicate right involved is subject, it will be indispensable to enter fully into the nature and object of the section quoted—and which, for brevity, I shall call the *guarantee section*—with the duties it imposes, and the rights it confers on the Federal Government. There is not another in the whole instrument more important; or, on the right understanding of which, the success and duration of our political system more depend.

The section contains three distinct stipulations and guarantees—that of a republican form of government, to every State of the Union,

271

that of protection to each against invasion, and that against domestic violence, on the application of the Legislature, or the Executive, when the Legislature cannot be convened. The States themselves are the parties—that is, the people of the several States, as forming distinct, sovereign communities, and organized under their respective governments. Such is clearly the meaning of the words in the section; and it is in this sense I shall use the words, *States, and People*, in this communication, unless otherwise explained. The language of the section is, "The United States shall guarantee;" followed by the three stipulations, or guarantees.

In order to ascertain the intention of the parties, in entering into them, we must turn to the preamble of the Constitution, which declares the objects for which it was ordained and established. Among them we shall find three specified—"to insure domestic tranquility, provide for the common defence, and to secure the blessings of liberty to ourselves and our posterity"—which have direct reference to the three guarantees; and to which they clearly stand as *means* to an *end*.

The framers of the Constitution were deeply versed in the history of free and confederated States; and knew well the dangers to which they are exposed from external and internal causes; and devised ample guards against them, among which these three guarantees are not the least efficient. In order to form a true conception of the mode in which they were intended to act, and to place a correct construction on the guarantees, it will be necessary to inquire, what are the quarters from which the peace, safety, and liberty of the States may be endangered, and against which the guarantees are intended to protect them. They may be, in the first place, from force or violence from within; against which, the guarantee of protection against domestic violence is clearly intended. They may be, in the second place, from hostile attacks from without; and against which, the guarantee of protection against invasion is as clearly intended. And finally, they may be from the ambition and usurpation of their governments, or rather rulers; against which, the guarantee of a republican form of government is intended, as I hold and shall hereafter show, as a protection.

Such being the quarters, from which the peace, safety, and liberty of the States may be endangered or destroyed, and against which the guarantees were intended to secure them, that construction of the *guarantee section*, which shall most fully meet, and most effectually guard against the dangers from these various quarters, and which may not be inconsistent with a fair interpretation of the language of the section, may justly be assumed to be the true one. Guided by this rule, I shall now state what I believe to be its true construction; beginning with the guarantee to protect each State against domestic violence.

I hold, that its object is, to protect the *Governments* of the States, by placing that of each under the protection of the united power of all the States, against such domestic violence or force, as might endanger or destroy it from *within*. It is clearly one of the means, by which the peace, safety, and liberty of the State itself may be endangered or destroyed; and hence it clearly falls within the class of objects, to which the guarantees stand, as means to an end, as has been stated. If to this be added, that it is difficult, if not impossible, to conceive how force or violence, from within, could be brought to bear against the State, except by being directed against its Government, it would seem conclusive that its protection is the immediate object of this guarantee. Any other would be violence offered by individuals against individuals; and would fall within the jurisdiction of the local authorities and Courts.

But if any doubt should still remain, that the protection of the *Government* of the State is the object, the wording of the guarantee would suffice to remove it. It expressly provides, that the protection shall be on the application of the Legislature of the State, or its Executive, if its Legislature cannot be convened; and thus vests in the *Government of the State*, and not the Federal Government, the right to determine whether there has been a case of domestic violence or not; and also of the necessity and propriety of applying for protection. It is only on such application that the Federal Government has any right whatever to interfere. This provision, of itself, would strongly indicate that the *Government* was the object of protection: but as strong as the indication is, of itself, it will be greatly strengthened by adverting to the reasons for inserting it, deduced from the character of our system of government.

In our complex system, the objects for which governments are instituted, are divided between the Federal and State Governments. The former is the common government of all the States; and to it is specifically delegated the powers necessary to carry into effect all the objects in which they have a common interest. The latter are the separate and peculiar governments of each; and to them and the people, all the other powers are reserved. Among them are embraced those that refer to the internal peace and safety of each State; to the governments of which, it exclusively belongs to determine what may endanger or destroy them; and the measures proper to be adopted to protect them. It is in strict accordance with this distribution, that protection, in case of domestic violence, should be on application of the Government of the State against which it is directed. What adds to the force of the reasoning is, that the provision is omitted in the other two guarantees, when the cause of inserting it does not exist. That it does not in the case of invasion, is clear; as all that appertains to the foreign or exterior relations of the States, belongs, in the distribution, to the Federal Government; and is accordingly embraced among the delegated rights. Hence, it is made its duty, to act, in that case, without waiting the application of the Government of the State invaded. The reason of its omission, in the case of the guarantee of a republican form of government—though less obvious, is not less strong, as I shall show when I come to consider it.

Such are my reasons for believing, that the immediate object of this guarantee, is the protection of the *Government* of the State, against force or violence from *within*, directed against it with a view to its subversion.

The next guarantee is, protection to each State against invasion. Its object is so clear, and it is so slightly connected with the objects of your inquiry, that I shall pass it over, without adding to the remarks I have made, incidentally, in reference to it, in considering the preceding guarantee.

I come now to the last, in the order in which I am considering them; but the first as they stand in the section; and the one immediately involved in the question under consideration—I mean the guarantee of a republican form of government to every State in the Union.

I hold that, according to its true construction, its object is the reverse of that of protection against domestic violence: and that, instead of being intended to protect the *Governments* of the States, it is intended to protect each *State* (I use the term as explained) against its Government; or, more strictly, against the ambition or usurpation of its rulers. That the objects of the Constitution, to which the guarantees refer, and liberty more especially, may be endangered or destroyed by rulers, will not be denied. But, if admitted, it follows as a consequence, that it must be embraced in the guarantees, if not inconsistent with the language of the section. But if embraced, it must be in the guarantee under consideration, as it is not in the other two. If it be added that, without this construction, the guarantees would utterly fail to protect the States against the attempts of ambition and usurpation on the part of rulers, to change the forms of their governments, and to destroy their liberty, (the danger, above all others, to which free and popular governments are most exposed), it would seem to follow irresistibly, under the rule I have laid down, that the construction which I have placed on the provision, as to the object of the guarantee, is the true one. But if doubts should still remain, the fact, that it fully explains why the provision which requires the application of the State, in case of the guarantee against domestic violence, is omitted, would place it beyond controversy; for it would be a perfect absurdity to require, that the party, against which the guarantee is intended to protect, should make application to be protected against itself.

There remains, indeed, one other quarter, from which the liberties of the States (one of the leading objects of the guarantees) can be destroyed: I mean the people themselves, constituting the several States, and acting in their political character, as citizens, and according to constitutional and legal forms. They may, acting in this character, if they choose, subvert the republican form of government, under which they entered the Union, and establish one of another form; and, thereby, abandon their liberty. I say, abandon it, for, according to the exalted conception of our ancestors, nothing was worthy of the name of liberty, but that which was enjoyed under free popular governments. Against this danger, there is, and can be no guarantee. The reason requires but little explanation. The States themselves are parties to the guarantee; and it would be absurd to suppose that they undertook to enter into a guarantee against themselves.

Besides, liberty, from its nature, cannot be forced on a people. It must be voluntarily embraced. If the people do not choose to embrace it, or continue it, after they have, it cannot be forced on them. The very act of doing so, would destroy it; and divest the State of its independence and sovereignty, and sink it into a dependent province. But, if it had been possible for it to be otherwise, even in that case, there would have been no guarantee against it. To provide one, would have been regarded as a superfluous precaution; for it was not in the heart of our free and brave ancestors, to conceive that any State of the Union would voluntarily abandon its liberty, by substituting for its republican government, one of a different form. Had such a proposition been made, it would have been regarded as an insult.

Such is the construction I put on the immediate objects of the three guarantees; with my reasons for it. As strong as they are, when the guarantees are considered separately, they are still more so, when viewed in connection as a whole. Thus viewed, according to my construction, they fully meet, and effectually guard against (as far as in the nature of things can be done) every danger, by which the peace, safety, and liberty of the States may be jeopardized or destroyed.

If lawless force, or violence of individuals, under whatever pretext, should be turned against the Government of the State, or its authority, from *within*, with the view of subverting them, the guarantee, to protect each from domestic violence, meets the case; if the attack should be from *without*, that against invasion meets it; and, finally, if the rulers should attempt to usurp power, and subvert the republican form of government, under which the State was admitted into the Union, the guarantee of a republican form of government to every State of the Union meets it. Thus, every door, through which danger may enter, that can in the nature of things be closed, would be closed, if the Federal Government should faithfully enforce the guarantees. Under no other construction, would it be the case; which is proof conclusive, that the construction which I place upon the section, is the one intended by the framers of the Constitution.

Having now explained my views of the nature and character of the guarantee section, it will not be difficult to assign my reasons for the answer I have given to the question under consideration. In determining what its duties are, under the section, the Federal Government must look to the whole; and take care that, in enforcing one of the guarantees, it does not violate its duties under another. It has been shown that the objects [*sic*] of the guarantee against domestic violence is, the protection of the *Government* of the State; but when the Government of a State ceases to be republican, it loses its right to protection. This, it has been shown, may take place, by the usurpation of rulers, or by the voluntary act of the people. It is clear that, in either case, the Government of the [United] States should withhold it; and of course it must have the right, in every case, to determine whether the application of a State for protection, be one of such cases or not. In the case of the usurpation of its rulers, it would be the duty of the Government, not only to withhold protection, but to unite its power with the people of the State, to suppress the usurpation. What would be its duty, in addition to withholding protection, in the other, I shall explain in the proper place, when I come to consider what would be the effect of a voluntary change of government, on the part of the people, from a republican to any other, on the relation of the State with the rest of the Union. But, while I admit the right, I also admit, that it is a high and delicate one; the highest and most delicate of any conferred on the Federal Government: and, I would add, the most dangerous, if I did not regard it subject to such restrictions, as left but little discretion in its exercise. What they are, I shall next proceed to consider.

The first, which I consider the foundation of all others, is to be found in my answer to your first question—that the Federal Government, in determining whether the Government of a State be, or be not republican, within the meaning of the Constitution, has no right whatever, in any case, to look beyond its admission into the Union. From this fundamental restriction, another, deduced from it, necessarily follows, of no little importance—that no change made in its Government, after its admission, can make it other than republican, which does not essentially alter its form, or make it different in some essential particular, from those of the other States, at the time of their adoption. In other words, the forms of the Governments of the several States, composing the Union, as they stood at the time of their admission, are the proper standard, by which to determine whether any after change, in any of them, makes its form of government other than republican.

But I take higher ground in reference to subsequent changes; and lay it down as a rule, that none such can fairly present the question, if the Federal Government should faithfully perform its duties under the guarantees, except such as may be made voluntarily by the people of the State, consistently with constitutional and legal provisions; and that, I have shown, would not be a case within the guarantees. So long as it performs faithfully its duties, it is manifest, from what has been stated, that no change in the form of Government of a State, can be made by force or violence from without or within, from invasion, or from domestic violence; unless it be such, as the united resistance of the Federal Government and that of the State, cannot overcome; and which, of course, would admit of no question under the guarantees.

The only remaining change that could be made, except by the voluntary act of the people, as stated, is that by the usurpation of the rulers of the State, for the time being—and this the ballot-box would put down, unless they should resort to force; when it would become, and not before, the duty of the Federal Government to enforce the guarantee, and suppress the usurpation. But this would be a case which would speak for itself, and admit of little doubt in determining; and would rarely, if ever, occur, if the Federal Government should do its duty, under the formidable difficulties which the guarantees oppose to such cases.

The remaining mode, in which a change of the form of government of a State may be made, from the republican to some other, is, by the voluntary act of the people of the State themselves, acting in their political character, and consistently with constitutional and legal provisions; and this, as I have shown, would not come within the guar-

277

antees. But, as it is intimately connected with the subject of your questions, I deem it proper to state what would be the effect of such an act, and the relation in which it would place the State, in reference to the others.

It would, in my opinion, be a clear case of secession—as clear as it would be for the State to do an act inconsistent with a fundamental principle of the Union; and to assume a character not compatible with her remaining in it. She would, in fact, be a foreign State; and would stand in the same relation to the others, as one foreign State does to another; and, of course, would have no right to claim any protection under the guarantees; or, if she did, the Federal Government would be under no obligation to grant it. There might, indeed, on such application, be a question, whether, in fact, the change was such, as to make the Government of the State other than republican, which would have to be decided under the restrictions I have stated. But, if doubt should still remain, the decision should be in favor of the State, when the consequence of deciding against her would be, to withhold protection, and place her out of the Union.

With these restrictions, this high and delicate power would be safe in the hands of the Federal Government; but without them, none could be more dangerous. Give to the Federal Government the right to establish its own abstract standard of what constitutes a republican form of government, and to bring the Governments of the States, without restriction on its discretion, to the test of this standard, in order to determine whether they be of a republican form or not, and it would be made the absolute master of the States. A standard more uncertain, or a greater or more dangerous power, could not be conceived. The Governments of one half of the States of the Union would not stand the test, which would be adopted by a large portion of the other half; and not one, that which many would adopt. The consequence would be, that, instead of tranquillity, safety, and liberty, anarchy, insecurity, and despotism would universally prevail; and the object of the guarantees be utterly defeated. Nothing but the most rigid adherence, in all cases, to the restriction laid down, can avert it. To relax in any, even the strongest, would open wide the door of unlimited discretion, and leave the Federal Government, without restriction, to fix on such a standard, as the caprice, ambition, party influence, or party calculations of those who, for the time being, might hold the reins of power, might dictate.

With this answer to your second question, I shall now proceed to reply to your third. It is in the following words: "After a State has been admitted into the Union, has the numerical majority of the people of such State the right to alter or abolish the Constitution, regardless of the mode prescribed for its amendment, if any; and where there is none, of the refusal or assent of such State?"

I answer—no; neither after, nor before admission. If the right exist at all, it must be either a natural or acquired right. It cannot be the former; because all such rights belong to man in what is called the state of nature, that is, in the state which is supposed to precede the existence of government, or, what is called, the political state. Although the human race cannot exist without society, nor society without government, yet, in the order of things, man must have existed before society, and society before government. And hence it has not been unusual for elementary writers on morals and politics, in treating of the rights and duties of man, to regard him in each of these states. In his natural state, he is considered simply as an individual, with no superior; and his rights and duties are deduced from those faculties and endowments, physical, intellectual, and moral, which are common to the race. Regarded in this state, all are equal in rights. In it, each individual is the sole master of his own actions; and there are neither majorities nor minorities, nor the rights of majorities and minorities. In the other, or political state, he ceases to be regarded in this isolated and independent character, and is viewed as a member of a body politic, or a State—that is, a society organized under a government, which represents its sovereign will, and through which it acts. It is in this state, and this only, that majorities and minorities are known, or have, as such, any rights. Whatever rights they possess, are political rights, the whole class of which are acquired, and are called conventional; that is, rights derived from agreement or compact, expressed or implied. How absurd, then, is it, to suppose the right of a majority to alter or abolish the Constitution is a natural right, a right belonging to man regarded as existing in a state of nature, when, in that state, majorities and minorities are unknown.

If, then, the right of the majority exist at all, it must be as a conventional right; and fortunately for the decision of the question, if it really exists in that character in our system, there will be no difficulty in finding it. The provident foresight of our ancestors has not left to conjecture or implication, in whom the right to abolish constitutions, or forms of government, resides; or how, for the most part, it is to be exercised. In every case (including the Federal Constitution) except New Jersey and Virginia, and recently Rhode Island, the authority by which it is to be exercised, and in what manner, is designated in the constitutions themselves. In all, if my memory be correct, the agency of the Government, in some form, is required, to alter or amend the Constitution. In a few, it may be done by the State Legislatures, according to the forms prescribed, without the express sanction of the people; but in all such cases, more than a mere numerical majority of the members is required. The most common form is, through a Convention of the people of the State, to be called by the Legislature thereof; and in the far greater number, two thirds of the Legislature are necessary to call a Convention; and, in all, the right of voting for the members of the Convention, or on the ratification of the Constitution, when submitted to the people, is restricted to those having the right of suffrage under the existing Constitutions. In one State, the votes of two thirds of the qualified voters are necessary to make the change. These various provisions clearly indicate the sense of the people of the United States, that the right of altering or changing constitutions is a conventional right, belonging to the body politic, and subject to be regulated by it. In not a single instance, is the principle recognized, that a mere numerical majority of the people of a State, or any other number, have the right to convene, of themselves, without the sanction of legal authority, and to alter or abolish the Constitution of the State.

Now, as the right, if it exists at all, must exist as a conventional right, that is, a right founded on express agreement or compact, or, in the absence of such an one, implied, it follows, from the statement, that it does not exist by express agreement or compact, in any of the cases, where provision is made for amending the Constitution: nor can it exist by implication, in any State, unless in the only two where Constitutions make no provisions on the subject.

That the right does not exist by implication in these States (New Jersey and Virginia), I hold to be equally certain. The fact, that their Constitutions do not provide for their amendment, cannot, by any force of reason, imply the right of the majority, to alter or abolish their Constitutions, without the consent of their respective Governments. Government, as has been stated, is the representative of a State, in its sovereign character, and the organ through which it acts. As such, it is vested with all powers necessary to the performance of its high functions, and which are not prohibited or expressly withheld by its Constitution, and among them, the most important of all, that of self-preservation. In our complex political system, the powers belonging to Government, as has been stated, are divided, a portion being delegated to the Federal Government, as the common representative of all the States in their united character; and the residue expressly reserved, to be exercised by the States, in their separate and individual character. Of this portion, the State Governments are the representatives and organs; and as such, are invested with all the powers not delegated, which properly appertain to Government, and which are not prohibited by their own, or the Federal Constitution. But they do not comprehend the power to make, alter or abolish constitutions, which, according to our political theory, belongs exclusively to the people; and cannot be exercised by Government, unless specially delegated by the Constitution. With these exceptions, the Governments of the States possess all others; and among them, that of proposing amendments to their Constitutions, and calling conventions of the people, for the purpose of amending, or proposing amendments, to be ratified by the people. That this power properly appertains to the functions of Government, and may be exercised without being delegated, will not be contested or denied. It has been uniformly exercised, and has never been questioned; and it is through its authority, whenever the Constitution provides for its amendment, that conventions are called, or propositions submitted for the purpose, are made. But being a power appertaining to government, it belongs to it exclusively; for government is not only the representative and organ of a State, in its sovereign character, but its sole and exclusive representative and organ; and it has, accordingly, ever been regarded, at every period of history, and under governments of every description, among the highest crimes, for unauthorized individuals to undertake to exercise powers properly belonging to it; and as such, it has been prohibited under the severest penalties.

If I do not mistake, your [Va.] Legislature has made the exercise of the very power in question, that of calling a Convention to amend the Constitution, without its authority, a high penal offence. If I mistake, you can correct me. But whether mistaken or not, surely none will deny, that it is within its competency, or that of the Legislature of any other State, to make it so.

But, it may be asked, if it be a power belonging to Government, and may be exercised without being specially delegated, why have the Federal, and all the State Constitutions, the two mentioned excepted, made provisions for their alteration and amendment? Why was it not left to the discretion of Congress, and the State Legislatures, to call conventions, or propose amendments to the people for their ratification? It is not because the power of doing either was doubted, but because those who framed them, while they were too wise not to see that amendments would become necessary, were, at the same time, too deeply impressed with the danger of frequent changes in the fundamental law of a State, to permit amendments to be made with too much facility. To meet the one, it was necessary that they should be left open to amendments; and to guard against the other, that restrictions should be imposed on the amending power; or, without them, the numerical majority of the Legislature might call conventions, or propose amendments at pleasure, to be adopted by a like majority of the people. The consequence would be, that Constitutions might be changed with almost the same facility as ordinary acts of the Legislature. It is to restrain this facility, that in all cases, where the Constitution provides for its amendment, it imposes restrictions on the power of amending, which would not otherwise exist. To impose such restrictions, was indeed the great object which their framers had in view, in prescribing the mode of amending; and it may be fairly doubted, whether without this, it would not have been left with the Government, as in the case of Virginia and New Jersey, to propose amendments and prescribe the forms for their adoption.

In denying, however, the right of the numerical majority, as such, to alter or abolish the Constitution of a State, regardless of the forms prescribed, or, where there are none, without the consent of the Government, I am far from denying that the people are the source of all power; and that their authority is paramount over all. But when political, and not natural rights are the subject, the people, as has been stated, are regarded as constituting a body politic, or State; and not merely as so many individuals. It is only when so regarded, that *they possess any political rights.* Viewed individually, as the elements of which the body politic is formed, they possess none but natural rights. Taken in either light, the people may alter or abolish their Constitution; but with this difference, that, in the former, they can only do it by acting according to the prescribed forms, where there are such, and when there are none, through the agency of its representative and organ—the Government of the State; while, in the latter, they act individually, and on individual responsibility. The one is a political, and the other a natural right—or as usually called, in such cases, *the right of revolution*—and can be resorted to, rightfully, only where government has failed in the great objects for which it was ordained, the security and happiness of the people; and then only where no other remedy can be applied. In such cases, the individuals who compose the community rightfully resume their natural rights; which, however restricted or modified they may be, in the political state, are never extinguished. But as a natural right, it is the right of individuals, and not that of majorities; although it may not be so safely and prudently exercised by one man, or a minority as a majority, it belongs to one as well as the other.

Such is my answer to your third inquiry, and my reasons for enter-taining the opinions I do on the question, in the general terms in which it is expressed. But I am of the impression that a more specific answer is required, to meet fully your intention in propounding it. Your question, as I conceive, presupposes a case of domestic violence, and of application, in due form, by the Government of the State, for pro-tection; and that the precise point, on which you desire my opinion, is, whether the fact, that the violence was under the assumed authority of the numerical majority, to alter or abolish the Constitution, would take it out of the guarantee, and make it the duty of the Federal Government to withhold its protection? And it is, as I understand it, with the view of obtaining an answer to it, in this form, that you have limited your question, as to the supposed right of a numerical ma-jority to alter or abolish its Constitution, to the case of a State after its admission into the Union. With this understanding of your object, I shall proceed to answer.

Whether the fact, that the violence was offered under the assumed authority of the majority, would take the case out of the guarantee, must obviously depend on the fact, whether it has the right assumed. If it has the right to alter or abolish the Constitution of the State, and to establish another in its place, the necessary consequence would be, that the one abolished would cease to be, and the one established would actually become rightfully the Constitution. It would, also, be a necessary consequence, after establishing the new, that those who might assume to exercise the functions of government under the old and abolished Constitution, against the new and actual, would be exercising it without constitutional or legal authority; and that, if the new government should undertake to put down the old by force or violence, and it should apply to the Federal Government for pro-tection, it would be its duty to withhold it. I go farther. If the old should resort to force or violence to suppress the new, and this should apply to the Federal Government for protection, it would be its duty to grant it, and suppress the old. But, on the contrary, if the numeri-cal majority has not the right, all this, of course, would clearly be reversed; and it would be the duty of the Federal Government to grant protection to the old, instead of the new; and, on its application, to put down those who might attempt to subvert it, under the au-thority of the new. They would, in fact, be a mere body of indi-viduals, acting without constitutional or legal authority; and with no more right to resort to violence against the Government of the State, than any other number of individuals, acting without pretext, against the authority of either.

That the numerical majority has not the right, in either of the cases supposed in your question, I have, I trust, established beyond controversy; and if so, it is no less unquestionable that, the fact of the violence being offered under its authority, cannot possibly take the case out of the guarantee, and make it the duty of the Federal Government to withhold its protection. Fatal, indeed, would be such a right. Its admission would be the death-blow to republican forms of government, or, what is the same thing, constitutional democracy.

Constitutions stand to governments, as laws do to individuals. As the object of laws is, to regulate and restrain the actions of individuals, so as to prevent one from oppressing or doing violence to another, so, in like manner, that of constitutions is, to regulate and restrain the actions of governments, so that those who exercise its powers, shall not oppress or do violence to the rest of the community. Without laws, there would be universal anarchy and violence in the community; and, without constitutions, unlimited despotism and oppression. This is true, be the form of government what it may. If the government of one man, or that of a few, would abuse its authority, if not restrained, as is admitted, there is no reason why that of the many would not do the same, if not also restrained. If, in a community of one hundred persons, forty-nine cannot be trusted with unlimited power over fifty-one, on what principle can fifty-one be trusted with unlimited power over forty-nine? If, unrestrained, the one will abuse its powers, why will not the other also? Can the transfer of a single individual, from the side of the fifty-one to that of the forty-nine, have the magic effect of reversing the character of the two, and making that unsafe, which before was trustworthy?

The truth is, the Government of the uncontrolled numerical majority, is but the *absolute and despotic form of popular governments*—just as that of the uncontrolled will of one man, or a few, is of monarchy or aristocracy; and it has, to say the least, it has [*sic*] as strong a tendency to oppression, and the abuse of its powers, as either of the others. Hence it is, that it would be the death-blow of constitutional democracy, to admit the right of the numerical majority, to alter or abolish constitutions at pleasure, regardless of the consent of the Government, or the forms prescribed for their amendment. It would be to admit, that it had the right to set aside, at pleasure, that which was intended to restrain it, and which would make it just no restraint at all; and this would be, to attribute to the simple numerical majority, an inherent, absolute, and paramount power, derived, not from agreement, compact or constitution, either expressed or implied, but a higher source. It would be, in short, to attribute to it the same divine right to govern, which Sir Robert Filmer claimed for kings; and against which, [John] Locke and [Algernon] Sydney so successfully combated. The argument, in both cases, is drawn from the same source, and leads to the same consequence. Admit political power to be *inherent*, it matters not whether in a dynasty, or in a numerical majority, and the consequence is inevitable, that it is absolute, and cannot be subject to constitutional restraints. It is only on the opposite theory, that all political rights are derived from assent or compact, expressed or implied, and are conventional, that government, be its form what it may, can be subject to constitutional restraints; and it is, accordingly, to this source, that Locke, Sydney, and other writers on the side of liberty, traced them. Fortunately for us, their doctrines became the creed of our ancestors, and the foundation of our free, popular, and glorious system of Governments, in which laws derive their authority from constitutions; and these, *from the free and united assent of the whole community, given expressly, or by a cheerful acquiescence.* Admit the opposite doctrine, the inherent and absolute right of the numerical majority, and all the restrictions which the Federal and State Constitutions impose on their respective Governments, and on the mode prescribed for their amendment, would be idle and delusive attempts to prevent the abuse of power, and to give a stability to our political system, inconsistent with the principles on which it would rest, and would prove utterly worthless in practice. There is, and always must be, a majority in, or out of power. If the one has a right to alter or abolish the constitution, the other must have an equal right to do so. If the majority out of power have the right to call, at their pleasure, a caucus or convention (the name is immaterial), and to alter or abolish the existing constitution or Government, and abolish others which would place them in power, surely the majority in power have the same right, by the same process, to alter or abolish all the restrictions which the constitution may place on their power, and make themselves absolute. And when it is remembered how irksome restraints are, who can doubt, if the right be admitted, but that it would soon become the established practice, when the tedious and cumbrous forms, which both the Federal and State Constitutions prescribe for their amendment, would be dispensed with. Once commenced, it would soon supersede entirely the prescribed forms; and when this was done, in a short time, the ceremony of calling a caucus or convention of the major party, be it out of, or in power, would be regarded as too tedious and troublesome, and the ordinary elections, or some still less certain evidence, would be regarded as sufficient to infer the will of the majority, and to supersede the Constitution; when the will of the numerical majority would take the place of Constitution and laws, and become the sole and absolute power.

This fatal process would be greatly accelerated, if the right of the numerical majority to alter or abolish constitutions, at pleasure, should be admitted, by the very guarantees, which were intended to secure the blessings of liberty, and give stability to our popular constitutional system. I have already shown that, if the right really exists, it would be the duty of the Federal Government, under the guarantee to protect the State against domestic violence, to aid always the side of the numerical majority to suppress the other. If it should be the majority *in power*, seeking to free itself from the restrictions imposed on the Government by the Constitution, it would be its duty to aid it, and to put down those who might attempt to resist the change; or, if it be the majority, *out of power*, seeking to alter or abolish the Constitution and Government, and substitute another, which would give them the power, the Federal Government would be equally bound to take its side, and to put down those who might attempt to uphold the authority of the Constitution and Government. The consequence would always be, to add the power and authority of the Federal Government to that of the majority in the State, seeking a change of Constitution and Government, be it in or out of power; and thus, instead of giving stability to the system, the guarantees would become the means of incessant changes and revolutions, and utterly destructive of the ends they were intended to effect.

Having now stated the reasons and principles on which I rest my answer to your third question, I shall proceed to reply to your fourth. It is in the following words:

"If one of the States of this Union, through her Government, should deny the right of a numerical majority of her people, to alter or abolish her Constitution at pleasure, and such majority should resort to force to effect its object, and the proper authority, under the Constitution proposed to be suppressed, should call on the Federal Government for protection, what would you regard as your duty, if President of the United States?"

My answer, after what I have already stated, is a matter of course. I would enforce the guarantee, and protect the State, to the extent of the authority vested in the President of the United States by the Constitution, and Acts of Congress made in conformity to it—provided (which, I presume, you assumed to be the fact) that the case, in all other respects, is within the provisions of the guarantee.

Your fifth question is, "If it should be deemed the right of the numerical majority to supersede the existing form of the Government of a State, at pleasure, and such majority should seek to establish another form of government, other than republican, what would be the remedy, and what the duty of the Federal Government?["]

As I do not deem it to be the right of the numerical majority, it will not be expected that I should answer the question: but I have, in answer to your second inquiry, stated what would be the effect if the people of a State, acting constitutionally and legally, should abolish their present republican form of government, and establish another of a different form, which will show what would be my opinion, if I thought the numerical majority had the right. If they had, it would make the numerical majority, in fact, the State; that is (as explained), the people, to the exclusion of the rest of the community; and, of course, would give to its act, abolishing the republican form of the government of a State, and establishing one of another form, the same effect, as if done by the people of the State themselves, acting constitutionally and legally.

I come now to your sixth and last question, which is in the following words:

"As these inquiries have grown out of the Rhode Island question, and that controversy out of the right of suffrage, I ask your opinion on the right of suffrage involved in the controversy."

As I understand the case, the question of suffrage involved was, whether the freehold suffrage, which existed under their form of government, should not be superseded, and the right be extended to the great mass of the community? It was, to express it in general terms, whether the right of suffrage should be restricted to freeholders, or be placed on a more liberal and enlarged basis?

My opinion is, and ever has been in favor of placing the right of suffrage on an extended basis. One of my first public acts was, to vote, as a member of our State Legislature, for an amendment of the State Constitution, to enlarge the right, and place it on the very liberal basis on which it now stands. The practical operation of the alteration has been good; and I have never had cause to repent my vote, or to change my early opinion. Thus thinking, my opinion and sympathy were on the side of, what has been called, the Suffrage Party, in Rhode Island, as far as the enlargement of the right was involved. The same remark is applicable to the other question involved in the controversy, whether the old form of government, under the Charter, should not be changed to one more analogous to that of the other States. But I regarded both as strictly domestic questions; and, as such, belonging to the State. Thus regarded, I hold that, so long as the controversy was confined to discussion and agitation, the Federal Government could take no cognizance of it; nor even, on a resort to force, until the Government of the State applied, in due form, for protection: and then, only, to determine whether the case came within the guarantee; and if so, to fulfil its duties. It had, even then, no right to take cognizance of the original cause of the controversy, or to be influenced by its opinion, in reference to it—unless, indeed, it should incidentally become necessary in determining whether the case came within the guarantee or not—which could scarcely be possible. Under this impression, I could not permit my individual opinion and sympathy, in reference to the original subjects of the controversy, to control or influence me, in deciding in my official character, on what would be the duty of the Federal Government, in a case involving so many, and such high and solemn constitutional questions, when viewed in, what may be called, the Federal aspect of the subject, in contradistinction to its domestic.

Having, now, answered your several questions, I deem it due, both to myself and the occasion, to state, in conclusion, what, according to the opinion I entertain, would be the effects of these guarantees, on the supposition that the Federal Government shall faithfully discharge the duties they impose.

The great and leading effect would be, to put an end to all changes in the form of government, and Constitutions of the States, originating in force or revolution; unless, indeed, they should be effected, against the united resistance of the State and the Federal Government. It would give to the Government and Constitution of each, the stability of the whole; so that no one could be subverted without subverting, at the same time, the whole system: and this, I believe to have been the intention of the framers of the Federal Constitution in inserting the guarantee-section. They were experienced and wise men, and did their work effectually. They had carried the country successfully through, by their wisdom and patriotism, the most remarkable political revolution on the records of history, and firmly established the Constitutions and Governments of the States, composing the Union, on the great principles of popular liberty, in which it originated. Nothing was left undone to perfect their great and glorious task, but to reconstruct, on more correct and solid principles, the common Constitution and Government of all the States, and bind them into one compact and durable structure. This was their crowning work; and how well it was performed, the Federal Constitution and Government will stand, more durable than brass, an everlasting monument of their wisdom and patriotism.

But very imperfect, indeed, would their task have been left, if they had not adopted effectual means to guard all the parts against the lawless shocks of violence and revolution. They were too deeply read in the history of free and confederated States, not to know the necessity of taking effectual guards against them; and for this purpose, inserted in the Constitution the guarantee-section, which will effectually and for ever guard against those dangerous enemies of popular and constitutional governments, if the Federal Government shall faithfully do its duty. They would, in such case, effectually close the doors, on every side, against their entrance, whether attempted by invasion from *without,* domestic violence from *within,* or through the lawless ambition and usurpation of rulers.

But while the framers of the Federal Constitution thus carefully protected the system against changes by the rude hand of violence and revolution, they were too experienced and wise to undertake to close the door against all changes. They well knew, that all the works of man, whatever may be their skill, are imperfect of themselves, and liable to decay; and that, in order to perfect and perpetuate what they had done, it was necessary to provide a remedy to correct its imperfections, and repair the injuries of time, by making such changes as the one or the other might require. They also knew that, if such changes were not permitted, violence and revolution would, in time, burst open the doors which they had so carefully closed against them, and tear down the whole system, in their blind and unskilful attempts to repair it. Nor were they ignorant that, in providing for amendments, it would be necessary, in order to give sufficient stability to the system, to guard against hasty and thoughtless innovations; but, at the same time, to avoid such restrictions as would not leave sufficient facility for making the requisite changes. And this, too, is executed with the same wisdom and skill, which characterized every other part of their work, in the various provisions contained in the Federal Constitution for amendments—which, while they afford sufficient guards against innovations, afford at the same time sufficient facility for the objects contemplated. But one thing still remained to perfect their work.

It might be, that the party in power would be opposed to all changes, and that, in consequence of the door being thus closed against force and revolution, and the restrictions imposed on the amending power, in order to prevent hasty innovations, they might make successful resistance against all attempts to amend the Constitution, however necessary, if no adequate provision were made to prevent it. This they foresaw, and provided against it an ample remedy; after explaining which, I shall close this long communication.

The framers of the Federal Constitution were not only experienced and wise men, but firm believers, also, in the capacity of their fellow-citizens for self-government. It was in the full persuasion of the correctness of this belief, that, after having excluded violence and revolution, or physical force, as the means of change, and placed adequate guards against innovation, they opened wide the doors, never to be closed, for the free and full operation of all the moral elements in favor of change; not doubting that, if reason be left free to combat error, all the amendments which time and experience might show to be necessary, would, in the end, be made; and that the system, under their salutary influence, would go on indefinitely, purifying and perfecting itself. Thus thinking, the liberty of the press, the freedom of speech and debate, the trial by jury, the privilege of *Habeas Corpus*, and the right of the people peaceably to assemble together, and petition for a redress of grievances, are all put under the sacred guarantee of the Federal Constitution, and secured to the citizen against the power both of the Federal and State Governments. Thus it is, that the same high power, which guarantees protection to the Governments of the States against change or subversion by physical force, guarantees, at the same time, to the citizens protection against restrictions on the unlimited use of these great moral agents for effecting such changes as reason may show to be necessary. Nor ought their overpowering efficacy to accomplish the object intended, to be doubted. Backed by perseverance, and sustained by these powerful auxiliaries, reason in the end will surely prevail over error and abuse, however obstinately maintained—and this the more surely, by the exclusion of so dangerous an ally as mere brute force. The operation may be slow, but will not be the less sure. Nor is the tardiness an objection. All changes in the fundamental laws of the State, ought to be the work of time, ample discussion, and reflection; and no people, who lack the requisite perseverance to go through the slow and difficult process necessary at once to guard against improper innovations, and to insure wise and salutary changes, or who are ever ready to resort to revolution, instead of reform, where reform may be practicable, can preserve their liberty. Nor would it be desirable, if it were practicable, to make the requisite changes, without going through a long previous process of discussion and agitation. They are indispensable means—the only school (if I may be allowed the expression,) in our case, that can diffuse and fix in the mind of the community, the principles and doctrines necessary to uphold our complex, but beautiful system of governments. In none that ever existed, are they so much required; and in none were they ever calculated to produce such powerful effect. Its very complication—so many distinct, sovereign, and independent States, each with its separate Government, and all united under one—is calculated to give a force to discussion and agitation, never before known, and to cause a diffusion of political intelligence heretofore unknown in the history of the world, if the Federal Government shall do its duty under the guarantees of the Constitution, by thus prom[p]tly suppressing physical force, as an element of change, and keeping wide open the door for the full and free action of all the moral elements in its favor. No people ever had so fair a start. All that is lacking is, that we shall understand, in all its great and beautiful proportions, the noble political structure reared by the wisdom and patriotism of our ancestors, and to have the virtue and the sense to preserve and protect it: and happy shall I be, if what I have written in answer to your inquiries, should contribute, in the least, to a better knowledge of it and through this, in any degree, to its perfection and preservation.

With great respect, I am, &c., &c., J.C. Calhoun.

PC in Crallé, ed., *Works*, 6:209–239; LS (fragment) in ScCleA. NOTE: This is one of the handful of important Calhoun documents for which the earliest complete text is that published by Crallé. Crallé did not give his source for this document, but stated in the "Preface" of the volume in which it appeared that "the Editor has felt himself constrained to adhere strictly to the original manuscripts of the author, in all cases where they could be procured. He regrets, however, to state that he has not always been successful in his efforts to obtain the originals." (Crallé, ed., *Works*, 6:v.) The surviving manuscript may be a fragment of the text from which Crallé worked. It differs from Crallé's text in incidentals of style, but not in content. The fragment consists of the last two pages (numbered 11 and 12) of the recipient's copy of the letter to Smith and its address leaf, with the text beginning in the middle of the seventh to last paragraph before the closing, the paragraph which begins: "My opinion is, and ever has been in favor of placing the right of suffrage on an extended basis." The manuscript fragment is in the handwriting of Thomas G. Clemson. It is signed by Calhoun, franked by Calhoun, and addressed in Calhoun's hand to Smith in Warrenton, Va. The fragment also contains a Pendleton postmark of 8/5 and Calhoun's AEU: "Discusses the Rhode Island case."

To A[ndrew] P[ickens] Calhoun, [Marengo County, Ala.]

Fort Hill, 6th July 1843

My dear Andrew, On my return from the mine a few days since, I received yours of the 11th June. I am much gratified to learn that all are well, and the prospect so fine. We are in equal enjoyment of health and have a promising crop. The corn, peas & potatoes are very fine. The wheat is of an excellent quality, but the yeild [*sic*] only middling. The oats ordinary. The Cotton forward and of good size & stand, but the squares, from some cause, have dropt more than I have ever known at this season of the year.

My Mine was not doing very well. I have been working on the surface, and in the slate principally about the mouth of the vein, without pursuing it down. I thought it better to do a safe business as long as I could; but as the surface and the state [*sic*] at the mouth of the vein are well near exhausted, I had determined to drive in a tunnel in order to draw off the water & pursue the vein. I expected when I left, that the tunnel would be finished in 10 days. It will determine whether the vein is rich below, or not. I think it doubtful. There are some indications favourable and others not. The vein and the whole formation ["is" *canceled and* "are" *interlined*] entirely different from any in the region. I am inclined to think, that there is a belt, ["of" *canceled*] extending the whole length of the lot and 50 or 60 yards wide with paral[l]el veins of greater or less richness in the whole extent; but it would be a work of time and expense to explore it.

Your Uncle John's [John Ewing Colhoun's] lot has again become productive. An under ground [vein] of great richness has been discovered. The extent not yet ascertained. I hope it may prove to be so extensive, as to relieve him from his embarrassment. Good Judges are of the impression, that there is an under ground of great extent and richness on the Obar, but that it lies so deep, that it will require the aid of Machinery to work it. The indications are strong in its favour, and I hope it may prove to be the case. If cotton should keep down, the mine may become of great importance.

We shall expect you as soon as Margaret [Green Calhoun] is able to travel and shall be happy to see you all. I expect John [C. Calhoun, Jr.,] out on a visit from the University [of Virginia], so that we shall all again be assembled except Patrick [Calhoun].

The letter you enclosed (Mr. Lewis'[s]) is very sensible and encouraging. I had a letter by the last mail from J[ohn] A. Calhoun. He speaks favourably of the indications in that quarter [of Ala.] and says that the prospect is daily brightening. My information from all quarters ["are" *canceled*] is favourable.

I enclose two copies of the Address of our Convention. Keep one for yourself and dispose of the other as you may judge best. It takes the only ground in reference to the Convention, that can be safely occupied. If the smaller States & the weaker portions of the Union should lose their control in the choice of the President, our whole system would go to wreck. Place the control of the ballot box, and the power, influence & veto of the Executive Department in the ["same" *canceled*] hands of ["the" *canceled*] a few large States, and the most odious despotism, that can be imagined would be the result.

All join in love to you, Margaret [Green Calhoun] & Duff [Green Calhoun]. Your affectionate father, J.C. Calhoun.

ALS in ScU-SC, John C. Calhoun Papers.

To EDW[ARD] DELONY, Clinton, La.

Fort Hill, July 6, 1843

I was absent from home when your letter [of 6/14] arrived, which will explain why it has not been acknowledged at an earlier period.

You are right in the opinion which you attribute to me on the subject of free trade. So far from desiring or aiming at substituting a system of direct or internal taxes for duties on imposts, as the means of supporting the Government, my object has been the very reverse, as I have often expressed in debate. One of the objections I have urged against high protective duties is, that it would hasten the period when a resort to a system of internal taxation would become necessary. I am, and always have been, of the opinion that the duties on imposts and the proceeds of the sales of the public land, are the legitimate sources of the revenue of the Union, and that it will prove a severe trial of the Federal Government, whenever it shall be forced to resort to internal taxes to meet its ordinary expenditures: under this impression, as well as for other powerful reasons, I have steadily opposed all schemes of alienating the revenue from the lands, or that were calculated to impair the source of revenue from the imposts.

PC in the Washington, D.C., *Madisonian*, August 26, 1843, p. 2; PC in the New York, N.Y., *Tribune*, August 26, 1843; PC in the Augusta, Ga., *Daily Chronicle and Sentinel*, August 25, 1843, p. 2; PC in the Norfolk and Portsmouth, Va., *American Beacon and Daily Advertiser*, August 30, 1843, p. 2; PC in the Petersburg, Va., *Republican*, August 31, 1843, p. 3; PC in the Alexandria, D.C., *Gazette and Virginia Advertiser*, August 31, 1843, p. 4; PC in the Richmond, Va., *Enquirer*, September 5, 1843, p. 3; PC in the Springfield, Ill., *Illinois State Register*, September 29, 1843, p. 2.

To R[OBERT] M. T. HUNTER, [Lloyds, Va.]

Fort Hill, 6th July 1843

My dear Sir, Your letter of the 16th June arrived while I was absent from home on business, which will explain the delay of my answer.

I entirely concur in the propriety of your suggestions; that our friends ought to organize on Congressional districts, and that candidates ought to come out at the proper time on our side, one in each District. But it appears to me, that some preliminary steps ought to be taken. If I do not mistake, we hold in our hand the means of forcing on the friends of Mr. [Martin] Van Buren in Virginia & N[ew] York the choice of delegates by District and the per capita mode of voting in spite of the dictation of General Drumgool [*sic*; George C. Dromgoole, Representative from Va.].

His friends (V[an] B[uren's]) have been forced, in order to escape from the awarked [*sic*; awkward] position, which [has been caused by] their attempt to have the Convention ["held" *interlined*] in Nov-[embe]r, to agree to leave the decesion [*sic*], as to time and place of holding it, to a majority *of the States*. You will see at once the advantage, which this gives us. It recognizes the principle, that the majority of the States is the proper authority to determine, all preliminary questions touching the Convention, where there is a division of sentiment among the friends of the candidates. It is a most important principle, better calculated to give a just control to the less populous States and sections of the Union, in making the nomination, than any other that could be devised; and, let me add, ["and" *canceled*] thereby to add proportionally to the stability of the Union and our free & popular institutions. Without it, the nomination, and through it the election, would be permanently consolidated in the hands of the great ["central" *canceled*] States lying contig[u]ous to the centre. Leave it to each State to determine, as Gen[era]l Drumgoole ["contends" *canceled and then interlined*], how the delegates shall be appointed, and how vote, how many shall be appointed and how their votes shall [be; "count" *changed to* "counted"], and it must be obvious, the [*one word canceled and* "central" *interlined*] & powerful States would control permanently the nomination, and thereby the election & the Executive Department, and through it the whole Government. It would, in fact, place the control of the ballot box and the executive power, patronage & veto in the same hands and ["thus" *interlined*] erect one of the most odious De[s]potism[s] that ever existed. It is, in fact, only when the Executive power is under the influence or control of the less populous States & section, that there is any balance in the system, and it is only then, as experience shows, that it works well. The value of the principle, in question, is that its certain tendency is to give them a just share of the influence & control over that Department. There is a large majority of the States, that are ["below" *canceled and* "under" *interlined*] the medium size & population, and if they are true to themselves, ["under" *canceled and* "they will under" *interlined*] the operation of the principle, ["will" *canceled*] establish the most equitable ["princip" *canceled*] rules for constituting the Convention & governing its votes & proceedings. It will be in the power of New England & the Southern & South Western States, to protect themselves ag[ai]nst the overwhelming vote of the mid[d]le & North western States.

We ought at once to acquiesce in the precedent & the principle it establishes, that the majority of the States is the proper authority to decide all preliminary questions, in reference to the Convention, and some one of the central Committees, say that of Maryland, or New Hampshire, ought to immitate [*sic*] that of Indiana, and call ["at the proper time" *interlined*] on the Committees of the several States to report to the same papers (Globe & Enquirer) the decision of their respective States, as to the mode of appointing delegates & how they shall vote. In the mean time, our friends in all quarters ought to be active by correspondence and discussion to call publick attention to the subject. I regard the establishment of the principle, that delegates shall be appointed by districts & that they shall vote per capita more important, as it regards the result of the election, & the future operation of the Government, than any other. Too much pains cannot be taken to establish it. It would be in fact, but a ["consumation" *canceled and* "consummation" *interlined*] of the great victory you effected last year, in the apportionment bill. The two would give a new lease to our institutions. Can you not put [Levi] Woodbury & our N[ew] England friends in motion on the subject? The thing is not only right of itself, but is calculated to be popular. What better authority can there be to settle preliminary questions than the majority of the States? Or what can be more fair & popular, than that the people shall choose their delegates, and have the control of their votes? Standing on such vantantage [*sic*] ground, and having their own authority & precedent, for what we propose, and the interest of a great majority of the States in favour of what we contend, we ought to succeed without failure. Our friends in this quarter will attend to the subject in the West & South west, leaving it to you & others to attend to other quarters.

My information from every quarter is favourable. I am pressed to visit the various sections of the Union, so much so, that it is hard to refuse compliance, but my feelings & judgement are strongly ag[ai]nst it. Yours sincerely & truly, J.C. Calhoun.

[P.S.] I send you a copy of our address in pamphlet form.

ALS in ScCleA; variant PEx (erroneously addressed to Thomas G. Clemson) in Jameson, ed., *Correspondence*, pp. 538–540.

From S A M [U E] L S T A R K W E A T H E R

Rochester [N.Y.,] 6th July 1843

D[ea]r Sir, I left the city of N[ew] York a few days since & have passed thus far through the State, carefully noticeing[?] the feelings of the democratic party, with a view to convey to you my opinion.

In N[ew] York [City] & along the river counties your friends are strong & gaining, but are not yet in the majority. At this place & in this region you have more strength than Mr. [Martin] Van Buren—no one else is thought of.

The Hon. Timothy Childs, formerly a member of Congress resides here. After a full interview with him, today, he allows me to say to you it is his opinion you should make a tour north, this Summer, Staying over a day or so at the more important places, as you pass & allowing your friends to call on you. I fully concur in that opinion & do not hesitate to say you can carry every vote in this district by such course. You will find well informed & discrete friends enough to accompany you & arrange all right. I return to N[ew] York [City] in a day or two, but not to remain long. Go thence to the interior until autumn. I recommend that you you [*sic*] keep clear of the taint of Tylerism. He has not any sincere friend in this State. Very truly yours, Saml. Starkweather.

ALS in ScU-SC, John C. Calhoun Papers.

To M[ICAH] STERLING, [Watertown, N.Y.]

Fort Hill, 8th July 1843

My dear Sir, I was absent from home when your letter was received, which will explain, why the answer has been so long delayed.

The information you give me relative to the state of things in N[ew] York and the other States in your section, corresponds with that, which I receive from other sources. Were it not for the old leaders & organs of the party, Mr. [Martin] V[an] B[uren] would be weak indeed; but with them, he is strong. All who held office, or had influence with him, while in power, are anxious for his restoration, and their union, skill & Zeal are the real, and almost exclusive source, of his strength. The young, & disinterested are to a great extent opposed to him; and, if things should take the turn, which your Ohio friend & correspondent anticipates, and which is not improbable, his defeat would be certain. The great point is, so to ["organize" *canceled and* "constitute" *interlined*] the Convention, that it shall speak truly the voice of the people, and not that of political managers; and that can only be done by choosing the delegates by Districts. It is all important, that our friends should insist on it. On none other is a Convention safe. It is the true Republican doctrine.

As to ["the" *changed to* "this"; "South" *canceled and* "section" *interlined*], I regard all South of Virginia as safe, and she would be among the most united and strong, were it not for the influence of [Thomas] Ritchie. Circumstances have given great influence & circulation to the Enquirer, which he conducts with great tack [*sic*; tact]. As it is, I regard the State as doubtful. If the delegates should be ["elected" *canceled and* "selected" *interlined*] by Districts, her vote would be much divided.

As to myself, I look on calmly. Personally, I care but little about the result. I have neither pride nor ambition to gratify. I regard the office, as a high, & responsible trust, to be undertaken, as a duty to be discharged, and not as a matter of vanity, or personal gratification. It is thus, that I should undertake it, if it should be the will of the people of these States to select me to fill the high trust. To preserve the Constitution & the liberty of the Country; to elevate the character of the Government & the people, and restore confidence & prosperity would be great objects, at which I would aim.

I am glad to learn, that the health of my name sake [John Calhoun Sterling] is so much better. I hope you will not abandon your intention of making me a visit. I would be happy to see both you &

him, and so would be, Mrs. [Floride Colhoun] Calhoun & my family. You are right, in supposing that I reside in a healthy region. There is perhaps none more so in the Union. It is perfectly safe at all seasons, even to Northern Constitutions. Yours truly & sincerely, J.C. Calhoun.

ALS in ScU-SC, John C. Calhoun Papers.

A. P. STINSON to Tho[ma]s G. Clemson, Fort Hill, Pendleton, S.C.

St. Joseph[,] Berrien Co[unty,] Mich., July 8, 1843
My dear Sir, Your Esteemed favor of 7th Ult[imo] came to hand p[e]r Due course of Mail. In reply to Which I have to say, that However much *my self* & the *friends* of Mr. [John C.] Calhoun may regret the Decision he has made, *not to travil North & West during* the Pen-den[c]y of the Presidential Campaign, we appreciate, highly appreciate the motives which have governed him in Deciding this Point. I agree with you Sir, that tis Little Else than a *"Show"* or at Least has been so heretofore. But It did seem to me, that *Mr. C[alhoun,]* Called upon as I knew he had been, might have Visited those Portions of the Country to Which he was a Stranger without being obnoxious to the Charge of "being on an Electione[er]ing Tour." He Could Sir, at Least have as good a Pretext as the *"Sage of Kinderhook"* [Martin Van Buren,] that of "Visiting his relatives"!

But this matter Mr. C[alhoun] has put a veto on, so I will as his friend submit. I have recently Rec[eive]d the *Honorable appointment* of Chairman of the Central *Calhoun* Committee of Correspondence for Berrien Co[unty], & have accepted the appointment. I Could have wished that my friend & Mr. C[alhoun']s friend, *Judge* [Thomas] *Fitzgerald* had been that Officer on several accounts, first that he is a more *prominent man* in Western Mich. than my self, second that he is *Post Master* & third that he wields a pen & Commands an Influence that few, if any, in our State do or Can. But he, (generous soul) bestowed this Honor on ["my" *changed to* "me"], saying, "It is Enough for me to be a Private in the *Calhoun Corpse* & I can Do much in that Sphere."

In our State they have recently been making, as you will have seen, a Stir for G[e]n[era]l [Lewis] *Cass* & I Should not be surprised If he Carry the State as a *first Choice*, though I believe If the People were to vote *Direct* to day for President Mr. C[alhou]n would have her vote. *Ohio* & *Indianna* are also moving for *Cass*. This I do not regret, as It is Drawing from Mr. Van Buren ["from" *interlined*] whom alone has Mr. C[alhoun] any thing to apprehend. I do not believe G[e]n[era]l *Cass* is, or can be in any Event *formidable*. Our People will go for him as the "Yankee Girl" ["Did" *interlined*] for her Beau who was rather annoying, Married him to get rid of him. Not Sir, that *Mr. Cass* is not a fine man & that he has not many good Qualities & many warm & Devoted friends, but he has not ["sufficient" *interlined*] *Energy* of Character, In my Estimation, for Chief Magistrate of this Nation. I have seen, as you will have Ere this reaches you, the Doings of the *N.H.* & *Maine* Conventions. My word for It Sir, The People are not with "Matty" in those States, notwithstanding the Doings of those "*Packed Conventions*." *Levi Woodbury* has something to say in these matters, & when he *speakes* his voice will be heard! Judge W[illia]m *Pitt Prebble* I notice was a Delegate in the Maine Convention. He is an "*Old 'un*", is the *Ajax* of the Party & if I Can Judge, is Decidedly in favor of "South Carolina[']s favorite Son." I Shall be Disappointed Indeed if Mr. Calhoun Does not Carry *Maine*[,] *N.H.*[,] *Conn.*, & Even the "Old Bay State" & a fair Chance for "Little *Rhody*". A[s to] *Vermont*, she is Antimason[,] Abolition & J[oin]ed[?] to her Idols. Let her alone. W[ill] not Sir, some of Mr. C[alhoun']s friends from the *South* visit the *North* & *West* & *Warm us up in the Good Cause*? We hope so. They Can Do It, without their motives being Impugned, or at Least without Compromitting Mr. C[alhoun] as making personal Exertions.

Had I the *Talent*[,] *Capacity* & *Means* I would visit Every *Village* & *Hamlet* in the "far off West" & Implore my Country men to be Just to Mr. C[alhoun], them selves, the Constitution & their Country, but as I have *neither*, I must Content my self to walk in a humble sphere & Do all I can for that Cause in which I have "Enlisted During War." Your friend In Great Haste, A.P. Stinson.

P.S. My Regards to Mr. C[alhoun] Please make ac[c]eptable & say to him that *Judge Fitzgerald* will soon write him.

ALS in ScCleA. NOTE: For other, and firsthand, commentary on the Maine Democratic convention, see the letters written by Leonard Jarvis from Bangor on 6/23/1843 to Edmund T. Bridge and D[aniel] D. Brodhead (ALS's in ScU-SC, John C. Calhoun Papers).

To W[ILLIAM] M. CORRY, ELLWOOD FISHER, J. L. VATTIER, STEPHEN HULSE, and W[ILLIAM] F. JOHNSON, Cincinnati

Fort Hill, July 9th, 1843

Gentlemen: I was absent from home when your letter [of 6/19] was received, covering the resolutions of a large and respectable meeting of the Democrats of Hamilton County, inviting me to visit them and the State of Ohio, which will explain why my answer has been so long delayed.

If any thing could induce me to depart from the course I have prescribed for myself, while my name is before the people for the highest office within their gift, it would be the invitation which you have so kindly tendered in the name of those you represent. The source whence the invitation comes, the grounds on which it is tendered, my desire, long entertained, to visit the great Valley of the Mississippi—the only portion of the Union I have never seen—and to meet the wishes of my friends who have so earnestly expressed their desire to see me, all strongly impel me to accept; but to these is imposed an objection which to me is insuperable—my conception of the proper course for me to pursue while occupying the position I do. Since I have been placed there by my friends, I have received frequent invitations from them in various portions of the Union, pressing me to visit their respective sections. In order to answer them, it became necessary that I should decide, on general principles, the course it would be proper for me to pursue. I accordingly gave the subject my deliberate consideration. The result was a conviction that I ought not to accept, and I have, therefore, declined all invitations of the kind.

I am aware that others, occupying the same position as myself, have come to a different conclusion, and that the practice, as you state, is different from that I have prescribed for myself. In adopting it, I intend no reflection on those who take a different view. It is a point which each has a right to decide for himself. I may be wrong, and they right. I may even expose myself to the charge of being fastidious, but as the conclusion to which I have come is the result of my deliberate judgment, after full reflection, I am bound to respect it. And I trust that such of my friends as think me wrong will pardon the error from respect to the motive which governs me.

With these remarks, and an expression of very sincere gratitude for the high estimate which my friends of Hamilton County have placed on my public services and the interest they feel for my success,

I would conclude my answer to your letter if I did not feel that something more than the bare statement of the rule I have adopted was due to them and to the occasion. I regard with great respect the relation which a public man holds to those who approve of his principles and conduct, and support his course. He is, in my opinion, bound, among other things, to pay great respect to their opinions and wishes, and when he cannot conform to them, it is his duty to assign freely and candidly the reasons which may prevent him. In compliance with that duty, I propose to assign briefly some of the more prominent of those which governed me in coming to the conclusion which compels me to decline the kind and pressing invitation of which you are the organ.

There are then in my opinion, strong considerations, both of propriety and expediency, why the office of President of the United States should not be sought by personal canvass or the usual modes of electioneering. Regarded merely in reference to feeling, the office, it seems to me, is too high and its duties too responsible to be the object of personal solicitation. Who, with the proper spirit, can contemplate the task of discharging its high duties without being inspired with a diffidence and awe calculated to suppress every feeling of the kind? When I look at the country as it now is, and compare it with what it was when I first entered the councils of the Union, as it relates to the population, wealth, improvements, and all the elements of greatness—and then look forward to what it will be when those who are now entering on the stage shall retire, provided our liberty, institutions, and union shall be preserved—and then reflect on the great and decisive influence which the powers vested in the President must have, in that respect, for good or evil, as they may be properly or improperly exercised, to me it seems to be the highest and most responsible office in the world—far too much so to be the object of personal solicitation, or sought by a personal canvass, or ever to be accepted on any other ground than that of duty.

Nor, in my opinion, are the considerations of expediency less strong. Regarded in that light, I hold it all important to the successful operation of our system of Government, that the highest office of the Union should be the exclusive reward of merit and services such as may be well known to the whole country—so as to enable the people at large to form a just estimate of their value, and of the character and motive of him who rendered them. In order to understand the force of the position, it will be necessary to bear in mind that no other cause has so powerful an influence in forming the character of a people under free and popular Governments, and, through it, over their destiny, as the means by which its offices and honors may be most successfully acquired. Whatever they may be—whether election-e[e]ring, management, intrigue, corruption, patronage or faithful and patriotic services—that will be the most carefully studied and cultivated by the aspiring and talented. And be it which it may, the influence which its study and practice will have on their character, will, by necessary consequence, extend in time to the mass of the community—either to debase and corrupt, or elevate and purify, as its tendency may be to the one or the other.

If this be true, as applied generally, to offices and honors, how much more strikingly must it appear to be so when applied, in our system of Government, to the office of President—the highest and most honorable by far of all, and having at its disposition many others much more valued than any in the gift of the States or the people. And how important is it, that it should be made the exclusive reward of services and merit—the only means by which it can be acquired, calculated to elevate and purify the character of those who aspire to its high distinction, and, through their example, the whole community—I might add, the only one by which it can be sought and acquired, which would not have a debasing and corrupting tendency. How important, then, it is, that all others should be discountenanced in the Presidential canvass, except an open and manly appeal to services and merit. Is it saying too much, to assert that the fate of our free institutions and the country, must, in no small degree, depend on a correct mode of thinking and acting on the part of the people, in reference to a subject of such magnitude?

Such are some of the considerations which have induced me to adopt the rule I have. There are others of much weight, which I forbear to press, to avoid prolixity. Acting in obedience to it, I must forego the pleasure which it would otherwise afford me to accept the invitation which you have so kindly tendered to visit your magnificent portion of the Union. Be assured that no feeling of indifference towards it, or my friends in that quarter, has in the least swayed me in declining to accept. I have ever had the kindest feelings towards the West, I have regarded its progress in population, wealth and improvement, with pleasure and admiration, and have omitted no opportunity to accelerate its growth. With great respect, I am, &c. &c., J.C. Calhoun.

PC in the Cincinnati, Ohio, *Daily Enquirer,* August 2, 1843, p. 2; PC in the Richmond, Va., *Enquirer,* August 15, 1843, p. 2; PC in the Washington, D.C., *Madisonian,* August 16, 1843, p. 2; PC in the Washington, D.C., *Spectator,* August 19, 1843, p. 2; PC in the Petersburg, Va., *Republican,* August 19, 1843,

p. 2; PC in the Charleston, S.C., *Mercury*, August 21, 1843, p. 2; PC in the Charleston, S.C., *Courier*, August 25, 1843, p. 2; PC in the Pendleton, S.C., *Messenger*, August 25, 1843, p. 1; PC in the Greenville, S.C., *Mountaineer*, September 1, 1843, p. 1; PC in *Niles' National Register*, vol. LXV, no. 1 (September 2, 1843), p. 11.

To R[obert] M. T. Hunter, [Lloyds, Va.]

Fort Hill, 10th July 1843

My dear Sir, I regret, that you could not take the Charge of the Spectator, but doubt not, that you have decided correctly all things considered. I think Mr. Smith would do well, and do hope he may assent. He would do much to hold the [Washington] Globe & [Richmond] Enquirer in check, & would have a fair prospect of obtaining at least a share of the publick printing. I think he could not do better.

I have given the subject of visiting the different portions of the Union on the invitation of my friends full & deliberate consideration, and the more I have reflected, the more thoroughly am I satisfied, the proper course ["viewed" *and one canceled word interlined*] every way is to decline; and I had, before I received your letter, written a formal letter declining the invitation of my friends of Cincinnati, to visit that place & Ohio. Laying aside all the higher considerations of propriety & general expediency, and viewing it simply, as bearing on the result of the election, and I feel confident, the weight of the argument is ag[ai]nst it. Take even, in that light, the most narrow view. To accept all or the greater part of the invi[ta]tions would engross my time & keep me continually on the route; ["which would be" *interlined*] alike exhausting to mind, body & character. Before the termination, ["I would" *interlined*] feel in my own estimation and would be regard[ed] in ["that of" *interlined*] the publick, to be a mere political electioneerer. On the other hand, to make a discrimination, and accept but a few, would give offence to all others. I could not go to the North, without offending the West; nor to both, without offending the South & South West.

But the truth is, if my opinion was different; if I thought, I could gain by it, and even secure the election, I could hardly bring myself to adopt it—certainly not, but from the ["wish &" *canceled*] respect I have for my friends ["and desire to meet their wishes" *interlined*]; so repugnant are my feelings to it. It may be pride, it may be fastidiousness, or a sense of propriety, or the whole combined; but so it is, and I cannot help it. I would be happy to travel quietly, as an individual to see my friends & converse freely with them; but I am adverse to ["being" *canceled and then interlined*] made a spectacle, or considered an electioneerer, or to take a step, that would, in the public estimation, indicate a personal solicitude about the office, which I do not feel. But enough of this.

I read the article in the Enquirer in answer to [George C.] Drumgool[e]'s miserable communication with pleasure. It does much credit to your Nephew [Muscoe R.H. Garnett?, later a Representative from Va.].

The nomination of [Martin] Van Buren in Maine, I regard as more a defeat, than a victory. To obtain [*one word canceled*] nominations ["by stealth" *interlined*] seems to be a part of his established policy. It cannot fail to react.

You are right, as to the course, that the Globe & the Enquirer intend to take. I see the Petersburgh Republican understands the game, and has taken good notice of it for a commencement. It is a point he [that is, Washington Greenhow, editor of the *Republican?*] may touch with great effect. The Mercury just at this time is quiet about the ["presidential" *interlined*] election, and it is perhaps proper ["be" *canceled and* "it" *interlined*] should be so. The elections are pending in Georgia, Alabama & Mississippi, where our friends for the most part are the candidates; and where the friends of V[an] B[uren], at least a part, would be glad to have any pretex[t] not to vote. Many of the old, inveterate hacks would prefer the success of the Whigs to any but their own friends, notwithstanding all the cant about harmony &[c.] &[c.].

I infer from an extract from a letter from Mr. [James] Buchanan, sent me by a friend [William Smith], that his feeling, ["are" *interlined and then canceled*] as you suppose, is adverse to Mr. V[an] B[uren].

The indications are, that the Whigs are beaten in Louisiana. If so, it will greatly damp the hope of [Henry] Clay's friends. I regard his case as hopeless; and, if such should prove to be the fact, it will be difficult to estimate ["the" *canceled and* "its" *interlined*] effect on the election. In shaping their course, our friends ought to take into the estimate, the probability of the fact. Truly & sincerely, J.C. Calhoun.

ALS in ScCleA; variant PC in Jameson, ed., *Correspondence*, pp. 540–542.

—— to [JOSEPH] GALES [JR.] and [WILLIAM W.] SEATON, [Editors of the Washington, D.C., *Daily National Intelligencer*]

New York [City], July 11, 1843

Messrs. Gales & Seaton: I observe that you have remarked upon the publication of Mr. [John C.] Calhoun's Speeches, by the Harpers of this city, and that in the course of your remarks you have laid some stress upon the publishers' "advertisement," which you seem to regard as having been furnished by the compiler of the work. Justice to that compiler and perhaps to Mr. Calhoun requires from me a correction of your mistake on this point.

The history of that "advertisement" [dated 6/1843] is very simple. The publishers wrote to me that they were about issuing the speeches, but that they had nothing in the shape of preface or introduction—for want of which the volume had a naked appearance; and they asked me to give them something to interpose between the title-page and the body of the work. They did not send me a copy, nor have I ever seen one. I knew nothing of the work except simply that it was to contain Speeches by Mr. Calhoun. With this knowledge, and no more, I "cooked up" the advertisement, specifically as a necessity of the publishing craft, and with no ulterior purpose whatever. I had to say something, and I said just what occurred to me as proper and decent for the purpose of the publishers.

Of course I have no remark to make on the fact that the book does not contain *all* Mr. Calhoun's speeches; for that the compiler is answerable; but I have thought it my duty to explain away whatever inferences might be drawn from the language of the publishers' preface or advertisement. Yours, very truly, &c. [unsigned.]

PC in the Washington, D.C., *Daily National Intelligencer,* July 15, 1843, p. 2. NOTE: The author of this letter is not identifiable with certainty. Compare Virgil Maxcy's letter to Calhoun dated 8/29/1843, below.

"Circular" from W[ILLIA]M HALE and JA[ME]S E. PLATT, "Private and Confidential"

Detroit, July 12, 1843

Dear Sir, The Calhoun Central Committee beg leave to call your attention to the propriety of an early and efficient organization of the friends of John C. Calhoun throughout the State. The preference of the State will doubtless be settled during the present season, and the claims of our favorite ought to be immediately brought before the people. It is not unlikely that the Presidential question will be agitated, perhaps disposed of at the next State convention in September. We feel therefore that there is no time to be lost.

As yet there has been but one committee formed[,] our own Central Committee at this place. To carry out our organization we propose the formation of a corresponding committee in each county, whose duty it shall be to communicate with us, and to whom we may also send communications. They will also furnish a convenient mode of distributing papers & documents. In forming these committees, it will not be necessary to hold public meetings; but it will be sufficient for a few of our leading friends in each county to consult together either in person or by writing & fix upon the persons to act as the Committee. It will be well for two of them at least to reside near the same place or near each other. Let the names of the committee as soon as it is formed be communicated to us.

Each County committee should then endeavor to get up a Township organization. For this purpose let them select one trusty friend in each town to act as a committee man in that town. Let it be his duty to transmit information to the Central County Committee and let all communications relative to his town be transmitted through him. Let the name of each Township committee man be forwarded to the Central Committee.

In this way perfect organization will be secured. We shall be able to ascertain our exact strength in every portion of the State. Whenever any thing is required to be done at a particular point, we shall have the means of being informed of it and thus a channel through which to accomplish it. We shall be able also to convey documents into every town, and to suggest one united movement throughout the State whenever the exigencies of our cause may demand it.

Our friends in this portion of the State are exceedingly active, and every day adds to the number of the advocates of John C. Calhoun. We beg leave to urge you to the utmost promptness, energy and activity, and hope that you will lose no time in forwarding to us the information, desired at your hands, and in carrying out in detail, the views & plans shadowed forth in this Circular. Truly Yours, Wm. Hale, ch[airma]n, Jas. E. Platt, Sec[retar]y.

DS (in Platt's hand) in ScCleA.

From JOEL BRANHAM and ROB[ER]T BLEDSOE

Eatonton, Geo[rgia,] July 13th 1843
Dear Sir, It is alledged [*sic*] by some of your political opponents in this section of the State, that you are the advocate of the protective Tariff system. Your political friends on the contrary, represent you to be the advocate of the free trade policy. Will you favour us with explicit answers to the following questions: Are you the Advocate of a Tariff for the protection of Manufactures? Does the party which favours your election to the Presidency support that policy? Your answers to these questions will oblige many of your friends here. Very respectfully &c., Joel Branham, Robt. Bledsoe.

LS in ScU-SC, John C. Calhoun Papers; variant PC in the Milledgeville, Ga., *Federal Union*, September 19, 1843, p. 3; variant PC in the Edgefield, S.C., *Advertiser*, September 27, 1843, p. 2; variant PC (misdated 7/19/1843) in the Augusta, Ga., *Daily Chronicle & Sentinel*, September 20, 1843, p. 2.

To A[NDREW] P[ICKENS] CALHOUN, Faunsdale (Marengo County), Ala.

Fort Hill, 16th July 1843
My dear Andrew, I am happy to learn by yours of the 27 [of June?], that you all continued well, & that the prospect was so fine. If your sea[so]n[?], since the date of your letter has been the same ["as" *canceled*] with you, as with us, it would exactly suit you. The weather has been extremely hot, and with the exception of one good rain, perfectly dry. My crop looks well; as good as I have ever had it at this season.

We shall look out with anxiety for your next letter, as we expect it will give an account of Margaret's [that is, Margaret Green Calhoun's] confinement. I hope she will have easy times, & get safely through, and that you will be able to set out by the end of the month or shortly after. You had better select some cool spell. Travelling would be intolerable, ["in" *interlined*] such weather as we now have & have had for the last ten days.

After my return from the mine, I received your letter, to which you refer in your last, containing the one from Mr. Lewis of Mobile, of which I informed you in mine in reply shortly after my return. I also stated, that my vein was not doing well. I have not yet heard whether they reached it below the water ["by" *canceled and* "through" *interlined*] the Tunnel.

John [C. Calhoun, Jr.] returned on a visit from the University [of Virginia] a few days since. I regret to say, that the affection of his throat is no better. He looks pretty well, but is subject to an almost continued hacking cough. We are all very uneasy about him. He is in other respects much improved. Anna [Maria Calhoun Clemson] had a letter a short time since from Patrick [Calhoun]. He was well and was to move with a detachment to establish a post at the False Washita [River, Indian Territory].

We shall all be happy to see you & family, when ["you" *interlined*] all will be again collected under the paternal roof except Patrick. I regret that the pressure[s] of the times are such, that it is advisable for him to continue in the Army. It is much ag[ai]nst my inclination.

You will of course have all the papers fully prepared for a settlement of our transactions with Mr. [Thomas G.] Clemson; and among others a conveyance in blank of his share of the land to us, & a list of [Ann] Ioor[']s negroes for the purpose of division.

All join their love to you, Margaret & Duff [Calhoun]. Your affectionate father, J.C. Calhoun.

ALS in ScU-SC, John C. Calhoun Papers.

To JOEL BRANHAM and ROBERT BLEDSOE, [Eatonton, Ga.]

Fort Hill, 17th July, 1843

Gentlemen, I had supposed that I would be the last man, to whom the questions you put to me [in your letter of 7/13], would be proposed. I had supposed my opinions on the subject were known to all; but as you desire an answer, I will give it.

I am decidedly opposed to a tariff for the protection of manufactories, both on the ground of expediency and constitutionality; and so far as I know, the party which supports my election, are also opposed to it. With great respect, I am &c. &c., John C. Calhoun.

PC in the Milledgeville, Ga., *Federal Union*, September 19, 1843, p. 3; PC in the Edgefield, S.C., *Advertiser*, September 27, 1843, p. 2; PC (misdated 7/27/1843) in the Augusta, Ga., *Daily Chronicle & Sentinel*, September 20, 1843, p. 2.

HARPER & BROTHERS to [Joseph Gales, Jr., and William W. Seaton, Editors of the Washington *Daily National Intelligencer*]

New York [City], July 17, 1843
Gentlemen: Our attention has been drawn to a publication under the head of "Political History," in your paper of the 8th instant, referring to a volume of Mr. [John C.] Calhoun's Speeches recently published by us.

The title to the volume, we are obliged to concede, (on having our attention called to it,) is capable of being misunderstood, when viewed apart from the two pages of Index to the Speeches, contained in the Life of Mr. Calhoun, published by us several weeks previously; which index it was intended should also have been published in the volume of Speeches issued separate from the Life. Our title-page hereafter will be "Speeches, &c. of the Hon. John C. Calhoun, *referred to in his Life."* The omission of these last words was an oversight; and you do us but justice, therefore, in acquitting us of an intention to mislead the public mind. It is due also to the gentlemen who made the compilation to say, that *we* are responsible for the Title-page and Advertisement to the volume, the copy of the title not having been received from the compilers until our first edition was printed. Respectfully, yours, &c., Harper & Brothers.

PC in the Washington, D.C., *Daily National Intelligencer,* July 21, 1843, p. 3; PC in the Petersburg, Va., *Republican,* July 26, 1843, p. 2.

From ALB[ERT] RHETT

Charleston, July 17, 1843
Dear Sir, An article will appear in the Mercury, a day or two hence, signed *South Carolina*—written, all but the very last part of it, by Brother B. [that is, Robert Barnwell Rhett]. You will recognise in the conclusion the views expressed to Col. [Franklin H.] Elmore in your letter of 4th June. Brother B. sent me his Article to publish, and I thought the substance of your letter would make a very fit conclusion to it, so I got your letter from Col. Elmore, and threw it into the form you will see. Hoping it will meet your approbation I am, in much haste, your ob[edien]t Serv[an]t, Alb. Rhett.

ALS in ScU-SC, John C. Calhoun Papers. NOTE: Calhoun's letter to Elmore of 6/4 has not been found. Some of the contents may be deduced from the article referred to by Albert Rhett, which appeared in the Charleston *Mercury*, July 19, 1843, p. 2, under the title of "The National Convention Again—The South Carolina Address." The article is a reply to criticism of the "South Carolina Address" by the Richmond *Enquirer*. The concluding paragraph, perhaps "the very last part" mentioned by Rhett, justified the "Address," adopted on 5/24/1843 by the S.C. Democratic Convention, in the following words: "In the meantime, without professing to speak *ex cathedra*, but believing we know almost as much of the designs of the South Carolina Convention as some others, we undertake to say— that the whole object of the Address thus put forth, was (as is clear from every paragraph) to assign the *reasons* for making the recommendations it did, both in respect to the candidate nominated, and the time and constitution of the National Convention. This it has done, in the most respectful manner, but with that candor and explicitness which is always due from one portion of the party to another, in deliberating on a matter of common concernment—the way to preserve and give success to its principles. Its object was to unite a friendly and free discussion on all the points of difference, in order that the course to be finally taken, might be chosen with all the lights before the party, that could be shed upon its counsels. The grounds brought forward against the plan to which it objects, are, if true, of deep import—they go to the very vitals of our political system, and touch on a Constitutional questions [*sic*] of the first magnitude. That they are true, the Convention had not itself doubt, and nothing has transpired since in the slightest degree to shake such a conviction, but it was reasonable and proper its final determination on them should be *suspended*, till they have been fully weighed and discussed—resolved as South Carolina is, to give the same candid consideration always to the reasons of others that she might presume to expect to her own. The Convention took this course, under the belief that the Republican party had no solid basis of union but truth, justice and the Constitution, and that what these demanded could be obtained only by free, full and fearless discussion. If this course be adopted by those States, which differ from us and the others concurring in the Maryland plan, the end will be either that the opposite reasons shall overrule ours, and convince us of error; or that our arguments will overrule their reasons and convince them of error; or, in any event, that such an approximation of sentiment would be brought about as will finally produce universal acquiescence in a common result. But if in this reasonable expectation we shall be disappointed; if instead of a free and fair discussion there should be denunciation and attack, and purposed suppression of the truth, and no decision can be come to, not involving abandonment of principle—it will *then* be time enough for us to decide how far it becomes a patriotic people to give up principles to party, and, in the eagerness for power, throw behind them all those rules of Constitutional obligation and public good faith, by which alone power when obtained, can ever be made available to an useful end." It is possible that the penultimate paragraph of the article, not reproduced here, also was a paraphrase of comments by Calhoun, though neither the last nor the next to last paragraphs much resemble Calhoun's style.

From F[RANCIS] W. PICKENS

Edgefield [S.C.,] 19 July 1843

My dear Sir, I enclosed you [Levi] Woodbury's letter [*not found*], & since it was written you see Maine & N[ew] H[ampshire] have gone for [Martin] V[an] B[uren]. I expected it. You will recollect I advised you in Washington ag[ain]st any active movement on the part of your friends, and expressly advised ag[ain]st the meeting in Charleston, and ag[ain]st starting a paper at Washington. You know the meeting in Philadelphia on 8th Jan[uar]y had nominated V[an] B[uren]—with [Andrew] Jackson's letter to back them. I thought our policy was to let the issues be made ag[ain]st V[an] B[uren], and as he was then put forward it would excite the jealousy of [Lewis] Cass'[s, James] Buchanan's & [Richard M.] Johnson's friends, and the fire would be drawn upon him—that we ought to make no move to divert that fire, or to create new issues. By making every thing turn upon him he could have been run down in the old Jackson ranks by this. Your position in the old Democratic or Jackson party was peculiar & had been for years. There was deep Jealousy & ill feeling towards you in it. Your great talents & services were just begin[n]ing to increase your popularity in that party. The old leaders & presses were drilled ag[ain]st you—the rank & file were just moving for you. Your policy was to stand still, & let V[an] B[uren] draw the secret opposition of all the other aspirants until he was run down & by that time your strength would be such as to secure an easy triumph. But if you attempted to move upon & make issues in advance in that old party they would become alarmed & all would move ag[ain]st you. I knew it was impossible to get up a paper with a list sufficiently strong to make any impression. Your talents & illustrious services were known to the rank & file—we ought to have waited events until they moved up upon the leaders. It was impossible for you to succeed without the aid of the old Democratic party. You will recollect these were my opinions then, & I think I was correct.

The moment a paper was started in Washington it drew the active hostility of All the old leading papers before we could be heard, & at a time when they were from circumstances to ["a" *interlined*] certain extent, muzzled before. That old party were not prepared to give us a fair hearing. The moves in Charleston with the Mercury & then our Convention alarmed them and they were worked upon by the idea of So[uth] Ca[rolina] dictation &c &c. This has been artfully managed & handled, & it has Given V[an] B[uren] & his friends an opportunity to escape from the false move they made in Ph[iladelphi]a on the 8th Jan[uar]y with Jackson.

If we could have kept the issue upon him & his moves instead of upon you & your ["moves," *canceled*] moves, it would have been better, as Cass, Johnson, & Buchanan would all have assisted us in that, & the old Democratic party would have been deeply divided, too much so, for V[an] B[uren] to succeed.

It will now take time & exertion to recover. If the Southern States take high ground, & if Ten[nessee] will go with us the game is yet ours. I will go to Athens [Ga.] & be there the 1st August. I expect ["to" *interlined*] see [Mark A.?] Cooper & others then. If they succeed this Fall Geo[rgia] can take a lead this Winter—so in Ala. & La.— & if Ten[nessee] could be brought up we would be safe. I shall start on Monday morning for Geo[rgia] & immediately after commencement I expect to go to the North. If you direct a letter to New York enclosed to J. Edward Boisseau[,] New York [City,] I will get it.

The weather is very hot—my three youngest children are at their Aunt Maria's [Maria Simkins Colhoun's]. She will take them to Pendleton in August. In great haste but truly, F.W. Pickens.

ALS in ScU-SC, John C. Calhoun Papers. Note: *Calhoun's AEU indicates that he answered this letter on 8/10 and addressed the reply to Pickens in New York [City] "as requested."*

From R[OBERT] B[ARNWELL] RHETT

[Beaufort, S.C.] 22d July 1843

My Dear Sir, At your suggestion I have taken up my pen, but here out of the way, I can not feel the interest which would induce either good or continual effort. The Piece signed "South Carolina" in the Mercury ["of the 20th" *interlined*; *sic*; that is, 7/19] is from me, treating of the Convention & the South Carolina Address. The Paper the next Day contains also a piece from me ["on the per capita voting" *interlined*], and I will send by this mail another piece on "State Rights & the National Convention." If I had been in Washington, I think I could have made the "fur fly"—but as it is, I am, from position, a poor, if not entirely a non combattant.

There can be no doubt your supposed opinions on the Rhode Island controversy, has been powerfully used to prejudice you in the minds of the Northern Democracy, by [Martin] V[an] Buren[']s friends. I understood in Washington that Mr. [William] Smith of Virginia had written Letters both to you & Mr. V[an] B[uren]—requesting your views on this subject, and that the Answers would be published. If this is so, why have not the Answers been published[?] V[an] B[uren] dare not take the ground that a brute majority irrespective of a written Constitution, can alter or abolish it, at its will. He ought to be made to speak out on the question.

I write merely [to] shew you that I was moving a *Little*—perhaps I might have done more but for the sickness of my family. Do remember us to all at Fort Hill—and believe Me Dear Sir Yours very truly, R.B. Rhett.

[P.S.] I hope you are writing your Book.

ALS in ScU-SC, John C. Calhoun Papers.

From A N D [R E] W P [I C K E N S] C A L H O U N

Cane Brake, [Marengo County, Ala.,] July 25th 1843 My dear Father[,] I have just been reminded that this is mail day and have only a few moments to spare before the mail usually closes.

Margaret [Green Calhoun] has been in delicate health since I last wrote, but is now doing better, and I trust will speedily recover. She was attacked on the third day with symptoms of puerp[er]al fever, which have continued untill the last day or two, and altho the disease has been removed, her strength has been prostrated. We hope to get off about the 20th next month for [South] Carolina and will take the upper route, in the mean time you will hear regularly from me.

Our crop is the finest in the county and infinitely the best we have ever had. The weed[?] has size[?], and I have never seen it so loaded with blooms[,] squares, and bolls, and there is no untoward cause operating against it so far. If we escape the worm, we must make a bale to the acre.

Judge [Henry B.?] Goldthwaite spent, with Col. Boyken [*sic*; Boykin], two days with me last week[;] they both requested to ride over the plantation, as they said they had heard a great deal of it. I took them all over our fields and they both said they had never seen any thing like it. The Judge has been in the State 20 years, and Boyken is a planter in Dallas. I met the Judge again afterwards in Demopolis, and in the presence of a crowd of gentlemen he said our

313

plantation exhibited the highest evidence of management he ever saw, and the most superior crop & &. I attribute the superiority of our crop to the thorough drainage of our plantation which has been of incalculable advantage this spring and summer when so much rain has fallen. At it regards corn we will make it without measure, at least 8 or 10,000 bushels, and we have a large quantity yet on hand of old.

We have had a warm canvass in this county for the last two weeks between Goldthwaite and Dillet [that is, James Dellet, Representative from Ala.]. The Judge is entierly [*sic*] the superior, and I never have seen such a victory in debate, as he obtained ove[r Dellet.] Goldthwaite is a very able m[an; if] elected I think he will head our delegation, not excepting [Dixon H.] Lewis. He [Goldthwaite] is a devoted friend of yours and averred in his speeches that you were the only man in the country who could reform it. It will be a close race but I am affraid [*sic*] Dellet will be elected as the whig majority at the last election was upwards of two thousand. The[re] are those who believe that Goldthwaite stands a good chance owing to the favourable impression he has made as a speaker.

We are all well, except Margaret. I have not had a Dr. on the place in 10 months except to see M[argaret] last week. Love to all. Your affectionate son, Andw. P. Calhoun.

ALS in ScU-SC, John C. Calhoun Papers. NOTE: This letter was addressed to Calhoun at Pendleton. Twenty-five cents was paid for its postage on 7/25 at Faunsdale, Ala.

From EDWARD DIXON

Alexandria [D.C.], July 25th 1843

Dear Sir, I send enclosed [*not found*], a letter which I received lately from Major [William W.] Wallace of Virginia, referring to a communication over the signature of "Ximenes," which I presume you have seen. I have expressed to him my firm conviction that the discussion of the Texas question at this time is injudicious. The condition of Texas is any thing but inviting, and I beleive [*sic*] that the public mind would revolt from the agitation of the subject. Indeed, it ought not in any manner to be connected with your claims. No such issue should be made between Mr. [Martin] Van Buren and yourself, because the admission of Texas into the Union would be regarded as a measure intended to ["stren" *canceled*] strengthen the slave-holding interest of the South, and in this view of the question, the non-slave-holding States would oppose your election. The South itself is greatly divided upon this subject, and that alone is a sufficient reason why your friends should stand aloof from it.

I have advised Major Wallace to call the attention of the public [in the Warrenton, Va., *Flag of '98*] to your general views upon the tariff and currency; these would be more popular topics of discussion, and they are questions in regard to which you have the whole Democratic party of the South with you. Major Wallace is a man of talents, your devoted friend, and can advance your interests in Virginia.

You are stronger in Virginia than Mr. Van Buren, and your popularity is daily increasing; your friends in that quarter are more active and zealous than the friends of Van Buren, who is generally regarded by the people as a cold, cunning, calculating, and selfish man. There is, however, among his friends, pretty good organization and discipline, but he is supported principally by the old party hacks. It is very generally beleived by the most enlightened of the Republican party in Virginia, that you will get the nomination. It is important that your friends in Virginia should be discreet, as well as active and industrious. If Virginia goes for you in the Convention, you will be sure to get the nomination. I regret that any of your speeches should have been omitted in the publication of them, for I do not think that it is calculated to produce a favorable result.

If it is not asking too much of you, please drop me a line in relation to the propriety of discussing the Texas question; if the agitation of the subject is injurious to your prospects, Major Wallace should not pursue the discussion of it any further. I would not trouble you with such a request but for the interest which I feel in your election, for I know that your very extensive correspondence must impose a heavy burden on you. If you write, please direct your letter to ["Fau" *canceled*] Warrenton, Fauquier County, where I expect to go in a few days. With very great respect, yours truely, Edward Dixon.

P.S. You will receive a number of the Alexandria Gazette in which you will find my reply to the notice that Mr. [Thomas] Ritchie took of the communication which I forwarded to you a short time ago. E.D.

ALS in ScU-SC, John C. Calhoun Papers.

To [JOSEPH] GALES, [JR.] and [WILLIAM W.] SEATON, [Editors of the Washington *Daily National Intelligencer*]

Fort Hill, July 28, 1843

Messrs. Gales & Seaton: I have just received from a friend the National Intelligencer of the 12th and 15th instant, containing your remarks on a volume recently published by the Harpers, of New York, entitled "Speeches of Mr. Calhoun, delivered in the Congress of the United States from 1811 to the present time." Your remarks are headed, "Political History—Suppressed Speeches of Mr. Calhoun." "Suppressed" is a strong word. The highest authorities define it to be, put down, destroyed, concealed; and your remarks leave no doubt that you intended to use it in the strongest and most offensive sense— that is, that they have been intentionally omitted in the compilation in order to give a partial and false view of my opinions; and, for that purpose, a false title was given to the volume. To the truth of this you pledge indirectly your word by heading your remarks "Political History." The charge is a grave one, and made in an imposing manner, and if true the imposition would deserve the public reprobation. The question, then, is, Is it true? Let facts answer.

The title is, indeed, false—false every way. It covers much not included in the volume, and omits much that is—reports, letters, and other writings. You have noticed the former, and called public attention to it, but not the latter, though equally obvious, and very material in determining whether the falsity of the title is a mere error or a fraudulent attempt at imposition. The one might, with some plausibility, be construed to be an attempt at imposition; but it is impossible for any ingenuity so to construe the other. It is impossible to assign to it a fraudulent object. But if the one is an error, why not the other? In fact the very grossness of both can leave no doubt that they are merely errors. It is not possible to open the volume without detecting them. The title covers all the speeches of Mr. Calhoun from 1811, when he entered Congress, till the present time, while the volume contains but one speech prior to 1833. Again: it omits to mention any thing but speeches, when of the four first of his productions of which the compilation is composed, only one is a speech. To make its grossness more palpable, all these are headed "Speeches." Has fraud ever been known to do its work in so clumsy a manner? It is idle to waste words on a thing so plain. The whole title is a gross blunder, of which I have much greater reason to complain than any one else. It looks much more like an attempt to injure me than to

316

impose on the public. I, however, can suspect nothing of the kind. How it happened I know not; nor is it material, so far as it relates to the object of this communication; but I deem it due to myself to state all that I know about it.

It so happens I have never yet seen the volume. I saw the title and the advertisement not long since for the first time. I was, as may be imagined, indignant at the blunder. I wrote immediately to a friend [Virgil Maxcy], who took an interest in the publication and corresponded with the publishers, and pointed out the blunders in the title and the objections to the advertisement, and suggested the corrections that should be made, which I requested him to have done forthwith. It was too late. I received his answer a few days since. He informed me that he had perceived the blunders before he got my letter, and had prepared a correction, but, owing to some delay in the transmission, it was not received in time. It may be proper to add, that the title I suggested (as well as I can recollect) was, "A selection from the speeches, reports, and other writings of Mr. Calhoun, subsequent to his election as Vice President of the United States, including his leading speech on the late war, delivered in 1811." It was drawn up to make it full and accurate—to cover the whole, and no more. So much for the title.

I come now to the selection or compilation; and here I take all the responsibility. It was done by me, and if there be any fraud or concealment, I am chargeable. In order that your readers may judge, I shall state the reasons which governed me in making the selection.

It is proper to premise that I have been urged from various quarters, in the last six or seven years, to have my speeches collected and published, and have during the same period received numerous applications for copies of my speeches in pamphlet form, with which I could not comply, because I had not spare copies. Since my name has been presented to the People in connexion with the Presidency, applications for copies have increased, and I have been more frequently urged to collect and publish my speeches, reports, and other writings on political subjects. I finally consented to the publication, because I believed it to be due to the People, in the position I occupy, to afford them the means of ascertaining the opinions and sentiments I entertain on all political subjects, particularly on those which have agitated the country of late, and on which the Presidential election will probably in a great measure turn. That I believed could best be done by publishing what I had said and written on those questions in a form which would make the work accessible to the People. It would give my opinions and sentiments in the fullest and most au-

317

thentic form, and in a manner much more consonant to my feelings than by popular speeches made for the occasion, or a personal canvass.

To effect the object, it was not only necessary that a selection should be made, but that it should be made from the later, and not the earlier of my speeches and other discussions on political subjects. To publish all I have said or written in the long period of thirty-two years, in which I have been without intermission in public life, would make the work too bulky and expensive to be accessible to the great body of the community; and to publish those of an early date instead of those of a late, would not give the information intended. I accordingly fixed on the termination of Mr. [James] Monroe's Administration, when I became Vice President, as the period from which to make the selection. That may be fairly regarded as the point of time in our political history which marks the end of an old and the commencement of a new order of things, in the midst of which we still are. From that to the present time is a period of eighteen years, being more than half of that in which I have been in the service of the Union. During the whole I took a prominent and responsible part on all important questions. Such was my leading motive for selecting the period I did from which to make the compilation.

There were others of a subordinate character which had their influence. It was the portion of my public life in regard to which information (as I believed) was most desired. I infer so, among other reasons, from the fact that the applications I have received for copies of my speeches were almost exclusively confined to it. There was another [reason] still stronger. It is the period in which my speeches and other publications contain my mature and settled opinions on the principles and policy of the Government; adopted after long experience and much reflection, which have modified, or changed, if you prefer, in many particulars, my earlier and less matured impressions. About the commencement of the period, my mind settled down in the views of the principles and policy of the Government I now entertain, and to which I have ever since adhered, regardless of personal consequences and uninfluenced by party considerations; thus giving the strongest proof possible of my deep conviction both of their truth and vital importance. By them I desire to be judged, and by them to stand or fall.

Guided by these motives, I compiled the volume in the first instance exclusively from that period; but afterwards yielded to the persuasion of friends, against my judgment, to include the speech already referred to, delivered in 1811. They urged it upon the ground that, as it was my first effort in Congress and on a subject of lasting interest, it was desirable it should be inserted, although a departure from the principle on which the volume was compiled.

But even within this period a selection became necessary to effect the object in view. To publish all my productions on political subjects during the period would make the volume still too bulky and expensive to be acceptable to the general mass of readers. Here, again, the leading reason which governed me in selecting the period, governed also in making the selection for the compilation. It is accordingly full on the subject of banks, sub-treasury, currency, tariff, distribution, State rights, and the principles and policy which should control in the administration of the Government. Those which discussed subjects of a more isolated character were for the most part omitted. But, after the compilation was first made within these restrictions, the work was thought to be still too bulky, and many were struck from it which it would have been desirable to retain.

Such are the facts in reference to the compilation. They show conclusively that the charge of suppression against it, is as unfounded as that of fraudulent imposition against the title. The very charge is absurd. How could the speeches be destroyed or concealed? They are to be found not only in the files of the Intelligencer, but in those of many other journals and publications of the day, where they are just as safe and as open to inspection as if placed among the public records. To attempt to keep them from the public eye would only cause them to be more greedily sought after. The very speeches you have published, as if they were new and unknown to the public, are the very ones which have been republished divers times, and have again and again been repeatedly referred to in Congress, in political harangues, and by newspapers; and that for the very purpose for which you now republish them. They are the very last which any one who was base enough to resort to a fraud would think of concealing. But why speak of them as being suppressed when they are referred to in the biographical sketch [*The Life of John C. Calhoun*] to which you allude, and which, it would seem from its index, [*sic*; contents?] was intended to be included in the work? Again, why speak of them as suppressed when all the speeches which I made during the war to rouse and animate the country to the defence of its rights and honor, and to sustain the burden and privations of the war with fortitude, and which are now unanimously applauded, are in the same predicament except one? Are they, too, suppressed or designedly concealed?

Why, indeed, should I attempt to conceal them, or any of my early speeches not contained in the volume, even those which contain opinions different from those I now entertain? What is there about

them that I should repudiate them? Do they not breathe lofty sentiments and devoted attachment to the country, and evince foresight
and firmness? Were they not applauded by the Republican party
at the time? And are they not now eulogized by you and other political opponents? Why, then, should I be ashamed of them, or cast
them away because they contain opinions in several particulars which
now, after more than a quarter of a century, I do not approve? Should
I be ashamed to acknowledge that I have lived to improve, and have
had the sense to see and the firmness to correct early errors? No; I
am far from repudiating these my more youthful efforts. Their very
errors lean to the side of the country. They belong to the times, and
grew out of ardent feelings of patriotism. The danger which then
threatened the country was from abroad. The overthrow of Napoleon was followed by a combination of the great sovereigns of
Europe, called the Holy Alliance. Its object was hostile to popular
Governments, and it threatened to turn its power against this continent in order to suppress the free States which had sprung out of the
old Spanish possessions. There was then no knowing at what moment we might be involved in a contest far more terrific than that
which had just terminated. It was in this state of things that Congress was called on to settle the peace establishment, on the termination of the late war with England. My attention was intently
turned to what I believed to be the point of danger; and I was anxious
to put the country in a condition to meet whatever might come. The
opinions I expressed in reference to manufactures, internal improvements, and a permanent system of revenue, kept constantly in view
my leading object—preparation for defence—as much so as what I
then said in reference to the army, the military academy, and the navy,
as the speeches themselves show.

The danger from without fortunately passed away, and that from
within began to disclose itself. I was not slow to see the strong
tendency the Government was taking towards consolidation, and that
many of the means which I had regarded as necessary to defend
against external danger, contributed not a little to increase the danger
within. That led to a reinvestigation, and that to the modification or
change of opinion which took place.

So far from casting away or desiring to conceal or keep out of view
my early speeches, I have long intended to collect and publish them.
I see you promise to publish freely from them. You cannot do me a
greater favor, and I hope you will not halt till you have republished
all. I was so careless as to neglect to preserve copies of my speeches
or other publications prior to my election as Vice President. Since

then I have been more careful. Your republication [on 7/8/1843 of my speeches of 1/31/1816 and 2/26/1816] will give me copies in a much more convenient form than that of manuscripts, and save me much time and trouble in collecting and some little expense for copying. I shall preserve carefully the two contained in the Intelligencer sent by my friend, and I shall take care to get such others as you may publish.

Let me, in conclusion, say, I wish you to understand that I make no complaint. So far from it, I feel rather obliged to you than otherwise. Be your motives what they may, you have afforded me an opportunity of giving an explanation made necessary by the awkward manner in which the volume has been introduced to the public, and in which I have been compelled to state much that ought to have appeared in a preface to the volume. With respect, I am, &c., J.C. Calhoun.

PC in the Washington, D.C., *Daily National Intelligencer,* August 5, 1843, p. 3; PC in the Washington, D.C., *Madisonian,* August 5, 1843, p. 2; PC in the New York, N.Y., *Herald,* August 7, 1843, p. 2; PC in the New York, N.Y., *Evening Post,* August 7, 1843, p. 2; PC in the Washington, D.C., *Globe,* August 7, 1843, p. 3; PC in the Richmond, Va., *Enquirer,* August 8, 1843, p. 2; PC in the Charleston, S.C., *Mercury,* August 9, 1843, p. 2; PC in the Charleston, S.C., *Courier,* August 9, 1843, p. 2; PEx in the Boston, Mass., *Post,* August 10, 1843, p. 1; PC in the Petersburg, Va., *Republican,* August 10, 1843, p. 2; PC in the Washington, D.C., *Spectator,* August 12, 1843, pp. 2–3; PC in *Niles' National Register,* vol. LXIV, no. 24 (August 12, 1843), p. 383; PC in the Milledgeville, Ga., *Federal Union,* August 15, 1843, p. 2; PC in the Raleigh, N.C., *North Carolina Standard,* August 16, 1843, p. 1; PC in the Edgefield, S.C., *Advertiser,* August 23, 1843, pp. 1–2; PC in the Greenville, S.C., *Mountaineer,* August 25, 1843, p. 1; PEx (in French) in the New Orleans, La., *Courrier de la Louisiane,* August 14, 1843, p. 2.

To T[homas] W. Gilmer, [Representative from Va.]

Fort Hill, 28th July 1843

My dear Sir, I agree with you in your estimate of the importance of placing before the people, at this time, ["the" *interlined*] information you suggest, and in the way you propose; and would, if my leisure would permit, cheerfully comply with your request. I hoped when I retired to find much more than I yet have, or fear will have. Between my correspondence, which is heavy, and my private and domestick concerns, I have but little left, and that little, I have appropriated for the present, and for some time to come. I trust, however, that my declining to undertake it, will not prevent you from doing it. I know no one more competent, and I am sure you cannot bestow your leisure moment[s] more usefully.

It is all important to keep Virginia right, and to expel the delusion, to which you refer, is an indispensible [*sic*] step. It is the strong hold of [Henry] Clay Whiggery. To storm it, is to break up the party in your State.

But will you [please] to permit me to say, that it is not the only indispensible step towards keeping Virginia right. Whiggery is not the only difficulty. Those who have lead [*sic*; led] in your State, since the death of [Thomas] Jefferson and his associates, have put and are endeavouring to keep Virginia in a false position. Her true political position; that in which Jefferson placed her; that which ["is alone" *canceled and* "only is" *interlined*] suitable to her old State rights doctrines of '98, and out of which they grew; that which ["alone" *canceled and* "only" *interlined*] can make her consistent & respectable, and, finally, that which only can give her influence & power, is to stand at the head of the South, and the weaker portions of the Union. It is *essentially a minority* position—one on the side of the limitations of the Constitution; yet it is the strongest of all positions, and will keep the power habitually in the hands of the State, that can from ["pos" *canceled*] her geographical position and weight in the Union take the lead in it, till the system itself shall fall into decay. The reason is obvious. It is the truly Democratick & popular position, and so long as our people cherish Democratick & popular sentiments, it must prevail over the opposite position; that which takes sides with power in contradistinction to ["the" *interlined*] limitations. That is essentially the Federal and aristocratick side, although naturally the majority side. The struggle is between the two sides, and ever will be so long as the sperit of our institutions is preserved; and the latter will hold its dominancy till it becomes extinct, if Virginia ["shall" *canceled*] should ["resume &" *interlined*] ste[a]dfastly hold to her true position. She is the only State that can take ["it" *canceled*], & steadily maintain it.

But she is and has been in a false one for years, & the effort now is to keep her there. She has associated herself with N[ew] York and the great central non slave holding States, and abandoned her old position of being at the head of the South & the weaker portions of the Union. It is a position, where she must ever act a secondary part; which must detach her from her old associates; alienate her from her old & glorious doctrines; and finally corrupt her morals & debase her character. She must yield to her new associates & compromise at every step her old principles & policy, till she herself will dispise [*sic*] & throw them away, as useless trumpery. This already has taken place to a great extent; and hence the formidable growth of Clay Whiggery in Virginia of late.

I regret to say, that the [Richmond] Enquirer has taken the lead in this false move; ignora[n]tly, I hope, but not the less dangerous on ["yo"(?) *canceled*] that account. It will be fatal to the State, and our institutions, if not arrested; and let me say, you & those of your age & influence, [*one word or part of a word canceled*] owe it to your-selves; to your State; to your section; and your country to arrest it. It can be effected now by union & vigour among yourselves, and no time ought to be lost in commencing the good work. Do not sup-pose that ["the interest," *interlined*] I may be thought to have in it, influences my judgement, or dictates what I say. Personally I feel no interest in the presidential election; and, if I did not believe, I could do much to reform the Gov[ernmen]t & restore the Con-stitution, I would not accept it, if tendered. You see I write you with-out reserve. I have entire confidence in your prudence & honor. I avail myself of the opportunity to express the pleasure I feel at your success in the recent election. Your presence will be important in the next Congress. Let the South understand one another & be bold & prudent; and they may reform the Gov[ernmen]t. Truly, J.C. Calhoun.

ALS in ViW, Tyler Scrapbook, p. 9; variant PC in *William and Mary Quarterly*, vol. XX, no. 1 (July, 1911), pp. 8–10. NOTE: Gilmer (1802–1844) had been Governor of Va. during 1840–1841 and was considered one of President John Tyler's chief spokesmen in the House of Representatives. In a public letter which had appeared in the Washington, D.C., *Madisonian*, the Tyler administra-tion organ, on January 23, 1843, he had drawn attention anew to the question of the annexation of the Texas Republic.

From W[illia]m Hogan

Nashua[,] N[ew] Hampshire, July 29th 1843
I have had the honor, Sir, of writing to you some months ago, in re-lation to the establishment of a Press ["here" *canceled*] in Boston.

My object in doing so, ["as" *interlined*] you must have known, from Mr. Colquit, [possibly Walter T. Colquitt, Senator from Ga.,] was to keep your name before the public, in as favourable a point of view, as could be, without alarming the [Martin] Van Buren Democ-racy of New England.

I hoisted the [John] Tyler flag, knowing that any recruits to that flag ["were" *canceled*] would be in time Calhoun men.

Assuredly, Sir, you must be aware that it was no easy task to enkindle a Calhoun fire here, while the engines of Nullification & Slavery, were playing on it from all directions. I have, however, succeeded beyond my expectations & though there is no blaze as yet, the fire is burning silently & had I the means, had I even the Government printing, which is given to other papers here, I would cause it to burn untill the whole fabric of Van Burenism fell into ashes.

The Boston Post, I presume, will now reap the benefits of my labour & it is for yourself, Sir, to say whether you will or will not trust the *Post party*; I would not. I know but two of them on whom you can rely; one is Mr. [David] Henshaw, whose feelings towards you he fully expressed to me nearly twelve months ago, & before he had any hopes of his appointment [as Secretary of the Navy by President John Tyler]. The other is Lemuel Williams Esq. a warm friend of yours & a worthy man with whom I am in daily intercourse.

As to your getting the vote of Mass., it is, in my mind impossible, unless the Press comes out *openly* for you.

The Post party will tell you the reverse, because they are unwilling ["to risk" *interlined*] their offices & expectations from [Martin] Van Buren, should he be elected, and elected ["he will be" *interlined*] by jug[g]lery of some kind unless the press comes out openly for *you*.

I have now, Sir, done all I could for you, without vesting more money and thereby straighten[ing] the circumstances of my family. None of the Departments of Government, have aided me, except Mr. [John C.] Spencer [Secretary of the Treasury], who to my *personal* knowledge is your uncompromising friend, and to whom I personally communicated my views in relation to yourself. He instantly gave me the Printing in his department, but the President has given me none. His sons have charged me with being a Calhoun man in disguise, but they are only boys & foolish ones too.

I will detain you no longer, Sir. Your Cause is now in the hands of those in whom you have confidence and I will only ask you for a letter to Mr. [Abel P.] Upshur [Secretary of State] telling him to give me a Consulship for which I have applied to him. If you think proper, Sir, to give me such a letter I shall expect it as soon as it is your convenience. One line from you to Mr. Upshur will ensure me success. I have the honor, Sir, to remain Very respectfully, Wm. Hogan.

ALS in ScU-SC, John C. Calhoun Papers.

From H[AYM] M. SALOMON

New York [City,] 31 July [18]43

Dear Sir, I wrote you a few days ago enquiring whether you had received the news papers and Letters which I occasionally forwarded.

And I now reiterate the expression of indignation which all your old friends are exclaiming on the subject of your alleged willingness (as stated by [newspaper editor Mordecai M.] Noah) to be sacrificed for ever by Mr. [Martin] Van Beuren [sic]—by permitting your name to be used under that of Van B[uren] for the V[ice] P[residency] thus defeating the expected views of your friends now[?] and the certain elevation if Mr. [Henry] Clay becomes elected thus thro[ugh] the bad conduct of Van B[uren]'s friends in the present contest.

Van B[uren']s office expectants are so desperate that *they propose* (that which to give[?] them a chance for their nominations will certainly condemn both parties to the compact and render a certain and final and fatal defeat to your pretensions hereafter), I.E., that *if you will permit* them to degrade your name and they Can succeed thereby Mr. V[an] B[uren] will resign the place [of President] after a ["twelve" *canceled*] year, and they have Carried thro' all their V[an] B[uren] nominations, and ["they" *canceled*] then you can manage for the next term.

When it was suggested to me I turned from them with the utmost disgust, knowing from past experience the odium that such bargaining produces and the effects it has on the unbiassed [sic] voters. It would sink your fair fame. The Consequences too would be similar to the indignation of the People in '24 when every body united on you and the others, *to oppose* (*a similar Caucus dictation*) as was seen in the protest of the Members of Congress headed by Col. R[ichard] M. Johnson in that year.

You may have noticed I have not been mistaken in my predictions of the consequences of certain ultra movements of party leaders in times past. The like causes will probably produce similar effects.

Let me therefore intreat you not to delay another mail in [my] receiving from you notice of your intention of Causing a proper rebuke to be given to such insidious enemies. Alex[ande]r Hamilton met me yesterday and said it was evident that Mr. Noah was trying now for the *third* turn in 12 Month[s]; I.E. to do all he Could for Van B[uren] and most insidiously defeat *your* friends in bringing you forward—but that no doubt you would immediately notice the slander.

Therefore Permit me to have inserted in one or two of the more prominent of the daily large and respectable papers, the notice on the other Side [of this page] which will put an end to the injury that those vile men are effecting. Respectfully, H.M. Salomon.

[The proposed notice:] We are Authorised to state most unequivocally that Mr. Calhoun will consent on no account or Condition whatever to permit his name to be used for the office of Vice President at the approaching election.

ALS in ScCleA. NOTE: Salomon was a son of the Revolutionary figure, Haym Salomon. A reply by Calhoun to the above letter has not been found. However, a letter written by Salomon to J[ames] W[atson] Webb, [editor of the New York, N.Y., *Courier and Enquirer*], dated 12/13/[1843], gives evidence that such a reply was written and indicates something of its contents. Salomon stated to Webb that [Mordecai M.] Noah and other N.Y. editors had frequently published the suggestion that Calhoun would accept a nomination for Vice-President on the ticket with Van Buren. Salomon considered this untrue, a "slander," and a calculated trick. He had written Calhoun about the matter, and Calhoun had written in reply a letter which Salomon now enclosed to Webb. He requested that Webb read and return the enclosed letter from Calhoun and then publish a statement that the editor had seen a letter "from an *unquestionable* source that Mr. Calhoun views with great indignation the proposal to place him on any ticket with Mr. Van B[uren] . . . ." (ALI in CtY, Sterling Library, Webb Papers.)

To Mrs. PLACIDIA [MAYRANT] ADAMS

[Pendleton, *ca.* August 1843?]

Dear Madam, I received the enclosed [*not found*] from my factor [John Ewing Bonneau] by the last mail, ["with" *canceled and* "& I have given" *interlined*] directions to my servant to leave it [at your home] as he goes & return for it when he comes from the Village with the mail.

Mr. Bonneau seems to put confidence in the promise of Mr. [George W.] Egleston, that he will pay punctually at the time specified; and, I am of the impression, that it would be better, as far as the order is concerned, to leave it as it stands.

As to the residue of the funds of the State in his hands, I would suggest, whether the better course would not be, to write to him for a statement, in detail of the amount that would be in his hands, after the debts, principal & interest are collected, and the stock sold & realized, deducting the amount to be paid on the order to me; and also at what time, or times the former could be collected & the latter realized, and to postpone any further step, in reference to the funds in his hands, till you hear from him. If his answer should be satisfactory, it would then, perhaps, be the the [*sic*] most advisable course, to give me an order on him, drawn to correspond with the times he would be in funds, which I could transmit to my factors for collection. With great respect, I am &[c.] &[c.,] J.C. Calhoun.

ALS owned by Holbrook Campbell, Springfield, Mass. NOTE: This undated letter has been assigned a tentative and approximate date because of its apparent relationship with a receipt which is presented below under date of 8/25/1843.

From J. KENRICK FISHER

New-York [City], August 1843

Sir: I am desirous to render such aid as I can to the cause of Commercial Freedom; and, as one means, to procure, for publication and wide circulation, a statement of what should be the ultimate policy of this nation and all nations, in reference to tariff imposts, and other checks upon trade. Such a statement would be most sure of a general and attentive reading, if it should come from a man already well known to the public; and if that man were so situated that his views might be regarded as a probable indication of the future policy of this country, its publication would produce considerable influence on the public feeling and the legislation in other countries. I believe you to be the man from whom such an outline, given as a personal opinion, would come with the best effect—if your views accord with the laws which nature has predetermined: and my object in addressing you now, is to beg you to inform me whether you would approve a total abolition of the tariff; for, to speak with the candor due to yourself and all others concerned, I should be painfully disappointed to learn that you are not ready, at any time, to abolish this mode of taxation, even without waiting for any other mode, save that indicated by the Constitution: but if you could sketch out a general policy, based on unqualified freedom of trade; and state what you deem the just claims of existing interests as to the *time* to be allowed for the transition; and also what means should be taken to induce other nations to adopt a reciprocal course; I should believe that I might render good service, by asking some of the friends of free trade to join in requesting your views, and in making arrangements to publish them in the way most likely to secure to them the attention of American citizens, and of the friends of free trade in other countries.

I would ask for your views on the course to be pursued, if, contrary to the belief of free traders, it should prove disadvantageous to us to admit goods free, while other nations do not reciprocate; because there are many, in both parties, who believe that *reciprocal*

327

free trade would be best for all; and who would join in the free trade movement if they thought that all fair means would be used to make other nations follow, with respect to us, any such liberal movement which we might make. Of course, it should not be proposed as a condition, but only as an opinion as to what is *the true policy*—which we are not to contrive, but to discover.

I would also ask how far—to what amount per year—we ought to make sacrifices for the general good of the world. The idea that each nation is to act for its own advantage exclusively, not regarding the influence of its example, is frequently inculcated by political teachers; but I apprehend that a loss, for a short time, of a few millions per year, should not deter us from being the first to adopt what we believe to be the true policy.

I have read the speech to which you referred [in your letter of 1/26/1843 to] the Committee of the Indiana Convention; which, though it fully answers the inquiries of that Committee, does not enable me to judge whether you would favor the views I wish to advance. Your obedient servant, J. Kenrick Fisher, 246 East Broadway, New-York.

ALS in DLC, Albert Kenrick Fisher Papers; PC in *Letters of William Gilmore Simms*, 6:68–69. NOTE: The letter to Calhoun from W[illiam] Gilmore Simms immediately below was written on the same paper as the above letter from Fisher.

From W[ILLIAM] GILMORE SIMMS

[New York City, August, 1843?]

Dear Sir, The writer of the above letter, Mr. J. Kenrick Fisher[,] is an amiable gentleman and an excellent artist, who is now engaged enthusiastically in concocting a scheme by which foreign art will be made familiar to our people. I am not so sure that it will be within your usual custom to respond to his application, but this is a matter which, of course, will wholly lie within your own judgment. Enough for me that I can assure you of the good faith with which his application has been made. He fancies that the slight but grateful acquaintance with which I have been honored by you will persuade you to regard his letter in an inoffensive light. With very great respect, I am Sir, your ob[edien]t & obliged Servant, W. Gilmore Simms of South Carolina.

ALS in DLC, Albert Kenrick Fisher Papers; PC in *Letters of William Gilmore Simms*, 6:68–69.

From DUFF GREEN

London, Aug[us]t 2nd 1842 [sic; 1843]
My dear Sir, I have been a close observer of events here and have had access to the most accurate sources of intelligence. There are a few facts which deserve your most serious consideration.

The Whigs went out of power and Sir Robert Peel came in on two propositions. The first to admit slave grown sugar in competition with British Colonial sugar, and the other a fixed duty on Corn. Sir Robert Peel in the debate on the sugar duties last year avowed that the purpose of this Government is to promote the abolition of slavery in Brazil, Cuba and the U[nited] States and Lord Brougham openly ["avowed" canceled] advocated his bill forbidding British subjects to purchase slaves on the ground that England having abolished slavery, and thereby raised the price of labor in her colonies was bound as an act of justice to her Colonial subjects to abolish slavery elsewhere.

The Abolitionists of Texas have deputed a Mr. [Stephen Pearl] Andrews as an agent, with a proposition to this Government for a loan to be applied to the purchase & emancipation of the slaves of Texas and Lord Aberdeen told Mr. [Ashbel] Smith the Texian Chargé that the British Gov[ernmen]t deem it so important to prevent the annexation of Texas to the United States, that they were disposed to support the loan if it should be required to prevent annexation.

It is now understood that the Queen is willing to reinstate the Whigs whenever Lord Melbourne says to her that Lord John Russell can organise a Government that can retain power and such a Government is in the progress of organisation. Lord Melbourne to occupy the same relation to the new Government that the Duke of Wellington now does to Sir Robert Peel's & his brother to be Sec[retary] for foreign affairs. Lord John Russell to be Premier. C[harles] Wood, (Lord Grey's soninlaw) President of the Board of Trade, ["Chas. Wood" canceled] Mr. F[rancis] Baring Chancellor of the Exchequer.

In this state of things Sir Robert Peel, is disposed to fold his arms & let ["things" canceled] events take their course. Becoming satisfied that he will not now do what he was anxious to do last year I resolved if I could to make his American policy, one of the points on which the new Ministers are to come in. I therefore obtained an introduction to Lord John Russell and had a full conversation on American Affairs and told him that I wished him to [make] up an issue with Ministers. He promised me to do so, and you will see in the Times which I will endeavor to send you, that he is the only speaker, on the side of the opposition who touched on the subject of America in the debate on the state of the nation.

I explained to Lord John Russell and to several who are to be his associates in the new ministry the relation of parties in the United States and the bearing which the slave question has on our policy. I am assured by them that during the recess of Parliament they will assail Ministers on their American policy and that upon coming into power they will go for free trade with America and an immediate adjustment of the Oregon Question, for the admission of slave ["grown" *canceled and then interlined*] produce, and non-interference in the domestic policy of other nations—that they will denounce the attempt to emancipate the slaves of Cuba[,] Brazil, the U[nited] States & Texas as an illegal & unwise interference. The most pregnant sign of the Times however is that the stock exchange are [*sic*] begin[n]ing to speculate for a fall in the price of Consuls [that is, consols] and hence any man who has Consuls can now get an advance upon them at short dates without interest.

The present ministers are sustained by the land holders—the established Church and the fund holders. A formidable Combination you will say—but it is a combination so sensitive to their own peculiar interests that they are ready to sacrifice any Government that endangers them[.] The Whigs understand this, and their measures are taken accordingly.

I remember to have heard you say that England will be compelled to establish free trade or to renew her system of plunder, and I find that a class of political economists connected with the funds are beginning to say that the true policy of England is to get up a general war. That the Continent and America have become her rivals in commerce & manufactures and that having the command of the Ocean, she can protect her manufactures and monopolise the Commerce of the World, and that a war in Europe would destroy the manufactures of the Continent. Do not these facts present a most serious question to you[?] What are you to do? Are you like Sir Robert Peel, to fold your arms and let events take their course? Are you to say that because the people have not given you the first office you will not give your influence where it might Contribute to Control events? If while you fold your arms and ["and" *canceled*] look on [Martin] Van Buren is elected and [Thomas H.] Benton comes into the State Department, how easy will it be for him to provoke a war on the Oregon question? Do you not see cause for apprehension in the late proceedings in Maine & New Hampshire favorable to Van Buren and the position which the Oregon question is assuming in the

West? I see that your friend[s] are pledging themselves to support the nominee of the [Democratic] National Convention and [it] is now rendered almost certain that Van Buren will be that nominee unless all other interests combine against him. Instead of this, [Richard M.] Johnson will compromise at any time for the Vice Presidency, and all the other candidates, I fear, will endeavor to weaken you under a belief that your friends will prefer any of them to Van Buren. Things will run on this direction until you are all handed over to Van Buren as so much political Capital in the hands of Col. Benton, unless you are wise in time. I have studied your position and I never was more fully satisfied as to what it is your duty to do. I am fearful that you are not yet prepared to see or to hear the truth as it is. I fear that it is the same case with the President [John Tyler]. Permit me however to say that great efforts are making to seperate you and Mr. Tyler—that you are embarked in a common cause and should stand by each other. United you may yet control events—divided you become ["a" *canceled*] prey to your common enemy and sacrifice the great cause for which you have so long labored and with it the best interests of your Country. I will be prepared in a few days to write to you more fully. In the mean time let me entreat you to ponder well over what I now say. What you have most to apprehend both as it relates to yourself and the country is that Van Buren, will be elected President & Benton be Secretary of State. If we are to have Van Buren the responsibility will rest on you, and you owe it to yourself, to your friends ["and" *canceled*] to your Country & the world to counteract as far as possible the evil consequences to be apprehended from his election.

I will endeavor to write to you more fully by the next steamer. If I do not and find things when I return right at Washington I may on my return come to see you. Please to write to me care of Mr. [Abel P.] Upshur [Secretary of State]. Your sincere friend, Duff Green.

P.S. It is now understood that Oconnel's [Daniel O'Connell's] next movement will be to compel the ["large" *canceled*] great landlord[s] to sell the land to the tenants by a combination to prevent the payment of ["taxes" *canceled and* "rents" *interlined*]—by an understanding that there shall [be] no bidders on a distress for rent.

ALS in ScCleA; variant PC (dated 8/2/1842) in Jameson, ed., *Correspondence*, pp. 846–849. Note: On 8/3/1843 Green wrote to Upshur, stating, in part: "I enclose herewith a letter to Mr. Calhoun. I have not sealed it because I wish you to read it, and that you should, after having submitted it to the President [John Tyler], seal it and send it to him at Pendleton. I have not time to make a copy." In his letter to Upshur, Green describes opposition of the British to

Texas annexation and rumors that the British government would recommend a loan to Texas to cover the cost of abolition of slavery. Green has met with British opposition leader Lord John Russell and others who have assured him that such a loan is impossible. "I have obtained already a full report of the proceedings of the Anti Slavery Convention here and there is an inexhaustable fund there which if properly used cannot fail to excite the indignation of the non slave holding as well as the slave holding States." ALS in DNA, RG 59 (General Records of the Department of State), Despatches from Special Agents, vol. 13, Duff Green, England (M-37:13, frames 1–2); PC in Frederick Merk, *Slavery and the Annexation of Texas*, pp. 224–225.

From ALBERT RHETT

Charleston, Aug. 3, 1843

My Dear Sir, I received your esteemed favour, some days since, and beg leave to express my acknowledgments for the kind terms, in which you are pleased to speak of me. Col. [Franklin H.] Elmore has seen your letter, and requests me to say to you that nothing but the pressure of business has prevented his being more active in ["carrying out" *canceled and* "executing" *interlined*] your suggestions. His Executive Committee will meet tomorrow, and I have drawn up something for their consideration, which you will probably soon see in the papers—carrying out the idea of your letter as to the Indiana mode of settling the preliminaries of the Convention. If you have read "South Carolina" in the [Charleston] Mercury, you saw your suggestion anticipated. That article seems to be waking up the [Martin] Van Buren ["men" *interlined*] once more. The New York Tribune is out upon it, and Old [Thomas] Ritchie ["is" *canceled*] bustling with vast preparation, but they can make nothing out of it. We are too plainly in the right.

I go tomorrow to Beaufort, to be absent about ten days. When I return, I will try to render you, ["or our cause rather," *interlined*] some service through the Mercury—as it is, almost every thing, political, that has appeared in it lately, proceeded from Brother B. [Robert Barnwell Rhett] or myself.

Mr. [John A.] Stuart sailed for the North yesterday—in a miserable state of health, and I shall be nowise surprised if he never returns.

The Executive Committee here, are, I regret to say, a very sluggish set of Gentlemen, not wanting interest in public affairs, but incorrigibly averse to work. They made such a clamour, last winter, about

332

the *Rhetts* having so much to do with your affairs, that I requested not to be put upon it, willing to let those, who thought themselves more patriotic and capable, take the honour and labour too, if they would. With the honour they are not dissatisfied—the labour, now as before, has to be done by others. But of this enough. If I did not feel, Sir, that a service rendered to you, however humble, was the best contribution I could make to the welfare of my country, I believe I should drop into the rear, and be done with this disgusting strife of selfishness & base intrigue. Pray excuse this, and believe me most sinc[erely] & resp[ectfully] yours, Alb. Rhett.

P.S. I will write to you, by your leave, whenever I have any thing ["worth" *interlined*] communicating, or desire information to be used for the good of our cause, but I beg, at once, you will never reply from a mere motive of politeness. I know the value of your time, and wish to take no part from the Public to as humble an individual as myself. Resp[ectfully] &c, Albert Rhett.

ALS in ScU-SC, John C. Calhoun Papers. NOTE: Albert Rhett was a graduate of Yale College and a member of the S.C. General Assembly, 1834–1843. He was a brother of Robert Barnwell Rhett and brother-in-law of John A. Stuart, editor of the Charleston *Mercury*. Albert Rhett died a few months later, on 10/29/1843, during a yellow fever epidemic in Charleston, at about the age of thirty-three, while Stuart, whose health was considered perilous, lived until 1852.

To "Col." [WILLIS H.] WOODLEY,
"Proctor, the University [of] Virginia"

Fort Hill, 4th Aug[us]t 1843
Dear Sir, I received a letter from Judge [Henry St. George] Tucker, informing me that the remittance of $70 which I had made my son [John C. Calhoun, Jr.] had been received since he left and has been applied to meet an advance of $100, which you had been so kind as to advance him. He requested me to remit the balance to you, which is herewith enclosed, in three ten dollars, South Carolina bank notes. I will thank you to acknowledge the receipt so that I may know that it has arrived safely.

For your kindness to my son in the affair you will please accept my thanks. With great respect, I am & &, J.C. Calhoun.

ALS in ViU, University Archives, Proctors' Records.

To R[OBERT] M. T. HUNTER, [Lloyds, Va.]

Fort Hill, 6th Aug[us]t 1843

My dear Sir, My impression is and has been, that it would be difficult, if not impossible to get up a general organization. It required the aid of office & patronage for Mr. [Martin] V[an] B[uren] to effect it; and cannot be effected in any other way, except through an opposition, such as [Henry] Clay heads, & which looks to plunder. Each State & section will have to act for itself. N[ew] England can readily organize.

Our strength lies in principles & position, in which we have altogether the advantage, so much so, that if we had the aid of a single central paper, of established influence, such as the Enquirer, or the Globe, there would ["be" *interlined*] no contest.

In nothing have we a greater advantage ["than that" *interlined*] of position ["than" *canceled*] in the question of the Convention. If that alone is well used, it would give us the control of the nom["ination" *interlined*] or force the friends of Mr. Van Buren to break up the Convention. We not only have truth, justice and the Constitution with us in reference to it, but what is not always the case, they are sustained by the plausible and the popular. The very fact, that our position permits us to appeal to a majority of the States to decide the preliminary questions, gives us a control over them; and through them over the nomination, if well used. The great point now is, to push the discussion in reference to it. In order to open it, I have, (inter nos & in strick confidence) aided in preparing an article in reply to Drumgoole's [*sic*; Representative from Va. George C. Dromgoole's] answer to the S[outh] Carolina address, which has been sent to the Petersburgh Republican for publication. You must follow it up.

There will be, I think, no difficulty in getting at the sense of the majority of the States. Most of them have already spoken through their conventions, or Legislatures, and central Committees, as in the case of the question of time, may speak for ["their States" *canceled and* "others" *interlined*], as was done on the ["In" *canceled*] appeal of the Indiana Committee; or it may be ["done" *canceled and* "taken" *interlined*], when the Convention meets, as you suggest. It would, however, in that case be advisable, that our friends every where, should send delegates from Districts. It would greatly strengthen our position. In a confederacy like ours, and on State rights principle, when States act as States, as the Richmond plan proposes, each is equal to the other, & ["the vote of" *interlined*] each counts but one.

I wrote to a friend in Boston, calling his attention to the subject, and suggested the propriety of their Convention making a move on the subject, when it meets next month. N[ew] England & the South have a deep interest in the question.

I received a letter from Mr. [William] Smith [former Representative from Va.] by the mail before the last, saying that he had received Mr. V[an] B[uren's] reply to his questions [on the Dorr Rebellion]. I sent mine by the last mail. I have had it prepared for a long time, and wrote him, that I would transmit it, as soon as he informed me, that he had received a reply from any one, to whom they had been addressed.

I have made ["it" *canceled and* "my answer" *interlined*] full; in fact, [*one or two words canceled*] covered the whole ground, and in a great measure exhausted the subject. I have requested him to show it to you, if an opportunity should offer. I would be very glad you could see it. My own impression has always been, that the best way was to meet the question; and, if it should be thought advisable, it can be done in no better form, than that in which the questions & answer place it. If he should conclude to publish, would it not be better to have ["it done" *canceled*] the correspondence put in pamphlet form first & sent to the various leading papers of the Union for publication[?] It would, I think give it a more general circulation, and more importance. Yours truly, J.C. Calhoun.

ALS in ScCleA; variant PC in Jameson, ed., *Correspondence,* pp. 542–544.

From V[IRGIL] MAXCY

Washington, 6 ["July" *canceled*] Aug[us]t 1843
My dear Sir, Your letter of the 30th July reached me here last evening. Tho' an invalid myself for 4 weeks past during which I have been held by the throat by the prevailing *Grippe,* (what an expressive name!) I seized the first moment the Doctor thought it right for me to leave Mrs. [Mary Galloway] Maxcy, to come over here. You will have learnt by my letters the annoyance I have felt at the conduct of the Harpers—which proceeds however rather from ["want of reflection &" *interlined*] neglect than bad feeling. I have received no answer [to] three strong letters I had written them on all the points touched in your letter—telling them in one of them, that if they required it, I would pay the expense of the alterations required. In one of them, I sent a draft of a letter, which I desired them to write to the Editors of the National Intelligencer, which however ["they" *inter-*

lined] did not do but wrote the meager note, which you no doubt saw in the Intelligencer. Not satisfied with this, I came here prepared to demand of the ["Editor of the" *interlined*] Intelligencer to insert a piece in my own name, presenting, in a manner not half so good, pretty nearly the same views, which your letter contains, and which appeared in the paper of the very day of my arrival here & prevented the necessity of any interview with the Editors. I am glad they have had the grace to get out out [*sic*] of the scrape by the ready insertion of your letter and the civil editorial remarks on the subject. Every body is delighted with your *characteristic* letter, & think with me it is calculated to [do] good in many respects as bearing your name, it will be copied every where and will compensate in some measure by the good it will do, for the ill effects of the Harpers blunders and will probably excite an eager curiosity to get the life & volume. I shall again write this evening to the Harpers to avail themselves of it & by putting a new title page ["and" *canceled*] &c. & binding up the biography with the copies they issue hereafter, (as they have done in 20 they sent to me,) atone for the past. I had previously to your letter containing the address of your factors [Mathewes & Bonneau] in Charleston requested them to send you 100 Copies to the care of Col. [Franklin H.] Elmore, supposing he would know how to dispose of them to get to you. If they had not already forwarded them they will on receipt of my letter send them to your agents. Altho' three weeks have now elapsed since Mrs. Maxcy's late attack of the "Grippe" passed the crisis & the Doctor pronounced her better, she recovers so slowly, that it was only the day before I left home that she was able to take a short ride, being carried—as she is still unable to walk—to the carriage. The Doctor has ordered me to take her to Saratoga as soon as she can travel. On my way I shall see the Harpers & if they shall not already have done what they ought under the influence of my letters, I shall endeavor to make them do better by coaxing— money or whatever I find the best means. Rely on it I shall spare no pains—for besides my desire that the publication should be serviceable to you, I feel in a measure personally responsible that I did not last winter or since consult with you & arrange a title before hand—so as to have prevented what has taken place.

   Besides the publication I intended for the Intelligencer, I had two other objects in view in coming over here. The first was to see Mr. [David] Henshaw [Secretary of the Navy] & Col. [Daniel D.] Brodhead of Boston, who came on with him. I wanted to ascertain the exact tack in which the former was sailing. I find he is all right. He came into the Administration, the *President* [John Tyler] *knowing he was a decided Calhoun man.* This being well known is the true reason for the personal malignant attacks of the Globe on him. He has long been the Leader of the Republican Party in Massachusetts and has contributed ["& raised" *interlined*] more money than any other man towards the establishment and support of republican papers in the State. The consequence of the attacks of the Globe has been that[,] of the 20 republican papers published in the State all have repelled them & sustained him except one—the [Boston] Bay State Democrat—and many of the papers in the other States of New England have denounced the arrogance of the Globe. All this is operating most powerfully against [Martin] V[an] B[uren] and Mr. Henshaw thinks will in the end probably bring New England right—tho' he nevertheless has his fears that, so strong is the old party machinery yet, that, V[an] B[uren] may nevertheless get a nomination, [by] hook or by crook at the coming September [Mass.] State convention. He will go on there however beforehand & be at the convention and use his utmost to prevent it. He says Silas Wright is to be there. Massachusetts has already adopted the District system & all the other New England States. He fears an appeal cannot be got up in that convention to the other States to express their opinion in favor of the District System. I shall continue my efforts to find out some mode of getting at it. Perhaps Mr. [Levi] Woodbury may help to devise some means. He I am happy to say ["he" *interlined*] has shaken off his lethargy & is now taking a political tour of the State. I find that just after my letter in June reached him pressing him to go to the Convention in N[ew] H[ampshire] Mr. Henshaw & Col. Brodhead paid him a visit & followed up the blow. Mr. Henshaw says it is absolutely necessary to keep the party together in Massachusetts ["or Clay takes the State" *interlined*] and therefore, that perhaps the only thing that can be effected, is to prevent the nomination of any one & adhere to the District system & per capita voting.

The other object I had in going to Washington was to meet [Robert M.T.] Hunter, to whom I had written begging him to meet me there to consult on the best mode of getting out an Expression of a majority of States in favor of the District System & per capita voting—to agree after consulting with Henshaw upon an Editor for the Spectator—& see if something could not be done to improve its pecuniary affairs. The Charleston Committee have sent in $500 only and without a considerable fund no editor can be got nor an extensive Circulation. Mr. Henshaw thinks it makes a very bad impression at the north that our friends are not strong enough to support an able daily paper, to meet daily the continual fire of the

Globe[,] Richmond Enquirer &c. ["I think" *canceled*] Hunter's family was sick & he could not meet me. As I am left to act by myself, I shall by a letter tomorrow make a strong appeal to Col. Elmore & the Charleston Committee on the subject of raising immediately a liberal sum—especial[ly] at this crisis, when New England from the force of recent circumstances is in a state of agitation and may by a powerful central organ at Washington receive a strong impulse in the right direction. Mr. Henshaw says money only is wanting to get an able editor immediately, who will build up the paper. He thinks $10,000 or $15,000 ought to be raised. Surely there must be found without much trouble 100 or 150 Carolinians who would contribute $100 apiece & the thing is effected. I fear that living in an atmosphere where there is but one current they are not sufficiently aware of the difficulties we have to struggle with in the middle & northern States, where purses are heavily taxed to oppose the common enemy in each of the States—& that they relax into negligence & forgetfulness.

[John] Heart complains bitterly that neither [Robert Barnwell] Rhett, who holds so ready a pen, [George] McDuffie[,] [Francis W.] Pickens, Elmore nor any of your Carolina friends have sent on any articles for the Spectator. Can't you rouse them[?]

When will Pickens come on [to Washington]?

Could not Rhett be induced to come on several months before the meeting of Congress & take up his residence at Georgetown[?]

I return to-morrow to West River [Md.], from which I shall take Mrs. Maxcy to Saratoga the moment she can travel. I shall give you notice of my movements by the first mail after I can foresee them myself.

With best regards to Mrs. Calhoun, Always faithfully y[our]s, V. Maxcy.

[Enclosure]
"Extract of Letter from V.M. to L[evi] Woodbury"

The efforts, which Mr. Van Buren's friends have made to obtain nominations for him in the New England States & the means resorted to to obtain them, ought to be fully exposed by an exhibition of all the facts. While their proceedings show how little regard to propriety they have in selecting their means to carry a point, they also prove their weakness: and if the facts were properly exposed, a re-action would be the necessary result—but without such exposure there is danger of great mischief from an exhibition of strength that does not belong to them.

The denunciatory course of the Globe in regard to the appoint-

338

ment of Mr. Henshaw has already prepared the press in Massachusetts to make the exposure required. Cannot the press in the other N[ew] E[ngland] States be induced to co-operate with that of Massachusetts?

Important however as the above movement of the Press in New England would be, there is another subject on which it seems to me still more necessary, that the press, not only in New England, but in all the smaller States should ring out a loud alarm, and that without delay—if they desire to maintain their proper & constitutional influence and importance in the union. I mean the justice nay necessity of an *uniform* system of appointing the delegates to the national convention & of voting there. All admit the necessity of a convention to produce harmony of action in the republican party against the common enemy. But all conventions and all political associations must be founded and constituted on principles of equal justice amongst the members, who compose them. To this uniformity in the mode of selecting the delegates and of voting, is absolutely essential. The majority of the smaller States are unquestionably in favor of the District System—and its corollary, voting per capita—to prevent the defeat of the true voice of the people by political intriguers & managers; a great majority if not all of them will adopt the District system, which will allow the voice of the minorities to be heard—but of what avail will the District system be for this purpose, if the large States are allowed to come into convention with an unanimous vote, the voice of the minorities in such States not only being drowned, but made to utter a sound in direct opposition to their wishes? What justice justice [*sic*] or equity is there in the formation of a convention, in which some States come in with an overwhelming unanimous vote, stifling the wishes of their own minorities, while the rest come in with a divided vote. Such a convention may produce discord & distraction & eventuate in the success of the common enemy but never can produce harmony in the party.

The coming convention being the first that ever had seriously the election of the President, so far as the party is concerned, confided to it, it is absolutely essential to the maintenance of sound principles and the just rights of the smaller but great majority of the States—that a right precedent should be set in its formation and mode of acting. Can't you get some of the leading New England presses to take up & push this subject vigorously at once?

The Richmond & Albany politicians have yielded the question as to time but manifestly with great reluctance and a bad grace and in getting out of the scrape of proposing a time in violation of *the usage of the party*, for which they claim to be such great sticklers, they have recognized a principle without fully comprehending it of vast importance to the smaller States. They appealed to the decision of a *majority* of the States to decide on the question of time, and thus recognized them as the proper tribunal to to [*sic*] decide on all preliminary questions relating to the convention. Of all the authorities, that could be selected, it is the most favorable to us. A great majority of the States—at least three fourths are deeply interested in the appointment by Districts & that their vote should be given per capita. If they can be made to understand the question, New England and the South would be united to a State. Richmond & Albany made their appeal thro the Central Committee of Indiana. Cannot you get a similar appeal made thro the central Committee of New Hampshire or some of the New England States? As Maryland took took [*sic*] the lead on the District System—thro their republican Legislative convention unanimously last winter, I would have had it done in Maryland, but our State having settled all the preliminary questions we have appointed no central State Committee and as there will be a great struggle by the whigs, *who have the money*, to get the State government, at the October election, we thought it best in order to avoid all collision on the presidential question, not to have either a State convention or Central committee but to organize ["in" *interlined*] each of the Counties for our State election & in the Congressional districts for the national Convention.

The Central committee of each of the different States or at least of such as have not already decided in favor of the District System to send their answers either to your central committee or to the Globe and Spectator. If this could be effected, a most important point will be gained. Indeed, it would be decisive of the contest. With the District System and its direct *logical* consequence, *per capita* voting, victory is certain. The whole south & southwest will rally on C[alhou]n & this system. Cannot N[ew] England be induced to do so also?

[Second Enclosure]

L[emuel] W[illiams] to Virgil Maxcy, West River, Md.

Boston, July 31st 1843

Dear Maxcy, Your letter of the 28th inst[ant] I received this morning. I regret to learn that Mrs. Maxcy is so ill & hope that she may soon be able to travel, when I have no doubt but a journey to the Springs will restore her health. Present to her my kind condolence, & to her & your family my best regards.

As to the suggestions of our friend I have only to say that ["as to" *canceled*] the mode in which Van Buren's friends have endeavoured to operate at the several conventions has not been of that character that any observations upon it would be productive of any benefit. But neither you nor our friend seem to understand the facts in relation to these conventions. At the New Hampshire State convention a motion was made to nominate Mr. Van Buren, which after an animated discussion *we negatived by a decided majority.* ["At the Maine" *canceled*] More than two-thirds of the members voting against his nomination. It is true that two "members at large" were chosen for the Baltimore Convention who are supposed to be friendly to Van Buren; yet we know the men, & know that they will vote with the majority of their State, which we hope will be for us in the final contest. The Charleston Mercury does not seem to understand the true facts of the New Hampshire Convention, but has represented it as favorable to Van Buren, & leads its readers to suppose that Van Buren got the nomination of that State. As to the Convention in Maine, Van Buren was nominated by a *minority* of the members. I send you a Maine paper containing an accurate account[?] of the proceedings of that Convention. At a recent convention in the seventh District of Maine a friend of Mr. Calhoun has been put in nomination for Congress, and another friend ["nominated" *canceled and* "chosen" *interlined*] for elector at the Baltimore Convention in May. *These facts may be confidently relied upon.* Maine will go for Calhoun or I am no calculator. The above statements have all been published in our papers, tho you & our distinguished Friend do not seem to be aware of them.

As to the mode of choosing electors for the Baltimore Convention, Maine & New Hampshire have both voted to *choose by Districts.* Maine has already chosen ["her" *canceled and* "two" *interlined*] electors at large & chosen one by Districts. New Hampshire has voted to choose by Districts, & has chosen two at large. In Massachusetts there will be no contest on this point. The District system will be adopted unanimously. The only contest will be for the two electors to be chosen at the Convention. *If the measures I wrote to you about,* are adopted, we shall carry the State, & if adopted in sum we can carry Rhode Island also. Until recently [Abel P.] Upshur has been opposed to the measures, which very much surprises me. I hear his opposition has now ceased. As to the editor of the [Boston] Post [Charles G. Greene] he is as you wish him, & will take any course that his friends think expedient. He has been doing much good by his able attacks upon the Globe, which I hope you have read. We have a majority of the Democratic papers in the State with us. *I wish you could enclose this letter to our friend* as he ought to have the facts, & I have not time to write to him just now. Send him also the paper which I send to you, & let him know that his friends are not asleep in New England. B. did not go to Washington until a week after you suppose he did.

The Attorney General [John Nelson] is as favorable to our cause as you yourself—*I know it.* Let me hear from you when you [*two words illegible*] at Washington & if you wish me to *do* any thing write. Yours truly & [*one word illegible*], L.W.

ALS with Ens in ScU-SC, John C. Calhoun Papers. NOTE: The first enclosure is an undated extract in Maxcy's handwriting; the second is an ALI.

From R[OBERT?] COCHRAN

[Fayetteville, N.C.?, *ca.* August 10, 1843] Sir, The [Congressional] election in North Carolina is over, but returns come in slowly. In this district (Fayetteville) Gen[era]l [Romulus M.] Saunders is certainly elected by 124 majority. Gen[era]l [James I.] McKay is certainly elected having no serious opposition. We are inclined to believe that Mr. [John R.J.] Daniel is also elected from the returns received, as well as Mr. [David S.] Reid *democrat.* But "Glory enough for One[?] day." Mr. [Archibald H.] Arrington is certainly elected, having defeated Edward Stanly some thousand votes. No returns received either from the upper district where [Francis B.] Craige & [Daniel M.] Barringer are running, or a lower one where Mr. [Kenneth] Rayner is opposed by Dr. [Godwin C.] Moore. Every thing looks well for North Carolina though the vote given on Thursday last [8/3?] is no evidence of the Democratic strength in the State. In this County alone the vote fell short more than 400 votes, the day was an uncommonly bad one, raining off and on from day light till dark. I am respectfully Y[ou]r Friend and Ob[edien]t Servant, R. Cochran.

ALS in George H. and Laura E. Brown Library, Washington, N.C. NOTE: This undated document has been assigned a tentative approximate date from its content.

"Organization of the National Convention," by "PENDLETON"

[Published at Petersburg, Va., August 12, 1843]

For the Republican[:] I am one of those, Mr. Editor, who have been from the first anxious to preserve the harmony of the party, and have witnessed with pleasure the growing tendency to union in its ranks, in relation to the questions which have arisen in reference to the Convention. Already, it may be said with confidence, that the question of the time of its meeting is definitely fixed for May 1844. Every portion of the party, even those who preferred the earliest period, have at length acquiesced. It is a great point gained. It affords ample time for mature deliberation, and closes a controversy, which, a short time since, alarmed our friends and animated the hopes of our opponents with the expectation of division and discord in our ranks.

But, as great as it is, it is not greater than another point, which may also be regarded as definitely settled; and that is, that a majority of the States is the proper authority to decide all preliminary questions relating to the Convention on which the party may unfortunately be divided. The appeal which Indiana made to this high authority on the important question of time, with the acquiescence of all the States, and the happy effects it has had in settling that question satisfactorily to all, already shows it to be the sense of the party, that it is the proper tribunal to decide all such questions. In fact, it is difficult to conceive how twenty-six States can get along in adjusting the many preliminary questions, which must arise in reference to the Convention, without some recognised tribunal to settle them; or conceive any other except that which can be resorted to for the purpose. It is conceived, the States are all equal, and that no one has a right to dictate to the rest, or force its own peculiar opinion on them. Hence the danger of division and discord, and the necessity of a common tribunal, which all respect; and hence, also, the importance I attach, as a friend of harmony, to the recognition by the party of the majority of the States as the proper tribunal to determine all preliminary questions touching the Convention.

It is at this time of greater importance from the fact, that there remain two such questions still to be decided of deep interest, and on which the party is much divided. They are more dangerous and more difficult to settle than was that of time, because they touch on important constitutional provisions. I refer to the mode in which the Delegates to the Convention should be appointed, and how they should vote when met. One portion insists, that their appointment should be by districts, and their votes counted *per capita*; that is, that the vote of every individual shall count one; while the other insists, that each State has the right to determine all preliminary questions for itself, and, of course, how their delegates should be appointed; how many their [*sic*] should be, and how they should vote. Elaborate arguments have been put forth on both sides; on the one, the South Carolina address, in support of the Maryland plan, and on the other, a communication published in the [Richmond] Enquirer on the 9th of June last, (said by the Editor [Thomas Ritchie] to be from the pen of a distinguished member of the Virginia Convention [George C. Dromgoole],) in reply to the South Carolina Address, and in support of the ground taken by the Virginia Convention. How can such an issue between leading States be settled without a common tribunal? But with such a one, recognised in the majority of the States, there will, I trust, be no difficulty or danger in settling it. Let the example already established be followed. Let a fair and full discussion, avoiding all personalities, enlighten the public mind on all the points involved in the questions; and when that is done, let some State, at the proper time, imitate the laudable and fortunate example set by Indiana, by appealing to the same high authority. The same happy consequence would follow. All the preliminary questions would be satisfactorily settled. No State that regarded the voice of the party would dare oppose. The Convention would meet in harmony; its decision acquiesced in; and the party rallied, to a man, would move forward to a glorious victory.

It is in my opinion, Mr. Editor, high time to open the discussion. The division exists. It is deep and extensive. Silence cannot heal it and delay will aggravate it. Under this impression, I have turned my mind to the subject and carefully examined the reasons on both sides; especially those contained in the address of the South Carolina Convention and the reply referred to in the Enquirer. The result is, a strong conviction that the grounds taken in the address are sound, and remain unanswered by the reply. In coming to this result, I have carefully guarded myself against all improper bias. I have taken truth, justice, and the Constitution, for my guides, and have implicitly followed wherever they lead; and what I now propose is, to assign the reasons for my conviction.

As wide as the difference appears to be between the grounds taken by the address and the reply, when they come to be fully compared, they will be found to be reduced to a single point. The former, indeed, insists that the delegates to the Convention should be appointed by districts, and that their votes should be given *per capita*, while

344

the other peremptorily demands for each State the right to appoint them, as she pleases, and to prescribe whatever mode she may think proper for their voting. Thus, on their face, the two are diametrically opposed; but when each comes to explain, the difference between them greatly diminishes. They both agree in the important point, that the proper relative weight of the States in the election, should be preserved in the nomination. The address assumes that, as a fundamental principle, and advocates the appointment by districts, and the vote *per capita*, mainly on the ground, that it is the only way that can be devised, by which the relative weight of the States in the nomination can be preserved; while the reply recognises the same principle, and admits, that the mode for which it contends, is limited by it. For after having laid down the broad and unqualified principle, that "each State must be left free and will be free" to decide on all preliminary questions for itself, it expressly says "We only insist, that no State shall exceed its relative weight in the actual election, in the popular mode of the Constitution," that is, as I understand the vague expression, in the Electoral college. I can see no other possible meaning which can be attached to it.

The limitation is an important one. It concedes expressly, that there is a qualification of the broad and absolute right previously demanded for each, to determine all preliminary questions for itself, and by implication, that the other States have the right to judge, whether the mode which may be adopted by any one State, for appointing delegates, and prescribing how they should vote, is not calculated to increase unduly the weight of the State; and if so, to *insist* that it shall not be adopted. These concessions fully vindicate the address of the South Carolina Convention. It is precisely what it has done, and for doing which it has drawn down the denunciations of the distinguished member of the Virginia Convention.

But it may be asked, if both are agreed that no State has a right to adopt any preliminary step calculated to increase unduly its relative weight in the nomination, wherein do they differ? It is as I have stated in one point only, but that an important one; the standard by which the relative weight of the States ought to be determined. The reply insists that the true standard, by which it should be, is their relative weight in the Electoral college; while the address contends, that it is by their relative weight in the election, comprehending the Electoral college and the eventual choice by the House of Representatives.

To have a clear conception of the difference, it must be borne in mind, that the Constitution provides, that the President shall be voted

345

for by electors; that each State shall be entitled to as many electors as it has members in the two Houses of Congress; that if any candidate should have a majority of all the votes, he shall be elected; but if not, then the House of Representatives shall elect the President from the three having the greater number of votes—the House to vote by delegations, the vote of each to be bestowed by the majority, and to count one. It will be seen at once, that the relative weight of the States, in the choice by the Electoral College and the House is very different. In the former, it is unequal; each State having a vote proportioned to its population, estimated in federal numbers, with the addition of two for their Senators; while their relative weight in the latter is equal, each State having one vote, without regard to population. What then the reply demands is, that the relative weight of the States in the Convention and nomination shall be determined exclusively by the Electoral College, while the address insists, that both shall be taken into the estimate. Such is the precise point of difference between them, stripped of all verbiage, and the question is, which is right?

The statement itself, unaided by argument, would seem to decide in favour of the Address. Why not take the whole provision for electing the President, as the true standard, instead of a part? Why should one part be taken to the exclusion of the other? Is not the nomination intended to be a substitute for both, as far as the party is concerned? Is not its avowed object, to concentrate the entire strength of the party, with the double view of defeating its opponents in the Electoral College, and of preventing the eventual choice by the House? It is on that ground almost exclusively, that it is argued and justified. Being then intended as a substitute for the entire election, on what principle of reason, justice, or the Constitution, can it be maintained, that the relative weight of the States should be different in the nomination from what it is in the election?

But this view is greatly strengthened, as strong as it is in the abstract, when taken in connection with the facts furnished by the history of the Convention, which formed the Constitution. It appears from them, there was great difficulty in fixing on any satisfactory provision for the election of the President. After many attempts, and long and persevering efforts, the present was adopted at a very late period. The real difficulty at bottom, was to fix, satisfactorily, the relative weight of the larger and smaller members of the Union. The present was adopted, as a compromise; and it was openly avowed and acted on, that the increased weight conferred on the small States, in the eventual choice by the House, was to compensate them for the undue weight assigned to the larger in the Electoral College. Neither could have been adopted without the other. The provision as it stands was taken as a whole, and could only be so taken. The portion relating to the eventual choice was adopted by ten States to one. Virginia voted with the majority. (See the Madison papers, 3d vol., from page 1499 to 1511.) I now ask, whether it would not be a gross fraud on the Constitution and palpable injustice to the smaller States, to attempt to deprive them, in the nomination of candidates, of their portion of the relative weight in the election, thus secured to them by the Constitution? On what possible ground can it be justified? On what the reply attempts to do it, I shall now proceed to state.

Its first ground is, that the election by the House, constitutes no part of the election of the President. It admits, indeed, "that the same relative weight of the States, as fixed by the Constitution in the election of President, and Vice President, should be preserved in the selection and nomination of the candidates," but without condescending to explain, it boldly assumes, that "this relative weight consists in the right of each State to appoint as the Legislature thereof may direct, a number of electors equal to the whole number of its Representatives and Senators;" that is in direct language, that the election consists in that by the Electoral College, to the entire exclusion of that by the House—What? Is that no part of the election, which the Constitution has expressly provided as a part? That no part, which, after a long and hard struggle between conflicting interests, was adopted as a compromise? That no part, which was so essential to the adoption of the very portion now asserted to be the whole election, that it could not be adopted without it?

The reasons for this extraordinary assumption, are not less extraordinary than the assumption itself. The first, stated in plain language, is, that it is contrary to the spirit and intention of the Constitution not to exclude the choice by the House, as a portion of the election, on the ground, that it is the intention of the Constitution, "that the popular principle shall operate in the election of the President and Vice President." Yes, certainly; no one denies that. It not only operates, but is the predominant principle in the election by the Electoral College, as is expressly stated and insisted on by the Address. But the question is not, whether the Constitution intended it should operate, but whether it was intended it should operate exclusively. The distinguished member himself will not venture to assert that such was the intention. He well knows, that it would be directly contrary to the facts; but, if such was not the intention, the argument falls to the ground.

His next reason is still more extraordinary—He says, that "no argument, or analogy, can be fairly drawn from that provision of the Constitution, prescribing the mode of electing the President by the House of Representatives. There is nothing like it, or akin to it in or out of the Constitution. It has no connection with the popular principle in the election of President and Vice President, and can have none in the nomination of candidates, upon whom that principle is to operate." I give his own words, because it contains the gist of his argument; but I must say, with due respect for the distinguished member, that I have never known an argument more unfounded in premises, or illogical in conclusion. What? Is there no connection between the election by the Electoral College and that by the House? No connection between what the Constitution so intimately unites, as to put them in the same provision? None between what so directly relate to each other, that the one was intended to correct the imperfection of the other, and so dependent, that the one could not have existed without the other? If these do not constitute a connection, I ask what does?

Not satisfied with the attempt to isolate, what are so intimately connected, the distinguished member takes bolder ground, and attempts to push the isolation far beyond. He asserts, that there is nothing like or akin to the election by the House, in or out of the Constitution; that is, that the mode of voting by States, when the election devolves on the House, is without example in our political history. Is it so? Has he forgot, in his over zeal, that it was the mode of voting in declaring independence; the mode in the old Congress of the Revolution and under the confederation; the mode in adopting the articles of confederation, and in the convention which formed the present Constitution; and finally, in its ratification by the States? Yes, it is to this anomalous and monstrous mode of voting, as it is now called, that we owe our birth and existence as sovereign and independent States; our Constitution; our liberty and greatness. It is the primitive and elementary mode, existing prior to all stipulations and compacts, and the only one known in their absence. It is the mode which ever prevails, when the States act as such; and it is the solid foundation, on which rests the glorious old States Right doctrine of '98. On the contrary, the mode, which the distinguished member would have us believe, is the sole and exclusive one known in our political history, with this single exception, is the mere creature of compact, having no existence but in consequence of positive stipulations, and is the sole ground on which, the doctrines of consolidation rest. Without the former, there would be no States Rights, and without the latter, no pretext for consolidation. If it was the exclusive mode, as the distinguished member would have it, the Government would be consolidated. But his conclusion is not less illogical, than his premises are false. Grant all he assumes, that there is no connection between the election by the Electoral College and that by the House, and that the mode of voting by the latter, is without example, and how would that prove, that it ought not to be taken into the estimate, in determining the relative weight of the States in the election? would the absence of connection, or precedent, make it less a provision of the Constitution? or would it diminish the weight, which it confers on the smaller States, in the election? And if not, why should it not be taken into estimate in determining their weight in it? Or why divest them of it in nominating candidates?

There is, indeed, a want of connection, but it is between the distinguished member's premises and conclusions. And there is, indeed, a mode of voting, which is not alike or akin to any thing in or out of the Constitution, but it is that prescribed by the Virginia Convention to vote by States, and count per capita. I challenge him to find an example of the kind, in the whole volume of our political history.

On this baseless and illogical argument, he undertakes to assert, that to take the vote by the House into estimate, in determining the relative weight of the States or "to compromise it, under the idea of an equivalent, falls but little short of an attempt to commit a fraud on the Constitution." What ought such an assertion to be called?— presumption or desperation! If to claim, as a right, that which the Constitution expressly confers, is to attempt to commit a fraud on it, what, I ask, ought the attempt to expunge virtually, an express provision from the Constitution, and to divest more than one half of the States of the right it secures, to be called?—Fraud, robbery, or what?

The truth is, that the distinguished member is hostile to the provision of the Constitution, which devolves the eventual choice on the House, as is manifest from the whole tenor of his remarks. He regards it as improperly trenching on the powers of the larger States in the election, and would, no doubt, gladly expunge it from the Constitution; but as that can not be done, he desires to supercede it in practise, through the instrumentality of a Convention. He almost acknowledges as much. He says in a note, that "it is almost a subject of wonder, that the South Carolina Convention did not object to a Convention of any kind," alluding to its insisting on taking into the estimate of the relative weight of the States, their weight in the election by the House. The remark clearly indicates, that the real value of a Convention in his eyes is to afford the means of depriving the smaller States of the advantage they have in the eventual choice by the House. His reply in reality, when properly viewed, is an attack on the Constitution itself, and it is not at all wonderful, that with such an object he should so signally fail in his argument. So much for the reasons of the distinguished member.

Standing on the frail grounds on which they place him, he undertakes to speak in the name of Virginia, and in the most dictatorial and author[it]ative manner says, "that Virginia uncompromisingly maintains her right to appoint her delegates to the National Convention in her own mode." And this too, after saying, Virginia insists, that no State, in nominating the candidates, shall exceed its relative weight in the election. Now, I trust, that Virginia will not object to concede to others, what she insists on for herself—She is too just to claim for herself, what she is unwilling to allow others. I now ask, what does the right involve, on which she insists, as the distinguished member says. It involves, in the first place, the right to decide on what is the proper standard of the relative weight of the States in the election; and of course, to determine whether it should be limited to the Electoral College exclusively; or should also include the election by the House. And in the next, the right to examine, whether the mode adopted by any one State, is not calculated to increase unduly its proper relative weight; and if so, to object to it. This is what she claims for herself, and can she object that Maryland, South Carolina, or any other State, should claim the same? Would it be just or honorable to do so? And if not, how can she uncompromisingly maintain her right to appoint delegates to the National Convention, in her own way, as is dictatorially claimed for her? No; I think better of our old Commonwealth. She is too just and honorable for that. She is willing to do as she would be done by; to mete to others, what she metes to herself. In spite of the assumption of her name, by the distinguished member, she will hear arguments on the points of difference, and after calmly and impartially weighing them, decide according to truth, justice, and the Constitution. She will do more. If, after such decision, there should be still a difference between her and any of her sister States, she will refer it to a majority of the States to decide, instead of dictating, or attempting to force her opinion on them. This is the true Republican course, and the only one becoming her elevated position and character. Any other would be sure to end in discord and distraction, and lay the responsibility of destroying the harmony of the party mainly at her door. [Signed:] PENDLETON.

PC in the Petersburg, Va., *Republican*, August 12, 1843, p. 2; PC in the Charleston, S.C., *Mercury*, August 18, 1843, p. 2; PC in the Washington, D.C., *Spectator*,

September 2, 1843, p. 1. Note: The two last cited sources both reprinted this document from the Petersburg *Republican*. In reprinting the article the *Spectator* commented as follows: "On our first page will be found an article which we have had on file for some weeks upon the principles which should govern the selection of delegates to the National Convention. Of the many arguments which the discussion of this important question has elicited, we consider this among the ablest. Its clearness of style, forcible arguments, logical conclusions, and thorough mastery of the subject, stamp its author as a man of no ordinary talent...." In a letter of 8/6/1843 to R[obert] M.T. Hunter, Calhoun said, "... I have, (inter nos & in strick confidence) aided in preparing an article in reply to [George C.] Drumgoole's answer to the S[outh] Carolina address, which has been sent to the Petersburgh Republican for publication."

From Nath[anie]l Bosworth

New York [City,] Aug. 13th 1843

Dear Sir, It is I believe about twelve years since I had the honour of calling on you at your mansion in Pickins [*sic*; Pickens District, S.C.], on my way to the Georgia gold mines, and receiving from you the attention characteristic of South-Carolinian hospitality. You will probably remember the occasion, as I dined that day with your neighbour J[ohn] E[wing] C[olhoun] in company with Hon. Warren R. Davis, whose demise we had soon after occasion to lament.

Our conversation on that occasion I have never forgotten, and I date my attention to national statistics from that period, since which, not a month, or week has passed without accumulating something in respect to the condition of society. The principal drift, and object of this research, was, to determine for myself, the operations, the relative condition, and structure of society; but while doing this, it was impossible not to notice the varied movements of ["the" *canceled*] National governments, and my attention has been particularly drawn to that of England, with her *moral machinery*, always under the banners ["of the cross" *canceled*] of the "cross"—of "freedom," and of "liberty"; yet ever denouncing free-men as slaves.

I am never moved at trifles, but I confess that from what I have seen from the date of Lord Ashbertons [*sic*; Ashburton's] advent to this country, with his "smiles and wine" the entre[e] into China—the Sandwich islands, the pretended steam packs [pacts?] between the two countries which were virtually instituted for *discipline*, and *sounding the channels*, the world[']s [antislavery] convention and the poison it has emit[t]ed, I am compelled to view England as a treacherous enemy, that ultimately intends to grasp this country with the rest of the world into her possession. I think she has her eye upon Cuba,

351

texas, and the Southern States, to begin to fasten on; and I offer an opinion, that to preserve our country with its fre[e]dom, it can in no way be done except by strengthening the South—we must set aside all sectional prejudice, and rally for the nation as a whole—let every man consider it as his own, and strengthen the weaker parts, defying the enemy at every point.

At an early period I studied, and practized [*sic*] the science of gunnery—wrote a treatise and published it on "sharp shooting for rifle and infantry practice." From 1817 to to [*sic*] 1823 I resided in Charleston, and on the sea shore experimented privately in long projectiles; and I am the first person that ever succeeded with gunpowder to throw a long projectile over three miles, the front end keeping foremost. In practice, such projectiles have always been found to tumble over—presenting a broad side to the direction of its course, and destroying its range. Viewing my success as a matter of importance, resolved to keep it to myself, until *war* should come to make it available for me in a letter of marque, or privateer. More than twenty years has elapsed without the occur[r]ence of any opertunity to benefit from the discovery. To dispose of it to a foreign country I have not consented—at home there has been nothing to do. The Texian squab[b]le with Mexico, was unworthy ["the" *interlined*] name of war.

Now Sir, as I am determined england shall never have this from me; and as the "secret archives" at Washington is *not certain to retain its secrets*; and as I have seen fifty seven years with no positive assurance of seeing fifty seven more, am desirous the subject first should not be lost; and second; that I cannot do a greater act of patriotism for my country than by placing this where private interest shall be above cupidity, in which case it will be likely to be preserved from a foreign enemy.

To do this I have thought of the States of South Carolina, and Virginia, in both of which I have spent many years; and I mean no compliment by attaching to them the highest civilization to be found in the Union.

In case of war—there is an arsenal at Richmond, and a Naval depot at Norfolk—Charleston has now every thing connected with this subject except the boring of guns. From these two States I should look for every thing that would save the south—and that saved, the Union would be preserved.

I have learned to trust to the honesty of men, where it is to *their interest* to be honest; and knowing the peculiar interest in the States mentioned—the attachment of families, the Pinckneys—Mydletons [*sic*]—Horrys—and others in Charleston—Maj[o]r [Charles] Yancey, and a host in Virginia—with some single suitable person in each place, I have thought the whole subject might be safely deposited, for use at the first important emergency. My first experiments were for extensive, accurate ranges—about nine years ago I renewed them for the purpose of making the projectiles more formidable by introducing percussion powder in their front end for tearing asunder the sides of a ship, &c—and here I proved that 2 ounces of percussion powder will devellope more electricity than is contained in an ordinary discharge of lightning, and will open a passage in the firmest structure of timber of five or six feet.

The size of the projectiles for war purposes is 6 to 8 inches calibre, their length four calibres. Projectiles of this size will range over 6 miles, and make a point plane shot at the distance of four miles. I would propose an armament of one gun only to a vessel not exceeding 300 tons for shore service, with steam, in addition to sailing power, 3 knots above the fleetest craft. We then can chuse [*sic*] and maintain our position *without* the range of the enemy's shot, keeping them *within* the range of our own. A few such vessels will save us, when *little dependence can be had upon the large clumsy steamers that have been made.* Capt[ai]n [Alden] Partri[d]ge is with me in such a view. I need not say more, in the first address of the kind I have ever thought proper to make, than *this*; that my proposition is *not for the purpose* ["of" *interlined*] *reward,* but to secure an important physical means, for the safety of the nation, should circumstances at a future time require it. I could not think of any southern gentleman more appropriate than yourself to address such a communication—not feeling very certain that you will attach much consequence to it. You will perceive that my course has been different from that of Mr. Stephens [Robert Livingston Stevens], with his shell—and of Capt[ai]n [Robert F.] Stoc[k]ton with his wrought iron gun and ball of 242 lbs.—all the particular excel[l]ences of which they have published to the world. I am not pleased with the structure of my letter and am aware that I ought to copy it but my situation at the moment will not allow of it, and not being fond of procrastination, will only say that I shall be pleased to receive from you an acknowledgement of its receipt.

I am dear Sir with the highest consideration for the very able and patriotic manner in which you have long defended the nation—Y[ou]r very ob[edien]t Serv[an]t, Nathl. Bosworth.

P.S. Since writing the above, have cut, and I now enclose a scrap from the New York Herald.

Please direct [your reply] to care of D. Sayre—25 New St.—New York.

ALS with En in Sc-Ar, Slavery—Letters, 201–50–1. NOTE: The En is a clipping containing one paragraph datelined "Sunday, August 13—6 P.M." concerning a circular distributed by the British government to all British representatives in the U.S. over the signature of Lord Aberdeen and requiring "the most minute and extensive information in relation to the blacks in the United States."

From A[BEL] P. UPSHUR, [Secretary of State]

Washington, Aug. 14, 1843

My Dear Sir, Your letter of the 6[t]h of August, is just received. Mr. Benj[amin E.] Green, son of Gen[era]l Duff Green, is going out to Mexico, immediately, as Sec[re]t[ar]y of Legation & will take all the dispatches which I have occasion to send. Of course, I have no occasion to employ any other person, in that service. But this does not prevent me from complying with your request, in regard to the Gen[era]l Green, of whom you write. As the Dep[artmen]t does not *need* a bearer of dispatches, it cannot *pay* any thing for that service; but it is a very common practice to give to citizens whose interests strongly require it, the facilities which are afforded by being made the bearers of dispatches, by simply entrusting to them a letter or packet of papers. This is a benefit to the citizen, & as he is paid nothing, it is not injurious to the government. This is, by no means, a general practice, but it is always done, in cases which clearly require it. Gen[era]l Green's case appears to be of this sort. I will therefore, whenever he shall desire it, give him that character, & will entrust to him, a letter strongly invoking the aid of Gen[era]l [Waddy] Thompson, [U.S. Minister to Mexico,] in behalf of his brother. This is all that I am authorized to do.

I have read Mr. [Ashbel] Smith's letter with very great interest. It confirms the information which I have received from a variety of sources, & upon which, I have already acted. Very strong letters have been written, to Gen[era]l Thompson & Mr. [William S.] Murphy, [U.S. Minister to Texas,] upon the subject, & I hope that some good will come of them. I have recently held very interesting conversations with Southern gentlemen, on this most interesting subject, & among others, with Mr. [Virgil] Maxcy. He promised that he would write to you in order to obtain your views, & that he would communicate them to me. But I hope that I shall be excused for availing myself of the present occasion, to ask them directly for myself. My own mind is very much disturbed on the subject of Texas, & I shall be much gratified to know from you, either that my apprehensions are well founded, so that I may act on them boldly, or that they are unfounded, so that I may no longer feel them. I ask leave, even at the risk of being tedious, to tell you what they are.

There can be no doubt, I think, that England is determined to abolish slavery throughout the American continent[s] & islands, if she can. It is worse than childish, to suppose that she meditates this great movement, simply from an impulse of philanthropy. We must look for a stronger motive for such an attempt, on the part of a great & wise nation. I can find no other motive than a desire to find or to create, markets for her surplus manufactures, & to destroy all competition with the labour of her colonies. I think there is a crisis in her affairs, which makes it necessary that she should go on; & the result will probably be, either that she will monopolize the commerce of the world, or that she will provoke other nations, to unite & destroy her. At all events, there are no backward steps, for her. The present attempt upon Texas, is the beginning of her operations upon us. If she should succeed, the slaves of Louisiana & Arkansas, will find an asylum in Texas, & it will be impossible to prevent them from seeking it. *This government will not do any thing to aid the slave-holder*, & of course, he will take the matter into his own hands. He will reclaim his slave by force, & this will lead to—*war*. The Northern States will not aid in ["such" *canceled*] a war, waged for such a cause, & this will lead to a separation of the Union. In this state of things, England will not be idle. The result cannot be calculated in degree, but it cannot be otherwise than disastrous.

Again. England will insist on, & will obtain, a commercial treaty, giving her decided advantages in the markets of Texas. Consequently, the ports of Texas will be filled with British fabrics, sent there with the express view to have them smuggled into the U[nited] States. The process will be easy; & thus the Southern & S[outh] Western States, will be filled with British fabrics, which will be sold at lower prices than those of our own country. The effect wil[l] be, 1. to injure the Northern manufacturer, by taking from him, the markets of Texas & the Southern States; 2. to injure the cotton grower, because the Northern manufacturer, not being able to sell, will not buy; & because the cotton of Texas will pay for the goods of England smuggled into our country, & of course, will take the place of so much of our own cotton. 3. To injure our revenue to the amount of all the duties on the smuggled articles. 4. To injure our navigating interest, in due proportion.

This is a mere out-line. If there be any thing in my views, you will carry them out, to their results, much better than I can. And if such would be the probable effects of the abolition of slavery, in Texas, under the auspices of England, is it, or is it not, probable that the thing will be done? It is impossible to contemplate the present condition of Texas, without being convinced that she is under an absolute necessity, to throw herself upon the protection of some stronger power. That power, must be either England or the U[nited] States.

What then, ought we to do? Ought we not to move immediately, for the admission of Texas into the Union, as a slave holding State? Should not the South *demand* it, as indispensable to their security? In my opinion, we have no alternative. To admit Texas as a non-slaveholding State, or to permit her to remain an indepen[den]t & sovereign ["State" *canceled*] non-slaveholding State, will be fatal to the Union, & ruinous to the whole country. I have no doubt that a proposition to admit her into the Union, would be received, at first, with a brush of repugnance, at the North; but the more the subject is reflected on, the more clearly will they see that the measure is absolutely necessary. To the South, it is a question of *safety*; to the North, it is one of interest. *We* should introduce rivals of our most productive industry, & should be, so far, losers; *they* would profit by that very rivalry. I have never known the North to refuse to do, what their interest required, & I think it will not be difficult to convince them that their interest requires the admission of Texas into the Union, as a slave-holding State.

Pray favour me with your views upon this subject, as much at large as you deem proper. Would it not be well, to break the subject to the people of the South, through the public prints? Both parties may unite in that, for it is a *Southern* question, & not one of whiggism & democracy. The southern people are far, far too lethargic upon this vital question. They ought to be roused, & made of one mind. The history of the world does not present an example of such insult, contempt & multiplied wrongs & outrages, from one nation to another, as we have received & are daily receiving, from our Northern *brethren!!* It is a reproach to us, that we [*one word canceled*] bear it any longer. We are *twelve States*, & we have a right to be heard & regarded, in a matter which concerns, not only our rights, but our safety. The present is a proper occasion, & this is a proper subject, on which to unite the South, as one man. Can nothing be done, to produce this result? Are there no idle pens in So[uth] Carolina, which would agree to be so employed? I trust that something will be done *among the people;* without their support, the government is powerless.

Presuming that you desire to have the enclosed letters, they are returned to you.

Pray let me hear from you, if you deem my suggestions worthy of consideration. With great respect, I am very sincerely & truely y[ou]r friend &c, A.P. Upshur.

ALS in ViW, Single Manuscripts Collection; PC in *William and Mary Quarterly,* second series, vol. XVI, no. 4 (October, 1936), pp. 554–557. NOTE: Calhoun's letter to Upshur of 8/6, to which the above is a reply, has not been found. Calhoun apparently had enclosed with it Ashbel Smith's letter of 6/19/1843 to himself. Though the passage is somewhat obscure in the absence of Calhoun's letter to Upshur to which the above letter is a reply, the latter part of the first paragraph seems to refer to a "General" Green other than "General" Duff Green mentioned earlier in the same paragraph. The remarks about the second "General" Green possibly relate to Gen. Thomas Jefferson Green of Texas, at this time a prisoner in Mexico.

From W[i]l[li]s H. Woodley, Proctor, University of Virginia, [Charlottesville], 8/15. "Your favor of the 4th Inst[ant] enclosing three ten dollar South Carolina bank notes, was received by last mail, which is in full [payment] of the advancement of one hundred dollars, made to your son [John C. Calhoun, Jr.] when he was about to leave this place." ALS in ScU-SC, John C. Calhoun Papers.

From JAM[E]S R. LAWHON

Dahlonega [Ga.,] August 16th 1843

Dear Sir, Your letter of [the] 6th Inst[ant] Enclosing an order on Mess[rs]. Sisson & Laurence in favour of Mr. [William?] Martin & myself for professional services rendered, has been rec[eive]d[,] presented & discharged for which you will please accept our thanks.

Mr. John Langston called on me a few days since & requested me to write you and obtain from you if possible a lease on your obar mine—he says that he knows of a vein on the lot that will yield well. Mr. Langston is a man that I have long known & deem him to be of irreproachable character. He thinks that if he had a lease on the lot that he could not only make it profitable to himself, but to you also.

He is willing to pay the Customary toll of the County & if the yield should be of an extraordinary Character he is willing to pay accordingly. Respectfully Y[ou]r ob[edien]t serv[an]t, Jams. R. Lawhon.

ALS in ScU-SC, John C. Calhoun Papers.

"The South Carolina Convention," by
A MEMBER OF THE CONVENTION

[Published at Charleston, August 16, 1843] FOR THE MERCURY. I observe that the *Richmond Enquirer* has renewed its call on the *Mercury* for explanation, in reference to the address of our [S.C.] State Convention [adopted on 5/24]. I am of the impression, that its call should be answered. I regard a clear and full understanding on all points of difference between the friends of the several candidates for the Presidency, as eminently desirable. It is the most certain way to prevent conflicts in the end, and preserve, throughout, the harmony of the party. Thus thinking, I am of the opinion, that if the address of our Convention should be thought by any respectable portion of the party to be ambiguous, it ought to be explained. The unfortunate ill health of the Editor of the *Mercury*, (Mr. [John A.] Stuart,) and his absence, in consequence, from his post, makes it impossible for him to answer, and would seem to devolve the duty on some of the members of the Convention. What I propose in this communication, is, to undertake the discharge of that duty.

The address, then, was intended to be perfectly explicit, and free from all ambiguity. It is not the character of the people of this State to disguise their sentiments on any subject. Manliness, at least, is one of their virtues. The object of the address, accordingly, as plainly stated, and openly avowed, is to RECOMMEND to the party of the other States, first, the candidate it preferred, and next, the mode of appointing delegates, and how they should vote in making the nomination, and to assign the reasons in a clear and respectful manner for its preference. The intention, as stated, is to elicit a free, full, and friendly exchange of opinions with the party in the other States, in the same way; in the hope that it would produce a concurrence of opinion, or if it failed in that, it would lead to the adoption of some means, by which the difference might be fairly and satisfactorily decided. All this is plainly expressed, or fully indicated.

But it seems that the *Enquirer* is not satisfied, and desires to ascertain, at this stage, what the friends of Mr. Calhoun intend, as their ultimate course. I, for one, (and I believe I may speak for the whole Convention,) am desirous of satisfying him. We desire no concealment on this, or any other point. We intend to be explicit, and will expect others to be equally so with us. But, as our *ultimate course must depend on the ultimate course of others*, and *especially Virginia*, it becomes necessary, before we answer, to ascertain what will be the *ultimate course* of the friends of Mr. [Martin] Van Buren in that State, on the points in the address of her Convention, connected with those in our address, on which the *Enquirer* asks for explanation. To enable me, then, to give the explanation desired, I ask the *Enquirer* for explanation on the following points.

1. *Do the friends of Mr. V[an] B[uren] in Virginia, intend to adhere "uncompromisingly" to the principle, that each State has the right to determine how its delegates shall be appointed, how many there shall be, and how they shall vote in the Convention, in making the nomination?*

2. *Are they willing to leave the decision of these and the other preliminary questions on which there are, or may be a difference of opinion, to the decision of the majority of the States, and to abide by their decision, ascertained by an appeal, similar to that made by the Indiana Central Committee, on the preliminary question as to the time of the meeting of the Convention?*

I hope the *Enquirer* will give an explicit answer to both, and say also—*if Virginia "uncompromisingly insists" on more than seventeen delegates, in the Convention?* I shall endeavor in the meantime, to acquire such full information, as will enable me to answer, explicitly, for the friends of Mr. Calhoun in this State. I know them to be sincerely desirous of preserving the harmony of the party. They believe, that its views of the policy which the Government ought to pursue, never were sounder, since the accession of Mr. [Thomas] Jefferson. It is the policy, which he and they have so long and boldly maintained, against fearful odds, and under the greatest difficulty. They look to the party to carry them out in practice. They desire its success for that purpose at the next Presidential election, and the harmony of the party to ensure its success. They have the deepest interest in it. But they believe that the harmony and success of the party depend on a strict adherence to the Constitution, and to truth, justice, and equity in all things; and they would regard success itself, as too dearly bought by their sacrifice. [Signed:] A MEMBER OF THE CONVENTION.

PC in the Charleston, S.C., *Mercury,* August 16, 1843, p. 2; PC in the Richmond, Va., *Enquirer,* August 22, 1843, p. 2. Note: Calhoun's authorship of this article is established by no direct evidence. However, it is included herein because of its close relationship to other documents which he is known to have drafted. This essay defends the "Address" adopted by the S.C. Democratic Convention on 5/24, which Calhoun at least partly drafted; further, after the above article was replied to by the Richmond, Va., *Enquirer,* in its issue of August 22, 1843, p. 2, Calhoun is known to have drafted another article signed by "A Member of the Convention," which appeared in the *Mercury* on 9/13. Compare the first paragraphs of the letters from Albert Rhett to Calhoun on 8/3/1843 and 8/17/1843; the second paragraph of Calhoun's letter to Robert M.T. Hunter on 8/26/1843; the third paragraph of Franklin H. Elmore's letter to Calhoun on 9/4/1843; the first paragraph of Albert Rhett's letter to Calhoun on 9/12/1843; and the article by "A Member of the Convention" printed below under date of 9/13/1843. If Calhoun did not draft the article above, then it perhaps followed closely suggestions he had made. It seems to carry traces of his thought and style.

From G. WALKER

Hamburg S.C., 16 Aug[us]t [18]43 D[ea]r Sir, I Send to the care of J[ohn] S. Lorton [at Pendleton] a h[ogs]h[ea]d Bacon for you[.] I had to pay cash for it. If it is Conven[ien]t I would be glad if you could Send me the am[oun]t of your acc[ount] or a part of it[.] Cotton is rather better this *week* than it has been for some time. Y[ou]rs Tr[u]ly, G. Walker.

ALS in ScU-SC, John C. Calhoun Papers. Note: On the same paper Walker noted an account due from Calhoun for the hogshead of bacon of $38.88. Calhoun's endorsement indicates that he sent in payment two twenty dollar bills, one on "the B[ank] of Hamburgh . . . & the other on the bank of Charleston." The same paper also contains Calhoun's calculations of how much was owed by himself, [Thomas G.] Clemson, and "Mr. Fredericks" for 619 pounds of bacon costing $46.20 that was to be divided in uneven portions between them.

From ALBERT RHETT

Charleston, Aug. 17, 1843 My Dear Sir, On my return to Town yesterday, I received your favour of the 5th Inst[ant]. You will see, by the Mercury of yesterday and today, that most of your suggestions have been attended to, and all will be, as far as is in my power, or I am permitted to exercise any agency in them. [Thomas] Ritchie, you perceive, has already altered his tone, for he offers now to publish any thing on both sides, without comments from himself, and only begs he may be personally exempted from attack. The ship is ["now" *canceled*] upon the right tack ["at last" *interlined*], and we have only to bear down steadily upon the foe, with all our canvass [*sic*] spread, and victory seems, to say the least, extremely probable. The inclosed [*not found*] has been handed me to read, & I have thought it might gratify you to read it. All our chances appear to me greatly strengthened by the result of the late elections, particularly those of Ten[n]essee, for the more formidable the Whigs appear the less the Democrats will dare ["to" *canceled*] undertake to beat them with ["Mr." *interlined*; Martin] Van Buren. Indeed I feel far from assured that Mr. Van Buren could under any circumstances, defeat such a candidate as Judge Maclean [*sic*; John McLean], though he might Mr. [Henry] Clay.

I agree with you, most heartily, that the District mode of electing Delegates to the [national] Convention we should under no circumstances surrender. To give it up would be to give up every thing—to give up all chance of the Presidency ["not only" *interlined*] now, but, for the smaller States, in all time to come; and to assign the Government over to the Albany and Richmond Juntos. Do others as they please, *you* cannot be instrumental in such a result, without impairing what I know you value more than the Presidential office, your fame with Posterity as a Patriot Statesman. Should we fail, in spite of all our efforts, having the National Convention constituted on the principles we have set forth, and this becomes appearant [*sic*] before the time of its meeting, you will then have, Sir, a great and solemn question to decide for yourself—whether you should not withdraw your name altogether from its consultations. It is a question I know you will decide honestly, and therefore, wisely. As I am not sounding your opinions, you will pardon the liberty of this suggestion, and let it pass for what it is worth. ["We are ren" *canceled.*]

We are renewing our efforts to raise money in order to make the [Washington] Spectator more efficient by converting it into a tri-weekly or daily Paper, and Col. [Franklin H.] Elmore tells me the prospects of success are good. Not being on the Committee or having personally any charge of the matter, I am able to speak only on the representations of others. As to getting men to wield their *pens*, it seems almost impossible, though, be assured I will make all effort in *my* power to rouse an interest in the discussion, now begun. So far, Brother B. [Robert Barnwell Rhett] and myself (chiefly he) have been the only writers in the Mercury. Will you not send me your suggestions freely, when you wish them to appear in the Mercury, and also any selections from other Papers you think advisable to republish. The Presidential election will be pretty well settled, I apprehend, by the movements and discussion of the next three months, and every hour, therefore, seems to me of the last importance. You will be pleased to hear that Mr. [John A.] Stuart, who is now at Saratoga, had, by the last advice, ["very much" *canceled and* "a good deal" *interlined*] improved, and we have strong hopes now of his recovery. I am, in haste, Dear Sir, y[ou]rs truly & resp[ectfully], Albert Rhett.

P.S. The accounts from Mr. [Virgil] Maxcy of your increasing popularity at the north, especially N[ew] England, are very encouraging.

[P.S.] Ought the article in the Petersburg [Va.] Intelligencer [*sic*; *Republican*] to have been signed "Pendleton"? I fear your hand will be recognised.

ALS in ScU-SC, John C. Calhoun Papers.

CIRCULAR by H[enry] Gourdin, F[ranklin] H. Elmore, and John S. Ashe

Committee Room of the Central Committee
CHARLESTON, AUGUST 18, 1843.
DEAR SIR: At a meeting of the Central Committee held to-day, the undersigned were appointed a Sub-Committee to address you on the important matters explained below, and to request your aid in effecting an object, which they deem of the greatest consequence to the country and to our own State more especially. The present condition of public affairs has given peculiar importance to the ensuing Presidential election. To the South it is of such magnitude, that all intelligent men of our own party, consider it a crisis in our Constitution and Government. Our foreign relations require the utmost care, integrity and firmness in their administration. Our domestic policy, so far as the planting States are concerned, was never on a worse footing, and more than ever requires reform. Yet we are in a state of lethargy; we do scarcely any thing to remedy our condition. In the coming Presidential election, events are involved which will shape our destinies for good, or for evil, perhaps for ages. At such a time, how vitally important to have at the helm of State, a man of purity, uprightness, ability and energy—of sagacity to perceive the exigencies before us—of wisdom to provide for coming events—of firmness and decision, to meet them? All of us may regard Mr. [Martin] V[an] B[uren] as a statesman, to whom, in the abstract, and in ordinary

times, the destinies of the country may be committed with safety. But we cannot forget, that he and those in whom he most confides, and who are most identified with him, have more than once yielded their own acknowledged principles, and sacrificed us by their acts.

The Tariff of 1828 was passed by the casting vote of Mr. Van Buren. We forgot it, and confided again. In 1842, the casting vote of Mr. Silas Wright, fastened upon us the present odious and oppressive Tariff, which has uprooted our commerce and ground our agriculture to the earth. Under these circumstances, can Mr. Van Buren or his friends be depended on to risk as much, or to labor as earnestly, effectually to reform this unconstitutional abuse of power, as one identified with ourselves? Nor are we as safe in his hands, as far as the protection of our domestic institutions is concerned. It is true, that he has pledged himself to veto any bill to emancipate slaves in the District of Columbia. It is true that he and his friends have made manful opposition to the abolitionists and their schemes. We feel grateful for this—but we apprehend that the utmost peril hangs over us from foreign, as well as domestic sources—that whilst incendiaries in our own country are instigating our slaves to abandon our service, and are aiding them to reach the British dominions, the ministry of England have declared that they shall not be surrendered up to our demand, under the late treaty, even though they have committed murder and robbery to effect their escape—that whilst the Tory Government holds this official language, and acts upon it, they are but doing as their Whig opponents will do, if they get into power—that now their abolition association, looking to the destruction of our system of slavery, embraces both Whigs and Tories, and has Prince Albert at its head. We know that at this very moment, the British Government have sent written questions to their Consul in Charleston [William Ogilby], (and we are informed the case is the same in every port where they have a Consul) inquiring most minutely into our laws and usages in regard to slaves; their condition, rights, labors, treatment, &c. We know enough of the dangers that attend every movement of that people and every act of their Government, not to apprehend that our safety calls for the sleepless vigilance, the profound wisdom, and the fearless determination of a great statesman— and we cannot but say that to Mr. [John C.] Calhoun alone of all this present generation, can we look with unbounded confidence for all that human wisdom and firmness can effect.

We have long felt the force of much that we now urge, but recent events have given far more importance to the subject. Our correspondence leads us to believe that Mr. Calhoun's prospects are fairer now than they have been at any time hitherto; and hence we should now press his claims, or at once relinquish the contest. The Hon. Virgil Maxcy, is an ardent, long tried and most faithful friend of Mr. Calhoun. He is one of those who at and near Washington in the recess of Congress are devoting themselves to Mr. Calhoun's services. A letter from him is now before the Committee, which contains views on this subject of so much interest, that they have been induced to put a copy into the hands of [*blank space*] to be shewn to you.

Under the impressions formerly entertained as to the importance to the country, of the election of Mr. Calhoun, and the aid which a properly organized and well conducted central press at Washington would give to that object, efforts were made to raise funds by general subscription, for the purpose of putting the [Washington, D.C.] Spectator on such a footing—they failed to effect any thing. After the [S.C. Democratic] Convention in May last, the Central Committee again earnestly appealed to the party, and sent a letter to each member of the Convention, urging them to give every aid in their power to collect subscriptions—the result has been a sum wholly inadequate, almost nothing in comparison with the object in hand.

Under these circumstances, the Central Committee has this day taken the subject again into consideration. They have determined to make one more effort in a different way to raise the funds required, according to the measures proposed by Messrs. Maxcy, [Robert M.T.] Hunter, [David] Henshaw and [Daniel D.] Brodhead; these measures receive the cordial support and approbation of the Committee. They have tried all other means, and if this fail they can but lament it, as an error which they think will exercise a fatal influence upon Mr. Calhoun's success. If this movement succeed, they entirely concur in the belief expressed by those gentlemen, that it will be attended by happy consequences, and conduce to the triumph of the great cause identified with Mr. Calhoun's election.

Thus believing, the Central Committee have opened a subscription, with a view to raise from $15,000 to $20,000, to be expended in spreading proper information among the people, and promoting thereby this most desirable event. They have amongst themselves subscribed from $500 to $1000 each. The undersigned have been appointed a Sub-Committee, specially charged to ask you to join us in the undertaking, by subscribing in shares of $500 each, payable by the 1st February next, subject to the conditions expressed in Mr. Maxcy's letter. Mr. [*blank space*] waits upon you for your answer. The exigency of the case requires that we should know as speedily as possible what is to be the fate of this last effort. Conventions are about to be assembled in New York, Massachusetts and North-Carolina, to settle the course of the Democratic party in those States, and doubtless others will follow soon after. Our measures should be such as to enable us to inform our friends at once what we can do, and also to arrange with them for our opperations [*sic*]. To do this effectually, to ensure concert and secure success, *it must be established, that we have provided means adequate to the end.*

The Sub-Committee will only remark in addition, that active measures are in progress elsewhere, to sustain this movement in South-Carolina, if it be an efficient one. One gentleman in Boston has already contributed $500, and is responsible for $350 more. One in Maryland has advanced $500, and large contributions are confidently promised if we but do our part in Carolina. In such a cause, where strangers are so warm and generous, can South-Carolina be cold and illiberal? Her honor and interests are deeply involved—she owes an unextinguishable debt of gratitude to the great Statesman, for whose cause—which cause is truly her own—this money is needed. For thirty-five years he has surrendered his private interests, and devoted all his best services to his country; to her already high renown, he has added imperishable glory; and we cannot permit ourselves to doubt that this appeal to you in a cause of so much importance to the whole country, but especially to us of the South, will be made in vain. We are, &c., H. Gourdin, F.H. Elmore, Jno. S. Ashe.

[Appended:]

V[irgil Maxcy] to Col. Franklin H. Elmore

WEST RIVER [Md.], 10th AUGUST, 1843.

MY DEAR SIR: I have just returned from Washington, where I went in the hope of meeting Mr. Hunter from Virginia, to consult what was best to be done in the matter of the Spectator. When Congress broke up, and afterwards, when I had the pleasure of seeing you at Washington, I was led to hope that something efficient would be done by the supporters of Mr. Calhoun's election in Carolina, for placing that establishment free from embarrassment, and issuing the paper three times a week, and to engage an able Editor, and after resisting a long time being made the depository of money contributed for it, as I could not be a resident in Washington, I finally consented, on its being intimated that it was absolutely necessary that some person should receive it whose character was known to the contributors. This was some three or four months ago. In the month of June, the amount of $500 was remitted to me by Mr. Gourdin, and immediately sent to the Editor or Publisher, Mr. [John] Heart, to relieve the most pressing necessities of the establishment and to keep it alive, as it would injure the cause after it had been proclaimed to be the organ of Mr. Calhoun's friends, to let it expire. Except this one sum, I have received not a cent, and by means of my own personal contributions and those of Col. Brodhead of Boston, the paper has been kept from going entirely down. I regret exceedingly that Mr. Hunter could not meet me at Washington, on account of sickness in his family; I found Col. Brodhead of Boston there however, and had the aid of his counsel and that of Mr. Henshaw, the new Secretary of the Navy. It is deemed by them highly important to the success of the cause, that the organ of Mr. Calhoun's friends should be put on a respectable footing without delay, and made a daily paper; that funds to the amount of $10,000 or $15,000 should be raised, not only for this purpose, but to employ an Editor of decided abilities, and to meet the expense for some time of a large gratuitous circulation; and they seemed to think it extraordinary, that one hundred Carolinians could not be found who would at once contribute $100 or more, a piece, especially from their unanimity at home, there can be but little occasion for the local contributors which are so heavy in other parts of the country. I am well aware, for I feel it myself, of the depressed state of the agricultural interest. But still it strikes me with strange contrast with the enthusiasm so justly manifested for Mr. Calhoun in Carolina, that so small a number with so moderate a contribution as the above, could not be found in or out of the Convention. The people in the North and in New England are greatly impressed by outward appearances, and the fact that the friends of such a candidate as Mr. Calhoun, cannot support but a weekly paper at Washington, to meet the daily and insiduous [*sic*] fire of such papers as the Richmond Enquirer and the [Washington, D.C.] Globe, necessarily indicates in their view great weakness, and seriously injures the cause. If any thing is intended to be done, and it is desired to produce the proper effect, *now* is the time for it. A State Convention is about to meet in Massachusetts, and another in New York, in September; and the attacks of the Globe on Mr. Henshaw, the true secret of which is, that he is a decided advocate for Mr. Calhoun, and was known to be so by the President [John Tyler], when he appointed him Secretary of the Navy, have brought out all the newspapers in Massachusetts except one, and many papers in the other New England States, in his defence, and against the arrogance of the Globe. It is thought particularly necessary that we should have a daily paper at Washington, with an able Editor this moment, to give a good tone to this state of things in the New England States, and cause a transfer of the odium which the Editor of the Globe [Francis P. Blair] has incurred to his favorite candidate, as well as to expose the dishonorable tricks and manoeuvres, by which a nomination of Mr. Van Buren has been obtained in Maine and New Hampshire. Until Carolina moves, no pecuniary aid can be expected from other States, whereas considerable subscriptions through the aid of her example, may probably be obtained in Boston, and perhaps other places. I verily believe that a fund of $15 or 20,000 judiciously applied in the establishment of a powerful central organ at Washington, and in aid of papers elsewhere, and in payment of able writers for the next six months, would decide the election in favor of Mr. Calhoun, and will his friends, with such a candidate, permit his cause to be endangered, and with it the vital interests of the South, and the best interests of the whole country, to be put to hazard for want of such a sum.

I trust, my dear sir, you will excuse the earnestness with which I speak on this subject. I claim no right to be importunate with our Southern friends from any fancied superior zeal in the cause of Mr. Calhoun. Though from early manhood a steady personal as well as political friend, who have [*sic*] cherished his character as the beau ideal of a perfect statesman and patriot, with an enthusiasm, which has never relaxed a moment, during a period of thirty-five years; yet it would be presumptuous in me to claim credit for more devotion to his cause, than his Charleston and other Carolina friends. But perhaps you may find some apology for my manifesting earnestness on the subject of this letter, in the fact, that I consented on the suggestion of its necessity, to be the depository for whatever sums might be sent on, and thereby exposed myself to constant importunities for money, which my private limited means have been entirely made to meet. And as the paper is now in great want and embarrassment, I feel it necessary for me to state its situation, that I may be informed definitively, whether any more funds are to be sent on by the Committee in Charleston, of which I believe you are the Chairman, or a member, and if so, as nearly as may be the amount to be relied on, and how soon.

Soon after Mr. [Dixon H.] Lewis and yourself left Washington, Mr. Hunter and myself had a meeting at Washington, the result of which was, as you have been informed, to separate Mr. [Joseph A.] Scoville entirely from the paper.

Mr. Hunter undertook to open a correspondence with the different States. Being a stranger, from absence, to the present political position and relation of even prominent individuals, other duties appropriately belonging to a Central Committee, were undertaken by me; for we found after the most diligent enquiring, that we could not make up a Central Committee out of residents at Washington, of the proper sort, nearly all of Mr. Calhoun's most respectable friends being holders of office, and therefore apprehending unfavorable consequences from taking an active part in politics.

It is right that you and our other friends, who may aid the paper with pecuniary means, to [sic] know what has been done by Mr. Heart, in order to satisfy them of his fidelity to the cause, and a right direction of the ["funds" handwritten into a blank space] of the paper. He has made a conveyance of the whole printing establishment, the cost of which was $1600, and outstanding claims on subscribers for an amount about equal to it, to John W. Maury, Trustee; in the first place, to secure the repayment of the sums of money advanced to it heretofore, of which I enclose a statement with its application, marked A., and also, for the repayment of whatever sums may hereafter be contributed. Schedule B. contains a list of the debts of the establishment. To secure Heart's fidelity, the Trustee is bound to sell all the property necessary to refund whatever is advanced or may be advanced, if required so to do in writing by Mr. Hunter and myself; and further, whenever the amount of contributions shall equal the above amount of debts, and the valuation of the property, the Trustee is required on a requisition by us, to convey the whole property of the establishment, the good will of the paper, and all its outstanding claims for subscription or advertisements, to any person to be named by us, and thereby deprive Heart of all connexion with the paper. Heart cannot associate with him, or employ any Editor without our sanction. Schedule C. shows the weekly expenses of the paper, and an estimate of what they would be if published tri-weekly or daily. After paying these expenses, if the subscribers list should so increase so as to afford a surplus, Heart is to receive one third of it, and the other two thirds to go towards the payment of an Editor, other expenses of the election, such as gratuitous circulation of papers, printing, &c., and the reimbursement of sums advanced to the establishment. The profits of any public printing that may be obtained of Congress, are to be appropriated in the same way, until December 1st, 1845, when on the repayment of one half of the sums contributed to the paper, Heart will be entitled, if then the publisher, to a conveyence in full property of one half of the establishment, and the other half is to be conveyed to an Editor, who may have served the cause well, on repayment of the other half of the subscriptions for its aid not reimbursed, and such other conditions as may be presented by Hunter and myself, or rather the contributors to the support of the paper, whose representatives we consider ourselves. From the above statements connected with the enclosed schedules, you will be able to form an opinion, whether adequate measures have been adopted to secure the faithful management of the paper. You can also ascertain the amount necessary to secure the paper from its debts and embarrassments—the weekly expenses of a weekly, tri weekly and daily publication, and after deciding on what footing the paper ought to be put, you can also decide, what fund it is expedient to provide for gratuitous circulation, for printing, aid to other papers, &c. The services of an able Editor, can be obtained until the Convention, for between two and three thousand dollars. A choice may be had I understand from Mr. Henshaw and Col. Brodhead, of Mr. Shadrach Penn, the Editor of the Missouri Reporter; Mr. [Benjamin F.] Hallett, a man of talents and education and an experienced Editor in Boston; a Mr. Knollton [*sic*; J.S.C. Knowlton], present Editor of the Worcester Palladium; and Mr. Hunter thinks, the services of the present Editor of the Petersburg Republican [Washington Greenhow] may be had. I am obliged to set off early next week to Saratoga, by order of Mrs. [Mary Galloway] Maxcy's Physician, who is in an extremely low state of health, and shall not return before the 20th of September. If money be sent on before that time, I must beg that it may be transmitted to John W. Maury, Trustee, Washington, who will have instructions from me as to its application. If funds should be forwarded sufficient not only for the relief of the establishment but to authorize the engagement of an Editor, I beg you will apprize Mr. Hunter of the fact, whom I shall request before leaving home, to attend and manage this matter in my absence. Write me I pray you to Saratoga Springs, what can and what cannot be done for the Spectator; I shall be in a state of much anxiety until I hear from you. Whatever shall be done or omitted, my time and exertions will be devoted in some form or other to the promotion of the great cause in which we are engaged, until the fate of the contest shall be decided. I shall not permit even the management of my own private affairs, to draw off my attention from the great object in view.

Our prospects in the East and North notwithstanding the fraudulent nominations of Van Buren, in Maine and New Hampshire, have brightened in the last month, and if we at the South do our duty, a great majority of the New England delegates will be with us. Much depends upon proper exertions in the next three months. Our prospects are fair in Maryland. In a word my spirits have risen many degrees within the last few weeks, and I look forward to the great result, if we do our duty with half the zeal of the supporters of Mr. Van Buren, with a high hope of confidence. With great respect and esteem, I remain Dear Sir, faithfully and truly yours, Signed, V. [Maxcy.]

[P.S.] I ought to have mentioned, that Heart is bound to render quarterly accounts to the Trustee, of the application of all funds received.

PDS with En in ScCleA; PDU with En in ScCleA. NOTE: Two printed copies of the above letter and its enclosure are found in ScCleA. One is signed, but badly mutilated; the other unsigned and slightly mutilated. The transcription presented above is a composite of the two extant copies, which appear to have been printed at different times and contain slight variations in punctuation and spelling. The statements mentioned as having been enclosed in Maxcy's letter have not been found.

From DUFF GREEN

London, Aug[us]t 18th 1843

My dear Sir, I write but to say that I have written to you making some suggestions which I hope will receive your favorable Consideration, but as they relate to the President [John Tyler] & to Judge [Abel P.] Upshur, and as they must Cooperate to carry these suggestions into effect I have enclosed my letter to Judge Upshur to be submitted by him to the President, ["and" *canceled*] with instructions not to forward the letter unless they both approve of the suggestions there made. Let me entreat you to deliberate well before you reject them. If under these circumstances my letter is forwarded it will [be] by their sanction and you will be at liberty to act as you deem best. They do not know that I have written this note. I have not time now or I would send you a copy. I may send you a Copy by next steamer.

I have only time to add, that I ["have" *canceled*] am encouraged to hope that I will get fund[s] here. Yours sincerely, Duff Green.

ALS in ScCleA. NOTE: A letter written by Secretary of State Upshur to Green on 9/25/1843 probably relates to the contents of the letter transcribed above. Upshur wrote: "The letter which you enclosed for Mr. Calhoun, I have not sent. The arrangement which you propose is wholly impracticable . . . ." ALS in NcU, Duff Green Papers (published microfilm, reel 5, frames 86–89).

From ROBERT HOUGH

Balt[im]o[re] Md., Aug [us]t 18, 1843

Dear Sir, I have always been a sincere admirer of your political course, my first vote was given to Gen[era]l [Andrew] Jackson in

1828 and from that period to the present I have acted with the "old Jackson party" and voted twice for Mr. [Martin] Vanburen [*sic*]. I differed with you upon the doctrine of nullification at the *time*, because I had not fully examined its merits. I am now a State Rights man in the general acceptation of the term, and believe you were right in the course you then pursued, as it has done more to check the consolidation of government by the force of public opinion than any thing else.

I do sincerely hope you may get the Democratic nomination at the May convention. Your freinds [*sic*] in this State are not without hope that you may get the vote of Maryland in the convention. In this city the leaders of the Democratic party are generally in favour of Mr. Vanburen, the same may be said of the up[p]er counties of the State, but on the eastern shore your freinds are very active, particularly in Talbott [*sic*] Co[unty] where [former] Governor [Samuel] Stevens [Jr.], the Lloyds and Martins are doing all they can to place your name before the convention. Other counties may be as active as Talbott but my information is not so decided, but it is generally conceded that you are the strongest man on the eastern shore counties.

I am also happy to state that you are powerfully supported in what we call here our *lower* counties[,] Charles, St. Marys, Calvert and Prince Georges, and if your freinds in the next Congress will organise and make a strong appeal to the people, Maryland can be brought over to your support, as I truly believe the only reason for the *shew* of preference for Mr. Vanburen is, that it *was* generally understood that he was to be the man; but every day he is getting weaker & Mr. Vanburen cannot add a *vote* to the party, but on the other hand many who left us are willing to come back. I have heard it stated that Mr. John V.L. McMahon, T. Yates Walsh [later a Representative from Md.] and other distinguished whigs are willing to take the *stump* under your banner [*ms. torn*; and?] not under Mr. Vanburen[']s.

Pardon me for the liberty I have taken, but what I have written is done honestly, as I am a merchant and have no motive in view, but your advancement to the Presidency, and I take this occasion to say I I [*sic*] go for you against the *world nominated* or *not nominated* provided your freinds think proper to run you. I am your very obedient Servant &C., Robert Hough.

ALS in ScCleA. NOTE: An AEU by Calhoun reads: "R. Hough[,] to be sent to [Virgil] Maxcy on his return from Saratoga."

From A. H. SNOWDEN

New York [City,] Aug. 18th 1843
My dear Sir, By direction of the State Central Calhoun Association of
N[ew] York, I have the honor to inform you of the receipt of communications from over one hundred similarly organized bodies in
this State, of the unalterable determination of your friends to firmly
insist upon the Convention in *May 1844* (the delegates to be chosen
by districts) to vote *per Capita.*

This we believe to be the most democratic mode of conducting
the next Presidential contest and one which in the end (if the people
will but be true to themselves) cannot fail to crown our efforts with
success, at the same time we shall have the proud satisfaction of having aided in elevating the democratic standard by sustaining the
author of the war report of 1812 (the sentiments of which in our
opinion are only secondary to the declaration of Independance) the
man who is more nearly identified with the great principles which
must sooner or later govern this great republic.

The numerous friends of James Kelly Esq[ui]r[e] of this City
(*who is one of your most ardent & active friends* in this Country) are
very anxious to know if you could not promote his views with Mr.
[Abel P.] Upshur [Secretary of State], who could be of great service
to him in his application now before the department of State. I have
the honor to be with great respect Y[ou]r mo[st] Ob[edien]t Ser-
v[an]t, A.H. Snowden, no. 5 Whitehall Street.

ALS in ScCleA. NOTE: An AEU by Calhoun reads: "Snowden[,] Send to Mr.
[Virgil] Maxcy when he returns."

From ROB[ER]T R. HUNTER

New York [City,] 21 Aug[us]t 1843
My dear Sir, I have been here during the last week aiding in the movements now making in this City in your favor, and this is the first
favorable opportunity I have had to reply to your highly valued letter
of the 8th June and to express my admiration of the excellence and
nobleness of its sentiments.

Some time ago, I purchased a press and intended to commence
the publication of a paper this month, supporting your claims to the
Presidency, but by the advice of our friends have concluded to defer

doing so at present, and to direct all our immediate efforts to the formation of Clubs—mixing with the people in their primary assemblages and by discussion get the Cause hearted in the breasts of those who do not read newspapers. This our friends think is the most judicious policy to pursue in order to defeat the office bestowing power of John Tyler and the wily subtleties and crafty fetches of the "Old grimalkin of Kinderhook" [that is, Martin Van Buren].

I felt much pleasure and pride in reading the expression of your approbation and admiration of the principles and doctrines of my late personal and political friend "Old George Clinton[.]" They are the principles and doctrines which I contended for 25 years ago when Martin Van Buren and myself were both members of the Legislature of this State—and those are the principles and doctrines by which I am still guided. I am rejoiced to find that [Moses H.?] Grinnell and other leaders of the Whig party who are extensively engaged in Commerce are openly declaring their preference for you over [Henry] Clay in consequence of his high tariff notions. I admire that delicacy which prevents your doing any act that might be construed as Electioneering for yourself; it proves that you are incapable of those little arts, which bring forward little men.

John Tyler is not now believed to be as honest a politician as he was once thought to be: there is constantly seen a ballancing [*sic*] of self interest and principle in his mind which gains him nothing but the contemptuous hatred of the whigs, and the disparaging suspicions of the Democrats. It is supposed that he will withdraw his name as a Candidate, *in which event, arrangements have been made to secure the forces he wields to your support.* The only reproach made against you by your friends here, is that you are *too honest* for the times. A system of national Corruption introduced by van Buren and his adherents now pervades the whole country, and which enables a man to raise himself, to an exalted station, without ability, integrity[,] wisdom or virtue. The doctrines of this school are that politicians are to be benefitted by political prostitution—that Government can be carried only by means of Corruption, and that the State must be given a prey to politicians. These are the maxims that are in vogue throughout the ranks of van Buren's adherents and encouraged by van Buren himself. I am thankful however that although this national Corruption has become general that it is not universal, that the funeral knell has not yet been channted [*sic*] to the remains of departed political virtue and patriotism.

Hoping we may be soon able by exalting you to the first Office in the Nation to restore to it the lustre and reputation which it has lost of late I remain Dear Sir, truly yours to Command, Robt. R. Hunter.

P.S. I leave this afternoon for Sandy Hill [N.Y.].

ALS in ScU-SC, John C. Calhoun Papers. NOTE: This letter was mistakenly addressed to Calhoun at "Fort Hill, Charleston, South Carolina."

From H[AYM] M. SALOMON

New York [City,] 21[s]t Aug. [18]43

Dear Sir, I send you again to day [*sic*] several of our [news]papers but would call your attention particularly to the long and marked editorials of the two principal commercial and respectable large papers of this City ["but" *canceled and* "and" *interlined*] of the U[nited] States respecting the real prostrated and degraded condition of your enemy as well as the bane of the best interests of the country[.]

That Mr. [Mordecai M.] Noah'[s] article was one of the most insidious paragraphs that could have been worded by your most malignant enemy is not less certain than that the drift of the whole paragraph was the best that his abilities could devise to serve that bane of our political Happiness Mr. [Martin] V[an] B[uren].

The disinterested position which these papers hold regarding the eligibility of the different democratic candidates makes their articles sent to day a Convincing proof of my declarations of yesterday and which when I penned the note to you I had not the most remote idea would be Confirmed in this manner—one of the Editors Mr. [James Watson] Webb [of the New York, N.Y., *Courier and Enquirer*] having just arrived.

I hope some of your friends may be induced to have them Copied into your country papers of the Southern States while the Canvass is progressing[.] Respectfully &c, H.M. Salomon.

ALS in ScU-SC, John C. Calhoun Papers.

From BENJAMIN F. PORTER

Tuskaloosa, Ala., 24 August 1843

Sir, I take the liberty of disregarding the ceremonies which might properly attend an address, from one, of whom you have no personal

374

knowledge. The danger which threatens the institutions of the nation; and the fact that you are looked to as capable of averting it, will I trust excuse an ardent friend, if he invades a strict conventional rule.

A number of your old State rights friends, with whose sentiments I am familiar, are uniting in Alabama, to give a proper direction to political events. By a proper direction, I mean one, which shall place the government in the hands of those possessed of virtue and intelligence; and whose views of [the Consti]tution are those of the State rights party, proper. We [*one or two words mutilated*] you and your political views long enough to know, that [the] country, and the integrity of the constitution are safe with y[ou.] We therefore, in our efforts to promote you to the Presidency [*word mutilated*] conscious of patriotic exertions in the cause of the South and [its] institutions. With your name we are effecting much. Its inf[luence?] was seen in our last elections. Whenever there has been a [Demo]cratic gain, it has been chiefly due to this influence. Fi[ve if?] not six of the members to congress owe their election to it [*about two words mutilated*] it is certain that if the issue had been alone between Mr. [Martin] Van Buren and Mr. [Henry] Clay the result would have been otherwise. Sixty four new members have been elected to the Leg[isla]ture; and we feel confident we can procure your nomina[tion] by that body. At the same time we have much to conte[nd] with. It is not necessary to allude to influences, which op[e]rate to defeat such a movement. Under these circumstances can you not make it suit your convenience to visit Tuscaloosa early in the month of December? I know it will immediately occur to you, that it would be attributed to electioneering motives. But if the salvation of our country; if the promotion and success of honest principles require it, is it not a patriotic duty to disregard this suggestion? In fact the disinterestedness of your position; and that of your supporters, would repel such an idea; and your presence here would be looked upon by all honest men as one necessary to the interest of the Country, not of a mere politician. I urge this matter upon your consideration the more earnestly, as I know the state of things in Alabama; and can see clearly the effect of your visit.

I write, of course, confidentially, because prudence requires it: And would be pleased, if your position does not forbid, that I may be favored with your views. [*Mutilation*]self, having embarked my pen, my political, and [*one or two words mutilated*] exertions in your behalf, I confess myself deeply [inter]ested, personally, in your visit here. But I am still more [conc]erned when I reflect, that your cause

375

is the cause of the [coun]try, and those sacred principles on which its safety and [pro]sperity rest. With high consideration Your Ob[edien]t Serv[an]t, Benjamin F. Porter.

ALS in ScCleA. NOTE: *An AEU by Calhoun reads, "Mr. Porter[,] Ans[were]d 3d Sep[tembe]r."*

Receipt by John C. Calhoun, Pendleton, 8/25. "Received of Mrs. Placidia [Mayrant] Adams on order on George W. Egleston Esqu[ir]e for $5000, which amount, or whatever part of it I may receive, I promise to account to her as soon as informed by my factors in Charleston [Mathewes & Bonneau], to whom the order will be transmitted for collection. J.C. Calhoun." *ADS owned in 1959 by Holbrook Campbell, Springfield, Mass.*

From T. P. ATTICUS BIBB

Bedford[,] Trimble County Ky., Aug. 25th 1843

D[ea]r Sir, You will confer a favour by sending me the names of those papers ["*especially*" *interlined*] advocating your election to the Presidency.

I have always been a warm admirer of yours and should you be the nominee of the Convention or run any way I shall take the "*stump*" for you in Ky.

That you may long be spared to continue ["to" *canceled*] your devotion & zeal to the cause of constitutional liberty & true Democracy Is the wish of your humble Ser[van]t & Fellow Citizen, T.P. Atticus Bibb.

[P.S. Henry] Clay[']s death-knell is ringing through Ky.—Five democrats elected to Congress.

ALS in ScCleA.

From R[OBERT] B[ARNWELL] RHETT

[Beaufort, S.C.] Aug. 25th 1843

My Dear Sir, I have been keeping up a pretty steady fire in the [Charleston] Mercury, and I think the enemy seems to feel it. I have sent down, from three to five Editorials every week, excepting the week I was writing my reply to Old [Thomas] Ritchie[']s Q[uer]ys. [James K.] Polk[']s failure in Tennessee is fortunate for us. If Georgia in the approaching election will give us a good majority, we will gain a strong position. The Elections in Virginia[,] North Carolina and Tennessee ["will"(?) *canceled and* "have" *interlined*] shewn that Mr. [Martin] V[an] B[uren; "must"(?) *canceled and* "cannot" *interlined*] run[?] in those States. Unless the Yankees can make him President themselves, they need not bring him forward, and that I am satisfied they cannot do. The late elections only shew I believe what is the temper of the People ever[y] where as to Mr. V[an] B[uren]. But the Politicians will hold on to him—to the death.

I was glad to see your letter declining visiting the West. I am satisfied it will do you much good amongst, the most valuable and patriotic Portion of the People every where. Beneath the cringing servility and personal canvassing of ambitious and low-minded individuals, the Presidency, is fast sinking in dignity, and at length may be so degraded [as] to be unworthy ["like the Roman purple" *interlined*] of Nero[']s horse.

The information I receive from the North is very encouraging— but I do not put much faith in it. I have heard so much, and seen so little from them, that I scarcely heed it. Virginia is our battle ground. Carry her and we carry the South—and if we cannot carry her, I do not see how we can succeed. I think, if there ["was" *canceled and* "had been" *interlined*] energy and life amongst ["our" *canceled and* "your" *interlined*] friends, we would long since have secured the victory—but both in this State and out of it, the little energy they appeared to possess seemed to be employed to injure you. Even now, they appear cold and indifferent: but I will forbear speaking all I think. I hope we are doing better, altho' I fear too late.

My kindest regards to Mrs. [Floride Colhoun] Calhoun & Mrs. [Anna Maria Calhoun] Clemson and believe me Dear Sir Y[ou]rs truly, R.B. Rhett.

ALS in ScU-SC, John C. Calhoun Papers.

To R[OBERT M. T.] HUNTER, [Lloyds, Va.]

Fort Hill, 26th Aug[us]t 1843
My dear Sir, Absence from home for a few day's [*sic*] has delayed till now the acknowledgement of your letter of the 4th Inst[ant].

You will have seen, if you take the Mercury, that the subject of an appeal to the Majority of the States has taken a new turn. A member of our State Convention [in the *Mercury* of 8/16] has propounded two questions to Mr. [Thomas] Ritchie, which will throw the onus on him. If he should, in his answer, yield to us, it will open the way to a joint appeal; but if his answer should be the reverse, then it will be for us to take our course. In my opinion, it should be bold & decisive, so as to make up the issue at once.

I am happy to inform you, that our friends in Charleston are acting with sperit in reference to funds. On the subject of an editor, I am not prepared to advise in detail. I have full confidence in yourself, [Virgil] Maxcy, & Gen[era]l [Nathan] Towson, who is a fast friend & has an excellent judgement & & [*sic*] who may be safely consulted on all points. We want ability, experience, tack [*sic*; tact], & sound principles on all points, with known devotion to the cause. It would be better that ["he" *canceled and* "the Editor" *interlined*] should be South of Mason & Dixon line. It will be difficult, if not impossible, to get all these combined in any one. Some must be sacraficed; but my impression is, that one thing is indispensible, that he should be *of us*, and *known to be devoted to our cause & principles*. We must fight the battle on our own ground, & those who join us, must rally under our standard. We must neither go over nor *seem* to go over to others, but they to come to us. Of ["the" *interlined*] two referred to by you, this indispensible requisite would seem to refer to [Washington] Greenhow, but what, in that case, would be done with the Petersburgh Republican? Who would take charge of it? Or would ["it" *interlined*] be transferred to Washington, & the two merged? How would C[ornelius] C. Baldwin do ["for an editor" *interlined*]? He has undoubted talents, & his position is good. If the gentleman recommended by W. should be thought of, ["his ought" *canceled and* "his" *interlined*] name should not for the present appear connected with the establishment. He is able & experienced, but would be wanting in the indispensible. It would be regarded as a coalition, and place us in a false position. I regard W. as a friend, & you would do well to speak explicitly ["with" *canceled and* "to" *interlined*] him. To stand fast on our own ground is indispensible to victory, or if defeat should be our lot, to prevent it from ["being" *canceled and* "becoming" *interlined*] an overthrow. Standing honestly & fearlessly on our own ground, we must ever have strength & command respect. That, you & all our friends must ["take care" *canceled and* "be cautious" *interlined*] not to take any step, which, by consequence, would lead to our abandonment ["of" *interlined*], really or appearently, from any calculation of increased strength, or victory.

378

I am glad, that you have opened a correspondence with Mr. L. He is an able & experienced man, and can do much. I hope he will be active. I read the article to which you refer. It is well done & will do good, and does credit to ["the author" *canceled and* "his son" *interlined*]. ["I Will" *canceled.*] I would be happy to hear from your young friend George [H.] Pendleton [later Representative from Ohio]. Will you say so to him? He will make a valuable correspondent in the West.

The result of the election in Tennessee & Kentucky is calculated to make a deep impression. It proves, that both Clayism & Jackson Van Burenism are worn out, and that a new order of things is approaching. It is the time for us to assume openly & boldly our ground. We have nothing to fear, defeated, or victorious, if we be but true to ourselves & our cause. The Mercury will henceforward take a bold and active part. The unfortunate sickness & absence of its talented editor [John A. Stuart] weakened it much for a time, but arrangement has been made to carry it on with vigour. Truly, J.C. Calhoun.

ALS in ScCleA; variant PC in Jameson, ed., *Correspondence*, pp. 544–545. NOTE: Calhoun mistakenly addressed this letter to "R.T.M. Hunter." As to the absence from home mentioned by Calhoun in his first paragraph above, Maria Simkins Colhoun wrote on 8/21/1843 from Fort Hill to James Edward Colhoun: "Mr. Calhoun went up to the mountains for your sister [Floride Colhoun Calhoun] Saturday [8/19] & they will return tomorrow." ALS in ScU-SC, James Edward Colhoun Papers.

From R[OBERT] B[ARNWELL] RHETT

Beaufort [S.C.,] Aug. 26th 1843

My Dear Sir, My Brother Albert [Rhett] arrived here yesterday with a Letter from the Committee in Charleston urging me in the strongest and most flattering terms to go on immediately to Washington, to put matters in a proper state there, and to see the funds they are at last raising, applied in a proper and efficient manner. When we could fight efficiently, they w[oul]d do nothing. In consequence of the Clamour at the last Legislature, in the Senatorial Election, my friends dared neither shew my Letters, earnestly pressing the necessity of sending on funds to us, nor to act strenuously themselves. No others w[oul]d act; and thus the important period when to act would have been to conquer, passed away. I fear now, it is too late for success— but it is never too late to strive in a good cause, whilst hope remains.

I shall therefore leave here for Washington on next Monday. Believe me yours sincerely, R.B. Rhett.

ALS in ScCleA. Note: The "clamour" in the Senatorial election involved the choice of George McDuffie to succeed William Campbell Preston, who had resigned.

From R[omulus] M. Saunders,
[Representative from N.C.]

Raleigh, Aug[us]t 26, [18]43

My dear Sir, I should ["have" *interlined*] written to you earlier, giving the results of our [N.C.] election, but that I wished to know the facts, as to the matter to which your letter refers. I was satisfied before the election, the [Martin] Van Buren leaders, would stand quiet as to my election, but supposed most of them would vote for me or not vote at all. The day was a very bad one—the Whigs were active & well organized & the result was what might have been expected. I cannot accuse them of bad faith, because at points where I know this feeling did not prevail the vote was a thin one. [John R.J.] Daniel [Representative from N.C.] too[?] was saved by a very large vote in Person [County], which is a Van Buren County. I ["came" *canceled and then interlined*] to the conclusion that all we have to complain of, is the want of activity, and the same apathy prevailed in [David S.] Reid[']s district, who is a Van Buren man. [William H.] Haywood [Jr., Senator from N.C.,] & [Louis D.] Henry both voted for me but I doubt not are gratified at the result. They got up a meeting in my absence, adopted resolutions & called a State Convention. The resolutions are objectionable, but I think I shall be able to put that matter right. I do not fear but we shall secure a majority of the Delegates to the National Convention. Still we have much to contend against. Our loss of the Western district is much against us. [Charles] Fisher [former Representative from N.C.] I doubt not could have done better than [Francis Burton] Craig[e]. As it is, he is yet absent & tho' [Michael] Hoke is decided[?], He is not active. He will be the Candidate for Governor, if it will serve your cause[,] otherwise not. I regret to say, that I very much fear the result in this State. With Van [Buren], we are certainly beaten & with you, if *they* prove even lukewarm, the result must be against us. Our getting the [Raleigh] Standard is much in our favour. Old [Thomas] Loring [the editor], has acted the dog—he is amongst the few who refused to vote for me, because of my being for you—but as far as I hear, he only carried one or two others.

Dr. [Samuel A.] Andrews whose letter you enclosed is an intelligent man—a warm friend—but as I think has not exactly informed himself as to the true course of certain characters. It was not actively for us, but not against us. Tho' they may not have urged others to attend the polls, I hardly think with but few exceptions, they advised any to stay away.

We are now taking the necessary steps for organizing & I shall have it in my power to take a more direct part. Very truly Y[ou]rs, R.M. Saunders.

ALS in ScCleA.

To [ABEL P.] UPSHUR, [Secretary of State], "Confidential"

Fort Hill, 27 Aug[us]t 1843

My dear Sir, You do not, in my opinion, attach too much importance to the designs of Great Britain in Texas. That she is using all her diplomatick arts and influence to abolish slavery there, with the intention of ["effecting" *canceled and* "abolishing" *interlined*] it in the United States, there can no longer be a doubt. The proceedings of the abolition meeting recently held in London, & the answer of Lord Aberdeen to the Committee, which, they appointed to call on ["him" *interlined*] in reference to the subject, taken in connection, fully establishe the facts on both points.

That her object is power and monopoly, and abolition but the pretex[t], I hold to be not less clear. Her conduct affords the most conclusive proof. No nation, in ancient, or modern time, ever pursued dominion & commercial monopoly more ["perseveringly &" *interlined*] vehemently than she has. She unites in herself the ambition of Rome and the avarice of Carthrage [*sic*].

If she can carry out her schemes in Texas, & through them her designs ag[ai]nst the Southern States, it would prove the profoundest & most successful stroke of policy she ever made; and would go far towards giving her the exclusive control of the cotton trade, the greatest branch, by far, of modern Commerce. This she sees and is prepared to ["effect" *canceled and* "exert" *interlined*] every nerve to accomplish it.

381

The danger is great & menacing, involving in its consequences the safety of the Union, and the very existence of the South; and the question is, what is to be done? On that you desire my views. I shall give them freely & frankly.

In my opinion, the first step ought to be a demand on the British Government for explination [*sic*]. There are sufficient facts to warrant it, before the publick, & I presume you have others unknown to it. The demand ought to be accompanied by a forcible statement, explanatory of the danger of the measure to our peace & security, and its certain tendency to involve the two countries in the most deadly conflict. That ought to be followed by a suitable representation to the Texian Gover[n]ment, tracing its hostile and dangerous character, both to them & us, accompanied by the expression of the most friendly feelings & disposition; and a communication to our Minister in Mexico apprizing him of the facts & the course adopted, with instructions to baffle, as far as it may be possible, the attempts of the British Gover[n]ment to draw ["it" *canceled and* "Mexico" *interlined*] into her schemes. In addition, an able minister, ["perfectly" *canceled and* "completely" *interlined*] identified with the South, and taken from South of the Potomack ou[gh]t to be sent to France, and be instructed to make suitable representations, explanatory of the ambitious & monopolizing sperit of Great Britain in this movement on Texas, and to show how far it would go to consummate her schemes of universal dominion & monopoly, should she succeed in her design. The like representation should be made to the Prussian Gover[n]ment, through our Minister at Berlin on the subject. The part of Germany under the control & influence of Prussia begins to be jealous of Great Britain, on the subject of commerce.

All these papers should be drawn up with the utmost care, & so as to be calculated to make a deep a deep [*sic*] impression on the publick mind generally, & to rouse the South, should they be called for at the next session, as they ought, if Great Britain should not explicitly disavow. In that event, the Message ["out" *canceled and* "ought" *interlined*] to take due notice of the subject.

In the mean time, I am of the impression, with you, that the attention of the people of the South ought to be turned to the subject, but not through the papers of this State. I have taken so prominent a stand on all subjects connected with abolition, that any movement, at this time, in this State would be ["regarding" *changed to* "regarded"] as intended for electioneering, & would do more harm, than good. I am decidedly of the opinion, that it ought to commence in Virginia, & through the Columns of the [Richmond] Enquirer, and that the opening & leading article, ["ought to" *canceled and* "should" *interlined*] be from your Department & pen. No one else, has the whole subject so fully before him, or can do it as full justice. You can have it communicated by some friend. They can be copied & followed up in the Southern papers.

I am of the impression, that the question of annexation ought not to be agitated till discussion has prepared the publick mind to realize the danger; but assurance ought to be given to the Texian Gover[n]ment of the hearty cooperation of the Executive towards effecting it, when the proper time arrives.

Connected with this subject, Cuba deserves attention. Great Britain is at work there, as well as in Texas; and both are equally important to our safety. Much can be done in France in reference to ["both" *canceled and* "each" *interlined*]. Would it not be well for our Gov[ernmen]t, & that of France to enter into a Gu[ar]anty of its possession to Spain, ag[ai]nst the interference of any other power? The overthrow ["of" *and an illegible word canceled and* "of" *interlined*] the British influence there & the ["establish" *canceled and* "establishment" *interlined*] of the French, would seem to be favourable to an arrangement of the kind. I throw it out for reflection. Would it not also be well, if the West should push the Oregon question, to unite with it the an[n]exation of Texas, in the shape of an ame[nd]ment ["of the bills" *canceled*], and, make them go hand in hand? With great respect yours truly, J.C. Calhoun.

ALS in DNA, RG 59 (Records of the Department of State), Miscellaneous Letters of the Department of State, 1789–1906 (M-179:102, frames 527–528); LS (retained copy in the hand of Thomas G. Clemson) in CtY, Beinecke Library, Western Americana Collection; PC in St. George L. Sioussat, "John Caldwell Calhoun," in *The American Secretaries of State and their Diplomacy*, edited by Samuel F. Bemis, 5:141–144.

From Stephen H. Branch

New York City, Aug: 28th, 1843

Dear Sir: As you will probably spend the next winter at Fort Hill, do you not want a Teacher of youth in your family, from October to May ensuing? or, if not, do you not know of some friend near you that desires one? I would strive to please you. I can learn a person to write a fair letter in twenty lessons, if he never saw a pen. Little children of six, and those of twenty, forty, and even sixty years of age,

I have taught with great success. In a short time I could, if disposed, effect a great change in your neighborhood in this department; but I would prefer confining my labors to your family, and to higher branches, though I would do any thing that you might desire. I teach systematically, thoroughly, and profoundly, imparting to my pupils the great foundation principles of human learning. Your society would be considered an ample equivalent for my services. You are advancing rapidly in age, and before God takes you from us, I am very anxious to commune with your lofty and unsullied genius, and to receive your invaluable counsels, to be consecrated, in my feeble way, to the glory of our country. I imagine myself unlike a portion of mankind, at least, in one regard: I appreciate the worth of the living: they, the dead. In my opinion, that will be a solemn hour for the American people when you are summoned to another existence. There will be a void that never, never can be filled. Who, then, would cast himself into the breach to save our glorious institutions? Who, then, would have the boldness, the independence, and the courage to adhere to right, amidst the almost universal frowns of his deceived countrymen? aye, amidst the gleaming bayonets, and thundering artillery of the foe? Who, then, would sacrifice the peace and happiness of his family, the warmest friendships, and the highest office beneath the sun, for the cause of truth and justice? What intellectual giant would then, solitary and alone, stand up proudly erect in the Senate assembly, and combat the legionary enemies of public liberty? aye, and vanquish them? Your philippics against the tyrants are worthy of the best days of Cicero and Demosthenes. The best evidence of their power is the signal victory you obtained in effecting *such* a compromise against *such* odds, and the final overthrow of those false systems that have seriously threatened to subvert the constitution itself—a victory unparalleled in political warfare, and deeply humiliating to the advocates of power and consolidation. Who, then, I say, would be the proud champion of twenty millions of freemen, contending manfully and fearlessly for the rights of these mighty, heaving, and unsophisticated masses, against the dangerous and ruinous encroachments of the cunning, designing, and interested few? There's not the man, living or dead, qualified for this important and momentous agency. [George] Washington had the virtue, but not the eloquence, abilities, or genius for the task. [Thomas] Jefferson would be disqualified, inasmuch as he was not an orator; but he now slumbers at Monticello, and can only speak in silence to his countrymen, whom he loved and served so well, through the enduring monuments of wisdom he left behind. But the combined wisdom of our Fathers, great as it is, could not resist the usurpations of the monied classes of this country, in the absence of the intrepid, energetic, and patriotic Calhoun; whose whole life is as pure and beautiful as a brilliant moonbeam, destined, ages hence, to shine as brightly and gloriously as the meridian sun, spreading its genial rays and healthful influence over the fertile and boundless fields of nature, of our country, and mankind. I trust that you will excuse me for this long and, I fear, tedious digression, in thus but briefly and imperfectly anticipating the impartial historian of this age.

In conclusion, I do hope that some arrangement may be made that will promote our mutual welfare. I would, of course, defray my traveling expenses; and produce unquestionable testimonials through any one in this city to whom you may refer. Please answer this letter on its reception, so that, if you conclude not to accept my proposition, I can arrange my affairs accordingly. I remain, With great respect, Your obedient servant, Stephen H. Branch.

ALS in ScCleA.

From V[IRGIL] MAXCY

Saratoga Springs [N.Y.,] 29 Aug. 1843

My Dear Sir, On my way here at New York [City], I called on the Harpers and I discovered, that what I suspected before was true— that what appeared bad conduct in them was in a great measure owing to [Joseph A.] Scoville. The moment I saw the first part of the proof sheets before the break with him, I wrote to him ["before you had said any thing on the subject" *interlined*] that I objected to have "Calhoun's Speeches" at the top of every page and begged him to get the Harpers to change it to the title of each speech. This the Harpers told me that he entirely neglected to do; of course when I afterwards wrote to him, it was too late to be corrected. They have promised however, when any more copies are struck off this shall be omitted— tho the name of each Speech cannot be put at the top of the Stereotype plates. The[y] tell me also that the Title & the advertisement, tho not written by him were submitted to him and received his approbation—and as the manuscripts were left with him & his name was used in making the contract, they supposed of course it was right to take his directions. This of course all took place before they knew that he had given up the contract—for as neither [Robert M.T.]

385

Hunter [n]or myself thought of informing them of it, he still affected to have the control. Perhaps they may do injustice to Scoville & throw more blame on him than he deserves, but such is their defence. I have induced them however to promise that they will print a leaf having the title page & Advertisement prepared by me on it, & cut out the present title & Advertisement from the unsold copies & put this new one in its place. But they say it will be impracticable now to put notes of reference ["at t" *canceled*] to the speeches at the bottom of the pages of the Biography. The Biography however they promise to have prefixed to all the copies hereafter sold. They told me that this had been done in the Copies sent to Col. [Franklin H.] Elmore for you ["to hi"(?) *canceled*]. They sent them to him on my suggestion, before you sent the address of your factors.

The day I stayed in New York [City] I was introduced to a gentleman named J. Fr[anci]s Hutton as a very warm friend of yours, who informed me that your friends in that city were at last organizing ["in earnest" *interlined*] & preparing to insist on the District System. I pointed out to him in as strong a manner as I could the injustice & impropriety of any other & urged them to go forward with their organization & try to get up the spirits of your friends in the different Congressional Districts to a sufficient point of zeal, to send a suond [*sic*] set of District delegates, ["to the National Convention" *interlined*] tho the Syracuse convention [of N.Y. State Democrats] which is to meet on the 5th Sept[embe]r should recommend the general ticket system. He thinks they can do it.

30th Aug[us]t
Having read yesterday in the Albany Argus a very artfully drawn up Article on the subject of State representation in the National Convention, copied from [Amos] Kendall's Expositor, and originally written I have no doubt for the purpose of supplying plausible arguments on the subject to the members of the Syracuse Convention, which meets the [*one word canceled and* "5th September" *interlined*] I sat down immediately—not to answer this piece ["directly" *interlined*] but to prepare another on the other side of the question & have it printed in a pamphlet or handbill for distribution among the members of the Syracuse Convention & else where & especially the Massachusetts Convention, which will meet on the 13th. Just after I had sat sat [*sic*] down to the work, (for Mrs. Maxcy is so much better, my mind was sufficiently at ease to undertake this, tho' it had been otherwise for a long time,) a gentleman sent up his name ["with" *canceled*] to my parlor with a request, that I would allow him to see me. It was the Mr. Hutton above-mentioned, who had come all the way from New

York [City] to talk with me about their organization and to tell me, that since I had seen him there had been a meeting of your principal friends in New York, who had determined to call a meeting in the Park of your friends on Monday next [9/4] partly with a view to instruct their delegates at the Syracuse Convention to vote for the District System &c—to pass resolutions on the subject of the National Convention & to nominate you for President.

I informed him ["of the" *and a partial word canceled*] how I was occupied, when he sent up to me. He said it was the very thing they wanted to furnish arguments to the Speakers & electioneerers on your side, and said immediately, if you will send down the manuscript to me I will have it put to press by the Harpers immediately and have it ready to send to the Syracuse convention and distribute all over the State. [*One or two words canceled.*] I accordingly as soon as it ["was" *canceled and* "is" *interlined*] half finished ["shall" *interlined*] send off the sheets to him (he returned to New York [City] after spending a day with me,) & the next day the rest of them. So that if he shall [*one word interlined and then canceled*] make arrangements as he promised he would for the immediate printing, it was [*sic*] there in time to have it done & sent to Syracuse, where the convention will assemble on the 5th Sept.

4th Sept.

All the manuscript had not been sent off before I received a letter from Mr. Hutton, begging me to prepare some resolutions for the meeting in the park. As soon as I had despatched the the [*sic*] last of the manuscript, which will make a pamphlet about as large as [Robert Barnwell] Rhett[']s appeal (the ideas of which I have freely made use of) I set about the Resolutions. I adopted for their basis the Maryland Resolutions & modified & added to them to suit the occasion & sent them off by mail day before yesterday. Whether they will be adopted by their committee without much change I can't say. If they do, they will adopt the Carolina views in toto. The meeting in the Park takes place to night. And day after tomorrow I shall get their proceedings which I shall send to you, tho' you will probably get them sooner direct from New York [City]. I expect at the same time some of the pamphlets, if they have been printed according to promise, and I will send you a copy.

I received some days ago a long letter from Col. Elmore in answer to mine on pecuniary matters & the [Washington] Spectator—and am rejoiced to say that instead of offending by its plainness & frankness ["as I feared my letter" *interlined and* "it" *canceled*] has roused up the committee to their duty. $5000 had been subscribed, conditioned however that $5000 should be obtained the means for which had been adopted. They authorize a tri-weekly Edition of the paper immediately & say that in a ["few" *canceled and* "two" *interlined*] weeks it will be known whether the $10,000 can be made up. I have written to Hunter, who with myself will be on the lookout for a suitable Editor. [Shadrach] Penn I don't like. Some of his principles I fear are not sound—too unsettled on Banking & Protection & moreover not a gentleman in the high sense we ought to have, to whom, as he must be the substitute for a central committee, all of us can write with perfect confidence &c. [Edmund T.] Bridge seems to me the best we can hear of, but he is useful where he is. We will be busy in our enquiries & Hunter & myself will decide the best we can.

Things I think, are taking a favorable turn in New England.

The mail is closing. Faithfully yours, V. Maxcy.

[P.S.] I am trying to get something done at Syracuse for taking the opinions of the several States on the District System.

ALS and ms. copy in ScCleA. NOTE: The pamphlet which Maxcy wrote to influence the N.Y. State Democratic Convention is apparently a rare 12-page item which was printed with the title *Democratic National Convention*, and with no publisher, date, or author indicated.

From J[OSEPH] A. SCOVILLE

Rotterdam, 29 Aug. 1843

My Dear Sir, Having an opportunity to send letters home via England, I cannot resist the temptation of dropping you a line. Since the date of my last letter to you, I have not heard a word about Am[erica]n politics.

I am really anxious to be in harness once more at home, and hope I shall make money enough here that I may be so, before six months are passed.

If there is any thing I desire in this world it is to see you President of the United States, and I believe you will be. I only regret that I am not able to be at home to add my mite towards your elevation.

I have got some curio[u]s documents to send you, when I get a chance. I have seen one on Government in manuscript which I should like much to be able to get hold of to send to you. I am sure you would be astonished when you see it. I will write you more about it in the course of a few weeks.

Please remember me to Mr. [Thomas G.] Clemson and Believe me, Yours &c, J.A. Scoville.

ALS in ScCleA.

From EDWARD EVANS

Philadelphia, August 30 [18]43
Respected & Learned Sir, Perceiving by "Niles['] Register" "1833—In the Number of Jan. 26," that on the 17th Jan., you offered *Resolutions*, the purport of which was that the States still possessed their Sovereignty and ["that" *interlined*] you delivered your opinions at that time upon it—I would therefore respectfully ask you if convenient, and if published in Pamphlet form to favour me with a copy, my reasons for wishing are, that I am now hearing a course of Lectures delivered on [the] Constitution of [the] U[nited] States and it seems to be the most interesting part. I would like therefore to obtain as much information as possible; on both sides and [as] I have the speeches of Mr. [Daniel] Webster & [John M.] Clayton on the *Federal* side I wish to see the *Democratic side* which I like the better.

Hoping you will pardon your young admiring friend for the liberty he has taken[,] I remain very truly &c, Edward Evans, Phila[delphia] P.O.

ALS in ScCleA. NOTE: The resolutions referred to can be found in *The Papers of John C. Calhoun*, 12:25–26.

From EDWARD J. BLACK, [Representative from Ga.]

Barnwell D[istric]t, S. Carolina, Sept[embe]r 1st 1843
My dear Sir, I would have written to you frequently before this—but I knew that you must be almost overwhelmed with correspondents of all sorts and descriptions. Do not believe, however, that my silence is indicative of forgetfulness of yourself individually, or of your political interests. Far otherwise. After I returned from Washington I exerted myself to get as many of our friends from lower Georgia into the [State] Convention as possible. I went, as a member, myself, and had the satisfaction to see our labours crowned with your nomi-

nation. The old cry of the triangular influence of [Walter T.] Colquitt, [Mark A.] Cooper [Senator and former Representative from Ga., respectively], & myself was raised by a few [Martin] Van B[uren] men with the hope of defeating you before that body. Judge Kennan [*sic*; Owen H. Kenan], Mr. [G.R.?] Hunter, of Crawford Co[unty] and a few other leading men, but most especially Col. [Howell] Cobb, of Clarke [County], one of our members elect to Congress made every effort to defeat you. For this opposition Cobb is mainly responsible, as he sustained and directed it. We laboured under some disadvantages in the Convention—neither Colquitt or Cooper were members. Cooper was not present, and was a prominent Candidate of a nomination for Gov[erno]r—and Colquitt did not arrive in Milledgeville until towards the last of our session. But notwithstanding these difficulties we turned out and measured our strength with these old Van B[uren] advocates—and they soon found that your name, even if it had been turned loose in the convention without a rider, would have run through, and distanced every Competitor. I assure you all that we had to do was to fix things a little, and then to hold in our young men, who, if let alone, would have been indiscreet in there [*sic*] ardour for you. After the nomination was made we succeeded, I think, in allaying the feelings of the great mass of our disappointed friends; and also succeeded in having the Geo[rgia] Delegates to the Baltimore Convention specifically *instructed* as to their votes, and that too without an *alternative*, that is, to vote for you, and for no one else. Now if Mr. Cobb, who is a delegate, will not obey those instructions he must resign, and his place will be filled by the remainder of the Delegation. I am very glad to see the Democracy succeeding in their elections, and I am also *glad to see that they are defeated in Tennessee.* Of course I do not speak thus publicly, but where I may say it with safety I do say it. It is well in my opinion that Democracy is temporarily defeated, just at this time, in Tennessee. It is to be hoped that it will operate as a sort of quieting dose to [Francis P.] Blair, and [Thomas] Ritchie. It will also serve to shew to the American people that there are other spokes in the Democratic wheel besides the "*old Hero.*" If you remember I got a letter from Mr. [John?] Boston, of Savannah, asking me to send the [Washington] Globe to him *if it was not unfriendly to you.* I sent the letter to Blair & Rives[?]—and they replied, in answer to Boston, at some length, and with much warmth, protesting their absolute neutrality until after a nomination. And privately to me they made the same professions, and Blair declared to me that he would not be guilty of forgetting *your* friends in the House who had helped him to the printing of the 26th Congress, in which I bore some part. But that as he was the central organ of the whole party he would support only the nominee of the Convention. How widely they have departed from their written promise to Boston, and their verbal promise to me. If it would result in no injury to our friends I would procure their letter to Mr. Boston, and publish it with an accompanying explanatory article. Their letter is very full and explicit, and indulges in some feeling because they were suspected of being averse to your election. How strangely their present position would contrast with that letter. I look forward with some satisfaction to the casting of my vote next winter for Printer, and I hope we shall have some friends in the House who will know how to *reward merit.*

Will we have many aspirants for the Speakership? It is a most powerful and important office, and I, for one, am not disposed to *give it away.* Without meaning to say that a man would be justifiable to buy support with the patronage of office, I am yet quite sure that whenever I have it in my power I shall so cast my vote, or patronage, if I have it, as to sustain those who sustain the principles upon which alone we must expect to succeed.

I read your letter [of 7/28/1843] to [Joseph] Gales & [William W.] Seaton, and it is just such a letter as you should have written; ["and" canceled] it has and ["will" *interlined*] increase the confidence of thousands in you. Your friends in Georgia regard it with the utmost satisfaction. We are in great hope of beating Geo[rge W.] Crawford in Georgia, and if we can succeed in keeping the Democracy together I think there can be no doubt of his signal defeat.

My dear Sir; I shall be at Washington this winter, and if I can serve you there in any way I hope you will not hesitate to call on me for my services. I propose to take some part in the action of the House and party during our session, and would not only be happy to render you any aid in my power, but to receive such suggestions as to our course and movements as your ability and experience entitle and enable you to give. I do not mean to impose any [*partial word canceled*] unnecessary additional burden of correspondence on you, but to signify my desire to sustain my portion of the struggle that is before us.

My family are in this District, spending their summer at a healthy spot, where we have the benefit of a school, and where I am occasionally with them. I am, my dear Sir, with great Respect, Your's [*sic*] very Truly, Edward J. Black.

ALS in ScCleA; variant PC in Jameson, ed., *Correspondence,* pp. 868–871. NOTE: George W. Crawford was the successful Whig candidate in the 1843 Ga. gubernatorial election.

From R[OBERT] M. T. HUNTER

[Lloyds, Va.,] Sept[embe]r 1st 1843

My dear Sir, I have not written to you for three or four mails because I heard through another correspondent that you were at Dahlonega and because too I had little news to communicate. Since that time however events begin to move more rapidly. The Charleston Committee promise funds and an editor is now the great want. There is a great difficulty in procuring an editor of sufficient general reputation to satisfy our friends at a distance. [Franklin H.] Elmore suggests [John A.] Stuart now at Saratoga where Mr. [Virgil] Maxcy is also for the present. I have written to Maxcy to make the proposition to Stuart. Should he fail I think [Edmund T.] Bridge is the next best chance[?]. I know nothing of his talents as a writer. But he is a first rate politician and I like his character—discreet[,] prompt & faithful. As I suggested to you before[,] the only objection to him with me is that he is so very useful in his present position. You know his office. Never has any man worked better. Next to him of the availables I like [Washington] Greenhow. He is doing well where he is, his paper is extending its circulation, and his decision[?] & boldness annoy [Thomas] Ritchie excessively. I think that with a writer[']s training in Washington under our friends he would become a first rate editor. But I do not like to propose to any one not generally known unless I know that he would be satisfactory. I should take the responsibility of proposing to Bridge if I thought he could be spared from his present place. Indeed if our N[ew] England friends had not expressed some fear as to his being taken away I should have endeavored to obtain him as an editor. His general knowledge of New England and his great influence with [Postmaster General Charles A.] Wickliffe would enable him to do much that he now does even if he were transferred to Washington.

Some of our Western friends have been writing to me for the Biography [of yourself], and desire to know why none are to be purchased in the West. The Harpers have managed this publication wretchedly and I have not thought it worth while to write to them about ["it" *interlined*]. I mentioned the matter however to Maxcy who was about to pass through N.Y.

I fear that [Martin] V[an] B[uren] is gathering strength in Pa. and that [James] Buchanan[']s measures are not strong enough to prevent him from acquiring the most[?] of his (B[uchanan]'s) friends. I am also of opinion that V[an] B[uren] cannot carry the State of Pa. even if nominated. The more I think of the matter the more impolitic does the renomination of V[an] B[uren] seem to me. If there be no recent disaffection to [Henry] Clay amongst the Northern & Eastern ["friends" *canceled and* "whigs" *interlined*] he will be not unlikely to beat V[an] B[uren].

Virginia may perhaps be carried for V[an] B[uren] and I incline to think that the majority of the party in this State prefer him but there is no doubt but that with your name the ticket would be vastly stronger before the people. There are changes I understand in our favor in the Albemarle district and in [William] Smith[']s old district. Of the district in which I live a large majority prefer you. It is only in Western Virginia that we are weak, that is to say we are weak precisely where Ritchie is strongest.

I have not heard a word from Smith in relation to your letter [on the R.I. controversy]. We do not live near each other so that I cannot see him. But I suppose he will not publish without letting me know something about it before hand. I suspect that Vans [*sic*; Van Buren's] answers are cloathed [*sic*] in generalities. Nothing decisive I imagine or I should have heard from him before this.

[Thomas W.] Gilmer [Representative from Va.] is with us. He is so understood to be in his district and I rather imagine that he is doing what he can without risk to himself.

Much depends upon the tone as well as the course of the South. I believe myself that we are more weakened by the secret idea that a slaveholder cannot be President than almost anything else. I have not heard anyone admit it to be sure. No northern ["man" *canceled and* "democrat" *interlined*] would express such a sentiment openly; no southern man would make the dastardly impression that he was willing to submit to all the consequences of such a state of public sentiment. Still I feel that the idea exists and that the Free States are quietly gaining all the moral and political strength which such an idea gives them, whilst the South looks on in apathy. We must arouse our Southern friends to that state of feeling which would reject a position in any party as *inferiors*. And yet how to do it I know not. Greenhow has spirit and talent, but he has not experience and might be deficient in tact if he were to attempt to execute it. We did wrong when we did not strike vigorously at the Rochester and Nantucket papers which first promulgated the notion. When I say we I do not mean to include you for I remember that with your usual sagacity[,] you saw the under current ["in public sentiment" *interlined*] of which their paragraphs were indicative. I throw out these suggestions to have your advice. Shall we ["attempt to" *interlined*] strike this c[h]ord in the Southern heart? Shall we handle the consequences of this anti slavery agitation upon our moral and political position? I begin to think it is time. Yours faithfully, R.M.T. Hunter.

ALS in ScCleA.

J. Fr[anci]s Hutton, New York [City], to R[obert] M.T. Hunter, Lloyds, Va., 9/1. Calhoun's friends in New York City have been busy. The [Martin] Van Burenites have spread a false report that Calhoun's friends are [John] Tyler men and are willing to support [Henry] Clay. According to an opposition newspaper, Calhoun's friends have carried, in the party primary assemblies, six wards out of seventeen and have elected four out of thirteen city delegates to the State convention. Hutton does not despair of starting a Calhoun newspaper soon. He met Virgil Maxcy, who is advised of the plans of Calhoun's friends and will speak to a meeting of Calhoun men of all wards. If the State convention disregards the will of the rank and file and elects a slate of delegates to the national convention under the unit rule, rather than providing for election by Congressional districts, Hutton suggests that Virginia should delay selection of delegates as late as possible. ALS in ScCleA.

From ROB[ER]T L. DORR

Dansville [N.Y.,] Sept. 2d [18]43

My Dear Sir: You know our State [Democratic] convention assembles at Sarycuse [*sic*] on the 5th Inst[ant]. You have probably seen by the papers that the Democratic portion of the party have prevailed in the appointment of delegates from the City of N[ew] York. In most other Counties it will be found that the Albany Regency have outmanaged the people, except perhaps from such Counties as Herkimer, Montgomery, Delaware, whose delegates will undoubtedly go for the broad Democratic doctrines advocated by South Carolina but for what candidate they will cast their votes at the National Convention is uncertain; their conversion to the South Carolina plan however, should such prove to be the case[,] may be taken as something of an indication of their *real* preference—tho' party drilling may induce them to do otherwise.

I have to say that I have used all reasonable exertions to become a delegate to the State Convention. I have written to & seen all the principal men of the County [of Livingston], without indicating to them my preference in the least, but the central power at Albany have had their *eyes and paws* upon me ever since I located here & knowing my preference, have adroitly outmanaged me. The warning too that not long ago issued from St. Lawrence County against the Young *Democracy* & in favor of the *discreet old lame ducks* of the party as delegates, was but a premonitory symptom, of the prominent features that *must & should* form the State Convention. I predict a considerable of a flare up at the convention, & know there would have been a worse one had I been there, & wait with much anxiety for the result. If they appoint the delegates at Sarycuse, I shall cause a meeting to be called in this District & appoint another delegate, will get the app[ointme]nt myself if I can, & will go to the National Convention. May God bless you. Much Respect, Robt. L. Dorr.

ALS in ScCleA.

From DUFF GREEN

London, 2nd Sept. 1843

Dear Sir, I have seen Mr. Goulbourn [*sic*; Henry Goulburn] the present Chancellor of the Exchequer and Lord Palmerston since I last wrote to you, and conversed with them both on the subject of American affairs, especially on the subject of the tariff, the Oregon & Texas questions. I have seen other influential men of the whig party who are prepared to rally against ministers on the question of slave grown produce, and especially on their policy of interfering with the question of slavery in foreign states.

I enclose you the Anti Slavery Reporter, the organ [of] the Anti slavery Committee and would call your attention to the sketches of Lord Brougham & Lord Aberdeen on the subject of Texas & the speeches of ["Lord" *canceled*] Sir Rob[er]t Peel on Lord Brougham[']s slavery suppression bill as well as to the comment of the Editor, and the Speech of Mr. [John] Bright. The latter is a quaker and his speech shows that a reaction has begun here. The Anti slavery party are losing their influence and if our Gov[ernmen]t can be induced to take strong ground on the question of [*one word or part of a word canceled*] Texas, the free trade [*one word canceled*] party here will rally for us against the fanatics and the whigs will make the refusal of ministers to meet the proposition of our Government a matter of serious assault.

I was most strongly advised to bring out an extract from your letter and also from a letter of Mr. [Abel P.] Upshur, that the people of England might know that you and he were in favor of an adjustment by treaty. It is believed that the effect will be to induce ministers to make the treaty or to so strengthen the popular sentiment ag[ains]t them as to bring in the whigs.

I am satisfied that it will do service here and in the United States. It will show that if all the questions between us be not satisfactorily adjusted the fault is not with us.

I hope that you will not disapprove of what I have done. I did it for the best and I am sure it will result in good.

I am progressing with my arrangements and hope to conclude them advantageously. I may get home in October, if not in Nov[embe]r.

[James Gordon] Bennett of the New York Herald is here. I have induced him to purchase all the Anti slavery documents, and have introduced him to influential parties here who have convinced him that the Anti slavery movement has nearly run its course, and he goes home prepared to take strong ground with the South on the Tariff and on Abolition. His paper [the New York, N.Y., Herald] will cooperate with us most efficiently and your friends may command it to the fullest extent.

I have seen your letter to the Ed[itors] of the [Washington, D.C., Daily National] Intelligencer and as you say you are under obligation to them. Your friend, Duff Green.

ALS in ScCleA; PC in Jameson, ed., Correspondence, pp. 871–872. NOTE: The extract from Calhoun's letter which Green "was most strongly advised to bring out" was from Calhoun's letter to Green of 6/7/1843. It appeared in the London Times on 9/1/1843. In a letter of 8/29/1843 to the President [John Tyler], Green related at length his efforts to secure an interview with the Prime Minister, Sir Robert Peel, in order to show him two letters [written to Green from John C. Calhoun] and Abel P. Upshur discussing matters "that will have an important bearing on the relations between" the U.S. and Great Britain. He did not see Peel, who had left London, but had an interview with [Henry] Goulburn, the Chancellor of the Exchequer, to whom he showed the letters from Calhoun and Upshur "in which they both express themselves favorable to an arrangement of the tariffs of the two countries by treaty, and explained to him the relation which the present parties in the United States bear to the tariff . . . ." Green further recounted to Tyler his plan to have extracts from the letters published in the London Times. FC or draft, Green to [Tyler], in NcU, Duff Green Papers (published microfilm, reel 5, frames 53–64). Green published extracts from Calhoun's and Upshur's letters in the London Times of 9/1 and the London Examiner of 9/23. Calhoun's reaction to this use of his letter has not been found. Upshur wrote to Green on 9/25/1843: "I have not seen the extract from my letter, which you have published & therefore cannot say whether I approve the publication or not. It is better however, not to bring me in that manner, before the public." ALS in NcU, Duff Green Papers (published microfilm, reel 5, frames 86–89).

NOTICE of a Calhoun Meeting, New York City

[Published September 2, 1843]
Democrats! Rally to the Park, all those in favor of *the Cause*—"Free Trade, Low Duties, No Debt, Separation from Banks, Economy, Retrenchment, and Strict Adherence to the Constitution"—*the man,* JOHN C. CALHOUN, as the Democratic Candidate for the Presidency of the United States, 1844—*the Country*—its System of Government—its Representative Institutions—the inalienable right of the people of each Congressional District to elect by their direct suffrages the delegate who shall represent them in the National Convention; also, the vote per capita, and that each vote shall be counted for the candidate to whom it is given, the same being consistent with the great Democratic principle that the Representative shall speak the voice and carry out the will of those he represents.

Friends of the Cause, the Man, and the Country: meet in the Park on MONDAY EVENING, September 4th, at half past 5 o'clock, rain or shine.

"Victory in such a cause will be great and glorious; much will it redound to the honor of those by whom it will have been won, and long will it perpetuate the liberty and prosperity of the country.["]
BY SPECIAL COMMITTEE. [Signed:] Dr. F.T. Ferris, James B. Scott, John Windt, Thos. D. Young, Isaac Hecker, James L. Stratton, James H. Brady, Henry S. Field, Dr. Nelson Stell, John Carnes, Clinton Roosevelt, Stephen Haley, J.F. Dieterich, Col. Joseph Le Count, C.S. Bogardus, John R. Brady, Ab[raha]m B. Purdy, Peter Smith, Francis Mallory, Thomas S. Gibbs, Ab[raha]m Moore, Philip H. Fink, H[iram] McCollum, Robert Walker, Wm. Mackie, Florence McArthy, J.J. Boyd, H.C. Martin, Edward Vincent, Major J.W. Forbes, Wm. Miles, Dr. Stephen Hasbrouck, Edmund S. Derry, James Wilson, R.B. Cuthbert, S.B. Andrews, Lathrop J. Eddy, J.W. Moore, John Heaney, A.D. Russell, George R. Ives, Joseph Hufty, George G. Glazier, R.B. Conno[l]ly, Dennis Mullen, S.R. Macnevin, Alex[ander] Lowry, David Egan, George Dixey, John B. Schmelzel, Edward Smith, E.J. Webb, L.B. Tompkins, John Commerford, Peter J. Sharpe, Jr., Warren Rowell, S.L. Jones, Henry P. Barber, Robert J. Reed, Eccles Gillender,

Timothy Daley, Charles A. Clinton, J.[L.]H. McCracken, G[eorge] E. Baldwin, J.S. Schultz, Dr. A[braham] D. Wilson, Edward Swords, Dr. M[iddleton] Goldsmith, John Mullen, Wm. F. Ladd, Wm. Francis, B.S. Hart, Cornelius Hoyt, John Hecker, E[manuel] B. Hart, J. F[rancis] Hutton, F.W. Guiteau, Robert Townsend, James Huey, A. Loubat, W.J. Bayard, Ab[raha]m T. Hilyer, J.B. Marsh, Daniel D. Smith, Mark Cohen, Edmund M. Young, F[itzwilliam] Byrdsall, S.P. Goldson, Hiram Niles, Samuel Earl, Edward Timpson, Robert Berney, Stephen J. Field, Joseph Cornell, George Harrall, John S. Gilbert, John Minos.

PC in the New York, N.Y., *Evening Post*, September 2, 1843, p. 2.

From F[RANKLIN] H. ELMORE

Charleston, 4 Sep[tember] 1843

My Dear Sir, I was prevented leaving the City (as I informed you you [sic] I would in my last) by an attack of the prevailing influenza. I have therefore had some more time to push our measures here. The opportunity has not been lost. Since I wrote we have succeeded in inducing Mr. [Robert Barnwell] Rhett to go to Washington with funds in hand & at his draft to put the Spectator into a daily if thought advisable & also, to make a movement for a paper in New York [City]. The Journal of Commerce has been of late doing us some kind service, but we must have a good[,] decided & able paper there if we can. Rhett left us last Wednesday. He was to stop a day or two in Virginia to see Mr. [James A.] Seddon [later a Representative from Va., Robert G.] Scott & other friends & members of the Central Committee—also to have an interview with [Thomas] Ritchie &c. He will probably be by this time in Washington. I had written to induce Gen[era]l [Romulus M.] Saunders, [Robert M.T.] Hunter, Mr. [Virgil] Maxcy, Mr. Broadhead [sic; Daniel D. Brodhead] & such others as they might think advisable to summon, to meet at Washington & make all proper arrangements for a systematic & regular plan of operations. Rhett had also written to Hunter. His plan adopted upon conference with our Committee of 15, is to first put the Spectator going & if possible to get Hunter to take it, he promising to remain & with or without Hunter, aiding to edit it. He also will go to N[ew] York [City] as soon as he can be spared to see if he cannot get a paper there. We have authorised him to say that we will raise $10,000 at least if our Northern friends will raise $5,000. All of what they raise, they may use in their own quarter. I have no fear of getting $15,000 if our friends in the country will do half as well as we are doing in the City [of Charleston]. We have suffered not a little in our operations by the prevailing influenza. My attack, & Alb[ert] Rhett's have both greatly impeded action. We would have had before now some one to visit [Francis W.] Pickens, [George] McDuffie[,] [James H.] Hammond & others to get their aid, but sickness in the family of Mr. [James] Simons our Secretary has stopped him. In a day or two we expect to get Mr. A[lexander] H. Brown off. He is a very warm friend of yours & will I hope visit you on his way. You will find him shrewd & sensible, but full of prejudices—yet on the whole well suited to the mission. We propose to send him first to Edgefield & thence to Abbeville, Pendleton, Chester, Fairfield, Sumter, Columbia[,] Orangeburgh & home. Alb[ert] Rhett was taken sick on his way to Beaufort after his Brother & was able to do nothing in that direction. Georgetown we must reach in some other way.

Our correspondence is becoming more active, but still it is not what it ought to be. I cannot do a tithe of what is needed. I endeavor to keep up something in that way, but it is but indifferently done. We have letters from your friends in Mobile & I think I will send you [John A.] Campbell's. A few days before I rec[eive]d his, one from Jos[eph] W. Lesesne (a son in law of Dr. [Thomas] Cooper[']s) was rec[eive]d by the Mercury asking much the same information that Campbell does. I wrote Lesesne, gave him a short history of our movements, let him understand the points in controversy with Ritchie & told him to keep his eye on that & he would easily understand what we should be going for. I also apprised him of Rhett[']s probable movement to Washington where I hoped some Central organization would be made & that he & our friends would know it if done. I also urged popular movements as widely as possible. Last winter they adjourned their [Ala. State?] Democratic Convention till the coming December. I said that now was the time to have county meetings to appoint Delegates, & one great movement should go off as a Leader with some strong exposition of our creed, resolutions declaring their preferences for the Presidency—District system[,] per Capita vote &c. I urged this as strongly as possible & inclosed the letter to [Dixon H.] Lewis with one to him insisting that he should go immediately up to Montgomery & Autauga & see Gov-[ernor Benjamin] Fitzpatrick & Mr. [James E.] Belser [Representative from Ala.] & form their plan of operations & set immediately about its execution. I have stimulated Gen[era]l Saunders [Representative from N.C.] as much as I can.

I have waited anxiously to hear from you since Mr. Ritchie[']s paper of the 22nd Aug. noticing "A Member of the Convention." I have prepared a short reply to his questions, but I will not put it in print for a day or two, waiting to hear from you. I hope you will not hesitate as soon as any thing appears in his paper requiring it, to let us have your views without waiting for us. You can see the course so much more clearly than we here who have so limited a scope of the field, that we would in all important moves rather greatly have your opinions before acting.

I hope today to hear from Rhett—if I do I will put in a post script to let you know what he says at Richmond. Would it not be well for you to drop your friend [Washington] Greenhow of the Petersburgh Republican a word of advice[?] He is too rough, too hasty, too unguarded. Mr. Ritchie gets greatly the better of him by his temper.

Two days ago I rec[eive]d a package of your lives & Speeches, some 3 or 4 Dozen I should suppose, bound togather [sic]. They came without letter or advice by the brig Tybee[?] & were here a month before I was notified. I opened them to see what they were & took one copy, as we have none here with your life in the same volume with the speeches. What am I to do with them?

I also send [John] Heart[']s last letter.

It is said in the [New York] Herald that a large Park mass meeting is called by your friends of the City Delegates to be held tomorrow or next day, & that all the [Lewis] Cass, [Richard M.] Johnson & [James] Buchanan men will join—he thinks 40,000 will be there. The [New York] Plebeian of the same day says there is a combination of traitors[,] friends of all the other candidates ag[ains]t Mr. [Martin] V[an] Buren & that it is time for his friends to throw aside all forbearance & to make war on the whole of you. The sooner he says Mr. V[an] B[uren']s friends draw the line the better. The Cincinnati Organ of his party holds the same language. What should our course be if this is done?

I must leave the City in a few days to be absent perhaps 2 or 3 weeks. Mr. [Albert] Rhett is again getting well enough to be on the alert, and I don't think much can be lost now by my absence. If you write to me any thing special for myself, within the next 10 or 12 days direct to Columbia. If for any thing to be done here direct to me & Alb[ert] Rhett. Very truly Yours, F.H. Elmore.

N.B. The letters in friday[']s [sic; Saturday's, Sept. 2] Mercury are from [Virgil] Maxcy of Maryland, [John A.] Campbell of Mobile, Detmold of N[ew] York & Dr. Ramsay [sic; James G.M. Ramsey] of

Tennessee. Ramsay wants to know if we desire any movement in Tennessee. I will write yes by all means.

I send also a copy of the letter to be sent to Mr. Picken[s,] McDuffie[,] [Armistead] Burt, J[ames] E[dward] Colhoun, Hammond, [James H.] Adams, [Frederick William] Davie, [Austin F.] Peay, [John M.] Felder, [William] McWillie, & [John P.] Richardson, & also to some dozen in the lower counties—[William] Dubose, Theo[dore] L. Gourdin[,] J[ohn] R. Mathew[e]s[,] R[obert] F.W. Allston, [Whitemarsh B.] Seabrook &c.

ALS in ScCleA; variant PEx in Jameson, ed., *Correspondence*, pp. 872–874. NOTE: The "copy of the letter" mentioned in Elmore's last paragraph has not been identified with certainty. However, it perhaps was related to soliciting funds for Calhoun's campaign. Compare the circular letter from Elmore, Henry Gourdin, and John S. Ashe which appears above in this volume under the date of 8/18/1843. Compare also the letters below from Henry Gourdin to James H. Hammond, 11/8/1843, and to James Edward Colhoun, 11/9/1843.

From H[ENRY] GOURDIN

Charleston, Sept. 4th 1843
Dear Sir, Mr. Wm. H. Brown of Charleston, but now residing in Philadelphia, is about publishing a work containing cuts executed by himself of eminent men in the United States, with a short biography of them, and is desirous of obtaining from such a short letter ["by wh" *canceled*] addressed to him expressing to him their opinion of his work, or on any other subject, that he may give a correct autograph of their signatures, and their style of writing.

Mr. Brown has written to me to request that I will ["obtain" *interlined*] such a letter from you. He says[:] "I want you to write to Mr. Calhoun, mention me, whom he knows, state to him what I am about doing, and request him to write me a letter for the purpose stated. I merely wish his opinion of a work got up splendidly as mine will be, and his opinion of the likenesses of our public men which he has often seen. Mr. Calhoun will not hesitate I know, for he bought 30 or 40 of different ones from me, and took a great fancy to my art. His likeness of a certainty will be one of my book."

Mr. Brown's likenesses I know possess much merit, and he is undoubtedly a man of considerable genius. If therefore you can oblige him in this matter, you will greatly ["oblige" *canceled*] serve him as well as myself.

I cannot but think that the cause in w[hic]h we are all so warmly interested is brightening, & had our friends in Charleston been as liberal three months since, as they have been in the last ten days, I have not the smallest doubt, that we should have carried every ward in the City of N[ew] York. What a trump Card this would have been in our hands? I hope however that it is not too late, and that well directed, and untiring exertions will yet secure us a glorious victory. I am Dear Sir Very resp[ectfull]y Your Ob[edien]t S[e]r[van]t, H. Gourdin.

ALS in ScCleA.

RESOLUTIONS of a Calhoun Meeting, New York City

[Adopted September 4, 1843]
Whereas—"It is all important to the successful operation of our system of government, that the highest office of the Union should be the exclusive reward of merit and services, such as may be well known to the whole country, so as to enable the people at large to form a just estimate of their value, and of the character and motives of him who rendered them." And whereas, at the present crisis of confusion of parties, agitation of principles, and of pressure upon the commercial and productive pursuits of industry, it has become indispensible to the general welfare, that a man be selected for the Presidency, who, in addition to the above-named requisites, presents to the consideration of his fellow citizens such enlightened views of public policy as would, if carried out, promote the most extensive commerce, invite the investment of capital, and impart new life to agricultural, mechanical and manufacturing pursuits; therefore,

Resolved, That contemplating to their full extent these great objects and grave considerations, we feel bound to declare our convictions, that John Caldwell Calhoun is preeminently qualified to administer the general government according to its true principles, and consistently with the best interests of the people, and the progressive spirit of the age.

Resolved, That in our manifestation of preference for one of the candidates for the Presidency of the United States, we have no wish or intention, to disparage any of his democratic competitors for that distinguished station. On the contrary, we are, as American citizens, proud of the great men of our country, (without regard to party or birth place,) as forming an element of its greatness. But we present Mr. Calhoun as the candidate of our choice, and we feel bound to set forth to our fellow-citizens of the Union, the following reasons which have induced this preference:

1. That Mr. Calhoun has given such proofs of his clear views of our system of government, of its constitutional provisions, and of State rights, as affords a guarantee that he would administer the functions of the Executive department within the limits of the Constitution.

2. That he has already avowed the measures of public policy he would pursue, both with respect to external and internal relations. "Free trade—low duties—no debt—separation from banks—economy—retrenchment, and strict adherence to the constitution;" and we believe that these measures are calculated to preserve the Union, and ensure the liberty and prosperity of the people.

3. That he has enlightened the popular mind with regard to primary or abstract principles, and shown the value of their application to all great questions of national debate which have come up during nearly thirty years. Mr. Calhoun has so impressed his pecul[i]ar intellect upon the national political mind, that there is a constant recurrence to those first principles now familiar as simple truths, which were formerly derided as his political abstractions.

4. That as the advocates of Mr. Calhoun for the Presidency, we do prefer and will sustain him, not because he happens to be from the north or south—not because he may or may not have the support of certain leaders—not because of any accidental preference—but because we know and estimate him as that enlightened statesman in whose keeping may safely be entrusted the welfare not of one section only, but of the whole country—because his high and chivalrous character will shield our country from the first advances of political error—because he has always stood forth as the champion of equal rights, and has always been ready to interpose himself equally to the untoward influence of a high tariff and monied oligarchy, and to the debasing doctrine of black mail tariff protection—and because he is the man of the people and for the people, and the prompt advocate of popular rights and human liberty. And, whereas, rotation in office is a cardinal principle of the Democratic theory of government; and as Mr. [Martin] Van Buren, in confirmation of this principle, has declared that "no one can expect, or should desire to be always in office under a government and institutions like ours, and that he has enjoyed that

privilege long enough to satisfy his utmost ambition;" and again, "with a political ambition more than satisfied by the many and distinguished honors which have already been conferred upon him, and with no higher aspirations, if there be higher, than to occupy the station, enjoy the privileges, and discharge the duties of an American citizen." We, therefore, responding to these laudable sentiments of Mr. Van Buren, are compelled to believe that the outcry of some of his friends for his restoration to office, and their strenuous exertions against the district plan of sending delegates to the national convention, and against the "equal and exact justice" of the vote, per capita, must be repugnant to his feelings, and are evidently more incited by selfish considerations than with any view to his wishes or advantages; for they are all well aware that "the same principle which demands his restoration, would demand, also, the restoration of all who held subordinate offices under him, from the cabinet minister down to the village post master."

Resolved, That the proposed reform of each congressional district electing, by the direct vote of the voters of the district, its delegates to the national convention, is not only consistent with the right of popular suffrage, but it is also the most simple and direct mode of ascertaining the popular will—

1. Because this reform is perfectly consistent with constitutional rights, as it enables each citizen to exercise with direct efficacy his conscientious preference in the choice of a delegate, and takes nothing from his right of suffrage by having others substituted to elect [a] delegate for him; in other words, to do that which he can do better and with less trouble to himself.

2. Because the usage of electing delegates to a County Convention to elect delegates to a State Convention, which shall elect delegates to the National Convention, results in a delegation no less than three removes from the people—And this political machinery to remove power, as far as possible from the hands of its rightful owners, is not consistent with democratic principles.

3. Because the Constitution of the United States allots Presidential electors to each State, equal in number to the members it sends to the House of Representatives, and two electors for the State at large. Hence the inference and the right is clear, that each Congressional district should also elect for itself a Presidential elector, while the State at large should elect the two who correspond with the State representation in the Senate of the United States. Therefore, in perfect consistency with the fundamental principles of these arrangements, each Congressional district should elect, in the most direct

manner, the delegate by whom it shall be represented in the National Convention.

Resolved, That the practice of voting and counting the votes, which has heretofore prevailed in our national convention to nominate Presidential candidates, is contrary to constitutional principles and repugnant to natural justice; for, to vote per capita, and then count by States, in other words, to vote individually, and then add the minority votes to the majority votes of each State, and count them all as majority votes, is such a violation of truth and right as has never prevailed in any legislature or deliberative body; and we believe, that this shameless despotism over minorities, has only been tolerated in this land of freedom, because of its not having been generally understood by the people.

Resolved, That justice and a regard for the equal rights of the States, require that the delegates from the several States, ought to be appointed in a uniform manner; that in a Convention of delegates from many States, the delegates from all be placed on an equal footing, that this equality is destroyed by one delegation being appointed by a State Convention voting a consolidated ticket, by which, the votes justly belonging to a minority in that State, (which may sympathize with a sufficient numbers [*sic*] of majorities in other States, to make a fair majority in the whole democratic party,) are not only silenced, but impressed into the service of the majority, made to utter a voice against their wishes, while delegations from other States are elected by districts, and voting per capita, are liable to be, and generally will be divided in their votes; that it is unworthy the character of the great State of New York, too strong from its own numbers to desire to increase its strength disproportionately by artificial combinations alike oppressive and unjust to the minority of their own political brethren in the State, and to other States having delegations elected by the people in districts, and liable, therefore, to be divided in their votes, and that on this account, as well as for the reasons already assigned; the State Convention about to assemble at Syracuse ought to decide that the New York delegates to the National Convention should be chosen by the democratic votes in the several congressional districts; one to each district, and that each delegate be allowed in convention to vote independently, according to the wishes of the district sending him.

Resolved, That we are utterly opposed to all such precedents as voting individually and counting by States, not only for the self-evident injustice of the principle, but because its practical operation enables two or three of the larger States in combination, to effect the nomination of such candidates as they prefer for the presidency and vice-presidency; thus forcing the smaller States to act as subordinates in the matter. We are opposed because there can be no harmony in the Democratic party when there is not "equal and exact justice." We are opposed because such despotism of the larger States, perfectly justifies the smaller States, in self-preservation, to take such steps as shall throw the election into the House of Representatives, where they can give the larger States "measure for measure."

Resolved, That while the friends of all the other Democratic candidates for the Presidency are favorable to the District plan of sending delegates, as well as the vote and count per capita in the Convention, we regret that many of the friends of Mr. Van Buren have taken a stand in opposition to arrangements so obviously constitutional and just. Have they any doubts of the real popularity of their candidate to make them fearful of trusting him to a Convention of the delegates elected by the people themselves—to a Convention democratically organized, and voting and counting the votes, like all other representative bodies?

Resolved, That while we reverence the true voice of the people, and would extend to the honest convictions of every American citizen the same respect which we claim for our own, yet we will not bow down to any false image of public opinion that the Nebuchadnezzers of party may set up: That while we are ready to yield much to the spirit of harmony and democratic brotherhood, we will yield nothing to political jugglery: And we would remind the opponents of popular representation, that should they succeed in excluding any portion of the party from a voice in the nomination of President, they must at the same time absolve the persons excluded from all obligation to support their nominee at the election.

Resolved, That it confirms our faith in the intelligence of the people to perceive the increasing popularity of Mr. Calhoun in all parts of the Union, the efforts of a cordon of organized presses, and the proscriptive re-echoes of a host of ejected officials to the contrary notwithstanding. We therefore recommend to the friends of Mr. Calhoun in every part of the United States to hold meetings in order to act in concert with each other for the sake of the cause, the man, and the country. And we call upon his friends in the several wards of this city, to organize themselves to act in vindication of their constitutional rights when necessary. Messrs. Robert Townsend, Edmund S. Derry, John Hecker, E[manuel] B. Hart, Stephen Hasbrouck, James L. Stratton, and George Dixey, are hereby appointed (with instructions to fill vacancies as they may occur in their number,) as a special committee to call meetings and assist in forming ward Democratic Constitutional Associations.

Resolved, That J.L.H. McCracken, Emanuel B. Hart and John Hecker be, and they are hereby appointed a Committee on behalf of this meeting to draft an address to the people of the United States, setting forth the grounds of preference for John C. Calhoun as the Democratic candidate for the Presidency.

PC in the New York, N.Y., *Evening Post,* September 6, 1843, p. 2; PC in the Boston, Mass., *Post,* September 11, 1843, p. 1; PC in the Charleston, S.C., *Mercury,* September 11, 1843, p. 2; Ms. (in the hand of Virgil Maxcy) in DLC, Galloway-Maxcy-Markoe Papers. NOTE: The New York, N.Y., *Evening Post,* September 5, 1843, p. 2, reported: "A large number of persons, say about two thousand, assembled in the Park yesterday afternoon, agreeably to invitation. The meeting having been called to order, the following officers were appointed: Dr. Stephen Hasbrouck, *President. Vice-Presidents,* J.H.L. [*sic*] McCracken, Denniss [*sic*] Mullens, John A. Stender, Edmund S. Derry, George G. Glazier, Robert Townsend, John W. Mitchell, Peter McLaughlin, Edmund M. Young, Robert Berney, M[iddleton] Goldsmith, Lewis P. Clover, John B. Schmelzel, John Leconick, Thomas S. Gibbs, John Hannorhan, Dr. F.T. Ferriss, Michael Gaffney, R.B. Cuthbert. *Secretaries*[:] John Commerford, S.R. MacNevin, Alexander Wells, J[ames] H. Brady, B.S. Hart, H[iram] McCollum. Mr. Henry [P.] Barber read a series of resolutions, when a candid and forcible speech was made by Jas. T. Brady, who was followed by Henry Barber and William [Ross] Wallace." Compare another first-hand account of the meeting, which appeared in the Charleston, S.C., *Mercury,* September 11, 1843, p. 2.

From EDWARD DIXON

Warrenton [Va.], September 5th, 1843

My Dear Sir, You will perceive by the paper which I send you, that there has been a public meeting of your friends in Fauquier County. In drawing up the resolutions, I may have omitted much that ought to have been added, but nevertheless, I hope they will meet your approbation. Major [William W.] Wallace delivered an able address on the occasion. A barbacue [*sic*] and sale in the neighbourhood on the day of the meeting prevented many from attending. We neglected to give notice of it in [the Warrenton *Flag of '98,*] our paper; the people of that neighbourhood say that if a notice of it had been published and some other day had been fixed upon, the company would not have fallen short of 150 persons. A very large majority or nearly all of the Republicans of that part of the County prefer you to Mr. [Martin] Van Buren. This preference is becoming general here and in some of the adjacent Counties. We have been compelled, however, to proceed with caution and skill and to feel our way before making any move, inasmuch as [Thomas] Ritchie and his co-adjutors have got the start of us in this State. If Van Buren's friends were to call mass meetings and make strong appeals to *party spirit*, they might override us, but it is our policy to call neighbourhood meetings in different sections of the County and gain a strong foothold before we get up a County meeting for the purpose of ascertaining the relative ["stren" *canceled*] strength of Mr. Van Buren and yourself in the County. We will not be afraid of the result after holding a few more meetings. Major Wallace and myself intend to call a meeting to be held on the 16th of this month in another part of the County, where we expect to have a full attendance. Of this, however, you may rest assured, that we will leave nothing undone which will be calculated to advance your claims. If you get Virginia in the Convention, you will receive the nomination. But ["it" *interlined*] is necessary that your friends in this State should be active and vigilant, for Mr. Van Buren has a strong and well organized party in Virginia. Major Wallace is exerting his talents effectively in support of your claims. His communication over the signature of "Ximenes" was intended for home consumption. You will observe that you are not committed by that article to any given course in relation to the question discussed. There is merely a presumption as to your opinions from your locality.

I shall continue to prepare articles for the press in support of your claims, but I am rather at a loss at present for topics of discussion. I would be pleased, therefore, to have a few suggestions from you in regard to this subject. If you can make it convenient, please let me hear from you. With sentiments of profound esteem, I remain very sincerely yours, Edward Dixon.

ALS in ScCleA.

From F[RANKLIN] H. ELMORE

Charleston, Sep[tember] 5, 1843

My Dear Sir, By a letter to Mr. A[lbert] Rhett rec[eive]d today I find you have not had the Rich[mon]d Enquirer of the 22 Ult[im]o cont[ainin]g Mr. [Thomas] Ritchie[']s notice of "A Member of the Convention.["] I regret this exceedingly as it will not do now to wait till I hear from you to answer his question. I will put in a reply in Thursday[']s Mercury to his single question, with some apology for the delay.

I was very much provoked at this number which I send to you & wrote to [John] Heart on the subject who has put my letter in full in the last [Washington] Spectator. The recent tone of some of Mr. [Martin] V[an] B[uren']s papers indicates that we can[']t hold terms long with them. We are defensive, but it seems to me we must show a readiness to repel & an ability to carry the war back upon them. Mr. V[an] B[uren] is too vulnerable on the Tariffs of '28 & '42 to come unscathed out of such a conflict. In these matters pray express your views without reserve. I have furnished the Mercury since Rhett has left us with some editorials & one I gave him today is a review of some of Mr. Ritchie[']s & the [New York] Plebeian[']s course lately.

The news from N[ew] York is so far highly encouraging. I re-c[eive]d two letters yesterday, one from Mr. [Fitzwilliam] Byrdsall the founder of their Free Trade association & one from Mr. E[manuel] B. Hart who[m] you may remember. Mr. Byrdsall refers me to you for information about him. He writes a very interesting letter, has hopes from the meeting to have been held [in New York City] last evening, but still writes in great anxiety. Hart is far more confident & says every arrangement is made for a great meeting. They will put themselves broadly in free trade, the District System & per capita vote & will in all likelihood express their determination to elect District Delegates let the Syracuse Convention say & do what it please.

I have not yet heard from [Robert Barnwell] Rhett. I hope to do so tomorrow. When I do you shall hear from me.

Your Knoxville editorial is I take it from our friend Ramsay [*sic*; James G.M. Ramsey] whose letter was in the Mercury a day or two ago. It appears tomorrow.

I trust you are not in any way in [Joseph A.] Scoville's power. Mr. Byrdsall *intimates* that he is not *true*, & an anonymous Correspondent of the Mercury from N[ew] York inquires with great anxiety what were your relations, as he says Scoville has been boasting of his cor-responding with you &c. & says Scoville is not reputable &c. I state these things that you may set them down at what they are worth. I think he *was as true to you* as such a man could be, but very indis-creet[,] unsteady & not reliable.

Your friends here are in fatter[,] better spirits. Many who had desponded are entertaining far higher hopes.

I leave Thursday to Saturday. Y[ou]rs truly, F.H. Elmore.

ALS in ScCleA. NOTE: The "reply in Thursday[']s Mercury" to Thomas Ritchie, mentioned by Elmore in his first paragraph, appeared under the name of "A Member of the Convention" in the Charleston, S.C., *Mercury*, September 7, 1843, p. 2.

From H[ENRY] MEIGS,
[former Representative from N.Y.]

New York [City,] Sep[tember] 5, 1843
D[ea]r Sir, Yesterday a meeting of several thousand persons was held in our Park where Resolutions were adopted very precisely expressing my sentiments.

My young friends Henry P. Barber & James [T.] Brady appeared on the stage and eloquently spoke the same doctrine. John B. Schmelzel one of the Vice Presidents, is a man of property—has been an Alderman and is respected as an old republican and good citizen.

The ninth ward—which is the most Republican of the city—gave a majority of *116* out of *1700 Republican votes—for J[ohn] C. Calhoun*. I have lived in that ward twenty five years—& have represented it in the Board of Aldermen, of which I was President.

I am now engaged in the American Institute. At our Fair in Oct. next I have provided for a Cotton Gin and have sent to John Rutledge of Charleston for a *Bale of Seed Cotton*. We have 250000 visitors at our Fair—of whom not one in 500 ever saw a *cotton gin in motion*.

The friends of John C. Calhoun have made up their minds *that they deserve success with their Candidate*—and are determined to abide the event. I am with great & true respect Y[ou]r Ob[edien]t Ser[van]t, H. Meigs.

ALS in ScCleA.

From ALBERT RHETT

Charleston, Sep[tember] 5, 1843
My Dear Sir, Your esteemed favour of the 2d has been received, and also your previous one, which I have been unable to answer from sickness. The Central Committee here prevailed on me to go to Beaufort and persuade Brother B. [Robert Barnwell Rhett] to go on to Washington, which, you know, he has done; I there got sick and have been out of bed only two days—["now" *interlined*] very much debilitated.

I most sincerely congratulate you on the improvement of our prospects. From all quarters the intelligence is most cheering, and if the mass meeting held yesterday in New York [City], by our friends, goes off prosperously, the effect will be electrical. I should be noway [*sic*] surprised if it deprive Mr. [Martin] Van Buren of his own State. Travellers just coming in from the North give the strongest representations of your increasing popularity, and Van Buren's decline. Perseverance, vigor and discretion, (backed with money) seems to me all that is wanting to give us the victory, and for us to lack in these would be shame indeed. In haste very resp[ectfully] & truly, Albert Rhett.

[Marginal P.S.] I am in hopes Brother B. is in New York [City] by this [time]. He determined to go there to establish a Press if possible.

ALS in ScCleA.

From M[ICAH] STERLING

Sharon, State of Connec[ticu]t, 5 Sept[embe]r [18]43
My D[ea]r Sir, I am on a visit to my Brother Ansel [Sterling] at this Place. You may remember him as a member of Congress with me in 1821 & [182]2. I am on my way to the sea side for health & recreation. My health is much better than it was tho I am not yet a perfectly well man. I think sea food & bathing will contribute to my health & happiness. I hope to see some of our old friends and classmates. Many are in their graves and among others my excellent friend Frank Winthrop. I think I shall go to New London and call on McQueen[?] who is I believe[?] a respectable clergyman at that Place.

Go where I will the main topic of conversation is the Presidential question, the more so I conclude because I am known as your Friend and many feel a deep interest in your success and nearly all would were it not for Party and the well known fact that you are opposed to the Tariff and attached of course to your own peculiar institution. At Great Barrington in Massachusetts I met Barsteron [*sic*; Gideon Barstow] from Salem whom you may remember as a member of Congress when I was. He thinks you would certainly be elected President were you not so much opposed to the Tariff but he says your ideas have undergone some modification upon that subject and to prove it quoted your letter to a gentleman in Louisiana upon the subject of sugar and seemed to think if you could favor the sugar of Louisiana you could upon the same principle favor the iron & the wool of the North. How that may be I cannot say but one thing I do hope that the present tariff will in its result operate so clearly for good or for

411

evil as to make us all think alike about it. If [Henry] Clay beats you should you two be the candidates it will be upon the ground alone that he is the great Champion of "American labor." All admit that it will be a fair fight between you and Clay and thousands are hoping that the contest will yet assume that shape. I yet hope that Mr. [Martin] V[an] Buren will have wisdom enough to withdraw from the contest and I believe he would if his friends allow him to but it is "neck or nothing" with them and they will not yield. Still V[an] Buren may find the opposition to him so violent & resolute as to deem it best to withdraw. He ought not to run unless the Party called for him almost unanimously. This is indeed far from the case. He can, I believe, force a nomination but I fear would be disgracefully defeated as in 1840. If the Convention is not constituted upon the right principles I do hope your friends will withdraw from the convention & give you a seperate [sic] nomination. As certain as you get into Congress, so certain are you elected for the Whigs at the North & the West prefer you to a man & will give you their support if compelled to abandon Clay. Are the Bonds of Party so strong that we are obliged to risk every thing to support it? Shall we nominate a man who we cannot elect merely to do justice to an individual[?] It may be we can elect him but I do not believe it for the opposition to him will be as violent here at the North, if not quite so strong as it was in [18]40 but how will it be at the South[?] Your friends will not go zealously into his support nor if you desire it can do much. He has had his day & ought to step aside—we want a new man with new men not the Albany & Richmond Regency over[?] again who were so disgracefully & shamefully defeated in 1840. I admit I have not patience to think that we are to be sacrificed as a great Party to support these men who care for little but themselves. *The South must contriv[e] to prevent it.* The men who take the lead in New York are his old friends and associates who are determ[ine]d to get into office again by supporting him. The People do not love them any more than they did in 1840 but they love Whigs less & have no hopes from that quarter. Still I do not believe they will again be willing to rally around the Regencies of Richmond & Albany. I do not believe the Party in N[ew] York will hearken[?] for a moment to the District system—they will be afraid that will give you a few votes & that they will not risk. This fact alone shows they mean to hold a convention for V[an] Buren & no one els[e.]

I may be prejudiced but I feel that to go sq[uare?] into the campaign with *the old story* of *Van Buren & Co.* will destroy all that zeal, ardor & enthusiasm so essential to success. If we really want again to be most shamefully & disgracefully defeated we will present for election the same candidate as in [18]40 and we will [be] sure of gaining our object.

Albany 14th Sept[embe]r

The foregoing letter was written in Connecticut. I fear you will hardly be be [*sic*] able to read it. Since then I have been to N[ew] York [City] & attended the Calhoun meeting on the 14th in[stan]t. It was large & respectable, tho the V[an] Buren presses make it out small & contemptible &c. But I saw it with my own eyes & think the estimate of ["$" *canceled*] 3,000 not far out of the way. I found much spirit & enthusiasm in your favor. Our class mate David Brush & other young lawyers take the lead. You will read the Proceedings in the Aurora & other papers. All are Whigs or V[an] Buren men here— it is head quarters as you know of the old Hunkers as they are called.

The resistance to the doings of the Syracuse Convention will be resolute, bold & zealous in this State. True we are in the minority but we have our rights and will endeavor to maintain them. I am quite alone in my country [of residence in northern N.Y.] but shall not fear to erect the Standard of Calhoun not withstanding. The People as a body are tired of V[an] Buren & Co. but they have the Presses and most of the leading men who have held office eternally & mean to get in again. I go hence to the center of our State to attend the great Fair of the State of N[ew] York at Rochester, where I think you have friends & I know you have some at Utica. We have passed the "Rubicon," have broken the ice. The Whigs do all they can to publish our doings, because they hate V[an] Buren & many of them highly esteem your character. What is to be the result God only knows—we will not be trampled upon & we shall look to the South for able support.

My health is improved tho I am still an invalid. Sea air, food & bathing have helped me much. The V[an] Burenites will denounce me but I care not for that. I have nothing to ask of them & nothing to expect from them.

We want an able, respectable Paper in the city of N[ew] York where all the World congregate[s]. Brush has agreed to attend to it & I think will succeed.

Sept[embe]r 16th. On my return to Watertown from Rochester I will write you again. I am in hopes to find some good friends at the West. M. Sterling.

ALS in ScCleA.

413

From JAMES WISHART

St. Clairsville [Ohio,] Sept[embe]r 5th 1843
My Dear Sir, Since I wrote to you in the early part of aug[us]t I have
seen your letter [of 7/9/1843] to the committee of Cincinatti [sic] appointed by a meeting of your friends. I am hi[gh]ly pleased with the
ground assumed by you, and if there is virtue enough left in the people to preserve the government, your reasons must prevail. Your
friends here, with the exception of myself, have urged an opposite
course, but are now convinced you are right.

I have now sold off my possessions here, and intend remaining
until it is settled by the Baltimore convention whether you get the
nomination. If you should succeed it will I think terminate the persecution of your friends by the old dynasty, if not it is my intention to
seek a new home, for I cannot live any longer in this community. For
thirteen years I have been regarded as the nucleus of Calhounism in
eastern Ohio. During that entire period an incessant warfare has
been maintained against me by the old organisation. Belmont is the
only co[u]nty in the State which has steadily refused to yield. Hence
your friends are more numerous here than other sections of the State.

The arguments of South Carolina in favor of electing delegates to
the Baltimore convention by districts, voting per capita, and the organisation of that body, are unanswerable, and will I hope ultimately
prevail. Yet that there is, as I believe, a settled and fixed design to
swindle you out of the nomination, need not be concealed. In the
great mass of our public men I have not the least confidence. Hence
I believe no reformation in the government will take place, should any
other candidate than yourself obtain the nomination. We carried one
of your friends for the legislature of the State, and one for county
treasurer, in our county convention for nominating candidates, in opposition to the official influence of Gov. [Wilson] Shannon and his
partner R[obert] I. Alexander, both of whom are [Lewis] Cass or
Johnston [sic; Richard M. Johnson] men as occasion may require, but
your old, tryed friend B.G. Wright who is superior to all the candidates offered, was defeated.

It is now known that, although the democratic press of the State,
so far as it has spoken on the subject, is in favor of the district system
of electing delegates to the Balt[imore] convention and the per capita
vote, the [Martin] Van B[uren] men will attempt to elect and instruct
delegates at the 8th of Jan[uar]y convention which according to usage
will then assemble to nominate a candidate for Gov[ernor] of the
State. This will be resisted—It is our intention to call a Calhoun

county meeting immediately after our election is over, when we will take our position on this and other important points. J[ohn] Brough[,] Auditor of [the] State[,] was called on to speak at our convention, and gave yourself and friends a stroke over the shoulders of [John] Tyler whose desertion of Gen. [Andrew] Jackson during his administration was denounced as an unpardonable sin against the democracy.

The friends of Mr. V[an] B[uren] think, and it is probably true, that a large majority of the democratic members of the next congress from the northern, eastern, and western States, is in favor of the election of that gentleman as the next president. Is it not probable that the [Washington] Globe and [Richmond] Enquirer are contending for an unfair and anti republican mode of electing delegates, to the convention, and consequently an unjust constitution of that body, with the intention to defeat the selection of any candidate, if they fail with V[an] B[uren] and thus throw the election of president into the House of rep[resentative]s under the impression that his majority there would secure his election?

I hope your friends will persevere. They have certainly the argument; and I believe all the people want is light. In the south you can hardly conceive the difficulty of giving that light in opposition to the will of the demagogues, and hence my fears of the result.

I have recieved [*sic*] nothing from Washington City but a subscription paper for the Spectator with a circular. I have seen since a private circular to B.G. Wright and a letter from Mr. [Robert M.T.] Hunter of Va. to him asking information on several points. I have not had any intercourse with the Calhoun central committee of Washington City, and know not who to address. This is partly my apology for writing to you in your present attitude, in addition to this I am anxious to keep you informed of contemplated movements of your opponents in this State, the motives by which they are governed, and the object they have in view as they may from time to time be develloped.

Beleiving [*sic*] I can best promote the interests of the country and the elevation of the human family by advancing your election, I shall continue, as I have done, to use all honorable exertions, feeble though they be, to secure an object so long and ardently desired. With the highest Respect, James Wishart.

P.S. I hope you will pardon me for adverting to one point in the contingencies of the future. In 1830 to 32 many rallied with your friends for principles as we thought, but afterwards left us for office and to avoid persecution. We now are greatly increased, and in the event of you getting the nomination many of those who persecuted you[r]self and friends will become your devoted friends. B.G. Wright ["and myself" *interlined*] are the only persons in eastern Ohio ["who" *interlined*] have adhered to the cause of true democracy and him whom we regarded as the embodiment and representative of the principles of the Union. Through good report and evil report we have never faltered, but steadily defended both the principles and the man. Is it too much to say that in this we have given evidence that we have not been actuated by unworthy motives or selfish considerations? In the event of your getting the nomination for president, which is regarded as being equivalent to an election, will you do us the honor to confer with us on any appointments you may desire to make in the eastern part of the State. This much I may I think safely say that such a course will not trammel your movements nor be detrimental to the public interest. This request will I trust however be regarded by you only as a suggestion of your true friends, who will not be disposed ["to" *interlined*] embarrass you in any manner, nor press any request unacceptable to yourself, neither will a reply to this request be anticipated before the spring of [18]45. J.W.

ALS in ScCleA.

From L[EMUEL] WILLIAMS,
[Collector of the Port of Boston]

Boston, Sept[embe]r 6th 1843

Dear Sir, Your letter of the 5th inst[ant] was duly received. If my anticipations regarding the movements of President [John] Tyler had been realized fully, & your friends had been placed, at an earlier period in situations of influence, we should have elected all the Delegates to the Baltimore convention from Maine (excepting two) friendly to you. But our opponents have had the advantage of party organization & will or have carried all the delegates excepting four; while I am assured, *upon the best authority*, that a decided majority of the Democratic party in Maine are favorable to you, including the most active & intelligent. The power of calling the conventions in the several States & counties lies with the committees who were appointed *under the old regime* & are in the interests of [Martin] Van Buren. Knowing the rapid progress your cause is making, they appointed meetings to be held at an early day & in that way have been successful; when if they had delayed calling these meetings until next Spring success would in almost every instance have been with you. Not content even with these proceedings, but fearing the effect which the developement of public opinion may have upon their own delegates, they have resorted to the expedient of instructing them to vote for Van Buren, thus violating a great principle adopted in fixing upon May rather than November for the time of holding the Baltimore convention. The reason for preferring May to November undoubttedly [*sic*] was that the later period would better enable the convention to judge with precision as to who was the most available candidate. By choosing delegates in August or September we lose the advantage of acting upon the information that we should be furnished with, from developements that will assuredly take place during the next session of Congress. The time between this & next May was intended for the benefit of observation & deliberation. These objects are lost by an early choice of delegates, bound too, by instructions. Our State convention is to be held at Worcester on the 13th inst[ant]; The contest is going on with great activity and no little virulence. I shall send you a few papers by which you will see that some of the towns are instructing their delegates to nominate Van Buren & others are instructing to keep the question of the Presidency *an open one.* Gov. [Marcus] Morton throws all the weight of his influence in favor of instructing the delegates to nominate Van Buren. Had he been friendly to you his position was such that with the aid of his influence we could have procured ["h" *canceled*] your nomination in Massachusetts, which would have powerfully influenced the action of the other New England States. As it is we shall nearly equal our opponents in convention, and we expect to defeat the plan of nominating Van Buren. I do not expect the convention will amount to more than about four-hundred members. We have elected 60 of the delegates from Boston favorable to you to 12 Van Buren. About the same proportion in Essex, 10 to 2 in Salem. Eight in Charlestown besides many other towns favorably heard from. One thing is certain—if the convention nominate Van Buren[,] Morton[']s vote will fall greatly short of what it was last year. We shall gain then *in any event.* If Van Buren is brought forward (as he assuredly will be) and fails of a nomination it will be evidence of his unpopularity. If nominated and Morton[']s vote is greatly diminished the same inference will follow. The meeting in the park has come off gloriously. Your cause is certainly looking up at the North. A week since I thought the nomination of Van Buren certain. Now I think your chance of a nomination is best. Your friends here are determined if Van Buren should receive the nomination to run you on an independent ticket. Your friend

[Orestes A.] Brownson thinks that we should have Whig votes enough to carry Massachusetts, Maine & New York & other Northern States which would follow the example of Massachusetts. I do not wish you to make any reply to this part of my letter whatever your sentiments may be. Your opponents are making a good deal out of your supposed sentiments upon the Rhode Island question. I should be glad to receive a statement from you on that head which I may show to some of our Democratic friends from that State. I was requested to day to procure one from you but not for publication or even to be copied. One other ground ["of" interlined; ob]jection is used with great effect by the Van-buren party which is this, that if you were elected president, your political friends would have nothing to look for, but the Whigs [would] be suffered to retain the offices obtained by thrusting out the Democrats. The [Portland, Maine,?] Eastern Argus has been very busy of late in propagating this notion. Now as Mr. Van Buren has always acted upon the policy of rewarding his friends, and Mr. [Henry] Clay has recently declared that he shall take care of his friends, some are deterred from adopting your cause from an opinion that if you are successful they would fare worse than the friends of either of the other successful candidates. Such motives will always operate on the selfish part of mankind who are but too numerous.

If the Southern politicians know, as I know, that one of the most objectionable means made use of by the Van Buren men here against you is your adherence to the domestic institutions of the South they would never consent to abandon your cause in any event. But more of this at some future period.

In relation to the Vice-Presidency it seems that [Levi] Woodbury will not be able to carry his own State & cannot of course, bring the least aid to your cause. Should Van Buren[']s friends hereafter conclude not to press his claims, or fa[i]ling to procure his nomination, withdraw his name, it seems to me that Silas Wright's ["of" canceled] name on your ticket as Vice President would give it more strength than any other. If Van Buren should not be withdrawn your friends would have to choose between [Lewis] Cass and [James] Buchanan. Would either of them consent to be run as Vice President?

I learn from intelligent gentlemen from the West that Cass has lost ground in that quarter by his controversy with [Daniel] Webster [over Cass's conduct while U.S. Minister to France]. Col. [Richard M.] Johnson is expected here on his northern tour & the friends of Van Buren here, & in N[ew] Hampshire are making extensive preparations to receive him. Their object is to persuade him to run with Van Buren for the Vice Presidency. Should they succeed it would greatly increase Van Buren[']s chances. Some think that Johnson[']s demonstrations are for the purpose only of making capital for the Vice presidency, while others who pretend to be well informed say that he will not run for the Vice presidency & that he calculates to go into the convention ["for the presidency" *interlined*] with the strength of ten States on the Oregon question. Are you correctly informed as to Johnson[']s views?

Sep[tember] 8

Since writing the above I have seen a gentleman who informs me that he has, within a few days, seen a letter from Col. Johnson stating that he will not *in any event* be considered a candidate for the Vice Presidency. *This is good news*, & in my opinion seals the fate of Van Buren. He must be defeated by a large majority on the first vote taken in the Convention. I was also informed yesterday from a source on which I can rely that four of the delegates to the Baltimore Convention chosen from Vermont are friendly to you. This we do not want known openly, as we should have to fear that they might be instructed adversely. The news from the Syracuse Convention [of N.Y. Democrats] received this morning has surprized us, *but agreeably.* I have seen many shrewd politicians to-day, & among others [former] Gov. [Isaac] Hill [of N.H.] & they, one & all, consider the fact that the Convention have chosen the delegate[s] to Baltimore ["as decidedly" *canceled*] as decidedly injurious, nay *ruinous* to the prospects of Van-Buren. It seems that he is afraid *to trust the people.* Your friends in that State will now rally & make choice of delegates by Districts. We hope the partizans of Van [Buren] will try the same thing here, whether successful or not, I have heard it whispered that they intend to do so.

Van Buren's friend Vanderpool [*sic*; Aaron Vanderpoel] was here, a few days since, endeavouring to buy up your friends. He was liberal, I am told, in his offers, promising to one the Post[?] office if ["his" *altered to* "he"] should succeed, & to my partner his former post of Naval Officer, &c &c.

I have just received a letter [of 9/5?] from our friend [Virgil] Maxcy, which as it is interesting I will send you a copy next week. I am going to Baltimore[?] next week for the purpose of [t]rying an important case there. I hope on my return to find a letter from you. With Sincere regard Y[ou]r friend, L. Williams.

P.S. As I write but an illegible hand I caused[?] my Son to copy the first part of my letter. Shall I keep you advised of the movements at the North?

LS in ScCleA; variant PC in Jameson, ed., *Correspondence*, pp. 874–878. NOTE: That portion of the above letter added on 9/8 is in Williams's handwriting.

From W[illia]m S. Hastie

New York [City,] Sept. 7th 1843
Dear Sir, Our Syracuse Convention has adjourned after electing Delegates to the Balt[im]o[re] convention, all friendly to the nomination of Mr. [Martin] Van Beuren [*sic*].

The system of electing by Districts, was lost by a vote of 103 to 19. A protest was entered on the minutes of the convention on motion of a friend of the District system by a majority of 4.

With the District system we could have shown considerable force in the State, could we have managed to divide with Mr. Van Beuren the vote of the State in the Balt[im]o[re] convention, Mr. Calhoun's friends would have been very sanguine of success, as we look for a strong pull from the New England States.

It is a hard case to be thus *cheated* out of our rights when the friends of Mr. Calhoun positively hold the balance of power in the State.

Mr. Van Beuren's friends have become alarmed at the demonstrations lately made in favour of Mr. Calhoun and have taken this mode of stifling their prospects.

"The meeting" in the Park [in New York City on 9/4] sent a Delegate to the convention with a report of the proceedings, and a Protest against choosing the members of the Balt[im]o[re] convention on any other plan than the District system.

The moment that messenger arrived at Syracuse with the intelligence that 5000 people had assembled in the Park as the friends of Mr. Calhoun, the fate of the District system question was settled instanter, "The Faithful" became alarmed, and well might they, for on so short a notice, New York has seldom witnessed such a meeting.

Had that meeting consisted of 500 instead of 5000 persons, the convention would have conceded every thing to the friends of Mr. Calhoun, as it was they saw the power was too great to be trifled with.

Although the effect has been unfortunate in our own State, the meeting was conceived in the true and proper spirit. The speech of

Mr. [James T.] Brady a young man who stands very high at our bar, and was formerly an active friend of Mr. Van Beuren[']s, was not only brilliant, but sound in argument, he made two very beautiful points. In speaking of want of consistency which he stated was often charged to Mr. Calhoun, he observed[,] "As it regards consistency I am pretty much of Dan[ie]l O'Connel[l]'s opinion, it is very well when we are right, but it becomes *obstinacy* when we are wrong.["] In alluding to the independence which has always characterised Mr. Calhoun's political course in politics, he repeated the following lines as Mr. C[alhoun]'s motto, with thrilling effect.

Thy spirit Independence! let me share,
Lord of the Lion heart and Eagle eye;
Thy form I'll follow with my bosom bare,
Nor fear the storm that howls along the sky.

For one at this early day I pin my hopes upon an election by the House, although we loose [*sic*] a few votes from this State, we have it in our power *to be dissatisfied at any moment.* At the same time we do not despair of making a respectable showing at the Balt[im]o[re] convention, provided the South is true to *herself.*

It is possible that two setts [*sic*] of delegates may claim seats at the Balt[im]o[re] convention, if this course is thought advisable a movement will be made in a few days.

I must apologise for the liberty taken in writing you, at the same time beg you will attribute it, to the proper feeling. I am Dear Sir With high respect &c, Wm. S. Hastie.

ALS in ScCleA.

From ALEX[ANDE]R JONES

192 Broadway, New York, September 7th 1843
Dear Sir, A few days since I sent you a copy of a weekly paper, published by an association of practical printers called the "Cynosure," which I concluded to edit for a few weeks, to see how I liked the business, and to pave the way, if possible, for a paper in your interest.

The articles on the "Annexation of Texas" were written by me, though with much haste, and amidst frequent interruptions. The article on the "Hanseatic League" was also written by me as well as several other articles. I also supplied daily, a commercial and money article, which the weekly sheet was too small to embrace. I send you a duplicate copy, with a copy of the daily also. I will send you a copy of the weekly to appear on the 9th Inst[ant].

The parties who own the paper, are poor, and are working with old type and therefore print ["my material" *canceled and* "my articles" *interlined*] very indifferently. They are very timid young men and ["of" *interlined*] rather limited education. I, therefore, volunteered my services. And were they not afraid, I could make it a Calhoun paper at once. They have however, offered to sell out one half of it to me, and invest the proceeds in new type—Enlarge the paper, and hoist your name at the mast head, "subject to the decision of a national convention fairly constituted." In this case I should assume the entire control of the paper, and endeavour to have it conducted in such a manner as best to promote your interest.

I have ["had" *interlined*] a conference on the subject, with some of your leading friends in N[ew] York, and they all concur in the opinion, that it is a matter of great importance to have a paper here devoted to your interest. I entertain a hope that among all hands, we may be able before ["long" *interlined*] to send you a paper with ["the" *interlined*] right heading to it. To sustain it, however, with useful success, we shall stand in need of all the aid your friends at the South can give us in the way of Subscription lists ["or"(?) *altered to* "with"; "any" *canceled and* "all" *interlined*] other aid in their power. We should have to contend against a powerful force, and meet it ["with" *interlined*] manly prudence and firmness. We should make the daily paper a two cent paper, And the weekly, better adapted to general country circulation, ["at" *canceled*] a $2.50 cents [per year] paper. This would be as low as a real good ["Com" *canceled*] Political & Commercial paper, with the usual general news, could be published at. The sooner we can commence the paper, if at all, the better. Your friends sadly need an efficient organ in New York at the present moment.

I congratulate you, however, on your brightening prospects in this part of the world. I am not accustomed to speak in public, or take an official part in public meetings, but, I can assure ["you" *interlined*] as far as my exertions ["go" *canceled*] can go, as a private citizen I am by no means idle.

My private residence is at 61 West Washington place, and in the 9th Ward, which ["is" *interlined*] the largest and most populous ward in the city, and I am happy to inform you that this is the strongest Calhoun ward in the city And that it has sent Calhoun delegates to the Syracuse convention, and will send ["a" *interlined*] Calhoun member, or two to the next State Legislature.

We have authentic information from Syracuse, stating a majority of the Convention being [Martin] Van Buren men, have by a large vote, adopted the election of delegates to the Baltimore [Democratic national] convention ["by general ticket" *interlined*], instead of ["by" *canceled*] the District system. Your friends in the convention, to the number of 19 entered their protest against the measure.

This course on the part of Van Buren and his freinds, will only tend to add strength to your cause. For now, your freinds, will organize and elect delegates to the same convention by Districts, who will also attend the Baltimore convention, and contest the seats of the ["other" *canceled*] Van Buren Delegates.

Your freinds here, want efficient organization, and an efficient paper. With these two arrangements, wonders may be done in New York in your favour.

Van Buren has no personal popularity And those most warm in his support, are the "old Hunkers" who held office under his late administration, and expect by his restoration to office, to simply regain their places. They support him without personal attachment, or from any love or admiration ["for" *canceled and* "of" *interlined*] the principles with which they ["expect to" *canceled*] profess to be governed. Your freinds on the contrary are conscious of rallying under another kind of man, and with higher motives and principles in view. Hence, among your freinds, ["here" *interlined*] are found, many of the most intellectual and promising young men of the city, with whom, are united a large number of the most retiring, quiet, respectable citizens of New York. As was evinced by the large meeting held in the Park the other day, ["which" *canceled and* "that" *interlined*] I attended. I there saw, one of the most genteel political public assemblages, I have ever ["seen drawn together" *canceled and* "witnessed" *interlined*] in this city. I saw, there, a great many faces, that are new at such places, and which seldom venture beyond the shades of the most [*one word canceled*] honorable private life. These are the proper kind of materials on which a man[']s claims and merit may rest with safety, and ["which" *interlined*] forms a sound bases [*sic*], for any party. With this class you have the Irish population mostly united in your favour, and it only wants a little judicious exertion, ["will" *canceled*] to succeed, in bringing over the ["entire" *canceled and* "all the" *interlined*] Irish ["population" *canceled*] of New York, to your support. And, I am happy, to inform you, that Mr. [John] Tyler's freinds, in the city, manifest a disposition to unite with your freinds, in promoting your interest.

The fact, is, Van Buren, is alarmed, and he is growing desperate in his games, and there is no telling what strategems, he may attempt. He must be closely watched, in all his movements. No body has any sincere confidence in him.

Should I go into a paper devoted to your support, I should desire to conduct it in such a way, as, for it not to prove ["and" *canceled and* "an" *interlined*] injury, instead of a benefit, and would be pleased with your aid and advice, as to the most prudent and efficient method of conducting it. And should to some, entent [*sic*], rely upon your freinds to supply it with manuscript materials—as well as with pecuniary patronage.

I shall be happy to hear from you at any time you may find ["it" *canceled*] a leisure ["moment" *interlined*] from your ["m" *canceled*] numerous calls and engagements to address me a line. While I have the honor to Remain your Sincere, though Humble Freind, Alexr. Jones.

P.S. I have been compelled to write the above, in the midst of the noise, confusion, & company, of a printing office. And in the greatest possible haste as the mail is about closing. A.J.

ALS in ScCleA. NOTE: Alexander Jones (1802–1863), author, physician, inventor, and journalist, was a North Carolinian by birth. He was later involved in organizing the New York Associated Press and in establishing telegraphic news service.

To DUFF GREEN, [London]

Fort Hill, 8th Sep[tembe]r 1843
My dear Sir, I have read with interest your letter [of 8/2]. It gives me much important information, which confirms my previous impressions. I have, in the present remarkable state of things, not been inattentive to the course of events in England, and have come to the conclusion, that it would take the turn you anticipate. England has but one alternative; to harmonize her interest with that of the other portions of the civilized world, or resort to force to maintain her preeminence. If she adopts the former, freedom of commerce and non interference with the institutions of other nations must be the basis of her policy; but if the latter, she must prepare for universal conflict with the civilized world. The danger is, that she will select the latter. If so, it will present a scene of struggle and violence unparalleled in the history of the world, which will end in her downfall; but if the former, it will open a new page of prosperity and civilization never before known on the Globe.

Strange as it may seem, the discussion of the corn law question and the sugar duties, will go far to decide this great issue. In the advanced state of commerce and the arts, the great point of policy for the older and more advanced nations is to command the trade of the newer and less advanced; and that cannot be done, but by opening a free trade in provisions and raw materials with them. The effect of the contrary policy is not only to cripple their commerce and manufactures, by curtailling [*sic*] exchanges; but to force the newer and less advanced portion to become prematurely their competitors. This England now sees and feels, and that to remedy the evil, the corn laws and the sugar duties in favour of her colonies, must be repealed, or that she must resort to force to maintain her commercial and manufacturing superiority. But, if force is resorted to, the blow will first be struck at the U[nited] States, Brazil and other slave holding countries. The reason is obvious. It is indispensible [*sic*] to give her a monopoly of the great staples they produce, and through them, a monopoly of the trade of the world. The abolition of slavery would transfer the production of cotton, rice, and sugar etc. etc. to her colonial possessions, and would consummate the system of commercial monopoly, which she has been so long and systematically pursuing. Hence the movements in Texas and elsewhere on the abolition subject at this time.

I see by your remarks, you have not formed a correct estimate of the state of things on this side of the Ocean. We are not ignorant of the danger to which you allude, but that is not our only danger. If there be danger from the spoils portion of the Democratick party, there is not much less from the Whig party, which is eagerly looking on to profit by any division in our ranks. It is necessary to guard against both, which requires great caution and makes the movements exceedingly complicated; the more so, from the position of Mr. [John] Tyler, who, I understand, is very sanguine.

In the mean time, the elections in Tennessee and Kentucky clearly indicate, the decay of the influence of both Mr. [Martin] V[an] B[uren] and Mr. [Henry] Clay, and a giving away of the foundations on which they stand. In Tennessee, the influence of V[an] B[uren,] Jackson and Polk was perfectly united without any disturbing cause whatever, and yet that is the only State, in which the Whigs have gained and the Democrats lost ground. As to Kentucky, the result speaks for itself and shows a great decay of Clay's influence.

As to myself, I am resolved, that let the election end as it may, I shall take care not to lose position. I shall abandon no principle, or any position, which I have heretofore assumed. Whether victorious, or defeated, it shall be on my own ground. Victory thus won will be worth having, and defeat, if it should come, will not be an overthrow. But within these limits, I shall exercise as much conciliation, as is consistent with preserving them. Of the two, I would rather risk defeat, than character.

PC in Jameson, ed., *Correspondence*, pp. 545–547.

From V[IRGIL] MAXCY

Albany [N.Y.,] 9 Sept. 1843

My dear Sir, I send you some slips from the newspapers, which I have picked up.

Notwithstanding the Syracuse Convention were united almost into unanimity, the Calhoun spirit is not dead. I received this morning a letter from one of the New York committee, saying, they were going to send off 200 Copies immediately to Boston of my Remarks on the National Convention [that is, my pamphlet, *Democratic National Convention?*] & that they should flood the whole State of New York with them. Followed up by the loud thunder which I presume we shall soon hear from your central committee at Charleston, I think the Van Burenites will be frightened and give way, as [Thomas] Ri[t]chie shews symptoms of doing already. Your committee ought to take pains to circulate the Address, which I take for granted, they will make to the people of the United States, far and wide in great numbers in every State & without delay. In great haste Truly y[ou]rs, V. Maxcy.

[P.S.] Address me hereafter, at West River [Md.].

ALS and ms. copy in ScCleA.

FLORIDE [COLHOUN] CALHOUN to Margaret M. [Green] Calhoun, [Marengo County, Ala.]

Forthill, Sept. 10th 1843

My Dear Margaret, You cannot be more disappointed than I am at your not paying us a visit this fall. I was so certain you would come, that I had every thing arranged for your comfort. Had my room down stairs fixed for you, and took Cornelia[']s [Martha Cornelia

Calhoun's], room opening into yours, to be near the Children, as Anna[']s [Anna Maria Calhoun Clemson's] are now so large as not to require me at night, I wish you could see how devoted a mother she is, and I think she has more experience now than I have with them. Both of her Children [John Calhoun Clemson and Floride Elizabeth Clemson] have suffered much with bowel complaints, and still require care in their diet. She desires much love to Eliza [M. Green], and yourself, and says she would like much to compare her Children with yours, but from what she hears, has no doubt but Duff [Green Calhoun] is the finest of all, Susan [Pickens] Calhoun spoke in the most extravagant terms of him, as well as his Grandfather [John C. Calhoun], when he returned [from Ala. in 1841]. Do when you see Susan again give my love to her, and [my nephew] James [Martin Calhoun]. Maria [E. Simkins Colhoun], and all of Francis [W.] Pickens['s] family, (including the Governess) have been spending three weeks with me. Francis is still at times gloomy [over the loss of his wife and a child]. Susan [Wilkinson Pickens] is quite tall and a fine girl. Her father takes her to Philadelphia next month. The three little girls are very sweet little creatures, they play on the Pianno, and Guitar really well. Francis speaks of taking them to Europe in a year or two. The house has been constantly full to overflowing for some time. We have had the Governor [James H. Hammond?] with us, he speaks of purchasing up here, he is so pleased with the climate. He offered to exchange his house in Columbia for Twelvemile. I assure you they are quite comeing out over there, Cuddy [Martha Maria Colhoun], has partys incessantly. She has improved very much from her visit to Columbia this winter. Her Aunt [Mary Cantey?] Hampton, has given her, and her mother [Martha Maria Davis Colhoun], the greatest quantity, of superb dresses, and other things. Also a great deal of pocket money. So much for rich kin. Brother John [Ewing Colhoun] is scarcely ever at home, he stays at the Gold mine [in Ga.], and I understand is doing fine business over there. Persons are finding gold in great abundance, at the mountains. I went up to stay during the hot weather there, and was so much pleased, that I have made Mr. Calhoun, promise when the roads are put in order, he will purchase a place up there for me to spend two months every year, instead of going to the Springs. The mountain scenery surpasses any thing I ever saw. I went to the top of the highest mountain, which is called the chimney top, which is seen from the spot I wish Mr. Calhoun to purchase. In fact there are nothing to be seen from the place, but the highest mountains all around. I had fresh venison, and delightful butter, and cream, which I enjoyed much. Mr. [William H.] Thomas the Indian agent is to have the roads put in fine order to the top of the mountains, two hundred Indians are to work on them. It will then be a trotting road all the way, and we can go easily in a day to our place from here. Andrew [Pickens Calhoun] was wrong to sell his mountain lands to Mr. Sloane [William Sloan?], he is now working gold there to advantage. Mr. [Thomas G.] Clemson, and John [C. Calhoun, Jr.], are now at the mines in Dahlonega, he has just written that they are doing fine business again. They will return next week. John goes to Charleston this winter, the Physicians think it will not suit him to return to the Virginia University, it is too cold for the effection he has of the throat. It does not affect his health, he looks as well as I ever saw him. His standing is very high at the University. We have now [at Pendleton] one of the finest male Academys in the country. James [Edward Calhoun] and William Lownde's [sic; William Lowndes Calhoun's] standing is hi[gh]er than any at the school. James is very tall, and much improved, in looks, and behaviour. He went down with his Aunt Maria [Simkins Colhoun], as my Brother James [Edward Colhoun] could not come up for her. She looks as well as I ever saw her, and her hands are entirely cured, they are now as delicately white as an Infants. I must not forget to mention that Mr. [John S.] Lorton has married the Widow [Amanda Whitner] Kilpatrick, with two Children, She is quite a suitable match for him. He is perfectly devoted to her. The Old Lady is pleased with his choice. They have built a fine house, on the same spot the other was burnt and expect to move into it next month. We are to loose [sic] the four Misses Bates. They have had a fine offer from Tallahassee to keep school, they will be universally regretted. It is said Dr. [William B.] Johnson, of Edgefield is to fill their place, and to preach in the Baptist Church. He now lies very low of congestive fever in Edgefield. Arthur Simkin[s]'s Wife has been ill, since her confinement, but is better. The child died, they have still a little boy left. They have not yet moved from Mr. Clemson[']s place, he crop[p]ed there this summer, as Mr. C[lemson], could not procure Negro[e]s in time to plant himself. But will take possession in October. I do not know what I shall do when they leave me. I will go down with them, and spend some time, between them and Francis Pickens. And perhaps I will visit Charleston. I must not forget to mention that Mr. William Sloan[']s Children, that were deaf, and dumb, have been restored to their hearing by Galvinism. I had it tryed on Cornelia, but I do not think she was benefited in the least. I sent to Charleston for an ear tube like Miss [Harriet] Martineau[']s, and she hears in a whisper through that. She is perfectly delighted with it, and wears it slung round her neck. She is as healthy as ever, and as amiable. She desires much love to Eliza, and yourself, and a kiss to the Children. If Andrew, and yourself, had come out, all the family but Patrick [Calhoun], would have been here together, which would have been delightful and I would not be surprised if Patrick comes on, his Father does not wish him to remain at [Fort] Washita, it is so unhealthy. He has had leave to quit if he chooses. I would be delighted to have Eliza with us, I know she would enjoy herself much with Cuddy, and my niece Eugenia Calhoun, who has been spending the summer with us. She is a sweet girl. Cornelia[']s doves are all alive still, She is perfectly devoted to them, and the Parrots. James has a pet Bear, which is a great curiossity and William Lowndes a Deer which is very beautiful with large branching horns, it begins to be troublesome, I intend getting several, and having a park arround the spring. We have made several improvements here since you left. Our fruit has been very fine this year, particularly peaches. I have been very busy preserving Quinces. I wish you were near enough to me to send you preserves. I loaded off Maria, and Lucretia Towndes [sic; Lucretia Calhoun Townes] with preserves of all sorts. I heard a short time since that Mrs. Kroft[?] of Greenville was extreemly ill, but I do not wish you to mention it to Elizabeth unless she has heard it. Give my love to her. I am affraid I have tired you out with this nonsensical epistle therefore will conclude with much love to all. And may a kind Providence, watch over you, and yours, is the sincere prayer of your devoted mother. Kiss the dear Children for me. Floride Calhoun.

ALS in ScU-SC, John C. Calhoun Papers. NOTE: On 9/20/1843, John C. Calhoun, Jr. wrote to Willis H. Woodley, Proctor of the University of Virginia: "As my health still continues delicate, father has concluded not to let me return to the University; but to send me to Charleston, where the climate is less changeable, and is therefore recommended as being more suitable to my disease." (ALS in ViU, University Archives, Proctors' Records.)

From HENRY A. COLE and Others

Clarksville [Tenn.,] Sep[tember] 10th 1843
Dear Sir, We address you as one of those distinguished leaders of the democratic party who by a long and devoted attachment to Democratic principles merit the esteem and respect of the Young Men Of America. To you and to others who have manifested thro-out long political Careers, unconquerable attachment to the great fundamental

principles of Equality of Rights We now direct our attention. The storm tossed Mariner looks With anxiety for some Beacon light whose Calm and Constant blaze points him to the Harbour of Safety. The Young men of America With equal eagerness Watch the political Course of those American statesmen Who are the inflexible advocates of the Inalienable Rights of Man, Cherishing the great principles of Democracy. *You* Cannot but look With anxiety upon the political Bias the minds of the Young men may take. The destinies of this Glorious republic Will ere long be in their Keeping. To You and to other distinguished democrats they look for exposition of the democratic Creed. The Federalists boast that at the last election in this State a majority of the Young men Voted With them, if this is true tis a melancholly [*sic*] truth and is Caused by a Want of investigation upon the part of the democratic Young men. Deeply feeling the importance of the extension of our Principles the Democrats of this County last monday held a meeting and passed resolutions proposing A Convention of the Young Men of Tennessee and the undersigned Were appointed a Committee of Arrangement for the occasion. The object of the Meeting is to Produce a more thorough promulgation of our principles. And now Sir In this emergency We look to you. Let the Democratic Young men of Tenn. know that you feel deeply interested in their behalf, that you Will be With them in Convention on 9th Novem[ber] 1843 at this place And We anticipate the happiest results upon the part of the democratic Young men. We therefore urgently solicit Your presence at our Convention, and respectfully ask an early response to this invitation So that if You Will attend we may Circulate the News far and Wide. With sentiments of the highest respect, We are Sir Your friends, Henry A. Cole, D.S. Newell, T. Rives, Sy.[?] T. Baughn, B.F. Moody, W[illiam] S. McClure, R.H. Moody, Ja[me]s N. Dortch[?], A.G. Wilcox, John S. Hart, John Parker, H.S. Garland, Ja[me]s Darrett, J.H. Hiter, D. Elliott, Isaac Brunson, Ed[ward] Howard, W[illia]m M. Shelton, John F. Couts, M.E. Wilcox, Ja[me]s [M.] Quarles, John Y. Jordan, W[illia]m J. Wynne, Geo[rge] Parker, J[?].M. Dye, Lo. O. Burden[?], L[ucien] B. Chase, "Committee of Arrangement."

LS in ScCleA. NOTE: An AEU by Calhoun reads: "Invitation to attend the meeting at ClarksVille Ten[nes]se[e,] Ans[were]d 20th Oct[obe]r." The answer has not been found.

"Address of the Committee Appointed by a Meeting of Democratic Voters in the City of New York, Held in the Park, 4th Sept. 1843," 9/11. This address was issued in the names of John L.H. McCracken,

Emanuel B. Hart, and John Hecker, the committee which had been appointed by the meeting of 9/4. [McCracken was Secretary of the New York Chamber of Commerce.] The address compares the claims of Martin Van Buren and Calhoun for the Presidential nomination and concludes that Calhoun has always been forthright and consistent while Van Buren has been the candidate of political managers and "has no personal popularity; he never had any; and the deliberate approbation, half negative, that we bestow on his public career is a thing as different from the genial feelings of friendship with which men speak of [Andrew] Jackson or Calhoun, as a certificate of good character is different from a cordial embrace." The address calls upon the citizens of N.Y. to overthrow the decision of the State Democratic Convention held at Syracuse on 9/5 as to the election of delegates to the Democratic National Convention. "The contract that puts the State of New York into the keeping of thirty-four men, to be delivered over, bound hand and foot, to Mr. Van Buren, must be annulled, for there are thousands upon thousands among its people who might have voted for him voluntarily, yet who will not be dragooned into it thus." PC in the New York, N.Y., *Evening Post*, September 12, 1843, p. 2.

To R[OBERT] M. T. HUNTER,
[Essex County, Va.]

Fort Hill, 12th Sep[tembe]r 1843

My dear Sir, I have no doubt, but that the course to which you refer has a powerful ["effect" *interlined*] in the North & North West; and that it has been secretly used by [Martin] Van Buren & his friends to weaken me. It ought to have been struck at vigorously when his papers first made a point of it aga[i]nst me, & the South, but that having passed, I do not think it ["will" *canceled and* "would" *interlined*] be advisable to move on the subject 'till some new occasion shall offer, which, if it should not before, it will be sure to do, ["so" *canceled*] during the next session of Congress. The slave question will then come up in some form, or another; either on the presentation of petitions, or in connection with Texas or the circular, said to be sent by the British Government to its consuls to acquire & report minutely on the condition of our slaves; when the friends of Mr. Van Buren will be compelled to show their hands. If my memory serves

431

me, the N[ew] York Legislature has not yet repealed the obnoxious act ag[ai]nst which the act of your Legislature was ["in part" *interlined*] directed, granting jury trial to fugitive slaves. If so, it will give a proper occasion to test the course of his friends on that vital question to the South. They have now, or will have a majority in both Houses of their Legislature, and will have no excuse, should they refuse to repeal the act. The question once opened ["the discussion" *interlined*] can ["then" *canceled*] receive the direction you suggest, & be connected ["itself" *canceled*] with the grounds taken by the N[ew] York Post, & the Rochester & Nantucket papers ag[ai]nst myself on the subject; and ag[ai]nst which, if I am right, Mr. [Thomas] Ritchie never raised his voice, or, if at all, in the feeblest tone.

I am of the impression, with you, that Mr. V[an] B[uren] is gain-[in]g strength in Pennsyl[vani]a, but ["that he" *interlined*] never can obtain sufficient to get the votes of the State. I never thought, that [James] Buchanan's hold on the State was strong. The great object of ["his friends there in" *interlined*] rallying on him ["there" *canceled*] was to wait events, and I am of the impression, that when the time comes, he will be too weak, or too timid to control the State; ["and" *canceled*] I have never calculated, accordingly, that he would have the control of ["the" *canceled and* "its" *interlined*] choice ["of the State" *canceled*]. It will go for the strongest, be he who he ["will" *canceled and* "may" *interlined*]; I mean, he who is most likely to succeed. I have no doubt, that Mr. Buchanan is in reality opposed to Mr. Van Buren, and would prefer the election of [*partial word canceled*] almost any other; but he will not seperate from the majority of the State, go which way it may. In a word, to control the State, *strength must be shown out of it.* If her votes can decide ["it" *canceled and* "the election" *interlined*] between V[an] B[uren] & any other, they will not be given to him.

It is now manifest, that the ["publick" *canceled*] sentiment of the party is in favour of appointing delegates by Districts and voting per capita. The indications are strong, that both Missouri & Tennessee will decide for that plan; and the question ["is" *interlined*], will N[ew] York & Virginia hold out for their plan? I say their plan, for it originated in Albany & Richmond. The politicians that control the two, will never yield but on compulsion. On ["mainting" *canceled and* "adhering to" *interlined*] it rests their scheme of power & ambition; and on defeating it, rests our hope of reforming the Gover[n]ment & restoring the Constitution. If they adhere, we cannot yield, and a split will be the consequence. In that case, I am decidedly of the opinion, our papers ought at once ["to" *interlined*] come out in a call on all, who are in favour of the rights of the people, and ["ag(ai)nst" *interlined*] the dictation of cliques & political managers, to select delegates in each Congressional District, where there are ["such" *interlined*] districts, as the only means left ["the people" *interlined*] of taking the power into their own hands, and out of those of their would be dictators and managers. I am also of the opinion, that the proceedings of the Syracuse Convention ought to be the signal ["to move" *interlined*], should it, in spite of the strong demonstration ag[ai]nst it[,] adhere to the plan. It ["would" *interlined*] make the crisis, which, if seized, would give us the control; but if not, it ["will" *canceled and* "would" *interlined*] pass from us to them. The bolder & more prompt[ly] it is seized the better & more safe. The Petersburgh Republican should come out without delay.

I fear my answer to [William] Smith's letter in ["reference to the Rhode" *canceled and* "reply to his" *interlined*] questions growing out of the Rhode Island affair, may have miscarried, as I, as well as yourself, have not heard from ["him" *interlined*], though, I requested him to let me hear from him, as soon as he received ["it" *canceled and* "my answer" *interlined*]. I wrote to him by the last mail, to ascertain whether he had got it, or not, and informed him, that if he had not, I would for[th]with transmit him a copy. I would be glad you could see my answer and that of the others. I am strongly inclined to think, that ["at" *interlined*] some stage of the contest, the answers ought to be published. The principles involved are vital, and it is right, that the sentiments of the candidates should be known. I have no fear, that I would be injured.

As far as I am informed every thing is going on well South of Virginia. Yours truly, J.C. Calhoun.

[P.S.] I am glad to hear, that [Thomas W.] Gilmer [Representative from Va.] is right. It is important that [Henry A.] Wise [Representative from Va.] should go with us. His letter to your dinner was kind. I read the proceedings at the dinner with interest. What is [William C.] Rives [Senator from Va.] doing?

ALS in ScCleA; variant PC in Jameson, ed., *Correspondence*, pp. 547–549.

From ALBERT RHETT

Charleston, Sep[tember] 12, 1843
My Dear Sir, I sit down only to acknowledge the receipt of yours covering the article in reply to Mr. [Thomas] Ritchie, which shall

appear in the [Charleston] Mercury tomorrow. Col. [Franklin H.] Elmore is absent up the Country. The article did not appear to me to need any correction or addition, and it will therefore be published as it is.

The Ball is now fairly opened and [Martin] Van Buren has led off, we must confess, boldly in the Dance; it will require equal boldness on our part to turn him in the figure, and trip up his heels, before he gets to the end. I am glad our friends in New York [City] appear of so determined a spirit; it should be our aim to confirm and stimulate them, for if they lose heart and give way, the torrent will roll over them and us, and all go down together. We have heard from Brother B. [Robert Barnwell Rhett] who has been waiting in Washington for Mr. [Robert M.T.] Hunter, but will be in New York [City] at the end of this week, furnished with funds to establish a Press, without which it is quite vain for us to expect to gain ground, or keep it if we gain it.

Our proper course seems to me to be to fight them before the People on the District System, and not break till we find we can[']t beat them and they are put clearly in the wrong. But I think we shall in no event go into a National Convention organised on the New York and Virginia Plan, for while we could gain nothing by it, the sanctioning such a precedent would inflict irreparable injury on the welfare of the country, and especially of the South. In one of the accounts given of the proceedings of the Syracuse Convention it is said that Col. [Samuel] Young (who went there by the way, as he confessed himself, representing only some 25 men) declared that if New York succeeded in putting in Mr. Van Buren, there was no doubt she could make Silas Wright his successor. The truth is that those men—the present Leaders, I mean, of the Democratic Party—are not going to let you be President ever, if they can prevent it, and no sort of reliance is to be placed on their promises and pledges—it seem[s] to be thought by them no disgrace in Politics to lie, whatever, but evidence of consummate skill to do so successfully. But I beg pardon for this garrulity. I am most resp[ectfully] & truly, Albert Rhett.

P.S. Mr. [John A.] Stuart returned today from the North—but, I am sorry to say, no better.

P.S. On the suggestion of Mr. [Virgil] Maxcey [*sic*], who will not be in Washington before the 20th, we shall forward immediately to our friends in Boston 500 copies of the S.C. Address. I strongly apprehend though that Van Buren will get a Convention nomination in New England.

ALS in ScCleA.

From I[srael] K. Tefft, "Corresponding Secretary" of the Georgia Historical Society, Savannah, 9/12. Tefft informs Calhoun that he has been elected an honorary member of the Society at a meeting on 9/11. The constitution, officers, and by-laws of the Society are printed on this document. An AEU by Calhoun reads, "I.K. Tefft announcing my appointment as honorary member of the Georgia Historical Society." PDS in ScCleA.

L[EMUEL] WILLIAMS to
[Virgil Maxcy in New York?]

Boston, Sep[t.] 12th 1843
Dear Sir, I have this morning received a letter from J. F[rancis] Hutton Esq. with a dozen pamphlets which I have caused to be circulated, among the members of the convention to be held to-morrow at Worcester. I have sent to Col. [Charles G.] Green[e] & [Daniel D.] Brodhead for their copies which I hope to obtain if they have arrived in the city. I have this moment received information from Col. Green[e], who received but few copies. I cannot learn that Col. Brodhead has received any. Your resolutions have not yet been received, & I fear will not.

I regret that a larger number of the pamphlets have not been forwarded, as they might have been circulated to advantage. Our convention will assemble at 9 o[']clock tomorrow & as the next mail does not arrive here until after the cars leave for Worcester I shall not receive your reloustions [*sic*] in time Which I very much regret.

You say you "fear the Van Buren machinery is unbroken in Massachusetts, & is too strong for us." I entertain no apprehension as to the result of the convention. My office has been crowded all day with the delegates from different parts of the State. We shall have over two hundred delegates, & many of our friends think a a majority. The chances are that we shall prevent a nomination of Van Buren, & perhaps a choice *at this time* of two delegates at large.

Calhoun's friends here are in high spirits & rejoicing at the good tidings from Maine, just received, by express. The nomination of Van Buren, by the Convention called to nominate a governor, has given great offence to the friends of Calhoun in Maine & [Hugh J.] Anderson[,] the Van Buren candidate will lose his election. [John] Fairfield[,] the democratic candidate was elected last year by about six thousand majority. This result will prove the unpopularity of Van Buren in Maine & has made a great impression unfavorable to the magician. In Cumberland County [former Governor Robert P.] Dunlap the Calhoun candidate to Congress has [been] elected by upwards of a thousand majority. The friends of Calhoun in Maine intend to rally next spring & instruct their delegates to the Baltimore Convention to vote for Calhoun, or they will choose new delegates. Calhoun[']s prospects never looked so well at the North as they do to day. Van Buren will never receive the nomination of the Baltimore Convention. Our strongest opponent I think will be Col. [Richard M.] Johnson. But of this when we meet. Why cannot you meet me in New York, where I wrote you I should be on Sunday morning on the arrival of the steamboat from the North & shall stop at the Astor House to breakfast & if I do not meet you shall proceed the same day to Philadelphia. I would wait at New York until monday for the purpose of seeing the Calhoun committee & ["making" *canceled and* "make" *interlined*] arrangements for the coming contest with them. There should be a concert among Mr. Calhoun[']s [friends] throughout the country. We intend to establish a Calhoun paper here, if the Post does not come out & take strong ground for us.

Wednesday [Sept.] 13[,] 12 o[']clock

I have this moment seen Col. Broadhead, who has just come into my office with the "Resolutions," which came here this morning. A fatality seems to have attended them. Why were they not sent yesterday? 50 copies of the Convention I received this morning which I should have been glad to have had sooner. Can your friends in New York have been informed of the time of the holding of our convention? I have this moment sent a messenger to Worcester with the resolutions to be put into the hands of one who will make use of them if not too late. They will reach Worcester at 3 O[']clock. I have also sent the pamphlets. I have great confidence that the Van Burenites will not be able to carry his nomination. The news from Maine has frightened many & strengthens our hands. Do leave a line for me at the Astor House indicating where you may be found, if you have left N[ew] York. In haste, yours truly, L. Williams.

P.S. I shall arrive in N[ew] York on Sunday & if you have left go on to Philadelphia[,] stop at the U[nited] States Hotel & leave P[hiladelphia] for Baltimore on Monday. Do stay in N.Y. & go on with me.

P.S. I intended to have written Calhoun but it will do as well for you to forward[?] him this letter which do *without* delay.

ALS in ScCleA.

From S. A. LAURENCE

New-York [City,] 13th September 1843

Dear Sir: The meeting *held* here on Monday week [9/4], was hastily, if not inconsiderately, got up; and neither shows the Character, nor number of persons friendly to your election, since many of the most respectable and influential were not apprised of the meeting in time. I was called upon on *Sunday*, and invited to serve as an Officer of a Meeting to be held the next day! without having seen the Call, or names of the Officers, or order of business and Resolutions; and of course declined—having long since laid it down as a rule, to understand *before-hand*, the principles, and contemplated proceedings, of political meetings, previous to sanctioning the same with my name.

The Chairman waited upon me the next day, and explained the manner of getting it up &c. I encouraged the effort, and suggested, for future operations, the *District plan* of calling meetings in this City. I also urged upon him—and now pray leave to present to your consideration—the necessity and importance of establishing in this City, a Democratic paper, friendly to your Election. It would, as I observed to him, do more good, than forty mass meetings! and recommended prompt and strong exertions for its establishment, which I think will be made with success. An issue of 2000 daily papers at Two Cents each, will be required to defray the expense, and sustain such a journal—1000 can be circulated in this City and State, and Subscriptions are now being obtained; for the balance foreign aid must be solicited, and can unquestionably be procured. Perhaps the most ready and easy mode of accomplishing it, is by furnishing the names of one or more prominent, influential friends in each State, who should be apprised of the importance of the enterprise (by a Central Committee of one or more members from each State, to be organized for the general purposes of furthering your Election) and invited to aid in its Circulation not only, but also to furnish Articles and Communications; and, if it can be so arranged, that a given number of papers shall be guaranteed to be circulated in each State, there would be little or no delay in its publication. The Pleb[e]ian is the only Democratic morning paper published in this City, and speaks for itself!

A strong Democratic morning paper, denominated the "United States Advocate," or some other appropriate name conducted by an able Editor, of great respectability, probity, and a high order of talent, advocating the *Union* & doctrine of Free Trade and sailors[’s] rights, is required in this City; and, in my opinion, would succeed, and yield a fair profit to the proprietor; and most assuredly, it would carry a

very great political influence and weight in your favor. It would unquestionably be the most useful and powerful engine, that can be
brought to bear upon the enemy, if worked adroitly upon the high
pressure System, and the Steam kept up, by editorial articles—communications—extracts from other papers [and] from your pamphlet—
remarks upon your patriotic conduct towards the [Martin] Van Buren
administration, in sacrificing private opinions and pregudices [*sic*] of
the man & with a single eye for the public good, throwing yourself in
the gap, & thereby saving his administration from dissolution, and
preserving the Union & integrity of the Democratic party—shewing up
his ingratitude in becoming your Competitor under such circumstances—his deception and want of honesty in professing to approve
the *one term* doctrine, and, at the same time, offer himself for a second
term! But, in his case, I am not surprised at any of these things; for
I have marked his entire political career. He, not having had the
benefit of a Classical Education, and all his time having been occupied in the practice of law, and the turmoil of politics, has had little
or no time for Reading or improvement, which has always operated
much against him—but he early acquired the character of an artful,
cunning, selfish politician, which he still retains. And these qualifications, with fugitive political principles, and much good luck, has
raised him to the high political position he now holds, and *nothing
else!* What great or good act, has he ever performed for this State,
or the United States? If any, I am ignorant of it!

The Irish vote in this City is very large; and a member of their
fraternity, observed to me a few days ago, that Mr. Van Buren would
not get 300 of these votes in this City & County! At the Syracuse
Convention, his friends had a majority, and as you'll observe have rejected the District plan, and adopted the old anti-republican system
of choosing delegates. The proceedings of the Convention are irreg-
ular; and they, in appointing Electors, have exceeded their powers!
& many members were received *without Credentials!* Four of our
delegates *protested*, and have called, or will shortly call a meeting of
our citizens friendly to the District System, and lay before them the
entire proceedings of the Convention, which will not—cannot be
sanctioned.

The inf[l]uence, I most fear, is the Anti Slavery Societies; and
should they act in concert, it will be a powerful vote, & *given* to the
Candidate who favors their principles. This subject, requires deep
consideration, and must be met, and controverted; its unjust, improper & dangerous tendencies, and their *fatal consequences* if carried
out, would be a Violation of the federal Compact, and cause a separa-

tion of the Union! Let it once be understood, that no President, shall hereafter come from a slave holding State, and the Rubicon is passed! But relying as I do upon the good sense, intel[l]igence, and patriotism, of the citizens of the U.S.—I hope for, and expect, a more favorable result. Pray excuse the liberty I take in addressing you, as above, but I feel a deep interest in the success of your Election, and a desire to do what I can to promote it; and have thought, that some of the ["preceeding" *interlined*] suggestions, may in some slight degree, benefit the Cause. With a tender of my services, which you may freely command I remain Very respectfully & truly Y[ou]rs, S.A. Laurence.

ALS in ScCleA; PC in Jameson, ed., *Correspondence*, pp. 878–881.

"The South Carolina Convention and Mr. Ritchie," by A MEMBER OF THE CONVENTION

[Published at Charleston, September 13, 1843] FOR THE MERCURY. *Mr. Editor*—The way in which Mr. [Thomas] Ritchie [in the Richmond, Va., *Enquirer* of August 22] has met my questions, has disappointed me, in matter and manner. I say Mr. Ritchie, because he has dropped the character of editor, and has come out in his individual capacity, which I regret, as it is calculated to give my notice of him more of a personal character, than I desire.

He has long and frequently called on the editor of the Mercury [John A. Stuart] to be informed, whether the friends of Mr. Calhoun in this State intend to adhere uncompromisingly to the recommendations of our Convention, and intimated in a pretty plain manner his suspicion, that South Carolina intended to take her own way, without regard to the course of her sister States. The absence of the editor of the Mercury from indisposition, made it impossible for him to reply, and I, as one of the members of our Convention, assumed to answer for him. He was told, that our ultimate course would depend on that of the other States, and especially Virginia, and that, in order to answer the questions of the [Richmond] Enquirer, it was necessary to know, what would be her ultimate course. To ascertain that, two great questions were asked in the plainest and most direct terms. The one, whether the friends of Mr. [Martin] Van Buren in Virginia would uncompromisingly adhere to the grounds taken in their Convention, and the other, whether they would abide by the decision of the ma-

439

jority of her sister States. They were put in good faith, without the least intention to embarrass, and with the sincere desire, that they should lead to a fair understanding on the important points involved. Mr. Ritchie, in putting the questions to us, gave us a right to put them back to him, preparatory to our answer. He did more. He gave us the just right to infer, that he was prepared to answer on his part the questions propounded to us, whenever called upon. To suppose otherwise, would be to attribute to him a trick, or gross impertinence, unworthy of his character and standing in the editorial corps.

Under these circumstances, I anticipated a plain, direct and manly response; but instead of that, he has evaded the questions; asked a half dozen or more irrelevent, or unnecessary questions, under the plea of explanation, shifted the responsibility of answering from himself to his correspondents, and shaped for them, the answers he desires, by leading questions and significant hints, in the form of comments. I say evaded, for he has undertaken, "in a manner," to use his own expression, to answer my first question, but instead of saying whether the friends of Mr. Van Buren in Virginia *intended to adhere uncompromisingly* to the plan of their Convention, which I desired to know, he has told us what that plan is, which is known to all.

To make good the assertion, that his questions, asking for explanation, are either irrelevant or unnecessary, it is only requisite that they should be quoted. After a long series of introductory remarks preparatory to publishing my questions, intended in his way to give the direction he desires to the attention of his readers, he says:

"Yet we wish to understand the proposition of 'A Member of the Convention,' in order that our appeal to the Republicans of Virginia may be better understood by them. How is the voice of the *"majority of the States"* to be collected? Are they all to count *one?* Is the smallest State to be on the same footing of equality with the largest? Is New York, with a population of 2,428,291, to have no more weight in a question, which is to decide the whole question in the Convention, than Delaware, with a population of only 78,085? That is, is New York, with 30 times as many people as Delaware, to have no more weight in the decision of the great preliminary problem? Is this the proposition? Does Pendleton, after claiming for the smaller States a vote in the Convention in a sort of compound, indefinable ratio, of the *electoral vote* before the people, and a contingent, uncertain right of *equality* of voting, before the H[ouse] of R[epresentatives] think it right, and does he appeal to the magnanimity of Virginia, her "elevated position and character," to refer the question "to a majority of the States to decide"—and abandon his compound ratio for a *simple equality* of votes? Is this what he means? But as it is possible, that we may not understand the proposition, we most respectfully call upon "A Member of the Convention" to answer at once. We must first ask the question of him, before Virginia can undertake to answer his questions. We, therefore, pause for a reply."

Had Mr. Ritchie not said, that this string of interrogations was intended to elicit explanation, in order to enable him to understand my second question, I certainly never should have suspected that was his object. Upon their face, they seem to be intended more for his readers and correspondents than for me; and much better calculated to forestall their opinion, than to call forth explanations. I shall, however, take him at his word, and answer them in the order they stand, although I am at a loss to perceive, what light the most full and explicit answers can reflect on the question, on which he says he desires explanation.

His first question is, "How is the voice of the *majority* of the States to be collected?" The question is somewhat equivocal, but I presume that its meaning is; How is the voice of the States to be ascertained? Taken in that sense, it is sufficient to say, that it will be time enough to decide that, after it is ascertained, that the friends of Mr. Van Buren are willing to abide by the decision of a majority of the States. In that case, the voice of the States could easily be ascertained by a mutual appeal to the other States, by the central Committees of South Carolina and Virginia, the manner in which the Indiana appeal was made, on the preliminary question of time. It would not be more difficult in this case, than in that.

The next question is, "Are they all" (each) "to count one?" Yes, certainly. They cannot be counted in any other way. A majority of the States means the greater number of the States, and the only way by which that can be ascertained is by counting all and taking the greater part.

The next is; "Is the smallest State to be on an equality with the largest?" yes; and such must be the necessary result on the Virginia plan, which assumes, that each State has a right to decide for itself, how the Convention shall be constituted. When States act as States they are all regarded as equal. Mr. Ritchie seems to forget, that ours is a Federal, not a National Republic, and that States, not individuals, are its constituent elements; and that in such a Republic, each, be it great or small, has an equal voice; unless where the Constitution provides otherwise.

Then follows the question; "Is New York with her 2,428,291 to have no more weight in a question, which is to decide the whole ques-

tion in the Convention, than Delaware with a population of 78,085?["]
yes, if N[ew] York should undertake to decide that question for herself, as a State. Acting as such, she has not a particle more right,
than Delaware. To decide otherwise, would be to destroy the foundation of State Rights, and to lay broad and deep, that of Consolidation.

Next follows the question, "Is New York, with 30 times the population of Delaware, to have no more weight in the decision of the
great preliminary problem." Not a particle more, if she undertakes to
decide as a State, just as she had no more, acting as a State, in framing
and ratifying the Constitution, which is the great organic law of Government, as the preliminary arrangements are of the Convention. The
principle, which governed in the one case, is equally applicable in the
other, and such was the decision of the friends of Mr. V[an] B[uren]
in New York itself, in the Indiana appeal on the great preliminary
question of the time of holding the Convention. The central Committee (the most authentic party organized in the State) acquiesced
in the postponement of the time from November to May, on the
ground, that such was the decision of the majority of the States. Such
too, only a short month since, was the opinion of Mr. Ritchie himself,
on the still greater question of holding a Convention. His opinion
may be found in the Enquirer of the 8th of August last, in the leading
editorial, headed "who is the Catechist." In answer to the question,
"does the State of Virginia intend to hold a National Convention in
November next?" he says, "she does not, she cannot form a National
Convention herself—nor does she wish to attempt one, with the concurrence of a minority of the States: *she is willing to sacrifice her own
wishes to those of a majority of her Sister States.*" Here we have the
deliberate admission, that it belongs to the majority to decide, whether
there shall be a National Convention or not, and that Virginia will
yield her wishes to the majority of her sister States; that is, in the
language of my question, she will abide by the decision of the majority
of the States, how the Convention shall be constituted; but which, if
we may judge from his course now, he utterly repudiates. How is this
sudden and total change to be accounted for?

His remaining questions are so perfectly and clearly irrelevant,
that I do not deem them worthy of a reply. They are plainly intended
for effect, and have nothing to do with explanation; so much so, that
I am surprised, that so experienced and dexterous a politician as Mr.
Ritchie, should put questions so little in accord with his avowed object, as to be calculated to call in question his candour and fairness.
But in declining to answer them, it is proper that I should repel the

insinuation, that the friends of Mr. Calhoun intend to insist on an equality of vote in making the nomination. There is no foundation whatever for it. They make a distinction between the preliminary questions and the nomination. In making the nomination they concede, as a fundamental principle, that every State should have the same relative weight, as is secured to it by the Constitution, in the election; meaning by election, the whole election, not a part, and including, as well the eventual choice by the House of Representatives, as that by the electoral college. What should be the standard by which the relative weight of each State should be determined, is, in their opinion, a question for deliberation. They believe the best practicable is, that the delegates should be chosen by districts, and that they should vote per capita, and on that account, and because it is the most popular and Democratic in its character, and best calculated to take the Convention out of the hands of political managers, they prefer it. The preliminary questions are such as in their nature require to be fixed in advance. They stand as has been said, to the Convention, as the Constitution does to the Government; and, both analogy and the reason of the thing demand, that the same authority which constituted the one, should, as far as practicable, constitute the other. It is thus only, that the analogy between the nomination and election can be preserved, and the just weight of the States in the election be maintained in the nomination.

But what has disappointed me most in Mr. Ritchie's course is, his attempt to shift the responsibility of the reply from himself to his correspondents. I say attempt; for what he aims at, will wholly fail him. The response of his correspondents will be regarded but as his echo. Indeed, he himself seems to regard them as of a very accommodating disposition; for his appeal to them is very little more than a letter of instruction, directing them what reply to make. Instead of submitting the two questions to which I ask his answer to them, as propounded by myself, without comment, for their decision, he has entirely changed them into leading questions of his own, accompanied by comments, which as clearly tell them what answer he desires, as the leading question of an experienced dextrous advocate, intended to extract from a witness a desired answer, tells him what it is. Not content with all these precautions, he reserves to himself the right of concealing the name of his correspondents, and publishing or not publishing their answers, and accompanying them with his glosses, as he pleases; and their answer is to be taken as the voice of Virginia.

A more unsatisfactory mode of taking it could not be conceived. Mr. Ritchie's own answer to our questions, on his direct personal responsibility, would have been much more satisfactory. If he really desired to have the voice of the people, why did he not call on them to express it through primary assemblies in the several counties, or take it through the agency of the Central Committee? Either would have been greatly preferable. But I shall not dwell upon the point. All I want is a response from Mr. Ritchie to my questions—a plain, direct and simple response. It matters little, whether it comes directly from him, or through him from his correspondents, so that he recognizes it as the voice of the friends of Mr. Van Buren in Virginia. What I want to know is, whether they are resolved to adhere, uncompromisingly, to the grounds taken by their Convention, and not to yield to the voice of a majority of the sister States.

There is much in this connection, in the course of Mr. Ritchie and some other of the friends of Mr. Van Buren, which requires explanation. They profess to care but little how the Convention shall be constituted. Their declarations would lead to the belief, that they are prepared to yield a ready obedience to the decision of the Convention, wherever and whenever held, and however constituted, and have even attempted to excite suspicion against the sincerity of those who do not subscribe to the same creed. They also profess to be the peculiar friends of compromise and concession—all for principles and nothing for men dwells on their lips. But when it comes to the test, they show a more stern, uncompromising disposition to have the Convention their own way, and less disposed to compromise and concession, than any other portion of the party. It is true, they have yielded on the question of time, but it was only on extortion, when the voice of the party proved so overwhelming against them, that they could hold out no longer.

Another point requires explanation. They profess to think that Mr. V[an] B[uren] is by far the most popular candidate with the mass of the people, and the columns of the *Enquirer* are filled with communications intended to make the impression that such is the fact; and yet, the editor and the friends of Mr. Van Buren are the most opposed of all others to leaving the decision to the mass of the people in their primary assemblies, and most strenuously in favor of the plan which takes it farthest from them, and leaves it most under the control of political managers. How are these apparent contradictions to be explained? [Signed:] A Member of the Convention.

PC in the Charleston, S.C., *Mercury*, September 13, 1843, p. 2. NOTE: The first paragraph of the letter of 9/12/1843 from Albert Rhett to Calhoun, above, seems ample evidence for Calhoun's authorship of this article.

From V[IRGIL] MAXCY

New York [City,] 14 Sept. 1843
My dear Sir, I believe in my last I mentioned that I had taken up the pen to write something on the subject of a National Convention, after I arrived at Saratoga, which might counteract an artful piece taken from [Amos] Kendall's Examiner [*sic*; *Expositor*] & republished in the Albany Argus on the same subject & designed to affect the proceedings of the Syracuse convention. I had not been engaged an hour before a member of the Calhoun Committee of this city called on me at Saratoga saying he had come from New York [City] to consult with me about their plans in New York & more especially the meeting to be called in the Park [on 9/4]. Calling his attention to the piece in the Albany Argus, I told him I had determined to write something to counteract it, when he urged me to do it immediately, that they might print it in New York [City] & send it to the convention at Syracuse. I accordingly did it and sent him the manuscript but a detention by the mail prevented their getting it printed in time to reach the Syracuse Convention. They then decided ["to stereotype &" *interlined*] to circulate them throughout the State to aid in exciting your friends to an organization in Congressional districts: and at my suggestion sent off a parcel of them to Boston for the Massachusetts Convention & circulation in N[ew] England. I send you a few copies [of *Democratic National Convention*]. The extreme haste in which I wrote must excuse the imperfections of the pamphlet. You will see I have not hesitated to make free use of the So[uth] Ca[rolina] Address [of 5/24/1843] & anything else on the subject that I thought appropriate.

On my arrival here yesterday the Calhoun Committee called to see me but made a mistake as to the Hotel & I received afterwards an invitation to meet them at a member[']s, Mr. [Emanuel B.?] Hart's house. I was delighted with the zeal that animates them. They are not at all frightened by the proceedings of the Syracuse Convention. They have called another meeting this evening in the Park, not exactly as a Calhoun meeting but of all opposed to the proceedings of the Convention. They are selling [*sic*; setting?] out the establishment of a newspaper, in which they have no doubt of succeeding. The Editors of the Commercial [*sic*; *Journal of Commerce*?], they think, could not be induced to make a partizan paper of their journal, and moreover think in its present attitude it is doing more good than in a partizan capacity, as it is essentially an advocate of the cause.

After receiving Col. [Franklin H.] Elmore's letter, respecting the Charleston movement to raise funds for the Spectator I wrote to L[emuel] Williams, in Boston & Col. [Daniel D.] Brodhead to sound [Charles G.] Greene of the Post & Mr. [Edmund T.] Bridge, whether either of them would undertake the Editorship, but they decline. I don[']t like [Shadrach] Penn, & I fear we will find it difficult to get precisely the man we want. I cannot find such a one here. I shall persevere. I go south tomorrow & hope to see [Robert Barnwell] Rhett & [Robert M.T.] Hunter in Washington. In haste Always yours, V. Maxcy.

[P.S.] Greene & Bridge both declined on the ground they were more useful where they are. Williams thinks so too.

ALS and ms. copy in ScCleA. NOTE: The Boston, Mass., *Post*, September 18, 1843, p. 2, carried a report of the New York City meeting which Maxcy indicated above was to take place "this evening." The meeting of 9/14 was attended by about 3,000. Not all of the leaders and speakers were previously identified as Calhoun supporters. The meeting passed resolutions supporting Calhoun for President, favoring the district system for electing delegates to the national convention (which had just been rejected by the N.Y. State Convention), and urged "the friends of the district system in every congressional district throughout the State, to hold meetings and organize, and select each their own representative to the Baltimore convention." On 9/26 Democrats of the Seventh Ward met in pursuance of the injunction to "organize," endorsed Calhoun and the district system, and appointed a committee to cooperate with that appointed on 9/4. (New York, N.Y., *Evening Post*, September 29, 1843, p. 2.) Another report of the meeting of 9/14 appeared in the New York, N.Y., *Evening Post*, September 16, 1843, p. 2. This stated, in part: ". . . the great leader of the custom house rowdies, Mike Walsh, who with his Subterranean band, have been supposed to stand at the head of the Tyler party and carry out the wise wishes of the principal officers of the government, made a speech and openly and avowedly announced himself a Calhoun man."

From J. F. G. MITTAG

Charlotte N.C., Sept[embe]r 15th 1843
Some difference of opinion prevails in this section of country in regard to your views on the subject of discriminating duties. I have always understood the State Rights Party to be in favor of what is called a horizontal Tariff and that only so far as an economical administration of the Government may require—and unwilling to recognize in the Federal Gov[ernmen]t the right to lay discriminating duties—in as much as the majority might throw the whole burthen of Gov[ern-

men]t upon a minority of a different Geographical interest—in short it would give Congress the right to lay any amount of duties upon articles of Southern consumption. I look upon yourself as being the only ["Candidate" *canceled*] individual whose name is before the American [people] for the office of Presidency that advocates this Constitutional barrier against the oppressive legislation of Congress.

If I am right in my opinion in regard to your views on this important subject I think it would be well to have it publicly known. I am satisfied that this point of difference between yourself and others ["democrats" *canceled*] who are now before the people does not at this time command due consideration. Yours Very Respectfully, J.F.G. Mittag.

ALS in ScCleA.

From ALBERT RHETT

Charleston, Sep[tember] 15, 1843

My Dear Sir, I received your favour of the 11th this morning. There have only twelve or fifteen copies of your "Speeches and life" come on, so that if I gave one to each of the committee, none would be left for yourself. I thought it would be as well therefore to deliver only four, to the four eldest members of the Committee—Mess[rs]. N[athaniel] Heyward, Ion [Jacob Bond I'On], [Ker] Boyce and [John S.] Ashe, and forward the rest, as you direct, and at the same time acquaint the younger members with the facts. The Books are always within their reach here to buy, and they will be as much pleased with the compliment from you in this form as the other. I was selfish enough ["though" *interlined*] to keep one for myself.

Mr. [John A.] Campbel[l]'s letter I will answer tomorrow.

Notwithstanding the Syracuse Convention, I think our prospects very fair at the North. The Papers of this morning show the evident symptoms of a ground swell already begun, that, if properly encouraged, will go nigh flinging [Martin] Van Bu[ren] and his "common cry of curs" into the skies. It was a bold move, but in truth he had no other, for to consent to the District system would have ["been" *interlined*] to lay his head deliberately on the Block, when the "Carolina" Axe would not have left him long in suspense. Every thing now depends on what can be done in New York [City], where Brother B. [Robert Barnwell Rhett] will be, at the end of this week, furnished

447

with funds to establish a Paper. It is remarkable *that the Plebeian declares it is the only Van Buren Paper in the city of New York.*

Old [Thomas] Ritchie, that arch Traitor, seems decidedly cowed by the thumping his own People have been giving him, for the impudence of issueing a circular, by ["whic" *canceled*] which to collect into himself, as the only legitimate reservoir, the whole public sentiment of Virginia, to be afterwards drawn off, to be sure, in just the quantities and ["in" *interlined*] the quality, that will suit the furtherance of his own views. The crack of the whip appears to encourage his ["sluggish" *interlined*] virtue and, I hope, ["therefore," *interlined*] we shall keep it unceasingly brandished over his recreant head. But as usual I am too talkative. Believe me Dear Sir, very truly & resp[ectfully], Albert Rhett.

P.S. Mr. [John A.] Stuart's health is very low, and his chance of recovery bad.

P.S. I have been, and am, as busy as my business will let me, in the Mercury; but am sorry I have so little time to spare from my profession, on which I have to depend for my livelihood.

ALS in ScCleA.

From L[EMUEL] WILLIAMS

Boston, Sep[tember] 15th 1843

Dear Sir, I intended to have written to you fully before my departure for Baltimore, whither I go to-morrow, but I have been so much occupied & interrupted by political visitors that I have not time to do more than refer you to my letters to [Virgil] Maxcy which I have requested him to forward to you. There ought to be more communication among your distant friends & I shall adopt some plan for that purpose immediately on my return from Baltimore, where I go to argue a case & shall be detained about ten days. I enclose you a letter r[e-ceive]d from Maxcy which will serve to show you that we have roused up your friends to a little more action at the South. Your friends can secure your election if they will. Your prospects were never so good before, & [Martin] Van Buren is considered at the North as already defeated. He cannot attain the nomination of the Convention. In haste but with great regard yours very truly, L. Williams.

[P.S.] My office is the resort of all your friends who come to Boston from the N[ew] England States. I have since commencing this letter seen several intelligent gentlemen from Maine who say that you will certainly have four at least of the votes of that State in convention.

[Enclosure]
V[irgil] Maxcy to Lemuel Williams, Boston

[Saratoga Springs, N.Y.] 5 Sept. 1843
My dear Williams, Read the enclosed letter to Col. [Daniel D.] Brodhead & if he is not in Boston, act in his place & see Mr. [Charles G.] Green[e] & get him to write to Mr. [Edmund T.] Bridge, if he rejects all idea himself of going to Washington.

Mrs. [Mary Galloway] Maxcy is much better for her visit here. With aff[ectiona]te regards to Mrs. W[illiams], Faithfully yours, V. Maxcy.

[P.S.] Now is the time for work. I have named you to Col. [Franklin H.] Elmore as one who will correspond with ["him or" *interlined*] the Committee at Charleston. Pray give him, as soon as you receive this as full an account of the state of things in New England— the different parts of it—as you can—and write to men who may be relied on in New Hampshire[,] Maine, Vermont[,] Connecticut & Rhode Island, to open a correspondence with Col. Elmore, directing the letters as above[?]. At the same time write to Col. Elmore the names, that he may have confidence in them.

[Second enclosure]
V[irgil] Maxcy to Col. "D.C." [*sic*; Daniel D.] Brodhead, Boston

Saratoga Springs, 5 Sept. 1843
My dear Sir, According to my promise when I had the pleasure to see you at ["Boston" *canceled*] Washington, I wrote a strong letter to Col. Elmore at Charleston, intended for the Central Committee, which was indeed so strong that I took for granted 9 out of 10 would take offence at it. On the contrary it has had the happiest effect in rousing them up—but I will give you the effect of it in Col. Elmore's words, "I got nine of our central ["State" *interlined*] committee together to day and after reading your letter, of which I made all possible use ["and" *canceled*] we got $5000 put down, eight of us raising $500 apiece and one good & true old patriot, Mr. Nat[haniel] Heyward giving us $1000. This is on condition that we get $5000 more of which I hardly doubt. We have an enlarged meeting on Monday of some 18 to 25 including the original 9 & we hope at that meeting to go a good way into the other $5000. We send our Secretary [James Simons] on a special mission out of the city into the Country to appeal to Mr. [George] McDuffie, [Francis W.] Pickens, Gov[ernor James H.] Hammond, Gov[ernor John P.] Richardson and some others for their

$500 each. I do not fear but we shall *now* get the money. But again as some are planters, & very short of money, till their crops come in, it may be, that all will not be paid up before the 1st Feb[ruar]y next ["to which" *canceled*], to which time we must give the planters, if they require it. Most of it will be paid, when called for—and the rest, if necessary put in the shape of notes and the money got on these out of our Banks. For all needful purposes consider the fund in hand. And now, my dear Sir, what may we look for elsewhere? Will our Boston & other friends now put their shoulders to the wheel and give the onward impulse to ["the Bank"(?) *canceled*] to our cause, never to be checked until the victory is won?"

"By getting a first rate man—one of character and standing, associated with [John] Heart, we may command the printing of one or both Houses and thus enable the press to aid, as I see is your intention, the procuring more of the sinews of war."

"Prudence, boldness, information and sagacity mark one man, that I had thought of viz: Mr. [Charles G.] Green[e] of the Boston Post, but Heart thinks he can hardly be got and that if he could, he is important where he is. Such a man would be a treasure and a host."

"We are not enough advised here as to how matters are progressing. We do not know what States to count on nor on whom to rely. We have few, very few correspondents. Letters to me addressed under cover to the Hon. I[saac] E. Holmes will be safely received or addressed under his cover to James Simons Esq: Secretary of the State central committee, Charleston. Could not Mr. Brodhead of Boston or Mr. Green or some other gentleman on whose statements and suggestions we could rely, be induced to enter into correspondence with us. Indeed, my dear Sir, we cannot have now too many, so they are of the right sort and well distributed."

"We have several thousand printed copies of the proceedings of our Convention & the address by it to the Party. Can you suggest how any can be usefully employed—would they do good think you at the New York Convention or the Massachusetts convention? and How? If to be used, direct and it shall be attended to."

Now, my dear Sir, will you shew this to Mr. Green[e], of the Post or any of the other of your friends, to whom you may state that my letter to Col. Elmore for the Central State Committee at Charleston, was principally on the subject of Pecuniary contributions for the establishment of the Spectator on a firm basis as our central organ, which it is desireable should at once be made into a daily paper: and the engagement of an able Editor. ["If Mr. Green cannot" *canceled*] Will you let me know as soon as possible what amount can be got subscribed—for these[?] purposes & as an election fund generally in Boston? I agree with Mr. H. we ought to have altogether $15000.

Mr. Green[e] would be preferred to all others, if he could be induced to go to Washington, but if not—Mr. [Edmund T.] Bridge, who, you thought at Washington could be induced to go there. [Robert M.T.] Hunter agrees with me in opinion as to him. I do not know his address. If there be no hope of Mr. Green[e], will you write to Bridge? With the aid which you can give at Boston, I think we may insure him the first year $3000. There can be no doubt a part at least of the public printing can be got. By our agreement with Heart, Hunter & myself can offer him one third of the net profits of this in addition—& one half after the election if success crown our efforts ["subject to a return of part of the direct advances for the paper(,) the purchase of it" *interlined*]. Unless he is resolved against resuming the editorial career, the prospect of emolument is very fair. It is desireable to have an answer immediately. If you can write in the course of a week from this date put your letter to me under cover to the Hon. Joseph R. Ingersoll, Philadelphia. If not till after the 12th direct your letter to West River Md. Send a copy of your letter to Mr. Hunter, whose post office is "L[l]oyds' P[ost] O[ffice,] Essex county, Va.["] We would both of us meet Mr. Bridge at Washington on any ["day" *interlined*] named, with 10 days notice to arrange matters. If this arrangement also is impracticable, let us know also immediately, that some other ["Editor" *interlined*] may be engaged.

Pray let me hear from you as soon as possible. Pray write to Col. Elmore & give him the names of confidential correspondents in Boston, & all the New England States. Send also the best news you can.

I am looking with anxiety to the result of the the [*sic*] meeting of yesterday in the Park at New York. Col. Elmore's ["address is" *canceled*] name is F.H. Elmore. He desires all political letters to him should be addressed to Albert Rhett in case of his absence. All under cover to the Hon. I.E. Holmes. Very truly yours, V. Maxcy.

[P.S.] Please do you or Mr. Green[e] write to some persons in N[ew] Hampshire, Maine, Vermont[,] Connecticut & Rhode Island— to open a correspondence with the Charleston Committee—d[itt]o Col. Elmore. Send their names before hand that they may have confidence.

If you desire any copies of the South Carolina Address—Please point out how & to whom they are to be sent.

ALS with Ens in ScCleA.

From THO[MA]S FITNAM

"Irish Emigrant Society Office"
62 Dock Street
Philadelphia, Sept[embe]r 16, 1843

Sir, The Hon. F[rancis] Mallory of Va. wrote me a short time ago a letter of enquiry concerning the strength and feelings of your friends in this section of Penn[sylvani]a, which I answered very favourably, giving him the result of a private conversation with Mr. [George M.] Dallas which I had on the subject.

I regret, however, to see the "Charleston Mercury" fall into unnecessary indiscretions about Irish affairs, denouncing "Repeal," &. when those things, if not directly advocated by your press, should, at least, remain unnoticed and unheeded.

You, sir, are the son of an Irishman, and your father's countrymen both here and elsewhere throughout the United States have looked upon your claims to the Presidency with favour; and, if those who happen to be your organs at the south, act the foolish and very indiscreet part of assailing those who have the power *and are willing* to aid you in the coming contest with Mr. [Martin] Van Buren, you must not look upon the efforts of those if they fail in strengthening your cause, as the result of an inherent weakness in ["their" *canceled*] either their power of doing good, or the means which they may employ of acquiring it.

Your friends here are very numerous, and all that is at all necessary to be done to make them efficient, is an organization—a beginning of some sort; this could be done if there was a press to advocate your nomination to the Presidency, and marshall your forces here in its support.

The support which is being given to Mr. [John] Tyler by the great body of the Irish democracy of the city and County of Philadelphia, is so much taken from Mr. Van Buren's ranks, and which tends to weaken them in the same ratio that Mr. Tyler's receives them. But, at the same time, that its operation is going on, your friends are receiving a *negative* support from it, as it must in the end tend to throw Mr. Van Buren altogether. The Irish have determined upon prostrating the Van Buren ticket here in October, and after that shall have been accomplished—as it most certainly will be, that faction will not be heard of afterwards.

If you and your friends cannot aid us in the cause of Repeal *directly*—which, if by any possibility could be done, without involving principles of a paramount character, would raise your stock at the

452

North one hundred per cent, do not allow either yourself or them to be betrayed into any act which might be construed by the *Greeks* as partaking of hostility to a cause to which their very souls seem centred[?] and irrevocably united. I have the honour to be, Sir, your obe[dien]t and very humble Ser[van]t, Thos. Fitnam.

ALS in ScCleA.

From A[lbert] Rhett

Charleston, Sep[t.] 18th 1842 [*sic*; 1843]

My Dear Sir, Your favours of the 14th & 16th (postmarked) both reached me today, and I hasten to answer them, as briefly as I can.

I put your piece [signed as "A Member of the Convention"] into the Mercury, notwithstanding the previous article by Col. [Franklin H.] Elmore, because one appeared to me a very good sequel to the other, and there was nothing in them to raise a supposition that they were not by the same hand, and designed to follow eachother [*sic*]. The last only covered the same ground, with the first, more fully and with a great deal more ability.

The plan of movements you suggest in your last is undoubtedly the true one, & you have seen, by this, that ["it" *canceled and* "the ground" *interlined*] has already been substantially occupied by the Mercury, so far as *it* is to play a part in the game, and there shall not be wanting the boldness and obstinacy necessary to maintain it. But as to that all important part of your suggestions, writing throughout the South and South West, I am sorry to say there may be serious difficulty. As I have mentioned to you before, I am not a member of the Central Committee, by whose authority it ought to be done, and it was so constituted that Col. Elmore is really the only person on it, sufficiently conversant with the present state of public affairs, to be able to conduct the correspondence prudently and in a manner to command confidence. Now he is absent, and will be so for some time, and the Committee ["is" *canceled and* "are" *interlined*] consequently in a state of paralysis, such as they were in, when I first wrote you early in the summer, and out of which had you not stirred them, they would have remained to this hour. I do not charge fault upon any one, but if there be any, it belongs, ["I think," *interlined*] to Col. Elmore, who had the whole control in the composition of it, at the [S.C.] Convention. He has always begged that when he was away, I should open his letters and manage the correspondence for him, but as I am not satisfied that he has any right to make me his Deputy, or that it would be agreeable to the Committee, I must decline thrusting myself into the position. I will deliver your letter to the Committee tomorrow, because I judge, from its terms, you meant it to take that direction. ["As" *canceled and* "So" *interlined*] far as depends on the Mercury, I will undertake that your wishes shall in this, as in all other matters, be immediately respected, but that the other parts of your recommendation shall be acted upon, with either the promptitude or the skill required by the occasion, I hope but I cannot promise. There is not a man on the Committee, I am convinced, who ["either" *canceled*] knows either whom to write to, or how precisely to express himself, or who, if he is able, takes interest enough in politics to undergo the trouble. I write to you, Sir, very frankly you perceive; because I know your [*sic; one word changed to* "are"] frank your self, and will not misunderstand me, nor let any thing I say to you go farther. Of course I do not express myself in the same way to others, ["and that" *interlined*] not because I am afraid but ["it" *interlined*] would be foolishly indiscreet, both as respects myself, and the public interests, which it is my duty to regard ["as"(?) *canceled; ms. torn;* "always"?] above myself.

The intelligence from New York continues very cheering, and remarkably illustrates your foresight in predicting the consequences to [Martin] Van Buren of rejecting the District system. I am rather of the opinion that the time is not yet ripe for our Central Committee to act in the manner you suggest, but had you not better prepare a suitable address, and let us hold it ready for the moment of action, which must arrive now before long? I beg you to excuse this scrawl and believe me Dear Sir most resp[ectfully] &c, A. Rhett.

P.S. I have received a pamphlet from N[ew] York on the "National Convention" and think I see your hand in it. Would you wish it published in the Mercury[?] It is very able, whoever be the Author. I see Brother B. [Robert Barnwell Rhett] is at work in the Spectator. We shall have a Paper in N.Y. very soon. A.R.

Sep[tember] 19. Since writing the above, the Committee have invited me to meet tomorrow in consultation with them on the matters contained in your letters, and to manage their correspondence for them. I shall not seek the duty, because I am unfeignedly distrustful of my ability to do it well, but neither will I refuse any part assigned me, in such a cause, however humble, or however high. A.R.

ALS in ScCleA.

454

From R[OBERT] M. T. HUNTER

[Lloyds, Va.] Sept[embe]r 19th [1843]
My dear Sir, I have just returned from Washington where I have been
to consult with our friends. Mr. [Robert Barnwell] Rhett I presume
has advised you of the proceedings there. He inclines to [Washing-
ton] Greenhow as an editor and so do I unless we should lose the
[Petersburg, Va.,] Republican by taking him away. Mr. Rhett is
probably this day in Richmond upon that business. He promised me
to consult [James A.] Seddon and the Richmond committee before
he saw Greenhow and in any event *not to destroy* the Republican
which is doing good service. I could not wait to see [Virgil] Maxcy.
He had ["not" *canceled*] then ["just" *interlined*] returned home from
the North where he published a pamphlet on the Convention said to be
very able. I have not yet read it but Maxcy writes well. [J. Francis]
Hutton writes me from N.Y. that our friends are in *high spirit.* They
mean to fight the battle in earnest and they will probably raise funds
in N[ew] York to establish an efficient Calhoun paper in that city. I
do not know who is to be the editor. Some assistance can be had from
Boston. I advised Rhett therefore not to offer funds from Charleston,
but when he visited[?] the North to urge them to establish the paper
in N[ew] York with their own funds. This I believe can be done. The
residue of the money raised in Charleston ought to be kept (I think)
for a document and contingent fund. Mr. Rhett will endeavor to
organize a committee in Washington to assist him. Gen[era]l
[Nathan] T[owson] thinks this will be difficult but I found one
["man" *interlined*] who will cooperate efficiently and others doubtless
may be had.

I found that Mr. Rhett had written you despondingly. I am no
prophet and of late I distrust my judgment as to future occurrences
more than ever. But I by no means despond. We may be beaten but
not if we fight with the proper spirit and judgment. The Syracuse
convention has given us a great advantage if our friends are staunch
and know how to use it. Our New York friends have taken the right
stand ["& we must sustain them" *interlined*]. We go for a district
convention and if the States known to be favorable to you will take
their stand upon this we will beat down the Syracuse plan and elect
our man. At least there would be fair chances for electing him. I
urged Rhett to write to [James] Buchanan at once. If [Richard M.]
Johnson[,] Buchanan & [Lewis] Cass unite with us on this position
we must either beat [Martin] Van Buren or there will be no Con-

vention. It is very desirable to have their aid but we had no time to wait. The Syracuse proceedings must be met at once. I fear however that B[uchanan,] J[ohnson] & C[ass] will keep up the old game of making us contest all matters with V[an] B[uren] so as to obtain the second place in the affections of his friends. But dispersed as we now are we had no time to play the game with them. It is very desirable that our friends all over the union should second the movement of our N[ew] York friends. It was made at Maxcy's suggestion who informed them that I had been endeavoring to prepare such a movement throughout the summer. So I have but God knows with little enough of success so far as organization is concerned. But they think that there is more of this last than really exists and the idea seems to inspirit them. The course of Georgia and probably of Mississippi will embarrass us. Early in the last spring I wrote to some of our friends in So[uth] Ca[rolina] and I think also to you to urge the propriety of districting Georgia as had been done in N[ew] Hampshire. Unfortunately for us two of our most reliable States have the general ticket system and there will be great difficulty in getting them to aid us in this movement. Gen[era]l T[owson] thinks this movement vital to our success. If our friends sustain in it there will be no Convention and New York will have the responsibility of defeating it. Will they aid us? You have seen by this [time] Rhett[']s article in the Spectator on this subject. I shall write tonight to urge Greenhow to sustain it. I have already written to young [Robert M.] McLane [son of Louis McLane]. This last writes me that our friends in the middle States are prepared to break up the Convention and he asked my opinion of the propriety of his ["defending" *canceled and* "advocating" *interlined*] the election by the House. I replied that to advocate an election by the House as good "per se" would do us mischief but he might well show that the evils coming from it would be less than that of a packed Convention or of one which like the Syracuse plan would destroy all the influence of the smaller States in the Presidential election.

As I came through ["Washington I" *canceled*] Baltimore last Saturday I saw [Harvey M.] Watterson [former Representative] of Tennessee who has been recently appointed to Buenos Ayres by [John] Tyler. He was just from a tour through 8 States. He says he thinks there is a growing impression amongst the Democrats that their only hope of success is in ["Congressi" *canceled*] an election by Congress. He says that in Tennessee since the election the party are convinced that they will be beaten in Tennessee if V[an] B[uren] is run. He was at the Hermitage about 4 weeks ago and Gen[era]l

[Andrew] Jackson told him that he would vote for you if nominated. He thinks that J[ackson] still prefers V[an] B[uren] but says he is now very silent about it. He was told by [James K.] Polk[']s brother in law [James Walker?] that you could take Tennessee but V[an] B[uren] could not. [Hopkins L.] Turney [former Representative from Tenn.] is now convinced that V[an] B[uren] cannot run successfully in Tennessee but talks about [Lewis] Cass. Johnson is gaining strength in the West and [Thomas H.] Benton it is said is alarmed. He says in his public speeches that it is "no mark of democracy to vote for Colo[nel] Johnson." [William] Allen [and Samuel] Medary & that set Watterson thinks are immovably for V[an] Buren, but they will be beaten (he thinks) in Ohio by the Whigs. In my own State Mr. [Thomas] Ritchie will have more difficulty than he expected. Your friends here do not yet know their own strength, but they are numerous and talented.

["But" *canceled*] I have so many letters to write this evening that I must reserve what I have further to say for another occasion. Yours truly, R.M.T. Hunter.

ALS in ScCleA; variant PC in Jameson, ed., *Correspondence*, pp. 881–884.

From V[IRGIL] MAXCY

Ellicotts Mills, Anne Arundel County
Maryland, 20 Sept. 1843

My dear Sir, I enclosed you a letter from Lem[uel] Williams, which shews after all my efforts that my pamphlet on the ["national" *interlined*] convention did not arrive in time to have any effect with the [Mass. State Democratic] convention ["at Worcester" *interlined*]. I found on my arrival at New York that in consequence of not getting the manuscript in time to have it printed for the Syracuse convention, they post-poned ["it till" *canceled*] the printing till after they should get the proceedings of the convention, supposing some modification might be wanted. ["Altho"(?) *canceled and* "Only" *interlined*] a few ["copies" *interlined*], about 60, instead of 200 got to Boston & that on the evening only before the convention. So that probably not one man had read it & the Calhoun men, blind to the consequences of allowing the general ticket to the large States, permitted the [Martin] V[an] B[uren] people to slip in the Resolution, just as the convention was breaking up, in favor of allowing every State to appoint their delegates as they please. I am mortified to death about it as Wil-

liams thinks if my pamphlet had arrived in time, it would have put
our friends on their guard & prevented the passage of [the] obnoxious
resolution. How much more active are evil than good spirits. I I [*sic*]
trust if [Charles G.] Green[e of the Boston *Post*] & the other democratic papers in New England republish the pamphlet as Williams
says they will, it may still do some good in doing away the mis[c]hief
of the obnoxious resolution in the Proceedings of the Worcester Convention.

The Court is sitting here & the Candidates (both sides) for the
H[ouse] of Delegates have been battling it before the people for
three days. I go down to my own neighborhood to morrow to attend
a great meeting there on Saturday & shall be on horseback & *on the
stump* for the next fortnight. Such are the delights of a Maryland
Canvass. In great haste Truly y[ou]rs, V. Maxcy.

[P.S.] Our friends say our republican ticket for the county will
succeed. I am too old to count chickens before they are hatched.

I spent an hour with Mr. [Robert Barnwell] Rhett on Sunday &
am delighted to find he has brought on the money & ["has no" *canceled*] is now probably gone to Petersburg to engage [Washington
Greenhow] the Editor of the Petersburg Republican to be Editor of
the [Washington] Spectator.

[Enclosure]

L[emuel] Williams to Virgil Maxcy, Baltimore

Boston ["June" *canceled*] Sep[t]. 14 1843

My dear Maxcy, I received your letter of the 12th ins[tan]t this morning. I regret that I cannot leave until Saturday & therefore cannot
meet you in Philadelphia, but I shall be at Baltimore about ten days
& will contrive to meet you there or Washington about the first of
October. I will not return north without seeing you, as I deem it
important, as you say, that we should meet. The result of the Worcester Convention [of the Mass. Democratic party] has been favorable
to us, & our friends are in high spirits. I regret the passage of the
third resolution which we introduced at the close of the proceedings
in the convention & just as the Convention was in haste to break up
in time to take the cars & was not duly considered, or rather its purport was not rightly apprehended. We had not sufficiently organized,
& our best managers ["from the Country" *interlined*] were shut out
of the convention by the management of the [Martin] Van Buren
voters.

The Van Buren men held a caucus the night previous, & agreed
upon a Chair & committees. A committee of 10 favorable to reporting
resolutions nominating Van Buren was named by the chair but upon

the motion of our friends an enlargement of the Committee to 25 was made, one for each county, & the resolutions favorable to Van Buren were rejected in committee & others substituted, with the (exception of the 3d resolution) which was afterwards introduced in the manner I have already stated.

The result of the convention then is the Van Buren's friends have failed of procuring his nomination, & we have shown a strength that has astounded them.

It is unfortunate that your pamphlets did not arrive sooner & in greater numbers, for then our friends would have prevented the passage of the 3d resolution. We here have adopted the *District system,* & of the electors at large we count on [Henry H.] Childs for Calhoun.

Your pamphlet [called *Democratic National Convention*] is acpetably[?] written & does you great credit. I have seen nothing on the subject equal to it. *The* [Boston] *Post will publish it* & it will be copied into all our Democratic papers at the north. Every one who has read, is lavish in its praise.

The news from Maine comes in favorable to us.

I will write you further about the editorship hereafter.

As I am restricted as to time send Calhoun this letter. Yours affectionately, L. Williams.

P.S. The resolutions which did not arrive in season at Worcester, I have not since received. I will procure them to day & forward to you or carry them with me to Baltimore. I stop at Coleman's Exchange [when in] Baltimore.

ALS with En in ScCleA.

From R[OBERT] B[ARNWELL] RHETT

[Georgetown, D.C.] Sept. 21[s]t 1843
My Dear Sir, Before receiving yours of the 12th Ins[tan]t I had written ["in the Spectator of" *interlined*] last week the article on the Compromises of the Constitution. I think the policy there laid down ["is" *interlined*] as far as we can go at present. The truth is the principles of a National Convention have not yet gone down to the People. They are not yet understood by the People. The proof of the fact, that the two arrangements in the Constitution, for electing the President, are a companion, altho' asserted, has *never* ["before" *interlined*] *been proved.* Accordingly [Amos] Kendall in his late

ingenious production on this subject, does deny it—and says that the election in the House, is only a dernier resort in the Constitution to elect a President—having no reference whatever to the arrangement of power under the Constitution. It seems to me we must have our grounds understood first, before we move, or we are in imminent danger with the whole Party press North & West in the hands of our opponents of being dire[c]tly run down. If we had two years ahead, we might stand that, but the time is too short. The truth is we have been sleeping, and now we must accommodate our policy to our position. It must come to this at last—that they will give up, their method of approving in the Convention, or we will blow up the whole concern; but there is policy in quarrelling as in every thing else, and we must endeavour first to let our grounds be understood in the Country, if we hope to be sustained in standing on them. Pray write to me after reading the article your further views.

I have just returned from Richmond, where I went to endeavour to obtain Mr. [Washington] Greenhow for the Spectator. I told them I did not want Mr. Greenhow, at the expense of ["that" *canceled and "the" interlined*] Paper in Petersburgh. That that must be efficiently[?] kept up; but if they could do this, and supply Mr. Greenhow[']s place at that point we would take him in Washington. They require until Sunday to answer, and ascertain if the necessary arrangement can be made.

[Robert M.T.] Hunter & [Virgil] Maxcy came here[;] the former stayed two days—the latter I saw about an hour. Hunter refuses to take the Paper, and I am left with every thing to do concerning it. Get an Editor—edit the paper, buy new[?] Press &c.

I [*illegible word*] for authority to Charleston, to enable me to set up a Press in N[ew] York. Our friends there, are determined, but somewhat cowed with the Syracuse Proceedings. They have raised I understand 5000$—to put up a press, but it will take 10,000$ at least to establish one—and 20,000$ to put up an efficient one.

Excuse this scrawl for I have a wretched head-ache and believe me yours truly, R.B. Rhett.

ALS in ScCleA. NOTE: The article referred to in Rhett's first paragraph above appeared in the Washington, D.C., *Spectator*, September 16, 1843. It was also issued as a pamphlet, *The Compromises of the Constitution Considered in the Organization of a National Convention* (No Place: no publisher, no date), 13 pages.

From E[LIZA] W. FARNHAM

New York [City,] Sept. 23d 1843

Sir, I embrace an early hour after my return from a sojourn of several weeks in the country to acknowledge the receipt of your very obliging answer to my inquiries. I scarcely dared hope, that with such a weight of public duties as devolves upon you [that] you would find it convenient to reply and this consideration [increases?] my sense of your kindness.

You observe that you have inherited a fine physical constitution from your mother but beleive [sic] that your intellectual endowments derive their leading character from your father. This is a very interesting fact, sir, and if clearly established it affords a striking exception to what is believed to be a general law of the transmission of mental qualities.

After completing the work on which I am now engaged I propose to undertake "Biographical Sketches" of the mothers of our great men from Mary Washington[']s time to the present period. I hope to make such a work useful in directing the ambition of my sex to the attainment of true ["and Exalted" *interlined*] *womanly* qualities instead of the phantasms of "Woman's Rights" and other follies of the time. Should I proceed with it may I look to you sir, for further detail[s] respecting your honored mother or for reference to some who enjoyed her acquaintance whose information will be authentic? Such kindness would place me under infinite obligations.

Meantime Sir, permit me again to express my profound respect for those talents and virtues which have not only added lustre to our country's greatness, but endeared you to the hearts of her sons and daughters. E.W. Farnham.

ALS in ScCleA. NOTE: An AEU by Calhoun reads, "Mr. [sic] Farnham." Eliza W. Farnham (1815–1864), a philanthropist and social reformer, wrote several books, the most important being *Woman and Her Era* (New York: A.J. Davis and Company, 1864).

From T[ILGHMAN] A. HOWARD

Rockville Indiana, 23d Sept. 1843

My dear Sir, I have been requested to ask your opinion of the best periodical published in the South—and particularly the character of a quarterly entitled I think ["entitled" *canceled*] "The Southern Review["]—and a paper entitled the Southern Literary Messenger. We desire to take a valuable southern journal and doubt not you can direct us to the most valuable. If there are two, or three, holding in your estimation the same rank, be pleased to mention them. Allow me to add a word on another subject which comes from my heart. It is said you are writing a work on government—if so, it may make up for your withdrawal from the Senate. That withdrawal neither diminished my confidence nor my affection, but it gave me great pain, because I regarded it as a public loss. My opinion is, that ["venerable" *interlined*] age, and ripe experience, ought never, without strong reasons, to voluntarily withdraw from the Senate of the U.S. It is in the structure of our government the great conservative body, and as such ought to have the characteristics I have mentioned. You, my dear sir, are in the ripeness of years—and that ripeness is the product of a maturity resulting from a long course of years of public service, and, like the fruit that ripens and comes to full maturity in the autumn, is not likely, prematurely to decay. I trust many years of active mental power, sustained by an equable health, the result of temperance and virtue, are yet in reserve to you, and those years belong to Mankind under Providence. Whether it is to be in the Presidency or else where it is in the future to disclose. I believe in the government of the Supreme, and He HAS ORDERED all these things.

> Chained to His throne a volume lies
> With all the fates of men.

It is a great mystery—*Fate* & *Freedom—accountability* & *necessity*—but it is true. I know not why I have got off into metaphysics—I mean to say, that no event *past*, nor any in the *future* must be allowed to take you from ["the" *interlined*] active counsels of your Country. I have been much ap[palled?] at the feelings that seem to be rising be[tween?] your friends & the friends of Mr. [Martin] Van Buren. I hope no evil may result from it. There are those ["who" *interlined*] feel very differently. Your best friends & his are not those who wrangle. You both belong to history—and *each must act a decided part in this crisis to give his character to history unimpaired.* I speak freely—not because I feel that I am worthy to advise, but because you, my dear Sir, know, that friendship is too cold a word to characterize my feelings towards you. I shall never forget our walks near the Capitol, and the conversation I had the privilege to enjoy. Part of this letter you will see on your own account should be regar[ded as?] confidential, and so shall y[ou]r answer. The other part respecting the periodicals is not of that character. Most truly, Y[ou]r friend, T.A. Howard.

ALS in ScCleA. NOTE: Howard, born in Pickensville, S.C., in 1797, was a Representative from Ind. in 1839–1840. A few words have been conjectured within brackets because of two slight mutilations in the ms.

To [J. F. G. MITTAG], Charlotte, N.C.

Fort Hill, Sept. 24, 1843

Dear Sir: You are right in reference to my opinions on the tariff. I deny the right of imposing any duties but for revenue, or to make any *discrimination* but on revenue principles. I also deny the right of raising revenue, but for the constitutional and economical objects of the Government.

I have recently expressed the same opinions [in a letter of 7/6/-1843] in answer to a letter from Louisiana, that I see has been published. You will find them fully and strongly expressed in my speeches, of which a volume has been recently published by the Harpers in New York [City]. With great respect, I am, &c. &c., J.C. Calhoun.

PC in the Washington, D.C., *Spectator*, October 28, 1843, p. 2; PC in the Baltimore, Md., *American and Commercial Daily Advertiser*, October 31, 1843, p. 2; PC's in *Niles' National Register*, vol. LXV, nos. 10 and 11 (November 4 and 11, 1843), pp. 160 and 178; PC in the Richmond, Va., *Enquirer*, November 7, 1843, p. 2; PC in the Petersburg, Va., *Republican*, November 11, 1843, p. 2; PC in the Nashville, Tenn., *Whig*, August 1, 1844, p. 2.

From ALB[ERT] RHETT

Charleston, Sep[tember] 24, 1843

Dear Sir, I send for your perusal the enclosed letter from Mr. [Virgil] Maxcy, which I have this moment received. You will see he makes the same suggestion, you did in the next to your last letter to me a few days since; and I beg you will consider it again, and write me your wishes. My own opinion has not changed—that it is not quite time yet to move *formally* through our Central Committee, but it will shortly be upon us, and we ought to be prepared. For this purpose allow [me] to renew the request that you will send us a proper Address, and give us your views farther, as to the time when to put it out.

I will send you tomorrow a copy of the circular I have drawn, at the desire of the committee, to circulate widely but confidentially among our friends, urging immediate, resolute, simultaneous popular action in favour of the District System, and in support of the position taken by our New York friends. Expect[ing] a speedy answer I am very resp[ectfully] & truly, Alb. Rhett.

[Enclosure]

V[irgil] Maxcy to F[ranklin] H. Elmore

New York [City,] 14 Sept. 1843

My dear Sir, I lost no time, after receiving your letter acquainting me with your success in regard to funds [in writing] to a warm friend of Mr. Calhoun & our cause in Boston[,] Lemuel Williams to sound [Charles G.] Greene, of the [Boston Morning] Post & Mr. [Edmund T.] Bridge on the subject of the Editorship of the ["Post" *canceled*] Spectator; both decline for reasons which you will find in Williams['s] letter [*not found*], which I enclose.

You will be furnished as you desired by Mr. Bridge & Mr. Williams with the names of correspondents in New England.

The Calhoun spirit, as you will perceive by the papers[,] is roused in this city & will extend—as soon as they get a paper going—to the country.

They are by no means frightened by the proceedings at Syracuse. I attended last night by invitation a meeting of the Calhoun Committee. They are full of zeal & determined to organize in the Districts. I send several copies of a hasty pamphlet I wrote ["at Saratoga" *interlined*] at their request for circulation, on the constitution of a National Convention. They hoped to have got it out before the Syracuse Convention—but could not. It was sent to Boston & the Massachusetts Convention at Worcester.

I go south tomorrow & hope to see Mr. [Robert Barnwell] Rhett & [Robert M.T.] Hunter at Washington next Sunday.

I hope to hear then that you succeeded in getting your Subscription List up to $10,000.

With perseverance, energy & activity we shall conquer, I see, from the Spirit that is getting up in the North & east. I expect soon to see your Central Committee out *in full thunder* on the proceedings of the Syracuse Convention. Now is the time to plant the Standard of equal rights on the rock of the District System—which must take with the people as it does with all reasonable Men. There ought to be no delay now. A full broad side must be poured out on the report & resolutions of the Syracuse Politicians. Speak plain & loud but a little cautiously as to [Martin] Van Buren personally—as his friends must in the end cooperate with ours. Excuse the scrawl & haste. Truly yours, V. Maxcy.

ALS with En in ScCleA.

From W[illia]m Smith

Warrenton [Va.,] Sept[embe]r 24th 1843
My dear Sir, I have this moment received yours of the 11th Ins[tan]t. Yours of the 3rd August, with its valuable enclosure [dated 7/3, on the R.I. question], came also duly to hand: And I take great blame to myself for not making the requisite acknowledgment. But I wished to read your views before I wrote you; Maj[o]r [William W.] Wallace however took them from me—then Judge [Thomas H.] Bayly got them & then Mr. [John S.] Barbour, so that I have but very [recently] reclaimed them; which with ten days indisposition, & an important criminal trial, which occupied me for a week, have prevented me from yet bestowing upon them that attention I wish.

I have, as yet, received no other reply than yours & Mr. [Martin] Van Buren's.

A few days ago I received from Mr. [Robert Barnwell] Rhett a letter, suggesting the propriety of withholding your views from the public. I wrote, in reply, that I concurred in opinion with him. With great regard Y[ou]rs truly, Wm. Smith.

ALS in ScCleA.

From A[lbert] Rhett

Charleston, Sep[tember] 25, 1843
My Dear Sir, I hope the annexed circular meets your views, as expressed in your last to me. Measures have been taken to send them

widely, but confidentially, wherever we have friends. The safest plan, we could think of, was to send them by parcels to a few leading & sure men in each of the Southern and South Western States—also into North Carolina and Virginia, and to Brother B. [Robert Barnwell Rhett] at Washington; and the same mail that bring[s] this will carry a package for you.

We are expecting every day, to hear from you on the suggestion of Mr. [Virgil] Maxcy's letter. My own opinion has not changed—that immediate declaration would be premature; I would rather wait on events a little longer. I wish to see the game in New York fairly played out—what kind of popular response the [Martin] Van Buren men will make to our late demonstrations. Every thing now augurs as well as we could possibly expect. Y[ou]rs most resp[ectfully] &, A. Rhett.

[Enclosure]

[Printed Circular:]

(Confidential)

Charleston, Sept. 23, 1843

Dear Sir, The undersigned are a Committee, appointed by the late South-Carolina Convention, and vested with the requisite powers, on behalf of the Democratic Party of this State, to advance by all proper means, the election of Mr. Calhoun to the Presidency of the United States; and we address you on the supposition that you heartily accord with us in feeling, and are ready to co-operate with us in the measures necessary to accomplish an end so very important to the welfare of our common country.

The events that have lately transpired in the Northern and Western portions of the Union, more particularly New-York, cannot have escaped your attention. The course of the Syracuse Convention in peremptorily rejecting the District mode of electing Delegates to the National Convention, and adopting the opposite, show at once a consciousness on the part of Mr. [Martin] Van Buren of his weakness before the people, and a fixed determination to have the Convention constituted, if he can, in his own way, without regard to fairness, to the analogies of the Constitution, or to the undoubted preferences of those by whose voices the election is to be decided. Perhaps the necessities of his position, more than deliberate choice, have brought him to this resolution; be that as it may, you cannot fail to see that the unavoidable consequence of the Van Buren portion of our common party, occupying this position, is that the friends of Mr. Calhoun, to give him any chance of success, must as promptly and decidedly assume the opposite. To submit to the dictation of the Syracuse Convention on this point, for one moment, would be to give up the contest without a blow. On the other hand, it appears to us that we have so clearly the popular side of the point at issue, and the whole strength of the argument, that we only have to obtain a hearing of the People, and it is impossible we can fail of a verdict in our favor. And, though from the shortness of the time, and the disadvantages under which we labor in striving to reach the popular ear, we should be defeated now, the intrinsic soundness of our principles will leave us a ground to rally upon for a future struggle, on which we cannot fail to achieve, ultimately, the most signal success.

We beg leave, therefore, to press upon you, most earnestly, the necessity of Mr. Calhoun's friends, every where, coming out at once, in denunciation of the policy indicated by the proceedings of the Syracuse Convention, as of dangerous tendency, disrespectful to the People, dictatorial and unfair. It should be done in every form calculated to rouse the attention and excite the indignation of the People—by personal converse—by public harangues—by popular expositions and resolutions—and, above all, by strong argumentative appeals through the Press. The ground should be distinctly taken, and resolutely and perseveringly maintained, that in all the States, where Congressional Districts exist, it is the right of the People, and *they will* elect Delegates, directly from themselves, to represent them in the National Convention, whatever may be done by unauthorized political managers to the contrary. Our friends, in the great State of New-York, have already taken this position, and are most gallantly maintaining it against fearful odds. It becomes us to give them, surely, no doubtful or lukewarm support in such a struggle, especially when we know that the cause we are battling is the cause of justice, safety, liberty and truth.

If by carrying out this defensive policy, with a firmness equal to the obstinacy that may be exhibited on the other side, a rupture of the Democratic Party ensue, either before or after going into the Convention, the fault and the blame will be, not with us, but with those whose political intolerance and selfishness have made them the aggressors, and who will consent to no union, the conditions of which are not inequitable to all but themselves, and involve an abandonment of the very principles on which the Democratic Party is founded.

We shall send this communication to our confidential friends in all the States, and warmly indulge the hope that it will have some effect in rousing them to immediate exertion, so as to produce an active simultaneous popular impulse throughout the Union, in favor of the District system, and Mr. Calhoun, as its champion, which shall result in the signal overthrow of our adversaries, and the establishment of the true principles of the Democratic faith. We are, most respectfully, &c., Jacob Bond I'On, Nathaniel Heyward, Sr., Ker Boyce, John S. Ashe, James Rose, Henry Bailey, F.H. Elmore, William Aiken, Henry Gourdin, William Dubose, John M. Felder, John L. Manning, William M. Murray, M.E. Carn.

ALS in ScCleA; En in ViU, Hunter-Garnett Papers (published microfilm of The Papers of Robert M.T. Hunter, reel 3).

J. Francis Hutton, New York [City,] to R[obert] M.T. Hunter, [Essex County, Va.], 9/26. Hutton reports in detail on the situation of Calhoun's campaign in N.Y. A recent Van Buren meeting was weak. Several men have arrived "from the West" to coordinate with the Calhoun committee. He has sent out a handbill showing the names and occupations of the signers of the call [to elect District delegates to the national Democratic convention in defiance of the N.Y. State Convention], and this has proved very effective. E[manuel B.] Hart is the treasurer and F[itzwilliam] Byrdsall the corresponding secretary of the Calhoun committee in New York City. Calhoun meetings will be held in several city wards and in Richmond County in the next few days, and western N.Y. will soon move to elect delegates to the national convention. Robert Tyler was recently in town and complained that the Charleston *Mercury* was making war on the [John] Tyler administration. ALS in Vi, Robert Mercer Taliaferro Hunter Papers; PC in Ambler, ed., *Hunter Correspondence*, pp. 64–65.

To A[lbert] Rhett, [Charleston]

Fort Hill, 27th Sep[tembe]r 1843

My dear Sir, When I suggested a prompt stand against the ground taken by the Syracuse Convention, it was from the apprehension, that if it was not so met by us, it might be acquiesced in on the part of our friends out of the State, untill it was ascertained what course we would take, and that silence on our part might be construed into acquiescence, which would have proved fatal. Things have taken a different, & better course. The prompt & sperited stand taken by our friends in N[ew] York, Superceded the necessity of any immediate movement on the part of our Committee, and, in fact, would make it unadvisable at present. I forthwith wrote to Mr. [Virgil] Maxcy to that effect, and stated my reasons.

I regard the course taken by our friends in N.Y. very fortunate [in] every way. It commences the resistance at the proper point, & in the proper way, and what is now wanting is, that it should be properly backed by our papers & friends every where. No opportunity should be omitted to back & encourage them, and denounce the proceeding of the Syracuse Convention. The Address of the N[ew] York meeting is excellent. It was drawn by Maxcy, who fortunately was in N[ew] York at the time. It ought to be published for[th]with in the Mercury, with proper commendation. That would endorse it on our part, and would, in a measure, make it a substitute for our address. Our papers generally should ["copy" *canceled*] publish it in and out of the State, not only for its intrinsick worth, but to show, that it is the ground on which we intend to rally. The Syracuse Convention should be denounced among other things, for the ground they have taken on the Tariff; and the course of Mr. [Martin] V[an] B[uren] & his friends should be shown to be as unsound, as that of Mr. [Henry] Clay & his friends, on that vital question.

It is highly important, that our friends in Virginia, ["N(orth) Carolina" *interlined*] & Tennessee should back the movement of our friends in N[ew] York, with promptness & energy; and as far as that can be effected by correspondence on the part of the Committee and our friends in Charleston, it ought to be done.

As you may not be able to put your hands on the Address of our friends in N[ew] York, I send you a copy.

The ball having now fairly started, it must be kept in motion, and the longer it can be kept briskly in motion, without the intervention of our Committee the better. The start is a good one; and, if kept up with animation[?], must be successful.

I do not think our Committee ought now to be in any haste; but to watch & wait events. I will endeavour to be prepared, so that they may seize promptly the proper moment, when it will be proper to make a movement.

Will you permit me to suggest, that, I think, the Mercury is deficient in not noticing sufficiently other papers, especially the prominent ones engaged in the same cause. Occasional notices in a favourable way of the [Mobile, Ala.?] Tribune, the Petersburgh Republican, the Spectator, when any article appears of great merit, would do much to stimulate them, and give them weight. The Tribune is admirably conducted of late. Its articles are excellent. Much of the skill & success of the [Richmond] Enquirer consists in judicious quotations, with suitable encouraging remarks, from papers engaged in the same cause with itself. The Mercury ought to be made the central ["of all" *canceled and* "point, from whence" *interlined*] the impulse of the party should come. Any relaxation there is sure to be felt throughout the whole circle of our friends over the whole Union. Yours truly, J.C. Calhoun.

[P.S.] I enclose an article from the N[ew] Haven Register which is judicious & well written. I think it would be well to publish as an extract all after the first paragraph.

ALS in NHi, Miscellaneous Manuscripts.

From DUFF GREEN

London, 29th Sept. 1843

My dear Sir, I send you the [London] Examiner's Comments on your letter. The article was prepared by one of the most influential members of Parliament who has at all times taken a most prominent lead in the Anti slavery movement, and I value it the more because you cannot fail to see that I have done much to remove from his mind the prejudice against the South, and especially on the questions of slavery and State rights.

I have also seen Lord Palmerston, and several other leading Whigs who were most disposed to go astray on that point and have done much to pledge them to free trade principles, without reference to the source from where the produce comes in exchange. Sir Robert Peel is sound in principle but it is now manifest that he will fold his arms and wait for events. The Anti Corn law league are making great progress and have enlarged their basis so as to go for free trade and against all monopolies. They have just made their report of the proceedings of last year, and have expended about $240,000 and propose expending 500,000$ more the next year in disseminating tracts, delivering lectures and prosecuting all bribery &C at elections.

The Tories were put into power by the free trade and liberal party, because they had no confidence in the Whigs. ["The Whigs" *and an illegible word canceled.*] Hence Sir Robert Peel was compelled to do more than the Whigs had promised to do. The Whigs are now prepared to go further than the Tories and hence the free trade and liberal party will support the Whigs ag[ains]t the Tories. What I have labored to do is to commit the Whigs in favor of free trade with America and of a favorable arrangement of our boundary. The article in the Examiner, which is one of the most influential of the Whig papers, is one step, and I propose before I leave to make arrangements for an active Correspondence, *through the press*, between the free trade party of England and the free trade party of the United States; I am to see Mr. [Richard] Cobden on ["Tuesday for this purpose" *interlined*].

As part of my arrangements Mr. [Nassau William] Senior one of the ablest and most influential writers for the Edingburg [*sic*] review has agreed to review your life and speeches and Judge [Abel P.] Upshur's review of Judge [Joseph] Story's book on the Am[erican] Constitution, and Mr. McGregor [*sic*; John MacGregor] has promised me that he will adopt and engraft our view of the Constitution and of trade in his great work which he is preparing under the order of the British Government on the Commercial systems of the world. His will be a standard work of great merit and altho he is not a lawyer, he will do much in disabusing the European Public as to our character and institutions.

I have written to Judge Upshur requesting him to forward to Mr. McGregor, and to Mr. Senior, copies of your Life & Speeches and of his review. It is of the first importance that these gentlemen shall be furnished with copies at an early day, & [I] hope that the Judge will attend to it.

I see that there is a movement for Judge [John] McLean and altho I do not learn any of the particulars I am prepared to believe that if [Martin] Van Buren is nominated Judge McLean will be the opposing candidate and if so he will be elected. I told ["you" *interlined*] that [William Henry] Harrison would be elected and you did not believe me. I advised you then to take the lead for Harrison and if you had placed yourself at the head of that movement you would have been the controlling member of the party. You thought yourself bound to go for Van Buren and you were defeated. If you do not now come into Mr. [John] Tyler's Cabinet and thus give to his friends & to yours some guarantee that they will be protected under Mr. Van Buren's administration, his friends in a body and many of yours will throw themselves against Van Buren. Indeed unless some such arrangements are made they will organise a third party out of the present opponents of Mr. [Henry] Clay and unite in getting up a nomination of Judge McLean. In that case Mr. [Daniel] Webster becomes a prominent and control[l]ing man in McLean's administration and you will be responsible for the consequences. [Marginal interpolation: And if Van Buren is elected, the Government, will fall into the hands of (Thomas H.) Benton, (Francis P.) Blair & (Amos) Kendall and you will also be responsible for the consequences which will be even more disastrous to you to your friends & to your principles. If you go into Mr. Tyler's Cabinet you can control events.]

It will not do for you to say that you cannot consent to take a subordinate station. That is placing yourself above the public interests. As a citizen of the republic you owe your services wherever they can be available. The crisis in which the relations between the United States and England are placed is such as to demand of you any sacrifice. I do not believe that there is any man who can render as much service to the country and especial[l]y to the cause in which you have so long labored, as you can do by coming into the State Department, and it is manifest that being there, whether Mr. Tyler, Mr. Van Buren or yourself be nominated your position will greatly contribute to secure the election of the nominee, and that being there you can do much, if you can not accomplish all that we desire in relation to England.

If you are in the State Department and invite this Government to send Commission[ers] and they fail to send them, or sending them fail satisfactorily to adjust all the points in difficulty between us, it will I am sure cause the over throw of the present ministers and bring in men prepared and pledged to grant us all that we ask both in relation to trade and to boundary. Indeed there is a powerful party here now prepared to sustain us if we will only couple the question of boundary with the proposition for a reduction of duties.

I fear that you will not see the importance & the bearing which your going into the State Dep[artmen]t would have on the negociations now pending between England & Spain & England & Brazil for abolishing slavery. England insists that all the slaves imported into Cuba since [one year canceled] 1820 have ["been" interlined] imported in violation of their treaty with Spain and demand their emancipation. They will exert them selves to abolish slavery every where else and will then press on as even a war will not stop them. Let us offer them free trade and we check mate them, especial[l]y if you do it. Let me entreat you to deliberate well before you reject this suggestion. Your sincere friend, Duff Green.

472

ALS in ScCleA; PEx in Duff Green, *Facts and Suggestions, Biographical, Historical, Financial and Political, Addressed to the People of the United States* (New
York: Richardson & Co., 1866), p. 85; PEx in Jameson, ed., *Correspondence*, pp.
884–885. NOTE: In the London *Examiner* of 9/23/1843 appeared an article entitled "England and the United States" which contained excerpts from letters
written by Calhoun and Upshur and which described Calhoun as a politician of
the "Old Virginia School," a "Conservative democrat," and not an advocate of
"numerical democracy." Green published letters in the London *Times* of 11/10
and 11/11/1843 in which he discussed the attitudes of various American leaders
toward the tariff and described Calhoun as "the decided and unqualified advocate
of free trade." Upshur's "review" of Story's *Commentaries on the Constitution*
was published as *A Brief Enquiry into the True Nature and Character of Our
Federal Government; Being a Review of Judge Story's Commentaries on the Constitution of the United States* (Petersburg, Va.: 1840).

From C[OLIN] M. INGERSOLL,
[later a Representative from Conn.]

New Haven [Conn.], Sep[tember] 29, 1843
Dear Sir, Enclosed I have [the] pleasure of sending you the proceedings of a Regularly called Democratic Meeting held in this city, at
which the Hon. Henry W. Edwards, Ex Governor of the State presided. The Delegates chosen at this meeting being called on to
express their preference in relation to the Presidential candidates
avowed the same at the meeting and were elected as being favorable
to your nomination for the Presidency. Great unanimity prevailed
at the meeting and the Resolutions passed with but two dissenting
voices. I trust we shall be able to give our friends in other States a
good account of our State Convention. I remain Respectfully Your
obedient Serv[an]t, C.M. Ingersoll.

ALS with En in ScCleA. NOTE: Ingersoll enclosed a clipping from the New
Haven *Columbian Register* of 9/28 that printed the resolutions adopted at the
meeting of "Democratic Republicans of New Haven." One resolution expressed
"especial praise and admiration to John C. Calhoun for his early attachment to
the Independent Treasury, when the democratic party were fearful of its results,
and for his early opposition to the distributions scheme . . . ." Another resolution
declared the meeting "decidedly in favor of the district system" for the selection
of delegates to the Democratic National Convention.

To R[OBERT] M. T. HUNTER, Lloyds
(Essex County), Va.

Fort Hill, 30th Sep[tembe]r 1843

My dear Sir, I agree with you, that we must back without hesitation the movement of our friends in N[ew] York. [Virgil] Maxcy did right in advising it; and we must make it our rallying point; & such as far as I can learn, is the unanimous opinion of our friends. I send you a copy of a circular [dated 9/23] of our central Committee [at Charleston], which will be, I understand, widely circulated.

I regard the proceedings of the Syracuse Convention most fortunate for us, and most unfortunate for Mr. [Martin] V[an] B[uren], if our friends shall act with the decision & boldness they ought. I do not apprehend much difficulty from Georgia, or Miss[issipp]i. They can both be put right in time.

We could not have a better issue, than we have; the people ag[ai]nst managers, & the Constitution ag[ai]nst a fraudulent Convention. It is safe every way, whether victorious, or defeated.

It is important, that our friends in Virginia should come out decidedly in favour of the people's side ["and" *canceled*]. As soon as the publick mind is prepared, there ought to be demonstrations in its favour.

I see the Globe and other papers in favour of Mr. V[an] B[uren] are begin[n]ing to give importance to [Thomas W.] Dorr, with the view of making capital out of him. I enclose an extract from a New Bedford paper. You know, I have always been desirous to meet the question [of the R.I. difficulties] directly. I have no doubt, it will become necessary, before the Canvass is over. It may be yet too early. I would be very glad if you could see the correspondence in [William] Smith's hand. I have not yet heard from him, whether he has received my answer, though I requested him to acknowledge it. I am somewhat surprised at it. If you could see the correspondence, it would enable you to form a probable opinion ["as to" *interlined*] what would be the effect of the publication in Virginia, which would go far to decide, whether it ought to be published, or not. Might it not be well to make the enclosed [clipping discussing the positions of Calhoun and Van Buren on the R.I. controversy], the basis of a communication to the Republican accompanied by a call on Mr. [Thomas] Ritchie to know, whether it is the opinion of Mr. V[an] B[uren], that the mere numerical majority of the people, including all others, as well as the qualified voters, have at all times the right of superceding the existing Constitution and Government, and establishing another in their place, without observing the forms ["of" *canceled and* "prescribed by the Con" *interlined;* "the Con" *canceled*] the Constitution, for its amendment, or of obtaining the sanction of the existing Government? If you should approve of the suggestion, I would be glad, that you would undertake its execution, but not otherwise. Yours truly, J.C. Calhoun.

ALS with Ens in ViU, Hunter-Garnett Papers (published microfilm of The Papers of Robert M.T. Hunter, reel 3). NOTE: Calhoun enclosed the printed circular issued by the Charleston committee on 9/23 and an unlabelled clipping, apparently from the "New Bedford paper."

To W[ILLIAM] H. BROWN, Philadelphia

[Fort Hill, September 1843]

Dear Sir, I take pleasure in bearing testimoney [*sic*] to your great aptitude in taking likenesses in your way, and the fidelity with which they are excecuted [*sic*]. I wish you great success in the work, which you are about to publish and do not doubt, but that you will make it worthy of the publick patronage. With great respect I am & &, J.C. Calhoun.

ALS in Art Reference Library, Munson-Williams-Proctor Institute, Utica, N.Y.; facsimile with Brown's silhouette of Calhoun in William H. Brown, *Portrait Gallery of Distinguished American Citizens, with Biographical Sketches, and Fac-Similes of Original Letters* (Hartford: E.B. and E.C. Kellogg, 1845). NOTE: This document, facsimiles of which are found in a number of libraries, is dated only by a "Sep[t.]" postmark.

OCTOBER 1-DECEMBER 31
1843

⫿

These months, outwardly, were among the quietest and most private that Calhoun had spent in years. They were passed entirely at home at Fort Hill, and during a good part of October Calhoun and family were sick with the prevailing "grippe." During this period, Calhoun made a formal settlement of his financial relations with his son-in-law, Thomas G. Clemson, which revealed, among other things, that Calhoun and his son Andrew were in debt to Clemson for $24,000. Yet, Calhoun was quite optimistic about the family's prospects. Given the richness and productivity of the Alabama lands farmed by Andrew, Calhoun wrote a relative on November 11, even allowing for the present depressed price of cotton he hoped to be out of debt within two years.

If Fort Hill was wrapped up in the routines of family, social, and plantation life, nonetheless it was a kind of focal point where centered the interest or hope of a great many people geographically quite remote from the South Carolina foothills. Calhoun's shrewder and more realistic friends were in the process of totting up the confusing welter of events and possibilities of the last few months of electioneering and drawing down to a bottom line. Doubtless it was a bottom line Calhoun had already foreseen, perhaps had always anticipated. The array of forces among the Democrats at the organization of the 28th Congress in early December dissipated the final hopes, revealing not so much the weakness of Calhoun's friends numerically as their inevitable incapacity for effective intra-party maneuver.

The bottom line was that there was no longer any reasonable hope that Calhoun could receive the Presidential nomination of those who were to represent the Democrats in convention in Baltimore in May of 1844. Calhoun, and, so it appeared at the time, all the other hopefuls, had been outmaneuvered by the sly old fox of Kinderhook. Almost everyone agreed that this was a pyrrhic victory which in the long run could only profit Henry Clay and the Whigs: Van Buren could not be elected.

476

The crystallization of defeat left responsibilities. There was honor to be vindicated, supporters to be advised, and influence to be preserved for another day. In defeat Calhoun always appeared at his best and displayed those Roman and republican qualities that many admired. About one aspect of the situation there was no difficulty. From the beginning Calhoun had rejected overtures as to a Vice-Presidential nomination with Van Buren in exchange for future support for the Presidency. Virgil Maxcy simply voiced Calhoun's own sentiments when, on December 10, he advised the statesman to scorn such overtures. "The first wish of my heart is to see you President," wrote Maxcy, "but I would rather see you lose a dozen Presidencies, were it possible, than to see the high honors of your great & pure name brought down so low and tarnished by such a polluting association. No; the more bold and lofty ground you take the better & the better chance you will have [of] forming a rallying point in better times for the virtue of the country." Even had such overtures been honestly intended, which was doubtful, they held no attraction.

There remained the question of how those political forces that looked to Calhoun for leadership were now to relate themselves to the party within which they had been acting and its future nominee. Some of Calhoun's friends had always distrusted the Democratic alliance. Remarked James Hamilton, Jr., "and what is the Democracy of the Union to which your friends have linked you? An immense mass of ignorance moved by the necessary momentum of knavery." Such a mass could never muster sufficient public virtue to put Calhoun at its head. Duff Green's sentiments toward the Democracy were not much different, but he was optimistic that, as he had always maintained, Calhoun could with the right combination of issues unite the Northwest to the South and still triumph. Most of Calhoun's "friends," though, especially the younger, wished not to sever completely the alliance with the Democracy, but to keep open that connection as the best hope for the future, both in policy and in the now-deferred prospect of seeing Calhoun at the head of the Union.

Calhoun did not presume to direct his supporters how they should deal with the situation, but "I am of the impression," he wrote, "our friends in Congress ought to have an understanding among themselves what course ought to be taken, and when they have decided, it ought to be made known to all who are disposed to act with us over the Union." A few days before Christmas he sent word to his supporters in Congress and to the central campaign committee in Charleston that under no circumstances would he allow his name to be put forward at the Baltimore Convention, and that he would give his faithful fol-

477

lowers time to decide upon their course of action before he made an announcement to the public. In an address to his supporters everywhere, drafted at that time, he criticized the bad principles governing the party machinery and the treason of a portion of the party on the tariff question. This document was not published until the next year however, and by then it had been revised at the earnest request of friends.

Having calmly said goodbye to his Presidential hopes, Calhoun's mind turned once more to the issues of the day that most provoked his concern. One of these was free trade. The other was now pressing itself steadily upon the attention of the country: Calhoun's correspondents—whether the Secretary of State, other influential men, spokesmen for public meetings, or private citizens—increasingly conveyed a sense of urgency in regard to the future of the Southwest. There, the Republic of Texas, settled largely by the sons, brothers, cousins, and former neighbors of Calhoun's friends and constituents, provided a point of intersection, potentially explosive, between the dynamism of America and the imperialist and abolitionist ambitions of Great Britain.

The effect that this would have on the Presidential election, and the role Calhoun soon would be called upon to play in the unfolding of events, could not fully be foreseen as the year 1843 came to an end. However, Calhoun had clearly been right in observing to Robert M.T. Hunter in October that "the Texan question will be forced upon the country" and that either the Executive, or failing that, the Congress, would have to begin to come to terms with it. In fact, at just about that time, the John Tyler administration had decided to reopen discussions with the Republic of Texas about annexation, which the Republic had several times previously sought, only to be rebuffed.

〚〛

From H[aym] M. Salomon

New York [City,] 1 Oct. [18]43
Dear Sir, Yours of 14 Ult[im]o came duly to hand, and the Tenor of its contents was such as might have been expected from your exalted character and worth and will but add still more to that fame as a patriot and statesman with which your name will be revered by posterity.

It cannot be denied that notwithstanding all the attempts and manoe[u]vers of the [Martin] Van B[uren] party the more you are understood, the more popular you become.

"The Pelebian" [i.e., the New York, N.Y., *Plebeian*] the only organ that was left him found not sufficient support and was sold away from [Levi D.] Slam[m] and bought by Mr. [Moses Y.] Beach ["of the Sun" *interlined*] for Mr. Rogers for a mere song.

The last great ["lie" *canceled and* "falsehood" *interlined*] it told was, that Mr. [Robert H.] Morris the Mayor *was to attend* the meeting of the V[an] B[uren] men, and speak to support. You are aware *I* knew better, and when I said that *he* would not countenance the meeting they thought me insane but Prudence kept me quiet.

I saw Mr. [Robert Barnwell] Rhett for a few minutes to day. Was obliged to introduce myself by showing *him* your letter disavowing the Humbug. ["Mr." *canceled.*] I waited for Mr. Morrell [John A. Morrill?] in vain to introduce me, and Mr. Rhett said he had not called on him yet. Very few of those who ever were active Van B[uren] men have my Confidence. They are to be suspected.

Be you and Mr. Rhett most cautious of [Emanuel?] M.B. Hart.

I send you to day [the New York, N.Y., *Examiner*, William Lyon] Mackenzie's new paper. Their [Van Buren's] faction is only to be killed by the bold exposure of such facts as he prints to day.

Mr. Rhett spoke to me of its violence and said that one ["a paper" *interlined*] ought to be established that would conciliate their party. If he had seen parties in *this State* as I have for forty years he would know that, *this* party as to character is an exception to every other that has preceded it. They are not to be conciliated. They are implacable. Their God is Van B[uren], as they worship him on the alter of official venality. The priesthood is limited in numbers, perhaps four or five men that have put him up and, will put him down, if it be an object to them.

I told him of the conduct of Harpers, and suggested that to establish an entire new paper was impolitic. They ought to buy one already with a few thousand regular Readers. [Mordecai M.] Noah, never had more than 500 or 700 at the most for his paper after the first number altho[ugh] it ["was the head of" *canceled and* "had" *interlined*] the patronage. He deceived the President [John Tyler] by printing and giving away 50,000 of the *first* number. Then, *he said* that *he circulated* that number of the paper—which was true but they were not ["paid" *canceled*] subscribed for.

Perhaps it would not be against the interest of this great cause, that you should send a line to Mr. Rhett, saying that he may have confidence in the sincerity of one who is uncon[s]cious of the principle of deceit and misrepresentation.

I may save them the loss of much money expended without any advantage—and save them the association with men undeserving of Confidence. In Haste, yours with great Esteem, H. M. Salomon.

P.S. It strikes me as possible that Mr. Rhett has been ["writin" *canceled*] reading some articles written by my son David [Salomon] (who is here for his health) as the correspondent of the [Mobile] Tribune of Alabama. They were very forbearing in their nature—and written ["after" *canceled*] the first day after his arrival from impressions made on him by some insidious partisans of the Van B[uren] School. After he had sent them he told me of it, but since that David has seen his error and the Alabama Tribune will have some other matter from this Quarter.

ALS in ScCleA.

SETTLEMENT OF ACCOUNT of
J[ohn] C. Calhoun and A[ndrew] P. Calhoun
with Tho[ma]s G. Clemson

Fort Hill [October 1, 1843]
Statement of Account between J.C. Calhoun[,] A[ndrew] P. Calhoun
& Tho[ma]s G. Clemson

Advanced by Thos. G. Clemson	$17,000
Advanced by J.C. Calhoun of T.G. C[lemson]	3,000
Interest on same for two years & ten months from the 1st of March when the advance was made to the 1st of Jan. 1842 when the contract expired	5,666.66
Advanced by J.C. Calhoun for T.G. Clemson on the 1st of March 1840	2,500

Interest on the same to the 1st Jan. 1842	458.33
Interest on $22,500 from the 1st of Jan. 1842 when the contract expired to the 1st of Nov. 1843 at 8 percent according to agreement	3,300
Then	[$]20,000
	5,666.66
	2,500
	458.33
	3,300
	$31,924.99
Due J.C. Calhoun on settlement on 16th Oct. 1842	$1,801.31
Due J.C. Calhoun on a note to John [S.] Lorton	1,109.66
Due J.C. Calhoun for advance made for the purchase of negroes	4,500
	7,410.96
Advanced J.C. C[alhoun] for Cook Judah	400
	[$]7,010.96
Due J.C. Calhoun & A.P. Calhoun[;] amount due Mrs. [Ann Mathewes] Ioor for assumption of said debt amounting to	2,000
	9,010.96
Due by J.C. C[alhoun] & A.P. Calhoun for T.G. Clemson's undivided share of Ioor's negroes	1,200
	$7,810.96
Deduct from the amount	[$]31,928.00 [sic]
The sum [of]	7,810.97 [sic]
[Balance due to Clemson]	[$]24,114.03

On settlement this day between J.C. Calhoun & A.P. Calhoun on one side & Thos. G. Clemson on the other there is found due by the two former (A.P. & J.C. Calhoun) to the latter on all transactions connected with the settlement of the Cane Brake place[,] Marengo [County,] Alabama the sum of twenty four thousand one hundred & fourteen dollars as appears by the above statement to which this is annexed. This amount has been liquidated by a due bill for $7,114 payable on demand & two promissory notes payable to order of Tho[mas] G. Clemson each for $8,500 due in March of 1845 & March of ["March" erased] 1846. The settlement includes the purchase money still due of six thousand dollars for certain negroes purchased of Mrs. Ioor & for which the said J.C. & A.P. Calhoun & T.G. Clemson gave their joint bonds [on 10/19/1839] to J[ohn] R. Mathewes the trustee of Mrs.

Ioor. In this settlement the said J.C. & A.P. Calhoun have assumed to pay the two thousand dollars being the one third part with the interest now due. [Signed:] J.C. Calhoun, Thos. G. Clemson, [and] Andw. P. Calhoun.

DS in ScCleA, Thomas Green Clemson Papers. NOTE: The date of this document is established by a letter from Thomas G. Clemson to John C. Calhoun, dated 10/14/1847, in ScCleA, Thomas Green Clemson Papers. The above document was written in the hand of Anna Maria Calhoun Clemson and signed by all three men.

From J. B. W.

New York [City,] Oct. 1, [18]43

Sir, Time alone can prove to you, the motives that dictates [*sic*] this communication which is to call your most special attention to a subject worthy of a true and benevolent mind. Which is now claiming the notice of the suffering portion of the community only—when it should be the engrossing one of all just men, both religious and political. And I fear not to say the man who omits to investigate the Social Science by Charles Fourier, is guilty of injustice to himself and his fellow man. I would not impeach John Calhoun to suppose he has not read these writings, no—no he never has; I am fully persuaded he has not. For had he, he never would allow himself to be the petty sport of a New York rabbal [*sic*] and a political faction where the lo[a]ves and fishies [*sic*] are the only impelling power. Good Sir, open your eyes and look at the state of your country as well as Europe and see what has been done for humanity by politicks. Read Fourier[,] he will tell you and more then [*sic*] all, he will show you where the evil lays. And now I come to the point not in words (I dispise them if they have not in every one of them meaning[)], well it is this Jhon [*sic*] Calhoun can rule the destinay [*sic*] and the happy dest[i]ny of this great nation. Note it Sir, it is now told you by a fe[e]ble illiterate old person, but remember ten years hence it will be a living truth that Charles Fourier has embodied the great truths of christianity when acted out will fulfill all the glorious promi[s]es of God to man, which is the true and second coming of Christ, to redeem man from evil, or as Fourier says place men in harmony with God[,] his fellow man and the universe. Sur[e]ly Mr. Calhoun has not lived till this day not to see that all is discord, though above his fellows he has had tallent [*sic*] wealth an[d] patriotism can he with a full and grateful heart Say I am happy.

No, it cannot be[.] The very unhappiness of my fellow man forbids it—and ever will till you make humanity part of yourself[.] But I am loosing [*sic*] myself, the object of this letter is to claim your notice to this one great and universal truth[,] the destiny of man.

Sir I have lived with you in all your political movements and perhaps among the few I have thought you honest to the good of the country. Now you have full oppertunity to prove it and how far you can act above the common herd of polaticians. What a feild [*sic*] for a great noble soul to range[.] Only read Fourier[,] what science what pure truth has he unfolded to the mind unshakled by false and selfish principles. May God lead you to examin[e] them. No third person will ever know of this letter unless you make it known and it is asked of you to let it rest in silence[.] Should I meet ever with Mr. Calhoun I may make myself perhaps known. I and [*sic*] would say that who ever at this day as President of the United States should believe in the writings of Fourier and seek to carry them in to full opperation would to all posterity be rememb[e]red as the greatest benefactor of man, and no doubt ensure his own ellivation and happiness. Think this not Sir the effussion of a distempered mind, though I know that is the impression of numbers, for the Gentleman [*"Albert Brisbane" interlined*] who first wrote on this subject is I am told consid[e]red a visionary and fanatic. If so I see it not in his Book titled Social Destiny of man. It is to this work I owe much but still more to a paper published in London titled the London Phalanx by Hugh Dougty [*sic*; Hugh Doherty]. It shows what politicks have done for the happiness and progress of humanity and what has it done? Look at the starving millions and the Bloatted Millioniars of the civillized world[,] one dying for what is the distruction of the other. Yet[?] is the wealthy and powerful using the gifts of God to develope their true being, and regulate their passions which was implanted in them for holy and blessed ends, but unless they awake to see where they stand their end is distruction and that speedely.

But may the true and Holy Lord arrouze some Master Spirit to the great cause of reform in this our favoured country and may it be John Calhoun. But if not I fear not to tell him the mantel [*sic*] which he could wear to the honour and glory of God—will rest on some other.

I close without apology. I know the motives that urged me to write[.] No man has bidden me[.] God is my judge and with him rests the results. And as ever God can use the weak things of the world to accomplish his purposes—and with this hope I subscribe myself your friend, J.B.W.

[P.S.] If I thought Mr. C[alhoun] would be governed by the

manner and stile of this letter I would say may he never[?] be President[.] All are not scholers but all may think and know God and should Mr. Calhoun like ["Namaan"(?) *canceled and* "Naaman" *interlined*] of old dip himself seven times in Jordan (I would in other words say make himself thouroughly [*sic*] acquainted with the doctrians of the social science in the writings of Fourier and his true deciples[)], my life upon it in his regeneration he in himself would be a host and how many noble but benighted minds might he lead to the fountains of light and truth and America be that favoured nation which is to be born in a day.

It is lik[e]ly Mr. C[alhoun] will never know from whence this comes, but if in another life he desires it, he may, and I know I shall not fear he should. The writer is old and fe[e]ble poor[,] poor in earthly goods even to ["say" *interlined*] with truth thay [*sic*] own not a cent[,] a person of one pair of shoes of one coat & &, but still has a society they would not exchange for the court of France. And more would rather be the poor obscur[e] Blank then the Czar ["of" *interlined*] Russia shrouded in ignorance[,] prid[e] and tyran[n]y, the victim of a false society without the feelings of humanity or the fear of God in his heart. But may the Lord of hosts visit us in this our day of need and give us a ruler who shall love him and do his will.

[P.P.S.] Washington guided the helm of political liberty[.] May Calhoun lead the industrial armies to victory and harmony.

ALI in ScCleA. NOTE: An AEU by Calhoun reads "Anonymous[,] relates to Fourier['s] social system." This letter was addressed to Calhoun in Charleston.

From F[RANKLIN] H. ELMORE

Columbia, Oct. 2, 1843

My Dear Sir, I have returned so far on my way to Charleston from the [Nesbitt] Iron works [in Union District, S.C.] & am as yet behind the current of events. I see by the papers that the great [Martin] V[an] Buren meeting in the Park [in New York City] has not been what his friends boasted. I should judge it was a failure.

An idea has crossed my mind that at this stage of the game we might make something by propounding inquiries from our committee to all of you who are before the Country for Pres[iden]t or V[ice-]Pres[iden]t calling for your views & opinions as to the mode of organizing the Convention on the District & per capita principles as distinguished from the Va. or N.Y. plan. The present indications of discord arising from the adherence of Va. to the plan of the Richmond Convention & the action of the Syracuse Convention, would warrant us in calling for these opinions in the hope that they may be such as may reconcile the points of difference by conforming to the true principles of the Republican creed. If you agree in my suggestions, & will put the questions & letter in such a shape as will draw out the answers fully, & forward it to me, we will act on it as soon as you may think it advisable. I write to [Robert] Barnwell Rhett on the subject also.

It is very late & I have not sufficiently considered the question you submit in your letter inclosing Gen[era]l [Romulus M.] Saunders['] letter & the one from Louisiana. I will confer with some of your friends in Charleston & write you on the subject. I go down in the morning.

Mr. [Alexander H.] Brown strained one of his feet so badly the day he reached here that he abandoned his enterprize until he is able to get about again. He returned to Charleston. The hurt I fear will disable him for some time. He had done well as far as he had gone. Y[ou]rs truly, F.H. Elmore.

ALS in ScCleA.

From [ESTWICK EVANS]

Wash[ingto]n City, Octo[be]r 3, 1843

Sir: I take the [*mutilation*] sent you the enclosed prospectus, with [*mutilation*] of gentlemen here.

Its purpose is [*mutilation*] you, but it cannot fail to me[*mutilation*] believe, strong, & thorough, & clear [*mutilation*]bation of the South, & also the [*mutilation*]able feelings of sensible & fair mi[*mutilation*]-duction is intended to be entirely gr[*mutilation*] but, withal, of some point.

I wish it to h[*mutilation*] on many accounts. Its influence upo[n; *mutilation*]ciples of the country cannot fail, as [*mutilation*] favourable. There is an appropriate notice [*mutilation*] yourself, & not a word on principle which w[*mutilation*] agreeable to you & your friends. It will hav[e; *mutilation*]able influence upon your doctrines, moti[*mutilation*] position: but at the same time without [*mutilation*] my part to produce a personal or party effect[?], inasmuch as my great object is political truth as it regards our institutions.

I will take upon myself, Sir, the freedom to say—not from policy, but from sincerity & fact & a natural openness of heart about me, & because, too, I desire to have it known to you & to all, as I believe it will be before long, on many great questions, that I am with the South in relation to their great constitutional rights, with moderation, yet with firmness & decision & thoroughly.

I refer you, Sir, to Mr. [Levi] Woodbury of Portsmouth New Hampshire, my native town. I wish for the countenance in the way of subscription of the South. To give you some confidence in [*mutilation*] I transcribe—not in vanity in the slightest, but with right, from [*mutilation*] from Mr. Woodbury in my behalf in 1829: "I have [*mutilation*] E[vans], & have ever considered him as a Gentleman whose [*mutilation*] & patriotism are of a high order." And then: "Mr. E. [*mutilation*] his principles & deportment."

I will only add, Sir, that I was led to write [*mutilation*] Mr. [Daniel] Webster's very celebrated speech [*mutilation*] have a very high opinion, of course, of Mr. [*mutilation*] constitutional learning, & have also the honor [*mutilation*] to & appreciated by him; but I cannot consid[er; *mutilation*]mise than most palpably erroneous in principle & il[*mutilation*] in reasoning. And, mark me, Sir, be [*mutilation*] is to be a revolution in publick sentiment [*mutilation*] quiet, yet strong; & it is to carry along [*mutilation*]t & benefit to the South on the great— the mo[*mutilation*]rilous subject of slavery. I do not know that [*mutilation*]larly moving, or has been, on the great subject of involving [*mutilation*] several other subjects of our national legisla[*mutilation*] of slavery—in fact involving *deeply* the spirit of our laws—that spirit which influences government & by which government & publick sentiment are influenced. It is my purpose to commence this work.

As to my style of writing—sometimes at least, I refer you, in confidence, to 14 No. over the signature of "A Marylander" in the [Washington] National Intelligencer just before the Presidential Election of 1840. Very few—even friends, know me as the Author. They created much of a sensation—much enquiry; & were attributed to Walter Jones &c. They are still a subject of reference & enquiry as to the writer in Maryland, & Virginia. My politics, Sir, are these: An old & thorough Democrat—Not an [John Quincy] Adams man—Not a [Andrew] Jackson man—Not a [Henry] Clay man—Not a [William H.] Crawford man—not suited in my opinion exactly. Acquiesced however, in the election of Adams, as he was the choice of the [*mutilation*] of my democratic friends in the Legislature of New Hampsh[ire; *mutilation*] member. I was a Whig: am so, generally, now; not [*mutilation*] to Clay: finally am for Democracy—true [*mutilation*] aristocracy on one hand & locofocoism on [*mutilation*] Mr. [Martin] Van Buren is out of the question, as to [*mutilation*] party, & his & their general policy. I am [*mutilation*] a political friend of Mr. Woodbury; but I [*mutilation*] have ever covered the true medium y[*mutilation*] think he was entirely at home under th[*mutilation*] or even of Mr. Van Buren. Mr. Woodbury[']s [*mutilation*]wise than agreeable to me. With very high [*mutilation*] am, Sir, your Obed[ient] Serv[an]t, [Estwick Evans.]

ALS (partly burned) with En in ScCleA. NOTE: An enclosed prospectus, dated 6/1/1843, announces the publication "next month" of "the first of a series" of "Essays in favor of State Rights" and lists nine residents of Washington who have subscribed: James Larned, George Wood, McClintock Young, J.N. Barker, Al[bio]n K. Parris, R.R. Gurley, John P. Van Ness, Alex[and]er Hunter, and John M. Moore.

ANNA [MARIA CALHOUN CLEMSON] to
Maria E. [Simkins] Colhoun, Terrysville, S.C.

Fort Hill, Oct. 5th 1843
Dear Maria, Supposing you are safely landed at Millwood ere this as your letter said you would be here goes an epistle for the P[ost] O[ffice] at Terrysville & if you don[']t get it soon it is no matter for there is or rather will be nothing of the least consequence in it that '*I knows on*' at present. Indeed I have so little to say that I have taken a perfect disgust to writing for the simple reason that I am sure my letters must be a task to read filled as they are with the same dull nothings & oft repeated excuses for said dullness. I would often delay writing or not write for this reason were I not afraid my correspondents would pay me in my own coin & therefore inflict my letters on all of you [*one word canceled*] on the regular barter principle for the consideration of a return. Generous! is it not?

The house is now quite vacant & dull after having been crowded for sometime. We had Andrew [Pickens Calhoun] here only for a week as he was anxious about leaving Margaret [Green Calhoun] & Eliza [M. Green] alone & did not stay a moment after his business was satisfactorily arranged. He[,] John [C. Calhoun, Jr.] & [my cousin] Eugenia [Calhoun] took their departure together. Andrew looks as well as I ever saw him[,] is in excellent spirits & uncommonly friendly so that his visit was a pleasant one. Margaret sent me the most splendid dress for little Sis [Floride Elizabeth Clemson] you ever saw with a very kind letter & Eliza sent her a beautiful [*ms. torn; a few words missing*] silk socks. Miss[?] Floride is lucky is she not? The [*ms. torn; one or two words missing*] long enough for me & I teased Eugenia to death telling her I was going to take it. Mr. [Thomas G.] Clemson left a few days since for Edgefield so that the family is very small for us but we have staying with us a Mr. [James] Wise a min[i]ature painter who brought father a letter from Mrs. Le Vert (the celebrated Miss Octavia Walton) & is taking his likeness. He has a picture of Mrs. Le Vert amongst others which is the most beautiful thing I ever saw both as to style & execution. I think his painting superior to anything I ever saw. He seems a retiring modest man devoted to his profession & will I hope take a good likeness of father.

Everyone is leaving Pendleton & I wish I was going too before cold weather sets in but I don[']t know when we shall get down now as we have to wait for a house. Mr. Clemson has gone down to hurry as much as possible. We expect our carriage in six weeks. It had to be built. The horses do admirably now except the tails. I have an idea of buying braids for them.

Mother [Floride Colhoun Calhoun] has been indisposed for a day or two from drinking too freely of cider. We have it so fine that she could not resist the temptation & you know acids always make her sick. She suffered a good deal of pain but nothing serious & will I hope be quite well in a day or two again. My children [Floride and John Calhoun Clemson] are almost well again & little Floride grows & improves in *beauty daily*. I have been suffering from ear ache & tooth ache for a day or two but not *very* severe. Father has been in the hands of [the] Grippe but is gradually escaping—so now you have a report of the board of health of Fort Hill [en]tire.

I [*ms. torn; a few words missing*]ly glad you left Susan [Wilkinson Pickens] in [school at?] Charles[ton; *ms. torn; one or two words missing*] so m[*ms. torn; one or two words missing*] your satisfa[ction]. Do write me from time to time how she likes the school & comes on. John & herself will be company to one another this winter. He carried her a large bag of chesnuts that James [Edward Calhoun] promised her. I expect they will cost her many a *stomachache*. Write her I say so & give my love to her. Eugenia said she would be sure to see her as she passed through on her way to Washington.

We are expecting a visit from Pat[rick Calhoun] sometime this month on his way to Washington where he will perhaps be stationed. He did not wish to apply to be exchanged till he could go on & see what they intended to put him at in Washington & so applied for leave of absence to go on there. If he gets it he will of course come by. I hope he may be stationed at W[ashington] as that would at least be within hearing distance & so much more pleasant for him.

Mrs. [Robert M.] Renick has arrived & mother & myself called on her but could not get much out of her. I suppose since you say she is deaf perhaps she did not hear us distinctly. She is quite pretty & does not look more than sixteen at the outside but did you ever see two such babies belonging to one person unless they were twins? It gave me great comfort to compare with her I assure you.

All are well at Twelve Mile but I suppose you hear from them oftener than from us for Aunt M[artha Maria Davis Colhoun] said the other day that uncle James [Edward Colhoun] & herself corresponded constantly.

I think for one who started with nothing to say I have said a good deal but I will release you now. All send love. Do write soon & often to cheer us in our solitude. Truly your [*ms. torn*] Anna.

ALS in ScU-SC, John C. Calhoun Papers.

From HENRY C. FLAGG

New Haven, Oct[obe]r 7th 1843
Dear Sir, Seven illustrious ["cities" *interlined*] contested the honor of Homer's birth place. The old bard however, had then slept so long with his fathers, that the dispute was of no more consequence to him, than was honor to Jack Falstaff's man who died on wednesday. Your name is connected with discussions of as great import *dum vivente*. In this, you have an advantage over the immortal Greek.

Two of the most ancient and honourable literary ["societies" *interlined*] in the nation, are now warmly contesting the honor of your membership. The Linonian Society of Old Yale have published your name in their catalogue and show it upon their records. The Brothers [in Unity] Society say you belong to them. The Linonians, (of whom I am one) have refer[r]ed to me for a decision which I am unable to give. The President ["is" *canceled*] in his letter to me upon the subject remarks—"It will be an important item in our cause, if we can at this time substantiate the fact, that the Hon. John C. Calhoun, was a member of the Linonian Society and that he has since been *her friend*. The Brothers in Unity impudently try to rob us of the honor of his name. You are his personal friend and acquaintance and are in possession of the facts. A brief certificate from your hand will be decisive on the question." I had the honor of addressing the Society by invitation, at their late anniversary, when the same request was renewed. I promised to write to you for the necessary information & to communicate your answer to the President at the earliest opportunity. ["In" *altered to* "I"] know it will afford you pleasure to relieve their anxiety.

I must trouble you with another question which I have been requested to solve. It comes from the "Young Democracy." "Who is the author of the Sub Treasury Scheme?" Did not Mr. [Martin] Van Buren in proposing ["it," *interlined*] use nearly the phraseology, to be found in one of your previous speeches upon fiscal concerns? It is strongly my impression that he did. But I cannot point it out; nor can it be found in Harper[']s selection [of your speeches]. This *is* a matter of importance. For Mr. Van Buren's friends, are more anxious to deprive you of the credit of anticipating him in the plan of an independent treasury, than are the Brothers to deprive the Linonians of the honor of your name as one of their members. These may be questions of some delicacy to you. But they are put directly to me; and I only ask such information as will enable me to give ["an" *interlined*] answer the responsibility of which will be entirely my own.

Col. R[ichard] M. Johnson was here on the 5th. The people were pleased with the old soldier's anecdotes. For his peace of mind hereafter, I hope he will not like our friend the Captain, mistake common curtesey [*sic*], for *political adhesion*. The Capt. has thrown away his trumps; and with a strange economy kept back his honors, until his adversaries have got the odd trick. He might have shown out, and yet is beaten!

I will not predict the result of the approaching convention to be held by the democrats; but I am confident, that if they express a preference for Van Buren, the whigs will carry this State [of Conn.] next spring. You are the decided preference here; and with the exception of Hartford, throughout the State. I spent a great part of the summer in New York & Ohio. In both of those States, as in this, all the guard will sustain you. In neither of them can Mr. Van Buren be sustained. I have had the best opportunities of judging. That portion of the Democracy who voted with the whigs in 1840, will in *no event* support Van Buren. You have many friends here among the whigs; and [*mutilation*; the New Haven] Herald still continues to give all the n[*mutilation*; yo]ur favor, besides throwing out useful[?] paragraphs, not wholly inconsistent wi[th?] her political position.

Your determination to remain at home during the great contest, meets with universal approbation. The people believe with [William] Lowndes, the office of President is of too great importance either to be sought or declined. Now as ever My dear Sir Your friend & Ob[edien]t Servant, Henry C. Flagg.

ALS in ScCleA. NOTE: An AEU by Calhoun reads "Mr. Flagg[,] Ans[were]d 20th Oct[obe]r 1843." Flagg was a member of the Yale class of 1811.

From R[OBERT] B[ARNWELL] RHETT

[Washington,] Oct. 7th 1843

My Dear Sir, I have just returned from New York whither I went to endeavour to establish a new Press ["there" *interlined*]. I am assured that it will go into operation next week; but I fear it will not have the means to employ such talent as to make it very useful. I went also to Richmond, and we have arranged that Mr. [Washington] Greenhow is to come here, so soon as his place is supplied in Petersburgh. Neither here nor at New York was any thing done before I came. Next week, I propose starting the Spectator as a triweekly Paper, I being the sole writer in it. I suppose you receive it, and see what I have done in it.

In New York our friends are very firm. If they can get up a vigorous press there we will accomplish a great deal. Last week without an effort we carried 9 out of the 17 wards, for nominating Candidates to the Legislature[,] Sh[eri]ff &c. Our side is moving I think both in that City & in New England. I saw also men from the interior of N.Y. A Press will shortly be set up in Utica. One is apt to be deceived from hearing only from one side, but I am strongly of opinion that we are gaining & Mr. [Martin] V[an] B[uren] is loosing [*sic*] ground. We will carry the District system in Connecticut, ["but" *canceled and* "and" *interlined*] may succeed in postponing the action of the approaching Convention in that State. [Harvey M.] Watterson [former Representative from Tenn.] was here last week and had a long conversation with [Richard M.] Johnson: and the result is, that he has written to [James K.] Polk that Johnson will take the Vice[-]Presidency on [the] V[an] B[uren] ticket. The rumor here to day is also that [Daniel] Webster & [Henry] Clay are again friends—and Webster is to be run as V[ice-]P[resident] on Clay[']s Ticket. The

Old Swiss [Albert Gallatin] is brought up again by the manufacturers. But this is not certain altho' likely.

If my views of the state of things are correct, it will not be wise to scale off from the Democratic or even V[an] B[uren] Party. It appears to me so plain that Mr. V[an] B[uren] cannot be elected, that a few months must convince stupidity itself. If he persists in his method of organizing the Convention, it will require no great effort to kill him. He will do that himself, and if it is necessary for us to do it, it will be time enough to take our way of doing it, when the time arrives for doing it. It is equally clear, that altho we are destroy[ing] him, we cannot succeed ourselves without Mr. V[an] B[uren's] friends. We have not yet reached the popular mind with our reasons for opposing a Convention, by a consolidated State Representation. We must have their ears; that when we move off we may move with power, and have the estimation of all impartial men, instead of violent prejudice to battle with. Hence I am for a moderate but firm tone. Fair and repeated discussion of principles. Repel attacks—but do it in such a way as to shew we are on the Defensive, and rather from our tone, than from our words let them understand where we will be found. Much [discussion?] of our future course in or out of the Convention will be wrong. Some of our friends I think have gone too fast in this respect. It will be time enough when the Convention is to meet to determine first whether we will go into it—and second what we will do in it. In my opinion, it is by no means improbable, that at this time Mr. V[an] B[uren] will be no Candidate. [Lewis] Cass will then be the most formidable man. If he would consent to take the V[ice-]P[residency] it would be the best arrangement. I have rec[eive]d proposals to that effect. What say you to it?

I am urged to return home to see my new Constituents this fall— and I am told that if I do not I may be opposed in the next election. My answer has been, that it was my design to visit my Constituents this fall; but that I am satisfied I am here doing them more service than by going to see them. If they will not believe this, they may turn me out, if they please. I shall stay here and work in their cause and the cause of the Country.

Remember me kindly to Mr. [Thomas G.] Clemson and believe me Dear Sir Yours truly, R.B. Rhett.

[P.S.] Mrs. [Elizabeth Washington Burnet] Rhett is still in So[uth] Ca[rolina].

ALS in ScCleA; variant PC in Jameson, ed., *Correspondence*, pp. 885–887.

From R[OBERT] B[ARNWELL] RHETT

Washington, Oct. 7th [sic; 8th?] 1843

My Dear Sir, I wrote to you yesterday [sic; 10/7], informing you of my going on to N[ew] York, and of ["the" *and a partial word canceled*] my efforts as to the Paper &c. I will add now but a few words [in reply] to yours of the 30th Sep[tembe]r just received.

Your grounds I think are just. We must sustain our position that a Convention organized on the Syracuse plan is entirely wrong & intolerable; and we will have to split upon it or they must succeed. But still, let us postpone splitting to the last, at the Convention, and let it be the consequence of their act. Nor need we say what we will do then. It will be sufficient to give it to be understood by discussion, that their plan of organization is false[,] unconstitutional and anti Democratic.

I wish you would immediately prepare an argument on the point of the ["organization of the" *interlined*] Convention. I wish to use it in the Democratic Review. That Review altho' very friendly to you, has come out strongly against our views. I will write an article with your aid which I am satisfied by going on to New York, I can get in by the next Number. Let me know if you will do this, that I might write to the Editor [John L. O'Sullivan] and inform him of my purpose. He has repeatedly asked me to write for his Review and I am satisfied will admit the Article. Go to work as soon as possible. I think together we can make a demonstration through that periodical which will cover us, as with a shield. In the mean time, I have, you know my hands full here editing the Spectator which next week we will commence as a tri weekly paper. [Washington] Greenhow is still in Virginia waiting ["the" *canceled*] for some one to supply his place in Petersburgh.

In politics I have ever been disappointed; but there is great enjoyment, in mere intellectual gladiatorship.

I have seen [David] Henshaw [Secretary of the Navy] this afternoon who is in bed with the Gout. He thinks as I do that our cause is rising in New England. [Robert M.T.] Hunter says, in answer to my goading, that they are going to move soon in Virginia. [John] Tyler is dreadfully jealous of you. Write soon and believe me Yours truly, R.B. Rhett.

[P.S.] I open this Letter to say that I have written to the Editor of the Democratic Review promising him the Article for the next Number. So you may help me by putting your pen to paper at once.

ALS in ScCleA. NOTE: This letter was postmarked in Washington on 10/8. No article such as that discussed in Rhett's third paragraph can be identified with certainty among the contents of the *United States Magazine and Democratic Review.*

From R[OMULUS] M. SAUNDERS, [Representative from N.C.]

Raleigh, Oct[obe]r 9[?] '43

My dear Sir, I duly rec[eive]d your favour with the inclosed address. *If* our friends in New York shall persevere, in their course & be sustained, then our cause may be successful, but I doubt, if the current in the State be not too strong for the City. There is great difficulty in bring[in]g the people up to the true question at issue. The [Martin] V[an] B[uren] party talk so much about harmony, that those who ought to take a part, are deter[r]ed from doing so. ["With"(?) *canceled*] Our people are decidedly for the district plan, yet they cannot be made to see, that in yielding to other States the right of selecting by General convention, they virtually surrender that principle. I had not thought the V[an] Buren men with us would have ventured to oppose it. But judging from the proceedings in Warren [County], where they beat us, I doubt not they will if they have the power in our State Convention. If they should *there*[?] will be the time & occasion for taking our stand. I am trying to rally for that event, but as yet, with but a single exception or two, nothing has been done in the west, where lies our strength. I fear [Michael] Hoke is neutralized in being proposed as Governor & [Charles] Fisher is now in Washington.

Our Treasurer [John H. Wheeler] & a few others, friends of Col. [Richard M.] Johnson, have invited the old man to visit this place. I did not sign the letter, but should he come, shall of course treat him with respect. His coming can do us no injury, but may the Van Buren party.

I cannot say things in this State are flattering, but they are not as bad, as might be supposed. I write in haste as I am in the midst of my circuit. Very truly, R.M. Saunders.

ALS in ScCleA.

494

From R[OBERT] M. T. HUNTER

L[l]oyds [Va.,] Oct[obe]r 10th 1843
My dear Sir, Since my last letter to you I have seen Mr. [Robert G.]
Scott of Richmond one of our central Calhoun committee. He told me
that in an interview with Mr. [Robert Barnwell] Rhett he had urged
him to advise you against the agitation of the Rh[ode] Is[land] question. He told me (but I had not time to question him particularly as
it was at a public meeting where we were both Speaking) that [Mar-
tin] V[an] B[uren]'s reply to [William] Smith [on the R.I. question]
consisted of a few lines only which I inferred were non-committal.
You may be right in supposing that the question will be forced upon
the candidates and that it will be made one of the issues. But I incline to think that the time has not yet arrived. Six or eight months
ago a public discussion might have been serviceable. But just now
it has effected all the injury of which it was capable and the reaction
is in our favor. If I am right in supposing that there is a reaction in
our favor we have no interest just now in opening[?] that question.
Upon the questions which now seem to be engrossing the ["public"
interlined] mind, we certainly have the advantage and although I do
not doubt but that with *ample time* for discussion you could make
capital out of the Dorr question[,] yet I fear there is not now time
enough. I am perhaps strengthened in the impression that we had
better not add this to the issues by the opinions of our N[ew] England
friends. [Edmund T.] Bridge is very discreet and a politician. His
energy is untiring and his services in N[ew] England have been
greater I think than those of any other of our friends as I may have occasion in another letter to explain. He is anxious that this question
should not now be mooted. The Van Buren tide is on its ebb. Every
gun has been fired. They have failed to carry every thing by a *general
sweep* which they expected to do. The reaction is slow but steadily
in our favor. I speak of N[ew] England. We have a majority of the
delegates in Vermont. We have strong hopes of securing[?] a majority in Maine[,] Massachusetts[,] Connecticut and Bridge even hopes
["fo" *canceled*] to carry Rhode Island! !! Rhett has just returned from
N[ew] York. He writes in high spirits. Our friends are beginning to
move and had we been organized for the effort we should have every
prospect for success. It is not too late even yet. If our friends in
Congress are judicious and active next winter and if we can maintain
our paper in N[ew] York, (the Spectator I regard as now safe) and
[*one or two words changed to* "place"] it in the hands of an able edi-

tor we may yet succeed. So far as Virginia is concerned I regard the issues which we now have and the Texas question (should it become one of present & immediate interest) as the best for us that could be presented. On the Rh[ode] Island question we could make capital in lower Virginia if the public attention could be roused to it. But there is difficulty in this and time would be required. The difficulty consists in the unwillingness of political leaders to get up questions upon which the Eastern & Western feelings are different. I wrote to Rhett a week since to beg him to endeavor to see the correspondence. Smith ["now" *interlined*] lives in Warrenton [Va.] about 40 miles from Washington. Your letter if directed to Culpeper C[ourt] H[ouse] his old residence has probably not reached him as yet. Smith is true to you, but he is disposed to preserve caste with his old political associates, most of whom are V[an] B[uren] men.

I presume you have heard from Mr. U. [Abel P. Upshur, Secretary of State,] on the Texas question. If so you know the grounds upon which he is disposed to press it. From my conversation with him I inferred that the President [John Tyler] was a little doubtful as to the expediency of pressing it. Should he concur with U[pshur], and should the question itself be vigorously discussed in the papers, the South must unite. Perhaps also the West or a portion of it will join us. The Petersburgh Republican has been developing cautiously on this question. I have been urging our Richmond Committee to write to our orators to take the stump on the questions of district representation &c and of the Presidential election. This Texas question might be urged by them with great effect. The difficulty now seems to be to make a graceful occasion for introducing our speakers. The organization of [Henry] Clay Clubs seems to me to present such an opportunity. But our friends still doubt. I shall write again to them this week.

The combinations in Christendom against the slave ["holding" *interlined*] interest, the course of English Diplomacy abroad, the state of Northern feeling at home and the present necessity for maintaining the balance of power between the free & slave holding States constitute a crisis which gives an importance to this question and also to the election of a Southern president which I think our papers and speakers might turn to good account. Yet it is not to be denied but that this question will do much to divide parties sectionally and you are better able to foresee its full effects than I am. Rhett, Up[shu]r & I agreed in Washington that our papers ought to take the initiative on this question and begin at once to develop cautiously.

["Let us" *changed to* "If we"] are wrong pray set us right at once—
we have not gone far as yet. Most truly yours, R.M.T. Hunter.

P.S. Smith lives at some distance from me and if I were to go to
his house my object would be [*two or three words canceled*] suspected. Every trip I have made to Washington has been the subject
of newspaper comment. This does not hurt me but it injures the
cause. I will however write to Smith.

ALS in ScCleA; variant PC in Boucher and Brooks, eds., *Correspondence*, pp.
186–188.

From CHARLTON POTTS

Philadelphia, (12 o:c[loc]k at night) 11th of Oct. [18]43
Dear Sir, The election in the city and County of Philadelphia, is over,
and the judges and Inspectors have just completed their counts. The
democratic Party, so called has been partially defeated; but the banner of *John C. Calhoun* and *free Trade*, floats Triumphant. The die is
cast, the edict has gone forth, and henceforth the democratic party,
in this section must rally with you as their leader, or else ["not rally"
canceled] not rally at all. It was made a question in all the districts
four in number which compose the city and county of Philadelphia.
Mr. Hutchinson [*sic*; James H. Hutchison] taken up by the democratic caucus in opposition to Mr. [Edward] Wartman, a friend of
yours and most excel[lent] man, was the open and professed friend of
Mr. [Martin] *Van Buren*, as wel[l; *mutilation*] the auditor and county
Treasurer. They have all been defeated [by] a majority of from
fifteen to eighteen hundred votes. The [*mutilation*] Commissioner
Taken up on the same ticket was your f[*mutilation*] though he had not
the manly independence to [*mutilation.*] He has been beat by a small
majority; [*mutilation*] many of your warmest friends used t[*mutilation*] the Ticket myself among the rest [*mutilation*] dispised [*sic*]
the Traitors, yet we wishe[d; *mutilation*] Triumphant. Mr. Vanburen[']s ["friends" *interlined*], as y[*mutilation*] of Juggling or Leger-
demain, for ["which" *interlined*] their l[*mutilation*] distinguished
carried the day in [*mutilation*] four officers on our Ticket [*mutilation*]ments, had to submit themselves [*mutilation*] the Sovereign
people—they have [*mutilation*] found wanting" and Philadel[phia;
mutilation] ascertained majority of upwa[rds; *mutilation*] Whigs. In
the first district Mr. [*mutilation*] and avowed[?] advocate of Van

Buren's [*mutilation*] in a district that commonl[y; *mutilation*; dem-o]cratic majority. In the [*mutilation*] the democratic candidate [*mutilation*.] In the Third district (Mr. John Randolph's Cradel of Democracy) *John T. Smith* the open fearless and manly advocate of *John C. Calhoun* and *Free Trade*, has been triumphantly elected by *nine hundred majority*, running as you will perceive about *three hundred ahead of his Ticket*. In 4th district, Mr. [Charles J.] Ingersoll, *a Jim Crow* of a fellow, has been barely elected, in a district that polls a Thousand democratic majority. I have no doubt, but that tomorrow he'll be a Calhoun man. I have seen and talked with many intelligent gentlemen from the interior of Pennsylvania who say that among the thinking portion of the honest husbandmen, you will have five votes to Mr. Vanburen[']s one. Enough of this for the present.

I see, Sir, by the papers, (which by the bye are not to be re[lie]d on) you intend to visit the middle and Northern [Sta]tes. It is candidly my impression, if you do so, that [*mutilation*] recollections of the past will be brought [*mutilation*]ds of the people. You was once the [*mutilation*; Pen*]nsylvania, and rest assured her Sons, [*mutilation*] will receive you with that warmth [*mutilation*] *great genius* and splendid acquire[ments; *mutilation*]and, from a noble, generous and [*mutilation*] citizens look to you and to you [*mutilation*] can successfully rally her [*mutilation*; p]leased to learn that you received, [*mutilation*] show[?] that the democratic prin[*mutilation*]tle yours. Excuse, for the Li[*mutilation*; ac]tuated by an honest zeal, and [*mutilation*; resp]ectfully to Remain yours, Charlton Potts.

ALS (partly burned) in ScCleA. NOTE: A mutilated AEU by Calhoun indicates that he answered the above letter, informing Potts that he did not intend to visit the North.

From JOHN A. TARVER

Lowndesboro [Ala.,] Oct. 11, 1843

D[ea]r Sir, I am informed by Maj. Nixon that he sent you some cotton seed of a new variety of which I was the first discoverer. Some highly important facts in my possession from cultivators of this cotton has [*sic*] induced me to obtrude this letter on you to learn the results of your experiment with the seed.

Abner McGhee of Mont[gom]ery one of the oldest, wealthiest and most practical planters of this State plants this year sixty acres from my seed. He affir[ms] that although his Petit Gulf seed was up [*muti-*

lation] mine was planted yet it matured a fortni[ght] earlier—that he will make half as muc[h; *mutilation*] more to the acre, that his hands are av[eraging] 50 pounds each ["a day" *interlined*] more from my cotton th[*mutilation*] common. Similar statements are given [*mutilation*] cultivating the seed[,] they being distri[buted?; *mutilation*] planters expressly to test their producti[on; *mutilation*]. Another established fact—this cotton pr[oduces?; *mutilation*] from 31 to 33 pounds nett from 100 pounds [*mutilation.*] Seed being an average of 4 pounds nett over [*mutilation*] Petit Gulf—28 pounds being the average of Pet[it Gulf] and 32 of mine. Therefore the quantity in the [*mutilation*] of Petit Gulf required to produce 100 b[ales; *mutilation*] weighing 500 pounds each would make op[*mutilation*] 115 bales of the same weight.

Any facts which I may state to you on this subject will be affirmed by the Hon[orab]l[e] Dixon H. Lewis. I venture the assertion that with those seed the product in cotton of your State would be increased one third. They are the only actual improvement ["in" *canceled*] as yet made in cotton seed. All others about here have been abandoned as humbugs.

I wish a corroboration of the statements of others from you Sir if it can be given by actual trial made, and my motive for asking it is to ship this winter what seed I shall have to Charleston say about six thousand [bus]hels. Pecuniary difficulties will break up [*mutilation*] planting business this winter and mine are [*mutilation*; o]nly seed that I would vouch for their [*mutilation.*] It would be a desideratum for your [*mutilation*] to get them. The demand for them here [*mutilation*] great but I have ["too" *canceled and then interlined*] many *friends* [*mutilation*]tly dealt with ["by them" *canceled*] in selling here. [Testimoni]als affirmed by Mr. Lewis as stated above [*mutilation*] had in any number. Please answer this [*mutilation*] direct to Lowndesboro[,] Ala. Respectfully y[ou]r friend, Jno. A. Tarver.

P.S. I first discovered a stalk from which all the cotton I plant has been produced in 1838 in a field of Petit Gulf of the first year. The same peculiarity that marked the original stalk is maintained unchanged up to the present. You will note that the Pericarp contains but four cells with few exceptions. The Petit Gulf has generally five cells which accounts for the bolls appearing smaller—but being nearly round when it opens the locks project beyond the point of the hulls. One grab removes the locks which accounts for the difference in picking out this cotton. It can be picked out ten p[e]r cent cleaner than other cotton. You will also observe that the fibres are curled being [*mutilation*] elastic and clinging together with g[reater tenac]-

ity than any other cotton. The staple [*mutilation*] equal if not superior to the Petit Gulf. J.A.T.

ALS (partly burned) in ScCleA. NOTE: An AEU by Calhoun reads "J.A. Taver [*sic*,] relates to the seed of his cotton."

From FRANCIS [WHARTON]

150 Walnut St., Philadelphia, October 11th 1843

Sir, I take the liberty to send you by the present mail, the October number of Hunt's Magazine. There are a few passages [in] the first article which it will give me great pleasure to submit [to] your attention.

I propose, as perhaps you may notice, to follow up the [*mutilation*] opened, by a series of papers on the commercial ["history"(?) *canceled and* "legislation" *interlined*] of [*mutilation*] States. To trace the history of those great principles of politic[al; *mutilation*] which you have developed and enforced with such [*one word or partial word canceled; mutilation*] ability, is my object; and though it will be out of place [*mutilation*] business magazine, to enter into their laboured defence [*mutilation*] to me that by exhibiting the futility of all plans of [*mutilation*] do not constitute the leading elements, their pro[*mutilation*] assisted. If you can favour me in reference to [*mutilation*] which I am next to enter, the tariff of 1816 [*mutilation*] which may assist me in discovering the tru[*mutilation*] or if you can tell me where I can find any [*mutilation*; of your speeches of] that date, if there are any truly reported, [*mutilation*.] Your obedient ser[vant,] Francis [Wharton.]

ALS (partly burned) in ScCleA. NOTE: Wharton's article, entitled "Sketches of Commercial Legislation," appeared in *Hunt's Merchants' Magazine,* vol. XIV (October, 1843), pp. 301–320. In a note which referred to Calhoun, Wharton observed: "We cannot but regret that so imperfect a record should remain of speeches uttered at a period so critical [that is, 1816], by a man whose efforts, under any circumstances, deserve study as much as they provoke admiration." Wharton (1820–1889) was admitted to the Philadelphia bar in 1843. He was subsequently a much-published legal scholar.

From "LeDuc," Bayou Goula, Iberville Parish, La., 10/12. In a long letter in French, "LeDuc" warns Calhoun of "une conspiration anglaise puissante et dangereuse" that also involves Roman Catholic clergy and foreign agents of England and of Louis Philippe, King of

France. Although he gives no definite information regarding the organization and aims of the plot, he claims that the plotters have been active in the administrations of John Quincy Adams, Andrew Jackson, and Martin Van Buren, and that he has written "un petit manuscrit, en receuil de lettres" that contains the names of the conspirators and their activities. He has given the manuscript to "Doctor Duperran" of New Orleans and has informed the president and members of a French mutual aid society in New Orleans of its contents. "LeDuc's" references to the conspirators' activities indicate that he believes they aim at securing the election of Martin Van Buren to the Presidency in 1844 because of his pro-English sympathies. According to "LeDuc," the plotters are willing to use methods "d'emprisonment, d'assassinat, de calomnies, de mensonges" to achieve their "Jesuitiques et criminelles" aims. "LeDuc" supports Calhoun's Presidential candidacy and offers to let Calhoun see his manuscript in order to secure himself from the plotters' machinations. ALS (partly burned) in ScCleA.

From W[illia]m [B. Rogers]

Univ[ersity] of Virginia, Oct[obe]r 12, 1843
Dear Sir, I have been commissioned by the Society of Alumni of this Institution to make known to you their earnest wish that you would honor them by your presence and by delivering to them a public Address on our next commencement day the fourth of July 1844.

In making this request I am aware that [*mutilation*] are asking a favour, for which however great th[e; *mutilation*] and instruction we should receive we are unable [*mutilation*] equivalent gratification in return. But we promi[se; *mutilation*] hospitable and cordial greetings of the Univ[ersity; *mutilation*] Soc[iety] of Alumni embracing many of the mos[t; *mutilation*] young men of the State, and of the large and [*mutilation*] which will be convened to listen to your A[ddress.]

Earnestly hoping that it m[ay?; *mutilation*] wishes[?] & your inclination to comply with [*mutilation*] asking the favour of an early notice of [*mutilation*] beg to tender you my best wishes & pro[*mutilation*]. Very truly [*mutilation*,] Wm. [B. Rogers,] Com[mittee] of [*mutilation*.]

[P.S.] I regret to learn that your son's [John C. Calhoun, Jr.'s]

501

health is still infir[m?; *mutilation*] me to him in great kindness. He won the good wishes of all [*mutilation*] him here & continues to be thought ["of" *interlined*] with lively interest & [*mutilation.*]

ALS (partly burned) in ScCleA. NOTE: An AEU by Calhoun reads "Prof[esso]r Rogers[,] Answered 23d Oct[obe]r." Rogers was Professor of Natural Philosophy at the University of Virginia and also Va. State geologist.

Toast by Calhoun at a meeting of the Pendleton Farmers Society, 10/12. At a dinner held in [Samuel] "Cherry's long room," Calhoun gave the following toast: "Agriculture: The most important, but the most oppressed branch of industry." PC in the Pendleton, S.C., *Messenger*, October 20, 1843, p. 2; PC in [C.L. Newmann and J.C. Stribling], *The Pendleton Farmers' Society* (Atlanta: Foote and Davies Co., 1908), p. 114.

From TH[OMAS DUNNE?]

Providence [R.I.,] October 13th 1843

Dear Sir, Understanding you are about to visit the North I take the liberty to address you in behalf of the Lyceum of this city to request you to address that Association, at such time as you may appoint. Our course of Lectures will commence in Nov. and be continued three months.

Should you consent to allo[w] your numerous friends and admirers in this place the gratification of heari[ng] you I will thank you to info[rm; *mutilation*] when you could come [*mutilation*] not be able to accept you[*mutilation*] be a sufficient answer [*mutilation.*]

Our compensa[tion; *mutilation*] services will be fifty D[ollars; *mutilation.*] I am with [*mutilation*] Your[*mutilation*] Th[omas?; *mutilation*] for [*mutilation.*]

ALS (partly burned) in ScCleA. NOTE: An AEU by Calhoun reads "Mr. Dunne[?]."

From E[STWICK] EVANS

Wash[ingto]n City, Octo[be]r 13th 1843

Sir: I take the gr[*mutilation*] to add a word to the letter [*mutilation*] myself the honour to write y[ou; *mutilation*] since.

I have just re[*mutilation*] the Hon[orabl]e Mr. [Levi] Woodbury, [*mutilation*] eight of the "Essay," expressi[ng; *mutilation*] sentiments entirely satisfact[ory; *mutilation.*]

But, Sir, [*mutilation*]ject in this communicati[on; *mutilation*] judging from my daily subscri[*mutilation*]ter[?] of those who favour me wit[h; *mutilation*] the subject of "States rights" is growing [*mutilation*] at least getting out a little from that [*mutilation*] I should say bitter prejudice, in which it has so long been laying, & which has always excited my deep indignation & sympathy; indignation at the error & the wrong, & sympathy for the individuals who became, more or less, victims to this prejudice, in consequence of having dared to advocate truth, reason, indeed our most essential liberties.

I have allowed myself [", Sir," *interlined*] to be in great haste; & have the honour to remain, with very great consideration, Your Obed[ient] Serv[an]t, E. Evans.

ALS (partly burned) in ScCleA.

From V[IRGIL] MAXCY

Tulip Hill [Anne Arundel County, Md.] 13th Oct. 1843
My dear Sir, Your two letters of the 18th & 27th Sept. came duly to hand. From having anticipated your wishes in two moves, I begin to have some confidence in my own judgment. But having changed my opinion in regard to an authoritative movement of your Central Committee, expressed to Col. [Franklin H.] Elmore & by him communicated to the ["Charleston" *canceled*] Committee I felt it a duty to write him a long letter, assigning my reasons for the change. I send you the rough draft, so that if you disapprove of the course I have recommended to them, you may write and counteract at once the little weight my views may have.

I am somewhat disappointed by our New England friends. They have not, I discover from a recent conversation with [David] Henshaw, made so rapid a progress as they led me to anticipate and are not yet prepared to take a bold stand. I don[']t believe the Boston Post even has ventured to re-publish my pamphlet [*Democratic National Convention*], tho [Lemuel] Williams informed me, that he promised to do it. These northern friends are characteristically cautious & must feel their way and operate covertly to get a majority first instead of coming out boldly at critical times & by decision[?] direct the current.

503

What is the meaning of Georgia coming out in favor of the Whigs? In haste truly Yours, V. Maxcy.

[P.S.] As I should like to keep a copy of my letter to Elmore, I should be glad if after reading you will return it.

Mrs. [Mary Galloway] Maxcy's health is much better than before she was taken ill, & I hope will leave my mind free to be devoted to our good cause. As I live near Annapolis & intend to remain here for the winter, I can go there often & perhaps do as much good as if a member of the Legislature, which w[oul]d necessarily give me other occupation, that would interfere with it.

[Enclosure]

V[irgil] Maxcy to [Franklin H. Elmore], "Rough Draft"

West River, Md., 10 Oct. 1843

My dear Sir, The last letter I ["wrote" *changed to* "sent"] from New York, I wrote under considerable excitement from the recent proceedings of the Syracuse convention and the confident expression of my expectation of hearing very soon some "Charleston Thunder" together with other strong indications of opinion, necessarily made the impression, that I was in favour of immediate & very decided action from your central committee. Subsequent developments in New York and more correct & full information of the state of things in New England have produced a considerable modification of my opinion as to the course of action which [South] Carolina ought to adopt at present. If man were a *reasoning* animal, I should still think that now was the time for "drawing the line" of separation between *hostile forces*, but he is a bundle of prejudices, pre-conceived and unexamined notions & selfish passions, and time must be taken to enlighten him and remove those prejudices and correct his erroneous opinions before you call on him to act decisively or ten to one he will act wrong. It is impossible for one accustomed to southern freedom of thinking and investigation only, to have a just conception of the strength of party drill ["at the north" *interlined*], by which ["the mass of" *interlined*] men have been almost converted into machines, whose motions receive their impulse ["entirely" *interlined*] from the touch of artful politicians. Every thing is done by caucus, and he who hesitates in his obedience to its decisions, is considered little less than a traitor to the constitution. Conventions for the nomination of Presidents have heretofore had little to do but ratify decisions previously made by public opinion and their action being in conformity to it nobody cared & therefore nobody inquired how they were formed. Even now, the mass of intelligent men are only beginning to inquire and it will require some time yet to divest the name "Convention" of its authority. Our newspapers must all take strong ground, must discuss & rediscuss & present ["in a strong light" *interlined*] the principles which ought to govern its formation and constantly urge the impossibility of permitting New York to control the nomination by its consolidated ticket. This is necessary to prevent the inference that we can in any case submit to her dictation: but if the South Carolina Central committee should now declare war, before the merits of the question are fully understood, it would drive off not only many who are now our friends but prevent others becoming so. Such a step now taken would lose us Maryland, [*one word canceled and* "where" *interlined*] with ["judicious" *interlined*] management we are sure of three fourths of the delegates & tho' she is not half so well drilled into obedience to Caucus as the more northern States. If New York persists in its stand, a rupture must come, but let us prepare the public mind to see that it is forced on us and that we could not submit without dishonor. I would still treat Mr. [Martin] Van Buren with consideration and avoid making his friends our enemies. Our object is not to defeat him, which can be done at any time, but to succeed ourselves, which we cannot do without the aid of those, who prefer him to Mr. Calhoun. Three States, Tennessee, Georgia & Maryland have gone over to the whigs, from indifference, if not aversion to Mr. V[an] B[uren; "who appears now to be the strongest candidate" *interlined*]—and I cannot but hope that not only his friends but himself will before long see that Mr. [Henry] Clay would beat him & that he is not an available candidate.

Nothing could prove more conclusively, that the principles on which a convention ought to be formed, are not at all understood yet, ["than" *interlined*] that, in the late Massachusetts State consention [*sic*], a Resolution ["in favor of" *canceled*] that every State has the [*one word canceled and* "right" *interlined*] to appoint delegates to the National convention in any way it pleases, passed ["without" *and an illegible word canceled and* "without one" *interlined*] of the 186 Calhoun members of that convention seeing its bearing & therefore did not oppose it. It is true that in accordance with the true spirit of Van Buren trickery, the resolution was smuggled in just ["before" *canceled and* "as" *interlined*] the convention was breaking up. Still it is passing strange that there was not one Calhoun man, who had his eyes open to its tendency.

I enclose an extract from the Democratic Review, the Editor [*sic*] of which, [Orestes A.] Brownson, is a friend of Mr. Calhoun, to shew that men of extraordinary intelligence like him, have not yet bestowed reflection or attention enough to the principles involved in the formation of a national convention to be fully aware of their importance.

Extracts from the Boston Post might be made to shew the same thing.

A conversation had on a recent visit to Washington with Mr. Henshaw, who avows himself & I doubt not sincerely a decided friend of Mr. Calhoun, ["which" *canceled*] satisfies me, that in New England public opinion must be enlightened before it will be safe to come to an open rupture. He assures me that Mr. Calhoun is gaining ground in Massachusetts & Maine but that in Massachusetts the democratic party is not strong enough to risk a division and that precipitation on the part of his friends would only have the effect to injure his cause.

Measures, which would be prudent in some States would be rash & injurious in others where there is a powerful Whig enemy to contend with. In this State a contest for the Legislature has terminated in our defeat. Three hundred votes would have saved the State. Eighteen more votes would have elected the ticket in my county, where in the hope of doing some good to Mr. Calhoun's cause, I had consented to be a Candidate. My own defeat in particular was brought about, as the polles [*sic*] of that part of the county shew, by the exertions against me of the manufacturers in the upper end of the County. Altho' I believe with many others, that the prospect of Mr. [Martin] Van Buren being the candidate of the Republican Party, caused an indifference and induced many voters to stay away from the polles in some parts of the State, I am bound to say in respect to my own defeat, I do not believe, ["notwithstanding" *canceled and* "that I lost votes from this cause or the neglect of the V(an) B(uren) Voters on account of" *interlined*] the *notoriety* of my sentiments in favor of Mr. Calhoun ["that I lost any votes from this cause" *canceled*]. Apart from the active opposition of the manufacturers, which are very numerous in one section of my County ["&" *canceled*] the loss of the ticket is attributable to excessive confidence in our strength.

I give you the above details to shew you, My dear Sir, how cautious we ought to be not to do any thing, that would divide our ranks, ["in the States nearly balanced between the two parties" *interlined*] before we have taken the necessary measures to satisfy the mass of the Democratic party of the clear justice of our cause and having in my letter from New York expressed ["strongly" *interlined*] an opinion in favour of prompt action in So[uth] Carolina, which I now think premature ["except as to newspapers" *interlined*] I take the more pains ["now" *canceled*] to shew the reasons of the modification of that opinion lest it might have ["had" *interlined and then canceled*] more weight, than it ought.

The movement has begun in the right place, New York, where our friends are zealous ["& respectable" *interlined*] but unfortunately, they have not wealth. A newspaper is absolutely necessary in New York, and altho' I understand, they have determined to set one up with the means they have ["collected" *interlined*] yet ["to make success sure" *interlined*] they stand in great need of assistance and I recommend strongly, that, as it is not thought necessary to make the [Washington] Spectator more than a tri-weekly paper ["for the present" *interlined*] that your central committee give Mr. [Robert Barnwell] Rhett a discretionary authority, to use $1000 of the funds placed in his hands, in aid of the establishment of a paper in the City of New York, if he should deem it necessary.

I think it ["would be" *canceled*] is essential that your committee be active in their correspondence with all parts of the U. States and in the circulation of pamphlets & newspaper articles calculated to enlighten the public mind on the subject of a National convention, by way of preparation for a final rupture, if that should become necessary as I incline to think it will be. I am now engaged with some friends in making out a list of persons ["in Maryland" *interlined*], in whose hands my hasty pamphlet published in New York may be placed in [*one word canceled*] the hope of its contributing to furnish reasons to the unreflecting but leading men of our party in this State & getting public opinion right before the meeting of our Legislature: and I will cause an immediate distribution to be made of any publication issued with you on the subject, if you will send them to me for that purpose. A packet too large for the mail would reach me, if sent to Baltimore to the care of Mr. Cooke & Son, 7 Light Street Wharf.

I beg you to excuse the length of this, I fear, tedious letter and believe me, My dear Sir Most truly Yours, V. Maxcy.

[P.S.] The Harpers have stereotyped my pamphlet on the "National Convention["] and will furnish any number to order, if deemed worthy of circulation out of New York at $15 per 1000 or 1½ cent[s] a piece.

ALS and copy with En in ScCleA.

From J[ames] Hamilton [Jr.]

Oswichee Bend [Russell County, Ala.,] Oct. 15[t]h 1843
My Dear Sir, I have designed visiting you for some time but some sickness in my family with a slight degree of suffering myself from in-

flamed eyes from excessive exposure to the sun have prevented me. Before I say a word on the subject of Politicks let me give you a brief summary of the information I procured of the Tal[l]apoosa [Ala.?] Mines.

They average a pennyweight to a Bushel of ore. Major Bradford[']s vein has yielded more. The Gold is found in Quartz enveloped generally in Slate. They run from N.E. to S.W. varying from 10 to 12 degrees. The dip of the vein varies from 35 to 50 Degrees with an horizontal width from 4 inches to 4 feet. The small veins are the richest. The depth of the veins ["are" *canceled*] is not yet known[;] already they have been worked 50 feet deep from the surface. The strip of Country through which the veins run is about one mile and have [*sic*] been traced about[?; *mutilation*] in length. Several of the mines [*mutilation*] have veins 40 feet wide. The average day[']s work to the hand is about ["8" *canceled*] eight Bushels[?] of ore p[e]r day.

Subsistence is cheap at the mines—Corn may be had at 40 Cents & Fodder at 95[?] Cents p[e]r hundred[?].

I have given you a very brief summary of the information I gleaned on the spot. But by 20[t]h Nov. I shall be able to speak more accurately as to results as I have 8 hands under a very competent & trustworthy agent making explorations for the purpose of ascertaining whether there is any thing of real value in the Country or not.

I understand you propose paying your son [Andrew Pickens Calhoun] a visit this autumn in this State. Your shortest & best route by which you will avoid passing through any large Towns will be to take the Stage at Madrid[?] via Franklin which [pa]sses on its route through a small place called Mount Jefferson where I will meet you on the 25th Nov. with my Carria[ge]. We can from that place drive to the mines in a day & return & take the Stage for Montgomery—to which place I [*mutilation*] accompany you on my way to [*mutilation*]. Drop me a line directed to Sa[vannah?] whether you will be able to meet [*mutilation*]. I should be delighted if Mr. [Thomas G.] Clemson [*mutilation*] ac[com]pany us as this judgment would be [*mutilation*].

Now as to politicks. [*Mutilation*] as slippery a subject as [*mutilation*] Gold. You will have seen the result of the Georgia Elections which on the first blush are calculated to exert an unfavorable influence on your prospects. Single handed, I am sure you are vastly stronger than [Henry] Clay in that State, & immeasurably so to [Martin] Van Buren. I shall attend the session for one week of the Georgia Legislature—and with [John H.] Howard consult what is best to be done to take off the effect ["of the disastrous defeat of the Democrats" *interlined*] whilst I shall endeavour to maintain my friendly relations with the Whigs at the same time, with Leaders of which party I am quite on ["friendly" *canceled and* "kind" *interlined*] terms—Many of whom would gladly support you but for the committment [*sic*] of the [*mutilation.*]

I have been applied to in [*mutilation*] Quarters to consent to go to Baltimore [*mutilation*] May. My answer is that as your friend I would go any where to serve you but [*mutilation*] anti Jacksonism[,] anti Blairism & [anti] Kendal[l]ism; they must reflect whether [*mutilation*]ld not do you more harm than good. That in the Democracy you were my Candidate *without an alternative* and that apart from your interests I did not feel the slightest interest in the election. Let me ["know" *interlined*] by directing *immediately* to Savannah how you think the game now stands. Will [Thomas] Ritchie[,] [Francis P.] Blair[,] [Amos] Kendal[l,] [Martin] Van Buren[,] [Thomas H.] Benton & the Albany Regency be able to stack the cards? If they are [Henry] Clay[']s election is certain. I remain My Dear Sir ever faithfully your friend, J. Hamilton.

P.S. I had a most gratifying visit from your nephew [John Alfred Calhoun] last week who lives at Upaloa [*sic;* Eufaula, Ala.] formerly Irwinton. He is highly regarded in this Com[m]u[ni]ty[?]. I need not say that he takes a deep interest in your political fortunes.

ALS (partly burned) in ScCleA. NOTE: This letter was postmarked in Columbus, Ga., on 10/16.

From R[OBERT] B[ARNWELL] RHETT

Washington, Oc[tobe]r 16th 1843

My Dear Sir, I find I will be compelled to leave this City and go home to bring Mrs. [Elizabeth Washington Burnet] Rhett, and I think I had better do it at once, so that I might be able to return the sooner, before the meeting of Congress.

The late Elections have very clearly shewn that the Whigs are very powerful—so powerful as to render it pretty clear that [Henry] Clay will beat [Martin] Van Buren. [Daniel] Webster it is now well understood will sink back into the Whig party—and they will be united. If Van Buren is run, Clay will beat him any how; but with the di-

visions & lukewarmness, (if no worse occurs[?]) which must neces-
saryly ["a" *canceled and* "follow a" *interlined*] nomination ["by a
Convention" *interlined*] constituted as Mr. V[an] B[uren's] friends
propose, it will ["be" *interlined*] desperate folly, to attempt to run him.
And yet if they persist in their method of organization, and we oppose or seceed [*sic*] from the Party, it is clear you cannot be elected;
for, there are sufficient V[an] B[uren] men in all the States, with the
Whigs, to defeat us. Indeed, if you were to get the nomination in the
present temper of Mr. V[an] B[uren's] friends, it would be useless, for
I am satisfied they would stand aloof and see us beaten. Van Buren
cannot succeed without us, ["&" *interlined*] we cannot succeed without his friends. Neither in their present mood will allow the other to
succeed; whilst we are conjointly too weak, to carry the election with
a nobody like [Lewis] Cass, or even [James] Buchanan. You are the
only man, who can beat Clay in the South, and the carrying of the
South has usually been the Presidency. As things now look, there
appears to me to be but one method for the Democratic Party to succeed, and that is, each portion of the Union running the man most
popular in each Section. Clay[']s chance is decidedly the best for the
next President.

All this mischief has arisen from Mr. V[an] B[uren] allowing himself, to be used by others who in flattering his vanity and ambition,
were only using him to keep you down. He will fail; and prove himself to be the heaviest curse of the Party. Had he not stepped in the
way, the whole Atlantic [sea]board would have united on you, and we
would have known none of the divisions which are the strength of the
Whigs.

I shall not leave here until Friday, and hope before I leave here,
to hear something definite from Mr. [Washington] Greenhow, who is
waiting for a fit person to take his place [in Petersburg]. In the mean
time I have written to [Robert M.T.] Hunter & [Virgil] Maxcy to aid
Mr. [John] Heart until I return, but to tell you the truth I calculate
but little on either of them, to contribute to the [*Spectator*] Paper.

The next Congress will be a very agitated one, and will doubtless
affect powerfully the Presidency. If the Democrats would play the
["protecti" *canceled and* "free trade" *interlined*] policy boldly out, and
sustain the Texas question—and run you; we can succeed. The zealots
at the North will oppose Clay because from the South, and in the
South you would beat him on ["that" *canceled and* "the Tariff" *interlined*] question, especially if his friends oppose the modifications
which we propose, as they will. But I fear there is little hope of such

a combination of wise results. The probability is, dissension and defeat.

Remember me kindly to Mr. [Thomas G.] Clemson and believe me Y[ou]rs, R. B. Rhett.

ALS in ScCleA; variant PC in Jameson, ed., *Correspondence*, pp. 887–888.

From DUFF GREEN

London, 18th Oct. 1843

My dear Sir, I have just returned from Manchester, where I have been to see parties with whom I am in negociation, and have not time to write to you in detail but I am so much impressed with the consequences that may follow an energetic course on the part of our Government, and so desirous that your influence should be enlisted in favor of the measures that I propose that I have enclosed this to Judge [Abel P.] Upshur with a request that he will cause the copy of my letter to him to be sent to you.

I have just seen a confidential friend from whom I learn the result of the interview late last night between the Brazilian Minister and the President of the Board of Trade. There will be no treaty because this [British] government demands, as a condition for the admission of Brazilian ["produce" *canceled*] sugar ["to" *canceled*] that Brazil shall emancipate her slaves. And after a very spirited debate, in which the necessity of admitting slave grown sugar ["was discussed" *interlined*] Mr. [William] Gladstone who represents Sir Robert Peel's views said that the Gov[ernmen]t will *not* admit slave grown sugar. It is the same as to Cuba as Brazil except that England insists that all African slaves and their descendants introduced into Cuba since 1824 are entitled to their freedom by virtue of the treaty with Spain. Let England succeed with Brazil & she will coerce emancipation in Cuba.

But the other aspect of the case is this—the free trade party, are now making alliances with all the discontents. The opponents of the *established* religion, the chartists, the disaffected in Scotland[,] in Wales and in Ireland are making common cause ["with the Whigs" *interlined*] against Sir Robert Peel, and he to protect himself in power has fallen back on his opposition to ["*negro*" *interlined*] slavery, as his last hope. The landlords and the Church [of England] united are compelled to call on fanaticism, and the consequence is that all the elements of opposition are uniting to denounce the hypocritical pretence of humanity, which to free the black man enslaves the white.

Shall we fold our arms or shall we avail ourselves of the present moment to do what we can do to promote such an adjustment of our relations with England as will quiet forever the political agitation of the question of slavery? The free trade party of England is a peace party. They desire free trade with us because they fear our competition as manufacturers and know that we will be their best customers as agriculturalists. ["Hence if" *canceled.*] One of the strongest arguments of the monopolists of England is that a relaxation of their system would not be followed by a relaxation on our part, and Mr. Abbot[t] Lawrence has been several times quoted to me as authority for the contradictory assertions that we can compete successfully with English manufactures—*without* protection—and that a repeal of the English Corn laws will reduce the value of land in England to a par with the price of lands in Ohio.

If we invite England to negotiate on the subject of the [Oregon] boundary & of the Tariff, Sir Robert Peel will refuse to send Commissioners to Washington, because it is understood that to carry his Canada Corn bill he was compelled to pledge himself that ["he" *interlined*] would make no further modification, and the effect of his refusal will be to enlist all parties opposed to him as the partisans of a favorable adjustment of all questions between us and to hasten the reorganisation of the ministry. The new ministers will settle the question of slavery by the admission of slave grown produce and thus end the agitation so prejudicial to our interests.

In this view of the case it is all important that our friends in New York and Charleston as well as every where else should raise the banner of free trade—we should make common cause with the free trade party of England, as laboring for a common principle. The late elections show that there will be a decided democratic majority in Congress, and that a democratic President will be elected in case there is no choice by the people. This breaks the force of the plea that is urged by [Martin] Van Buren's partisans and I hope that your friends will not permit themselves to be made the dupes of his intrigues. Your sincere friend, Duff Green.

ALS in ScCleA; PC in Boucher and Brooks, eds., *Correspondence,* pp. 188–190. NOTE: In regard to the transmittal of this letter to Calhoun, see below the letter from Abel P. Upshur dated 11/8/1843.

From James Wishart

St. Clairsville [Ohio,] Oct[obe]r 18th 1843
My Dear Sir, I Have the honor to acknowledge the receipt of two letters from you in answer to mine of prior dates. Your first dated the
28th Aug[us]t reached me about ten days after my second was mailed,
and the one dated the 27th Sept[embe]r, on the 11th inst[ant], the
day after our annual election.

Three weeks ago Dr. [John G.] Miller editor of the administration
paper at Columbus, and brother-in-law of Mr. [John] Tyler, called o[n
me] on his way to Washington City, to induce me to us[e?; *mutilation*]
up a State convention in Nov[embe]r in behalf of the Pr[*mutilation*]
break down Mr. [Martin] V[an] B[uren]. I stated to him that I
[*mutilation*] to such a movement, but was satisfied no [*mutilation*;
Democrat]ic candidates could alone contend with h[im?; *mutilation*;
suc]cessfully so far as the nominating conventio[n; *mutilation*] Ohio
was his strong hold for the nom[*mutilation*] could not get the electoral
vote of th[e; *mutilation*] him successfully we must in add[ition; *mutilation*] proposed by him get an expression of [*mutilation*] the district
system and the per cap[ita system?; *mutilation*] against the demagogues. The distr[ict system?; *mutilation*] convention plan, and thus
the battle [*mutilation*] successfully than on any one candida[te; *mutilation*] a letter, within a few days past, from [*mutilation*] some effect,
which I shall answer in [*mutilation*] convinced of the error of my
views on this [*mutilation*] you favor me so far as to give me the bene-
f[it; *mutilation*] on this point.

I have the pleasure of informing you that w[e; *mutilation*] carried
the election of the three friends on our [*mutilation*] ticket, although
much effort was made by some of [the] V[an] B[uren] men to defeat
their election. In this county [of Belmont], always close, we succeeded in our entire ticket. But in other counties where Van Burenism was made a test of democracy we have been defeated.

Returns from the State sufficient to show the complexion of the
legislature, and members of congress, have been received. The democrats have four of a majority in the senate, and the whigs a like
majority in the lower house. The democrats have elected twelve members of congress, the whigs nine. In the Chil[l]icothe district ex-Gov.
[Robert] Lucas has lost his election, so also with [William] Medill in
the Lancaster district and Barker in the [Mc]Connelsville district
south of Zanesville. Van Buren [*mutilation*]ese and other places was
made the test of democracy [*mutilation*] rise of the legislative session
we anticipate a [*mutilation*] in the public mind. The people will now

[*mutilation*; Wilson] Shannon is now out openly against V[an] B[uren; *mutilation*]ing to support is very uncertain.

[*Mutilation*] the editor [John Dunham] of the [St. Clairsville] Gazett[e] wrote the biograph[y; *mutilation*] in that paper. He often writes a very [*mutilation*.]

[*Mutilation*; loo]ks brighter than it did some months [*mutilation*] made by the friends of V[an] B[uren] could not. [*Mutilation*] better adapted to promote the advancement [*mutilation*; "they are" *canceled and* "it is" *interlined*]. If he does not recede, ["the election" *canceled*; *mutilation*] probably go to the House of Rep[resentative]s and there [*mutilation*] to be apprehended is another "union between [the puritan] and the blackleg" [as in 1824]. With great Respect &C, James Wishart.

ALS (partly burned) in ScCleA. NOTE: An AEU by Calhoun reads "Dr. Wisha[rt]." The "biography" referred to in the fifth paragraph was an article on Calhoun which appeared in the St. Clairsville, Ohio, *Gazette*. It was reprinted in four columns in the Pendleton, S.C., *Messenger*, September 15, 1843, p. 1.

From ALB[ERT RHETT]

Charleston, Oct. 19, 1843

My Dear Sir, Your friends here have been deliberating on the plan of calling a Convention of the Young men of the U[nited] States favourable to your election to the Presidency—the place Washington or Richmond—the time—early in January. Letters will go in every dire[ction; *mutilation*] today, to our friends elsewhere to [*mutilation*] their views and propose them [*mutilation*]ment. We think the propos[al?; *mutilation*] come first from New York. [*Mutilation*] be here today or tomorrow [*mutilation*] to take his family on, and [*mutilation*] his views. In the mean [time; *mutilation*] assigned to me to lay the [*mutilation*] you and request as imme[diate; *mutilation*] as you can furnish desc[ribing; *mutilation*] of the scheme generally and [*mutilation*] as to form, time—place & [*mutilation*].

The late Democratic reve[rses?; *mutilation*] my mind, at all impair our c[*mutilation*; ul]timate success, on the contrary [*mutilation*] than by making it too clear that Mr. [Martin] Van Buren never can rec[eive; *mutilation*] vote of a majority of the country. [*Mutilation*] only to press steadily & vigorously on. [*Mutilation*] yours most truly & resp[ectfully; *mutilation*,] Alb[ert Rhett].

ALS (partly burned) in ScCleA.

From Ch[arles] Aug[ustus] Da[vis]

New York [City,] 21 Oct. 1843

My D[ea]r Sir, I took the liberty of giving a Mr. Cornell of this city a letter of introduction to you at the request of his Father, a highly respectable citizen. The object of the young man[']s [*mutilation*] to your quarter is regarding some land situ[ated; *mutilation*] land known to or own'd by you—and it [*mutilation*] local knowledge and kind advice that [*mutilation*] ask'd.

Political affairs in th[is; *mutilation*] to warm up a little, as our elections [*mutilation*] yet it is very difficult to determine how [*mutilation*] the actual question of the ["Presidenency" *altered to* "Presidency"] is [*mutilation*] recognized in the *Voting* yet. They learn[?] that [*mutilation*] year.

The doctrine of *internal improvement* has taken a deep hold of our people in all this quarter. The very first interest (among all those prostrated by late events) that lifted its head was the *Rail road interest*—and that is not a very great [*mutilation*] of political parties—but is a party *sui generis*. [*Mutilation*; m]easures. To this may be added the *protective* [*mutilation*] now extend the doctrine of protection to [*mutilation*; every] *where*—not only over Cotton spindles [*mutilation*; cur]rency and credit. They urge that the [*mutilation*] planter is best promoted by inducing [*mutilation*; m]anufacture cotton for themselves. As we[?; *mutilation*] extend its *consumption* by means of extending [*mutilation*] consumers to pay by exchanges at home [*mutilation*] not applicable in paying abroad. This doctrine [*mutilation*] home industry is very captivating with the mass[es]. I took the liberty of stating at a meeting of friends the other evening—that on looking back it w[oul]d be found that the oldest *father* of the promotion of *home industry—now living*—was yourself but not to let it run over and crowd out all other interests—that you regarded a Ship as much an implement of home labor as a spindle or a loom.

This is the Season of our [commercial?] fairs—and [*mutilation*] here are truly wonderful. They are thro[*mutilation*] and nightly and every ev[enin]g addresses are [*mutilation*] multitudes. This is a tremendous eng[ine?; *mutilation*] power.

The hesitation and [*mutilation*] of the Democracy to risk the *distric*[*t* system; *mutilation*; "be" *interlined*] sadly against them. The inference being [*mutilation*] pretend to rest exclusively on the People [*mutilation*] pack them in masses. They don[']t like the [*mutilation*] so well as "the grand army" system—which by [*mutilation*] a few *field marshalls.* Y[our] fr[ie]nd & ob[edien]t Ser[vant,] Ch[arles] Aug[ustus] Da[vis].

ALS (partly burned) in ScCleA.

From W[ILLIAM] H. MAR[RIOTT]

Baltimore, October 21[s]t 1843
My Dear Sir, The news papers will have informed you before the receipt of this, of the result of the Election for a Mayor of this City, which took place on Monday last. Although I obtained a larger Vote than was ever before given to any D[emocratic] Candidate, from the year 1800 to the p[resent; *mutilation*; never]theless I was defeated, by the treach[*mutilation*] who claimed to belong to the party [*mutilation*] laying, ["so"(?) *canceled*] well understood in oth[*mutilation*] Coon party, & extensively practi[*mutilation*] on Monday last. The late cont[*mutilation*] severe and untiring[?] before the elec[tion; *mutilation*] close of the Polls than was ever [*mutilation*] that in 1800 between the late [*mutilation*] & Winchester. Such were the [*mutilation*] of the Coon party [that is, the Whigs] & their plans to [*mutilation*] in favor of "Harry of the West" [Henry Clay] as de[*mutilation*] throughout the contest, that not less [*mutilation*] were expended (according to the declarati[on; *mutilation*] of their prominent leaders) to obtain suc[*mutilation*] although in *some measure* denied by them, th[*mutilation*] obliged to admit, that a larger number of Votes were received than they expected, and openly to acknowledge that they believed themselves defeated, *before* the close of the Polls. Persons from Philadelphia & Washington were brought here by the Coons & voted, and our Judges were so [w]eak and timid as to receive only the affidavit [*mutilation*] voter, without requ[iri]ng[?] other proof as to [*mutilation*; reside]nce. I have been defeated, but not [*mutilation*] manly fight & although our [*mutilation*] was extremely defective, I assure [*mutilation*; Dem]ocratic party were never in [*mutilation*], and have already determined [*mutilation*] for the contest next fall. [*Mutilation*] promise you that the discipline to [*mutilation*] of the party shall be effectual [*mutilation*] to elect a Democratic Mayor [*mutilation*] on Monday ["next" *canceled*] last[?] was only to [*mutilation*] vacancy by the resignation of Col. [Solomon] Hillen. [*Mutilation*; M]ayors election next fall will be for [*mutilation*] and the Democratic Candidate [*mutilation*] elected, will not be embarrassed by [*mutilation*] free holders, as all now in office will be removed by the Coon

Mayor, & if we succeed next fall of which I entertain no doubt, the Mayor will then be enabled to look to the entire party to make the *best selections*, which no doubt will be done. I am entirely satisfied with the result, & it shall be my care & pleasure, as well as my duty, to lend my constant aid towards [*mutilation*] *regulations* & Government, *as a party*[?; *mutilation*; *one word illegible*] them on Monday last) as to ins[*mutilation*] the next trial. The friends of M[*mutilation*] with us, and I believe generally [*mutilation*] & gave me their aid & assistance [*mutilation.*]

I have written this hasty [*mutilation*] you the *true reasons* of my de[feat; *mutilation*] the favor to let me hear fr[om; *mutilation*] My Dear Sir, I am for[?] th[*mutilation*] & O[bedien]t [*mutilation,*] W.H. Mar[riott,] Saturday.

ALS (partly burned) in ScCleA. NOTE: An AEU by Calhoun reads: "Gen[era]l Marriott." Marriott, a prominent Baltimore Democrat, had been Speaker of the Md. House of Delegates and President of the Md. Senate. In 1844 he was appointed Collector of Customs at Baltimore by President John Tyler.

From F[RANCIS] W. PICKENS

Charleston, Sunday Morning [Oct. 22, 1843]

My dear Sir, On my arrival here day before yesterday I found your friends in some excitement. I heard that you were determined to refuse immediately to go into a convention at all, and that you desired the central Com[mittee] here to take the stand openly unless N[ew] York receeded [*sic*] from the Syracuse Convention &c &c. I saw [Franklin H.] Elmore, [Ker] Boyce[,] [Henry W.] Conner[,] [James] Gadsden[,] [Henry] Gourdin[,] [John S.] Ashe &c &c, but could get nothing very definite or certain, except they seemed to be in confusion. Elmore then shewed me a letter from [Robert Barnwell] Rhett at Washington, in which the first sentence was, "I entirely disapprove of the course advised by Mr. Calhoun & Mr. [Virgil] Maxcy," and then goes on to give excellent advice and full of good sense according to my judgement; but I could not understand what yours and Maxcy's advice was, & Elmore could not tell me, only that he understood it was to refuse to go into convention &c &c. This was all strange to me. Rhett is to be here to-day & Elmore is to have us all together to-morrow to consult freely. I think nothing ought to be done decisive until Congress meets and let every friend of ours be on the ground at least 5 days before the meeting and let them consult together freely,

517

and give the most authentic information as to the true state of things in their different States. My own opinion is that we ought to give up the Speakership if we can get the Printer—in the present state of the country it ["is" *interlined*] more important to us. But I would give up neither unless they would liberally & cordially give to us the Printer. It will strike a decided blow at the [Washington] Globe & [Richmond] Enquirer. If they will not agree, then push [Dixon H.] Lewis—or I would still rather take a [James] Buchanan [supporter as] Speaker if they will act with us & the whigs & give us the Printer. But I fear Lewis might not like this, as I hear he is eager for the Speakership. But of one thing I am sure[:] the most decided moves ought to be made at the opening of Congress. And in the consultation tomorrow I shall take decided grounds ag[ain]st doing any thing ["dec" *canceled*] final at present, but wait the meeting of Congress. I think [Henry] Clay is stronger than he was for[merly?]. I have no idea that any portion of the whigs will ever support you as long as there is the slightest chance for him. I have just seen Col. Hanson from Milledgeville [Ga.]. He was with [John M.] Berrien [Senator from Ga.] day before yesterday at Savannah, and has recently been all through Geo[rgia]. You know he is whig but personally a friend of yours. He says that State will undoubtedly go for Clay, and that the Democratic party are split & that a new convention will be called & nominate [Martin] V[an] B[uren] &c. I rec[eive]d a letter from Col. I[saac] W. Hayne of Montgomery [Ala.] & also one from [your nephew] J[ames] M[artin] Calhoun [of Selma, Ala.] the other day. They both say that they think the Democratic party will nominate V[an] B[uren] this winter at Tuscaloosa [Ala.]. Now this may come from their fears & their peculiar position.

If N[ew] York acts upon what our friends have moved there—that is to elect Dist[rict] Representatives to the Convention[—]this will bring up the question directly, and we may have a separate Dist[rict] Convention, but I hardly think it will *break the organization* of the Democratic party & will only throw off our own State. The consequence may be to give us also N[orth] Ca[rolina], at least to keep it from V[an] B[uren], but this would not take you to the House. I think it very probable it might elect Clay.

Do tell Mr. [Thomas G.] Clemson that Dr. [Eli] Geddings tells me, there will be no vacancy in that Professorship [at the Medical College of Charleston] & that he would allways [*sic*] be pleased to aid him when an opportunity occurs. In great haste but Truly, F.W. Pickens.

ALS in ScCleA; variant PC in Jameson, ed., *Correspondence*, pp. 889–890.

From WHITEMARSH B. SEABROOK

Columbia [S.C.], Oct. 23d 1843
Dear Sir, In reference to the subject upon which we very briefly conversed at your house, I beg leave to say, that any action on the part of
the Committee *at this time* would, in my judgment, be premature and
highly injudicious. That at some future period it will become their
duty to announce to the people of the [*mutilation*] that S.C. will not
go into Convent[ion; *mutilation*] the New York plan be abandon[ed;
mutilation] District system adopted, I en[*mutilation*] when ought this
to be done [*mutilation*] question. If now, you woul[d; *mutilation*]
accused of creating a schism [*mutilation*; Democra]tic ranks, and
probably some [*mutilation*] might be dissatisfied with [*mutilation*].
When Congress assembles, your [*mutilation*] doubtless take the matter into [*mutilation*] and after a full and free confe[rence deter]mine
the course which you sho[uld; *mutilation*]. It is not improbable too,
that [*mutilation*; New] York & the other States favorable [*mutilation*]lectial[?] system may yet yield [*mutilation*] of the majority of the
States, & adop[t; *mutilation*] mode of election. I therefore think
[*mutilation*] wait the progress of events is your true [*mutilation.*] It
is nevertheless due to the people, and to the maintenance of the elevated position you have so long occupied, that your determination
should, at a proper time be made known. On my arrival in Charleston, I shall converse with Col. [Franklin H.] Elmore & others on the
subject. Very respectfully your obedient Servant, Whitemarsh B.
Seabrook.

[P.S.; *mutilation*] and probably Pennsylvania, are con[sidered?;
mutilation] a declaration on the part of the [*mutilation*] the New
York plan *at this* ["plan" *canceled*; *mutilation*; ag]ainst you in those
States? While [*mutilation*] it appeared to be generally conceded
[*mutilation*; Pennsylv]ania would ultimately give you her [*mutilation.*]

ALS (partly burned) in ScCleA. NOTE: Seabrook became Governor of S.C.
during 1848–1850.

To FRANCIS WHARTON, [Philadelphia]

Fort Hill, 23d Oct[obe]r 1843
My dear Sir, I am much obliged to you for the number of Hunt's
Magazine, which you were so kind as to send me, and have read the

article to which you refer with pleasure. I am glad, that you are engaged on the subject of the commercial legislation of the U[nited] States. It is one of deep interest and badly understood. Since the termination of the late war with Great Britain, that Great branch of industry has been most harshly treated by the Government, to use no stronger language.

Of all the acts ever passed by Congress, I regard the [tariff] act of '28 as the most indefensible and misch[i]evous. It grew out of the contest between the friends of Gen[era]l [Andrew] Jackson and Mr. [John Quincy] Adams for political power, and the Constitution and the interest of the Union was [sic] wickedly and shamefully sacrificed to party considerations. A full and accurate history of its origin, its passage and its disasterous [sic] consequences is a desideratum in our political history. I have often alluded to it in debate, but never fully. You will find a reference to it, which will give you some facts, in my life, published by the Harpers, beginning at page 32; and also in the volume of speeches etc. printed by the same, beginning at page 36 and again beginning 264, and again 372 (it perhaps would be well to begin with 366); but you will find the fullest account in a speech, not included in the volume, delivered in the month of March, I think, 1837 on a bill introduced by Mr. [Silas] Wright to repeal certain duties in violation of the compromise act. You will find it, I think, in a file of the [Washington Daily National] Intelligencer of that day.

These references will give you much of the information you desire in reference to that flagitious act. To realize, however, fully its flagitious character, it must be borne in mind, that the high duties which had been previously imposed, had been mainly to pay the debt of the revolution and the late war, and that the country had submitted to them in the first instance, and had continued to bear the heavy burthen, because they approved of the object. When that was accomplished, on any principle of honor, honesty and justice, they ought to have been reduced to the lowest point, consistent with the economical and necessary wants of the Government, for its current expenses, after the debt was discharged. Instead of that, by this act of wickedness and folly they were doubled on many of the necessary articles of general consumption, and the burthen of the people, instead of being reduced by the discharge of the debt has been heavier since than they ever had been before in time of peace. It is a curious fact, that in the only instance in which a heavy funded debt has been paid, that I recollect, instead of being followed by reduction of taxes and revenue has been followed by an increase of both, and that in the most popular Government in the world! And what adds to it is the fact, that the party by whose agency it was effected, was that which professed the most popular doctrines, and the portion of the party which professed par Excellence to be the Democracy! I mean Mr. [Martin] V[an] Buren and Mr. Wright and their friends.

I shall be gratified in having an opportunity of perusing the subsequent articles from your pen, that may appear in the Magazine. I am not a subscriber to the work.

PC in Jameson, ed., *Correspondence*, pp. 550–551. NOTE: The speech mentioned by Calhoun at the end of his second paragraph, as having been delivered about 3/1837, was actually that of 2/23/1837. (See *The Papers of John C. Calhoun*, 13:454–467).

To R[OBERT] M. T. HUNTER, Lloyds, Essex County, Va.

Fort Hill, 24th Oct[obe]r 1843

My dear Sir, I readily acquiesce in the opinion of my friends, as to the Rhode Island question. I defer entirely to their opinion, ["as the best judges," *interlined*] on the probable effect of the publication of the correspondence [with William Smith] on publick opinion; although, I think, it to be regretted, that any one of the important questions, which come fairly into the present issue, should not be fully discussed. If the people should ever become thoroughly acquainted with the principles of our Government, & fully competent for self Government, it will be by drawing into the Presidential canvass ["all" *canceled*] and fully discussing, all the great questions of the day. One of my [*partial word canceled and* "strong" *interlined*] objections to the caucus system is, that it stiffles [*sic*] such discussions, and gives the ascendency to intrigue & management over reason & principles. It is, in fact ["a" *canceled and* "an admirable" *interlined*] contrivance to keep the people ignorant and debased.

I take for granted, that the Texan question will be forced on the country. The movements of the British government in Texas, and the outrages committed on the country in the instructions said to be given to her consuls in reference to collecting information, relating to our slave population, cannot be passed over in silence by the President [John Tyler]. But, if it should, it will be due to the South, that one of its members should call for information, as to the facts, & the steps taken by the Executive.

The result of the recent elections must put the whigs in high sperits; and, if Mr. [Martin] V[an] B[uren]'s friends could see things as they really are, they would be equally depressed. I do not doubt, the efficient cause for the ["reason"(?) *canceled and* "recent" *interlined*] change, is, the belief that he will be the candidate of the party, which has prevented the large body of our party, which went off in '40, from changing their position.

I see you have commenced in your State an organization aga[i]nst the whigs. Will it not, unless you are firm and decisive in your course, throw you into the hands of Mr. [Thomas] Ritchie? It seems to me, that our true policy is to oppose the whigs with Zeal & vigour. We are their real opponents; but without yielding an inch of ground, that we have taken aga[i]nst the N[ew] York plan or in favour of the Maryland in reference to the Convention.

The Messenger is waiting & I must close my letter. Yours truly, J.C. Calhoun.

ALS in ViU, Hunter-Garnett Papers (published microfilm of The Papers of R.M.T. Hunter, 1817–1887, reel 3).

To I[srael] K. Tefft, Savannah, 10/24. Calhoun accepts "with great pleasure the Honorary Membership" conferred on him by the Georgia Historical Society. He accompanies his acceptance with his best wishes for the success of the society "in promoting the important object for which it was instituted." ALS in ScHi, Prioleau Collection.

From F[ELIX] BOSWORTH

Lake Providence, parish of Carroll, Louisiana
October 28th 1843

Dear Sir, I have the honor to inform you, that in a large democratic meeting, mostly of the farmers, mechanics, and laborers, of the parish of Carroll, Louisiana, this day held, I have been commissioned to present you, as one of those distinguished Democrats spoken of for the Presidency, with the enclosed emblem, the American Eagle as a fit *rallying sign* for the Democra[*mutilation*] Union in 1844—and to ask of you [*mutilation*; accept]ance, and thereby your consent to [*mutilation*] honorary member of the "Demo[cratic Assoc]iation of Carroll."

While we entertain the best [*mutilation*] and kindness for yourself, and [*mutilation*] support you for the first gift in [*mutilation*] the great people of these United States, if [*mutilation*] Nominee of the Democratic National [*mutilation*; Convention] yet we desire not *division*, or [*mutilation*] *defeat*. We therefore trust that you [*mutilation*] with us (and not only you, but [*mutilation*] body of the Democracy of the Union [*mutilation*] keeping alive a high and proper sense [*mutilation*] *Union*, and *strength*, in our Ranks [*mutilation*] readily and fully accede to the wish [*mutilation*] cordially expressed, that you should become an honorary member of the "Democratic Association of Carroll"—and join with us and all our democratic friends in aiding under this flag to elevate the great principles of Democracy through the person of that *man* for President of the United States who may be selected by the Democratic National Convention, of May 1844.

With the best wishes for your good [*mutilation*] and happiness, and their long [*mutilation*]nce, I am very respectfully, your ob[edien]t serv[an]t, F. Bosworth.

LS (partly burned) with En in ScCleA. NOTE: Enclosed with the above letter is a printed picture of an American eagle and the motto of the Democratic Association of Carroll, "Under this flag we will conquer in 1844." An AEU by Calhoun reads "The Democratick meeting in Carroll."

From S[TEPHEN] H. BRANCH

New York City, Oct[obe]r 28th, 1843
Dear Sir: Accompanying this letter is the New York Evening Post, of Oct[obe]r 27th, '43, in which you will find an Article addressed "To the Democracy of the Union," written by myself, which, I sincerely trust, may meet with your cordial approbation. I do hope that some scheme may speedily be devised, by which our alarming divisions may be healed[.] I h[ave] conversed with many of our friends here, wh[*mutilation*; them]selves warmly in favor of my proposition. [*Mutilation*]culate on reaping a glorious harvest from the [*mutilation*] already too deeply sown in our ranks. I thin[k; *mutilation*] we moved in this matter. To prolong the qu[*mutilation*] I think, would be fatal to our hopes. Indee[d; *mutilation*] opinion, that unless an immediate and de[*mutilation*] to produce peace and harmony in our cou[*mutilation*] overwhelmed by our enemies. Moreover, I as[*mutilation*] everything depends on the course of yours[elf; *mutilation*; and Martin Van] Buren. If, in the exercise of your wonted [*mutilation*] would boldly and magnanimously declare [*mutilation*] cheerfully acquiesce in the decision ["of the Conven(tion)" *interlined*], be it w[*mutilation*] would not only do an act for which a

523

grat[*mutilation*] would hold you in eternal remembrance [*mutilation*] the glorious institutions of our beloved Coun[*mutilation*] conciliation, and concession inscribed upon o[*mutilation*] would elect you by a tremendous majority, against the most potent combinations and machinations of our adversaries. And, in conclusion, I do hope, that your answer will, at once, effect the glorious consummation that we all have so much at heart, inspiring the democracy, from Machias [Maine] to Saint Mary's [Ga.] with the most sanguine hopes of victory in '44. An early reply is respectfully solicited. I remain, With distinguished consideration, S.H. Branch.

ALS (partly burned) in ScCleA.

From V[IRGIL] MAXCY

New York [City,] 28 Oct. 1843

My dear Sir, Finding they were very tardy in the establishment of the newspaper [the New York, N.Y., *Gazette*] they talked to me so much of, when I passed thro' this city from Saratoga and it being a convenience to my son in law [Capt. George W.] Hughes, that I should meet my daughter [Ann-Sarah Maxcy Hughes] at Philadelphia on her way home, as he was not yet relieved from his post at Albany where he has been surveying the river with a view to the improvement of its navigation, I determined to leave her a few days at Mr. [Charles J.?] Ingersoll[']s in Philadelphia and come on here. I found ["them"(?) *canceled*] our friends here very zealous & animated and they say they have made such arrangements for the issue of their paper, that it will now appear in the course of a week. The election for their general assembly approaches very near, and our friends have deemed it best policy not to attempt to run a ticket of their own, by which, if defeated, they would be charged with dividing the party, but to let [Martin] Van Buren candidates be appointed, that it may be seen, that whenever V[an] B[uren]'s friends are opposed by the Whigs the latter will beat them, which is expected to be the case in this city, and indeed many here [*one word changed to* "think"] the whigs will have a majority of the assembly. If so I hope it will teach Mr. Van Buren himself & his immediate friends, or rather supporters, what is already from the falling off of four States manifest to all others—that he is not an available candidate in opposition to Mr. [Henry] Clay and that he had better retire from the field before the battle commences with as

524

much grace & dignity as he may in preference to submitting to a second ignominious defeat.

The usual trickery of Mr. V[an] B[uren]'s managers has been resorted to in Connecticut and he has obtained[?] a nomination of Van Buren ["Electors" *canceled and* "Delegates" *interlined*] in their convention by a general ticket. It is said that two or three hitherto avowed Calhoun men, ["by s" *canceled*] members of the convention, were by some exercise of magic or other, suddenly converted into Van Buren men: and I begin to think, there is no safety in the District System, in the States where he has the press and the political machinery at his command, which seems to be the case in the north where every thing is governed by caucus. Nobody doubts that a majority of the people in Connecticut is for you and yet you see how powerful still is the old organization. Unless this can be broken up there is not much hope that even the people, if delegates were to be appointed from the congressional districts by popular vote, will not be wronged or cheated in some way or other.

I have as yet learnt nothing of the particulars of the convention proceedings except what you see in the enclosed paper.

Immediately after the paper is out here and the Election to the Assembly is over, our friends here will, they say, take vigorous steps for organizing in each of the congressional districts for appointing delegates to the National Convention. Our friends here are miserably deficient in the sinews of war.

I shall set my face southwardly day after to-morrow & after staying a day or two in Philadelphia proceed homeward immediately. Faithfully yours, V. Maxcy.

[P.S.] A new Edition of your Speeches are [*sic*] coming out. The Harpers tell me the first is exhausted.

ALS in ScCleA.

From [ROBERT BEALE,
Assistant Doorkeeper of the Senate]

Frederic[k], MD, Oct. 30 [18]43

My Dear Sir, It has been some time since I wrote you. I have been waiting to see what was the feeling in this section of country growing out of the controversy between Mr. [Martin] Van Buren's & your friends. I find there is a great deal ["of" *interlined*] irritation &

th[*mutilation*] are making all of the capital out of [*mutilation.*] In my travel in the [railroad] cars & boats [*mutilation;* ex]ceedingly busy in trying to infl[uence; *mutilation*] your friends against Mr. Van Bu[ren; *mutilation*] but for him you would have h[*mutilation*] and that his policy is deadly hosti[le; *mutilation*] interests, & your personal enemy & [*mutilation*] upon a Van Buren man they attribute [*mutilation;* diffi]culties to you & your friends & th[e; *mutilation*] your ambition ["are" *canceled*] will sacrafice [*sic; mutilation*] your friends intend to go for Mr. [*mutilation*] succeede upon the ground that [*mutilation*] as high a tariff man as Mr. Van Bu[ren; *mutilation*] men who are playing this game pretend [*mutilation*] your friends or the friends of Mr. Van Buren as it suits their purpose. Many of your sinceere [*sic*] friends express their alarm at the present prospect of affairs. I travelled from Baltimore to this place with Mr. Guin [*sic;* William M. Gwin, Representative] of Mississippi, he is unquestionably your friend but he is evidently full of apprehensions—he thinks that Col[o]n[el Richard M.] Johnson is more likely to get the nomination [than a]ny one else & that after that you stand in a [*mutilation*] than any other candidate. There is a [*mutilation*] by very many of the Democratic party [*mutilation;* pr]esent mode of electing electors in [*mutilation*] Clay if we run more than one [*mutilation*] a plurality in a large majority [*mutilation*] will give him the vote in the [*mutilation*]eges; how this can be I don[']t under[stand; *mutilation;* Cla]y[']s friends in this State are the [*mutilation*] & active men I ever met with—they [*mutilation;* confi]dently of his success as tho he never[?; *mutilation.*] You are much stronger with [*mutilation;* office]rs than I had any idea. I have been [*mutilation*] of the posts w[h]ere the officers are stationed [*mutilation*] great unanimity for you. You have no doubt seen the accounts of Col. Johnson[']s reception in the east. I saw one of the letter writers in the cars & he is a devoted Clay man & he says it was alarming to see the enthusiasm with which the old Col[o]n[el] was received in the east—he says he has more fear of this military mania than any thing else.

I received a letter some 8 or 10 days since from Mr. [Levi] Woodbury & he says that you & Col. Johnson are evidently going a head in his section [*mutilation.*]

I hope Mrs. [*mutilation*] & your sons. Your sinc[ere; *mutilation;* Robert Beale.]

P.S. Mr. Van Buren is evidently loos[*mutilation*] New York & the whole east.

ALS (partly burned) in ScCleA.

526

From [ESTWICK EVANS]

Wash[ingto]n City, Octo[be]r 31, 1843
Sir: Your letter [*mutilation*] answer to mine, was received yesterday; [*mutilation*] respectful & kind notice taken of my e[*mutilation.*]

It is by n[o; *mutilation*] to covet the honour of a further cor[respondence; *mutilation*]pose to myself to write you a few ad[*mutilation*] in far too great a hurry to accord wit[*mutilation*] with, Sir, the consideration I owe to you.

Allow me [*mutilation*] will ever find me of a sincere & candi[d; *mutilation*] never be in favour of, but against, any thing [*mutilation*] unkind, or ungenerous. The whole cas[*mutilation*] on State Rights—particularly the first, [*mutilation*] write in the first instance in order to [*mutilation*] truth of the country, & the public ["good" *interlined*]; & 2nd for [*mutilation*; pecu]niary advantage. With respect to the first, [*mutilation*] the deep wrongs & grievous vexations of the south [*mutilation*] the interference of the North with her institutions of slavery, the only shield against which is the inherent, & unalienated[?], & unalienable[?] principle of State sover[e]ignty.

But the subject of State rights is the only security in fact of the States of the North—equally with the South; & the former may lament their wanton disregard of this vital principle of our political being.

But how difficult is it to do any thing like justice, in a few lines, to this broad & mighty subject! I desist, & pass on to say a word more of myself—but merely as I would speak of another & not in vanity; & also a word or two upon the present political as[pect]s of the country. I am, by nature, & in practice, entirely Democratic [*mutilation*] before the war. I witnessed your *vigour* during that epoch. I [*mutilation*] the election of Mr. J[ohn] Q[uincy] Adams—nor for that [*mutilation*] your[?] objections to both. I latterly opposed the Admin[istration; *mutilation*] & also that of Mr. [Martin] V[an] Buren. I wrote a great deal [*mutilation*] N[ational] Intelligencer—probably not less than one [*mutilation*; comm]unications. I rejoiced in the success of the Whigs [*mutilation*]ent of necessity for strong & unqualified condem[nation; *mutilation*] I am still opposed to Mr. Van Buren. I wish [*mutilation*] of the Whigs. I have kindly sympathies for Mr. [Henry] Clay; but [*mutilation*]osed with him. I think there is some body else in the world [*mutilation*] I am one of the number. There is very little if any thing be[*mutilation*] little—very little. In God's name I love him; [*mutilation.*]

[*Mutilation*] see[?], Sir, how natural it is for me to speak openly.

[*Mutilation*; ex]pense[?], perhaps, of the strictest taste. As to the op[*mutilation*] I trust V[an] Buren will fail. But I have no political [*mutilation*]. I consider the Whigs a pretty fair party; & I agree in [*mutilation*]ions: Distribution not—Districting not—[*mutilation*] not. I know not, Sir, how you have been on these points [*mutilation*]m-ous[?] to me to be otherwise. I should still speak thus [*mutilation*] some regard to any thing of discourtesy in it.

But there might be a more perfect party—a real Democratic party—free from locofocoism—the democracy of the time of Jefferson—keeping locofocoism, in the general, at bay—the dem[ocr]acy of [James] Madison &c &c.

I have faith—faith in my Essay [on State rights]—in its true & unsoiled[?] ground. This first may be folly; but what is a man without faith! I hope—what is a man without hope! I hope to *renovate* our political elements by defining & illustrating them.

Again with respect to the coming election, my impression at present is—an impression, however, by no means fixed—that between Mr. V[an Buren] & Mr. Clay—the latter will prevail. But if Mr. V[an Buren] should be laid aside by conse[n]t[?] or events, & you, Sir, should have the start[?]—by a now[?] gradual advance—I think it most highly probable that yourself & Mr. Clay would be the only competitors in the [*mutilation*] the Democratic party would prevail—for those on the migh[*mutilation*] after all. I pray, Sir, that you will excuse the [*mutilation*] I wish to express my opinions; & yet I am extrem[ely; *mutilation*] by my honesty.

I do not know by wha[t; *mutilation*] & yours have been combined; but I should thin[k; *mutilation*] North in this, very politic; & I have no [*mutilation*] administration would be one of entire safe[ty; *mutilation*] to yourself. Sir, *allow* me to say that I have long [*mutilation*] wrong done you, through *ignorance* & prejudice as to State [*mutilation*] right, & I *rejoice* in the RIGHT, in insisting[?] on [*mutilation*.]

I conclude, Sir, by saying that I [*mutilation*] political condition[?], & with entire per[*mutilation*] Y[ou]rs [*mutilation*; Estwick Evans.]

P.S. Suffer me to add, Sir, what I omitted to say, [*mutilation*] expectation, perhaps too sanguine, to get up through[ou]t the country a [*mutilation*] & also a strong party against the interference of the North in the Sta[tes; *mutilation*] provided, of course, I can be duly encouraged in it. It strikes me [*mutilation*]ment in my first letter, that none but a Northern man can do th[*mutilation*.] With great resp[ect; *mutilation*] E. [Evans.]

ALS (partly burned) in ScCleA. NOTE: An AEU by Calhoun reads "Mr. Evans." Estwick Evans' "Essay" mentioned above was his *Essay on State Rights . . . The*

Object of Which Is To Define and Illustrate the Spirit of Our Institutions and of Liberty, and To Renovate Our Political Elements (Washington: W. Greer, 1844).

From R[OBERT] B[ARNWELL] RHETT

[Washington, November, 1843]
My Dear Sir, I have rec[eive]d your two Letters on my arrival here—the one on our course as to the Presidency generally—the other on the subject [of] a Convention for the Democratic Review. The treatise on the Convention ought to be general, but considering the grounds taken in the Syracuse Convention, and the Democratic Review.

As to the policy on the Presidency I will write to you at large so soon as I have had an opportunity to confer with the members of Congress. We cannot fight within them, and my impression is, our party even in the South, are very far from being prepared for the stern measures you recommend. Have you remarked the course of our friends in Alabama lately? I shall strive for a separate organization at the approaching Congress both for Speaker, Clerk & Printer. It will test of what materials our Party is composed. To all your friends I shall communicate your views.

I leave W[ashington] for N[ew] York in the morning. Y[ou]rs Dear Sir, R.B. Rhett.

ALS in ScCleA. NOTE: This undated letter was postmarked in Georgetown, D.C., on a November day that is not legible. The year is determined by the contents.

From C[OLIN] M. INGERSOLL, "Private"

New Haven [Conn.,] Nov. 1, 1843
Dear Sir, Since the receipt of your last letter we have held our State convention and the result[s] perhaps you have learned ere this. On the question of referring the election of the Delegates to the several congressional Districts we were voted down by a m[ajority] of eight among about three hundred, [*mutilation*] had the vote been taken at an [*mutilation*] of the Convention before many [*mutilation*] had returned home, the Distr[ict; *mutilation*] I have reason to believe, have [*mutilation*] vote of the convention. In the [*mutilation*] sixteen on Resolutions, both the [*mutilation*] favor of the Gen[eral] Ticket sys-

tem [*mutilation*] the one expressing a preference [*mutilation*] the committe[e] were divided eq[ually; *mutilation.*] The whole force of party man[agement?; *mutilation*] was used in the getting up and [*mutilation*]ting of this convention, and its [*mutilation*] I fear will be the loss of the Sta[te; *mutilation*] at the next election.

New Haven county to a man a[*mutilation*] with the advocates of the Dist[rict] sys[tem; *mutilation*] and had we not been dissappointed [*sic; mutilation*] those from other parts of the State fro[m] whom we had a right to expect support we should have come out of the convention in triumph—but such have been the means employed, that the very men whom we looked ["to" *interlined*] to sustain our positions—men who before the convention had assured us of their preferences for our favorite candidate &c by some means or other were induced to remain passive or openly oppose us.

[T]hree of the Delegates elected—Messrs. Billings [*mutilation*] and J[ohn] C[otton] Smith Jr. were considered ["Calhoun] men" and yet they suffered them[selves; *mutilation*] elected as the advocates of the [*mutilation*] of Mr. [Martin] V[an] Buren a third time to [the Presiden]cy. Mr. Smith wrote me previous [*mutilation*]tion to be on the grounds and [*mutilation*; ag]ainst Mr. V[an] Buren and his guard [*mutilation*] understood him to be (as he had [*mutilation*] presented himself to me) *on the Day* [of the con]*vention* the advocate of the nomi[nation of] Calhoun for the Presidency—and yet [*mutilation*] as it may appear he came before [the conv]ention and said he would consent [*mutilation*] the Baltimore Convention pledged [*mutilation*] of Mr. V[an] Buren!

[*Mutilation*; The De]mocracy of New Haven are justly in-[censed?] at the course pursued by the Demo[cra]ts in the Convention and at a general meeting have passed unanimously a resolution sustaining the course of the New Haven Delegates in the Convention. Great efforts are now making by the Van Buren presses throughout the State to make it appear that the convention passed off harmoniously, but such is not the fact, we shall all I trust support the State ticket at the next spring election but I doubt if so much can be said for the election that is to follow if [*mutilation*] Van Buren is the candidate—he [*mutilation*] the *heart* for the American [*mutilation.*] I remain with great [*mutilation*] Your ob[edien]t se[rvant,] C.M. Inge[rsoll].

ALS (partly burned) in ScCleA.

From ——, New York [City], 11/4. In "behalf of the New England Society in the city of New York," six or seven persons whose signatures are mutilated beg Calhoun's "acceptance of an invitation to unite with the Society on the 22d Dec. next, in celebrating the anniversary of the Landing of the Pilgrims. The Hon[ora]b[l]e Rufus Choate," [Senator from Mass.], will deliver the "address on the occasion." LS (partly burned) in ScCleA.

From JOSEPH SMITH

Nauvoo, Ill., Nov. 4th 1843

Dear Sir, As we understand that you are a candidate for the Presidency at the ensuing Election; and as the Latter Day Saints, (sometimes called Mormons, who now constitute a numerous class in the school politic of this vast Republic,) have been robbed of an immense amount of property, and endured nameless sufferings by the State of Missouri, and from her borders have been driven by force of arms, contrary to our National Covenant, and as, in vain, we have sought redress, by all constitutional[,] legal, and honorable means, in her courts, her Executive Councils, and her Legislative Halls; and as we have petitioned Congress to take cognizance of our sufferings without effect, we have judged it wisdom to address you this communication, and solicit an immediate, specific, & candid reply to *What will be your rule of action*, relative to *us, as a people*, should fortune favor your ascension to the Chief Magistracy.

Most Respectfully, Sir, Your Friend and the friend of peace, good order, and Constitutional Rights, Joseph Smith. In behalf of the Church of Jesus Christ of Latter Day Saints.

Received copy in ScCleA; FC in USlC, Historical Department; PC in the Nauvoo, Ill., *Neighbor*, January 10, 1844, p. 2; PC in the New York, N.Y., *Herald*, January 26, 1844, p. 2; PC in the New York, N.Y., *Evening Post*, January 27, 1844, p. 1; PC in *Niles' National Register*, vol. LXV, no. 23 (February 3, 1844), p. 357; PC in the New Orleans, La., *Courrier de la Louisiane*, February 10, 1844, p. 3; PC in the Norfolk and Portsmouth, Va., *American Beacon and Daily Advertiser*, February 22, 1844, p. 2; PC in *The Voice of Truth, Containing General Joseph Smith's Correspondence with Gen. James Arlington Bennett; Appeal to the Green Mountain Boys; Correspondence with John C. Calhoun, Esq. . . . Also, Correspondence with the Hon. Henry Clay* (Nauvoo, Ill.: Printed by John Taylor, 1844), p. 21; PC in *Correspondence Between Joseph Smith, The Prophet, and Col. John Wentworth . . . and The Honorable John C. Calhoun . . .* (New-York: Published by John E. Page and L.R. Foster, 1844), p. 11; PC in *Americans, Read! ! ! Gen. Joseph Smith's Views of the Powers and Policy of the . . . Government of the United States . . . Correspondence with the Hon. John C. Calhoun . . .* (New-York: E.J. Bevin, printer, 1844), p. 26; PC (addressed to Henry Clay) in [Henry Mayhew,] *The Mormons: Or Latter-Day Saints. With Memoirs of the Life and Death of Joseph Smith, the "American Mahomet"* (London: Office of the National Illustrated Library, [1851]), p. 143; PC in *The Prophet Joseph Smith's Views on the Powers and Policy of the Government of the United States. To which is appended the Correspondence between the Prophet Joseph Smith and the Hons. J.C. Calhoun and Henry Clay, Candidates for the Presidency of the United States in 1844* (Salt Lake City: Jos. Hyrum Parry and Co., 1886); PC in Jameson, ed., *Correspondence*, pp. 890–891. NOTE: Both the manuscript copy received by Calhoun and the one preserved at Salt Lake City were written by Willard Richards and signed by him for Joseph Smith. Richards was one of Smith's secretaries in 1843. The received copy was addressed to Calhoun at Pickens Court House, S.C., where it was apparently received on 11/23 and forwarded to Calhoun. Calhoun's AEU on this same document reads "Joseph Smith." Smith had been in Washington during 11/1839–2/1840 and had met Calhoun and other notables at that time.

From V[IRGIL] MAXCY

Philadelphia, 6 Nov. 1843

My dear Sir, In a day or two after I wrote you from New York, I came on here. It was almost *certain*, that the Whigs would get the members to the Assembly at the Election, which takes place I think tomorrow, and I really wish they may get the whole State, as it is the only thing, that would give me any hope, that Mr. [Martin] V[an] Buren, would be withdrawn from the list of candidates.

I regret to find that in consequence of the impression gaining ground, that neither you nor Mr. V[an] B[uren] could be nominated at the Convention, from the bitterness, which the contest between your respective friends is engendering, can be nominated with a hope of success, people are beginning to talk of putting an end to discord in the party by taking up Gen[era]l [Lewis] Cass. Should this be the case, Mr. [Henry] Clay will take the prize, as he probably would, if both you & Mr. V[an] B[uren] should be run.

I am quite at a loss to decide what ought to be done with a faction like V[an] B[uren]'s friends who neither carry any thing nor expect to carry [any]thing but by trick & management. When they were beaten off from an early convention, they resorted, as a substitute[,] to getting an early appointment of the delegates to the nominating convention. This, they effected in Maine, by getting a convention to nominate a Governor &c, to take measures for the early appointment of delegates, tho' they had no authority to act on the subject. In New Hampshire a regular State convention refuse to nominate Van Buren, & his friends, in violation of what are called the usages of the party for which they affect to be great sticklers, turn round from the convention to a caucus of the democratic members of the Legislature, who are drilled into a nomination of Mr. V[an] B[uren]. In Massachusetts, just as the convention was breaking up and while the ["first" *interlined*] bell for the [railroad] cars, that were to take off the greater part of the members was already ringing, a resolution declaring that each State had a right to appoint delegates to the convention in the way it likes, ["was introduced" *interlined*] and passed without being examined, debated or understood. In Connecticut, the Convention, refusing to submit the appointment of delegates to the people, decide that they would elect the two State delegates themselves & then that the *representatives* from each congressional district should nominate ["&" *changed to* "a"] delegate & the whole convention should afterwards vote for them. Wherever ["in fine" *interlined*] the friends of Mr. V[an] B[uren] have come to act on the Presidential question, their whole conduct is marked by trick & deception, & every body now begins to think in this part of the world, that V[an] B[uren] will out manoeuvre you & certainly get the nomination ["whether the delegates to Convention be appointed one way or the other" *interlined*]. What is to be done with such a set of men? There is no safety in acting with them and there is great danger, by refusing to do so, that the odium of breaking up the party will be thrown on your friends: but this is the question that must be solved and if you have made up your mind as to the course to be taken I wish to be informed of it & be instructed how to act. I consider it settled that a fairly constituted convention ["whether by districts or general ticket" *interlined*] unless V[an] B[uren] should be defeated in New York *State*, & retire, is an impossibility.

I go home day after tomorrow, where I hope to find letters from you.

The circumstance, that Georgia has appointed delegates by a *general ticket* is used with great effect against you & the District System. Cannot that State be induced to re-trace her steps? Faithfully yours, V. Maxcy.

ALS in ScCleA; PC in Boucher and Brooks, eds., *Correspondence*, pp. 190–191.

H[ENRY] GOURDIN to
    Governor [James H.] Hammond

Charleston, Nov: 8th 1843
Dear Sir, You were made acquainted some time since of an effort that was making on the part of the Calhoun Central Committee of this

State, aided by several other gentlemen of this City to raise a sufficient fund to place the Spectator in Washington on a permanent, and efficient footing, and to publish and disseminate documents in advocacy of the election of Mr. Calhoun for the Presidency of the United States.

In order to make a stronger appeal to the leading and prominent friends of Mr. Calhoun in the interior, we sent (some time since) Mr. Alexander H. Brown with a communication to each, which was delivered in person, and I am pleased to say that in every instance the call was responded to. Mr. Brown was directed to call on you especially, being one of Mr. Calhoun[']s friends and occupying the highest office in the State, but he deemed it respectful to wait on you at your residence, which an accident prevented his doing at that time, and I have consequently in behalf of the Committee to ask that you will waive the ceremony of a formal messenger, and contribute to the subscription which we have commenced. It is needless for us to do more than to request your pe[r]usal of the enclosed Circular, and annexed we hand [you] a list of the gentlemen who have thus far subscribed to the fund. I am Dear Sir, very resp[ectfull]y Your Ob[edien]t S[er]v[an]t, H. Gourdin, Act[in]g Ch[airma]n, Special Com[mitt]ee.

[Appended List]

Mr. N[athaniel] Heyward	$1000	paid
Col. [Jacob Bond] I'On	500	"
Ker Boyce Esq.	500	"
W[illiam] Aiken	500	"
Col. [John S.] Ashe	500	"
Col. [Franklin H.] Elmore	500	"
Edward Frost Es[q].	500	"
Henry Bailey Esq.	500	"
H. Gourdin	500	"
Hon. R.B. Rhett	500	"
Hon. G[eorge] McDuffie	500	"
Hon. F.W. Pickens	500	"
Hon: R.F.W. Allston	500	"
Col. [John L.] Manning	500	"

[*Added by Hammond:*]

J.H. Hammond	500	Pd. F.H. Elmore

ALS in DLC, James Henry Hammond Papers, vol. 10. NOTE: The enclosed circular has not been found, but was probably that from Gourdin and others dated 8/18/1843.

From F[rancis] W. Pickens, Edgewood, [Edgefield District, S.C., *ca.* 11/8/1843]. Pickens sends an unidentified document so that Calhoun "may see what is said at Milledgeville [Ga.]. Be so kind as to enclose it back again." (This letter is dated only by a postmark.) ALS in ScCleA.

From A[BEL] P. UPSHUR, [Secretary of State]

Washington, Nov[embe]r 8, [18]43
My Dear Sir, I transmit a letter [of 10/18] addressed to you by Gen[era]l [Duff] Green, & sent to me open, with a request that I would read it. I also send an English newspaper which accompanied it. The copy of Mr. Green's letter to me [of 10/17], will be sent as soon as it can be prepared.

The affairs of Texas are every day, assuming a deeper interest. I have given unceasing attention to them & think that nothing is now wanting, but the consent of Texas herself, to a treaty of annexation. That it will be violently assailed, is beyond doubt, but I have as little doubt that it will be more & more approved, the more it is considered. Will you favour me with your views upon the subject, to be held in as strict confidence as you may direct? Is there any difficulty, so far as the Constitution is concerned? I shall feel greatly obliged to you for any suggestion which you may offer touching the subject in any of its aspects. In my opinion, it is emphatically, *the* question of the day. It involves consequences which startle me in contemplating them. In my view of it, the preservation of the Union, & the salvation of all its great interests, depend on the annexation to it, of Texas as a slaveholding territory.

I have acted on your suggestion in regard to England. But Mr. [Edward] Everett [U.S. Minister to Great Britain] I fear, is from the wrong side of Mason & Dixon. We should be represented in England, by some one who understands domestic slavery as it exists among us, & who can properly appreciate its bearing, upon other great interests of the U[nited] States. Very truely y[ou]r friend &c, A.P. Upshur.

ALS with En in ScCleA. NOTE: The enclosed letter from Duff Green to Calhoun appears above under its own date of 10/18/1843. "The copy of Mr. Green's letter to me," that is, Green's letter to Upshur dated 10/17/1843, appears below as an En to Upshur's letter to Calhoun of 11/30/1843.

H[ENRY] GOURDIN to James E[dward] Colhoun,
Terrysville, S.C.

Charleston, Nov: 9th 1843

Dear Sir, Finding it absolutely necessary to establish a Calhoun paper in the City of Washington on a permanent and efficient footing, a number of Gentlemen in this City subscribed some six weeks since the sum of $5500 towards that object in sums of $500 & $1000 each, but made it a condition that not less than $10,000 sh[ould?; *mutilation.*] Unassisted therefore all our efforts here, wil[*mutilation*] and in order to obtain aid from the friends [*mutilation*] in the interior, the Committee some time [*mutilation*] Mr. A[lexander] H. Brown into the interior, to mak[e; *mutilation*] application to his prominent friends, who [*mutilation*] means, and whose interest in his success, and [*mutilation*] of our principles, would render them willin[g; *mutilation*] to our fund. I am pleased to say [*mutilation*] whom he made application, responded to [*mutilation*] through some misapprehension he did n[ot; *mutilation*] you, and having met with an accident [*mutilation*; com]-pelled him to return to the city, the Committee now ask that you will ["dispense with" *canceled*] permit them to dispense with the ceremony of a personal application, and that you will, if in your power, add to our efforts your aid in carrying out the great objects we have in view, viz. the election of Mr. Calhoun to the presidency & through him to obtain for us the triumph, and permanent establishment of principles, essential to the security of the political existence of the southern States, and their peculiar institutions.

I hand annexed a list of the names of [*mutilation*] who have subscribed—also, you will find [*mutilation*] from the Committee, to which [we] crave [*mutilation*]tion. I am Dear Sir, Very resp[ectfull]y, H. Gourdin, Ch[airman] Act[in]g Com[mitt]ee.

ALS (partly burned) in ScCleA. NOTE: The appended list of contributors and sums was the same as that printed above with Gourdin's letter to James H. Hammond of 11/8/1843. To the list, in another hand, is added J[ames] Edward Colhoun's name with the sum of [$]500.

From DAVID LEE CHILD

New York [City,] Nov. 11, 1843

Sir, In pursuance of a duty of *free* citizens of the United States to inform themselves of the opinions and [*mutilation*] (if elected) of thier [*sic*] candidates [*mutilation*] I beg leave for myself [*mutilation*;

be]half of friends and fellow ci[tizens(?)] who sympathize with me, [*mutilation*; res]pectfully to inquire of you [*mutilation*] is your opinion of the justice [*mutilation*] expediency of the annexatio[n of] Texas to the United States. Respectfully y[ou]r ob[edien]t S[er]v[an]t, David Lee Child, Ed[itor,] N[ational] A[nti-]S[lavery] Standard.

ALS (partly burned) in ScCleA. NOTE: An AEU by Calhoun reads "Mr. Stanard [*sic*], About Texas." Child was subsequently the author of *The Taking of Naboth's Vineyard, or History of the Texan Conspiracy, and an Examination of the Reasons Given by the Hon. J.C. Calhoun, Hon. R.J. Walker and Others, for the Dismemberment of the Republic of Mexico* . . . (New York: S.W. Benedict & Co., 1845).

To "Col." JAMES ED[WARD] COLHOUN

Fort Hill, 11th Nov[embe]r 1843

My dear Sir, I saw Mr. [Armistead] Burt & find, that the whole amount credited by my order, was paid by Robert Anderson, and that your statement of what I owe you was correct. Annexed [*not found*] you have a due bill for the amount. I reminded Andrew [Pickens Calhoun] of the sum he owed you, & informed him, that his note was in Mr. [John Ewing] Bonneau's hand. He said he would attend to it. He took Charleston in his route, & made arrangement, while there, to ship to Mathew[e]s & Bonneau 100,000 pounds of clean cotton, to meet a payment of $7000 due to Mr. [Thomas G.] Clemson, with a farther understanding, if more should be needed to square accounts with them, the amount will be remitted on the sale of the balance of our crop in Mobile.

He calculated to make certain[ly] 400 bales of 500 pounds each, and probably 450. We have got a superb place. It is rich, durable & healthy, with upwards of 800 acres, in one body, cleared & ditched & in the highest order. The times have been bad since we purchased, but we feel ourselves now safe, in meeting our engagements, even at 7 cents for cotton. If there be no mishap, two years at that price will square accounts with the world after the present crop.

We have all had the prevailing influenza, except Anna [Maria Calhoun Clemson] & James [Edward Calhoun], but are pretty well over it now.

All join in love to you & Maria [Simkins Colhoun]. Yours truly, J.C. Calhoun.

ALS in ScCleA.

To C[olin] M. Ingersoll, [New Haven]

Fort Hill, 11th Nov[em]ber 1843

Dear Sir, The facts you state, prove, conclusively, that had those on whom we had reason to calculate stood firm, the result of the proceedings of your [Conn. State Democratic] Convention would have been very different. They also conclusively prove how easily Conventions may be managed, and how little they are to be relied on, as the exponents of public opinion.

That N[ew] York, Pennsylvania, ["and" *canceled and* "or" *interlined*] other larger States, should be the advocates of the appointment of delegates by the mass, is not surprizing but it is strange indeed that Connecticut and the other New England States should give it the least countenance. Of all the schemes ever devised it is that which is best calculated to divest them of all influence, and render them perfectly insignificant.

It is the more strange in Connecticut than any other, for it was owing to her influence, more than to that of any other State of the Union, that the Constitution was so modified, as to give to the smaller States in the eventual choice of the President & V[ice] Pres[iden]t, an equality with the large States. It is to the sagacity of your [Roger] Sherman and [Oliver] Ellsworth, that we owe that, and many other of the provisions of the Constitution, which constitute the main pillars of States rights.

I fear ["that" *canceled*] the day for sagacious and patriotic statesmen has passed, and that the country is doomed to be the victim of juggling politicians. I rejoice that a portion of the State so enlightened as the County of New Haven has stood firm and erect on so important a question. With great respect I am & &, J.C. Calhoun.

Copy in NcU, Tucker Family Papers. NOTE: The ms. copy of Calhoun's letter transcribed above was made by Ingersoll and discussed and enclosed by him in correspondence with John Randolph Tucker in 5/1887.

To Tho[ma]s Ritchie,
[Editor of the Richmond, Va., *Enquirer*]

Fort Hill, 12th Nov. 1843

Dear Sir: I write this to correct the mistake you made, in supposing, that, in my letter to a gentleman of North Carolina [J.F.G. Mittag, dated 9/24/1843] on the subject of the Tariff, (published in the [Richmond] Enquirer of the 7th instant) I referred to my letter to Mr. [Robert Carter] Nicholas of Louisiana, published in the same article. The letter referred to [by me] was to Mr. Delaney [*sic*; Edward Delony] of Louisiana [on 7/6/1843], and was in answer to one containing an enquiry similar to one addressed to me from N[orth] Carolina. The answer to Mr. Nicholas was to one on a very different subject. If you had adverted to dates, you would have avoided the mistake. The North Carolina letter refers to one recently written. It is dated the 24th September last, and the letter to Mr. Nicholas 7th May, 1842, more than fifteen months before.

I regret the mistake. Unauthorised liberty has been taken with my letter to Mr. Nicholas, by printing portions in Italics, and the word protecting in glaring Capitals, calculated to make the impression that I, too, am the advocate of the protective policy; and that, too, by editors professing to be opposed to protection and friendly to me, as well as those in favor, and politically hostile to me. By such means, hasty readers of newspapers have been led to believe, that I admit the right of protecting the Louisiana sugar planters against foreign competition by the imposition of duties on the foreign article for that purpose, directly against the plain import of my letter. The protection of which I spoke is expressly stated to be, not against foreign competition, but "against the machinations of the opponents of slave labor." I intended simply to say, that I would resist, in adjusting the Tariff, any attempt that might be made to take off or reduce the duty, that foreign sugar ought fairly to pay, on revenue principles, on the ground of discouraging the domestic article, because it was the product of slave labor.

What I regret in your mistake is, that it is calculated to strengthen the false impression made by the unauthorised Italics and Capital letters, not only by publishing my letter with them, but still more strongly, by publishing it as the one referred to in my North Carolina letter, in confirmation and elucidation of my opinion on the subject of protection.

As it is my wish to be fully and explicitly understood on that and all other public subjects, I must request you to publish what I have written, in the Enquirer. With respect, I am, &c, &c, J.C. Calhoun.

PC in the Richmond, Va., *Enquirer*, November 24, 1843, p. 2; PC in the Washington, D.C., *Madisonian*, November 25, 1843, p. 2; PC in the Petersburg, Va., *Republican*, November 25, 1843, p. 2; PC in the Alexandria, D.C., *Gazette & Virginia Advertiser*, November 25, 1843, p. 3; PC in the Washington, D.C., *Spectator*, November 28, 1843, p. 3; PC in the Baltimore, Md., *American & Com-*

mercial Daily Advertiser, November 28, 1843, p. 2; PC in the Washington, D.C., *Globe,* November 29, 1843, p. 3; PC in the Raleigh, N.C., *North Carolina Standard,* November 29, 1843, p. 3; PC in the Augusta, Ga., *Daily Chronicle & Sentinel,* December 1, 1843, p. 2; PC in *Niles' National Register,* vol. LXV, no. 14 (December 2, 1843), p. 218; PC in the Edgefield, S.C., *Advertiser,* December 6, 1843, p. 2; PC in the Anderson, S.C., *Gazette,* December 9, 1843, p. 2; PC in the Pendleton, S.C., *Messenger,* December 15, 1843, p. 1; PC in the Springfield, Ill., *Illinois State Register,* December 22, 1843, p. 2. NOTE: In printing the above letter, the *Enquirer* began: "To remove any incorrect impressions, which may have been undesignedly produced by our remarks, we cheerfully lay before our readers, the following letter from Mr. Calhoun—received by yesterday morning's mail." Calhoun's letters to Mittag and Delony appear above in this volume. His letter to Nicholas can be found in *The Papers of John C. Calhoun,* 16:273–274.

From GARVIN & PATERSON

"Anglo American" Office
6 Ann St., New York [City]
Nov[embe]r 13, 1843

Sir, By this day's mail we have the honor to forward an early copy from an engraved portrait of the Immortal Washington, of which we respectfully request your acceptance. The plate is accurately copied from the original portrait by [Gilbert] Stuart which now adorns the State House at Hartford, Conn. It has carefully and steadily occupied the burin of the able artist [John Halpin] who executed it, during the last eight months; and, by many who are of sufficient seniority to remember the features and figure of the great "Father of his country" it is pronounced an excellent likeness.

This specimen of American skill, which we flatter ourselves is unsurpassed by any in the same department of art, has been executed for presentation to the Yearly Subscribers to "The Anglo American" a weekly Journal published in this city, and of which we are the proprietors. We offer you the copy now sent, in token of respect; should it meet your approbation we shall be abundantly satisfied. We have the honor to be Sir Yours very obed[ien]tly, [E.L.] Garvin & [A.D.] Paterson.

LS in ScCleA.

From V[IRGIL] MAXCY

Tulip Hill, West River [Md.,] 13th Nov. 1843
My dear Sir, Being detained in Philadelphia by the indisposition of
Mrs. [Ann-Sarah Maxcy] Hughes on my return from New York, I did
not receive your letters of the 20th & 24th [of October]. I write a
line now only to acknowledge their receipt, and to say that by the
next steamer I will send the copies of your Speeches with the life prefixed with the corrected title to [Henry] Wheaton [U.S. Minister to
Prussia] & Gen[era]l [Duff] Green [in London]. I shall suggest to
Wheaton, if he cannot get some eminent Frenchman to undertake it,
to write a Review of them himself in French & have it published in a
leading review in Paris. And leaving Gen[era]l Green to get some-
body to write an article for the Edinburgh or Westminster Review. I
will myself write to Mr. [Nassau William] Senior, the celebrated Political Economist[,] & endeavor to get him to review them.

I think it highly important that your opinions on the [Dorr] affair
in Rhode Island should be given to the Public at some period or other.
It is for you to judge, whether it is prudent to do it *now* or not. All
our political friends in Rhode Island, Massachusetts & even in *New
York* have run perfectly wild on this matter.

Do not apprehend any indiscretion on my part in regard to your
going into convention on the Albany or Richmond plan. I find on
this ["point" *canceled*] essential point I have acted as I shall continue to act, entirely in accord with your views. [*A few words canceled.*] In New York & every where else I have uniformly given it as
my decided opinion that your friends could not & ought not in any
event to consent to go into a convention of this sort, & that if a split
must come, this was the dividing point. I have urged strongly on our
friends in New York on my recent visit & especially Mr. [Alexander]
Jones, who is to be the Editor of the Statesman, which is to hoist your
banner, to take this ground & to maintain it without flinching or yielding an inch. My fear now is—fraud has so uniformly marked every
step taken by [Martin] V[an] B[uren]'s friends, from the surrepti-
tious nomination in Maine, the violation of all *usage*, which they affect to ["be" *canceled and* "consider" *interlined*] sacred, in N[ew]
Hampshire, down to the Syracuse, Massachusetts & Connecticut conventions—that if the District System or any other System whatever
of forming the Convention should be adopted, they would cheat you
out of the nomination by some means or other. I hear that N[ew]
York city has elected the greater part of the ticket, notwithstanding my

impressions, when I left there. If [sic] am apprehensive therefore that Mr. V[an] B[uren] will not have the benefit of the warning of a Whig Victory in the State.

Finding the Harpers had sent you only a small part of the copies you were entitled to, I requested them to forward the rest, as soon as they came out with their second edition with the corrected title & advertisement. If they have already sent off all I will take a half a dozen out of 20 I have still on hand of those I subscribed for, & can paste in the correct title & advertisement. In haste Faithfully y[ou]rs, V. Maxcy.

ALS and ms. copy in ScCleA.

From CHA[RLE]S H. POND

Milford (Con[n].), Nov[embe]r 13, 1843
D[ea]r Sir, Herewith I send you "The Norwich News" which contains the particulars of our late [State] Democratic Convention held at Middletown on the 25[th] ult[imo]. You see *they* made me President pro tem[pore], but would have a known friend of Mr. [Martin] Van Buren for the organized President. I was on the committee to prepare Resolutions for the Con[ventio]n. From the complexion of the Conven[tio]n, I well knew that our best course was to avoid expressing [*mutilation*] preference for any Presidential candidate, & [*mutilation*] report in favor of choosing the delegates to [the] Baltimore convention by districts. In committee [we] discussed those matters fully & freely: the com[mittee] consisted of sixteen: on one point there was a [ma]jority of one against us, & on the other there was [*mutilation.*] The Chairman of the committee was the Hon. [Perry Smith,] late M[ember of] C[ongress] & who, rumor says, is to go into [*mutilation*; the Cab]inet, or some other good place, *when* Mr. V[an Buren is] elected. The Chairman was ardent; & persist[ed in] bringing before the convention the point on [which] the committee were tied. After this had b[een] done, I knew there was no chance to stop the passage of the Resolution, & under all circumstances saw that it was best to dispose of the subject as harmoniously as practicable. For much discussion would certainly have jeopardized our next election, & unless we carry the next election, *probably*—we may not carry the State for any democratic candidate. Mr. [Isaac] Toucey & his friends through the columns of the Hartford Times had been very active in bringing their peculiar friends into the convention.

It may be gratifying to you to know that on *the committee* was the brother of Gov[erno]r [Chauncey F.] Cleveland & the executive Secretary; & both of them went with us on the votes respecting the disputed & vexed points. You have strong & true friends in this State, but as you know Mr. V[an] B[uren]'s friends are [a] majority, at present; ["in this" *canceled*] mainly ["with" *canceled and* "for" *interlined*] reasons [conn]ected with the Tariff subject; the fact that Mr. V[an Buren] was defeated in defending democratic measures [and prin]ciples, & cheated out of his election; a desire to [*mutilation*] him triumph over his slanderers; & the circumstance [that] he is a native of New York. We shall have [*mutilation*] work to carry our spring election, & as "union, [*mutilation*]tion & concert of action" are our watch words, [*mutilation*] we have to steer our course accor[dingly.] If the democrats prevail we shall have [a ch]ance to speak again during the session of [the] Legislature (if not before) which sits early [in] May.

An eventful crisis is approaching & the result will be long felt. In the course of the winter cannot some plan be devised, honorable to you & your friends & also to Mr. V[an] B[uren] & his friends, by which all of your respective friends can unite in carrying into the Presidential chair some democratic Republican? If the whigs can only be defeated at the coming election they will *stay defeated* for many years; very many years—if the Republicans only act wisely. What that arrangement is to be & how it is to be brought about, no man in this great country knows better or can be more instrumental in bringing it about than the illustrious individual to whom these hasty lines are addressed. Among very many others, I ardently hope that such an arrangement may be made.

In four or five States the elections have [not] gone as well as they might have gone. But [on] the whole the grand result is certainly ver[y] gratifying. There is a large Republican m[ajor]ity on the popular vote. Some *how or other* the majority ought, & must act together on the [*mutilation*] contest. I suppose that you will smile at [*mutilation*] eagerness. But I do want to see the democra[ts tri]umph at the coming Presidential election.

I know that your time must be m[uch] taken up. Yet I should like to hear from you now & then. I have seen it stated often [that] you was [*sic*] coming Northward: is it so? I saw your [*mutilation*] but know not that special reasons may have changed your mind. Excuse this hasty letter & believe me sincerely, Your friend & very hum-[b]le se[rvan]t, Chas. H. Pond.

ALS (partly burned) in ScCleA.

From F[RANCIS] W. PICKENS

Edgewood, 14 Nov: 1843, Wednesday evening
My dear Sir, I rejoice to say to you that I have just returned from Millwood [in Abbeville District] and that I have negotiated for the sale of Col. J. Edward's [that is, James Edward Colhoun's] lands & place at *$60,000* Sixty thousand dollars. Dr. [Thomas A.] Anderson, who you recollect went to England to make arrangements with some British capitalists for emigrants, has been at my house, & I took him to Millwood. He was at once struck with the water power &c. &c. He never was in So[uth] Ca[rolina] much before & is astonished to find it so rolling and pleasantly situated. He is making selections in Tenn: and is not authorised to make a final purchase of lands in So[uth] Car[olina] but has no doubt that it will be concluded on their part on his representations. We will know certainly in three months. I hope & trust it may be so, for the place will ruin the Col. if he keeps it. He is full of the [*one word or partial word canceled*] sale and thinks I have done wonders for him. I had to do every thing—even [*partial word canceled*] shew the lands—and make out the papers &c— he seems to have so little time for practical business. He & Maria [Simkins Colhoun, my sister-in-law] will be at my house this day week, and he will make his arrangements to move down here. It will be a great blessing to my children, and I know it will be far better for him. Dr. Anderson is a fine intelligent gentleman. He goes to the Nashville Convention, and I have advised him to urge our friends to follow up the N[ew] York move & protest ag[ain]st the nomination of delegates by the convention, and then to start a candidate in each Congressional Dist[rict]. Appeal to the people & present, if they can[,] delegates thus chosen and we can act upon the issues thus made according as events develope themselves. I wanted him to go and see you but he had no time. He says [James K.] Polk is dead ag[ain]st us. I go to Columbia the first week of the [S.C. General Assembly] Session—have to go to Charleston first. In great haste but affectionately, F.W. Pickens.

[P.S.] I was glad to learn from Mr. [Thomas G.] Clemson that all settlement with Andrew [Pickens Calhoun] was made so satisfactory to all & I rejoice at it.

ALS in ScCleA.

From DUFF GREEN

London, 18th November 1843

My dear Sir, I send you a copy of my letter [dated 11/16] to Judge [Abel P.] Upshur and have directed Mr. [Charles G.] Greene of the Boston Post to send you copies of his paper contain[in]g my letters to the [London] Times, and such as may contain extracts from the English papers commenting upon them.

I cannot here go fully into a detail of all the considerations which induced me to publish the extracts from your letters. Suffice it to say that I saw that they could not prejudice you at home and influential ["parties" *interlined*] here were very anxious that they should be published here to aid them in the struggle which is now progressing in this country. Parties are hanging as it were in a balance. The opening of the Chinese trade seemed to give more confidence and it was deemed very important that the real state of the American question should be given. The abolition feeling here is expiring. This is clearly proved by several [*one or two words canceled*] facts. Not the least striking is the fate of Lord Brougham's bill, which began in the pretence of suppressing slavery & the slave trade & ended in legalising slave dealing.

Again, in the case of Zelueta [*sic*; Pedro de Zulueta], an eminent merchant, the proof was conclusive that he purchased a ship that had been engaged in the slave trade, captured and condemned as such, for a correspondent known to be engaged in the slave trade, fitted her out, took on the charter party, furnished the goods with the old captain & sent her to the slave dealing port in Africa. He was prosecuted[,] the proof was clear, but being an eminent merchant, the mercantile interest of London rallied, and altho the proof was conclusive, he was acquitted [in 1840] and the Times denounced the antislavery party & the prosecutors.

["They" *canceled*.] My letters have excited much more interest than I anticipated. They have been the theme of the week[.] They have been noticed in almost every paper and in some ["for" *interlined*] several days successively, they give a leading article. My object here is accomplished. The French press has taken up the subject also, and the eyes of the Continent will now be directed to the pretence & objects of England.

An American gentleman [Henry Wikoff], on reading my letter to the [Boston?] Morning Post, in reply to [the Rev. Joshua] Leavitt came to me, and proposed to establish a paper in New York [City]. He says that he has 25,000$ that he will invest if I will give him

545

["my" *canceled*] the use of my name as Editor and prepare the leading Articles. I have the subject under consideration and think it probable that I will devote one year at least to the paper. He will allow me a liberal salary, and the privilege of becoming a partner if I desire it. The paper is to advocate free trade, and be thoroughly democratic and State rights. One object with me will [be to] give you that support, which can be better given from New York than any where else. You will see that in reply to the [London Morning] Herald I have said that you know that I think that Justice to Mr. [John] Tyler would give him the preference. This will put me in a stronger position. My preference for you no man can doubt, and as Mr. Tyler can not get the nomination, it will enable me to vindicate your claims as opposed to [Martin] Van Buren[']s with more effect. You may expect that whether I go to New York or not I will take an active part in the election, & these letters will give more strength at home.

You will see from my letter to Mr. Upshur what my views are. I have written to Gen[era]l [Lewis] Cass and believe that he can be induced to run on your ticket for Vice President. Your friends should look to this. Yours sincerely, Duff Green.

[Enclosure]
Duff Green to A[bel P.] Upshur, "Copy"

London, 16th November 1843
My dear Sir, I send the [London] Times of the 10th[,] 11th & 14th of this month, and the [London Morning] Herald of the 11th & 14th. In the Times of the 10th and 11th you will see two letters from me & in that paper of the 14th you will see their comments on my third letter which third letter they refuse to publish. This suppressed letter will appear in the [London?] Globe of friday and Saturday. I will send you a copy if I can get it in time for the mail, that you may see why they suppress it.

You will see in the Herald of the 14th that their second article is written in a very different spirit, making several very important admissions not the least of which is the danger of collision on the Oregon question and that in case of war, we will be united, and the war popular.

I have cause to believe that the course of the Times was dictated by the position of pending negotiations with Brazil and Holland, and that the article in the Herald was prepared by some one connected with the Government.

As was fully explained in Mr. [Joseph] Hume's letters, Sir Robert Peel came into power nominally by opposing a reduction of the duty on slave-grown sugar, and hence he feels extremely anxious to accomplish something in the treaty now progressing here, for the abolition of slavery in Brazil. He is also pressed, by a negotiation, or rather a remonstrance from Holland, on account of the measures, now reduced to a system, adopted by the Authorities in British Guiana to induce the slaves in Dutch Guiana to emigrate to the British Colony, where they are protected and made the Agents of persuading others to desert their masters, thus transferring the labor from the Dutch to the British Colony. The Times a few days ago had a curious article in reference to Brazil to which I call your attention.

But I have ascertained that one difficulty in forming a new ministry consists in the position of Lord Palmerston, who is the Brother-in-law of Lord Melbourne, and who is deeply committed on the slave question, and much disposed to interfere in the domestic matters of other nations, in opposition to the basis on which Lord John Russell & others wish to organise the new ministry. He has the controul of the Chronicle, and seeing that in truth the Oregon is the point on which the policy of the present, or the new ministers is to have the greatest difficulty, has commenced, in that paper the discussion of that subject so as to throw difficulties in the way of its adjustment. The purpose is manifest. If the present ministers enter into any negotiation or the new ministry are organised in reference to it, to his exclusion, he stands ready to condemn. That question is his political stock in the bargain for power, and backed as he will be by Lord Melbourne, who it is said has the ear of the Queen, and next to the Duke of Wellington has most influence with her, he relies on his position, and the influence of the Chronicle to place him again in the foreign office. In the mean time the free trade and liberal party are progressing. They are for peace and free trade. Sir Robert Peel, it is believed is himself much inclined in that way, and is controlled by the peculiar state of parties, and not by his own views of what is best for England. If he could adjust the Irish Question, and the Corn and Sugar questions he would have plain sailing. There is a strong war party in England. The prejudice and ignorance are inconceivable. The bigotry, arrogance, selfrighteousness, insolence and avarice of this people cannot be conceived by one who has not witnessed it. But they have an instinct as to their interests which constitutes a controlling principle. Jealous as they are of our growing strength and prosperity, much as has been done to misrepresent and depreciate our institutions, and national character, much as they desire to blot out the remembrance of the past, there is an influence in the middle classes, that sympathises with us, because they feel that they are doubly interested in preserving peace, and establishing Commerce with us, and the new ministry must be organised on this basis, or it cannot be sustained. Hence an effort is making to create a Combination, which will exclude Lord Palmerston, by putting another near relative of Lord Melbourne into the foreign Office. His Lordship will probably go to France or Russia. I have assurances on which I can rely that on a change of Ministers, we will have no difficulty on the slave question, or the Oregon. That this Government will meet our's [sic] in the most liberal spirit, and that the leading members of the opposition will make their issues with ministers so as to prepare public opinion for yeilding to our views on the slave question, and the Oregon; on the ground that it is the interest of England to make these, and even greater concessions, for the sake of peace and to secure our trade.

I conferred freely with persons in whom I have confidence and they urged me to make a communication to the Times, so as to prepare the way for their own movements. Looking to the state of things here, and at home, and believing that it would greatly aid you in any measures you may be taking in relation to Texas, or the Oregon, I availed myself of the occasion, which the letters and comments of the Times offered, to place the real questions in issue between the United States, and England, before the British public, in such terms as to arrest the attention of other Governments, interested in them, as well as of the American, and British, people. The refusal of the Times to publish my third letter, and the comments on the series, have excited much enquiry; and the present state of the public mind here will throw (throw) upon ministers the responsibility of failing to preserve peace.

The bearing of these letters on the measures of our Government must be beneficial. They identify the American abolitionists with the attempt of England to monopolise the trade and commerce of the world, and cannot fail to unite our people by the exposure of the hypocritical pretence of British philanthropy.

The comment on Lord Brougham's bill will be illustrated much more (fully) & forcibly when I get home. I will be detained here until the 5th December, and will sail in the Hibernia.

I hope that the part I have taken here will be approved of by my friends at home, and that the President [John Tyler] will not permit himself to be annoyed, by the attempt of the [Henry] Clay press, to charge that I am here on a diplomatic mission &c. I am prepared to meet all that when I get home, and will show that I have on all proper occasions negatived such assertions. We must unite the democratic party; past dissentions must be healed—We must rally the people, and the measures and policy of England must be urged, as requiring a sacrifice of all considerations of minor, or personal, interest. Yours Sincerely, Duff Green.

P.S. 17th Nov[embe]r. Since the above was written, I have seen [Edward Baldwin?] the Editor of the Herald, which paper is one of the two organs of the present ministers. I have had a very interesting conversation with him, and have enlisted him against the Times, and Chronicle. I threw into my letter, which you will see in that paper, of this date, the intimation about Lord Palmerston, & the Chronicle, as an inducement to him to publish it. You will see that he has seized upon the idea, and urged ministers to close the negotiations upon the subject of the Oregon. So far so good. We cannot relinquish our claim up to the line of 49° N. Lat[itude]; and if you press our claim up to the Russian boundary, they will be glad to compromise on 49°.

Ministers would gladly delay all action on the subject. They look to the chapter of accidents. The Irish and Russian questions put them in that position that they cannot quarrel with us now. It is well understood that the movement in Greece, was an English movement, intended to establish a free government there, where public matters should be freely discussed in the press, and in their Legislative assemblies, as a check to Russian influence. England sees that Russia is moving towards Constantinople, and that she will be prepared to act, in case of a war with America. Now therefore, is the time to press our measures. Annex Texas, and urge our rights to Oregon, while the question of our Trade, is the subject of agitation, and made the prominent measure on which the opposition rely for bringing them into power. Let me entreat you, annex Texas, and insist on the Latitude 49° N., as the limit. Claim to the Russian boundary, but do not take less than Lat[itude] 49°. The N.W. fur Company are making arrangements to throw into the [Oregon] Country a body of emigrants. Russia will be in position, and willing, to aid us—and our Minister there should be instructed to prepare the way for it. Let our measures be firmly taken, and time and circumstances, will work for our advantage. Your friend, Duff Green.

ALS and En in ScCleA.

From THOMAS L. JONES

Prison Milledgeville Georgia, 18th Nov[embe]r 1843
Dear John, Am here, under peculiar circumstances, desiring to address the leading spirits of the State. Upon the *end* they may pass it

as you did, without supposing there was any thing more in it than an every day[']s occurrence, and one of those common vagarys [*sic*] that should be hooted[?]. Shall endeavour to maintain equanimity. Wish you were here that I might try your nerve, a little more truely, altho it was tolerably done in my call upon you. I might have a thousand & one things to say to you, if I dare speak to you as one man should with another, and I was not too proud to write to[?] great or small. You would hard[ly] suppose your moral likeness was taken while there yet surely it was[.] You should recollect, I was nearer a real *stranger*, than any one who had ever called upon you. I want you to be an original man therefore will with[h]old the many suggestions of improvement, you should make in your morals. Must therefore just enjoin upon you the study & practice of the Bible, & be sure you stop not short of the faith of the *Son* of *God*. Your daughter named our church, now adorn it by a proper walk & *Godly*, conversation. We cannot bear[?] the truth, with one another, however loving & kindly it may be suggested. Therefore had better not write than write a lye [*sic*]. You can hardly think what a world of delinquency I saw about ye. Altho was fed & lodged well & talked to reasonably well, yet my dear John there was a void after all this which I regret, as I wanted to accord you the palm. If worlds was [*sic*] given me [I] could not do [so], as I am used for higher purposes. Do not mean any thing here as a disparagement with others, but with what [to] me might or should be, to be, a moral man cannot be counterfeited & one moral man can tell another as soon as they touch. I just have to stop or I shall offend you & all which I have no desire to do, as you suppose you treated me so kindly in common parlance & so I speak of it. But faith or virtue[']s friendship calls upon us to read another page.

My honor & the honor of the South is in jeopardy, for the non payment of a Bill of one dollar, raised against me in your State, which should not have been done. Wrote your Governor [James H. Hammond] to adjust it, see that it is done. May [be] put in jeopard[y] again here, as I [can] not exactly see how my horse is to come from the stable, nor when I am to get away. Did you ever go on a Spiritual Mission, of high dignity, upon its own excellency. If you did not, as I know you have not, study well before you do. I meet with many new things, but what are they to a man like you, who is made up of lives & likenesses. If you know Judge [James M.?] Wayne [Associate Justice, U.S. Supreme Court] you should teach him some thing about charges to Juries. Thomas L. Jones.

[Marginal P.S.] Tell Mrs. [Floride Colhoun] Calhoun & Daughter not to let that woman be hung in your State, it would blight your prospects.

P.S. This is written upon H[ugh] L. White[']s Mot[t]o, he who speaks plainest to him of his infirmities is his best friend. L.J.

[Marginal] P.S. You should not sleep untill a young man who is imprisoned for 10 years should be released. Post office concerns brought it about.

ALS in ScCleA.

From J[AMES] H. RION

Pendleton [S.C.,] Nov. 18th 1843

Sir, Being desirous of obtaining an appointment to the United States Military Academy, I take the liberty to ask your assistance to procure it, if you should deem my recommendations, such as, entitle me to the fostering care of the government.

I will be 16 years of age, on the 17th of April next. I have studied [Jeremiah] Day's Algebra, Euclid's Geometry, and Day's Mathematics comprising Logarithms, Mensuration of surfaces, solids, h[e]ights and distances, Trigonometry, Surveying and Navigation; and [Charles] Anthon's Caesar, Virgil, Sal[l]ust, and Cicero's Orations and a part of Anthon's Greek Reader, together with several French works under Mr. E[lliott] Pynchon, Savannah; and also Conic Sections, Legender[']s Geometry, and French under Mr. [Robert M.] Renick[,] Pendleton, letters from both of which gentlemen I have enclosed. Very Resp[ec]t[fully] y[ou]r Ob[edient] s[e]r[vant], J.H. Rion.

ALS with Ens in DNA, RG 94 (Records of the Adjutant General's Office), Application Papers of Cadets, 1805–1866, 1843, 234 (M-688:149, frames 93–94, 101, 107–108). NOTE: Rion enclosed with his letter to Calhoun two testimonials, one from Elliott Pynchon, principal of Chatham Academy, Savannah, Ga., dated 5/1/1843, and another from Rob[er]t M. Renick, principal of the Pendleton Male Academy, dated 11/18/1843.

To "Col." JAMES ED[WARD] COLHOUN

Fort Hill, 19th Nov[embe]r 1843

My dear James, Dr. [Thomas A.] Anderson will find in my life, page 26, a summary of the result of my economical reforms in the Army proper. The same sperit of reform was carried through all other branches; the Ordenance [*sic*], the Engineer, the Indian, and what may be called the civil disbursements of the [War] Department. The reduction in all these were [*sic*] proportionally great; but they were never collected & reduced to tabular form, and it would be a work of vast labour to collect & compare them with expenditures of like kind, before or since. As the Doctor may not have seen the sketch of my life published by the Harpers, I herewith transmit a spare copy, which you or Francis [W. Pickens] may transmit to him ["put up" *interlined*] in pamphlet form, which will make the postage but a trifle. If I were to transmit it direct, it would not reach [him] in time for the Nashville Convention; and I prefer its going through you or him.

I am much gratified to learn, that you have made a conditional sale of your Millwood property on such favourable terms. I think you have done well to sell. It took more capital than you could command to Develope its resources.

We are all well except colds & all join their love to you, & Maria [Simkins Colhoun]. Affectionately, J.C. Calhoun.

ALS in ScCleA; variant PC in Jameson, ed., *Correspondence*, pp. 551–552.

From C[HARLES] A. WICKLIFFE, [Postmaster General]

Washington, Nov. 20[t]h 1843

My dear Sir, Your favour of the 11[t]h is just at hand. In answer to the enquiry you make in relation to the law supposed to have passed at the last Session granting the Franking privileege to Ex Vice Presidents, I can inform you that a Bill for that purpose passed the Senate but was not acted upon in the H[ouse] of R[epresentatives].

I shall interpose no obstacle to the passage of such a Bill, tho I apprehend the Franking privileege with its abuses in this country and the private exp[*mutilation*] will ultimate[ly] prostrate this Department and put it upon the Treasury.

With you I anticipate an excited Session and no good to the country ["and" *canceled*] I ["regret to" *interlined*] find the prophecy of Alex[ande]r Hammilton [*sic*] too soon fulfilled "that every interest State and national is made subservient if not lost sight of in the contest for the Presidency."

The Democracy with Mr. [Martin] Van Buren as its head is

destined to be overwhelmed and demolished by [Henry] Clay & his followers and woe betide the country[,] its interests[,] its purity, when he and his followers shall have uncontrolled sway. An issue of $200,000,000 of Gov[ernment] stock to pay State Debts, which stock is to constitute the capital of a U.S. Bank: the public lands given away. We shall have no more need to discuss the Tariff question, a Tariff for Revenue then will be high enough in God[']s name for for [*sic*] protection. But enough of this. I hope ["yet" *canceled*] common sense will assert her empire and guide the friends of Democratic principles into a choice of a man upon whom the *whole* Democracy can unite. They never will unite on Van Buren. Your friend, C.A. Wickliffe.

ALS in ScCleA.

To A[NDREW] P[ICKENS] CALHOUN, Faunsdale, Marengo County, Ala.

Fort Hill, 21st Nov[embe]r 1843

My dear Andrew, I received by the mail of yesterday yours from Charleston. I feel satisfied, that the arrangement is the best, that can be made, and I hope, that the 200 bales will more than cover the advance to Mr. [Thomas G.] Clemson. It is our interest to have them sent on as early as practicable, in order to stop interest. You say nothing of what Mr. [John Ewing] Bonneau thought of the quality, or whether you made any arrangement for his advancing for John [C. Calhoun, Jr.], what he might want.

It is probable, that the residue of our crop may be disposed of to the best advantage in Mobile; but on comparing the last quotations in the [Mobile] Tribune with those in the [Charleston] Mercury, I find the difference of a cent, ["between" *canceled and* "in" *interlined*] the highest quality in favour of Charleston; but you will be best able to form a correct opinion, where we should sell, by keeping your eyes on the average prices of the two places for the residue of the season.

Mr. Bonneau writes me, that another payment has been made on Mrs. [Placidia Mayrant] Adams['s] order of upwards of $2000; so that the balance remaining due on our note in bank in Charleston is something less than $1000. Six hundred more is to be paid on the 1st Jan[uar]y, & I have little doubt the whole will be paid & the note discharged in a short time.

Mr. Clemson, who is now absent at Edgefield, I learn by his conversation is still desireous of getting Glover's place. I hope you will see Glover as soon as it may be convenient, and write him on what terms he may get it. I would not be surprised, if he gets a good offer for his Edgefield place, that he should sell it & purchase Glover's, if the terms are not unreasonable. I find, that his objection to our proposition was, that it would leave him nothing to do. He would have accepted, I infer from, what he says, if the management of Glover's place had been left under his ["management" *canceled and* "control" *interlined*], with your advice.

I trust you will be able to make a satisfactory arrangement about Mathew's place. It would be a great acquisition to our's. You ought to give it your early attention.

The weather continues fine, and I hope on your return, that you found great progress had been made in getting in the cotton. I shall be anxious to hear how much is got out, how much will probably be made, & what will be the general quality of the crop.

We are all well & all join their love to you, Margaret [Green Calhoun] & family.

Mr. [James] Wise succeeded in making an admirable likeness. The family say the best that has ever been painted. Your affectionate father, J.C. Calhoun.

ALS in ScU-SC, John C. Calhoun Papers.

From J[AMES] HAMILTON, [JR.]

Milledgeville [Ga.,] Nov. 21st 1843

My Dear Sir, On my arrival at this place I found a most unfortunate state of things in regard to the *Democratic party*—which is broken[,] routed & disunited. The old Union Flank of the party attribute their defeat to your friends bringing forward the nomination at the June Convention and selecting [Mark A.] Cooper [former Representative from Ga., as a candidate for governor] instead of some one from their own ranks. The truth is the old Unionists are deeply tainted with Van Burenism, and if some means are not taken to unite the party it can never be rallied again by its old Leaders. I think the party is panic struck with their overwhelming Defeat & here I can find but one man in the right spirit and that is [John H.] Howard. We have both written for [Matthew H.] McAllister who has more influence with the

Union portion of the party than any man in Georgia, to come here & consult with us what it may be best to do.

The District system will be engrafted in the Constitution of Georgia in the composition of her Senate & H[ouse] of R[epresentatives] and for her Congressional Representation. The Democrats have called a Convention to meet here on the 2d Monday in Dec[embe]r expressly in reference to the Presidential election. The [Martin] Van Buren men desire by its means to reconfirm the present Delegates to the Baltimore Convention ["by" *canceled and* "but" *interlined*] to leave them unfettered by[?] instructions *to vote for you* ["but to vote as they deem best at the Convention" *interlined*]. Howard & your friends will of course if they are strong ["enough" *interlined*] come out with an open nomination of yourself—or if this cannot be carried Refer the choice of new Delegates to the Districts which the amendment to the Constitution will lay off. I have advised this ["Latter" *canceled*] latter course most strenuously because I know that it is more in conformity with your own views. Connecticut & N.H. having gone against us & Mr. Van Buren[']s triumph in N.Y. have dishearte[ne]d your friends exceedingly in this State, and with the exception of Howard & a few other staunch spirits, the opinion seems to be gaining ground that you ought to withdraw, which I have discountenanced with utter scorn—as a pusillanimous retreat before even the Battle is commenced. Judge [Walter T.] Colquitt [Senator from Ga.] I am sorry to say seemed to incline to this opinion that he doubted if Dick Johnson [that is, Richard M. Johnson] runs whether you would be one of the *three* highest to go into the House, and if you did go in, he thought you could get no other, than the States that sent you *there*. In other words that in the House Van Buren had already a majority secured or if not, that [Henry] Clay would be elected. By retiring Colquit[t] thinks in 4 years you would be the man chosen by the people of the U.S. above all other Candidates if you were *now* to make yourself so acceptable to the Democracy as to withdraw from distracting it any further. As I regard such a retrograde movement ["as not to be entertained" *interlined*] which would be construed as ["resulting rather from a sense of" *interlined*] weakness ["rather" *canceled*] than a magnanimous concession to your opponent Mr. Van B[uren]—who has no right to ask or expect it at your hands[,] I have set my face resolutely ["to" *canceled and* "against" *interlined*] your backing out as has our friend Howard. The truth is My Dear Sir the Democratic party of Geo[rgia] composed as it is [is] not worth the paper on which its obituary might be written—and what is the

Democracy of the Union to which your friends have linked you? An immense mass of *ignorance* moved by the necessary momentum of *knavery*. I never believed the Leaders & organs of the party would have the public vertue [*sic*] & discernment to select you as their man. Your friends have committed a great & fatal mistake in committing you to the Democracy & of bringing you out *eo nomine* under its banner. You should have stood on your own ground as a War Republican of 1812, and in your place in the Senate *still have been at the head of* ["*the*" *canceled and* "a" *interlined*] *Great Southern party*. I believe this Session of Congress would have not passed without your having a Republican party around you which would have given you a primary strength not inferior to your Competitors. But they have attempted to bind you hand & foot & to throw you in the midst of our old subtle & implacable [*one word canceled and* "foes" *interlined*] the Old [Andrew] Jackson party of the Kitchen & Bed Chamber happily uniting the morals of [Amos] Kendal[l] with those of Mrs. [Peggy] Eaton. I was cursed by your friends for my London Letter. I wrote it I confess to you to give you a Plantform [*sic*] to stand upon in this coming contest which I knew you could only occupy with strength on some middle ground, which your speech in 1835 on the Currency & your last speech on the Tariff must amply [have] afforded. If we had had a distinct party formed between the extreme restrictive rigor of Mr. Van Buren['s] school ["which means hypocracy covering licentiousness" *interlined*] & the extreme licence of Mr. Clay['], I believe the Country might have been carried under the lead of your genius & public vertue. But it is too late now. Your friends have brought you out as a Democrat & under that Flag with a divided Empire you will have to fight.

I have told our friends here, that nothing now remains but to *agitate* and to *agitate deeply* & *extensively*. At a meeting of our friends in Charleston it was agreed on my suggestion that we should get up a Young's [*sic*] Man['s] Convention to meet at Columbus[,] Geo[rgia,] calling on all ["the" *canceled*] Young men among your friends to hold meetings ["all over the South" *interlined*] & send Delegates early in the spring to that place [to] take into consideration the best means of promoting your election. The question was from what point the invitation should come for the assembly of such a body. It was agreed it ["could" *canceled and* "should" *interlined*] not come from So[uth] C[arolina] & the Season of the year forbid [*sic*] all hope of its coming from New York as Delegates would not travel to N.Y. during the inclement weather of the ensuing winter &

early spring beyond which the Convention could not be postponed. It was agreed that if possible the invitation should come from Georgia which our friends will endeavour to effect before the adjournment of the Legislature, if it can be ["effect" *canceled and* "compassed" *interlined*] with harmony & perfect concord, which can alone give authority to such a move. It is not to be concealed, that the old Union party ["of Geo(rgia)" *interlined*] desire to *repress every token in your favor for fear it may prejudice Van Buren.* It is still *confidently* believed in a fair issue before the people of Georgia you could beat any man in the U[nited] States but between Clay & Van Buren it will scarcely be a contest—as I believe the Struggle all over the Union will turn out if it should happen that Van Buren is the Nominee of the Baltimore Convention. From the progress of events, I am more reluctant than ever to go into that "Den of Thieves." Let me know your own views of *our* best course, and whether you have determined on *your own.* My advice to you may be comprehended in a single [sen]tence. *Stand firm & wait the progress of events.*

I shall leave this next week ["for the Chattahoochee" *interlined*] therefore[?] write fully & without reserve to Major Howard as to the posture of the affairs of our party throughout the Union & in this State. Address me at Fort Mitchell (*Ala.*) to which place I shall return next week prepared to give any impulse in any quarter you may desire.

Having disposed of this public matter let me advert to another. Do you ["not"(?) *canceled and* "know" *interlined*] that I think that our friend Howard has started a Question upon which the highest interests of the South may be involved to wit—whether Texas as an integral part of Louisiana is not *de jure* ["a po" *canceled and* "now" *interlined*] in the Union. If under the treaty of 1803 between France & the U[nited] States she was comprehended in the Limits of Louisiana & as such was admitted into the Union, the Gen[era]l Gov[ernmen]t could not cede any portion of the Territory of a State without violating its territorial soverei[gn]ty. This was overlooked by you all in Mr. [James] Monroe[']s administration when the Florida treaty was concluded. But no lapse of time can consecrate a Usurpation on the part of the Federal Gov[ernmen]t. If this be a true view of the subject Louisiana according to Howard[']s ["view" *canceled and* "opinion" *interlined*], Louis[ian]a [*sic*] has nothing to do but to extend her jurisdiction over Texas & she is *de jure* & *de facto* in the Union. Let me hear from you immediately on this point. Yours faith[full]y, J. Hamilton.

P.S. Major Howard is at my Elbow since closing this Letter & begs me to say emphatically to *you hold on.* He will be exceedingly gratified to hear from you.

Howard may move on the Texas question [in the Ga. legislature] in a few Days.

ALS in ScCleA; variant PC in Jameson, ed., *Correspondence*, pp. 891–894.

From DIXON H. LEWIS

Lowndesboro [Ala.], Nov. 21st 1843

My Dear Sir, Herewith I enclose you a letter from Mr. [John L.] O[']Sullivan [Editor of the *United States Magazine and Democratic Review*], & I send in another envelope, the rough sketch of my answer to it, that, you may see the general course of my reflections on it. I submit the whole matter to you, hoping to hear from you fully when I reach Washington, to which place I shall start in a day or two. Write me *confidentially* or otherwise, in reference to it.

You will see the letter is dated Oct. 30th. It never reached me till the 15th [of November] & was I have no doubt, first sent to [Martin] V[an] Buren at Kinderhook [N.Y.], & then returned & sent on to me. The same intimations have before been thrown out in the Democratic Review & the N[ew] York Evening Post & have no doubt been well considered at Head Quarters. Hoping to hear from you frequently during the coming session I am truly your friend, Dixon H. Lewis.

P.S. Please return after you write [*sic*; read?] O'Sullivan's letter & the rough draft of my answer. D.H.L.

ALS in ScCleA. NOTE: Lewis's correspondence with O'Sullivan has not been found. However, a letter from O'Sullivan to [Martin] Van Buren, dated 12/8/-1843, sheds considerable light on it. O'Sullivan reports his recent conversations in Washington with Lewis and other friends of Calhoun: He urged that they withdraw Calhoun from the "distracting and weakening competition" with Van Buren for the Presidential nomination and content themselves for the present with Calhoun's nomination as Vice-President, thus unifying the party and placing Calhoun in an advantageous position for the future. O'Sullivan did not find Calhoun's friends to be favorably disposed toward this proposition (although he found that Van Buren's friends received it with great favor), but still believes that Van Buren ought to conciliate them and hopes that the results of the convention will do so by the nomination of Calhoun or "some secondary man of the same school and stamp." Lewis told O'Sullivan that Calhoun's friends regarded a particular system of organization of the convention and a reduction of the tariff as *sine qua non* to their support for Van Buren's nomination. O'Sullivan believes they will yield the first point but not the second and hopes that the present Democratic majority in the House of Representatives will take satisfactory action on the tariff. "In that case I have no doubt they will come in heartily to their station in the severe encounter we have to fight from now till next November. Otherwise, I do not believe they will, and I shall, I cannot but confess, tremble for the consequences." ALS in DLC, Martin Van Buren Papers, series 2, Letterbook 48 (Presidential Papers Microfilm, Van Buren Papers, roll 27).

To Col. [JOSEPH G.] TOTTEN, [War Department]

Fort Hill, 21st Nov[embe]r 1843

Dear Sir, I transmit the enclosed [letter from James H. Rion, dated 11/18/1843] to you, because I am personally acquainted with the applicant, and Mr. Renwick [*sic*; Robert M. Renick], writter [*sic*] of one of the accompanying letters. He is the teacher in our Academy, himself a graduate of the Military Academy, and a gentleman of intelligence & worth. From what I know of Master Rion, he is entitled to all Mr. Renwick says of him. He is the son of a widow in very humble situation, who devotes most of her means to the education of her son.

I feel assured, that the patronage of the Gov[ernmen]t could not be better bestowed, than by giving him an appointment. With great respect, I am & &, J.C. Calhoun.

ALS with Ens in DNA, RG 94 (Records of the Adjutant General's Office), Application Papers of Cadets, 1805–1866, 1843, 234 (M-688:149, frames 93–94, 97–98, 101, 107–108).

From CHARLES WHITTELSEY

Charleston, Nov. 22, 1843

Dear Sir, There is due the Estate of Jno. E[wing] Colhoun (of whom your wife is the daughter about) $140 and as executor of S[amuel] B. Colhoun $75 or there about in all something over two hundred Doll[ar]s, this sum I can collect without much delay. I have spoken with Mr. H[enry] A. Dessassure [*sic*; DeSaussure] of this city Ex[ecutor] of [Henry] W[illia]m Dessassure who was Ex[ecuto]r for Mr. Colhoun's estate, & offered to collect it for one third of the amount collected. Mr. Dessassure to whom I have communicated the nature of the debt does not think my charge unreasonable, but is unwilling to act unless authorized or requested by you so to do, it is but a small sum to be sure to you, but perhaps it may not be amiss to say, though a stranger to you, that the commission for the collection would be very acceptable to me, though trifling in your view. I hope therefore that should you think the matter too trifling to attend to on your own ac[count] You may be induced to do so knowing that you will benefit me, though a stranger without injuring yourself. To Mr. D[eSaussure] I will give such references as will be satisfactory. The am[oun]t is due from the United States & has been unclaimed since the death of Mr. Colhoun. A line ["at a period as early as suits your convenience" *interlined*] through the P[ost] Office directed to me will be promptly attended to. I shall leave this place in Ten or twelve days or two weeks at furthest. Respectfully Yours, Charles Whittelsey.

ALS in ScCleA.

From HENRY P. BARBER

New York [City,] 11 Chambers Street, Nov. 24, 1843
Sir, Copies of the accompanying [printed] circulars are now in progress of despatch throughout the United States. The Circular for the State of New York (a copy of which you will receive with this) has likewise been extensively disseminated throughout our State and I trust will be productive of some good. We have some two thousand of each ready for distribution: what the Committee now most require is the *names of prominent individuals* throughout the United States favorable to our cause—of course it is necessary to obtain these in order to distribute the Circulars. With this view I have written to the Central Committee at Charleston—also to the editor of the [Charleston] Mercury and of the Washington Metropolis [*sic*] requesting information on that head. Trusting that success may crown our persevering efforts I remain Your Ob[edien]t Ser[van]t, Henry P. Barber, Sec[retar]y Correspond[in]g Com[mittee].

[First enclosure]

NEW-YORK, Nov. 22d 1843
SIR: At a meeting of the "DEMOCRATIC REPUBLICAN CENTRAL COMMITTEE OF NEW-YORK," held at Washington Hall, in the City of New-York, on Monday Evening, the 23d October, the undersigned were appointed a "Central Committee of Correspondence," to communicate with the various sections of the United States, as to the best mode of a general organization, to procure the nomination of the Hon.

JOHN C. CALHOUN of South Carolina, for the President of the United States, and a suitable person for the Vice President, by the Convention to be held at Baltimore in May next. In furtherance of these objects, the Committee recommend to the friends of the cause, the District System of appointing Presidential Delegates—a regular organization of the whole country, into State, County, Town, and District Committees, or associations—and to secure the co-operation of the Press, so far as possible, to disseminate the political principles, doctrines, policy, and character of this distinguished Statesman. Mr. Calhoun, for the first time since the death of the "Father of his Country," is the free candidate of the People, resting his claims to their support upon the firmness and purity of his Democratic Republican principles, his consistent course, and patriotic services, tested by over thirty years' experience in high and responsible offices; his intellectual attainments and high order of talent, and an unsullied private character. In addition to these, we may likewise recognise the claims which he justly has upon his country, for the valuable and exemplary services rendered to the cause of freedom by his family during our revolutionary struggle.

The prospects of Mr. Calhoun in this quarter are flattering, his interests evidently increasing, and the plan of raising the revenue necessary to an *economical* administration of the government from duties imposed on foreign imports, having always a reference to the various interests of the Union, in the arrangement of a just and equal tariff, and a liberal commercial policy, are measures calculated to increase that interest here and elsewhere.

A Daily Democratic Paper, called the Gazette, advocating the District System of choosing Delegates and the claims of Mr. Calhoun to the Presidency, is just established in this city—subscription $6 per annum for the daily, and $3 for the weekly paper. It is expected to be an official organ of the party, interesting for its commercial and literary matter; and the Committee solicit your patronage and aid in procuring subscriptions and a wide circulation. Address "To the Editor of the Gazette, 6 Tontine Buildings, New-York City."

The Committee are directed to propose the following questions, to which they request an early answer forwarded (either franked or post-paid) to S.A. LAWRENCE, New-York City.

I. What is the political bias of the Democratic party in your State and its various sections, with reference to a Presidential candidate?

II. Have you appointed Delegates to the Baltimore Convention? If so, how many, in what manner, and what are their political preferences for the Presidency?

III. If those Delegates are not appointed according to the District System, is it probable that your State will annul the appointment, and proceed to choose others by the District System, in time for the Baltimore Convention?

IV. Will the friends of Mr. Calhoun in your State send Delegates to that Convention, elected by the District System—provided those opposed to that system, shall refuse to annul the former appointment of Delegates?

Let the answers to the above queries convey the *most accurate* information you can obtain. And the Committee would likewise feel grateful for any other information which you may be able to furnish of the public sentiment in your State. Yours respectfully, S.A. Lawrence [*sic*], F.T. Ferris, F[itzwilliam] Byrdsall, H.P. Barber, W[illia]m Francis.

[Second enclosure]

NEW-YORK, Nov. 24, 1843

SIR, The undersigned DEMOCRATIC REPUBLICAN CENTRAL COMMITTEE OF CORRESPONDENCE OF NEW-YORK, in favour of the District System, respectfully requests your co-operation in the great political movement now in progress, of each Congressional District in the State [of N.Y.], electing its own Delegate to the National Convention for nominating candidates for the Presidency and Vice Presidency of the United States—a movement so evidently democratic in principle, and so obviously necessary to the future harmony and united action of the Democratic Republican Party in the contest of 1844, as to require no argument to show its "equal and exact justice"—no special pleading to evince its propriety and expediency.

Precluded by the approaching winter season from holding a State Convention to consult with our Democratic brethren from the State at large, we are authorized by the Park Meeting in favour of the District System, in September last, and subsequently by the Central Committee, to present the following plan, as the one most advisable under present circumstances:

1. That each Congressional District of the State shall hold a convention of delegates from the several towns in the District, in April next, whose duty shall be to elect, or cause to be elected, a delegate to the National Convention at Baltimore in May next.

2. The delegates so chosen from the several Congressional Districts, shall meet in Tammany Hall, in the city of New-York, on Thursday, the 23d day of May next, and elect two delegates for the State at large.

Upon the foregoing simple and democratic plan of proceeding—simple because of its requiring not the usual political machinery, and democratic because of its affording a true means of giving effect to the popular will—we presume it is unnecessary to offer any comment. We have therefore only to request from you an answer on the following points:

1. What prominent or active men do you know of, in your county, or in any other County of the State, who are favourable to the election of delegates by Congressional Districts? Please give us their names and nearest Post Offices.

2. What is the general sentiment of the Democracy in your section of the State, in relation to the premeditated caucussed usurpation of the Syracuse Convention, in choosing thirty-six delegates, no less time than nine months before the meeting of the National Convention, in total disregard and open violation of the rights of the people?

3. What are the probabilities and prospects of your district being induced to co-operate with the other districts, in choosing its own delegate to the National Convention?

We cannot believe that a Democratic Republican National Convention, constituted by direct representation, will countenance delegates appointed by a State Convention, and no less than three removes from the people; and we are well assured that a decided preference will be given to delegates from the Congressional Districts, because this is perfectly consistent with the great vital principle, upon which our Governments, both State and National, are founded.

We request replies at your earliest convenience. Please address, franked or post paid, to S.A. LAWRENCE, corner of Wall and New streets. Yours respectfully, S.A. Lawrence, F.T. Ferris, F[itzwilliam] Byrdsall, H.P. Barber, W[illia]m Francis.

ALS with Ens in ScCleA; PC's of Ens in the Charleston, S.C., *Mercury*, November 29, 1843, p. 2. NOTE: The dates on the circular letters were filled in by hand in blank spaces left for that purpose. The Norfolk and Portsmouth, Va., *American Beacon and Daily Advertiser*, October 28, 1843, p. 2, reprinted a report from the New York, N.Y., *Express*, which is relevant to the above documents: "Calhoun Committee. Committees in favor of the District system, and of John C. Calhoun for the next President, are forming in every portion of the State. On Monday evening the New York Committee, consisting of sixty five leading democrats of the city met at Washington Hall with a view to organization." The article reported the names of the officers and active members of this movement and stated that a committee "was appointed to correspond throughout the Union with the friends of Mr. Calhoun."

From F[RANCIS] W. PICKENS

Edgewood, 24 Nov: 1843

My dear Sir, I re[ceive]d yesterday yours enclosing one from Gen-[era]l [Duff] Green. I fully agree as to the importance of the Texas question in all its bearings. I think we are bound to take the highest and most decided grounds. I think the possession of Texas as a British colony would be just cause of war, and if the nonslaveholding States oppose its admission upon the ground of its strengthening the slave holding interests &c, we will be bound in self respect & self-preservation to join Texas with or without the Union. It is a grave and a momentous question in all its bearings, and I am ready to pledge all that I am and all that I hope to be on its issues.

I have not seen [George] McDuffie and suppose I shall not, as I hear that Maj. [Armistead] Burt [Representative from S.C.] passed to Columbia & says that McDuffie will not start [for Washington] until the last of next week when he is to go on with Mrs. [Martha Calhoun] Burt and to meet in Charleston Monday week. I do not know his sentiments now on Texas but hope they are sound although I fear it, particularly as he was so ultra on the Oregon question, and I am sure it is our policy to unite the two questions together, & thus seperate [*sic*] the Non slaveholding N[orth] West States from the Northern States. If both our Senators [McDuffie and Daniel E. Huger] should go wrong (& they will not seperate) it will be a bad thing for So[uth] Ca[rolina]. If the Legislature were to pass resolutions it might look like instructing McDuffie as he was so strong ag[ain]st us when Gov[ernor], and yet I cannot see how the State can avoid moving if the Pres[i]d[en]t[']s [John Tyler's] message is strong. I should dislike to do any thing to wound his feelings. I hope some development will be made.

I shall not be in Columbia until next Thursday. I will write you from there.

Col. J[ames] Edward [Colhoun] has gone to Charleston & to Columbia, and he and his wife [Maria Simkins Colhoun] will be with me all Christmas. Now it would be very delightful to me if you & Cousin Floride [Colhoun Calhoun] & [Martha] Cornelia [Calhoun] with Anna [Maria Calhoun Clemson] & Mr. [Thomas G.] Clemson would visit me at that time too. A little excursion would be agreeable to you all then, and I know of no persons whom it would give me more sincere pleasure to see than your family.

I do hope you will come down. I am enlarging my house &c &c,

and I know Cousin F[loride] delights in such things, & I would be too happy to have her at my house.

Drop me a line to Columbia and let me know if I can expect you. If you will come I will go to Charleston from Columbia & order up oysters, fish & fruit of all sorts for the occasion, and give you a full specimen of old fashioned So[uth] Ca[rolina] hospitality &c.

Present me affectionately to all. Yours very truly, F.W. Pickens.

ALS in ScCleA; variant PEx in Boucher and Brooks, eds., *Correspondence*, pp. 191–192.

From Geo[rge] McDuffie, [Senator from S.C.]

Cherry Hill, [Abbeville District, S.C.] 25th Nov. 1843

My dear Sir, I enclose you ["two letters" *interlined*] from a writer unknown to me, & as he appears to have loose notions of political morality, I have not answered him. I set off in the morning for Washington & as I write with much labor, I can say but a few words. As I do not correspond with any person on politics, I would be glad to receive a letter from you at Washington giving your views & the information you have received as ["to" *interlined*] the prospect before us. My fear is from all I see that a sufficient number [of Martin] V[an] B[uren]'s friends will support a protective tariff to prevent an adjustment & reduction of it, & that he, as a reward, will be nominated by the [Democratic National] Convention, receiving the votes of all the Democratic tariff men.

I should have paid you a visit, but the pressure of my business has constantly prevented it. My kind regards to Mrs. [Floride Colhoun] C[alhoun,] Mr. [Thomas G.] & Mrs. [Anna Maria Calhoun] Clemson & all the family. Yours sincerely, Geo: McDuffie.

ALS in ScCleA.

From Geo[rge] N. Sanders and Others

Ghent, Carroll Co[unty,] Kentucky, 25 November 1843

Sir, In accordance with a resolution contained in the accompanying proceedings, we present ourselves before you, as one of the distinguished gentlemen, to whom the eyes of the people are now directed, as the possible successor to the Presidential chair.

Our citizens have not heretofore, been awake to the importance of the relations between Texas and the United States. Indications however lead us to the conclusion, that the time has come when the whole nation will deem them of paramount importance. The Presidential election being near at hand, it becomes matter of deep solicitude to the nation, to be made aware of the sentiments of the probable candidates for that office. Hoping that from your elevated position, we may receive from you, forcible illustrations of this all-important measure, we confidently await your reply. Your Fellow Citizens, Geo[rge] N. Sanders, H[enry] Ramey, J[u]n[io]r, Frank Bledsoe, E[lisha] B. Campbell, W[illiam] B. Lindsay, Ja[me]s P. Cox.

[Enclosure]

Mass Meeting in Carroll County.

Annexation of Texas.

Democrats and Whigs have impartially called a general meeting at the town of Ghent, in Carroll county, Kentucky, on Saturday the 25th November, 1843, for the purpose of taking into consideration the importance of admitting Texas into the United States, Lawrence Ashton was called to the Chair, and Bartlett Searcey appointed Secretary.

Whereupon *George N. Sanders* offered the following preamble and resolutions:

We, citizens of Carroll county, Kentucky, in mass assembled, without distinction of party, present to our fellow citizens of Kentucky, and the other United States of America, our earnest and deliberate views in regard to our sister country, Texas—and to the statesmen of the Union, our solemn and unalterable opinion as to the importance and necessity of her immediate admission into our confederacy.

The territory of Texas formerly belonging to the United States, having been unwisely and prodigally ceded to the government of Spain, has, notwithstanding, asserted the claims arising from its near neighborhood and neglected advantages, by becoming the residence of the Anglo-Americans, who are now the rightful owners of the soil, both by conventional engagements and the laws of nations. By a similar train of events they erected the free State of Texas, as we became the free States of America. They have declared and maintained their independence, now acknowledged by Great Britain, France, and the United States. They have asked to become, what they always should have been, sharers of the blessings which the virtues of their and our fathers won for the vast dominion we claim as the United States territory. Respecting the increased extent of territory which the annexation of Texas produces, (urged as objectionable by some,) we clothe our ideas in the just and beautiful language of Mr. Calhoun, in his letter to our county in 1840: "In taking the course I have, I was governed by a deep conviction that our system of government, fairly understood, excells in beauty and wisdom all that has preceded it; that if administered according to its true construction and the intention of its framers, it might embrace our wide-spread territory to its utmost limits, and endure to the latest generation." He concludes by observing that when the creed and system of Thomas Jefferson shall be securely established, "our free institutions, including the General and State Governments, each in its assigned orb, diffusing light, and heat, and happiness, will become the wonder and the admiration of the world." Can any of our sister States be so selfish, so heartless, so obstinately blind to the harmony and interest of all, as seriously to determine to shut out the genial sunshine of our constitution, from any of our fellow creatures who may ask to gladden their soil in its warmth, whether on the Rio Del Norte or the bottoms of the Sabine? If we are deeply penetrated with the elevating tendencies of our code of laws, neither generosity nor humanity can go with us in our churlish refusal to admit to the same board the brothers who have eaten and drunk from their childhood in our "father's house."

Our patriots, our orators, and our press have constantly proclaimed the loveliness and majesty of a system of government which left the individual States independent, while it brought it into a harmonious union with an affiliated corps of independencies, differing, however, widely from it in climate, products, or internal policy. And it argues a want of faith in our professions to show any hesitancy to receive a people, "bone of our bone, flesh of our flesh," reared up under our own glorious institutions, and admiring them as we do, they ought to be received with a joyful welcome. Any reluctance on our part now must diminish the good feeling which ought to exist between us after our reunion. Circumstances may hereafter arise, which will compel us to do that amid storms and terrors, which we have now the opportunity of doing in peace and with deliberation.

The futile objection of the mother country's negation of the independence of Texas, had much better be urged against the introduction of Florida without the approbation of the Seminoles, they being in fact the occupants of the soil.

A line drawn from the mouth of the Rio Del Norte, thence along the Cordilleras till it cuts the Arkansas river, is plainly the most natural and suitable boundary between the United States and Mexico. To harmonize the Northern and Southern sections of the United

States, we suggest to the Texans that they make the 20th degree of longitude west from Washington city, till it strikes the Colorado, thence to its mouth, the limit of slavery in Texas. The free States of Texas would thus have a border for two thousand miles along the Mexican frontier, giving them all the advantages of the trade along that extended boundary. They would own five-sixths of the new territory, and have an equal sweep along the Gulf coast. They would interpose between white slavery in Mexico, and negro slavery in the United States, and probably form a continuous chain at no distant day from Maine to the Gulf of Mexico. The laws of the United States against the importation of slaves would put a stop to that traffic as lately carried on between Texas and the West Indies. This circumstance will have weight with those abolitionists in the North who are actuated by mistaken benevolence, and not by interested motives, or degrading subserviency to British dictation. Of the weighty, and, to the Southern States, solemn matters connected with the slaves, we have prepared ourselves to speak with the seriousness with which they are fraught. The accession of Texas would bring in a vast tract of country separating them from the interference of a foreign people. Whereas, should we, by our supineness, force the republicans of Texas to accept the aid of the wily diplomats of Britain, it requires no prophetic fire to light us to the inevitable fate of Texas, and all that we have to dread in her fall. Clenched in the silver vise of the British abolitionists, she may sigh in vain over foul machinations against her kinsmen and former associates—the slaveholders of the United States. Is there anything in the fierce and unceasing denunciations of Englishmen against slaveholders, where the life-stake of the white man is forgotten in the idolatry for black blood? anything in our own recollections of British warfare on the United States territory? anything in the daily cry from the trampled and devastated countries of the old world, to lead the Southern States to hope for any more honorable policy towards them than a system of household murder, stimulated by the zealots who would insidiously thrust the faggot and the knife into the hands of a people ignorant of what they would have, and infatuate them with the belief that the assassinations of the kind white friends whose hands have ministered to them in sickness, and who have watched their infant steps and trembling age with a tenderness of which England would in vain seek to boast towards her own oppressed multitudes, will be as a holocaust, to the God of the Christians.

The new and unsettled States of Texas would offer an extensive market to the eastern manufacturers, and a large carrying trade to the shipping of the great commercial cities, Boston, New York and Philadelphia; while the products of the West, which now too often glut the New Orleans market, would be carried off to Texas free of the onerous taxes which now fetter our trade. Our intercourse with Santa Fe would be greatly facilitated. It could not be long before the West would receive for her manufactured articles a greater influx of specie from that source than from any other.

We are anxious that the approaching session of Congress should act resolutely on the subject, and free the nation from all difficulties of the question before the next Presidential election—therefore,

Resolved, That we invoke our fellow citizens of the 7th Congressional District to join us in instructing our representative, the Hon. William P. Thomasson, [a Whig,] to urge upon his colleagues in Congress assembled, the speedy adjustment of Texas' claim for admission into the Union; and that Benjamin Jackman, R.T. Lindsey and Elisha Campbell be appointed to correspond with and forward to him a copy of these proceedings, and to know of him whether he will require a majority of the district to petition directly, before he will favor the annexation.

Resolved, That where the vital interest of the nation, or any part of it, is involved, we are opposed to all temporizing sacrifices to any narrow views of political strategy, and that we trust our own noble State will be foremost in a unanimous and heart-stirring appeal to her sister States from Maine to Louisiana, to come forward now, fearlessly disregarding how their action will operate on this or that man's prospects for the Presidency, avow their determined resolution on this subject momentous, as it may be, to our very existence as a nation.

Resolved, That we will, to the utmost of our ability, concentrate all our energies—yield all our prepossessions—harmonize all dissensions— for the accomplishment of this weighty and essential proposition. If necessary for a compromise, we are willing that the Bank, the Sub-Treasury, and the Distribution Bill, may sleep for the next four years, and the Tariff remain undisturbed.

Resolved, That we will frown upon any aspirant to the Presidency who shall prove so recreant to the highest glory and to the best interests of his nation, as to endeavor to retard the admission of Texas, by entangling it with any minor considerations of home policy.

Resolved, That a committee of six be appointed by the Chair to communicate our views to each of the distinguished gentlemen who are spoken of for President and Vice President of the United States, also those who are spoken of for next Governor of Kentucky, with a request that they will make known to us, or to the public, their views as to the policy of admitting Texas into the United States.

Resolved, That a copy of our proceedings be transmitted to President [John] Tyler, and to General [Samuel] Houston, President of independent Texas.

Resolved, That our fellow-citizens now forming the Republic of Texas, are requested to make known to their brethren, the *people* of the United States, through the press and by public meetings, their particular views in regard to the proposed union with us.

Resolved, That in our own name, as men, as republicans, and as Americans, we invite the nation of Texas home to our bosom; and we pledge ourselves for the whole Union, that her lone star shall be received into the "star spangled banner." Let her therefore come forward boldly with her constitution in her hand, and knock at the Halls of Congress for admission. We will not call a blush of shame for our Representatives by doubting her success. Let not the man who would oppose it dare to return to the State he degrades by his refusal. His very mother, and wife, and sister would turn from him in sorrowful rebuke.

Resolved, That copies of these proceedings be sent to the Intelligencer, Globe and Madisonian, Washington city, to the Journal and Advertiser, Louisville, and to the Yeoman and Commonwealth, Frankfort, with a request that they be published with the opinions of the Editors.

After a few remarks from Messrs. Ashton, Sanders, and others, the question was put, and the preamble and resolutions were unanimously adopted.

The Chairman appointed the corresponding committee three from each of the great political parties, viz: Geo[rge] N. Sanders, Elisha Campbell, William B. Lindsey, Henry Ramsy, jr. [*sic*], James P. Cox, and F. Bledsoe.

The meeting then adjourned. Lawrence Ashton, Ch[airma]n, Bartlett Searcey, Sec[retar]y.

LS with printed En in ScCleA; another LS (headed "Copy") in ScCleA. NOTE: An AEU by Calhoun reads: "Texas[.] Want my opinion on the annexation." See below the letter from Sanders of 1/20/1844.

From B[UCKNER] H. PAYNE

Plantation near "Pecan Grove" Post office
Parish of Carroll[,] La., 26th Nov[embe]r 1843
Dear Sir, Although a stranger to you personally, I nevertheless took the liberty of addressing a letter to you this past summer at your

residence, feeling well assured that we had a common interest, in the safety and perpetuity of the Institutions of our Common Country. I do not know whether my letter ever reached you, if it did I have never rec[eive]d any answer. I will however remark that the events which have since transpired have only Confirmed the views then expressed, to wit: that the manoeuvers of Mr. [Martin] Van Buren, were all intended to bring about a *"Stacked"* National Convention, in which you would have no fairness dealt out to you by the party & yet *seemingly* that appears as the main principle with him & his friends.

You will not only be *cheated out* of the nomination for Presidency but you are the very man that he can most successfully play off his tricks & knavery upon. He knows you would not stoop or condescend to any trickery or double dealing—that your character is far above its practice ["yourself" *canceled*] & that you would equally discountenance it in others, whilst on the other hand, he is *only* in his *element* when *chicanery, trickery* & *double dealing* for his own selfish ends can be rendered available to his success. In these he is greatly, *greatly* in advance of you & will always *remain so.* But to my purpose in now writing—A great Democratical meeting & Barbacue came off in this Parish in the neighborhood of Providence (our Parish town) on the 28th Ultimo to which were invited specially Gen. [John B.] Dawson member elect to Congress from this District & the other members of Congress from this State—all democratic. I knew last spring that Gen. Dawson was violently opposed to you, and equally violent a partizan of Van Buren. Previous to the meeting I perceived that great efforts were being made to *"trick"* the Democracy of this parish and District into a nomination of Van Buren, notwithstanding his known unpopularity—accordingly when Gen. Dawson arrived (he came from New Orleans) he was attended by several partizans equally warm for V[an] B[uren] and opposed to you, accompanied also with Badges pledging one & all to support the Baltimore nomination let it be whom it may. Having this accomplished and their wire workers distributed among the people, it was then proposed that a vote by *Ballot* should be taken as to who the Democracy would *then* prefer for President. Under the previous party drilling you got few or no votes—Van Buren got nearly all & that too [*illegible word*] it is well known he has neither popularity or strength, and *this game is being played all over the State.* The wire working gentlemen were [al]ready supplied with Ink, paper & pencils to write the desired name upon the ticket and I am assured, that names were written down directly adverse to the wishes of the applicant, and the ballot used. Your friends looked with scorn upon such base & contemptible doings.

Under these circumstances they feel that you can have no fair chance with such a man as V[an] Buren.

Many of them differ with Mr. [Henry] Clay, but feel assured that he like yourself, is above all trickery & that he is an honest man, and will prefer him to V[an] B[uren] on that account. They feel assured that should V[an] B[uren] be even[?] elected to the Presidency, that he will sell himself & his party to any one else sooner than advance your prospects ["& with them the interest of the country" *interlined*] if by so doing he could advance himself in *any way*. Under these circumstances, as Mr. Clay having distinctly avowed that he goes only for a tariff for Revenue incidental to protection, & on the currency there is no great difference in your views & he is in favor of limiting the Presidential incumbent to one term, is it not a sacrifice that our common country should at this time command our support of him, rather than see the destinies of 17 millions of people committed to the keeping of so unprincipled a man & political *trickster* as Martin Van Buren. *We must keep the the* [*sic*] *Presidential office* if possible confined as yet to the slave States. Whenever we have traveled out of them ruin & confusion have been the result. By your friends taking position with Mr. Clay now[?] you will most certainly be his successor in office. This will give time for abolitionism &c to wear itself out. By remain[in]g where they now are, they can render you ["nor the country" *interlined and then erased*] no service—their country no service, & Mr. V[an] B[uren] will trick himself into a *nomination* but he will be beaten, badly beaten and in his fall you will be seriously injured & the country suffer for want of your integrity [*mutilation*] proper place and in all human probability [*mutilation*; Silas?] Wr[ight? wil]l be the suc[c]essor. Under these circumstances [*one word mutilated*] friends [have?] but one of two courses to adopt— either to [*one word mutilated*] out & support Mr. Clay or stand neutral. They cannot support Mr. V[an] B[uren] with a knowledge of his trickery. Ne[u]trality would do no good towards accomplishing the objects of bringing the Gen[eral] government to a strict construction of the Constitution—and yet it is equally certain that if V[an] B[uren] gets the nomination that it will not do for you to take the field, as thousands & tens of thousand[s of] honest men will never see the tricks by which they have been duped by a *stacked* Convention, and as far as my limited understanding will allow me to judge, the true policy of your friends at this time would be to throw down the gauntlet at once & take sides openly for Mr. Clay. In this way the country may be saved & the wishes of your friends gratified. Your friends are filled with solicitude to know what is best to be done. I thought it due to you to write what I have so that you may be advised of what is going forward. Very respectfully, B.H. Payne.

ALS in ScCleA.

From THEOPHILUS FISK

Portsmouth, Va., Nov. 29, 1843
Sir, May I dare to presume so far upon your kindness as to beg that you will favour me with a letter [of introduction] to any friend you may have in Europe, that you may feel at liberty to make me acquainted with. Should it meet your convenience and approbation to grant this request, you will please add to the obligation by addressing it to me at Washington, under cover to the Hon. D[ixon] H. Lewis. I expect to sail for England or France about the middle of December as bearer of despatches from our government.

I take the liberty of forwarding you [*not found*] the proceedings of the late meeting of our district Convention, to elect a delegate, or delegates, [to the convention] to be held in Baltimore in May next. You will perceive that it adjourned without going into an election, in consequence of three of the Counties in this district, being unrepresented. The motion for adjournment was made and carried by your friends, and they have gained great credit for their magnanimity, as we outnumbered the [Martin] Van Buren delegates [*"just"* canceled *and* "more than" *interlined*] two to one! And that too with but little effort on our part, while they moved earth and sea to pack the Convention with their exclusive friends. We shall lose nothing by adjourning, as Princess Anne and Surry Counties will elect delegates friendly to yourself, and the other (Southampton) will, it is thought, do the same. The votes of the Counties will stand in the Convention—

Calhoun		*Van Buren*	
Norfolk County,	2	Sussex	1
Norfolk borough,	1		
Isle of Wight,	1	*doubtful*	
Nansemond	1	Southampton	1
Surry	1		
Princess Anne	1		
	7		

I very greatly fear that the Convention at Baltimore will be any thing rather than a true exponent of public opinion. Indeed I have feared this from the very first, as Mr. [Francis W.] Pickens and Mr. Lewis can both testify. Knowing the trading politicians who draw the wires for Mr. Van Buren, as well as I do, I could not trust them so far as to meet them in Convention; this made me so anxious to unfurl your banner "subject *only* to the decision of the American people." I ventured to do this; it met the approbation of all our friends here; but other papers devoted to your interest thinking it best to say "subject to the Baltimore Convention" I very reluctantly yielded my preferences. I hope that your friends will never again consent to submit their claims to any other body than the sovereign people.

We have gained a very considerable accession to our numbers by the "Tyler meeting" which was held here some six or eight weeks ago. The [Henry] Clay and Van Buren men united and established a new paper here in opposition to the "Old Dominion"; to counteract their base designs, your friends united with those who were friendly to Mr. [John] Tyler and held a large public meeting—the proceedings of which have been so basely misrepresented by the whig papers, as being of an unfriendly character to yourself. These gentlemen continue to act with us in good faith, and will do so at the polls, when they see that there is no hope of his re-election. Pardon the liberty I have tak[en; *mutilation*] believe me With the highest respect Your ob[edien]t ser[van]t, Theophilus Fisk.

ALS in ScCleA; PC in Jameson, ed., *Correspondence*, pp. 895–896. NOTE: Fisk had been editor of the Portsmouth *Old Dominion*.

From A[BEL] P. UPSHUR, [Secretary of State]

Washington, Nov[embe]r 30 1843

My Dear Sir, I have now the pleasure to enclose a copy of the letter from Gen[era]l [Duff] Green, alluded to in my last to you. I submitted the letter to the President [John Tyler], at Gen[era]l Green's request, & he took it with him to Virg[ini]a, from which place he has only recently returned. This accounts for the delay in transmitting the copy.

I thank you for your suggestions in the matter of Texas; & am happy to see that they support my own views. I have reason to think that nothing more is necessary to insure success, than that the South should, be true to itself. I trust that no Southern representative will be found, so blind or so tame of spirit, as not to be worthy of the present great occasion. Very truly & resp[ectfull]y yours &c, A.P. Upshur.

[Enclosure]

Duff Green to [Abel P. Upshur]

London, 17th October 1843

Dear Sir, I take it for granted that you will receive through Mr. [Edward] Everett [U.S. Minister to Great Britain] regular files of the [London] Times and the [London] Chronicle and that you will thus be informed of whate transpires through the press—the ratification of the treaty with China has given an impulse to trade which, coming as it does on the moment when two favorable harvests have greatly increased the supply and reduced the price of food, and when the reaction in commerce was giving a new impulse to the manufacturing industry of this country, will give more confidence to the landlords and the monopolists interests associated with them which may protract the struggle which must end in the adoption in their broadest sense of the principles of free trade.

The Election in the city of London, if it goes against the Government may be considered as deciding the question of monopoly and ousting the Tory ministry. It is as I think more than doubtful, but the friends of [James] Pattison are sanguine—when we remember that in this country, the will of Parliament is supreme—that might is right— that the tendency of the movement is to abolish *all* monopolies & that the city of London is made up of monopolies, the oft repeated gratuities won or purchased of successive Kings, it is cause of special wonder that the anti corn law league ["dares" *interlined*] thus to beard the Lion in his den—to meet the patronage of the union—the wealth and influence of Mr. [Alexander] Baring [Lord Ashburton] and his class, when those on whom they are to operate are themselves monopolists, extorting large sums from the masses by virtue of corporate grants which Parliament can repeat and which must give way before the movement which threatens to go backe to the very foundation and strip the Hierarchy themselves of the spoils accumulated through successive centuries. The election of Pattison will give new life and vigor to the League—who having hoisted the banner of *free trade* now occupy a platform that permits the opponents of the Tory administration to rally with them, and those who seek *power* as well as those who seek wealth, will make common cause with them. It is no longer a question between the manufacturers and the landlord. It is now a question between free trade and monopoly, on which the many are enlisted against the few. [Richard] Cobden, and the League are progressing—they are the assailants, the monopolists are the besieged, beleaguered party.

Let Cobden and free trade triumph here in London, and then it will be for them to dictate terms to the conquered aristocracy—when the alliance between the landlord and the Church can no longer protect them against the progress of liberal principals, each will endeaver to make for themselves the best terms they can. What those terms will be it is now impossible to foresee. There are influences at work connecting the artificial state of society in Protestant England with the artificial state of the roman Catholic monarchies of Europe, which require to be well understood, before we venture an opinion as to final results. Yet I think that I can see even in those elements, that which should arrest the attention of American Statesmen whose duty it is to protect our own interests and free institutions from those evil tendencies apparent on the surface and which if left to take their course must end in combinations greatly to our prejudice, and which may by a wise and energetic course on the part of our government not only be defeated but substituted by other interests more in accord with ours and which will seek to identify themselves with us as their natural ally and chief support.

(I had written thus far when the times [newspaper] of this day came to hand. I beg to refer you to the speeches of Mr. Labruchere [sic; Henry Labouchere] and of Mr. Baring in confirmation of what I have written & will only add that should Mr. Pattison be defeated it will rally the country against these London *Monopolies*, and that altho the end may may [sic] be delayed, it is the no less certain). So much by way of Parenthesis. The position of England is such that she has no alternative but free trade. The effect of the Treaty with China will be to give a new impulse to her manufacturing industry, but you will see in the proclamation of the Chinese Government that the same commercial privileges are to be given to other countries and it requires but little knowledge of human nature to see that the national vanity and self love which placed this declaration in that important document will secure to their competitors a more friendly intercourse because conceal it as they may, the documents show that the English will be considered as intruders, while all other nations are invited guests. They are admitted per force—we are introduced by way of relieving the national vanity from the morti[fi]cation of being coerced by England. Under such circumstances the intelligent commercial and manufacturing interests of England see that they enter the Chinese market at a disadvantage, and that of all others they have most to fear from american competition, if by an adherence to the to the [sic] present restriction systems, the two Governments combined to force the surplus Capital and labor in the United States into manufactures, instead of affording it the natural inducements of a free trade which would cause it to be employed in agriculture. They see that free trade would not only greatly increase the american consumption of British manufactures, but by preventing an unnatural stimulus to manufactures, which must soon create a surplus in our market, relieve them from that competition which they most fear in China.

Under such circumstances you will find the free trade party of this Count[r]y sympathising with the free trade party in America and ready to sustain those measures which are so essential to the peace and prosperity of both countries that nothing but the artificial state of society fostered and matured by the class legislation of both Countries can be opposed to their adoption.

You will see that ministers have at length attempted to arrest the *repeal* movement by their proclamation against the Clontarf meeting is admitted to be unconstitutional, the arrest and prosecution of Mr. Oconnell [*sic*; Daniel O'Connell] and his associates may be fatal to them. The proclamation was harsh and ill timed as well as unconstitutional. The arrest and prosecution of Mr. Oconnel may become the question on which ministers are to retain office.

It is admitted Ireland has cause to complain of grievous injustice— Oconnel content that all his proceedings have been strictly legal and constitutional.

He has on all occasions protested his devotion to the Queen [Victoria] and his loyalty to the throne. His monster meetings were in progress during the sitting of Parliament when ministers admitted their legality and failed to ask for new laws forbidding them or granting them authority to suppress them. If under such circumstances Mr. Oconnel is co[n]victed will he be punished?

If he is punished he will become a martyr and the discontent in England as well as in Ireland will manifest itself so strongly and will become so much a part of the general sentiment as to oust the [Sir Robert] Peel ministry. If he is acquitted then ministers will be compelled to come before the next session of Parliament and ask for new powers to suppress the repeal agitation which will have received a new impulse by their failure, and by the measures which they then propose must they stand or fall. I am by no means disposed to doubt that this is the issue they seek. Indeed I can find no other rational explanation of the delay in taking their final action. It is now announced by authority that arrangements have been made with the King of Hanover [Ernst August] for 20000 troops, and the tone of French *ministerial* press shows that the King of the French [Louis Philippe]—roman Catholic, though he be, came to an ["to an" *canceled*] understanding with the Queen or Lord Aberdeen, that the movement in Ireland was of a character so revolutionary that it was for the interest of *his Dynasty* to discourage it.

In other words, the anti liberal and monarchical party of Europe find it their interest to prevent the *national* independence of Ireland. The repeal of the Union is a hopeless and obsolete idea, but it by no means follows that all redress to Ireland will be denied. The moment that the question of repeal is disposed of, then comes up the other question of justice to Ireland; and who can foresee what will be the consequence when the whig opponents of Sir Robert Peel are enabled to consolidate, the friends of Ireland—the friends of freedom in trade and the ["friends of" *interlined*] freedom of religion in a common sentiment of opposition to the Peel ministry. Oconnel and Ireland never can coalesce with Sir Robert Peel. His hatred to the Tories will force him upon the Whigs. Sir Robert Peel is compelled to take upon himself all the odium of the strong measures necessary to suppress the repeal agitation, and in doing so necessarily drives all the Irish members into a cooperation with the whigs. To me it is obvious therefore that the Tory ministry cannot retain power beyond the next session of Parliament or if they do so, it must be accompanied by extraordinary concessions forced upon them by surrounding difficulties.

I know that a dictum of [George] Washington's suited to our infant condition has induced our people to believe that we have no interest in progress of other nations. But we should remember that the infant of that day has grown into a powerful commercial nation, whose interest[s] are diffused over every quarter of the globe, and that the purpose for which the federal Government was constituted was to protect those interests. You cannot look into an English newspaper that does not bear upon its face proofs that this great nation look to us as the only rivals whose competitions they have cause to fear. England feels that she depends upon her manufacturing supremacy for the maintenance of her relative position among the great nations of the world. The treaty with China opens to her new prospects, and she will be enabled to diminish the oppressive burden of her national debt if she can give activity to her manufacturing industry. A modification of the commercial systems of England and the United States which will enable them to consume the products of our agriculture & us to consume their manufactures, will identify our interests and make us deeply interested as the manufacturers of England themselves in every measure which may increase the consumption of the products of English manufacturing industry, or promote the wealth or prosperity of the mother country. When the material interests of England and the United States are thus consolidated we may confide in the friendship of British statesmen. Until this be done, we may expect them to be jealous of our growing strength and that who ever may be in power, their measures will be taken in reference to their interests. If we could have induced the Tory ministers to repeal their restrictive measures it would have been better for us first because they are now in power and we are compelled to look to them, and to them only only [*sic*] for that measure—and next because being the monopoly interest all concessions made by them may be considered as permanent. But failing to obtain from them such a modification of their tariff as will permit a fair exchange of the products of our labor for their manufacturies, we are compelled to take our measures in reference to parties as they exist here.

This brings me to consider the bearing which the present struggle in this country necessarily has in our interest. By refer[r]ing to the speeches of Mr. Baring and Mr. Pattison and the speeches of Mr. Cobden & Mr. [John] Bright and the comment of the press on the canvass now progressing in London, You will see that the duty on Brazilian & Cuban Sugar is a prominent question. I refer you to the comment of the Sunday Times in confirmation of whate I have before written on the subject of the anti slavery movement. It is now well understood that Tory sympathy for the negro is but another name for Tory oppression of the white labour of England and you may rest assured that all that is wanting to give the last blow to this humbug is for the Government of the United States to take a decided stand upon this subject. Not in favor of the slave trade, but in sup[p]ort of existing institutions—not in favor of slavery in the abstract, but against the impertinent interference of England in the domestic institutions of the United States[,] of Cuba & Brazil. When it is palpable to all the world that under the mask of humanity to the black race she seeks to enslave the white—that under the pretence of opposition to slave labor she seeks to make all the world dependent upon her for the supply of sugar[,] Coffee[,] Rice &c. I have before given you my views as to the British attempt to convert Texas into a refuge for runaway slaves and thieves. I would urge upon the Government that now is the time to make common cause with Brazil & Cuba, and that it becomes the present administration to exert themselves for the counteraction of the avowed determination of England to accomplish the abolition of slavery there. I have heard from an unquestioned source that France is about to indemnify the growers of Beetroot sugar, and that a treaty is now in progress if it is not already concluded whereby France stipulates to admit Brazilian sugars & other articles Cotton & will no doubt be included. Brazil admitting french manufactures at reduced rates of duty. I hope that you will not sleep over this question—that you will not fail to see in the position which England has assumed towards Brazil a conclusive argument why the United States & Brazil should act together against the insolvent pretension of Sir Robert Peel, that he is bound as the advocate of humanity to demand the emancipation of the slaves of Brazil.

I have just seen an intelligent friend who is just returned from a tour through Scotland and he tells me that all Scotland to a man are prepared to sustain *free trade*—that all parties there, whig and Tory, demand an abrogation of the duty on sugar—that they ridicule and denounce the pretense of humanity on which Sir Robert Peel and his partisans pretend to justify it, and that if our Government act with firmness & especially if they ask Sir Robert to send Commissioners to the U.S. to adjust the boundary and confer on the subject of the Tariff, and he refuses as ["they" *interlined*] believe he will, it will enable those who desire to identify the interests of the two countries, when they come into power, as come they soon must do, to arrange all matters pending between us on more favorable terms.

Not having heard from you, I cannot know what you have done because for reasons which I will explain to you I have not co[n]versed with Mr. [Edward] Everett on his instructions from home, but I am so deeply impressed with the importance of the measure, whether I consider it in reference to the state of parties at home or here, that I must renew my entreaty to you to instruct Mr. Everett to invite this Government to send a Commission to Washington charged with the settlement of the N[orth] Western Boundary as well as the adjustment of the tariff. There is a time for all things and there never was a time more favorable to the United States than the present for the settlement of these questions, and to neglect to improve the occasion will be a culpable neglect of a most solemn duty.

I have much to say to you in confirmation of of [*sic*] these views which is reserved until I see you personally which I hope will be in a few weeks after you receive this. Your sincere friend, Duff Green.

ALS and En in ScCleA; FC of En in NcU, Duff Green Papers (published microfilm, roll 5, frames 101–116); PC of letter and PEx of En in Frederick Merk, *Slavery and the Annexation of Texas*, pp. 257–258, 234–236.

Pamphlet campaign biography of John C. Calhoun, published at New York City, *ca.* 11/——. This 24-pp. pamphlet, illustrated with woodcut drawings, presents an account of Calhoun's life and a defense of him. Much space is devoted to the Revolutionary war services and frontier bravery of Patrick Calhoun and the Caldwell uncles of the statesman. Calhoun's leadership and steadfastness during the War of 1812 are also recounted and praised, as are his services as Secretary of War. Common charges against Calhoun, such as sectionalism and being "ultra" on free trade are argued against. Calhoun's private character is praised for charity, purity, fairness, honesty, and intellectual sincerity. The pamphlet concludes: "In conclusion, fellow-citizens, we recommend John C. Calhoun to you, conscious that, if he were personally as well known over the whole country as he is to his immediate acquaintances, he would be as much beloved by the whole nation as he is by them. We recommend him to you as a long-tried and faithful public servant—as an honest man—as a true patriot and upright citizen—and as a man every way qualified for the *Presidency of the United States.* Then let us give three cheers for the memory of *old Patrick Calhoun*—three cheers for the *three Caldwells*— and nine cheers for *John Caldwell Calhoun.*" The pamphlet's tone and appearance suggest it was intended for a relatively unsophisticated audience. There is a Preface signed only "The Author," and dated at New York [City], November, 1843. The Preface states that Calhoun's public and private life are not "as fully known among the mass of our fellow citizens" as they deserve to be; that he has suffered from many "prejudices and false impressions, cast around him by over zealous opposition"; and that he is the only present candidate for President whose family "took any active part in the Revolutionary War." Information on the title page indicates that the pamphlet was priced at 6¼ cents and that it was available for sale at specified addresses in New York City, Boston, Philadelphia, Baltimore, Albany, and New Orleans, "and by booksellers and periodical agents throughout the United States." [*The Calhoun Text Book,* published shortly afterward, states on p. 31 that this *Life* was published at the office of the New York, N.Y., *New World,* "under the superintendence of the Calhoun General Committee of New York city."] PC in Anonymous, *Life and Character of the Hon. John C. Calhoun, with Illustrations: Containing Notices of His Father and Uncles, and Their Brave Conduct During Our Struggle for Independence, in the American Revolutionary War* (New York: J[onas] Winchester, New World Press, [1843]).

The Calhoun Text Book, published at New York City, *ca.* 11/——.
This 36-pp. campaign pamphlet contains an unsigned introduction

dated Baltimore, 11/15/1843. The title page contains a quotation from Calhoun predicting the "final triumph" of the "popular party" which will achieve a low tariff, the elimination of public debt, separation of the government and banks, retrenchment, and strict adherence to the Constitution. The "text book" consists largely of reprinted articles from publications praising Calhoun and analyzing favorably his prospects for and potential performance in the Presidency. Articles included are from the New York, N.Y., *Journal of Commerce*; the New Haven, Conn., *Register*; the Washington, D.C., *Spectator*; *Hunt's Merchants' Magazine*; the Chambers, Ala., *Herald*; *Southern Quarterly Review*; the Charleston, S.C., *Mercury*; the Washington, D.C., *Globe*; the *Life and Character of the Hon. John C. Calhoun* . . .; the Milledgeville, Ga., *Union*; the New York, N.Y., *World*; the *Independent Democrat*; the New York, N.Y., *Evening Post*; and perhaps other sources not fully identified. Some writers are identified, some are unidentified. Information on the title page indicates that the pamphlet was available at specified publishers or booksellers in Philadelphia, Boston, Charleston, New Orleans, and Mobile. PC in *The Calhoun Text Book* (New York: Herald Office, [1843]).

Announcement of the Pendleton Female Academy, 12/——. The trustees announce to the public that James F. Gould and his daughters will open this school on 1/1/1844 and describe the curriculum and costs. John C. Calhoun is among the citizens listed as references for the enterprise. Printed circular or broadside in ScU-SC, Pendleton Female Academy Papers.

From R[OBERT] B[ARNWELL] RHETT, [Representative from S.C.]

[Georgetown, D.C.] Saturday, Dec[embe]r 2d 1843

My Dear Sir, I told you I would endeavour to make a separate organization of those opposed to Mr. [Martin] Van Buren, in the Election of Officers of the House [of Representatives]; and that I thought this would give us a pretty good test of their mettle and character. I have been at this, for the last three weeks. We had determined to run [for Speaker] Mr. [William] Wilkins of Pen[n]sylvania; and by keeping out of caucus, it was sure we would succeed. After a show—to day they have been w[h]ipped in[?]–the Pen[n]sylvanians go into caucus–and of course, there can be no opposing organization. It would be useless for your friends to keep out. So you see, it is as I feared. I shall myself, however, not go into the caucus, and let them place me where they please on the Committee. A Van Buren Speaker and Printer will be elected and it will be hailed, as an authoritative endorsement of his pretensions to the Presidency. What can we do with soldiers who will not fight? Yours Dear Sir, R.B. Rhett.

[P.S.] I will write again in a few Days.

ALS in ScCleA.

To JOSEPH SMITH, [Nauvoo, Ill.]

Fort Hill, 2d Dec[embe]r 1843

Sir, You ask me what would be my rule of action, relative to the Mormons, or Latter day Saints, should I be elected President, to which I answer; that, if I should be elected, I would strive to administer the Government according to the Constitution and the laws of the Union; and that, as they make no distinction between citizens of different religion [*sic*] creeds, I should make none. As far as it depends on the Executive Department, all should have the full benefit of both, and none should be exempt from their operation.

But, as you refer to the case of Missouri, candour compels me to repeat, what I said to you at Washington; that according to my ["views" *altered to* "view"] the case does not come within the Jurisdiction of the Federal Government, which is one of limited and specific powers. With respect I am &c &c, J.C. Calhoun.

CC in USlC, Historical Department; PC in the Nauvoo, Ill., *Neighbor*, January 10, 1844, p. 2; PC in the New York, N.Y., *Evening Post*, January 27, 1844, pp. 1–2; PC in *Niles' National Register*, vol. LXV, no. 23 (February 3, 1844), p. 357; PC in the New Orleans, La., *Courrier de la Louisiane*, February 10, 1844, p. 3; PC in the Norfolk and Portsmouth, Va., *American Beacon and Daily Advertiser*, February 22, 1844, p. 2; PC in *The Voice of Truth, Containing General Joseph Smith's Correspondence with Gen. James Arlington Bennett; Appeal to the Green Mountain Boys; Correspondence with John C. Calhoun, Esq. . . . Also, Correspondence with the Hon. Henry Clay* (Nauvoo, Ill.: Printed by John Taylor, 1844), pp. 21–22; PC in *Correspondence Between Joseph Smith, The Prophet, and Col. John Wentworth . . . and the Honorable John C. Calhoun . . .* (New-York: Published by John E. Page and L.R. Foster, 1844), pp. 11–12; PC in *Americans, Read! ! ! Gen. Joseph Smith's Views of the Powers and Policy . . . Government of the United States . . . Correspondence with the Hon. John C. Calhoun . . .* (New York: E.J. Bevin, printer, 1844), pp. 26–27; PC in [Henry Mayhew,] *The Mormons: Or Latter-Day Saints. With Memoirs of the Life and Death of Joseph Smith, the "American Mahomet"* (London: Office of the National Illustrated Library, [1851]), pp. 149–150; PC in *The Prophet Joseph Smith's Views on the Powers and Policy of the Government of the United States. To which is appended the Correspondence between the Prophet Joseph Smith and the Hons. J.C. Calhoun and Henry Clay, Candidates for the Presidency of the United States in 1844* (Salt Lake City: Jos. Hyrum Parry and Co., 1886). NOTE: The manuscript transcribed above is possibly a copy or extract made from Calhoun's ALS.

To PETER HAGNER, Third Auditor, Washington

Fort Hill, 3d Dec[embe]r 1843

My dear Sir, The enclosed is, I presume, ["from" *interlined*] one of those agents who prowl about the Treasury to pick up & collect old claims.

If it would not put you to too much trouble, I would take it as a favour, if you would ascertain, or put ["it" *interlined*] in the hand of some officer, who would ascertain, whether there is any, and if any, what amount standing to the credit of John E[wing] Colhoun [Sr.], and to inform me how to proceed to obtain it.

I am at a loss to conjecture how there should be a balance in his favour, unless it should be for what may be due him, as a Senator in Congress, as that is the only ["office" *canceled and* "place" *interlined*] he ever held, as far as I am aware, under the Government of the U[nited] States. He died, while Senator, in the summer of 1802.

I make this request, because I would rather lose, whatever may be due to his estate, than to give a cent to one, who makes it his business to hunt up old claims against the Government.

I will thank you to return the enclosed with your answer.

I hope you & your family continue to enjoy good health.

With best respects to Mrs. [Frances Randall] Hagner I am Yours truly, J.C. Calhoun.

ALS in DNA, RG 217 (Records of the General Accounting Office), Third Auditor: Miscellaneous Letters Received, 1843. NOTE: An EU indicates that the enclosure was a "letter of Chas. Whittlesey [to Calhoun, dated 11/22/1843] relative to amount due Estate of Jno. E. Colhoun." Another states that Calhoun's letter was received on 12/13 and that it was answered on [12]/14.

From V[IRGIL] MAXCY

Tulip Hill[,] West River [Md.,] 3rd Dec. 1843
My dear Sir, I duly received your letter of the 14th Nov. some days
ago and should have gone over [to Washington] immediately to consult with Mr. [Robert Barnwell] Rhett on the expediency of a congressional consultation for the purpose of preventing a split in the
party, but circumstances occurred which prevented my doing so. I
have concluded therefore to present the conclusions to which my mind
has been brought by a view of the past. It would not be safe to go
into any convention, however formed, with the Richmond & Albany
politicians. And it would not be consistent with principle to give
countenance to any one, not formed on the District system. And as
there is no reason to expect that the friends of Mr. [Martin] V[an]
B[uren] will alter their course in regard to this, it appears to me, that
you ought at some period—what period future events must decide—
to publish thro' the medium of a letter to a friend, written for publication or in some other mode, your reasons for determining not to
produce division by allowing your name to be presented before a convention, formed in whole ["or in part" *interlined*] on any other plan
than a direct representation of the people in Districts. Such a course
would place you higher than ever before the country ["which is getting sick of caucus or Convention dictation" *interlined*], and preserve
your lofty name & character as a rallying point in the future, whereas
if you went into the convention and should be rejected, as you undoubtedly would be, it would lower your character & destroy in a
great measure the influence of your name in rallying the good men of
all parties, when a new organization of parties shall take place as it
will undoubtedly do after Mr. [Henry] Clay[']s term is out. I say
after Mr. Clay's term is out: for such is the dissatisfaction & ill feeling
now produced in the different portions of the ["republican" *interlined*] party by the base fraud, which has procured every one of the
nominations of V[an] B[uren,] that I do not believe that if he should
be withdrawn even you could be elected. The treachery of the V[an]
B[uren] men would produce your defeat, if nothing else. I do not
think that any consultation of the republican members of Congress
would do any good. A majority of them are for Van B[uren] & determined I believe to persevere as they have begun. Our friends in
New England have greviously [*sic*] misled us, and painful as it is to
say so, yet as I feel it a sacred duty of friendship to give my opinions
without reserve, it does appear to me, that there is nothing left but
["that" *canceled and* "to decide how" *interlined*] you should be with-

drawn so that you may be preserved for the country in future. There is one event & but one, it appears to me, that can alter this state of things, & that is, the immediate calling up of the Texas question, which may possibly unite the South & ["by weakening Clay" *interlined*] bring the Southern candidate into the House. Whether this will take place or not cannot be known before the meeting of Congress, a day or two after which I will go over to Washington & write you again. Faithfully yours, V. Maxcy.

ALS in ScCleA; variant PC in Jameson, ed., *Correspondence*, pp. 896–897.

To GEORGE McDUFFIE, [Senator from S.C.]

Fort Hill, 4th Dec[embe]r 1843

My dear Sir, You did right in not answering the letter [*not found*] you enclosed to me [in yours of 11/25]. The writer is, as you supposed, one of lo[o]se political notions, as is the case with almost the whole body of politicians in Pennsylvania. I regret much that you could not make me a visit. I had much to say, that could be better said in conversation, than by letter.

You are right in supposing that many of the friends of Mr. [Martin] V[an] B[uren] are against us on the Subject of the Tariff. Indeed, they have long been so, and that, in fact, has been the cause of all our difficulties since 1828 'till the present time. It was he and his friends, who formed and passed the Tariff of '28, and it was that measure which gave Gen[era]l [Andrew] Jackson's administration a false direction, and controlled events 'till the suspension of the Bank in 1837. Mr. [Silas] Wright is the real author of that Tariff. He was on the Committee of manufactures, which concocted and reported it, and was its leading member. It was passed in the Senate by the vote of Mr. V[an] B[uren], Col. [Thomas H.] Benton and his other friends, added to that of the National Republicans. The consequences of that wicked and oppressive measure is [*sic*] to be found recorded in the political history of the country since. To it, all the disasters, which have befallen the country and the party may be distinctly traced.

After the suspension of '37, when V[an] B[uren] and his friends fell prostrated, we refused to cooperate with them, except on the Subtreasury and other measures, which we had supported; or to join them in an Address, till they agreed explicitly to renounce the protective policy, and adopt our principles and policy generally. This they did in two consecutive addresses to the party.

After the defeat of Mr. V[an] B[uren] in 1840 the whole party boldly and openly took our ground against a protective Tariff, and all the connected measures. No one was more openly and apparently sincerely opposed than Mr. Wright. He continued so till within a short time before the passage of the bill of '42. It was not till within three or four days of its passage, that we heard for the first time, that he and Mr. [James] Buchanan had determined to vote for it, to our great surprise. They put their votes on the false and flimsy ground, that the revenue made it absolutely necessary that some bill should pass, and that was the only one which could, when they could not but know, it would diminish, rather than increase the revenue, as it then stood.

Since then, there have been three State conventions held in N[ew] York; the last of which was the Syracuse, which nominated Mr. V[an] B[uren]. They have all adopted resolutions on the subject of the Tariff as unsound as the doctrines of Mr. [Henry] Clay and his friends on the same subject. Indeed, Mr. Clay in his late letters has come up almost to the identical language held by the Syracuse convention.

If to this we add, the vague language held by Mr. V[an] B[uren] himself on the same subject, there can be no doubt that we shall again be betrayed, as we were in '28, should he and his friends again get the control. We may rest assured, that those who will play false to get power, will play false to retain it. And let me add, another betrayal would, if possible, be still more fatal to the South, than that of '28. It would demoralize and break us down. The worse that could befal[l] us, would be to put into power the portion of the party opposed to us on the Tariff. They would on that question be supported by the Whigs, which would make all opposition to it hopeless, whereas if a Whig should be elected President, the whole of the Democratick party would take sides with us to expel him from power.

But, my dear Sir, there is another objection to Mr. V[an] B[uren] and his friends not less fatal, in my opinion, than the Tariff; I mean the mode, on which they dictatorially insist to constitute the [Democratic national] Convention. It is calculated and intended to give the control of the nomination, to the large central States, and through that of the election, as far as the party is concerned. If it be permitted, it will give to them the entire control of the Executive Department, which, added to the like control in the House of Representatives, would give them the control over the whole Government. It would unite the ballot-box, the vote and the patronage in the same hands, and leave the Government without a check.

With a clear conception of these results, it will be impossible for me, with my principles and conception of duty, to permit my name to go before the Baltimore Convention, constituted as it now must be. It would be to betray the Constitution and the smaller States, and weaker portions of the Union, that is the South. On that point, I have made up my mind; and I wish my friends so to understand it, in determining what course they ought to persue. I am of the impression, our friends in Congress ought to have an understanding among themselves what course ought to be taken, and when they have decided, it ought to be made known to all who are disposed to act with us over the Union. If they should decide, that they cannot act with those, whose opinions accord much more with the Whigs, on the vital question of the Tariff, than with us; and who insist on constituting the Convention on such false and dangerous principles, I shall stand by them, be their number ever so few, even if we should carry not a single State; but if they should decide otherwise, it will cause me no mortification or pain to stand alone, on the ground which I feel it my duty to occupy. The approbation of my own conscience, and the preservation of my character, are dearer to me, than any office that can be bestowed on me. In writing as I do, I do not desire to dictate to my friends. My object is simply to inform them of the course which I will feel it my duty to take.

All that has since occurred, prove[s] the wisdom of the resolution [for a Constitutional amendment] you long since moved, to District the States for the election of the Chief Magistrate, and give the election directly to the people. The smaller States would do well to yield the eventual choice by the House, in order to break up that general ticket system, in choosing electors. The introduction of that system has done much to disorder and corrupt the Government, and country. In fact, where many choose many it is no election at all. It creates the necessity of making nominations, and those who make the nomination virtually control the election. I do hope that you will again introduce your resolutions at this session. It will give you a fine field in which to exercise your talents and eloquence, and display your principles and patriotism.

I see the subject of Texas is destined to be one of the first magnitude. The interference there by Great Britain in order to act on our Southern institutions has presented it in a new and most important aspect, and so changed it, that those who were formerly opposed to the annexation, may well support it now. I think no alternative is left us, and that if the Executive should take a stand for it, he ought to be unanimously and decidedly supported by the South.

I can have no objection to your showing this confidentially to your colleague [Daniel Elliott Huger], or any other friend. Give my respects to him, and say to him I shall be happy to hear from him. I hope to hear [*missing*] from you, even if your letters should have to be short.

PC in Jameson, ed., *Correspondence*, pp. 552–555. NOTE: While Representative from S.C. in 1825, McDuffie had proposed a Constitutional amendment to provide for a uniform system of districts in all the States for voting for President and Vice-President and to repeal the reversion of the Presidential election to the House of Representatives in case of the lack of a majority in the Electoral College.

To A[NDREW] P[ICKENS] CALHOUN,
Faunsdale, Marengo County, Ala.

Fort Hill, 5th Dec[embe]r 1843
My dear Andrew, The Mail of yesterday brought your letters to Mr. [Thomas G.] Clemson & myself, contain[in]g a copy of the conditional purchase of Glover's place for him. When they were received he had two wagons standing loaded in the yard, ready to start for his Saluda [river] place, with furniture and other articles preparatory to taking possession. He expects to follow in a day or two himself, & to be prepared ["shortly" *interlined*] to take possession with his family. He has already expend[ed] in purchasing negroes and other expenditures a large portion of the credit negotiated for him with Mathew[e]s & Bonneau, which will put it out of his power to take the purchase, unless he can dispose of his Saluda place, without too great a sacrafice [*sic*]. He is satisfied with the terms ["of the Glover purchase" *interlined*] and would be glad to take it; & if he can possibly make a sale of his Saluda place, when he goes down, will go forthwith to Alabama to look at ["the" *canceled and* "Glover's" *interlined*] place before he closes the purchase. He will write you soon after his arrival at his Edgefield [District] place.

If Mr. Clemson cannot take it, it would be a very desirable purchase for us, if we could conveniently command the means. But ["I" *interlined*] do not think we can. I have heard nothing farther from Mr. [John S.] Barbour, and conclude, he has had some difficulty in realising the funds he expected to ["receive" *canceled*] have. As we cannot venture on the purchase of ["that" *canceled and* "Glover(')s tract, should Mr. C(lemson) decline," *interlined*] it becomes more important, that we should secure Mathew's place. I hope you will not neglect to give ["it" *canceled*] your early attention to the subject.

I hope you are making good progress in getting in your cotton crop, and that the yield will equal expectation. The last account from Europe was not so favourable; but as I regard it now pretty well ascertained, that the crop will not exceed an average, I have confidence that the recent prices will, at least, maintain themselves. What intelligence have you about our Havana[?] Shipment? I hope it is favourable, and that we will have a balance of two or three thousand dollars coming to us from the last year[']s crop.

I recently made a visit to my [gold] mine [in Ga.]. It has not been doing much for the last three months, and I fear I cannot rely on it, & that I shall be compelled to draw on our Alabama crop for about $1000. I hope I will be able to meet my engagements and get through with that amount. Would it not be the best to add say 30 bales to meet what I may need, to the 200 we have agreed to ship to ["him" *canceled and* "Mathew(e)s & Bonneau" *interlined*]? It would suit me, as it would enable me to draw on them from time to time as I might need. If you can conveniently make the arrangement to do so, I would be glad that you would drop them a line to that effect.

What you write, as to the proceedings of the [Martin] V[an] B[uren] party in Marengo [County], does not surprise me. They have played the same trick every where. I do not believe from all I hear, that the Baltimore convention, will really represent ["the vote of" *canceled*] ⅓d[?] of the party. The whole affair is a gross fraud, and I intend to wash my hands of it. I have written to friends [*part of a word canceled*] in Congress, that I cannot permit my name to go before the Convention, as it must now be constituted, and that I deem it my duty to inform them of the fact, in order, that they may take it into the estimate in making up their decision on the proper course to be pursued. I ["have" *canceled*] also stated, that I did not see how we, of the free trade party, could act in concert with those, whose opinions accorded much more with the Whigs, than with us, on [the] all important question of the Tariff. I also s[t]ated, that there was no time to be lost in coming to a decision, ["as to" *interlined*] what course they intended to take; and that, if they accorded with my opinion, I would stand by them however far [they] might go along, but, if not, I would rather stand alone, than to enter into a contest for power with those, who differed from us on such essential points.

I contemplate addressing a formal letter to them, stating the grounds on which I shall be compelled to act, with my reasons and if they shall have the sperit ["of raising" *canceled and* "to raise" *interlined*] the banner of free trade & the people against monopoly & political managers, we shall have a glorious cause to rise or fall by. I believe the people to be ready for such an issue. I would be glad to see an article in the [Mobile] Tribune to that effect, as early as possible. I am sorry to hear, the ["boys are" *canceled and* "children" *interlined*] have been so much indisposed. I hope they have ere this recovered. All join love to you & Margaret [Green Calhoun]. Your affectionate father, J.C. Calhoun.

ALS in ScU-SC, John C. Calhoun Papers. NOTE: On 12/12/1843, Thomas G. Clemson wrote Andrew Pickens Calhoun, thanking him for his "kind offices" in making arrangements for the purchase of "the Glover plantation" in Ala. However, Clemson stated, he would not be able to purchase until he sold his place in Edgefield District, S.C. On 12/21/1843 Clemson wrote again to A.P. Calhoun, informing him that he had no buyer for his Edgefield place and could not pursue the purchase in Ala. Clemson also stated that he wished a payment due to him to be made in January rather than in March as previously indicated. He added that there was much sickness, especially scarlet fever, at Fort Hill and in its neighborhood, and that Mr. Fredericks [John C. Calhoun's overseer] had been bitten by a rabid dog and had to have a finger amputated. (ALS's in ScCleA, Thomas Green Clemson Papers.) Calhoun's mention of "the children" in his last paragraph referred presumably to his grandsons, Duff Green Calhoun, aged four years, and John Caldwell Calhoun, aged five months.

From ALEX[ANDER] JONES

New York [City]
61 West Washington Place
Dec[embe]r 7th 1843

Dear Sir, I owe you an apology for not sooner acknowledging the receipt of two letters I had the honor to receive from you a short time since. Unfortunately for us they came to hand too late, to be introduced, in the short popular life accompanied with illustrations, published by the Calhoun central committee of this city. It appeared to be a matter of great importance to them, to publish the life if possible before the New York election about the 1st ult[imo]. The M.S. was accordingly placed in the hands of [Jonas] *Winchester* the publisher, a few days previous to the election, and when about half in type it was discovered a considerable portion of the M.S. had been stolen, and had to be rewritten in great haste, and that without previous notes to refer to. When it was ready to go to press, the proof sheets were read with haste, but all errors were carefully corrected, yet when the work appeared, we regretted to find, many errors which had been noted, and corrected, remained unchanged by the compositors—["which we sincerely regretted" *canceled*]. It was intended for circulation

591

among the mass, and so far, it has, ["as it is" *canceled*] answered a good purpose, and I have no doubt been the means of greatly augmenting your strength in this city. The whole edition of several thousand which we had engaged at 3 cents each, was struck off before your letters came to hand, otherwise the valuable and interesting additional particulars they contained would have been introduced. Should another eddition [*sic*] be ["call" *canceled*] determined on, the necessary corrections will be made, and the additional matter introduced.

All my time and energies have been absorbed for ["a month" *canceled*] two or three months endeavouring to get up and sustain our Free trade paper, notices of which you have seen ["as well as we trust" *canceled*]. As we mail the paper to your address, you can also judge of its tone and merits. I am only one of the three gentleman [*sic*] engaged in conducting it, and consequently, have had to yield many points, to their better judgement. I was in favour of placing your name at the head of the columns, which they did not deem to be necessary, as the other large and respectable party papers of the city had not done ["so" *interlined*] with regard to their favourite candidates. We have endeavoured to bring the justice and Democracy of the District system prominently before the people, and to make a strong point on free trade, or a reduction of the present Tarriff [*sic*], to a revenue standard. We have reason to believe that your strength ["at" *canceled*] with the Democratic party at the north is gradually on the increase. Your freinds [*sic*] have greatly augmented within the last three months. The Syracuse Convention, and the proceedings growing out of it, has lost Mr. Van Buren many freinds among the people, especially in this State. Our freinds here are now making an effort to cause delegates to be elected to the Baltimore convention by the District system from this State, and under encouraging prospects of success thus far.

I am extremely sorry to inform you however, that the existence of the *"Daily Gazette"* is in great jeopardy at this time, and you need not be surprized to hear of its temporary discontinuance. In the first place, we succeeded in obtaining a subscription amounting to about $2000 Dollars. In addition to which we were promised, or were led to expect a contribution from Mr. [Robert Barnwell] Rhett of $500 more. Of the two thousand, we have so far only been able to avail ourselves of about $1300 or $1400 Dollars. ["With" *canceled*] This amount was placed by Mr. [John L.H.] McCracken in the hands of a Mr. E.B. Clayton, the publisher of the New York price current, with the understanding, that he would go on and publish the *"Gazette,"* till he himself had expended as much in materials[,] house rent &C as was advanced to him to commence the publication. With the funds paid over to him he purchased a Napier printing press, ["and n" *canceled*] at $650 doll[ar]s, and new type and other materials amounting altogether to the sum of about 13 or ["$" *interlined*] 1400 dollars. After ["conducting the" *canceled*] issuing the paper two, or three weeks, he has come forward with a claim of $600 or $700 against the ["papers" *altered to* "paper"], and refuses to proceed in its publication beyond this week, unless money is raised and advanced to him to expend in carrying it forward. Mr. Clayton[,] unfortunately for us, is a whig Alderman representing the first ward in this city and withall, a very fickle[,] temporizing[,] timid man, and wholly disregards all verbal engagements. The plan on foot now, is, if possible to pay off Clayton's liabilities and for Mr. Kittell [Thomas P. Kettell?] and myself to take charge of all the materials, and raise money, and carry it forward *exclusively* on our own account. To bring this about if Mr. Rhett, ["wl"(?) *canceled*] will aid us with the $500 expected, & for which we have authorized Mr. McCracken to solicit from ["Mr. Rhett" *canceled and* "him" *interlined*], I am willing to add $500 in addition to what I have already given. And we expect a freind of Mr. Kittell[']s may be able to loan him about $1500 for the same purpose, these sums united will enable Mr. Kittell and myself to proceed in the publication of the paper for six months, when we have no fear, but it will be so firmly established as to require no further aid, and will be placed in a position ["to" *canceled*] not only [to] go on, but to refund all the means contributed to establish it. If however, we fail in making these arrangements, or old Mr. Clayton, refuses either to go on himself, or to permit ["hi" *canceled*] us to go on, in the manner stated, or we should be disappointed in raising the necessary additional means, I see no chance, but the paper must stop for a short time at all events—which should it happen I shall most sincerely regret. Of the result, you will soon learn, or within a few days at farthest.

I am sorry to trouble you with these unpleasant details; but in case the paper should ["have" *interlined*] suddenly stopped, I thought it best you should be in possession of the cause which led to it.

We were ["led" *interlined*] to trust to Clayton from the highest recommendations bestowed upon him by some of our respectable Calhoun men in the city, and sadly have we been disappointed in his course. The paper has met with as much success probably as any new paper ever started in New York for the time it has been in existence, and has continued up to the present moment to increase the number of its city subscribers, and as far as ["we" *canceled*] it has had time to become known in the country, we receive flattering accounts of its reception, and of a disposition on the part of the people to subscribe for it. Your strength in the city of New York, is more in point of numbers, than in wealth, and our free trade freinds in New York have not come forward with the liberality we had just reasons to expect. Could the paper live till time be had to canvass the Southern States for subscribers to the weekly paper, I feel confident a liberal support might be obtained.

In all the Southern States at present we have not two dozen subscribers either for the Daily or weekly. To obtain the support of our Southern freinds, it will be necessary for me to go forth among them in person, once the paper is sufficiently advanced to enable me to leave it, and let it go on while absent. Your freinds in this city till ["the in" *canceled*] the month of September or October last never had an ["organizat"(?) *canceled*] organization, when I appointed a meeting for ["or" *canceled*] arranging a central committee, when only a small number attended, some six or seven; we appointed a Chairman, Secretary &C, and proceeded to add members as delegates from the different wards; till the present *Calhoun Committee*, consist of 51—active members—composed of 3 delegates from each of the 17 wards of the city, who meet regularly on the first Tuesday of each month. And so far, our progress is onward. Wishing you every Happiness & successful prosperity through life, I have the Honor to Remain your Sincere Friend & ob[edien]t Serv[an]t, Alex[ander] Jones.

ALS in ScCleA. NOTE: In regard to the pamphlet, *Life and Character of the Hon. John C. Calhoun, with Illustrations* . . . , printed by Winchester, further information is given in a letter from Winchester to H[aym] M. Salomon of N.Y., dated 12/11/1843. Winchester complained that Calhoun's *"friends"* had failed to take delivery and pay for most of the 3,000 copies of the pamphlet he had produced. Winchester threatened to make "an exposé of the conduct of these gentlemen, so injurious to the interests of the man of their choice—and withal not exactly honest." (ALS in ScCleA.) No other documents that have been discovered shed any light on the merits of Winchester's claim or indicate how his letter to Salomon came to rest among Calhoun's papers.

From GEO[RGE] COX

Huntsville Ala., Dec[embe]r 8, 1843

Sir, Believing that you feel a lively interest in the promotion of the contemplated work, the undersigned takes the liberty of sending you, per this day's mail, the Report [*not found*] adopted at a Meeting held on the 30th Instant [*sic*]. If you can aid the undertaking by your counsel & advice, we shall be happy to receive any communication from you on this subject, & remain [*mutilation*] very respectfully, Your Ob[e]d[ien]t Serv[an]t, Geo. Cox, one of the Committee of Correspondence &c.

[Enclosure]

Huntsville, Ala., November 21st 1843

Sir, A meeting of our citizens was held on Saturday last, to adopt such preliminary measures as were thought expedient to promote a connection between the Tennessee Valley and the Atlantic seaboard, by means of a Rail Road from the Tennessee to the Coosa River; and, ultimately, by an extension of this Rail Road southwardly, a connection between the Tennessee River and the waters of the Mobile Bay. A committee was appointed by the Chairman to make a Report, embodying all the information on the subject that could be obtained, to be laid before a meeting appointed for the 30th instant, and also to invite the co-operation of all who are interested in the completion of the proposed great works.

It will afford us pleasure if you will attend the meeting on the 30th, and any aid or information relative to the subjects before the meeting will be acceptable. Very Respectfully, Your ob[edie]nt serv[an]ts, B.M. Lowe, W.J. Mastin, J[ohn?] H. Lewis, Clement C. Clay, Jr., D[aniel] B. Turner, Geo[rge] P. Beirne, J.C. Thompson, A[rchibald] E. Mills, J.J. Donegan, J.J. Fackler, Geo. Cox, Committee.

ALS with printed En in ScCleA. Note: This letter was addressed to Calhoun at "Mt. Hill, Abbeville District, South Carolina."

From R[OBERT] B[ARNWELL] RHETT

[Georgetown, D.C.] Dec[embe]r 8th 1843

My Dear Sir, I told you in my last written in great haste & disgust, that I would shortly write to you again.

For a month before Congress met I was labouring to effect an organization of all opposed to Mr. [Martin] Van Buren, and thus control the election, ["of" *canceled and* "in" *interlined*] the House of Representatives. I thought, if this was accomplished, it would shew such a decided opposition to him, as to put him out of the question for the Presidency. For this purpose I saw Mr. [George M.] Dallas [later Vice-President of the U.S.] of Philadelphia[,] the Brother in Law of

Judge [William] Wilkins [Representative from Pa.], and disclosed to him my views. The Judge fell into our policy. We were to run him for Speaker, ["if he could" *canceled*] keep out of all caucusses [*sic*] and with the Pen[n]sylvanians & ["the" *canceled and* "our" *interlined*] Southern men with the [Richard M.] Johnson men control events. Johnson who has been for some time in Washington fell into our views. Every thing went on well until [Charles J.] Ingersol[l] [Representative from Pa.] & [James] Buchanan [Senator from Pa.] arrived in Washington. The former by an active, and the Latter by a negative influence, scared the Pen[n]sylvania Delegation, and they broke ground. Our Southern friends who were trembling before at the boldness & hazards of this policy, soon gave up also. As soon as this was ascertained on Saturday [12/2] I returned home and wrote to you my last Letter informing you of this result and my determination to have nothing to do with the Caucus. Near Sun-set however [Dixon H.] Lewis sent a Gentleman with a hack[?] to me, to beg me to return to Washington, to consider with our friends some new measures. I went, and found the proposition, to force on the Caucus, the ⅔ principle of nomination, or to seceed [*sic*]. To carry this, I was strongly urged to go into the Caucus. I consented at last[,] went into the Caucus and carried it. The rest you will have learned from the Papers. We were obliged to stand to the nominations when made according to our own rule. The Georgians tried hard to make one of their Citizens Clerk. It failed and I was glad of it.

The effect of the organization of the House and indeed all late events bearing on the Presidency is undoubtedly, to make Mr. Van Buren the nominee of the Party. Indeed, if you could obtain the nomination, as I stated to you before, it would be useless in the present temper of things. The Van Buren People would defeat you as they did [Mark A.] Cooper [as gubernatorial candidate] in Georgia. And unless the ["revision of the" *interlined*] Tariff is properly supported by the Party, it is equally impossible for Mr. V[an] B[uren] to be elected. Our friends will undoubtedly defeat him. Our policy at present is, to keep things as they are. Push on our principles as to the Tariff & the organization of the Convention, and take position in future as circumstances render necessary. Strive to control events for good for the present—and as to the future to keep you in position to be head of the Party if it dissolves by defeat—or should even succeed. Time will devellop [*sic*] what we shall do, and when we shall do it. We are going to be beaten, most dissasterously [*sic*], with Mr. Van Buren; and I trust there will be [an] end of the cursed and cursing influence of the old [Andrew] Jackson Clique. On you we must rally—and you must keep yourself in position, to enable us to do so. The Whigs are sanguine & buoyant of success, I think with good reason.

And now my Dear Sir, in communicating to [you] once more the sad tydings [*sic*] of failure, I know you will appreciate the efforts of your friends, whilst you will probably regret results so far as you are concerned probably less than any of them. Let us cheer up our hearts with the remembrance and consolation, that if God regards the interests of individuals, he must much more regard the movements of nations—and that in him we are safe. To labour with energy and cheerfulness, but to submit with humility to his decrees, is the dictate of the truest philosophy as well as the requisition of our peace. You have heard of my mighty affliction in the loss of my Brother [Albert Rhett]. In him is gone the chief personal reward I looked to in my public labours—lifting up this great and virtuous mind to ["the" *canceled and "a" interlined*] sphere of usefulness congenial to its powers. God has said, "I forbid it"—and calls him home to himself. I bow I trust with a proper submission,—and may I not hope, that I shall meet you hereafter, if no more on earth, with him, in the mansions of rest. Let me implore you, my aged friend and political Father, seek God in Christ. I have found him, and you will find him also if you will seek him. Excuse me, if it is presumption, in thus speaking to you, and attribute it, to a sincere and affectionate interest in your temporal and spiritual welfare. That God will bless and visit you and yours with his salvation is the prayer of Your friend, R.B. Rhett.

P.S. Mrs. [Elizabeth Washington Burnet] Rhett who is working at the table makes me take up my pen to send to you her kindest remembrance.

ALS in ScCleA; variant PC in Jameson, ed., *Correspondence*, pp. 898–900.

From FRANCIS WHARTON

Philadelphia, Dec. 9th 1843

My dear Sir, I take the liberty to send you a number of Hunt's [Merchants'] Magazine, containing a paper on commercial legislation, which you were good enough to express a desire to see, and another on the doings of congress, from the same pen. The magazine itself has a large and increasing circulation, chiefly among the businessmen of the commercial cities, and through the medium it affords, a large portion of society, generally most inaccessible to either the theories of the economist or the schemes of the politician, is touched and worked upon. I take it, however, that a bold vindication of the principles of free trade would be looked upon by such men with suspicion. It is by exhibiting the *working* of the protection leaven in its different bearings, by shewing the infamous log-rolling by which the various tariffs have been pushed through, and the abominable oppression in which they have resulted, that the work can be best effected. We have only to speak history in order to shew the whole system in its native deformity. It is my hope that by the clues which abler and older heads may afford me, I may be of some humble use in thus assisting the developement of those great principles both of trade & banking ["of" *canceled*] which it has been your lot to revive and apply. The number I send you now is much more unsatisfactory than I could have wished, not only from the distance of the time, but from the barrenness of the subject. There was one great object to make, & that was to justify the south for the course it took [in 1816] in relation to the passage of the [tariff] bill. If that object is met, I shall be for the present fully satisfied. ["If" *canceled and* "As soon as" *interlined*] my professional occupations give me ["some" *canceled*] margin for the work, I propose to take up the bill of 1828, to which you were kind enough to allude in your letter. If you can open to me any fresh materials in that connection, you will continue to confer on me very great obligations.

I have just sent on to the Democratic Review, a review of your speeches, lately published by Harper. It will comprise about ["thirty" *canceled and* "20" *interlined*] pages of print, and pretends to be a criticism of the *literary* merits of [*one word canceled and* "arguments" *interlined*] which I believe to be the most remarkable of modern times. I was obliged, however, on account of the *Catholic* character of the review, to steer clear of the presidential question, but from the tone of impartiality which is assumed in relation to that great contest, it may be that the positions I assumed will have more weight than if they were professedly directed to a partizan object. I shall make bold to send you the review when published, in the hope that it may give you an half hour's amusement.

If there is any other way in which my pen may be useful to the great cause of which you are the head, you will have only to command me. I remain with great respect Yours truly, Francis Wharton.

ALS in ScCleA. NOTE: Wharton's review of the *Speeches of John C. Calhoun* appeared anonymously, under the title "Mr. Calhoun's Parliamentary Eloquence," in the *United States Magazine and Democratic Review*, vol. XIV, no. 68 (February, 1844), pp. 111–130.

From V[IRGIL] MAXCY

Washington, 10th Dec[embe]r 1843
My dear Sir, I wrote the enclosed letter [to you dated 12/3] a few days ago, but missing the hour of departure of the mail from West River, I brought it over here and have concluded to send it to you. If I write now under feelings of less discouragement, I do it under those of greater mortification from the events, that have taken place here. You have no doubt received various accounts of them from your friends here, who participated in them. I am glad I did not get here till after the final caucus, in which your flag, tho' not struck down, as represented by the correspondent of the Richmond Enquirer, was nevertheless not held up by your friends, in defiance of the violent gale that was blowing, with the unflinching firmness it ought to have been, ["I" *changed to* "for"; "have(?) sooner been here" *canceled and* "fear" *interlined*] as I could not have changed the current of things, my excitement might have led me into indiscretions, that might have excited the resentment and ill-feelings of some of our friends without doing any good, as my private station would have given me neither the right nor the opportunity at the suitable moment to interfere or remonstrate.

I have now been here four days and have been endeavouring amidst conflicting accounts, (from the desire of those who participated in the movements here to cast blame from themselves upon others,) to find out the truth, which I believe is as nearly as follows.

Mr. [Robert Barnwell] Rhett, as he, no doubt, has informed you, had taken a journey to Philadelphia & New York partly with a view to form a coalition among the friends of the candidates for nomination opposed to Mr. [Martin] Van Buren for the purpose of making Mr. [William] Wilkins Speaker [of the House of Representatives], who I understand without hesitation gave the necessary pledges in regard to Committees, the 23rd rule &c. Rhett thought he had succeeded in forming a combination sufficiently strong, with the aid of the whigs to elect Wilkins and to refuse to go into caucus. Among the allies were the Pennsylvania delegation & some of [Richard M.] Johnson[']s friends. If all had remained firm, Wilkins would have been elected, but it is said that [James] Buchanan [Senator from Pa.] after his arrival had not firmness enough to keep his friends up to the sticking point. Your friends then, I understand yielded so far, as to go into the caucus in the expectation of being able to prevent the election of the Van Buren Speaker by requiring ⅔rds of the number to effect a nomination. The Van Buren men unexpectedly agreed to this proposition and obtained the majority required on the first vote—thro' the aid, as Gen. [Alexander O.] Anderson [former Senator from Tenn.] who is here informed me, of three votes from your men, who from weakness dreamed of *conciliation* ["of the V(an) B(uren) men" *interlined*] to the last. Even our friend [Dixon H.] Lewis is charged with want of firmness in resisting the torrent and did not, as he might have ["kept" *canceled and* "done, keep" *interlined*] one or two of his delegation straight. Mr. [William W.] Payne [Representative from Ala.] is the only name I recollect of the three, except Mr. [Archibald H.] Arrington, [Representative] of No[rth] Carolina, who are said to have voted for [John W.] Jones [Representative from Va., for Speaker]. It was now [*one word canceled*] too late to retrieve the false step of going into Caucus at all, and all the officers fixed on by the V[an] B[uren] men were elected.

Some indiscreet remarks by Mr. [James E.] Belser, one of your friends from Alabama, to the effect that "constituted as the national convention would be Mr. Calhoun's friends had not the slightest expectation of a nomination" have been the ground of the false representation by the correspondent of the Richmond Enquirer.

The result of all has been to place you in a false position and make the impression on the public, that you were given up as a Candidate and, that your friends were disposed to fall in with the current in favor of V[an] B[uren]. One or two only, I am told, are suspected of a disposition to fall down & worship Moloch but the rest are deeply mortified at the course of events and now would be glad, if they had taken a different stand in the beginning. You will see from the [Washington] Spectator the turn which Rhett is endeavoring to give of the matter with a view to rectify public opinion in regard not only yourself but of your friends' disposition to give way to the violence & despotism of the Albany politicians. I have given it as my opinion, that something more was necessary than newspaper declarations, and that some of those known to possess your confidence should come out and in their own names & contradict the false representations of surrender on the part of your friends or that there should be a meeting of your friends & an expression of opinion given by it, which should relieve you from the false position in which they have placed you. Whether any thing will be done or not I cannot even give an opinion, but I am rather disposed to think, that some occasion, that may arise in some of the proceedings of congress will be taken to set public opinion right. At first I was of opinion that you ought to come out in proper person and avow your opinions on the subject of a Convention, constituted as it evidently will be and the impossibility of your even permitting your name to be placed before it or giving in any way your sanction to the protective doctrines of the Syracuse convention ["or their mode of forming a national convention" *interlined*]. I now think if this course had been firmly taken before the assembling of congress it would have been best, as to do it now *immediately* would be attributed to the recent events. But my opinion now is that it would be best to wait until the [John Tyler] Administration are prepared to make a communication to Congress on the subject of Texas, which Mr. [Abel P.] Upshur thinks will be in about three weeks—and then come out on all these grounds together.

With this last gentleman I have had several free & most confidential communications, with permission however to communicate what I please to you. These communications have revived my hopes and put me in better spirits, than when I wrote the enclosed letter. He, as well as all your friends, with whom I have conversed are of opinion, that convention nomination will still have such force, even in the Southern States as to preclude the hope, that a rally can be made against Mr. V[an] B[uren] on the anti-tariff protective principle alone, there are so many even of Southern men, who yield to the doctrine of discrimination ["for incidental protection" *interlined*] being admitted into a revenue Tariff. It is necessary therefore to have some more exciting topic connected with it and this will be the annexation of Texas.

In this opinion I concur, & think that your manifesto, whenever it shall come out, should embrace the three topics of Convention, Tariff & Texas.

Mr. Upshur informs ["me" *interlined*] in the strictest confidence however except to you, that the terms of a treaty between him & the Texan minister [Isaac Van Zandt] have already been agreed on & written out, & that the latter only waits for instructions from President [Samuel] Houston, which are expected in two or three weeks. But some of the suspicions of the treachery of this Houston, which you have seen circulated in the newspapers, ["are" *canceled and* "it is" *interlined*] feared, have some foundation and instructions may possibly be refused—in which case Mr. U[pshur] thinks the Texan Minister, convinced as he is of the almost unanimous desire of the people of Texas to come into the Union, may be induced to sign a treaty ["without instructions" *interlined*] and go home & throw himself on the protection of the People of Texas. The President [John Tyler] is ["so" *canceled*] resolved, that he will communicate such a treaty to the Congress, & if the minister has not firmness to sign, he will adopt some other mode of bringing the matter before Congress. Mr. Upshur is of opinion, that ["it"*and a partial word canceled*] this is the only matter, that will take sufficient hold of the feelings of the South, to rally it on a Southern candidate and weaken [Henry] Clay & Van Buren so much there as to bring the election into the House [of Representatives], where the Southern States would not dare to vote for Mr. V[an] B[uren] or C[lay]. This is the ["effect" *canceled and* "result" *interlined*] I alluded too [*sic;* "&" *canceled and* "as" *interlined*] inspiring the only hope I now had in the latter part of the enclosed letter. The President has some hopes, that he may become that Southern Candidate. But Mr. U[pshur] considers you as the only one, that can be taken up & with a view to your availing yourself of the first moment, after the Executive communication to Congress on Texas, to place before the public your views on the question, that all, who concur with you, may at once rally upon you, you ought at once to write a letter as if in answer to one from myself making inquiries of you as to your opinions on the subject, in case ["the subject" *canceled and* "it" *interlined*] should come up, which letter I should at once publish after the communication by the Executive should be made—for which purpose he would write me as to the time of coming over to Washington to have the letter published.

I beg to say, that I mention my own name as the person to be written ["to" *interlined*], simply because Mr. Upshur did, tho' I think it would be better to choose some more conspicuous person for your correspondent. I will only add, that if you choose to address it to me, I beg you to believe I shall fear no consequence, ["from" *canceled*] of proscription in consequence of my name being identified with this subject as well as the others I have above suggested to you to join with them—as it is possible may be the case with some of your more important ["& more ambitious" *interlined*] friends, who I have heard with grief & mortification have yielded to the idea of your running on the ticket with V[an] B[uren] as *Vice President*, in order to secure the successor-ship! ! ! The first wish of my heart is to see you President but ["with the" *canceled*] I would rather see you lose a dozen Presidencies, were it possible, than to see the high honors of your great & pure name brought down so low and tarnished by such a polluting association. No; the more bold and lofty the ground you take the better & the better chance you will have [of] forming a rallying point in better times for the virtue of the country.

I had a number of other things to say, but the time has come for my going to the rail road by which I go to Annapolis this evening on my way home. General Anderson is here, who concurs in all my views

& would have written to you but from an injury to his hand which disables him from doing it.

With kindest regards, with those of my daughter Mrs. [Mary Galloway Maxcy] Markoe to Mrs. [Floride Colhoun] Calhoun & yourself, I remain faithfully yours, V. Maxcy.

ALS in ScCleA; variant PC in Jameson, ed., *Correspondence*, pp. 900–904.

From R[obert] B[arnwell] Rhett

Dec[embe]r 9th [*sic*; 10th?] 1843

My Dear Sir, I enclose you at the request of Mr. [William A.] Harris ["a former member of Congress" *interlined*; from Va.] a Letter he has written to me.

The organization of the Committees [of the House of Representatives], shew[s] that we are to be put aside & the Pen[n]sylvanians to be conciliated. From the Committee of Ways & Means, I expect nothing ["as to the Tariff" *interlined*]. [George] McDuffie [Senator from S.C.] will soon move in the Senate—where at present alone efficient movement can be made.

Mrs. [Elizabeth Washington Burnet] Rhett joins me in her warmest remembrance. Yours Dear Sir, R.B. Rhett.

[Enclosure]

W[illiam] A. Harris to R[obert] Barnwell Rhett

Washington, 10 Dec[embe]r 1843

My dear Sir: I should esteem myself very deficient in a proper appreciation of your kindness, if I did not, before I leave the City, express to you my very sincere and very grateful ["sense" *canceled and* "feelings," *interlined*] for your friendly intentions towards me, in the late election of Clerk of the House [of Representatives]. And, although my hopes were not crowned with success, it increases, if possible, my abiding sense of your goodness, and imposes and [*sic*] additional obligation upon me to acknowledge it.

I avail myself of the occasion also, to say a word or two upon another subject, in the magnitude and importance of which, my own inconsiderable personal affairs, are swallowed up and lost. The developments of the last few months, have left us no room to hope, that that matchless statesman and incomparable man, Mr. Calhoun, can receive the nomination for the presidency. Mr. [Martin] Van Buren is carried along by the force of circumstances, as inexorable and as resistless as fate, and, so far as we are permitted to judge, will as certainly be nominated by the Baltimore Convention, as that body meets. What then? Can he be elected? I believe that the most sanguine of his friends, consider his success at least doubtful; but, for myself, I look upon his defeat as almost certain. The truth is, that although he may receive the nomination, yet he cannot, in my opinion be elected without the aid of Mr. Calhoun. I do not mean the mere acquiescence, or even the willing cooperation of Mr. Calhoun's friends in that nomination; but the moral influence of his own great name and services, must be thrown into Mr. Van Buren's scale, to give it sure and effective preponderance. How shall this be done? The only conceivable way that this can be achieved, as I apprehend, will be to place Mr. Calhoun on the ticket with Mr. Van Buren, as vice president. I have suggested this thing within the last six weeks, repeatedly amongst the people of the country, and it was hailed on all occasions by the most enthusiastic acclamation.

The spontaneous declaration was instantly made, that it would not only secure the complete success of the democratic ticket now, but that it would as certainly secure Mr. Calhoun's election at the end of four years, with the most hearty and cordial approbation of the party.

Most justly *entitled* as he is, in the estimation of many—and certainly *meriting* in the opinions of all, the chief honors of the republic, yet in the present posture of affairs, to make this noble self sacrifice, and to forego his claims to the first, and for the sake of harmonizing his party and ensuring its success, to take the second place, would be such a glorious example of devoted patriotism, as would call forth the plaudits and the enduring gratitude of the whole party. It would forever put to flight too, the unjust aspersion, that his impatient ambition, failing of its gratification, would seek to destroy his own party. It would in fact, as I have before said, not only secure our complete success in '44, but, would as certainly and inevitably insure his own triumphant elevation to the presidential chair in 1848. His just claims, arising from his long services, his unequalled ability, his pure and elevated political morality, and spotless character, are admitted by all, and his pride for a moment may revolt at being placed in the position indicated; yet, when the consequences of consent or refusal, will almost inevitably be such as I have described, I cannot but hope, that an elevated patriotism will swallow up every feeling of repugnance and pride. My humble counsels, I know, can exercise no influence upon him. You and others, however, may well approach him on this subject. He will not resist your solicitations. But, this I will say, that if unmixed servitude on my part, for a period of time, equal

604

to that expended by Jacob for both of his wives, would induce him to take this course and insure his success hereafter, most cheerfully and willingly would I undergo it. The bare *hope* that I shall yet see him advanced to a station, upon which his brilliant powers would shed such unfading honors, constantly serves to stimulate and impel me in my prudent exertion, to accomplish that glorious result. I beg your serious consideration of this matter. It is the prudent course—it is the safe course—and, it is almost the only proper or successful course, now left us. If we pursue it, success is certain—nothing can resist us. If we do not form such a ticket, we are divided—beaten—struck down and scattered, for many years to come.

I trust to God that he will not be inattentive to the suggestions of even his humblest friends. It is true, that our views may be limited—our eyes are near the ground; but ["it" *interlined*] may be for that very reason, that we may see things more plainly than those whose mental vision is raised to things of a more extended range and of greater elevation. Let this position then, be carefully and well considered, and if possible, adopted. I am, most truly and sincerely, Y[ou]r friend [and] ob[edient] Ser[van]t, W.A. Harris.

ALS with En in ScCleA. NOTE: Rhett appears to have erroneously dated his letter, since its En is dated a day later. Rhett's letter was postmarked on 12/13.

From THOMAS W. GILMER,
[Representative from Va.]

Washington, Dec: 13, 1843
My Dear Sir, At the instance of a mutual friend I venture to drop you a line, not to speak of the chances, calculations & chapter of accidents of a presidential election—(for these I have very little appetite)—but to remind you of a conversation we had nearly a year since on a subject, which as I then predicted, is beginning to attract general & deserved attention. I allude to the annexation of Texas to our Union. I have not doubted for some time that this question would soon assume a practical shape & that its results would ultimately ["(if not immediately)" *interlined*] enure to the peace, perman[en]ce & prosperity of the Union. If the question were free from some prejudices (which by the way apply with equal force to a portion of the Union as it is) it would not be approached for a moment as one of only local importance. It is indeed a great American question & involves the

["first" *interlined*] principle of American independence. The efforts of European powers which have been or may be made to establish an influence in Texas prejudicial to our commercial interests & ["free" *canceled and* "republican" *interlined*] institutions, will probably aid in giving this question a national aspect ["somewhat" *interlined*] sooner than could be hoped from its intrinsic merits. You remember I asked you last winter to turn your mind to this subject in all its bearings and to be ready to meet it. As a candidate for public favor, I would not have you or any other to be committed on this question in advance. I do not therefore approach you as one of those now in the public eye as candidates for the chief magistracy, but as an illustrious citizen whose opinions would ["in fact" *canceled*] derive no additional force from any station, ["and which" *canceled and* "as" *interlined*] I believe ["they" *interlined*] would not be influenced by ["any" *canceled and* "a" *interlined*] desire to obtain it. I have no doubt you *have* bestowed much reflection on this particular subject. While I am not at liberty, (nor am I informed) ["indeed)" *canceled*] to speak of the precise state of this question at present, I will say to you that negotiations have been commenced, the object of which is to annex Texas to the Union. On a question of such magnitude, it is not meet, that a voice which for more than thirty years has been heard with so much interest on all public questions, should be silent. I will esteem it a favor ["& so will many others" *interlined*] if you will give us the benefit of your counsels now. They shall be regarded as confidential if you chuse [*sic*], or otherwise. You are familiar with the negotiations, correspondence &c. between our gover[n]ment and Spain from 1805 to 1819 with regard to the boundaries of Louisiana ["as claimed by us" *canceled*] under the treaty with France. The effect of annexation on the interests (domestic & foreign) of our country, however, is the point to which public attention will be chiefly directed. The test will be practically applied, whether the compromises of the constitution are to be regarded, or the union endangered by violating rights secured under the compact of 1787.

Excuse this liberty, I beg you, and allow me to subscribe myself with sincere esteem & very high consideration your friend &c, Thomas W. Gilmer.

ALS (retained copy) in ViW, Tyler Family Papers; PC in Lyon G. Tyler, *Letters and Times of the Tylers*, 3:130–132; variant PC in Jameson, ed., *Correspondence*, pp. 904–906. NOTE: Jameson apparently transcribed this letter from the now missing recipient's copy.

From R[OBERT] M. T. HUNTER

L[l]oyds, Essex [County, Va.,] Dec[embe]r 13th 1843
My dear Sir, I am a delinquent in relation to your last letter, not from negligence or indifference but because I was dispirited. Everything seemed to have taken so untoward ["a" *interlined*] direction, and the course of events was so unpropitious for the country that I had no heart to take the pen when of necessity some reference must be made to circumstances so disagreeable. In this state I have had no serious hopes since the convention last March in which our friends were so completely outmanaged. Your apprehensions in relation to the clubs in this State were not unfounded but alas we can do little towards turning the tide. What might have been done was not done in time.

In the East our friends have been sadly deceived if they believed what they wrote to me. If there had been more union between the friends of [James] Buchanan[,] [Richard M.] Johnson[,] [Lewis] Cass and ourselves much more might have been done. As it is I see nothing to hope except from vigorous and skil[l]ful action from our friends in Congress, or else from a more determined spirit in the South than it will exhibit. The section which pursues its object with the strongest will, must succeed and that section just now is the West. In this quality I fear the South now stands last. The majority feeling in the free States has been roused against us ["in the free States" *canceled*] on the Rh[ode] Island and other questions. The sectional feeling of the west on the Oregon question and our principles does not permit us to offer douceurs in the way of appropriations to harbors and rivers. All this makes it the more important that we should draw the lines upon States right and republican principles that we may at least rally all who have a vital interest in them.

But our friends in Congress will I trust consider all these things and take whatever course is best. I could almost wish that you were back again. But for your own fame it is perhaps better as it is. Yours faithfully, R.M.T. Hunter.

ALS in ScCleA.

From P[ETER] HAGNER,
[Third Auditor of the Treasury]

Washington, Dec. 14, 1843

Dear Sir, I received on yesterday your letter of the 3d Inst[ant] with its inclosure, and as you therein request have made the necessary inquiry at the appropriate office (The Register of the Treasury) as to any credits standing to the account of John E[wing] Colhoun [Sr.] & S[amuel] B. Colhoun and have been informed that there is standing to the credit of the former the Sum of 134^{22}⁄$_{100}$ & to the latter 57^{86}⁄$_{100}$ both being for unclaimed Interest on the old funded debt. These I presume to be the credits referred to by your Correspondent, tho' not agreeing in amount. Payment will be made at the Treasury to the legal representatives of the deceased—if it be most convenient to establish by letters of administration[,] that course might be adopted & duly authenticated transcripts forwarded with directions how the amount is to be transmitted. It can be remitted direct to the Administrator or other legal representative by the Treasurer of the United States on being so instructed. I will with pleasure attend to the business for you if you desire it. The letter [of Charles Whittelsey] is returned inclosed. With kind rem[em]brances to Mrs. C[alhoun] in which I am joined by Mrs. [Frances Randall] H[agner,] I remain Very respectfully D[ea]r Sir yours, P. Hagner.

ALS in ScCleA.

From V[IRGIL] MAXCY

Tulip Hill, West River [Md.,] 14 Dec. 1843

My dear Sir, Yours of the 5th is just received. You will perceive from a letter written [by me] a few days ago [on 12/10] from Washington, that I recommended essentially the same course as the one on which you ask my opinion—the only difference ["is that" *interlined*] in addition to your taking ground on the formation of the convention & the tariff you ["should" *interlined*] join with them the Texas question, to ["do" *interlined*] which with most effect would require you to wait till the Executive [John Tyler] shall take the initiative by a communication to Congress. This I concluded from my conversation with Mr. [Abel P.] Upshur he would probably make in the course of a month. Some of your friends at Washington I fear would hesitate at taking issue with Mr. [Martin] V[an] B[uren] & Mr. [Henry] Clay on what they consider your extreme notions on the subject of a Tariff alone, and for that reason to prevent the possibility of a schism ["I thou" *canceled*] or any faltering in the ranks it seemed to me expedient to strengthen your position and your hold on them by the addition of the Texas question. This course would I think strengthen you throughout the South, where I should hope there would be no division on the Texas question tho' on the subject of a protective tariff, there are still some, who ["think that" *canceled and* "feel a toleration for" *interlined*] discrimination, not only for revenue, but for the purpose of incidental protection or *encouragement* of manufactures. I think it would be right that you should prepare your paper immediately so as to have it ready to be published immediately after the President shall make his communication & address it to your friends in Congress instead of to me as suggested by Mr. Upshur.

I think moreover, that it would be right for you to prepare the paper you thought of & suggested to me, showing that Mr. V[an] B[uren] has done more than Mr. Clay to injure & corrupt the sentiments of the Republican party, but this paper I do not think should be published under your signature, as in such case, it would be considered to originate in personal motives & dislike.

I will attend to your wishes in respect to the transmission of a copy of your Speeches [abroad] to Messrs. [William Pleydell] Bouverie, [Richard] *Cobden* & [John] M[a]cGregor. I have already sent two copies to [Henry] Wheaton [U.S. Minister to Prussia] & one to Mr. [Nassau William] Senior with a letter a copy of which I enclose. I directed three others to be sent to General [Duff] Green, but left it optional with Mr. Upshur to send them or not according to the information he should receive by the mail of the steamer which has just come from England as to his return. I have just received a note from Mr. Upshur which renders it probable he [Green] is on the ocean on his way home. When he arrived [*sic*] I will get him to write to some of his friends to write a review of it & I asked Wheaton to do it in French or get some Parisian to do it. In the copies I sent I cut out the old Title & Advertisement & pasted on it the new. All had your Life in them.

Mrs. M[axcy] joins in kindes[t] remembrances to Mrs. [Floride Colhoun] C[alhoun] & yourself. Faithfully yours, V. Maxcy.

[Enclosure]

V[irgil] Maxcy to [Nassau William] Senior, "Copy"

Tulip Hill[,] West River [Md.]

My dear Sir, Thro' the kindness of the Secretary of State [Abel P.

Upshur] I am enabled to send you, in his despatch bag to our Minister, a Volume, containing a Sketch of the Life and a selection of the Speeches and other writings of Mr. Calhoun, which I beg you to accept.

Mr. Calhoun is the most profound and philosophical Statesman we have, [Daniel] Webster not excepted. He is the Head of the Republican or State rights as Mr. Webster is of the Federal or consolidation or, as now called, Whig School—which latter term, by a strange fortune, means here precisely the reverse of its import in England and indicates the class of our politicians opposed to popular doctrines.

I found but few persons in Europe, who had a right conception of the nature of our complex political system, on the relative powers of which, between the State & federal governments is founded the distinction of our parties. As the best commentary on them by a deep original thinker I can confidently recommend many of the speeches in this book, while others, not connected with Constitutional Law, present in the clearest and strongest light the principles and policy of the Republican Party on subjects, deeply interesting to Englishmen. The members of this party are advocates of free trade both from convictions of ["policy" *canceled*] expediency and constitutional obligation. Some few American Books are now, I believe, considered worth reading on your side of the water. Of the whole of them I unhesitatingly & confidently pronounce this the most worthy not only of perusal but of study by an enlightened foreign Statesman, desirous of understanding the true nature and Spirit of the institutions which have been adopted by a large portion of the Anglo-Saxon family.

If your opinions on the merits of this publication after a careful perusal correspond at all with mine, I think you will deem it worthy of notice in the Edinburgh or Westminster Review. Any Review ["of it" *interlined*] taken from either of these periodicals would now circulate universally throughout the United States amongst all parties and while it would make the name of the Reviewer familiar to all the intelligent and reading class of our country would contribute largely and usefully to the propagation of the doctrines, which ought to govern the commercial relations between England & our Union.

I know no one in England so capable of comprehending the profound views of political Philosophy, which abound in Mr. Calhoun's Speeches, so well as yourself and it would give him, who is well acquainted with your character, reputation & writings, as well as his friends high gratification, if you would undertake the task above-suggested and in case this would not suit your convenience or inclination, if you would induce some one of your friends to engage in it.

Mrs. Maxcy, whose health is better than it was in Europe, and my daughter Mrs. [Mary Galloway Maxcy] Markoe, both of whom have a lively recollection of the kind civil[it]ies of Mrs. Senior & yourself desire to join me in cordial remembrances to you both. With high respect & esteem I am dear Sir most faithfully Y[ou]rs, V. Maxcy.

ALS with En in ScCleA; PEx of ALS in Boucher and Brooks, eds., *Correspondence*, pp. 192–193. NOTE: This letter was postmarked in Washington and was franked by R[obert] B[arnwell] Rhett. Nassau William Senior (1790–1864) was a noted British economist and writer. No review by Senior of Calhoun's *Life* or *Speeches* has been found.

From W[ILLIA]M W. WILLIAMS

Aiken [S.C.,] December 16th 1843
Dear Sir, I have once more concluded to write you on the subject of my claim before Congress. I have just written to R[obert] B. R[h]ett requesting him to have the goodness to renew my peti[ti]on and stated to him that I should ask the favour of you to give ["your" *interlined*] opinion and such information as you was in possession of. I therefore hope if it is not an intrusion on your time and convenience that you, would drop him a few lines stating such facts and circumstances as may come under your knowledge and urging his assistance in my ["half" *altered to* "behalf"], also if agreeable that ["you would" *interlined*] write the Hon[ora]ble George McDuffey [*sic*] giving him simmaler [*sic*] information and directions and requesting his Co-opperation [*sic*] in getting my claim passed. Your attention to the matter will Confer an other strong obligation on your friend and humble Servant, Wm. W. Williams.

[P.S.] Don[e] in great haste.

ALS in ScCleA. NOTE: For Williams's claim, based on his father's Revolutionary War services, see *The Papers of John C. Calhoun*, 14:122 and 15:395.

From S[AMUEL] A. ANDREWS

Goldsboro, N.C., Dec. 19 [1843]

D[ea]r Sir, I did myself the honor to report to you the position of political parties in our State as I supposed them to exist at our August elections. I now in the same spirit offer my observation on our present state. The last week I spent in Raleigh having the honor to be selected as one of the Deligates [*sic*] to represent this county (Wayne) in our Democratic State Convention.

The convention was organized on Thursday by the appointment of Louis D. Henry as President. The committee who reported the Officers for the convention consisted of 9[,] 1 from each Congressional District. 5 were the decided friends of Mr. Calhoun[,] 1 gave a preference to Col. [Richard M.] Johnson & 3 were for [*sic*; *illegible word altered to* "friends"] to the renomination of Mr. [Martin] Van B[uren]. Mr. Henry you are aware was the democratic candidate for Gov. in our last election. He is supposed to be in favor of a renomination of Mr. Van B[uren]. Yet in the spirit of conciliation & kindness the committee reported & he was re[ceive]d as the Pres[iden]t of the convention. 2 friends of Mr. Calhoun were reported for Vice [presidents] & 1 Johnson man & 1 Van B[uren]. In making the great committee for business the presiding officer consulted the Vice Presidents & that committee was constituted thus[:] 11 for Mr. Calhoun—6 for Mr. Van B[uren] & 1 for Col. Johnson. There was little difference of oppinion [*sic*] on the committee & after a free discussion & interchange of opinions they united in perfect harmony in the Report a copy of which I have the honor herewith to transmit (see [the Raleigh] Standard sent by to day[']s mail).

You will perceive sir that to preserve harmony & retain our full force every vote being needed in this State—your friends have conceded much—possibly *too much*—but we hope our course will lead to beneficial results.

The ["Candidate" *canceled*] nominee for Gov. [Michael Hoke] is a devoted friend to Mr. Calhoun & his opinions were freely canvassed in our body—& no man—even the most impracti[ca]ble but re[ceive]d the nomination with heartfelt Joy. Of Mr. [Charles] Fisher[,] our first deligate to Baltimore I need say nothing[;] his long tried & fervent affection for Mr. Calhoun is known to every man in our State. Of Mr. Henry our 2nd deligate I *will* say nothing. He boasts no man knows his preference—but every *man* considers him a Van Buren *man*. His address on taking the chair was admirable, being entirely in defense or support of ["what" *canceled*] democratic principles. The famous motto on the Calhoun flag was his text, & gloriously did he discourse it.

The convention was thought to [be] the largest (business) convention ever assembled in our State. Perfect kindness & unanimity existed throughout & we separated in better spirits & confidence than has existed among us in many years.

A different course would have given us another vote (probably) in Baltimore—but would have precluded all possibility [*one word canceled and "of" interlined*] success in the election—be the nominee *who* he may.

In my communication of 1st[?] August I freely gave oppinions connected with the course of some leading men *calling* themselves democrats which endangered the election of every member of Congress running from a Calhoun district. My recent observations justify ["my" *canceled*] the assertions I then made. And however humiliating the confession—truth obliges me to say your friends are compelled to yeild [*sic*] to a *minority* or forego every prospect of success.

My appology [*sic*] for addressing you Sir in the familiar manner I have done is contained in my former letter—trusting you will forgive many faults in a devoted friend to *you* & your principles. S.A. Andrews.

ALS in ScCleA; PC in Boucher and Brooks, eds., *Correspondence*, pp. 193–194. NOTE: The proceedings of the N.C. State Democratic Convention are described in the Raleigh, N.C., *North Carolina Standard*, December 20, 1843 (weekly edition).

From R[OBERT] M. T. HUNTER, "(Private)"

L[l]oyds, Essex [County, Va.,] Dec[embe]r 19th 1843
My dear Sir, Since my last to you I have learned from Washington ["through an" *canceled*] from a *source entirely reliable*, that a Treaty for the annexation of Texas will probably be submitted to the Senate this winter. Nothing but [Samuel] Houston[']s refusal can prevent it (as I am informed) and it is supposed that he *dare* not *refuse*. He will probably impose the condition upon the Texian minister that there shall be a probability of its ratification in our Senate. [Isaac] Van Zandt[,] the present representative of Texas in Washington[,] is anxious for the treaty and will probably be easy to satisfy that there is a chance for its ratification. These things I was requested to com-

municate to you concealing the name of my author[?] which is entirely unnecessary as you will readily guess it. It is thought to be a matter of great importance by the administration, as I suppose it is, to do all that is possible to secure the Senate. Of the effects of such a measure both as to principles and men you will be better able to judge than I can be. It will be something if we can really make an issue with the antislavery feeling and arouse the public mind to its importance. Can this be done? Will not the Presidential question absorb it and will not [Thomas] Ritchie et id omne genus do all that they can to give the question the "go by" and divert public attention from it? If it could be made one of the real issues of the day I think I foresee many consequences to flow from it which will be interesting to you in more than the public point of view. Would it not force you again ["into public life in some" *canceled*] upon the theatre of public action[,] let the question terminate as it might[?] Could the South look to any other man to conduct it through such a crisis?

I learn orally that the Ritchie wing of the Democracy affect to be anxious for you to be placed on the [Martin] V[an] B[uren] ticket as Vice President. Some of their papers hint at the same thing. Perhaps I ought not to make any conjectures as to the meaning of all this. I am too remote from the active theatre of public affairs to form reliable opinions, but I suspect that there is no friendly design in these *intimations*. [Thomas H.] Benton and [Silas] Wright would neither be willing to see you V[ice-]P[resident] and Ritchie would not move against their wishes. He would not elect you if you really desired it, (which I am far from presuming to be the case) if he could in any other manner secure V[an] B[uren]. The danger I fear is to bring down upon you the jealousies of the other aspirants [Richard M.] Johnson[,] [James] Buchanan[,] [Lewis] Cass[,] [James K.] *Polk* &c &c and to prevent any combination between their friends and yours. The V[an] B[uren] men begin to be afraid that they have pushed things too far in the recent organization. Speaker[,] printer[,] clerk and even doorkeeper—all[,] all have they grasped and now frightened at the prospect of reaction they wish to soothe your friends by an act of pretended friendship which will at the time render all the candidates for the V[ice-]Presidency and all the expectants of the Presidency after the next term more jealous of you than of V[an] B[uren]. They have coquetted with Polk until they have killed him and now they strike at higher game. Perhaps after all these suspicions are too refined. It may be that they really desire such a combination to secure V[an] B[uren]'s reelection but I doubt them.

The course of things in Washington has dispirited our friends at a distance very much. I have been asked the reason but having heard nothing from [Dixon H.] Lewis or [Robert Barnwell] Rhett, ["beyond" *canceled*] since the commencement of the session I have nothing to give but surmises. I suppose that the friends of Buchanan and Johnson being unwilling to oppose the majority of the party in any thing our friends thought it useless and imprudent to make an unavailing contest, and thus drew down upon themselves the whole odium of the division.

And yet as it is I fear their course has driven all the timid and wavering of our friends into the arms of Van Buren.

Unless some explosion should take place in Congress to arouse the South I fear that V[an] B[uren] will get the nomination from a convention constituted on his own terms and I suppose the resistance which he will experience in the party will be rather passive than active. Such seems to me to be the present tendency of events. In this view of the case I look to the probable ["future" *interlined*] course of public affairs with deep despondency. I have struggled ["I believe" *canceled*] for the South and ["for what I believed to be" *interlined*] the true interests of my native State not long it is true but through the best years of my life and I have had an uphill time of it even at home. I have not regarded the difficulties on my own account but it is a source of the deepest mortification to me to see ["the" *interlined*] hands into which Virginia is about to fall.

I hope that your contemplated work [on principles of government] goes bravely on and I assure you that I contemplate with the greatest pleasure the prospect of such a monument as I hope it will rear to your fame. Yours truly, R.M.T. Hunter.

[P.S.] The antislavery men in Washington are supposed to be in entire ignorance of this move in relation to Texas. Nor are there more than two men in Congress informed of the real state of the case. I mention these facts to you that you may be guarded in your communications to your friends. The administration is anxious (I am informed) that nothing should be known of the movement in Washington until the Treaty is made.

ALS in ScCleA; variant PC in Jameson, ed., *Correspondence*, pp. 906–908. NOTE: The unnamed person in Washington who had communicated with Hunter about the likely treaty with the Texas Republic was very possibly Secretary of State Abel P. Upshur.

From F[RANCIS] W. PICKENS

Edgewood, 20 Dece[mbe]r 1843

My dear Sir, I suppose you have been kept regularly informed of every thing that has taken place both [in the S.C. General Assembly] at Columbia & Washington. I found things not exactly right on the Texas question. [Benjamin F.] Hunt the chairman of the comm[ittee in Columbia] was very wrong. But I found a majority of the comm[ittee] sound. Many were covering[?] themselves under the former views of [George] McDuffie, and from what I heard I fear he is still wrong. I have quit writing to him as he appeared so indifferent.

I think our friends managed with but little tact at the opening of Congress. I have just heard that the Ala. Convention at Tuscaloosa nominated [Martin] V[an] B[uren] by a majority of 17 votes. This is what I expected & so wrote you this Fall. The people have not yet been scourged enough to learn wisdom. My impression is that if V[an] B[uren] is run he cannot be elected without great difficulty, & [Henry] Clay may succeed. If so you will command the Future—if your friends pursue a dignified and [one word or partial word canceled] wise course. I saw Sturges the defeated candidate for Clerk at Charleston. He says that they are moving every thing at Washington to compromise between you & V[an] B[uren] by writing[?] both on one ticket &c. He says there was a strong feeling for it amongst many, and that the N[ew] Y[ork] members made all sorts of pledges as to the Future. He says also it was talked of to withdraw V[an] B[uren] and run you & [Silas] Wright on a ticket &c. Wright is a far more dangerous man than any North[erner] to our interest in the South.

I regret very much you & Cousin Floride [Colhoun Calhoun] could not come down [to this place in Edgefield District]. I had set my heart on it. Mr. [Thomas G.] Clemson left here & will tell you about John [C. Calhoun, Jr.?] &c.

I [one word canceled and "was" interlined] with Susan [Wilkinson Pickens] a great deal in Charleston and am delighted with her school & improvement. It is a delightful school & the ladies very accomplished. If it were not that I have Miss Elizabeth [Barksdale Pickens?, my cousin,] with me I would take the other children down also, and spend most of the winter with them. I shall at any rate put them all there at school next Fall, and travel myself, as I have long desired to do. I have but little to interest me in home, and much to oppress my feelings at times.

Mr. Clemson told me of the fine offer he has had in Ala: in his profession, and I think he ought to accept it as I have always feared he never will be contented at his plantation. [*Manuscript torn*] wished to sell his place but I do not desire to purchase at all as I am [*manuscript torn*] with land. Col. J[ames] Edward [Colhoun], to my surprise, when he heard you & the family were not coming Christmas, went to Millwood & took Maria [Simkins Colhoun] with him while I was in Charleston. I hear he has been quite sick at home.

Present me kindly to all and accept for yourself the highest esteem of yours very truly, F.W. Pickens.

ALS in ScCleA.

"THE ADDRESS OF MR. CALHOUN TO HIS POLITICAL FRIENDS AND SUPPORTERS" (First Version)

Fort Hill, 21st Dec[embe]r 1843

I have left it to you, my friends and supporters, through whos[e] favourable estimate of my qualifications, my name has been presented to the people of the United-States for the office of Chief magistrate, to conduct the canvass on such principles, and in such manner, as you might think best. But I did not waive, in so doing, my right to determine, on my individual responsibility, what course my duty might compel me to pursue ultimately; nor have I been an inattentive observer of the canvass, and the course you have taken.

It affords me pleasure to be enabled to say, that on all leading questions, growing out of the canvass, I heartily concurred with you in the grounds you took, & especially in those relating to the mode, in which the delegates to the proposed Convention, to be held in Baltimore, should be appointed and ["how" *canceled and* "in what manner" *interlined*] they should vote. You have in, my opinion, conclusively shown, that they should be appointed by districts, and vote per capita; but your reasons as conclusive as they are, have proved in vain. Already New-York and some other States have appointed delegates en masse by State Conventions, and one State (Virginia) has resolved, that the votes of her delegates should be given by the majority, ["and count per capita" *interlined*]. Their course would necessarily overrule that, which you have so ably supported, should you go into Convention, and would leave you no alternative, but to yeild [*sic*] yours and adopt theirs, however much you may be opposed to it on princi-

617

ple, or to meet them on the most uneaqual [*sic*] terms; with divided against united and concentrated forces.

The question then is, what course under such circumstances should be adopted? and that question you will be compeled speedily to decide. The near approach of the time, for meeting of the proposed Convention, will not admit of much longer delay. But, as your course may depend, in some degree, on that which I have decided to take, I deem it due to the relation subsisting between us, to make mine known to you without further delay.

I, then, after the most careful and deliberate survey of the whole ground, have decided, that I cannot permit my name to go before the proposed Convention, constituted as it must now be, consistently with the principles, which have ever guided my public conduct. My objections are insuperable. As it must be constituted, it is repugnant to all the principles, on which, in my opinion, such a Convention should be founded. What those principles are, I shall now proceed briefly to state.

I hold then, with you, that the Convention should be so constituted, as to utter fully and clearly the voice of the people, and not that of political managers, or office holders and office seekers; and for that purpose, I hold it indispensible, that the delegates should be appointed directly by the people, or, to use the language of Gen. [Andrew] Jackson, should be "fresh from the people." I also hold, that the only possible mode to effect this, is for the people to choose the delegates by districts, and that they should vote per Capita. Every other mode of appointing must be, controlled by political machinery, and place the appointments in the hands of the few, who work it.

I object, then, to the proposed Convention, because it will not be constituted in conformity with this fundamental article of the Republican creed. The delegates to it will be appointed from some of the States, not by the people in districts, but as has been stated by State Conventions en masse, composed of delegates, appointed in all cases, as far as I am informed, by county or district Conventions, and in some cases, if not misinformed, these again composed of delegates appointed by still smaller divisions, or a few interested individuals. Instead, then, of being directly or fresh from the people ["these delegates" *altered to* "the delegates to the Baltimore Convention"] will be the delegates, of delegates, of delegates, and, of course, removed in all cases, at least, three, if not four degrees, from the people. At each successive remove, the voice of the people will become less full and distinct, until at last, it will be so faint and imperfect, as not to be audible. To drop ["metaphor" *canceled and then interlined*], I hold it impossible to form a scheme, more perfectly calculated to annihilate the control of the people over the Presidential election, and vest it in those, who make politics a trade, and who live, or expect to live, on the Government.

In this conviction, I object not less strongly to the mode ["in which" interlined] Virginia has resolved her delegates shall vote. With all due respect, I must say, I can imagine nothing more directly in conflict with the principles of our federal system of government, [partial word canceled] or to use a broader expression, the principles on which all confederate communities ["must be" canceled and "have ever been" interlined] united. I hazard nothing in saying, that there is not an instance in our political history, from the meeting of the first Revolutionary Congress to the present day, of the delegates of any State voting by majority and counting per capita; nor do I believe an instance of the kind can be found, in the history of any confederate community. There is ["indeed" interlined] something monstrous in the idea of giving the majority the right of impressing the votes of the minority [illegible word canceled and "into" interlined] its service, and counting them as its own. The plain rule—that which has ever prevailed, and which conforms to the dictates of common sense is, that when a State votes, as a State, by a majority of its delegates, the votes count one; be they few or many, or the States large or small. [Illegible word canceled and "On" interlined] the contrary, where the votes of all the delegates are counted, they vote individually and independently, each for himself counting one; ["it is however" canceled and "and it is" interlined] to be noted, that where ever this ["latter" interlined] mode of voting exists among confederated States, it is, in all cases, founded on compact, to which the consent of each State is required.

In the absence of compact, the invariable mode of voting in ["all cases, is" altered to "such States is in all cases"] by the majority, ["and" canceled] their votes counting one. The course, which Virginia has resolved to take, is in violation of this plain and fundamental rule, and ["if it should become the settled practice would be" interlined] destructive of the foundation, on which the whole structure of the State Rights doctrine, is reared.

I hold it in the next place to be an indispensable principle, that the Convention should be so constituted, as to give to each State, in the nomination of a candidate, the same relative weight, which the Constitution secured to it, in the election of the President, making due allowance for its relative party strength. By the election, I mean the whole—the eventual choice, when it goes into the House of Representatives, as well as the primary vote in the electoral college. The one is as much a part of the election, as the other. The two make the whole. The adoption of the one, in the Convention which framed the Constitution, depended on the adoption of the other. Neither could possibly be adopted alone. The two were the result of compromise between the larger and smaller States, after a long and doubtful struggle, which threatened the loss of the Constitution itself. The object of ["*giving to*" canceled and "*placing*" interlined] the smaller States ["*on*" interlined] an equality with the larger, in the eventual choice of the House, was to counterpoise the preponderance of the larger in the electoral College. Without this, the smaller would have voted against the ["*whole*" interlined] provision, and its rejection would have been the consequence. Even as it stands, Delaware voted against it. In confirmation of what I state, I refer to Mr. [James] Madison's Report of the proceedings of the Convention.

Having stated what I mean by the election, it will require but a few words to explain my reasons for the principles I have laid down. They are few and simple; and rest on the ground, that the nomination is, in reality, the election, if concurred in, as far as the party is concerned. It is so intended to be. The leading reason assigned for making it is, to prevent a division of the party, and, thereby prevent the election going into the House, where the smaller States would have the advantage, intended to be secured to them by the Constitution, by being placed on an equality with the larger.

Such being the intended object and effect, I now submit to every candid mind, whether the Convention ought ["*not*" interlined] to be so constituted, as to compensate in the nomination, for the important advantage in the election, which the smaller States would surrender, by going into a Convention.

Would it not be unfair—a palpable want of good faith, and subversive of the compromise of the Constitution, to with[h]old it? Or, if demanded, would it be short of an insult to refuse it? Can it be thought, that the smaller States are so debased and absorbed in the party politics of the day, as to permit themselves to be thus indirectly stripped of a right, which their high minded and patriotic ancestors held so dear, as even to prefer the loss of the Constitution itself, rather than surrender it.

I object, then, to the proposed Convention, in this connection, because it makes no compensation to the smaller States for the surrender of this unquestionable and important Constitutional right. Instead of that, its advocates peremptorily and indignantly refuse any and treat with scorn every attempt to secure it. Some have even gone so far, as to deny, that the eventual choice of the House constitutes any portion of the election, and to manifest open hostility against the provision of the Constitution, which contains it.

If there was no other objection, the one under consideration would be insuperable with me. I differ utterly from the advocates of the proposed Convention, in reference to this provision. I regard it as one of the first importance; not because I desire the election to go into the House, but because, I believe it to be an indispensable means, in the hands of the smaller States, of preserving their just and Constitutional weight in the Presidential election, and through that, in the Executive Department and the Government itself, which I believe to be essential to the preservation of our sublime federal system. I regard the adjustment of the relative weight of the States in the Government, to be the fundamental compromise of the Constitution, and that on which our whole political system depends. Its adjustment constituted the great difficulty, in forming the Constitution. The principle on which it was finally effected was, that while due concession should be made to population, ["some" *canceled and* "a" *interlined*] provision should be also made, in some form, to preserve the original equality of the States, in every department of the Government. The principle was easily carried out in constituting the legislative department, by preserving the equality of the States in one branch (the Senate) and conceeding [*sic*] to population its full preponderance in the other. But the great and difficult task of reducing it to practice was in the Executive department, at the head of which there ["was but one" *altered to* "is but a single"] officer. So great was it, that it occupied the attention of the Convention, from time to time, during the whole session, and was very near causing ["a" *interlined*] failure at last. It would have been an easy task to constitute that department, either on the principle of equality of the States in the Government, or that of population. To combine the, two in the election of a single officer, was quite a different affair; but however difficult, it had to be performed at the hazard of loosing [*sic*] the Constitution.

It was finally accomplished, by giving the larger States nearly the same preponderance in the electoral College, as they have in the House; and to the smaller, in the event of a choice by the House, the same equality they possess in the Senate; thus following closely the analoge of the legislative department. To make it, as close as possible, it was at first proposed to give the eventual choice to the Senate, instead of the House, but it was altered, and the present provision adopted, for reason which did not affect the principle.

It was believed by the framers, that the practical operation of the provision would be, that the electoral College, in which the influence of the larger States preponderates, would nominate, and that the House, voting by States, where there [*sic*] equality is preserved, would select, who should be the President. To give it that operation, in practice, the provision, as it originally stood, in the Constitution, was, that each elector should vote for two individuals, without discriminating which should be President, or Vice-President, and, if no one had a majority of the whole votes, then out of the five highest, the House, voting by States, should elect one, and the person not elected, having the highest number of votes, should be the Vice-President. It has been since altered, so that the electors should designate, which should be President and which Vice-President, and the selection of the House was limited to the three highest. It is manifest, that, if this provision of the Constitution had been left to operate by itself, without the intervention of caucusses or party conventions, between the people and the electors, that the practical operation would have been, such as I have stated, ["and" *interlined*] as was clearly intended by the framers of the Constitution.

The object intended is important. The preservation of the relative weight of the States, as established by the Constitution in all the departments, is necessary to the success and duration of our system of Government; but it may be doubted whether the provision, adopted to effect ["it" *interlined*] in the Executive Department, is not too refined for the strong, and, I may add, corrupt passions, which the Presidential election will ever excite. Certain it is, that, if the practice of nominating candidates for the Presidency by Conventions, constituted as the proposed, shall become the established usage, it will utterly defeat the intention of the framers of the Constitution, and would be followed by a radical and dangerous change, not only in the Executive Department, but in the Government itself.

This danger was early for[e]seen, and to avoid it, some of the wisest and most experienced Statesmen of former days, so strongly objected to Congressional caucusses to nominate candidates for the Presidency, that they never could be induced to attend them; among these, it will be sufficient to name Mr. [Nathaniel] Macon and Mr. [William] Lowndes. Others, believing that this provision of the Constitution was too refined for practice, were solicitous to amend it, but without impairing the influence of the smaller States in the election. Among these I rank myself. With that object, resolutions were introduced, in 1828; in the Senate by Col. [Thomas H.] Benton, and in the House by Mr. [George] McDuffie, providing for districting the States, and for refering the election back to the people, in case there should be no choice, to elect one from the two highest Candidates. ["These were introduced, because the amendment they proposed was believed to embrace" *canceled and* "The principle, which governed in the amendment proposed, was to give" *interlined*] a fair compensation to the smaller States for the surrender of their advantage, in the eventual choice by the House, and ["further(?) because they were assumed to be more in conformity to the" *canceled and* "at the same time to make the mode of election of the President more strictly in conformity with the" *interlined*] principles of our popular institutions, and ["to be" *interlined*] less liable to corruption, than the existing ["provisions" *canceled and* "provision" *interlined*]. They received the general support of the party, but were objected to by a few, as not being a full equivalent to the smaller States. The principle ["they" *canceled*] embraced is identical with that, on which you proposed to constitute the Baltimore Convention; but which has been so dictatorially objected to by some, who there took so prominent a part in its favour. If you have not succeeded, there is at least some consolation in reflecting, that, if others have since changed, you now stand where you ["then" *interlined*] did, in the purer and better days of the party. I was in favour of it then, as I am now; not ["that" *canceled and* "because" *interlined*] I consider the ["resolutions" *canceled and* "amendment proposed" *interlined*] as perfect, theoretically, as the existing provisions of the Constitution, but because, I believed, it would in practice more certainly accomplish, what the framers of the Constitution intended. But, while the provision stands as it does, I would regard myself, as little short of a traitor to that sacred instrument, should I give my assent, directly or indirectly, to any practice, which would have the effect of divesting the smaller States of the due weight, which is secured to them in the Presidential election, whether designed or not. And here let me add, that as objectionable, as I think a Congressional caucuss for nominating a President, it is, in my opinion, far less so, than a Convention constituted as proposed. The former had, indeed, many things to recommend it. Its members, consisting of Senators & Representatives, were the immediate organs of ["the" *canceled*] State legislatures, or the people; were responsible to them respectively, and were, for the most part, of high character, standing and talents. They voted per capita, and what is very important, they represented fairly the relative strength of the party, in their respective States. In all these important particulars, it was all that could be desired, for a nominating body, and formed a striking contrast to the proposed Convention; and yet, it could not be borne by the people, in the then pure days of the republic. I, acting with Gen.

623

Jackson, and most of the leaders of the party at the time, contributed to put it down, because we believed it to be liable to be acted on and influenced by the patronage of the Government—an objection far more applicable to a Convention, constituted as the one proposed, than to a Congressional caucus. Far ["however" *interlined*] was it from my intention, in putting that down, to substitute in its place, what I regard, as an hundred times more objectionable in every point of view. Indeed, if there must be an intermediate body, between the people and the election, unknown to the Constitution, it may be well questioned, whether a better, than the old plan of a Congressional caucus can be devised.

In taking the ground I have, in favour of maintaining the right secured to the smaller States, by the compromise of the Constitution, I am actuated by no partisan feelings, or desire to conciliate their good opinion. If the case was reversed, and the right of the larger, instead of the smaller, was invaded, I would, with equal readiness and firmness, stand up in their defence. I am the partisan of neith[er] one, nor the other, but simply of the Constitution, and what I believe to be just and fair. I regard the Constitution, as the only ark of safety for all, and ["believe" *interlined*] that in defending it, I defend the interest and safety of each & all—the greater, as well as the smaller—the States invading the rights of the others, as well as the States whose rights are invaded.

I laid down the principle, on which I rest the objection in question, with the limitation, that the relative weight of the States should be maintained, making due allowance for their relative party strength. The propriety of the limitation is so apparent, that but a few words in illustration with [*sic*; will] be required. The Convention is a party Convention, and professedly intended to take the sense of the party, which cannot be done fairly, if States having but little party strength, are put on an equality with those having much. If that were done, the result might be, that a small portion of the party from States the least sound politically, and which could give, but little support in Congress, might select the candidate and make the President, against a great majority, from the soundest and on which the President and his administration would have to rely for the support ["of his measures" *canceled*]. All this is clearly too unfair and improper to be denied. There may be a great difficulty ["remedying it" *altered to* "applying a remedy"] in a Convention, but I do not feel myself called upon to say, how it can be done, or by what standard the relative party strength of the respective States should be determined; perhaps the best would be, their relative strength in Congress at the time.

In laying down the principle, I added the limitation for the sake of accuracy, and to show how imperfectly the party must be represented, ["in which" *canceled and* "where" *interlined*] it is over looked. I see no provision in the proposed Convention to meet it.

But in order to realize how the Convention will operate, it will be necessary to view the combined effects of the objections, which I have made. Thus viewed, it will be found, that a Convention so constituted tends irresistibly to centralization—centralization of the control over the Presidential election in the hand of a few of the central, large States at first, and finally, in political managers, office holders and office seekers; or to express it differently, in that portion of the community, who live, or expect to live on the Government, in contradistinction to the great mass, who expect to live on their own means, or their honest industry ["which last are in a political sense" *altered to* "& who are, political(ly) speaking"], emphatically the people.

That such would be the case, may be inferred from the fact, that it would afford the means to some six or seven ["States" *interlined*] lying contiguous, and not far from the centre of the Union, to control the nomination, and through that, the election, by concentrating their united votes in the Convention. Give them the power of doing so, and it would not long lie dormant. What may be done by combination, where the temptation is so great, will be sure, ere long, ["to" *interlined*] be done. To combine and conquer is not less true ["as a maxim" *interlined*], where power is concerned, than to "Divide and conquer." Nothing is better established, than that the desire for power can bring together and unite the most discordant materials.

But the tendency to centralization will not stop there. The appointment of delegates, en mass[e] by State Conventions, would tend at the same time, and even with greater force to centralize this control in the hands of the few, who make politics a trade. The farther the Convention is removed from the people, the more certainly the control over it will be placed in the hands of the interested few; and when removed three or four degrees, as has been showed it will be, where the appointment is by State Conventions, the power of the people will cease, and the seekers of Executive favour will become supreme. At that stage, an active ["trained &" *interlined*] combined corps will be formed in the party, whose whole time and attention will be directed to politics. It will be their sole business. Into their hands the appointment of delegates, in all the stages, will fall; and they will take special care, that none but themselves, or their humble and obedient dependents, shall be appointed. The ["State and central" *altered to* "central and State"] Conventions will be filled by the most experienced and cunning; and after nominating the President, they will take good care to divide the patronage and offices, both of the General and State governments among themselves and their dependents. But why say *will?* Is it not *already the case?* Have there not been many instances of State Conventions, being filled by office holders and office seekers, who after making the nomination, have divided the offices in the State among themselves and their partisans, and joined in recommending to the candidate, whom they have just nominated, to appoint ["accordingly. If such" *canceled and* "them to the offices, to which they had been respectively allotted? If such" *interlined*] be the case in the infancy of the system, it must end, if such Conventions should become the established usage, in the President nominating his successor. When it comes to that, it will not be long before the sword will take the place of the Constitution.

Such are my objections to the ["mode in which the" *interlined*] proposed Convention ["is to be constituted" *interlined*] and reasons for entertaining them. They are such, that I cannot refuse to obey them, without renouncing the principles, which I have often avowed, in public and in private, and which have guided me through the whole course of my public life.

In coming to this conclusion, I have not passed over, without careful examination, the reasons assigned by its advocates, for constituting the Convention, as they propose. They have not diminished the force of my objections. I propose to notice ["one or two of" *canceled*] the most prominent.

That which they have urged with the greatest confidence is, that each State has a right to appoint delegates, as she pleases. I meet it by utterly denying that there is any such right. That each State has the right to act, as it pleases, in whatever relates to its self exclusively, no one will deny; but it is a perfectly ["new" *canceled and* "novel" *interlined*] doctrine, that any State has such a right, when she comes to act in concert with others, in reference to what concerns the whole. In such cases, it is the plainest dictate of common sense, that whatever affects the whole, ["shall" *canceled and* "should" *interlined*] be regulated by the mutual consent of all, and not by the discretion of each. That the appointment of delegates to the proposed Convention is a case of this description, I trust, I have conclusively shown. I have, I also trust, shown more; that the supposed right is perfectly deceptive, for while it claims for each State, the right to appoint delegates, as it pleases, it, in reality, gives the larger States, the right to dictate, how the others shall appoint. If for example, the Empire State, as it is called, adopts the mode of appointing ["(which she has done)" *al-*

tered to "(as she has)"] which will concentrate her whole strength, what discretion would she leave to others, if they go into Convention, but to appoint, as she has appointed, or to be ruled by her? It is, then, neither more nor less, than a claim to dictate, under the garb of a right; and such its exercise has proved, in the present case. It has left no option, but to conform to her course, or be over rulled [sic], or refuse to go into Convention.

I regret this ["as"(?) canceled and "because" interlined] I sincerely desire to preserve the harmony of the party. I had strong hope, that the rally, after the defeat of 1840, would be exclusively on principles. This hope was greatly strengthened, by the truly republican and noble stand, taken at the extra session [of Congress in 1841], and the earlier portion of the succeeding regular session. During that period of rigid adherence to principles, perfect harmony pervaded the ranks of the party. I beheld it with joy. I believed the moment highly fav[o]urable for the thorough reformation of the Government, and the restoration of the Constitution. To the Republican party, I looked for the accomplishment of this great work, and I accordingly felt the deepest solicitude, that the stand taken and the harmony which existed, should be preserved. In order that it should, I made up my mind to voice the objection, which I had long entertained to any intermediate body ["known" altered to "unknown"] to the Constitution, between the people and the election of the President, in the hope, that the proposed Convention would be so constituted, that I might consistently with my principles give it my support. In this, I have been disappointed; and being so, am compelled to decide, as I have. The same motives, which impelled me to seperate from the administration of Gen. Jackson, in the plentitude of its power, and to come to the rescue of Mr. [Martin] Van-Buren's, at its greatest depression, compels me now to withhold my name from the proposed Convention.

It is not only, however, in reference to the mode of constituting the Convention, that I have been disappointed. I have been not less so, in reference to the vital question of the Tariff. I had a right to anticipate, from the grounds taken by the party in their address [of 7/6/-1838], after the suspension of the Banks in 1837, and before their defeat in 1840, that they would forever abandon the protective policy. This anticipation had become almost a settled conviction, from the strong and general opposition, manifested by the party to the protective policy, at the extra session of 1841, and at the succeeding regular session, until within a very short time, prior to the passage of the highly protective ["Tariff" interlined] of 1842. Even then, I had good reason to suppose, from the declaration of the portion of the party, (especially in the Senate) whose votes, united with the whigs, passed the bill, that they were compeled to vote for it, strongly against their inclination, from the supposed necessity of the treasury. But subsequent events have expelled, whatever hopes I once entertained. I intend to speak freely and plainly. Duty to myself, to you and to the country demands it.

I, then, have ceased to hope, that the party will unite against the protective policy. The grounds taken, on this all important question by the Syracuse Convention, which nominated Mr. Van-Buren, connected with that taken, by the two preceeding [*sic*] Conventions in the same State, and the almost unanimous vote of the legislature of Pennsylvania, including both parties, in favour of a protective tariff, have convinced me, that a large and influential portion of the party, still adhere to that odious and oppressive policy. With such divisions in the ranks of the party, there can be no hope, it can be put down. A much smaller and less influential portion, by uniting with the whigs, can enact, or prevent the repeal at pleasure of a protective tariff, as sad experience proves. It would be idle to deceive ourselves. The Free-Trade battle is to be fought over again, not simply with the whigs (there would be in that little difficulty) but ["which" *canceled and* "what" *interlined*] is far worse, with them united with a portion of the party. It was by such ominous union, that the Tariff of 1828 was passed—the most detestable and fatal measure, ever adopted by the Government; and by the same ["union" *interlined*] that of 1842, its twin brother in iniquity; and what is to be noted, by the same portion of the party, ["and" *canceled*] I might almost say, by the same individuals. I call them twin brothers, because they are of the same parentage, and of the most striking likeness. The only material difference between them is, that the elder was boldly and openly ushered into the world, as a protective tariff; while the younger was surreptitiously, as a tariff for revenue, with incidental protection; and yet, as if to let us know what was meant by such a tariff, this junior offspring, passed under the plausible profession of revenue, reduced, instead of increasing the revenue, and openly carried the protective policy to prohibition, on a greater number and those more important articles, than its more honest senior brother! With such an instance of practice against profession to admonish us, what faith can be put in the latter, or what possible advantage can we hope, from ["the" *canceled and* "a" *interlined*] change of names, without a change of things. We are ["called upon" *canceled and* "justified" *interlined*], by such an instance, to be vigilant, and even jealous. To use the language of an eminent citizen [Littleton W. Tazewell], at the time Senator from

Virginia, in reference to the tariff of 1828, we have been deceived, (not once as he said but) twice, that was your fault; if we should be deceived again, it ["is" *canceled and* "will be" *interlined*] ours.

I wish not to be misunderstood. I believe, that the great body of the party is sound, on this vital question; but what does that avail, practically, when a considerable portion agree ["on it" *canceled and* "in reference to it" *interlined*] much more with the whigs, than with us; and who, when their vote is necessary to pass or retain a protective tariff, fly off and join them? What greater harm could they do, were they rallied under ["an" *canceled and* "the" *interlined*] opposite flag? Could they do half as much? Can anything be more fatal, than the desertion of a part of the forces in the midst of the battle? Would it not be better by far to meet them, as open foes, belonging to the ranks of our ["enemies" *canceled and* "opponents" *interlined*]?

But to come to the point; How can we of the Free-Trade party go into Convention with those ["whose" *interlined*] practice and opinions agree with the whigs, on this all important question. I say whose practice and opinion agree with them, for when it comes to the pinch, we find them steadily voting together; and after a full and careful examination of the grounds taken by the Syracuse Convention, in reference to the protective policy, I can find no distinction, favourable to us, between their opinions, and those of [Henry Clay] the father of ["that policy" *canceled and* "the American system" *interlined*], as contained in his letters to his friend, which have been recently published. I regard both, as thoroughly protective, and though skilfully dressed, in order to be as little offensive as possible to us, consistently with the avowal of the principle of protection. The garb is nothing. It was put on for the occasion, and will be put off whenever the occasion requires it. Of one thing we may be assured, that those who assume a garb to get power, will be sure to keep it on, if necessary to retain power.

Having made these remarks, I again repeat the question; How can we go into a Convention with those, who agree with the whigs, on this all important subject? Would we go into one with the whigs, if they agreed with us on all other questions? And where is the difference between that, and going into Convention with a portion of the party, who agree with them on it? Does it make a difference to what party they nominally belong—Democrate or whig, so long as they differ from us, on this vital question? I call it so, because I regard it as the great question of the day. If any one measure of that system of policy advocated by the whigs, may be called the parent measure, it is a protective tariff. Should it be overthrown, in the present state of things, there would be no danger from any other of the whole batch; but if continued, it would draw in its train all the rest. It is, in truth, the real question at issue, between the two parties; I might almost say, under circumstances, the only one. If not overthrown, there will be neither reform of the Government, nor restoration of the Constitution; be the result of the next election, what it may. But, if it should be, both would follow, almost as a matter of course.

Now I hold, that the protective policy can never be overthrown, so long as a portion of the party, bearing the name of Republican, shall adhere to a measure, so thoroughly and essentially belonging to the creed of the whigs. So long as that is the case, there is no hope, whether the whigs are defeated or not. In either case, the union of a portion of the party with them, ensures a majority for protection. It is a desperate game, for the advocates of Free-Trade to engage in, as experience of 20 years has shown. Let who will win, they are sure to lose. I, as one of its advocates, cannot consent to play it, and must, therefore, withold my name from going before the Convention, or pledging my support to its proceedings, when the friends of the protective policy will constitute so influential a portion. To do so, with the evidence before me, would be to declare, practically, that I regard the protective policy to be an open question, as far as the party is concerned, which I would consider a virtual abandonment of the cause of Free-Trade. That can never be; I have done and suffered too much for it, when its friends were few and feeble[,] to abandon it now— now when the auspices every where, on this and the other side of the Atlantic proclaim the downfall of protection, and the permanent triumph of Free-Trade. I, who upheld it against monopoly and plunder, in the worst of times, and branded [sic] the menaces of administration and op[p]osition, when backed but by a single State, will not—cannot abandon the glorious cause now, when its banner waves in [*illegible word*; proud?] triumph over the metropolis of the commercial world. No, I shall maintain immovably the ground, which I have so long occupied, until I have witnessed its great and final victory, if it shall please the Disposer of Events to spare my life so long. It will be indeed *a victory*—the harbinger of peace to nations, and the dawn of a new, and brighter civilization.

It will, I know, be objected, that my course is calculated to defeat the party. To this I answer, that, if my views are correct, (which I cannot doubt) the opposite course is calculated to sacrifice the principles of the party. Now, it has been a rule with me, which I have followed without hesitation or deviation during my long political life, whenever party and principles come into conflict, to take the side of principle against party. In doing so, I believe that I have been faithful to both; for the strength of the Republican party, according to my opinion, depends on adhering to its principles, and its weakness in departing from them. Whenever it departs from them, it is better by far, that it should be defeated, than that it should succeed. Defeat in such cases, leads to reformation and a return to principles, and these, again, to victory. The effects of success are the reverse. It sanctions in the mind of the party, its departure from principle; corrupts its doctrines; gives a wrong direction to its policy, and confounds all distinction between it and its opponents. These are followed by the loss of the confidence of the people, and, finally, by irretreivable [sic] overthrow. If, I am right, such would be the character and consequences of a victory won under the flag of the proposed Convention, associated with the false colours of the protective policy. Indeed, the only victory worth having, and which in the end will not prove a curse, instead of a blessing, is one founded on principle; that is one, in a contest on a true issue, embracing all the principles and doctrines of the party, & excluding all belonging to the creed of its opponents. Such was the issue in the contest of 1800, which led to the great victory, that first brought the Republican party into power. From that issue, the protective policy was especially excluded & denounced by the Republican party of that day. Its admission since, has been the bane of the party, and the leading cause of its recent defeat & disasters.

At no period was a victory won, as that, ever more needed, than the present; nor would any one rejoice more, than myself, to witness it. I am totally opposed to the whigs, bothe in principle and policy. I believe theirs to be hostile to the genius of our free, popular, federal system and that their permanent ascendency would end in its destruction.

If harmony and union be desirable to ensure the success of the party, and the defeat of the whigs, in the present contest, they may easily be had, as far as I am concerned. Let the false and dangerous principles, on which it is proposed to constitute the Convention, be abandoned, and let the odious, oppressive, anti-republican and unconstitutional system of monopoly and plunder, called protection, be openly denounced and disavowed by the party, and let their acts correspond with their words, by beginning at once the repeal of the last of its progeny, the Tariff of 1842, and substituting in its place, an honest revenue tariff, which shall impose no duty, and make no discrimination, but for revenue; and raise no revenue, but what the wants of the Government econommically administered, may require. Let this be done, and there is no sacrifice, which I would not cheerfully make to ensure harmony and union. I would even rejoice to make any and every sacrifice. I would esteem it a greater honour to do so, if needed for its success, than any honour, which it can confer. But, without that, I would regard the success of the party a curse in disguise—as but a step to its future overthrow, and the permanent ascendency of the whigs.

I have now made known to you frankly and freely the course, I have decided to take, with the reasons, which have governed me. I have stated them more fully than I otherwise would, that you might clearly understand my motives in taking a step, which may possibly effect the political relations existing between us. I, on my part, dearly cherish them, and would consider it, a great misfortune, should they be changed. In deciding on my course, I assume no right to decide for you. I recognize in each of you the same right to decide for himself, which I claim for myself. If you should concur with me in opinion, and rally on the grounds I have taken, of Free Trade, the people and the Constitution, against Monopoly, Political Managers; and caucus Conventions, I am prepared to stand by you, be your numbers few or many; but, if not, I shall be neither pained, nor mortified, to stand alone. I would infinitely prefer ["that" *interlined*] where my judgment and conscience approve, than to act with the majority where they condemn. [Signed:] J.C. Calhoun.

DS in NcU, Robert Barnwell Rhett Papers; DS (fragment) in NHi, Miscellaneous Manuscripts. NOTE: The 36-page manuscript document transcribed above is dated and signed by Calhoun. It is a nearly finished copy in an unidentified hand with a few corrections in Calhoun's hand. Calhoun stated in letters below that he sent copies of the "Address" to his friends in Congress and to the "Central Committee" in Charleston. The manuscript now among Rhett's papers is possibly the copy sent to Washington. The manuscript fragment cited secondly above corresponds to approximately the last eleven pages of the complete manuscript. The fragment is in the hand of Anna Maria Calhoun Clemson, is signed by Calhoun, and is a rougher copy—perhaps a surviving portion of a draft. Calhoun apparently transmitted the "Address" to the committee in Charleston enclosed in the letter to Jacob Bond I'On and others which appears directly below in this volume. However, by the time that letter and the accompanying "Address" were published in the Charleston newspapers on January 29, 1844, the "Address" had been the subject, as is reflected in many letters below in this volume, of extensive discussion and advice from Calhoun's "political friends" and had undergone revision. See below Calhoun to Franklin H. Elmore, January 16, 1844, and compare the manuscript document transcribed above with the public version of the "Address" under date of 1/29/1844 below. In preparing his edition of Calhoun's *Works*, Richard K. Crallé did not have access to Calhoun's manuscript. He printed the later version of the text probably taken from a contemporary newspaper, and he commented in a preface that many of Calhoun's original manuscripts "are now irretrievably lost; and amongst them that of the *Address to his political friends and supporters,*—which is the more to be regretted as the Editor has reason to believe it contained some important matter which does not appear in the printed Copy." (Crallé, ed., *Works*, 6:v.)

To JACOB BOND I'ON and "Other Members of the Committee," Charleston

Fort Hill, Dec. 21, 1843
Gentlemen—I herewith enclose you, as the organ of those who nominated me for the Presidency in this State, subject to a Convention fairly constituted, an Address to my political friends and supporters, assigning my reasons for not permitting my name to go before the proposed Convention to be held in Baltimore in May next. I transmit it to you, because I deem it respectful and proper to make it known to those to whom it is addressed, through you, and in order to afford you an opportunity to take such measures in relation to it, as you may deem proper, if indeed, you should deem any necessary. All I have to request is, that its publication should not be unnecessarily delayed. With great respect, I am, &c. &c., J.C. Calhoun.

PC in the Charleston, S.C., *Mercury*, January 29, 1844, p. 2; PC in the Charleston, S.C., *Courier*, January 29, 1844, p. 2. NOTE: Calhoun enclosed with this letter the first version of his address to his supporters, which appears herein under the date of 12/21/1843. However, by the time the above letter was published along with the "Address," the document had undergone considerable revision, as will appear below in this volume. Calhoun's letter above first appeared in the two Charleston newspapers cited. It was reprinted along with the "Address" in dozens of other contemporary newspapers that are not cited.

From LEWIS E. HARVIE and DAVID MCCOMAS

Richmond, Dec. 21st 1843
Dear Sir, One of us has been appointed by the Democratic members of the Virginia Legislature to draft an Address to the People of Virginia to be submitted to the ["Committe" *canceled*] Convention of the Democratic party which is to assemble in this City in February next, for its adoption. That portion of the address which will refer to the adjustment of the Tariff policy of the Federal Government, is

in our opinion by far the most important and knowing the great attention that you have bestowed on the subject & your deep devotion to Southern interests, we take the liberty to ask you to prepare su[ch] an exposition of your views on th[e] subject as you would wish to be embodied in the Address. We would desire it to be so worded that it may be inserted in the address, without a change even of its phraseology. We believe there is a general concurrence of sentiment on this subject, amongst the Democracy of Virginia at this time. And there is no doubt that an Address *decidedly* denunciatory of the Protective Policy will meet with general support in the Convention. We hope that your name will be before the people as an exponent of these principles, and we desire to place the people of Virginia in such an attitude on this subject that their opinions will be identified with yours. You may rest assured, if you accede to this request, that no liberty will be taken with your name, that the manuscript will be destroyed, and the knowledge of your participation in the address will be confined within our own breasts. Should your time and ["othe" *canceled*] engagements admit of it, of course we would be *much* pleased to receive your views upon such other matters, as in your opinion should be contained in the Address. We are sure at all events that you will understand and duly appreciate the motives that have prompted this request. With great Respect, Lewis E. Harvie [and] David McComas.

LS (in Harvie's handwriting) in ScCleA.

From J[ohn] P. King, [former Senator from Ga.]

Charleston, Dec[embe]r 21[,] 1843

My dear Sir, It has been some time since we have corresponded on a subject of much interest to us both and in fact to the whole South Atlantic and Gulph States—I may add in fact to the *union*, so far as the whole can be interested in cheap milatary defences of each part. I have made such arrangements as have induced me to venture on a *vigorous* prossecution of our [rail]road to Whitehall [near Athens, Ga.,] provided we can receive the aid of a remission of duties [on iron]. Most[?], is said to be apprehended from the democratic party, in the House [of Representatives]. I am told New England will go for it, ["I am told" *canceled*] and certainl[y] a part of the west. May I ask that you w[ill] by letter use your influence with such individ[ual] members, as you could most likely influence, [*mutilation*] who would have influence in the House [*mutilation.*] In favor of all Roads *commenced*[?] *under the* [*mutilation*] of government, it is certainly nothing but jus[*mutilation*] the principal roads at the north, have had the benef[it] of it, and are now enjoying it. It is only those that have been compelled to begin *from their weakness,* that ["have" *canceled*] are soon[?] *stopped,* in their *embarrassments* by this prohibitive duty. It *is policy* for the government to encourage *all such improvements*; for they effect a *great national object* at the expense of individual capital. The advantage of these improvements in a time of war, could scarcely be estimated; especially those connecting the Coast with the Western [that is, Mississippi] valley. The completion of *our*[?] *enterprize* to the Tennessee river, affording a speedy & cheap transportation of *the whole resources* of the valley, to the Atlantic & Gulph Coast would be of more real value in defending our e[x]tensive ["Coa" *canceled*] *and unprotected Coast* than a standing army of *200,000*; verbum sat. *Please help me all you can in your own way.* I shall be at Washington in a few days, and shall try and push the question to a decission. Your Spartanburg [i]ron Companies have memorialized for the remmission [*sic*], and I am told others at the North will do so. [Th]ey are certainly much interested *in the repeal of* [*mutilation*] *Duty*[?] *law intended for their protection.* The duty [*mutilation*] no protection to them and by impeding the progress [*mutilation*; Ra]il Roads they lose the supply of spikes [*mutilation*; pre]liminary[?] Casting &c which is so profitable [*mutilation*] them[?]. Y[ou]r friend, J.P. King.

N.B. Whatever action our [Ga.] legislature takes, *the road will go on quite as fast as it ought, till connections are made.* Suppose you flatter [Representative Edward J.] Black of our State with a letter. He has an itching[?] to abuse monopolies and corporations. You can say to him here however that Rail Road priviledges [*sic*] are not enviable, they are only the priviledge of *monopolizing loss for the benefit of the Community.*

ALS (partly burned) in ScCleA. NOTE: King was president of the Georgia Railroad and Banking Company.

To [LUCIUS LYON, Representative
from Mich., Washington]

Fort Hill, 21st Dec[embe]r 1843
My dear Sir, I have requested my son, Lieut[enant] P[atrick] Calhoun, to deliver the accompan[y]ing letter [*not found*], addressed to

the Hon: I[saac] E. Crary [former Representative from Mich.], to you. It contains papers of value, and which are necessary to foreclose a mort[g]age, which one of [my] neighbours has on lands in Michigan. In order that they may go safe, you will oblige me by putting the letter under cover, and addressed & franked to Mr. Crary. I have requested my Representative in the House, the Hon: Mr. [Richard F.] Simpson, to let you have $20 to be forwarded to Mr. Crary to meet expenses, which I will thank you to send at the same time with the letter to him. I regret to put you to so much trouble, but feel assured you will excuse me.

ALU in MiU-C, Lucius Lyon Papers.

To R[OBERT] M. T. HUNTER, L[l]oyds, Va.

Fort Hill, 22d Dec[embe]r 1843

My dear Sir, It is some time since I have heard from you, which I attribute to the fact, that you had nothing agreeable to communicate. Those who expect to live on the Govt. have proved stronger than the people, & political machinery stronger than arguments.

I write now to say, that I have prepared an Address to my political friends & supporters; and have sent one copy to our central Committee in Charleston, & the other to our two Senators [George McDuffie and Daniel Elliott Huger], with a letter addressed to my friends & supporters in Congress. The Address contains my reasons for declining to permit my name to go before the Baltimore convention. I object to the mode in which it is constituted, and the Tariff principles of an influential portion of those, who will be represented in the Convention (principally N.Y. & Pennsy[lvani]a). I have reasoned both grounds pretty fully, & taken high grounds for my course. I have taken the ["stept" (sic) interlined] on my own individual responsibility, leaving my friends free to say, whether they will support the stand I have taken or not. My course is irrevocably taken.

I have sent the two copies in advance of of [sic] the [one word canceled and "publication" interlined] of the Address, to afford the Committee & my friends in Congress an opportunity to decide on their course, before it appears, but have requested the former not to delay its publication unnecessarily. I presume it will be published in 8 or 10 days at farthest.

I hope you will be able to make a visit to Washington, to aid in the deliberation of our friends. I have written to [Virgil] Maxcy to the same effect. For myself, I have no solicitude as to their decision. I am content to stand, where my Address places me, and to terminate my political life with it, if they decide so; but there ought to be a rally to save our principles. A run[?] between Mr. [Henry] Clay & Mr. [Martin] V[an] B[uren] on the issue, which will be made up between them, will utterly demoralize the South, ["to be followed by" *interlined and "to" canceled*] the final loss of the good old State rights doctrines. I think, I have shown that clearly in the address, not directly, but by inference. The object now is, not victory, but to preserve our position & principles; the only way, under circumstances, by which we can preserve our influence & the safety of the South. They can beat us in management, but there, if true to ourselves, we can beat them. If [Henry A.] Wise, [William C.] Rives & [Thomas W.] Gilmer could be brought to act with Zeal & concert with you, ["your" *interlined*] weight will be felt in Virginia. The South has nothing to hope from V[an] B[uren]. He is in my opinion a doomed man, and there is no obligation on us to share his fate. We could not sustain him on our own issue, and much less could we do it on the issue ["with" *interlined*] which he must now go into the contest. I honestly believe, that his defeat is necessary to save the party, not by ["our" *interlined*] joining the Whigs, but by standing fast & rallied on our own ground. Yours truly, J.C. Calhoun.

ALS in ScCleA; variant PC in Jameson, ed., *Correspondence*, pp. 556–557.

From WILSON LUMPKIN,
[former Senator from Ga.]

Athens [Ga.,] Dec. 22d 1843

My dear Sir, Since I wrote to you last, I have mingled more with the people (or rather politic[i]ans of Ga.) than usual, & have several letters from Washington, since the meeting of Congress, and without attempting to enter upon the details which have led to my conclusions, I feel it my duty, to suggest to you my present views, in connection with passing events, so far as you are necessarily personally concerned. This is due to personal friendship, as well as the high estimation which I place on your public & private character. And first, let me say, it is obvious & clear, that the seeds of discord, confusion & division, have become too deeply rooted, in what we call the

637

Democratic party, for any thing like general union & harmony [to] be brought about speedily. Every thing is chaos.

The office holders, office seekers & corrupt press, [are] at the foundation of the intended Baltimore con[vention.] If they meet at all, every thing is already [arranged]. They meet simply for the purpose of forcing [the] whole party into the support of Mr. [Martin] Van B[uren].

Under these circumstances, I shall regret to [see] your name go before such a convention. [It] ought not to be permit[t]ed. And I believe, the [good] of the country will be most promoted, by it being known at once, that there is a portion of the party at least, too pure & patriotic, to be used as the mere tools of political schemers.

Should you concur with me, in the suggestions above made, I submit to your better Judgment as to the best mode of a public annunciation of a determination not to submit to the intrigues & management of selfish aspirants & managers.

I think this matter requires decision & action; it will be folly to expect, to overturn corruption, by any [compromise?]. The old combination of office seekers, are again linked together, & having unity of motive, can easily be brought to union of action. I don[']t know what is to be the result. I fear we shall again be under the yoke of Federalism. Mr. Van Buren can never again be elected President of the U.S.

Since I last wrote to you, I have been surprized, to find in Georgia, N[ew] York & Virginia influence so widely spread in this region. I have only time to add, my unabating friendship & sincere regard for your welfare. Wilson Lumpkin.

ALS in ScCleA; variant PC in Boucher and Brooks, eds., *Correspondence*, pp. 194–195. NOTE: A few words and parts of words have been supplied in brackets in the above transcription where the margin of the ms. is slightly mutilated.

To A[RMISTEAD] BURT, [Representative from S.C.], Washington

Fort Hill, 23d Dec[embe]r 1843

My dear Sir, I am much obliged to you for the information you give me, and I hope I shall hear from you frequently & fully. There is now no doubt, that political management & political machinery are too strong for the people. They have forced [Martin] V[an] B[uren] on the party against the real wishes of three fourth[s] of the party, and when the workers of the machinery must see, at the hazard of a defeat & the overthrow of the party.

I have decided to Address my friends & supporters, and to assign my reasons for not permitting my name to go before the Baltimore convention. One copy has been sent of my Address to the central Committee in Charleston, & the other under cover to our Senators. I have written to [Robert Barnwell] Rhett, [Dixon H.] Lewis & [George] McDuffie, & for fuller particulars I refer you to what I have said to them.

We have nothing to hope from the two great factions that are now contending for the spoils, they have extorted from us. The leaders of the Democratick portion are more hostile to us, than to the Whigs, to whom they are much more nearly allied in policy & principles than to us. If they should ever be put to the test, such will prove to be the fact.

The object now is not so much victory, as to preserve our position & principles, and that can only be done by keeping our flag flying. The object of my address is two fold; to put my self rectus, & the next to afford those, who agree with me, [*partial word canceled*] a point on which to rally. I have done my duty, it rest[s] with them to do theirs.

I regret to hear, that Martha [Calhoun Burt] has been so unwell. I hope she is ["well" *canceled and* "recovered" *interlined*] ere this. I am glad you are in so pleasant a Mess. It will add much to yours & Martha's pleasure during, what I anticipate will be a very long session.

All join in love to you & her. Yours truly, J.C. Calhoun.

ALS in NcD, John C. Calhoun Papers; PC in Jameson, ed., *Correspondence*, p. 557.

To "Col." J[AMES] ED[WARD] COLHOUN, [Abbeville District, S.C.]

Fort Hill, 24th Dec[embe]r 1843

My dear James, I have ascertained, that there stands to the credit of your farther [*sic*; your father, John Ewing Colhoun, Sr.], and Samuel B. Colhoun, on the Books of the Treasury a small amount, say $160 or there abouts for interest on unfunded stock. Samuel B. Colhoun was an elder brother of yours who died young & long before your memory.

639

It will require a power of attorney to receive it[,] from you & your brother [John Ewing Colhoun, Jr.]. A simple letter, I presume will be sufficient from you, authorising me to receive your share of whatever sum of money may be standing to the credit of your deceased farther John E. Colhoun & deceased brother Samuel B. Colhoun. As soon as I receive yours & your brother's authority I will make application through the proper office for payment.

We have had a gread [*sic*] deal of wet weather, but I learn from the west they have had much more. The general impression there is, that it will greatly diminish the cotton crop, which I cannot but think will cause a rise in the price.

The scarlet fever has become very prevalent. Your brother's family has suffered much, both whites & blacks. Some of the cases have been very severe, but there has been no death, and I understood from Martha [Maria Davis Colhoun] yesterday they were all on the recovery.

We have had a good many among our negroes, but all have been light but one case & that not dangerous.

I have prepared an Address to my political friends & supporters declining to permit my name to go before the Baltimore Convention, and assigning my reasons for the same. I have sent a copy to the Central Committee in Charleston, requesting that it should be published without any unnecessary delay. I suppose it will appear in 8 or 10 [days]. I object to the mode of constituting it, & the tariff principles of an influential portion ["of the party" *interlined*], who will be represented ["there" *canceled*] in it.

All join in love to you & Maria [Simkins Colhoun]. Yours affectionately, J.C. Calhoun.

ALS in ScCleA.

To THOMAS W. GILMER,
 [Representative from Va.]

Fort Hill, 25th Dec[embe]r 1843
My dear Sir, My opinion has long since been made ["up" *interlined*] and often expressed on the important subject, to which your letter [of 12/13] refers. I believe the annexation of Texas to be necessary to the peace & security of both countries, and [that it] will be beneficial to

the rest of the civilized world, including Mexico herself. That it is obviously so for Texas and the Southern portion of our Union must be admitted by all, who will calmly & fairly examine the subject. That she will contribute vastly more to the general wealth & prosperity of the commercial world, without endangering the peace or independence of any other nation, by being annexed to our Union, than without it, I hold equally clear, if Mexico be not an exception. I hold that she is not. To my mind, it is clear, that if Texas, in her independent, state should become a bone of contention between us & England, it is almost impossible, but that Mexico would be involved as a party with England, & that her subjugation would follow, almost as a matter of course.

As to the other portions of our Union, North & North west, her annexation would open a wide & valuable market for their products, while in a political point of view, it could not more than compensate, for the vast extension ["of" *canceled and* "opened to" *interlined*] the non slave holding States to the Pacifick on the line of the Oregon.

The objection, that it would extend our domestick institutions of the South, it must be met as a direct attack on the compromise of the Constitution; and the highest ground ought to be taken in opposition to it, on our part. You will find one of my resolutions moved on the subject of abolition in ["the" *canceled*] '38 or '39, I think, directly applicable to the case. I think it was the last of the 5 I then moved. I do not think, that there is any thing in the ground, that we acquired the country under the Treaty of Louis[i]ana, and had no right to cede it away, & that therefore it is still ours. It seems to me the true ground is, that the interest and safety of both countries require it, and that it ["is" *canceled and* "would" *interlined*] not be detrimental to any other. Under such circumstances, no nation has pretex[t] to interfere except it be Mexico, & she none fairly considered. The same principle, as was applicable to the Union of England & Scotland, or Ireland, or of these States is applicable to the Union of Texas with us. The proper course in all such cases is to take openly & boldly the true ground, and to maintain it ["at" *interlined*] all hazard. In such a case, I would rely on no refinement, or unimportant argument; but take the broad, plain, general ground.

I do not wish, what I write to be published. I think, it would rather do harm than good to publish any thing from me on the subject, under existing circumstances. It would give it too much the air of a mere presidential movement. Besides, I have ever been averse to appearing in the papers, when I could avoid it. But I have no objection that my views should be known & that you should show this to any friend you may think proper. With great respect I am yours truly, J.C. Calhoun.

ALS in DLC, John Tyler Papers, series 2 (Presidential Papers Microfilm, Tyler Papers, reel 2); PC in Lyon G. Tyler, *Letters and Times of the Tylers*, 2:296–297; PC in Jameson, ed., *Correspondence*, pp. 559–560. NOTE: For Calhoun's "resolutions moved on the subject of abolition," see *The Papers of John C. Calhoun*, 14:31–33.

To FRANCIS WHARTON

Fort Hill, 25th Dec[embe]r 1843

My dear Sir, I am much obliged to you for the Magazine, and have read your article with pleasure. It will do good, especially in reference to the great object you had in view; to justify the South for its course on the passage of the [tariff] bill of 1816. She was actuated by the most liberal and patriotick motives on the occasion, and much she has suffered for it. Even those who gained by it, and have turned what was then conceded to them into the means of unbounded extortion, have turned round and accused her of inconsistency because she would not quietly submit to be plundered.

Your plan is exceedingly judicious, and you have been very successful in its execution; you will reach by it the understanding of many, which could not be in any other way. I hope you will find leisure to continue your valuable labour. The cause is great. Free trade and intercourse, with the facility which modern improvements afford both, are destined to work the greatest and most happy change, which have ever taken place in the condition of our race. Its reaction on politicks, morals and religion will be powerful and most salutary.

I am much gratified that you have prepared an article for the Democratick Review on the volume of my speeches. I could not desire it to be in better hands. I shall be anxious to see the article. If you have an European correspondent through whom you could have it reviewed there, in some of [t]he quarterlies of established reputation, you would add to the obligations, under which you have already placed me. The conception on that side of the Atlantic is universally false in referance [*sic*] to our system of Government. It is indeed a most remarkable system; the most so, that ever existed. I have never yet discussed it in its higher elementary principles, or rather, I ought to say, in reference to higher elementary principles of political science. If I should have leisure, I may yet do it.

I have prepared a paper addressed to my political friends and supporters, assigning my reasons for refusing to permit my name to go before the Baltimore convention. I object to the mode in which it is constituted, and the principles of a large portion of the party who will be represented there in reference to the political policy. It will probably appear in 8 or 9 days. I mention this however in confidence, as I do not wish it to be spoken of till the address appears.

PC in Jameson, ed., *Correspondence*, pp. 558–559.

From F[RANCIS] W. PICKENS

Edgewood, 27 Dec[emb]er 1846 [*sic*; 1843]
My dear Sir, Patrick [Calhoun] arrived & stayed a day & two nights &c. with me. I think he has improved. I read with great interest & care your Address and would have gone to Charleston on account of it if I could possibly have left home, but just at the new year I am so busey [*sic*] that I could not possibly leave—particularly as I am about to change my overseers & somewhat my system. I have not got out near all my cotton yet.

Your refusal to allow your ["nae" *canceled*] name to go before the Convention & the reasons will produce a profound impression in the country. My impression is that it of course kills [Martin] V[an] Buren, and I rather think elects Mr. [Henry] Clay. It is a very powerful paper—but I shall write you freely & candidly—as a sincere friend ought to do. The first objection will be made as to its time. It ought to have been much sooner, and your friends ought ["not" *canceled*] never to have agreed to go into a convention. Their position in the So[uth] Ca[rolina] Legislature a year ago and for the last two years will weaken the moral force of the address. The second objection will be that it bears the aspect of being too personal ag[ain]st V[an] B[uren]—particularly that quotation from [Littleton W.] Tazewell "*that he had decieved* [*sic*] *us once*" &c. Perhaps that quotation from [Andrew] Jackson's expression of its "*being fresh from the people*" had better not [have] been made. You need the aid of no living man to give weight or authority to whatever truth you may advance and much less the aid of a living enemy.

I fear again that if we should be compel[l]ed to take ultra or extreme measures ag[ain]st the Tariff that ["it" *canceled*] disappointment may be attributed to us & it may be said that we have become desperate &c. They may say that you saw the result in 1842 and the votes then on the Tariff, & if it is as you say then you ought to have remained in the Senate and given the alarm from your place & taken your final stand then or immediately afterwards. These are the views & feelings of a friend who may be extremely sensitive for your welfare, & perhaps others may not take these views. I have fears as to Clay's election & power. I fear it may end in keeping on the present Tariff, & also in adding thereto a Bank. I do not think it possible for a high tariff to stand permanent without a Bank to swell the local currency so as to indemnify for the increased cost of production. Without a Bank to [*one word or partial word canceled*] create expansion a high Tariff must run down. I fear also that when the rally is made on your [*"name" interlined*] now and on the issue of Free Trade that under existing circumstances and as parties are now[?] organized at this late period of the Canvass, that the advocates of free trade will appear much weaker than they really are, and that it may produce & [*sic*] unfavourable impression ag[ain]st us.

But yet I am clear that your ["posi" *canceled*] position must be sustained—it is ["dute"(?) *canceled*] due to you and to the State. ["It must" *canceled*.] You must be supported in your move with calmness and dignity, and [I] have so written to [Franklin H.] Elmore[,] [Ker] Boyce & our other friends. I trust in God, you may not be injured. I hope for the best. I am confident of one thing[,] that it will break up the [Democratic] party at present as far as success is concerned, and can not say what will be the final and permanent effect. If it were not for Clay—I am sure it would in the end be all for the best. As it is, I cannot clearly see the future. I hope you will take the earliest opportunity to write a full exposition of the true principles of free Trade[,] its present prospects—and its future hopes. It is due to you—to the country—& to all mankind. A virtuous people will finally sustain you, and posterity will bless your name, let a corrupt and degenerate country take what course they may as to the present. I never felt so much anxiety for you as at present. I wish now you had not resigned, and yet I saw many[?] great difficulties in your being there.

I wrote you as to the school in Pendleton, & wish to take the boys up to it.

Present me very kindly to all and accept for yourself the affectionate regards of yours, F.W. Pickens.

ALS in ScCleA.

From James Wishart

St. Clairsville [Ohio,] Dec[embe]r 28th 1843
My Dear Sir, The letter with which you favored me, dated 4th and
Post-marked 14th ult[imo], reached me on the 1st inst[ant]. I have
defer[r]ed writing to you that I might see the development of public opinion, in reference to the course of events. Belmont [County]
seems to be the only green spot in Ohio, as you will see by our proceedings in the [St. Clairsville] Gazett[e] of this week, which I send.
They are not what I desired them to be, but as good as could be
obtained.

I shall give you public opinion, as I see it, and also my own views,
freely; assured that you will be guided by wiser counsels than any I
feel myself able to give, and therefore satisfied you will not be misled
by them, if erroneous. It is now almost universally believed that the
Baltimore convention [will] be packed—That arrangements for this
purpose were mad[e; *mutilation*] ago—And that it is useless to make
an effort to prevent [*mutilation*; Martin] Van Buren from being nominated, as it is believed h[e will?] be, by a large majority on the 1st
ballot. It is thought t[*mutilation*] a settled point that in the contingency of Mr. [Henry] Clay an[d; *mutilation*] being the candidates,
Mr. [John] Tyler will, also, be in th[e; *mutilation.*] But it is believed,
in that contingency, the contest [*mutilation*; set]tled in the electoral
college, in favor of Mr. Clay, by a [*mutilation*] large majority. Some
of your friends here are opposed to yo[ur] being a candidate unless
you get the nomination of the Baltim[ore] convention. Others are
afraid to let the election go to the House of Rep[resentative]s lest the
consummation of a bargain which it is believed was made, when Mr.
V[an] B[uren] was learning Mr. Clay to plant cabbage in the shades
of Ashland. But the impression is very general that if a number of
democratic candidates run, Mr. V[an] B[uren] will not even get into
the electoral college, and consequently cannot enter the House.

It appears to me that the alternative of electing a whig in the
electoral college or a democrat in the House of Rep[resentative]s, is
presented, for the first time, to the democratic party, in the contingency that Mr. V[an] B[uren] is the choice of the Baltimore convention, of which I now have no doubt.

The want of concert, the divisions and consequent weakness of
the south, have discouraged your friends here, so that I fear no further
effort will be made. If the south does not rely [on] herself she has no
hope. For principle is cast, by both [par]ties, in ["the" *interlined*]

645

north, to the moles and the bats, and if salvation does [not] come, to the democratic party, from the south, we are lost. [James Bu]chanan, [Lewis] Cass and Johnston [*sic*; Richard M. Johnson] with their friends have been look[*mutilation*] and not presenting any formidable objections or opposition [*mutilation*; di]rection[?] of Mr. V[an] B[uren] under the delusive hope that their [*mutilation*] would be the compromise candidate of the party. [*Mutilation*; ho]pes are I think now dissipated, and ["a" *interlined*] more general [*mutilation*] of opposition to Mr. V[an] B[uren] will spring up than has heretofore existed. But I do not think it will resist the nomination of the convention, however unrighteously obtained—All will succumb to the party despotism however arbitrary.

Admit[t]ing that Clay, V[an] B[uren] and Tyler should run, will [the] free trade men support either, and consent to lay aside their principles and be unrepresented in the contest of [18]44?

There are but a few copies of the [Washington] Spectator taken here, and the people were ignorant on the subject of the constitution of the Baltimore convention. The Gazett[e] had published little or none from that or any other, on the subject. A few numbers, hastily and imperfectly written, were submitted by ["the" *altered to* "me"], over the signature of Junius, for the Gazett[e], and the people are now right on that question. I also wrote in continuation of those numbers, two, 5 and 6, on the tariff, but discontinued them for the present because I did not wish, at this time, to place you in opposition to the other democratic candidates on that question. Although I believe this State is right on the tariff, yet such is our devotion to men, that the man without the principle, if he suits the leaders, will be prefer[r]ed to the man with it, if prejudice intervenes. Few men in this and other we[stern] States know your true character. The whig press has abused you [and] the democratic press has vilified and slandered you. You [*mutilation*] therefore but little known, and where you are, it is dis[advan]tageously, excepting a few who understand and du[ly? appre]ciate it. There are more persons in this county inform[ed; *mutilation*] point than in the residue of the State.

If Clay, V[an] B[uren] and Tyler are the only candida[tes; *mutilation*] my opinion, impossible to prevent the success of the wh[igs in] 44. The alternative I have stated above has never been [*mutilation*]ed to the V[an] B[uren] men, for the reason that they would regard [or] pretend to regard it as a proposition to divide the party. The V[an] B[uren] faction here believe that their object is accomplished for 44, and now raise the huzza for [Thomas H.] Benton in 48. They believe their party machinery is omnipotent—and it looks indeed very like it. I have little doubt that the consolidated State convention vote will be given to V[an] B[uren] but if he is the candidate he will loose [*sic*] the electoral vote of the State by from 20 to 40 thousand. He will also loose Penns[ylvani]a. Can he carry New York? If not, then Clay will want but 53 electoral votes, besides the 85 given by these three States, to elect him.

It is no use to preach conciliation toward V[an] Buren[']s friends here. Their course is and has been so bitter and proscriptive that all who have differed with his friends as to the policy of bringing him forward, look for as much honesty, lenity and forbearance, from the whigs as from [th]em. When they get the power, the ax will be used freely, [a]nd this idea alone will break him down, if there [wa]s no other obstacle to his election.

[W]ill the south do her duty to the country? Will she [*mutilation*] down her own diminished strength by a foolish [*mutilation*]d to her own peculiar interests? Will the south unite [*mutilation*] own[?] free trade candidate? This alone in my opinion [*mutilation*] save us. Will 48 be any more propitious? I fear [*mutilation*.] Believe me as heretofore most devotedly and Respectfully Yours &c, James Wishart.

ALS (partly burned) in ScCleA.

From HENRY P. BARBER

New York [City,] Dec[embe]r 29th 1843
Dear Sir, Your favor of the 3rd instant has just reached me owing partly probably to a delay of the mails and partly to a slight mistake on your part in directing it [to] Henry P. Baber instead of Henry P. Barber ["owing to which" *canceled*] on account of which it was not brought to me by the postman but suffered to remain in the Post Office and advertised. I am happy to hear that you approve of our circulars—some pains were certainly taken in getting them up and they were well considered before publication. Numbers of them have been sent throughout every part of the United States principally to the various postmasters and I think I may say their operation has been in some instances successful. We have received answers from various quarters—generally however (for I would not wish to deceive you but give the most correct information) the answers have not been so satisfactory as your friends could have wished. That proscriptive party organization which under the cool[,] calculating[,] selfish and

most treacherous policy of Mr. [Martin] Van Buren has fettered as it were the very souls of political men is hard[,] very hard to break. We find it so every day: in addition all the thirsty bloodsuckers of public plunder who under that dynasty have ever carried on the most shameless and disgraceful peculation expect to rise again with their soulless leader who to the lust of popularity and power would not hesitate to sacrifice every feeling of rectitude. Impelled by principles of self-interest the strongest motive power of action for men such as these[,] they watch with an Argus eye every attempt made to disenthral the great masses of the People from this abject slavery. Every man who refuses to bend the knee to their Baal to worship that Nebuchadnezzar whom they have set up is instantly proscribed and the dreaded cry of disorganization raised against him. Here it is eminently so and the yelling pack are led on first and foremost by Levi D. Slamm [editor] of the Plebeian—the personification of contemptible ["meaness" canceled] meanness and base treachery. These may be strong terms but for him there is no language sufficiently expressive of the loathing and disgust which every highminded and honorable man must feel. In spite however of this there are a few bold spirits whom this cry has not alarmed and who are doing every thing in their power to advance your interests and the cause of those great principles for which you contend. There was a time when the name of Mr. Van Buren was the only one heard in old Tammany [Hall]—but lately we have given cheer after cheer there for John C. Calhoun and no one dared to say Nay! [Illegible word canceled.] The Democratic party here have just elected their Old, Young Men[']s & Ward Committees for the ensuing year. In the young men[']s Committee consisting of 85 there are at least 20 on whom we can depend to advocate your principles and cause. I may say without vanity the talent and perseverance is decidedly with them. In the Old Men's Committee consisting of 51 you have several friends though I cannot yet state their number—neither of the Committees having yet organized. Among the Old Men[']s Committee is James T. Brady one of the most talented lawyers at our bar and one of your firmest friends—a host in himself. He defeated Peter Crawford[,] Mr. Van Buren[']s Baltimore delegate in his own ward by an immense majority. In the young men[']s Committee are Mr. Francis W. [sic; Fitzwilliam] Byrdsall and myself[,] two humble individuals whom you may rest assured will watch over your interests there—nail your flag to the mast and fight while a plank remains. In the ward which I represent, the Van Buren men knew that I wished to be a member of the Young Men[']s Committee and proscribed me on account of my being a "Calhoun man." The night before [the] election I went to some of my friends[,] made up a ticket consisting of five firm and tried friends of yours—["and" *canceled*] defeated *two* tickets opposed to us in the ward and returned the entire delegation to the Committee. We shall fight the tariff in the Committee pari passu with your friends [in] Washington & in addition strain every nerve for the adoption of the District System. I have heard a rumor whether well authenticated or not I am ignorant[,] that there is a proposition on foot to unite you with Mr. V[an] B[uren] as Vice President in furtherance of your obtaining the Presidency in 1848 in case (and so far as that goes without) Mr. V[an] B[uren]'s success. The V[an] B[uren] men I know would jump at the idea; and I presume his nomination by the Convention is now hardly problematical. [James] Buchanan's resignation has removed one obstacle & Pennsylvania *may* cast her vote for Mr. V[an] B[uren]. We have fought hard and well—we have battled every inch of ground—we have contested every debateable [*sic*] point and if the worst comes to the worst—["I trust(?) that" *canceled*] if your friends are at last not conquered but borne down by party organization and fraudulently packed conventions I trust that you will not at once reject the proposition without mature deliberation. In the hope of seeing you president[,] I for one would suffer much & I speak the sentiments of thousands of others. However disagreeable might be the cold selfishness[,] the soulless egotism of Mr. V[an] B[uren] surely a master spirit like your own could even with him direct the wheels of government. I presume the resignation of Gen. [Lewis] Cass will be the next news we hear & another obstacle to Mr. V[an] B[uren]'s ambition is removed. I do not however wish for a moment—nor would I on any account give up the fight till the last moment. Presenting as we do a bold front impervious alike to scorn[,] adulation and ridicule we now hold a position that commands and enforces respect, even from our bitterest opponents. They *may* ridicule but they *do* dread. Should the result to which I have referred happen it would no[t] be on our side but ["yours" *canceled*] theirs that the request would come. [We] should not appear as suppliants— No! The friends of Mr. V[an] B[uren] wou[ld] gladly accord to that salutary dread with which we have inspired them—what at the same time they would most gladly deny if they dared! I have no doubt that at this moment the most earnes[t] prayer of Tom Benton, Buchanan, & Silas Wright, is that you may refuse. The information I received I state to you merely as a rumor and not as coming from any authentic source—but positive I am that the V[an] B[uren] men would rush to accept it. They would sacrifice any thing except "their Lord and master." The documents to which you refer I will shortly forward and attend to your instructions concerning them. A propòs of the [New York] "Gazette"[;] In consequence of some difficulties ["amon"(?) *canceled*] between the Editors and Publisher it has been suspended for a while and is now in Chancery [court]. I trust however that it will ere long be revived again when I will gladly comply with the request conveyed in your letter. Of any *private* political matters here I will keep you faithfully advised—and the public political topics here you doubtless often see in the Charleston Mercury of which I am a correspondent from this place under the signature of "Henry." Having already trespassed too long on your valuable time allow me to subscribe myself Your devoted friend, Henry P. Barber.

ALS in ScCleA; PC in Boucher and Brooks, eds., *Correspondence*, pp. 195–198. NOTE: In regard to the New York *Gazette*, the obviously hostile New York *Herald*, December 13, 1843, p. 2, commented, under the title "Another Newspaper Abortion": "The new daily paper called the 'Gazette,' published by Alderman [E.B.] Clayton, and edited by Mr. [John L.H.] McCracken, exploded yesterday after a rickety existence of two weeks and one day. This was the paper that was started on a fund of $2,500 by some of the silly friends of Mr. Calhoun in this city, in order to revolutionize the democratic party, and write up free trade— alias free humbug. It has spent all the money and given up the ghost before it got fairly on its legs. Poor thing! We appoint Mr. [William Cullen] Bryant, the sweet poet, to sing its requiem, Mr. [Thomas] Ritchie of Richmond to pronounce its funeral sermon, and the editor of the Charleston Mercury to write its biography. Mr. Calhoun and his friends are thoroughly acquainted with the principles of free trade, but when will they learn the principles of common sense?"

By Dr. William L. Jenkins, [Pendleton], 12/31. Jenkins records in his medical daybook a visit to the Calhoun household: "Hon. John C. Calhoun. To visit & Medicine (Mrs. [Floride Colhoun] C[alhoun]). [$]2.25." Entry in ScCM, Waring Historical Library, William L. Jenkins Daybook, 1840–1848, p. 29.

From V[IRGIL] MAXCY

Washington, 31 Dec. 1843

My dear Sir, I received a letter day before yesterday from Mr. [Abel P.] Upshur pressing me to come over here. I found him very anxious to have your friends here to unite in an address to the people of the people of the [*sic*] United States taking ground against the packed Baltimore convention and otherwise "defining their position." He moreover pressed me very much to prepare the address. I told him ["that" *canceled*] that I feared very much it would ["be" *interlined*] considered presumptuous ["in me" *canceled and* "for me" *interlined*], who had no public station here, ["for me" *canceled*] to do it. He did not consider that a sufficient excuse. I still urged that it would come much better from some other person, and looking over the list of your friends here, I thought [George] McDuffie would do it much better and much more would have weight enough to induce every one here friendly to you to sign it. He finally consented, that I should see Mc-Duffie on the subject. I did so and altho he would not give his positive consent, he promised to visit Mr. Upshur tomorrow morning, and Mr. Upshur from whose [*sic*] I have just [come] thinks he will without doubt induce him to undertake it.

At McDuffie's I was told that your Address to your friends and ["supporters" *interlined*] had just been received and he read it to myself & Gen[era]l [Duff] Green who accompanied me. The grounds you have taken on the subject of the convention are perfectly unanswerable and must be so considered by every mind open to conviction. But Mr. Upshur, to whom with McDuffie's permission I took it, concurs in opinion with me, that it would be better to omit all you say on the subject of the Tariff, because the great object being to assign the reasons, why you cannot permit your name to be brought before a convention constituted as it will be, it seems proper to confine yourself to that subject: for as you had consented to go into a convention properly constituted, it does not seem quite logical to assign now as a reason for not doing it, that a part of those ["which" *changed to* "who"] will be members, do not entirely concur in your opinions on the subject of the Tariff, which has nothing to do with the formation of the convention and into which the same persons would have been admitted without objection, if the district system in forming it had been adop[t]ed. We both of us think therefore that what you say on the subject of the Tariff would be more suitable to be brought into the address of your friends here.

We both of us think moreover, that it would be better for your friends to take the initiative, instead of you, as personal motives would be immediately attributed to you, the whole [Martin] Van Buren Press would be opened upon you & some of your weaker friends might be fright[e]ned off from signing the address. Whereas if they should precede you in coming before the public, they would manifest from their numbers a strength, which would show them they ["(the partizans of Mr. V[an] Buren[)]" *interlined*] could not succeed ["you" *canceled*] without ["your" *changed to* "them" *and* "add"(?) *canceled*]. This would deter that press from attacking you.

651

As it is now 12 o[']Clock & I have to go to New York at 6 in the morning, I cannot write any more at present. Gen[era]l [Alexander O.] Anderson, who is still here concurs in all respects in the views taken by Mr. Upshur himself. I have promised Mr. Upshur, ["if he desires it," *canceled*] to come immediately back here, [*one or two words altered to* "from"] New York, if he desires it. I am so fatigued & sleepy I hardly know what I have written. Faithfully yours, V. Maxcy.

ALS and variant copy in ScCleA. NOTE: This letter was addressed to Calhoun in Pendleton. An AEU by Maxcy on the address page reads, "If not at home to be forward[ed] immediately."

JANUARY 1–MARCH 31
1844

〽

Except for a visit to his gold mine, Calhoun was at home in January. The South Carolinian let go of his Presidential prospects easily. For himself, he had no regrets. Honor was intact. He was far more concerned that the political scramble had eroded the seemingly firm position that the Democratic party had but a few years earlier taken on the tariff and abolition—and about the country's foreign relations, which involved grave and potentially explosive questions in regard to the future of the vast territory of Oregon and the vast Republic of Texas. As to himself he took a long view. The time was not right for the kind of leadership he could offer. If the time were ever to become right, he would try to be ready.

"The publick mind is greatly debased," Calhoun wrote Orestes Brownson. "The first step toward any effectual reform, is to put down and disgrace party machinery & management. No devise ever was adopted better calculated to gull the community; to put down all individuality & manliness of feeling, & keep the people in ignorance. It originated with Aaron Burr, & has been carried to perfection by the New York politicians. With them Democracy is but a profession, which is laid aside whenever it stands in the way of obtaining political power."

At last, on January 29, the campaign committee published in the Charleston press and thus released to the world Calhoun's statement that he would not allow his name to be considered by the convention of Democrats set to convene in Baltimore in the spring. Beyond this, what stand should his friends take in the Presidential contest? There was about this a large and conflicting volume of advice. Many wanted to collaborate with the Democracy as the lesser evil and in the hope of preserving a base for the future. Duff Green, as always speculating on a grand scale, projected a convention to meet in Philadelphia on the Fourth of July, in which the friends of President Tyler and independent men of all parties would unite with the friends of Calhoun to nominate a ticket that would compete favorably with the Demo-

653

*crats and Whigs. Calhoun considered the first suggestion an aban-
donment of principle and the second an illusory hope which could
only end in failure and embarrassment. His own conclusion was out-
lined to Robert M.T. Hunter on February 1: "Let our friends take this
high & impregnable position; & refuse all pledges, except the conditional one, that they will support Mr. V[an] B[uren], if those
pledges so solemnly given be in good faith fully redeemed, before the
meeting of the Convention, but not otherwise." The solemn pledges
referred to were the public statements made by the party in Congress
before the election of 1840, in favor of a revenue tariff and of the exclusion of slavery from the federal arena.*

*It was just in regard to those issues that many felt the lack of Cal-
houn's leadership in Washington. In February Calhoun was informed
that the junior Senator from South Carolina, Daniel E. Huger, who
had been elected to fill Calhoun's unexpired term and was in bad
health, would gladly resign, there being little question that the Governor, James H. Hammond, would appoint Calhoun to the seat. But
before this proposal could be dealt with, events had moved beyond it.*

On the 28th day of February, the United States warship Princeton
*took on board a large party of Washington notables, including the
President and Cabinet, their ladies and friends, and many others, for
an excursion down the Potomac to Mount Vernon and back. One of
the highlights of the trip was to be the demonstration of the huge
cannon which was the personal design and pride of Capt. Robert F.
Stockton. The gun exploded, killing a number of seamen and by-
standers. Among the dead were Secretary of State Abel P. Upshur,
the newly-appointed Secretary of the Navy Thomas W. Gilmer, and
David Gardiner of New York, who was to become the President's
father-in-law in a few weeks. Upshur was a friend and ally of Calhoun, but the greatest loss to him in the disaster was a private citizen,
Virgil Maxcy, whom Calhoun had loved as a brother since youth.
Upshur and Maxcy may well have been discussing Calhoun when
they were taken away by an act of that Providence to which Calhoun
always, in the final analysis, referred human events. Also on board
was the Carolinian's son, Lt. Patrick Calhoun of the Army, who could
have become one of the casualties had not the lady he was accompanying declined his suggestion to go nearer the gun.*

*The tragedy left vacant the headship of the Department of State
at a moment at which all recognized that serious questions of foreign
relations were impending. Calhoun had been sounded out before,
under more theoretical circumstances, about his willingness to take*

the post. He was now sounded out again, through Senator George McDuffie of South Carolina. In his reply, Calhoun indicated his unwillingness to undertake such an arduous labor as the head of a department. If called upon as a matter of duty, he might be willing to take charge of the pending negotiations with Great Britain in a special capacity, or to take the department for a limited time. But before this reply was written, much less could be received in Washington, events had moved on once more. The President had taken the matter into his own hands, unknown to Calhoun, and put the appointment on a basis which he knew the South Carolinian could not refuse. On March 6 Calhoun's nomination to be Secretary of State was sent to the Senate. It was confirmed the same day, without dissent from any Senator of either party.

Calhoun, rightly, took this event as a tribute, considering the controversiality and importance of the issues facing the country, and also as a call to duty that could not honorably be refused. Once more, as so often before, Calhoun made what arrangements he could for the management of Fort Hill and set out for the distant capital of the confederacy. Arriving at Charleston on March 26, though he had already refused a congratulatory dinner, he was met by a welcoming committee of one hundred mounted men, given a speech by the Attorney General of the State, and carried through thronged streets in a carriage drawn by four matched grays to the city hall, where he received another speech from the Mayor. When he departed the city next day on the mail boat for Wilmington, North Carolina, there were more crowds and a salute from the guns on the Battery. In Wilmington there was another cannonade and reception before Calhoun took the railroad north, and during the pause at Petersburg there was yet another public demonstration.

He arrived in Washington on March 29 and put up at Fuller's Hotel. Shortly before, J. Pinckney Henderson had reached the city after a two-week journey from the Texan capital of Washington-on-the-Brazos. Henderson carried instructions to join the Republic's representative already there, Isaac Van Zandt, in negotiating a treaty of annexation. The administration had indicated its willingness to take up that matter, and with this in mind, on the same day that Calhoun had been nominated, Tyler had named a new Minister to Mexico, Governor Wilson Shannon of Ohio. Another recent arrival in Washington was Richard Pakenham, who had presented credentials from Whitehall authorizing him to settle fully the outstanding question between Britain and America—Oregon. Calhoun dined with

Pakenham and members of the Senate Foreign Relations Committee on the day that he arrived, and, as reported in the press, used the occasion "to declare emphatically that he was for peace."

On March 30, a Saturday, Calhoun took the oath of office, preparatory to entering upon his duties on Monday, April 1. Some might have considered this an inauspicious day, but there was no trace of superstition in the mind of the South Carolinian, who was, in some respects, a survivor of a vanishing Age of Reason.

॥

From "A Friend of State Rights"
[JAMES H. HAMMOND]

[1844?]

You will probably recognize, in what I am about to say, the voice of one, who, tho' once provoked to retort the asperity, with which you thought proper to treat such States Right men, as could not make up their minds to join you in ["the" *canceled*] supporting Mr. [Martin] Van Buren, has yet always held your talents and virtues in the highest respect. There is reason to believe that you are now sensible of the mistake of which, at that time, I desired to convince you. You are sensible that no reliance can be placed on the word or principles of Mr. Van Buren; that he habitually plights his faith but that he may break it; and that whatever principles he may profess are but assumed to enable him to break his faith with advantage to himself.

I beg you to pardon whatever of ["seeming" *interlined*] arrogance there may be in thus charging error upon you. I have no right to censure it, for I am bound to confess that I, and others with whom I acted, were at the same time betrayed into an opposite mistake, of the like kind. Against this we too were warned, and warned by you. I can cast no censure against you which will not recoil upon myself. ["All th" *canceled and* "Much" *interlined*] Even ["what" *canceled and* "that" *interlined*] I said in the exciting struggle of that day rises up in judgment against me now. You, I have little doubt look on the past and the present with like feelings. So should all States Right men who took an active part on either side of the great controversy of 1640 [*sic*; 1840]. Heated by the strife into contention with those with whom *we* had been before identified, we all said much that we should be eager to recall lest our anathemas should fall on our own heads.

"It is but seemly, that where all deserve,
And stand exposed, by common peccancy
To what we all endure, there should be peace,
And brethren in calamity should love."

It is no time for mutual reproaches, but rather for ["candid" *canceled*] a restoration of harmony & confidence, and candid consultation on the best means of averting what may, and of mitigating, what cannot be avoided. Let me hope then, that remembering the past only as a source of ["the" *canceled*] wisdom for the future, you will not be disinclined to receive the suggestions of one who, without ever asking ["or" *interlined*] hoping ["or wishing" *canceled*] any thing for himself, has ever laboured, as an humble and private individual, for the maintenance of the great principles with which you are now identified. In saying this of myself I do not mean to make a parade of disinterestedness. I only announce the result of a conviction long since impressed upon my mind, that he who devotes himself unreservedly[,] faithfully and without compromise to those principles destroys his own hopes of advancement beyond a point of no very great elevation. If his ambition aspires to more than this, he must labour to rise above his station, and by the display of wisdom[,] ability[,] integrity[,] fidelity to principle, ["and" *canceled*] disinterestedness and magnanimity, to win for himself ["honours" *interlined*] higher than station can confer.

Trust me, Sir, this is sometimes an easier task than is commonly supposed. When the fortunes of a State are on the increase, the people intelligent[,] enterprising[,] frugal[,] industrious, devoted to the pursuits of honest industry and not yet corrupted by prosperity, to be ["place" *canceled*] called to the conduct of the affairs of such a people, is to be securely placed in a high niche in the Temple of Fame. The natural growth of things and the natural course of events achieve every thing for a ruler who does not by perverseness and folly manifestly counteract the working of these causes. But when the course[?] of advancement is drawing to a close, when the resources of the country have been developed or anticipated, when energy has subsided into sloth, when frugality is exchanged for luxury, and simplicity for ostentation, when ["the work of" *canceled*] corruption is ["in progress" *canceled*] at work, great men striving to advance themselves and not their country, and the multitude dissatisfied with the gains of honest industry ["grow" *canceled and* "and" *interlined*] restive under the curb of Law, it is no longer Fame to be identified with such a State. In the earlier ages of the Roman Republic the energy and virtue and genius of the people achieved greatness for all to whom the conduct of her affairs was committed. To ["name" *canceled and* "enumerate" *interlined*] the men of those days whose names will forever live in history is to call over the list of her consuls for three hundred years. But when Conquest had done its perfect work, & filled the State with the wealth and the vices of the conquered, we hear no more of greatness but that achieved by crime. In two ["successive" *interlined*] generations we hear of none great at the head of affairs but Marius & Sylla[,] Pompey & Caesar. These by turns were the State[,] identified with it in all but this, that in accomplishing their own ends they destroyed their country. And yet, with all their marvellous endowments, what is the honour which these men won for themselves compared with that which posterity has with one voice accorded to two others, of whom one was deficient in talent, the other in courage? I speak of Cicero and Cato, whose glory it was that they wished to have saved their country, and only failed to do so because their country rejected their services. So ["all" *interlined*] men have said ["so some have thought" *interlined*] and so ["th they" *canceled and* "all" *interlined*] have tried to think. For myself, I confess, ["that" *canceled*] I hardly ["think they would" *canceled and* "believe" *interlined*] that, had they been placed at the head of affairs, they could have resisted the course of events and the operation of causes all tending to destruction. But this ["is only" *canceled*] opinion, ["is rare" *interlined*] and the most sceptical still gladly accords them a praise in comparison with which the glories of their more successful antagonists ["is" *altered to* "are"] but splendid infamy. How much better for their fame is this fate than to ["have" *canceled and* "have been placed in public stations, but to" *interlined and* "shared" *altered to* "share"] the sort of honour which the imperial purple conferred on the well meaning Galba[,] "All would have pronounced him worthy of empire, had he never reigned." So says History of Galba, and so might it have said of the virtuous Cato, or the philosophic & eloquent Cicero. I will not run the parallel between that case and our own. I simply congratulate you, Sir, that when the contest is between a factious populace led on by ["the" *canceled and* "a" *interlined*] savage Marius and his creature Cinna, ["thirsting" *canceled and* "burning" *interlined*] for revenge, and a no less factious Aristocracy headed by an ambitious Sylla, you have been quietly put aside as unfit for the purposes of either of the two great factions whose ["purposes" *canceled and* "ends and aims" *interlined*] are alike fatal to the ["liberty" *canceled and* "freedom" *interlined*] and happiness of the Country. When all that shall be left to the friends of constitutional Liberty shall be ["but" *canceled*] to take up the lamentation of the Poet, and exclaim *"fuit Ilium—fuimus Troes"* then the highest praise that History can award will be for him of whom it can be said[,]

> *"Si dextera Pergama*
> *Defendi possint, etiam hac defensa fuissent."*

It is in this thought that I find consolation for the conviction long since established in my mind, that however the principles of States Right Men may be respected and valued, even by those who do not avow them, they can never be the declared and active principles ["for the time being" *interlined and then canceled*] of any actual dominant majority in the United States. The love of power will not permit it. Majorities in power are not apt to recognize any principles which at all restrict the right of Majorities to do their will in all things. The same individuals, when in minority could readily feel that Majorities may be unjust[,] arbitrary and oppressive, and that there can be no right in ten ["mens" *altered to* "men"] to bind according to their will and pleasure nine others in any matter in which the nine have ["not" *interlined*] consented to be so bound. But when they find themselves in a Majority they forget all this, and think only of retorting the injury, ["than ref" *canceled*] instead of guarding against its recurrence by an authoritative condemnation of the principle in which it took its rise. Observe, I pray you, Sir, how eagerly the [Democratic?] majority in the present Congress have appropriated to themselves all the arbitrary ["prof" *canceled*] precipitate[,] indecent and ["insol" *canceled*] insolent modes of proceeding, of which the very same men so loudly and justly complained two years ago. It is a saying as old as the present division of parties in England, that Whigs in opposition are Tories in power. ["With" *canceled*] How much more persuasive are the influences operating here to make it true in like manner, that States Right men in opposition are Centralists in power. The administration of the federal Government for four and twenty successive years by the acknowledged leaders of the States Right party ended in total oblivion or profound contempt ["for" *canceled and* "of" *interlined*] the principles of that party. It was during that time that you yourself came into public life, and modestly, as became your youth, took your place as a pupil at the feet of the men then recognized as the fathers of the Constitution the founders of the States Right School, the purest & wisest of our Statesmen. You studied their principles in their practice: and what did you learn from that that your own subsequent inquiries did not convince you was totally at variance with those principles. Was Louisiana to be purchased? Mr. [Thomas] Jefferson could find in the Constitution an authority for it. Was the Habeas Corpus act to be suspended in time of profound tranquillity? Mr. [William Branch] Giles could ["find" *canceled and* "furnish" *interlined*] an argument in support of it. Was the public money to be partially applied to internal improvements for the benefit of favoured portions of the Union? None of the party could see any objection to the plan, and all who did object were denounced as *federalists*. Was a bank to be chartered? Mr. [James] Madison could find (what none else could) an answer to his speech in Congress in 1792, and to his resolutions and report in 1798–9. Was a Tariff of protection required for the farther benefit of the manufacturers, who during the war had fattened on the blood ["is those who were warring" *canceled and* "shed" *interlined*] in his defence? Every man who hinted at the Constitution was ["dra" *canceled*] stigmatized as a traitor, and enemy to his Country. The mild precepts of Christianity are not more at variance with the crimes perpetrated in its name, than are the practices of States Right Men in power, with the principles by which they profess to be guided. In both cases the result has been that words have changed their meaning, and are used to sanction the very things they were intended to condemn. And in both cases the reason is the same. A bad life and a bad faith are reciprocally causes of each other. The Pope while, in obedience to his Master, he called himself "Servant of Servants," claimed to be King of Kings, and a respect[?] to the rights of the States is manifested by trampling on their authority and scoffing at their Sovereignty.

Are there then none remaining who may be justly called *States Right Men?* I thank God there are. I doubt whether we may say, with the prophet, that there are yet "seven thousand men in our Israel who have not bowed the knee to Baal." But there is still a persecuted and scattered remnant of that true but suffering Church. If ever the broken fragments, shivered like a glass snake by the wand of the arch magician, ["are" *interlined*] again united ["themselves" *canceled*], you will be again ["your" *and* "their" *canceled and* "their" *interlined*] head. But it is the office of the head to seek them out, to combine them again together each in its proper place, each with its due organization. That office belongs to you Sir, and it is on the duty of performing it, and the manner in which the task should be performed, that I propose ["in a future letter" *interlined*] to offer some thoughts to your consideration. *A Friend of State Rights.*

ALU in DLC, James Henry Hammond Papers, vol. 23. NOTE: This document is in Hammond's handwriting, found among Hammond's papers, and addressed to Calhoun. Whether it was sent to Calhoun is unknown. If intended for publication, no such publication has been found, nor has any subsequent letter signed with the same pseudonym been found. The undated document has been given a conjectual date of early 1844 from its content.

From E[STWICK] EVANS

Wash[ingto]n City, Jan. 2, 1844

Dear Sir, I have noticed, with regret—& something a little sterner, the manner in which certain parties or shreds of parties are disposed to crowd you out of the field—availing themselves of the old grudge about State rights &[c] to effect their object. Permit me to say that I hope your friends will hold on & dispute the ground inch by inch—until better auspices—which I hope may come extremely soon & very suddenly. The elements of your case are those of the country; this is an *eventful* world; & many things may soon turn up to put a new face on things. I rather believe—not with absolute certainty, however, by any means, that Mr. [Henry] Clay would beat Mr. [Martin] Van Buren; but I believe the only certainty—or certainty to a large extent, depends on the party of the latter taking up a [*one word canceled*] man, strong in the true general elements of the country & liberty—& having a *freshness* in relation to the public feeling. Mr. Van Buren is not himself a man of vigour—has been long before the public mind—& *in* the public mind—& is beside[s] a candidate for the second term.

I do not consider Mr. Clay's grounds altogether sound in view of the *popular sentiment.*

["A" *altered to* "I"] have requested Mr. [Levi] Woodbury to do me the favour to enclose this to you. I consider Mr. W[oodbury] as having very favourable political relations: they are the basis of his *very* general success.

Delayed as the Essay [on State Rights] has been, it is now delivering[?] its proofs—& will be out I think in a week or ten days. I go into the war with a sense of power & understanding of the subject. You & Carolina, as Carolina was—the true Carolina, will find passing notice. I have spoken of my consciousness of power, because I mean also to say that you will expect from no man, in this day of light & talent[?], any miracle in the way of [*one word canceled*] writing. If you should, on a careful perusal, with which I hope to be honoured, find it calculated to enlighten & arouse the *Popular* Elements of the country, be pleased to have it noticed in the papers of the country & give to it a run[?]. I think I have said enough of what is favourable to ["to" *canceled*] you & State Rights—you espec[ia]lly—for the entering wedge. If then this goes well, I shall strike strong & home—& with hard[?]—though with the silk glove of dignity & courtesy in a 2[n]d No. of the series—which is read[y] for the press & can be out immediately after the first is on its track.

I hope your friends will nail your colours to the mast—(not to *say* so of course) but to do so & to let it be seen—by the deeds themselves that they do so. Glory will attend you—if you could well[?]—even *if* you should die in struggling for the Goal—without reaching it—for the reason that your elements of mind, & soul, & public labours, are glorious. With very high consideration, Y[ou]r f[rie]nd & Ob[edien]t S[ervan]t, E. Evans.

ALS in ScCleA.

From JOSEPH SMITH

Nauvoo, Illinois, Jan[uar]y 2, 1844

Sir, Your reply to my letter of last November, concerning your rule of action towards the Latter Day Saints, if elected President, is at hand: and, that you and your friends of the same opinion, relative to the matter in question, may not be disappointed as to me, or my mind, upon so grave a subject, permit me, as a law abiding man: as a well wisher to the perpetuity of constitutional rights and liberty, and as a friend to the free worship of Almighty God, by all, according to the dictates of every person's conscience, to say *I am surprized*, that a man, or men, in the highest stations of public life, should have made up such a fragile "view" of a case, than which there is not one on the face of the Globe fraught with so much consequence to the happiness of men in this world, or the world to come. To be sure[,] the first paragraph of your letter appears very complacent, and fair on a white sheet of paper, and who, that is ambitious for greatness and power, would not have said the same thing? Your Oath would bind you to support the Constitution and laws, and as all creeds and religions are alike tolerated, they must, of course, all be justified or condemned, according to merit and demerit—but why, tell me why, are all the principle [*sic*] men, held up for public stations, so *cautiously careful*, not to publish to the world, that *they will judge a righteous judgment*—

law, or no law: for laws and opinions, like the vanes of Steeples, change with the wind. One Congress passes a law, and another repeals it, and one statesman says that the Constitution means this, and another that; and who does not know that all may be wrong? The opinion and pledge therefore, in the first paragraph of your reply to my question, like the forced steam from the engine of a Steamboat, makes the show of a bright cloud at first, but when it comes in contact with a purer atmosphere, dissolves to common air again.

Your second paragraph leaves you naked before yourself, like a likeness in a mirror, when you say that "according to your *view*, the Federal Government, is one of limited and specific powers," & has no Jurisdiction in the case of the Mormons. So then, a State can at any time, expel any portion of her citizens with impunity and in the language of Mr. [Martin] Van Buren, frosted over with your gracious *"view of the case,"* "though the cause is ever so just, government can do nothing for them, because it has no power."

Go on, then, Missouri, after another set of Inhabitants, (as the Latter Day Saints did) have entered some two or three hundred thousand dollars worth of land, and made large improvements thereon: go on, then, I say, banish the occupants or owners, or kill them, as the mobbers did many of the Latter Day Saints, and take their lands and property as a Spoil: and let the Legislature, as in the case of the Mormons, appropriate a couple of hundred thousand dollars to pay the mob for doing the Job, for the renowned senator from South Carolina, Mr. J.C. Calhoun, says, the powers of the Federal Government are so *specific and limited that it has no Jurisdiction of the Case!* Oh ye people who groan under the oppression of tyrants, Ye exiled Poles, who have felt the Iron hand of Russian grasp: Ye poor and unfortunate among all nations, come to the "Asylum of the oppressed": buy ye, lands of the General Government, pay in your money to the Treasury, to strengthen the Army and Navy: Worship God according to the dictates of your own consciences; pay in your taxes to support the Great Heads of a *glorious* nation; but remember, a *"Sovereign State"!* is so much more powerful than the United States, the parent government, that it can exile you at pleasure, mob you with impunity; confiscate your lands and property: have the Legislature sanction it; yea, even murder you, as an edict of an Emperor, *and it does no wrong*, for the noble Senator of South Carolina, says, the power of the Federal Government, is *so limited and specific, that it has no Jurisdiction of the case!* What think ye of *Imperium in imperio*[?]

Ye Spirits of the blessed of all ages, Hark! Ye shades of departed Statesmen, listen! Abraham, Moses, Homer, Socrates, Solon, Solomon, and all that ever thought of right and wrong, look down from your exaltations, if you have any, for it is said in the midst of counsellors there *is safety,* and when you have learned that fifteen thousand innocent citizens, after having purchased their Lands of the United States, and paid for them, were expelled from a "Sovereign State" by order of the Governor, at the point of the Bayonet: their arms taken from them by the same authority: and their right of migration into said State, denied under pain of imprisonment, Whipping, Robbing, Mobbing, and even Death, and no Justice or recompence allowed: and from the Legislature, with the Governor at the head, down to the Justice of the Peace, with a Bottle of Whiskey in one hand and a bowie knife in the other, hear them all declare that there is no Justice for a Mormon in that State, and Judge ye a righteous Judgment, and tell me when the virtue of the States was stolen; where the honor of the General Government lies hid; and what clothes a Senator with Wisdom? O nullifying Carolina! Oh little tempestuous Rhode Island! would it not be well for the great men of the nation to read the fable of the *Partial Judge,* and when part of the free citizens of a State had been expelled contrary to the Constitution, Mobbed, Robbed, Plundered, and many murdered, instead of searching into the course taken with Joanna Southcott, Ann Lee, the French Prophets, the Quakers of New England, and Rebellious Niggers in the Slave States, to hear both sides and then judge, rather than to have the mortification to say, "Oh it is *my* bull that has killed *your* Ox—that alters the case! I must enquire into it, *And if, and if*"?

If the General Government has no power, to re-instate expelled citizens to their rights, there is a monstrous hypocrite fed and fostered from the hard earnings of the people! A real "Bull Beggar" upheld by Sycophants; and altho' you may wink to the Priests to stigmatize; wheedle the drunkards to swear, and raise the hue and cry of *Imposter, False Prophet, God dam*[n] *old Joe Smith,* yet remember, if the Latter Day Saints are not restored to all their rights, and paid for all their losses according to the known rules of Justice and Judgment, reciprocation and common honesty among men, that God will come out of his hiding place and vex this nation with a sore vexation—yea, the consuming wrath of an offended God shall smoke through the nation, with as much distress and woe, as Independence has blazed through with pleasure and delight. Where is the Strength of Government? Where is the Patriotism of a [George] Washington, a [Joseph] Warren, and [John?] Adams? and where is a spark from the Watch fire of '76, by which one candle might be lit that would glimmer upon the confines of democracy? Well may it be said that one man is not a State; nor one State the nation. In the days of General [Andrew] Jackson, when France refused the first instalment for spoliations, there was power, force, and honor enough to resent injustice and insult, and the money came. And shall Missouri[,] filled with negro drivers, and white Men Stealers, go "unwhipt of Justice" for tenfold greater sins than France? No; verily no! While I have powers of body and mind; while water runs and grass grows; while virtue is lovely and vice hateful; and while a stone points out a sacred spot where a fragment of American Liberty once was, I, or my posterity, will plead the cause of injured innocence until Missouri makes atonement for all her sins—or sinks disgraced, degraded and damned to hell—"where the worm dieth not and the fire is not quenched."

Why Sir, the power not delegated to the United States, and the States, belongs to the people, and Congress[,] sent to do the people's business, have all power—and shall fifteen thousand citizens groan in exile? Oh vain men, will ye not, if you do not restore them to their rights and $2,000,000 worth of property, relinquish to them, (the Latter Day Saints) as a body, their portion of power that belongs to them according to the Constitution? Power has its convenience, as well as inconvenience. "The world was not made for Cäesar alone, but Titus too."

I will give you a parable: A certain Lord had a vineyard in a goodly land, which men laboured in at their pleasure; a few meek men also, went and purchased with money from some of these Chief Men that labored at pleasure, a portion of land in the vineyard, at a very remote part of it, and began to improve it, and to eat and drink the fruit thereof, when some vile persons who regarded not man neither feared the Lord of the Vineyard, rose up suddenly and robbed these meek men and drove them from their possessions, killing many. This barbarous act made no small stir among the men of the vineyard, and all that portion who were attached to that part of the Vineyard where the men were robbed, rose up in grand council with their Chief Man, who had firstly ordered the deed to be done, and made a Covenant not to pay for the cruel deed but to keep the spoil, and never let those meek men set their feet on that soil again neither recompense them for it. Now these meek men, in their distress, wisely sought redress of those wicked men in every possible manner and got none. They then supplicated the Chief Men who held the Vineyard at pleasure, and who had the power to sell and defend it, for redress and redemption, and those men, loving the fame and favor of the multitude, more than the glory of the Lord of the Vineyard, answered, "your cause is just, but we can do nothing for you, because we have no power." Now, when the Lord of the Vineyard saw that virtue and innocence was not regarded and his vineyard corrupted by wicked men, he sent men and took the possession of it to himself and destroyed those unfaithful servants and appointed them their portion among hypocrites.

And let me say, that all men who say that Congress has no power to restore and defend the rights of her citizens, have not the love of the truth abiding in them. Congress has power to protect the nation against foreign invasion and internal broil: and whenever that body passes an act to maintain right with any power: or to restore right to any portion of her citizens, *it is the supreme law of the land* and should a State refuse submission, that State is guilty of *insurrection or rebellion,* and the president has as much power to repel it as Washington had to march against the "Whiskey Boys of Pittsburg," or General Jackson had to send an armed force to suppress the rebellion of South Carolina!

To close, I would admonish you, before you let your *"candor compel"* you again to write upon a subject, great, as the Salvation of man, consequential as the life of the Savio[u]r, broad as the principles of eternal truth, and valuable as the Jewels of Eternity, to read in the 8th Section and 1st Article of the Constitution of the United States, the *first, fourteenth* and *seventeenth* "Specific" and not very "limited powers" of the Federal Government, what can be done to protect the lives, property and rights, of a virtuous people, when the administrators of the laws, and law makers, are unbought by bribes, uncorrupted by patronage, untempted by gold, unawed by fear and uncontaminated with tangling alliances—even like Caesar's Wife, not *only unspotted but unsuspected!* and God, who cooled the heat of a Nebuchadnezzar's furnace, or shut the mouths of Lions for the honor of a Daniel will raise your mind above the narrow notion, that the General Government has no power—to the sublime idea that Congress, with the president as executor, is as Almighty in its sphere, as Jehovah is in his. With great consideration I have the honor to be Your obed[ien]t serv[an]t, Joseph Smith.

FC in USlC, Historical Department; PC in the Nauvoo, Ill., *Neighbor,* January 10, 1844, pp. 2–3; PC in the New York, N.Y., *Herald,* January 26, 1844, p. 2; PC in *Niles' National Register,* vol. LXV, no. 23 (February 3, 1844), pp. 357–358; PC in *The Voice of Truth, Containing General Joseph Smith's Correspondence with Gen. James Arlington Bennett; Appeal to the Green Mountain Boys; Correspondence with John C. Calhoun, Esq. . . . Also, Correspondence with the Hon. Henry Clay* (Nauvoo, Ill.: printed by John Taylor, 1844), pp. 22–26; PC in *Correspondence Between Joseph Smith, The Prophet, and Col. John Went-*

worth . . . and the Honorable John C. Calhoun . . . (New-York: Published by John E. Page and L.R. Foster, 1844), pp. 12–14; PC in *Americans, Read!!!* *Gen. Joseph Smith's Views of the Powers and Policy of the Government of the United States. . . . Correspondence with the Hon. John C. Calhoun . . .* (New-York: E.J. Bevin, printer, 1844), pp. 27–32; PC in [Henry Mayhew,] *The Mormons: Or Latter-Day Saints. With Memoirs of the Life and Death of Joseph Smith, the "American Mahomet"* (London: Office of the National Illustrated Library, [1851]), pp. 150–153; PC in *The Prophet Joseph Smith's Views of the Powers and Policy of the Government of the United States. To which is appended the Correspondence between the Prophet Joseph Smith and the Hons. J.C. Calhoun and Henry Clay, Candidates for the Presidency of the United States in 1844* (Salt Lake City: Jos. Hyrum Parry and Co., 1886). NOTE: The manuscript of this document transcribed above is in the handwriting of Thomas Bullock, one of Joseph Smith's secretaries in 1844. It is signed by an unknown individual, not Bullock, imitating Joseph Smith's signature, and is addressed mistakenly to "Hon. J.C. Calhoun, Fort Hill, Charleston, South Carolina."

To Gov[erno]r [JAMES H.] HAMMOND, Columbia, S.C.

Fort Hill, 3d Jan[uar]y 1843 [*sic*; 1844]
My dear Sir, The writter [*sic*; Joseph W. Farnum?] of the enclosed was the Essayer [*sic*] for the Mint at Dahlonega [Ga.]. I know him well. He is well qualified for the place for which he applies. None can be had better, and [he] is withal a most excellent man. I would be gratified to see him appointed.

I have decided not to let my name go before the Baltimore Convention and have prepared an Address & transmitted a copy to the Central Committee at Charleston for publication, assigning quite fully my reasons for doing so. It will I presume soon appear. I have acted on my individual responsibility. The paper is addressed to my political friends & supporters, who I have left free to sustain the course I have taken or not, as they may deem their duty to dictate. With my principles, it was impossible for me to take any other course. I hope the paper, when it appears, will meet your approbation. Truly, J.C. Calhoun.

ALS in DLC, James Henry Hammond Papers, vol. 10; PC in Jameson, ed., *Correspondence*, pp. 560–561. NOTE: The enclosure has not been found, but the person most likely referred to was Joseph W. Farnum, who was Assayer of the U.S. Mint at Dahlonega during 1837–1843.

From DIXON H. LEWIS, [Representative from Ala.]

Washington, Jan[uar]y 3rd 1844

My Dear Sir, I have received since I reached this place your two letters, the last coming to hand three or four days since, and have for the first time ["today," *interlined*] seen a copy in manuscript of your Address [dated 12/21/1843] to the Central Committee. I regret that I have been so much confined to my bed with two attacks of Erysipelas since the meeting of Congress, that I have not written to you sooner, and in fact, before you wrote your Address. I should have suggested to you some modifications, founded on the state of things here, which if the Document is not published before this reaches you, I hope you will still make.

I agree with you fully as to the propriety of your not suffering your name to go before the Convention as at present constituted, and I am more than satisfied with the sound reasoning on which you base your refusal. It is such as will fully justify you before the Country, while it free[s] you and your friends from the thraldom of a corrupt system, which unopposed, would have been a precedent, for the most corrupt bargaining not only for the Presidency but the succession to it, and which at present can answer no other purpose than to pledge the Democratic Party to Mr. [Martin] Van Buren. That his friends have the power in that Body to nominate him, there can be no doubt, & that nothing but his acknowledged want of availability will prevent them from doing so is equally certain. Nevertheless I feel great doubts, if the developements of public opinion before the first of May, do not drive them from it. The sentiment that he will be beaten, is almost as universal out of the range of a few of his devoted friends, as that he will be nominated. His friends have not a little added to this conviction by their suicidal course on the subject of Abolition petitions and the Tariff, and if they do not speedily change their course, the evidences will become so strong as to arrest the conviction of his most devoted followers. They can in no event hope to elect him without the aid of thousands who prefer you, and any measure therefore on your part which would look to assuming a position independent of, and out of the pale of the Party, would furnish them with a hope of separating your friends from you, and thus by the force of Party obligation of uniting them to Mr. Van Buren. Unless this can be done, I hardly think they will have the boldness to follow [Thomas H.] Benton into a nomination, more particularly under circumstances which on the subjects of the Tariff & abolition will not even leave them a foot to stand on in the South. The question then recurs what will they do? They have already tried the force of a Convention, & have unfortunately committed most of your friends to its decision irrespective of the mode of its organization. On that subject, you can make an issue with them so far as to refuse to let your name go before the Convention, but your friends who have not ["so" *interlined*] generally insisted on the conditions of District representation & per Capita voting as they perhaps ought to have done, cannot. Hence it is important that while you refuse to go into the Convention, you make no move which shall look like getting up an opposition to the nomination merely on the ground of your objections to the Convention. On the contrary, I think you should expressly state, that while your objections are so decided against the manner of constituting the Convention, and while its decisions should impose on you no obligations, you should not on account of a difference with your party on a question of party proceeding, however objectionable, separate yourself from them, but would so far from ["separating" *canceled*] allowing your name to be used to defeat your own principles, ["use your strenuous efforts to" *canceled and* "support" *changed to* "would" *and then canceled*] support any candidate going into the contest distinctly pledged to & truly supporting those principles. You might in this way prescribe ["the" *canceled*] terms to Mr. Van Buren & his friends on the Tariff during the present session of Congress, with a distinct avowal that if the great Democratic Principle of Free Trade was not openly sustained by the Nominee your name or your aid was at the service of any portion of your friends however small who might under a distinct nomination wish to rally under that Flag.

The advantages of a position so taken would be[:]

First—It would enable you to break down any such Convention in future, without breaking with your Party.

Secondly—It would not only secure but greatly increase that sympathy, which I know is felt for you by a large portion of the Party, which makes you the first choice of many of them, who by the constraints of the Convention will go for Van Buren, & the second choice as I beleive [*sic*] already of two thirds, and the prominent man for the succession with four fifths of them.

Thirdly—It will ["put" *interlined*] V[an] Buren & his Party here before he is a Candidate, under a whip you yourself will hold over them, & for the slightest departure from the line of faith which you will draw, they will be thrown overboard, ["as unavailable because of their departure," *interlined*] & you yourself ["will" *canceled*] probably from your position, will be the Nominee. The Tariff, Abolition, & the Texas question will be a narrow line for them to track any how, and ["for" *canceled*] in case of a failure, your chances will be only strengthened for the reason, that you do not consider yourself a Candidate.

4th. If V[an] Buren runs & is beaten you gain rather than lose the sympathy of your Party by such a course & thus put yourself in a position to supplant a wing of the Party which by such second defeat will become odious. He will certainly be beaten even by [Henry] Clay.

5thly. If he is nominated without any concession to the Free Trade portion of the Party, the Convention can give him no power because it cannot render his election even probable & then as the *Free* Trade Candidate you can get the support of Thousands who now do not foresee the perfidy of his course on that question—and who at present are pampered by a Convention, which you will disarm of all of its power, the moment you refuse to go into it, without breaking with your Party, which you can do by basing your support or opposition not on the *nomination* but on the *Principles* of the Candidate selected.

6thly—Should V[an] Buren be elected under pledges which will satisfy you & your friends on the Tariff ["which is hardly possible" *interlined*], you will have a control over that administration in spite of him, which will make you omnipotent with the Party & for the succession. Benton & his loose Tariff friends will be bridled, and the honours of the Party will enure not to Partisans but to those who support in good faith Democratic Principles. The very manner of electing him will break the collars of Party men in future & break up Party machinery.

These are my views fully & honestly given. I fear your letter will be published before they reach you & I regret that painful illness has prevented me from giving them to you earlier. I shall show this letter to no one. It is well considered however, and I hope you will take it as the honest advice of one who always has & always ["will" *interlined*] sustain you to the extent of his power, in what he believes are sincere efforts to save the Institutions & Liberties of the Country. It is not a very wide departure which I advise from the course you have already taken, but it is better guarded as I believe, & more calculated to [*one word or partial word canceled*] sustain that confidence & estimation, which I know the great body of the Party have for you— and above all, is the course which will enable your friends to sustain you with most effect—Many of whom are too deeply pledged to the Convention now to make war on it. If I hear nothing in reply I shall fear, you intend by your silence to reprove a freedom on my part in giving my advice, which nothing but my friendship for you could have emboldened me to offer. I am very truly your friend, Dixon H. Lewis.

ALS in ScCleA. NOTE: On the same date as the above letter, Lewis wrote twice to Franklin H. Elmore in Charleston, urging him to withhold Calhoun's "Address" from publication until revised and giving his reasons at length. See below the enclosure and note with Elmore's letter to Calhoun of 1/9/1844.

From Geo[rge] McDuffie, [Senator from S.C.]

Washington, 3rd Jan[uar]y 1843 [*sic*; 1844]
My dear Sir; Your address was duly received, & after awaiting the return of Judge [Daniel Elliott] Huger [Senator from S.C.] from New York it was read to the assembled delegation who all approved of your course & the reasons of it, Judge Huger most decidedly. He regards the exposition of your grounds as perfectly unanswerable & as exhausting the argument, & thinks it will place you on very high grounds before the country. Judge [Abel P.] Upshur entertains the same opinion & is warmly your friend. He suggested that it might be well to rest your withdrawal of your name upon the organization of the Convention alone, leaving the tariff to be urged by your friends in case [Martin] V[an] Buren's friends do not enable us, by co-operating in good faith, to reduce the tariff to a fair revenue standard. We have yet some hope that they will do so, as they are pretty well satisfied that Mr. Van Buren will get but a very small vote in the South & S[outh] West, even against Mr. [Henry] Clay, if they do not. They clearly have the power, ["to do it" *interlined*] & must know that the South, twice deceived already by them, will take no other evidence of Mr. Van Buren's & their sincerity.

Under these circumstances we have deemed it our duty to take no position at present, which will destroy the hope, that your friends may ultimately vote for Mr. Van B[uren] if his friends co-operate faithfully on reducing the tariff. Indeed if we were to take that position, it would be confined to a portion of our own delegation. Even Mr. [Dixon H.] Lewis says he could not ["now"(?) *canceled*] sustain himself in taking such a position now. There is an impression here that the administration are negotiating for the annexation of Texas, but nothing certain or definite has transpired. My own opinion is that nothing, but a very high state necessity will justify the measure either on the score [of] justice or policy. It would be *ipso facto* making war on Mexico, if done without her concurrence, & there would be a hazard that Great Britain would take part with Mexico. Make my best regards to Mrs. [Floride Colhoun] C[alhoun] & the family. Very sincerely your friend, Geo: McDuffie.

ALS in ScCleA; variant PC in Boucher and Brooks, eds., *Correspondence*, p. 198.

From FRANCIS WHARTON

Philadelphia, January 5th, 1844

My dear Sir, Your letter of the 25th of January [*sic;* December] was brought me yesterday. I am most happy to find that the [p]lan[?] of the papers in Hunt's magazine meets with your approbation. My own great hope is that they may contribute to remove from the minds of the mercantile community, that marvellous ignorance of their own position, which is as derogatory to their intelligence as it is dangerous to their safety. Let the delusion once be removed, and we will have supporters in each of the great cities most active, & most powerful. One single, well organized, commercial establishment, will do us more good at an election, than all the Tippecanoe Log-Cabins or Tammany wig-wams in the country. There is nothing harder, however, than to reach the minds of the mercantile classes. Their ears are dull & gross to all reasoning that smacks of oratory[?]. Generally speaking, also, I can say almost universally, they hate, & with justice, the name of Democracy. There is something in the Democratic war-cries, in this State, that makes a man of property either in possession or expectance, shiver[?] and shake. There is a careless way of talking contracts, and credit, which terrifies and rep[*mutilation*] I am very anxious that the conservatism [*mutilation*] trade theory should be proved for the general [*mutilation*] of the trading community, and perhaps as g[*mutilation*] doing so as any that we have, is by shewing [*mutilation*] infamous fraud, & trickery, & lawlessless [*sic*] by which tariffs have been distinguished.

I shall await with great anxiety, the appearan[ce; *mutilation*] your retirement address. It strikes me that on its [*mutilation*] & bearing depends the future destiny of our youn[g &] great country. If its influence should be such as [to] divide the republican party, I fear the dawn of th[*mutilation*] will be still longer postponed. It may be that we a[re] fated to remain still longer in the night watches—I am convinced that nothing will be ["so much" *interlined*] calculated [to] accelerate the success of the principles for which w[e] contend, as ["present" *interlined*] harmony among those within our pa[rty?] limits. There is something meanly destructive, something as grovelling as it is demagoguical [*sic*], in the conduct of the [Albany] regency leaders, but for all that, we must bear it. We must condescend to use them, and in order to do so, we must make up our minds not to be shocked by their habits of mind or body. If we break off from them now, & give them reason to believe that ["they"(?) *canceled and* "by" *interlined*] our revolt[?], Mr. [Henry] Clay's election is clinched, they will never have the generosity to forgive us. Allow me to say this much, because I wait with longing eyes for your election to the presidency, and because I despair of that great consummation unless we obtain the aid of the New York politicians. Let Mr. [Martin] Van Buren sulk[?; *mutilation*] full, and then drop off from the capitol inert[?; *mutilation*]ted. It is now settled that he either must go there again [*mutilation*]is appetite is to be whetted by another [*mutilation*] people. I see no other course than for u[*mutilation*]it. We must coöperate with them, in [*mutilation*]o make them coöperate with us. If you can [*mutilation*], make up your mind to give Mr. V[an] Buren, unworthy [though] he is, a complete support as you did before, I do [b]elieve I shall have the delight of seeing you, if I live, and I am young enough so to do, in the white house [*mutilation*] for eight years.

The review I mentioned to you of the Harper[*mutilation*; v]olume is in Mr. [John L.] O'Sullivan's hands, under [*one word canceled and* "a" *interlined*; *mutilation*; pr]omise six months old to publish whatever [I s]end him. I suspect it will appear [in the *United States Magazine and Democratic Review*] in February, [if] things go smoothly, but it is very ardent, and [may] perhaps be longer postponed. I believe Mr. O'Sul[*mutilation*]st, but those wily N.Y. politicians ab[out] him are on the alert. I trust it will soon [*mutilation*] as it is a tribute, which, were it only as able in its style as it is warm in its estimate, would be of value to our cause. With very great respect I am yours resp[ectfull]y, Francis Wharton.

ALS in ScCleA. NOTE: This letter is torn on both its right and left edges.

From D[UFF] GREEN

Washington, 6th Jan[uar]y 1844

My dear Sir, I wrote to you from London that I had made arrangements to publish a paper [the *Republic*] in New York [City]. The party associated with me [Henry Wikoff] places in trust subject to my order ample funds to sustain the paper & I have absolute & unlimited editorial control.

Upon reaching New York, I found that the delegation from the City to the Syracuse Convention had protested against the organisation of the convention and against the appointment of delegates to the Convention at Baltimore, that they had reported their protest to a meeting of the people who had organised a committee with full powers to call another meeting or to act as they deemed best—that this committee wished your friends in Congress to prepare and publish an address denoun[c]ing the Baltimore Convention and the caucus system, to which they would respond through a meeting of the people.

I came on here and found your friends greatly at a loss to know what to do. They were in utter despair of your ever being sustained, and unwilling to lose their own position in the party. They need urging that it would not do to close the door ["in" *changed to* "of" *and* "the" *canceled*] hope in the face of [Martin] Van Buren's friends so long as they indicated a willingness to act with us on the Tariff and the slave question. I took my ground that I would go on to New York, and denounce the whole concern, that we must make a movement from the people against caucus and the dictation of party, that Mr. Van Buren if nominated cannot be elected and that ["it" *canceled*] we must protect the democratic party from the influences which have usurped the control and now dictate the candidates to be voted for.

I propose to go to New York tomorrow and will ["will" *canceled*] move immediately. We will call a meeting of the people[,] we will denounce the Caucus, we will recommend the nomination of anti caucus electoral candidates in every district in the United States. We will charge that the effect of adhering to the Baltimore nomination will be certain defeat of the democratic party and throw on Van Buren[,] [Thomas H.] Benton & Co. the responsibility of disorganisation & disunion by proposing that a convention to be chosen by districts & to vote per capita, shall meet at some suitable place and at some day to be agreed on say July[,] August or September to select a candidate for whom the electors shall vote.

If Van Buren is nominated we will run our own ticket. Van B[uren]'s election is defeated and we will occupy the democratic anti caucus platform and be prepared for the next election.

The tendency in the public mind is against caucus—the reaction will be in our favor & we will control events. I have consulted Judge [Abel P.] Upshur & the President [John Tyler] and they approve of the movement. The President has consented to make common cause with you, and I am going to see him to night & will urge on him to tender you the Treasury Dept. to be made vacant on Monday [1/8] by the nomination of Mr. [John C.] Spencer to the [U.S.] Supreme Court. I do not hesitate to say that he will tender you the office nor do I hesitate to say that you ought to accept it. It will enable you to be on the spot here, to control and guide your friends & to place yourself and your party right on the question of the Currency.

I will write to you from New York. ["I have" *canceled.*] Mr. [George] McDuffie read me your address. The points are well taken. Mr. [Dixon H.] Lewis tells me that he has written to you to modify it so as to leave a hope that you and your friends will support Van Buren if they go for a reduction of the Tariff. My objection to it is that it is too much so now. You should stand on your objection to the organisation of the convention, to the illegal and unconstitutional control of the party caucus. You have done yourself too much injury by attempting to conciliate the party. Benton has resolved to rule or ruin and you have nothing to hope by concession—by placing yourself on the objection of the organisation of the caucus you occupy impregnable ground and you weaken yourself by any other issue. Should Mr. Tyler offer you the Treasury Dept. you ought to accept it. Do not reject it. Your friend, D. Green.

ALS in ScCleA; PC in Boucher and Brooks, eds., *Correspondence,* pp. 199–200.

From D[uff] Green

Washington, 6th Jan[uar]y 1844
My dear Sir, After dispatching my letter of this date I called on Judge [Abel P.] Upshur and after conversing with him I am so much impressed with the view which he presented of the bearing of that part of your address ["which relates to the tariff" *canceled*] that I [*two words canceled*] deem it my duty to urge you to omit all that part which relates to the tariff—because you are now making an issue on the organisation of the Baltimore convention, and we believe that by introducing the tariff you will greatly weaken the force of your Constitutional objection to the caucus. We must present a platform on which the anti caucus feeling of the country can be ralli[e]d and we fear that it will be charged that by introducing the question of the tariff ["it will be charged that" *canceled*] you are refusing to go into the convention not because you object to its organisation but because

675

you have ascertained that you cannot get the nomination, and that, as you must have anticipated that ["there" *canceled*] persons in favor of the protective tariff would be members of the convention, and that question was not before presented as a subject to be considered in the organisation ["of the convention" *canceled*], it is now presented as an after thought, and would ["not" *interlined*] have been mooted had you not been satisfied that you would not receive the nomination.

The single issue on the organisation is enough to justify your refusal to place your name before them, and as that is the strongest issue and the issue on which we must organise the anti caucus movement we do hope that you will strike out every thing else and leave us to make the battle on that issue and on that alone.

As the question of the tariff was not presented as ["any" *canceled*] constituting an element in the organisation of the convention to whom it is understood you had consented to submit your pretensions, it will be said, by your enemies that you have no right now to raise the question, ["now" *canceled*] since you had been previously committed, ["not" *canceled*] to acquiesce ["to" *canceled and* "in" *interlined*] the decision of the convention if elected so as to fairly represent public opinion without reference to the tariff.

The issue of the tariff can be made here after, when ["whe" *canceled*] we shall have been organised and that and other issues which must arise cannot fail to ["make" *canceled*] give us a controlling influence for good if we do not triumph. Yours sincerely, D. Green.

ALS in ScCleA.

From PERCY WALKER

Mobile [Ala.,] January 6th 1843 [*sic*; 1844]

Dear Sir, Your letter of the 23rd ultimo, addressed to your "friends and supporters in Mobile," was placed in my hands a few days since by Col: [James S.?] Deas, with the request that I should make such use of it, as I thought proper. I have submitted it to several gentlemen, and am happy to inform you that your determination, not to permit your name to go before the Baltimore Convention, meets the unqualified approval of your friends in this place. It has been a matter of regret with us that you did not take the step at an earlier day. But we ["will"(?) *canceled*] welcome the announcement of your purpose, and are prepared to sustain you, with all the zeal and ability, at our command. We regard the movement as the only one by which the unity of the Free Trade State-Rights party can be preserved. We have ce[ased?; *mutilation*] to pay any heed to the professions of the great [*mutilation*] of the northern Democrats, on the Tariff qu[estion; *mutilation*] and are satisfied that they have been and s[*mutilation*] deserting us and ranging themselves und[er; *mutilation*] of "Protection." We have been long convi[*mutilation*] unsoundness of the Northern Democracy. [*Mutilation*] vital question & have therefore felt but [*mutilation*] at certain late developments.

It is manifest, that the "protective in[terest; *mutilation*] increasing in power and influence, a[*mutilation*] South looks well to herself, and acts w[ith; *mutilation*] and decision, utter ruin awaits us.

The conviction that *you* and *you alone*, can awaken her to a sense of her danger, causes us to rejoice at the stand you have determined to take, & to look with much anxiety & impatience for your "address."

For the purpose of preparing our friends in this State for it, I have written an article, which appears in the [Mobile] "Alabama Tribune" of this morning, and which I herewith send you. I have endeavoured to frame it, as if I had no knowledge of your intention. It may test the allegiance of our friends & for that purpose I wrote it. I have however, no fears of them. They will not, I feel assured, falter or hesitate.

Unknown as I am to you, it may be expected that I should tender an apology for addressing you. As your letter, was placed in my possession, I felt [*mutilation*] duty to inform you of the reception it meets [*mutilation*] from your "friends & supporters in Mobile," and [*mutilation*] you that they will not prove derelict in [*mutilation*] to you, to themselves & the Country. With the greatest respect & esteem, I remain Y[ou]rs, Percy Walker.

ALS in ScCleA. NOTE: One corner of the ms. is torn away. Percy Walker, who was Representative from Ala. during 1855–1857, was a physician and lawyer and the son of John W. Walker, one of the first Senators from Ala.

From V[IRGIL] MAXCY

Tulip Hill, West River [Md.,] 7 Jan[uar]y 1844
My dear Sir, I wrote you from Washington on the 30th ult[im]o [*sic*; the 31st] the state of things there and what Mr. [Abel P.] Upshur and my opinions were as to the course your friends there ought to adopt.

On my return home from New York this evening I found your letter of the 22nd Dec. I promised Mr. Upshur when I parted with him, that I would keep on from Baltimore, on my return from N[ew] York, to Washington, if I should find a letter from him there, saying my presence would be useful. I found a letter in Balt[imor]e from him of which the following is an extract. "I have been hard at work here ever since you left me, but with what success is yet uncertain. The Southern members are absolutely asleep. I have never known any thing like their infatuation. I have promises, that something shall be done: but I find men always prone to fall back into their old delusions. I will let you know the result."

A servant of mine will go over tomorrow. I shall write to Mr. Upshur, that, unless your friends shall take the course themselves, which was recommended, when I was at Washington, promptly & most decidedly on both the grounds of your address, I am of opinion that your own address should be published without the loss of a day: for I perfectly agree with you, that it is not consistent with your character to leave your position at all equivocal and if your friends at Washington think it best not to take the initiative at once, your address should be published and then let the responsibility rest where it ought.

[*Marginal interpolation*:] I beg you to believe that the opinion I expressed in my last against your taking ground against the Tariff was not for the purpose of keeping your opinions ["out" *interlined*] of view on this subject. Indeed that would be impossible, so well are they known, but simply because it was not exactly applicable as a reason for not going into a convention. I have seen Gen[era]l [Duff] Green, who has confided to me all his plans. He agrees with Mr. U[pshur] & myself as to the course your friends ought to take.

We thought we perceived a disposition in some to say with [Daniel] Webster, "where are we to go"? but that if a man with so much authority as [George] McDuffie should prepare an address to the country and propose to your friends to sign it that they would do so & afterwards remain firm to their principles; but that if you should come out first that the whole of the [Martin] V[an] B[uren] press would come out in full volley upon you—denounce you as the destroyer of the Republican Party, impute to you motives of personal hostility to V[an] B[uren] for becoming so, and that some of our weaker brethren might be frightened out of the true path. Perhaps we are wrong in this apprehension of their want of firmness. At all events if your friends do not move at once you ought to do so in my opinion & shall urge its adoption on Mr. Upshur. If I do not hear something is done in the course of this week I shall go over to Washington. I was frequently ask[ed] the question by our friends in N[ew] Y[ork] what course are we to take? Why do not Mr. C[alhoun]'s friends at Washington tell us?

I found from Mr. [John] McKeon [former Representative from N.Y.], a warm friend of Gen[era]l [Lewis] Cass, that his friends had begun to entertain strong hopes, that the convention, would be convinced of the impossibility of electing V[an] B[uren] and take up him. I told him very freely, if Gen[era]l Cass did not denounce the formation of the convention & refuse to go in it he could by no possibility be taken up—even in the case you should decline.

I am sorry I did not hear your son [Patrick Calhoun] was at Washington. Mrs. M[axcy] joins in aff[ectiona]te regards to Mrs. [Floride Colhoun] C[alhoun] & yourself. Faithfully y[ou]rs, V. Maxcy.

ALS in ScCleA; variant PEx in Boucher and Brooks, eds., *Correspondence*, pp. 200–201.

From EDWARD J. BLACK,
[Representative from Ga.]

Washington City, Jan[uar]y 8th 1844

My dear Sir, Your letter of the 27th Ultimo was rec[eive]d yesterday, and I have reflected anxiously on its contents. The reasons you present for a remission of duties on the iron for our Rail Roads are the only arguments to sustain a discrimination in their favour. They were of such weight with me that I would not vote against the application of the Petersburg road to the last Congress. That application failed, I think, for the want of southern support. I have carefully Collated & compiled the am[oun]t that has been remitted to rail Roads & Corporations north & East of Mason's & Dicksons line, and in addition to the views you present, it can be shewn that they have received from the government, in this way, a much larger Sum than has ever been granted to the South—and we might at least balance accounts with them before we apply rigidly to ourselves a rule they have always rejected for themselves.

I have read your address, and prepared as I was by feeling, and inclination, and judgment to approve what you might do in that regard, I was most thoroughly satisfied, after I had read it, with every word you have written. Now that your position with regard to the party is not what it was some months since, I am more at liberty than I ever ["have" *canceled*] have been to tell you with what devotion and singleness of purpose I have aspired to your success, not only politically, but personally. Principles *and* men is the true version of

679

the old maxim, and Mr. [John] Randolph was right when he said, you might as well talk of marriage without women, as principles & *not* men.

After maintaining my family in Comfort at home, and sustaining the country in my political relations creditably and honorably, I have no other motive, that I know of, but to assist in my humble way, in advancing you to the Presidency—and you only—for there is no other prominent man in whom I have any confidence. That event would gratify my personal feelings, and assure the consummation of what I hold to be true in politics. With deep ["feel" *canceled*] feelings of regret and indignation I have been forced to the conclusion that we cannot succeed in our hopes & efforts at the approaching election. I now look to the election in 1848, and my efforts shall be directed to the Contest that will take place then. With that view what you have written about the Baltimore Convention is right, and so far as I am individually Concerned, I am disposed to defy them openly—but I suggest that while you condemn the principles on which that Convention is about to be assembled (as you have properly done) that you simply *protest* against the mode and manner of its election, and its proposed action. That will leave us where we are, firmly and consistently Standing on our principles, without subjecting us to the imputation of abruptly denouncing the *Party*. It will clear your skirts of the Convention, without your seeming to denounce the Party.

In relation to the Tariff, & the policy heretofore maintained by the [Martin] Van B[uren] Democrats upon that subject nothing could have been written more forcibly than what you have said in your address. The instances you have adduced of their double dealing must Carry Conviction to every honest man, and all that you have referred to to sustain your Suspicions of the Van B[uren] men would be doubly Confirmed by what has transpired during this session of Congress. What more convincing than the votes on Mr. [Robert B.] Rhet[t']s resolution, on my revenue resolution, & on Mr. McDowal's [*sic*; Joseph J. McDowell's, Representative from N.C.]? Rhet[t]'s was lost by a large majority & mine by one vote, & that too when we have a Dem[ocratic] majority of more than 60 votes in the House.

Doubtless you have watched the proceedings of the House on the Abolition question. The South has lost more during the short month we have been in session than we have since the days of Henry L. Pinckney. Every step we have taken has been retrograde. The Massachusetts memorial to abolish our ["two thirds" *canceled*] three fifth's Slave representation has not only been received, but referred to a Select Committee, headed by Mr. [John Quincy] Adams. The Petition of a free negro has been received, & referred—& to cap the Climax a Van B[uren] Dem[ocratic] Speaker has appointed a Committee on Rules—and after deliberate Consultation they have, in Committee, stri[c]ken out the 21st Rule—& that too by the aid of the votes of two Van B[uren] Democrats ([Samuel] Beardsl[e]y of N[ew] York, and Doctor [John W.] Davis of Indiana). When their report was brought into the House, the Van Buren members tried to stave it off, first by endeavouring to postpone the Consideration of the report indefinitely. When that did not Succeed Drumgoole [*sic*; George C. Dromgoole, Representative from Va.], with the hope of avoiding a *teste* moved to recommit it—but as good luck would have it, I got the floor, and moved to amend his motion by *instructing* the Committee to report the 21st Rule to the House as one of the Rules for its government. We are yet debating that motion of *instruction*, & we have them in a tight place. Beardsl[e]y[,] [Hannibal] Hamlin [Representative from Me.], Davis, all V[an] B[uren] Democrats have been Compelled to come out, and have made out and out abolition speeches—openly denouncing the rule.

None of the papers have reported my speech. Particularly has the Globe cut it up and misrepresented it. I gave the party warning that their votes upon that subject would be looked to by the South as a test of their truth and loyalty to Democracy. That if they faltered they would be lost, and that I made the motion for the express purpose of making them shew their hands. I will write out my speech, and thus defeat [Francis P.] Blair in his attempt to suppress it.

There is no doubt but that if Van [Buren] was out of the way you would be nominated by an overwhelming majority of the party, and although the majority of the party seem to be at this time in favor of Mr. Van B[uren] yet the course adopted by his northern friends here in relation to the 21st Rule and the Tariff (particularly the latter) is producing some excitement among the better part of the Western Representatives. These symptoms, encourage me to hope that we are not yet excluded entirely. This Democratic Congress may yet kill Mr. Van B[uren]. If all your friends would stand up in the House, yield not an inch of ground, or a particle of principle, and by Concerted action force this Congress to a definite shewing on these two great questions, I believe there would yet be a great revulsion in the Country. Your friends have not yet had even a meeting for consultation as to their course in the House. I am endeavouring to bring about a meeting of that sort. But I fear I have tired you, so I must beg you to believe that all I have written is prompted by the most ardent feelings for you, & your success, and submitted always to your better judgment. As occurrences take place here I will let you know; and if I can serve you in any way here let me know it, and if I do not succeed, it will not be for want of zeal, or an effort, on my part in your behalf; and I shall always be glad to receive your letters. Yours very Truly, Edward J. Black.

ALS in ScCleA; variant PC in Boucher and Brooks, eds., *Correspondence*, pp. 202–204. NOTE: The three resolutions mentioned in Black's fourth paragraph above all were aimed at instructing the House Committee on Ways and Means to prepare revisions of the tariff toward a revenue basis. Rhett's and Black's resolutions were defeated on 1/3 by votes of 57 to 112 and 83 to 84, respectively. McDowell's was defeated the next day by 84 to 102.

From [2nd Lt.] PATRICK [CALHOUN, U.S. Army]

Washington D.C., Jan. 8th 1844

Dear Father, I arrived here only a few days since, and have not as yet been able to suit myself with rooms. I find it difficult in the part of the City near the Departments to get a room of any description, all having been engaged before this; by going a little way off I might get some of an inferior kind, but these do not suit me. On inquiry I find that it will be equally, if not more expensive to take furnished rooms, than to board at Fuller's Hotel which as far as situation goes is as convenient as any other. The charge here is forty dollars a month, every thing found[?] which I think is quite moderate, and if I can get a good room I will remain here at least for a month or so.

I was called off before I could finish my letter, and have not had an opportunity to resume it until to day, Jan. 11th. In the meantime I have changed my quarters. Mr. Fuller who keeps the Hotel of that name, promised me on my arrival to let me have in a day or two, one of the best rooms in his house, this he delayed doing from day to day, for six or seven days, when finding that there was but little probability of my getting any other than the one I had, I changed my quarters. I have taken a room in a house opposite to Fuller[']s, in which two of my brother officers live, one of whom (Li[e]ut[enant Thomas L.?] Ring[g]old) I have known for some years, which renders it more agreeable than to be amongst strange[r]s[.]

I take my breakfast in my room, and dinner and tea at the Hope Club, which is very near and is composed, with the exception [of] Gen. [Daniel] Parker Chief Clerke of the War Department, entirely of officers of the Army. I cannot tell yet how I shall like this arrangement; it is objectionable however from my having to leave the house to get some of my meals. Living in this way will cost me from thirty to thirty five [dollars] a month.

I have been out but little as yet although most of the families appear desirous of showing me attention; in future I shall go out more, indeed as much as circumstances will allow. I attended a large party the other evening at Mr. Governor's[?] and was much pleased with it.

On my arrival, hearing that Gen. [Duff] Green and family were in the City I called on them. As the Gen. intended leaving the next morning & had some business of importance to attend to, I had only a few moments['] conversation with him. After leaving his boarding House, I walked with him a little way in the street. During the walk he informed [me] that he had just finis[h]ed a letter to you, in which he had explained the state of things here, and the necessity of your presence in Washington. He informed me of several other things, which it will not be necessary for [me] to mention, as I suppose you have received [his let]ter before this.

I have called upon most of the delegation from So[uth] Carolina, but as we are living at different ends of the City I have not seen much of them.

I have as yet done nothing in the line of my duties as Prof[esso]r [James P.] Espy [meteorologist in the War Department] informed me that he had nothing for me to do for sometime. I find both Mr. Espy and his wife very agreeable people, and having an unbounded[?] admiration for yourself.

I feel so badly to day that I cannot write all intended—indeed I fear that I am going to have and [*sic*] attack of the influenza, as I have a soar throat and bad cold, the first thing of the kind that I have been attacked with for several years. There has been many inqui[rie]s about you since I have been here. Love to all, Your affec[tio]nate son, Patrick.

P.S. I have heard from home but [once?] since I left; that was a letter from Sister A[nna Maria Calhoun Clemson].

ALS in ScU-SC, John C. Calhoun Papers. NOTE: In a letter of 11/17/1843, Patrick Calhoun, then at Fort Towson in the Indian Territory, had been informed by Roger Jones, Adjutant General of the U.S. Army: "The services of an officer being required by Mr. Ja[me]s P. Espy, charged with collecting and arranging meteorological observations for the Government . . . you have been selected for that duty. Should the detail be agreeable to you, you will consider this an order to repair to Washington to enter upon your duties in the Meteorological Bureau attached to the Surgeon General's Office." FC in DNA, RG 94 (Records of the Adjutant General's Office), Letters Sent (Main Series), 1800–1890, 20:33 (M-565:13, frame 336).

From F[RANKLIN] H. ELMORE

Columbia, 9 Jan[uar]y 1843 [*sic*; 1844]

My Dear Sir, I have just rec[eive]d yours of the 3rd inst[ant] forwarded to me from Charleston. I have not been to the city since I met Lieut[enant Patrick] Calhoun. I was taken next day with grippe & prostrated for several days & since then have been here much engaged in private affairs, which have harrassed me exceedingly & incapacitated me for almost every thing. I, as soon as I was able to attend to it, inclosed your address to Col. [Jacob Bond] I'On, Mr. [Henry] Gourdin & Mr. [Ker] Boyce. The two latter only were in town. Mr. Gourdin writes me that he took out & read letters from Gen[era]l [George] McD[uffie] & Mr. [Robert Barnwell] Rhett to me after reading y[ou]r address, which had been submitted to the Delegation. They approve your ["declinin"(?) *canceled*] withholding y[ou]r name from the Convention & think you should publish the address with some modifications. What he does not say. I have a letter from [Dixon H.] Lewis of the same date as yours begging me earnestly, if y[ou]r address is not published to stay till I hear from you as he had written very fully to you giving his views as to an important modification. I had in my letter to the Committee in Charleston taken the same view expressed by Mr. Lewis. I send you ["as he requests" *inserted marginally*] his letter, begging you to send it back to me when you have read it, with your views. The address I expect to find in proof when I get down tomorrow. I wrote to Mr. G[ourdin] that I hoped the Committee would be in the City by that time & we could have a meeting. His letter to me was dated the 6th & mine in reply went next day to him. He told me that Mr. Boyce was the only one of the Committee in the City since he rec[eive]d the address. He & Mr. Boyce seemed to express the same opinions that Lewis has stated so strongly.

It will not I trust be out of place to express to you the impression made on my mind in one respect by the address. It is liable to be used by Mr. [Martin] V[an] B[uren]'s friends to your disadvantage with the party & to be made the means of holding you up as the cause of that defeat which they are bringing on themselves. You know there are some of their leaders who hate you & who have the control of their presses. No sense of justice or fairness will restrain them & the fire you have poured out upon their selfish unprincipled conduct & treachery they will convert into attacks on the Party & before you or your friends can stem the torrent, they will have raised up such a current against you, that ["the" *canceled*] you will be discarded by thousands who are honest & who are truly your friends. The grounds you have taken in withdrawing your name from the Convention are such as your friends will sustain in all their extent if you decide on them and yet I think they would[,] as far as I have had the means of ascertaining, be more pleased that you should take a course which will not endanger you with the mass of the Democratic Party. One which will give you all the strength of your present course without subjecting you to any fair ["char"(?) *changed to* "or"] plausible charge of having broken them down. The ground Lewis suggests I confess strikes me as the best & under my present opinions I think it would give you a position of great power—perhaps the entire control of the matter.

Lt. Calhoun in some sort misapprehended me in one particular—the Tariff proceedings were only a part of ["what I thought subsequent" *canceled*] developments subsequent to your writing, which I thought might have commanded your attention. The Abolition & Texas questions were also referred to. They are every day assuming so important a position in politics, ["that" *changed to* "and"] the course of certain of our professed friends has been such that they or the first of them at any rate, I thought should have been treated of in your address. I intended to have written to you next day, but the attack I was subjected to was first confined to my head ["& eyes" *interlined*] & was so painful & depressing, that I was unable to do any thing & fearing too much delay ["as soon as I was able" *interlined*] I inclosed the papers to the Committee for their action. This was prevented by the intire absence of the Committee.

I go down [to the lowcountry] in the morning. A few days more will make no great difference & if I don't hear from you in consequence of Lewis'[s] letter, (which I suppose you have had before this,) when I get down, I will propose to the Committee to wait even a few days more, having the address in type to [*one word canceled*] be ready the moment we hear from you for any course.

I write this immediately on receiving yours & Mr. Lewis'[s] letters tonight, after a day of much fatigue & in so desultory a way as nothing but the urgency of the occasion will excuse.

If Mr. [Thomas G.] Clemson is with you do say to him I will answer his letter from Charleston. Yours truly, F.H. Elmore.

[Enclosure]

Dixon H. Lewis to F[ranklin] H. Elmore, [Charleston]

Washington, Jan[uar]y 3rd 1843 [*sic;* 1844]

My dear Sir, I have just read Mr. Calhoun's address to the Central Committee & proceed to give you my opinions. So far as Calhoun's withdrawal & the reasons growing out of the Convention are concerned, it is just the thing—first because it disconnects him and his friends from a vicious system of selecting a candidate, and secondly because he stands no earthly chance of the nomination, and as long as his name is held up, it is a means of exciting against him & his friends all the *jealousies*, without any of the *chances* of a Candidate. Mr. [Martin] V[an] Buren will be nominated as sure as the Convention assembles unless his friends become convinced of what every one now begins to think that he will as surely be beaten as he is nominated. In that event they may look to [Lewis] Cass or Calhoun for more availability and will do it the sooner, because they are not in the way of his nomination. I have no doubt the sensible part of them are now looking around for a mode of retreat & by abandoning ["a contest(?) in the" *interlined*] the Convention, you give them a chance to do so. But while not competing ["for" *canceled and* "with" *interlined*] them for the nomination, it should not appear that Mr. Calhoun's friends have withdrawn him or that he withdraws himself from the Convention the more certainly to be a Candidate against the nomination. On the contrary while the mode of constituting the Convention is decidedly condemned & they are given to understand, that as constituted it does not now, and never can hereafter control the action of Mr. Calhoun's friends, & therefore cannot at a future ["day" *interlined*] be brought up as a precedent, still I think we should rest our course of whether we shall support or oppose Mr. Van Buren on the ground, of whether he shall truly come up to our principles on the Tariff and the Texian questions. We should declare him at present *out* of position on the Tariff & require of him to disavow in *terms* & his friends by their votes during the present session to put their veto on the Syracuse Tariff resolve, & on the course of Mr. [Silas] Wright last session.

I would advise this course because Mr. Calhoun, though he cannot be nominated enjoys so much of the sympathy & confidence of those who will nominate Mr. Van Buren, that it is important by no act of his own he should lose it. He can in fact by a course of moderation prescribe terms to Mr. Van Buren & the Party. The moment he withdraws from the Convention, with an avowal nevertheless that though opposed to the organization too much to make himself a Party to it, he stands ready to support the Candidate of the ["Convention" *canceled*] Democratic Party not because of his *nomination*, but because of his anti tariff ["Principles" *canceled*] & other Democratic Principles, and that he stands also ready to oppose any Candidate not coming up to this standard, either by suffering his own name to be used for that purpose or rallying on any other name, irrespective of ["the" *canceled*] Whig or Democratic nominations—& his friends sustain him in this course, that moment his power will be felt & acknowledged & the Democratic Party will either force V[an] Buren to comply or will throw him overboard.

["Washington, Jan(uar)y 3rd 1843" *canceled.*]

Let Calhoun then withdraw his letter & suit it ["to" *interlined*] this aspect of the case, which can be easily done while at the same time he can be as decided as he now is against the mode of constituting the Convention & against the Tariff. Let him throw aside all taunts & cuts at Van Buren & with that frankness & goodnature [*sic*] which belongs to him take this course & one of the following results must take place—either

first he will destroy the *power* of the Convention without breaking with the Democratic Party.

2ndly—He will draw attention to ["Van Bu" *canceled*] the only suitable mode of constituting the Convention in future & place himself beyond its present or future control unless it is modified to suit him, & will also draw attention to V[an] Buren's Tariff principles & force him to modify them or be thrown overboard.

3rdly It will give him a position with the Democratic Party—which will force them to conform to his standard before the election—and afterwards place V[an] Buren if elected in his power, & whether elected or not will make him the Candidate of the Democratic Party the next time[.] The fault of Calhoun's letter is in taking it for granted, that the Democratic Party will with Van Buren go wrong on the Tariff—when a majority of the Party are as sensitive on that subject as he is—& by his making it the "sine qua non" of his support or opposition to the Candidate they may bring out, gives him complete control over the question & sinks the weight and importance of their Convention machinery.

If therefore his letter is not published, which I trust in God it is not, return it to him with these views & with it if you choose this letter. I have been sick or I would have written to you & him also at an earlier day. This course will give him control over the Convention, instead of arraying that power against him & in the mean time, with his power augmented he will stand on an armed neutrality, ["untill" *canceled*] ready to profit by the chapter of accidents, untill the course of public opinion shall be more distinctly seen on the Convention, on V[an] Buren's availability on the Tariff & the Texas question & then if V[an] Buren shall be found even in the estimation of many who now support him unequal to the occasion, he can be made the Candidate and the more readily & easily, because ["of" *canceled*] he has not chosen to consider himself as such against the wishes of a majority of his Party. Truly your friend, Dixon H. Lewis.

[P.S.] I think some part of Calhoun's letter wants temper—& is rather personal. I am just able to be in my seat [in the House of Representatives] having been confined by Erysipelas.

P.S. Calhoun's friends here are most all committed to the nominee of the Convention—& can only sustain him effectively in the course I have reccommended [*sic*]. I shall write to Calhoun tomorrow but nevertheless, if you choose send him this hasty scrawl.

[Marginal P.S.] Don[']t publish the Address untill you write fully to Calhoun.

ALS in ScCleA; variant PC in Jameson, ed., *Correspondence*, pp. 908–910; ALS of En in NHi, Miscellaneous Manuscripts Collection. NOTE: The actual date of the En was perhaps 1/2 rather than 1/3, because Lewis stated that he would write to Calhoun "tomorrow" and his letter to Calhoun is dated 1/3, as is a second letter from Lewis to Elmore. In this second letter, Lewis mentions the earlier letter which he "hastily" sent Elmore "last night." The second letter, also dated "1843," is brief and more considered. Lewis repeated his urging that Calhoun's address be withheld from publication temporarily. Wrote Lewis to Elmore, in part: "If he can keep out of the Convention, without breaking with his Party he kills the Convention dead, & at the same time takes a position which makes him omnipotent now, & in future, whether Van [Buren] is elected or beaten. . . . let the Party understand, that if V[an] Buren & his friends put themselves on their best behaviour on the Tariff & Texas question—their *principles* shall save them from an opposition which their Convention was well calculated to provoke." Lewis stated further that two-thirds of the party now feels that Van Buren cannot be elected. "Dread not that they will not look on this course of Calhoun as a magnanimous concession. The report is rife every where that he has written that he will not submit to the Convention. This is all however which is known. They look for war behind this, & if they find an olive Branch, on the simple condition, that their Candidate shall prove true to their avowed principles— they will rejoice & at once require evidence which *cannot* be mistaken. Old [Thomas] Ritchie will bellow at the top of his voice for a compliance which shall ensure peace in the South." (ALS in NHi, Miscellaneous Manuscripts Collection.)

From L[EMUEL] WILLIAMS

Boston, Jan[uar]y 9th 1844

My dear Sir, Your letter of the 24[th] Sep[tember] was received by my family during my long absence at Baltimore where I was employed during nearly the whole month of October in the trial of an important action, & immediately after my return the sickness of my family occupied my attention for several weeks; & lat[t]erly business, which was necessarily neglected, has prevented me from replying to your interesting communication which on all points was entirely satisfactory. I regret that your views on the Rhode Island question were not given to the public & think now they ought to be in some form or other; as they would correct a representation which has been industriously circulated.

The course taken by the Van Buren party in forcing an early nomination of delegates to the Baltimore Convention, has defeated, in a great measure, the object in postponing the time of holding the Convention to May next. It remains to be seen whether your friends or the friends of the other candidates will submit to have the question forestalled. Had no election taken place until this time the result would have been very different at the north at least. Aside from the old party organization you were decidedly the most popular man in all New-England. A few days before the Connecticut Convention Judge [Andrew T.] Judson (of the District Court of Connecticut) told me that three fourths of that State were in your favour, yet at the Convention where the delegates had been chosen many months previous, & chosen ["with" *canceled and* "for" *interlined*] another purpose Van Buren rec[eiv]ed an equal number of votes. I mention this among a great many instances of unfair practice on the part of our political opponents, of which I suppose you may be well informed.

It seems to be the general opinion of the best informed politicians that Van Buren can in no event succeed if nominated. While I was in Baltimore I saw many well informed gentlemen from whom I learned that Van Buren could not expect to carry Maryland, but that you could carry it against all opposition. [John Van Lear] McMahon who presided at the Convention which nominated [William H.] Harrison told me that he was ready to come out in your favor, & that large numbers of planters who had not recently taken any part in the elections were ready to buckle on their armour under your banner.

I have some business at Washington which will call me there in a few days, where I shall see your friends, & shall be better informed of their & your views than I am at present.

I should be glad to have from you letters of introduction to Mr. [Isaac E.] Holmes or Mr. [Robert Barnwell] Rhett, & [George] McDuffie of your State. I can procure introductions to them at Washington from others from others [*sic*], but should prefer being introduced by your letters, that they may commune with me confidentially. If you will send me letters enclosed in an envelope to me & under cover to Henry Williams of the House of Representatives [from Mass.] I can meet them at Washington where I expect to be in a little more than a week.

I saw Gen. [Duff] Green on his disembarkation at this place, & had an interesting conversation with him relating to you. He had not then recently heard from you. With unabated regard & esteem I remain yours, L. Williams.

ALS in ScCleA; PEx in Boucher and Brooks, eds., *Correspondence*, pp. 205–206.

To GEORGE COX, [Huntsville, Ala.]

Fort Hill, 10th Jan. 1844

Dear Sir: You are right in supposing that I take a deep interest in the completion of the Rail Road to connect the Tennessee river with the Southern Atlantic ports. I am of the impression, that one of its branches ought to terminate at Gunter's Landing [in Ala.], where your address proposes, and that branch (in connection with the river and the Decatur Railroad) ought to connect with the Mississippi at Memphis; and with the Cumberland at Nashville. The completion of the whole, I regard as of the utmost importance in every view; commercial, political and social, and am prepared to render every aid I can towards it. It will effect a revolution in the trade of the Great Valleys of the West.

From some delay of the mail I did not receive your [letter of 12/-8/1843 and your] circular till after your proposed meeting. I would suggest as the best means of giving a decided impulse to the great enterprise, that efficient measures should be taken to obtain a full attendance from the Southern Atlantic States, and those in the Great Valley, at your proposed meeting in May next. There is not a State in the Valley of the Mississippi, that has not a deep interest. There ought to be put out a pressing call, stating some of its principal advantages, and urging a full attendance of all concerned, which should be widely circulated. It would afford me great pleasure to attend and give my support to it every way, if I should not be unavoidably prevented by my engagements, and if a full meeting shall be called. With respect, I am your obedient servant, J.C. Calhoun.

PC (from the Huntsville, Ala., *Democrat* of unknown date) in the Charleston, S.C., *Mercury*, February 23, 1844, p. 2; PC in the Pendleton, S.C., *Messenger*, March 8, 1844, p. 1; PC in the Milledgeville, Ga., *Federal Union*, March 19, 1844, p. 3. NOTE: The *Mercury* reprinted part of an editorial from the *Democrat* that accompanied its publication of the letter. "It will be seen that Mr. Calhoun intends to be present at the meeing to be held here on the 20th of May next, provided a general meeting is called and his engagements will not prevent his attendance. We trust that every exertion will be made to get him here on that occasion; for we believe a mighty impulse will be given to the spirit of internal improvement. Every part of this State, of Georgia, of South Carolina and Tennessee, should send delegates. The people of Huntsville will be proud of the occasion to offer their warm hospitality, and at that delightful season our village and the neighborhood are particularly attractive and picturesque." The May meeting involved incorporation of the Tennessee and Coosa Railroad Company.

From A[mbrose] H. Sevier, [Senator from Ark.]

Washington, Jan[uar]y 11th 1844

My dear Sir, Your letter of the 20th ult[imo] reached me in the midst of a violent attack of Bilious fever and influenza, combined. I was then, as I had been for three weeks, confined to my bed, but I handed your letter, *confidentially,* to my colleague [William S. Fulton, Senator from Ark.], who is on the Post office committee, to read, and requested him to introduce a resolution upon the subject to which your letter refers. ["He" *canceled and then interlined*] did so, and the subject is now before that committee. I am now so far recovered as to be able to go to the Senate and will give it my special attention, not forgetting, in so doing, to bear in mind, your injunctions upon the subject.

You will see by the papers that we are all sold to "the *Sage of Lindenwald*" [Martin Van Buren]—and the consequence of which is, so far as I can judge, that our party will receive a worse drubbing, than it did in 1840. Well, after that I suppose, some of our ultra leaders will be satisfied—as their fortunes are inseperably connected with his and as they will share his fate. I regret that you left the Senate; we need you greatly upon the subject of the Tariff. I suppose we shall obtain some modification of it, but not to the extent to afford much relief to the South, or much aid to an exhausted treasury—and yet, we see all the South going, for those who are advocating protective duties, positive or incidental. Even Arkansas has joined the crowd, much to my astonishment, and regret. Yet, it should be understood, that the nominations in that ["State" *interlined*] were carried by a close vote, and it should also be borne in mind, that there [were] but *sixteen* counties, in attendance with their delegates, out of forty five (45) and but 30 delegates out of 77, & this minority, made the nomination. Whether it will be acquiesced in or not, is still a matter of doubt, as there is now much discussion going on in regard to it.

I shall always be glad to hear from you, and if I can be of any service to you, command me freely. Your friend, A.H. Sevier.

ALS in ScCleA. NOTE: Ambrose H. Sevier (1801–1848) was a grandnephew of John Sevier, Governor of Tenn., and represented Ark. as Territorial Delegate and Senator from 1828 to 1848. Sevier's first paragraph probably relates to a resolution introduced by William S. Fulton, Senator from Ark., on 1/8, concerning extension of the franking privilege to former Vice-Presidents. This resolution was referred to the Committee on the Post Office and Post Roads, from which it apparently never emerged.

From P[HILEMON] WATERS

Mobile [Ala.,] Jan[uar]y 11 [18]44
Dear Sir, When about Eighteen years of age I had the honor of an introduction to you. I think it was in Newberry district [of S.C.]— my birth place. My object in addressing you is to solicit your influence in favor of [my brother] Robert Waters, who was one of the unfortunate [Texas] prisoners taken at [the battle of] Mier. Robert is the grandson of Mrs. Gillum [*sic*; Elizabeth Caldwell Gillam], who I believe was a sister of your mother. He is a high minded, honourable man[,] one that you could not help respecting if you were personally acquainted with him. I hope you will use your influence, to have him released from prison. I sent to Mr. W[addy] Thompson [Jr., U.S. Minister] at Mexico, on the first of this month two hundred dollars for Robert[']s use.

When [Gen. Antonio López de] Santa An[n]a passed through the U.S.A. [in 1837] you probably became acquainted with him, and can approach him directly on the subject. At all events I have no doubt but that through the influence of yourself, and friends, you can procure his liberation. Please to acknowledge the receipt of this and oblige Your Ob[e]d[ient] S[er]v[an]t, P. Waters.

ALS in ScCleA.

Advertisement for the Pendleton Male Academy, 1/12. The trustees announce the continuation of this school under the charge of R[obert] M. Renick as Principal and F.M. Adams as Assistant Teacher. Renick is a graduate of the U.S. Military Academy and Adams of Yale College. The curriculum offered includes "English grammar, Geography, History, Logic, Rhetoric and Composition; Natural, Moral and Intellectual Philosophy; the Greek, Latin, and French Languages, comprising a thorough course of the authors read in our Colleges; Mathematics, pure and mixed, commencing with Arithmetic and concluding with the application of Algebra and Geometry to the Sciences of Surveying, Astronomy, Optics, and Mechanics; Chemistry, Mineralogy and Geology, Electricity and Magnetism," plus, for certain students, a "full course of Military instruction." The trustees mention the improved system of discipline at the school. "Genteel" neighbourhood families offer boarding for $75 per year; tuition charges will be $4, $6, and $8 per quarter, depending on classification. Signing as trustees are R[obert] A. Maxwell, J[ohn] C. Calhoun, J[ames?] F. Stuart, F[rederick] W. Symmes, J[esse] P. Lewis, O[zey] R. Broyles, T[homas] M. Sloan, E[dward] Harleston, and J[oseph] V. Shanklin. PC in the Pendleton, S.C., *Messenger*, January 12, 1844, p. 3, and six subsequent issues.

From DUFF GREEN

New York [City,] 12th Jan[uar]y 1844
My dear Sir, "The democratic republican voters of the city & county of New York" held a general meeting in the Park on the 14th September 1843 for the purpose of receiving the report of their delegates to the Syracuse Convention, who protested against the organisation of the Baltimore Convention, and appointed a committe[e] with power to take such measures as they deem expedient in relation to that Convention. That committee, [with] Col. Cha[rle]s A. Clinton, the son of Gov[erno]r [De Witt] Clinton in the chair, ["and" *canceled*] have just unanimously adopted an address to the people of the United States prepared by me at their request, in which I have denounced the organisation of the Baltimore Convention, asserted that no candidate nominated by that Convention can recieve [sic] their ["votes" *canceled*] support, and recommending the people in each congressional district to elect one delegate, and the delegates thus chosen in each State to elect two for such State to be delegates to a convention to be held in Phil[adelphi]a on the 4th of July next, in the place and on the anniversary of the day on which our ancestors declared their independence of King George then & there to declare our independence of King Caucus and to nominate a candidate to recieve the support of the people.

693

I have argueed [*sic*] the question, and show that as 275 is the whole number of electoral votes and 138 a majority and as 7 States towit New York, Pen[n]sylvania[,] Ohio, Virginia, Massachusetts, Tennessee & Kentucky, give 139—the majorities in which added together make but 75, the effect of the principle adopted by the Syracuse Convention is to ["give a"(?) *canceled*] enable seven States, and 75 delegates to control the choice of the candidates of the party. I have made the address pungent enough, and I feel that it is the commencement of a revolution which will break up the Baltimore Convention. But I was compelled to assume the ground that our purpose was not to divide and defeat the party but to propose an organisation of a convention which will enable us to unite and concentrate the wishes and energies of the party and to invite the the friends of all the candidates to unite with us ["in" *interlined*] the spirit of harmony and conciliation that we may be united.

You will see that this movement constitutes an element of great strength, if our friends every where are on the alert. The address will appear in the [New York, N.Y.,] Evening Post of Monday next [1/15]. I will cause copies to be sent to you and to some of your prominent friends and they should every where recommend the immediate action on the recommendations of the Committee. [Martin] Van Buren obtained the organisation of the Baltimore Convention[;] it will be our fault if they obtain the control of this.

I found the party dead and dispirited. I have infused new life into it, and if your friends elsewhere do their duty as we will do ours here all will be well, but you *must* come to Washington. You ought to go into the Treasury Department. The tariff question is secondary to the currency. Free trade is making such rapid progress in England that its establishment in this country will soon follow. Van Buren cannot be elected and you cannot be unless you are at Washington. I have urged Mr. [Abel P.] Upshur to send Mr. [George] McDuffie to Paris that you may come into the Senate, if you will not consent to come into the Treasury. My own opinion is that Mr. Packenham [*sic*; Richard Pakenham, British Minister in the U.S.] is authorised to settle the Oregon [question] & that he will probably require some concessions on the question of the trade. Sir Rob[er]t Peel is so situated that he must wish to make favorable arrangements with us as to our tariff. He has failed in his treaty with Brazil. Mr. Rebiero [*sic*; José de Araújo Ribiero] told me that England had required him to agree to abolish slavery and that he was going back without making a treaty. Sir R[obert] Peel cannot ["retain" *canceled*] re-enact the discriminating duty on slave grown sugar, (it is enacted from year to year,) and ["that by"(?) *canceled and* "a" *interlined*] repeal of the partnership between the monopolists is to that extent broken up and he will ["be" *interlined*] forced into free trade with us, or quit office, and Mr. [Henry] Clay does not love office more than Sir R[obert] Peel does. These questions, the Oregon, Texas, the Tariff, a commercial treaty, all demand your presence at Washington and you will suffer in the opinion of the people now, and in the page of history hereafter if you escape them under a delusive hope that by doing so you can be elected President. The only way to be elected is to be at Washington in the discharge of your duty in such position as may be open to you. I say in the Treasury, if not there in the Senate. I know your confidence in Gen[era]l [Nathan] Towson & send this [to Washington] under cover to him to be forwarded for the double purpose of letting him know what I am doing & that he may unite with me in saying that you cannot safely entrust your reputation or your interests in the hands of the young men who now represent you at Washington. Yours, Duff Green.

[P.S.] I hope to get my [news]paper under way early next week with ample funds and a good organisation.

ALS in ScCleA. NOTE: Ribiero, the Brazilian Minister to France, had been in London at the same time as Green to negotiate a commercial treaty, looking toward the reduction of British import duties on sugar. Negotiations ended when the British Ministry insisted on linking abolition of the slave trade to any commercial agreement.

From F[RANKLIN] H. ELMORE

[Charleston] Jan[uar]y 13, 1844

My Dear Sir, I have but a moment to drop you a line. I will endeavor tomorrow or next day to do more.

I was detained a day in Columbia longer than I expected when I wrote you by indisposition. I got down in miserable weather. I found no members of the Committee in Town except Mr. [Henry] Bail[e]y, [Henry] Gourdin, [Ker] Boyce & [Edward?] Frost. Gen[era]l [James] Hamilton [Jr.] was here & I met Mr. [Barnard Elliott?] Bee on the road who told me of it. I saw him immediately—and last night we got all we could of the Committee with Gen[era]l Hamilton, Mr. [Charles M.] Furman, [Alexander] Mazyck & [Henry W.] Peronneau to gather & read your address. They were told of Mr. [Dixon H.] Lewis['s] Letters & there were before them some rec[eive]d from other quarters. I send you one from Mr. [John A.] Campbell & one from Gen[era]l [Duff] Green. From [George] McDuffie & [Robert Barnwell] Rhett we also heard. The substance of their letters was that beyond the So[uth] Ca[rolina] Delegation & a very few others, to nominate & run you ag[ains]t the Baltimore Convention w[oul]d produce such an irreconcileable breach with the Democrats that you would lose many very many of them who are warmly & truly yours. That you would lose in all respects a position which may yet be one of controlling power even on the adjustment of the Tariff at this Session. They do not say so but from the tenor of their letters I think both of them w[oul]d rather that you should postpone the publication of your address until the course of the party shall be more definitively fixed.

Of your friends here, none will fail to stand up to whatever course you adopt. If you publish at once or postpone, as it is or with alterations I believe you may count on their standing by you. At the same time, however, they direct me to say to you that they feel a great reluctance to your taking any position, which is not necessary, that will cut you off from the next canvass. They partake greatly of the feeling of Mr. Campbell. They think if any act of Providence should before the election open a way to the Presidency for you, that you should not by any step not absolutely called for, put a barrier in your way. That if Mr. [Martin] V[an] B[uren] is defeated, as he in all probability will be, that to you the Party will surrender, if you have not before hand, made that impossible. That in your hand they may be purified & victorious & that you with them may restore the purity of the Government. Under these circumstances five of the seven present [( )& Boyce today added his vote[)] concurred in directing me to say to you that if you could reconcile it to yourself to decide not to publish at present your reasons, but simply to withhold your name from the Convention, promising or not your reasons hereafter, & stating that you would be governed by circumstances hereafter in their conduct as to your support of the Party, that it would perhaps be best. But as I said before, if you say otherwise the paper will be ready for the press the moment you say so.

If it is to be published they also suggest that you allow some of those portions which may be considered as bearing to[o] strongly on individuals & the party where it will not weaken or alter the argument, & may prevent the misconceptions that ["the" canceled] your enemies will endeavor to circulate that your feelings have influenced your course. The instance you alluded to as to Mr. [Littleton W.] Taz[e]-well[']s remark is one—there is one or two which Mr. [Silas] Wright might feel & make the excuse for arraying hostility in the ranks of the party ag[ains]t you. Will you my Dear Sir pardon us for the freedom we take & give some discretion to such of your friends here as you may designate to do this for you? I know it is a delicate point in us to interpose, but you may rest assured that it is only the strongest friendship that would *venture to ask for such responsibility*, and I would far rather that you should blame us than the *hopes of the whole South* & the Country['] s welfare should be destroyed or even endangered. I must confess that the comparison of opinions last night & the letters we had have even made me more fearful of the result & more anxious that you should think again before it is too late, if this movement may not be pretermitted or at least postponed. I remain as ever Yours truly, F.H. Elmore.

P.S. On one point more I was directed to say a word. If the Treasury Dep[artmen]t is in a proper way tendered to you, that you might accept it. By a proper way is understood such a way as would put the Gov[ernmen]t in your control. A year is a short lease, but in that time you could do much to give spread to your principles, exhibit your policy[,] see, & give consistency to the action of your friends—in short prepare a harvest here after without violating any of ["your" *canceled*] the rules you have prescribed for yourself as a public man. Y[ou]rs truly, F.H.E.

[Enclosure]
J[ohn] A. Campbell to Franklin H. Elmore, Charleston

Tuskaloosa [Ala.,] Jan[uar]y 4th 1844
My Dear Sir, I fear this letter will reach you too late, but in hopes that you may receive it in time I write it. I have received information that Mr. Calhoun is about to publish an address. That the object of that address is to rally the free trade State rights party in opposition to [Henry] Clay & [Martin] Van Buren. That his name is to be placed before the people for what it is worth &c.

I should have been pleased if this course had been taken at first. It is now too late. *The reasons you assigned in a late letter to me are unanswerable.* We have addressed the democratic party as members of it. We are members of it *so far at least as to prevent us from* from [*sic*] *contesting the plain and manifest declaration of that party in favor of Van Buren.* We are concluded at least so far as to prevent the nomination of a candidate on our part. We have waited too long. We have pledged ourselves to too much to allow such a course to be taken. There has hardly been a meeting in which the pledge to abide a convention has not been given. The few of us who have refused it, in an honest deference to our opinions & principles have been compelled to act in regard to it so that no separation from the party should be occasioned.

I say then Mr. Calhoun[']s course is ruinous to himself and will ["advance"(?) *canceled*] prejudice the cause. I say that the time is an insuperable barrier to it.

What shall we do? The northern democrats will dodge the questions arising on the Tariff—and they evidently intend to take advantage of the fact that Clay is a slave holder. I feel that is the case. You cannot have a worse opinion of the tortuous course of New York democratic politicians than I have. *So much the better for us.* The course of events will throw the South together. Mr. Calhoun and his South Carolina friends are the men on whom it must repose. The truckling course of the northern politicians will have the effect to unite us.

Van Buren I have always felt would receive this nomination. He has been in the eyes of men. ["Their mouths are familiar with h" *changed to* "They have been accustomed"] to hurrah for him.

The majority neither know, or care for his delinquencies. They hear of them from opponents & disbelieve them. He has a party popularity tho he has been rejected by its thinking truthful men. Mr. Calhoun has had but a small party. That party has taken but little pains to spread its peculiar principles—and the spread of principles has been made by the democratic party & the necessity ["of" *changed to* "on"] the leaders of that party to ["adopt their" *canceled*] examine & promulgate them. You must not loose [*sic*] advantage. You must not isolate yourselves *or rather we must not isolate ourselves.* We are growing too fast. We have too bright prospects before us to allow them to be thrown away. We must maintain our connexions with the democratic party and bestir ourselves to infuse the principles of our own section among the meritorious of that party.

The isolation of Mr. Calhoun in 1831 has done infinite mischief to the Southern States. It has done much mischief to himself. Do not permit this to occur again. At all events do not allow this to be done under circumstances that will frustrate every hope of a resuscitation of his name & interests. The country is not prepared for this course. It will revive all the feeling that exists in the public mind that he is instable[,] capricious[,] versatile. I approve his feelings. *They must* ["however" *interlined*] *be controlled.*

Politicians are worthless who manage this contest for the democratic party. Mr. Van Buren is a man of ["petty" *interlined*] policy & employs base instruments ["he may say" *interlined*]. Take all this for granted. We have no confidence in him or in the friends about him. It is a choice of evils between him & Mr. Clay and both are equally bad. ["Let this be granted" *interlined.*] We contemplated the possibility of his nomination nay the practicability of it. Our friends have expressed confidence & have agreed to aid in his elevation. We have concluded that for the good of the party we would under certain circumstances support him. The will of the party is manifest. Van Buren will be the nominee & would have been under any state of facts. The thing is clear & palpable.

I would say we should not have come to such a condition ["as we are in" *interlined*]. You in whom I have more confidence than in my own judgement on this subject say yes, we have done right. Let us not avoid the plain consequences of our own conduct.

Can *we* carry out Mr. Calhoun[']s views[?] I say no. *I am willing, even now* to do it—for I am under *no committal* & have spoken *with freedom.* I will stand by you. Will [Richard B.] Walthall[,] [David] Hubbard[,] [Henry] Goldthwaite[,] [Governor Benjamin] FitzPatrick[,] [Thomas S.] Mays[,] [Isaac W.?] Hayne[,] [William S. or Philip] Phillips[,] [Francis S.] Lyon[,] McLung [*sic*; James W. Mc-Clung,] [John] Erwin[,] [William O. or John A.] Winston[,] [Jeremiah] Clemens and others in our State? Some of them have already acted. Some have sought places on electoral tickets & others have come under direct pledges *with a full knowledge of the facts* relied on by Mr. Calhoun. You cannot *wean* men from their party in a moment.

In our State we have a good party—the best party. Mr. Calhoun is the choice of both parties after Van Buren & Clay—and to his own party ["members" *canceled*] belongs every conspicuous man in our own ["(democratic)" *interlined*]. Look at the map of Alabama. Every county east of the Alabama & Coosa save one is his. Every county South of Tuscaloosa is his save one. For cowardice in Wilcox[,] Dallas[,] Perry[,] Montgomery & neglect in Marion, lost the State nomination. The northern counties will have to be acquired but we have the means to do it.

We shall raise Calhoun[']s name in 1845 the 5th ["May" *changed to* "March"] & we can commence in time and can commence with the democratic party. We have the officers of the State and they will speak freely then which they did not do in this contest. We shall have no competitor against Mr. Calhoun in any Southern State—At least we ought not to have. Van Buren must either do nothing if elected or follow in Mr. Calhoun[']s footsteps. He will do nothing. I therefore say that we can and will maintain our feelings and we shall have no opposing sentiment to commence the next campai[g]n with.

Now Van Buren I think will be defeated. Mr. Calhoun cannot be elected and the only consequence of their withdrawal ["of Calhoun from the party" *interlined*] will be the ruin of ["their" *changed to* "those"; "very best" *canceled*] who look to him to preserve the country.

I write you freely, and in the confusion of the Sup[reme] Court. I have conversed with the Governor. You know his good sense. He says that this movement will injure no one but Mr. Calhoun & his friends. That it will make no serious division in the democratic party in this State. That our men are all committed. Walthall says the same thing. They go for peace with the party in this contest and for instant action after it to be now announced.

I say then let Mr. Calhoun[']s friends withdraw his name. Let them declare they will support the candidate of the democratic party on the principles set forth in 1840—or if they do not choose to do that let them simply withdraw his name. It appears to me that Mr. Calhoun[']s position allows this. He has not sought the office. His friends have sought it for him. They no longer ask it. We do not need a name to[?] rally us. We can well afford to wait.

We can employ this year in making our principles known and in directing the contest on those principles. I would prefer myself that no pledges should be given—but of that you are the best judge.

I write you freely as I have said. I have submitted what I have written to the Governor who approves. If you conclude that Mr. Calhoun shall be a candidate I will give you aid, but it will be a fruitless effort. I say it is too late for this course & should not now be adopted. Yours very Respectfully, J.A. Campbell.

[Second enclosure]
D[uff] Green to "Gen[era]l Ellmore"

Washington, 6th Jan[uar]y 1844
My dear Sir, After consulting Judge [Abel P.] Upshur I am convinced that the publication of that part of Mr. Calhoun's address which relates to the Tariff will do us great injury. I leave here tomorrow to go [to] New York to organise an anti Caucus movement. We propose to call a meeting of the people and to denounce the organisation of the Syracuse [and; "Baltimore" *interlined*] Conventions and the manner in which they are to vote at Baltimore.

We propose to get up ["an" *canceled*] anti caucus electors in every district and to throw on Mr. [Martin] Van Buren & Col. [Thomas H.] Benton the disorganisation and disunion of the Democratic party by proposing to hold a convention to be elected by districts, to designate a candidate to be voted for by the anti caucus Electors. If Van Buren receives the Baltimore nomination in the face of our invitation to union the responsibility will be on him. If

700

we fail to get the proper men as electors and as delegates to the convention to be held in August or September then the fault will be ours.

Mr. Calhoun did not require that the delegates to the convention should be anti tariff. He consented to abide by the nomination if the convention were properly and fairly constituted. We fear that his enemies will say that he [has] no right now to ["re" *altered to* "object"] to the nomination because the party are not right on the tariff and that the publication of that part of his address which relates to the tariff will enable his enemies to produce an impression he is actuated by selfish ["motives" *interlined*] and regardless of the interests & harmony of the party.

I have written to Mr. Calhoun directed to Pendleton and I write this hoping that you will delay the publication until he can be heard from unless you feel authorised to omit all ["but" *interlined*] that ["does" *canceled and* "which" *interlined*] relates to the simple issue of the organisation of the convention.

The question of the tariff can be here aft[e]r fully & properly presented and that & other issues speedily to come up will give us a commanding if not a controlling influence hereafter if they do not secure our present triumph. The publication of that part of Mr. Calhoun's letter relating to the tariff will greatly embar[r]as[s] our movement in N[ew] York which will be followed in Pen[nsylvani]a & Ohio and should be actively responded to throughout the entire south. Yours sincerely, D. Green.

ALS with Ens in ScCleA; variant PC in Jameson, ed., *Correspondence*, pp. 911–913. NOTE: Among the people mentioned by John A. Campbell in his letter, David Hubbard and Francis S. Lyon were former U.S. Representatives; Richard B. Walthall and John A. Winston were Ala. State Senators; James W. McClung, Jeremiah Clemens (a future U.S. Senator), William S. and Philip Phillips, and William O. Winston were Ala. State Representatives; Henry Goldthwaite was a Justice of the Ala. Supreme Court; and Thomas S. Mays was elected in 1844 a Judge of the Montgomery County Court. John A. Campbell, son of Duncan G. Campbell who died while a nominee to be Governor of Ga., was a noted lawyer and was subsequently Associate Justice of the U.S. Supreme Court (1853–1861) and Assistant Secretary of War of the Confederate States.

To DUFF GREEN

Fort Hill, 15th Jan[uar]y 1844

My dear Sir, I have received by the same mail your two letters to day; and as I expect to leave home tomorrow morning early on business and to be gone 8 or 9 days you must excuse a short letter, especially as it is now 10 o[']clock at night and I have several letters on my table to answer.

I have modified my Address as far as I could consistently with the principles on which I act, to meet the views of my friends. I omitted all the part which treats of the Tariff as one of the grounds for not going before the Convention, although I do not concur altogether in the objections taken to it.

Its appearance has been accidentally delayed. I presume it will appear now in a short time.

I wish you great success in your New paper [the New York, N.Y., *Republic*]. The position is a commanding one, and with your great experience, and the advantage of the popular side of the question, I cannot doubt you will make a deep impression. If the party machinery and the spoils principles be not put down, the Govt. is lost.

But while you war against them, I hope you will not be silent on the subject of Free Trade. It is destined to triumph and is now popular in the West and a large portion of the North. Nor on the subject of abolition. Your assailing them at the same time you attack the Caucus system will strengthen your position, while it will make your fire more destructive to those against whom it is directed.

Let me hear from you frequently and send me your paper when it appears.

PC in Jameson, ed., *Correspondence*, pp. 561–562.

From V[IRGIL] MAXCY

Washington, 15th Jan[uar]y 1844

My dear Sir, I came here five days ago at the invitation of Mr. [Abel P.] Upshur and Gen[era]l [Alexander O.] Anderson to consult with them and if it should be thought expedient to prepare an Address to the people of the United States either ["before & after" *canceled*] to precede or follow your address, as [George] McDuffie, I understood, after consenting to write one had on reflection declined, as he found those who ought to join in it very much divided in opinion as to the good policy of taking that step *now*. [Silas] Wright & others of Mr. [Martin] V[an] B[uren]'s friends have been making fair promises as to the tariff. Timeo Danaos et dona ferenteas and I put no faith in their sincerity and our friends who have ["yielded" *interlined*] to the belief that they will be fulfilled, will regret, I fear, their credulity, when too late. Even three of the Carolina delegation positively refused to sign any paper whatever under present circumstances. Mr. U[pshur], Gen[era]l A[nderson] & myself came unanimously to the opinion therefore, that it was not expedient for us to prepare ["an address" *interlined*] or any longer to urge the signing of one, where there ["was" *canceled and* "is" *interlined*] so much halting among those, who we believe will before long be freed from their delusion & do what is right.

You, I understand have been informed from various sources, of what has passed here and therefore will have all the different views of your friends, who sadly want a leader of sufficient authority & energy to control & harmonize their action. Some have even gone so far as to desire that you would so modify your address ["so" *interlined*] as ["to" *interlined*] intimate that you ought to ["intimate" *canceled and* "say" *interlined*], that you will support the nominee of the Convention, if Mr. V[an] B[uren]'s friends, will cordially aid in passing a proper tariff! This of course you neither can nor ought to do, but I could wish, that whenever you come out on the Tariff whether in your address or in a letter to be hereafter published, when the treachery of those who heretofore joined the Whigs in subjecting the country to the robbery of a protective ["tariff" *canceled and* "system" *interlined*] that you would omit ["the" *canceled and* "to" *interlined*] *name* Mr. V[an] B[uren], if in other respects you do not think it proper to moderate the expression of your indignation, which, like electric[it]y in a surcharged body, throws out sparks from every sentence, if not every letter of your Address. We all think, I mean those who *toe the mark* without quailing or doubt, that the use of the words *Syracuse convention* is sufficiently specific, while naming Mr. V[an] B[uren] might lay you open to the charge of personal motives. But all these suggestions, *I even hope*, are too late for I wish that your address may have been already published. Not a moment ought now to be lost in blowing that trumpet, which no one but you can fill to a tone loud enough to wake Southern men from the sleep into which they have fallen.

I have just heard the strange report, that Mr. V[an] B[uren] has sent on here a letter to be published in the Globe, himself declining a nomination by the convention. Tho' I intended to have gone home to day, where I have a pressing call to return, I will stay two days longer if necessary to trace this report & give you the result before I close this letter.

[January] 16th

As far as I can discover as yet the above report is an idle rumour, ["but" *canceled*] & tho I shall remain here to-morrow and write you again on the subject, if I see any ground for it, I now send off this letter at once to communicate to you what has surprised me full as much as it will you. On my way thro' the passage of the State Department to see Mr. Upshur my son in law [Francis] Markoe met me and immediately called me into his room to tell me, that the Senate in Executive session last night had rejected Mr. [David] Henshaw and that Mr. Upshur had asked him (Markoe,) whether he thought I would consent to be nominated as Secretary of the Navy Department, telling him that he was very anxious for it and meant this morning to go to the President [John Tyler] to propose it to him as the most popular appointment he could make! ! ! He meant of course in this latter part of his conversation, that my nomination would be received with great favor on account of the indication it would give of the course the President meant to pursue, now he has given up the idea of an election himself. Now, My dear Sir, as I consented last autumn to stand as a candidate for the humble post of member of the House of Delegates of Md. almost solely with a view to be placed in a position, where I might be useful to you, so in the *barely possible* case, that something serious may grow out of this partiality of Mr. Upshur & the President may offer this ["post to me" *canceled*] important post to me, [*one word or partial word canceled*] my principal inducement to accept it would be to enable me more effectually to aid in my humble way the great cause in which you are engaged and I therefore hasten to ask you before-hand on account of the distance we are apart your views on the course I ought to take—whether to accept or refuse: and if the latter on what ground. Let me hear from you by return mail & believe me always Faithfully yours, V. Maxcy.

[P.S.] Gen. Anderson, whom I have just met in the rotunda of the Capitol told me he had just come up to the House to urge Mr. [Henry A.] Wise [Representative from Va.] to support Mr. Upshur[']s view, in regard to me, tho' there had been no concert between him & Mr. U[pshur].

ALS and copy in ScCleA. NOTE: David Henshaw of Mass. had been serving as Secretary of the Navy for six months when the Senate rejected his nomination. Thomas W. Gilmer of Va. was appointed by President John Tyler to the post on 2/15/1844, and, like Maxcy himself, was killed two weeks later in the explosion on the *Princeton*. Francis Markoe was a senior Clerk in the State Department.

From EUSTIS PRESCOTT

New Orleans, 15th Jan[ua]ry 1844
My Dear Sir, You will undoubtedly ere this have seen the proceedings of our State convention—declaring that the first choice of the people of this State for President, is Mr. [Martin] Van Buren—my object in now addressing you is to express my firm conviction that such is not the fact, altho it is very difficult to ascertain popular feeling in so scattered a population, and I am confident that conventions are rarely fair exponents of the public will. One fact I have ascertained, that *you* are the first choice of a majority of the Democratic members of the Legislature, but I fear *they* have committed themselves by becoming members of this convention.

I have deprecated its action from the first, but could not persuade your friends, many of whom are as warm in their attachment to you as myself, from taking part in it. From the onset I have urged an appeal to the people in the Congressional Districts to elect delegates for each direct, to the National convention, but some of our friends could not be induced to deviate from the former practice of the party, and a few of them are Delegates, instructed to cast their vote first for Mr. V[an] B[uren] and next for you.

The only good which the Convention has done for us, is an unanimous declaration in favor of our principles, and instructing the delegation to sustain them in the convention, if they do this manfully—as I know some of them will—it may produce discord, and change the aspect of affairs. I am satisfied that there is no cohesion between Northern & Southern Democrats, and that the friends of Free Trade will ultimately have to rally under their own flag—when, they will receive important strength from eastern whigs—as well as many, in the south and west.

I have taken some pains to ascertain the feeling in the parishes, in one, Mr. V[an] B[uren] had a majority of *one*, in a general meeting of the party, in another *two*, and in a third *four*, but in very few parishes was there even this test.

When in New York & Massa[chusetts] last summer I urged upon our friends concert of action, the appointment of a central corresponding committee &c, and also here on my return, but altho all were anxious, still they were afraid of dissevering the party. Now, as then, they complain of not knowing your views & feelings on the subject, not probably reflecting sufficiently on the delicacy of your situation.

F[elix] Bosworth, Parish Judge of Carroll, has some time since I learn addressed letters to Gen[era]l [Lewis] Cass, Col[o]n[el Richard

M.] Johnson, Mess[rs]. [James] Buchanan, [Martin] Van Buren & yourself [dated 10/23/1843], announcing your election as honorary members of the Democratic Association of Carroll—accompanied by a badge—to these, replies have been received from all but yourself—and in them, each pledges himself to sustain the nominee of the National convention—whoever he may be. I think these have been used to your disadvantage, and also a report that you had written [*not found*] to a Mr. Shepherd [possibly F.B. Shepard] of Mobile, that you considered it entirely unimportant to the south, whether Mr. Clay or Mr. V[an] B[uren] were the succes[s]ful candidate.

I have written you my dear Sir with the candor of a warmly attached friend of many years and should be gratified to receive a reply, which if I should be so favored shall be strictly confidential, or such portions of it communicated to our friends as you might suggest. I never can cordially support Mr. V[an] B[uren] and Mr. Clay[']s principles are too antagonistical to mine ever to permit me to vote for him.

I hope that the present session of Congress may eventually lead to some beneficial results, but the present prospect is gloomy, and I am really at a loss to know what ought to be our next course—if submission to the dictates of King Caucus & the Baltimore convention, I suppose we must do it with the best grace we can. Believe me to remain My Dear Sir Very sincerely your Obed[ien]t Serv[an]t, Eustis Prescott.

ALS in ScCleA; PEx in Jameson, ed., *Correspondence*, pp. 913–914. NOTE: This letter was wrongly addressed to Calhoun at "Fort Hill, Abbeville District," S.C.

From WHITEMARSH B. SEABROOK

Edisto Island [S.C.], Jan. 15th 1844
Dear Sir, As it is now nearly certain that, in reference to the Presidential election, the will of the people will be defeated by the political managers, it becomes a very grave question, what course it is advisable you should pursue. Without professing to be skilled in these matters, I give it as my deliberate conviction, that the true policy of your supporters is to continue in the field with your flag in their hands. Rather than submit to the dictation of the New York clique, it would be far better to encounter the risk of a decision by the H[ouse] of R[epresentatives], ["which perchance may elect Henry Clay, than"

canceled and "altho Henry Clay may in consequence be elected" *interlined.*] A choice by the people seems out of the question. Unless a great reformation, which I do not anticipate, should take place, I apprehend that the *freemen* of this country will never again put their Chief Magistrate into office. Of this power they appear to have been completely divested by the demagogues and wily statesmen of the day. As this is undeniably true, I view with feelings of the deepest emotion the contest between them and their opponents. It is vitally important, then, if the former are to be defeated, that it be done, not by surrendering their standard at the bidding of the Kinderhook tactician [Martin Van Buren], but after manfully contesting every inch of ground. Voluntarily to yield would be death to our Institutions. Let the Committee, therefore, at once declare that, as defenders of the people and the States, the federative features of the government, and the compromises of the Constitution, while you are ready to submit to the judgment of the citizens of the U.S., you will not abide by the decision of a Convention constituted on the Syracuse plan. The effect of such a declaration will be at once to rally your friends throughout the country, and to disabuse the public mind as to the probability of your retiring from the contest. Other favorable results, especially in relation to the legislation by Congress, would ensue. Under Van Buren[']s administration the Tariff question will not be settled; on the contrary, ["its" *altered to* "the"] burden of paying heavy taxes on the articles ["with" *canceled*] for which we exchange our staple products, may be fastened on us permanently. Our national affairs are indeed wearing a gloomy aspect. So[uth] Ca[rolina] must again prepare for resistance, as I have no confidence in the ["acts"(?) *canceled and* "doings" *interlined*] of other States, she must rely ["alone" *interlined*] on the indomitable energy, & patriotism of her own sons, in a word, we must again unfurl the banner of '33, with a resolute determination promptly to adopt such measures as will *insure* a permanent restoration of our rights, or an open collision with the Federal Government. We cannot, my dear Sir, continue longer in our Colonial condition; the people are ready for a decisive movement, be the consequences what they may. The spirit of abolition too is abroad, & the power of the government will in a few years be transferred forever to the West. Never was one man more anxious than I was to see you in the Presidential chair. I desired ["it" *interlined*] not for your gratification, but the safety of my country. Of all the statesmen of the Union, you alone seem fitted by nature & education to ["restore" *altered to* "reestablish"] & maintain the true principles of the Federal Compact. I shall despair of the Republic, if the decision of the people be against you. But will they have a voice in the matter? No! Shall we then allow the *corrupt* politicians of *hostile* States effectually to deprive us of our birth right, & to ["soil &" *canceled*] trample ["under foot" *interlined*] the sacred work of our Fathers? The answer is at hand. Be ready for the death struggle, for come it must, & that soon.

I have written *currente calamo*, but ["the" *altered to* "my"] opinions are honestly entertained & candidly expressed. Very respectfully yours, Whitemarsh B. Seabrook.

ALS in ScCleA. Note: Seabrook was Governor of S.C. during 1848–1850.

From R[ichard] F. Simpson, [Representative from S.C.]

House of Rep[resen]t[ativ]es, Jan[uar]y 15, 1844
My dear Sir, Judge [Edward] Cross [Representative from Ark.] a particular friend of yours from Arkansas, handed to me some seed of the osage orange & desired me to send them to you which I now enclose. He will write to you soon and give you whatever discription [*sic*] of its uses you may desire. I understand however from him that it is a beautifull [*sic*] evergreen yard tree and that when trim[m]ed makes an excellent hedge, with this peculiarity, that if a part of the hedge dies, as it may, the dead stalk will dry up and stand for years as strong as when alive.

I also now inform you that I attended to your request with Mr. [Lucius] Lyon [Representative from Mich.] and advanced him the $20. And will take a pleasure to attend to any business or request that you may desire me.

I have delayed the communication of the above particulars with the hope I could accompany them with some information from Congress that might be interesting to you. In a conversation with Mr. [Dixon H.] Lewis this morning he said I might say to you that the Committee of Ways & Means of which he is a member, he thinks will in a few days Report in favour of ["a" *altered to* "an"] ad valorem duty but not so low as ["to" *canceled*] for revenue alone. And that the committee are more sound than Van Buren[']s friends in the House.

I think from all the evidences yet given by his friends in the House the conclusion is a fair one that they do not intend to do any thing on the reduction of the Tariff until after the the [*sic*] Baltimore convention—nor make a decission [*sic*] of the question on the Rules [as to abolition petitions] either.

Now I will submit to your better discretion for I will not pretend to advise *you*, whether the evidences already given that they do not intend to come to the principles laid down by the Democratic Conventional Report of 1840, are not already sufficient to authorize you to come out at once, and place your position as well on the present course of Van Buren[']s friends on these two questions, as on the improper organization of the convention to meet in May next. I think I may safely say that among some of the friends of V[an] B[uren] or rather among some of [the] Free trade portion of those who are pledged to his nomination, there is now existing a considerable doubt of ["of the prospects for" *canceled*] his success if nominated, and a desire to drop him and take up some other, & that other is [Lewis] Cass—that is with that portion of them who would like to drop V[an] B[uren] mostly from Ill[inois,] Ind[iana, and] M[ichigan].

Now I do feel a very great desire that the position you may think best to take, may be so done as not to depress you and your future prospects in the minds of the American People. Yet I do not feel capable of advise [*sic*], but only of caution, satisfied that you are fully capable of taking the correct view, when all the facts are before you. Then whether will it be your interest to be placed as a candidate? I am satisfied your *un*pledged friends will hold on to you in any event. And the only course I am anxious about is that one which will place your ulterior prospects to greatest advantage.

I feel that my inexperience in political struggles & true positions of political parties, gives me no other right, than that resulting from my friendship, towit [*sic*] to suggest.

I am anxious to furnish you with any [*mutilated word*] documents that you may desire for information and I would be glad you would ["name any" *apparently canceled*] that you may be necessary to give you all the information that any of them may contain.

Present my respects to Mrs. Calhoun and accept for yourself my best wishes. Very respectfully, R.F. Simpson.

ALS in ScCleA. Note: An AEU by Calhoun reads "Hon. Mr. Simpson." Richard Franklin Simpson (1798–1882), a Pendleton lawyer and planter, during 1843–1849 represented the Congressional district in which Calhoun resided.

To F[RANKLIN] H. ELMORE

Fort Hill, 16th Jan[uar]y 1844

My dear Sir, I hasten to answer your letter, which I have just received. I have prepared a modification of my Address [originally dated 12/-21/1843] intended to meet the views of all my friends as far as I possibly can consist[ent]ly with the principles which govern me.

What I propose is, to strike out all after the first part, which treats of the mode of constituting the convention, and insert in its place the enclosed [*not found*]. To avoid mistake, I will quote the concluding part of the sentence of the portion to be retained, and the begin[nin]g of that to be struck out. The first is in the following words "and to come to the rescue of Mr. [Martin] V[an] Buren's at its greatest depression compels me now to with[h]old my name from going before the proposed Convention"; and the other in the following; "But it is not only in reference to the mode of constituting the convention." The former ends a paragraph & the latter commences one.

In making the change, I cheerfully yield to the wishes of my friend[s], which I always do, when I can consistently with what I regard my duty. Some of my Washington friends have urged me to omit all that relates to the Tariff, as not strictly belonging to the object of the Address. I meet their wishes by omitting it, as part of my reasons for not going into the Convention, and limiting what I say in reference to it, to the form of a mere decleration of one of the grounds, which will govern me in deciding on giving my support ["to" *interlined*] a presidential candidate. By giving it that form, it enables me to comply with the object, which Mr. [Dixon H.] Lewis has in view, as well as what I understand to be yours & that of some of my Charleston friends; and to avoid at the same time, what I regard an insuperable objection to his views. It would be impossible for me, after the strong grounds I have taken to the convention, to bring my mind to declare, that I would support its nominee on any condition. There seems to me to be something incompatible in the two, which I avoid by taking the course I have, while at the same time, I increase the pressure, on which he so much relies. To add to it, and give a promin[en]ce which is due to a still more important subject, I add to it abolition. But be this as it ["may" *canceled and* "may, it" *interlined*] is the nearest approach, which I can make to his views. I hope it will be satisfactory.

Now let me add, if I have taken stronger grounds than what you and other friends approve, it is because I have lost all confidence in

Mr. V[an] B[uren] & his friends, I mean his influential friends. They have never failed to betray us, whenever we have trusted them for the last 16 years. I had hoped the disasters of '37 would reform them, and that hope had increased untill the passage of the Tariff of '42; but since then, their entire course, especially in reference to the Tariff & abolition has been one of treachery, and violation of pledges. As soon, as they believed, that the Whigs were beaten through our exertions, & we trammelled by the machinery of party, they turned round and courted the Tariff & abolition parties at our expense. It is the game they have always played and played at our expense, till we are nearly ruined in property & character. They played it in '28. Mr. V[an] B[uren] & Mr. [Silas] Wright are the real authors of the Tariff of that year; and that is the real cause of all the calamity which has since befallen the country & the party.

Let me, now, entreat you and the Committee to take your ground boldly. While you avoid giving offense, as far as possible, cover firmly the ground on which you ought to stand. Conciliate the party, as much as you can, but not at the expense of principle, or in the vain hope, you can compel Mr. V[an] B[uren] and his friends to go right, except through fear. Your resolutions and Address, if you should conclude to make one should take strong grounds, on the Tariff & abolition; and should insist on the party to fulfil[l] their pledges in reference to both. You will ["find" *interlined*] strong pledges for both in their two Addresses before the election of '40, and in addition, in reference to abolition, in many resolutions on that subject, the four first of which were unanimously adopted by the vote of the party ["in the Senate" *interlined*]. You will find the resolutions in my life published by the Harpers. On the Tariff, the omitted portion of my Address will furnish a good deal of materials. I hope there will be [a] full meeting of my friends; and the Address read and the resolutions adopted as suggested in my private letter [*not found*] to the Committee. A delay of a few days, in order to have all well done, will be of no importance.

I will thank you to return the copy of my ["original" *interlined*] Address, or what I would prefer, if it has been put in type, a printed copy. Truly, J.C. Calhoun.

ALS in NHi, Miscellaneous Manuscripts. Note: The revisions of his "Address" which Calhoun enclosed have not been found, but see the version of that document which appears below under date of 1/29/1844.

From [Brig. Gen.] N[ATHAN] TOWSON,
[U.S. Army]

Washington, Jan[uar]y 16th 1844
My dear Sir, I received the enclosed [letter to you from Duff Green,
dated 1/12] yesterday, and called at the Dept. of State to shew it to
Mr. [Abel P.] Upshur, but could not obtain an interview as he was
engaged. I left it with a note for him and it was returned this morning without remark. We shall probably meet at the drawing room
this evening and if he says any thing on the subject I will communicate it to you.

The movement in New York is a bold and important one, calculated in my judgement, to produce a change in the democratic arrangements for nominating a candidate. It will alarm the friends of
Mr. [Martin] Van Buren and may convince them, that the party cannot be united on him, they ["must" *interlined*] be already convinced
that without union he cannot be elected. I agree with Gen[era]l
[Duff] Green, that so far as your fortunes may ["to"(?) *canceled*] be
affected by the change this movement may produce, will depend on
your coming to Washington. I would not however, advise you to accept a place in the Cabinet if it should be offered to you, of which I
have strong doubts, for I do not beleive [*sic*] the Senate will agree to
Mr. [John C.] Spencer[']s transfer from the Treasury to the Supreme
Court. Mr. [David] Henshaw was rejected yesterday [as nominee
for Secretary of the Navy] and Mr. [James M.] Porter[']s fate [as
nominee for Secretary of War] is doubtful; but you cannot in justice
to yourself, accept either of the vacancies, nor do I think you could
any office or appointment within the gift of the present administration
unless it be, for the purpose of negotiating a treaty with a foreign
power. The Senate is of all places the one in which you could be most
serviceable to the country and to yourself and I do not think you
should hesitate ["a(?) hesitate" *canceled*] a moment if the arrangement Gen. Green proposes for Mr. [George] McDuffie can be effected.
I always thought you should have remained in the Senate and I beleive ["all" *interlined*] your friend[s] *now* concur in that opinion.

I have no reason to doubt the attachment of the friends Gen[era]l
Green alludes to in his last paragraph, on the contrary beleive they
ardently desire your elevation to the Presidency, but have long
thought they considered the prospect hop[e]less, and I think they
have shewn a want of judgement and tact in not making the most of
your political capital both for you and for themselves. They yeilded
[*sic*] every thing in going into caucus for speaker [of the House of

Representatives] and received nothing in return, not even thanks! Out of caucus they could have dictated to it; in it they were worse than powerless. True, Mr. Van Buren[']s friends could have elected their officers without the aid of your friends; but they could not have made the impression on the public that the latter had been whipped into his support, which is much more important than the election of a speaker. Had your friends remained free they would have been courted[;] now they are spurned. There is however one advantage in it, having found by experience, that they are to receive no personal or political favor for submitting they will be more firm hereafter.

Gen[era]l Green thinks Mr. [Virgil] Maxcy should go to Balt[i-mor]e. I do not beleive he can be induced to do so. At all events it can only be done by you. This is an unfavorable time for a movement in Maryland as the Congressional Elections take place next month and any division in the democratic ranks will certainly give the State to the whigs. The probability now is, that the whigs will carry five out of the six districts. The State is democratic, but there has been such an apathy in the party ever since the Syracuse Convention that the whigs have triumphed in all the elections. Our friend [Elias?] Brown can be elected if he gets the party nomination but I fear Mr. Van Buren[']s friends will oppose it.

I saw Patrick [Calhoun] a day or two since[;] he was in health and enjoying the gayety of the season.

Please make my respects to Mrs. Calhoun. I shall be glad to hear from you soon. Yours truly, N. Towson.

ALS in ScCleA; ALS (copy) in DLC, Duff Green Papers; PEx in Boucher and Brooks, eds., *Correspondence*, pp. 206–207. NOTE: As predicted by Towson, President John Tyler's nominations of John C. Spencer of N.Y. to the Supreme Court and James M. Porter of Pa. to be Secretary of War were both rejected by the Senate. Towson (1784–1854), a Marylander, was Paymaster General of the Army from 1822 until he undertook a field command during the Mexican War.

To J[ohn] H. Logan, A[ugustus] T. Broyles, and R[ichard] W. Denton, Committee

Fort Hill, 17th Jan[uar]y 1844

Gentlemen, My numerous and heavy engagements prevent me from accepting the honor conferred on me by the Clariosophic Society of the South Carolina College, by electing me to deliver the annual Oration. They are such, as to leave me no spare time, which I hope the Society will accept as an apology for declining the office I have been elected to discharge. With great respect I am &c, J.C. Calhoun.

FC in ScU, University Archives, Clariosophic Society Papers, Minutes, 1842–1849, p. 106.

From R[OBERT] M. T. HUNTER

L[l]oyds, Essex [County, Va.] Jan[uar]y 19th 1844
My dear Sir, I was very glad to receive your last letter and you were right in ["suppo"(?) *changed to* "your"] conjecture as to the cause of my silence. I had so little that was pleasant to tell you that I had not the spirit to write. I did not go on to Washington to see your letter [to your supporters] because I could not well leave home at that time and I supposed that it was in any event to be published as written. I live so remote from the scene of action that I should scarcely ["know what to advise" *canceled*] confide in my own opinion upon a subject of so much importance as that of your letter. I was not surprised to learn that you had refused to place your name before the Baltimore Convention. In your strictures upon its probable organization I have no doubt but that I should concur. The course of the New York Democrats in the present Congress deserves to be damned by every honest man in the Country but I fear your motives would be misconstrued should you give utterance to such sentiments. Upon this matter however I cannot judge ["without seeing the letter" *interlined*] as I know language to be ["the" *interlined*] most flexible of human instruments as I have often heard you say and I know also that you have a mode of delivering truth without offending others which is almost peculiar to yourself. But I confess that I think it safest and most prudent that in this letter you should not give countenance to the idea of running a separate ticket for yourself. Under present circumstances I fear that as against ["such" *canceled*; "a" *changed to* "the"] nominee of the convention such a ticket would not receive a tithe of the votes of those who really prefer you. In this I may err. I am not well informed as to the state of public sentiment and your judgment is much better than mine. You doubtless have considered the question. But I should dislike very much to see your name before the people and the State of So[uth] Carolina alone voting for you. Your popularity is worth preserving not only for your own sake but for that of the South. To whom else shall we look for a defender?

In the Congressional district in which I live we have succeeded so far in preventing the party from pledging itself to the nominee of the Baltimore Convention. But it is the only district in the State in which your friends have made an approach to a successful fight. How long they will hold out here I cannot tell as the people are fast coming to the conclusion that Mr. [Martin] V[an] B[uren']s nomination is inevitable. In this State some of the leaders amongst your friends may hold off but the mass I think incline to support the nominee, not because he is the nominee of the Baltimore Convention but from their desire to defeat [Henry] Clay. At the same time I believe that they will hold aloof from the Baltimore Convention. In our State Convention in Feb[ruar]y next the V[an] B[uren] men will probably propose a pledge to support the nominee of the B[altimore] Conven-[tio]n—as a test of Democratic fellowship. If so there will be a split in the party in this State. Most of your friends will refuse any such pledge and attack ["it" *canceled and* "the" *interlined*] organization of that Convention. In that event a separate ticket will probably be run in this State. I was in Richmond ten days since. Some of the first ["young" *interlined*] men in the State are warmly your friends— undecided as yet as to a separate ticket but determined to refuse a pledge to the nominee [of the Baltimore Convention] should an attempt be made to exact it. Amongst them are [James A.] Seddon[,] [Thomas T.] Giles (a son of Wm. B[ranch] Giles) and [John S.] Caskie. [Robert G.] Scott is an older man[,] active[,] able and zealous. Seddon I think inclines to a split. He says he would not propose it because he fears it would be fatal to your future prospects and he thinks it a question for your own decision only. Should you be willing to risk it he would not hold back. I have promised to attend this State Convention. Our course is as yet undecided except as to refusing the pledge to sanction the Baltimore convention no matter how organized. [Former Representative from Va. William F.] Gordon and [William?] Taylor [Representative from Va.] I am told will give such a pledge but your friends generally will not do it. We hope to have a general consultation amongst our friends at that time. Should the attempt be made to force this pledge from us we shall issue an address to the people of Virginia. It will be prepared [for this] contingency. Mr. [Thomas] Ritchie is very a[ngry and] very arbitrary. Towards us at least his an[*mutilated*] tact. I should be very glad to hear from you before this convention. To meet me in time your letter ought to be directed to me at Richmond under cover to James A. Seddon who will take care ["of it" *interlined*] should it arrive before or after the Convention. Our friends in the ["Va." *interlined*] legislature will move resolutions on the subject of the Tariff, the 21st rule and the negro petition from the District of Columbia. I advised them to do so *at once*. They will move them without previous consultation with the V[an] B[uren] Democrats in Caucus—so much do they distrust them. Queries will probably be sent to Mr. V[an] B[uren] to ascertain his opinions upon the course of the N[ew] York Democrats in the present Congress. Yours sincerely, R[obert] M.T. Hunter.

ALS in ScCleA; variant PC in Jameson, ed., *Correspondence*, pp. 914–916.

From GEO[RGE] N. SANDERS

Grass Hills, Carroll Co[unty] Kentucky, 20 January 1844
My Dear Sir, Guided by a feeling of certainty that in your present retirement from the national councils you retain all the solicitude for your country[']s best success that before inspired your eloquence, I feel anxious to lay before your consideration a paper upon the settlement of Oregon, the original of which, I have recently forwarded to the President of the United States [John Tyler].

Our foreign relations never had a more interesting aspect than at present, never have they demanded more thoughtful and yet more vigorous action than now. With them, I consider the settlement of Oregon, as well as the various threads spinning out from the Amalgamation, Abolition and slave interests as more or less intimately entwined. All the advantages flowing from a plan embracing this favourable offer to the blacks, cannot be immediately foreseen. While it promises so much to the blacks themselves, and to their disinterested friends among the whites, its successful passage through Congress, will also alarm the political Abolitionist and his co-adjutors among the free blacks, into their proper senses; and vindicate the power of the slave States yet to protect themselves against the prophecies and machinations of their enemies.

I was one of a committee deputed by a meeting held at Ghent in this county, in November last to address you on the Texan Annexation. As we have not as yet received your letter in reply, I forward copies of the letter [of 11/25/1843] and proceedings in company with this, upon the supposition that the others have not been received, they having been directed to Charleston.

The democratic candidates for the Presidential nomination are as was antic[i]pated, reducing in number, as the time of the convention draws near. Mr. [James] Buchanan having positively declined, and several others who have been talked of, now being scarcely mentioned. With most of the Kentucky delegates, you are (Col. [Richard M.] Johnson out of the question) the first choice and as they believe the strongest man. If Mr. [Martin] Van Buren comes out against the Annexation of Texas, it will at once turn the whole Mississippi val[l]ey against him.

If it does not as yet meet your views to make a public declaration of your sentiments on the Annexation of Texas, I would be most happy to receive from you a letter on the settlement of Oregon, to be made public, if not otherwise directed by you. I send you the [Frankfort] Kentucky Yeoman of the 11th inst[ant] containing the letters of Mr. [Levi] Woodbury, [Robert B.] McAfee and [John M.?] McCalla to the Ghent committee on Texas. Next week[']s Yeoman will have answers from Messrs. Buchanan, Johnson, [Charles A.] Wickliffe & [William O.] Butler—replies have not yet been received from Messrs. Van Buren, [Henry] Clay, [Lewis] Cass, [Winfield] Scott, [John] McLean, [Daniel] Webster, [John] Davis, [James K.] Polk, [William R.] King, [Robert J.] Walker, [Nathaniel] Tallmadge, [Thomas H.] Benton or Sargeant [*sic*; John Sergeant] all of whom have been addressed on the subject.

Allow me in subscribing myself your friend with every sentiment of esteem for your moral excellencies, and the highest veneration for your intellectual endowments to declare the gratification it would afford me to give my individual efforts towards your elevation should the Democratic party be so fortunate as to receive your name as the candidate for President. Geo. N. Sanders.

[Enclosure]

Geo[rge] N. Sanders to President [John] Tyler, "Private, (Copy)"

Grass Hills, Carroll Co[unty] Kentucky, 15 January 1844

Sir, It has occurred to me that some of the most difficult and agitating issues now before the people of the United States, might be absorbed in the settling of the Oregon Territory. The United States to form a Territorial Government west of the Rocky mountains, wherein should be established perfect equality of colour, with the protection of the Government pledged against all molestation. Arthur Tappan or some other distinguished abolitionist to be Governor.

Let a general rendezvous be named somewhere on the Missouri River; from there, the government should defray the expenses to the end of the journey, and provide rations for one year for all who are not worth five hundred dollars. A half section of land to be granted to each and eve[r]y person who may emigrate previous to the year

1850. The principle of perfect equality to be guarantied to the blacks even to the military organization, a branch of the Army to be formed there, manned and officered without regard to colour.

The slave States might pass laws which would without injustice, make it the interest of the free blacks under fifty within their borders to join the new colony, thus draining the south of an abundant source of evil. Those who are anxious to manumit their slaves, might be bound to provide for their being sent in comfort to Oregon, and provided for, for one year from the time of their arrival.

A few of the advantages that occur to me from this scheme, shall be stated as concisely as possible. It presents a bar to the machinations of political abolitionism, which might by it be diverted and distracted from its present reckless career, while to ["the" *interlined*] conscientious of that party, it offers the most advantageous field whereon to carry out their benevolent schemes to the fullest extent. The Liberia colony has proved in a great degree a failure. The American Blacks are no longer Africans in constitution, habits or tastes; and the great expense of transportation, must always render the emigration to that country a difficult and doubtful experiment. Now in the Oregon plan, the cost is reduced to a comparatively small sum, and the painful necessity of expatriation is av[o]ided. A healthy and genial climate, and a grateful soil, invite the settlers; who at the end of their journey, find themselves still under the protection of the United States, and inhabiting a portion of their native land. The proposition of intermarriage could there be acted on without interfering with the customs of an established community, or subjecting the participants to ignominy in the estimation of their associates. The mighty barriers between us and the new colony, would relieve the Southern States of all apprehensions in regard to any tampering with the slaves from that quarter. Nor would the slaves themselves, attached as they usually are to their homes, feel any undue anxiety to depart to so great a distance, without the protection and encouragement of their masters in the undertaking. This plan, if vigorously carried out, might also at some day afford a solution of the trying question—"What is to become of the excessive slave population of the South?" and without exterminating or oppressing this Israel in Egypt, we might gradually be freed from any danger to ourselves, arising from their liberation, insurrection or increase.

Mr. Tappan is now I believe poor, and his business connections with this part of the country, must be in in [*sic*] a great measure broken off. If you would write to him to visit Washington, and prevail on him to enlist in the cause, his exertions would give a powerful impetus to the enterprize. The Blacks have confidence in his wisdom and his good will for them. They would rally around him from every part of the Union; while his reputation and standing in society, w[oul]d make his name a lode-star to those whites who coincide with his opinions in regard to the American Africans. The blacks would be placed in a more favourable position for their own elevation, than they have ever been at any period of their existence, either here or in their own country; and they would have the most ample means of developing those abilities, claimed for them by their admirers of the Liberty party.

Should this proposition upon your own mature deliberation, so far meet your approbation as to induce you to present it in some form to congress, with additional development and remark, I cannot deny to myself the hope that great good may result therefrom. The sums of money now expended in various ways by the abolitionists, would if concentrated to one practical aim, be enough to carry a rail way from the Missouri to the top of the Rocky Mountains. We should endeavour to relieve the government from any onerous charge in the undertaking by exciting the rich abolitionists as well as slave holders to unite their means in carrying it forward.

The several States might enact laws sentencing to transportation thither, those free blacks who were habitual vagrants, or convicted of light crimes. In the event of a war with Great Britain we would have some suitable place to which to transport those free blacks who were found guilty of favouring the British cause.

From all that I can anticipate of popular sentiment from any source, I cannot but feel the utmost certainty, that if this mode of settling Oregon Territory, together with the annexation of Texas to the United States, should be urged forward and carried through by your address and zeal, it would shed a glory around the present administration unequalled by the lustre of any that has preceded it. Believe me Sir, with respect and regard, your fellow citizen, Geo. N. Sanders.

ALS with Ens in ScCleA. NOTE: In addition to the copy of his letter to Tyler, Sanders enclosed a second copy of the letter of 11/25/1843 which he and others had addressed to Calhoun. Sanders (1812–1873), was a horse breeder and the grandson of George Nicholas, Va. Revolutionary leader and early settler of Kentucky. Sanders subsequently enjoyed a picturesque career as lobbyist, speculator, advocate of "Young America" and of Stephen A. Douglas's Presidential aspirations, U.S. Consul in London (briefly in 1853), confidant of Kossuth, Garibaldi, and other European revolutionary leaders, and Confederate agent abroad.

From JACOB BOND I'ON

[Charleston] Jan[uar]y 24th 1844

My dear Sir, I was absent from Charleston from the 2nd of Jan[uar]y untill the 10th of the same month, when I returned, & have continued here ever since, but did not know of the address, untill monday last the 22 Ins[tan]t. Col. [Franklin H.] Elmore in the morning of that day called on me & left that paper, together with Letters from our friends at Washington & other papers, to which I gave a hasty perusal. A meeting of such members of the Central Committee, (as could be assembled,) and a few other persons friendly to our purposes, was had in the evening; and after consultation, it was determined, to publish the address in the daily Papers, so soon as a preface could be drawn up, & submitted to a meeting of the Comm[it]te[e], to examine the same. I shall do all in my power to hasten this publication, & think it will be made in the course of the current week. You are aware, that an alteration, has been made in the address by omitting a portion of the 6th[?] Sheet, & substituteing a paragraph, prepared (as I understand,) in conformity to the advice & desire of your friends at Washington & elsewhere, by yourself. I will submit your favour of the 14th Ins[tan]t to the committe[e], & endeavour to hasten it's action, being well aware of your delicate position, & the importance of laying the Address before the Nation. Having just perused your Letter, I have indited these few lines to relieve, as far as in my power, your mind, from doubt & uneasiness; you will find me always prompt in my communications with you, and no man more scrupulous, to sustain your feelings & carry out your wishes. I request you to present my aff[ectiona]te regards to your family & ["accept" *interlined*] assurance of my respect & friendship to yourself—faithfully yours, Jacob Bond I'On.

[P.S.] This is written in haste.

ALS in ScCleA.

To Mrs. A[NNA] M[ARIA CALHOUN] CLEMSON, Mount Willing, Edgefield District, S.C.

OBarr Mine, 26th Jan[uar]y 1843 [*sic;* 1844]

My dear Anna, I arrived here about one o[']clock the third day after I left home and found all well, but doing very indifferent business. I have concluded to lease and expect Mr. [Benjamin M.] Milner over today & hope to conclude my arrangement with him & leave tomorrow for home.

I found the road not near so bad as I expected, and had fine weather 'till I had nearly reached here, when it began to rain a little. The next night and day it rained very hard. The streams have been very full in consequence. It is now clear & cold, with a high wind from the North west & the prospect of a cold ride home.

I hope you found the road better than anticipated, & the journey much less tedious & disagreeable than you expected; and also that ere this reaches you, that you ["are" *canceled and* "will be" *interlined*] right comfortably quartered. You & Mr. [Thomas G.] Clemson will be kept as busy as bees for some time; but will not be the less happy on that account. With all of the discomforts of a new s[e]ttlement, the employment & the improvement make it far from disagreeable. That at least is my experience, and I hope it will be your's [*sic*] & his. The place, if I do not mistake, is a good one, & will well justify being improved. I do not doubt it will well repay all the labour & expenditures which may be judiciously bestowed on it.

That you & he & the family may be prosperous & happy on it is the prayer of your father.

Give my love to Mr. Clemson & kiss [John] Calhoun [Clemson] & little sis [Floride Elizabeth Clemson] for me. Write me as soon as you receive this. Your affectionate father, J.C. Calhoun.

[P.S.] I have leased the lot to Mr. Milner. He is to pay ¼ toll, and I am to have the liberty to to [*sic*] put in when I please any number of hands I please not exceeding his, paying my proportional share of the expense. I leave tomorrow for home.

ALS in ScCleA. NOTE: This letter was postmarked at Dahlonega, Ga., on 1/28.

From DUFF GREEN

New York [City,] Jan[uar]y 26th 1844

My dear Sir, I have not heard from you since I came home. I wrote to you from Washington and again from here. The rumor of the day is that Mr. [John] Tyler has gone over to [Henry] Clay, that the [Washington] Madisonian has been purchased up by a few office holders who hope to protect themselves by going over [to the Whigs] with [William C.] Rives [Senator from Va.].

This is true I believe to a certain extent only. I fear that young Tyler has been engaged in very improper speculations, and that he and a few desperate men are playing a very desperate game. You ought to be at Washington. By leaving the Senate you have left [Thomas H.] Benton in command. [George] McDuffie is operated through [Andrew] Stevenson & [Martin] Van Buren, and he controls all the younger men. If you were there *now* there ["are" *changed to* "is"] excellent material to organise upon. The young men from the West are the men who are to control events, they are honest and ardent. They would rally around you and you could yet recover the ground we have lost. The movement of the New York committee recommending the convention to be held in July at Philadelphia will enable your friends to take ground against the Baltimore Convention that will drive [Martin] Van Buren's friends in Congress to to [*sic*] take strong southern ground on the tariff and on abolition. If your friend[s] in South Carolina respond to the movement there will be popular meeting[s] got up every where to the north & west and Van Buren will [be] driven into the 4th of July convention or else ["will" *canceled*] to withdraw from the contest.

If Mr. Tyler has resolved to go for Mr. Clay he will not make a vacancy in the Senate by nominating Mr. McDuffie [to a diplomatic post], but the necessity of availing himself of your aid to support his treaties with England & with Texas is so apparent that—unless he is resolved to go for Mr. Clay[—]he will not hesitate to do so.

I have written to the President and to Mr. [Abel P.] Upshur and have recieved [*sic*] no answer from either. Your friends here are anxiously awaiting ["your" *canceled*] the publication of your letter, and its appearance will be the signal for popular meetings.

Do let me hear from you and should any occasion offer for your return to Washington let me entreat you to avail yourself of it. Your friend, Duff Green.

ALS in ScCleA. NOTE: Green's reference to "young Tyler" is presumably an ironic contrast of the President with his father John Tyler, Governor of Va. during 1808–1811. Green's projected Philadelphia convention is mentioned further in a letter to Richard K. Crallé, January 20, 1844 (LS in DLC, Duff Green Papers; PEx in Moore, ed., "Calhoun as Seen by His Political Friends," p. 420).

From JAMES GADSDEN, [President of the South Carolina Railroad]

Charleston S.C., Jan[ua]r[y] 27, 1844

My Dear Sir, I have for the last 4 weeks been absent from the city on a visit to Florida. On my return on the 24 inst[ant] I heard for the first time the position in which you have been placed. If not anticipated, it was not unexpected. I have been among the few in this State, who have for the last ["six" *canceled and* "12" *interlined*] months looked upon the movements made on the political check[er]boa[r]d with very great distrust. Your resignation from the Senate I considered a mistake. To trust [Martin] Van Buren & his corps of political plundere[r]s was a still greater mistake, but to consent to go into convention with his division of assumed Democrats was a fault. The issue has been, as I expected, and how for us advocates of Free Trade to get back to the position we occupied some 12 or 18 months since I confess is beyond my ken. Prospects then looked encouraging. We had a little band united & moving onward. But in an evil hour you retired from the only position in which you could then aid our cause & the one you had so long battled for, & by intimating a willingness to ["allying"(?) *changed to* "ally"] with Traitors we have or may be made to suffer from their treachery. Indeed our position is delicate. Professing to be Democrats we are accused of desertion of party; and that because we cannot carry our Candidate. Whatever the enlightened may think, the mass believe that no other motive actuates Carolina, but to carry her favourite, & that disappointed in securing his nomination before the Democratic convention, is the sole motive for refusing, if we do, going into that convention. You will understand me; I speak of what I hear & having mingled much among the citizens South & West of late I hear the above asserted in all quarters. It would not deter me however, any more than I know it will not you, for still adhering to our principles let the impugning of motives be what they may. But in adhering to [our principles] we wish to see these principles triumph and having got a check of late, it becomes a question of moment how can we recover our lost ground. Again rally our little Spartan band & move onward once more for victory. As things now stand, we have nothing to do with the Presidential election. [Henry] Clay, will be successful, but he is our open opponent. Van [Buren] we cannot trust & ought not to contribute to his success. Indeed our cause will ultimately be safer in his defeat than his election. Success now will secure the power to a party indeed I may call it a faction: who have no principle to contend for: & who as you once said are held "together by the attractive cohesion of plunder." Alliance with them is death, their defeat is necessary to the ultimate triumph of our cause. But to succeed even hereafter we must keep our force embodied & in the field: and encouraged with the hope yet of victory. To do this we must have a rallying point, and it is with no motive to flatter that ["on" *interlined*] you & you alone can we rally or depend. You must return then to the Senate. There to keep before the Community & the Government our principles, & not permit our forces to be distributed between Clay & Van Buren, because they have no hope. It has been intimated that sh[oul]d [John C.] Spencer[']s place as Sec[re]t[ary] of Treas[ur]y be vacated, the tender will be made to you. Should this be the case, I hope you will not hesitate in accepting. The Sec[re]t[ary] of the Treasury is at this time the government. It is the place of all others which would enable you to bring before our people in bold relief those principles of free Trade for which we are contending. The shortness of [John] Tyler[']s administration may be an objection, not giving time for such a report & its circulation as would & must awaken the People of the U.S. to their true interests. A People of all others most deeply interested in the success of free Trade. A Long session [of Congress] however which now seems inevitable, would give you an opportunity & as Sec[re]t[ary] of the Treasury, with the whole government as completely at your disposal, as if you were President you might, ere a new administration comes in make such an impression as to force either who may obtain the power to come to our principles. I really hope you may take the view I do, of this all engrossing subject, and will not reject the opportunity & the position, which seems to me of all others at this crisis best calculated to restore our forces to the place they have lost and to rally us with renewed hope & confidence in an ultimate triumph. If you do not, if you are resolved to remain in retirement, I fear nothing that you can do, no manifestos or no communications from Pendleton will stir us up but despairing many will like you go into retirement, while others wanting firmness to quit the high places they occupy will rally under a pretended democracy & join the assumed W[h]igs. We Free Traders will literally have no party & no leader & without an army & a General what cause can expect to triumph[?] I have my Dear Sir for 18 months past looke[d] with such distrust on events & movements, that I have rather avoided taking any part in the political movements: and fearing what now seems inevitable I was unwilling to be committed to a support of a man in whom I never have had any trust: or to a party which he professes to represent. Indeed it did seem to me as if some of our friends were blindly sacrificing everything for which they professed to battle. If with present prospects we must disband & await future times to rally; the cause of Free Trade is dead and I must confess that if we have not the spirit to resist the oppressive exactions on our industry by the selfish restrictionists of the Country, I for one would convert these exactions to my benefit by demonstrating to the North that we have advantages in manufacturing & fully equal to theirs: & that we may be both producers & manufacturers & enjoy the protection on both. But to return to the subject[?] which has elicited these remarks. Let me have your views as to the future & say how or by what means are the Free Traders to be kept together & encouraged in future efforts in their cause if they have no rallying point, no incentives to future action. To you we look & I really hope that should Mr. Tyler acknowledge his inability to govern, by virtually resigning the government, you will not decline administering it, if it be but for the brief space of 12 months. It will give you time at all events, to throw before the Public & in an official form, something to think on, which must produce action: and will at least prove to the nations abroad that there is a party & no inconsiderable one who will rally with them in the great cause. You well said once "names are nothing[,] things everything." The Secretary of Treasury at this crisis is virtually the President, in the hands of one who understands the present condition of our country & who comprehending its great interests will promote them without regard to sectional & selfish influences.

With a hope of hearing soon from you I remain as ever your friend, James Gadsden.

[P.S.] Your letter or communication I understand is to appear in both [Charleston] papers on Monday. ["But" *canceled.*]

ALS in ScCleA; variant PC in Jameson, ed., *Correspondence*, pp. 916–919.

From ALEX[ANDE]R JONES

New York [City,] Jan[uar]y 28th 1844
Office of the *Republic*

Dear Sir, I have the honor to acknowledge the receipt of your letter by due course of mail. At the time of its receipt I had corresponded with Gen[era]l [Duff] Green on the subject of reviving the Free Trade paper, having heard that he contemplated starting a paper in New York. He accordingly came to New York on the 8th of this month, and became the purchaser of the materials of the late daily Gazette, and as you no doubt already know has his paper "the Republic" under way.

He has engaged the services of *Mr.* [Thomas P.] *Kettell* as the writer of the financial and money articles of the paper, at a standing salarary [*sic*] of $1500 Dollars per annum, allowing him at the same time the priviledge of writing commercial articles for ["some of the" *canceled*] "Hunts Merchants Magazine", and ["for" *interlined*] "the Democratic review", he has ["proposed to" *interlined*; "engaged" *changed to* "engage"] me as the travelling Agent of the paper for the Southern and western States, ["and" *canceled*] at a salary of $1200 Dollars per annum, and to pay my reasonable travelling expenses. It is possible I may accept his proposals, and if so, shall set out on my tour next week.

You will perceive by the movement of your friends ["in N.Y." *interlined*] that, they have taken a stand preparatory to the reception of your letter, and will on its arrival immediately call a meeting ["to sustain" *canceled*] and adopt resolutions to sustain your views.

The prospect of being able to get up a Democratic Convention in Phil[adelphi]a on the fourth of July next, seems to brighten as we progress. Could the times have favoured the plan at an earlier period, I think it would have been attended with greater success.

I know little of Gen[era]l Green personally. My knowledge of him, has been derived entirely through the public press. And I beg leave to state to you that I fear his success in his new position. This I ["do" *canceled and* "state" *interlined*] in strict confidence of course, and without intending any disrespect for the Gen[era]l, and hence my hesitation at entering into his service, with a ["view" *canceled and* "prospect" *interlined*] of permanent employment. He tells ["me" *interlined and then canceled*] Mr. Kettell, that Mr. Wycoff [that is, Henry Wikoff], late of Philadelphia, & who accompanied Fanny ["Ellsler" *canceled*] Ellesler, in her Theatrical tours, and is a man in wealthy circumstances[,] has agreed to advance the funds to establish the Republic, and has with this view entered into an agreement with ["him" *interlined*] (Gen[era]l Green,) by which he becomes the Agent for the Proprietor, and Editor of the said paper. To secure the necessary funds, say from $20 to $25000 Dollars, Wycoff has executed a mortgage on about $60000 Dollars worth of property in Philadelphia & has advanced $3000 in cash, with which the paper has been commenced, that Wycoff now in Europe is to return to this country himself, within a few months, and probably become the business man of the paper, as well as its proprietor.

It is not so much on account of funds I fear Gen[era]l Green[']s success—as ["to" *canceled*] the interference of [*word obliterated*] schemes he has in View, and which he has in part unfolded to me, and which; I communicate to you, in great confidence. It appears while in England, engaged in negotiating a loan on his coal Lands in Maryland, he formed an extensive plan of an Emigration and General

Insurance Association, intended to have branches ["wh"(?) *canceled*] in various places both in this country and in Europe. For such a company, or Association he expects to obtain a charter from the Government of Texas at the present session of Congress, ["granting" *interlined and* "with" *canceled*] the priviledge of entering or purchasing ["s" *canceled*] public land at a stipulated price. Persons who hold wild lands; to have the priviledge, of ["entering" *canceled*] subscribing them, or conveying them to the Company, and receive in return certificates of their value in stock. The company in the mean time, to make arrangements for an extensive plan of emigration, by means of which it is expected the value of the lands will be greatly enhanced, and afford handsome dividends to the company. The company are likewise to engage in the purchase and entry of wild lands in the United States in the same manner, in conversion for stock, to which ["increased emigration is to be" *canceled*] emigrants are to be led in the same manner. The same company are to become a kind of universal Insurance Association[.] The head of the company for this continent is to be fixed in New York, and in London & Paris for Europe. In unfolding this scheme the Gen[era]l proposed I should at once proceed to Texas to press the charter before Congress, which I have determined to decline. I believe he has engaged a Mr. Todd [John G. Tod?] of Washington to proceed on that errand. Here is a scheme that can engulph from $100,000 to $500,000 Dollars, and is of sufficient scope to engage the united attention of a dozen able men, without allowing leisure for other pursuits.

The scheme may be feasable, and if well carried out by men and means, may even end in profit to the parties engaged. As to this I am not capable of judging. But one thing I do know, that to make a large daily paper succeed in New York, will require the entire and undivided attention, of an able, industrious, and single minded business man. No capital can supply the place of such a man, or of such a head. The competition in the news paper Press in New York is immense. With a strictly & single minded business man to ["mang" *canceled*] manage it, $25000 Dollars is an ample sum to establish a new paper on a permanent bases [*sic*]. Without such a man's services, I cannot name any sum that will be necessary. It may be possible Wycoff may be a business man. This, however, I should hardly be led to suppose, else, why should he enter the service of a travelling dancing woman, and follow her over the world? If he has property in Philadelphia worth $60,000, it has of course been left him as a patrimony to which he has not probably added a dollar to its value. My fear is, therefore, that after a brief existence, the $25000 will be spent,

Wycoff lose his money, and the paper come to an end. Such are my fears, though I trust they may turn out to be groundless. Under such circumstances I ["cannot" *canceled*] consider my engagement with the paper at present *as only temporary*. I am to be paid my salary at the end of each month, and to be at liberty to withdraw at any time after three months shall have expired.

The friends of Mr. [Martin] Van Buren in this quarter are becoming much alarmed, They begin to admit that he cannot by any possibility be elected. And I should not be surprised if some of his friends were to urge his withdrawal. As to general movements at Washington you are fully advised. Your friends here, ["as" *canceled*] are as warm, and as steadfast as ever. They will support you, and stand by you, through good and evil report. Though not over powerful, they will yield to none in the ardour of their devotion, ["and" *canceled and* "or (*"the" canceled*) in the" *interlined*] sincerety of their attachment.

The weather in New York is intensely cold. The Thermometor yesterday, outside of my window, stood at 4° above 0°, and this morning at 3½°. The Rivers & harbours in the vicinity are full of Ice. Ingress and Egress from and, to, the ocean is almost cut off.

I should be pleased to hear from you in reply. Address me care of Mr. Rowe, "Office of the Republic" N. York, While I have the Honor to Remain Your Sincere Friend & Ob[edien]t Serv[an]t, Alexr. Jones.

ALS in ScCleA. NOTE: Henry Wikoff (1811–1884), a wealthy Philadelphian and notable bon vivant who spent much time in Europe, had put up the funds for Green's short-lived New York *Republic.* He was an author, a friend of Louis Napoleon, and in 1846 became owner of the *United States Magazine and Democratic Review.* Wikoff's *Reminiscences of an Idler* (1880) contains observations and anecdotes about Calhoun's career.

From W[ILLIA]M D. MERRICK,
[Senator from Md.]

Washington, January 28th 1844

Dear Sir, Your valued favor of the 27th Ultimo was duly received, but severe domestic afflictions, with which I was visited about that time, have prevented my returning so prompt an answer, as under ordinary circumstances I certainly should have done. I did myself the honor some days since of forwarding to you a copy of the Bill I have lately introduced, on the subject of mails & postages, in which you will find the views you expressed in your letter are fully met by an express provision, at the same time that it is proposed greatly to abridge the franking privilege generally. The facts in your case are so striking, that it would be of great service in the discussion of this provision, to be authorized to state them, but this I can not do under the restrictions you have impo[sed.] I seize the occasion to assure you, that you do me no more than justice in supposing, that I have every disposition to oblige you; for besides a warm personal attachment, formed in the days of my early manhood, I have constantly cherished towards you sentiments of lively gratitude for preeminent services to our common Country.

No right minded man, it seems to me, who may have enjoyed opportunities equal to my own, of observing you nearly, (however he may dissent, as I have done, from some of your views of public policy,) can fail to cherish in grateful remembrance, your noble bearing, your invariably dignified and courteous manner, your splendid talents, and your selfsacrificing devotion to what you considered the true interests of your Country.

There is a secret comfort in feeling authorized to assume the liberty of speaking thus to a high minded independent Patriot, long pursued and in some measure victimized by wily artifices & base intrigues; & there is still more comfort in believing that the time for retributive justice must come.

Be pleased to tender my most respectful compliments to Mrs. [Floride Colhoun] Calhoun, & believe me to be With Very Great respect your Friend & Ob[e]d[ien]t Ser[van]t, Wm. D. Merrick.

ALS in ScCleA. NOTE: On 1/22 Merrick had introduced Senate Bill No. 51 (28th Cong., 1st Sess.). Among other provisions, the bill reduced postal rates and limited the franking privilege to five items per day per official. The bill passed the Senate on 4/29/1844, but was not acted on by the House of Representatives. See below Orestes A. Brownson's letter of 2/5/1844 to Calhoun.

"THE ADDRESS OF MR. CALHOUN TO HIS POLITICAL FRIENDS AND SUPPORTERS"
(Published Version)

[Published at Charleston, January 29, 1844]
I have left it to you, my friends and supporters, through whose favorable estimate of my qualifications, my name has been presented, to the people of United States for the office of Chief Magistrate, to

conduct the canvass on such principles, and in such manner, as you might think best. But, in so doing, I did not waive my right to determine, on my individual responsibility, what course my duty might compel me to pursue ultimately, nor have I been an inattentive observer of the canvass and the course you have taken.

It affords me pleasure to be enabled to say, that on all leading questions, growing out of the canvass, I heartily concurred with you, in the grounds you took, and especially in those relating to the mode in which the Delegates to the proposed Convention to be held in Baltimore, should be appointed, and how they should vote. You have, in my opinion, conclusively shown, that they should be appointed by Districts and vote *per capita*; but your reasons, as conclusive as they are, have proved in vain. Already New York and some other States have appointed Delegates en masse by State Conventions, and one State (Virginia) has resolved that the votes of her Delegates should be given by the majority, and be counted *per capita*. Their course would necessarily overrule that which you have so ably supported, should you go into Convention, and would leave you no alternative, but to yield yours and adopt theirs, however much you may be opposed to it on principle, or to meet them on the most unequal terms, with divided against united and concentrated forces.

The question then is, what course, under such circumstances, should be adopted? And that question, you will be compelled speedily to decide. The near approach of the time for meeting of the proposed Convention will not admit of much longer delay. But as your course may depend in some degree on that which I have decided to take, I deem it due to the relation subsisting between us, to make mine known to you without further delay.

I, then, after the most careful and deliberate survey of the whole ground, have decided, that I cannot permit my name to go before the proposed Convention, constituted as it must now be, consistently with the principles, which have ever guided my public conduct. My objections are insuperable. As it must be constituted, it is repugnant to all the principles, on which, in my opinion, such a Convention should be formed. What those principles are, I shall now proceed briefly to state.

I hold, then, with you, that the Convention should be so constituted, as to utter fully and clearly the voice of the people, and not that of political managers, or office holders and office seekers; and for that purpose, I hold it indispensable, that the Delegates should be appointed directly by the people, or to use the language of Gen. [Andrew] Jackson, should be "fresh from the people." I also hold, that the only possible mode to effect this, is for the people to choose the Delegates by Districts, and that they should vote *per capita*. Every other mode of appointing would be controlled by political machinery, and place the appointments in the hands of the few, who work it.

I object, then, to the proposed Convention, because it will not be constituted in conformity with this fundamental article of the Republican creed. The Delegates to it will be appointed from some of the States, not by the people in Districts, but, as has been stated, by State Conventions en masse, composed of Delegates, appointed in all cases, as far as I am informed, by County or District Conventions, and in some cases, if not misinformed, these again composed of Delegates appointed by still smaller divisions, or a few interested individuals. Instead then of being directly, or fresh from the people, the Delegates to the Baltimore Convention will be the Delegates, of Delegates; and of course removed, in all cases, at least three, if not four degrees from the people. At each successive remove, the voice of the people will become less full and distinct, until, at last, it will be so faint and imperfect, as not to be audible. To drop metaphor, I hold it impossible to form a scheme more perfectly calculated to annihilate the control of the people over the Presidential election, and vest it in those, who make politics a trade, and who live or expect to live on the Government.

In this connection, I object not less strongly to the mode in which Virginia has resolved her Delegates shall vote. With all due respect, I must say, I can imagine nothing more directly in conflict with the principles of our federal system of government, or to use a broader expression, the principles on which all confederated communities have ever been united. I hazard nothing in saying, that there is not an instance in our political history, from the meeting of the first Revolutionary Congress to the present day, of the Delegates of any State voting by majority and counting *per capita*; nor do I believe an instance of the kind can be found in the history of any confederated community. There is indeed something monstrous in the idea of giving the majority the right of impressing the vote of the minority into its service, and counting them as its own. The plain rule, that which has ever prevailed, and which conforms to the dictates of common sense, is, that where a State votes as a State, by a majority of its Delegates, the votes count one, be they few or many, or the State large or small. On the contrary, where the votes of all the Delegates are counted, they vote individually and independently, each for himself counting one. And it is to be noted, that wherever this latter mode

731

of voting exists among confederated States, it is in all cases founded on compact, to which the consent of each State is required. In the absence of compact, the invariable mode of voting, in such States, is, in all cases, by the majority, their vote counting one. The course which Virginia has resolved to take, is in violation of this plain and fundamental rule, and if it should become a settled practice, would be destructive of the foundation on which the whole structure of the State Right doctrine is reared.

I hold it, in the next place, to be an indispensable principle, that the Convention should be so constituted, as to give to each State, in the nomination of a candidate, the same relative weight, which the Constitution secures to it in the election of the President, making due allowance for its relative party strength. By the election, I mean the whole—the eventual choice when it goes into the House of Representatives, as well as the primary vote in the electoral college. The one is as much a part of the election as the other. The two make the whole. The adoption of the one, in the Convention, which framed the Constitution, depended on the adoption of the other. Neither could possibly be adopted alone. The two were the result of compromise between the larger and smaller States, after a long and doubtful struggle, which threatened the loss of the Constitution itself. The object of giving to the smaller States an equality with the larger in the eventual choice by the House, was to counterpoise the preponderance of the larger, in the electoral college. Without this, the smaller would have voted against the whole provision, and its rejection would have been the consequence. Even as it stands, Delaware voted against it. In confirmation of what I state, I refer to Mr. [James] Madison's report on the proceedings of the Convention.

Having stated what I mean by the election, it will require but a few words to explain my reasons for the principles I have laid down. They are few and simple, and rest on the ground, that the nomination is in reality the election, if concurred in, as far as the party is concerned. It is so intended to be. The leading reason assigned for making it, is to prevent a division of the party, and thereby prevent the election from going into the House, where the smaller States would have the advantage intended to be secured to them by the Constitution, by being placed on an equality with the larger.

Such being the intended object and effect, I now submit to every candid mind, whether the Convention ought not to be so constituted, as to compensate in the nomination for the important advantage in the election, which the smaller States would surrender by going into a Convention. Would it not be unfair—a palpable want of good faith and subversive of the compromise of the Constitution to withhold it? Or, if demanded, would it be short of an insult to refuse it? Can it be thought, that the smaller States are so debased and absorbed in the party politics of the day, as to permit themselves to be thus indirectly stripped of a right, which their high minded and patriotic ancestors held so dear, as even to prefer the loss of the Constitution itself, rather than surrender it.

I object, then, to the proposed Convention in this connection, because it makes no compensation to the smaller States for the surrender of this unquestionable and important constitutional right. Instead of that its advocates peremptorily and indignantly refuse any, and treat with scorn every attempt to secure it. Some have gone even so far, as to deny, that the eventual choice of the House constitutes any portion of the election, and to manifest open hostility against the provision of the Constitution, which contains it.

If there was no other objection, the one under consideration would be insuperable with me. I differ utterly from the advocates of the proposed Convention, in reference to this provision. I regard it as one of the first importance, not because I desire the election to go into the House, but because I believe it to be an indispensable means, in the hands of the smaller States, of preserving their just and constitutional weight in the Presidential election, and through that, in the Executive Department and the Government itself, which I believe to be essential to the preservation of our sublime federal system. I regard the adjustment of the relative weight of the States in the Government to be the fundamental compromise of the Constitution, and that on which our political system depends. Its adjustment constituted the great difficulty in forming the Constitution. The principle on which it was finally effected was, that, while due concession should be made to population, a provision should be also made, in some form, to preserve the original equality of the States in every department of the Government. The principle was easily carried out in constituting the legislative department, by preserving the equality of the States in one branch, (the Senate) and conceding to population its full preponderance in the other. But the great and difficult task of reducing it to practice was, in the Executive Department, at the head of which there is but a single officer. So great was it that it occupied the attention of the Convention, from time to time, during the whole session, and was very near causing a failure at last. It would have been an easy task to constitute that department, either on the principle of the equality of the States in the Government, or that of population. To combine the two, in the election of a single officer, was quite a different affair; but however difficult, it had to be performed, at the hazard of losing the Constitution.

It was finally accomplished, by giving to the larger States nearly the same preponderance in the electoral college, as they have in the House, and to the smaller, in the event of a choice by the House, the same equality they possess in the Senate; thus following closely the analogy of the Legislative Department. To make it as close as possible, it was at first proposed to give the eventual choice to the Senate, instead of the House, but it was altered and the present provision adopted, for reasons which did not affect the principle.

It was believed by the framers, the practical operation of the provision would be, that the electoral college, in which the influence of the larger States preponderates, would nominate, and that the House voting by States, where their equality is preserved, would elect who should be the President. To give it that operation in practice, the provision, as it originally stood in the Constitution, was that each elector should vote for two individuals, without discriminating which should be President, or Vice President, and if no one had a majority of the whole votes, then out of the five highest, the House voting by States, should elect one, and the person not elected, having the highest number of votes, should be the Vice President. It has been since altered, so that the electors should designate which should be President, and which Vice President, and the selection of the House was limited to the three highest. It is manifest, that if this provision of the Constitution had been left to operate by itself, without the intervention of caucusses, or party conventions between the people and the election, that the practical operation would have been such as I have stated, and such as was clearly intended by the framers of the Constitution.

The object intended is important. The preservation of the relative weight of the States, as established by the Constitution in all the Departments, is necessary to the success and duration of our system of Government; but it may be doubted, whether the provision adopted to effect it in the Executive Department, is not too refined for the strong, and I may add, corrupt passions, which the Presidential election will ever excite. Certain it is, that if the practice of nominating Candidates for the Presidency, by Conventions constituted as they proposed, shall become the established usage, it will utterly defeat the intention of the framers of the Constitution, and would be followed by a radical and dangerous change, not only in the Executive Department, but in the Government itself.

This danger was early foreseen, and to avoid it, some of the wisest and most experienced statesmen of former days so strongly objected to Congressional caucusses to nominate candidates for the Presidency, that they never could be induced to attend them; among these it will be sufficient to name Mr. [Nathaniel] Macon and Mr. [William] Lowndes. Others, believing that this provision of the Constitution was too refined for practice, were solicitous to amend it, but without impairing the influence of the smaller States in the election. Among these, I rank myself. With that object, resolutions were introduced, in 1828, in the Senate by Col. [Thomas H.] Benton, and in the House by Mr. [George] McDuffie, providing for districting the States, and for referring the election back to the people, in case there should be no choice, to elect one from the two highest candidates. The principle which governed in the amendment proposed, was to give a fair compensation to the smaller States for the surrender of their advantage in the eventual choice by the House and at the same time to make the mode of electing the President more strictly in conformity with the principles of our popular institutions and to be less liable to corruption than the existing provision. They received the general support of the party, but were objected to by a few, as not being a full equivalent to the smaller States. The principle embraced is identical with that on which you proposed to constitute the Baltimore Convention, but which has been so dictatorially objected to by some, who then took so prominent a part in its favor. If you have not succeeded, there is at least some consolation in reflecting that if others have since changed, you now stand where you then did, in the purer and better days of the party. I was in favour of it then, as I am now, not because I consider the resolutions as perfect, theoretically, as the existing provisions of the Constitution, but because I believe it would in practice more certainly accomplish what the framers of the Constitution intended. But while the provision stands as it does, I would regard myself as little short of a traitor to that sacred instrument, should I give my assent, directly [or] indirectly, to any practice which would have the effect of divesting the smaller States of the due weight which it secures to them in the Presidential election, whether designed or not. And here let me add, that as objectionable as I think a Congressional caucuss for nominating a President, it is in my opinion, far less so, than a Convention constituted as is proposed. The former had indeed many things to recommend it. Its members consisting of Senators and Representatives, were the immediate organs of the State Legislatures, or the people; were responsible to them, respectively, and were for the most part, of high character, standing and talents. They voted per capita, and what is very important, they represented fairly the relative strength of the party in their respective States. In all these important particulars, it was all that could be desired for a nominating body, and formed a striking contrast to the proposed Convention; and yet, it could not be borne by the people in the then purer days of the Republic. I, acting with Gen. [Andrew] Jackson and most of the leaders of the party at the time, contributed to put it down, because we believed it to be liable to be acted on and influenced by the patronage of the Government—an objection far more applicable to a Convention constituted as the one proposed, than to a Congressional caucus. Far however was it from my intention, in aiding to put that down, to substitute in its place what I regard as an hundred times more objectionable in every point of view. Indeed, if there must be an intermediate body between the people and the election, unknown to the Constitution, it may be well questioned whether a better than the old plan of a Congressional caucuss can be devised.

In taking the ground I have, in favor of maintaining the right secured to the smaller States by the compromise of the Constitution, I am actuated by no partisan feeling or desire to conciliate their good opinion. If the case was reversed, and the rights of the larger, instead of the smaller, were invaded, I would with equal readiness and firmness, stand up in their defence. I am the partisan of neither one, nor the other, but simply a supporter of the Constitution, and what I believe to be just and fair. I regard the Constitution, as the only ark of safety for all, and I believe that in defending it, I defend the interest and safety of each and all—the greater, as well as the smaller—the States invading the right of the others, as well the States whose right[s] are invaded.

I have laid down the principle, on which I rest the objection in question, with the limitation, that the relative weight of the States should be maintained, making due allowance for their relative party strength. The propriety of the limitation is so apparent, that but a few words, in illustration, will be required. The Convention is a party Convention, and professedly intended to take the sense of the party, which cannot be done fairly, if States having but little party strength, are put on an equality with those which have much. If that were done, the result might be, that a small portion of the party from States the least sound, politically, and which could give but little support in Congress, might select the candidate, and make the President, against a great majority of the soundest, and on which the President and his administration would have to rely for support. All this is clearly too unfair and improper to be denied. There may be a great difficulty in applying a remedy in a Convention, but I do not feel myself called upon to say how it can be done, or by what standard the relative party strength of the respective States should be determined; perhaps the best would be their relative strength in Congress at the time. In laying down the principle, I added the limitation for the sake of accuracy, and to show how imperfectly the party must be represented, when it is overlooked. I see no provision in the proposed Convention to meet it.

But, in order to realise how the Convention will operate, it will be necessary to view the combined effects of the objections which I have made. Thus viewed, it will be found, that a Convention so constituted, tends irresistibly to centralization—centralization of the control over the Presidential election in the hands of a few of the central, large States, at first, and finally, in political managers, office holders and office seekers; or to express it differently, in that portion of the community, who live, or expect to live on the Government, in contradistinction to the great mass, who expect to live on their own means, or their honest industry; and who maintain the Government, and [are,] politically speaking, emphatically the people.

That such would be the case, may be inferred from the fact, that it would afford the means to some six or seven State[s] lying contiguous and not far from the centre of the Union, to control the nomination, and through that the election, by concentrating their united votes in the Convention. Give them the power of doing so, and it would not long lie dormant. What may be done by combination, where the temptation is so great, will be sure ere long to be done. To combine and conquer, is not less true as a maxim, where power is concerned, than to "Divide and conquer." Nothing is better established, than that the desire for power can bring together and unite the most discordant materials.

But the tendency to centralization will not stop there. The appointment of delegates en masse by State Convention, would tend, at the same time and even with greater force, to centralize this control in the hands of the few, who make politics a trade. The farther the Convention is removed from the people, the more certainly the control over it will be placed in the hands of the interested few, and when removed three or four degrees, as has been shown it will be, where the appointment is by State Conventions, the power of the people will cease, and the seekers of Executive favour will become supreme. At that stage, an active, trained and combined corps will be formed in the party, whose whole time and attention will be directed to politics. It will be their sole business. Into their hands the appointments of delegates in all the stages will fall, and they will take special care that none but themselves or their humble and obedient dependants shall be appointed. The central and State Conventions will be filled by the most experienced and cunning, and after nominating the President, they will take good care to divide the patronage and offices, both of the General and State Governments, among themselves and their dependents. By why say *will?* Is it not *already the case?* Have there not been many instances of State Conventions being filled by office holders and office seekers, who, after making the nomination, have divided the offices in the State among themselves and their partisans, and joined in recommending to the candidate whom they have just nominated to appoint them to the offices to which they have been respectively allotted. If such be the case in the infancy of the system, it must end, if such conventions should become the established usage, in the President nominating his successor. When it comes to that, it will not be long before the sword will take the place of the Constitution.

Such are my objections to the mode in which the proposed Convention is to be constituted, and my reasons for entertaining them. They are such, that I cannot refuse to obey them without renouncing the principles which I have often avowed in public and private, and which have guided me through the whole course of my public life.

In coming to this conclusion, I have not passed over, without careful examination, the reasons assigned by its advocates for constituting the Convention as they propose. They have not diminished the force of my objections. I propose to notice the most prominent.

That which they have urged with the greatest confidence, is, that each State has a right to appoint Delegates as she pleases. I meet it, by utterly denying that there is any such right. That each State has the right to act as it pleases, in whatever relates to itself exclusively, no one will deny; but it is a perfectly novel doctrine, that any State has such a right, when she comes to act in concert with others in reference to what concerns the whole. In such cases it is the plainest dictate of common sense, that whatever affects the whole should be regulated by the mutual consent of all, and not by the discretion of each. That the appointment of Delegates to the proposed Convention is a case of this description, I trust I have conclusively shown. I have, I also trust, shown more; that the supposed right is perfectly deceptive, for while it claims for each State the right to appoint Delegates as it pleases, it in reality gives the larger States the right to dictate how the others shall appoint. If, for example, the Empire State [of New York], as it is called, adopts the mode of appointing (as she has) which will concentrate her whole strength, what discretion would she leave to others, if they go into Convention, but to appoint as she has appointed, or to be ruled by her. It is then, neither more nor less than a claim to dictate, under the garb of a right, and such its exercise has proved in the present case. It has left no option, but to conform to her course, or be overruled, or refuse to go into the Convention.

I regret this, because I sincerely desire to preserve the harmony of the party. I had strong hope that the rally after the defeat of 1840 would be exclusively on principles. The hope was greatly strengthened by the truly republican and noble stand, taken at the extra session and the earlier portion of the succeeding regular session. During that period of rigid adherence to principle, perfect harmony pervaded the ranks of the party. I beheld it with joy. I believed the moment highly favourable for the thorough reformation of the Government and the restoration of the Constitution. To the Republican party, I looked for the accomplishment of this great work; and I accordingly felt the deepest solicitude, that the stand taken, and the harmony which existed, should be preserved. In order that it should, I made up my mind to waive the objection, which I have long entertained to any intermediate body, unknown to the Constitution, between the people and the election of the President, in the hope that the proposed Convention would be so constituted that I might consistently with my principles give it my support. In this I have been disappointed, and being so, I am compelled to decide as I have done. The same motives which impelled me to separate from the administration of Gen. Jackson, in the plenitude of its power, and to come to the rescue of Mr. [Martin] Van Buren's at its greatest depression, compels me now to withhold my name from the proposed Convention.

Having now assigned my reasons for refusing to to [sic] permit my name to go before the Baltimore Convention, it rests with you who have placed it before the people, and assented to abide by a Convention fairly constituted, to determine what course you will pursue.

Be your decision what it may I shall be content. But I regarded it as due to the occasion, to you and myself, to declare that under no circumstances whatever shall I support any candidate, who is opposed to free trade, and in favor of the protective policy, or whose prominent and influential friends and supporters are. I hold the policy to be another name for a system of monopoly and plunder, and to be thoroughly anti republican and federal in its character. I also hold that so long as the duties are so laid as to be in fact bounties to one portion of the community, while they operate as oppressive taxes on the other, there can be no hope that the Government can be reformed, or that its expenditures will be reduced to the proper standard.

Were I, with the evidences before me, to say otherwise of my course, it would be, practically, to declare that I regard the protective policy to be an open question, so far as the party is concerned; which I would consider, on my part, a virtual abandonment of the cause of Free Trade. That can never be. I have done and suffered too much for it, when its friends were few and feeble, to abandon it now—now, when the auspices everywhere, on this and the other side of the Atlantic, proclaim the approaching downfall of protection and the permanent triumph of Free Trade. I, who upheld it against monopoly and plunder, in the worst of times, and braved the menaces of Administration and Opposition, when backed but by a single State, will not—cannot abandon the glorious cause now, when its banner waves in proud triumph over the metropolis of the commercial world. No, I shall maintain immoveably the ground I have so long occupied, until I have witnessed its great and final victory, if it shall please the Disposer of Events to spare my life so long. It will be, indeed, *a victory*—the harbinger of a new and brighter and higher civilization.*

Much less, still, can I give my support to any candidate, who shall give his aid or countenance to the agitation of abolition in Congress or elsewhere; or whose prominent and influential friends and supporters shall. I doubt the sincerity of any man, who declares he is no abolitionist, whilst at the same time, he aids or countenances the agitation of the question, be his pretext what it may. If we have a right to our slaves, we have the right to hold them in peace and quiet. If the Constitution guarantees the one, it guarantees the other; and if it forbids the one from being attacked, it equally forbids the other. Indeed the one stands to the other, as means to an end, and is so avowed by the abolitionists; and on the plainest principles of morals, if the end be prohibited, the means of effecting it also are. Of the two, I regard the deluded fanatic far less guilty and dangerous than he, who, for political or party purposes, aids or countenances him, in what he knows is intended to do that, which he acknowledges to be forbidden by the Constitution.

It is time that an end should be put to this system of plunder and agitation. They have been borne long enough. They are kindred

* Editor's note. In the Pendleton, S.C., *Messenger* version of this "Address," published on February 9, 1844, and apparently corrected by Calhoun from earlier newspaper printings, this sentence read: "It will be, indeed, *a victory*—the harbinger of peace to the world and a new and brighter and higher civilization."

measures and hostile, as far, at least, as one portion of the Union is concerned. While the tariff takes from us the proceeds of our labour, abolition strikes at the labor itself. The one robs us of our income, while the other aims at destroying the source from which that income is derived. It is impossible for us to stand patiently much longer, under their double operation, without being impoverished and ruined. [Signed:] JOHN C. CALHOUN.

PC in the Charleston, S.C., *Mercury,* January 29, 1844, p. 2; PC in the Charleston, S.C., *Courier,* January 29, 1844, p. 2; PC in the Columbia, S.C., *South-Carolinian,* February 1, 1844, p. 2; PC in the Petersburg, Va., *Republican,* February 1, 1844, p. 2; PC in the Richmond, Va., *Enquirer,* February 1, 1844, p. 2; PC in the Washington, D.C., *Spectator,* February 1, 1844, p. 2; PC in the Washington, D.C., *Daily National Intelligencer,* February 2, 1844, pp. 3–4; PC in the Washington, D.C., *Globe,* February 2, 1844, p. 2; PC in the Washington, D.C., *Madisonian,* February 2, 1844, pp. 2–3; PC in the New York, N.Y., *Evening Post,* February 3, 1844, pp. 1–2; PC in the New York, N.Y., *Herald,* February 3, 1844, p. 1; PC in the New York, N.Y., *Tribune,* February 3, 1844, p. 2; PC in the Philadelphia, Pa., *Pennsylvania Inquirer and National Gazette,* February 3, 1844, p. 2; PC in the Milledgeville, Ga., *Federal Union,* February 6, 1844, p. 2; PC in the Camden, S.C., *Journal,* February 7, 1844, p. 1; PC in the Edgefield, S.C., *Advertiser,* February 7, 1844, pp. 1–2; PC in the Raleigh, N.C., *North Carolina Standard,* February 7, 1844, pp. 2–3; PC in the Athens, Ga., *Southern Banner,* February 8, 1844, pp. 1–2; PC in the Greenville, S.C., *Mountaineer,* February 9, 1844, p. 1; PC in the Anderson, S.C., *Gazette,* February 10, 1844, pp. 1, 4; PC in *Niles' National Register,* vol. LXV, no. 24 (February 10, 1844), pp. 372–374; PC in the Jackson, Miss., *Southern Reformer,* February 12, 1844, p. 2; PC in the Nashville, Tenn., *Union,* February 13, 1844, p. 2; PC in the Knoxville, Tenn., *Register,* February 14, 1844, p. 1; PC in the Grand Rapids, Mich., *Enquirer,* February 23, 1844, pp. 1–2; PC in the Springfield, Ill., *Illinois State Register,* March 1, 1844, p. 3; slightly variant PC in the Pendleton, S.C., *Messenger,* February 9, 1844, pp. 1–2; slightly variant PC (dated February, 1844) in Crallé, ed., *Works,* 6:239–254; PEx's in Thomas H. Benton, *Thirty Years' View,* 2:596–599; PEx's in Arthur M. Schlesinger, Jr., ed., *History of American Presidential Elections, 1789–1968,* 1:808–813. NOTE: The version of Calhoun's "Address" above is the one published in the Charleston *Mercury* and *Courier* on January 29, 1844, and copied into other newspapers. It was, thus, the version known to the public at the time. This newspaper version of the "Address" carried no date. Compare it with Calhoun's original draft above in this volume under the date of December 21, 1843. The published version substitutes a briefer and considerably altered concluding passage for the last pages of the draft. This alteration was apparently embodied by Calhoun in a no-longer-extant manuscript which he enclosed to Franklin H. Elmore in his letter of 1/16/1844 above. Since Calhoun's manuscript revisions are missing, it is not completely clear whether the published version was entirely his or whether the final product may have received other revisions from the "central committee." The significant differences between the draft and the newspaper version begin with a paragraph following the paragraph that begins in each: "I regret this . . . ." In publishing the text on 2/9/1844, the Pendleton *Messenger* stated: "Some slight inaccuracies which had crept into the original publication of Mr. Calhoun's address in the Charleston papers, have been corrected by himself in the copy from which we make the re-publication which appears in our paper today." The differences between the *Messenger* text (which was the one used by Crallé) and the Charleston text were indeed "slight." These involved paragraphing, punctuation, and less than ten minor verbal changes. The most important of these changes has been described in an editor's note near the end of the text. Published with the address, by way of preface or announcement, were Calhoun's letter to Jacob Bond I'On and others, dated 12/21/1843 (above in this volume), and an unsigned note from the "Central Committee" in Charleston. This note stated that the "Address" had been transmitted to the committee by Calhoun, was being submitted to the public in accordance with his wishes, and had been delayed in publication because of the absence of a quorum. This statement was dated 1/23/1844 in the *Courier* and 1/3/1844 in the *Mercury*, the latter perhaps a typographical error.

To T[homas] G. Clemson, Mount Willing, Edgefield [District], S.C.

Fort Hill, 30th Jan[uar]y 1842 [*sic*; 1844] My dear Sir, I returned from the [gold] mine day before yesterday after an exceedingly cold ride. I found all well, but that Mr. Frederick[s] had lost his second son in my absence. It is uncertain whether it was the scarlet fever or worms.

I wrote Anna [Maria Calhoun Clemson] from the mine and informed her that I had leased the OBarr to Mr. [Benjamin M.] Milner. It had scarcely covered expenses since the last settlement when we were over. I paid Mrs. Worsham $5 on your account for the things you got of her husband & which she said you had not paid. She was about to leave for Tennessee, and as I suppose the fact was as she stated (she spoke with confidence) I thought it was best to pay it.

I have not heard from [Franklin H.] Elmore yet, which however I attribute to the failure of mail from Charleston to day. Should I hear in time I will attend to your request. I found the note you left for Mr. [W.G.?] Lawrence to be sent to him by Bill, sealed on the mantle piece, where I presume you left it. Shall I send it or not?

I am glad to learn by Tom, who got up safely, that you had a pleasant trip down[,] all things considered. I hope you found all doing well, & that you are getting on satisfactorily.

Tell John [C. Calhoun, Jr.] that his box from the University [of Virginia] came this evening, if he should be with you. I have not had time to examine its contents. If he desires it, or any thing it contains to be sent to him he must write me immediately.

You must excuse so short and uninteresting a letter, as it is very late & night and I am very much pressed with bring[ing] up my correspondence.

We greatly miss you all. The House looks empty & lon[e]some, when the boys are at school.

All join in love to you & Anna. Tell [John] Calhoun [Clemson] he must not forget his grand Father. Your affectionate father, J.C. Calhoun.

ALS in ScCleA. Note: While Calhoun seems to have written "1842" in the date-line of this letter, the correct date is very clearly 1844 from the content and from the fact that the letter is addressed to Clemson in Edgefield District.

By John E[wing] Colhoun, Pendleton, 1/31. "I authorize the Hon[ora]ble J.C. Calhoun to receive, as my agent, whatever sum may be due to me as one of the heirs of my dec[ease]d Father and brother, viz. John Ewing Colhoun [Sr.] and Samuel B. Colhoun, ..." The remainder of the sentence written by Colhoun, "Being a balance due from the first U.S. Bank, on shares held in their name," has been canceled and the following interlined in the handwriting of John C. Calhoun: "& stand[ing] unpaid on the Books of the Treasury." ADS in ScCleA.

To the Rev. O[RESTES] A. BROWNSON, [Boston?]

Fort Hill, 1st Feb: 1844

My dear Sir, I am much gratified, that you have revived your Review [in Boston as *Brownson's Quarterly Review*], and wish you to put my name on your list of subscribers. I trust you will be well sustained, & think the prospect is favourable. The publick mind is greatly debased, but, I think, I see the commencement of a reformation. I speak politically.

The first step, towards any effectual reform, is to put down and disgrace party machinery & management. No devise [*sic*] ever was adopted better calculated to gull the community; to put down all individuality & manliness of feeling, & keep the people in ignorance. It originated with Aaron Burr, & has been carried to perfection by the New York politicians. With them Democracy is but a profession, which is laid aside whenever it stands in the way of obtaining political power. Their reliance is on the spoils & party machinery.

I had hoped, that the disaster of '37 would have reformed them;

but their conduct for the last 18[?] months has satisfied me that we have nothing to hope from them. My remarks are limited to the leaders. The great body of the party, I believe to be sound; and, if left to themselves, would go right. It is essential to success, while assailing the one, to do justice to the other.

You will of course understand, that what I write is intended for yourself.

I read your first number with pleasure, especially the two ["articles" *interlined*] of a political character. What you say in reference to myself, in connection with nullification, I heartily approve. It is the portion of my publick conduct, that I should rather be rescued from oblivion, than any other. Yours truly, J.C. Calhoun.

ALS in InNd, Orestes A. Brownson Collection (published microfilm, roll 2, frames 233–234); variant PC in Henry F. Brownson, *Orestes A. Brownson's Early Life: From 1803 to 1844*, pp. 361–362. NOTE: The first issue of *Brownson's Quarterly Review* (vol. I, no. 1) was dated January, 1844. The two articles mentioned in Calhoun's last paragraph above were apparently Brownson's essay on "Demagoguism" (pp. 84–104) and his review-essay on Calhoun's recently published *Life and Speeches* (pp. 105–131).

To R[OBERT] M. T. HUNTER, [Richmond?]

Fort Hill, 1st Feb: 1844

My dear Sir, I have just received your's [*sic*] of the 19th Jan[uar]y, and hope that this may reach you at Richmond before the meeting of your State Convention.

Our friends ought by no means [to] give a pledge ["unless conditional" *interlined*] to support the nominee of the Baltimore convention. They ought to take the ground boldly and adhere to it, that they cannot support Mr. [Martin] V[an] B[uren] or act with his friends, till they redeem fully the pledges given after the catastrophy of '37, and before the election of '40, in their Addresses, especially in reference to the tariff & abolition; and, also, their pledge in reference to the latter in ["adopting" *interlined*] the resolutions, I offered in the Senate, in relation to ["it" *canceled and* "abolition" *interlined*]. You will find them in my life, prepared by yourself, & published by the Harpers. The four first were adopted by the unanimous vote of the party, if I recollect aright. You know the fact, I presume, that I, in particular, and, I believe, our friends generally refused to act with them as a party untill these open & solemn pledges were given. The

744

reosutions [*sic*] take the high ground, that the Constitution prohibits the agitation of the subject of the abolition either in the District of Columbia, or elsewhere, on the ground, that where the end is inhibited the means are so, & that ["we" *canceled*] the right to ["the" *canceled*] property includes the right of enjoying it without molestation; and yet, in the face of these pledges, the great majority of the N[ew] York delegation, including the confidential friends of Mr. V[an] B[uren] have acted as they have, in the H[ouse] of Representatives, ["this session" *interlined*] & the Albany Argus has openly endorsed the course of the most prominent of them, Mr. [Samuel] Beardsley. It is a case of political treachery almost without example; and to ask our friends, ["with" *canceled*] under such circumstances, to pledge themselves to support the nomination of Mr. V[an] B[uren], is nothing short of an insult.

It will be time enough to ask them, after these pledges are redeem[ed]—after a tariff bill strictly for revenue has been reported by the V[an] B[uren] Committee of the House, & voted & passed by his friends ["in the House" *canceled and* "there" *interlined*], & the 21st rule restored by the same vote. Nothing short of it, ought to be taken, after such an example of treachery; nor ought any distinction to be admitted between Mr. V[an] B[uren] & his friends; I mean his prominent and influential ["friends" *interlined*]. After the repeated instances of treachery, from the passage of the tariff of '28 untill the ["action(?) of this(?) Congress" *canceled and* "the present time" *interlined*], *we ought to be done with promises. Nothing ought to be taken but performance.*

Let our friends take this high & impregnable position; & refuse all pledges, except the conditional one, that they will support Mr. V[an] B[uren], if those pledges ["so solemnly given" *interlined*] be in good faith fully redeemed, before the meeting of the Convention, but not otherwise. ["They" *canceled and* "His friends" *interlined*] have ample time to redeem them ["before that" *interlined*], and if they do not, we have a right to conclude, that they do not intend to do so. If ["it" *canceled and* "the position" *interlined*] be taken, as it ought, the effect will be decisive & happy; ["but" *interlined*] to give a positive pledge to support the nominee, under existing circumstances, would subject us and our cause to the ["deserved" *interlined*] scorn of the whole Union. Our friends have already done much to expose ["us" *interlined*] to scorn by their timidity. They seem to forget, that a good cause is all powerful, when boldly defended, in the sperit of truth; but is feebleness itself, if defended with timidity or hesitation. The sound portion of Virginia must now stand fast, or agree to take the yoke. [Thomas] Ritchie & his associates are resolved to put it on them. I trust that even Gen[era]l [William F.] Gordon [former Representative from Va.], will refuse to pledge himself, except conditionally, after what he has witnessed during the present session.

One thing I do hope, that our friends will ["not" *interlined*] permit their course to be in the least sewayed by any consideration in reference to myself or my future prospects. They ought not to weigh a particle, where the rights & safety of the South and the preservation of our free institutions are involved; and I shall be deeply mortified, if they should yield an inch of ground on their account. Indeed, it would be a great mistake, if they should suppose, that they would promote my interest, either now or hereafter, by it. The higher the ground they take, & the more resolutely they defend it, the better for me, as well as the cause of the South & the Constitution. Let them forget me, & look exclusively to the cause, and they will act in the manner best calculated to advance both.

I am of the opinion, they ought not to think of rallying on me at the next election, unless it should be found to be indispensible to keep our flag a flying, in order *to preserve our position.* It will be time enough yet to decide on that; provided our friends take they [*sic*] stand they ought, in your convention, & refuse to give pledges. ["But" *interlined*] Unless Mr. V[an] B[uren]'s friends ["p"(?) *canceled*] shall redeem their pledges, and make up an issue thereby ["which" *canceled*] with Mr. [Henry] Clay & his friends, which we can support on our own principles, it appears to me a seperate rally will be indispensible to save them. A run between him & Mr. Clay, on the issue as now made up between ["them" *interlined*], would demoralize & ruin the South, whatever side we may take. Truly, J.C. Calhoun.

ALS in ScCleA; variant PC in Jameson, ed., *Correspondence,* pp. 562–564.

From FRANCIS WHARTON

Philadelphia, February 1st 1844

My dear Sir, You will receive by the present mail, or at all events very soon, the February number of the Democratic Review. I have just glanced over the leading article, about which I have already spoken to you, but I can scarcely put it into your hands without expressing my sense of the inadequacy & feebleness of the tribute it bears. It may be

of some use, however, among the class of politicians who have eyes, &
see not, and hearing, but do not understand. It may be that a few
["even" *interlined*] of the narrowest of the Albany politicians, may
["finding" *canceled*] be led to read it ["from"(?) *canceled and* "for"
interlined] the sake of the magazine in which it is contained, and may
thus be obliged to stare full in the face at opinions from which they
have always hidden and skulked. I hope and trust, and I take it that
my trust is not vain, that the day will soon come when hiding and
skulking will be over. The worst sign I see now, is Mr. [James]
Buchanan's equivocations, both about the tariff & the presidency.
The great danger is that a few designing manufacturers in this city
and in the coal district, will succeed in placing the republican party
in the State in a false attitude. Such a ["danger" *canceled and* "step"
interlined] would be attended with consequences almost fatal to our
ultimate success, more however, from its reaction on the South, than
from its local bearings. I am afraid that the friends of free trade in
the South—the *true* friends, by which I mean *your* friends—will become disgusted with the vacillations & ignorance of many of our northern leaders, and will refuse to act in concert with them in matters of
general policy. Be assured that a severance of the republican ["party"
interlined] will be now fatal. There is not one of our great measures
which we can carry if we refuse to accept of the qualified aid of even
the [Albany] regency politicians. They offer us their hand under the
proviso that they are not to go beyond a certain mark. Let us seize
hold of it and see whether when we once get them out of their ambush,
we may not commit them to the whole figure. Mr. [Martin] Van
Buren himself is susceptible of being forced, on a great emergency,
to go all lengths, as the sub-treasury measure showed. Let us get him
out of his hole, and then when he is fairly uncovered, he will have to
fight fairly, or run away. If he runs away, his apostacy will be no-
torious, and he will leave us the possession of the field indisputed,
without the incumbrance of the feeble & treacherous alliance he has
lately professed. If he really fights, ["we" *canceled and* "he" *interlined*] will ["fight" *interlined*] in *our* cause, and for *our* victory. I am
most anxious to see your expected letter. I trust & believe that nothing in it will have the tendency, to exasperate the northern section of
the party. Withdrawal from the Baltimore convention I think is
right, but I am most anxious that it should be such a withdrawal as
will conciliate, & not repel, the aid of the Democratic party in the
north for the subsequent campaign. Mr. V[an] B[uren] is lost already. Pennsylvania is tottering. The South is gone. If we kick him

now, never will the jackalls who are awaiting the ["re" *interlined*]organization of the Kitchen cabinet forgive us. I look upon the next election as his state funeral, and at such a ceremony, our attitude should be such as to avoid unnecessary offence to the mourners who will attend his interment. I can ["not" *interlined*] forbear therefore, repeating my hope, a hope in which your friends here—I wish they were as many as they are warm—join to a man, that your position for [the] present may be such as to give the venomous & [*manuscript mutilated*]trous feelings of the Albany politicians ["now" *canceled and* "no" *interlined*] f[ield of exer]cise. If we would use ["them," *interlined*] as we hope to do, we [must] avoid ruffling them. With great respect, I am yours &, Francis Wharton.

ALS in ScCleA; variant PC in Jameson, ed., *Correspondence*, pp. 919–921. NOTE: The article referred to in Wharton's first paragraph was his anonymous "Mr. Calhoun's Parliamentary Eloquence," a review-essay of the *Speeches of John C. Calhoun*, which appeared in the *United States Magazine and Democratic Review*, vol. XIV, no. 68 (February, 1844), pp. 111–130.

From V[IRGIL] MAXCY

Annapolis, 2 Feb. 1844

My dear Sir, Your address has just been received here and I am glad to find you have modified it. It has not yet been generally read and of course I cannot form an opinion as to the effect it will produce ["here" *interlined*]. It will, I have no doubt, enrage the [Martin] Van Buren men at first but I cannot help hoping, as there is nothing directly denouncing such of them as support the protective tariff ["or rather those, who who (*sic*) do not think the ground taken by V(an) B(uren) in the Syracuse Convention as sufficient reason for deserting him," *interlined*] as whigs, that it will shame & frighten them back to the true faith after their passion subsides, and ["that they will" *interlined*] gradually disown their having departed from it, whereas if a mark has been set on them by a direct denunciation ["in your address" *interlined*] and no locus penitentia had been left, they would have nourished a strong tho' secret hostility to you personally ["&" *interlined*] be inclined ["hereafter" *canceled*] to do all they could to prevent your being a rallying point hereafter.

Under cover of attending to the progress of a Bill here [in the Md. legislature], which I have an interest in seeing passed, I have been trying to find out the currents that are setting here, since it has been considered probable, that you would be out of the field. And tho' I have been sorry to perceive, that the chains of party discipline are still very strong and that there is not as yet sufficient moral courage even among those who prefer you, to break and denounce ["them" *interlined*], I have been gratified to see, that there is a general disgust at the course V[an] B[uren] has pursued and that there is very little attachment felt for him by those, who advocate him. The consequence is, as there is a strong desire on the part of both your friends & his to hit upon some expedient, (as it is now next to certain that [Henry] Clay will have a majority in this State & of course all the electors) to hit upon some expedient [*sic*], by which we may not be divided in our *State* elections next autumn, for success in which there is some hope. A current therefore is strongly setting in favor of a nomination by the republican members of our legislature ["in favor" *canceled*] of Gen[era]l [Lewis] Cass, not in the expectation, ["of(?) not" *canceled*] of choosing Cass electors but of preventing any discussions arising between your friends & ["the supp" *canceled*] those of Mr. V[an] B[uren], which might dampen our united efforts to save the party in our State elections, which come on a month before our presidential election.

Would you approve of a nomination of Cass here? [*One word or partial word canceled.*] What would be its effect on our prospects for 1848? I have as yet neither discouraged nor promoted the idea, but in the state of things now existing here, altho' I might not be able to prevent a nomination of Cass, I believe I can exert influence enough to ensure it, if you approve of it.

Hoping to hear from you soon ["on this subject" *interlined*] I remain in haste faithfully yours, V. Maxcy.

[P.S.] A passenger came in the [railroad] cars yesterday ev[e-n]ing from Washington who reported here that there was a general talk at Washington of my being nominated Secr[etar]y of *War*, not of the *Navy* as when I wrote you, since [James M.] Porter[']s rejection & I [*one word canceled*] received a message from Gen[era]l [Alexander O.] Anderson to hold myself in readiness to go over to Washington ["at a moment(')s notice" *interlined*]. Still I consider the thing as a bare possibility, yet these rumours make me anxious to get an answer to my letter written from Washington, containing your views on this matter.

ALS in ScCleA; variant PEx in Boucher and Brooks, eds., *Correspondence*, pp. 207–208.

From CHA[RLE]S H. POND

Milford (Con[n.]), Feb[ruar]y 2, 1844

D[ea]r Sir, Your frank & acceptable letter of Dec[embe]r 4th was duly rec[eive]d; it's contents carefully read; but my answer has been delayed until I could watch & note certain political movements.

I agree with you that the Whigs are more formidable than they were last year, & we also agree as to the cause of their increase. But we know that *they* are yet less numerous than the Republicans; who can (if united) have things in their own way.

I think that the House (at least) will revise the Tariff so as to do more justice to the Agricultural & Commercial interests: & thus make it more of a revenue Tariff. All agree that Government is to be supported by duties on imports; & the proceeds of the public lands will be applied to the same object by the Democrats. The main point of difference seems to be the *principle* by which the Tariff shall be framed. You know the feelings of the North on this subject. Those feelings however are changing. But one thing is certain—that hereabouts Mr. [Henry] Clay['s] friends are stronger than any body else for a prot[ective] Tariff.

I also agree with you that the mo[de of] choosing delegates to the B[altimore] convention is objection[able—]very. The district mode should have been foll[owed;] it would have been more satisfactory & more just to the parties concerned. And had this been done the nominee would have been unanimously supported & certainly elected.

But so it is; & the question arises what shall be done now. In view of these movements & their incidents, as an old friend I ask leave to submit a few candid remarks. Many thousands of Democrats at the North would have been better pleased if these delegates had been chosen in a way which would have more clearly evidenced popular sentiments; & if some other things had been differently done so as to have given your friends better chances to express their feelings & wishes. These friends however do not yet view it as absolutely certain who will be the nominee at the democratic B[altimore] convention. New events may occur before the latter part of May. Your friends therefore hope & trust that although you may disapprove of certain occurrences; yet it is very clear that all State rights democratic Republicans should & must so far keep together as to prevent the federal whigs from succeeding; & then [br]inging on your friends & ours a *grievous* Adminis[tra]tion. Admitting then that justice has not *yet* [been] done you; yet you may confidently rely [up]on it, that after all[,] your numerous friends [in] this region are democratic

Republicans, who [would?] heartily rejoice to see you in the Presi-[dential] chair & will continue to do their utmost to effect this desideratum. And although *your friends* may complain that more justice has not been done you, yet we (meaning many influential Democrats in various States) ardently hope that *they* will wait & see the doings of the B[altimore] convention. In the mean time your friends in Washington & elsewhere will learn what is to be expected *ultimately*. Do have patience even under injuries; for we firmly beli[e]ve that right & justice towards you will finally take place. Hoping that these friendly suggestions will be duly weighed by you; & ardently hoping that the glad time will yet arrive; hoping also that you will write me soon, as this is a critical juncture I remain, D[ea]r Sir, sincerely Your friend, Chas. H. Pond.

N.B. On reading over what I have written I find that I have spoken as frankly as one brother would address another. Please accept this as the effusion of a warm heart & for the sake of patriotism & righteousness do continue to use your great influence—probably the controlling influence—to keep whig[g]ery down & Republicanism up. Truly yours, C.H.P.

ALS in ScCleA. NOTE: In the letter above a few words and parts of words have been supplied in brackets where the ms. is torn.

"Address, Directed to be Published by a Meeting of the Friends of John C. Calhoun, Delegates to the [Va.] State Democratic Convention ... to the Democratic Republican Party of Virginia," adopted at Richmond, 2/3. This long and ably argued document discusses in detail the objections of the signers to the formation of the prospective Democratic national nominating convention, which they find to be hostile to the Constitution, to the rule of the people, and to the interests of the South. However, because of the need to defeat the Whigs, and with assurances of the "complete accord and concurrence of the whole Republican party of this State" upon the "Tariff and Abolition questions," they expect to support the nominee of the Convention. For the present, the signers will "forego the high gratification of rendering the imperfect tribute of our suffrages to that distinguished statesman, John C. Calhoun, whose pre-eminent abilities, profound political sagacity, and enlarged experience have extended the wisdom and illustrated the annals of his age. ..." The signers of the document describe themselves "as the constituent admirers of the greatest living champion of the Constitution and the rights of the States." The address is signed first by the members of the committee which reported it (Lewis E. Harvie, R.M.T. Hunter, James A. Seddon, Wm. O. Goode,

Washington Greenhow, Ro[bert] G. Scott, and Wm. F. Gordon), and
then by other delegates to the Convention. These were Sam[ue]l C.
Anderson, David M[c]Comas, Jno. R. Taylor, J.L. Gordon, R. Herbert
Tatum, J[ohn] S. Barbour, N.M. Taliaferro, Tho[ma]s T. Giles, Jno.
B. Todd, James H. Cox, Thomas S. Bocock, John B. Ailsworth, Jno.
Washington, Rich[ar]d H. Colman, Austin M. Trible, M[uscoe] R.H.
Garnett, John B. Young, W.H. Sims, Wm. S. Fontaine, Eustace Con-
way, P[eter] Carr, Francis W. Scott, Geo. L. Nicholson, John P. Young,
Charles F. Osborne, John S. Caskie, Anthony Thornton, James Alfred
Jones, Charles H. Edwards, Thomas M. Isbell, John H. Walker, and
Wm. Robertson Jr. The preface of the address stated that it was
adopted at a meeting held after the adjournment of the convention,
so "that all of our friends did not have an opportunity of seeing and
signing it. . . ." PC in the Petersburg, Va., *Republican*, February 6,
1844, p. 2; PC in the Washington, D.C., *Spectator*, February 10, 1844,
pp. 1–2; PC in the Richmond, Va., *Enquirer*, February 10, 1844, pp.
1–2; PC in the Richmond, Va., *Whig and Public Advertiser*, February
13 and 16, 1844.

From J[AMES] H. HAMMOND, [Governor of S.C.]

Silver Bluff, [Barnwell District, S.C.] 3 Feb. 1844
My Dear Sir, I received your letter inclosing an application [of Joseph
W. Farnum?] for the appointment of Assayer & forwarded the latter
to the President of the Bank [Franklin H. Elmore]. The power of
appointing to that office is vested in the President & Directors of the
Bank of the State. I received by last mail the papers containing your
letter withdrawing from the Baltimore Convention. I concur entirely in all the views expressed in it & I have no doubt it will meet
the approbation of all your friends throughout the U.S. & of all *honest*
men. I think too it will do good. The fact of your withdrawing, as
well as the striking & unanswerable argument against the Convention,
must produce a strong impression, & will have I trust a powerful influence in recalling the country to the Constitution. I am beginning to
fear however that there is small chance for the perpetuity of a Constitutional Government. The great body of the people neither know
nor care any thing about the Constitution, & nine tenths of the politicians are nearly as ignorant & still more regardless of it. No class
of people except we South Carolinians ever seem seriously to object

to any thing because it is unconstitutional. Established precedents have far more influence whether constitutional or not than the Constitution itself. And sectional & political interests & convenience are rapidly building up a practical system of Government which has already superceded in many essential particulars that formed in '89 & is destined I fear in no long time to supercede it altogether. We Constitutionalists will soon be denominated the *"Ancien Regime"* & laid on the shelf—if we are not wise enough to lay ourselves there beforehand—as behind the age. All that a great & wise man can do is to develope on pages that will outlive the times, the beauty & wisdom of the Constitution, & pave the way for its revival after ["the" *canceled*] some future revolution. I have great confidence in the ["Spirit" *canceled*] Love of Liberty which still pervades all classes in this country & I trust that that & the advance of knowledge—which every thing should be done to promote—will rescue those who come after us from any Government much worse than the present. Very truly & sincerely Yours, J.H. Hammond.

ALS in ScCleA; retained copy in DLC, James Henry Hammond Papers, vol. 11; PC in Boucher and Brooks, eds., *Correspondence*, pp. 208–209.

To Geo[rge] N. "Saunders," Grass Hill, Ky.

Fort Hill, 3d Feb. 1844
Dear Sir, I received by the Mail of yesterday your letter with its enclosures. The one from the Committee, in reference to Texas, of which you enclosed a copy, was received some time since. I did not reply, not from want of respect to the Committee, but because there was reason to believe, that the subject of annexation was in discussion between the two Governments and that the agitation of it might be embarrassing, without doing any good. The reason still continues, which I hope the Committee will regard as a sufficient explanation for my silence. It is well known, that I have been from the first in its favour.

I can by no means agree with you on your Oregon plan. I regard it as neither Constitutional, nor expedient. We of the slave holding States must never compromise with the fell sperit of abolition. The slave question is one exclusively for our own decision, and all attempts at interference by others ought to be promptly and indignantly repelled.

For your kind feeling of regard for me, please accept my thankful acknowledgments. With respect, J.C. Calhoun.

ALS in DLC, John C. Calhoun Papers; PC in *The Political Correspondence of the late Hon. George N. Sanders, Confederate Commissioner to Europe during the Civil War. To Be Sold on Wednesday, May 13th, 1914* (New York: American Art Association, [1914]), unpaged. NOTE: Calhoun erroneously addressed his letter to "Saunders" rather than Sanders.

From ALEX[ANDE]R JONES

61 West Washington Place
New York [City,] Feb[ruar]y 4th 1844

Dear Sir, Since writing to you last my departure for the South has been delayed to the end of this month, and very possibly it may be postponed altogether. It seems that Gen[era]l [Duff] Green himself is only the agent or servant of Mr. [Henry] Wyckoff [*sic*; Wikoff] the proprietor of the paper, at a standing salary. The Gen[era]l showed me the written agreement drawn up between Wyckoff and himself, in which the latter [*sic*; former?] engages to ["pay" *interlined*] him $4,000 per annum, as Editor of the paper, for one year. And on his arrival here, ["engages" *interlined*] to place property he holds in Philadelphia in the hands of Trustees to a sufficient amount, to raise $20,000 Dollars with which to establish the paper. But, I could not discover in the agreement any provision whereby Gen[era]l Green was authorized to make a written engagement or contract similar to the one he has made with me. Still I proposed to Gen[era]l Green to go forward and canvass the Southern States, with all the energy[,] industry and perseverance in my power, and to pay my contingent travelling expenses from my own purse; if ["you" *canceled*] he ["will" *canceled and* "would" *interlined*] place $50 or $100 dollars on ["a"(?) *canceled*] guarrentee [*sic*; "to" *canceled*], at three, or six months ["to my" *interlined*] credit ["to my" *canceled*] on account. This he refused to do, but still insisted that I should go forward on the business of the paper, ["bu" *canceled*] pay all my ["own" *interlined and then canceled*] expenses from my own means, and trust to him and his agreement with Wyckoff and the paper for reimbursement of expenses, and payment of salary. On my declining to do this[,] the Gen[era]l has grown rather cool and cross. He is also unfortunately surrounded with some persons, who are most *precious humbugs*, who talk much, and yet are persons of no kind of responsibility whatever. They are pretended friends of yours, and ["m" *canceled*] induced me to go forward last fall, and advance money for circulars & handbills, in reference to public meetings &C. under a promise to divide the expense with me, yet ["they" *interlined*] meanly backed out from their engagements, and left me to pay the whole amount. In one instance, the sum was $20.00 Dollars, and in another $35.00. In the first case *F. Birdsall* [*sic*; Fitzwilliam Byrdsall] and *J. F[rancis] Hutton* engaged to divide the expense with me, yet neither of them has ever paid one cent. Their credit in New York, I find, is not good for a *hat* or a *pair* of *Boots*. In the latter case the $35 dollars, I paid for wood cuts, on the promise of *Robert Berney*, that he would see the ["the" *canceled*] amount refunded to me, yet when the time came he utterly refused to do so. And, if I had not sold the wood cuts to the publisher, I should have lost the whole amount. These are small matters, and I only mention them to show you what kind of people Gen[era]l Green has surrounded himself with. He has made a kind of business man or *Cashier* of *Birdsall*! ! while *Hutton* is one of his *confidential advisers*! ! They of course dislike me, a man, ["whom" *interlined*] they have kept bad faith with ["me" *canceled*], and they, hence, pursuade Gen[era]l Green, that he has agreed to pay me too much, and that one like themselves would serve him and the paper for a great deal less, and that he ought to annull the contract made in writing between us! ! The result, is, that I have agreed to wait the arrival of Wyckoff, who is expected to sail ["sail" *canceled*] from Liverpool this day, in the Steam Ship for Boston: and will probably arrive in New York on the 21st or 22d Inst[ant] when the agreement ["be" *canceled*] will be submitted to him for his approval. Should he confirm it, I shall at once proceed to discharge the duties agreed upon. If he dissents from it, I shall then be left to shape my course according to circumstances. ["Such" *canceled*.]

I have thought it might be well for me to explain to you my present position with the paper. Should I ever ["have" *canceled*] have the opportunity of visiting South Carolina I trust I may have the honor and pleasure of giving you a call, ["as" *canceled*] on my passage through the State.

I have been highly gratified at reading your able letter. Your reasons and conclusions to ["my" *interlined*] mind, seem irresistable and I have no question will carry conviction to all disinterested[,] candid and honest men. I hope and trust your freinds [*sic*] will be led to pursue a course best calculated to sustain your views and position. Whatever stand they ["mak" *canceled*] may take, they should if *con-*

sistent and *firm* in their *principles,* stand by the doctrines you have proclaimed.

Free Trade, a *Sacred regard for the Constitution, and* opposition to the *fanatical crusade against* the *inst[it]utions* of *the South,* must be the cardinal points in the creed of every sincere freind to his country, and to the perpetuity of the Union. He that is not with us, on these points, is against us, and by their success we must be prepared to stand, or fall. It is better to fall with our *principles,* for a time, than to float with the tide of corruption; to gain temporary success. History & posterity will finally judge all men by their *principles*—and condemn or approve as they may have been right or wrong, good or evil. With the most sincere and ardent good wishes for your health[,] prosperity and happiness[,] I ["have" *canceled*] claim the Honor to be, now & forever more, Your Sincere & Devoted Friend, Alexr. Jones.

ALS in ScCleA.

From V[IRGIL] MAXCY

Annapolis, 4 Feb. 1844

My dear Sir, Four or five of our friends came to my room last evening, to compare notes on the effect of your address. The first impression as might be expected was to excite the ire of the few [Martin] V[an] B[uren] men, who have been weak enough still to believe that their leader might be elected. Those, who thought it only a possible thing & are not excited by any warm feeling, as is the case with 9/10th[s] of them, now have made up their minds, that since the appearance of your letter, V[an] B[uren's] prospects are hopeless. The effect of this already is to increase the force of the current, that, in my letter of yesterday, I told you, was setting in favor of taking up [Lewis] Cass as a pis aller. Your friends & those of V[an] B[uren] are disposed to unite in this expedient in order to prevent discord in our ranks, which would defeat beyond all question the election of Governor next ["Autumn" *canceled*] October. I am now inclined to the opinion that I should not be able to prevent the republican members of both sides, taking up Gen. Cass & nominating him in a Convention of the republican members of the Legislature & that the only thing I could do, would [be] to get a V[an] B[uren] man to take the lead in the movement, if you should think it better than that one of your friends should do it, committed as Cass is in favor of a Tariff discriminating for protection as well as Van Buren. The only difference in this particular is that the latter is thus committed by a solemn act of his friends in Convention and the other in a letter I believe.

Pray write me by the ["first" *interlined*] mail after getting this on this subject. Direct your letters in future, West River, *via Annapolis*.

In great haste Truly y[ou]r[s], V. Maxcy.

[P.S.] The Republican members of the Senate here are equally divided between you [&] V[an] B[uren] & tho that can[']t be ascer-[tained] with perfect certainty I believe that is about the case in the H[ouse] of Delegates also.

ALS and copy in ScCleA.

To FRANCIS WHARTON, [Philadelphia]

Fort Hill, 4th Feb: 1844

My dear Sir, Before this reaches you, you will have seen my Address. I hope "the tone and bearing" may meet your approbation. I confess, it required great effort to restrain my indignation at the course of Mr. [Martin] V[an] B[uren] and his friends. It has been treacherous and mean beyond any example in the political history of our country.

We stept forward, generously and patriotickly, to save him and them from utter prostration at the extra session of 1837; not, indeed, for his or their sake, but for that of a measure, on which he was thrown by the course of events. We refused to go one step farther in his support, untill his friends pledged him and themselves twice, openly, in their Address [of 7/6/1838], before the election of 1840, to our principles and policy generally, and especially on the subjects of the Tariff and Abolition. To make the pledge more binding in reference to the latter, I move[d] a set of resolutions in reference to it in the Senate, as strong as I could draw them, condemning agitation itself as a violation of the Constitution. The four first of which were adopted by the unanimous vote of the party. You will see them in my life published by the Harpers. Under the force of these pledges, we supported his election and saved him from complete and final prostration. Without our aid, he would have got scarcely the vote of a single State. We did more. After his defeat, we took the lead in the overthrow of the Whigs; I acting as chairman of the Standing Committee in the Senate, which plan[n]ed and carried on the campaign [during the special session of Congress in 1841]. Our success was complete. The Whigs were routed in two months, and would have remained so, if Mr. V[an] B[uren] had not been brought forward. Now, after all this, and profiting by our aid, to turn round in violation of all these open and solemn pledges, to court the Tariffites and Abolitionists, after they had secured our support, as they thought, by obtaining a majority of the Convention, is an instance of treachery hard to be equalled.

But it is not the only instance, in which they have been guilty of flagrant treachery. The [tariff] act of '28 was passed by the same party (Mr. [Silas] Wright taking the lead in the House and Mr. V[an] B[uren] in the Senate) by a violation of pledges not less strong, though less open—an act which deprived the country of the fruits of the great victory achieved over the national party that year, and to which the disasters which have since befallen the country and party may be clearly traced. After such repeated examples of perfidy, it is impossible for me to repose the least confidence in any promise, which they may hereafter make; and it required no little exertion on my part and no small influence on the part of my friends to restrain me from saying so. No consideration, or influence could restrain me from saying less. With my views of the Constitution, I could do no act that could countenance a usage, as they call it, intended to supercede in practice the fundamental compromise of the Constitution. To *destroy or supercede that would be to revolutionize the Government.*

The present indication is, that Mr. V[an] B[uren] will be defeated. It is impossible for me or my friends to support Mr. [Henry] Clay and the Whigs. We are the opposites in all things; but I am not certain whether his success is not necessary to save the Republican party. Certain it is, that his course has raised the Whigs to their present power, and I fear if he succeeds it will but contribute to the entire discredit of the Republican party and the permanent ascendency of the Whigs. I see the Democratick Review has not published your article. I suppose political reasons have prevented it. I do hope that if it refuses, you will not let it be lost. I am sure the Southern or some other liberal Review would be glad to publish it.

PC in Jameson, ed., *Correspondence,* pp. 564–566.

From [ORESTES A. BROWNSON]

Boston, Feb. 5, 1844

Dear Sir—I have just received through your attention, a copy of the printed Bill reported by Mr. [William D.] Merrick [Senator from Md.]

in relation to the post Office. I like many features of it, but some I think are rather severe. I am the publisher of a periodical [*Brownson's Quarterly Review*], and I naturally look to see how the new rates would affect my business. About one half the copies I circulate are through the mail, and something more than one half the remittances I receive, are through the post masters. The new Bill would effectually prevent the circulation of the work through the mail, and ["require" *canceled*] deprive me of the channel through which I now receive my remittances. As the law now stands post masters may make these remittances free of charge, and they may also send me subscribers' names; the new law will prohibit this, and the result will be I must stop my Magazine. The new law reduces the rates of postage indeed on Letters, but ["it" *canceled*] it actually raises them on periodicals. Those of us who publish periodicals will be seriously injured by the change. A copy of my Review fresh from the press, will weigh not less than six ounces, the postage on which will be thirty cents, nearly half the price of the work, instead of ["fifteen" *canceled and* "twenty one and a half" *interlined*] cents as now. This would make the work come to distant mail subscribers, allowing ten cents on the letter ordering it[,] come [*sic*] at Four dollars and thirty cents a year, when the subscription price is but three dollars. While the new Bill is liberal to Letters and newspapers, it is very severe, according to my reading, on periodicals of the class to which mine belongs.

I see also no provision for free exchanges. Now news papers are allowed to receive one copy of any paper in the country free of charge. Periodicals, very improperly[,] are ["all" *canceled*] not allowed this privilege. The policy of the law seems to be to encourage newspaper literature, but periodical literature it seems to regard as a luxury, and a species of literature which will have to be taxed heavily, yet works of the class to which mine belong[s] are the ones most needed in the community, and the most difficult to sustain. The higher order of literature most needs ["the" *canceled*] encouragement, and in our country can least bear being taxed.

I do not like the restrictions placed on the franking privilege of the members of Congress. It is a reproach upon them, and will be found in practice so [e]xtremely inconvenient that they will not submit to it.

The mail is intended I suppose to be a public convenience. Its importance cannot be estimated. It is the business of government to have charge of it. It will not do to let it fall into the hands of private companies. To prevent it, the rates of postage on *all mailable matter* must be reduced, and I am inclined to think ["to a" *canceled*] even lower than the Bill proposes. What if it does at first become a tax on the government? In a short time, [in] a country so rapidly filling up as ours, the increase of mailable matter, will make up the deficiency. But I did not intend to travel out of my line, and to discuss a subject which the Senator to whom I write understands in all its bearings, so much better than I do or can. Forgive the liberty I have taken in sending you the thoughts which [*and here this incomplete manuscript ends.*]

ALU (incomplete) in InNd, Orestes A. Brownson Collection (published microfilm, roll 2, frames 238–239).

From BENJ[AMIN] F. PORTER

Tuscaloosa [Ala.], 5 Feb. 1844

Dear Sir, I have been wishing for some time to address you, but desired, first, to see what course would be taken by your friends in this, and other States. The tame submission of many, upon whose firmness I relied much, to the action of the Convention, in Alabama, has given a plain indication of what may be expected in the course of the Baltimore convocation. Had I been in this Convention, I would have firmly called upon your friends to secede, and led the way. But the resolutions of the [Martin] Van Buren men to coerce, while still pretending to conciliate; to deceive us with frankness; were too well concocted, to admit of opposition. You may have perceived, that some of your friends in the convention, from different parts of the State, were selected as delegates and electors. I could have received this favor, if I had chosen to connect it with promis[es of] acquiescence in the action of the Convention: that is, take a Calhoun [ap]pointment, with Van Buren instructions. I was sorry to see your friends [sub]-mitting to this course. I should have indignantly rejected it. The wh[ole] matter has, however, settled down to this, that Alabama must vote for [Mr.] Van Buren: this proposition settles another, to wit, that after Mr. Van B[uren,] she is bound to the succession of Mr. [Thomas H.] Benton. I know the men [here so] well, who have originated and pressed this affair. I know so perfectly [the] train of circumstances, and motives, and opinions of those concerned, as to see that this event is arranged.

Your friends here will take different steps. Some will support Mr. [Henry] Clay, as the only course to secure ["the" *canceled*] a healthy action in Alabama: Some will remain neutral: Some support Mr. Van

Buren. Whatever direction I may give my own efforts, I pray you, be assured, I shall neither abate a tittle of the general principles upon which I have endeavoured to extend your popularity in Alabama, nor cease to admire your public and private character.

The state of things in this State I have more than once endeavoured to inform you of; You will understand me when I say, the connection of one person with the Van Buren ticket, has effected these results. The men who to day reject you for Mr. Van Buren, will to morrow set you aside for Mr. Benton. Self interest is a powerful lever in the actions of men: And impels them to do often what conscience condemns. Foreseeing, as I think, the arrangements made here, for the future, I shall feel it my duty to mingle with any honorable opposition to defeat it; looking to the virtue of the people, under the direction of Providence for the success of those main principles, on which rest the safety of our common country.

For the kindness with which you have received my suggestions, I return my grateful thanks. My communications have been governed by motives of patriotism: And I hope the day is not distant when my Country will feel the same enthusiasm in the prospect of your elevation, that I do.

I need not say, that this letter is considered due to my previous professions in your favor; and is written in the same confidence with which you have received my others. Very respectfully Your Ob[edien]t Serv[an]t, Benj. F. Porter.

ALS in ScCleA; variant PC in Jameson, ed., *Correspondence*, pp. 921–922. NOTE: Several words or partial words have been furnished in brackets where the margin of the ms. is torn.

From JAMES A. SEDDON

Richmond, February 5th 1844

Dear Sir, Tho' not honored with your personal acquaintance I am induced to trespass on your indulgence in accordance with the request of Mr. R[obert] M.T. Hunter for the purpose of giving a brief explanation of the course pursued by your friends in the late Va. Convention and the motives which induced it. This duty I am aware could have been much more appropriately and ably discharged by that Gentleman himself but that circumstances compelled him to leave the City before an opportunity was afforded him of Communicating with you except by a hasty letter. Promising that however unknown, in profound appreciation of your abilities and Virtues and in sincere devotion to the great principles of which you are alike the best exponent and ablest Champion, I yield to no friend or adherent you have in this State, I shall proceed in my assumed duty in a spirit of the fullest Candor and freedom.

Your late letter reached here only the day before the session of our convention and to it was immediately given the grave and anxious Consideration of all your leading friends who had then reached the City. It was immediately perceived that the juncture had arrived, when some decisive line of policy must be adopted for the guidance of your friends in the approaching Contest for the Presidency—and that on us had devolved the grave responsibility of determining it. With the noble boldness which has ever characterized your public Career, you had struck a heavy blow against the wretched system of Party organization and packed Conventions, by which public opinion had been so long at the will of selfish cliques of interested partizans either manufactured or smothered, but at the same time with no less generosity, had left to your friends the option of taking such course as they might deem under the circumstances most advisable. Even before the receipt of your letter we had become satisfied, and the reports of our country friends as they came in confirmed the conviction that for the present the arts and machinery of party leaders here as in many other States of the Union had proved too strong for the cause of Truth and merit, and that to persist in presenting your name as a Candidate for the Presidency at the next election would almost certainly result in present failure and the utter sacrifice of your future prospects of enlisting the whole Republican Party. It was I believe certainly true that your friends held in this State at least the balance of power and might had they deemed it wise or politic have prevented the Vote of Va. from being Cast for any other republican Candidate—more they Could not do, nor indeed Could they have rallied one half of those who really entertained a decided preference for you over all Competitors, for such under the working of a Corrupt system of party organization established for many years were the influences of hope and fear and the apprehensions of distraction and defeat artfully induced and pressed on the minds of the people, that in a "triangular" Contest, a large proportion of your friends would have been seduced or drawn from your support to that of the Competitor sanctioned by the Corrupt usages of the party. Such a result, deemed by us inevitable would have been most unfortunate both for your own future prospects with the promotion of which the best interests of the Country are identified and the State rights party of which you are the acknowledged leader. Ever afterwards that result would have been Considered as Exhibiting the strength both of yourself and your Cause, and such Conviction however untrue would have been productive alike of mortification and of serious mischief in the future struggles of parties. It was not to be disguised either that notwithstanding the truckling and disgraceful Course ["of a p" *canceled*] so justly rebuked by you of a portion of the Northern Democrats on the questions vital to the South of the Tariff and Abolition, a great majority of your friends in this State thought much was to be gained in a Contest between Mr. [Henry] Clay and any Democratic Candidate by the Election of the latter, and much reluctance was felt to pressing any third Candidate even yourself to the extent of destroying the ascendancy of the democratic party and ensuring the triumph of the Whigs.

We all felt likewise that in the event of your being pressed as a candidate and the democratic party sustaining defeat, the whole odium of the result would ["have" *canceled*] be dextrously Cast on you and your friends and your own weight and efficiency ["in the party" *interlined*] as well as the great good to be attained by the whole Country from your future elevation would be utterly lost—perhaps forever. Neither we your friends, nor the South Could endanger or sacrifice you, for so long as you remain as a rallying point and stand ready as a leader we can ["enforce" *canceled*] inspire apprehensions and enforce respect and protection to our rights. We also felt that under the stalwart blow you had given to the selfish oligarchy of political Intriguers and their infamous machinery, they must totter and that if time were given, for the inculcation of the views of your letter, sanctioned by the full weight of your character as one of the undoubted Leaders of the party and weakened by no suspicion of personal ends and especially if the whole prostituted press of the party (the Richmond Enquirer among them) could be muzzled against attack upon them or their author, they must be in another contest with you as a leader be utterly subverted. This was an end of prime importance, involving restoration of purity ["to" *canceled and* "in" *interlined*] the practical exercise of the elective franchise and release from infamous party thraldom to the Country and ourselves and to attain it, we were willing to make some sacrifice.

All these considerations, as you will readily perceive my dear Sir, inclined most of your friends to acquiesce in the painful necessity of relinquishing for the present the cherished hope of elevating you to the presidency, but opposed to such a course were all the predilections of our nature—our deep and ardent admiration of your talents—our devotion to your principles and Character. In this struggle I for one and many others with me were willing to have risked all—Cheerfully resigned every personal aspiration and been Content to fall battling for our principles and our Choice, ["had not" *canceled*] and would have done so but that similar Considerations themselves forbade that we should by abuse of your own generous permission to use your name peril the ultimate attainment of the destiny for which you were intended and cut off all the immense advantages to the South and the Union which we believed would result from your administration of the government at a future day. These latter considerations, I believe I may safely assure you alone prevailed with the mass of your friends, whose feelings might else have proved too strong for the sober Convictions of Judgment.

In accordance with the views above were the resolves of a meeting of your friends[,] Delegates to the Convention and members of the Legislature, held at my rooms on the night of the receipt of your letter. They determined to attend the Convention and when there to require and obtain the adoption and recognition in full of the soundest State rights principles upon all the questions in agitation in the Country (including the Tariff and abolition questions) as constituting the Creed of the whole party in the State, and that such principles in all their extent should be pressed with all the influence of Va. on the whole party of the Union. That those principles having been fully sanctioned, We should withdraw your name as our Candidate and issue an address (separate from that of the Convention) announcing our solemn Convictions against the proposed constitution and organization of the national convention and assailing it in the ablest manner we could, but at the same time consenting not to press the decision of that issue at this time in consequence of the danger of division to the party and success to our opponents therefrom. In this address, we also determined to rest our support of the Candidate of the Republican Party not upon the nomination, but treating that as an objection, upon its apparent necessity under the peculiar Circumstances of the time, provided we could feel assured by the pledges of the Candidate or the action of those who supported and nominated him that by his election we should promote the principles expounded in the resolutions of the Convention. These resolves of your friends were frankly made known by a Committee appointed for the purpose to the leading adherents of Mr. [Martin] V[an] Buren, and they were received in a spirit of ready acquiescen[c]e that denoted the seriousness of their previous apprehensions. An informal understanding was then had that our resolutions avowing the principles of the party should be adopted fully. That no pledges to sustain the Convention or vote for the nominee should be exacted. That our address should be issued and opposition to the Convention avowed without severance ["from" *canceled and* "of" *interlined*] the party, exclusion from its conmunion or censure imputed to the principles of your letter, your course or our own. Upon this basis, the proceedings of the Convention were concluded smoothly and harmoniously. Our demands were Complied with and in effect we Controlled tho' we could not Command the Convention. At the same time the best spirit prevailed especially towards yourself. The merit of your withdrawal and the sacrifice made by your friends redounded to your elevation in the Confidence and affections of the whole party. The secret feelings of many, heretofore smothered by party influence, burst forth in your favor, and with it Cooperated the gratitude of Mr. V[an] B[uren]'s blindest partizans, so that I am thoroughly Convinced at no previous time have you ever been more securely fixed in the esteem and Confidence of the Republican Party of Va. This fortunate state of things must daily be enhanced. Your friends constituting most of the speakers of the party, will conduct, (as indeed all the republican speakers from the adoption of the resolutions by the Convention will be forced to do also) the Canvass on your Principles. Your authority—your arguments must be duely avouched and familiarized to the people, and now that all personal motives of detraction are removed, your character will be more highly appreciated, and your services and talents more justly estimated than ever heretofore. From all these causes many just auguries may be adduced of the Course of future events— and if the firm resolves and best exertions of a host of able friends can aid their realization, they shall certainly be so wrought out as to fill the measure of ["your" *interlined*] Honors which now ["only" *canceled*] fall short ["only" *interlined*] of your fame. To yourself who have already done enough for glory to your name and State, this may be a matter of comparative indifference but to your friends, it must constitute a matter of deep anxiety and lively anticipation, and to none more truly than to Yours with Sentiments of unfeigned esteem, James A. Seddon.

ALS and ms. copy in ScCleA; variant PC in Jameson, ed., *Correspondence*, pp. 923–927. NOTE: Seddon was later a Representative from Va. and Secretary of War of the Confederate States. His activities in support of Calhoun's campaign in Va. can be followed in letters to Hunter, some found in ScU-SC, James Alexander Seddon Manuscripts, and others printed in Ambler, ed., *Correspondence of Robert M.T. Hunter.*

From R[OBERT] M. T. HUNTER

Tuesday, L[l]oyds, Essex County, Feb[ruar]y 6, 1844

My dear Sir, I addressed you a hasty note before leaving Richmond to advise you ["in part" *interlined*] of the motives of your friends in the Va. Convention. Before this reaches you I hope you will have seen our address as it is expected to appear in the [Petersburg] Republican this morning. Your letter reached us the morning before the Convention in the Mercury. The same paper contained an editorial taking your name from the head of its column and announcing the terms upon which the candidate of the Dem[ocratic] party might receive the suffrages of So[uth] Ca[rolina]. So at least we understand it. Under the circumstances to have nominated you would have been a great injustice as we believed to your fame and popularity. Such a ticket would not have received near all of those who really prefer you. To have assumed a neutral position would have disbanded your friends. The mass would have divided, some voting for [Henry] Clay but more voting for [Martin] V[an] B[uren] or whoever is the candidate. The object was to take such a course as we believed would most advance your popularity and our common principles. We determined to issue an address taking our position against the ["Baltimore" *interlined*] Convention, announcing our intention to support the candidate of the party if we could promote the principles of the Dem[ocratic] Rep[ublican] party as announced in the *resolutions of our convention* which you will perceive are *good principles* and leaving it undetermined what we would do in the other event. Such seemed to be the position of the Mercury; such seemed to us the true position. Our object was to drive the friends of Mr. V[an] B[uren] as far [as] possible on the right line and to maintain ["& advance" *interlined*] your popularity in the party. It was distinctly understood with [Thomas] Ritchie that there was to be no attack on you or your letter, and I publicly told him that if the issue should be disastrous to the South the *responsibility* would rest upon him and Mr. V[an] B[uren]'s southern friends who had insisted upon him. In the private meeting, your friends determined upon preserving their ["opposition" *canceled*] organization and upon hoisting[?] your name immediately after the next presidential canvass was over without regard to conventions; ["such" *canceled*] unless they would give us such an organization as we claimed in justice. In the meantime we have determined to use every means to increase your strength and extend your popularity. Our object was to bring you in next time if you would permit it and to raise up a Southern party upon true and Southern principles. You will see the bearing our address has upon this point. When the convention adjourned many[,] very many of the supporters of V[an] B[uren] assured us of their determination to support you next time. They said our course had strengthened you and that the party would be disgraced if it did not take you up on the next occasion. Mr. Ritchie assured me privately and in confidence that he had seen lately letters from V[an] B[uren] which would satisfy me and the South as to his disposition upon every point. I did not see those letters and therefore cannot vouch for their existence. He pledged himself to use all the means short of actually renouncing V[an] B[uren] to drive his friends to the right line of action and that he thought our course would be useful to this end. What he will do I know not. But we have a position in the party which will make it a matter of political life or death with him to do so. Your friends I believe were activated by a most sincere desire to ["aid you" *canceled*] raise your name and popularity and to preserve a position in which they could defend your principles and the South. I do believe that our movement will make you the strongest man in Virginia should it not be disapproved by yourself. We also considered its effects upon the South and our principles. To have supported Clay would have been utterly inconsistent and ruinous. To have remained neutral would have destroyed the leaders and disbanded the mass of your friends; nothing was left us but to declare our determination to go in ["with the Democrats" *interlined*] if we could promote our principles by doing so and to throw the responsibility of selecting V[an] B[uren] upon those men in the South who have forced him upon us. What shall we effect by it? We shall ["kill" *canceled*] put an end to such national conventions as have been heretofore organized. We have induced the *whole party* in Va. to adopt the resolutions which express your principles; we have I believe greatly strengthened you in Virginia and I hope in the union and we have preserved a position in the mass which will enable us I think to force the ["quondam" *interlined*] leaders to go on properly or else *break them down.* If Mr. Clay had been elected through the neutrality or with the active cooperation of your friends it would have been destructive to you and them. If he should now be elected the Dem[ocratic] party must rally upon you next time—at any rate we have a position in which we can better unite the South upon your principles. The movements we have taken in all their attending circumstances have been amongst the most painful of my life. I need not say why. I never was more decided in my life as to the propriety of the course. The apprehension has been least [*sic*] you should disapprove it. I most earnestly trust not. Should you do so, my position will be painful indeed. In the meeting of our friends, I told them I was governed entirely by your ["private" canceled and "public" interlined] letter ["which they had seen" interlined] and my own views of what was proper. That I did not even know what course you would desire us to pursue, but that I felt to run you under such circumstances would have been cruel injustice towards you. That I knew you would be perfectly willing to the sacrifice if you thought our common principles would be advanced by it. But ought we to be willing to ask such a sacrifice? I think they were all of opinion that such an idea was not to be entertained. ["They" canceled.] You will perceive that your friends have prominent positions on the electoral ticket. I did not advise this course. But as every other in the private meeting seemed to think it highly important I did not express my doubts. They offered me the post of elector which I declined. They then appointed me an assistant ["which I also decline" canceled] without my knowledge. I left a letter in Richmond declining this also. My doubts were as to the chance of our prominent friends becoming real V[an] B[uren] men from the habit of defending him. But when it was determined to be important that they should take these posts I then suggested (and it was so understood) that your friends on the ticket would take the ground that the resolutions of the convention (expressing in fact your principles and drawn by your friends) should be held up as the party creed, that the Whigs and their candidate should be attacked for their opposition to this creed and that the Dem[ocratic] Candidate should be defended where he approached the creed ["the" canceled] more nearly than the Whig, and that no departures from it in him should be justified.

Before seeing your letter I had prepared an address in the event that ["they" canceled] the V[an] B[urenites] should present as a test a resolution pledging us to the nominee. They offered none such and in some respects it was changed. The argument against the ["Baltimore" interlined] Convention and on the true position of Va. was from myself, the three first and the three or four last pages in the manuscript were from [James A.] Seddon. After our course was taken and shortly before the convention ["adjourned" interlined] a letter reached ["us" canceled and (Washington) "Greenhow" interlined] from Duff Green urging us to nominate you on a separate ticket. Our course had been previously taken, nor did we presume that he was acting under your advice as the Mercury ["& Spectator" canceled] had ["both" canceled] taken down your name and as we thought too that such an act would be ruinous to you, as it would close your political life under ["circumstan" *canceled*] appearances which would do the greatest injustice to your ["real" *interlined*] popularity and estimation amongst the people; and which would be false if taken by posterity (as they would be) as evidences of your true strength and popularity.

I shall look with great anxiety for a letter from you; if we have done wrong let us know it and if the error is of a character to be repaired ["let us know it" *canceled and* "tell us how" *interlined*]. If you should disapprove our course because you apprehend disastrous consequences to ourselves we are willing to meet them and encounter all the hazards. Should you disapprove ["however" *interlined*] because you think the course may be injurious to you we should be grieved indeed. Our position was difficult and painful. The exhibitions of feeling on the part of your friends were deep and nothing I believe restrained them but the fear of injuring you and the settled determination to make you the President next time should God spare you to us so long. If our course should be approved by yourself and friends elsewhere I believe we can do it. I am my dear Sir most truly yours, R.M.T. Hunter.

ALS in ScCleA; variant PC in Jameson, ed., *Correspondence*, pp. 927–931. NOTE: Hunter's statement that "We have induced the *whole party* in Va. to adopt the resolutions which express your principles," refers to the fifteen policy resolutions adopted by the Va. State Democratic Convention. As reported in the Richmond, Va., *Enquirer*, February 6, 1844, p. 2, these affirmed that the federal government was one of limited powers and that internal improvements, assumption of State debts, and a national bank were unconstitutional. They also opposed the protective tariff, abolition agitation, and any restriction of the Presidential veto power, and called for the separation of the government from banks. The committee of seven which reported the resolutions to the convention included two allies of Calhoun, Robert G. Scott and James A. Seddon.

From WILSON LUMPKIN

Athens [Ga.,] Feb[ruar]y 6th 1844

My dear Sir, I have now read with care & consideration, your late address to your friends. And most of your true & patriotic friends will approve of it. The true principles which you advocate, must meet the approbation of sensible men, who love their Country, more than men, or party.

For myself, your address consoles & strengthens me; because I find views and principles which so entirely coincide with my own, in my present secluded mode of life. My Zeal for *party*, is nearly or quite extinguished. What is called the Democratic party, pretending to Represent the old Republican party, has become so corrupt, in many of its leading members, that I cannot sympathize with its destiny. I only prefer it to the Whig party, because it is less corrupt & dangerous, to the liberty of the Country & perpetuity of our institutions.

I have been very much disgusted, with the conduct of a large portion of those called Dem[ocrats] in Congress, since the commencement of the session. The conduct of many of these members, upon the subjects of the Tariff, Abolition, & public expenditures, Western Waters, Oregon &C. &C. has been so obviously designed to opperate [*sic*] on President making, that I cannot ["reading"(?) *canceled*] read the proceedings of Congress, without the strongest abhorrence of the corruption of the times. The Veil is too thin to hide the real object from the most common, attentive observer. For the destiny of a great nation to [be] in such hands, is really alarming. I discover however, that the leading managers have become somewhat alarmed, & surprised, if they now endeavor to keep the subjects of the Tariff & Abolition in *statu quo*, until after the presidential election.

Your address will have the effect, to check the so called Democrats, in their demonstrations in favor of protective Tariffs & the encouragement of the Abolitionist. I enjoy good health, stay at home closely, attend diligently to ["my" *interlined*] humble private affairs, read a great deal, & think more—but have just entered upon the 62d year of my age, & am too old, stout as I feel, to enter again upon the bustling field of political strife. You nor myself, never have, nor never will, hold an office, which has to be sought through the management and intrigues, of corrupt caucuses & conventions. Our services will only be desired, when it is seen & felt, that the Country needs them. It is impossible from the nature of things, that we can be favorites with a party, the majority of whose leaders are corrupt selfish men. I must be pardoned for my selfish indelicacy, as I neither seek or desire to recommend myself to public notice by any thing I say on this subject. I write to you, with the freedom of confidence & friendship. Sincerely y[ou]r friend, Wilson Lumpkin.

ALS in ScCleA.

To "Col." JAMES E[DWARD] COLHOUN, Calhoun's Mill, Abbeville District, S.C.

Fort Hill, 7th Feb. 1844

My dear Sir, I have written to the Editor of the Mercury to correct the statement, that my name was withdrawn by myself. I could not do it consistently with the position I occupied, which was a passive one (neither to decline or seek the office); nor with my Address, which simply withheld my name from the Baltimore convention, leaving my friends & supporters to decide what course ought to be taken, under circumstances, in reference both to themselves & myself. Indeed, my principal object in transmitting it to the central Committee of the State, was to give them, as the representative of my friends & supporters ["of" *canceled and* "in" *interlined*] the State, an opportunity to decide in advance, what that course ought to be. I have concluded to make ["up" *interlined*] my mind to abide by its decision, be it to support me or not; and be their motive what it might; for it would be in vain for my name to be continued before the people, unless heartily supported by ["the" *canceled*] my friends in the State. In its decision I must be content; but it must be *their* decision, & so *announced*; and I have accordingly requested the Mercury to state the fact, if the withdra[wa]l was made on its authority. To that extent, it is my duty to go, but I can go no farther. To go beyond, and insist on my friends to hold on, would be, on my part, inconsistent with my position & Address, and, with my deference for your opinion, improper. Not that I doubt, that the true policy for my friends would be to hold ["on" *interlined*] & to keep our flag a flying; not ["however" *interlined*] from any hope of ["my" *interlined*] being elected; but for the important object of *keeping our position & preventing ourselves and cause from being merged in a wretched struggle, who should have the spoils plundered from ourselves.* Be assured, that you are deceived, if you should think, that any thing beyond that, is to be hoped for in the contest. I am the last man, that can be elected in the present condition of the country. I am too honest & patriotick to be the choice of anything like a majority. The Philadelphia convention will be an abortion, &, if it should not, it ["would be" *canceled and* "will" *interlined*] present a miserable struggle between [Richard M.] Johnson's, [Lewis] Cass['s], [John] Tyler's & my friends, for a barren nomination. I can never consent for my name to go before a convention, after what I have seen. No; our only course is to rally on our own ground, be our number few or many; or to withdraw & stand aloof from the fraudulent game. The great point for me, is to *preserve my character*, in these corrupt & degenerate times. That may be of service hereafter; not to run again as a candidate, but in some greater emergency. Things cannot go on in the direction they are taking much longer. A split between us & the Northern Democracy is innevitable, unless we should prove [to; "be" *interlined*] the most base & submissive ["rival"(?) *canceled and* "people" *interlined*] on earth, or they should reverse their course on the Tariff & slave questions, which I do not expect. You need not fear, that I shall ever permit disgust to influence me. I am proof against that. All other impulses have long since been [sub]merged with me, in my publick conduct, except ["those from" *interlined*] duty & devotion to country. If I know myself, I would cheerfully lay down my [*mutilation*; life?] and glory in it, to preserve our free institutions, or ["preserve" *canceled and* "save" *interlined*] the South from distruction.

As to the result of the present contest, I see nothing that can prevent the success of the whigs, as things stand. I have no doubt, but [Henry] Clay will easily beat [Martin] V[an] B[uren]; &, perhaps that result, though we cannot aid it, is the only way by which the Republican party can be purged of ["the" *canceled*] spoils men & be regenerated.

All join in love to you & Maria [Simkins Colhoun]. Truly, J.C. Calhoun.

ALS in ScCleA; variant PC in Jameson, ed., *Correspondence*, pp. 566–567. NOTE: Calhoun's letter to the editor of the Charleston *Mercury* mentioned in his first paragraph has not been found, but see the reply from J. Milton Clapp on 2/11/-1844.

From F[RANCIS] W. PICKENS

Edgewood [Edgefield District, S.C.] 7 Feb[ruar]y '44
My dear Sir, From a letter John [C. Calhoun, Jr.] rec[eive]d from you yesterday I learn that you have returned from Georgia. I regret that your address was so long kept back, but I suppose it was for correction, as I see it is very much altered. I think perhaps a little too much altered as to the Tariff. I understood from [Franklin H.] Elmore, who was here a few days ago, that [Dixon H.] Lewis, [Robert Barnwell] Rhett, [Robert M.T.] Hunter & [Virgil] Maxcy all wrote the most urgent letters to have it altered &c &c. If this is so, I regret that they let it out first to all the letter writers at Washington, for I saw in

the N[ew] York Herald an exact synopsis of the address as I first read it, & it was stated that the writter [sic] got it from a friend of yours at Washington. This was injurious to you, but I suppose the person who spoke of it supposed at the time that it would not be altered & that it would soon be published. I do not know any thing about it, but suppose the Mercury has acted by the advice of yourself & friends in Charleston in hauling down your name entirely. I see the editorials are upon the same policy &c. Now I was under a very different impression when I saw you & when I first read the address. I thought those who chose would run you upon an independent basis. It may be perhaps that the course pursued is the more prudent & as it has been adopted by those who are well informed as to all the points I have nothing to say. But I wrote to Ala. & N[orth] Ca[rolina] very different letters as to the course to be pursued—& also to [Alexander O.] Anderson in Tennessee.

I have not rec[eive]d a letter from Washington since I saw you, and do not know the under currents there, but I hear from others who receive letters from Mr. [Armistead] Burt [Representative from S.C.] that it is understood the Tariff is to be reduced to the revenue standard by the Democratic party as far as their votes can do so—& that they are to take some new & strong stand ag[ain]st Abolition, & that this is to conciliate our support &c.

I fear this will come too late, for it will be difficult now to save the election of [Martin] V[an] B[uren] under any circumstances. I am one of the Delegates to the Baltimore convention appointed by the ["State" *interlined*] Convention, but I shall not attend it. Elmore is the other & he passed on through in a hurry, but said to me he wanted to consult with me about it &c. I shall not go. I see in Miss: & Louisiana the Democratic conventions have nominated V[an] B[uren] by large majorities. I hope you are now above all these events and that, resting upon honor unsullied and the calm dignity of intellectual fame without a rival, you look to the Future and to posterity to do your name that honor which a corrupt & degenerate age seem disposed at present to refuse. I re[ceive]d a letter from poor [Hiram] Powers at Florence as to your statue &c. I enclosed by the last steamer to him $1,100 on account of it. Yours very truly & affectionately, F.W. Pickens.

P.S. John seems to look very well & has improved since he came here, but sometimes it distresses me to hear him cough. He is reading steady[?], & I advised him to read light reading.

ALS in ScCleA. NOTE: On the same day that he wrote the above letter, Pickens wrote also to J[ames] Edward Colhoun, from whom he had received letters about

Calhoun's Presidential effort. Pickens wrote: "I rec[eive]d your two last, and as to what you say about Mr. Calhoun's address I know nothing of the matter. Mr. C[alhoun] has put himself so entirely into the hands of a few gent[lemen] for the last two years to consult with & to advise of his course that nothing has been left me but to follow & do the best I can. I think he ["he" *canceled*] has been cruelly treated by those who have professed exclusive friendship. Whenever I saw this Fall that [Robert Barnwell] Rhett had visited old [Thomas] Ritchie & the movements afterwards I said the game was up. As to a move here I find not a human being taking the least interest in politics, and a move of the kind you desire would only split the State and produce such division as to destroy us. It would produce the bitterest feelings in the State—Besides I take it for granted that the gent[lemen] in Charleston have acted under the advice & consultation of Mr. Calhoun himself. The fatal step was his resigning his seat in the Senate at the request of selfish friends." Pickens's financial situation will not allow him to buy at this time the Negroes offered to him by Colhoun. He hopes to see James Edward and Maria [Simkins] Colhoun soon. (ALS dated 2/7/1844 in ScU-SC, Francis W. Pickens Papers.)

From S[TEPHEN] H. BRANCH

New York City, Feb. 8th, 1844

My Dear Sir: I am studying Mnemo-Phrenotechny, or the art of acquiring memory, with every possible facility afforded me for its most critical mastery. Men of science say that it is the most wonderful and useful discovery of the age. If convenient, I purpose coming to Carolina's genial and friendly skies to impart it to yourself and children as a slight testimonial of my regard for you. I am happiest when tendering my sincerest homage to distinguished integrity and genius. I love to sacrifice at virtue's hallowed shrine. Palsied, indeed, be my humanity when I cease to cherish the immortal patriots and godlike intellects of my country. I know you will be highly pleased with this new science, you are so alive to all that glorifies the mind. I remain, With profound respect, S.H. Branch.

ALS in ScCleA.

From L. P. FERRY, S[AMUEL] S. MORSS, and JOSEPH MORGAN

Fort Wayne (Indiana), February 8th 1844

Hon[ora]bl[e] Sir, Deeply impressed with the importance of unanimity among our political friends in the Coming presidential Canvass and relying upon your Known Character for Candour we have taken the liberty of laying aside any question of delicacy and address you directly upon the subject.

It would perhaps be unnecessary for us to say, that the Delegation in Convention in may next will be verry nearly Equally divided between Mr. [Martin] Van Buren and yourself, and what is perhaps most to be apprehended is that the favoritism of your mutual friends may become Excited to that degree that the antagonistical feelings of Each Could not Easily (if at all) be reconciled to the nomination of Either.

If our apprehensions in this particular should become realized— The question of what should then be done? is a verry important One to Every person in whose opinion the success of our party is identical with the prosperity of our Common Country—but it is more important when addressed to the many Eminent Gentlemen whose names have been mentioned in Connection with the Presidency.

In the Event alluded to the idea has suggested itself to us that a unity of all Conflicting interests, and una[ni]mity the only bond of security Can alone be secured by selecting some person who will at the same time that his name will Command the Confidence and support of our party, not be Identified with any dissensions which now Exist among us relative to the selection to be made by our Convention.

In such a result, the object of this letter is to obtain from you not only your own, but the feelings of your friends—as to the propriety of forming that unity on Col. Thomas H. Benton of Missouri.

We write this Enquiry in a spirit of frankness that we have Every hope will be placed by you in its true light, and Every Confidence that you will respond to it in a like spirit.

The Contingency which we apprehend may never occur. It is to be hoped not. If it does not, if yourself or any of the gentlemen who Command the tithe of the admiration or respect for their Character as you do of ours we shall most Cheerfully accord our support to the selection. With sentiments of respect & Esteem, L.P. Ferry, S.S. Morss, Joseph Morgan.

LS in ScCleA.

To JAMES M. BUCHANAN, Baltimore, Md.

Fort Hill, 9th Feb: 1844

My dear Sir, I had supposed, that my paramount attachment to State rights Republican principles was too well known for any friend of mine to suppose, that my support could be given to any one, except in obedience to them. So far from giving it to Mr. [Henry] Clay, I shall give it to no one, who does not come fully up to the standard. I do not recognize the principle of availability or choice of evils. On the contrary, I believe that nothing will so certainly destroy the Republican party as acting on it. It has already well near effected it.

Your letter was received by the mail of yesterday, which will explain, why it was not answered in time. With great respect I am & &, J.C. Calhoun.

ALS in DLC, Personal Miscellany.

From V[IRGIL] MAXCY

Washington, 9 Feb. 1844

My dear Sir, Day before yesterday a matter of private business brought me here, very much against my inclination, when I found your letter of the 18th [of January], having received yours of the 16th at home together with its enclosure, which I have read with great interest. If published and widely circulated, it must produce a deep sensation. But it is absolutely essential, that its authorship should not be known. How can this be ["done" *canceled and* "avoided" *interlined*]? If published at the Spectator office, it will be inferred. Nothing strikes me as better, than to send it to New York [City] to Gen[era]l [Duff] Green, & yet—perhaps I ought not to say it—I have some doubts of his discretion. Pray let me have your opinion on this subject.

You will perceive that the Globe and the Richmond Enquirer are disposed not to quarrel with you. Suppose they do not attack you, *when* must it be published? Your letter seems to make it depend on a conflict between [Martin] Van Buren's friends & yours. Suppose it should not take place, what then? I am sorry to say, that it seems to me from what I see, your friends here seem *too* anxious to avoid a conflict, and I am exceedingly fearful, that some of the members from the South from whom better things ought to be expected, will not stand up boldly when the trial comes on & demand of the V[an] B[uren] men a strictly revenue Tariff. Ought not then your history of V[an] B[uren] desertion of principle to appear at once to stimulate the South & frighten his northern friends ["of V(an) B(uren)" *can-*

celed]? You must decide these questions. I go home tomorrow and will immediately prepare ["it"(?) *canceled*] for publication ["tho" *canceled*]. I do not see the necessity of much change, except some few verbal alterations and of course, it can be prepared in a very short time. It seems to me that it would be a good thing to attach to the publication, when it comes out by way of appendix a comparative view in a table of the duties imposed on the leading articles of commerce in the principal commercial countries of Europe. I have not the materials or I would prepare the table, if you approved of it.

I am extremely obliged by the advice, which you were good enough to give me on the subject of a seat in the Cabinet, in the possible case of Mr. [Abel P.] Upshur's wishes prevailing with the President [John Tyler]. I had before receiving it made up my mind to do precisely what you recommend—in case of a necessity for acting before I got the benefit of your opinion. But it has turned out as I expected. It was opposed by the President, rumour says, for I know it from no other source, having avoided conversing ["seriously" *interlined*] with any human being on the subject, except Gen[era]l [Alexander O.] Anderson, and he does not know exactly where the opposition came from. I consider the whole matter at an end. The report to day is that [Thomas W.] Gilmer of Va. will take the War office & [William] Wi[lkins] the navy. Since the appearance of your Address the President[']s weak brain has been more disturbed than ever with the hope of the Presidency, it is said. I have not seen the President for six months.

It is very late & I have written as you probably perceive half asleep. Always yours, V. Maxcy.

[P.S.] Why was your flag at the head of the Mercury hauled down immediately on the appearance of the address? It seemed to me premature.

Mr. Upshur, whom I have seen since writing the above in order to guard against any possible indiscretion of Gen[era]l Green suggests that he should send the manuscript after I have written out the manuscript form, to Gen. G[reen] and to say it was written by a gentleman whose name he was not at liberty to mention. I shall not shew the manuscript to Mr. U[pshur] till I have copied it & made such alterations as I may think suitable.

ALS and ms. copy in ScCleA.

From ARCH[IBAL]D BOWMAN

Andersonville [S.C.,] 10 Feb. 1844
Sir, I had my boat sunk & lost making the last trip [on the Savannah
River?] and am now using a hired boat, for a trip or two, and, have
two loads engaged—it is therefore verry uncertain when I cou[l]d take
your load—not before about the 1 Ap[ri]l at best—but shou[l]d you
arrange otherwise I will send up as soon as possible. Verry Respectfully &c &c, Archd. Bowman.
P.S. Shou[l]d you depend on me you will please let me know.

ALS in ScCleA.

To DUFF GREEN

Fort Hill, 10th Feb. 1844
Dear Sir, I received by the last mail yours of the 26th Jan[uar]y. I
did not answer yours of an earlier date, in consequence, in part, of
my absence from home when it was received, and waiting, after my
return, for the publication of my Address and to see what course
events would take.

In conformity with your urgent desire and that of several other
friends, I omitted the part, against my own judgement, in reference
to the Tariff. Your wish, and those who thought with you on that
point, was limited to that; but not so with a much larger portion of
my friends. They entertained the hope (a vain one I am sure) that
they could compel the friends of Mr. [Martin] V[an] B[uren] to redeem their pledges, in reference to the Tariff and Abolition, and were
adverse to taking any step, which would lead to a seperation. This
giving away, was so extensive at Washington and acted with such
force from that point on this State, or rather on the Committee in
Charleston, that I soon saw there was little hope, that the position
I took would be backed by the Committee. The result is such as you
have seen. The withdrawal of my name was without authority from
me, and was neither consistent with the Address or the position that
I had taken in the canvass. It was for them and my friends and supporters to withdraw it, and not myself, if they should think proper.
I have written to the Editor of the Mercury to correct the error; not
that I wish my name to be continued before the publick (far otherwise) but I wish to avoid the imputation, to which the unauthorised

withdrawal on my authority might expose me. I write this, however, in strict confidence, as I wish no conflict with the Committee or any of its members.

I am now disentangled from the fraudulent game of President making, and hope never to have to do anything with it again. It is abhor[r]ent to my feelings and taste. The truth is, that both of the great parties have degenerated from their original standard so far, that they have ceased to represent their original principles. The Whigs are the old federal party turn[ed] demagogue—a thing most abhor[r]ent to their original character; the Democrats are the old Republican party turn[ed] spoils men, a thing equally abhor[r]ent to their original character. It would be still more in conformity to facts, to say that they, or at least the V[an] B[uren] wing, are the legitimate offspring of the [Aaron] Burr school of politicks, and that in his and their triumph, the school of Burr has triumphed over that of [Thomas] Jefferson.

I cannot think in the present state of parties of entering again on the political arena. I would but waste my strength and exhaust my time, without adding to my character, or rendering service to the country, or advancing the cause for which I have so long contended. I feel no disgust nor do I feel disposed to complain of any one. On the contrary, I am content, and willing to end my publick life n[ow]. In looking back, I see nothing to regret, and little to correct. My interest in the prosperity of the country, and the success of our peculiar and sublime political system when well understood, remain without abatement, and will do so till my last breath; and I shall ever stand prepared to serve the country, whenever I shall see reasonable prospect of doing so.

I write you in the confidence of an old friend.

PC in Jameson, ed., *Correspondence*, pp. 568–569. NOTE: Green perhaps referred to this letter when he wrote from New York City to Charles Stewart (who had been occasionally mentioned as a Presidential candidate) in Philadelphia on 2/18/1844: "I have just received a very important letter from Mr. Calhoun, and his friends in this City will in a few days make a very important step on the Presidential question." FC in NcU, Duff Green Papers, Letterbook, vol. 11 (published microfilm, reel 25). A meeting of Calhoun supporters in New York City had been held on 2/8 at which Lathrop J. Eddy, John A. Morrill, J[ohn] L.H. McCracken and Green had spoken. This meeting resolved that Calhoun's "able and masterly address to the people" deserved to be heeded by "every one who is attached to our republican institutions" and that "we cannot recognize" the proceedings of the Baltimore Convention "as binding on the party." (New York, N.Y., *Herald*, February 9, 1844, p. 2.) As to the future meeting projected by Green, the *Herald*, February 19, 1844, p. 2, reported that a meeting of Calhoun's friends was to be held "To-morrow evening," with the probable purpose of electing delegates to the Fourth of July Convention in Philadelphia. However, that this meeting did not materialize is implied by Green's letter to Calhoun of 2/24 below and by the fact that no such meeting was reported.

From A[MBROSE] H. SEVIER, [Senator from Ark.]

Washington, Feb. 10th 1844
Dear Sir, Your letter of the 1st inst[ant] reached me last evening. No apology was necessary for not answering my letter, of a previous date, at an earlier moment. Multiplied and multifarious as your correspondence must be, I shall not expect prompt replies to any thing I may write you. But, at your moments of leisure—when you have nothing else to do—and are in the humour for it, I shall ever esteem it an honor to receive, upon any subject, a line or two from you.

Your declining to go into convention, I think a wise determination. You and all others, would have been defeated there, by the friends of Mr. [Martin] Van Buren. In your present position, as you are, (where I think you ought not to have been,) out of the Senate, you can do more to accomplish your favourite measures, than you could have done, while a candidate for the Presidency. This, I think, certain. Our friends are note [*sic*] sanguine, in supposing, that they will be able, to retain the 21st rule; and of accomplishing, what, at this moment, is probably more important, an essential modification of the Tariff. I have reason to think, that a Bill will pass, with a maximum duty upon no article of importation, exceeding 30 per cent, ad valorem—and upon others, of southern consumption of not more than 25 per cent advalorem. This, though short of our standard, will be something worth fighting for—and more particularly, as the free trade principle is a growing principle in the country, and requires only time & intelligence to make it popular. [George] McDuffie and [Levi] Woodbury [Senator from N.H.] have made masterly efforts upon this subject, and have happily, succeeded, in putting the "Protectors," in a panting, blustering and raging mood, greatly to my amusement, I assure you. Such a bill, as I anticipate; and the retention of the 21st rule, will, I hope, enable you, and our friends generally, how ever, reluctant with many, to support Mr. Van Buren against Mr. [Henry] Clay. This, I desire, not only for the sake of the party, but ["for" *interlined*] your sake also. I should regret, to see you, *even in appearance*, separated from your party. In the worst, aspect, they can be presented, there are certainly degrees of good between the *ma-*

jority of the democratic party and whig[g]ery. The majority of the Democratic party are certainly *sound* upon *somethings,* and the whigs upon *nothing,* that I know of. We are compelled to make a choice between the two, as we are, at present, too weak to set up shop for ourselves upon our own capital. We should do the best we can, under the circumstances of our position—and abide, with patience, our time, which will, I think, roll round to us in 1848. These are my opinions, hastily expressed, but honestly given—and being *my own* opinions, and honestly entertained, I hope, they will be received by you in the spirit which dictates them—and not censured because obtruded unsolicited. Verry respectfully your friend & ob[edien]t ser-[van]t, A.H. Sevier.

ALS in ScCleA.

From J. MILTON CLAPP

Mercury Office [Charleston,] Feb. 11, 1844
Dear Sir, Your note of the 6th inst. directed to the Editor of the Mercury, was received last evening. Deeply perplexed as to the means of effecting your wishes without giving our enemies occasion to say there was distraction and misunderstanding and weakness among your nearest friends, I have thought a brief statement of the reasons of the course of the Mercury, ought to be made to you before I attempt to do what I really at present feel incapable of doing with any grace or propriety. I had been under the impression, till the receipt of your letter, that you were immediately informed of the action of the Committee with their reasons for it, and I cannot doubt you will receive such explanation before this reaches, as it was distinctly understood that their views should be communicated to you without delay. I met them but once, on the occasion when they decided upon the manner of publishing the Address, and it was but a few days before that, that I saw for the first time the original draught of it. I said at once, on reading it, that we must either break with the party, or desert Mr. Calhoun, or the Address must be modified somewhat on the plan suggested by Mr. [Dixon H.] Lewis. Nearly all your friends were in favor of the last. When the modification of the Address was received, I was invited to and attended the meeting of [the] Committee to decide upon the position we must occupy and the duties that devolved upon us. There were conflicting opinions as to the call

of a public Meeting—but after full conference, the decision was against it, from a general impression that under present circumstances we could neither count upon enthusiasm nor unanimity—that it might give the best opportunity to the mongrel politicians of the city—whose qualities you know—to raise factions for their own private purposes and bring utter disgrace and irreparable injury on our cause. There were men believed ready in such a case to present to the people the issue—a breach with the party to make a hopeless organization in favor of Mr. Calhoun, or a pledge to abide the ["th" *canceled*] will of the majority—who could tell how many office-hunters, suddenly moved by a generous self-devotion, might discover that good faith required them to yield their individual preferences, and by no means incur the reproaches and displeasure of the majority! Others there were, likely to take advantage of the warm resentment of a great part of the people, to invoke an open declaration of war against Van Buren and a decla[ra]tion of preference even for Mr. Clay, and the extent to which they might succeed in embarrassing the occasion no man might say. Such were some of the reasons that decided the Committee against a public meeting.

The next point was, how do we stand toward the party by this demonstration. It was answered—that the reasons urged by your friends in Washington in favor of the modification, and to which you had yielded, were, that we ought not yet to take the action of the party on the Tariff and Abolition as final—that they might yet satisfy us on those points—and that the only power we could exercise over them, was to make their action on those subjects, absolutely the conditions of support or opposition—that to organize separately was at once to give up that power and withdraw those conditions, and to continue your name before the public as a Candidate for the Presidency, after it had been withdrawn from before the only nominating agency recognised by the great body of the party, of itself would be a separation from the party and involve all the consequences of an open organization against it. The Address too, it was further urged, implied that you might yourself give support to the candidate of the party on the same conditions proposed by your friends at Washington, and to adopt now a separate organization, would contradict that implication and render impossible that support. Your nomination it was further said, was only the presentation of your name to the consideration of the Baltimore Convention, and your Address annulled that nomination. We then as an organized portion of the party, were left without a candidate for the Presidency, and waiting its action to determine whether we should support or oppose it. Our connection with it now referred not to men, but wholly to measures. Having proposed conditions, we must repudiate our own proposition, or give them time to act up[on] it. If they go wrong, then in opposing them we shall be fulfilling, not breaking our pledge. These were the consequences it was thought, that flowed from the views of our friends at Washington, and it was decided that the Mercury, as well as the Committee, should submit to them.

The manner of announcing the position was then considered, and it was thought best that I should do it simply as Editor. What I wrote was submitted to and approved by Members of the Committee to whom that duty was referred.

If on consideration it shall be ["thought" *interlined*] that an unwarrantable liberty was taken with the Address, it will be cause of deep mortification and regret to me. God knows with what sincerity and ardor I have sought to do some service to my country by contributing with however feeble powers to the elevation of him in whom I have recognised and honored the representative of just government. I have almost lost hope that there may be found in the country any capacity to comprehend the uses of honesty in high places. On every side vociferous profession and mean performance. In North Carolina all was lost by a quarrel for the Senatorship. In Georgia nothing was held worth considering but the interests of the leaders and the State was thus surrendered to the Whigs. We are on the eve of a wretched and distracting contest for the Governorship in our State, that will end, I fear, in disgracing and ruining our party and our cause. But I am thrusting in things that belong not to the purpose of this letter. You will, I feel sure, excuse the liberty I have taken in addressing ["your" *altered to* "you,"] and will have a proper consideration for the embarrassments of my present position. I am sure too you will not doubt the perfect respect and warm devotion to yourself in which I subscribe myself your friend and Ob[edien]t Ser[van]t, J. Milton Clapp.

ALS in ScCleA. NOTE: Calhoun's letter to "the Editor of the Mercury" of 2/6 has not been found. Clapp, a native of Ohio and a graduate of Yale College, was associate editor of the *Mercury* from 1837 to 1/1845, when he became editor, and had probably been acting editor for some time before that during the prolonged illness of John A. Stuart.

From Benja[min] M. Milner

Feb. 11th 1844
Dahlonega[,] Lumpkin C[oun]ty Ga.
Dear Sir, I write according to promise and I have to say to you that I shall have some six weeks work more to do before I can know whether I can do as big work as I expected to do[.] I shall have to take out a great portion of this old work before I can venture under it and if I find what I expect to find I shall then have to run a large drain tunnel before I can do much work[.] I have not struck a lick towards searching for my rich place yet on the account, of havving so much old dirt to remove but you shall hear from me just as soon as I can determine when it will be to your advantage[.] I believe there are some men in this country that are getting very uneasy and if there is any body that knows or understands more of this place now than I do I do not know who it is[;] in short I shall do all I can for you sir on all your mines[.] I want to know verry much what to do for you in the sale of your cane creek lots 747 & 798[.] If you have not written you must write or send an agent so that I can have it in time[.] Yours Truly, Benja. M. Milner.

ALS in ScCleA.

To Richard H. Baptist, Christianville, Mecklenburg [County], Va.

Fort Hill, 12th Feb. [18]44
My dear Sir—I remember the facts as you state them, that in the session of 1841, you consulted me on the question of the obligation of the Legislature to fill the vacancy in the Senate of the U[nited] States, when it occurs; and that I gave my opinion in a letter [of 2/1/1841] addressed to you, that it was. I also remember, that I showed the letter to Mr. [William H.] Roane [then Senator from Va.], and that he concurred in the opinion. I deem the case too clear to admit of a doubt, and you are at liberty, if you should think proper, to use this letter, and the one alluded to, if you should succeed in finding it. With great respect, I am truly yours, &c., John C. Calhoun.

PC in the Richmond, Va., *Enquirer,* March 29, 1844, p. 4; PC in the Richmond, Va., *Enquirer,* April 15, 1845, p. 4. Note: Baptist had been attacked by fellow Democrats for having refused to collaborate in delaying the election by the Va.

legislature of a U.S. Senator. (William C. Rives, a Whig, was elected.) Baptist used in his defense Calhoun's opinion that a legislature was Constitutionally obligated to fill vacancies in the Senate.

From ANNA [MARIA CALHOUN CLEMSON]

Canebrake [Edgefield District, S.C.] Feb. 12th 1844
Dear father, Mr. [Thomas G.] Clemson wrote you last Sunday which prevented me from answering your kind letter from Dahlonega but as he never had an opportunity of sending his letter & I have a little leisure to-day I will delay no longer even tho' my epistle should have to wait as long, that you may see the fault is not in us if you do not hear regularly.

I do not write because I have anything to say for this is a poor place to furnish wherewith to make an interesting letter & when I have told you that we are all well the children especially & wonderfully so considering all the exposure & discomfort they have had since we left home, that we can get nothing to live on for love nor money for this is a regular cotton region & they do not go for comfort we cannot even get milch cows[,] that every body & every thing myself included are as busy as busy can be trying to restore this dilapidated place to something like order I have exhausted the Canebrake news. To add to every thing else we have but little prospect of getting into our new house before fall. It is impossible to get lumber. We send twenty five miles & then sometimes only get half a load & that of the wrong sort one half the time & have had to dismiss our white carpenter for the want of materials. William has hardly enough to employ him & if this continues till they commence planting which is shortly now how we are to contrive about the lumber I know not. This is right provoking especially when we can ill spare the waggon & team at best but we are all well & these are but trifles anyhow & I only mention them because I know you will be interested in all our distresses. We want you sadly to assist us with your advice & counsel.

John [C. Calhoun, Jr.] has not come yet nor can I conceive the reason. When we came down we should have sent for him the first suitable day but Mr. Humphreys (our overseer) told us it was useless for John told him positively that he would borrow a horse from cousin Francis [W. Pickens] & come down the very first suitable day. This kept us easy the first ten days for the weather was so dreadful that we concl[ud]ed that prevented him especially as he knew how comfortless the house was. Then Arthur Simkins on his way from Hamburg came through Edgefield & John told him he would be up in a day or two & thus we have been kept constantly expecting him & not much surprised that he did not come for the weather has been so cold or so wet that there have never been two consecutive days when he could come with comfort but now we have had two delightful days & to-day is equally pleasant & yet no news of John. We should send off immediately but that Mr. Clemson only waits for a letter from you before he starts for Charleston & will go this week or the very first of next whether he hears or not. He will go in the waggon to Edgefield & send John back in it & on his return Spencer will meet him in Hamburg with the horses & he will come up in the carriage which has been there ten days but the roads have been so dreadful we would not send for it. I write all this because Mr. Clemson & myself are hurt & mortified lest you should think us negligent in sending for John but the case has been as I tell you & had you been in our place I think you would have acted in the same way for tho' we should have been pleased to have seen him at any time & done all we could to make him comfortable we did not like by sending to urge him to come to such a barn in unsuitable weather when we had every reason to suppose he would come as soon as the weather became fit. We know he is well for a gentleman saw him in Gen. [Milledge L.] Bonham's office [in Edgefield town] a day or two ago but did not speak to him. He might at least have written us as he knew from his messages we would be certainly expecting him.

Saturday. I had got so far day before yesterday when John arrived. He had been detained by the weather first & then waited till F[loride Noble] Cunningham who was on a visit to Edgefield left. He looks very well & coughs less I think than he did in Pendleton. His spirits are very good & he has taken to hunting with great zest. Is out all day this fine weather. Tho' there is nothing of any consequence in this letter & Mr. Clemson's goes at the same time yet as much time has now elapsed since I received your letter I will send it lest you think me negligent & not write so often yourself.

I have been really indignant at the course pursued with regard to your Address but you know I thought before I left there was too much holding back among your friends & that they wanted spirit to carry out the thing as it should be done. I consider the State as disgraced & wish I was out of it.

The children [John Calhoun Clemson and Floride Elizabeth Clemson] send kisses to Grandma & Grandpa & Calhoun often talks of you & Pendleton. Floride does not walk yet but crawls all about & is gaining strength every day. My love to all & do all of you write often.

[P.S.] I wrote mother [Floride Colhoun Calhoun] by Mr. Miller who is I hope on his way back. My love to mother & tell her I hope he mentioned to her that I wished her to send me some yeast cakes to start my yeast. I have not been able to have raised bread yet for the want of it. I have often regretted I did not bring down the nice corn beef you offered me & indeed had I known how difficult it was to get things here I should have brought many things I thought useless. Ever your devoted daughter, Anna.

ALS in ScCleA.

To VIRGIL MAXCY, West River, Md.

Fort Hill, 12th Feb. 1844

My dear Sir, I received day before yesterday, too late to answer by the return mail, yours of the 2d, & today, that of the 4th Ins[tan]t, which I answer without loss of time according to your request.

I am decidedly of the opinion, on the point on which you desire my opinion, that the proper course of my friends and you especially is to take no active part. Let publick opinion take its own direction. It is now clear, that the race will be between Mr. [Martin] V[an] B[uren] & Mr. [Henry] Clay, and I see no motive to induce us to interfere to attempt to prevent it. Our present position, if properly maintained, is calculated to command the respect of both parties, and may be used with some effect, I hope, to advance our principles & policy. Let what will come of the election, if we should act as we ought, the cause for which we contend, will be stronger than it has ever been. I feel relieved by being fairly out of the wretched scramble; and now, that my correspondence will be less onerous, I have recommenced the continuation of [*two words canceled*] what I had commenced writing on government more than 12 months ago. It requires much reflection and my progress will have to be slow. If I can execute it satisfactorily, I hope to lay a solid foundation for the science of gov[ernmen]t. It is, indeed, strange, that should not have been laid long since. Constitutions are human[?] contrivances, and what man does and ["*the*" *canceled*] his reasons for it, surely ought not to be beyond his capacity fully to comprehend.

I enclosed a packet, to Judge [Abel P.] Upshur, Addressed to you some considerable time since, containing an Address to the Republican party, explaining the cause of the their [*sic*] defeat in 1840, & their probable defeat in 1844. I hope you have received ["it" *interlined*] and yet I fear you have not, & that it has miscarried, as you mention nothing about it. Let me hear, without delay, whether you have or not, & if you have not, do call on the Judge and ascertain whether he received it or not.

It is probable, that the course of events will take such a turn, as will make its publication unnecessary; but still I would be glad if perfectly convenient to you, that you ["will" *canceled and* "would" *interlined*] rewrite it as I requested. If not now, it may be necessary to publish something of the kind hereafter. It gives an account of a deeply important portion of our political history, and one necessary to be understood, to ["understand" *interlined*] the causes, which have produced the present state of things.

I would be glad, if you would return me the original, at your leisure.

Mrs. Calhoun joins in kind regards to you & Mrs. Maxcy. Mr. [Thomas G.] Clemson & Anna have left us for their home in Edgefield about 30 miles from us. Truly, J.C. Calhoun.

ALS in DLC, Galloway-Maxcy-Markoe Papers, vol. 48.

From FARISH CARTER

Milledgeville [Ga.,] Feb[ruar]y 13th 1844
My Dear Sir, I have your esteemed favour of the 4th before me. I should have written two months since but in comeing from Florida the horses ran off and I was thrown out of the stage waggon on the 27th Dec[embe]r at Bainbridge [Ga.] 200 miles from this ["and" *canceled and* "had" *interlined*] the whole of my right side litterally stove in nearly all my ribs being either broke or fractured and I have not been able to leave my room yet, but am now mending fast and hope to be out in a few days. It is only recently that I have been able to set up and write.

In consequence of this accident I knew that I should not be able to be at Da[h]lonega next month and as Major [J.] Hansell was interested in the sale of some lots at the same time and by the same commis[s]ioners we determined to have it put off until May or June. He will be at Lumpkin [County] court an[d] will attend to it. We have written to our agent on this matter.

I can assure you that in the event of a sale I shall protect your interest as much as my own. The reason for getting the order of sale is that the lotts are constantly being worked and you and I get but little or nothing of the tole [*sic;* toll] and I think we have been wronged long enough by Capt. [Henry M.] Clay and his agents.

I have re[a]d with great care your able and lucid address. I am in hopes it will open the eyes of our stupid people, but this is hard to do. I will write you again as soon as I get able. Yours truly, Farish Carter.

ALS in ScU-SC, John C. Calhoun Papers. NOTE: Farish Carter (1780–1861) was one of the wealthiest planters and most active entrepreneurs of Ga.

From [FRIEDRICH LUDWIG, Baron VON] ROENNE

Berlin, February 13th 1844

My dear Sir, Mr. [Friedrich] von Raumer, the celebrated historian, who will have the honor to hand these lines to you, is about to visit the United States. He is most anxious to make the acquaintance of one who stands so prominent in the United States and whose life must afford a double interest to an historian like Mr. von Raumer. I need not tell you that he is full of admiration for you—how could it be otherwise! The great kindness which you have always shown me, makes me hope, that you will kindly receive Mr. von Raumer. My love and esteem for you will never cease, believe me ever most truly and sincerely your most obed[ien]t serv[an]t, Roenne.

ALS in ScCleA; PC in Jameson, ed., *Correspondence,* pp. 931–932. NOTE: Von Roenne had been the Prussian Minister to the U.S. during 1834–1843, and in 1844 he became head of the Prussian *Handelsamt* or Ministry of Trade.

To "Col." JA[ME]S EDWARD COLHOUN, Charleston

Fort Hill, 14th Feb. 1844

My dear Sir, I did not receive your letter till after my return from Georgia. While there, I leased my mine to [Benjamin M. Milner] one of the most experienced & skil[l]ful miners in the country, as well as the most responsible. I have little faith in those, from whom Dr.

[Alexander B.] Arnold obtained his information, and after their unfair course, under the former lease, had no inclination to lease to them
again. The gentleman to whom I leased knows about as much about
the mine, as they do, and is a much more skil[l]ful & successful miner.
He thinks it rich; but I fear he will find it much less so, than he expects.
The vein is a very unceartain [*sic*] & difficult one to pursue. I have
more confidence in an under deposite, which I think exists, and, if it
does, will probably prove to be very rich. My Lessee is to try it. So
much for the mine.

The course you are for taking, I have no doubt is the one, that
ought ["at first" *interlined*] to be taken, and I had prepared my Address on that supposition; and urged on the Committee a prompt
publication. But I soon found, it was altogether too high to be sustained by a large portion; much the ["great" *canceled*] majority; and
among them many the most intelligent & devoted. I modified, as far
as I could consistently with my principles my Address to meet their
views, and relieve them from embarrassment. I could not do less,
without still farther deviding, distracting & weakening ["of" *canceled*]
the South.

But, whether the course was right, or wrong at ["the" *canceled*]
first, it is now entirely too late to be thought of, and cannot be taken
without doing great mischief to the cause & causing much embarrassment and injury to myself. My mind is so decisively made up on the
point, that I cannot permit it, and should it be persisted in, I should
feel myself compelled to come out in disapprobation of it. I hope,
therefore, that the proposed meeting in Abbeville will not take place,
and if it should, that there will be no action such as you suggest; and
I rely on your friendship to arrest it, or give a different direction to its
proceedings, if it be too late for that.

The great mass of my friends & supporters, who disagree with the
course you are in favour of, still hope, that the party will redeem their
pledges, both in reference to the tariff & Abolition; and that the pressure to compel them to do so, will be greatly increased by the ground
we now occupy. They farther think, that it will be time enough to
take hostile ground, & rally under our own flag, after it ["is" *interlined*] ascertained, that their pledges will not be redeemed. I confess,
that I have little faith, that they will, or that any effective rally can be
made, if they should not be; but still, as I cannot doubt their fidelity
& sincerity, I am certain, that our true policy, under existing circumstances, is to give to those, who take the view, time & opportunity to
give it a fair trial. If it fails, as I apprehend it will, in both particulars, one thing is certain, it will lead to the defeat of [Martin] V[an]

B[uren], by the universal disgust it will excite against the perfidy of his friends.

Let me, now, entreat you, to give up your contemplated movements, & to remain quiet for the present, at least. There can be no movement, in this State ["at least" *canceled*], at this time, which would not call in question my sincerity in making the decleration [*sic*], that I would be content let my friends decide as they would. Every movement in the State, which would indicate discontent, would be attributed to me. You cannot oblige me more, than in acquiescing in these views. I must preserve my character above all suspicion for candour & fair dealing. It is all important to myself & to our cause. I care nothing for the Presidency, except for my friends & the country, but much for my character & standing both now & hereafter.

I shall be anxious to hear from you. Write without delay. Truly & affectionately, J.C. Calhoun.

ALS in ScCleA; variant PEx in Jameson, ed., *Correspondence*, pp. 569–570. NOTE: This letter was addressed to Colhoun "care of Col. J[ames] Gadsden," in Charleston.

From J. H. JONES

Union Town[,] Fayette Co[unty]
Penn[sylvani]a [*ca.* February 14, 1844?]

Hon. Sir, I have been much pleased an[d] instructed by the reading of your recent Letter[.] Having been always your friend Sir I was much gratifyed at your course. The policy of the [Martin] Van Buren men in this State[,] their organization[,] The a[c]tivity of the old Office holders & the favored Editors was such that ["th"(?) *canceled*] had the contest been between Van Buren & [James] *Buchanen* Van Buren would have had the intire vote of *Pennsylvania,* intirely owing to the course of electing Delegates by *Gen[eral]* Ticket[.] Van Buren and his old officers & Editors are a *dril[l]ed* army whose weapons are *Trickery* and primiry *Treachery.* The Abolitionists are taking grounds for V[an] B[uren]. If however they Take up a candidate the effect will be to assist V[an] B[uren]. The Demo[cratic] part of them will sup[p]ort V[an] B[uren] while the whig part will s[u]pport their own man[.] V[an] B[uren] has already gained ["&" *canceled*] great advantage over Buchanan & yourselfe—by the conduct of V[an] B[uren] writing private letters to such friends as he can confide in and the[y] will show ["th" *canceled*] parts of these letter[s] but refuse to

791

give copies and indeed the Abolitionists them selve[s] appear to favour the secrecy. [Henry] Clay of course is denounced by the (abolitionists Demo[crats] & whig)[.] They know they cannot expect anything from Clay and V[an] B[uren] being a New Yorker and the promices of his Friends ([Samuel] Beardsley) and others) they will favor him[;] they have at least s[u]pported him in opposition to your selfe[, Lewis] Cass[,] Buchanan[, Richard M.] Johnson. They are also workin[g] a deap scheam to induce the States to Elect by *Gen[eral]* Ticket and if they are successful (holding the ballenc of power in the larger States) They will return to Congress from N.Y.[,] Pa[.,] & Ohio 83 Black hearted Abolitionists. The resuld of the pending question in Congress in relation to the (Gen[eral] Ticket men) will determine them. I hope that your letter will awaik reflection among the Souchern members[.] Your arguments are uqually applycabl to the District system as to the mode that you recom[m]end for Electing Delegates[.] How can they Elect Delegates by Districts If the State Elect by Gen[eral] Ticket[?] Then a State convention will controle the State & *cunning men* the Convention[,] The Large States the Small ones and The North the South[.] This your Letter clearly proves[.]

Some effort is ["ness" *canceled*] necessary by Southern men to Defeat the policy of New Hampshire[,] Georgia[,] Missouri & Mississippi and sustain the act of last Session if it was passed by the whigs.

Expecting your efforts I am yours most truly, J.H. Jones.

ALS in ScCleA. Note: This letter is undated, but the content fixes the year as 1844, and a nearly-illegible postmark seems to read "Feb. 14." The postmark is that of Washington, D.C.

To JAMES A. SEDDON, Richmond

Fort Hill, 16th Feb: 1844

My dear Sir, I am much obliged to you for your full and satisfactory account of the motives, which governed my friends in your convention. The last mail brought me their Address, which I have read with much pleasure. It is manly, able & exceeding well written, and covers fully the grounds, that I could not well occupy. The two taken together, make up the full argument, with the exception of one or two points only, against the Baltimore Convention. I ought, perhaps, to say against any convention, or intermediate body, except that provided by the Constitution, between the people & the object of their choice; and of the propriety of even that, I doubt. I hold it to be a mistake, that such intermediate bodies, be it a Convention, or a Congressional Caucus, is necessary to the harmony of the party. It is, whether one or the other, a source of discord, in my opinion, rather than of harmony, through the intrigue & corruption to which it will ever lead, when resorted to. Without their instrumentality, the party would be compelled to rally on principles to save itself; and to do do [*sic*] that, to rally on their ablest & most faithful exponent.

The position, which my friends in Virginia have taken is very strong & commanding and gives me more hope of ["again" *canceled*] seeing the old Commonwealth again in her true position, at the head of the South, and the weaker portion of the Union. It is one not only of great power, but also highly favourable to the developement of patriotism, & all the manly virtues. However paradoxical it may seem, I regard ["it" *interlined*], not only as strong, but the strongest position, which any State in the Union can occupy. Faithfully taken by the leading State of the South, it would unite the entire section, and that, would always secure a sufficient support in the other sections ["sections" *canceled*] to ensure a majority. Let Virginia do her duty, and all will come right. Every thing has gone wrong since she sunk down from her former elevated position to become the subordinate of N[ew] York.

As strong & commanding as is the position of our friends in Virginia, I fear it will be lost in the canvass. In your ardour to defeat Mr. [Henry] Clay & the Whigs, which I approve, I fear you will from the force of circumstances be compelled to excuse, or at least pass in silence, the improper course, which I apprehend the prominent & influential friends of V[an] B[uren] will pursue in Congress, both in reference to the Tariff & Abolition. It is possible they may redeem their pledge in reference to the former; but from indications, it is hardly to be hope[d], that they will in reference to the latter. Mr. Clay is a slave holder, and they are determined to turn that circumstance against him & to the advantage of Mr. V[an] B[uren] in the non slave holding States. It is a dangerous game to us, and ought not to be permitted to be played, even if our resistance to it, should lose the election. No political consideration should induce the south to permit *that question* to be tampered with.

I see some of our friends will be members of the Baltimore Convention. Much will depend on their course. Yours truly, J.C. Calhoun.

ALS in ScU-SC, John C. Calhoun Papers; ms. copy in ScU-SC, James Alexander Seddon Manuscripts. Note: The ms. copy cited was incorporated by Seddon in a letter he wrote to R[obert] M.T. Hunter on 2/29/1844. In this letter Seddon discussed political affairs in Va. at length and commented: "Mr. Calhoun is almost too noble and elevated for the evil times we live in but how he challenges our admiration and confidence!"

From J A M E S W I S H A R T

St. Clairsville [Ohio,] Feb[ruar]y 18th 1844
My Dear Sir, About the 28th of Dec[embe]r I addressed a letter to you stating the course which the Ohio State convention would take, and acknowledging the reception of your letter of the 4th of Nov[embe]r. After I became satisfied that the district system would not be adopted, I was prepared for the course you have pursued, as you occupy the ground I expected you would, in your letter to your friends in Charleston, but I must confess I was not prepared for the step they took in consequence of your withdrawal from the Balt[imore] convention.

I do not claim the same intimate and confidential relation to you which they no doubt occupy, and yield to them in natural as well as acquired ability. They also have sources of information from which I am cut off. Hence thier [*sic*] decission [*sic*] may be correct, but on this point I am not yet satisfied. A letter from the representative from this district in congress says that we must go for a protective tariff otherwise the democratic party will be defeated. This, in part, unfolds the policy of your friends should your withdrawal be but temporary. If it is final and irrevocable however, I must say I regret it exceedingly. It is with me a settled point that northern candidates will not suit the south, nor southern ones suit the north. To secure them both, candidates from both sections are requisite. But the point which would decide whether this policy would be good or not is, can Mr. [Martin] V[an] B[uren] reach the House [of Representatives], should he have northern democratic competitors as well as southern ones—And next can he command a majority of States in the House of Rep[resentative]s when there. If these points are settled in the affirmative, then I can acquiesce in the decission of your friends. While I do this however, I think the cause of democracy, the constitution, free trade and the great principles, of which you alone, of all the candidates named for the presidency, are the representative, will suffer, should your friends be compelled to sustain candidates opposed to them in principle without a hope, in doing so, that they might thus secure your election. A total withdrawal on your part will leave them in this hopeless condition.

Mr. V[an] B[uren] got seven States in [18]40. On the supposition that Messrs. [Henry] Clay, [Lewis] Cass, [John] Tyler, Van Buren and yourself were candidates, could Mr. V[an] B[uren] get more than two of that number—and if not he cannot reach the House, and this would secure your success.

Several years ago I expressed to you my opinion of the importance of the present election; in this I believe I did not differ from your sentiments. Passing events have not changed that opinion—I submit to the superior knowledge of yourself and friends, and in all things else than a devotion to the cause of which you are the representative, ["yield" *interlined*]. And hope you will still continue to regard me as a sincere friend, let the result of the present contest be what it may, and whether you consent to be a candidate or not, *you will still remain my first choice against all competitors.* Accept the assurance of my high regard, James Wishart.

P.S. Your friends here altho, so situated that they can do little for you are grieved on account of your withdrawal, but console themselves with the reflection that your friends are governed by wise counsels, which will ultimately secure the object we have in view.

If the alternative should be presented to us of choosing between Clay and Van Buren we can hope for no amelioration in either. The first is repugnant to every democrat—nor can we expect to brake [*sic*] down, by it, the old organisation of Jacksonism, by any number of whig victories. If we select the latter, we participate in fastening the fetters of party despotism on the people, and destroy the elective franchise.

I have written twice to Dixon H. Lewis but have no answer. I have, since, made an attempt to open a correspondence with Mr. [Robert Barnwell] Rhett in order to relieve my anxiety in relation to the policy of your friends.

The St. Clairsville Gazett[e] has published very few articles from the [Washington] Spectator, but is right on the district system, the tariff and abolition. ["but" *canceled*] I could ["not" *interlined*] get your address published. He [John Dunham, the editor of the Gazette] is very unstable, and very uncertain as to the future. J.W.

[P.P.S.] Gov[ernor Wilson] Shannon, rumor says, will get the mission to France. There is a contest going on in the legislature of this State on Banks and hard money which will blow up V[an] B[uren] in the State, and will I hope aid [in] prostrating him and his friends every where.

ALS in ScCleA.

To VIRGIL MAXCY, West River, Md.,
   via Annapolis

Fort Hill, 21st Feb: 1844

My dear Sir, I am much releived [*sic*] by yours of the 9th to learn, that you have received mine of the 16th [of January] with its enclosure. Not having heard of its reception, I expressed my fears in my last to you written a few days since [on 2/12], that it had miscarried, which would have been unfortunate.

I wish it to remain entirely with you from whom it came, or at least with you & Judge [Abel P.] Upshur.

It is a question, which deserves much reflection, under present circumstances, where it should appear. After due reflection, I am inclined to think ["it should" *interlined*] in Brownson's Review, from which it could be copied into such papers as might be inclined to publish it. There are objections to publishing it in the paper you mention. If published in Brownson's Review, it is desirable, that it should appear as his own; and if you should concur with me, that that would be the best disposition, that can be made [of] it, you could send it to him, as so much materials out out [*sic*] of which to make an article for his next number. You might, I would suppose, safely trust it to our friend [Lemuel] Williams to be placed in the hands of Mr. Brownson. It might be transmitted to him under the frank of Judge Upshur.

I hold it important, that the country should be made fully acquainted with the real cause of the disaster, through which it has passed, & who were in fact its authors. It will never get right till it does, and unless it should, the fall of our government is innevitable. It is in this point of view, that I regard its publication as important.

I think it would command more attention, should it appear in a Review, than in any paper, which would probably publish it.

I fear you have not taken sufficient liberty with it in rewriting it. I bestowed but little pains on any thing, but the matter.

Should you concur with me, it ought to be sent without delay to be in time for the next number. Yours truly, J.C. Calhoun.

ALS in DLC, Galloway-Maxcy-Markoe Papers, vol. 48.

From R[OBERT] B[ARNWELL] RHETT

Washington, Feb[ruar]y 21st 1844

My Dear Sir, I did not write to you advising you as to your course, as to your address, knowing that you would have advisers enough, and being prepared to support any position you should take. Supposing the course of the Charleston Mercury, after the long delay and correspondence with you, the course determined on, I have followed it. I think however it would have been better, if you had authorised us here to act in the matter.

Matters here are pretty bad. McCay [*sic*; James I. McKay, Representative from N.C.,] the Chairman of the Committee of Ways & Means shewed me a few Days ago a huge bill, being a reduction and modification of the [tariff] Act of [18]42. It reduces the duties to 30 per cent ["ad valorem" *interlined*]—some below thirty to twenty five and twenty, but without any good reasons, and when the Bill, if such a Bill is reported reaches the House whether as a Revenue or protective Bill, the injustice of discriminating, and putting some [imported articles] at greater disadvantage than others, will run all up to the 30 per cent. It then adds three per cent More, by adding ten per cent on the foreign cost—thus making the reduction to 33 per cent. It leaves the free list of the Act of [18]42 amounting to many millions, for the benefit of the manufacturers and tea and coffee. It retains specific duties on iron and sugar and a few other articles, and it has no prospective reduction to a distinct revenue standard like the act of [18]33 to 20 per cent. Do write to me at once what you think of such a Bill?

I told Gen[era]l McCay that in my opinion such a Bill was only a modified protective Tariff Bill, and as such I should oppose and denounce it. Mr. [Levi] Woodberry [*sic*; Woodbury, Senator from N.H.,] spoke to me in favor of it—and Gen[era]l McCay told me [George] McDuffie [Senator from S.C.] approved of it. I told Mr. Woodberry, that such a Bill would be the grave of the free-trade cause for ever—That after a protective Tariff ["Bill" *canceled*] is made by the Whigs, and only modified by the Democrats—the principle will be supposed to be surrendered by both Parties. That I would resist and oppose it with all my might, if such a Bill was reported to the House.

The truth is, the rotten portion of the Party with Silas Wright [Senator from N.Y.] at its head, is trying to cover[?] themselves by the Report from the Committee. They dare not, take position with the Whigs, and move to shape a Revenue Tariff into a protective

Tariff. They want the Committee to perpetrate a lie; and under the guise of a revenue Tariff—report such a protective Tariff as they can stand on—and put us to the position of voting and moving in the House, against the report of the Committee which they will say, is voting against the Party.

Do write to me, what you think of such a Bill, and what Bill we ought to support. Ought we to vote for any Bill which is not pretty clearly a revenue Bill—which has for instance a prospective reduction to 20 or 25 per cent[?] Send me your views at once, for the Committee is expected to report next week. Had we all stood firm, we would have commanded.

My best remembrance to M[rs. Floride Colhoun] Calhoun[,] Mrs. [Anna Maria Calhoun] Clemson & yourself. Yours truly, R.B. Rhett.

ALS in ScCleA; variant PEx in Boucher and Brooks, eds., *Correspondence*, pp. 209–210.

From DANIEL E. HUGER, [Senator from S.C.]

Washington, Feb[ruar]y 22d 1844
Sir, You have been kept informed no doubt of the march of events here. The spirit of abolition has become rabid—not only the District of Columbia but the U.S. must be sacrificed to its fury.

Sectional Interests are encroaching more and more on the general wellfare. The manufacturing interest will not be satisfied with less than all it can exact from the Planting States. The Planting States are distracted. There is no one in Congress on whom they have been accustomed to rally—and rally they must or be destroyed.

The services of every Southern man are now required—and they should be employed too in the very position in which they are most available. Your State demands your services in the Senate of the U[nited] States, and I now call upon you in the name of South Carolina, to ["accept" *canceled and* "take" *interlined*] the position I now hold and afford to your Country the benefit of your experience and influence.

Permit me to assure you, that as far as I am concerned, the greatest favour you can confer, is to afford me an *immediate* opportunity of performing a high duty to my Country. I have the honor to be with the greatest respect Yours &, Daniel E. Huger.

ALS in ScCleA; PC in Boucher and Brooks, eds., *Correspondence*, p. 210; PC in the Columbia, S.C., *State*, June 16, 1895, p. 4.

From Geo[rge] McDuffie, [Senator from S.C.]

Washington, 22nd Feb: 1844

My dear Sir, Our friend Judge [Daniel E.] Huger—as he will inform you by a letter which will go by the mail which carries this—has come to a very decided conclusion in his own mind, that the political circumstances of the country are such as demand your services in the Senate. Prompted, therefore, by that perfect self-devotion ["the" canceled] to South Carolina & the whole country, which has so preeminently distinguished his course, he proposes to resign his seat immediately, if you will consent to take his place. He entertains no doubt that the Governor [James H. Hammond] would appoint you, as a matter of course, upon being assured of your acceptance, & considers it your duty not to withhold your services in the existing emergency, so deeply involving the interests of all the slave holding States on two great & vital questions. At his request I shall write to Governor Hammond confidentially on the subject, & shall expect an answer from him by the time yours may be received. I will add that I know that Judge Huger would feel it a personal gratification to be assured that such an arrangement would be agreeable to you. Permit me then to suggest that, you at least go so far as to say, that if Judge Huger is determined to resign & the Governor should tender you the appointment, it will not be declined. We have a reasonable prospect of reducing the tariff very nearly to the average of the compromise, with specific duties of 20$ a ton on iron & 2$ a hundred on sugar, as the only specific duties & no other above 30 p[e]r c[en]t ["as"(?) canceled] on the foreign cost. ["My" canceled] My best respects to Mrs. C[alhoun] and the family. Sincerely your friend; Geo: McDuffie.

P.S. Judge Huger has been quite unwell for a week or ten days but is now much better. This matter should be kept secret of course at present.

ALS in ScCleA; PC in Jameson, ed., *Correspondence*, pp. 932–933; PEx in the Columbia, S.C., *State*, June 16, 1895, p. 4.

To Francis Wharton, [Philadelphia]

Fort Hill, 22d Feb: 1844

My dear Sir, I have read the article in the Democratick Review with much pleasure. The manner and the matter both do you much credit. If a half a dozen men of leisure and education, North of the Potomac, would follow your example a revolution might be made in the publick sentiment of that portion of the Union, which would save the country and our truly wonderful and sublime system of Government. As it is their fate is doubtful. One thing, however, is certain, things cannot much longer progress, as they have for the last fifteen years. In consequence of the false direction the Albany party have given, the overwhelming majority which brought Gen[era]l [Andrew] Jackson into power has wasted away. They have done more to raise up the Whigs and depress the Republican party, than all the other causes combined. They have even made [Henry] Clay formidable in the South; a thing that nothing else could have done.

I hope, that my Address has not departed far from the line you approve. To meet the wishes of a large list of friends, I modified it as far as I possibly could, without losing my position, and becoming a partisan, which nothing could induce me to do. Had I consulted my own feeling and judgement, I would have tendered the issue at once and specifically, fulfil[l] your pledges or lose our support. Nothing, I fear, but another defeat still more signal can reform the Albany wing of the party. They are essentially spoils men.

PC in Jameson, ed., *Correspondence,* p. 571.

By Dr. William L. Jenkins, [Pendleton], 2/23. Jenkins records in his daybook services rendered to the Calhoun household: "Hon. John C. Calhoun. To mercurial ointment & Peruv[ian] Bark. [$]1.25." Entry in ScCM, Waring Historical Library, William L. Jenkins Daybook, 1840–1848, p. 30.

From W[illia]m Smith

Warrenton Va., Feb[ruar]y 23rd 1844
My dear Sir, Your esteemed favour of the 4th Ins[tan]t is before me. I shall be in Washington next week, when I will return your views on the R.I. question, through the channel you have specified. Lewis is however, very anxious to get them; & I shall probably let him have a peep at them; but you shall nevertheless have them as stated.

I approve your reasons for withdrawing from the convention. But I trust, & so do an immense majority of your friends in this State, that you will not allow any thing to weaken your connection with the

Democratic party. The course of the N[ew] York & Pennsylvania democrats particularly, is false & disgusting; but still the tye [*sic*] which holds you to the party, *as a whole,* must not be weakened or sundered, as the succession if nothing more, must, with prudence be inevitably yours. For my part I am against all Presidential Conventions. And, I think I shall take open ground against them as soon as the approaching election is over.

The fates will not let me stick to my private pursuits. Rapidly accumulating a heavy [law] practice, indispensable to my family, I find myself seriously disturbed by my new position, forced upon me ag[ains]t my earnest remonstrance, and by the approaching election. Already letters are pouring in upon me claiming me for future appointments &C; and I am no little perplexed as to my line of duty. The appointment of [Presidential] elector I have accepted, as it would have produced a bad effect for me to have declined it. But distant ["engage" *canceled*] invitations I am declining, in consequence of my inability to bear the burdens their acceptance would impose.

In this State we shall have an unparrelled [*sic*] contest; but I have no doubt we shall give her vote to the candidate of the party. With sincere & cordial regard I remain Y[ou]rs most truly, Wm. Smith.

ALS in ScCleA.

From D U F F G R E E N

New York [City,] 24th Feb[ruar]y 1844

My dear Sir, You will see from the Republic that I have anticipated your wishes—that I understood your position. There are a chosen few in this city who are prepared to risk every thing in the cause of correct principles and we would have made a demonstration that would have driven Mr. [Martin] Van Buren's friends in Congress into our terms if your friends in the South had not given way. With the 4th of July Convention impending over them they would have reduced the tariff and taken the most decided grounds on abolition, but the withdrawal of your name and the acquiescence of [Robert M.T.] Hunter in Virginia relieved them from the pressure of your friends and left Van Buren open to the overtures from the Abolitionists whose leaders are now seeking offices, and are ready to bargain. In this alternative I have siezed [*sic*] upon the defection of the [Washington] Madisonian to suggest that Mr. [John] Tyler[']s friends having refused to go into the 4th of July Convention we should hold it as a Convention of State rights democrats, and for the avowed purpose of organising the party and giving that direction to the weight and influence of the party which will best promote the maintenance of our political principles. If we find it necessary and proper to unite in support of the nominee of the Baltimore Convention[,] the 4th of July Convention will sanction it. If on the other hand we find it necessary to run a State rights candidate, the 4th of July Convention will be our warrant for doing so.

I have recieved your letter [of 2/10?], and am encouraged to hope that you will not only sanction the 4th of July Convention but that you yourself will be one of the delegates in case the action in Congress, and the resolutions adopted by the Baltimore Convention are such as to make it proper that your friends should sustain Mr. Van Buren. In that case the action of that Convention, espec[i]ally if you were a member would unite the party on our principles and place you and our cause in a most favorable position during Mr. Van Buren's term. It will also furnish you a suitable occasion to visit the north, and you should travel through the northern and Western States. I have written to Mr. [Armistead] Burt urging him to induce the [Washington] Spectator to take the ground that the 4th of July Convention is indispensable as a means of organising the State rights party, and hope they will do so.

This is as I verily believe the only hope we have in our present emergency. By coming north you can organise your friends. Coming under such circumstances the democratic party every where will recieve you with open arms. You will do more to defeat [Henry] Clay than Van Buren and all his fr[ie]nds can do and by preserving proper relations to Clay, many of his friends will be prepared to rally on you, after the next election. You should remember that the next election puts both Van Buren & Clay aside—that the pressure which has prevented Clay[']s friends from [*word canceled*] supporting you heretofore will be removed and that all that is wanting to induce many of them to do so is for you to pass through the Country and make a demonstration. You could not travel under so favorable auspices as this. Your progress would be a triumph every where. ["It will" *canceled*] The announcement that you are a delegate to the Convention will bring your friends the ablest men of every State into it—and thus give a character and weight to it which no other Convention since that of 1776 ever had. And your progress through the ["Congress" *canceled and* "country" *interlined*] will get up an enthusiasm that elect[s] Van Buren & the part you will have had in his election will have given you such strength in the party & in the country that no man can resist you. Again you can arrange a correspondence with Van Buren that will so far commit him as to make his election the triumph of your principles. If he fails you will have no competitor in the party. I have often undertaken to advise you. I was never more fully convinced that in this case I am right. Your sincere friend, Duff Green.

ALS in ScCleA; FC (addressed only to "My dear sir") in NcU, Duff Green Papers, vol. 11 (published microfilm, roll 25, frames 39–40). NOTE: No significant files exist of the short-lived New York, N.Y., *Republic* which Green was editing at this time. Probably the best source for the fortunes of the *Republic* is the letterbook labelled "Volume 12" in NcU, Duff Green Papers (published microfilm, reel 25). Some perhaps biased accounts of Green and of other Calhoun supporters in New York City can be found in the New York, N.Y., *Herald*, March 3 and 4, 1844. See also the Charleston, S.C., *Mercury*, March 8, 1844, p. 2.

From JOHNSON BROWN

Feb[r]uary the 25th 1844
State of georgia Lum[p]kin county

Mr. Calhoun[,] I went to Mr. Mills last week[.] I found him in Polk county Tenn[.] He had bought him self a track of land and is a going to farming[.] I shewed him that note[;] he said that he would not pay it and would not ack[n]owle[d]ge to any of the debt only said that he owed some rent gold but he said he done work on the lot enough to pay for the rent gold and said for you to make him pay it if you can[.] I made him draw of his ac[c]ount so that I Could send it to you[.] Look [*one or two words imperfectly erased*] at his ac-[c]ount he has against you on the other paper [*not found.*] I could do nothing more with him[.]

He liv[e]s on the duck town trail four miles the other side of the State line on the Tennessee side[.]

No more but remains your friend, Johnson Brown.

ALS in ScCleA. NOTE: An AEU by Calhoun reads: "Mr. Brown[,] Relates to my ac[coun]t against Mills for toll gold & & &." This letter was postmarked in Dahlonega.

From [the Rev.] AARON FOSTER

Boston, Feb[ruar]y 26, 1844

D[ea]r Sir, This winter has been spent in N.H., Mass. & R.I. I am thinking of a journey in N.Y. & perhaps in the west & South west. I lecture of war [and] peace, of the prophetic future &c. I am continually with the common people. As to yourself you know my opinions from early life, & lately they have not changed. All classes & with great curiosity enquire after Mr. Calhoun. I am sure your candor will bear with me when I speak of conversations with this class, the voters, who are not leaders nor expectants, but they would be pleased to see your name & a line from you as to your health, happiness & family. There were some promising *young* sons when I was in your family. Our talk of Mr. C[alhoun] is like this[.] Of his youth, of him & family at home & as a neighbour, of his 30 or 32 official winters ["in succession" *interlined*] at Washington & of this winter as the first spent in retirement since he was 32 (I believe) years old. As to talent none object when Mr. C[alhoun] is placed equal to the highest. Is he not *ambitious?* And I speak of his unrivalled popularity when first elected V[ice-]P[resident] & of the immense self sacrifice in defending the country against the popular high tariff. Of opinions always expressed ["fearlessly" *changed to* "fearless"] of personal popularity. I ask what other states man but [George] Washington has done this? Besides you do not hold it a crime to aspire to the highest *confidence* of your countrymen? For then you will condemn all the high officers. All this is granted. It cannot be denied. But has not Mr. C[alhoun] changed his politics? Or it is asserted that he has. Well, Times change, our country changes, the world changes. Our relations with other countries change, & here I repeat the principles of the letter on the published & unpublished speeches. At this day of revolution 32 years is equal to many centuries 1000 years ago. In agriculture he who always follows the same track is not talked of as the wisest man. He is a fool who makes war on his neighbour for changing his opinions. On this point some who are silenced are not satisfied. Private morals & religious views are matters of enquiry. As to the correctness of these I never have heard one doubt expressed, & this is more than can be said of Washington, & [Benjamin] Franklin or [Thomas] Jefferson, or [Andrew] Jackson or [Martin] Van Buren or [Henry] Clay or [Daniel] Webster, (I am grieved for Webster.) Still christians know that in the political high life it is hard & rare to "seek *first* the kingdom of God & justification by faith in the Mediator" & they remember the saying of Jesus, "not many noble are called," ["My own" *changed to* "Mr. C(alhoun)'s"(?)] view of the tariff is the stumbling block of the north, which cannot be removed. Few of the northern people agree with Mr. C[alhoun] on the *principles* of slavery, but the great majority *as yet* do on the principles of the *compact*.

At the end of conversations like the above it is common for whigs & democrats to say "I prefer Mr. C[alhoun] to any other man.["] This is a general sentiment among good & reflecting men over 30 years old. But organization ["&" *canceled and* "with" *interlined*] the press govern the 99, a part of whom ["will" *interlined*] stay at home on election day, if they see no successful way of voting for Mr. C[alhoun]. I never had confidence in Mr. Van Buren & dread his return as a public calamity. We much need an original[,] experienced, practical, independent, *upright* man whose powers can reorganize the disjointed materials of government. To bring the car of state into upright action would be a harder service than even that which reduced the war department to order from the chaos of Mr. [James] Madison[']s term. Public confidence in the capacity & integrity of the President would give *security* to every man's *interests in his own mind.* I am quite sanguine that a fair majority & much the better half, at this time feel that not another man lives equally competent to this herculean work, & that their votes would say so if the ballot box could be reached free from the influence of previous party organizations. It is devoutly to be wish[e]d that this spell of party might be so broken that men may cast votes agreeable to judgements & hearts. We then might see in office the man whom circumstances [*mutilation*] to our country have too long prevented [*mutilation*] people from electing.

Let us not despair of the divine protection & let us not cease to pray for the public happiness as I do not my dear Sir, for your own. We know that democracy divorced from christianity cannot be trusted. All history says so. Neither is it more safe to unite them in the form of church & state. Intellectual education is properly the work of government but the religious education must be the free will offering of its friends. The divine purpose in protestant divisions may be to work out the divorce of religion from the state, & rest it on its own independent resources.

Permit me to expect a line as to yourself & family (if soon let it be directed to Albany care of E.P. Prentice). Yours devotedly, A. Foster.

[P.S.] We have 4 little daughters in good prospects. My health had so far failed that I had been on a farm for several years also[?] with a parish & have recruited. Our friends in Pendleton keep us informed of some of the changes. Many here think that the gold mines are making you the richest man in the nation. Mrs. F[oster] sends a most affectionate remembrance to Mr. C[alhoun] & Lady & says when you are President & make the tour of the north we may have the honour to offer our entertainment. I join this to Mrs. Calhoun.

I know of no occasion when I shall write again. Therefore *fare well*. I shall never cease to love you, & by the grace of God, may we meet in the world of happy immortality. Aaron Foster.

ALS in ScCleA. NOTE: The Rev. Aaron Foster (1794–1870) was a native of N.H. and a graduate of Andover Theological Seminary. He had been pastor of the Presbyterian church at Pendleton during 1825–1828, had held other pastorates in S.C., and had returned to the North in 1832.

From JAM[E]S R. LAWHON

Dahlonega [Ga.,] Feb[ruar]y 26th 1844

Dear Sir, Your letter of the 4th Inst[ant] came to hand by due course of mail, & should have been answered ere this but that I received a letter from Col. [Farish] Carter by the same mail in which he stated that he had given you the information you desire. In consequence of an oversight in Gen[era]l [J.] Hansell in not embracing all the [gold mining] Lots held in Common in the order taken at the last term of the Court, the Sale will not come on till June next, at which time it will be Col. Carter[']s purpose to be present; at this term of our Court which will come on next week, the order will be enlarged & a[d]vertised accordingly. Dr. [Joseph J.] Singleton[,] Mr. [William?] Woods & myself are the Commissioners appointed by the Court. I will forward you a copy of the order immediately after Court. Your case with Mr. [Johnson?] Brown will be attended to promp[t]ly. Y[ou]rs Respectfully, Jams. R. Lawhon.

ALS in ScCleA.

From [2nd Lt.] PATRICK [CALHOUN]

Washington D.C., Feb. 28th 1844

Dear Father, I have only time to write you of the most dreadful accident that I have ever known to happen. You will however I dare say see it in the papers as soon as this reaches you.

That you may the better understand the whole affair I will begin at the begin[n]ing. Capt. [Robert F.] Stoc[k]ton who commands the steam ship Princeton, and has gained himself some noterity by his inventions, and large *guns*—brought that vessel round here, for the purpose of having her examined by the authorities. He has given several entertainnets on board, and to day invited the ladies and gentlemen of the city on board. The President [John Tyler] and most of the Cabinet Minister[s] attended. The entertain[m]e[n]t was a splendid one, and every thing went on delightfully until the second time one of the large guns was fired just, as ["we" *canceled*] the vessel was brought round off M[oun]t Vernon. Understanding that the large gun was to be fired the second time, and being anxious to see how she was managed, I was making my way on deck, when I was stop[p]ed by a lady of my acquaintence, and asked to see her on deck, which of course I did. On coming on deck, I requested her to go near the gun that we might the better be enabled to see her. She declined doing so, saying that the report was disagreeable to her. We therefore tur[ne]d around to leave the vicinity of the gun, and had advanced only a few paces, when the gun was touched off. On looking around I saw a man apparently almost lifeless, and bleeding profusely not far from the gun. The lady exclaimed, great God! some accident has happened, do go and see. On approaching the cannon, I found that she ["was" *canceled*] had bursted, and some five or six lying dead around. I of course stooped to examine, and found Judge [Abel P.] Upshur [Secretary of State], Mr. [Thomas W.] Gilmer Secretary [of the] Navy, Com[m]od[o]re [Beverley] Kennon, Mr. [Virgil] Max[c]y, and Mr. [David] Gardiner, of New York were the persons killed—and some ten or twelve wounded. Amongst the injured, are Col. [Thomas H.] Benton, and Capt. Stoc[k]ton, how severely I do not know; Mr. Benton appeared considerably so. The most terrible state of confusion ensued that you can imagine of, many of the ladies fainting, and others almost beside themselves. Mrs. [Anne Baker] Gilmer who was on board, became frantic and remain[e]d so up to the time of her leaving. Cousin Martha [Calhoun] Burt was in company with Mrs. Gilmer and was much affected. Altogether it is the most awful accident that I ever heard of, and has cast a deep gloom over the City. We did not return until 7 o[']clock[,] every one of course feeling most awfully—when I sat down to write you, for fear that you might be uneasy in seeing the accou[n]t in the papers, supposing that I might be on board. I cannot write any more. Love to all. Your affecti[onate son,] Patrick.

ALS in ScU-SC, John C. Calhoun Papers.

Account of "John C. Calhoun with E[noch] B. Benson & Son," Pendleton, *ca.* 2/——?. This pocket-sized book contains nine pages of entries for charges to Calhoun. The entries are for purchases of goods and provisions and repairs to household and farm utensils. The first entry is dated 11/21/1842 and the last 2/13/1844. As of 1/1844, Calhoun owed $97.11. Manuscript volume in ScU-SC, John C. Calhoun Papers.

From JOHN BINNS and Others

Philad[elphi]a, March 1st 1844

Dear Sir, A numerous company of Irishmen and the friends of Ireland purpose to dine together in this City on Monday the 18th of March to commemorate St. Patrick[']s Day. Never was the situation of Ireland more deeply interesting than at this time.

The truly astonishing spectacle of a nation of more than nine millions of People in the enjoyment of all of the blessings of Temperance, A nation who while their hearts pants for Independence and they claim it with all earnestness, yet cannot be provoked into a breach of the peace or the commission of a crime. Such a nation in such a commanding and moral position cannot but awaken the sympathies of the friends of Independence. To gather together some of the most influential and powerful of her friends is now greatly desired. With this in view we very earnestly and anxiously pray that you will honour us with your Company on this interesting oc[c]asion.

With sentiments of high Consideration & respect we are Dear Sir yours respectfully, John Binns, W[illia]m Dickson, John Maitland, Joseph Diamond, Myles D. Sweeny, Hugh O[']Donnell, E.F. Brady, W[illia]m A. Stokes, R.W. Dunlap, John G. Thompson, James Faye, C. McCaullay, Bart[holome]w Graves, Committee.

LS in ScCleA. NOTE: The writer of this invitation signed for all of the members of the committee. An AEU by Calhoun reads simply "Philadelphia."

From J[AMES] H. HAMMOND, [Governor of S.C.]

Silver Bluff, 1 March 1844

My Dear Sir, I have just rec[eive]d a letter from Gen. [George] McDuffie advising me confidentially that Judge [Daniel E.] Huger has expressed to you a desire to resign his seat in the Senate if you will take ["it" *interlined*] & inquiring of me whether it would meet my views to concur by appointing you to the vacancy. I can hardly suppose that any doubt could be entertained as to my course in such an event; but perhaps it may not be amiss in me, to save time, to say that in case you accept of Judge Huger's proposal you can make your arrangements at once & by giving me a few days['] notice, your Commission will be ready for you in Charleston. I have always looked on you for the first vacancy in the Senate in case you were not elected President. I did not however expect that the offer of one should come from Judge Huger. It is a noble instance of self-denial & personal sacrafice [*sic*] for the ["for" *canceled*] sake of the country. Very truly & sincerely Yours, J.H. Hammond.

ALS in ScCleA.

From GEO[RGE] MCDUFFIE, [Senator from S.C.]

Washington, 1st March 1844

My dear Sir; You will have received, before this reaches you, the astounding intelligence of the sudden death of Mr. [Abel P.] Upshur, Sec[retar]y of State, Mr. [Thomas W.] Gilmer, Sec[retar]y of the Navy & other distinguished men, by the bursting of one of the large guns on the Steamer Princeton. By this melancholy event a great calamity has fallen upon the country & especially upon the South. At the moment when one important & delicate negociation was coming, as I have reason to believe, to a close, & another was about to commence, poor Upshur, the main pillar of the executive government & poor Gilmer the only member of the cabinet who could be depended upon to aid him, were stricken down. The first question asked by every one—after the overwhelming shock produced by this disaster had in some sort ceased—was what is Mr. [John] Tyler to do? What *can* be done to obviate the hazards growing out of the critical state of our foreign relations?

Mr. [Henry A.] Wise called upon me to day to say that he believed you were the only man in the country who could meet all the exigencies of the crisis, & to request that I would immediately write to you to know whether if the office of Secretary of State should be tendered ["to" *interlined*] you unsolicited & with no party views whatever, you would not put aside all personal considerations, & accept the appointment? He expressed in the strongest terms his deep conviction that your services were imperiously demanded by the country & especially by the Southern interests now so deeply involved in the questions ["now" *canceled*] to be decided by negociation, and that you ought not to refuse them. Gen[era]l [Alexander O.] Anderson of Tenn[esse]e has the same views, & I have reason to believe they occurred to all your Southern friends without communication from one to another. In expressing my entire concurrence in them to Mr. Wise as I now do to you, I added that it must be distinctly understood that this is a proceeding, in which your personal friends have had no agency. He replied that he would take care that there should be no misapprehension on that point.

As I write in haste I will only ["to" *canceled*] say in conclusion that if the office is tendered, ["I think" *interlined*] you ought to accept it & *to come on immediately.* Mr. Wise says he will urge the President to bring Mr. [Robert M.T.] Hunter of Va.—your warm friend—into the Navy Department. Let me hear from [you] as soon as possible. Sincerely your friend, Geo: McDuffie.

ALS in ScU-SC, John C. Calhoun Papers.

From F[RANCIS] W. PICKENS

Charleston, 3 March 1844
My dear Sir, I came here & found things in much confusion. I think your immediate friends in this city managed very badly, and the country gentlemen were very much excited (many of them being in to the races). I called a meeting or caucus to consult to-gether. [Franklin H.] Elmore introduced resolutions—which I did not approve, & I moved a substitute & carried them. The main point of which was that 1st we should not go to the Balt[imore] Con[vention] & 2d that your friends should distinctly hold your name in reserve and under control—and that it might be our sacred duty to vote for you finally &c &c. Upon consultation I found that we had to temper a little at present as to the Convention, for fear small meetings would be forced up in places to appoint delegates as from the people &c. So we called a meeting of the Com[mittee] for the 18 March so that we could gain time & the developements in Congress, and by then there would be no division as to our course in the State. It was suggested by Elmore that we might find it politic to go into Convention as to the future &c, but I said this was folly & they would laugh at us as their

810

victims, & that our keeping out would produce no impression in two years time however much they might pretend to be offended now.

The great difficulty was to get your name back again. You see the article in the Mercury yesterday (Saturday). It was presented to me and was drawn up to meet the general views of my resolutions in Caucus. It does so but with more policy, as they say to prevent a meeting in this city to be called immediately by [Henry L.?] Pinckney. They say the meeting is now killed, but I ["shall" *canceled*] tell them if he calls one, let our friends attend and either move to lay on the table & adjourn or vote down the resolutions. I think there has been some bad moves & I hope it has been from bad judgement rather than from any thing else. [George] McDuffie has written that every thing will be done for us that we desire on the Tariff &c. So writes [Robert Barnwell] Rhett & [Dixon H.] Lewis. But [Isaac E.] Holmes writes differently. I fear McDuffie has been imposed on.

You see the dreadful ["catastrophe" *canceled*] accident at Washington & deaths. I hear some of our members have written to day here that I am to be offered a place in the Cabinet &c, but of course this must be premature, & even if so, I shall refuse. In haste, but truly, F.W. Pickens.

ALS in ScCleA; variant PC in Jameson, ed., *Correspondence,* pp. 933–934.

From KER BOYCE

Charleston, March 4th 1844

My dear Sir, I have felt that I ought to have wrote to you long since, but have put off untill now. Col. [Francis W.] Pickens has been hear [*sic*] and he will be able to give you a full statement of the course which I took in the Committee, as to your ad[d]ress. I never could get to see the Editorial which ac[c]ompaneyed your letter and little did I expect to see your name so uncer[e]mon[i]ously took down from the Mercury, but [it] is now too late to say any more on that point. I cannot but believe that those friends who advised you to withdraw from the Senate of the United States, gave you very bad advice—to say the least off [*sic*] it, ever since that perriod you have fell back, and as farr as my observation in matters of this kind, I find that as soon as a man with draws from the publick station, that he begins to fall back unless he travels from town to town thr[ou]ghout the countrey but anoyhf [*sic*] on this point.

I have another ["matter" *interlined*] which I have to sujest[?] to you and that is from the melencolly Cotephrey[?] which has took place whare you have lost some of your best friends[,] the two Secretarys [of State and Navy, Abel P. Upshur and Thomas W. Gilmer] & Mr. [Virgil] Maxcy. It leaves the countrey in a[n] awfull state whare two very important negociations are now depending, and whare [*sic*] is the man now to carry them on to the advantage of the South & the West. I can see no man but yourself who can now do justace to this countrey, and I have to beg you to deliberate, upon this matter as it is not unlikely you may be called to that post, and should that be the case, I do hope you will ac[c]ept if only to make the two Treatyes the An[n]exation of Texas and the Oregon Treaty which Mr. Packingham [*sic*; Richard Pakenham] has been sent to this countrey to make. I know that the President [John Tyler] is weak, but you are strong and what ever credit would be gained that would be awarded to you and again place you on that front rank whare you ought to stand in this countrey. If you should be applyed to you can accept, for the purposes above mentioned and as soon as that was ac[c]omplished you might retyire[?]. I know, that a letter left here[?] yesterday to Washington to M[r. Isaac E.] Ho[l]mes to have the president to appoint you and I have no doubt but the President, will be glad to call you to his aid under such trying times with him.

I know I have presumed much in taking a liberty of writing you and giving you my views on any subject but that interest I have allways felt, for you and my countrey. I have allways spoke candidly to you as one who[se] only interest is you, to see you at the head of this great nation whare you could serve the countrey with so much interest. I have been induced[?] to write you on this subject as you have allways treated my letters with such respect, as to give me confidence [to] give you the opi[ni]on of plain men Honestly! With sentiments of great regard I remain your most obedient Serv[an]t, Ker Boyce.

ALS in ScCleA.

To the Rev. A[aron] Foster, Albany, N.Y.

Fort Hill, 5th March 1844
My dear Sir, I am very much obliged to you for your kind letter, and the interest you take in my welfare, here and hereafter.

I am sure it will afford you happiness to learn, that my health, and that of Mrs. [Floride Colhoun] Calhoun & all my children remain good, except my third son, John [C. Calhoun, Jr.], who is troubled with a cough, which, though he looks well, gives me uneasiness. My oldest son [Andrew Pickens Calhoun] is settled in Alabama and is a large & successful planter. He is married and has two children. My oldest daughter, Anna [Maria], is also married to a gentleman of the name of [Thomas G.] Clemson, has also two children, and resides in this State, about 80 miles from my residence. My second son [Patrick Calhoun] is in the Army, & the rest of the family are still with me, the two youngest going to school.

As long as I have been in publick life (35 years continuously including the State & Union) my habits have never changed. I find full employment both of body & mine [*sic*], and have not the slightest desire to return to publick life again. Indeed, nothing but a sense of duty could induce me to return. I look back on the past with calmness and satisfaction. I can lay my hand on my heart and say, that I have in every act of my publick life acted in obedience to my judgement and the obligations of what I believed to be my duty. I have looked to them, and not to popular favour; and when most censured, no one has ever heard me utter a word of complaint. I censure no one, but I deplore the condition of the country. Government has gone wrong, and it has corrupted and debased the country. I have long seen it; I have raised my voice and struggled against it; but I fear in vain. It is now more than a dozen of years since I said in a publick Address, in which I stated my opinion on the relation of the States to the Federal Government, that if I am right, the Government will go on from bad to worse, unless its course should be changed, untill it would fall into utter disorder; but if not, that it would progress with prosperity, & that I was willing to leave time to decide. I fear its decision will be in my favour and against the country. We have committed many & great errors—too many & too great to escape with impunity.

I hope you & your family have enjoyed good health in the long interval since I saw you. Mrs. Calhoun joins her kind respects to you & Mrs. Foster. Yours truly, J.C. Calhoun.

Photostat of ALS in DLC, Personal Papers—Miscellaneous.

To [JAMES H.] HAMMOND, Governor [of S.C.]

Fort Hill, 5th March 1844
My dear Sir, I have answered Judge [Daniel E.] Huger, and informed him, that I could not obtain my own consent to return to the Senate,

should he resign, & the place be offered to me. I am willing to make any & every sacrafice to save the country; but I do not think, in my present position and under existing circumstances, I could be of any service in the Senate. It is in the power of the [Martin] V[an] Buren leaders in Congress to settle the only two questions of pressing importance, as they please; I mean the tariff & abolition. They will settle both simply in reference to the presidential question. If they should conclude, that the chance is, that Mr. V[an] B[uren] will get more votes by favouring the abolitionists & the friends of the Tariff, they will be settled in their favour, against any thing that I can do and in violation of all their pledges, were ["they" *interlined*] ten times more numerous than they are. My opinion may appear uncharitable; but it has been forced on me by a thorough knowledge of the party, founded on long observation & much experience. I have lost all faith in them, I mean, the leaders. If we wish to control them, there is but one way; and that is to satisfy them how many votes they have to gain or lose by taking this or that way on any question, in which we have an interest. We must show, as fixed a determination to defend our property & our safety, as the friends of the tariff & the abolitionists do to assail them, which I fear, from all I can see, is far from being the case. If I thought the South would sustain ["me" *interlined*] in taking the course, which the occasion demands, I would make the sacrafice and brave the hazard, as great as they might be, to repel the attacks on their property [and] safety. But I see no prospect of that at present, and am unwilling to exhaust the few years, that remain to me, in vain efforts. I hope to appropriate them more satisfactor[il]y to myself, and more useful to them in the quiet of a private station, in which I am content to spend the rest of my days. Yours truly, J.C. Calhoun.

ALS in DLC, James Henry Hammond Papers, vol. 11; PC in Jameson, ed., *Correspondence*, pp. 571–572.

From JAMES G. HOLM[ES]

Charleston S.C., 5th March 1843 [*sic*; 1844]
My dear Sir, The very important Southern interests involved in pending negotiations point at once to yourself as the fittest successor to Mr. [Abel P.] Upshur and in advance of any offer which may be made, those of your friends here who have together spoken of the subject

concur in the hope that you may view as they do the services you could render.

I may say to you that Mr. [Ker] Boyce, Mr. Alfred Huger[,] Mr. James Rose and Mr. [Alexander] Mazyck are those with whom I have particularly conversed. Some of us as you know are no politicians; we do not enter into the arena but we entertain and on proper occasions express our opinions on the interests of our country.

At the Instance of the two first named gentlemen I wrote on Sunday last to my Brother [Representative Isaac E. Holmes], expressing the hope that you might be called to the head of the State Department and that you would accept.

I have never before taken the liberty of address[ing] myself directly to you on any public event, but [*manuscript mutilated*] the present is an occasion which will excuse if [*manuscript mutilated*] not justify my course. With the highest respect & esteem [*manuscript mutilated*] Yours truly, James G. Holm[es.]

ALS in ScCleA.

From GEO[RGE] MCDUFFIE, [Senator from S.C.]

Washington, 5th March 1844

My dear Sir; I write this merely to say that I have had an interview with the President [John Tyler] to day, at Mr. [Henry A.] Wise's request, on the subject of your acceptance of the appointment of Secretary of State. The President is very anxious that you should accept & come on immediately, as the Texas negociation admits of no delay, & requested me to say so to you. The moment you communicate your willingness to do so, your name will be sent in to the Senate, & I, therefore, wish you to write to me immediately. I now repeat the opinion I expressed in my last, that it is my decided opinion & that ["of" *interlined*] your friends here that your acceptance would be regarded by the country as a magnanimous offering at the shrine of patriotism, & that you ought not to hesitate. I mention to you in confidence that the Texas question is in such a state, that in ten days after your arrival the Treaty of annexation would be signed, and from poor [Abel P.] Upshur's count 40 senators would vote for it. The President says he has hopes of the acquiescence of Mexico. It is a great occasion involving the peace of the country & the salvation of the South; and your friends here have ventured to say for you, that no party or personal considerations would prevent you from meeting the crisis. Very sincerely yours, Geo: McDuffie.

ALS in ScCleA; PC in Jameson, ed., *Correspondence*, pp. 934–935; PEx in the Columbia, S.C., *State*, June 16, 1895, p. 4.

From R[OBERT] B[ARNWELL] RHETT

[Washington] March 5th 1844

My Dear Sir, You have many Days since doubtless heard of the nation[']s loss in the death of [Abel P.] Upshur[,] [Thomas W.] Gilmer & [Virgil] Maxcy. We of the State Rights Party, who believe that the salvation of the Country, and the safety of the South depends on the enforcement of our principles in the Govt. must especially mourn. I really know not how our loss is to be repaired, in Virginia and Maryland and if I did not look higher than mortal agencies, I should despair of the country.

It is understood that the office of Secr[etar]y of State will be offered to you. It was plainly stated to me ["by one in the President's confidence" *interlined*], that the honours of the Cabinet would be placed at our disposal provided we would go into [John] Tyler[']s Convention in May, and support him for the Presidency. Of course the President will not intimate any such conditions to you, but that he and his friends will expect should you take any appointment from him, that you and your friends should support him for the next Presidency, I have no doubt. The Country especially the ["South" *interlined*] is in a very dangerous state. The annexation of Texas to the Union—the [*one word canceled and* "course" *interlined*] of Great Brittain towards us—the consequences which may follow the annexation of Texas—The Oregon Question, (which by the by Upshur told me he had no hopes of adjusting with the Brittish Minister)—make the position of Sec[retar]y of State a most responsible one. To be a component part of Tyler's administration, it appears to me will not do for you. You can with propriety at your time of life, and after your services hold but two situations[,] President of the U.S. or a U.S. Senator. Yet if the President will offer you the position of a special Minister Plenipotentiary to adjust our difficulties with England, and to treat with Texas, I think you might accept of it with propriety. And you might even take the place of Sec[retar]y of State pro: tem, to effect these objects, if it is understood that as soon as they are accomplished, you are to retire. A temporary connexion with the administration, for a particular great public purpose, will not be unbecoming of you. A permanent connexion as a regular part of the administration, would not be consistent with your present position in the Country.

I hear that [Henry] Clay is opposed to the admission of Texas—and also [Thomas H.] Benton—the latter I doubt; Upshur told me, that a Treaty could pass the Senate with ease. But if Clay takes ["a" *interlined*] decided stand against it, can it pass? I doubt it. But I also doubt, his taking any stand against it.

I have thus written to you frankly in consequence of the talk here. I wish what I have said to be rather the intimations of a freind [*sic*], than advice. You are far more capable of judging of the state of the Country, and your own duty than I can be. Believe me Yours very truly, R.B. Rhett.

ALS in ScCleA.

From W[ILLIA]M ANDERSON

Washington City, March 6, 1844
Dear Sir, You have been nominated to the Senate as Secretary of State, and ["no doubt" *canceled*] you ["will" *canceled*] have been unanimously confirmed, without reference [to committee].

Excuse me for introducing the expression of my opinion. The vast, the momentous interests of the country demanded the nomination and, in my humble judgment, imperatively calls [*sic*] for its favorable reception at your hands—at a crisis so awful, so full of the most important results. And omnipotent, all-wise Providence clearly appears to have carved out the way—inviting and urging you to accept it. Sir, those feelings of patriotism which I believe to exist in your bosom high above every consideration of self will I trust, induce you patiently to listen to me while I urge some of the mighty motives which accumuelate [*sic*] to support your acceptance of the office.

The country North, South, East & West will hail with an almost unanimous delight, your acceptance of this office at this most extraordinary juncture; the most momentous, in my view, that has existed since the 4th of July 1776. Does the country want peace, and does she want it on honorable terms; you, Sir, are the man who by your comprehensive views will most effectually of all men that the country furnishes, cooperate with the President [John Tyler] in the attainment of these great objects—and best advance the interests and reputation of the whole country.

You will carry with you into that Department a weight of character beyond what any other man that could be chosen for it ["would" *canceled*] from this vast confederated republic; and available to the best political interests of the nation. I cannot see how you can, consistently with your principles, forego the glorious opportunity. Consider the interests—the whole interests of that South (as well as of the other parts of the country) which you have ["it" *interlined*] now in your power, as it were unwillingly, and by most extraordinary providences—presented before you—to preserve and to advance to an immeasurable degree. No one can even with a semblance of plausibility charge upon you any other coalition than one of patriotic effort to maintain the true interests of the country. Your friends *know*, all upright and intelligent men believe—that you would accept the office only upon high public considerations. Suppose you were to refuse. The negotiation and all the vast relations over which, if you accept, you could exert a controlling influence would necessarily fall into less competent hands in that Department—less competent by reason of inferior ability and less competent by reason of deficiency in that commanding confidence which a vast majority of the country feels in your integrity and talents. Would you not then be justly answerable for any failure, any depression of Southern or other interests which your refusal might bring on in relation to Southern, and other national interests[?]

It would be a magnificent, sublime spectacle to see you engaged in this juncture in adjusting in a satisfactory manner the vast pending questions—involving as they do the universal interests of man, with which as you said in your noble speech on the Treaty, the relations of Great Britain and the United States were intimately interwoven. For this destiny I hope Providence designs you. I am, Sir, very respectfully Your Ob[edien]t Serv[an]t, Wm. Anderson.

ALS in ScCleA. NOTE: William Anderson was son and brother, respectively, of Joseph Anderson and Alexander O. Anderson, two former Senators from Tenn., and had been a Clerk in the 1st Comptroller's office of the Treasury Department since 1820.

From A[aron] V. Brown,
[Representative from Tenn.]

H[ouse] of Rep[resentatives,] March 6th 1844
Dear Sir, The news comes to us from the other end of the Capitol, that your name has been sent to the Senate as Secretary of State. You may well immagine the conversation that would spring up amongst your friends as to wheether [*sic*] you ought or would accept in the event of confirmation which no one doubts. I know you will excuse any thing I may say on this subject whatever your determination may be. I have not hesitated to say that as an appointment to meet a *great exigency,* you ought not to decline accepting not as *a permanent* acceptance but for & during such exigency. All this could be set right in your correspondence with the President. This *exigency* of course relates in part if not chiefly to the *Texan* & Oregon *questions,* besides some others having reference to our relations with Great Britain. Now every one knows precisely your views & opinions about Texas & the other question about fugi[ti]ves from Florida. As to the Oregon subject, you have no doubt noticed the strong *Western* anxiety that has been gotten up. Now if the course which you would feel at liberty to take with that subject—should be *in accordance* with this Western feeling—you could not fail to disarm your enemies, or some of them & largely increase the circle of your friends.

Much I think depends on this point & if your course would be one which would meet the state of Western feeling your acceptance could not fail to result in a manner gratif[y]ing to your friends[,] agreeable to yourself & of great importance to the country.

Now you will see that this is a hasty letter written in the bustle of business in the house. I will only add that from what I have learned & indeed know that the question about Texas is in a condition to take up your pen & go right on in drawing out the Treaty. In haste expecting no answer I remain yours &C, A.V. Brown.

ALS in ScCleA.

From Hu[gh] A. Haralson,
[Representative from Ga.]

Washington, 6th March 1844
My dear Sir, It is understood this morning that you will be nominated by the President to the Senate as Secretary of State. This must have

been done without any knowledge of yours since that office has been vacated now only six or seven days. It is therefore the more complimentary. That in the present crisis of our political affairs you should have been looked to as the proper individual to conduct our delicate foreign relations and negotiations is not a matter of surprise to your friends. Indeed there are those of us who believe that no other man could have been selected suited to this important period in our history. It is feared however that you may not be willing to quit the retirement of your own private family residence again to mingle in the strife of political life, especially, in discharging the duties of an office no way necessary to your fame. Perhaps you would even be subjecting your already well earned reputation to some Censure by doing so. But my dear Sir it will not be the first time that you have shown yourself willing to subject yourself to Censure for your Country[']s sake. The censure of the world will have no terrors to you when your Country's interest is at stake. Now that your Country[']s interest is at stake there is no doubt. Our delicate relations with Great Britain, Mexico & Texas—our own perhaps still more delicate domestic relations, require your aid in conducting them. Pardon me for taking the liberty I do. Nothing but considerations of patriotism could induce me to urge upon you the acceptance of this office. I have conferred with no man upon the subject—have only expressed the hope to your friends Mr. [Isaac E.] Ho[l]mes of S.C. and [Dixon H.] Lewis of Ala. that you would accept it. To you I now express the same. [*Illegible words altered to* "I trust"] that you will make the sacrifice—accept the appointment for your Country[']s sake and show to the world that you are *always John C. Calhoun.* Your friend (in haste), Hu. A. Haralson.

[P.S.] Since writing the above I understand your ["nomination" *interlined*] was unanimously confirmed by the Senate. I have also heard several of our Southern friends express their great pleasure ["at your nomination" *interlined*] and earnest hope that you would accept. ["It is the" *canceled.*]

ALS in ScCleA.

From I[saac] E. Holmes,
[Representative from S.C.]

Washington, March 6th [18]44

My Dear Sir, I wrote you yesterday [*not found*]. To day y[ou]r nomination has gone into the Senate. This step you may think premature. But—Let me say, I acknowledge *I* advised it with others. My reasons are—That it would be a just compliment to you—It w[oul]d shew, That, when the country was in danger, It naturally looked to its greatest man. It draws Cincin[n]atus from his Farm. It shews that no condition was attach'd. The Whigs & Democrats other than the [Thomas H.] Benton Democrats are delighted. Benton will no doubt *rage*. Nay—He will take ground ag[ai]nst Texas. For I learn'd that He was raising an opposition to the annexation upon the ground that it was a Calhoun measure. [Ephraim H.] Foster of Tennessee, who is a Whig Senator[,] told me that He rejoiced at the appointment. You will effectually defeat y[ou]r Enemies & gather around you y[ou]r ancient friends. Y[ou]r Enemies rejoiced at y[ou]r retirement. I know they thought that a great light would be hidden. I applied to you in a speech I made at Charleston—The lines of Gray— and in response to y[ou]r foes, ["Think ye, fond, Impious men" *canceled*] "Fond impious men, Think ye yon sanguine cloud, raised by ["thy" *canceled and* "your" *interlined*] breath can quench the *orb* of *Day*: Tomorrow, He repairs his Golden flood & warms the Nations with redoubled ray.["] Dear Sir, Don[']t falsify my prophesy—come and cheer us with redoubled rays. Sincerely & with respect Y[ou]rs Truly, I.E. Holmes.

ALS in ScCleA.

From DIXON H. LEWIS, [Representative from Ala.]

House of Rep[resentative]s, March 6th 1844
My Dear Sir, I have just heard in a manner, which leaves no room to doubt its correctness, that your name has been to day sent to the Senate, as the successor of Mr. [Abel P.] Upshur to the Office of Secretary of State, & that the name of John Y. Mason [*Marginal interpolation*: "some say James M. Mason of Winchester. Silas Wright has been offered the judgeship in the Supreme Court. He waits to accept, I *think*, until he finds whether you will."] of Virginia has also been sent in as the suc[c]essor of Mr. [Thomas W.] Gilmer in the Navy Department.

In effecting this result, your friends here have had no agency, and are in no way responsible. Many of them were unconsulted & entirely ignorant in relation ["to it," *interlined*] untill the rumour has this moment reached this House. Others have in reply to the general designation of your name to the station, expressed doubts whether you would accept it. So far as I know or believe none have solicited the place for you. In reply to frequent inquiries addressed to me, as to whether you would accept—(enquiries in some instances coming from those, who I supposed had the ear of Mr. [John] Tyler)—my uniform reply has been—that if it were a mere question of whether you would accept the office of Secretary of State under Mr. Tyler, I did not beleive you would accept of a station, which could confer no honour on you, and which would consume much of your time at an advanced age, which would not likely be requited either by an advancement of your own reputation, or the interests of the Country, but that if by the death of Mr. Upshur, & the state of the Texas & Oregon questions there was an exigency which required your services, I knew you too well to doubt that considerations of duty & patriotism would control you in this, as I believed it had on all other questions—and that at any personal sacrifice you would accept. This opinion so often expressed, contains my deliberate view not only of what you *will*, but what you *ought* to do in this matter. I am of course ignorant of the true state of both the above mentioned questions, but I take it for granted that Mr. Tyler will disclose to you fully their actual state. If I am not mistaken in my conjectures, the Texas question has already been reduced to a Treaty—waiting only to be submitted to, & receive the confirmation of the Senate. The opinion of *all* is, that the question is imminent, & in the present condition of the Country, to confirm a Treaty at all—& to do it under circumstances which will not involve us in a double war with ["Texas" *canceled and* "Mexico" *interlined*] & Great Britain—will be a most difficult matter. If the Treaty be rejected, I consider the Union at an end. It may not at once suffer absolute disruption, but the interests & sympathies of a large portion of the Union must be stronger in favour of an Union with Texas, than with a confederacy, which in the midst of unceasing plunder by Taxation, is waging a relentless war against their Institutions, & making those Institutions the avowed ground of objection to a political Union with those who in every other respect are, bone of our bone & flesh of our flesh.

In this veiw of the question in the opinion of all, it is important that the question should be under the charge of one having the confidence of every party both for intelligence & patriotism. I have taken some pains to ascertain the state of public feeling—and I am glad to say—that I have never seen stronger evidences of *complete unanimity* on any public question, than that, you are the man, & as most of them say, the only man to meet the crisis. The rumour of your nomination at once created here, a great stir. Men neglectful of business were talking about in groups. I left my seat to gather public opinion. I heard a general expression not only of approval but of satisfaction. Many in their anxiety urged me to write, & beg you to accept. [Representative William W.] Payne of Alabama, says "accept by all means, to meet a great crisis, but to base your acceptance on that crisis & to limit your acceptance to the crisis." I think your acceptance ought to be put on that high ground, & that your continuance though not strictly limited by it, ought not to ["be" *interlined*] much beyond the period you are actually & necessarily engaged in what all consider the *extraordinary* duties of the station. I take it for granted Tyler will give you a *carte blanche* as to the two great questions.

While writing [Francis P.] Blair [editor of the Washington *Globe*] has come to my seat & asked me good naturedly what I was doing. I answered that I was writing to you. He said he had come to beg me by all means to earnestly advise you to accept. He says he goes [to] his death for Texas & wants you to manage the matter—that you are the man, & that you have the confidence of all parties. He said further that by taking this position you would build up a reputation with the Democratic Party which would make you impregnable at another time. He evidently however betrayed a little anxiety, that in your position you should do nothing, to weaken & divide the Party, as he expressed it but which of course meant, to dislodge Mr. [Martin] Van Buren. I give you this for what it is worth. Dr. Martin is in ecstasy at your appointment—& comes to tell me that Joe Gales [that is, Joseph Gales, Jr., editor of the Washington *Daily National Intelligencer*] has just said to him, that the appointment meets his entire approbation. The Whigs all say so.

I have written this, to give you a better idea of the state of feeling. The Senate have just confirmed your appointment unanimously without referring it to a Committee. Every body is delighted & are expressing themselves so. The evidences are so strong it is needless for me to write more.

I must however say that this matter proves the truth of what I wrote you before this winter, that you have a strength & consideration in the Democratic Party which should prevent you from doing any act which would separate you from that Party. The extent of this feeling was never so obvious as now. Men are expressing ["themselves" *interlined*] without reserve & it is almost universal even among those whom party machinery have unwillingly united to Mr. Van Buren. The Leaders I have no doubt dislike you & dread you & this day has been a dark one to them—but of the Van Buren men as they are called numbering a *majority* of this House, I beleive that three fourths of them are more friendly to you than to him & if left free would rather run you as the Candidate. The other fourth are however so bitter that I beleive in no event could they be brought to support you—& therefore I am for not risking your name in a contest in which I fear a majority of the voters are already inclined to [Henry] Clay even if V[an] Buren's friends are wise enough to back out from him. Still I agree with the opinion expressed so often to day—that in the position you are about to occupy, you can place yourself in a position which will make you impregnable in 1848. It may be however that a ground swell from the people themselves growing out of the Texas question may roll you into the position of a Candidate. If so no one would be more delighted than myself, but I mean to say that no action in my opinion on the part of yourself or your friends ought now to look to that result. Let Van [Buren] run & be beaten as he *certainly* will & then the Party will be purified of him & his clique. Let them be forced to withdraw him & run an indifferent man & then his organization is destroyed & you must be the man four years hence.

These are my views given to you to cover every aspect of the question as to your acceptance. If the *occasion* calls for your services—accept. If not—decline but in any event look to the effect which your course may have on a popularity in the Democratic Party—which will at another time prove stronger than a corrupt Party organization which manacles your friends at present, but which has received its ["quiet"(?) *canceled*] death wound by your withdrawing from the Convention, & which will be doubly killed & damned by the certain defeat of V[an] Buren[,] [Thomas H.] Benton &c in the coming election. I am truly your friend, Dixon H. Lewis.

P.S. Enclosed is a letter from [Representative John A.] Mc-Lernard [*sic*; McClernand] of Illinois, who says, that he writes the sentiments of every member from that State except two & of four fifths of the Democracy of the State[;] yet they are all considered good V[an] Buren men. The Oregon question is one on which I beleive a deep feeling exists in the West. Benton's shams have some foundation in fact. The Oregon is a question now only second to the Texas Que[stion.]

P.S. [Robert Barnwell] Rhett showed me a letter from you on the Tariff. I am on the committee & have forced them to bring in a better tariff than Rhett hoped for. With the exception of sugar & Iron no duty to exceed 25 per cent ad valorem—& the *price abroad* the basis of valuation. I think 25 per cent with the foreign valuation exclusive of charges equal to 20 per cent with the home valuation. Many important articles of coarse woolens at 20 per cent. I think the Bill will be equal to the compromise [of 1833], except Iron & sugar on which we consent to yield to pass the Bill.

P.S. I think we will have a clause in our Tariff Bill which as a substitute for the warehousing system will be equal to a reduction of five per cent.

P.S. I beleive we will drive the Party into an earnest effort to pass the Tariff Bill, & we will be able to draw the lines so closely as to read any man out of our ranks who does not go for our Bill. All of our friends have consented to a relaxation on sugar & Iron—but our Report will go the whole length against Protection.

P.S. Make such avowals as will satisfy all you do not intend to mix the Presidency with your position. This is your *true* policy even if you were playing for the Presidency.

P.S. I have been scribbling this hastily written letter under constant interruptions since 1 o[']clock. My object has been to show you the *"res gesta,"* as it presents itself to me.

ALS in ScCleA; PEx in Jameson, ed., *Correspondence*, pp. 935–938.

From JOHN A. MCCLERNAND, [Representative from Ill.]

House of Representatives
Congress U.S., March 6th 1844
Dear Sir, Having studied your official Career with interest and edification, and having enjoyed the pleasure of an introduction to you, some years since, (which however is now no doubt forgotten by you) I have taken the liberty to address you a few lines upon the subject of your nomination to the State Department of the General Government of which I am advised this morning.

The foreign relations of this Government at this time are in some respects in a critical state. I refer to the questions of the Annexation of Texas, and the adjustment of the Controversy about Oregon. I believe the people of the West ["of" *canceled*] generally, and of Illinois ["in particular" *interlined*] are in favor of efficient and decided measures on the part of this Government, in relation to both.

Allow me to say, sir, that a prominent instrumentality on your part, in procuring the annexation of Texas, and the ejection of Great Britain from Oregon, together with your just and liberal course upon the subject of the public lands, would efficiently serve to fortify the favorable position you now occupy in the affections of the people of the West. Praying your forgiveness for intruding upon your notice with these suggestions, I subscribe myself, Your ob[e]d[ien]t Serv[an]t, John A. McClernand.

ALS in ScCleA. NOTE: McClernand (1812–1900), a native of Ky., was Representative from Ill. during 1843–1851 and 1859–1861 and Major General in the U.S. Army during the Civil War.

From GEO[RGE] McDUFFIE, [Senator from S.C.]

Washington, 6th March 1844

Dear Sir; Your ["nomiation"(?) *canceled*] nomination to the office of Secretary of ["State" *interlined*] has come in this morning, & I have no doubt will be unanimously confirmed before I close this letter. The whigs who consider the peace of the country jeoparded by the oregon question are anxious that you should accept & come on as soon as possible. Such was [Senator from Va. William S.] Archer's language to me, who will call up the nomination for immediate confirmation. The confirmation by the Senate will give this the character of a national call; & when we consider the public emergency, is a very high & flattering testimony of the public confidence.

Mr. [Walter T.] Colquit[t, Senator from Ga.] has just requested me to say that he strongly concurs with your other friends in urging your acceptance—½ past 3 o[']clock. Your nomination has just been unanimously confirmed. Sincerely yours, Geo: McDuffie.

ALS in ScCleA; PC in the Columbia, S.C., *State*, June 16, 1895.

From SAM[UE]L S. PHELPS, [Senator from Vt.]

Senate Chamber, March 6, 1844

Sir, Although a very humble member of the Senate of the U. States I have yet the good of our common country at heart—and although our political opinions have been antipodes that very circumstance induces me to address you in the present emergency. A tremendous calamity which had nearly carried me into eternity as it did better and more useful men has deprived the president [John Tyler] of two very worthy confidential advisers. The supplying of their places was and still is a matter of extreme anxiety to all. Your nomination to the office of Secretary of State relieved me and many if not all of my political friends from deep anxiety. The ready and harmonious confirmation of that appointment by the Senate is the most decisive proof to you of their cordial approval.

I can not presume to offer you my advice; but I may be permitted to express my own deep sense of the obligation resting upon you to consult in your acceptance or refusal of the appointment the common wish of all parties here and the political necessities of the country.

You are aware of the critical condition of the Origon question and of the the [*sic*] tremendous consequences which may follow an injudicious selection of the individual who shall conduct that negociation. Save us then if you can from indiscretion and folly and from a war engendered in national pride and of course bitter[,] relentless and in its spirit ["inte" *canceled*] and consequences interminable. Sir I will not enlarge on this subject—you apprehend the nature of the crisis better than I do. My object is to assure you that in the present emergency could you accept the office you will be sustained in your efforts which I doubt not would be sincerely and zealously made to extricate us from this embarrassing question by considerate and prudent men of all parties and especially of the [Whig] party to which I belong. Very respectfully Yours, Saml. S. Phelps.

ALS in ScCleA; variant PC in Boucher and Brooks, eds., *Correspondence*, pp. 212–213.

From ALBERT SMITH,
[former Representative from Maine]

Washington, Mar[ch] 6, 1844

My dear Sir, You have this moment been nominated for the State Department. In this present state of our Foreign relations it is of much importance, that you accept of this appointment. I have not heard, from any individual, of any party, a dissent from this opinion, & your *friends* are quite anxious that you should be at this metropolis. Most faithfully your friend, Albert Smith.

ALS in ScCleA. NOTE: Smith had been Representative from Maine during 1839–1841 and then had become a member of the Northeastern boundary commission.

From [President] JOHN TYLER, "Confidential"

Washington, March 6th 1844

My dear Sir, After a free and frank conversation with our friends, Governor [George] McDuffie and Mr. [Isaac E.] Holmes of South Carolina, and in full view of the important negociations now pending between us and foreign Governments, I have unhesitatingly nominated you this day as Secretary of State in place of my much lamented friend, Judge [Abel P.] Upshur. I have been prompted to this course by reference to your great talents and deservedly high standing with the Country at large. We have reached a great crisis in the condition of public affairs, which, I trust, will assume the place of a commanding epoch in our Country's history. The annexation of Texas to the Union, and the settlement of the Oregon question on a satisfactory basis, are the great ends to be accomplished: The first is in the act of completion and will admit of no delay. The last had but barely opened, when death snatched from me my lamented friend. Do I expect too much of you when I, along with others, anticipate at your hands, a ready acquiescence in meeting my wishes, by coming to the aid of the Country at this important period?

While your name was before the Country, as a prominent candidate for the Presidency, I could not have urged this request without committing alike an offence to yourself and many others; but now, since your friends have withdrawn your name from that exciting canvass, I feel it every way due to the Country to seek to avail myself, in the administration of public affairs, of your high and exalted talents.

I hope the action of the Senate will be as prompt as my own, and that you will immediately be at my side. John Tyler.

LS in ScCleA; PC in Jameson, ed., *Correspondence*, pp. 938–939.

From [President] JOHN TYLER

Washington, March 6, 1844

My D[ea]r Sir; I wrote you this morning a letter informing you of the circumstances which had led me to nominate you to the Senate ["as Secretary of State" *interlined*]. I now write to say that the Secretary of the Senate [Asbury Dickins] has this moment brought me the intelligence of your confirmation. Thus it is D[ea]r Sir, that the country unites with me in the call which I have made upon you. I may leave the rest to the promptings of your own patriotic feelings.

Be assured of my high regard. John Tyler.

ALS in ScCleA.

Commission of Calhoun as Secretary of State, Washington, 3/6. President John Tyler, "with the advice and consent of the Senate," appoints Calhoun to be Secretary of State. This document is signed by Tyler and John Nelson, Secretary of State *ad interim.* DS in ScCleA.

From FRANCIS WHARTON

Philadelphia, March 6th 1844

My dear Sir, It gives me much pleasure to see by your letter that the paper in the Democratic Review received your approbation. Very conscious am I of its inadequacy, and the only sure consolation I have is the belief that it will lead to the increased study of a volume [of your *Speeches*] which I consider to be the most important of the generation. Whatever I can do is at your command. If there is any service of which my pen is capable, tell me, and it will give me the sincerest pleasure to accomplish it. It may be enthusiasm, it may be something better, but I believe that I can render no better service to my country, next to the dissemination of the truth of the gospel, than by advocating the true republican principles in the only way in which they can successfully be advocated—through the person and under the guidance of a leader with whom they are identified.

I was very much struck with your letter on the Baltimore convention, as much with its consummate dignity, as with its irresistable [*sic*] force. It has cowed the Albany leaders in this city. Mr. [George M.?] Dallas, with whom I had a conversation immediately after its appearance, and who told me that ["the" *canceled and* "he" *interlined*] concurred with me in considering the speeches in the Harper volume as the models of senatorial eloquence, spoke as if a load had been removed from his mind, and intimated that now the only obstacle to a thorough reunion of the republican party in reference to the term which will succeed the next [*sic*]. The leaders here absolutely hate Mr. [Thomas H.] Benton. The old federalists, such as Mr. H[enry] D. Gilpin and Mr. [John K.] Kane, are Mr. [Martin] V[an] B[uren]'s only true friends, and even they are cold. It is to the *succession*—four years off, it is true, but still near, and of paramount interest—that the eyes of men are turned. To Mr. V[an] B[uren] will be awarded the compliment of a second defeat, and by that defeat the hermaphrodite school to which he belongs will be finally overwhelmed. Here, we will be up & doing. I shall write to you again on the subject of a system of primary agitation. ["among" *canceled and* "The" *interlined*] most of the young men here are determined opponents of V[an] Burenism in either of its phases. I only fear that the [Henry] Clay enthusiasm may lap up from our ranks a few who will find it difficult to get back.

Let me repeat, that if in any way my pen can be useful to you, you have only to command me. Yours with great respect, Francis Wharton.

ALS in ScCleA.

From C[HARLES] A. WICKLIFFE, [Postmaster General]

Washington, ["Feb." *canceled*] Mar[ch] 6 1844 D[ea]r Sir, I urged the President [John Tyler] to your appointment as Sec[retar]y of State. I did this without knowing whether you would accept. But sir I believe you to be a patriot and how can you refuse your services to your country at this time. Remember the Texas and Oregon questions. Mind what I say to you[,] the Texas question overrides all others, and I will not allow myself (under the belief that you are out of the Presidential race) to think for one moment that you will refuse to aid us. Give me Texas and I care not who may dispense the patronage of this government for four years we have our union safe and we can then say to these intermed[d]lers of the north Stand back. I will say no more. Your friend, C.A. Wickliffe.

ALS in ScCleA.

From EDWARD J. BLACK, [Representative from Ga.]

House [of] Representatives, March 7th 1844 My dear Sir—Yesterday Mr. [John] Tyler sent your name to the Senate as Sec[retar]y of State, and it is understood here that you were instantly Confirmed, unanimously. This Certainly is a high Compliment to you personally, to your principles, and your friends. For myself, individually, I hope you will accept the office—not that it is necessary to your fame as a man, a patriot, or Statesman—but for the sake of the Country. I beleive that the ultimate prosperity—perhaps the very existence, of the South depends in a great degree upon the measures to be adopted during this year by this government towards the republic of Texas. Of course these measures must depend almost wholly upon the incumbent of the State department. It will give you, too, an opportunity of confirming all we have said of your abilities of administration, and to reform any errors you may, & doubtless will, find there. If you were Secretary of State Mr. [Henry L.] El[l]sworth would promulgate no more high protective Tariff doctrines through the medium of his "patent reports," and the country at large would feel safe in its foreign relations. Last, but not least, you would be *here*; *with us*. During all this winter your friends, in this City, have acted without ["without" *canceled*] preconcert. If we have agreed in our public demonstrations it was only by the ["cohesive prin" *changed to* "cohesion of"] our common principles. There was ["was" *canceled*], & is, no Chief among us—and while we would maintain our individual equality, we yet have Certainly felt the want of that Concert which, perhaps, your your [*sic*] presence alone could produce among us.

Pardon me for these crude & hasty suggestions—they are prompted by the interest ["the interest" *canceled*] I take in your prosperity, and success; and are submitted, ["with" *canceled*] only as my reflections, to your better Judgment.

The universal hope here is that you will Come. The government is without character—and your presence ["this" *canceled*] will elevate it, and make it of high consideration, at home and abroad. Your acceptance would be regarded as a special mission for the good of your Country. This want of Character is attributed to the present administration by the ultra Whigs, & [Martin] Van B[uren] Democrats— while many others, among whom I profess to be one, regard Mr. Tyler as an honest man—disposed to do right, & peculiarly fitted, Just at this time, by the circumstances which surround & control him, to be made the recipient of ["Just" *canceled*] such advice as your friends believe you would give him. I write this in great haste in a Confused House. Very Truly, Your friend, Edward J: Black.

ALS in ScCleA; variant PC in Boucher and Brooks, eds., *Correspondence*, pp. 213–214.

From JOHN J. FLOURNOY

Wellington, (Athens P[ost] O[ffice]) [Ga.,] March 7 1844
Hon[ora]ble Sir: You would doubtless excuse this epistolary communication of one, utterly, (by *audit*) insensible to all but the loudest
sounds—who by no means can converse by oral discourse, except only
to the degree of his understanding labial motions—and your cognizance of his deafness will not, ["I" *canceled and* "he" *interlined*]
hopes, have any detracting influence on whenever truth he may be
fortunate enough to convey to your perception. A deaf man by continued experience, I know, the world regards as a *natural inferior*, and
men are unwilling that he should presume to instruct or advise *them*.
His place they think is in natural obscurity, in perpetual privacy; and
every effort he makes to take a philosophic survey of things, or to
speak with the authority of one, they regard as want of modesty and
bold assumption, and if he ever offer to enter any career of usefulness,
they instantly repel him into the Shades of private life, with the indignation of offended pride!

Thus thought of by the world, particular and at large, remote and
near, I should quietly regard myself as belonging to the inert mass of
["the" *canceled*] animal life—should drop forever the pen and resign
myself to the slumbers of a nullity of all effort to do good in my day
and generation, or only exercise whatever power of body or spirit I
have in the operations of a secular economy. But I thank God I am
above such ignorant supineness. I know the superiority of mind to
matter, and notwithstanding bodily imperfection, will exercise the
powers of the soul. I know also that popular ignorance and perversion, are the parents of their prejudice against me, and I should be a
son purely of folly only, were I to encourage them in their dismal infatuation against me. In the eye of Religion not of their Preachers—
but of God himself, they are only dead in sin and blindness, and shall
I succumb to the degrading ["attitude" *canceled*] attitude of throwing myself a way to suit the confounded ideas of such blind Sinners?
No Sir, Philosophy the handmaid of Religion, tells me, too, that men
must be effectually checked in their own perversions and follies or
their Liberties can never stand the shocks of time, or ["the" *canceled*]
endure the alembic of that experiment upon which all original freedom had to be founded.

In addressing myself to you I believe I am addressing one who has
the superior wisdom to overlook corporal defects and to listen to
truth from whencesoever it comes.

Already in advising you of how the popular will treats me, I exhibit the growing depravity of our people. If they be no better than this and such like—they do not deserve to be freemen, and I am sure but regret it, will not long continue to be. The best moral and political Philosophers in every age from that of the Immortal Socrates to that of Dr. Thomas Cooper late of Columbia S.C., have put the duration of Liberty upon popular virtue, and that, too, not alone politically, but socially or personally. The public itself has to be strictly just and wise—if the independence of the Republic is to continue. But the people in private life are grossly unjust to one another, malice occupying almost the thoughts of every man—and their wisdom is at so low an ebb, that they yes, this wretched people of America! cannot but insult any one who offers to do them a service, as if they would alter the Laws of natural integrity and constitute Deafness a crime! If "straws show which way the wind blows"—these indications are certainly straws of no ordinary magnitude, And Socrates and Dr. Cooper, and the vicissitudes of Republics being Judge, our Liberty cannot last a full century at any rate—unless some reform greater and deeper than a mere Presidential Change be interposed among or *upon* this people!

There are errors enough left in our structure of General and State Governments, which at the outset the wisest minds of our fathers, amid the multiplicity of their arrangements in the Constitution, could not discern. They made the structure as free as it were possible for the Genius of Thomas Jefferson, aided by James Madison to conceive, but then the country is left a prey for Demagogues. A constitution with Madison for its master spirit, was framed upon the most philanthropic scheme benevolence could actuate—yet that instrument itself is the ultimatum only of the most variant and irritable interpretations that construing pragmatists, could invent! ! !

While touching on the Constitution and apparently speaking from its *horns*, a hundred parties are formed in this country, or at least two obstinate constructives—*making destruction with their constructions*—embittering too by a thousand heartless Editors of perverse papers, the public heart and confusing its mind, the private people themselves are agreeing upon nothing with so hearty a good will, as in the strength of their mutual hatred. I mean not party or political ["hatred" *canceled*] but personal hatred. The fracas and murders constantly happening in our country tells the dreadful tale too much plainer than I.

Well then Sir, this is our *country* and these our *countrymen*. What must be done to remedy evils, not only constitutional in the Government, but *constitutional* in the people, themselves? In vain can statesmen ["by" *interlined*] regulating systems, or cutting down political or commercial errors, or designs, arrive at the established point, after which improvements be no longer vitally necessary. A vitiated people will despatch vicious men to Congress, or place them in power—and men thus malignant, mercenary, soulless in the exercise of prerogatives, would not consult either the parchment of the Constitution or the popular welfare. The compact of the Union under such auspices is a dead instrument—is kick[e]d into the fire—during the period of their reign—and if at every recurring Election a morbid people reelect them, or men still of their *kidney*, the transmutation of the Republic into a Despotism would be effected by insensible graduations, until the change become complete, by the exertion of the people's will against themselves. The effort to restore the original purity of the civil establishment, or to renovate the soul of Liberty, would as has been the result wherever such an effort was made in other Empires be attended with civil feuds. The restoration itself if successful has to be thro' a virtual Revolution!

I almost Despair of the Republic. Liberty does not seem to be natural to man—(for nature by the fall from Eden is polluted—there is no health in nature until God helps!—) but she is a boon from On High—and to prolong her stay mankind, whenever she lights among them, have to be virtuous, honest, *peaceable*, pious and attendent, on and observant to conform to the Divine Will. God is the source the centre of all Good—and Liberty is the good *"let alone* policy" of philanthropy. She therefore must only exist by connection of men with the Eternal. Not otherwise.

Look at the Nations that have risen and fallen, and that yet continue with tower and spire to catch the tints of the rising sun. Which of them have come down to the 19th century with the unbroken radiance of freedom—["not on" *canceled*] from immemorial time? Not one—all former Republics are sunk or faded with the times that produced them. Which of them founded as a monarchy in the first ages, have continued to this day to exhibit the Colossal Sceptre of Royal Dominion?—there is China—There are Persia and Great Britain, herself. Republics altho' that of Rome existed 500 years are rather short liv[e]d. Monarchy seems to be the legitimate and settled order of Government. If duration be the test of legitimacy ["they" *canceled and* "it" *interlined*] alone is legitimate. But Philosophy and the Bible teaches us that so far from being legitimate by the ordination of the fitness of things or by Heaven's will, the Royal System is an upstart of the perverted human will—and has been continued only by the natural wickedness of men. Monarchy is the natural ["state" *in-*

terlined] of the world, as it is in Sin—in the fallen state. But sin itself is not legitimate, of course; then its system of Government cannot be—altho by settling down to the natural state of folly, like a sediment, a Government may exist under despotism. A Republic on the contrary is an elevated attitude of men, a benevolent guaranty to all of their just Rights—and it has not been maintained, because Liberty cannot live in a vicious atmosphere like ["the" *interlined*] Absolutism of the human will. Freedom supposes a superior order of things and men actuated by better and holier resolves. So long as men be thus actuated the freedom of the Land will remain—but when men decline from the severe virtues necessary to propitiate and perpetuate the Heavenly principle upon Earth, that principle will return to the God who gave it, and leave us amid the natural consequences of that stable and settled system which acknowledges one mortal or a few as better than all the world besides! A system too which has been always till of late years, or since the French Revolution the fruitful parent of discord, and of the wars that have from time to time marked their bloody courses of desolations over the face of this globe. Even our wars, that of the Revolution and the last, accrued from the arbitrary exertions of Monarchy against our Country. The Napoleonian contests had their basis in Europe in the same systems—he fought to make himself Emperor. It was the same actuating principle—Kingly rage or ambition. Excepting the Crusades, the Ancient Conquests of Rome, and some civil wars in Greece—excepting these alone and the ["petty" *interlined*] Indian wars of our Republic—Monarchy has been the cause of all war.

Thus we perceive how inestimable is Liberty—how legitimate and Divine! But our people are, amid their mercenary operations and political favoritisms, forgetting the principles upon which ["their" *changed to* "the"] continuance of freedom can depend. They are gradually becoming a wild, a licentious and rabid race—unmindful as individuals of any ["corn" *canceled*] concern but money getting and forgetful of every other principle but their own petty, but ["destructive" *canceled*] mutually destructive malignancies. Such a people cannot ensure Liberty to themselves, they will force her out of the Land. They will but banish her one day by these exe[c]rable irregularities. Then what shall continue true in civil Government, but that ancient dogma that *"Man is incapable of self government"*! [To] a patriot like yourself whose endea[v]ours have been directed to equal and exact justice between all parts of the Republic—such a state of things cannot but be mortifying and full of desponding reflections. Meditations on this subject will ever be melancholy, until some great movement be made to animate the grand masses of our people as Individuals, to a lively sense of their duties and responsibilities, and their majesty as Sovereigns, to whose keeping and upon whose votes are committed the welfare, or the peril of centuries yet to come.

In a nother Letter I would do myself the honour of suggesting some remedies which I cannot ["beut" *canceled*] but believe may be conservative if they could be applied. Having weighty arguments to lay before you, I could not abbreviate them—as I went on, and altho intending to have written but one letter, like many others, I found a second one necessary to clearly express my mind—for which intrusion I hope your pardon. Very Respectfully Hon[orable?] Sir Your Very obedient humble Servant, John J. Flournoy.

ALS in ScCleA.

From DAVID HALE, "Editor [of the] Journal of Commerce"

New York [City,] March 7 1844

D[ea]r Sir, I trust you will pardon me for expressing to you my own feelings and the feelings which have been excited in this city by the announcement of your appointment as Secretary of State. It has sent a thrill of joy through the community and those whose party prejudices have made them in general your decided opponents, speak in terms of the warmest gratific[ation] that the country may hope for your help in a time when some master mind is evidently wanted to inspire confidence in the administration. I have hardly ever witnessed so strong and unanimous an expression of real regard. You know sir as well as any man how changable [*sic*] is public favor, yet it is a gratification to your friends to perceive that whatever party interests may put on externally, the real opinion of the people does you some justice, and is a basis upon which you ma[y; *mutilation; one word missing*] in resuming the responsibilities of office. In no case has our country more distinctly called for the aid of any distinguished citizen and never ["have" *altered to* "has"] it been more distinctly felt that the obligation would be more entirely on her side. Pardon me for adding to the thousands who will press upon you, my wish that you will not deny the unanimous request of the nation. I am Sir yours very truly, David Hale, Editor[,] Journal of Commerce.

ALS in ScCleA. NOTE: An AEU by Calhoun reads "David Hale." This letter was franked and forwarded from Washington by R[obert] B[arnwell] Rhett.

From R[OBERT] B[ARNWELL] RHETT,
[Representative from S.C.]

[Washington, *ca.* March 7, 1844]
My Dear Sir, It certainly appears here that your friends are pretty unanimous ([Armistead] Burt and [Dixon H.] Lewis included), that you should accept of the appointment of Sec[retar]y of State. The manner in the Senate, of confirming your nomination, was highly gratifying, and the Whigs and Democrats both seem to desire your acceptance[?]. I think it proper to advise you of the state of opinion & feeling with respect to you in this matter.

I understand that the power to make a treaty with Texas, is expected daily. The Minister [Isaac Van Zandt] informs me, that on receiving his communication, informing them that a Treaty would pass ["the" *canceled and* "our" *interlined*] Senate, the Congress of Texas unanimously passed Resolutions of instruction directing the President [Samuel] Houston to forward the necessary power. He also stated to me that preliminary conditions had been forwarded which had been assented to by [Abel P.] Upshur. Yours truly, R.B. Rhett.

ALS in ScCleA. NOTE: This letter is dated only by its postmark.

From J[ACOB] THOMPSON,
[Representative from Miss.]

House of Rep[resentative]s, March 7, 1844
Dear Sir, I wrote you on yesterday but failed to get my ["letter" *interlined*] to the office before the closing of the southern mail.

Your nomination by the President [John Tyler] to the office of Secretary of State and the complimentary promptness with which the nomination was confirmed by the Senate, was very gratifying to all of your friends. All parties are now eager to learn what course you will pursue, and all seem as anxious that you should accept the office. The feeling on all sides is that the emergency demands of you to make some sacrifice for your country. Every body has higher hopes and greater confidence that the honor and true interests of the country will be maintained should you undertake this high charge. The Texas & Oregon questions must be met and you are the man for the occasion. Under your lead, we feel confident of an honorable termination to these most exciting and most embarrassing questions.

Let me then with that kind feeling which you know I entertain for you and for [your] future name urge you to accept this station. Providence has afflicted a grievous calamity upon the country, by which this vacancy has been made and it would be a great relief to the whole people of the United States, to know that thereby you had been called from your retirement and induced to ["give" *canceled*] take an important part in guiding the ship of state in the difficult passes through which she is now ["passing" *canceled and* "running" *interlined*]. I hope you will lay aside your private interests and again sacrifice your personal ease and take charge of this office so freely and so unexpectedly offered to you. The Country will never forget her faithful & patriotic citizens. With high regard Your Ob[e]d[ien]t Ser[van]t, J. Thompson.

[P.S.] This morning both the Globe & Intelligencer express their gratification at your nomination.

ALS in ScCleA.

By an UNKNOWN PERSON, "For the Madisonian"

Washington, March 7: 1844

Mr. Editor, I heard a speech of one hour this morning in the H[ouse] of R[epresentatives] by Mr. Bun Kum (alias [Thomas L.] Clingman of N.C.) in reply to a previous speech as stated by the gentleman ["from" *canceled and* "made by" *interlined*] Dr. [Alexander] Duncan of Ohio ["made" *interlined and then canceled*] professedly (by the Dr.) to Bun Kum. Among all the ramblings and girations [*sic*] of the Representative of Bun Kum, he told how terribly the Democracy were to be beaten at the next election ["under any leader" *interlined*] by a gentleman whose qualities he enumerated, and whom he ultimately named Henry Clay. He said among other things to make him what he wished his hearers to believe him to be, that he was one of the *first advocates of the last war*, and carried away by the belief that the picture he had drawn of the man was true, he said "he had never forsaken a friend or fled a foe." Now Mr. Editor all this very easy to talk [*sic*] but let us see how it quadrates with the facts. On a certain [day] in 1842 [*sic*; possibly 1841] I was witness of proceedings in the Senate of the U.S. to the following effect. The [Alexander] McLeod question was under discussion. Mr. Clay in speaking upon it declared the matter a "mere baggatelle" and scouted the idea of the

Senate gravely ent[ert]aining it for a moment, saying he did not take the position he did from any fear of a collision with Great Britain. He trusted his whole life would absolve him any suspicion on that head. He could appeal as proof to his course in relation to the last war, and there was one *gentleman present* who who [*sic*] could bear testimony to that course."

When Mr. Clay had finished his remarks Mr. Calhoun arose and said: that upon the question he was decidedly opposed to the position assumed by the gentleman from Kentucky, and went to declare his sentiments that the destruction of the Caroline was a wanton outrage upon the law of nations—that the acknowledgement or assumption of the act after the fact was no sanctification—that it only made two culprits instead of one, the first McLeod by the act and the government accessory by adoption if we put a strict construction upon it. He said suppose this McLeod had come into Charleston and commenced tampering with their Negroes inducing them to treason and rebellion, would we not have hung him up under the State Law. It need not be supposed that if England, just as we had got ready to execute the culprit under sentence, would be permitted [to] assume the act as a national act and thereby procure his liberty. No Mr. Speaker we would have ["him" *erased and* "punished" *interlined*] him under the State law and if Great Britain felt aggrieved she could have sought her redress. But ["he" *interlined*] continued I am called upon, I presume so, at least, for I am the only person in this Senate who was in the H[ouse] of R[epresentatives] with the Senator from Kentucky at the declaration of the last war [in 1812] (Mr. Calhoun paused) I perceive I am the witness. I am extremely thankful Mr. Speaker for this opportunity, the first which has presented itself in the long time which has elapsed of correcting the impressions which have widely obtained in relation to the active person in that declaration—and before I can give such testimony as has been called for, or I am able to give, I will ask the Senator from Kentucky the favor of answering me two questions—they are these—

1st Did not he, the Senator from Kentucky on the night the Declaration of war was, the House with closed doors, come down from the Speaker's Chair which he held, and speak from 9 o'clock P.M. untill 11 o[']clock *against* the Declaration?

2d Did I not reply to him from 11 o[']clock P.M. until 3 o'clock A.M. and on the conclusion of my speech was not the vote taken and war declared?

Mr. Calhoun here paused. Mr. Clay sat still, silent. Mr. Calhoun said, I am answered. I will now do that justice which the gentleman desires—by bearing testimony as I have on all occasions, to ["the" *canceled and* "his" *interlined*] able and efficient services in sustaining the country *after the Declaration.*

As to the other assertion of Mr. Bun Kum in regard to Mr. C[lay]'s fidelity to friends and effrontery to foes, I refer him to that small transaction of Mr. [John Quincy] Adam[s]'s election, his ["opposition to" *canceled*] speech in opposition to the United [States] Bank, before his change, and lastly, I should like to when [*sic*] he answered the published charges of one Mr. [William L.] Brent a former confidential friend and associate, made in the newspapers far and wide in 1842.

ALU in ScCleA. NOTE: John B. Jones was editor of the Washington, D.C., *Madisonian* at this time. This document was probably sent to Calhoun and apparently was never published.

From JAMES M. BUCHANAN

Balt[imore,] March 8th 1844

My Dear Sir, Classing myself among the most ardent though perhaps among the most humble of your friends I trust you will not be offended if I add my feeble voice to that of the whole nation and beseech of you to accept of the appointment recently offered to you.

I know it can add nothing to your already exalted character but it may put you in a situation to render the most important services to the Country. I am with the highest regard and respect Your fr[ie]nd, James M. Buchanan.

ALS in ScCleA.

To T[HOMAS] G. CLEMSON, "Oakland (P.O.)," Edgefield District, S.C.

Fort Hill, 8th Feb. [*sic*; March] 1844

My dear Sir, The mail of Sunday [3/3] brought me yours of the 11th Feb: & Anna's [Anna Maria Calhoun Clemson's] of the 19th, long subsequent to the receipt of the two preceding of the 19th, & even subsequent to that of the 28th.

On the receipt of the last, I dispatched a note to Mr. [James]

Laurence, and requested him to call on me in reference to Bill. He called day before yesterday, and at my request, [*one word or partial word canceled*] in order to avoid mistakes, he wrote me the enclosed note, containing his terms. You will see, that he has risen to $600 cash, and that if it is not accepted, he requests that you should give him a pass to return home.

I stated to him that your understanding was, that there was a positive trade between you ["and him" *interlined*] & that you were to have him at $556 on a year's credit. This he denies, as you will see by his note. He said that he has made up his mind about the price, and that he will take nothing less; that he was offered that sum in cash for him in Hamburgh lately, & that he could dispose of him for a much larger sum, and would do so, were he not disposed to accommodate Bill. I said to him, that he might ["not" *interlined*] come if a pass was given him, and ["asked him" *interlined*] what was to be done with him in that case? He said he had no doubt he would come; but ["I" *interlined*] understood ["him" *interlined*], if he did not he would fetch him.

You have now all the facts, and can better decide what you ought to do, than I can advise you. The price is very high; but you can by this time judge from what you have seen of him, whether, under circumstances, you had better give it or not. As to standing a suit on what you regard as the original bargain, I would by no means advise it, unless your proof is strong. Other testimony would be required, you know, than your own recollection. In fact, I would hardly advise it, with any proof; for it would cost you, probably, in the long run a sum equal to the difference, besides the vexation. If you should give him a pass, & he should refuse to return, I would advise you to inform Mr. Laurence of the fact without delay. It might otherwise subject you to improper imputations, & be construed in addition, ["in addition" *canceled*] to an implied assent to take him at the $600.

You must have had a great deal ["of" *interlined and then canceled*; "trouble &" *canceled and* "of" *interlined*] difficulty & trouble in commencing your settlement. I hope the worst has passed, and that you will find every day less & less. The country must be singularly destitute of means. I am distressed to think, that you have found it so hard to get ordinary supplies. If I had supposed it possible, I would have insisted on you to take down some milch cows at least. We have turned out four or five, rather than to feed them. If I had now an opportunity, I would sen[d] two or three, as inferior as they are, & liable to die by the distemper by going below.

We will let you have what hams & shoulders we can spare. I hope it will be sufficient for your family use. I know of no opportunity, however, by which they can be sent. If you should know of any let me know.

I know of no other way by which you can get the mail route of which you speak, except by petition on the part of those interested; the Villagers of Edgefield, & Newberry and the citizens along the route. The petition should be ["sent" *canceled*] in duplicate; one for your member, Mr. [Armistead] Burt, & the other to Mr. [George] McDuffie [Representative and Senator from S.C., respectively]. They should be addressed to Congress, & their attention requested by private letters.

I am doing much to put my place in order. The substantial outside fence has added much to its appearance, & the two division fences, ["through" *canceled*] one up to fort Hill, & the other through the big bottom will add still more. I have made many other improvements. When all are finished, the place will really look well.

Tell Anna, I will answer her letter shortly. I am happy to hear the children [John Calhoun Clemson and Floride Elizabeth Clemson] have been so well & look so hearty. Tell Calhoun he must not forget Grandfaddy [*sic*], & kiss both for me. Love to Anna. Your affectionate father, J.C. Calhoun.

[P.S.] Jack's family & himself have not been yet sold. I find you expect Mr. Miller to take you down a supply of corn. I infer from what Mr. Fredericks heard him say, that he did not understand that there was any definitive arrangement between you. I mention it as you might otherwise be disappointed. J.C.C.

ALS in ScCleA.

From R[OBERT] M. T. HUNTER

[Lloyds, Va.,] Friday, March 8th 1844
My dear Sir, I never was more gratified than at the receipt of your last letter. Not that I doubted the propriety and policy of our course but I feared least [*sic*] at that distance you might not understand all the circumstances under which we acted. You are satisfied and we can now carry out our plans in Virginia with zeal and certainty[?]. We will give you this State next time. I have heard [Martin] V[an] Buren men (some from whom I did not expect it) say that the party

would be forever disgraced if it did not nominate you next time. The difficulty which you suggest as to our men on the electoral [college] ticket I foresaw and still feel. But I believe we can manage it. We came to the determination in Richmond before we parted to conduct the canvass on our own grounds and not to defend palpable delinquencies. The resolutions passed in Richmond offer an admirable platform ["upon" *interlined*] which we will endeavor to place every Democratic association in the State. We have other plans ["of" *canceled*] which I will develop hereafter. Our friends write me that I shall have to take a hand. I shall do so cautiously you may be sure and with an eye to our *ultimate object.* I believe I did not communicate to you the fact that our friends in their meeting passed a resolution to run you without regard to a convention for the next term and to take measures to announce you as soon as the present canvass is over[?]. [William O.] Goode [former Representative from Va.] and I said nothing against it, but we concluded that we ought to be guided by what might seem at the time ["the" *canceled*] to be best calculated for ensuring the election. ["The" *canceled.*] We therefore thought it was well ["to get them" *canceled*] for them to pledge themselves but not to publish it so ["soon"(?) *changed to* "long"] beforehand. Your friends here will be ripe for starting you next winter should it be deemed adviseable and are now in position to run you despite all conventions. We have secured that by our course. We have done more[;] we have ["made our course" *canceled*] so shaped our course and address as to throw the whole merit of the sacrifice on you. We have treated it as the natural result of your letter, it is so esteemed by the Democracy in this State and will be so esteemed elsewhere and you are acquiring more of their sympathies by it.

You may rely upon it that V[an] B[uren] will now do his best to get his Northern friends to mould [*sic*] their measures to suit you. Whilst he feared a Republican rival in the South he endeavored to enlarge the basis of his strength in the Free States, now that this fear is removed he will (if in his power) take a course to conciliate the South. *Of his dispositions* I was convinced in Richmond. I wrote to [Franklin H.] Elmore immediately upon my return from Richmond explaining our course and begging him to keep up the Calhoun organization in the South as far as possible and also if he could do it conscientiously to sustain our address. I have received no answer. You have a gallant set of friends ["in" *canceled and* "amongst" *interlined*] the rising generation in this State. Your life and speeches ["sale" *canceled*] are sold at our universities faster than they can be supplied. Some weeks since one was set up at an auction of a dead man[']s effects and the students ran it up to three or four times the bookstore price.

I got strange news from Washington this evening. You are nominated and confirmed Secretary of State. There[?] the Intelligencer compliments the appointment. I enclose you [Henry A.] Wise's letter. It is a subject upon which I am not sufficiently informed to advise. What his reasons are I know not. I imagine they are connected with Texas. The Oregon question I fear is more difficult than it is supposed to be. The British will agree to no treaty which [Thomas H.] Benton will not attack and plausibly I fear. [John] Tyler too may be obstinate. But you are the best judge and perhaps if I knew the whole ground I should think it wise and politic for you to accept. The state of feeling in Washington would seem to indicate that the acceptance would be popular and perhaps a necessary act of patriotism. But I am uninformed and as I said before inept to advise. I have so much faith in your powers ["to surmount difficulties" *interlined*] that I shall have not much fear if you accept. Still I feel apprehensive of every move which might impair in the least your strength. We mean to make you president next time, and if we manage this old commonwealth by next ["winter" *canceled and* "fall" *interlined*] as we hope to do, our friends further South must not only cease their croaking but give us help. We are in the right line.

I send you Wise[']s letter. He evidently thinks it a great move for you. How I do not exactly perceive. Most truly your friend, R.M.T. Hunter.

P.S. Our poor friend [Virgil] Maxcy was one of the sufferers in the Princeton as you have seen. I suspect he had letters from you which ought to be returned. His sons in law are Whigs.

[Enclosure]

Henry A. Wise to R[obert] M.T. Hunter

Washington, March 7th 1844

My dear Hunter, As soon as [Abel P.] Upshur was killed I turned at once to Mr. Calhoun. I advised with Gen[era]l [George] McDuffie who said he thought he ought to & would accept the State Departm[en]t. I went forthwith to the Pres[iden]t who most promptly & generously towards Mr. C[alhoun] nominated him to-day and the Senate confirmed his nomination immediately. Let me congratulate you, and ask you at once to write to him & urge him to accept. I have'nt time to give you the reasons why—the mail is closing—you *must* act as I ask instantly, for reasons the most *imperative*. I leave

here friday. Ever yours, Henry A. Wise [Representative from Va.].
[Marginal P.S.] I have written to Mr. C[alhoun] & am told the
whole S.C. delegation have a joint letter.

ALS with En in ScCleA.

From R[OMULUS] M. SAUNDERS,
[Representative from N.C.]

Washington, March 8, [18]44
My dear Sir, Altho' your friends have entire confidence in your own
discretion as to what you ought to do in the highly delicate situation
in which you have been placed—still I suppose you will be glad to
have the opinions of those, who are entitled to respect. With this
view I enclose the letter of Mr. Louis McLane. He expresses the
public sentiment—as to the wish that you should accept. But whether
you will do so or not, will depend on the fact, whether or not you
shall believe you can do the public any service—of this you will be the
best judge after being advised of the true state of the pending questions. Of course we are all anxious on the matter of Texas. How
would it do for you to come here before you decide? As to what Mr.
McLane says about the navy, I presume that is disposed of—at all
events after what has transpired, I could not accept of it, unless I
knew that you would *certainly* come in & then with the view of
sustaining you. I fear Mr. McL[ane]'s suspicions of the Attorney
General [John Nelson] are but too well founded—atleast[?] it is
proper for you to be put on your guard. For I regret to say we have
found too many, who have proved themselves but politicians in the
recent transactions.

We shall wait with much anxiety to hear your decision. Very truly
y[ou]rs, R.M. Saunders.
[Enclosure]
L[ouis] McL[ane] to "Gen[era]l" [Romulus M.] Saunders
Baltimore, March 7, 1844
My dear Sir, I am sincerely gratified at the appointment of Mr. Calhoun; and I have no idea that he will fail to see the advantage of the
position assigned him both for the Country & himself. The President
deserves more credit for the sagacity of this act, than for any other,
or all the others of his administration. The appointment will com-

mand universal confidence, and this with the probity, no less than the intellect of Mr. C[alhoun] will give new power to the adm[inistratio]n and to the result of the negotiation. It ought ["to" *canceled*] at once to place Mr. C. at the head of all that is valuable in the old Dem[ocratic] party, and give us once more a rallying point; if not for the present, certainly for the future. It may now be hoped that out of that appalling disaster, from which I confess I have not recovered, an inscrutable, but all wise, *God* will be pleased to bring good for the Country.

Now, my dear Sir, if you could be called to the vacancy in the Navy, my wishes would be fully gratified. And why should it not be so? Will not Mr. Calhoun have something to say on that head? Certainly; & then can there be any doubt that he would prefer a friend to a man of doubtful politics?

Now, in addition to what I have here said, one purpose of my writing this letter is, in strict confidence, to put you on your guard & to request you to put Mr. C[alhoun] on his guard, respecting the present Attorney General [John Nelson]. Mr. C[alhoun] ought to know that he is not only not his friend, but an enemy as efficient as such a man can be. Watch him well—for I tell you his conceit is not his worst quality, as I have had reason more than once to know. If Mr. C[alhoun] do[es] not understand him, he ought to do so, without much delay. Believe me most sincerely y[ou]r friend, L. McL.

ALS with En in ScCleA. Note: McLane was a former Senator from Del., Secretary of State and Treasury, and Minister to Great Britain.

From FRANCIS WHARTON

Philadelphia, March 8th, 1844
My dear Sir, The news of your appointment & confirmation as Secretary of State has just reached Philadelphia, and I am going to take the liberty of telling you that the hope & trust of your friends in this section of the country is that you should accept the appointment. Independently of the conviction that no other than a master mind can adjust the Oregon negotiation, that such a labour requires the whole of that great intellect which can only be found in two men in the country of whom you are one, that there is but one man who can unite to such an intellect a character which precludes the supposition of fear, favour, & affection, & that that man is yourself—independently,

I say, of such reasons, I cannot doubt that your appearance once more in public life, in a catholic attitude, will awaken [*one or two words canceled*] in the ["feelings" *canceled and* "men" *interlined*] of the middle & ["southern" *canceled and* "northern" *interlined*] States, the feelings of pride & attachment with which they looked upon you in 1812, & 1816. The parenthesis of nullification, misunderstood as it is by the great majority at the North, will be merged, even in minds of the most prejudiced, into the whole context of your history. Believe me, looking at you once more as the representative of the union as a whole will open the old fountains of affection. There was a time when Pennsylvania would have voted for you by acclamation—that time may come again. I may be sanguine, but who would not be sanguine ["with the" *canceled and* "when so" *interlined*] great a consummation as the restoration of the North to the true republican creed, has become for the first time for twenty years probable? The Secretaryship of War made you the second man in the affections of the nation: the Secretaryship of State will make you the first. With great respect I remain your, Francis Wharton.

ALS in ScCleA; variant PC in Jameson, ed., *Correspondence,* pp. 939–940.

To A[RMISTEAD] BURT, [Representative from S.C.], Washington

Fort Hill, 9th March 1844
My dear Sir, In answer to your question, I have to say, that Gen[era]l [Duff] Green, as far as I know, is acting on his own responsibility in reference to the proposed convention at Philadelphia. He is, at least, not acting under my advice or countenance, nor shall I take any part whatever in reference to it.

The conduct of the Northern wing of the Democrats appears to me to be outrageous on the abolition question, after the solemn pledges which they gave before the election of '40, in reference to it; and I must say, that I regard with surprise, that the deceptive vote of laying the question on the table by one vote, should be regarded as a triumph by some of our Southern friends. It is very obvious, that it is but a trick, in the infamous scheme of endeavoring to catch the abolition votes, without offending the South, and ought to be so treated. I am glad to see, that you took the high ground you ought in your speech. It would be better by far to bring the question at once to issue, than that we should be made the dupes & victims of a fraudulent game. Sound policy & self respect leave to the South but one course; to hold Mr. [Martin] V[an] B[uren] & his friends to their pledges, both in reference to the tariff & abolition. It would be the extreme of weakness and folly to attempt to exact new pledges, while the old, openly & solemnly given, remain unredeemed.

Mrs. [Floride Colhoun] Calhoun & the family join their love to you & Martha [Calhoun Burt]. Yours truly, J.C. Calhoun.

ALS in NcD, John C. Calhoun Papers; PC in Jameson, ed., *Correspondence*, pp. 572–573.

From DAVID HENSHAW, "Private"

Boston, March 9, 1844

My dear Sir, I am rejoiced as are all your friends here that you have been tendered the important post of the State Department. It is the undivided opinion of your friends in this quarter, so far as I can learn that opinion, that you should accept the office. The important questions concerning the Oregon and Texas renders it highly desirable that you should have the immediate charge of those questions. There are other considerations which will readily suggest themselves to the mind that make it equally important that you accept.

With an earnest hope that you will let no considerations deter you from taking the office and a firm belief of your success in it I am dear Sir very truly your Ob[edien]t S[er]v[an]t, David Henshaw.

ALS in ScCleA.

To [GEORGE MCDUFFIE, Senator from S.C.]

Fort Hill, March 9th 1844

My dear Sir, No one has greater cause to be distressed by the astonishing events, of which your letter conveyed the intelligence, than myself, except the families and the immediate connections of those, who fell by the fatal explosion [aboard the U.S.S. *Princeton* on 2/28]. It deprives me of old and tried friends, to whom I was strongly attached, and whose places, I can never hope to supply. But my loss, as great as it is, is nothing compared to that of the publick, especially the South, and by the death of Mr. [Abel P.] Upshur, at this critical moment. No one feels it more, in that respect, aside from our personal relations, than I do; and among other reasons, that his death, at this time, should, in your opinion and that of other friends, create a necessity for my returning again to publick life.

When I resigned my ["seat" *canceled*] seat in the Senate, I intended ["it" *canceled*] to close my publick life, unless the voice of the people should freely call me to take charge of the administration of the Government, ["on" *changed to* "or"] the occur[r]ence of some great calamity should clearly demand ["my return to" *interlined*] it, as a duty; neither of which had I any reason to anticipate. Acting in conformity with this fixed intention, I have appropriated the rest of my days to my entire satisfaction; and among other things, to a task, which I am very desirous of executing, and to do which, would engross all the spear [*sic*; spare] time, on which, at my period of life, I have a right to calculate. No consideration of a personal character could possibly induce me to break my arrangement, and return to publick life. As far as I am concerned, mine is closed, to my entire satisfaction. I have done my duty to the country. I have devoted the prime of my life to ["it" *canceled*] its service, and to the best of my abilities endeavoured to promote its interest. I have done so, because it was my duty, without looking to any reward beyond; and aside from duty, neither Government nor people can bestow any reward on me, which could induce me to return to publick life.

Whether, then, I ought to accept the place [of Secretary of State], to which you refer, if offered, is with me exclusively a question of duty. To do so would be a great personal sacrifice. In addition to the reasons already assigned, it would breake up for a temporary employment all my family arrangements, and what adds to the difficulty, I have no hope that I could possibly induce Mrs. [Floride Colhoun] Calhoun again to return to Washington.

But as a question of duty, I do not feel, that I prossess [*sic*] the requisite information to decide satisfactor[il]y. The only possible reason I can see for accepting the [State] Department, should it be offered, as far as duty is concerned, is limited to the pending negotiations relating to Texas and Oregon. They are both, I admit, of vast importance; especially to the West and South; and if a satisfactory termination of one or both should be thought on reasonable grounds, to depend on my accepting or not, I feel it would be a strong case of duty. But is there any such reasonable grounds? Is there reasonable hope, that a tr[e]aty for annexation, such as *ought* to be acceptable to both Governments can be made with Texas, and that the Oregon question, can be settled on grounds, that *ought* to be mutually acceptable to the United States and Great Briten [*sic*]? And if so, is there reasonable ground to believe, that ["*that*" *canceled*] any service of mine would be important either in the negotiation of the tre[a]ties, or in carr[y]ing them through successfully? If so, I do not see how I cou [*sic*] could withould my services, if required by the President [John Tyler]; and if he should desire it, I leave it to you and General [Alexander O.] Anderson, who has also written, and with whom you have consulted, with such friends as you may think proper to consult, to decide for me. If, in that case, you should decide, that my service is important, I will give it to the utmost of my abilities to the administration and the country.

But the way in which it should be given is a matter of no small importance, at least to myself. I have stated, that I could see no motive, which could induce me to go into the State Department, except the pending negotiations. It seems to me, that if my services should be required as important in reference to them, it would be better, at least it would be far more agreeable to me, and break less on my arrangements, to take charge of the nego[ti]ations, or aid in conducting them, without taking charge, at the same time, of the State Department. I can see no such necessary connection between them, as to require both to be united in the same person. On the contrary, there appear, to me to be strong reasons, why a Secretary, who has just entered on the duties of his office, and who is unacquainted with its duties, should not be exclusively charged with such high and onerous duties, as ["*the*" *canceled and* "*that of*" *interlined*; "discharge" *changed to* "discharging"; "*of*" *canceled*] the duties of his office and ["*the*" *canceled*] conducting of two such negotiations would impose on him. It would be impossible for him, under such circumstances, to discharge them all satisfactorily; as it has been a rule with me, not to undertake to perform, what I could not well and conveniently exe[c]ute. With my impression I would have strong, if not insuperable objections to undertake to discharge the duties of the Department under such ["*considerations*" *canceled*] circumstances.

What then would be altogether the most acceptable to me, should my service be deemed important, would be to receive an appointment to take charge of the negotiations, either seperately or in conjunction with whoever might be appointed Secretary of State, ["*or*" *canceled and* "*as*" *interlined*] might be the most agreeable to the President and him. Either would be equally so to me. The ["questions of the double" *canceled and* "two" *interlined*] negotiations would be as much as I would feel disposed to undertake.

If the additional expense should be thought to be an objection, I would willingly make such arrangements ["on that head" *canceled and* "in reference to it" *interlined*], as would remove all difficulty. The pay would be nothing to me, compared to having no more of my time appropriated, nor any farther derangement of my plan of dis- [*sic*] disposing of it hereafter, than ["ought to" *canceled and* "might" *interlined*] be necessary to the accomplishment of the object intended, and which only [*and here this incomplete manuscript ends.*]

DU (incomplete) in ScU-SC, John C. Calhoun Papers; PEx in Jameson, ed., *Correspondence*, pp. 573–576. NOTE: This document is an apparent draft, written in an unidentified hand, possibly that of Martha Cornelia Calhoun, with a few corrections by John C. Calhoun. The extant part of the ms. is neither signed nor addressed, but both its content and provenance establish it clearly as a reply to McDuffie's letter of 3/1/1844 to Calhoun.

To Mrs. VIRGIL (Mary Galloway) MAXCY, [West River, Md.?]

Fort Hill, 9th March 1844
My dear Madam, The mail of yesterday bro[ugh]t me the intelligence of the heartrending occurrence on board the Princeton, and the heavy stroke of affliction which has fallen on you.

I will not attempt to offer consolation, where I know it is impossible. All I can do is to mingle my grief with yours. The stroke which deprived you of the kindest & best of husbands deprived me of the most faithful of friends, and whose place I can never hope to supply.

It is now ["almost" *interlined*] forty years since our acquaintance commenced, During that long period, not an instance ever occurred to impair our friendship. Throughout the whole period, [*several illegible words, possibly canceled*] in all the vici[ssi]tudes, through which it has been my fortune to pass, I ever found him a true & devoted friend, taking not less interest in what concerned me than I did myself. This friendship was not unreciprocated. I loved him, as a brother; and felt the stroke which seperated us as if it seperated a brother from a brother. To my last breath, I shall ever cherish his memory and bear a kind affection to all that is his. With the deepest sympathy your aff[ectiona]te friend, J.C. Calhoun.

Ms. copy in DLC, Galloway-Maxcy-Markoe Papers, vol. 48.

From H[ENRY] M. BRACKENRIDGE

Tarentum [Pa.,] March 10th 1844

D[ea]r Sir, I am confident you will not be offended at my sending you one of my political speeches, in the contest last Fall [for election as Representative from Pa.], with Mr. [William] Wilkins, the democratic candidate. Your name is mentioned in it, but I hope with that liberality and respect, which I have always entertained for your eminent talents and honourable motives. When men honestly differ, the difference itself is often not so great as it is with those who dishonestly differ. The opinions of men are often the result of the positions which they occupy; change those positions, and the opinions will change. If I were a South Carolinian I might see things as you do, and if you were a Pennsylvanian, you might think as I do. In one thing, I flatter myself with being like yourself, in being open, undisguised, and frank in my opinions, as well as fearless and regardless of consequences. If I could consent to look upon antimasonry as any thing but a humbug, and abolition anything but ignorance, folly and wickedness, I should *now be the Whig candidate for Congress, and without doubt elected.* But it was ["said" *interlined*] that my opinions were too freely and decidedly expressed; it was therefore thought more prudent to choose some one who could get antimasonic and abolition votes. It is not likely that I shall ever appear again as a candidate for the suffrages of the people. My antimasonic rival, Mr. [Neville B.] Craig, is now taken up as the abolition candidate, and there seems to be an increase of this mischievous fanaticism. It will undoubtedly make progress in a certain portion of society, *between* the labouring classes, with whom it can never be popular, and the higher class of intelligence, with the exception of a heated fanatic here & there, or an intellectual *sui generis* like Mr. [John Quincy] Adams. It is *between* the two classes of the common laborers, mechanics &ca, who hate the negro race, and the highest intelligence, that abolition looks for its partizans. This middle class consists of the materials for mischievous fanatics to work upon. It requires some degree of intelligence, and to be tolerably well off in the means of livelihood, to be susceptible of this kind of false benevolence heated to enthusiasm; and to be free from actual distresses of their own, to indulge in the luxury of suffering for others' woe, whether it be for the condition of the poor heathen cannibal of Madagascar, the negro of the Southern plantation, or the Irish repealer. This fanaticism can never be popular with the numbers, with the materials for mobs in our cities and towns. The finely dressed black gentlemen and ladies, as they pass along our streets, are regarded with disgust and hatred by our plainly dressed labourers and mechanics. There is no doubt that the spirit, with which the South resents the impertinent interference of abolition, tends to give it strength and consistency; and yet I am aware that it is almost impossible to treat it differently.

I hope you will not consider it flattery when I say that, as an american, and a lover of my country, I rejoice to see you where you are. I lay all circumstances aside—it is enough for me that you are there, and I believe that in the present juncture, your appointment would be as unanimously ratified by the people of the United States, as it was by the Senate. It has come with an agre[e]able surprise on every one, especially as it will now be necessary to settle the Oregon question. We ought to have what is ours, even if it be arsenic. We might split the difference between the mouth of the Columbia [River], and the 49° of latitude. The Hudson's Bay Company might be permitted to occupy their trading Forts for a period of ten years, admitting our right of soil, and exempting them within certain limits from our jurisdiction. The main thing is to settle the question of right, even if that of exclusive occupancy be postponed. The entrance of the Columbia river is bad; a more Southern port[,] that of S[an] Francisco, would be of much greater value to us. A settlement and local government on the Columbia, or Pacific, would be of immense importance as a means of communicating with China, and the East Indies, even if it were only for the purpose of intelligence, and also as respects the countries bordering on the Pacific, and our shipping employed on that Ocean. This is the chief present value of the Oregon [Territory] to us in a national point of view. There ought to be a line of Posts, and contiguous settlements to form the chain of connection, in the manner of the Russians to Siberia and to the borders of Tartary. They might be placed within sixty, and even thirty miles of each other, surrounded with two or three hundred families, quite sufficient for protection against the nomadic tribes. In this way, information could be obtained in four months at Washington direct from China, and in two from the Pacific. I have amused myself with planning, and *locating* a line of Stockades, and settlements across to the Pacific, having in early life hunted towards the source of the Missouri [River], and since directed my attention to everything which concerns the subject. I shall look with great interest to the settlement of the important question, and in your hands every one feels that it is safe, not meaning any disrespect to the memory of your lamented Predecessor Judge [Abel P.] Upshur, whose ability and integrity was unquestioned. You will find in Mr. Wilkins [the newly-appointed

Secretary of War], a man not only of very polished manners, but excellent practical sense, and I think peculiarly fitted for the department which he fills. He will be highly popular with the army. Although we have taken opposite sides in politics, there never has been any unfriendly feeling between us.

I hope you will not consider this letter as offensive; or obtrusive. Nothing of the kind I assure you ["wa" *canceled*] is intended by me. Since our first acquaintance my feelings have warmed towards you, in part perhaps from the belief on my part that you entertained a favorable opinion towards me. I am with great respect Your most obed[ient] S[ervan]t, H.M. Brackenridge.

ALS in ScCleA. NOTE: Henry M. Brackenridge (1786–1871) was a son of Hugh Henry Brackenridge, author of *Modern Chivalry*. The younger Brackenridge had held a variety of public offices and was the author of *A Voyage to South America* (1819) and other works. "One of my political speeches," which Brackenridge mentioned in his first paragraph that he was "sending," was probably *Speech Delivered in Broadhurst's Grove on the Evening of the 6th October, 1843* (Pittsburgh: Pittsburgh Daily Advocate, 1843).

From J[AMES] GADSDEN

Charleston, March 9[t]h [*sic*; 10th] 1844

My Dear Sir, We have just heard of your nomination & unanimous confirmation as Secr[etary of] State. Your friends one & all seemed more than gratified & really hope you will not permit this opportunity to escape to enable us to recover our lost ground & you placed in a position in which you can render such essential benefit to your Country, and to the Great Cause in which you have so long contended. I have no time for argument, or reasons why or wherefore as it is Sunday & the mail is now closing. As one of your most devoted friends; as one who thinks, by bad management on the part of some we are in a fair way of being politically cheated; I say you must accept. If you do not our Party, "Free Trade[,] Low duties[,] economy[,] retrenchment" &c & are broken into fragments. We cannot rally or recover our ground without our Leader is again in the Field. To your Tents o Issrael—To your Post—as we shall all feel encouraged to make one more effort in the cause of victory. If you do not, I repeat discontented, and deceived (and in this I speak my own feelings) by those with whom we should never have communed, our Free Trade Party will be broken up & enter the Presidential canvass on personal feeling. Some will keep aloof, but many will go [*ms. torn:* for Henry]

854

Clay & console themselves [*ms. torn*: with Martin] Van Buren[']s defeat. I therefore repeat, go to Washington, settle the Oregon & the Texian question[s] & make a commercial Treaty on Free Trade principles & leave the rest to us. If you accomplish the above before fall, the political horizon will bear a very different aspect from what it now does. Your friend, J. Gadsden.

ALS in ScCleA. NOTE: March 10, 1844, was a Sunday, suggesting that Gadsden misdated this letter.

From GEO[RGE] MCDUFFIE

Washington, 10th March 1844

My dear Sir; I received your letter of the 3rd of March yesterday, & confess myself quite surprized at Mr. [Robert Barnwell] Rhett's letter relative to [Representative from N.C., James I.] McKay's bill for reducing the tariff & your own views upon the subject. And frankness requires me to say to you that I now regret as I have long done, that you have made such a man ["as Rhett" *interlined*] your confidential adviser. You could not have selected a worse, not excepting Duff Green. He is vain, self conceited, impracticable & *selfish in the extreme*, & by his ridiculous ambition to lead & dictate in every thing, has rendered himself odious both in Congress & in the State. I know of no man who is injuring you so much. Every thing he does in Congress & writes in the [Washington] Spectator is ascribed to you. If you should accept the State Department as I sincerely hope you will, I think the Spectator should be stopped. In any event it ["does" *canceled and* "will do" *interlined*] nothing but mischief, as now conducted. Even if McK[ay]'s bill were as represented by Rhett I differ with you (as do the whole delegation except Rhett [*closing parens canceled*] & perhaps [Isaac E.] Holmes) as to the propriety of supporting it. By doing so we gain much, *very much* & surrender *nothing*. We shall have as perfect a right & a much better chance of bringing it to our own standard one or two years hence than if we do not touch the tariff of 1842. You speak of the *hold* we have on both parties, as if it was in our power to make them do as we please; whereas it is a mere rope of sand. Did it prevent the whigs & democrats from passing the act of 1842? Why was not the bond then enforced upon them? And now when we are about to accomplish the greatest free trade victory ever achieved since 1816 not excepting the compromize of 1833, are ["we" *interlined*] to stop short and refuse to vote for & support the measure because ["the" *canceled*] we have the pledge of two faithless parties to reduce the tariff still lower? If we had been weak enough to follow Mr. Rhett's lead, & threaten Mr. [Martin] V[an] Buren's friends instead of reasoning with them, it is certain the tariff never would have been touched this Session. And if McK[ay]'s bill is defeated I fear the responsibility will rest upon Rhett & those he can influence.

McK[ay]'s bill, as you will see, lays the duty on the *foreign* cost without adding the usual 10 p[e]r c[en]t. But how much better would even the 10 p[e]r c[en]t be than the *home* valuation of the compromize, which you know was very near causing me to vote against that law? McK[ay]'s bill comes down after one year to 25 p[e]r c[en]t as the maximum, ["&" *interlined*] I regard ["it" *interlined*] as better than the compromize with the home valuation. A large amount of dutiable imports are placed at 20 p[e]r c[en]t & under.

As to tea & coffee I have always [thought] that you & the democratic party committed a great error in voting against the duty proposed by the whigs. Those democrats in Georgia & elsewhere who voted against these duties then & turned out their opponents who voted for them, dare not now vote to impose the duties. Upon the whole we have done all that can be done, & my only fear is that [the] bill reported may not pass though I have [*mutilation*; very?] strong hopes it will.

You will see by the papers that no event which has occurred for many years, has produced such a simultaneous & general burst of congratulation & applause as your appointment to the State Department. I hope you will be able to gratify the national wish, as I am sure it will promote ["your" *canceled*] the public welfare & extend your own fame & popularity. Sincerely your friend, Geo: McDuffie.

ALS in ScCleA; variant PC in Boucher and Brooks, eds., *Correspondence*, pp. 214–215.

From H[AYM] M. SALOMON

New York [City,] March 10th [18]44
Dear Sir, We have to day the an[n]unciation of your appointment.

I send by this mail the [New York] C[ourier] & Enquirer and you doubtless have also seen the [Washington] National Intelligencer. For what other citizen could such generous remarks have been made unless for one whom providence had reserved an occasion for universal respect amidst the most extraordinary and unexampled political strife that could have been remembered by the most aged of our Citizens.

The Nomination *by Mr.* [*John*] *Tyler*—The *manner* of Confirmation—The warm expressions of *satisfaction* by the principal respectable journals of *both* great parties, all taken together form a circumstance in the incidents of your long political Life that must at this day be not only pleasing in the highest degree to your amiable family ["but" *canceled*] as well as to your constant political friends but seem as one of those rare events in which may be traced the shield of protecting omnipotence over a name heretofore so basely abused by certain evil intentioned citizens.

To accept this, the highest post in the cabinet Council of the nation, from the present Incumbent binds you to no bias in favour of either of the Great parties. For the President Ostensibly favours none.

The unanimity in the senate on this matter proves that the whig majority was satisfied that the profound indignation which you ["so" *interlined*] justly entertained ["and expressed while a senator" *interlined*] in common with every other good and wise Citizen at the unjustifiable course which brought Mr. [Martin] Van Beuren by the most gross corruption to supercede you as chairman of that illustrious Body—has not been lessened by the ["unjustifiable" *canceled*] combinations lately exhibited to impose again on the nation as their chief one who by his inherent principles of moral action is so entirely unfitted. And that they in their best judgements really thought you not that factious political plastic which the [Mordecai M.] Noah organ and its adjuncts wished to represent you in the restoration of a slander of which I gave you timely notice[,] I.E. that you too had conde-[s]cended to be again duped with offers and promises [of the Vice-Presidency] which in Mr. Van [Buren's] last pilgrimage had been first *offered* and accepted by [James K.] Polk—Then *tendered* and accepted by Mr. [William R.] King—then *guaranteed* to Col. [Richard M.] Johnson—and now *claimed* by Mr. [Andrew] Stevenson. And which from the timely disavowal to me under your own hand has done more towards placing you in an upright position before the principal [Henry] Clay leaders here than you can imagine unless you are aware in how eminant a degree the insane friends of Van B[uren's] reelection permit themselves to be deceived by every report of the adheasion and combination of distinguished men to their impure views.

The unanimity of the senatorial Body for gra[n]ting you the *highest* station *in their gift* is enhanced in its gratification to yourself and true friends by the recol[l]ection that Mr. Clay[']s nomination for the same post was permitted to pass by a very slender majority.

Permit one again who has had a long and uninter[r]upted regard for your interests and those of the country connected with your final advancement to intrude a few humble hints as to the future.

Mr. Clay if elected would not think of removing you if he Could for the reason of his own knowledge of your intrinsic merits and from the fact of his having no pretence himself for a reelection. Besides if no circumstance should arise ["which"(?) *canceled*] preceding the ensuing contest by which the nation could ["be" *canceled*] happily claim you as their *next* chief[,] your retaining ["such an" *interlined*] office under him would enable you on many accounts to become so popular from your *Central* position and connection with his adminis-t[r]ation that you would most likely be the successor after him for one term but like [Thomas] Jefferson your selfish enemies would be finally silenced and you would go in on the second term 164 to 14!

And that you could not ["then" *interlined*] be properly opposed is evident from the uniform expressions of Confidence that the honest organs of the Ante Van Beuren party are now so generally publishing.

And for the good reason I humbly think that you so patriotically withheld yourself from the late proffered embrace of one of the most venal, dangerous and destructive factions ["that" *canceled*] with which this or any other nation was cursed. Very respectfully, your Sincere Friend, H.M. Salomon.

P.S. As a proof of ["the" *canceled*] in point of the Jacobinical and [*one word canceled*] destructive propensity of the faction after attaining power in one State[,] you have seen the hatchet of execution has even been raised to the benches of our high courts of Justice. One Van der pool [*sic*; Aaron Vanderpoel, former Representative from N.Y.] an ignorant Van B[uren] Lawyer was elevated last winter to our superior Court so unfit to replace the exemplary man whom he superceded that the Bar unanimously petitioned the Legislature to abolish the court in order to rid the bench of the Judge.

And just now we have seen that they have cut off from the Bench of Common pleas and from the Bench of Marine Juridicature two of our most distinguished jurists—Men who from their great Learning[,] Integrity and respectability would be no disgrace to the Supreme Court at Washington—and these men have been superceded by such characters as Cause the the thoughtful part of the Bar to shudder for the future purity of the Ermine of justice.

ALS in ScCleA.

From W[ILLIA]M W. WALLACE

Warrenton [Va.], March 10 1844

Dear Sir: You must pardon the intrusion of this note upon your attention, from the deep interest I feel on the subject of your accepting the appointment of Secretary of State. I am aware that the mere office can add nothing to your fame; but in the present crisis of our affairs, the negotiations on which that department is about to enter, first as to the annexation of Texas to the United States, and secondly the adjustment of the Oregon question with Great Britain, are of the highest importance to the whole country. No questions can be fraught with greater interest. I am credibly informed that the last is believed in Washington seriously to threaten the peaceful relations between Great Britain and the United States; and that a just sense of what is due to the country in such a crisis has had no little agency in your appointment. Upon the other, I need say nothing. You no doubt appreciate its importance to the South. Let me then at once urge you my dear sir to accept the appointment at least for the sake of the country. It will be in the highest degree satisfactory to all parties; and will materially advance your prospects in future. The adjustment of these questions will give ["you" *interlined*] a new claim on your country, both north and south. I know nothing which would give me more regret than intel[l]igence of your refusal to accept the charge of that department under present circumstances & at this crisis. Yours truly, Wm. W. Wallace.

ALS in ScCleA.

CHARLES DOUGLAS to William W. Payne, [Representative from Ala.], Washington

New London [Conn.], March 11, 1844

Dear Sir, I am highly pleased to inform you that the appointment of Mr. Calhoun to the office of Secretary of State, meets the entire approbation of the people here. It is equally acceptable to both political parties, all being satisfied that the rights and interests of the nation are in safe hands, and will neither be compromitted nor endangered for party or other purposes. Unquestionably the selection was wise and fortunate at this eventful crisis, as the peculiar position of Mr. Calhoun, aside from other considerations, is altogether favorable for conducting successfully the Oregon negociation. Brought into office by the united action of both parties, he is placed beyond the control of influences, which, under different circumstances, might operate injuriously upon him. He now has the confidence of both, without the danger of being dictated to by either, and consequently can move in a far more ample circle than otherwise he would have occupied, and exercise an influence commensurate with the advantageousness of his position. Thus favorably circumstanced, and in view of the present condition of our foreign affairs, the necessity of having a skilful pilot at the helmn at such a time, and in compliance with the wishes of the people that he should take the helmn, I hope Mr. Calhoun will not hesitate to accept the important trust, satisfied that by so doing he will greatly benefit the country. I am, most respectfully, your friend and servant, Charles Douglas.

ALS in ScCleA. NOTE: This letter was forwarded to Calhoun by D[ixon] H. Lewis with the following AES: "I have received another letter of the same kind from the same writer."

From F[RANKLIN] H. ELMORE

Charleston, 11 March 1844

My Dear Sir, I write you in the midst of the business of a very busy day at the urgent instance of many of your oldest & warmest friends, to express to you what I am warranted in saying is the universal desire of your friends here in regard to your recent appointment to the State Department. Every man concurs in the earnest request that you will accept. So many & so important questions are to be in the charge of that Department in which the Union at large is deeply interested & in which the South most especially is vitally affected, & in the arrangement of which you will command more of confidence & have a greater ability to serve the country, that all look on it as the most desirable event that could happen. For your own fame no position they think could be more propitious. Mr. [James E.] Belser [Representative] of Alabama passed through yesterday. I did not know it till today. Mr. [Ker] Boyce, who is now sitting with me, saw & conversed with him. He tells me that Mr. Belser says all your friends at Washington are earnestly hoping your immediate acceptance. He says the Western members most especially are warmly for your acceptance. He say[s] that they freely declare that altho' they know you do not altogether agree with them on that point, that you are the *only man* who can settle ["it" *canceled and* "the Oregon question" *interlined*] satisfactorily—for they know your justice & fairness & will be content to stand to whatever you will agree to, and that if you settle it & the Texas questions, nothing could possibly confer a greater benefit on them, nor give you a higher claim upon their gratitude.

Col. [James] Gadsden has just stepped in & says he wrote you yesterday, and today he has had more opportunities of knowing the opinions of the people. All think you cannot do a greater service to the Country than the present occasion offers the opportunity for. I am my Dear Sir In the utmost haste Yours truly, F.H. Elmore.

ALS in ScCleA; variant PEx in Boucher and Brooks, eds., *Correspondence,* pp. 215–216.

From W[illia]m J. Grayson,
[Collector of the Port of Charleston]

Charleston, March 11th 1844

Dear Sir, I cannot resist the temptation of expressing to you my hope that the appointments announced by the paper of this morning may find acceptance with you.

The manner in which it has been confirmed by the Senate, and received by the people of all parties throughout the Country does so much honour to the Nation, as to render its completion by your consent, desirable as a National gratification.

I will not presume to add the considerations of duty springing from the condition of our foreign relations, and the infinitely important and vital consequences to our own section of Country, which might flow from a failure to settle our differences with England. To these you are fully alive.

I trust, my dear Sir, you will ascribe my letter to the anxiety which I feel in common with all to see an important negociation in the best hands, and to the sincere esteem and admiration with which I have always regarded you. I am with great respect Your Ob[edien]t Serv[an]t, Wm. J. Grayson.

ALS in ScCleA.

From A L E X [A N D E] R J O N E S

192 Broadway
New York [City,] March 11th 1844

Dear Sir, I congratulate you and the country upon your appointment as Secretary of State. Your friends in this quarter are rejoiced at both the appointment and the complementary manner in which it was conferred. Not only do your personal and political friends ["seem" *canceled and* "appear highly" *interlined*] gratified; but, in no instance, have I heard a single voice raised in disapprobation; but on the contrary, every single newspaper without exception, and every man of all political parties, with one accord have approved of the appointment in the most earnest and emphatic manner. The universal desire, is, that you will accept the appointment. We know the place itself cannot confer any honor upon ["you" *interlined*] higher than your country has already awarded you, and if you consent to fill the station assigned you, it will be from a *sense* of *patriotism*, which we all know, is a higher principle with you, than the love [of] office, for the [*word or words accidentally omitted at the end of a page?*] of its empty honors, or emoluments.

I regret to state that since Mr. Wyckoff's [*sic*; Henry Wikoff's] arrival in this city from England, about the 20th ult[imo], difficulties have grown up between him["self" *interlined*], and Gen[era]l [Duff] Green, which have led, to their separation.

Wyckoff, expressed much ["dissaction"(?) *canceled*] dissatisfaction at the arrangements made for publishing the paper, previous to his arrival, in reference principally I believe, to the pecuniary outlay.

My ["active" *interlined*] connection with the *"Republic"* ceased, as I before informed you, some two or three weeks before Wyckoff came on; subject to a renewal, or confirmation by him. He has failed to offer any satisfactory arrangement, and hence; I am at present, wholly unconnected with the Republic, and wholly out of immediate employment of any kind whatever. I have some thoughts of paying a visit to the west, to look at the country, and to see if any thing may present itself, in which I may be able to engage with safety. I am much pleased with St. Louis, as a place of business: but fear it is already overdone.

In confidence, I think Gen[era]l Green's greatest difficulty grows out of his want of *business tact*. In other words, he seems to want talents for managing with success and profit *pecuniary affairs*. I think him a man of many amiable traits of character, and that he designs to be strictly honest and fair in his dealings; ["but" *canceled*] if others suffer by transactions with him, it arises more from his *car[e]lessness*, than from his disposition to injure any one. He is also, credulous, and liable to be imposed upon by designing men, and bears impatiently the *frank expressions* or *advice* of *a friend.* He is also a man of strong feelings, ["a" *canceled and* "and" *interlined*] liable to be strongly biased, or prejudiced, in his feelings, either for, or against others. *Such men are always more dangerous as friends, than formidable* as *enemies, unless governed by a parament* [*sic;* paramount?] *share* of *prudence.* If guided by *prudence and* and [*sic*] *reflection,* they *never fail* to make the *best,* and most *steadfast friends* we can ever have.

I speak this without the least ill feeling or disrespect for Gen[era]l Green. I am sure he has no friend who would be more rejoiced at his prosperity. I think him intrinsically a far better man than Wyckoff. But, notwithstanding this feeling towards him on my part, I fear he does not fully reciprocate it, on his part, owing to the influence, of one, or two unworthy persons, such as I hinted at in my last letter, who obtained his confidence, and who seemed to think the only means of maintaining their position, was by alienating the Gen[era]l's regard for me. This individually, I felt to be of no consequence to me, and let it pass in silence.

Since the explosion of the Gun on board the Princeton, I have taken the pains to examine into the character and history of *Wrought Iron Cannon,* and I have arrived at the conclusion, that *no wrought iron cannon,* can ever be made *perfectly* ["safe" *interlined*] from the changes the material undergoes by concussion. Wrought ["Iron" *interlined*] possesses, within itself, intrinsic and ["uns" *canceled*] insuperable difficulties, which wholly disqualifies it for such purposes.

Inclosed [*sic*], I send you a short article on this subject which I wrote for the *"Journal of Commerce"* over the signature of *"A.B."*

These are important facts, and at least might challenge the examination of Gover[n]ment, before the construction of other wrought Iron Guns are ordered.

Wishing ["you" *interlined*] all the health, happiness and prosperity, this world can afford, I have the honor to Remain, your Sincere Freind [*sic*] & Very Humble & Ob[edien]t Serv[an]t, Alex[ande]r Jones.

ALS in ScCleA.

From ROB[ER]T W[ILLIA]M ROPER

Charleston, 11th March 1844

My dear Sir! The important intelligence of Your appointment as Secretary of State & flattering Confirmation by the Senate has filled all parties in Charleston with unfeigned delight. Altho sensible I may be guilty of some presumption in wielding my pen on such an occasion I hope I may be pardoned the indulgence of my Individual feelings in expressing the particular pleasure I experience at your appointment. Besides the gratification of my pride & partiality I am impressed with a deep concern at the strait in which our national interests are involved on the Texas[,] Oregon & Tariff questions & do hope You will leave Your retirement & descend from the pin[n]acle on which your moral worth & great talents, so universally accorded & reposed in by the whole nation have elevated You, to rescue us from the embarrassments of our position. And that You will contribute in promoting the permanent happiness of a Young people, testing the capabilities of a republican form of Government. Let me assure You the general wish is that You will accept this appointment & express my ardent hope's to that effect from which I could not refrain, tho not prominent in political life. Again apologising for the freedom I have assumed, permit me to add the high esteem of Y[ou]r Ob[edien]t Ser[van]t, Robt. Wm. Roper.

ALS in ScCleA. NOTE: This letter is written on paper with a Calhoun campaign letterhead such as is described in *The Papers of John C. Calhoun*, 16:673.

From C[HARLES] C. PINCKNEY

Eldorado [on] Santee [River, S.C.] 13th March 1844

My dear Sir, The paper received here this morning informs me of your nomination to the Department of State & the very handsome confirmation by the Senate. Apprehending that you might hesitate under your peculiar circumstances, I take the liberty of sending you the opinion of one whose memory I know you hold in respect. When my Father [Thomas Pinckney] was appointed a Major Gen[era]l by Mr. [James] Madison at the commencement of the last war, he received a letter from Mr. [William] Polk, asking him his plan, he having received a similar nomination, & being adverse to the administration. The reply was, that the call of a Government he had never supported, was not the call of a Party, but the call of his Country, that it was the duty of every citizen to obey such a call without hesitation. I sincerely hope & trust that such may be your determination. Had my Father declined there were good men & true, to take the place: but if you decline, the Administration falls into the hands of enemies of the South in every particular. Mr. [Daniel] Webster would probably be the next nomination.

I trust you will excuse this trusspass on your time, & believe me Yours respectfully & Sincerely, C.C. Pinckney.

ALS in ScCleA. NOTE: Charles Cotesworth Pinckney (1789–1865) was a part-time resident of Pendleton, and had a son, Charles Cotesworth Pinckney (1812–1899) who was an Episcopal clergyman also well known in the Pendleton vicinity. "Eldorado" was located in St. James Santee Parish, Charleston District.

From J[AMES] H. HAMMOND, [Governor of S.C.]

Silver Bluff, 14 March 1844

My Dear Sir, I received your letter declining the appointment of Senator & entirely concur in the propriety of your doing so. In fact I was of that opinion from the first. To-day[']s papers confirm what has been before rumoured. I see that you are appointed & confirmed as Secretary of State. Like every one else, I am inclined to the opinion that you should accept. No man in America I imagine will regard it as any honor conferred on you, or that you can accept for any other purpose than to serve the country in a critical period. Nor will any one suppose that in accepting it from Mr. [John] Tyler you place yourself under any obligation to support him. He only binds himself to support you. He will be too glad to throw himself into your arms & if you will allow him the semblance of authority & the management of small matters, you will be virtually President for the next year & may do much good in many ways, even with such an incubus ["as Tyler on" *canceled and* "as him upon" *interlined*] you. In the settlement of our relations with Texas, Oregon & it may be arranging a commercial treaty with G[reat] Britain, you can render ["invaluable"(?) *canceled and* "inestimable" *interlined*] services. And services which I think no other man can render.

In accepting the office & taking on your shoulders ["even as to foreign affairs" *interlined*] an administration without a party; ["&" *canceled and* "as" *interlined*] well as in the great delicacy & exciting character of the negociations in which you will be involved you will certainly encounter great difficulties. They would be sufficient to deter an ordinary man who had any thing to lose from taking such a position. But they are just such obstacles *you* are capable of contending with & converting into causes of triumph. I have entire confidence that you will be able to do so & hope that you may see proper to incur the risk. Very truly & Sincerely yours, J.H. Hammond.

ALS in ScCleA.

From R. R. SMITH

Raleigh [N.C.,] 14th March 1844

My dear Sir; I sincerely hope you will excuse the liberty I have taken in venturing thus unceremoniously to trespass upon your valuable time, & my apology must be found in the great interest I feel in whatever relates to your present & future political Course.

Your recent nomination by the President [John Tyler] & Confirmation by the Senate to the Office of Secretary of state, seems to give universal satisfaction in all quarters & to all parties, & I most ardently hope before now, you may have Accepted the appointment. At first, I thought in your present position you could not honorably Accept it; but upon deliberate reflection pardon me for saying, I think you Ought by all means to do so.

In filling this highly honorable post, you will have it in your power to adjust & definitely settle the Texas & the Oregon questions, more to the satisfaction of your Country, than any Other man in it. This, of itself, ought to be a very strong inducement, but when it appears that all your Democratic friends, far & near, as well as the whigs, universally, Call loudly upon you to Accept this Office, I really do hope for the good of the Country & your own fame, that you will at once consent to do so, without hesitation.

The fact is, I understand the manner of this nomination & Confirmation, is entirely unprecedented in the annals of the Country, & Cannot fail to reflect the highest honor upon you as a patriot & statesman.

To be thus honored by the President, & both parties in the Senate of the U. States, represen[ting] Twenty millions of free people, is *more honorable* in my opinion, at this particular juncture, than to be elected President by a party.

Under these highly honorable Circumstances, all your friends of the Democratic party, together with the whigs, in this quarter, join in One universal expression of hope, that you may Accept the high office tendered to you by the President of the U. States.

The fact is, my dear Sir, I should not myself, have addressed you at all on this subject, having such unbounded Confidence in your wisdom & discretion in matters of this kind; but I have been so urgently requested by our Democratic as well as whig friends to write & urge your Acceptance of the office, that I Could hesitate no longer.

Please pardon our presumption, & believe me, as ever, yours with the highest respect & Consideration, R:R: Smith.

ALS in ScCleA.

To Mrs. A[NNA] M[ARIA CALHOUN] CLEMSON, Edgefield District, S.C.

Fort Hill, 15th March 1844

My dear Anna, I find by looking at the date of your letter and this my acknowledgement of its receipt, that the Cane Brake and Fort Hill are nearly as far a part, as far as the intercourse by mail is concerned, as if they were on the opposite sides of the Atlantick.

I wrote Mr. [Thomas G.] Clemson last week on business, and informed him, that I would write to you in a few days. I hope he has got my letter. As ["mine" *interlined*] to him was confined to business, I shall endeavour to make this one of news, which however is a scarce article in this part of the world at this season of the year. I begin with the strictly domestick.

Your Mother [Floride Colhoun Calhoun], then, has got Mrs. Ryan [*sic*; Mrs. Margaret Hunter Rion] for a House keeper. She seems to me to understand her place and business well, and thus far has given much satisfaction, and there is, I think, good [reason] to hope she will continue to do so. Thus far, it has made a happy change. Every thing has been going on with great harmony about the House.

Your Uncle James [Edward Colhoun] has written to your mother, so urgently that she cannot decline, to go to Edgefield to bring up Maria [Simkins Colhoun], or if that cannot be done to be with her there during her confinement. She will set out on Monday next, if the weather and the state of the roads will permit.

The next item of news relates to myself, and is to me far from being of an agreeable character.

I have been offered the State Department, and owing to the two important negotiations now pending, in reference to the annexation of Texas & settling the Oregon question, and ["I am" *interlined*] strongly appealed to through Mr. [George] McDuffie and others to accept. The appeal is to my patriotism and magnanimity, & in behalf of the South. My repugnance to accepting is every way great. I have in answer stated strongly such leading reasons for wishing to decline, as I could with propriety, with the expression, in strong terms, of the hope that I might be spared the sacrafice; but that, if on a review, my friends should think my services cannot be dispensed with, without hazard, that I would accept an appointment to negotiate the treaties, seperately from the Department, if such an arrangement could be made with propriety; but if not, I would accept the latter, as averse as I am to it, with the understanding, that I should be at liberty to resign as soon as the negotiation was over. On a full survey of all circumstances, I did not see, that I could, without loss of character & standing give any other answer; but I accompanied that, with a strong wish, that the President [John Tyler] might be able to make some other satisfactory arrangement.

I expect to hear the result in 12 or 13 days. If I cannot get off, I shall set out as soon as it is announced, that my name is before the Senate, and in that case, as soon as you & Mr. Clemson see it announced, ["you" *interlined*] must make your arrangement to meet me at Col. [Francis W.] Pickens'[s] allowing me about three or four days, after the information ["would" *interlined*] reach me to be there. I wish to meet John [C. Calhoun, Jr.] also with you.

Now I believe, I have very little more to add, except that weather is exceedingly wet, & the spring fairly started. Our peach trees have just begun to blos[s]om.

I hope you will not fail to visit your mother at Edgefield, as soon as you hear of her arrival, or at least to write to her affectionately. She is somewhat hurt, at not having got, but one short letter from you by Mr. Miller, and thinks that you have evinced coldness towards her. You must not hesitate to take ["the" *canceled*] proper steps to remove it, as I hope Mr. Clemson will also to produce kinder feelings between him & her. I trust, the former unpleasant state of things have passed, not to return, & wish to see harmony all around. We are all well & all join their love to you all. I trust you all continue well, & that [John] Calhoun [Clemson] & Floride [Elizabeth Clemson] daily grow & improve. Kiss them for Grandfather. May God bless you all. Your affectionate father, J.C. Calhoun.

ALS in ScCleA; variant PEx in Jameson, ed., *Correspondence*, p. 576.

To T[homas] G. Clemson, Cane Brake, Edgefield [District, S.C.]

Fort Hill, 16th March 1844

My dear Sir, I wrote Anna [Maria Calhoun Clemson] by the last mail down, and among other items of news, gave her what had occur[r]ed in reference to the State to [*sic*] Department, and ["suggested" *interlined*] the possibility I should be forced to accept, however reluctant. Very unexpectedly the next mail up, brought me the intelligence of my nomination & confirmation, accompanied by twenty or thirty letters, one from a Whig New England Senator [Samuel S. Phelps], urging in the strongest terms my acceptance, and saying that it was the unanimous sentiment of all parties, that I ought.

Under all the circumstances, I do not see how I can decline, without loss of character, and I have accordingly answered the President [John Tyler], that I accepted; but that as nothing short of the crisis caused by the pending negotiations could induce me to do so, that I accepted, on the condition, that as soon as they should be concluded, I should be at liberty to retire.

I expect to set out this day week, or at farthest day after tomorrow week, by stage, and will be at Col. [Francis W.] Pickens['s] on tomorrow (Sunday) week, or Tuesday week, as the case may be, and have enclosed this to him, with the request, that he should send it to you, so that you may certainly get it in time. I wish you to send up your carriage to meet me and to have it at the fork of the road to Col. Pickens['s] on Sunday when the stage passes, & if I should not be in it, on tuesday at the same time, so that I may go directly to his house, without going to the Village, & thence to the Cane Brake, or what I would prefer, if you & Anna can make it convenient, that you & she & John [C. Calhoun, Jr.] & the children [John Calhoun Clemson and Floride Elizabeth Clemson] should meet me there. It would save me a day, which is important, as I am urged to lose no time.

We are all well & all join love. Your affectionate father, J.C. Calhoun.

[P.S.] Say to John I wish him to bring up my trunk, as I shall want to exchange trunks.

ALS in ScCleA; variant PEx in Jameson, ed., *Correspondence*, pp. 577–578.

To [President JOHN TYLER]

Fort Hill, March 16th 1844

My dear Sir, I received by the Mail of yesterday your letter of the 6th Inst[ant] written in the Morning, and informing me that you had nominated me to fill the vacancy in the State Department occasioned by the lemented death of Mr. [Abel P.] Upshur, and your note of the same date written in the evening, that the Senate had unanimously confirmed the nomination.

I highly appreciate the honour you have confer[r]ed on me, in selecting me to fill the Department, ["as so importante" *canceled and* "at" *interlined*] a crisis, when two such importante negotiations are pending, and the very flattering manner the nomination was confirmed.

It is with great reluctance, that I return again to publick life; but, under all the circumstances, I do not feel myself at liberty to decline the appointment. But as nothing short of the magnitude of the crisis, occasioned by the pending negotiations, could induce me to leave my retirement, I accept on the condition, that when they are concluded, I shall be at liberty to retire.

I shall forthwith commence making my arrangements to leave home for Washington, and hope to be able to take my departure this day week or day after tomorrow week at fartherest, by the speed[i]est conveyance. With great respect Yours truly, J.C. Calhoun.

Retained copy in ScCleA; variant PC in Jameson, ed., *Correspondence*, p. 577. NOTE: The ms. transcribed above is in an unknown hand, possibly that of Martha Cornelia Calhoun, and is labelled "(Copy)." An AEU by Calhoun on the ms. reads: "The President's letter informing me of my nomination and its confirmation by the Senate, to the State Dep[artmen]t with a copy of my acceptance."

To A[NDREW] P[ICKENS] CALHOUN, Faunsdale, Marengo County, Ala.

Fort Hill, 17th March 1844

My dear Andrew, You will have seen by the papers, that the State Department has been tendered to me. I have been compelled, most reluctantly, to accept. Indeed, my nomination was placed on such grounds by the President [John Tyler] and confirmed in such a manner by the Senate & the appoint[ment] has been so received by the country, & pressed on me by my friends, that I did not feel myself at liberty to decline.

Immediately after the death of Judge [Abel P.] Upshur, I received letters from [George] McDuffie and other friends at Washington, indicating that the appointment would be offered, & pressing me, if it should be, not to decline. They put their opinion on the ground of the importance of the pending negotiations, in reference to Texas & Oregon to the South & the peace of the Union. I replied expressing the greatest reluctance to accepting & the strongest hope, that some one else should be selected; but said that if my service should be deemed indispensable, I would greatly prefer to take charge of the negotiation seperated from the State Department, to accepting, which I had almost insuperable objections.

The impatience was too great to wait my answer, and the appointment was made before it was received. It was made and unanimously confirmed without the usual formality at once. By the ["last" *interlined*] mail ["of yesterday" *canceled*] I received twenty or thirty letters announcing the fact, and pressing me to accept. They state it to be the wish of all sides and of all quarters. Although I regret the necessity, yet I cannot but be gratified, at this evidence of universal confidence.

I answered the President's letter by the mail that takes this ["t"(?) *canceled*] accepting the appointment, but with the condition, that when the negotiation is concluded I shall be at liberty to retire. I shall set out on my journey on the 24 or 26th Inst[ant], so that your next letter to me must be addressed to Washington.

Your mother [Floride Colhoun Calhoun] leaves home for Millwood [in Abbeville District] day after tomorrow, & from thence to Col. [Francis W.] Pickens['s], with your Uncle James [Edward Colhoun], in order to be with Maria [Simkins Colhoun], who is there, during her confinement, which it is expected will be in a few weeks. It is very inconvenient for both to be absent at the same time, but fortunately we have got an excellent Housekeeper, Mrs. Ryan [Mrs. Margaret Hunter Rion], who will take charge of the establishment during the [*and here this incomplete ms. ends.*]

ALU (incomplete) in ScU-SC, John C. Calhoun Papers.

From J[OHN] R. MATHEWES

Habersham Co[unty, Ga.,] 17 March 1844

My Dear Sir, It seems that providence yet battles for us oppress[e]d people of the South and in the face of envy, Jealousy, Hatred, malice & all uncharitableness—rough hew our ends as our enemies ["may" *interlined*,] he shapes them. The last papers brought me the gratifying intelligence of a nation[']s unanimous ["call" *interlined*] for the uses of your virtue & Talents to rescue her from the mire & filth which ["which" *canceled*] a poney[?] Club of office seekers have conspired to plunge her in. The Earthquake of circumstances preceeding this honour, they have ["been" *interlined*] compell[e]d to offer you, at once convinces me that God alone could have changed so suddenly the tide of distruction which was so fast approaching most especially the southern shores of this confed[e]racy—and England[']s suppress[e]d pleasure will be of short moment when your appointment will so soon follow the news of the truly shocking effects from the bursting of Capt[ai]n [Robert F.] Stockton[']s gun. You have gain[e]d more in one moment than your showy rivals [Henry] Clay & [Martin] Van Buren have obtain[e]d their whole lives. No president since the time of [George] Washington has rec[eive]d such an expression of Public hope & confidence in the mental powers of one man—yourself—and at such ["a" *interlined*] Crisis too. When every crowned head in Europe is anxiously looking for the hoped event of our national discord & consequent disgrace.

So much of prologue, you will say. I know that your time is precious & have little time to read my letters therefore I will proceed to state to you my humble views in this business which as on former occasions said[,] if of any account you are welcome to them; if not throw them in the fire & their will be an end of it and no harm done I hope. I am interrupted by company & therefore you are so blessed as to have a shorter letter than I intended. A cardinal point in this British negociation is to knock from under her feet the eminence on which she so proudly exults at our civil discord. She knows she has a trump Card in her hand—Abolition—a fanatical party in this Country to fight her battles as Gen[era]l [Andrew] Jackson had the Union party in So[uth] Ca[rolina] for his purpose, when with the same feelings he was to act against our State. As long as England is in possession of this weapon she will negociate with the word of promise to your ear, fan the flame in this ["country" *interlined*] & when the pear is ripe—to us will most cruelly break it to the sense—remember in treating with any nation her policy is to take advantage of time &

circumstances. She will if she can distroy your reputation & this nation with another constructive treaty, & call in the New England States to sustain her in her interpretations of its articles. Her abolition paw is on our necks—she invites the attention of every Crown[e]d ["head" *interlined*] in Europe to see her successfully use us as a Cat does a mouse—first play & then stay. We must not let her know that we know her game. Our Gover[n]ment talks too much—tells too much—writes too much & does too little—carefully & prudently instruct our northern folk, of the intentions—the war in disguise of England to dismember this nation first & then use us as she has done Portugal & all others that she allows to govern themselves "by & with her advice." I repeat to you that no treaty can be formed with England till she ceases to hope to sustain her annihillating views towards this only republic that she dreads as a successful Rival—by sustaining her abolition army in this Country—then only will she treat in peace & in truth. I have more to say but am interrupted[,] in the meanwhile accept the assurances of my most cordial wishes for your happiness & success & remain most respectfully & sincerely yours, J.R. Mathewes.

[P.S.] I know your acceptance will be at the sacrafice of much happiness & Domestic pleasure & comfort but you cannot decline it—it is the spontaneous call of a nation & there would be as much in declining it as were you call[e]d to save her at the Crisis of a Battle.

ALS in ScCleA.

F[ITZWILLIAM] BYRDSALL to Dixon H. Lewis, "(Confidential)"

New York [City,] March 18th 1844

My Dear Sir, The Enclosed you will please hand to Mr. [John C.] Calhoun when he arrives in Washington. Should he however not accept the appointment of Secretary of State, you will please forward the enclosed to him, as a testimony that his friends here will support him in any political station he may be in, so long as he is an exponent and a vindicator of those principles we cherish, and which lie at the foundation of our political fabric.

You will please read them, i.e. the enclosed proceedings of the Calhoun Central Committee of New York. They were passed unanimously after some opposition, ["from E.B. Hart and J.J. Coombes" (?)

canceled]. We have here some good & true Calhoun men of the State rights breed. Permit me to say that you and some others at Washington were rather imposed on by the [Joseph A.] Scovil[le] tribe.

We hold it a matter of propriety to advance to the support of Mr. Calhoun even in anticipation of his acceptance of the premiership. We wish him to know when he arrives in Washington that his friends in New York are ready, aye ready to stand by him in any department of Government. It is something of a proof of our estimation of him that while east[,] west and south of us, some have fallen and others have bent down before [Martin] Van Buren yet that we in this city with three administrations (United States, State and city) against us have stood firm and uncompromising, almost alone defying the party organization in its strongest Citadel.

Never had so strong a man such weak partizans as Mr. Calhoun's Southern friends with a few exceptions. I say weak because of their want of energy and perseverance in the cause. Had they arose with enthusiasm and activity and spoken with determination to the people of the North[,] East & West, such confidence would would [*sic*] have been given to his friends in Maine, Mass.[,] N.H. & Con[n]. as well as in the Western States ["that" *canceled and* "as" *interlined*] would have ["sent" *canceled and* "elected" *interlined*] other delegates to the Baltimore Convention. To no movement of his friends here has the South responded. Languor and laziness is doing the destiny of the South. She is now compelled to compromise her candidate for the sake of Tariff and twenty first rule. Power never shews justice or magnanimity to the opponent who is not in a formidable position ["nor to the" *canceled*] nor to the rebell who indicates his weakness by grounding his arms and trusting to ["justice or magnimity" *canceled*] the fairness of those who have the power in their hands.

I shall be much pleased at Mr. Calhoun's acceptance of the premiership provided he shall be able to settle the Oregon question and the annexation of Texas. If he shall acquire additional reputation on these subjects, he may yet be president but not otherwise, for the South can[']t, because it won[']t go through the necessary exertion.

As regards the tariff that is sure to come right in a few years because the agricultural population of the north & West are beginning to find it is not profitable to them. As to Texas the people who gave twenty millions for Louisiana and five millions for Florida will undoubtedly take Texas without cost. It is not in the race of Anglo Saxon Land robbers to refuse that which of all other things is the object of the master passion of the race. There may be some talking on the subject on the score of Abolition, but American abolition is about equal to British justice[,] always a tremendous affaire when it *costs* nothing but display. The best way to argue with these hypocrites is to give them trouble about their own institutions. Titles or rights to Slaves are as good as tittles to lands—both are creations of human law. Why not have petitions for the abolition of land titles?

Write me frequently. I am well acquainted with men and things here. Yours Resp[ect]f[ull]y, F. Byrdsall.

[Appended]

New York [City,] March 15th 1844

At a special meeting of the Democratic Republican Central Committee of the City and County of New York, held at Washington Hall on Thursday Evening the 14th March, the following Preamble and Resolutions were unanimously adopted.

The Central Committee representing the Democratic Republican Voters of the City & County of New York favorable to the election of John C. Calhoun to the Presidency of the United States, avail themselves of the occasion of his appointment as Secretary of State, to survey the position of public affaires, that they may determine what it becomes them to do in the present crisis.

Should Mr. Calhoun accept this appointment, it follows that his doing so raises a new relation between him and the President of the United States [John Tyler]. Hence it becomes our duty to examine what that relation is.

This Committee is pledged to support the nominee of a National Convention properly Constituted and fairly Organized—in other words, we are pledged to sustain the candidate nominated by a convention chosen by Congressional Districts & voting per Capita. But it is now known that the large States of New York and Virginia have violated the condition on which Mr. Calhoun's name was to be submitted to the Convention, and that instead of being a general Convention of the party, the assemblage at Baltimore will be a meeting of the personal partizans of Mr. Van Buren representing a minority of the party, and so organized as to defeat the will of the majority. To sustain the nominee of that Convention would be to sanction the fraud that deprives us of our preference, and to confirm the usurpation of a corrupt party organization.

We do not believe that either Mr. Van Buren or Mr. [Henry] Clay is the preference of a majority of the people. The leaders have resolved to so use the party machinery as to compel ["the people" *canceled*] the people to choose one of two unpopular candidates. The question as between them is not which most deserves the public confidence—we are not permitted to elect whom we would support—

they would compel us to say whom we must oppose—they would make the election depend, not upon the merits, but the demerits of the respective candidates, and thus by an abuse of the prerogatives of party, these party leaders would deprive us of our dearest birth right—the right of suffrage.

It is in this crisis, that the acceptance by Mr. Calhoun of the appointment as a member of the Cabinet, will create a new relation between us and the president. As a State rights Democrat he opposed a single vote to the Force Bill. As a strict constructionist of the Constitution, his vetoes again and again defeated a national Bank. With Mr. Calhoun in his cabinet, we confidently believe that he will accomplish treaties for the adjustment of the Oregon question—for a favorable modification of our trade with England and for the annexation of Texas to the United States.

As members of the Democratic party it is our duty to support the measures which accord with our principles and which will best promote the public interests as the surest means of regenerating the Democratic party and of restoring to the people their legitimate controll in the operations of Government.

Therefore

Resolved, that this Committee Protests against the manner in which the Syracuse Convention appointed delegates to the National Convention and the manner in which the latter convention is to be organized, as a fraudulent attempt to Controll the choice of a presidential candidate; and that as members of the Democratic party we are not bound to recognize as binding upon us, any nomination made thereby.

Resolved, that as Citizens of the United States it is our duty to give an independent and zealous support to those measures which are in accordance with a strict construction of the Constitution of the United States, which tend to promote the public interests and preserve the rights and liberties of the people.

Resolved, that we will judge the present administration by its measures and hold ourselves at liberty to pursue that course which justice to the President and our own sense of public duty may require.

Resolved, that the proceedings of this meeting be signed by the chairman and Secretary and that they forward copies thereof to the President of the United States, and to Mr. Calhoun. [Signed:] Edm[un]d S. Derry, Chairman of Calhoun Central Committee of N[ew] York. F. Byrdsall, Sec[retar]y protem.

ALS with En in ScCleA; variant PC in Jameson, ed., *Correspondence,* pp. 940–942. NOTE: An AEU by Calhoun on this letter reads: "The Proceedings of the

State right party in N[ew] York." Jameson mistakenly named Calhoun as the recipient of this letter, which was undoubtedly forwarded to him by Lewis. On the same day that the above resolutions were adopted by the Calhoun committee in New York City, the Calhoun committee of Charleston also met and adopted resolutions calling upon members of the party to refuse to send delegates to the Baltimore convention. (Charleston, S.C., *Mercury*, March 19, 1844, p. 2.)

From A. W. H. CLAPP

Portland [Maine], March 19, 1844

Sir, I take the liberty of recommending for your favorable consideration Mr. Jere[miah] O'Brien of Brunswick Me., a gentleman of intelligence, and high standing, and a firm, & able advocate of Free Trade. Should an opportunity offer by which you could give him a situation in your Department, it would be highly gratifying to your friends in this State. With Sentiments of respect Your Ob[edien]t Serv[an]t, A.W.H. Clapp.

ALS in DNA, RG 59 (General Records of the Department of State), Letters of Application and Recommendation during the Administrations of Martin Van Buren, William Henry Harrison, and John Tyler, 1837–1845, O'Brien (M-687:24, frame 364).

To "Col." JAMES ED[WARD] COLHOUN, [Abbeville District, S.C.]

Fort Hill, 19th March 1844

My dear Sir, I write to say, that I have been compelled most reluctantly to accept the State Department, but I have done it on the condition, that when the negotiations are concluded, I shall be at liberty to retire. The grounds on which the nomination was placed, the manner it was confirmed, and they [*sic*; "way" *interlined*] it has been received by the people left me no option.

I expect to leave on Saturday or monday [March 23 or 25], probably the former, and will stop probably a day at Francis [W. Pickens's residence in Edgefield District], either Sunday night & part of monday, or Tuesday night and part of Wednesday, as the case may be. I would be very glad to meet you there and hope you will make your arrangement so that we may meet. I hope to be absent not more than three or four months. Yours affectionately, J.C. Calhoun.

ALS in ScCleA.

877

From JA[ME]S GILLAM

Abbeville Court House [S.C.,] 19 Mar[ch] 1844
It is the business of this to inform you that I ["have" *interlined*] just
rec[eive]d intel[l]igence that my nephew Rob[er]t Gillam Waters is
a prisoner in Mexico and inur[e]d to labor on the streets of the city,
and to ask you what course his friends should take in order to procure
his release, with any hope of success.

He was born in in Newberry Dis[tric]t[,] remov[e]d ["to" *interlined*] Alabama thence to Texas, joined the Army, was in the Mier expedition, and of course can have claims from the Gov[ernment] of
the U.S.

Under these circumstances, it seems to me that the prospect for his
release is surrounded with difficulties, and I can see no chance likely
to prove successful.

The task would be too delicate to ask the public functionaries of
this country to interfere in the matter or perhaps to interest themselves personally in his behalf.

Should you receive this before your departure for Washington (As
we have learn[e]d of your recent appointment and acceptance) Please
to drop me a few lines to Lodi P[ost] O[ffice] and give me your views
on the subject.

My family in health, and also Mr. [Thomas G.] Clemson's on our
last intel[l]igence. respectfully Yours, Jas. Gillam.

ALS in ScCleA.

From ROBERT HANNA, [former Senator from Ind.]

Indianapolis, 19th March 1844
Sir, Allow me to congratulate you, and the whole Country on your
appointment to the State Department. The present Posture of our
foreign relations requires a clear head, and an honest Heart, besides
the unanimity with which your appointment has been concur[re]d in,
not only by the Senate, but the Country every whare; must be agre[e]-
able to yourself and your numerous Political friends. Aside from all
this, the strength that your appointment will bring to this much
abused Administration is a peculiar gratification to me.

Your bold and fearless letter withdrawing yourself from all connection with the "packed and preconcerted V[an] B[uren] Conven-

tion" binds you closer to my heart, it came too late however, to suit my notions of propriety. I endeavoured to put you on your guard in due time, because certain movements with which I was acquainted convinced me of what was in progress. After the meeting of the District & Circuit Courts in May next I expect to be in Washington when I will do myself the pleasure to make my respects to you in person, mean time believe me your friend and always very much at your service, Robert Hanna.

ALS in ScCleA. Note: Robert Hanna (1786–1858) was a native of Laurens District, S.C., had been Senator from Ind. during 1831–1832, and had held a variety of other public offices.

D[ixon] H. Lewis to
[Richard K. Crallé, Lynchburg, Va.]

House of Rep[resentative]s, March 19th 1844
My Dear Sir, Yours of the 8th reached me, & I showed it to Judge [Robert G.] Scott of Richmond, who was one of the signers of the Calhoun Address. He says the concessions were *mutual,* but that [Thomas] Ritchie suppressed those made by him & his friends & published [in the Richmond *Enquirer*] only the concessions of Mr. Calhoun's. It had a most fatal effect among our friends *out* of Virginia, by whom it was looked on as *unconditional* surrender, which so discouraged them, that it led almost to a general disbanding of our forces every where.

But it is of no Consequence. Every thing depends on the Texas question, which is an element of Power so much stronger than [Henry] Clay, [Martin] V[an] Buren & their Conventions—that it unsettles all calculation as to the future course of men & parties. It is the greatest question of the *Age*, & I predict will agitate the Country more than all the other public questions ever have. Public opinion will boil & effervesce & eructate more like a volcano tha[n] a cider Barrel—but at last it will settle down with *unanimity* for annexation in the South & West & a large majority in the North. It will in the mean time *unite* the *hitherto divided South*, while it will make Abolition & Treason synonimous & thus destroy it in the North.

The beauty of the thing is, that Providence rather than [John] Tyler has put Calhoun at the head of this great question, to direct its force & control its fury. It is understood by letters from him that he accepts [appointment as Secretary of State].

Thus you see that instead of my going into a Department & offering you a Clerkship Calhoun will do it. Greene [that is, Duff Green] has already spoken to Tyler about it & he wants you to ["come on" *canceled and* "be the man" *interlined*]. Of course you know Calhoun will prefer you. It will be two or three days before he gets here, & in the mean time as the heat of the battle will be *as soon as he gets here,* (the Texian special Minister being expected about the same time) if you take part, as I hope for your *own fame* you will—you must be here *at once. Come then* & *come quickly.* Let some friend bring on Mrs. [Elizabeth Morris] Cralle but *don*[']*t fail to be here* in a day or two after Calhoun arrives. I had rather have my name identified with that event than any other in our history—a word to the wise is enough. Patriotism[,] your own fame & the more cherished fame of our great Leader, demands your *immediate presence.* Don[']t delay or dally in "getting a family"—as you say in your letter, but as soon as you can shave, & bundle your clothes up, & Kiss Madam, be on the way. You know how glad I shall be to see you & my old Leader on this great occasion, "riding on the Whirlwind & directing the storm."

Keep this letter which you may look upon more as a rhapsody than otherwise, but if I am not mistaken, our children will read it with some pleasure, when you & I are dead & gone. Put it away in your secret Archives. I want to see how it will stand the test of Time, which will either prove or disprove its prophecies. Your friend in great haste, D.H. Lewis.

P.S. It is understood the pretiminaries [*sic*] of the Treaty have already been arranged & only awaits [*sic*] the special minister who is daily expected.

ALS in DLC, Richard Kenner Crallé Papers; PEx in Frederick W. Moore, ed., "Calhoun as Seen by His Political Friends," *Publications of the Southern History Association*, vol. 7 (1903), pp. 421–422. NOTE: Duff Green had written to Crallé on 3/18 that he had already "written to Mr. Calhoun that I *know* that you will accept the situation of Chief Clerk [of the State Department] and urged your appt. . . . There are others pressing for the place—The President wishes you to get it." (LS in DLC, Duff Green Papers; PEx in Moore, "Calhoun as Seen by His Political Friends," 7:421.)

From W[ILLIA]M P. PREBLE

Portland [Maine], March 19, 1844

Sir, Jeremiah O'Brian [*sic*] esquire of Brunswick in this State is desirous of obtaining the situation of a Clerk in the Department of State, if you can, consistently with your own views, find a place of the kind in your gift to bestow. Without wishing myself to interfere in the least degree with any arrangement of your own in this matter, I beg leave to assure you that, living as I do in the vicinity of Mr. O'Brien, I have full confidence in his integrity and uprightness, and in his qualifications for the employment he wishes to obtain; and that, as one of your friends in Maine, I should be pleased with his appointment, if made by you. With very great respect I am, Sir your obedient servant, Wm. P. Preble.

ALS in DNA, RG 59 (General Records of the Department of State), Letters of Application and Recommendation during the Administrations of Martin Van Buren, William Henry Harrison, and John Tyler, 1837–1845, O'Brien (M-687:24, frame 365). NOTE: Preble had been U.S. Minister to the Netherlands and one of the Maine commissioners for the settlement of the Northeastern boundary.

From RICH[AR]D HAWES

Paris Kentucky, March 21, 1844

Sir, I presume so far on ["the" *canceled and* "our" *interlined*] acquaintance formed at Washington to address you on the subject of the annexation of Texas, to the U. States. I am induced to this particularly, from the information, that you have been nominated & confirmed as Secretary of State, an appointment which I hope you may be willing to accept.

It is known to you that there is a belt of country extending across our continent peculiarly adapted to the production of cotton, and perhaps the only portion of the Globe, where it can be successfully & extensively cultivated, and that it is a staple which in value far transcends any other to which human labour can be applied. I am firmly persuaded that it is our policy to own all the cotton lands of North America if we can. I fear that Texas cannot subsist as a separate nation, and that she must become by incorporation, or by alliance of some kind [united] with some foreign power, if we decline to be united with her.

Her people are our brethren, our neighbours, fathers, sons,

brothers &c &c and we should & will sympathise with every suffering they endure, & must be embroiled in all her quarrels & wars. While this state of things exist[s] is it not best that she should at once be united in the Confederacy with us? If she should form a foreign alliance, will not the natural bonds of friendship ["to us" *interlined*] be dissevered, and like all family quarrels will it not be turned into a most virulent hatred, which will be constantly aggravated by commercial rivalry in the cotton market?

If as I suppose she will if rejected by us be driven to a foreign alliance, will not that alliance necessarily conform to the miscalled & distempered philantrophy of the day, and be based on the abolition of slavery in Texas[?] In this event Texas will be a den of run away slaves from the south & South west &c &c.

The Northern States now have pos[s]ession of the markets of the U.S. in cotton manufactures, and will ultimately get ahead of England & France with foreign nations. Is it not to their ultimate interest that we should own the country & the whole country which produces the raw material?

Is it not a miserable truckling to abolitionists to allow their interference with our slave property under the hypocritical cant of liberty, to alarm us out of a great national policy?

Is it not disreputable to the spirit of the South & West, to be bullied by the North in a question of slave & non slave holding political ascendency?

Let the treaty be once made, and the gallant enthusiasm of the South & West, with the whole influence of the army & navy will accomplish the confirmation of it. It may be deferred & defeated at first, but it must be ultimately confirmed. The constitutional question, the great extent of Territory, &c urged against annexation, are mere bug bears. The North is quite willing to get up any agitation to the North, so as to get ["the" *interlined*] Canadas, and when the canadians are ripe for such an event, they will drive us into a war on that matter to a certainty.

There is no danger of a war with England—she is constantly despoiling India, & china, & she cannot part with our commerce, much less can she allow our manufactures to ripen into that maturity, which a war would inevitably produce.

I make these hasty & loose suggestions, which will pass with you for what they are worth. They are only a part of what might be urged.

The only difficulty in the entire success of annexation is its association with party. Mr. [Henry] Clay is against it, and he is a host with his friends, but let the treaty be once made, and the national pride, &

the ardor of the south & west, coming in unison with their sympathies, & interests will do the work. Very Resp[ectfull]y y[ou]rs, Richd. Hawes.

ALS in ScCleA; variant PC in Boucher and Brooks, eds., *Correspondence*, pp. 217–218. Note: Richard Hawes (1797–1877) had been Representative from Ky. during 1837–1841 and became the Confederate Governor of Ky. during the Civil War.

From Rob[er]t Semple

Alton (Illinois), March 22, 1844

Dear Sir: From personal motives, I am induced to ask a favor at your hands. I boast of no high-toned Patriotism in my present application. I have a constitution which will not bear a Northern climate and my fortune is not sufficient to afford me a residence in the South, and under a thorough conviction that I am quallified and willing to perform the duties of a government officer with honor to myself and my country, I am induced to ask you, if it should be in your power, to give me the appointment of Consul, Vice Consul, or even commercial agent for some of the Ports of South America or Mexico. I know of no Vacancy, nor do I wish any to be created on my account.

On the score of politics, I am and always have been a thorough "State Rights" man, and was one of 73 men that resolved, in the event of an open rupture [in 1832–1833], to go from Kentucky to assist South Carolina in her struggle for Liberty. I have never asked for office from any administration, but I feel more at liberty now that I have done, and my state of health admonishes me that it is best for me to get South.

I would refer you for my character and qualifications to my brother [James Semple], one of the Senators from this State; to Hon. Mr. [Sidney] Breese, [and] Hon. Robert Smith, [Senator and Representative] of Illinois; and to Hon. George A. Caldwell, and Hon. W[illia]m Thomasson [Representatives] of Ky.

Should it be convenient for you to give me such an appointment, you will confer a lasting favor upon me, and no effort of mine shall be wanting to make it an honorable one to the State. Very Respectfully your ob[edien]t Serv[an]t, Rob[er]t Semple.

ALS in DNA, RG 59 (General Records of the Department of State), Letters of Application and Recommendation during the Administrations of Martin Van Buren, William Henry Harrison, and John Tyler, 1837–1845, Semple (M-687:29, frames 622–624).

To [the Rev.] W[ILLIAM] B. SPRAGUE, Albany, N.Y.

Fort Hill, 22d March 1844

Dear Sir, I would gladly furnish any material in my power, which might tend to illustrate the character of one, for whose memory I have so much respect, as I have for Dr. [Timothy] Dwight, but I can call to memory no anecdote, calculated to aid you in your laudable task.

I was only two years in [Yale] College, and knew him more in the capacity of an instructor, than any other. In that, his character was marked by great dignity and kindness. It was free from all peculiarities and excentricities [*sic*]. It was in all respects a model for instructors; and, perhaps, on that account, in a great measure exempt, from anecdotes. With great respect I am & &, J.C. Calhoun.

ALS in ScU-SC, John C. Calhoun Papers. NOTE: Sprague became the author of a "Life of Timothy Dwight" that was published in Jared Sparks, *Library of American Biography*, 2nd series, vol. IV (1845).

From GARRET D. WALL, [former Senator from N.J.]

Woodbury [N.J.], March 22, 1844

D[ea]r Sir, I take the liberty of introducing to your acquaintance Dr. Franklin Lippincott, of this place who will be the Bearer of this. Dr. Lippincott is a native of the County of Gloucester, a member of a very respectable family, much esteemed in this county, of unexceptionable character and of very respectable attainments in his profession and a gentleman in feeling, manners and education. The feeble state of his health has induced him, in the hope of restoring it to seek a Consular appointment, in some clime which will afford him [*one word canceled and "a" interlined*] change [*"of climate" interlined*]. I have great pleasure in assuring you, that any aid which you may deem it in your power to afford him, will be bestowed on a worthy Gentleman, who will never disgrace his friends or our Country. With great respect Y[ou]r ob[edien]t Ser[van]t, Garret D. Wall.

ALS in DNA, RG 59 (General Records of the Department of State), Letters of Application and Recommendation during the Administrations of Martin Van

Buren, William Henry Harrison, and John Tyler, 1837–1845, Lippincott (M-687:19, frame 489). NOTE: Lippincott was appointed U.S. Consul at Cienfuegos, Cuba, on 9/5/1844.

From WILSON LUMPKIN

Athens [Ga.,] March 23d, 1844

My dear Sir, That the destiny of men & nations are under the controuling influence of an *All-wise* Providence, has long since been one of the set[t]led *Tenets* of my *faith*. And it is thus, that I account for your being placed in the position which you now occupy, in connection with the great interests of our beloved Country. I know, that your present position has not been anticipated by you, or your friends. I hope, trust & believe, that the recent changes, however deeply mingled, with calamity, woe & regret, may be overruled for the good of our country. At this particular juncture, your post is the most important one under the government.

Upon an enlarged consideration, of the permanent interest of our confederacy, we have nothing at this time of equal importance, to that of the great Territorial questions, of *Texas & Orregon*. Upon these questions I entertain no doubt, of the correctness of your views, as well as of the views of President [John] Tyler, and therefore trust, you may be the honored instruments of bringing these vexed questions to a happy & successful issue. As regards the adjustment of the Oregon question, you know & will do what is best to be done on that subject.

Upon the subject of *Texas*, allow me to say, that Country, must speedily become a part & portion, of our great confederacy—or the abolition spirit, will destroy our beloved institutions. The peaceable acquisition of Texas, will go further to ensure & perpetuate the general welfare & permanent union of our Confederacy than any thing which has transpired, since the acquisition of Louisiana. I have no special knowledge of the exact relation of things, touching this subject at present. I have however a very accurate knowledge, of a large number of the leading and most influential men of Texas, & of the true character & feelings of the great body of the population of that Country. My eldest son [Pleides O. Lumpkin] emigrated to that Country about 10 years ago, & has continued to live there ever since. He has a wife & children, is a steady sensible, educated man—and has several times been a member of the Legislature of Texas. I am intimately acquainted with [former] President [Mirabeau B.] Lamar, Gen[era]l [Thomas J.] Rusk & various other Georgians who have become prominent in that Country. Therefore through these associations I have continued to know more, & feel more in regard to Texas, than most men.

The great body of the people of Texas, ardently desire to come into our Union. Any opposition which may appear to annexation, whether from President [Samuel] Houston or others, I am well assured is altogether selfish & factious.

Anxious as I am, to know the state of our negociations & prospects, upon this subject, your present position forbids my making many enquiries which might be suggested, if I considered you at liberty ["to" *interlined*] confer with a private citizen upon a subject, which may at the present moment require the most profound silence, out of the council chamber.

I could easily write an Essay, or volume, upon the great importance of the annexation of Texas, but deem the multipl[ic]ation of words upon this subject, when addressing you, altogether useless— because I know you will ["will" *canceled*] duly appreciate its magnitude in all its bearings.

I would willingly make any sacrifice of my quiet, ease & inclination, to aid in furthering and consum[m]ating this all important object. And if I find the state of things touching this subject, should in the course of the present year, open a door for useful & efficient service, I have it [in] view to visit the Country. If Texas should become a part of the U.S. It will be a matter of vital importance, to the entire South, that all the incipient steps, touching the establishment of the local institutions of that Country, should be based & founded in wisdom, & that far seeing forecast, so necessary to the permanent prosperity & harmony of the whole Union.

Any thing, that may be proper for me [to] know, at any time, on the subject of Texas, will be rec[e]ived with thankfulness. For your health, happiness, & success in your present labors, my poor prayers & best wishes await you. As Ever y[ou]rs, Wilson Lumpkin.

ALS in ScCleA; variant PC in Jameson, ed., *Correspondence*, pp. 942–944. Note: This letter was addressed to Calhoun in Washington and was postmarked in Athens on 3/26[?].

From A[ARON?] MILHADO

Norfolk, Mar[ch] 23d 1844

You will I am sure my Dear Sir, pardon me for expressing my great gratification at your accepting the important office to which you have just been called.

The momentous Questions now agitating the Union will I feel assured be settled upon terms alike hon[orabl]e to yourself and the Country at large.

When the news first reached here of y[ou]r appointment, it brought forcibly to my mind the Dream, (which doubtless ere this you have forgotten) that I related to yourself and Gov[erno]r [Littleton W.] Tazewell at the Dinner given you at French's Hotel during y[ou]r late visit to Norfolk [in 3/1843]—relative to a close conversation between Pres[iden]t [John] Tyler & yourself—you replied, Dream no more Sir; Dream no more—for I have had only one close conversation with Pres[iden]t Tyler, & that was at the *commencement* of the [1841] Extra Session of Congress—to which I rejoined— well it doesn't follow, in consequence of that; that you will not have another towards the *close* of his term—from the present aspect of things, I am very much inclined to believe my Dream, will be verified.

With my best wishes for y[ou]r continued health & happiness I have the hon[o]r to subscribe myself Y[ou]r f[rien]d & O[bedien]t S[ervan]t, A. Milhado.

ALS in ScCleA.

From G[EORGE] ROBERTSON

Lexington Ky., 23rd march 1844

Dear Sir, Presuming that you have accepted the Secretaryship of State, allow me to congratulate you and the Country on an event I consider so ["just and" *interlined*] auspicious to that long abused Country and to you.

The position itself, the crisis, and the circumstances of your appointment made an appeal to both the head and the heart which, in my humble judgement, neither patriotism nor prudence could resist. And placed where, as I presume, you now are, you may right the rudderless ship of State, and, in righting that, *may also right yourself.*

That you may be the blessed instrument of effecting both ends is my sincere and ardent wish.

Have not the Character of our Government and the popular Confidence, at home and abroad, in the efficacy and stability of it's fundamental institutions been cruelly and alarmingly impaired by the fatal predominance, for years, of factious combinations of unprincipled placemen, selfish *politicians,* and their ignorant and licentious tools? And should it not be the *paramount* object of every lofty patriot who consults either his own fame or his countrie's weal, to restore that lost Character and lost confidence by endeavoring to place in power, of all grades, men of probity and talents and frown out of Countenance the humiliating, corrupting, and enslaving practise of rewarding ["vice"(?) *canceled*] duplicity, charlatanism, and unscrupulous prostitution? Is not this *now* the great *comprehensive* question—*"the one thing needful"?* And this atchieved—will not all other attainable blessings follow? And is not an honest effort to accomplish this great moral and political revolution as much the interest as it is the duty of every wise and patriotic American? Your concurrence, head and heart, in these sentiments I *will* not doubt. And with this conviction I salute you cordially as Secretary of State of the United States; and ["will" *interlined*] cherish a hope that you may—by ["sti]cking to this text," and by illustrating it as *you* are so well qualified to do, advance our countrie's prosperity, elevate it's character, and add to your own renown.

Interpret rightly, I beseech you, and *therefore* excuse this frank, though laconic, communication from an ancient friend who is neither "Nullifier" nor "Democrat" in the perverted sense of locofocoism, ["or" *interlined*] Van Burenism, or Bentonism, or any other *-ism* than Americanism, Constitutional, conservative, moral, *intellectual.* Neither holding nor desiring ["party"(?) *canceled*] office, my only motive is friendship, my only purpose good—good to you, good to all honest men, good to our character and our union as people, as States, as a nation. And I trust that *"auld lang sine"* will relieve me from the suspicion of any sinister end as well as from the imputation of officiousness or presumptuousness in thus uttering such sentiments and intimating such counsel, at such a time, and to one so ripe in years and matured in all the knowledge befitting the highest place and the most exalted aspirations. Believe me, I have no selfish object, no occult meaning, no indirect or sinister purpose. And give me credit for Candor and some prophetic sagacity when I assure you that I have no doubt that if—looking at the petty game of "party" as below the dignity and honor of a lone Statesman and regarding, at this momentous crisis, (especially), all diversities of opinion as to politico-economical expedients as comparatively trifling and postponable—you add the weight of your influence in behalf of the great *moral* revolution to which I have alluded, a most glorious triumph is sure—triumph to our institutions and our name as an united nation—and ultimate triumph to yourself as signal as it will be honorable. And all this will, as it seems to me, accord as well with your principles and policy as with your patriotism and honorable ambition. Yours respectfully, G. Robertson.

LS in ScCleA. NOTE: George Robertson (1790–1874) was Representative from Ky. during 1817–1821 and professor of law at Transylvania University, 1834–1857.

From EDWARD EVERETT, [U.S. Minister to Great Britain]

London, 25 March 1844

Dear Sir, I beg leave to recommend to your friendly attention the gentleman who offers you this letter, Professor [Friedrich] Von Raumer of the University of Berlin, who I doubt not is well known to you by reputation, as the author of several popular and valuable works. I am indebted for his personal acquaintance to [Friedrich Ludwig,] Baron [von] Roenne [former Prussian Minister to the U.S.] and Mr. [Henry] Wheaton [U.S. Minister to Prussia], who have recommended him to me in the warmest terms.

Professor Von Raumer in company with his son proposes to visit the United States with a view of studying their institutions, manners, social and economical condition. He carries with him the kindest dispositions towards our Country, and the calm and impartial spirit of a philosopher, (I use the language of Mr. Wheaton) whose talent for observation has been perfected by travels in different countries of Europe, the results of which have been already communicated to the public.

Any assistance you may be able to render him in his enquiries, and any good offices toward him, will be bestowed on a gentleman of great personal worth as well as literary respectability, who unites to his individual claims the circumstance of being a citizen of a country, in which a kindly feeling toward the United States is widely diffused, and where a respectable American traveller would be sure to meet a hospitable reception. I have the honor to be, Dear Sir, with great respect, very faithfully yours, Edward Everett.

LS in ScCleA. NOTE: An AEU by Calhoun reads: "Mr. Everett[,] introducing Von Raumer." The address leaf of this letter is missing, but it is clear from his official dispatches at this time and later that Everett was not aware of Calhoun's appointment as Secretary of State when he wrote.

From ALBERT SMITH,
[former Representative from Maine]

Washington, Mar. 25th 1844

The undersigned, having been long & intimately acquainted with Jeremiah O'Brien most cheerfully bears testimony to his high character for intelligence & integrity. Should it be in the power of the Secretary of State, consistently with his other engagements, & the public interest to give Mr. O'Brien the appointment [as a State Dept. Clerk] his friends solicit, the undersigned would be personally obliged. Albert Smith.

ALS in DNA, RG 59 (General Records of the Department of State), Letters of Application and Recommendation during the Administrations of Martin Van Buren, William Henry Harrison, and John Tyler, 1837–1845, O'Brien (M-687:24, frames 357–359). NOTE: Smith's letter was appended to a letter to Smith, dated 3/21/1844, from John C. Humphreys, Alfred J. Stone, and A.B. Thompson, recommending O'Brien.

From H[ENRY] BAILEY, "Chairman"

CHARLESTON, MARCH 26, 1844.

Sir: Your acceptance of the important trusts of the State Department of the Union, and your passage through our city to the seat of government, have afforded to the citizens of Charleston, and its vicinity, a grateful occasion, of which they have availed themselves with feelings of enthusiasm, to present to you a public testimonial of the profound regard, admiration, and esteem, which they entertain for you.

Fixed as you have long been in their affections, there needed nothing to increase their attachment to you, or to enhance their estimate of either your abilities, or your virtues. For more than thirty years you have been identified with the history of your country, and those of its pages are most luminous with your name, on which the eye of patriotism, philanthropy, and virtue, will most delight to dwell; and although had you exhibited less of those transcendant abilities, those lofty powers of intellect, and those exalted moral qualities, which have guided, sustained, and distinguished your entire public career, and even added lustre to the virtues of your private life, we should still have felt that we, and our successors, had incurred to you a debt of gratitude, as enduring and imperishable, as the liberties and institutions, of which you have been the bold yet patient, sagacious, undaunted, and we trust, eventually, the successful defender.

But, sir, you have, by your recent and prompt acceptance of the difficult, although highly distinguished position, to which you have been called by the unanimous voice of your countrymen, greatly enhanced the measure of your obligations, and added yet another, and striking testimonial of the justness of the estimate we had made of your character. We cannot but be aware that the appointment tendered to you, however important to the country, and with whatever circumstances of honor conferred upon you, was yet one which you must, as far as yourself was concerned, have been most reluctant to accept. Whilst it could not add to the honors and distinctions which have already in rich profusion gathered around your name, it was a summons to abandon that retirement and repose, of which you were in the enjoyment, and which we know you must earnestly have desired, and whilst it involved other sacrifices, painful, irksome, and annoying in themselves, it presented only difficulties to be encountered and responsibilities to be incurred, rather than honors to be won. Such, sir, seems to have been the general estimate of the duties you have been called upon to assume. The conviction has been universal, that the highest interests of our country were to a very great extent, dependent upon the conduct of the department to which you have been called; and it was because of the momentous importance of the interests which are in question, and because, whilst the duties of the State Department, in the present emergency, required abilities of the highest order, guided by a mature wisdom, stern integrity, and a lofty patriotism—they at the same time involved responsibilities which might peril the most exalted reputation, that all eyes, through the length and breadth of the land, were turned upon you. This, sir, is a tribute to your character, the more valuable, not only from its being the spontaneous offering of the whole nation, stifling for a moment the voice of party, but because it may well be described as involuntary and instinctive. And it has in no way surprised us, without reference to this tribute of honor, that you "could not resist this call upon your patriotism," but that you unhesitatingly determined to obey it, at any and every personal sacrifice; yet neither is the obligation on this account diminished, nor the emotion of our admiration and grateful esteem, the less excited by this new and eminent instance of the self-devoted patriotism which has characterized your whole life.

Nor, in making a just estimate of the difficulties of the charge you have undertaken, would we wish to be understood as holding the language of despondency. We cannot indulge the apprehension, that your sacrifices on this occasion will be without their reward; but we fervently trust that they will receive, in the successful termination of your official labors, that only recompense which you covet, the advancement of the best interests of your country. We might say, with the ancient wanderer, *"Nil desperandum Teucro duce;"* but we have a far higher hope than that which is founded in a reliance upon the mere ability or good fortune of any individual; and we do trust that the same moderation, where principle is not involved, and that intrepid, unyielding and sacred adherence to the principles of truth, justice, national honor and constitutional liberty, which have heretofore sustained you in so many conflicts, and under so many difficulties, will here also be crowned with a triumph grateful to humanity.

Impressed and animated with these convictions, your fellow-citizens of Charleston, of all parties, with a unanimity perfect and enthusiastic, have seized the present occasion to give expression to their feelings. At a recent public meeting, as you have been already apprized, a committee of one hundred of their number was appointed, in concurrence with the municipal authorities, to welcome your arrival in Charleston, and tender to you the hospitalities of the city; and the same committee were also specially instructed "to convey to you the feelings of the meeting, and their estimate of your public course and character, and to invite you to partake of a public dinner." This grateful duty I have now the honor to perform, on behalf of the committee, and as their organ; and it only remains, in the name of the citizens of Charleston, respectfully to invite you to meet them at the social board, and partake of a public dinner, at such time as may suit your convenience.

Please, sir, to accept the assurance of the committee and myself, of the high personal regard and esteem with which We have the honor to be Your obedient servants, H. Bailey, Chairman.

PC in the Charleston, S.C., *Courier,* March 29, 1844, p. 2; PC in the Milledgeville, Ga., *Federal Union,* April 2, 1844, p. 2; PC in the Washington, D.C., *Spectator,* April 4, 1844, p. 3; PC in the Jackson, Miss., *Mississippian,* April 10,

1844, p. 3; PC in the Nashville, Tenn., *Union*, May 4, 1844, p. 2. NOTE: Henry Bailey (1799–1849) was Attorney General of S.C. during 1836–1848. He was perhaps chosen to head Calhoun's welcoming committee because he was the highest ranking State official present in Charleston at the time.

To H[ENRY] BAILEY

CHARLESTON, 26th March, 1844

Sir—I exceedingly regret, that the arrangements which I have made, and the time I have fixed for my arrival in Washington, will not permit me to accept the invitation of my fellow-citizens of Charleston, to partake of a public dinner, which you, as the organ of their committee, have so acceptably tendered.

You are right in supposing, that I left my retirement with great reluctance. When I resigned my seat in the Senate of the United States, I intended so to close my public life, unless the voice of my country should call me into its service. I had accomplished my full tour of duty. I had served the public for thirty-five years, continuously in various capacities, according to the best of my ability, and I anxiously desired repose. But I hold, that when the voice of the country, distinctly pronounced, demands the service of any citizen, he is bound to obey, be the sacrifice what it may. In my case I feel the responsibility to be great. The pending negotiations, which I have been unanimously called upon to take charge of, have never been exceeded in their importance by any since that which sealed our Independence, excepting that, which so honorably terminated the late war [of 1812]. I can scarcely hope, that I shall be able to terminate, by any effort I can make, the duties which I have to perform, with the same unanimity with which I have been called on to undertake them. I shall, however, omit no exertions to preserve that high and general confidence, which has led to my appointment, and should deeply deplore, should it be my misfortune, to have it impaired in any degree. But as greatly as I should regret it, I shall not be deterred from doing, what I may honestly believe to be right, even by that sacrifice. My duty and my country shall be my guides, and I shall faithfully follow them, lead where they may.

It is well known that I am the advocate of peace—peace with all, and especially with that great country, from which we draw our origin, and of whose renown we may well be proud. There are no other two countries which can do more harm to each other, or confer greater

893

benefits, the one on the other. But as highly as I value peace, I hold it subordinate to the honor and just rights of the country; whilst, on the other hand, no consideration shall induce me to sacrifice the peace of the country, by claiming more, in the discharge of my duties, than I shall honestly believe, that the honor and rights of the country demand. Her true honor and interests consist, according to my conception, in claiming nothing but what is just and right, and in accepting nothing that is not.

Permit me, in conclusion to say, that no language, which I can command, can suitably express the feelings excited in my bosom by the honors, which the citizens of this ancient, and honored commercial metropolis of the State, have conferred upon me, and by the highly acceptable manner, in which you, as their organ, and the Honorable the Mayor of the city [John Schnierle], as that of the Corporation, have so kindly tendered them. They, and the many heretofore bestowed upon me, and the steady support, which I have ever received from my fellow-citizens of Charleston, in all the trials and difficulties through which it has been my lot to pass, have imposed a debt of gratitude, which I shall ever remember, but which I shall never be able adequately to discharge. With high respect, I am, &c., J.C. Calhoun.

PC in the Charleston, S.C., *Courier*, March 29, 1844, p. 2; PC in the Charleston, S.C., *Mercury*, March 30, 1844, p. 2; PC in the Washington, D.C., *Spectator*, April 1, 1844, p. 3; PC in the Richmond, Va., *Enquirer*, April 2, 1844, p. 2; PC in the Milledgeville, Ga., *Federal Union*, April 2, 1844, p. 2; PC in the Alexandria, D.C., *Gazette and Virginia Advertiser*, April 2, 1844, p. 2; PC in the Philadelphia, Pa., *Pennsylvania Inquirer and National Gazette*, April 2, 1844, p. 2; PC in the Washington, D.C., *Madisonian*, April 3, 1844, p. 2; PC in the Raleigh, N.C., *North Carolina Standard*, April 3, 1844, p. 3; PC in the Norfolk and Portsmouth, Va., *American Beacon and Daily Advertiser*, April 4, 1844, p. 2; PC in the Pendleton, S.C., *Messenger*, April 5, 1844, p. 2; PC in *Niles' National Register*, vol. LXVI, no. 6 (April 6, 1844), p. 85; PC in the New Orleans, La., *Courrier de la Louisiane*, April 6, 1844, p. 3; PC in the New York, N.Y., *Evening Post*, April 6, 1844, p. 1; PC in the Greenville, S.C., *Mountaineer*, April 12, 1844, p. 2; PC in the Jackson, Miss., *Southern Reformer*, April 13, 1844, p. 2; PC in the Nashville, Tenn., *Union*, May 4, 1844, p. 2.

From [the Rev.] W[ILLIAM] CAPERS

Charleston, Mar[ch] 26, '44

Honored Sir, While your fellow citizens are crouding [*sic*] around you with eager emulation to do you honor—and especially in view of this last act of yours, in consenting to serve, under present circumstances, as Secretary of State of the U.S.—I dare persuade myself it will not offend if one of my habits & calling should approach you in this private manner.

Permit me then, to assure you of my best wishes; & my prayers to God for you, that it may please Him long to preserve your life & health; & that long as you live, you may have his grace to prevent & assist you, that your example may still prove strongly on the side of virtue & religion—a guide to our youth, & an encouragement to all good men.

Believe me, honored sir, that in my prayers to Almighty God for his blessing on "all who are in authority," I charge myself always to remember you.

I am, honored Sir, very sincerely, Your friend, & most humble servant, W. Capers.

ALS in ScCleA. NOTE: Capers (1790–1855), notable for his missionary work among the Creek Indians and S.C. slaves, became a bishop of the Methodist Episcopal Church South in 1846.

From N[ATHANIEL] CHAPMAN, M.D., "Professor &c in the University of Pennsylvania"

Philadelphia, March 26, 1844

It affords me great pleasure to bear my testimony, in common with many of his friends, to the respectability of the character and standing of Dr. Franklin Lippincott of New Jersey. For several years I knew him well, as a student in our Medical School, where he was distinguished by his talents, and gentlemanly deportment, and finally graduated with distinction, as a Doctor of Medicine. Being now, in delicate health, he is desirous to remove to a warmer climate, and I have no doubt will prove an acquisition to any community in which he may settle. N. Chapman, M.D., Professor &c in the University of Pennsylvania.

ALS in DNA, RG 59 (General Records of the Department of State), Letters of Application and Recommendation during the Administrations of Martin Van Buren, William Henry Harrison, and John Tyler, 1837–1845, Lippincott (M-687:19, frames 490–491).

From JOHN A. JONES, "Private"

Fairie Known[,] Paulding c[oun]ty Ga., 27th March 1844
Sir, An opinion has gone abroad since the publication of your letter
withdrawing your name from the consideration of the Baltimore convention for May that you refuse in any event or in any manner to permit your name to be run for the Presidency. How such a construction
could be put on that letter, I am at a loss to conjecture, for I gave it
a very different reading[.] I understood you to refer that matter to
your friends thereby intending it to be distinctly understood that the
advocates of free trade might freely make you instrumental in carrying out doctrines which you & they believe essential to the prosperity
& happiness of the people & to the preservation of the union. I am
one of those & I desire to know from you if we are to understand that
you forbid the effort to be made by & through our exertions & your
instrumentality to preserve the institutions of the republic & the rights
of the South. If leisure & inclination affords a reply to this ["be" *interlined*] pleased to put it in a shape for publication if it should be
deemed expedient to give it that course. I am very respectful[l]y
your ob[e]d[ien]t S[er]v[an]t, John A. Jones.
P.S. As an entire stranger it may possibly not be improper to say
to you Messrs. [William H.] Stiles & [John H.] Lumpkin of the
Georgia delegation [in the U.S. House of Representatives] can inform
you who I am. J.A. Jones.

ALS in ScCleA. NOTE: An AEU by Calhoun reads: "Mr. Jones[,] Relates to
withdrawing my name."

From N. NEWTON, JR., E. M. STONE, and O. JENNY

Norwalk, Huron Co[unty], Ohio, March 27, 1844
Sir, We take this method of recommending to your favourable notice
Mr. Benj[amin] T. Brown ["of" *canceled*] as a proper person to be
employed in your Department. Mr. Brown is a resident of this place,
a Student at Law, a gentleman of good talents; and his relations who
reside in Michigan, are some of the most respectable and intelligent
citizens there.

Should you deem it proper to give him an appointment, we have
no doubt that you would find him to be a gentleman of strict business

habits, of well disciplined mind, and every way worthy of your high regard. And while the station would be conferring a favour on him personally, it would at the same time, be esteemed by your friends in this part of Ohio no less a mark of your regard towards them. We have the honor to be your sincere friends, N. Newton, Jr., E.M. Stone, O. Jenny.

LS in DNA, RG 59 (General Records of the Department of State), Letters of Application and Recommendation during the Administrations of Martin Van Buren, William Henry Harrison, and John Tyler, 1837–1845, Brown (M-687:3, frames 417–418).

REMARKS AT CHARLESTON

[March 27, 1844]

On reaching the City Hall, Mr. Calhoun was received with loud and repeated cheers by the citizens, and met by the Mayor [John Schnierle] and Council, with their staves of office; and his Honor, the Mayor, in a strain of warm and impassioned greeting, tendered to the illustrious guest the hospitalities of the city and the welcome of her citizens. Mr. Calhoun made a brief and animated response, in which he alluded to the spontaneous welcome of his reception, without distinction of party, as one of the most gratifying events of his long public career. He spoke, too, of his call to the State department, with the concurrence of all parties, as a mark of confidence he might well be proud of; and declared that it would be his object, in administering it, to conciliate all parties—especially in reference to the too [*sic*; two] delicate and important negotiations now pending—not exceeded in importance by any since that which ratified our independence. He added that he had no intention of making a speech—indeed, he was without the material for one—the mode of his reception rendered party politics a sealed book to him—and he concluded with cordial and ardent wishes for the prosperity of Charleston and her citizens.

From the Charleston, S.C., *Courier*, March 27, 1844, p. 2; partly printed in the Baltimore, Md., *American and Commercial Daily Advertiser*, March 30, 1844, p. 2. NOTE: Calhoun's rather triumphal visit to Charleston and the preparations for it are amply reported in the Charleston, S.C., *Mercury*, March 22, 23, 25, 26, 27, and 28, 1844. His reception when he landed at Wilmington, N.C., to take the railroad is reported in the *Mercury* of March 30.

From J[AMES] HAMILTON [JR.]

New Orleans, March 28th 1844

My Dear Sir, I enclose you the within Letter which I understand is from a worthy applicant for a Consulate in Cuba whom Mr. [Abel P.] Upshur had he lived would have appointed.

I leave for Texas this morning & will write you on my return to this place in the course of [*one number canceled and "14" interlined*] Days. I remain with esteem Yours ever, J. Hamilton [Jr.].

[Enclosure]

Isaac Stone to Gen[era]l James Hamilton

New Orleans, 27th March 1844

Dear Sir, I address you the present at the suggestion of my friend Mr. James Reed tho' I hope to have the pleasure of seeing you this evening and explaining to you more fully than I can on paper my object in requesting of you the favor indicated by him. My wish is to obtain the Consulate of "San Juan de los Remedios" in the Island of Cuba— and about mid way between Matanzas & Muriatos[?]—it is a small post, but being well situated and in a thickly settled part of the Island I think that a considerable & profitable trade may be built up there— and I wish the appointment solely for the protection it will afford to myself and the interests of our countrymen engaged therein—the emoluments of this office would be no object to any one. I have applied for the appointment and judging by my letters from Washington I suppose I should have received it ere this but for the sad catastrophe on board the Princeton and death of Mr. [Abel P.] Upshur. I am now advised that it will be well for me to get a letter to Mr. Calhoun & with this in view I went to see Mr. Reed in order to get him to inquire of you *where* I should direct a letter in order to have it reach Mr. [Joel R.] Poinsett—with whom I had the pleasure of being on intimate terms during his residence in Mexico—where next to him I held the most important post, in the gift of our government (the Consulate at Vera Cruz) & I know he would cheerfully render me any aid in his power to accomplish my wishes—at the same ["*time*" *interlined*] I was fearful that he might not be on friendly terms with Mr. Calhoun which would place him in an unpleasant position. Under these circumstances Mr. Reed suggested that I should apply to you for the favor of a letter— and proffered his friendly services in my behalf. Should you grant my request you will confer a favor & I beg to assure you that your recommendation shall suffer no dishonor from Very Respectfully Sir Your mo[st] ob[edient] Servant, Isaac Stone.

ALS with En in DNA, RG 59 (General Records of the Department of State), Letters of Application and Recommendation during the Administrations of Martin Van Buren, William Henry Harrison, and John Tyler, 1837–1845, Stone (M-687: 31, frames 413–417). NOTE: Stone received the appointment requested in 8/1844.

From I[SRAEL] K. TEFFT

Savannah, 28th Mar[ch] '44

Dear Sir, I avail myself of the kindness of my friend W[illia]m B. Hodgson Esq., who will leave here this ev[enin]g for Washington, to forward your Diploma of honorary membership of the Georgia Historical Society, and for your acceptance copies of the two vols. of its Collections—the receipt of which I beg you will do me the favor to acknowledge. I have the honor to be with great respect & regard Your Ob[edien]t Serv[an]t, I.K. Tefft.

ALS in ScCleA.

From JAMES WISHART, "Private"

St. Clairsville [Ohio,] March 28th 1844

My Dear Sir, Your letter of the 8th inst[ant] did not reach me until the 23rd[.] Before that time the opinion that you would accept the office of Secretary of State, was prevailent, and seemed to give great and universal satisfaction. Although there are some circumstances connected with it, not as we might wish them, yet I rejoice that you are again at the centre of action, in the present critical situation of affairs.

At the time I wrote the letter to which yours is an answer I was laboring under the influence of great mental depression occasioned by the course of your friends at Washington and elsewhere, but it is a source of high gratification to know that your opinions correspond with my own. Presuming that your correspondence is very laborious, I have abstained from addressing you as often as I wished, and only wrote when I ["wished" *canceled and* "desired" *interlined*] to communicate information which I deemed important, or make a point on passing events. Your letters have uniformly been very pleasant, and acceptable to me, and if I could obtain them more frequently without imposing on you the labor of writing them, my pleasure would be greatly enhanced.

In the intercourse which has taken place between us I think you have had some evidence that I am neither a parasite nor sycophant. I shall assume, for the present at least, that such is the fact. I have seen enough I think to justify the conclusion, that although, all of your southern friends of whom I have any knowledge, are men of talents, and statesmen of a high order, there is not a general or a leader of commanding ability among them, unless Mr. [Robert B.] Rhett may have some claims to such designation. You have given ample evidence, more than enough to satisfy me that you can see further and more clearly into the future, and take a more comprehensive view of things than any man with whom I ["have" *interlined*] had intercourse—while your powers of analysis are unequaled by any writer ancient or modern. You say in your last letter to me, it is not in my nature to do that through others which I could not, with propriety, do myself. This is a noble sentiment, and shows a mind without guile, but even in the purest mind, will not admit of universal application. A member of my family may be a corp[se], the duty of sepulture is mine, while its offices are more properly performed by others. Now as the south requires the best tallents she can produce to save her in the crisis which is upon her, unless you will act, the united efforts of all other southern men are futile; as we have seen within the last six months. You may rest assured my dear Sir I would not advise to any act which would tarnish your character or detract from your well merited fame, for I glory in both, and both are very dear to me. What I propose is that you act yourself as generalissimo of the campaign. Make me, or any other you may deem more suitable, your channel of communication, and thus shield yourself from the assaults of your enemies. Your secret will be with me inviolable, and the object secured by its operation, a great, and very probably a lasting benefit confer[r]ed on the human family. This proposition is made because I have lost confidence in the generalship and ability of all other southern men but yourself, to effect anything, and if any southern man but yourself were to offer he would find few to follow in the north and west. Should this suggestion meet your approbation please to give me your thoughts on it, if not let it be forgotten.

B.G. Wright Esq[ui]r[e] showed me a letter addressed to Mr. [Robert M.T.] Hunter of Va. dissenting from the course of your friends there. Mr. [William P.?] Simpson informed me he addressed one of similar import to Mr. [George] McDuffie. It was, I know, from the character of the man, rough, strong and pointed. None of these have elicited any reply, except my own to Mr. Rhett; and that was two [*sic*] short to give the information desired. I wrote to him a few days ago, but I think he will not show you my letter.

Since [18]32 we have made several rallies for democratic principles ["here" *interlined*]. Often we have elected men to office who could never have risen but by our aid, such for instance as Gov[ernor Wilson] Shannon but so far every man, so elevated, has deserted us when elected. Every new rally has been with new men, chiefly, as the old had deserted. If we are now disbanded and have no leader to hold us together, I believe there will not be again a rally for the south. Men have become worn out with ["the" *canceled*] a conflict which leaves them between two fires, the whig on the one side, and the old organisation on the other. I have been and am odious to both, and in order to wreak their veng[e]ance upon me, they have united to break down my professional business, and though I do not fall behind the profession, I believe, they have so far succeeded in a war of thirteen years duration, as to have sunk about the half of all I was worth. I am preparing to leave this [place] in the spring of [18]45, because I feel unable, in justice to my family, to bear any further sacrifices. I state this to show the south how little ground it has to calculate on northern aid. But if the south, to win back the organisation from its alliance with the abolitionists and protectionists of the north will agree to take back all she has said against the organisation of the Baltimore convention, and reward with the Presidency, Mr. [Martin] Van Buren, and sacrifice her own sons in doing so, she merits the doom that awaits her. After aiding the old organisation to rivet the shackles of party despotism on the limbs of the people, her moral power will, as it ought, depart from her. The south is not, I hope, prepared for this, but it would seem, some of her simple sons were meditating such a catastrophy. Let them not suppose that any amount of party subserviency will secure, either now or hereafter, the nomination of a southern democrat worthy the name by any convention, however constituted, or his election by the electoral college. If they ever elect a southern democrat it will be by the House of Rep[resentative]s.

If, as I suppose is the fact, and as Mr. Rhett informs me is the case, Mr. V[an] B[uren] has secured a majority of States in the House of Rep[resentative]s, the next question is can he reach the House with three or four democratic competitors? The opinion has been prevailent in the west that he would fail to secure a single electoral vote, but this is perhaps going beyond the mark. He obtained but seven States in [18]40. Can he now carry New Hampshire, Virginia, South

Carolina, Alabama or Arkansas. And are not even Missouri, Illinois and Michigan doubtful? He certainly will not get Ohio and Penns[ylvani]a. Can he secure New York. If this too [is] doubtful, will there ever come a time when the chance of the south will be better? Your friends have lost confidence by the retrograde movements in the south, can any thing be done to regain our ground?

I hope the senate will not confirm the nomination of Gov. [Wilson] Shannon [to be U.S. Minister to Mexico], or that the President will withdraw his name, and thus save unpleasant ["reflections" *canceled*] reflections at a future day. My reasons I will give you confidentially. He is not a diplomatist by either nature or art, and will be an unskillful and inefficient representative at a foreign Court. If his nomination is confirmed it will not be the reward of merit, but the wages of folly or worse. His treachery to us in [18]38 when we brought him out, and secured his election, and since, on every occasion we have trusted him, has prevented the deffusion [*sic*] and success of our principles in the State. Last spring, he and R.J. Alexander professing to act with your friends, defeated my nomination and consequent election to congress, which was regarded by us as decissive of the vote of the State in the House of Rep[resentative]s should the election of President as it might, be terminated there. Should he be confirmed by the Senate these items may not be useless to you in your official intercourse with him. I hope ["you" *interlined*] will ["excuse" *interlined*] this long letter, and let me be favored by as early an answer as more important duties will permit. With High Respect, James Wishart.

ALS in ScCleA.

From JOHN T. WYMBS

New York [City], March 28th 1844

Sir, I take the liberty of inclosing to you letters of Introduction [dated 3/29/1844] from some of my ["Frien" *altered to* "intimate"] Friends [Edmund S. Derry and John McKeon] supporting me in an application for the Consulship of Paris in France, having heard that the present incumbent [Lorenzo Draper] was likely to be removed. I had the honour to make the acquaintance of the Hon. John C. Spencer last winter who can inform you of the respectability of my Friends and their influence in the Democratic Party, as well as his Opinion of my Capability to fill that office with intelligence. I trust that my reference to him will be a Sufficient excuse for this abbrupt intrusion upon your attention.

A perfect knowledge of the French Language and a residence of 12 years in that city where I have been established and acquainted with most of the influential public men of France, would enable me to render efficient service to the minister who would be appointed to that country. I could also afford usefull and [*one word altered to* "valuable"] information to the Treasury Department with regard to the business relations of that Nation and ours. You will please accept in advance my thanks and the assurance of my sincere gratitude [*sic*] for the interest you may take in my behalf. Very Respectfully your most ob[e]d[ien]t servant, John T. Wymbs.

ALS with Ens in DNA, RG 59 (General Records of the Department of State), Letters of Application and Recommendation during the Administrations of Martin Van Buren, William Henry Harrison, and John Tyler, 1837–1845, Wymbs (M-687: 35, frames 249–254).

From EDM[UN]D S. DERRY

New York [City], Mar[ch] 29, 1844

Dear Sir, Permit me to introduce to your favorable consideration the application of Mr. John T. Wymbs for appointment as Consul to Paris. I have known him for many years, he is of the proper political stamp and is, I believe, well qualified to discharge the duties of that post. It will afford me pleasure to have secured for him, the kind assistance which it may be in your power to bestow beyond his right to claim my endorsement of his political character and personal merits, a long existing friendship increases my desire that he Should be successful. With much respect Your very ob[edien]t Serv[an]t, Edm[un]d S. Derry.

ALS in DNA, RG 59 (General Records of the Department of State), Letters of Application and Recommendation during the Administrations of Martin Van Buren, William Henry Harrison, and John Tyler, 1837–1845, Wymbs (M-687:35, frame 254).

From R[OBERT] P. DUNLAP and JOSHUA HERRICK, [Representatives from Maine]

House of Representatives, Mar[ch] 29, 1844

Sir, We would respectfully recommend Jeremiah O'Brien Esquire of Brunswick, Maine, as a gentleman well qualified to discharge the

duties of a clerk in the Department of State. We have the honor to
be with great respect Your Ob[edien]t S[er]v[an]ts, R.P. Dunlap
[and] Joshua Herrick.

LS (in Dunlap's handwriting) in DNA, RG 59 (General Records of the Department of State), Letters of Application and Recommendation during the Administrations of Martin Van Buren, William Henry Harrison, and John Tyler,
1837–1845, O'Brien (M-687:24, frame 361).

From JOHN MCKEON,
[former Representative from N.Y.]

New York [City], March 29, 1844
Dear Sir, I take great pleasure in recommending to your favourable
consideration the application of Mr. John T. Wymbs for the appointment of Consul at Paris. Mr. W[ymbs] is a gentleman who is an
American by birth but has spent a large portion of his time in France.
He is well acquainted with mercantile affairs & is also well informed
in general politics and if appointed would discharge the duties of
Consul with great advantage to the country. I have known him since
childhood. His private character is irreproachable. With my best
wishes for his success I remain Your Obed[ient] Ser[van]t, John
McKeon.

ALS in DNA, RG 59 (General Records of the Department of State), Letters of
Application and Recommendation during the Administrations of Martin Van
Buren, William Henry Harrison, and John Tyler, 1837–1845, Wymbs (M-687:
35, frames 251–253).

From D[ANIEL] RAYMOND

Cincinnati, March 29, 1844
Dear Sir, There is as you are aware a very large German population
in Ohio and in all the Western States. For the accommodation of
these people, there is very much needed a German Consul in these
States for the purpose of preparing and authenticating documents
which they are constantly under the necessity of sending to Germany
for the purpose of receiving money &c &c. They are now under the
necessity of sending such documents to New York or Baltimore for
authentication. This is attended with trouble and expense.

Michael Dumbroff Esq. a Gentleman with whom I am well acquainted has made application through his friends in Germany to the Gov[ernmen]t of Bavaria to be appointed Bavarian Consul for the States of Ohio, Kentucky, Ind[ian]a, Ill., Mo., M[ichiga]n and the Territories W[isconsi]n & Iowa. They inform him that the King of Bavaria will readily appoint him provided the Pres[iden]t of the U.S. will authorise Mr. [Henry] Wheaton our Minister at Berlin to inform the Gov[ernmen]t of Bavaria that the appointment of Mr. Dumbroff would be agreeable to the Pres[iden]t.

The object of this letter therefore is to request you to obtain from the Pres[iden]t permission to make such a communication to Mr. Wheaton.

Mr. Dumbroff is as well qualified for the office as any man in the Western Country. He was a lawyer in Bavaria before he emigrated to the U.S. He has been in the country about ten years. He has studied our laws and has been admitted to the Ohio Bar and is now in the practice of the law in Cincinnati. He is a man of liberal education—of strict integrity and unblemished character and in every respect well qualified to discharge the duties of the office. His appointment would be very gratifying to our German population. Permit me therefore to bespeak your friendly offices in his favor. Permit me at the same time to congratulate you and the Country on your accession to your present important and responsible office. With great regard I have the honor to be your friend & Ob[edien]t S[er]v[an]t, D. Raymond.

P.S. If the enclosed letter is approved, it may be forwarded to Mr. Wheaton. D.R.

ALS in DNA, RG 59 (General Records of the Department of State), Miscellaneous Letters of the Department of State, 1789–1906 (M-179:104, frames 110–111).

From C[LAUDIUS] CROZET

New Orleans, March 30th 1844
Sir, Presuming on the advantage I had to be known to you while at West-Point, I hope not unfavorably; and that what you may have learned since, from time to time about me, will not have diminished your confidence, I take the liberty to address you on the subject of the collectorship of N[ew] O[rleans], to which I have once more removed since the prostration of Engineering in Virginia.

The President [John Tyler] Knows me personally well enough to be convinced of the safety of my appointment to the above office; I am, I believe sufficiently popular to be acceptable in this place; and I am certain of the support of the Louisiana Senators if presented. With these advantages of position, I should not doubt of success if you thought it expedient to give me the weight of your own recommendation and support for this now vacant office.

Allow me to improve this opportunity to renew the assurance of the high respect with which I have ever been Your most obed[ien]t Serv[an]t, C. Crozet.

ALS in DNA, RG 56 (General Records of the Department of the Treasury), Applications for Appointment as Customs Service Officers, 1833–1910, box 56, C. Crozet.

From JOSHUA HERRICK,
[Representative from Maine]

House of Rep[resentatives,] Washington, March 30th 1844
Sir, I herewith inclose two letters from Portland, Maine, recommending my friend Jere[mia]h O'Brien, Esquire, of Brunswick in that State for an appointment in your Department. I have the honor to be Your Ob[edien]t Serv[an]t, Joshua Herrick.

ALS with Ens in DNA, RG 59 (General Records of the Department of State), Letters of Application and Recommendation during the Administrations of Martin Van Buren, William Henry Harrison, and John Tyler, 1837–1845, O'Brien (M-687:24, frames 362–365). NOTE: Herrick enclosed two letters, one from A.W.H. Clapp, and one from W[illia]m P. Preble, both addressed to Calhoun and dated 3/19/1844.

OATH OF OFFICE as Secretary of State

[Washington, March 30, 1844]
I John C. Calhoun, having been appointed Secretary of State of the United States solemnly swear that I will support the Constitution of the United States, and well and faithfully execute the trust committed to me. [Signed:] J.C. Calhoun.

Subscribed and sworn this 30th day of March 1844, before me. [Signed:] W[illiam] Cranch.

DS (in Cranch's hand and signed by Calhoun) in DLC, Harwood Family Papers.

SYMBOLS

〚〛

The following symbols have been used in this volume as abbreviations for the forms in which papers of John C. Calhoun have been found and for the depositories in which they are preserved. (Full citations to printed sources of documents, some of which are cited by short titles in the text, can be found in the Bibliography.)

Abs   —abstract (a summary)
ADI   —autograph document, initialed
ADS   —autograph document, signed
ADU   —autograph document, unsigned
AEI   —autograph endorsement, initialed
AES   —autograph endorsement, signed
AEU   —autograph endorsement, unsigned
ALI   —autograph letter, initialed
ALS   —autograph letter, signed
ALU   —autograph letter, unsigned
CC   —clerk's copy (usually not for retention by the writer)
CCEx   —clerk's copy of an extract
CtY   —Yale University Library, New Haven, Conn.
DLC   —Library of Congress, Washington, D.C.
DNA   —National Archives, Washington, D.C.
DS   —document, signed
DU   —document, unsigned
EI   —endorsement, initialed
En   —enclosure
Ens   —enclosures
ES   —endorsement, signed
EU   —endorsement, unsigned
Ex   —extract
FC   —file copy (usually a letterbook copy retained by the sender)
InNd   —University of Notre Dame Library, South Bend, Ind.
LS   —letter, signed
LU   —letter, unsigned
M-   —(followed by a number) published microcopy of the National Archives
MH   —Harvard University Library, Cambridge, Mass.
MHi   —Massachusetts Historical Society, Boston
MiU-C   —William L. Clements Library, University of Michigan, Ann Arbor
NcD   —Duke University Library, Durham, N.C.
NcU   —University of North Carolina Library, Chapel Hill
NHi   —New-York Historical Society, New York City

NNC	—Columbia University Library, New York City
PC	—printed copy
PDS	—printed document, signed
PDU	—printed document, unsigned
PEx	—printed extract
PHC	—Haverford College Library, Haverford, Pa.
PHi	—Historical Society of Pennsylvania, Philadelphia
RG	—Record Group in the National Archives
Sc-Ar	—South Carolina Department of Archives and History, Columbia
ScCleA	—Clemson University Library, Clemson, S.C. (John C. Calhoun Papers in this repository unless otherwise stated)
ScCM	—Waring Historical Library, Medical University of South Carolina, Charleston
ScHi	—South Carolina Historical Society, Charleston
ScU-SC	—South Caroliniana Library, University of South Carolina, Columbia
TxU	—University of Texas Library, Austin
USlC	—Historical Department, Church of Jesus Christ of Latter-Day Saints, Salt Lake City, Utah
Vi	—Virginia State Library, Richmond
ViU	—University of Virginia Library, Charlottesville
ViW	—College of William and Mary Library, Williamsburg, Va.
WHi	—State Historical Society of Wisconsin, Madison

BIBLIOGRAPHY

〚〛

This Bibliography is limited to sources of and previous printings of John C. Calhoun documents in this volume.

Alexandria, D.C. and Va., *Gazette*, 1808–.

Ambler, Charles Henry, ed., *Correspondence of Robert M.T. Hunter, 1826–1876*, in the *American Historical Association Annual Report* for 1916 (2 vols. Washington: U.S. Government Printing Office, 1918), vol. II.

Americans, Read! ! ! Gen. *Joseph Smith's Views of the Powers and Policy of the Government of the United States. An Appeal to the Green Mountain Boys. Correspondence with the Hon. John C. Calhoun. Also a Copy of a Memorial to the Legislature of Missouri*. New York: E.J. Bevin, printer, 1844.

Anderson, S.C., *Gazette*, 1843–1855.

Anonymous, *Life and Character of the Hon. John C. Calhoun, with Illustrations: Containing Notices of His Father and Uncles, and Their Brave Conduct During Our Struggle for Independence, in the American Revolutionary War*. New York: J[onas] Winchester, New World Press, [1843].

Athens, Ga., *Southern Banner*, 1831–?.

Augusta, Ga., *Chronicle and Sentinel*, 1785–.

Baltimore, Md., *American*, 1799–.

[Benton, Thomas H.,] *Thirty Years' View; or, a History of the Working of the American Government for Thirty Years, from 1820 to 1850 . . . .* 2 vols. New York: D. Appleton & Co., 1854, 1856.

Boston, Mass., *Post*, 1831–.

Boucher, Chauncey S., and Robert P. Brooks, eds., *Correspondence Addressed to John C. Calhoun, 1837–1849*, in the *American Historical Association Annual Report* for 1929 (Washington: U.S. Government Printing Office, 1930).

Brownson, Henry F., *Orestes A. Brownson's Early Life: From 1803 to 1844*. Detroit: H.F. Brownson, publisher, 1898.

Brown, William H., *Portrait Gallery of Distinguished American Citizens, with Biographical Sketches, and Fac-Similes of Original Letters*. Hartford: E.B. and E.C. Kellogg, 1845.

[Calhoun, John C.,] *Speeches of John C. Calhoun. Delivered in the Congress of the United States from 1811 to the Present Time*. New York: Harper & Brothers, c. 1843. [Some copies of this work have the alternate title page: *A Selection from the Speeches, Reports, and Other Publications of John C. Calhoun, Subsequent to His Election as Vice-President, (Including Also His First Speech in Congress in 1811), and Referred to in His "Life."*]

The Calhoun Textbook. New York: Herald Office, [1843].

Camden, S.C., *Journal*, 1826–1891?.

Charleston, S.C., *Courier*, 1803–1852.

Charleston, S.C., *Mercury*, 1822–1868.

Cincinnati, Ohio, *Daily Enquirer*, 1841–.

Columbia, S.C., *South-Carolinian*, 1838–1849?.

Columbia, S.C., *The State*, 1891–.

Correspondence between Joseph Smith, the Prophet, and Col. John Wentworth, Editor of "The Chicago Democrat," and Member of Congress from Illinois; Gen. James Arlington Bennet, of Arlington House, Long Island, and the Honorable John C. Calhoun, Senator from South Carolina. In Which is Given, a Sketch of the Life of Joseph Smith, the Rise and Progress of the Church of Latter Day Saints, and their Persecutions by the State of Missouri: with the Peculiar Views of Joseph Smith, in Relation to Political and Religious Matters Generally; to Which is Added a Concise Account of the Present State and Prospects of the City of Nauvoo. New York: published by John E. Page and L.R. Foster, 1844.

Crallé, Richard K., ed., *The Works of John C. Calhoun.* 6 vols. Columbia, S.C.: printed by A.S. Johnston, 1851, and New York: D. Appleton & Co., 1853–1857.

Edgefield, S.C., *Advertiser*, 1836–.

Grand Rapids, Mich., *Enquirer*, 1837–1863.

Green, Duff, *Facts and Suggestions, Biographical, Historical, Financial and Political, Addressed to the People of the United States.* New York: Richardson & Co., 1866.

Green, Thomas J., *Journal of the Texian Expedition Against Mier; Subsequent Imprisonment of the Author; His Sufferings, and Final Escape from the Castle of Perote. With Reflections upon the Present Political and Probable Future Relations of Texas, Mexico, and the United States.* New York: Harper and Brothers, 1845.

Greenville, S.C., *Mountaineer*, 1829–1901.

[Hunter, Robert M.T.,] *Life of John C. Calhoun, Presenting a Condensed History of Political Events from 1811 to 1843.* New York: Harper & Brothers, 1843.

Jackson, Miss., *Mississippian*, 1832–1865.

Jackson, Miss., *Southern Reformer*, 1843–1846.

Jameson, J. Franklin, ed., *Correspondence of John C. Calhoun,* in the *American Historical Association Annual Report* for 1899 (2 vols. Washington: U.S. Government Printing Office, 1900), vol. II.

"John C. Calhoun to Thomas W. Gilmer," in *William and Mary Quarterly,* first series, vol. 20, no. 1 (July 1911), pp. 8–10.

Knoxville, Tenn., *Register*, 1816–1863.

Life of John C. Calhoun, Presenting a Condensed History of Political Events from 1811 to 1843. Together with a Selection from His Speeches, Reports, and Other Writings Subsequent to His Election as Vice-President of the United States, Including His Leading Speech on the Late War Delivered in 1811. New York: Harper & Brothers, n.d.

London, England, *Examiner*, 1808–1880.

London, England, *Times*, 1785–.

[Mayhew, Henry,] *The Mormons: Or Latter-Day Saints. With Memoirs of the Life and Death of Joseph Smith, the "American Mahomet."* London: Office of the National Illustrated Library, [1851].

Merk, Frederick, *Slavery and the Annexation of Texas.* New York: Alfred A. Knopf, 1972.

Milledgeville, Ga., *Federal Union*, 1830–1872.

Moore, Frederick W., ed., "Calhoun as Seen by His Political Friends: Letters of Duff Green, Dixon H. Lewis [and] Richard K. Crallé During the Period from 1831 to 1848," in *Publications of the Southern History Association,* vol. VII (1903).

Nashville, Tenn., *Union,* 1835–1875.

Nashville, Tenn., *Whig,* 1838–1855.

Nauvoo, Ill., *Neighbor,* 1843–1845.

[Newman, C.L., and J.C. Stribling,] *The Pendleton Farmers' Society.* Atlanta: Foote and Davies Co., 1908.

New Orleans, La., *Louisiana Courier,* 1807–1860.

New York, N.Y., *Evening Post,* 1832–1920.

New York, N.Y., *Herald,* 1835–1924.

New York, N.Y., *Tribune,* 1841–1924.

Niles' Register. Baltimore: 1811–1849.

Norfolk and Portsmouth, Va., *American Beacon,* 1815–1861.

Oliphant, Mary C. Simms, Alfred Taylor Odell, and T.C. Duncan Eaves, eds., *Letters of William Gilmore Simms.* 6 vols. Columbia: University of South Carolina Press, 1952–1956, 1982.

Pendleton, S.C., *Messenger,* 1807–?.

Petersburg, Va., *Republican,* 1843–1850.

Philadelphia, Pa., *Pennsylvania Inquirer and National Gazette,* 1842–1860.

The Political Correspondence of the late Hon. George N. Sanders, Confederate Commissioner to Europe during the Civil War. To be Sold on Wednesday, May 13th, 1914. New York: American Art Association, [1914].

Proceedings of the Democratic State Convention, Composed of Delegates from the Several Districts and Parishes of the State of South-Carolina, Assembled at Columbia, on the 22d of May, 1843. Columbia: printed at the South Carolinian Office, 1843.

The Prophet Joseph Smith's Views on the Powers and Policy of the Government of the United States. To which is Appended the Correspondence between the Prophet Joseph Smith and the Hons. J.C. Calhoun and Henry Clay, Candidates for the Presidency of the United States in 1844. Salt Lake City: Jos. Hyrum Parry and Co., 1886.

Raleigh, N.C., *North Carolina Standard,* 1834–1870.

Richmond, Va., *Enquirer,* 1804–1877.

Richmond, Va., *Whig,* 1824–1888.

Schlesinger, Arthur M., Jr., ed., *History of American Presidential Elections, 1789–1968.* 4 vols. New York: Chelsea House, 1971.

Sioussat, St. George L., "John Caldwell Calhoun," in *The American Secretaries of State and their Diplomacy,* 5:[125]–233, c. 1928.

Springfield, Ill., *Illinois State Register,* 1836–1918.

Tyler, Lyon G., *The Letters and Times of the Tylers.* 3 vols. Richmond: Whittet & Shepperson, 1884–1896.

Upshur, John A., ed., "Letter of A.P. Upshur to J.C. Calhoun," in *William and Mary Quarterly,* second series, vol. 16, no. 4 (October 1936), pp. 554–557.

The Voice of Truth, Containing General Joseph Smith's Correspondence with Gen. James Arlington Bennett; Appeal to the Green Mountain Boys; Correspondence with John C. Calhoun, Esq.; Views of the Powers and Policy of the Government of the United States; Pacific Innuendo, and Gov. Ford's Letter; a Friendly Hint to Missouri, and a Few Words of Consolation for the

"Globe;" also, Correspondence with the Hon. Henry Clay. Nauvoo, Ill.: printed by John Taylor, 1844.

Washington, D.C., *Daily National Intelligencer,* 1800–1870.

Washington, D.C., *Madisonian,* 1837–1845.

Washington, D.C., *Spectator,* 1842–1844.

Washington, D.C., *The Globe,* 1830–1845.

INDEX

⓪

Anne Arundel County, Md.: mentioned, 506. *See also* Annapolis, Md.; West River, Md.

Anthon, Charles: mentioned, 551.

Antimasonry: mentioned, 244, 256, 299, 852.

Appeal to the Democratic Party: mentioned, xviii, 387.

Appointments and removals: of federal officials, vii, xxii–xxiii, xxv–xxvi, 36–37, 73–74, 83, 114, 118, 125, 138, 156–157, 159–162, 167, 185, 190, 192, 217, 219, 227, 230, 237, 244, 246, 254, 259–260, 297, 324, 330–331, 336–339, 354, 366, 368, 372–373, 403–404, 415–416, 418–419, 423, 446, 456, 472, 517, 542, 654–656, 667, 675, 694–695, 697, 704, 712–713, 722, 724–725, 749, 752, 777, 795, 801, 804, 809–812, 814–831, 836–838, 840, 844–851, 853–862, 864–881, 883–885, 887, 890–891, 896–899, 902–906. *See also* Executive patronage.

Archer, William S.: mentioned, 826.

Argentina: mentioned, 456.

Arkansas: mentioned, 355, 708; politics of, 691–692, 780–781, 902.

Arkansas River: mentioned, 567.

Army, U.S. *See* Calhoun, Patrick (son); United States Military Academy; War Department, U.S.

Arnold, Alexander B.: mentioned, 789–790.

Arrington, Archibald H.: mentioned, 342, 600.

Art and artists: 257, 264, 268–270, 328, 401, 475, 488, 540, 554, 580–581, 755, 773. *See also frontispiece.*

Ashburton, Alexander Baring, Lord: mentioned, 351, 575, 576, 579.

Ashe, John S.: from, 362, 466; mentioned, 212, 401, 447, 517, 534.

Ashton, Lawrence: mentioned, 566, 569–570.

Assignments: by Joseph A. Scoville, 123, 239.

Assumption of State Debts. *See* State debts and stocks.

Astor House: mentioned, 436.

Athens, Ga.: mentioned, 264, 312, 390, 637, 769, 832, 885–886.

Athens, Ga., *Southern Banner*: document in, 729.

Atkinson, Archibald: mentioned, 177.

Attorney General, U.S.: mentioned, 237, 254, 845–846.

Augusta, Ga., *Daily Chronicle and Sentinel*: documents in, 293, 307, 308, 538.

Autauga County, Ala.: mentioned, 399.

Bacon: mentioned, 360.

Bacon, T.I.: from, 254.

Bailey, Henry: from, 466, 890; mentioned, 212, 534, 655, 695; to, 893.

Bainbridge, Ga.: mentioned, 788.

Baldwin, Cornelius C.: mentioned, 378.

Baldwin, Edward: mentioned, 549.

Baldwin, George E.: mentioned, 398.

Baltimore, Md.: Democratic National Convention at, 129, 193, 199, 211–212, 234, 341, 371, 390, 414, 416–417, 419–421, 423, 436, 446, 476–477, 509, 542, 555, 557, 561–562, 571, 573–574, 588, 590, 592, 604, 612–613, 617–618, 623, 636, 638–640, 643, 645–646, 648, 650, 653, 667, 674–676, 680, 689, 693–694, 696, 700, 706, 709, 714–715, 722, 730–731, 735, 739, 744, 760, 766, 768, 771, 773, 779, 782, 792–794, 802, 810, 829, 874–875, 877, 896, 901; mentioned, xx, 129, 176, 187, 192, 218, 259, 371, 419, 448, 456, 458–459, 507, 516–517, 526, 581–582, 677–678, 688–689, 713, 840, 845, 904.

Baltimore, Md., *American*: documents in, 463, 538, 897.

Bangor, Maine: mentioned, 299.

Banking. *See* Currency and banking.

Bank of Charleston: mentioned, 360.

Holmes, Isaac E.: from, 820; mentioned, 450–451, 689, 811–812, 815, 820, 828, 855.

Holmes, James G.: from, 814.

Holy Alliance: mentioned, 30.

Homer: mentioned, 489, 663–664.

Horry family: mentioned, 353.

Horses: mentioned, 116, 264, 267, 458, 488, 550, 655, 719, 785–786, 788.

Hough, Robert: from, 370.

House of Representatives, U.S.: Calhoun's career in, xi, xvi, xxiii, 3, 5, 11–37, 42, 105–107, 111, 118, 121, 223–224, 316–321, 372, 500, 527, 556, 581, 659–660, 838–840, 847; Clerk of, 529, 596, 614, 616; elections to, 118, 126, 134, 159, 171–172, 175–177, 180, 186–188, 220, 229, 262, 304, 314, 323, 342, 375–377, 379–381, 390, 425, 436, 456, 497–498, 508–509, 513–514, 613, 713, 792, 852, 902; freedom of debate in, 101; librarian of, 146; mentioned, 48, 70, 323, 390–391, 411, 492, 518, 529, 552, 555, 558–559, 569, 582–583, 586–587, 595–596, 599–600, 603, 614, 616, 634–636, 680–682, 688–689, 704, 708–709, 712–713, 716, 729, 745–746, 750, 758, 780, 794, 797–798, 819–825, 830–831, 837–839, 847–848, 855–856, 896, 903; role of in Presidential election, 43–44, 137, 167, 201–202, 204–206, 208, 240, 343–351, 404, 406, 412, 415, 421, 440, 443, 456, 459–460, 514, 518, 555, 586, 588–589, 595, 602, 619–623, 645, 706–707, 732–736, 794, 901–902; Speaker of, 19, 25, 192, 391, 518, 529, 582–583, 595–596, 599–600, 614, 681, 712–713.

Houston, Samuel: mentioned, 570, 601, 613, 837, 886.

Houston, Texas: letter from, 176.

Hovis, ——: mentioned, 116.

Howard, Edward: from, 429.

Howard, John H.: mentioned, 233–234, 246–247, 508, 554–555, 557–558.

Howard, John P.: mentioned, 158, 161.

Howard, Tilghman A.: from, 461.

Hoyt, Cornelius: mentioned, 398.

Hubard, Edmund W.: mentioned, 134.

Hubbard, David: mentioned, 699, 701.

Hudson's Bay Co.: mentioned, 853.

Huey, James: mentioned, 398.

Hufty, Joseph: mentioned, 397.

Huger, Alfred: mentioned, 815.

Huger, Daniel Elliott: from, 798; mentioned, 564, 589, 636, 654, 671, 799, 808–809, 813–814.

Huger, Francis K.: mentioned, 182.

Hughes, Ann-Sarah Maxcy: mentioned, 219, 524, 541.

Hughes, George W.: mentioned, 524, 844.

Hulse, Stephen: from, 248; mentioned, 251; to, 300.

Hume, Joseph: mentioned, 546.

Humphrey, Harvey: mentioned, 257.

Humphreys, —— (overseer): mentioned, 785.

Humphreys, John C.: from, 890.

"Hunkers": mentioned, 413, 423.

Hunt, Benjamin F.: mentioned, 616.

Hunter, Alexander: mentioned, 487.

Hunter, G.R.: mentioned, 390.

Hunter, John: mentioned, 214.

Hunter, Robert M.T.: document signed by, 751; from, 175, 186, 245, 392, 455, 468, 495, 607, 613, 714, 766, 842; mentioned, xi, xiii–xiv, xvii, xx, xxii, xxiv–xxv, 3–4, 116, 118, 132, 147–148, 215–216, 218, 220, 263–264, 269, 337–338, 351, 360, 364–369, 385–386, 388, 398, 415, 434, 446, 451, 460, 464, 478, 493, 510, 654, 761, 772, 801, 810, 900; to, 115, 126, 132, 135, 147, 171, 180, 228, 294, 303, 334, 377, 394, 431, 474, 521, 636, 744, 765, 793, 844.

xiv–xv, xxi, 354, 396, 400, 582, 650, 773, 779, 803.

New York, N.Y., *Journal of Commerce*: mentioned, xxi, 398, 445, 582, 836, 863.

New York, N.Y., *National Anti-Slavery Standard*: mentioned, 537.

New York, N.Y., *New World*: mentioned, 581–582.

New York, N.Y., *Plebeian*: mentioned, xvii note, 157, 400, 409, 437, 448, 479, 648.

New York, N.Y., *Price Current*: mentioned, 592.

New York, N.Y., *Republic*: mentioned, xxi, 673–674, 695, 702, 725–728, 754–756, 776, 796, 801, 803, 862–863.

New York, N.Y., *Sun*: mentioned, 479.

New York, N.Y., *Tribune*: documents in, 293, 729; mentioned, 332.

Niagara Falls, N.Y.: mentioned, 179, 256.

Nicholas, George: mentioned, 719.

Nicholas, Robert Carter: mentioned, 411, 539–540.

Nicholson, George L.: document signed by, 751.

Niles, Hiram: mentioned, 398.

Niles' National Register: documents in, 225, 300, 316, 463, 531, 538, 583, 662, 729, 893; mentioned, xxvi, 389.

Nixon, Maj. ——: mentioned, 498.

Noah, Mordecai M.: mentioned, 214, 325–326, 374, 479, 480, 857.

Nomination: possible independent Presidential (*see* National Convention: independent nominating).

Norfolk and Portsmouth, Va., *American Beacon and Daily Advertiser*: documents in, 293, 531, 583, 893; mentioned, 563.

Norfolk and Portsmouth, Va., *Herald*: mentioned, 113.

Norfolk County, Va.: mentioned, 573.

Norfolk, Va.: mentioned, 113, 177, 352, 573, 887.

North: political practices of, xii–xiv, 114, 147–148, 152–154, 162, 173–174, 179, 191, 214, 217–218, 225–226, 236, 249, 255–257, 296, 298, 303, 338, 366–367, 369, 373, 377, 415, 434, 482, 497–498, 503–506, 515, 521, 525, 530, 532–533, 538, 541, 571, 585–587, 647–648, 689, 698–699, 707–708, 723, 745, 747–748, 758, 791–792, 843, 857, 901.

North American Review: mentioned, 70.

North Carolina: politics of, xviii note, 182, 192, 232, 235, 342, 365, 377, 380–381, 399, 424, 446–447, 463, 466, 469, 485, 494, 518, 538–539, 600, 612–613, 655, 680, 682, 773, 783, 797, 838, 845, 855–856, 866–867, 897.

Northeastern boundary: mentioned, 827, 881.

Northeastern Boundary Commission: mentioned, 827.

Norwalk, Ohio: mentioned, 896–897.

Norwich, Conn., *News*: mentioned, 542.

Nullification: doctrine of, 52, 54–65, 67–72, 78, 230, 240, 324, 371, 503, 643–644, 707; period of, 56–57, 61–73, 92, 108, 196, 223, 384, 389, 415, 554–555, 581, 627, 630, 661, 664, 666, 698, 707, 723, 740, 744, 804, 847, 872, 876, 883, 901.

Nullifiers: as a party, 50, 64, 70–71, 74, 78, 92–93, 247, 656–661, 888.

Oak trees: mentioned, 142.

Oath of office: Calhoun's as Secretary of State, 906.

Oats: mentioned, 241, 292.

Obar Mine: mentioned, 113, 116, 123, 129, 136, 140, 235, 241, 262, 264, 292, 307–308, 357–358, 428, 590, 653, 720–721, 742, 772, 784, 788–790, 803, 806.

O'Brien, Jeremiah: mentioned, 877, 881, 890, 903–904, 906.

South Carolina Railroad: mentioned, 722.

Southcott, Joanna: mentioned, 664.

Southern Literary Messenger: mentioned, 462.

Southern Quarterly Review: mentioned, xvi note, 462, 582, 758.

Southfield, N.Y.: mentioned, 150.

Southworth, Edward, Jr.: mentioned, 159.

Spain: mentioned, 30, 46, 320, 383, 472, 511, 566, 606.

Sparks, Jared: mentioned, 884.

Spartanburg District, S.C.: mentioned, 635.

Specie Circular: mentioned, 88–89.

Specie Resolution of 1816: mentioned, 34, 90.

Speculation and speculators: 75, 83–84, 102, 108–109, 253, 261, 330.

Speech before the Passage of the Tariff Bill (August 5, 1842): mentioned, 149, 171.

Speeches of John C. Calhoun: abstracted, 223; advertisements for, 223–225; described, xv–xvii, 3; mentioned, 104, 112–113, 123–124, 149, 151, 163–164, 171, 183–184, 232, 239, 241–242, 305, 309, 315–321, 335–336, 385–386, 400, 447, 463, 471, 490, 520, 525, 541–542, 598, 609–611, 642, 673, 744, 746–748, 757–758, 799–800, 804, 829, 843–844.

Speech on the Bill for the Occupation and Settlement of the Territory of Oregon (January 31, 1843): mentioned, 149.

Speech on the Treaty of Washington (August 19, 1842): mentioned, 146, 818.

Speight, Jesse: to, xii.

Spencer (slave): mentioned, 786.

Spencer, John C.: mentioned, 244, 324, 675, 712–713, 724, 902–903.

Spoils. *See* Executive patronage.

Sprague, William B.: to, 884.

Springfield, Ill., *Illinois State Register*: documents in, 293, 538, 729.

Stages: mentioned, 73, 508, 788, 869.

Stanly, Edward: mentioned, 342.

Starkweather, Samuel: from, 296.

State debts and stocks: mentioned, 85–87, 98–99, 198, 242, 326, 553, 769.

State Department, U.S.: appointments in, vii, 118, 125, 219, 237, 254, 259, 324, 330–331, 354, 372, 456, 472, 654–656, 694, 722, 795, 877, 879–881, 883–885, 890–891, 895, 897–899, 902–906; business of, 237, 354–357, 370, 381–383, 418, 478, 496, 535, 548–549, 574–580, 601–602, 606, 608–610, 613–615, 671, 692, 753, 809–810, 812, 814, 816, 819–820, 822, 825, 828, 831, 837–838, 846, 848–850, 855, 859–860, 878, 886, 893, 904–905; Calhoun as Secretary of, vii–viii, xxv–xxvii, 254, 654–656, 712, 846, 854, 860–861, 865–873, 876–899, 902–906; Calhoun's appointment as Secretary of, 114, 471–472, 809–810, 812, 814–831, 836–838, 840, 844–851, 853–862, 864–879, 881, 885, 887, 890–891, 895, 897–899; Calhoun's commission as Secretary of, 829; Calhoun's oath of office as Secretary of, 906; Calhoun's papers as Secretary of, vii–viii; mentioned, xx note, 24, 269, 704, 712; Secretaries of (*see* Legaré, Hugh S.; Upshur, Abel P.).

State Historical Society of Wisconsin: document in, 266.

Staten Island, N.Y. *See* Richmond County, N.Y.

Staten Island, N.Y., *Richmond County Mirror*: mentioned, 149–150.

Statesmanship: Calhoun on, 79–81, 92–93, 105, 108–109, 111–112.

Steck, P. Roman: from, 183.

Stell, Nelson: mentioned, 397.

Stender, John A.: mentioned, 407.

Sterling, Ansel: mentioned, 411.

Sterling, John Calhoun: mentioned, 240, 297–298.

Sterling, Micah: from, 139, 156, 239, 411; mentioned, xxiii; to, 297.